Language

INTRODUCTORY READINGS

SEVENTH EDITION

Language

INTRODUCTORY READINGS

EDITED BY

Virginia Clark
Paul Eschholz
Alfred Rosa

University of Vermont

Beth Lee Simon

Indiana University–Purdue University

BEDFORD/ST. MARTIN'S

BOSTON ♦ NEW YORK

For Bedford/St. Martin's

Developmental Editor: Stephanie Butler
Senior Production Editor: Harold Chester
Production Supervisor: Andrew Ensor
Marketing Manager: Adrienne Petsick
Art Director: Lucy Krikorian
Text Design: Anna Palchik
Copy Editor: Kay Kaylor
Cover Design/Cover Art: Trudi Gershenov
Composition: ICC Macmillan
Printing and Binding: Haddon Craftsmen, Inc., an R.R. Donnelley & Sons Company

President: Joan E. Feinberg
Editorial Director: Denise B. Wydra
Editor in Chief: Karen S. Henry
Director of Development: Erica T. Appel
Director of Marketing: Karen Melton Soeltz
Director of Editing, Design, and Production: Marcia Cohen
Managing Editor: Shuli Traub

Library of Congress Control Number: 2005934868

Manufactured in the United States of America.

2 1 0 9 8 7
f e d c b a

For information, write: Bedford/St. Martin's, 75 Arlington Street, Boston, MA 02116   (617-399-4000)

ISBN-10: 0-312-45018-4
ISBN-13: 978-0-312-45018-2

Acknowledgments
Acknowledgments and copyrights appear at the back of the book on pages 873–76, which constitute an extension of the copyright page.

Preface

Language matters. It is an instrument through which we see and know ourselves and others, and it affects how we experience our world. Through language—in all its modes—we become ourselves, know our own thoughts, and construct our ideas. It is a given that we communicate knowledge through language, but it is also important to recognize just how thoroughly events in the world are shaped by language use. Dialects signify where and how we live and the cultures we have encountered. We conform to, rebel against, or even change societal expectations with the words and phrases we use. At times, biases are reflected in our speech. And, increasingly, specific languages—English, for instance—take on new roles, becoming common to diverse peoples, and bridging countries, economies, and histories. The seventh edition of *Language: Introductory Readings* focuses on language as a necessity for participating in and understanding the world.

The book begins by defining language and moves through the most important subfields of linguistics. Part One presents fundamental ideas about language itself—what it is and how it developed. Parts Two through Four are concerned with language structures and meaning; Parts Five through Nine discuss language history, regional and social variation, and human language behaviors based in culture and identities. Finally, Part Ten looks specifically at language throughout the world and Part Eleven at its role in education.

This edition also addresses contemporary ideas and new scholarship in the study of language. Carefully selected readings provide an authoritative yet inviting introduction to the essential issues of language study. Classic, foundational texts are complemented and balanced by the best contemporary pieces. As a whole, the volume offers an inviting, coherent, student-centered introduction to the current theories, issues, and research in the field of language.

New to This Edition

New readings complement classic selections and illustrate linguistic study's real-world applications. Almost half of the selections are new, and these, together with articles from earlier editions, represent the theories, research, and ideas that make up the foundation for the study of language and human behaviors in the twenty-first century. Familiar essays like Harvey A. Daniels's "Nine Ideas about Language" present time-honored discussions of the study of language. Even as students build the groundwork for studying linguistics in the first four parts of the book, new essays demonstrate how an understanding of the field's basic concepts applies to the world at large. For instance, alongside essays on phonology and syntax is "Mc-: Meaning in the Marketplace," Genine Lentine and Roger Shuy's description of how they used a morphemic study of advertisements and business names as evidence in a trademark infringement lawsuit involving McDonald's.

New readings also reflect the increasingly multilingual, multinational world students live and work in today. An entirely new part addresses globalization and English; it includes discussions of the growth of English worldwide and how that phenomenon results in whole new varieties of English. This edition of *Language* also draws on studies of languages other than English, and new readings throughout the book examine European, Asian, Aboriginal, pidgin, and creole languages. These essays illustrate the fascinating interaction between language and culture.

The second half of *Language* concerns itself largely with the study of language as it relates to a number of social constructs and builds on the linguistic groundwork of the first four parts. George Lakoff and Mark Johnson's highly influential ideas about metaphor, cognition, and culture are here. Language variation, especially based on region, race and ethnicity, and gender, are explored. Following Lee Pederson's article on the development of American regional dialects, John Rickford applies linguistics to a landmark moment in U.S. social history when a school board proposed using Ebonics to help students use Standard English. Two classic pieces by Deborah Tannen about the differences in the way men and women communicate are now complemented by more recent discussions by Mary Talbot and Fern L. Johnson, who offer a comparative look at gendered language behavior in several countries.

Expanded and updated apparatus assists students in applying linguistics to their own learning experiences, to issues in their communities, and to their everyday interactions. In this edition, readings and apparatus work to illuminate how a rich understanding of language offers a window to the world, so the Questions for Discussion and Review for each essay and projects at the end of each part have been heavily reworked. The book encourages students and instructors to call on their own backgrounds and experiences in order to illustrate how language is a primary way of being in and knowing the world. Projects also take advantage of new information technologies—such as professional Web sites and blogs—as sources of information and as tools for linguistic study. We believe instructors will find that they need not have a technical background in linguistics to work with this volume beneficially.

The pedagogical apparatus is designed to be used flexibly and allows instructors and students enough contextual information to work sequentially through each part for a complete and in-depth study of a field or with individual pieces to supplement other course materials. The introductions to each part provide a broad overview, and headnotes preceding each essay serve as an up-to-date framework for understanding the author's background and the piece's intention. The heavily revised bibliographies offer entry to the latest ideas, theories, and data. In order to accommodate both the wealth of information available and the ways in which students learn and research today, these bibliographies provide extensive online and multimedia references in addition to book and journal information. Entries reflect a range of levels of sophistication. The new glossary reflects changes in terminology and includes key phrases used in new linguistic scholarship.

Language and its study is presented in a systematic, coherent, and welcoming way. This means the volume can provide a semester course of study or be used in part for specific goals. Our intention is to provide students with a broad and deep introduction to language as a fundamental way to understand the world, in academic settings and beyond. This approach to the study of language, we hope, bridges the gap between the classroom and "real life."

Acknowledgments

Generous assistance came from the staff of the Department of English and Linguistics at Indiana University Purdue University, and in particular, Kate Butler was instrumental in coordinating text exchanges with the publisher. Michele Devinney prepared all the annotations for the bibliographies for this edition. The edition as a whole benefited from the valuable comments, criticisms, and suggestions of our colleagues around the country: Naomi S. Baron, American University; Theodora Helene Bofman, Northeastern Illinois University; Brigittine M. French, Grinnell College; K. Seon John, Columbus State University; Rea Keech, Anne Arundel Community College; Rebecca A. Litke, California State University at Northridge; Pat McGrath, University of Hawaii; Betty Samraj, San Diego State University; Susan Kay Shear, University of Florida; Chad Thompson, Indiana University–Purdue University; Matthew Weltig, University of Nevada at Reno.

Bedford/St. Martin's editorial staff, especially editors Stephanie Butler and Carolyn Lengel, provided excellent guidance. Judy Voss lent her excellent ear and writing talents to the apparatus and her incisive questions helped us hone the text. The text was deftly copyedited by Kay Kaylor, and Harold Chester and Andrew Ensor ably guided the project from manuscript to bound book. We would also like to thank those linguists who wrote articles specifically for previous editions of *Language: Introductory Readings* or offered previously published pieces to enhance the discussion of various topics in this edition, R. Edward Callary, Karen Emmorey, Jeannine Heny, Frank Heny, William Kemp, and Roy Smith.

VIRGINIA CLARK
PAUL ESCHHOLZ
ALFRED ROSA
BETH LEE SIMON

Contents

PART SIX
LANGUAGE VARIATION AND SOCIAL INTERACTION
371

PART SEVEN
LANGUAGE AND CULTURE
449

Language

INTRODUCTORY READINGS

LANGUAGE AND ITS STUDY

Language is not only the principal medium of human communication, but also what binds us to one another, to our various cultures, and to our remarkably interconnected world. To understand our humanity, we must understand how language helps to make us human. The study of language, then, is a practical, as well as challenging, pursuit. In beginning this study, we will consider some fundamental questions: What is language? What are its origins? What are its unique characteristics? What common misconceptions about language impede our understanding of it? How are signs and symbols of language organized in the brain? The selections in Part One explore these questions and suggest some answers.

Most people take their language abilities for granted; knowing and understanding language seem as natural as breathing and sleeping. But human language is extremely complex. In the first selection, "Nine Ideas about Language," Harvey A. Daniels discusses his nine ideas about language that most contemporary linguists believe are demonstrably true. Although Daniels first published these ideas years ago, they remain a useful way to begin discussing perceptions, and misperceptions, about language. His ideas will also enhance your understanding and enjoyment of selections throughout the book.

In "Language: An Introduction," W. F. Bolton discusses the basic characteristics of human language and the intricate physiological adaptations that make speech and hearing possible. He points out that all languages are systematic and that no language is simple or "primitive," and he warns us against ethnocentric attitudes.

In "Sign Language," Karen Emmorey demonstrates that speech, which nondeaf people might assume is fundamental to human communication, is not a necessary component of language. She draws exact parallels between the sound system, word formation, and word order rules of spoken language and their equivalents in signed languages such as American Sign Language (ASL).

In "Nonverbal Communication," George A. Miller explores the role of various types of body language—adornment, ritualized gesture, spatial positioning, and eye contact—in human communication systems. These nonverbal signals vary from culture to culture, and they are as necessary as words and sentences to our understanding of, and communication with, one another.

Finally, Jean Aitchison analyzes the biological origins of human language and examines data from three different linguistic sources: primate vocalization, the processes of human language acquisition, and the formation of pidgin and creole languages. She finds, in "chimps, children and creoles," that each of these offers a possible basis for the origins of language but that no single theory provides a fully satisfactory explanation. Thus, Aitchison concludes that language may well have developed from multiple sources.

1

Nine Ideas about Language

Harvey A. Daniels

In the following chapter adapted from his book Famous Last Words: The American Language Crisis Reconsidered *(1983), Professor Harvey A. Daniels presents nine fundamental ideas about language that are widely accepted by contemporary linguists. In doing so, he dispels a number of myths about language that are all too prevalent among Americans. The ideas introduced here provide a foundation for readings in later parts of this book, where they are discussed in more detail.*

Assuming we agree that the English language has in fact survived all of the predictions of doom which have been prevalent since at least the early eighteenth century, we also have reason to believe that current reports of the death of our language are similarly exaggerated. The managers of the present crisis of course disagree, and their efforts may even result in the reinstatement of the linguistic loyalty oath of the 1920s or of some updated equivalent ("I promise to use good American unsplit infinitives") in our schools. But it won't make much difference. The English language, if history is any guide at all, will remain useful and vibrant as long as it is spoken, whether we eagerly try to tend and nurture and prune its growth or if we just leave it alone.

Contemporary language critics recognize that language is changing, that people use a lot of jargon, that few people consistently speak the standard dialect, that much writing done in our society is ineffective, and so forth—but they have no other way of viewing these phenomena except with alarm. But most of the uses of and apparent changes in language which worry the critics *can* be explained and understood in unalarming ways. Such explanations have been provided by linguists during the past seventy-five years.

I have said that in order to understand the errors and misrepresentations of the language critics, we need to examine not only history but also "the facts." Of course, facts about language are a somewhat elusive commodity, and we may never be able to answer all of our questions about this wonderfully complex activity. But linguists have made a good start during this century toward describing some of the basic features, structures, and operations of human speech. This section presents a series of nine fundamental ideas about language that form, if not

3

exactly a list of facts, at least a fair summary of the consensus of most linguistic scholars.

1. Children learn their native language swiftly, efficiently, and largely without instruction. Language is a species-specific trait of human beings. All children, unless they are severely retarded or completely deprived of exposure to speech, will acquire their oral language as naturally as they learn to walk. Many linguists even assert that the human brain is prewired for language, and some have also postulated that the underlying linguistic features which are common to all languages are present in the brain at birth. This latter theory comes from the discovery that all languages have certain procedures in common: ways of making statements, questions, and commands; ways of referring to past time; the ability to negate, and so on.[1] In spite of the underlying similarities of all languages, though, it is important to remember that children will acquire the language which they hear around them—whether that is Ukrainian, Swahili, Cantonese, or Appalachian American English.

In spite of the commonsense notions of parents, they do not "teach" their children to talk. Children *learn* to talk, using the language of their parents, siblings, friends, and others as sources and examples—and by using other speakers as testing devices for their own emerging ideas about language. When we acknowledge the complexity of adult speech, with its ability to generate an unlimited number of new, meaningful utterances, it is clear that this skill cannot be the end result of simple instruction. Parents do not explain to their children, for example, that adjectives generally precede the noun in English, nor do they lecture them on the rules governing formation of the past participle. While parents do correct some kinds of mistakes on a piecemeal basis, discovering the underlying rules which make up the language is the child's job.

From what we know, children appear to learn language partly by imitation but even more by hypothesis-testing. Consider a child who is just beginning to form past tenses. In the earliest efforts, the child is likely to produce such incorrect and unheard forms as *I goed to the store* or *I seed a dog*, along with other conventional uses of the past tense: *I walked to Grandma's*. This process reveals that the child has learned the basic, general rule about the formation of the past tense—you add *-ed* to the verb—but has not yet mastered the other rules, the exceptions and irregularities. The production of forms that the child has never heard suggests that imitation is not central in language learning and that the child's main strategy is hypothesizing—deducing from the language she hears an idea about the underlying rule, and then trying it out.

My own son, who is now two-and-a-half, has just been working on the *-ed* problem. Until recently, he used present tense verb forms for all

---

[1] Victoria Fromkin and Robert Rodman, *An Introduction to Language* (New York: Holt, Rinehart and Winston, 1978), 329–342.

situations: *Daddy go work?* (for: *Did Daddy go to work?*) and *We take a bath today?* (for: *Will we take a bath today?*). Once he discovered that wonderful past tag, he attached it with gusto to any verb he could think up and produced, predictably enough, *goed, eated, flied,* and many other overgeneralizations of his initial hypothetical rule for the formation of past tenses. He was so excited about his new discovery, in fact, that he would often give extra emphasis to the marker: *Dad, I swallow-ed the cookie.* Nicky will soon learn to deemphasize the sound of *-ed* (as well as to master all those irregular past forms) by listening to more language and by revising and expanding his own internal set of language rules.

Linguists and educators sometimes debate about what percentage of adult forms is learned by a given age. A common estimate is that 90 percent of adult structures are acquired by the time a child is seven. Obviously, it is quite difficult to attach proportions to such a complex process, but the central point is clear: schoolchildren of primary age have already learned the great majority of the rules governing their native language, and can produce virtually all the kinds of sentences that it permits. With the passing years, all children will add some additional capabilities, but the main growth from this point forward will not so much be in acquiring new rules as in using new combinations of them to express increasingly sophisticated ideas, and in learning how to use language effectively in a widening variety of social settings.

It is important to reiterate that we are talking here about the child's acquisition of her native language. It may be that the child has been born into a community of standard English or French or Urdu speakers, or into a community of nonstandard English, French, or Urdu speakers. But the language of the child's home and community *is* the native language, and it would be impossible for her to somehow grow up speaking a language to which she was never, or rarely, exposed.

2. Language operates by rules. As the *-ed* saga suggests, when a child begins learning his native language, what he is doing is acquiring a vast system of mostly subconscious rules which allow him to make meaningful and increasingly complex utterances. These rules concern sounds, words, the arrangement of strings of words, and aspects of the social act of speaking. Obviously, children who grow up speaking different languages will acquire generally different sets of rules. This fact reminds us that human language is, in an important sense, arbitrary.

Except for a few onomatopoetic words (*bang, hiss, grunt*), the assignment of meanings to certain combinations of sounds is arbitrary. We English speakers might just as well call a chair a *glotz* or a *blurg*, as long as we all agreed that these combinations of sounds meant *chair*. In fact, not just the words but the individual sounds used in English have been arbitrarily selected from a much larger inventory of sounds which the human vocal organs are capable of producing. The existence of African languages employing musical tones or clicks reminds us that the forty phonemes used in English represent an arbitrary selection from hundreds of available sounds. Grammar, too, is arbitrary. We have a rule in English which requires most adjectives to appear before the noun which they modify (*the blue chair*). In French, the syntax is reversed (*la chaise bleue*), and in some languages, like Latin, either order is allowed.

Given that any language requires a complex set of arbitrary choices regarding sounds, words, and syntax, it is clear that the foundation of a language lies not in any "natural" meaning or appropriateness of its features, but in its system of rules—the implicit agreement among speakers that they will use certain sounds consistently, that certain combinations of sounds will mean the same thing over and over, and that they will observe certain grammatical patterns in order to convey messages. It takes thousands of such rules to make up a language. Many linguists believe that when each of us learned these countless rules, as very young children, we accomplished the most complex cognitive task of our lives.

Our agreement about the rules of language, of course, is only a general one. Every speaker of a language is unique; no one sounds exactly like anyone else. The language differs from region to region, between social, occupational and ethnic groups, and even from one speech situation to the next. These variations are not mistakes or deviations from some basic tongue, but are simply the rule-governed alternatives which make up any language. Still, in America our assorted variations of English are mostly mutually intelligible, reflecting the fact that most of our language rules do overlap, whatever group we belong to, or whatever situation we are in.

3. All languages have three major components: a sound system, a vocabulary, and a system of grammar. This statement underscores what has already been suggested: that any human speaker makes meaning by manipulating sounds, words, and their order according to an internalized system of rules which other speakers of that language largely share.

The sound system of a language—its phonology—is the inventory of vocal noises, and combinations of noises, that it employs. Children learn the selected sounds of their own language in the same way they learn the other elements: by listening, hypothesizing, testing, and listening again. They do not, though it may seem logical, learn the sounds first (after all, English has only forty) and then go on to words and then to grammar. My son, for example, can say nearly anything he needs to say, in sentences of eight or ten or fourteen words, but he couldn't utter the sound of *th* to save his life.

The vocabulary, or lexicon, of a language is the individual's storehouse of words. Obviously, one of the young child's most conspicuous efforts is aimed at expanding his lexical inventory. Two- and three-year-olds are notorious for asking "What's that?" a good deal more often than even the most doting parents can tolerate. And not only do children constantly and spontaneously try to enlarge their vocabularies, but they are always working to build categories, to establish classes of words, to add connotative meanings, to hone and refine their sense of the semantic properties—the meanings—of the words they are learning. My awareness of these latter processes was heightened a few months ago as we were driving home from a trip in the country during which Nicky had delighted in learning the names of various features of the rural landscape. As we drove past the Chicago skyline, Nicky looked up at the tall buildings and announced "Look at those silos, Dad!" I asked him what he thought they kept in the Sears Tower, and he replied confidently, "Animal food." His parents' laughter presumably helped him to begin reevaluating his lexical hypothesis that any tall narrow structure was a silo.

Linguists, who look at language descriptively rather than prescriptively, use two different definitions of *grammar*. The first, which I am using, says that grammar is the system of rules we use to arrange words into meaningful English sentences. For example, my lexicon and my phonology may provide me with the appropriate strings of sounds to say the words: *eat four yesterday cat crocodile the*. It is my knowledge of grammar which allows me to arrange these elements into a sentence: *Yesterday the crocodile ate four cats*. Not only does my grammar arrange these elements in a meaningful order, it also provides me with the necessary markers of plurality, tense, and agreement. Explaining the series of rules by which I subconsciously constructed this sentence describes some of my "grammar" in this sense.

The second definition of *grammar* often used by linguists refers to the whole system of rules which makes up a language—not just the rules for the arrangement and appropriate marking of elements in a sentence, but all of the lexical, phonological, and syntactic patterns which a language uses. In this sense, *everything* I know about my language, all the conscious and unconscious operations I can perform when speaking or listening, constitutes my grammar. It is this second definition of grammar to which linguists sometimes refer when they speak of describing a language in terms of its grammar.

4. Everyone speaks a dialect. Among linguists the term *dialect* simply designates a variety of a particular language which has a certain set of lexical, phonological, and grammatical rules that distinguish it from other dialects. The most familiar definition of dialects in America is geographical: we recognize, for example, that some features of New England language—the dropping r's (*pahk the cah in Hahvahd yahd*) and the use of *bubbler* for *drinking fountain*—distinguish the speech of this region. The native speaker of Bostonian English is not making mistakes, of course; he or she simply observes systematic rules which happen to differ from those observed in other regions.

Where do these different varieties of a language come from and how are they maintained? The underlying factors are isolation and language change. Imagine a group of people which lives, works, and talks together constantly. Among them, there is a good deal of natural pressure to keep the language relatively uniform. But if one part of the group moves away to a remote location, and has no further contact with the other, the language of the two groups will gradually diverge. This will happen not just because of the differing needs of the two different environments, but also because of the inexorable and sometimes arbitrary process of language change itself. In other words, there is no likelihood that the language of these two groups, though identical at the beginning, will now change in the same ways. Ultimately, if the isolation is lengthy and complete, the two hypothetical groups will probably develop separate, mutually unintelligible languages. If the isolation is only partial, if interchange occurs between the two groups, and if they have some need to continue communicating (as with the American and British peoples) less divergence will occur.

This same principle of isolation also applies, in a less dramatic way, to contemporary American dialects. New England speakers are partially isolated from southern speakers, and so some of the differences between these two dialects are maintained. Other factors, such as travel and the mass media, bring them into contact with each other and tend to prevent drastic divergences. But the isolation that produces or maintains language differences may not be only geographical. In many American cities we find people living within miles, or even blocks of each other, who speak markedly different and quite enduring dialects. Black English and midwestern English are examples of such pairs. Here, the isolation is partially spatial, but more importantly it is social, economic, occupational, educational, and political. And as long as this effective separation of speech communities persists, so will the differences in their dialects.

Many of the world's languages have a "standard" dialect. In some countries, the term *standard* refers more to a *lingua franca* than to an indigenous dialect. In Nigeria, for example, where there are more than 150 mostly mutually unintelligible languages and dialects, English was selected as the official standard. In America, we enjoy this kind of national standardization because the vast majority of us speak some mutually intelligible dialect of English. But we also have ideas about a standard English which is not just a *lingua franca* but a prestige or preferred dialect. Similarly, the British have Received Pronunciation, the Germans have High German, and the French, backed by the authority of the Académie Française, have "Le Vrai Français." These languages are typically defined as the speech of the upper, or at least educated, classes of the society, are the predominant dialect of written communication, and are commonly taught to schoolchildren. In the past, these prestige dialects have sometimes been markers which conveniently set the ruling classes apart from the rabble—as once was the case with Norman French. But in most modern societies the standard dialect is a mutually intelligible version of the country's common tongue which is accorded a special status.

A standard dialect is not *inherently* superior to any other dialect of the same language. It may, however, confer considerable social, political, and economic power on its users because of prevailing attitudes about the dialect's worthiness.

Recently, American linguists have been working to describe some of the nonstandard dialects of English, and we now seem to have a better description of some of these dialects than of our shadowy standard. Black English is a case in point. The most important finding of all this research has been that Black English is just as "logical" and "ordered" as any other English dialect, in spite of the fact that it is commonly viewed by white speakers as being somehow inferior, deformed, or limited.

5. Speakers of all languages employ a range of styles and a set of subdialects or jargons. Just as soon as we accept the notion that we all speak a dialect, it is necessary to complicate things further. We may realize that we do belong to a speech community, although we may not like to call it a dialect, but we often forget that our speech patterns vary greatly during the course of our everyday routine. In the morning, at home, communication with our spouses may consist of grumbled fragments of a private code:

Uhhh.

Yeah.

More?

Um-hmm.

You gonna...?

Yeah, if...

'Kay.

Yet half an hour later, we may be standing in a meeting and talking quite differently: "The cost-effectiveness curve of the Peoria facility has declined to the point at which management is compelled to consider terminating production." These two samples of speech suggest that we constantly range between formal and informal styles of speech—and this is an adjustment which speakers of all languages constantly make. Learning the sociolinguistic rules which tell us what sort of speech is appropriate in differing social situations is as much a part of language acquisition as learning how to produce the sound of /b/ or /t/. We talk differently to our acquaintances than to strangers, differently to our bosses than to our subordinates, differently to children than to adults. We speak in one way on the racquetball court and in another way in the courtroom; we perhaps talk differently to stewardesses than to stewards.

The ability to adjust our language forms to the social context is something which we acquire as children, along with sounds, words, and syntax. We learn, in other words, not just to say things, but also how and when and to whom. Children discover, for example, that while the purpose of most language is to communicate meaning (if it weren't they could never learn it in the first place), we sometimes use words as mere acknowledgments. (*Hi. How are you doing? Fine. Bye.*) Youngsters also learn that to get what you want, you have to address people as your social relation with them dictates (*Miss Jones, may I please feed the hamster today?*). And, of course, children learn that in some situations one doesn't use certain words at all—though such learning may sometimes seem cruelly delayed to parents whose offspring loudly announce in restaurants: "I hafta go toilet!"

Interestingly, these sociolinguistic rules are learned quite late in the game. While a child of seven or eight does command a remarkably sophisticated array of sentence types, for example, he has a great deal left to learn about the social regulations governing language use. This seems logical, given that children *do* learn language mostly by listening and experimenting. Only as a child grows old enough to encounter a widening range of social relationships and roles will he have the experience necessary to help him discover the sociolinguistic dimensions of them.

While there are many ways of describing the different styles, or registers, of language which all speakers learn, it is helpful to consider them in terms of levels of formality. One well-known example of such a scheme was developed by Martin Joos, who posited five basic styles, which he called *intimate, casual, consultative, formal,* and *frozen*.[2] While Joos's model is only one of many attempts to find a scale for the range of human speech styles, and is certainly not the final word on the subject, it does illuminate some of the ways in which day-to-day language varies. At the bottom of Joos's model is the *intimate* style, a kind of language which "fuses two separate personalities" and can only occur between individuals with a close personal relationship. A husband and wife, for example, may sometimes speak to each other in what sounds like a very fragmentary and clipped code that they alone understand. Such utterances are characterized by their "extraction"—the use of extracts of potentially complete sentences, made possible by an intricate, personal, shared system of private symbols. The *intimate* style, in sum, is personal, fragmentary, and implicit.

The *casual* style also depends on social groupings. When people share understandings and meanings which are not complete enough to be called intimate, they tend to employ the *casual* style. The earmarks of this pattern are ellipsis and slang. Ellipsis is the shorthand of shared meaning; slang often expresses these meanings in a way that defines the group and excludes others. The *casual* style is reserved for friends and insiders, or those whom we choose to make friends and insiders. The *consultative* style "produces cooperation without the integration, profiting from the lack of it."[3] In this style, the speaker provides more explicit background information because the listener may not understand without it. This is the style used by strangers or near-strangers in routine transactions: co-workers dealing with a problem, a buyer making a purchase from a clerk, and so forth. An important feature of this style is the participation of the listener, who uses frequent interjections such as *Yeah, Uh-huh,* or *I see* to signal understanding.

---

[2] Martin Joos, *The Five Clocks* (New York: Harcourt, Brace and World, 1962).
[3] Ibid., 40.

This element of listener participation disappears in the *formal* style. Speech in this mode is defined by the listener's lack of participation, as well as by the speaker's opportunity to plan his utterances ahead of time and in detail. The *formal* style is most often found in speeches, lectures, sermons, television newscasts, and the like. The *frozen* style is reserved for print, and particularly for literature. This style can be densely packed and repacked with meanings by its "speaker," and it can be read and reread by its "listener." The immediacy of interaction between the participants is sacrificed in the interests of permanence, elegance, and precision.

Whether or not we accept Joos's scheme to classify the different gradations of formality, we can probably sense the truth of the basic proposition: we do make such adjustments in our speech constantly, mostly unconsciously, and in response to the social situation in which we are speaking. What we sometimes forget is that no one style can accurately be called better or worse than another, apart from the context in which it is used. Though we have much reverence for the formal and frozen styles, they can be utterly dysfunctional in certain circumstances. If I said to my wife: "Let us consider the possibility of driving our automobile into the central business district of Chicago in order to contemplate the possible purchase of denim trousers," she would certainly find my way of speaking strange, if not positively disturbing. All of us need to shift between the intimate, casual, and consultative styles in everyday life, not because one or another of these is a better way of talking, but because each is required in certain contexts. Many of us also need to master the formal style for the talking and writing demanded by our jobs. But as Joos has pointed out, few of us actually need to control the frozen style, which is reserved primarily for literature.[4]

Besides having a range of speech styles, each speaker also uses a number of jargons based upon his or her affiliation with certain groups. The most familiar of these jargons are occupational: doctors, lawyers, accountants, farmers, electricians, plumbers, truckers, and social workers each have a job-related jargon into which they can shift when the situation demands it. Sometimes these special languages are a source of amusement or consternation to outsiders, but usually the outsiders also speak jargons of their own, though they may not recognize them. Jargons may also be based on other kinds of affiliations. Teenagers, it is often remarked by bemused parents, have a language of their own. So they do, and so do other age groups. Some of the games and chants of youngsters reflect a kind of childhood dialect, and much older persons may have a jargon of their own as well, reflecting concerns with aging, illness, and finances. Sports fans obviously use and understand various abstruse athletic terms, while people interested in needlecrafts use words that are equally impenetrable to the uninitiated. For every human enterprise we can think of, there will probably be a jargon attached to it.

---

[4] Ibid., 39–67.

But simply noting that all speakers control a range of styles and a set of jargons does not tell the whole story. For every time we speak, we do so not just in a social context, but for certain purposes of our own. When talking with a dialectologist, for example, I may use linguistic jargon simply to facilitate our sharing of information, or instead to convince him that I know enough technical linguistics to be taken seriously—or both. In other words, my purposes—the functions of my language—affect the way I talk. The British linguist M. A. K. Halliday has studied children in an attempt to determine how people's varying purposes affect their speech.[5] Halliday *had* to consider children, in fact, because the purposes of any given adult utterance are usually so complex and overlapping that it is extremely difficult to isolate the individual purposes. By examining the relatively simpler language of children, he was able to discover seven main uses, functions, or purposes for talking: *instrumental, regulatory, interactional, personal, heuristic, imaginative,* and *representational.*

The *instrumental* function, Halliday explains, is for getting things done; it is the *I want* function. Close to it is the *regulatory* function, which seeks to control the actions of others around the speaker. The *interactional* function is used to define groups and relationships, to get along with others. The *personal* function allows people to express what they are and how they feel; Halliday calls this the *here I come* function. The *heuristic* function is in operation when the speaker is using language to learn, by asking questions and testing hypotheses. In the *imaginative* function, a speaker may use language to create a world just as he or she wants it, or may simply use it as a toy, making amusing combinations of sounds and words. In the *representational* function, the speaker uses language to express propositions, give information, or communicate subject matter.

Absent from Halliday's list of functions, interestingly, is one of the most common and enduring purposes of human language: lying. Perhaps lying could be included in the representational or interactional functions, in the sense that a person may deceive in order to be a more congenial companion. Or perhaps each of Halliday's seven functions could be assigned a reverse, false version. In any case, common sense, human history, and our own experience all tell us that lying—or misleading or covering up or shading the truth—is one of the main ends to which language is put.

As we look back over these three forms of language variation—styles, jargons, and functions—we may well marvel at the astounding complexity of language. For not only do all speakers master the intricate sound, lexical, and grammatical patterns of their native tongue, but they also learn countless, systematic alternative ways of applying their linguistic

---

[5] M. A. K. Halliday, *Explorations in the Functions of Language* (London: Edward Arnold, 1973).

knowledge to varying situations and needs. We are reminded, in short, that language is as beautifully varied and fascinating as the creatures who use it.

6. Language change is normal. This fact, while often acknowledged by critics of contemporary English, has rarely been fully understood or accepted by them. It is easy enough to welcome into the language such innocent neologisms as *astronaut, transistor*, or *jet lag*. These terms serve obvious needs, responding to certain changes in society which virtually require them. But language also changes in many ways that don't seem so logical or necessary. The dreaded dangling *hopefully*, which now attaches itself to the beginning of sentences with the meaning *I hope*, appears to be driving out the connotation *full of hope*. As Jean Stafford has angrily pointed out, the word *relevant* has broadened to denote almost any kind of "with-it-ness." But these kinds of lexical changes are not new, and simply demonstrate an age-old process at work in the present. The word *dog* (actually, *dogge*), for example, used to refer to one specific breed, but now serves as a general term for a quite varied family of animals. Perhaps similarly, *dialogue* has now broadened to include exchanges of views between (or among) any number of speakers. But word meanings can also narrow over time, as the word *deer* shrank from indicating any game animal to just one specific type.

The sounds of language also change, though usually in slower and less noticeable ways than vocabulary. Perhaps fifty years ago, the majority of American speakers produced distinctly different consonant sounds in the middle of *latter* and *ladder*. Today, most younger people and many adults pronounce the two words as if they were the same. Another sound change in progress is the weakening distinction between the vowel sounds in *dawn* and *Don*, or *hawk* and *hock*. Taking the longer view, of course, we realize that modern pronunciation is the product of centuries of gradual sound changes.

Shifts in grammar are more comparable to the slow process of sound change than the sometimes sudden one of lexical change. Today we find that the *shall/will* distinction, which is still maintained among some upper-class Britishers, has effectively disappeared from spoken American English. A similar fate seems to await the *who/whom* contrast, which is upheld by fewer and fewer speakers. Our pronouns, as a matter of fact, seem to be a quite volatile corner of our grammar. In spite of the efforts of teachers, textbooks, style manuals, and the SAT tests, most American speakers now find nothing wrong with *Everyone should bring their books to class* or even *John and me went to the Cubs game*. And even the hoary old double negative (which is an obligatory feature of degraded tongues like French) seems to be making steady, if slow progress. We may be only a generation or two from the day when we will again say, with Shakespeare, "I will not budge for no man's pleasure."

While we may recognize that language does inexorably change, we cannot always explain the causes or the sequences of each individual change.

Sometimes changes move toward simplification, as with the shedding of vowel distinctions. Other changes tend to regularize the language, as when we de-Latinize words like *medium/media* (*The newspapers are one media of communication*), or when we abandon *dreamt* and *burnt* in favor of the regular forms *dreamed* and *burned*. And some coinages will always reflect the need to represent new inventions, ideas, or events: *quark, simulcast, pulsar, stagflation*. Yet there is plenty of language change which seems to happen spontaneously, sporadically, and without apparent purpose. Why should *irregardless* substitute for *regardless*, meaning the same thing? Why should handy distinctions like that between *imply* and *infer* be lost? But even if we can never explain the reasons for such mysterious changes—or perhaps *because* we can't—we must accept the fact that language does change. Today, we would certainly be thought odd to call cattle *kine*, to pronounce *saw* as *saux*, or to ask about "thy health," however ordinary such language might have been centuries ago. Of course, the more recent changes, and especially the changes in progress, make us most uncomfortable.

But then our sense of the pace of language change is often exaggerated. When we cringe (as do so many of the language critics) at the sudden reassignment of the word *gay* to a new referent, we tend to forget that we can still read Shakespeare. In other words, even if many conspicuous (and almost invariably lexical) changes are in progress, this doesn't necessarily mean that the language as a whole is undergoing a rapid or wholesale transformation.

However, once we start looking for language change, it seems to be everywhere, and we are sorely tempted to overestimate its importance. Sometimes we even discover changes which aren't changes at all. Various language critics have propounded the notion that we are being inundated by a host of very new and particularly insidious coinages. Here are some of the most notorious ones, along with the date of their earliest citation in the *Oxford English Dictionary* for the meaning presently viewed as modern and dangerous: *you know* (1350); *anxious* for *eager* (1742); *between you and I* (1640); *super* for *good* (1850); *decimate* for *diminish* by other than one-tenth (1663); *inoperative* for nonmechanical phenomena (1631); *near-perfect* for *nearly perfect* (1635); *host* as in *to host a gathering* (1485); *gifted*, as in *He gifted his associates* (1660); *aggravate* for *annoy* (1611).[6]

If we find ourselves being aggravated (or annoyed) by any of these crotchety old neologisms, we can always look to the Mobil Oil Corporation for a comforting discussion of the problem. In one of its self-serving public service magazine ads, Mobil intoned: "Change upsets people. Always has. Disrupts routine and habit patterns. Demands constant adaptation. But

---

[6] With many thanks to Jim Quinn and his *American Tongue and Cheek* (New York: Pantheon, 1981).

change is inevitable. And essential. Inability to change can be fatal."[7] And Mobil inadvertently gives us one last example of a language change currently in progress: the increasing use of sentence fragments in formal written English.

7. Languages are intimately related to the societies and individuals who use them. Every human language has been shaped by, and changes to meet, the needs of its speakers. In this limited sense, all human languages can be said to be both equal and perfect. Some Eskimo languages, for example, have many words for different types of snow: wet snow, powdery snow, blowing snow, and so forth. This extensive vocabulary obviously results from the importance of snow in the Eskimo environment and the need to be able to talk about it in detailed ways. In Chicago, where snow is just an occasional annoyance, we get along quite nicely with a few basic terms—snow, slush, and sleet—and a number of adjectival modifiers. Richard Mitchell has described a hypothetical primitive society where the main preoccupation is banging on tree-bark to harvest edible insects, and this particular people has developed a large, specialized vocabulary for talking about the different kinds of rocks and trees involved in this process. In each of these cases, the language in question is well adapted to the needs of its speakers. Each language allows its speakers to easily talk about whatever it is important to discuss in that society.

This does not mean, however, that any given language will work "perfectly" or be "equal" to any other in a cross-cultural setting. If I take my Chicago dialect to the tundra, I may have trouble conversing with people who distinguish, in Eskimo, ten more kinds of snow than I do. Or if one of Mitchell's tree-bangers came to Chicago, his elaborate rock-and-bark vocabulary would be of little use. Still, neither of these languages is inherently inferior or superior; inside its normal sphere of use, each is just what it needs to be.

There is a related question concerning the differences between languages. Many linguists have tried to determine the extent to which our native language conditions our thought processes. For all the talk of similarities between languages, there are also some quite remarkable differences from one language to another. The famous studies of American Indian languages by Benjamin Lee Whorf and Edward Sapir have suggested, for example, that Hopi speakers do not conceptualize time in the same way as speakers of English.[8] To the Hopi, time is a continuing process, an unfolding that cannot be segmented into chunks to be used or "wasted." The words and constructions of the Hopi language reflect this perception. Similarly, some languages do not describe the same color spectrum which we speakers of English normally regard as a given

---

[7] "Business Is Bound to Change," Mobil Oil advertisement, *Chicago Tribune*, January 5, 1977.

[8] See Edward Sapir, *Culture, Language, and Personality* (Berkeley: University of California Press, 1949).

physical phenomenon. Some of these name only two, others three, and so on. Are we, then, hopelessly caught in the grasp of the language which we happen to grow up speaking? Are all our ideas about the world controlled by our language, so that our reality is what we *say* rather than what objectively, verifiably exists?

The best judgment of linguists on this subject comes down to this: we are conditioned to some degree by the language we speak, and our language does teach us habitual ways of looking at the world. But on the other hand, human adaptability enables us to transcend the limitations of a language—to learn to see the world in new ways and voice new concepts—when we must. While it is probably true that some ideas are easier to communicate in one language than another, both languages and speakers can change to meet new needs. The grip which language has on us is firm, but it does not strangle; we make language more than language makes us.

It is also important to realize that a language is not just an asset of a culture or group, but of individual human beings. Our native language is the speech of our parents, siblings, friends, and community. It is the code we use to communicate in the most powerful and intimate experiences of our lives. It is a central part of our personality, an expression and a mirror of what we are and wish to be. Our language is as personal and as integral to each of us as our bodies and our brains, and in our own unique ways, we all treasure it. And all of us, when we are honest, have to admit that criticism of the way we talk is hard not to take personally. This reaction is nothing to be ashamed of: it is simply a reflection of the natural and profound importance of language to every individual human being.

To summarize: all human languages and the concept systems which they embody are efficient in their native speech communities. The languages of the world also vary in some important ways, so that people sometimes falsely assume that certain tongues are inherently superior to others. Yet it is marvelous that these differences exist. It is good that the Eskimo language facilitates talk about snow, that the Hopi language supports that culture's view of time, and I suppose, that Chicago speech has ample resources for discussing drizzle, wind, and inept baseball teams.

8. Value judgments about different languages or dialects are matters of taste. One of the things we seem to acquire right along with our native tongue is a set of attitudes about the value of other people's language. If we think for a moment about any of the world's major languages, we will find that we usually have some idea—usually a prejudice or stereotype— about it. French is the sweet music of love. German is harsh, martial, overbearing. The language of Spain is exotic, romantic. The Spanish of Latin Americans is alien, uneducated. Scandinavian tongues have a kind of silly rhythm, as the Muppet Show's Swedish chef demonstrates weekly. British English is refined and intelligent. New York dialect (especially on Toity-Toid Street) is crude and loud. Almost all southern American speakers (especially rural sheriffs) are either cruelly crafty or just plain dumb. Oriental languages have a funny, high-pitched, singsong sound. And Black English, well, it just goes to show. None of these notions about different languages and dialects says anything about the way these tongues function in their native speech communities. By definition—by the biological and social order of things—they function efficiently. Each is a fully formed, logical, rule-governed variant of human speech.

It is easy enough to assert that all languages are equal and efficient in their own sphere of use. But most of us do not really believe in this idea, and certainly do not act as if we did. We constantly make judgments about other people and other nations on the basis of the language they use. Especially when we consider the question of mutually intelligible American dialects, we are able to see that most ideas about language differences are purely matters of taste. It isn't that we cannot understand each other—Southerners, Northerners, Californians, New Yorkers, blacks, whites, Appalachian folk—with only the slightest effort we can communicate just fine. But because of our history of experiences with each other, or perhaps just out of perversity, we have developed prejudices toward other people's language which sometimes affect our behavior. Such prejudices, however irrational, generate much pressure for speakers of disfavored dialects to abandon their native speech for some approved pattern. But as the linguist Einar Haugen has warned:

> And yet, who are we to call for linguistic genocide in the name of efficiency? Let us recall that although a language is a tool and an instrument of communication, that is not all it is. A language is also a part of one's personality, a form of behavior that has its roots in our earliest experience. Whether it is a so-called rural or ghetto dialect, or a peasant language, or a "primitive" idiom, it fulfills exactly the same needs and performs the same services in the daily lives of its speakers as does the most advanced language of culture. Every language, dialect, patois, or lingo is a structurally complete framework into which can be poured any subtlety of emotion or thought that its users are capable of experiencing. Whatever it lacks at any given time or place in the way of vocabulary and syntax can be supplied in very short order by borrowing and imitation from other languages. *Any scorn for the language of others is scorn for those who use it, and as such is a form of social discrimination.* [Emphasis mine.][9]

It is not Haugen's purpose—nor is it mine—to deny that social acceptability and economic success in America may be linked in certain ways to the mastery of approved patterns of speech. Yet all of us must realize that the need for such mastery arises *only* out of the prejudices of the dominant speech community and not from any intrinsic shortcomings of nonstandard American dialects.

---

[9] Einar Haugen, "The Curse of Babel," in Einar Haugen and Morton Bloomfield, *Language as a Human Problem* (New York: W. W. Norton, 1974), 41.

9. Writing is derivative of speech. Writing systems are always based upon systems of oral language which of necessity develop first. People have been talking for at least a half million years, but the earliest known writing system appeared fewer than 5,000 years ago. Of all the world's languages, only about 5 percent have developed indigenous writing systems. In other words, wherever there are human beings, we will always find language, but not necessarily writing. If language is indeed a biologically programmed trait of the species, writing does not seem to be part of the standard equipment.

Although the English writing system is essentially phonemic—an attempt to represent the sounds of language in graphic form—it is notoriously irregular and confusing. Some other languages, like Czech, Finnish, and Spanish, come close to having perfect sound-symbol correspondence: each letter in the writing system stands for one, and only one, sound. English, unfortunately, uses some 2,000 letters and combinations of letters to represent its forty or so separate sounds. This causes problems. For example, in the sentence: *Did he believe that Caesar could see the people seize the seas?* there are seven different spellings for the vowel sound /ē/. The sentence: *The silly amoeba stole the key to the machine* yields four more spellings of the same vowel sound. George Bernard Shaw once noted that a reasonable spelling of the word *fish* might be *ghoti: gh* as in *enough, o* as in *women,* and *ti* as in *nation.* In spite of all its irregularities, however, the English spelling system is nevertheless phonemic at heart, as our ability to easily read and pronounce nonsense words like *mimsy* or *proat* demonstrates.

Writing, like speech, may be put to a whole range of often overlapping uses. And shifts in the level of formality occur in writing just as they do in talk. An author, like a speaker, must adjust the style of her message to the audience and the occasion. A woman composing a scholarly article, for example, makes some systematically different linguistic choices than those she makes when leaving a note for her husband on the refrigerator. Both writers and speakers (even good ones) employ various jargons or specialized vocabularies that seem comfortable and convenient to the people they are addressing. Rules change with time in both writing and speech. Most obviously, changes in speech habits are reflected in writing: today we readily pen words which weren't even invented ten or a hundred years ago. And even some of the rules which are enforced in writing after they have been abandoned in speech do eventually break down. Today, for example, split infinitives and sentence fragments are increasingly accepted in writing. Our personal tastes and social prejudices, which often guide our reactions to other people's speech, can also dictate our response to other people's writing.

Our beliefs about writing are also bound up with our literary tradition. We have come to revere certain works of literature and exposition which have "stood the test of time," which speak across the centuries to successive generations of readers. These masterpieces, like most enduring published writing, tend to employ what Joos would call formal and frozen styles of language. They were written in such language, of course, because their authors had to accommodate the subject, audience, and purpose at hand—and the making of sonnets and declarations of independence generally calls for considerable linguistic formality. Given our affection for these classics, we quite naturally admire not only their content but their form. We find ourselves feeling that only in the nineteenth or sixteenth century could writers "really use the language" correctly and beautifully. Frequently, we teach this notion in our schools, encouraging students to see the language of written literature as the only true and correct style of English. We require students not only to mimic the formal literary style in their writing, but even to transplant certain of its features into their speech—in both cases without reference to the *students'* subject, audience, or purpose. All of this is not meant to demean literature or the cultivation of its appreciation among teenagers. It simply reminds us of how the mere existence of a system of writing and a literature can be a conservative influence on the language. The study, occasionally the official worship, of language forms that are both old and formal may retard linguistic changes currently in progress, as well as reinforce our mistaken belief that one style of language is always and truly the best.

The preceding nine ideas about language are not entirely new. Many of them have been proclaimed by loud, if lonely, voices in centuries long past. It has only been in the last seventy or eighty years, however, that these ideas have begun to form a coherent picture of how language works, thanks to the work of the descriptive and historical linguists. It is their research which has been, I hope, accurately if broadly summarized here.

A look at the history of past crises offered a general kind of reassurance about the present language panic. It suggested that such spasms of insecurity and intolerance are a regular, cyclical feature of the human chronicle, and result more from social and political tensions than from actual changes in the language. The review of research presented in this section broadens that perspective and deflates the urgency of the 1983-model literary crisis in some other ways. It shows us that our language cannot "die" as long as people speak it; that language change is a healthy and inevitable process; that all human languages are rule governed, ordered, and logical; that variations between different groups of speakers are normal and predictable; that all speakers employ a variety of speech forms and styles in response to changing social settings; and that most of our attitudes about language are based upon social rather than linguistic judgments.

And so, if we are to believe the evidence of historical and linguistic research, our current language crisis seems rather curious. This is a crisis which is not critical, which does not actually pose the dangers widely attributed to it. If anything, the crisis is merely a description of linguistic business as usual, drawn by the critics in rather bizarre and hysterical strokes. It seems fair to ask at this point: What's the problem?

$$\equiv$$

FOR DISCUSSION AND REVIEW

1. In presenting his "nine ideas about language," Daniels attempts to dispel some commonly held but inaccurate beliefs about language. List as many of these myths as you can. How successful is Daniels in dispelling them?

2. As Daniels notes, children learn relatively late the "rules" about the kinds of speech that are appropriate in various circumstances. From your own experience, give some examples of children's use of language that, given the social context, was inappropriate.

3. You probably would describe a particular event—for example, a party, a camping trip, an evening with a friend—differently to different people. Jot down the way you would tell a good friend about some event. Then write down the way you would describe the same occurrence to your parents. When you compare the two accounts, what differences do you find? Are they the differences Daniels leads you to expect?

4. Daniels believes that most people have "some idea—usually a prejudice or stereotype"—about different languages and dialects. Define the terms *prejudice* and *stereotype*. Then test Daniels's theory by asking five people what they think of (a) the languages and dialects or (b) the speakers of the languages and dialects Daniels mentioned under point 8 on pp. 16–17. Study the responses, and describe any prejudices or stereotypes you find.

5. Daniels notes that many different dialects exist within American English. Are you aware of dialect differences? For instance, do you drink pop but know other people who drink soda? List some words or phrases you use that you know have an alternative in another part of the United States. If you can, do the same for other languages you or your classmates use.

Language: An Introduction

W. F. Bolton

The ability to use language is the most distinctive human characteristic, and yet most people take this ability for granted, never considering its richness and complexity. In the following selection, from his book A Living Language *(1981), Professor W. F. Bolton analyzes the intricate physiological mechanisms involved in speech production and in speech reception, or hearing. Especially interesting is his discussion of the differences between "speech breathing" and "quiet breathing." Professor Bolton also explains the "design features" that characterize human language; this explanation is important for understanding many of the later selections in this book. His concluding warning against ethnocentricity remains important today.*

Language is so built into the way people live that it has become an axiom of being human. It is the attribute that most clearly distinguishes our species from all others; it is what makes possible much of what we do, and perhaps even what we think. Without language we could not specify our wishes, our needs, the practical instructions that make possible cooperative endeavor ("You hold it while I hit it"). Without language we would have to grunt and gesture and touch rather than tell. And through writing systems or word of mouth we are in touch with distant places we will never visit, people we will never meet, a past and a future of which we can have no direct experience. Without language we would live in isolation from our ancestors and our descendants, condemned to learn only from our own experiences and to take our knowledge to the grave.

Of course other species communicate too, sometimes in ways that seem almost human. A pet dog or cat can make its needs and wishes known quite effectively, not only to others of its own species but to its human owner. But is this language? Porpoises make extremely complex sequences of sounds that may suggest equally complex messages, but so far no way has been found to verify the suggestion. Chimpanzees have been taught several humanly understandable languages, notably AMESLAN [American Sign Language] and a computer language, but there has been heated debate whether their uses of these languages are like ours or merely learned performances of rather greater subtlety than those of trained circus animals. If the accomplishments of dolphins and chimpanzees remain open questions, however, there is no question but that human uses of language, both everyday and in the building of human cultures, are of a scope and power unequaled on our planet.

It seems likely that language arose in humans about a hundred thousand years ago. How this happened is at least as unknowable as how the universe began, and for the same reason: there was nobody there capable of writing us a report of the great event. Language, like the universe, has its creation myths; indeed, in St. John's Gospel both come together in the grand formulation, "In the beginning was the Word, and the Word was with God, and the Word was God." Modern linguists, like modern cosmologists, have adopted an evolutionary hypothesis. Somehow, over the millennia, both the human brain and those parts of the human body now loosely classed as the organs of speech have evolved so that speech is now a part of human nature. Babies start to talk at a certain stage of their development, whether or not their parents consciously try to teach them; only prolonged isolation from the sounds of speech can keep them from learning.

Writing is another matter. When the topic of language comes up, our first thoughts are likely to be of written words. But the majority of the world's languages have never been reduced to writing (though they all could be), and illiteracy is a natural state: we learn to write only laboriously and with much instruction. This is hardly surprising, since compared with speech, writing is a very recent invention—within the past 5,000 years. Still more recently there have been invented complex languages of gesture for use by and with people unable to hear or speak; these too must be painstakingly learned. What do the spoken, written, and sign languages have in common that distinguishes them from other ways to communicate?

PROPERTIES OF LANGUAGE

Perhaps the most distinctive property of language is that its users can create sentences never before known, and yet perfectly understandable to their hearers and readers. We don't have to be able to say "I've heard that one before!" in order to be able to say, "I see what you mean." And so language can meet our expressive needs virtually without limit, no matter how little we have read or heard before, or what our new experiences call on us to express. Another way of describing this property is to say that language is *productive*. We take this productivity for granted in our uses of language, but in fact it is one of the things that make human communication unique.

Less obvious is the fact that language is *arbitrary*: the word for something seldom has any necessary connection with the thing itself. We say *one, two, three*—but the Chinese say *yi, er, san*. Neither language has the "right" word for the numerals, because there is no such thing. (It might seem that a dog's barking, or a blackbird's call, were equally arbitrary, as both might be translated into various languages as "Go away!" or "Allez-vous-en!"—but within the species the sound is universally understandable. A chow and a German shepherd understand each other without translation—unlike speakers of Chinese and German.)

Even the sounds of a language are arbitrary. English can be spoken using only 36 significantly different sounds, and these are not all the same as the sounds needed to speak other languages. These 36 sounds are in turn arbitrarily represented by 26 letters, some standing for two or more sounds, others overlapping. (Consider *c*, *s*, and *k*.) And the patterns into which these sounds, and indeed words, may be arranged are also arbitrary. We all know too well what *tax* means, but, in English at least, there is no such word as *xat*. In English we usually put an adjective before its noun—*fat man*; in French it's the other way round, *homme gros*. This patterning is the key to the productivity of language. If we use intelligible words in proper patterns, we can be sure of being understood by others who speak our language. Indeed, we seem to understand nonsense, provided it is fitted into proper patterns—the silly nonsense of doubletalk, the impressive nonsense of much bureaucratese.

This ability to attach meaning to arbitrary clusters of sounds or words is like the use and understanding of symbolism in literature and art. The word *one* does not somehow represent the numeral, somehow embody its essence the way a three-sided plane figure represents the essence of triangularity. Rather, *one* merely stands for the prime numeral 1, giving a physical form to the concept, just as the word *rosebuds* gives a physical form to the concept "the pleasures of youth" in the poetic line, "Gather ye rosebuds while ye may." Thus the sound /wʌn/, spelled *one*, has a dual quality as a sound and as a concept. This can be seen from the fact that /wʌn/, spelled *won*, matches the identical sound to a wholly different concept. This feature of *duality* is both characteristic of and apparently unique in human communication, and so linguists use it as a test to distinguish language from other kinds of communication in which a sound can have only a single meaning. (Such sounds are called signs, to distinguish them from the symbols that are human words.)

Sounds can be made into meaningful combinations, such as language, only if they are first perceived as meaningfully distinct, or *discrete*. We can find an analogy in music. Musical pitch rises continuously without steps from the lowest frequency we can hear to the highest, sliding upward like the sound of a siren. But most of music is not continuous; it consists of notes that move upwards in discrete steps, as in a scale (from *scalae*, the Latin for "stairs"). This is why we can talk about notes being the same or different, as we could not easily do if all possible tones from low to high were distributed along a continuous line. Similarly, in speech we can slide through all the vowels from "ee" in the front of the mouth to "aw" in the throat—but then how could we tell *key* from *Kay* from *coo* from *caw*? Likewise we distinguish between *v* and *f*, so that *view* is different from *few*. But these distinctions are arbitrary. They are not even common to all languages. For example, in German the letters *v* and *f* both represent the sound /f/, the letter *w* represents the sound /v/ — and there is no sound /w/. What all languages do have in common, however, is the property of discreteness.

These four properties, or "design features," of language were first set down by Charles Hockett in 1958 as part of an attempt to see how human language differs from animal communication systems. There are of course other design features — their number has varied from seven to sixteen but these four (discreteness, arbitrariness, duality, and productivity) appear to be the most important. Among the others:

Human language uses the *channel of sound*, generated by the vocal organs and perceived by the ear, as its primary mode. As a consequence, speech is *nondirectional*: anyone within hearing can pick it up, and we can hear from sources which we cannot see. Our hearing, being stereophonic, can also tell from what direction the sound is coming. Also, our language acts *fade rapidly* (unless recorded on tape or in writing). We do not, as a rule, repeat these acts the way animals often do their signals.

In human language, *any speaker can be a listener and any listener can be a speaker*, at least normally. Some kinds of animal communication, such as courtship behavior, are one-way. And we get *feedback* of our own utterances through our ears and through bone conduction. Nonsound animal communication, like the dances of bees, can often only be invisible to the originator of the message.

Our language acts are *specialized*. That is to say, they have to do only with communication; they do not serve any other function. For example, speech is not necessary for breathing, nor is it the same as other sounds we make, such as a laugh or a cry of pain or fear. Of course, such sounds can communicate, but only by accident to those within earshot. Their main purpose is a reflexive one: they happen more or less involuntarily, like the jerk of a tapped knee.

Italian children grow up speaking Italian; Chinese children learn Chinese. *Human language is transmitted by the cultures we live in*, not by our parentage: if the Chinese infant is adopted by an Italian couple living in Italy, he or she will grow up speaking perfect Italian. But a kitten growing up among human beings speaks neither Italian nor Chinese; it says *meow*. Its communication is determined by its genetic makeup, not by its cultural context.

THE PHYSIOLOGY OF SPEECH

Speech is a kind of specialized exhalation, so it follows that we breathe while we speak. But the two sorts of breathing are not at all the same. "Quiet" breathing is more rapid and shallow than breathing during speech. Quiet breathing is also more even and restful than speech breathing, for during speech the air is taken in quickly and then expelled slowly against the resistance of the speech organs. Quiet breathing is mostly through the nose, speech breathing through the mouth. These differences, and others, would normally affect the accumulation of carbon dioxide (CO_2) in the blood, and the level of CO_2 is the main regulator of breathing—the rate or volume of breathing responds to the level of CO_2 so as to keep us from getting too uncomfortable. If we consciously use "speech" breathing but remain silent, we resist this response and our discomfort grows rapidly. That discomfort does not take place during actual speech, however; some other mechanism comes into play.

> Thus, it is quite clear that breathing undergoes peculiar changes during speech. What is astonishing is that man can tolerate these modifications for an apparently unlimited period of time without experiencing respiratory distress, as is well demonstrated by the interminable speech with which many a statesman embellishes his political existence. Cloture is dictated by motor fatigue and limited receptivity in the audience—never by respiratory demands.[1]

Our neural and biochemical makeup is in fact specially adapted so that we can sustain the speech act. Other animal species are equally adapted to their systems of communication, but none of them can be taught ours because ours is species-specific, a set of abilities that have evolved in humankind over a very long time. The evolution has included the most intricate adaptations of the body and its workings, particularly the neural system (including, above all, the brain); the motor system (especially the muscles that the neural system controls); and the sensory system (especially hearing, of course, but also touch).

The speech act involves an input of meaning and an output of sound on the part of the speaker, the reverse on the part of the listener. But a great deal takes place between the input and the output, and it takes place in the brain. That means that the organ for thinking, the brain, is by definition the seat of language. And the brain is also the control center for the intricate virtuoso muscular performance we call speech, commanding the vocal activities and—most important—ensuring their coordination and sequencing.

The brain is not just an undifferentiated mass in which the whole organ does all of its tasks. The different tasks that the brain does are localized, and in a more general way, the whole brain is lateralized. In most people, the right half (or hemisphere) controls the left half of the body and vice versa, and many brain functions are also lateralized. Language is one of them; it is localized in several areas of the left hemisphere. The language centers are not motor control centers for the production of speech. Instead, they are "boardrooms" in which decisions are

---

[1] Eric H. Lenneberg, *Biological Foundations of Language* (New York: John Wiley & Sons, Inc., 1967), 80.

made, decisions that motor control centers in both hemispheres of the brain implement by issuing the orders to the body. The orders are carried by electric impulses from the central nervous system (brain and spinal cord) into the peripheral nervous system (activating the muscles).

Wernicke's area lies in the left hemisphere of the brain, just above the ear. It takes its name from the German Carl Wernicke (1848–1905), who in 1874 showed that damage to that part of the brain leads to a disrupted flow of meaning in speech. A decade earlier the Frenchman Paul Broca (1824–1880) had shown that damage to another area of the left hemisphere, several inches further downward, led instead to disrupted pronunciation and grammar. There are also differences in the areas when it comes to receptive ability: damage to Broca's area does not much affect comprehension, but damage to Wernicke's area disrupts it seriously.

These differences suggest that the two chief language areas of the brain have functions that are distinct but complementary. It seems that the utterance gets its basic structure in Wernicke's area, which sends it on to Broca's area through a bundle of nerve fibers called the *arcuate fasciculus*. In Broca's area the basic structure is translated into the orders of the speech act itself, which go on to the appropriate motor control area for implementation. In reverse order, a signal from the hearing or the visual system (speech or writing) is relayed to Wernicke's area for decoding from language to linguistic meaning. Broca's area, which seems to write the program for the speech act, is not so important to listening or reading as Wernicke's area is.

All of this, naturally, is inferential: the evidence as we know it points to these conclusions, but no one has ever actually seen these brain activities taking place. The conclusions are also incredible. It is difficult to imagine all that activity for a simple "Hi!" But those conclusions are the simplest ones that will account adequately for the evidence.

All sound, whether a cat's meow, a runner's "Hi!," or a sonar beep, is a disturbance of the air or other medium (water, for example) in which it is produced. When the sound is speech it can be studied in terms of its production (articulatory phonetics), its physical properties in the air (acoustic phonetics), or its reception by the ear and other organs of hearing (auditory phonetics). The first of these is the easiest to study without special instruments, and it is the only one of the three that directly involves the motor system.

The vocal organs are those that produce speech. They form an irregular tube from the lungs, the windpipe, the larynx (and the vocal cords it contains), and the throat, to the mouth (including the tongue and lips) and nose [Fig. 2.1]. All the organs except the larynx have other functions, so not all their activities are speech activities. The lungs are central to breathing, for example, to provide oxygen to the blood, and so many animals that cannot speak have lungs. In that sense speech is a secondary function of the lungs and of all the vocal organs; it has been said that they are "vocal organs" only in the sense that the knees are prayer organs. The

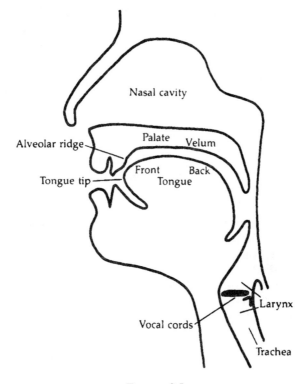

FIGURE 2.1

action of forming the sound we write with the letter *p* is very similar to that of spitting, but *p* is a part of a language system while spitting is not.

Nonetheless, to regard the speech function of these organs as secondary is to overlook the profound language adaptation of the whole human anatomy. The language functions of the motor system are not simply "overlaid" on their other functions, for the language functions in many ways conflict with the others: the tongue is far more agile than is needed for eating, the ear more sensitive than is needed for nonspeech sounds, and the esophagus much too close to the pharynx for safety (hence the need for the Heimlich maneuver). In human beings, there is nothing really secondary about the speech activities of the vocal organs.

The lungs produce a steady stream of exhaled air which the other speech organs specialize into speech. For vowels and for many consonants, the air is set into rapid vibration by the vocal cords in the larynx or "Adam's apple." The more rapid the vibration, the higher the pitch of the speech. The air can also be set in motion by a partial constriction farther up the vocal tract in the mouth, or by a complete stoppage followed by an abrupt release. The vocal cords produce a buzzlike vibration, constriction produces a hissing sound, stoppage and release produce a small explosion. A buzz alone gives us one or another of the vowels, such as the *u* in *buzz.* A stop without buzz will be like the *p* in *stoppage,* with buzz like the *b* in *buzz.*

Whether buzzing or not, the column of air driven by the lungs next passes through the pharynx, a tube that extends from the larynx through the back of the mouth as far as the rear opening of the nasal cavity. The nasal cavity itself is a chamber about four inches long, opening in front at the nostrils and at the rear into the pharynx. The nasal cavity is divided in two by the septum. The nostrils cannot open and close, but the entrance into the pharynx is controlled by the soft palate or velum. The velum is open for *n* and *m* (and often for sounds adjacent to them), closed for other sounds. You can probably feel, or with a mirror even see, the velum open at the end of a word like *hang.*

Within the mouth, the air column is molded by the tongue and the lips. The lips can cause constriction or stoppage; they constrict the air when the upper teeth touch the lower lip to make an *f* or *v* sound, and they stop the air when they close to make a *p* or *b* sound. They also close for the *m* sound, which is emitted through the nose, not the mouth. The lips can further mold the air by rounding, as they do when making the vowel sound in *do* or the consonant sound in *we,* among others.

The tongue—which has a surprising shape for those familiar only with the tip and the upper surface of it—can cause constriction or stoppage of the airflow at any point from the back of the teeth to the roof of the mouth near the velum. Like the lips, the tongue is involved in making both vowel sounds and consonant sounds. It makes both with the tip in a word like *eat.* Or the rear of the tongue can arch up toward the roof of the mouth to make a "back" consonant or vowel. It makes both in a word like *goo.* The tongue can approach the roof of the mouth in other positions farther forward as well, and it can change the shape of the oral cavity in other ways without actually approaching or touching the roof of the mouth.

So the speech sounds are formed in the larynx, in the mouth, and in the nasal cavity. They are formed by the action of the larynx, the velum, the tongue, and the lips. The lips may touch the teeth, and the tongue may touch the teeth or the roof of the mouth. That sounds a trifle complicated, but it is only a small part of what goes on in the motor system. To begin with, all the vocal organs are controlled by muscles, from those that cause the lungs to inhale and exhale air to those that shape the lips in speech. These muscles are not single—a lung muscle, a lip muscle, and so forth—but arranged in intricate groups. In reality, the vocal organs are not only those that articulate but those that activate the articulators.

Other parts of the anatomy too are involved in articulations although we do not usually think of them as vocal organs. The pharynx changes shape as we talk, and so do the cheeks. Some of the vocal organs move in ways that coordinate with articulation but do not seem to be part of it: the larynx moves up and down, for example, in speaking as it does more obviously in swallowing.

Finally, all the vocal organs are in constant motion during speech. The vowels in *house* and in *white* are formed by a change of position in the mouth, not by a single position. And as the mouth moves from the first consonants in these words, through the complex vowel sound, to the final consonants, it is always in motion. What is more, these actions must be coordinated. To take a simple example, the buzz of the larynx must be "on" for the first sounds of *mat* but "off" for the *t*; meanwhile, the mouth closes and the velum opens for the *m*, but they reverse roles for the *a* and *t*. The whole performance adds up to a virtuoso display that far exceeds in complexity . . . the minute adjustments required for even the finest violinist's playing. To observe that "The cat is on the mat" is, from the standpoint of the motor skills required, so demanding that we would think it impossible if we paused to analyze it. We usually do not.

THE SENSORY SYSTEM

In a way, the main sensory system of language, hearing, is the reverse of speech. Speech turns meaning into sound, while hearing turns sound into meaning. Speech encodes meaning as language in the brain, and the brain sends neural messages to the motor system for action; the motor system produces speech. Hearing turns the speech sounds back into neural messages which go to the brain where they are decoded into language and interpreted for meaning.

Sound, as we have seen, is a disturbance of the air—a kind of applied energy. The ear is designed to pick up and process that energy, often in incredibly small amounts. The ear is good not only at amplifying small sounds but at damping loud ones, within limits: a very sudden, very loud noise, or even sound that is not sudden (if it is loud enough), can cause damage to the sensitive sound-gathering mechanisms of the ear, damage which if severe or prolonged can be permanent.

What we usually mean by *ear* is the appendage earrings hang from, but that is only the ear's most visible part. In fact it has three divisions: the outer ear, which extends into the eardrum; the middle ear; and the inner ear. The outer ear collects the sound, passes it through the ear canal, and focuses it on the eardrum. The eardrum is a tightly stretched membrane which is set into motion by the vibrations of sound energy; it is really a "drum" in reverse, for while the bass drum in a marching band converts the energy of motion (a blow from a drumstick) into sound waves, the eardrum converts sound waves into motion energy which is picked up in the middle ear. That motion is carried through the middle ear by three tiny bones; here weak sounds are amplified and very strong sounds are damped. The last of the three bones delivers the sound motion to a membrane called the oval window, which is smaller than the eardrum; the difference in size helps to concentrate the sound energy.

The oval window divides the middle ear from the inner ear. The inner ear is composed of several cavities in the bones of the skull; in one of these, the cochlea, the energy that arrived at the outer ear as sound, and is now motion, will be converted by a set of intricate organs into electrical impulses and fed into the central nervous system for delivery to the auditory center of the brain. The remaining steps in the process are then neural, not sensory.

The process here described, and our idea of hearing in general, relates to sound that reaches us from outside by conduction through the air, water, or other medium. But there is another way in which we can receive sound. A vibrating tuning fork held against the skull will be "heard" by conduction through the bone itself, even if the ear-hole is effectively plugged. Bone-conduction helps us monitor our own speech by providing continuous feedback; thus we can pick out our own words even when surrounded by loud conversation or noise. Bone-conduction has a different sound quality from air-conduction, which is why your voice sounds to you one way when you are speaking and another when you hear it played back from a tape. And bone-conduction can sometimes substitute for air-conduction—for example, when a hearing aid "plays" sound waves directly into the bones of the skull.

LANGUAGE AND CULTURE

Language is species-specific to humankind. By *humankind* we mean the genus *Homo*, species *sapiens*—no other species of this genus survives. Any smaller subdivisions, such as sex or race, may differ among themselves in other very visible ways, but the neural, motor, and sensory equipment necessary to language is common to all. Not that the equipment is identical, otherwise everyone would speak at about the same pitch. But racial, sexual, or individual differences in the shape and size of the nose and lips, or of the internal speech organs, do not override the structural similarity of the vocal organs among all human groups, and they definitely do not result in any functional differences. The members of any group, that is, have the vocal organs to articulate any human language with complete mastery. The same is true of other genetic factors: the intellectual ability to use language is the same in all the varieties of humankind and in all normal individuals.

That is not the same as saying that adult individuals can learn a foreign language as easily as they learned their own in childhood. The physiological habits of the speech organs are complex, and they are learned early. We observe that a native speaker of Chinese has difficulty with the sound of *r* in *very*, a native speaker of Japanese with the sound of *l* in *hello*. That is because their native languages have given them no opportunity to practice those sounds. On the contrary, the languages have reinforced other sounds that tend to crop up when the Chinese speaker attempts English *r* or the Japanese speaker English *l*. The problem, however, is one of habit and not heredity. An American of Chinese ancestry has no trouble with the sounds of English, including *r*, while a person of European ancestry raised to speak Chinese would.

Our virtuosity in our own language carries with it other commitments, some easily understandable and some less so. Speakers of English easily handle a system of pronouns that distinguishes among masculine (*he*), feminine (*she*), and neuter (*it*) forms. They may have trouble with a language like German, however, where the nouns, adjectives, and articles (equivalents of *the* and *a*) make a similar three-way distinction, often in apparent disregard of the sex of the noun—a *maiden* (*das Mädchen*) is neuter, [but changes to feminine] when she becomes a *wife* (*die Frau*)—or with a language like French which makes only a two-way distinction between masculine and feminine, so that *table* is feminine (*la table*) but *floor* is masculine (*le plancher*).

We should not rush to conclude, however, that the Germans and the French see sexual characteristics in inanimate objects or concepts, or do not see them in people. Rather, their languages have grammatical features that English lacks. True, words like *he*, *she*, and *it* do reflect the sex of their antecedent (except for a few oddities, like referring to a ship as "she"). But their equivalents in French and German refer not to sex but to *gender*, which is an entirely linguistic, and therefore arbitrary, matter. No French speaker regards a table as having any feminine properties other than grammatical ones.

In more remote languages the differences are still greater. When a Chinese speaker counts items, he or she puts a "measure word" between the number and the item: "one [measure word] book," and so forth. There is nothing quite like this in English, although when we arrange numbers in order we signify that we are ordering rather than counting by inserting expressions like *number, No.*, or #: "We're number 1," "Love Potion No. Nine," and the like. But our practice is invariable, while the Chinese measure word is not; it varies according to the thing being counted. The most common one is *ga*, "one *ga* book." But for flat objects it is *zhang*, "one *zhang* table"; and for other kinds of objects there are many other measure words. Sometimes it is far from obvious what the objects have in common that makes them take a common measure word: the measure word *ba* is used for both chairs and umbrellas!

This all sounds formidably difficult, but only to us—not to the Chinese. The Mandarin variety of Chinese is the native language of over half a billion people in the world today, and they all master their language at the same rate and by the same age as English speakers do. No language, no matter how strange and difficult it may seem to outsiders, is too hard for its native speakers to master. All languages are systematic, which makes their complexities intelligible to their native speakers, but each system is arbitrary in its own way, which makes it something of a closed book to others.

Equally, no language is especially "simple," if by that word we mean lacking complexity in its phonological and grammatical systems. More likely, people who speak of simplicity in language have a restricted vocabulary in mind. But even this judgment needs to be well-informed if it is to be at all valid. Of course, some languages have larger vocabularies than others; English may comprise half a million words, depending on your manner of counting, while a small tribal group out of touch with the complexities of industrial and urban civilization would probably have a markedly smaller vocabulary. But that vocabulary might be more subtle than English in those areas of thought and experience vital to its users. For example, Eskimos have many different words for different kinds of snow. Moreover, the tribal vocabulary could rapidly expand to deal with new needs as they come along, by borrowing or creating new words. Borrowing, indeed, is one of the most important ways that the English vocabulary has grown to such size. (And, of course, no individual speaker of English has all its half-million words at his or her disposal.)

So the equation of language with culture, one we tend to make, has two possibilities of misleading us. First, we are likely to judge another culture as "simple" because we do not understand it or even know much about it; cultural anthropologists would quickly remedy that error for us. Second, we are likely to think that a "primitive" culture has a primitive language. Yet such remote languages, we now know, seem forbiddingly complex to outsiders who try to learn them.

These attitudes are forms of *ethnocentricity*—a point of view in which one culture is at the center of things and all others are more or less "off the target," either because they never got on target (they are too primitive) or they have wandered away from it (they are decadent). Language is very fertile ground for ethnocentricity. We are quick to judge even small differences from our own variety of English as "wrong," either laughably or disgustingly. When another people's language is different in more than just small ways, we are inclined to doubt the native intelligence of those who use it, its adequacy for serious purposes, or both.

A more enlightened and indeed more realistic view is the opposite of ethnocentricity. It often goes by the name of "cultural relativism," but learning the name is not the same thing as adopting the view. Only an objective eye on the facts, and a careful eye on our own attitudes, will raise us above ethnocentricity.

To compare linguistics with the study of other forms of human behavior is instructive, but a still grander comparison comes to mind: In many ways the study of language is like the study of life itself. Languages, like species, come into being, grow, change, are sometimes grafted to each other, and occasionally become extinct; they have their histories and, in the written record, their fossils. The origins of both life and language, and their processes, are mysteries that can be penetrated (if at all) by reasoning from incomplete and perhaps ultimately inadequate evidence. And linguists, the scientists of language, study language and its environment with a biologist's care and intensity in order to approach an understanding of the nature of language itself—the most characteristic attribute of all humanity.

FOR DISCUSSION AND REVIEW

1. Why is the fact human language is *productive* one of its most distinctive properties? In answering this question, consider both your ability to create sentences you have never seen or heard before and also your ability to understand such sentences.

2. Another important property of human language is that it is *arbitrary*. Discuss the several aspects of language characterized by this property.

3. Two other significant "design features" of human language are *duality* and *discreteness*. One way to be sure that you understand these concepts is to try to explain them in your own words to someone else. Write brief explanations of these two concepts, and ask a friend to evaluate the clarity of your explanations.

4. Review the seven additional "design features" discussed by Bolton. Do they seem to you to be of equal importance? Why, or why not?

5. How does human physiology support the conclusion that speech functions are not simply "overlaid"?

6. Summarize the differences between "quiet" breathing and "speech" breathing. *Without speaking*, use "speech" breathing for at least a minute. Write a brief description of your physical sensations.

7. Explain the functions in the hearing process of (a) the outer ear, (b) the middle ear, and (c) the inner ear.

8. For what reasons does Bolton insist that "all languages are systematic" and that "no language is especially 'simple'"? How is an understanding of these principles important to our understanding of different cultures and their peoples? What is *ethnocentricity*?

9. Bolton asserts that "we seem to understand nonsense, provided it is fitted into proper patterns." Consider the following "nonsense," the opening stanza of "Jabberwocky" by Lewis Carroll (Charles Lutwidge Dodgson [1832–1898]):

> 'Twas brillig, and the slithy toves
>   Did gyre and gimble in the wabe;
> All mimsy were the borogroves,
>   And the mome raths outgrabe.

What do you "know" about the meaning of this stanza? For example, can you identify any nouns? Any verbs? Do you know that something will or did happen? If so, what is that something? Try to describe *how* you "understand" these and other aspects of the stanza.

3

Sign Language

Karen Emmorey

Sound appears to be one of the most obvious properties of language. People speak; people listen and hear. One major branch of linguistics analyzes sound patterns in language; another studies the physiological attributes that allow human beings to produce and receive those patterns. It was a long-held belief that the deaf were disadvantaged in their linguistic capabilities—that sign language was a poor second best to spoken language. In the following 1994 essay, originally published in the Encyclopedia of Human Behavior, *Karen Emmorey, Professor of Speech Language and Director of the Laboratory for Language and Cognitive Neuroscience at San Diego State University, decisively lays to rest the myth that sign language is an inferior form of communication. Basing her conclusions on a study of American Sign Language (ASL), Emmorey finds that sign language shares—albeit in a different format—all the characteristics and complex structural patterns of spoken languages.*

Sign languages are used primarily by deaf people throughout the world. They are languages that have evolved in a completely different medium, using the hands and face rather than the vocal tract and perceived by eye rather than by ear. They have arisen as autonomous languages not derived from spoken language and are passed down from one generation of deaf people to the next. Deaf children with deaf parents acquire sign language in the same way that hearing children learn spoken language. Sign languages are rich and complex linguistic systems which conform to the universal properties found in all human languages. As with spoken language, the left hemisphere of the brain is critically involved in processing sign language, indicating that the general brain basis for language is modality independent. American Sign Language (ASL) is the language used by deaf people in the United States and parts of Canada.

MYTHS ABOUT SIGN LANGUAGE

Myth 1: Sign language is universal. Sign language is *not* a universal language shared by deaf peoples of the world. There are many different sign languages that have evolved independently of each other. Just as spoken languages differ in grammatical structure, in the types of rules that they contain, and in historical relationships, signed languages also differ along these parameters. For example, despite the fact that American Sign Language (ASL) and British Sign Language are surrounded by the same spoken language, they are mutually unintelligible. Sign languages are generally named for the country or area in which they are used (e.g., Austrian Sign Language, German Sign Language, Hong Kong Sign Language). The exact number of sign languages in the world is not known.

Myth 2: Sign language is made up of pictorial gestures and is similar to mime. An important property of human language is that the form of words is generally arbitrary. For example, there is no relation between the English word "frog" or the French word "grenouille" and an actual frog. In contrast, many signs have a discernible relation to the concepts that they denote. For example, the sign for "tree" in American Sign Language is made with the forearm held upright with the fingers spread wide. One could say that the forearm represents the trunk and the fingers represent the branches of the tree. In Danish Sign Language the sign for "tree" differs from the ASL sign, but it also bears a perceptible relation to a tree: the two hands outline the shape of a tree starting with a round top and ending with the trunk. Although both of these signs are iconic and resemble mime, they have been conventionalized in different ways by the two sign languages.

Although some signs have iconic properties, most signs do not bear a clear resemblance to what they denote. For example, the ASL sign for "apple" is made with the knuckle of the index finger touching the cheek and bears no resemblance to an apple or to eating an apple. For most signs, the relationship between the form and the meaning is not transparent. In addition, the iconicity of signs is generally irrelevant to the way the language is organized and processed.

Furthermore, pantomime differs from a linguistic system of signs in important and systematic ways. The space in which signs are articulated is much more restricted than that available for pantomime. For example, pantomime can involve movement of the entire body as well as any part of the body. In contrast, signing is constrained to a space extending from just below the waist to the top of the head, and the entire body is never involved. In addition, sign languages have an intricate compositional structure in which smaller units (such as words) are combined to create higher level structures (such as sentences), and this compositional structure is found at all linguistic levels (phonology, morphology, syntax, and discourse). This complex and hierarchical compositional structure is not present in pantomime.

Myth 3: Sign language is a pidgin form of spoken language using the hands and has no grammar of its own. American Sign Language has been mistakenly thought to be "English on the hands." However, ASL has an independent grammar that is quite different from the grammar of English. For example, ASL allows much freer word order compared to English. English contains tense markers (e.g., -*ed* to express past tense), but ASL (like many languages) does not have tense markers that are part of the morphology of a word; rather tense is expressed lexically (e.g., by adverbs such as "yesterday"). There are no indigenous signed languages that are simply a transformation of a spoken language to the hands.

One might ask "If sign languages are not based on spoken languages, then where did they come from?" However, this question is as difficult to answer as the question "Where did language come from?" We know very little about the very first spoken or signed languages of the world, but research is beginning to uncover the historical relationships between sign languages, as has been done for spoken languages. For example, part of the origin of American Sign Language can be traced to the establishment of a large community of deaf people in France in 1761. These people attended the first public school for the deaf, and the sign language that arose within this community is still used today in France. In 1817, Laurent Clerc, a deaf teacher from this French school, established the first deaf public school in the United States and brought with him French Sign Language. The gestural systems of the American children attending this school mixed with French Sign Language to create a new form that was no longer recognizable as French Sign Language. ASL still contains a historical resemblance to French Sign Language, but both languages are mutually unintelligible.

Myth 4: Sign language cannot convey the same subtleties and complex meanings that spoken languages can. On the contrary, sign languages are equipped with the same expressive power that is inherent in spoken languages. Sign languages can express complicated and intricate concepts with the same degree of explicitness and eloquence as spoken languages. The linguistic structuring which permits such expressive power is described in the next section.

LINGUISTIC STRUCTURE OF AMERICAN SIGN LANGUAGE

American Sign Language is one of the most widely studied sign languages. A brief description of ASL structure is provided here—a complete description would require a large volume (the full characterization of any grammar is lengthy). The description is designed to illustrate that signed languages exhibit the same properties and follow the same universal principles as spoken languages and that signed languages provide unique insight into the nature of language itself.

Phonology

Phonology is the study of the sound patterns found in human languages; it is also the term used to refer to the system of knowledge that speakers have about the sound patterns of their particular language. But do sign languages have a phonology? Is it possible to have a phonological system that is not based on sound? In spoken languages, words are constructed out of sounds which in and of themselves have no meaning. The words "cat" and "pat" differ only in the initial sounds which have no inherent meanings of their own. Sounds may be combined in different ways to create different words: "bad" differs from "dab" only in how the sounds are sequenced. Similarly, signs are constructed out of components that are themselves meaningless and are combined to create words.

Signs are composed of four basic phonological parameters: handshape, location, movement, and palm orientation. American Sign Language contrasts about 36 different handshapes, but not all sign languages share the same handshape inventory. For example, the "t" handshape in ASL (the thumb is inserted between the index and middle fingers of a fist) is not used by Danish Sign Language; Swedish Sign Language contains a handshape formed with an open hand with all fingers extended except for the ring finger which is bent—this hand configuration is not used in ASL. Figure 3.1A illustrates three ASL signs that differ only in handshape. Signs also differ according to where they are made on the body or face. Figure 3.1B shows three signs that differ only in location. Movement is another contrasting phonological parameter that distinguishes minimally between signs as shown in Figure 3.1C. Several different path movement types occur in ASL, e.g., circling, arc, straight; and signs can contain "internal" movement such as wiggling of the fingers or changes in handshape. Finally, signs can differ solely in the orientation of the palm; for example, the sign WANT (signs are notated as English glosses in uppercase) is produced with a spread hand with the palm up, and FREEZE is produced with the same handshape and movement (bending of the fingers and movement toward the body), but the palm is facing downward. These meaningless phonological elements are combined and sequenced to create lexical signs.

ASL exhibits other phonological properties that were once thought to be only found in speech. For example, ASL contains phonological rules similar to those found in spoken languages. ASL contains deletion rules in which an element (such as a movement or a handshape) is deleted from a sign and assimilation rules in which one element is made more similar to a neighboring element. ASL signs also have a level of syllabic structure which is governed by rules similar to those that apply to syllables in spoken languages. The fact that signed languages exhibit phonological properties despite the completely different set of articulators (e.g., the hands vs. the tongue) attests to the universality and abstractness of sublexical structure in human languages.

Morphology

ASL contains the same basic form classes as spoken languages, nouns, verbs, adjectives, pronouns, and adverbs, but it has a very different system

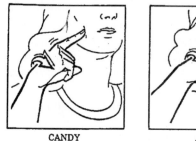
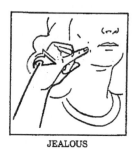

CANDY   APPLE   JEALOUS

Signs contrasting only in hand configuration

FIGURE 3.1A

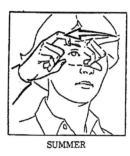

SUMMER   UGLY   DRY

Signs contrasting only in place of articulation

FIGURE 3.1B

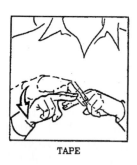
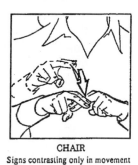

TAPE   CHAIR   TRAIN

Signs contrasting only in movement

FIGURE 3.1C

FIGURE 3.1   Illustration of Part of the Phonological System of American Sign Language. These signs contrast the different phonological parameters of ASL, which are themselves meaningless but can be combined to create lexically meaningful signs.

of word formation. In English and in most spoken languages, morphologically complex words are most often formed by adding prefixes or suffixes to a word stem. In ASL, these forms are created by nesting a sign stem within dynamic movement contours and planes in space. Figure 3.2A

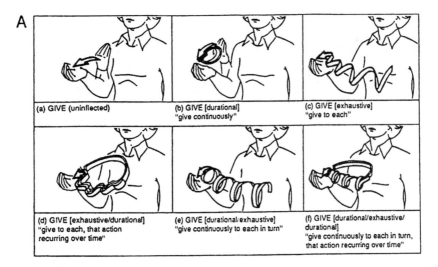

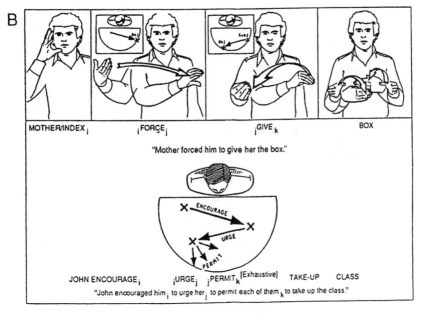

FIGURE 3.2 Morphology and Syntax in American Sign Language (A) The uninflected sign GIVE is illustrated in (a), and GIVE with single inflections is shown in (b) and (c). The figure shows different embedded combinations of inflections which have distinct meanings (d, e, and f). Note that these inflections are produced simultaneously rather than as prefixes or suffixes. (B) Syntactic spatial mechanisms in ASL. The figure illustrates the association of nouns with loci in space (indicated by subscripts), and movements of verbs between these loci (indicated by arrows). The spatial endpoints of these verbs agree with the spatial loci established for the subject and object of the sentence.

illustrates the base form GIVE along with several inflected forms which can be embedded within one another and which convey slightly different meanings. ASL has many verbal inflections which convey temporal information about the action, e.g., whether the action was habitual, iterative, or continual. These inflections do not occur in English, but they are found in other languages of the world.

Another set of inflections applies to a subset of ASL verbs and indicates the subject and/or object of the verb (see Fig. 3.2B). In ASL, noun phrases are associated with points in a plane of signing space, and verbs can move between these spatial points to indicate the subject or object. For example, if MOTHER has been associated with a point on the signer's right and BOY with a point on the signer's left, then if the verb FORCE moves from right to left, it would mean "She forces him" (see Fig. 3.2B). If the verb were to move left to right, it would mean "He forces her." The first spatial endpoint of the verb agrees with the subject, and the final endpoint agrees with the object; thus, these verbs are called "agreeing" verbs. Other inflections can also be added to indicate plural objects or reciprocal ("each other").

Like English, ASL has rules that govern how compound nouns and verbs are formed. An example of an English compound is the word "blackboard" which does not mean a board that is black (blackboards can even be white) and which has a different stress pattern than the phrase "black board." ASL compounds also have different meanings and stress patterns compared to noun phrases. For example, the ASL compound BLACK-NAME which means "bad reputation" is formed by combining the sign BLACK with the sign NAME. In isolation the sign NAME contains two beats, but within the compound it contains only one beat. Compounding is a common morphological process in ASL, as it is in many languages.

Finally, ASL does not have many prepositions, and instead encodes spatial relations through morphological devices. ASL uses a system of classifiers which are pronominal forms that classify an object according to its semantic and/or visual-geometric properties. Many of the world's languages have classifier systems (especially Bantu languages) in which a different pronoun is used for humans, for animals, for inanimate objects, etc. ASL classifiers are embedded in verbs of motion and location which describe the movement and position of objects and/or people in space. For example, to express "the bicycle is beside the fence" a vehicle classifier is used for bicycle and is positioned in space next to a visual-geometric classifier for fence ("long-sectioned-rectangular object"). The ASL expression tends to be much more explicit compared to the English preposition "beside" because the ASL classifier verbs of location also indicate the orientation and precise location of the fence and bicycle with respect to each other (e.g., whether the bicycle is close to the fence, facing the fence, etc.). Again, although this system appears mimetic, it is not. ASL expressions of location and motion have an internal structure comprised of a limited set of movements, locations, and manners of movement which are constrained by linguistic rules.

Syntax

The basic canonical word order for ASL is subject–verb–object; however, ASL word order is much more flexible compared to English. ASL morphology can mark the relationship between words, and ASL does not need to rely on word order to convey grammatical relations such as subject or object. For example, the object of the verb can appear as the first word of the sentence, if it is morphologically marked as a topic, e.g., CAT (topic), DOG CHASE. "As for the cat, the dog chased it." Topics are distinguished by a specific facial expression (see below). Similar to Italian and unlike English, ASL allows "subjectless" sentences. For example, it is possible to sign the following: TODAY SUNDAY. MUST VISIT MY MOTHER. In English these two sentences would require subjects (subjects are bolded): "Today, **it**'s Sunday. **I** must visit my mother." The constraint on overt subjects is just one of the ways in which the syntax of ASL differs from English (but is similar to other languages).

Personal pronouns in ASL are expressed with either a flat handshape (fingers together) to indicate possessive case ("my," "your") or with a closed fist and extended index finger (pointing) to indicate nominative ("I," "you"). For referents that are physically present, the pronominal sign is directed at the physical referent; thus, first-person reference is made by the signer pointing to his or her own chest, and second-person pronominal reference is made by pointing to the addressee's chest. Similarly, when referents are actually present, third-person pronouns are produced by pointing to the appropriate persons. Although these pronoun signs appear to be simple pointing gestures, they are not. The ASL system of pronouns has the same grammatical properties found in spoken languages. For example, the pronominal signs are compositional, unlike pointing gestures, and the component parts convey different grammatical distinctions. Hand orientation indicates grammatical person (e.g., first vs. second person), handshape contrasts grammatical case (e.g., possessive vs. nominative), and movement (an arc vs. pointing) indicates grammatical number (plural vs. singular).

Many of the syntactic functions that are fulfilled in spoken languages by word order or case marking are expressed in ASL by spatial mechanisms. For example, when noun phrases are introduced into ASL discourse, they may be assigned an arbitrary locus in the plane of signing space. Once a referent has been associated with a locus, the signer may then refer to that referent by using a pronominal sign directed at the locus. In addition, verbs can move with respect to these loci to indicate subject and object relations. Generally, these loci remain fixed in space, but under certain discourse conditions, the loci can *shift* such that they are associated with different referents. In addition, spatial loci can be embedded within different subspaces of the reference plane, and there is evidence for more than one signing plane (e.g., nonspecific reference and counterfactuals may use diagonal and/or higher planes of space). Overall, the syntactic system of ASL is used to express the same linguistic *functions* found in the world's languages, but the *form* these functions take is explicitly spatial. The use of space for syntactic functions is a unique resource afforded by the visual modality of sign language.

Linguistic and Emotional Facial Expression

The face carries both linguistic and emotional information for ASL signers. Both hearing and deaf people use their face in the same way to convey emotional information—these expressions (e.g., happy, sad, angry) are universal. However, ASL signers also use facial expressions to convey linguistic contrasts. Linguistic and emotional facial expressions differ in their scope and timing and in the face muscles that are used. Grammatical facial expressions have a clear onset and offset, and they are coordinated with specific parts of the signed sentence. Emotional expressions have more global and inconsistent onset and offset patterns, and they are not timed to co-occur with specific signs or parts of a signed sentence. Examples of linguistic facial expression include marking for adverbials, topics, questions, conditionals, and relative clauses.

Grammatical facial expressions are critical to the syntax of ASL because they distinguish several different syntactic structures. For example, consider the following two ASL clauses: TODAY SNOW, TRIP CANCEL ("It's snowing today; the trip is canceled"). These are two coordinate main clauses. However, if the first clause is produced with a conditional facial expression (the eyebrows are raised, the head is tilted slightly to the side, and the shoulders move slightly forward), the syntactic structure is altered. The first clause becomes a conditional subordinate clause, and the meaning changes to "If it snows today, the trip will be canceled." The only difference between the two structures is the facial marking that co-occurs with the first clause. Facial behaviors also represent adverbs which appear in predicates and carry different specific meanings. For example, two ASL sentences may have exactly the same signs and differ only in the facial adverbials which co-occur with the signs. The facial expression "mm" (lips pressed together and protruded) indicates an action done effortlessly; whereas the facial expression "th" (tongue protrudes between the teeth) means "awkwardly" or "carelessly." These two facial expressions accompanying the same verb (e.g., DRIVE) convey quite different meanings ("drive effortlessly" or "drive carelessly").

Researchers are studying facial expressions in ASL for insight into the interface between biology and behavior. Emotional expressions are produced consistently and universally by children by 1 year of age.

Emotional facial expressions also appear to be associated with specific neural substrates that are distinct from those involved in language. How does the linguistic system underlying the use of grammatical facial expressions interact with the biologically programmed use of emotional facial expressions? Current research suggests that different neural systems may subserve linguistic and emotional facial expressions—the left hemisphere appears to be involved in producing linguistic facial expressions, whereas the right hemisphere is important for producing emotional facial expressions. In addition, although deaf children produce emotional facial expressions very early (as do hearing children), they acquire linguistic facial expressions later and with a quite different pattern of development, which reflects their (unconscious) analysis of these facial signals as part of a linguistic system.

Fingerspelling and the Manual Alphabet

The manual alphabet used in ASL consists of 26 different hand-shapes which correspond to the 26 letters of the English alphabet. Other signed languages have different fingerspelling systems; for example, British fingerspelling uses a two-handed system. Fingerspelling is often used when there is no existing ASL sign (e.g., for place names) and is somewhat separate from the grammar of ASL—grammatical rules do not apply to *novel* fingerspelled words.

However, fingerspelled words can become "lexicalized" or enter the sign vocabulary if they are used repeatedly in one or several contexts. These fingerspelled signs are quite distinct from fingerspelled English words because they have undergone significant phonological reshaping and have become incorporated into the ASL grammar over time. For example, N-O was a fingerspelled word meaning "no" which has been incorporated into the ASL lexicon. The sign #NO (the # indicates a lexicalized fingerspelled sign) has a different movement than the fingerspelled word (N-O moves to the right slightly whereas #NO moves forward slightly), and #NO contains modified alphabet handshapes such that neither the N nor the O handshapes appear as they do in the original fingerspelled word. Further evidence that the sign #NO is part of the ASL lexicon is that it can undergo a morphological rule which creates a verb which can be inflected. The verb SAY-NO-TO is derived from #NO and can inflect for subject and object as an agreeing verb.

Dialects, Accents, and Language Use

Very often speakers in different geographic regions or from different social groups show systematic differences in language use, and these groups are said to speak different dialects of the same language. The same phenomenon occurs for signed languages. For example, ASL signers from the Northeast and Southern regions of the United States often use different signs for the same object (compare British and American dialectal differences in word use: gas/petrol, diaper/nappy, elevator/lift). Southern signers also produce the two-handed form of signs more often than non-Southerners (some signs have both one-handed and two-handed forms that do not differ in meaning). The deaf black community in the United States also has its own dialect of ASL. Certain signs (e.g., FLIRT, SCHOOL) have black forms which originate from the time when schools for the deaf were racially segregated. These signs are used most often when black deaf individuals interact with each other and form part of the culture of the black deaf community. Both regional and black signing dialects also differ phonologically, but these systematic differences in pronunciation have been less well studied. In some regional dialects, the thumb may be extended while producing certain signs without changing meaning (e.g., FUNNY, BUTTER); this difference in pronunciation may be perceived as an accent. Similarly, when signers of Chinese Sign Language learn ASL, they may have an accent derived from small phonetic differences between CSL and ASL. For example, the closed fist handshape is slightly different for ASL and CSL. In ASL, the hand is relaxed and only the very tip of the thumb protrudes above the fist, but in CSL the fist is more rigid, and the entire top joint of the thumb protrudes. When CSL signers produce ASL signs, they may maintain the handshape from CSL, and this phonological difference may be perceived as a foreign accent.

In addition to regional and social dialects, different "situational dialects" or language styles can be found for users of ASL. The signing style used for formal lectures differs from that used for informal conversations or narratives. Formal ASL is slower paced, uses a larger signing space, tends to use two-handed variants of signs, and shows less coarticulation. In contrast, for casual or informal signing, signs that are made near the face may be produced lower down, one-handed signs predominate, and signs are often articulated such that they "overlap." For example, the sign THINK is made with an "l" handshape touching the forehead, and the sign PLAY is made with a "Y" handshape (thumb and pinky extended, other fingers closed). When THINK occurs before PLAY in casual signing, the signer may "anticipate" the handshape for PLAY and produce THINK with a "Y" handshape and extended index finger. This kind of anticipation or coarticulation does not occur as frequently in formal signing. These phonological and lexical changes are not unlike those found for formal and informal speech.

Sign Poetry and Song

Poetry and song are forms of artistic expression that make use of linguistic patternings of sound, rhythm, and grammar. How are poems and songs expressed in a language without sound? ASL poetry exhibits some internal structuring that is parallel to that found in oral languages, but it also contains poetic structure that is intrinsic to its visual-spatial modality. Like spoken poetry and song, ASL can rhyme by manipulating the phonological structure of words. Signs can rhyme if they share the same handshape or the same movement, and a poem may contain signs that all share a single handshape or group of handshapes that are formationally similar. Rhythmic structure within a sign poem can be created by manipulating the flow of movement between signs and by rhythmically balancing the two hands. The use of space is a poetic device that is intrinsic to the visual modality. Signs move through space and are clustered and separated within space to produce an additional dimension of structure within a poem. Sign poetry also takes advantage of the visual modality by using "cinematic" techniques such as zooms, close-ups, and visual panning.

The poetic and literary tradition for English is hundreds of years old. For ASL, this tradition is developing within our generation through organizations such as the National Theater of the Deaf. The nature of ASL literature is similar to the "oral" literature of storytelling and poetry that exists in communities which do not have a writing system. Songs and stories are passed down from generation to generation which reflect the culture of the society. Similarly, deaf culture is strongly reflected in the themes of ASL stories and poems. For example, poems and stories often express the value of sign language to the deaf community—a common language is a major determinant of any culture. Other themes include the origins of the deaf community, the relationship between hearing and deaf people, and shared cultural experiences such as growing up in a residential school for the deaf.

SIGN LANGUAGE ACQUISITION

A child acquiring a sign language appears to be faced with a quite different task than a child acquiring a spoken language. A completely different set of articulators is involved, and the language is perceived with a different sensory system. Do the properties of sign languages affect the course and timing of language acquisition? For example, do the iconic properties of sign languages aid in their acquisition? Do the spatial properties of sign language present special challenges for the acquisition process? Recent research has added these questions, and the results are briefly described here. This research is based on deaf children acquiring ASL as a native language from their deaf parents. The general finding is that deaf children acquire sign language in the same way as hearing children acquire a spoken language: both groups pass through the same linguistic milestones at the same time. These findings suggest that the capacities which underlie language acquisition are maturationally controlled and that the psychological, linguistic, and neural mechanisms involved in language acquisition are not speech specific.

Babbling and First Signs

Just as hearing babies babble prior to producing their first word, deaf babies babble with their hands prior to producing their first sign. Babbling occurs between about 7 and 10 months of age, and is characterized by a rhythmic syllable organization for both speech and sign. Just like vocal babbling in hearing infants, manual babbling is produced with a subset of manual phonetic units found in sign languages of the world and is produced without meaning or reference. The fact that babbling occurs in babies exposed to sign language suggests that babbling in general is not simply a result of the maturation of the motor system governing vocal articulation, but rather babbling may be the product of the maturation of a modality-neutral linguistic capacity.

Children acquiring both spoken and signed languages go through a stage in which isolated single words are produced. There is some evidence that first signs in ASL emerge earlier than first words in English. First signs have been reported as early as 6 months, whereas first words tend to appear between 11 and 13 months. The apparent early appearance of first signs is not tied to iconicity since the majority of first signs are not particularly iconic. For example, MILK, which is a frequent first sign (and first word) is made with movements similar to milking a cow. While this sign may be iconic for adults, it is not iconic for children. The ostensible early appearance of first signs may be due to the early motor development of the hands compared to the vocal tract. However, some recent research has questioned the early appearance of first signs and has suggested that first words and signs may appear at about the same time.

Similar to spoken languages, early lexical signs tend to be uninflicted, i.e., just the stem or base form of the word is produced. In addition, children often make phonological substitutions and alterations within their first signs. Thus, just as hearing children acquiring English might say "baba" for "bottle," deaf children simplify and alter adult signs; e.g., the "baby" sign for MOMMY is often produced with an "l" handshape (loose fist with index finger extended) rather than the correct spread hand (fingers not touching) and contact to the chin is with the index finger rather than the thumb. The phonological alterations in both sign and speech tend to reflect articulatory ease, with more difficult sounds and handshapes acquired later.

The semantic relations that are expressed in children's early word combinations are also the same for speech and sign. Children sign and talk about the existence and nonexistence of objects, actions on objects, possession of objects, and locations of objects. The expression of semantic relations occurs in the same order for both signed and spoken languages: existence relations appear first, followed by action and state relations, then locative relations. The last semantic expressions to emerge for both types of languages are datives, instruments, causatives, and manners of action.

Acquisition of Morphology and Syntax

All children make "mistakes" when learning language, and deaf children learning ASL make the same kinds of errors that hearing children make when acquiring English. For example, English-speaking children go through a stage in which they overgeneralize the past tense marker *-ed*, producing forms such as *comed*, *goed*, and *broked*. Similarly, children acquiring ASL overgeneralize verb morphology. For example, once children have learned to inflect verbs for subject and object, they may overextend this marking to verbs which do not permit this inflection. These "mistakes" provide a view into the child's developing grammar and indicate that children do not simply imitate adult utterances but instead have an internal system of rules that may or may not match the adult grammar.

Children learning English (and other spoken languages) make errors with personal pronouns, substituting "you" for "me" and vice versa. Pronoun reversals are not that surprising in child speech, given the shifts that occur between speakers and listeners using "I" and "you." Children often construe "you" as a name for themselves. For ASL, one might predict a different course of acquisition for these pronouns because of their iconic properties, i.e., "you" is indicated by pointing to the addressee and "me" is indicated by pointing to oneself. Both hearing and deaf children use pointing gestures prelinguistically. This raises the question of how deaf children move from prelinguistic gestural communication to linguistic–symbolic communication when the form (pointing) is virtually identical. Is the acquisition of pronouns early and error-free for children acquiring ASL—do they capitalize on the iconic nature of ASL pronouns? The surprising answer is no; despite the transparency of pointing gestures, deaf children do not use ASL pronouns earlier than children acquiring English, and they make pronoun reversals in early signing. Children acquiring ASL seem to go through three stages: (1) the use of gestural (nonlinguistic) pointing, (2) the use and misuse of pronouns as lexical signs (i.e., "you" as a name), and (3) the correct use of pronouns within a grammatical system.

Children acquiring ASL must master the syntactic use of space, which is quite intricate and complex (see Syntax above). At age 3, children do not use spatially indexed pronouns to refer to people or objects that are not physically present. By age 4, children begin to associate noun phrases with abstract loci in space, but they make errors. For example, children may fail to correctly maintain the unique association between a locus and a noun phrase, producing sentences in which it is not clear who is doing what to whom. Similarly, children acquiring English produce sentences with unidentified "he's" and "she's." By age 5, ASL learning children provide an abstract locus for noun phrases when one is required, and generally maintain this association appropriately. Verb agreement between these loci is also produced correctly. The complete spatial reference system (including shifting space) is not acquired until age 7 or 8—the same age at which English-speaking children master the reference system of English.

Understanding the nature of language acquisition for a signed language has provided important and profound insight into the nature of human language and the human capacity for language. The maturational mechanisms underlying language are not tied specifically to speech but appear to be linked to a more abstract linguistic capacity such that the acquisition of visual–manual and aural–oral languages are acquired according to the same maturational time table. Furthermore, linguistic symbolic systems are essentially and fundamentally arbitrary, and children acquiring ASL ignore its potential iconicity and construct linguistic rules according to grammatical principles which are not grounded in form-meaning similarities.

Acquisition of Sign Language Late in Childhood: Evidence for a Critical Period for Language Acquisition

The majority (90 percent) of deaf children are first exposed to sign language later in life—only deaf children who have deaf signing parents are exposed to sign language from birth. Children who have hearing parents who do not sign may have no effective language exposure in infancy and early childhood. These children typically acquire sign language when they enter a residential school for the deaf and become immersed in the language, using it to converse with other deaf children and adults. Some children may not enter a residential school until high school. Unfortunately, deaf children rarely acquire competence in English and often have no primary language until they acquire a sign language. This population of deaf signers provides a unique opportunity to investigate the "critical period" hypothesis for language acquisition. Essentially, this hypothesis posits that a child must be exposed to language within a particular critical or sensitive period in development in order to acquire language normally and completely. Exposure to language past this critical period will result in imperfect and abnormal language acquisition. Because most individuals are exposed to their native language from birth, this hypothesis has been difficult to test.

Recent research with deaf adults who were not exposed to sign language until late in childhood or adulthood supports the critical period hypothesis for language acquisition. There is a nearly linear relationship between the age at which a deaf person was first exposed to ASL and their performance on tests of ASL grammar and processing—the later the exposure to language, the worse their grammatical knowledge and performance. Crucially, these differences are not due to the number of years of signing experience—the native signers and the "late" signers in these studies were equated for the number of years of practice with ASL, and most had been signing for 20 or 30 years. The production and comprehension of ASL morphology are strongly affected by age of acquisition, with those exposed to the language early in life outperforming those exposed at later ages. Late learners of ASL are not entirely incompetent in their use of ASL morphology, but they lack the grammatical analysis and highly consistent use of linguistic structures that is displayed by native signers. Similar critical period effects have also been found with spoken languages for second-language learning. Researchers hypothesize that these effects are due to the maturational state of the child at the time of language exposure. A precise account of the mechanisms underlying the maturational change involved in the critical period for language acquisition remains a goal for future research.

BRAIN ORGANIZATION FOR SIGN LANGUAGE

Sign language exhibits properties for which each of the cerebral hemispheres of hearing people shows different predominant functioning. The left hemisphere has been shown to subserve linguistic functions, whereas the right hemisphere subserves visual–spatial functions. Given that ASL expresses linguistic functions by manipulating spatial relations, what is the brain organization for sign language? Is sign language controlled by the right hemisphere along with other visual–spatial functions or does the left hemisphere subserve sign language as it does spoken language? Or is sign language represented equally in both hemispheres of the brain? Recent research has shown that the brain honors the distinction between language and nonlanguage visual–spatial functions. Thus, despite the modality, signed languages are represented primarily in the left hemisphere of deaf signers, whereas the right hemisphere is specialized for nonlinguistic visual–spatial processing in these signers.

Damage to the left hemisphere of the brain in deaf signers leads to sign aphasias similar to those observed with spoken language. Aphasias are disruptions of language that follow certain types of brain injury. For example, adult signers with left-hemisphere damage may produce "agrammatic" signing which is characterized by a lack of morphological and syntactic markings and is often accompanied by halting effortful signing. For example, an agrammatic signer will produce single sign utterances which lack the grammatically required inflectional movements and use of space. Similarly, "agrammatic" aphasia in spoken language is characterized by effortful speech and a lack of grammatical markers, such as the past tense *-ed* or plural *-s* in English. Lesions to a different area of the left hemisphere produce a different kind of aphasia characterized by fluent signing or speaking, but with errors in the selection of grammatical markers and syntactic errors. A signer with this type of lesion may sign fluently but will not correctly utilize syntactic spatial loci and will produce incorrectly inflected signs. Differential damage within the left hemisphere produces differential linguistic impairments, and these impairments reflect linguistically relevant components for both sign and speech.

In contrast, right-hemisphere damage produces impairments of many visual–spatial abilities, but does *not* produce sign language aphasias. When given tests of sign language comprehension and production, signers with right-hemisphere damage perform normally, but these same signers show marked impairment on nonlinguistic tests of visual–spatial functions. For example, when given a set of colored blocks and asked to assemble them to match a model, right-hemisphere damaged signers have great difficulty and are unable to capture the overall configuration of the block design. Similar impairments on this task are found with hearing, speaking subjects with right-hemisphere damage. In contrast, left-hemisphere damage does not impair performance on most visual–spatial tasks for either signers or speakers. The poor performance of right-hemisphere damaged signers on nonlinguistic visual–spatial tasks, such as perceiving spatial orientation or understanding spatial relations between objects, stands in marked contrast to their unimpaired visual–spatial linguistic abilities. The brain exhibits a principled distinction between linguistic and nonlinguistic visual–spatial functions.

The brain organization for sign language indicates that left-hemispheric specialization for language is not based on hearing and speech. The underlying basis for left-hemisphere specialization is the fundamental nature of linguistic functions rather than the sensory modality which conveys the language. Investigations of the neural under-pinnings of signed and spoken languages are currently making use of *in vivo* techniques which can probe linguistic and visual–spatial processing in the intact brain. By contrasting signed and spoken languages, these studies can illuminate in greater detail the determinants of brain substrate for language and visual–spatial cognition.

BIBLIOGRAPHY

Klima, E. S., and U. Bellugi. *Signs of Language*. Cambridge: Harvard University Press, 1988.

Newport, E., and R. Meier. "The Acquisition of American Sign Language." In *The Crosslinguistic Study of Language Acquisition*. Ed. D. Slobin. Vol. 1. Hillsdale, NJ: Erlbaum, 1985.

Padden, C. "Grammatical Theory and Signed Languages." In *Linguistics: The Cambridge Survey*. Ed. F. Newmeyer. Vol. 2. New York: Cambridge University Press, 1988.

Poizner, H., E. S. Klima, and U. Bellugi. *What the Hands Reveal about the Brain*. Cambridge: MIT Press, 1987.

Reilly, J., M. McIntire, and U. Bellugi. "Faces: The Relationship between Language and Affect." In *From Gesture to Language in Hearing and Deaf Children*. Ed. V. Volterra and C. Erting. New York: Springer-Verlag, 1991.

=

FOR DISCUSSION AND REVIEW

1. Review the four prevalent myths about sign language. How might each have arisen? How is each refuted?

2. The phonological elements of spoken language are based on patterns of sound. What characteristics of sign language are analogous to the phonology of spoken language? For help in answering questions 2, 3, and 4, refer to the figures accompanying the article. For more detailed definitions of phonology and morphology, see the Edward Callary essay "Phonetics" in Part Two and "The Minimal Units of Meaning: Morphemes" from The Ohio State University Language Files in Part Three.

3. How are morphological form changes created in English and most spoken languages? How are they created in ASL?

4. In English, as in most spoken languages, syntax is based largely on word order. Explain how the use of spatial mechanisms makes syntax more flexible in ASL. You might also refer to "Syntax: The Structure of Sentences" by Frank Heny in Part Three for a more detailed definition of syntax.

5. How are facial expressions used in sign language? How do they differ from normal expressions of emotion?

6. How are regional dialects and foreign accents perceived in ASL?

7. Just as hearing babies babble using sound, deaf babies babble using gesture. What does this suggest about the nature of the maturational process represented by babbling?

8. Identify some of the important parallels between the acquisition of language by hearing children born to hearing parents and by deaf children born to deaf parents.

9. What are the disadvantages of deaf children born to hearing parents? What does their experience suggest about language acquisition?

10. What does research show about the differences and similarities of language functions in the brains of speakers and signers? What do these findings imply about the nature of language?

11. Although sign language appears to differ drastically from oral language, the similarities between them are striking. List the most fundamental characteristics of human language shared by sign languages and oral languages.

4

Nonverbal Communication

George A. Miller

Anthropologist Edward Sapir once described nonverbal behavior as "an elaborate and secret code that is written nowhere, known by none, and understood by all." Certainly we study nonverbal behavior in a number of scholarly fields, but our understanding of it is far from complete, perhaps partly because popular writings have oversimplified the subject of body language, suggesting that we easily read the nonverbal signals people unconsciously send. In fact, people from different groups often misunderstand one another because they have different nonverbal systems—postures, gestures, facial expressions, and so on. In the follow-ing selection from his classic Communication, Language and Meaning: Psychological Perspectives *(1973), George A. Miller, the Princeton James S. McDonnell Distinguished University Professor of Psychology Emeritus, uses a variety of examples to explain how necessary it is to understand both the languages and nonverbal systems of other cultures.*

When the German philosopher Nietzsche said that "success is the great-est liar," he meant that a successful person seems especially worthy to us even when his success is due to nothing more than good luck. But Nietzsche's observation can be interpreted more broadly.

People communicate in many different ways. One of the most impor-tant ways, of course, is through language. Moreover, when language is written it can be completely isolated from the context in which it occurs; it can be treated as if it were an independent and self-contained process. We have been so successful in using and describing and analyzing this special kind of communication that we sometimes act as if language were the *only* kind of communication that can occur between people. When we act that way, of course, we have been deceived by success, the greatest liar of them all.

Like animals, people communicate by their actions as well as by the noises they make. It is a sort of biological anomaly of man—something like the giraffe's neck, or the pelican's beak—that our vocal noises have so far outgrown in importance and frequency all our other methods of signaling to one another. Language is obviously essential for human beings, but it is not the whole story of human communication. Not by a long shot.

Consider the following familiar fact. When leaders in one of the less well developed countries decide that they are ready to introduce some technology that is already highly advanced in another country, they do not simply buy all the books that have been written about that technology and have their students read them. The books may exist and they may be very good, but just reading about the technology is not enough. The students must be sent to study in a country where the technology is already flourishing, where they can see it firsthand. Once they have been exposed to it in person and experienced it as part of their own lives, they are ready to understand and put to use the information that is in the books. But the verbal message, without the personal experience to back it up, is of little value.

Now what is it that the students learn by participating in a technology that they cannot learn by just reading about it? It seems obvious that they are learning something important, and that whatever it is they are learning is something that we don't know how to put into our verbal descriptions. There is a kind of nonverbal communication that occurs when students are personally involved in the technology and when they interact with people who are using and developing it.

Pictures are one kind of nonverbal communication, of course, and moving pictures can communicate some of the information that is difficult to capture in words. Pictures also have many of the properties that make language so useful—they can be taken in one situation at one time and viewed in an entirely different situation at any later time. Now that we have television satellites, pictures can be transmitted instantaneously all over the world, just as our words can be transmitted by radio. Perhaps the students who are trying to learn how to create a new technology in their own country could supplement their reading by watching moving pictures of people at work in the developed industry. Certainly the pictures would be a help, but they would be very expensive. And we don't really know whether words and pictures together would capture everything the students would be able to learn by going to a more advanced country and participating directly in the technology.

Let me take another familiar example. There are many different cultures in the world, and in each of them the children must learn a great many things that are expected of everyone who participates effectively in that culture. When I say they are taken for granted, I mean that nobody needs to describe them or write them down or try self-consciously to teach them to children. Indeed, the children begin to learn them before their linguistic skills are far enough developed to understand a verbal description of what they are learning. This kind of learning has sometimes been called "imitation," but that is much too simple an explanation for the complex processes that go on when a child learns what is normal and expected in his own community. Most of the norms are communicated to the child nonverbally, and he internalizes them as if no other possibilities existed. They are as much a part of him as his own body; he would no more question them than he would question the fact that he has two hands and two feet, but only one head.

These cultural norms can be described verbally, of course. Anthropologists who are interested in describing the differences among the many cultures of the world have developed a special sensitivity to cultural norms and have described them at length in their scholarly books. But if a child had to read those books in order to learn what was expected of him, he would never become an effective member of his own community.

What is an example of the sort of thing that children learn nonverbally? One of the simplest examples to observe and analyze and discuss is the way people use clothing and bodily ornamentation to communicate. At any particular time in any particular culture there is an accepted and normal way to dress and to arrange the hair and to paint the face and to wear one's jewelry. By adopting those conventions for dressing himself, a person communicates to the world that he wants to be treated according to the standards of the culture for which they are appropriate. When a black person in America rejects the normal American dress and puts on African clothing, he is communicating to the world that he wants to be treated as an Afro-American. When a white man lets his hair and beard grow, wears very informal clothing, and puts beads around his neck, he is communicating to the world that he rejects many of the traditional values of Western culture. On the surface, dressing up in unusual costumes would seem to be one of the more innocent forms of dissent that a person could express, but in fact it is deeply resented by many people who still feel bound by the traditional conventions of their culture and who become fearful or angry when those norms are violated. The nonverbal message that such a costume communicates is "I reject your culture and your values," and those who resent this message can be violent in their response.

The use of clothing as an avenue of communication is relatively obvious, of course. A somewhat subtler kind of communication occurs in the way people use their eyes. We are remarkably accurate in judging the direction of another person's gaze; psychologists have done experiments that have measured just how accurate such judgments are. From an observation of where a person is looking we can infer what he is looking at, and from knowing what he is looking at we can guess what he is interested in, and from what he is interested in and the general situation we can usually make a fairly good guess about what he is going to do. Thus eye movements can be a rich and important channel of nonverbal communication.

Most personal interaction is initiated by a short period during which two people look directly at one another. Direct eye contact is a signal that each has the other's attention, and that some further form of interaction can follow. In Western cultures, to look directly into another person's eyes is equivalent to saying, "I am open to you—let the action begin."

Everyone knows how much lovers can communicate by their eyes, but aggressive eye contact can also be extremely informative.

In large cities, where people are crowded in together with others they neither know nor care about, many people develop a deliberate strategy of avoiding eye contacts. They want to mind their own business, they don't have time to interact with everyone they pass, and they communicate this fact by refusing to look at other people's faces. It is one of the things that make newcomers to the city feel that it is a hostile and unfriendly place.

Eye contact also has an important role in regulating conversational interactions. In America, a typical pattern is for the listener to signal that he is paying attention by looking at the talker's mouth or eyes. Since direct eye contact is often too intimate, the talker may let his eyes wander elsewhere. As the moment arrives for the talker to become a listener, and for his partner to begin talking, there will often be a preliminary eye signal. The talker will often look toward the listener, and the listener will signal that he is ready to talk by glancing away.

Such eye signals will vary, of course, depending on what the people are talking about and what the personal relation is between them. But whatever the pattern of eye signals that two people are using, they use them unconsciously. If you try to become aware of your own eye movements while you are talking to someone, you will find it extremely frustrating. As soon as you try to think self-consciously about your own eye movements, you do not know where you should be looking. If you want to study how the eyes communicate, therefore, you should do it by observing other people, not yourself. But if you watch other people too intently, of course, you may disturb them or make them angry. So be careful!

Even the pupils of your eyes communicate. When a person becomes excited or interested in something, the pupils of his eyes increase in size. In order to test whether we are sensitive to these changes in pupil size, a psychologist showed people two pictures of the face of a pretty girl. The two pictures were completely identical except that in one picture the girl's pupils were constricted, whereas in the other picture her pupils were dilated. The people were asked to say which picture they liked better, and they voted in favor of the picture with the large pupils. Many of the judges did not even realize consciously what the difference was, but apparently they were sensitive to the difference and preferred the eyes that communicated excitement and interest.

Eye communication seems to be particularly important for Americans. It is part of the American culture that people should be kept at a distance, and that contact with another person's body should be avoided in all but the most intimate situations. Because of this social convention of dealing with others at a distance, Americans have to place much reliance on their distance receptors, their eyes and ears, for personal communication. In other cultures, however, people normally come close together and bodily contact between conversational partners is as normal as eye contact is in America. In the Eastern Mediterranean cultures, for example, both the touch and the smell of the other person are expected.

The anthropologist Edward T. Hall has studied the spatial relations that seem appropriate to various kinds of interactions. They vary with intimacy, they depend on the possibility of eye contact, and they are different in different cultures. In America, for example, two strangers will converse impersonally at a distance of about four feet. If one moves closer, the other will back away. In a waiting room, strangers will keep apart, but friends will sit together, and members of a family may actually touch one another.

Other cultures have different spatial norms. In Latin America, for example, impersonal discussion normally occurs at a distance of two or three feet, which is the distance that is appropriate for personal discussion in North America. Consequently, it is impossible for a North and a South American both to be comfortable when they talk to one another unless one can adopt the zones that are normal for the other. If the South American advances to a distance that is comfortable for him, it will be too close for the North American, and he will withdraw, and one can chase the other all around the room unless something intervenes to end the conversation. The North American seems aloof and unfriendly to the South American. The South American seems hostile or oversexed to the North American. Hall mentions that North Americans sometimes cope with this difference by barricading themselves behind desks or tables, and that South Americans have been known literally to climb over these barriers in order to attain a comfortable distance at which to talk.

Within one's own culture these spatial signals are perfectly understood. If two North Americans are talking at a distance of one foot or less, you know that what they are saying is highly confidential. At a distance of two to three feet it will be some personal subject matter. At four or five feet it is impersonal, and if they are conversing at a distance of seven or eight feet, we know that they expect others to be listening to what they are saying. When talking to a group, a distance of ten to twenty feet is normal, and at greater distances only greetings are exchanged. These conventions are unconscious but highly reliable. For example, if you are having a personal conversation with a North American at a distance of two feet, you can shift it to an impersonal conversation by the simple procedure of moving back to a distance of four or five feet. If he can't follow you, he will find it quite impossible to maintain a personal discussion at that distance.

These examples should be enough to convince you—if you needed convincing—that we communicate a great deal of information that is not expressed in the words we utter. And I have not even mentioned yet the interesting kind of communication that occurs by means of gestures. A gesture is an expressive motion or action, usually made with the hands and arms, but also with the head or even the whole body. Gestures can occur with or without speech. As a part of the speech act, they usually emphasize what the person is saying, but they may occur without any speech at all. Some gestures are spontaneous, some are highly ritualized and have very specific meanings. And they differ enormously from one culture to another.

Misunderstanding of nonverbal communication is one of the most distressing and unnecessary sources of international friction. For example, few Americans understand how much the Chinese hate to be touched, or slapped on the back, or even to shake hands. How easy it would be for an American to avoid giving offense simply by avoiding these particular gestures that, to him, signify intimacy and friendliness. Or, to take another example, when Khrushchev placed his hands together over his head and shook them, most Americans interpreted it as an arrogant gesture of triumph, the sort of gesture a victorious prize fighter would make, even though Khrushchev[1] seems to have intended it as a friendly gesture of international brotherhood. Sticking out the tongue and quickly drawing it back can be a gesture of self-castigation in one culture, an admission of a social mistake, but someone from another culture might interpret it as a gesture of ridicule or contempt, and in the Eskimo culture it would not be a gesture at all, but the conventional way of directing a current of air when blowing out a candle. Just a little better communication on the nonverbal level might go a long way toward improving international relations.

Ritualized gestures—the bow, the shrug, the smile, the wink, the military salute, the pointed finger, the thumbed nose, sticking out the tongue, and so on—are not really nonverbal communication, because such gestures are just a substitute for the verbal meanings that are associated with them. There are, however, many spontaneous gestures and actions that are unconscious, but communicate a great deal. If you take a moving picture of someone who is deeply engrossed in a conversation, and later show it to him, he will be quite surprised to see many of the gestures he used and the subtle effects they produced. Sometimes what a person is saying unconsciously by his actions may directly contradict what he is saying consciously with his words. Anthropologists have tried to develop a way to write down a description of these nonverbal actions, something like the notation that choreographers use to record the movements of a ballet dancer, but it is difficult to know exactly what the significance of these actions really is, or what the important features are that should be recorded. We can record them photographically, of course, but we still are not agreed on how the photographic record should be analyzed.

---

[1] Nikita Khrushchev, Soviet premier from 1958 to 1964, met with then Vice President Richard Nixon in 1959, first in Moscow and again in the United States, where he made this now famous gesture. Khrushchev was instrumental in an initial relaxing of U.S.-Soviet relations during the Cold War. —Eds.

Finally, there is a whole spectrum of communication that is vocal, but not really verbal. The most obvious examples are spontaneous gasps of surprise or cries of pain. I suspect this kind of vocal communication is very similar for both man and animal. But our use of vocal signals goes far beyond such grunts and groans. It is a commonplace observation that the way you say something is as important as what you say, and often more important for telling the listener what your real intentions are. Exactly the same words may convey directly opposite messages according to the way they are said. For example, I can say, "Oh, isn't that *wonderful*" so that I sound enthusiastic, or I can say, "Oh, isn't *that* wonderful" in a sarcastic tone so that you know I don't think it is wonderful at all. Because the actual words uttered are often misleading, lawyers and judges in the courtroom have learned that it is sometimes important to have an actual recording and not just a written transcript of what a person is supposed to have said.

Rapid and highly inflected speech usually communicates excitement, extremely distinct speech usually communicates anger, very loud speech usually communicates pomposity, and a slow monotone usually communicates boredom. The emotional clues that are provided by the way a person talks are extremely subtle, and accomplished actors must practice for many years to bring them under conscious control.

A person's pronunciation also tells a great deal about him. If he has a foreign accent, a sensitive listener can generally tell where he was born. If he speaks with a local dialect, we can often guess what his social origins were and how much education he has had. Often a person will have several different styles of speaking, and will use them to communicate which social role he happens to be playing at the moment. This is such a rich source of social and psychological information, in fact, that a whole new field has recently developed to study it, a field called "sociology of language." . . .

One of the most significant signals that is vocal but nonverbal is the ungrammatical pause. . . . In careful speech most of our pauses are grammatical. That is to say, our pauses occur at the boundaries of grammatical segments, and serve as a kind of audible punctuation. By calling them "grammatical pauses" we imply that they are a normal part of the verbal message. An ungrammatical pause, however, is not a part of the verbal message. For example, when I . . . uh . . . pause within a . . . uh . . . grammatical unit, you cannot regard the pause as part of my verbal message. These ungrammatical pauses are better regarded as the places where the speaker is thinking, is searching for words, and is planning how to continue his utterance. For a linguist, of course, the grammatical pause is most interesting, since it reveals something about the structure of the verbal message. For a psychologist, however, the ungrammatical pause is more interesting, because it reveals something about the thought processes of the speaker.

When a skilled person reads a prepared text, there are few ungrammatical pauses. But spontaneous speech is a highly fragmented and discontinuous activity. Indeed, ungrammatical pausing is a reliable signal of spontaneity in speech. The pauses tend to occur at choice points in the message, and particularly before words that are rare or unusual and words that are chosen with particular care. An actor who wanted to make his rehearsed speech sound spontaneous would deliberately introduce ungrammatical pauses at these critical points.

Verbal communication uses only one of the many kinds of signals that people can exchange; for a balanced view of the communication process we should always keep in mind the great variety of other signals that can reinforce or contradict the verbal message. These subtleties are especially important in psychotherapy, where a patient tries to communicate his emotional troubles to a doctor, but may find it difficult or impossible to express in words the real source of his distress. Under such circumstances, a good therapist learns to listen for more than words, and to rely on nonverbal signals to help him interpret the verbal signals. For this reason, many psychologists have been persistently interested in nonverbal communication, and have perhaps been less likely than linguists to fall into the mistaken belief that language is the only way we can communicate.

The price of opening up one's attention to this wider range of events, however, is a certain vagueness about the kind of communication that is occurring—about what it means and how to study it. We have no dictionaries or grammars to help us analyze nonverbal communication, and there is much work that will have to be done in many cultures before we can formulate and test any interesting scientific theories about nonverbal communication. Nevertheless, the obvious fact that so much communication does occur nonverbally should persuade us not to give up, and not to be misled by our success in analyzing verbal messages.

Recognizing the great variety of communication channels that are available is probably only the first step toward a broader conception of communication as a psychological process. Not only must we study what a person says and how he says it, but we must try to understand why he says it. If we concentrate primarily on the words that people say, we are likely to think that the only purpose of language is to exchange information. That is one of its purposes, of course, but certainly not the only one. People exchange many things. Not only do they exchange information, but they also exchange money, goods, services, love, and status. In any particular interaction, a person may give one of these social commodities in exchange for another. He may give information in exchange for money or give services in exchange for status or love. Perhaps we should first characterize communication acts in terms of what people are trying to give and gain in their social interactions. Then, within that broader frame of reference, we might see better that verbal messages are more appropriate for some exchanges and nonverbal messages for others, and that both have their natural and complementary roles to play in the vast tapestry we call human society.

FOR DISCUSSION AND REVIEW

1. According to Miller, why is reading about some advanced technology developed in another country not enough? Why must students actually *go* to the country? In answering this question, try to use specific, original examples.

2. Miller asserts that, along with their language, children also learn certain nonverbal "cultural norms" that "are communicated to the child nonverbally." Drawing from your own experience, describe three of the cultural norms American children learn.

3. Keep track for a day of how people you meet use their eyes to make or avoid eye contact. Write a brief description of the behavior you have observed. Do your findings agree with Miller's statements about how Americans use their eyes? If not, what are the differences?

4. Miller offers two examples of using clothing to communicate. Based on your own experience, give two additional examples.

5. Spatial norms vary from culture to culture. Describe any differences you have noticed between norms of your own culture and those of other cultures either within your own country or outside it.

5

Chimps, Children and Creoles: The Need for Caution

Jean Aitchison

Despite the many hypotheses on how human language developed, the hard facts are fragmentary and come from different fields, such as anthropology, sociobiology, and physiology. Understanding the origins of language may help us understand what language is, to what extent language abilities are natural, and the relationship of language to other kinds of human cognition.

Originally presented as part of a conference on the biological origins of language, Jean Aitchison's essay draws on three kinds of linguistic data: the intentional sounds and gestures of primates, the cognitive processes children use to acquire language, and the social circumstances that allow pidgin and creole languages to develop. After considering data from these different sources, Aitchison, Rupert Murdoch Professor of Language and Communication at Oxford, concludes that no single source should be used when developing hypotheses about the origins of human language.

INTRODUCTION

"There are certain areas of scholarship . . . where the scantiness of the evidence sets a special challenge to the disciplined mind. It is a game with very few pieces where the skill of the player lies in complicating the rules. The isolated and uneloquent fact must be exibited within a tissue of hypothesis subtle enough to make it speak" (Murdoch, 1969:171). This quotation is particularly apt for studies on the origin of language where facts are few, but hypotheses are multifarious and contradictory: a researcher who tried to list the "principal theories" came up with a total of 23 (Hewes, 1977).

Consequently, today, as a century ago "The greater part of what is said and written upon it is mere windy talk" (Whitney, 1983:279). However, the genesis of human language is an important topic. We therefore need to distinguish the "windy" hypotheses from the possibly substantial ones. An essential preliminary step is to examine the fragmentary sources of evidence at our disposal, and to establish two things: first,

61

to what extent these are reliable; second, what inferences can be drawn from them.

Evidence for the origin of language comes from two types of source, external and internal. An "external" source is one which makes use of non-linguistic clues, such as archaeological evidence relating to the anatomy of the vocal tract in early humanoids. An "internal" source is one which utilizes linguistic information, such as child language.

In this paper I want to discuss some commonly used sources of linguistic evidence: primate vocalization and signing, child language, pidgins and creoles. Superficial parallels among these linguistic phenomena are often taken—wrongly—as evidence that they are all similar in nature. Consequently, researchers tend to seize random examples from any of them in order to justify some point they are making. I therefore want to look more carefully at some of the similarities and dissimilarities, and to see to what extent we are justified in drawing inferences about language origins from them. For the purpose of this paper, I take language to be a rule-governed communication system in which discrete symbols are combined creatively.

The paper is organized as follows. First, I will outline the various types of evidence, and highlight some of the problems involved. Second, I will point out some apparent similarities in the linguistic output from these sources. Third, I will show that surface similarities may speak deeper differences by examining the nature of repetitions and omissions in each type of data. Finally, I will discuss what conclusions about the origins of language we may reasonably draw from the data under discussion.

LINGUISTIC EVIDENCE: SOME SOURCES AND THEIR PROBLEMS

This section considers some frequently quoted linguistic sources of evidence for language origin, and points out why each of them might be misleading unless used with caution.

Primate Vocalizations

Primates naturally have a set of vocal signals in which each call, or occasionally combination of calls, means something different. A number of people claim that these calls represent a step on the ladder towards human language.

The vervet monkey tends to be quoted most frequently in this context (Struhsaker, 1967). This animal reportedly has 36 vocal calls—a number slightly inflated by the inclusion of sneezing and vomiting. The vervet's main claim to fame, however, lies in its alarm calls, in which it distinguishes between different types of predator: a *chutter* warns of the presence of a snake; a *rraup* is uttered when an eagle is spotted; a *chirp* is used for lions and leopards; and a call which creates less panic, an *uh!* occurs for spotted hyenas and Masai tribesmen. An early suggestion that the vervets are simply distinguishing between the intensity of different types of danger appears to have been ruled out by a subsequent experiment in which a concealed loudspeaker played recordings of the different alarm calls. A *chutter* caused the vervets to stand on their hind legs and look around for a snake; a *rraup* made them dive into the undergrowth, as if hiding from an aerial predator; and a *chirp* sent them all up trees (Seyfarth, Cheney and Marler, 1980). It is therefore at least arguable that these sounds are used as symbols for the various types of predator.

The cotton-top tamarin, a marmoset monkey, has a different type of sophistication in its call system: it can modify an original alarm call by combining it with a second signal. An alarm call normally causes the animal's mane to stand erect. However, mane-raising fails to occur when the alarm signal is combined with an alerting "Watch out" squeak. This double call tends to occur some time after an initial alarm call, when the monkeys are standing still, warily scanning the landscape around them, so is interpretable as a general call for vigilance (Cleveland and Snowdon, 1982; reported in Demers, 1988). From the linguistic point of view, this sequencing might be regarded as an elementary syntactic operation.

These abilities are interesting, but they should not be overinterpreted, for two reasons. First, primate vocalizations may not be directly comparable to human language. They may represent a common substrate of calls which humans still in part possess, and which are most directly observable in infancy, when the various cries of hunger, anger, pain are recognizable across cultures. If this point of view is correct, then primate calls are distinct from language, which must then be regarded as a secondary system superimposed on a more primitive one. At the moment, the question is still open. A second reason for caution is the danger of subconsciously selecting evidence which fits a private hypothesis. Anyone who simply scans primate calls, looking for signs of "language" is likely to find some chance resemblances, since sound systems often coincidentally develop in similar ways in quite different species: a survey of a wider range of animals reveals that birdsong, rather than primate calls, is the nearest system to human language in terms of shared characteristics (Nottebohm, 1975). For these reasons, primate calls should be treated with caution in arguments about language origin.

Ape Signing

In recent years, a number of primates, mainly chimps, have been taught to manipulate a language-like system. The systems differ from language in that they involve visual signals, rather than auditory ones, since an ape's vocal apparatus is unsuited to making language-like sounds. Some of the animals use sign systems (Washoe, Lana, Koko, Nim, Chantek), others manipulate tokens (Sarah, Lana) (for summaries of their abilities, see Aitchison, 1989a; Dingwall, 1988). Leaving aside Sarah, a chimp who was taught only to respond to instructions, all the animals show considerable ability in the productive use of their systems.

The animals are clearly able to symbolize: all of them have some arbitrary symbols which refer to a particular object, action or quality: Nim tapped his stomach with the palm of his hand for the color "blue" (Terrace, 1979). Lana's keyboard token for "eat" is a diamond super-imposed on a circle inside a rectangle against a blue background (Rumbaugh, 1977). Furthermore, they can generalize these symbols effectively. For example, Washoe extended the sign for *key* to a wide variety of keys, including car ignition keys (Gardner and Gardner, 1969). All of them are able to combine symbols, and to do this creatively: Washoe used the novel combination *Go sweet* in a request to take her to the raspberry bushes (Gardner and Gardner, 1969); Lana reportedly referred to a cucumber as *banana which-is green* (Rumbaugh, 1977); Nim spontaneously requested *Tickle me* (Terrace, 1979). Some doubts have been cast on the extent of the symbolization and creativity: more signs are iconic than arbitrary, and some reported instances of creativity may have been chance juxtaposition or due to prompting (Pettito and Seidenberg, 1979). But it is nevertheless clear that symbolization, generalization, combination of symbols and creativity are within the animals' capability.

There is, however, no evidence as yet that these sequences are struc-tured. Lana was able to produce symbols in a fixed order (Rumbaugh, 1977), but this is what she had been trained to do: even pigeons can be taught to peck at boxes in a particular sequence. Those animals who were allowed to produce symbols freely did not show such a strong predisposi-tion to order them, even though certain mild preferences emerged. Nim, for example, tended to put any food he was requesting at the beginning of a sequence (e.g. *Grape eat Nim*), but this was not a strong enough trend to be labeled a "rule." And a fuller, computer analysis of Nim's output showed the combinations to be more random than had appeared at first sight (Terrace, 1979). Washoe's trainers claim that she settled down to signing in a consistent order, but this apparent organization may be an artefact of the analysis, since her trainers omitted repeats of words within the same "utterance". Koko's trainer admits that her ordering of signs is inconsistent, partly because she sometimes signs with both hands simul-taneously (Patterson, 1978). It is unclear whether the observed inconsis-tencies are due to the nature of sign language (as some claim) or the character of apes (possibly the majority verdict).

Ape signing can therefore be used to show that these animals are capable of symbolization, generalization of these symbols, and the cre-ative combination of signs. But it would be premature to conclude that ape signing is rule-governed in any meaningful way.

Child Language

Children start babbling at around six months, go through a "single word stage" at around 15 months, and begin putting words together at the age of approximately 18 months. They start adding endings onto these words at around two years. Utterances then gradually increase in length and sophistication until adult-type competence is acquired. This is the "normal pattern," judging from the majority of books on child language. There is no doubt that a number of English-speaking children do behave in this way (e.g. Brown, 1973). But it would be unwise to regard it uncritically as an inevitable pattern which must have been paralleled in the birth of language in humankind.

Caution must be used, for a number of reasons. First, researchers tend to pick children who are easy to comprehend. Others have been reported in the literature who do not fit words together like building bricks: they produce intonation patterns into which indistinct words are slotted at intervals (e.g. Peters, 1977). The "normal" pattern may not therefore be the norm, it may be the pattern which fits in with our preconceived ideas, especially as the range of variation found in child language is now much wider than was once assumed (e.g. Wilson and Peters, 1988). Secondly, the hypothesis that ontogeny recapitulates phylogeny cannot be adopted uncritically. The evidence from ethology suggests that ontogeny [development of an individual of a species] *may* recapitulate phylogeny [evolutionary development of the species], but that parallelism is not inevitable. A third reason for caution is that children have a model to follow: they deduce rules by paying attention to the speech of those around them. The originators of language had no such model. The structure of the existing language inevitably influences the paths children follow. We must therefore be careful not to draw conclusions about humankind from the speech of a few English-speaking children.

The main general conclusion which can be drawn from child language is that children seem to have an innate knowledge that language is structured. At an early stage they express semantic relations consistently (such as possessor-possessed, verb-object), even though the way they do this varies from language to language: structure is commonly signalled via word order, but can be marked by word endings in languages where these are regular and transparent (Slobin, 1985).

Pidgin

A pidgin can be defined as a subsidiary language system used by people with no common language. It is usually overtly derived from one base language, though may contain substantial admixtures of other languages (Mühlhäusler, 1986; Holm, 1988). A stable pidgin is not just a substandard version of an existing language, but a new system whose rules are unpredictable from a knowledge of the base. Stable pidgins are simpler (more regular) and more impoverished (having fewer resources) than "full" languages, and are regarded by some as embryo languages whose characteristics are similar to those found in the early stages of language in the human species.

However, pidgins cannot be regarded as direct reflections of the early origins of language primarily for two reasons: first, pidgin speakers already have a first language of their own, so they tend to fill in gaps in the pidgin with components from their own language. In some cases pidgin constructions turn out to consist of lexical items imported from the base grafted onto structures which have been borrowed from the substrate languages (e.g. Keesing, 1988). Second, pidgins are continuously developing systems, with a large amount of variation involved: it is therefore almost always possible simply to pick the examples one requires from the wide range available. Indeed, the variety of language systems labeled "pidgins" have led some people to suggest that we should not seek to define an elusive ideal "pidgin," but should instead clarify the process of "pidginization," the development of a simplified system from full languages (e.g. Mühlhäusler, 1986).

As a generalization, however, a stable pidgin can be characterized as a rule-governed system which relies mainly on content words, and so uses word order to express semantic relationships. Morphology and embedding are either absent, or very limited in extent.

Creoles

A creole can be defined as a pidgin which has become someone's first language. The children who acquire this system are inevitably learning a less than full language and have no other one at their disposal. According to some researchers, they are therefore driven back on their innate linguistic capacity which will convert the subsidiary system into a "real" language: "All members of our species are born with a bioprogram for language which can function even in the absence of adequate input" (Bickerton, 1981:xiii). This claim is superficially strengthened by the observation that widely separated creoles show surprising similarities. A creole is therefore sometimes regarded as constituting evidence for a biologically programmed core of language.

Once again, caution is necessary. The generation who begin to convert the pidgin into a "full" language are working with a language-like system in the first place. Many of the developments are not new impositions by the learners, but the implementation of potentialities that are already in the system (Aitchison, 1983). A large proportion of creolization involves the stabilization of structures already used intermittently by the pidgin speakers (Goodman, 1985). Second, the creole does not leap fully fledged into existence in the mouth of each toddler: it takes years, sometimes even generations for the creole to stabilize, as speakers interact with one another (e.g. Arends, 1986). Furthermore, the similarities noted in the speech of various creoles are statistical probabilities, not absolute necessities. A creole often starts out being fairly heterogeneous in nature, then gradually narrows down to the statistically likely constructions for reasons which may not be strictly linguistic ones (Aitchison, 1989b).

In spite of these cautions, the process of creolization is undoubtedly an interesting one for discovering how the human mind elaborates a simple and impoverished system, in particular how separate items get combined and reanalyzed as novel structures.

SIMILARITIES AND PSEUDO-SIMILARITIES

This brief overview of commonly quoted sources of linguistic evidence for language origin indicated first, that all of them need to be treated with caution. Second, it showed that we are dealing with disparate phenomena. This section will consider to what extent they contain similarities.

The only feature which the various data types have in common is that they are all used for communication, and all use discrete signals. Chimp vocalizations are fairly unlike the rest: they do not definitively involve symbolization, combinations are few, and there is no evidence of creativity. They are to a large extent innate, and learning is minimal. If these vocalizations are left aside, then some further similarities are evident in the remaining sources.

Ape signing, child language, pidgins and creoles, all involve symbolization, ability to generalize, and creative combination of signals. In all of them, the communication behavior requires a considerable amount of learning. A further similarity is that the symbols represent mainly "content" words: they stand for objects, actions and qualities which occur in the external world. However, creoles differ in that the content words are linked together in a far more sophisticated way than the other three, with a semi-developed morphology, some function words, and elements of embedding. They are therefore more comparable to "full" languages.

Superficially, the systems which look most similar to the casual onlooker are ape signing, child language and pidgins, since all three involve output which is "telegraphic," in that content words are juxtaposed with no overt links, as in *me eat* (chimp), *Bobby juice* (child), *mi hangri* (pidgin). But (as already noted) there is no firm evidence of structure in the ape output, so only child language and pidgins can be regarded as genuine rule-governed systems—and as will be shown, these differ quite considerably. However, since all three phenomena are sometimes quoted indiscriminately in relation to claims about language origin, it may be useful to demonstrate that the likenesses are to a great extent illusory, in that the various surface structures reflect mechanisms which are fairly different at a deeper level. This will be illustrated by the treatment of two phenomena found in all three sources of data: repetitions and omissions.

TREATMENT OF REPETITIONS

Repetitions of various types are found in ape signing, child language and pidgins. This section will show that the types of repetition found are quite dissimilar, suggesting that it would be misleading to regard the superficial similarities between the data sources as indicating a common origin. The term repetition is here taken to cover both iteration, i.e. repetition of a whole word, and reduplication, i.e. repetition of part of a word, since the two overlap in the data under discussion.

Repetitions in Ape Signing

For most of the apes, repetitions have simply been omitted from the published samples (Pettito and Seidenberg, 1979). Nim is the only chimp whose output has been fully analyzed, and in his speech the repetitions seem to be structureless and random (Terrace, 1979).

Most of Nim's speech consisted of fairly short utterances, and his MLU [Mean Length of Utterance] was consistently under two signs. His two sign combinations showed no evidence of structure (e.g. *eat Nim* occurred 302 times, and *Nim eat* 209), even though certain positional preferences were apparent: for example, the signs *more* and *give* tended to be the first of two, with *more* occurring in first position 85% of the time, and *give* 78%. Part of this preference was due to a gradually increasing tendency to imitate his trainers. Longer sequences were rare, and he showed no increase in his average utterance length in the last two years of training. When he did produce longer utterances, these were often partial or total repeats of shorter ones: 9 out of his 26 most frequent 3 sign-combinations involved repeated items, as in *nut Nim nut, Nim eat nut*; and all 21 of his most frequent 4-sign combinations involved repetitions as in *eat Nim eat Nim, Nim eat Nim eat, me eat me eat, grape eat Nim eat, me gum me gum, banana eat me Nim*. The repetitions may have been produced partly in order to please the trainers: Nim and the other apes could have adopted a strategy "the more signs the better"; but they may also be due to ape nature. It has been suggested that: "Repetitive, inconsistently structured strings are in fact characteristic of ape signing" (Pettito and Seidenberg, 1979:186), a claim which seems to be borne out by Nim's longest utterances: "Give orange me give eat orange me eat orange give me eat orange give me you." In conclusion, there seems to be no communicative reason behind ape repetitions, beyond a possible desire to please the other participant in the conversation.

Repetitions in Child Language

Repetitions within utterances are not a notable feature of child language, even though whole utterances may be repeated ad nauseam when a child persists in demanding something he or she wants: "Biscuit! Biscuit! I want a biscuit!". Within utterances, repetitions are mostly syllabic reduplications, and have three main sources. The first of these are neutral "babbles," *babababa, mamama*, and so on, which occur from around six months onward, and are often seized on by adults and reinforced as words such as *mama, dada, papa* (Jakobson, 1962). A second source of reduplication occurs in adult babytalk. "Words" such as *gee-gee, quack-quack, itty-itty, choo-choo, wow-wow* are learnt from English-speaking adults, who often encourage such repeats. Phonological processes provide a third source of repeated syllables. A number of characteristic processes occur in the speech of young children (Ingram, 1986). Some lead to reduplication, in particular when consonant and vowel harmony are combined (e.g. *kuku* for "kudu"; *gugu* for "Dougal," *lili* for "really"). The reduplications from the third source do not seem to serve any useful purpose, and appear primarily to be due to the child's immature phonetic/phonological system, as when there is a discrepancy between a stored representation and the ability to reproduce this accurately (Vihman, 1978; Aitchison, 1987b). In conclusion, early infant babbling may be similar to some of the unstructured repetitions in ape signing. But elsewhere child reduplications which are not copied from adult models mostly reflect an intermediate stage through which children pass en route to a mature sound system.

Repetitions in Pidgins

Repetition in pidgins almost always occurs for a purpose, such as disambiguation, or the enlargement of a limited repertoire. The examples quoted below are from Tok Pisin (Papua New Guinea), though similar examples can be found in other pidgins (e.g. Todd, 1984:9, who quotes examples from Cameroon pidgin; cf. Holm, 1988:88f).

Homonymy is sometimes avoided by reduplication. Pidgins have a smaller repertoire of sounds than full languages, potentially leading to multiple homonyms. In Tok Pisin the English-based words "ship" and "sheep" would fall together, so would "fish" and "piss." The potential ambiguity has been solved by reduplication, with *sip* retained for "ship," but with reduplicated *sipsip* for "sheep." Similarly, *pis* is the normal word for "fish," but *pispis* is used for "urinate."

Iterative or durative actions in pidgins are frequently expressed by repetitions, as in *em i krai i krai* "He kept on shouting." In Tok Pisin a repeated verb may be replaced by the repetition of *i go i go: mi slip i go i go* "I kept on sleeping, I slept on and on." Sometimes a repeated verb occurs together with *i go: mipela wok long singaut singaut i go i go i go* (Laycock, 1970:54). "We set on wailing and wailing and wailing."

Intensification may also be expressed by repetition, as in *bikpela bikpela pis* "a really big fish," and so may distribution, in the sense of "each, one by one": *ol i go wanpela wanpela* "they went one by one."

Repetitions, then, are dissimilar in the three types of data. In ape signing, they are random and unstructured iterations. In child language, some are early babbles, which may be comparable to the ape repeats. Others are either copied from adults, or are due to processes typically found in immature phonetic/phonological systems. In pidgins, repetitions clarify or enrich an impoverished system.

OMISSIONS

The types of words omitted are also dissimilar in the various sources.

Omissions in Ape Signing

The omissions found in Nim's signing seem essentially motiveless: he appeared to be equally likely to omit the subject, verb or object (Terrace, 1979). Among his 25 most frequent two-sign combinations, we find *Nim eat, eat Nim* (omission of object), *gum eat, grape eat* (omission of subject), *banana me, banana Nim* (omission of verb). Among his most frequent three-sign combinations, we find *eat me Nim, eat Nim eat, Nim me eat, Nim eat Nim* (omission of object), *nut Nim nut, sweet Nim sweet* (omission of verb). Such extreme variation suggests that the omissions were simply random.

Omissions in Child Language

Children in the early stages of speech omit the "little words," such as pronouns, prepositions, copulas, articles. A recent theory has suggested that English children omit subject pronouns because they have "set a parameter" wrongly under the false assumption that English is a language such as Italian which allows pronouns to be dropped at the beginning of sentences (Hyams, 1986). This theory, however, does not explain why children omit items, not just subject pronouns. A more traditional, and more plausible view is that children primarily leave out unstressed items, which are insufficiently salient (Gleitman and Wanner, 1982). They have possibly heard them, but attend selectively to the stressed items. Since child omissions are often based on prosodic factors, considerable ambiguity can arise, as when a child says: *Mummy car* to mean either "Mummy's car" or "Mummy's in the car."

A further reason of child omissions is that children tend to adopt a strategy: "One word for each unit of meaning," a principle widely acknowledged in the literature (e.g. Clark, 1987, who refers to it as the "Principle of Contrast"). If they are unable to assign a consistent meaning to a segment, then they ignore it. For example, English children have been found to omit the verb *be* from the progressive at a time when they already include it as a copula. They say: *Mummy coming* for "Mummy is coming" at a time when they already say: *Daddy is a doctor* (Brown, 1973). The apparent reason is that they cannot assign a meaning to the verb *be* partly because they do not expect discontinuous constructions (Slobin, 1985).

Overall, children's omissions are attributable to the immaturity of the child. He or she pays selective attention to salient aspects of the utterance, and omits "mini" items which cannot be assigned a clear meaning.

Omissions in Pidgins

Omissions in pidgins are somewhat difficult to classify, since it is easier to speak of optional insertions, rather than omissions. For example, "pastness" or "anteriority" may optionally be expressed in Tok Pisin by the preverbal marker *bin* or the post-verbal marker *pinis*, but it is not essential to do so.

There is no particular tendency to omit unstressed items, since plenty of these occur in any text, such as the so-called "predicate marker" *i*, and pronouns *em* "he, she, it," *ol* "they." Omissions occur primarily when a subject or object is redundant:

> *ol i kilim em. Kilim em na olgeta i go bek nau long ples* (Dutton, 1973: 267). 'They killed him. [They] killed him and all went back to their village' (redundant subject).

> *em i lukim wanpela liklik torosel em i karim wanpela banana, wanpela, em i karim na i go pundaun gen* (Laycock, 1970:59). 'He saw a little tortoise carrying a banana, a single one, he was carrying [it], and fell down again' (redundant object).

Omissions, therefore, differ in each data source. The chimp omissions are random. Child language omissions occur primarily for prosodic reasons, though may also be found when a child cannot assign a meaning to a linguistic form. Pidgins tend to omit redundant items.

DISCUSSION

In the previous sections, ape signing, child language, and pidgins were shown to be dissimilar in nature, in spite of occasional surface similarities. Omissions and repetitions in these data sources highlight the following points:

1. Ape signing lacks structure.
2. Children have an inbuilt understanding of structure, but they are immature speakers who cannot cope fully with either the sound patterns or the syntax. They therefore pay selective attention to some items at the expense of others.
3. Pidgin speakers are fully aware of the resources of language, and use these to clarify and enrich an impoverished system.

In view of the disparity of the data, one might at first sight abandon these sources of evidence, and return to a situation in which the topic of the origin of language was considered speculative and pointless. But this is unnecessary. Inferences can be drawn from these sources, if this is done with caution.

Judging from the animal world in general, significant behavioral developments come about in a number of stages:

1. There is a substrate of abilities which are common to a wide range of animals.
2. In a few of these animals, some of these abilities converge in a new kind of behavior, which is more than the sum of the original parts. The convergence occurs either as a response to some challenge in the environment, or is brought about by some independent additional development.
3. Once a new type of behavior has occurred, its presence fluctuates for a time, and it may disappear. But if it persists, its initial nature lays down the possible paths along which it can develop.
4. A number of the possible paths may be tried out, but some of them lead to dead ends. Those which prove fruitful become reinforced.

If we look at this pattern in relation to the origin of human language, we can glean information about some basic primate abilities by considering primate call systems. We note, for example, that discrete sound signals can be used for communication, and that there is a potential for modifying them in various ways. We can make further observations about primate abilities by noting which facets of human language apes find easy to grasp, such as the ability to symbolize.

The crucial difference between ape signing and child language is that children instinctively structure their utterances. We can then make hypotheses as to the convergences which led to this development, and its possible causes. Perhaps, due to the development of an upright posture, humans became capable of making many more sounds (Lieberman, 1984). This may in turn have led to the coining of numerous "lexical items." At a certain point, the number may have become too large for easy memorization: of the various possible ways of coping with these lists of items, perhaps the "structure" option was the one which proved viable.

Pidgins can then be examined to see which options are open to a simple system which relies on content words and word order. Those permanently selected are likely to involve strategies which reinforce one another, and which are easy to parse (Aitchison, 1987a). Finally, creoles can show how the options chosen by a pidgin can be elaborated into a full language. This will occur partly for structural reasons, partly because of pragmatic and psychological ones (Aitchison, 1989b).

Of course, we are still a long way from understanding exactly how language developed in the human race. But the course of action proposed above will narrow down the options to those which are consistent with the various kinds of evidence. This "constructionist" viewpoint might in the long run be able to explain why languages are the way they are: it cuts across essentialist and evolutionist arguments, since it provides an evolutionist account, but one which allows development to occur in leaps.

CONCLUSION

This paper began by noting that hypotheses on the origin of language were numerous and contradictory, and suggested that this was partly because a number of disparate sources of evidence were lumped together uncritically. In this situation, it was always possible to select convenient examples in order to support any point, as in one tenet of Murphy's Law: "Enough research will tend to support your theory."

The paper therefore considered some of these sources: primate vocalizations, ape signing, child language, pidgins and creoles. It showed that these were heterogeneous in nature, and that not one of them could be regarded as a true reflection of the early origins of language. The heterogeneity was demonstrated in particular by considering the repetitions and omissions in each type of data.

Finally, the paper suggested that it was possible to put forward cautious hypotheses which were in accordance with these disparate data sources by following a constructionist viewpoint: using evidence from them, one could first of all observe a substrate of basic primate abilities. Hypotheses could then be put forward as to how and why convergence might have led to a leap forward in a communicative system. Finally, one could then consider the options available to simple systems, and, by studying pidgins and creoles show which ones are likely to be permanently adopted by human languages, and which ones abandoned.

REFERENCES

Aitchison, J. 1983. On roots of language. *Language and Communication* 3:83–97.
_____. 1987a. Other keyholes: language universals from a pidgin-creole viewpoint. In *Noam Chomsky: Consensus and Controversy* ed. by S. and C. Modgil, pp. 93–103. Lewes, Sussex: Falmer Press.
_____. 1987b. *Words in the Mind: An Introduction to the Mental Lexicon.* Oxford: Blackwell.
_____. 1989a. *The Articulate Mammal: An Introduction to Psycholinguistics.* 3rd ed. London: Unwin-Hyman.
_____. 1989b. Spaghetti junctions and recurrent routes: some preferred pathways in language evolution. *Lingua* 77:209–229.
Arends, J. 1986. Genesis and development of the equative copula in Sranan. In *Substrata versus Universals in Creole Genesis* ed. by P. Muyskens and N. Smith, pp. 103–127. Amsterdam: Benjamins.
Bickerton, D. 1981. *Roots of Language.* Ann Arbor, MI: Karoma.
Brown, R. 1973. *A First Language.* Cambridge, Mass.: Harvard University Press.
Clark, E. V. 1987. The principle of contrast: a constraint on language acquisition. In *Mechanisms of Language Acquisition* ed. by B. MacWhinney, pp. 1–33. Hillsdale, N.J.: Erlbaum.
Demers, R. A. 1988. Language and animal communication. In *Linguistics: The Cambridge Survey.* Vol. 3, ed. by F. J. Newmeyer, pp. 314–335. Cambridge: Cambridge University Press.
Dingwall, W. O. 1988. The evolution of human communicative behavior. In *Linguistics: The Cambridge Survey.* Vol. 3, ed. by F. J. Newmeyer, pp. 274–313. Cambridge: Cambridge University Press.
Dutton, T. E. 1973. *Conversational New Guinea Pidgin (Pacific Linguistics D-12).* Canberra: Australian National University.
Gardner, R. A. and B. T. Gardner. 1969. Teaching sign language to a chimpanzee. *Science* 165:664–672.
Gleitman, L. R. and E. Wanner. 1982. Language acquisition: the state of the state of the art. In *Language Acquisition: The State of the Art* ed. by E. Wanner and L. R. Gleitman, pp. 3–48. Cambridge: Cambridge University Press.
Goodman, M. 1985. Review of Bickerton (1981). *International Journal of American Linguistics* 51:109–137.
Hewes, G. W. 1977. Language origin theories. In *Language Learning by a Chimpanzee: The LANA Project* ed. by D. M. Rumbaugh, pp. 3–54. New York: Academic Press.
Holm, J. 1988. *Pidgins and Creoles.* Vol. 1. Cambridge: Cambridge University Press.
Hyams, N. M. 1986. *Language Acquisition and the Theory of Parameters.* Dordrecht: Reidel.
Ingram, D. 1986. Phonological development: production. In *Language Acquisition.* 2nd ed., ed. by P. Fletcher and M. Garman, pp. 223–239. Cambridge: Cambridge University Press.
Jakobson, R. 1962. Why "mama" and "papa"? In *Child Language: A Book of Readings* ed. by A. Bar-Adon and W. F. Leopold, pp. 212–217. Englewood Cliffs, N.J.: Prentice-Hall.
Keesing, R. M. 1988. *Melanesian Pidgin and Oceanic Substrate.* Stanford, California: Stanford University Press.

Laycock, D. 1970. *Materials in New Guinea Pidgin (Coastal and Lowlands) (Pacific Linguistics* D-5). Canberra: Australian National University.

Lieberman, P. 1984. *The Biology and Evolution of Language.* Cambridge, Mass.: Harvard University Press.

Mühlhäusler, P. 1986. *Pidgin and Creole Linguistics.* Oxford: Blackwell.

Murdoch, I. 1969. *The Nice and the Good.* Harmondsworth: Penguin.

Nottebohm, F. 1975. A zoologist's view of some language phenomena with particular emphasis on vocal learning. In *Foundations of Language Development: An Interdisciplinary Approach* ed. by E. H. Lenneberg and E. Lenneberg, pp. 61–103. New York: Academic Press.

Patterson, F. G. 1978. The gesture of a gorilla: language acquisition in another pongid. *Brain and Language* 5:72–97.

Peters, A. M. 1977. Language learning strategies: does the whole equal the sum of the parts? *Language* 53:560–573.

Pettito, L. A. and M. S. Seidenberg. 1979. On the evidence for linguistic abilities in signing apes. *Brain and Language* 8:162–183.

Rumbaugh, D. M. 1977. *Language Learning by a Chimpanzee: The LANA Project.* New York: Academic Press.

Seyfarth, R. M., D. L. Cheney and P. Marler. 1980. Monkey responses to three different alarm calls: evidence for predator classification and semantic communication. *Science* 210:801–803.

Slobin, D. 1985. *The Crosslinguistic Study of Language Acquisition.* Hillsdale, N.J.: Erlbaum.

Struhsaker, T. T. 1967. Auditory communication among vervet monkeys (Cercopithecus aethiops). In *Social Communication among Primates* ed. by S. A. Altmann, pp. 281–324. Chicago: University of Chicago Press.

Terrace, H. S. 1979. *Nim.* New York: Knopf.

Todd, L. 1984. *Modern Englishes: Pidgins and Creoles.* Oxford: Blackwell.

Vihman, M. M. 1978. Consonant harmony: its scope and function in child language. In *Universals of Human Language* ed. by J.H. Greenberg, pp. 281–334. Stanford, California: Stanford University Press.

Whitney, W. D. 1893. *Oriental and Linguistic Studies.* Vol. 1. New York: Charles Scribner's Sons.

Wilson, B. and A. M. Peters. 1988. What are you cookin' on a hot? Movement constraints in the speech of a three-year-old blind child. *Language* 64:249–273.

=

FOR DISCUSSION AND REVIEW

1. When discussing the call systems of primates, Aitchison mentions the cries of human infants. What point is she making about primate calls?

2. A number of primates have learned signed languages and use them not in imitation but on their own in ways that are typical of human language. Give some examples from the signed languages of Washoe, Lana, Koko, and Nim. Taken together, why are such examples considered indications of real language use?

3. What seems to be true of all children in the early stages of acquiring a language? Is this true of primate signing as well? Explain.

4. What is a *pidgin* language? How does it differ from a "full" language?

5. What is a *creole,* and how does it develop? Why does Aitchison suggest it is worth looking at the process of creolization?

6. How are repetitions different in the three types of data Aitchison analyzed?

7. In regard to omissions in child language, explain the principle "one word for each unit of meaning." Why might children say *Mommy sleeping* even though they also say *Daddy is a fireman?*

8. According to Aitchison, what are some of the significant differences between primate signing, child language development, and pidgin languages? How should we use these sources to construct theories about the origins of language?

Projects for "Language and Its Study"

1. Harvey A. Daniels presents, "nine fundamental ideas about language." List the nine one-sentence ideas, and show them to five people who are not in your class. Summarize their reactions. Are some of the ideas more controversial or less accepted than others?

2. On pages 15–16, Daniels briefly describes the Sapir-Whorf hypothesis: that the structure and vocabulary of a people's language influences that people's cultural patterns, social organization, and worldview. In class, explore this hypothesis.

Form small groups. Each group should take one part of the grammar of a language they know (such as pronouns) or a set of related vocabulary items and try to make an argument that the language either influences or reflects a cultural worldview. For instance, one group might consider whether verb tenses *reflect* cultural notions of time, making a counterargument to the Sapir-Whorf hypothesis. A second group might try to support Sapir-Whorf by arguing that culturally specific notions of time *influence* a language's verb tenses. Other groups might construct pro or con arguments involving sets of vocabulary items.

An excellent summary of such arguments can be found in Danny D. Steinberg's *Psycholinguistics: Language, Mind and World*. See also "Mentalese," in *The Language Instinct* by Steven Pinker and Geoffrey K. Pullum's, *The Great Eskimo Vocabulary Hoax and Other Irreverent Essays on the Study of Language*. (All are listed in the bibliography at the end of this section.)

3. In "Language: An Introduction," W. F. Bolton points out that "perhaps the most distinctive property of language is that its users can create sentences never before known, and yet perfectly understandable to their hearers and readers." He calls this property "productivity."

Test the validity of this claim. Pair off with someone you don't know well. Take turns creating sentences that are not likely to have been made before. These sentences should be grammatically correct but may seem silly (for example, *I put the lamp in my shoe* or *Even moths drink milk after dark*). Is the recipient able to understand? Discuss how that is possible. Try writing something never written before and exchange it. Is it possible to read something new? Try writing a very complicated sentence. Discuss how it is possible to construct new, grammatically complicated sentences.

4. Your instructor will show an image, such as a photograph or cartoon, to the class. Working individually, write a sentence describing the image. Then read the sentences out loud and compare them. How different are they? What does this project demonstrate about the property of productivity?

5. Discuss the relationship between human physiology and the production and perception of sound-based human language. Use the essays in this part and Part Two, as well as materials from the selected bibliographies, to inform your discussion. If possible, invite a university expert or community professional to join you in class. How important are the vocal organs for human speech? What about conduction of sound and the auditory nerve in the inner ear?

6. In his 1982 book *The Word-A-Day Vocabulary Builder*, lexicographer Bergen Evans states:

> Words are the tools for the job of saying what you want to say. And what you want to say are your thoughts and feelings, your desires and your dislikes, your hopes and your fears, your business and your pleasure— almost everything, indeed, that makes up you. Except for our vegetable-like growth and our animal-like impulses, almost all that we are is related to our use of words. Man [sic] has been defined as a tool-using animal, but his most important tool, the one that distinguishes him from all other animals, is his speech.

Do you agree with Evans's statement? Is it possible to think without language? Can people do some creative activities without speech? Write a brief essay defending your position.

7. Harvey A. Daniels's book *Famous Last Words: The American Language Crisis Reconsidered*, from which "Nine Ideas about Language" is taken, disputes the idea that the English language is deteriorating and argues that language change is not only natural but also unavoidable. Scholars and others, from politicians to parents both past and present, have strong opinions on this issue and on the question of "correct usage." This is your opportunity to join the debate.

Divide into three groups. Each group should research one of the following positions: (a) the English language is deteriorating; (b) the English language is not deteriorating; and (c) there exists an objective, unchanging standard for "correct" English. Base your group's argument on solid information, and prepare a logical, well-documented position paper. For starters, you might consider Edwin Battistella's *Bad Language: Are Some Words Better Than Others* (2005; see bibliography) for an insightful and entertaining discussion.

8. Select a country with an official national language—a language recognized in that country's constitution or by another national agency. (Use a reliable source such as ethnologue.com to find the official languages for any existing nation.) Find out when that country gave recognition to the language. If a country has more than one national language, what are they, and were they named at the same or different times? Does the country have a government agency that monitors the development or use of the national language? What is the mission of this agency, and what kinds of activities does it sponsor? Find media coverage of changes

to language policies in the country. Write a brief summary of the information you find. Some countries to choose from are Angola, Canada, Croatia, Finland, France, Iceland, India, Indonesia, Iran, New Zealand, Pakistan, Serbia, Spain, Sudan, and Switzerland.

9. Consult at least four introductory linguistics textbooks (such as those included in the bibliography at the end of this section), and jot down the definition of *language* that each gives. Compare the definitions carefully, and write up your results. Use a graph or chart to show all the characteristics of language from all the definitions you analyzed and the source(s) of each characteristic. Doing so will reveal the characteristics possessing substantial agreement.

10. Some American schools for the deaf use a form of signed language called "Signed English" instead of American Sign Language (ASL). Research these two languages, and write a short paper on the differences and similarities between them. Be sure to include information on why some schools have such a strong preference for one language or the other. A good place to begin your research is at the Web site for the PBS documentary *Through Deaf Eyes* (www.pbs.org/weta/throughdeafeyes), which contains a history of sign language in America.

11. Technologies for hearing are advancing all the time. Write a report on the latest designs and equipment for hearing. In your report, include responses by proponents of signed language. For instance, one of the more popular current devices is the cochlear implant, which is considered controversial among some sign language users. Discuss the arguments for and against using such technological developments. A discussion of these implants is included at the *Through Deaf Eyes* Web site (see project 10).

12. Individually or in small groups, prepare answers to the following questions for a class discussion: (a) What are your three most common gestures? What are your instructor's three most common gestures? What conclusions (about personality, setting, etc.) can you draw from these? (b) In a conversation, how do you know when someone is losing interest? Is not losing interest? (c) What aspects of a person's appearance cause you to feel (at least initially) friendly? Hostile? (d) In what ways do you act differently at home from the way you do at a friend's? Why?

13. George A. Miller claims that our ability to interact with each other relies on knowing and understanding a variety of nonverbal communication behaviors. Using images from a Web site devoted to nonverbal communication, such as Professor Dane Archer's at University of California–Santa Cruz (nonverbal.ucsc.edu/), discuss the culturally defined meanings and uses of what you see. Make and defend claims about specific facial gestures, body positions, proxemic arrangements, and personal appearances.

14. Jean Aitchison looks for the origins of human language by examining different linguistic behaviors and processes. Other researchers examine nonlinguistic developments and their possible link to language

in humans. In his book *Laughter*, for instance, Robert Provine asserts that becoming upright and bipedal was a necessary condition for language:

> In quadrupeds, there is a one-to-one correlation between breathing pattern and stride because the lungs must be fully inflated to add rigidity to the thoracic complex (sternum, ribs and associated musculature) that absorbs forelimb impacts during running. Without such synchronization, the thorax is weak and unable to absorb the impact. When primates stood and walked on two legs, the thorax was freed of its support function during locomotion, breaking the link between breathing patterns and stride. This flexibility enabled humans to regulate breathing and ultimately, speak.

Divide into four groups. Two groups should take the position that language developed from linguistic origins and the other two take the position that language developed from nonlinguistic origins. Then each group should research and develop a ten-minute presentation arguing for its position. In class, each group should present its argument; then, hold a brief debate using the information provided in each presentation.

Selected Bibliography

Ager, Simon. *Omniglot: Writing Systems and Languages of the World.* 2007. <www.omniglot.com>. [An online resource with information on writing systems and languages of the world; features a user blog for information exchange.]

Akmajian, Adrian, Richard A. Demers, Ann K. Farmer, and Robert M. Harnish. *Linguistics: An Introduction to Language and Communication.* 5th ed. Cambridge, MA: MIT Press, 2001. [An introductory text that demonstrates how the fields of linguistics and communication interact rather than viewing them as isolated concepts.]

alphaDictionary. 2006. The Lexiteria Corporation. <www.alphadictionary. com/langdir.html>. [A one-stop guide to thousands of languages and dialects.]

Axtell, Roger, ed.. *Do's and Taboos around the World.* Hoboken, NJ: Wiley, 2003. [A guide to international behavior and protocol.]

Battistella, Edwin. *Bad Language: Are Some Words Better Than Others?* Oxford: Oxford UP, 2005. [A study of what constitutes "good" and "bad" language that includes a discussion of attitudes toward immigrant foreign language speakers.]

Baynton, Douglas C. *Forbidden Signs: American Culture and the Campaign against Sign Language.* Chicago: U of Chicago P, 1996. [Documents the social and historical difficulties encountered by American Sign Language users.]

Bolinger, Dwight. *Language: The Loaded Weapon.* New York: Longman Group, 1980. [A short but insightful introduction to language, with an emphasis on the importance of meaning.]

Burling, Robbins. *The Talking Ape: How Language Evolved.* Oxford: Oxford UP, 2005. [A readable account of the evolution of language over millions of years.]

Carstairs-McCarthy, Andrew. *The Origins of Complex Language: An Inquiry into the Evolutionary Beginnings of Syllables, Sentences and Truth.* Oxford: Oxford UP, 1999. [A well-received and controversial study of the evolution of language and why humans are the only animals to use verbal language.]

Chapman, Siobhan, and Christopher Routledge, eds. *Key Thinkers in Linguistics and the Philosophy of Language.* Oxford: Oxford UP, 2005. [An accessible reference to the key figures in language study and philosophy.]

Costello, Elaine. *Signing: How to Speak with Your Hands.* New York: Bantam Books, 1983. [A comprehensive guide to American Sign Language.]

Crystal, David. *The Cambridge Encyclopedia of Language.* 2nd ed. Cambridge: Cambridge UP, 1997. [Collection of essays includes numerous illustrations and charts.]

Deacon, Terrence W. *The Symbolic Species: The Co-Evolution of Language and the Brain.* New York: W. W. Norton, 1997. [Deacon's background in neurology and anthropology provides a unique perspective on human language and development.]

Exploring Nonverbal Communication. University of California–Santa Cruz. <http://nonverbal.ucsc.edu>. [Includes links for exploring and testing nonverbal communication understanding.]

Finegan, Edward. *Language: Its Structure and Use*, 4th ed. Belmont, CA: Heinle, 2003. [Edition includes a greater focus on political and social aspects of language.]

Fromkin, Victoria, Robert Rodman, and Nina Hyams. *An Introduction to Language*. 7th ed. Boston: Thomson Wadsworth, 2003. [One of the enduring introductory textbooks, appropriate for all levels and aspects of the study.]

Gould, Stephen. J. *The Panda's Thumb*. New York: W. W. Norton, 1980. [A collection of essays on evolution written for the American Museum of Natural History.]

Hulit, Lloyd M., and M. R. Howard. *Born to Talk: An Introduction to Speech and Language Development*. 3rd ed. Boston, MA: Allyn Bacon, 2001. [An accessible introduction that addresses such topics as bilingualism and social, cultural, and gender differences in language.]

Jackendoff, R. *Foundations of Language: Brain, Meaning, Grammar, Evolution*. Oxford: Oxford UP, 2002. [An updated assessment of Noam Chomsky's research on linguistics.]

Kenneally, Christine. *The First Word: The Search for the Origins of Language*. New York: Viking Press 2007. [Journalist traces biological beginnings of language.]

Langer, Suzanne K. *Philosophy in a New Key: A Study in the Symbolism of Reason, Rite and Art*. 3rd ed. Cambridge, MA: Harvard UP, 1956. [A classic work on the human symbol-making process and its relationship to language.]

Liddel, Scott. *Grammar, Gesture and Meaning in American Sign Language*. Cambridge: Cambridge UP, 2003. [Includes discussions of sign grammar and spatial uses of sign.]

Lieberman, Philip, and Sheila E. Blumstein. *Speech Physiology, Speech Perception, and Acoustic Phonetics*. Cambridge Studies in Speech Science and Communication. Cambridge: Cambridge UP, 1988. [An accessible yet thorough introduction to the study of speech.]

"LinguaLinks Library." *Ethnologue*. 2007. SIL International. <www.ethnologue.com/ll_docs/contents.asp> [A collection of electronic reference materials designed to support language fieldwork.]

Linguistic Society of America. Linguistics Society of America. <www. lsadc.org>. [Links to student resources and LSA bulletins, publications, and directories.]

Marcus, Gary F. *The Birth of the Mind*. New York: Basic Books, 2004. [A discussion of how genetics determines brain function and how that affects our learning of languages.]

McElree, B., S. Foraker, and L. Dyer. "Memory Structures That Subserve Sentence Comprehension." *Journal of Memory and Language* 48 (2003): 67–91. [Examines how the memory system impacts sentence comprehension.]

Nonverbal Behavior: A University of California Video Series. Dir. Dane Archer. Videocassette. Berkeley Media, 1991–2000. [A comprehensive series that explores various issues in nonverbal communication, including cultural differences, gender issues, and individual self-image.]

Pinker, Steven. *The Language Instinct: How the Mind Creates Language*. New York: Morrow, 1994. [See especially ch. 3, "Mentalese," for arguments against linguistic determinism.]

———. *Words and Rules: The Ingredients of Language*. New York: Basic Books, 1999. [An enthusiastic study of language and the relationship between how we communicate and how we think.]

Poyatos, Fernando. *Cross-Cultural Perspectives in Nonverbal Communication.* Lewiston, NY: C. J. Hogrefe, 1988. [Interesting study includes gestures, painting, photography, clothing, and architecture.]

Pullum, Geoffrey K. *The Great Eskimo Vocabulary Hoax and Other Irreverent Essays on the Study of Language.* Chicago: U of Chicago P, 1991. [A lively and sometimes whimsical collection.]

Puppel, Stanislaw, ed. *The Biology of Language.* Amsterdam & Philadelphia: John Benjamins, 1995. [A collection of essays on evolution and the origins of language.]

Rowe, Bruce M., and Diane P. Levine. *A Concise Introduction to Linguistics.* Boston: Pearson Education, 2006. [Emphasizes linguistic anthropology.]

Rumbaugh, S., Stuart G. Shankar, and Talbot J. Taylor. *Apes, Language and the Human Mind.* Oxford: Oxford UP, 1998. [A study of Kanzi, a male bonobo taught to communicate through the use of lexigrams.]

Saussure, Ferdinand de. *Course in General Linguistics.* 1915. Trans. Wade Baskin. Ed. Charles Bally and Albert Sechehaye. New York: Philosophical Library, 1959. [Based on lecture notes collected by former students, this text outlines what is typically considered the beginning of modern theoretical linguistics.]

Schwartz, Jeffrey H., and Ian Tattersall. *The Human Fossil Record*, four volumes. New York: Wiley-Liss, 2002. [A comprehensive guide to the study of evolution through fossil evidence.]

Steinberg, Danny D., Niroshi Nagata, and David P. Aline. *Psycholinguistics: Language, Mind and World.* Upper Saddle River, NJ: Pearson, 2001. [This study of language acquisition includes discussions of deaf language education and bilingualism.]

Through Deaf Eyes. March 2007. Corporation for Public Broadcasting. <www.pbs.org/weta/throughdeafeyes/index.html>. [Accompanies the PBS documentary of the same name; contains a history of sign language in America and a discussion of deaf culture.]

Tserdanelis, G., and Wai Yi Peggy Wong. *Language Files: Materials for an Introduction to Language and Linguistics.* 9th ed. Columbus: Ohio State UP, 2004. [An introductory text with useful exercises at the end of each section.]

Whorf, Benjamin Lee. *Language, Thought, and Reality.* Ed. John B. Carroll. Cambridge, MA: MIT Press, 1956. [A classic work on the relationship between language and culture.]

Wilson, Edward O. *On Human Nature.* Cambridge, MA: Harvard UP, 2004. [A well-written follow-up to Wilson's classic 1975 text, *Sociobiology*.]

PART TWO

THE SOUNDS OF LANGUAGE: PHONETICS AND PHONOLOGY

To study language, we investigate the interrelated topics of language structures and language use. The differences between these two are understood by asking two questions: What does it mean to *know* a language? What does it mean to *communicate in* a language? The former is a question about linguistic knowledge—the components of language. The latter concerns language use in the real world.

The answers to these questions are, of course, also interrelated: to use a language, we need knowledge of it. However, when examining language, we usually focus on *either* linguistic components *or* language use. While focusing on these two major fields of investigation, linguists have developed many subfields of inquiry. Here are some of the main ones:

1. Phonetics and phonology—the study of the sounds of a language and the possible relationships between its sounds.
2. Morphology—the study of the formation and structure of words and of their relationships to each other.
3. Syntax—the study of the arrangement of words in phrases and sentences.
4. Semantics—the study of the meaning of individual words, phrases, and sentences.
5. Pragmatics—the study of meaning within specific contexts.
6. Discourse—the study of how text and speech are understood and used as communicative tools.

Parts Two through Four of this book will aid your understanding of the components of language. They cover, in turn, the subfields of phonetics and phonology, morphology and syntax, and semantics and pragmatics.

Part Two introduces phonetics and phonology. Phonetics seeks to describe the physical properties of language: how sounds are formed and the patterns of their arrangement. Different languages include different sounds, and no language includes all possible sounds. Languages that include the same sounds often have different patterns for combining them. While phonetics is concerned with spoken language as a whole, phonology is concerned with the sound patterns governing individual languages and with accounting for similarities in the sound systems of different languages. As these selections show, describing the physical properties of individual sounds and explaining the patterns of relationships among sets of sounds are interrelated. In fact, current research indicates that the boundary between phonetics and phonology is not clear-cut. Investigating phonological issues calls for phonetic descriptions, and examining the features of sounds presumes phonological analysis.

In "Phonetics," Edward Callary introduces the study of speech sounds by discussing *articulatory* phonetics (the production of speech sounds) and *acoustic* phonetics (the features of the sounds themselves). He also presents the principles of phonetic transcription, which allows us to accurately represent the specific sounds of any language. The exercises within the article give readers an immediate opportunity to apply phonetic concepts to words in spoken and written American English.

In the next selection, "The Form of the Message," Nancy Bonvillain relies on contemporary research methods emphasizing interviews, onsite observations, and recordings of natural language to discuss how we produce, respond to, and understand the full range of sounds that make up a language. Her discussion helps form the bridge between phonetics and phonology by emphasizing the purpose of isolating phonetic features of human language as a basis for communicative behavior.

Finally, in "What Is Phonology? Language Sounds and Their Rules," we turn to one of the most successful approaches to describing general linguistics. The *Language Files* began as a collection of lecture notes, exercises, and other materials developed by Ohio State instructors for teaching language study at the undergraduate level. In this selection, from the ninth edition, we are guided in doing phonological analysis, forming hypotheses about how sounds influence each other, and investigating the systematic nature of language sounds.

6

Phonetics

Edward Callary

Phonetics is one of the most studied subfields of linguistics because some knowledge of phonetics is essential for understanding other areas of this discipline. Written especially for the third edition of this book (1981), the following selection, by Professor Edward Callary of Northern Illinois University, still provides a valuable introduction to articulatory and acoustic phonetics. Callary explores two aspects of the grammar of phonetics, both known by all native speakers of English: (1) the permissible sequences of sounds in English and how they can be described in terms of general rules and (2) the regular changes in sounds speakers make due to the contexts of the sounds. The exercises that appear throughout the essay reinforce and clarify the author's points, and you can use them to discuss applications of these principles and methods for interpreting other sound systems.

Phonetics is that part of linguistics concerned with the sounds and sound systems of language; it deals with how sounds are produced, their physical properties, and how the rules of language organize and change sounds from one context to another.

The study of phonetics provides information with practical applications in a variety of areas. Knowledge of how sounds are produced, perceived, and understood is necessary for clinicians who diagnose and remediate speech disorders; for language specialists who teach a nonnative language; for engineers who design more efficient telephones and create voice-based identification and security systems; and for linguists who analyze the properties common to all human languages.

As part of their work, phoneticians (people who study phonetics) analyze the characteristics of the sounds that make up the syllables, words, and sentences of spoken language. For a particular language, they ask the following: How many sounds are there (this is not as easy to answer as it sounds)? What is the best way to describe these sounds? How does the language organize sounds (how do the sounds change from one situation to another and how are they added to or deleted from words)? Ultimately, phoneticians want to know not only about individual languages but about language in general—those characteristics that are common to all languages and what they reveal about the structure and functioning of the human mind.

Since this is an introductory selection, the examples and the problems are simplified and English examples are used almost exclusively; however, the principles are applicable to all languages, since human languages differ only in their details, although the details themselves are infinitely interesting.

It is extremely important to keep the following point in mind while reading this selection: many of the ideas about language that we have assimilated are in conflict with the facts of how language actually works. In this essay on phonetics, it is especially important to emphasize that language is *sound*, not *writing*. As educated people who have spent years learning to read and spell correctly, we may have the mistaken notion that writing is somehow "real" language and that speech is an often poor attempt to express the sounds that letters naturally possess. The idea that letters "have" sounds is not only mistaken but misleading as well, since it tends to blind us to the principles and rules of our spoken language. Rather than saying, for instance, that the letter *c* has the sound [s] or [k], it is truer to the facts of language to say that, in the English spelling system, the sounds [s] and [k] are sometimes represented by the letter *c*. (For the sake of clarity, square brackets enclose sounds, and italics indicate letters of the regular alphabet.) Remember, we learn to speak and understand a complex language well before we learn to read or write that language. Many languages, even those in use today, have never been recorded in writing and are just as legitimate (and just as phonetic) as those that have been written for centuries.

ENGLISH SPELLING AND THE PHONETIC ALPHABET

In order to communicate sounds in print, we need to be able to represent them in a way that all readers can understand. This is why alphabets were invented in the first place, to assign a permanence to the ephemeral air of speech. Unfortunately, the alphabet we already know and have spent such a long time learning, the familiar ABCs or Roman alphabet, is not adequate for this task.

The relationship between sounds and their spellings is not perfect in any living language, but in English it is particularly deceiving. If you have studied a language such as Spanish or Swahili, you know that your chances of correctly pronouncing a word on first sight are quite good and, conversely, your chances of correctly spelling a word on hearing it the first time are also good. But in English there are so many different ways to represent sounds and so many unsystematic spelling "rules" that reading mistakes and spelling mistakes are common.

While there are reasons for the many discrepancies between sound and spelling in English, two are particularly important. First, with the introduction of the printing press in England in the fifteenth century, spelling began to be standardized and standard spelling reflected the pronunciation of that time. However, pronunciation has changed dramatically in the past 500 years and spelling has not. Many of the "silent letters" in contemporary English represent pronunciations of the past; for instance, the *gh* of *light*, the *k* of *knee*, and the *h* of *whale* were pronounced in earlier times.

Second, today we often have either multiple spellings for the same sound or instances where the same letter represents first one sound and then another because of adoption. When we adopt a word from a foreign language, we often adopt its spelling as well. For example, the letter *i* represents one sound in *ice* (a native English word) and a completely different sound in *police* (adopted from French).

There have been a number of attempts to modify English spelling in order to bring it into line with English pronunciation, such as writing *night* as *nite* and *though* as *tho* (the *Chicago Tribune* of the 1930s and 1940s was an especially active advocate of spelling reform); but these have come to naught and, with the advent of the spell checker, there is even less motivation for spelling reform than before, despite the fact that attempts to represent the approximately forty sounds of English using the twenty-six letters of the regular alphabet are bound to create problems.

The inconsistencies of English spelling require an unambiguous alphabet with a consistent relationship between sound and spelling—where a given sound is always represented by the same symbol and where a given symbol always represents the same sound. Such an alphabet is called a *phonetic alphabet.* Many phonetic alphabets have been devised over the years (unfortunately the symbols they use are not consistent from one phonetic alphabet to another). The phonetic alphabet this text employs is based on the most famous phonetic alphabet currently in use, the International Phonetic Alphabet (IPA), which was developed by a group of European phoneticians toward the end of the nineteenth century. One of the developers of the IPA was the English phonetician Henry Sweet, the model for Professor Henry Higgins in George Bernard Shaw's *Pygmalion* (and its musical offspring *My Fair Lady*). Higgins, who devises a universal alphabet in the play, could (according to Shaw) identify more than 130 vowels! The IPA is complex; it has been revised several times and now contains more than 100 symbols, plus diacritics and other specifying marks. This text uses far fewer symbols, since the aim is to represent the sounds of only a single language, English, and not to attempt to provide symbols for every sound in all languages, as the IPA does.

The symbols of our phonetic alphabet that represent English consonants follow, along with several words illustrating their sound values.

Notice the different ways in which many of the sounds are spelled. Most of the symbols are already familiar to you, since they have the values you might expect from the way they are represented in the regular alphabet. Five symbols use modified Roman letters: ǰ, č, š, ž, and ŋ. Since these are single sounds in English, a single letter represents each one.

PHONETIC SYMBOL	AS IN:	PHONETIC SYMBOL	AS IN:
p	pit, happen	θ	thin, bath
b	bit, rubber	ð	this, bathe
t	bet, thyme	s	sincere, science
d	did, maddest	z	haze, lose
k	sheikh, catch	š	sure, shine
g	gone, ghost	ž	treasure, azure
f	stuff, phone	č	itch, concerto
v	of, savvy	ǰ	jam, gem
m	thumb, simmer		
n	none, foreign		
ŋ	bring, thanks		
l	pale, tall		
r	berry, rhythm		
y	yet, million		
w	with, suede		
h	help, who		

The consonant symbols shouldn't present problems, since most of them are drawn from the regular alphabet and are closely related to the values we might expect. The vowels, however, present some difficulties because there are not enough vowel letters to cover all sound values. As you can see from the list below, contrary to what you learned in elementary school, there are more than a dozen vowels in English, not five. Look at the symbols and their sound values and try to pronounce the sounds (not the words) several times. Pay particular attention to the symbol [ə]; this symbol is called *schwa* and it represents one of the most frequent sounds in English. In the regular alphabet schwa is spelled using all the vowel letters: *a*bility, blasph*e*my, eas*i*ly, c*o*nnect, c*u*p and by using many combinations of vowel letters.

PHONETIC SYMBOL	AS IN:	PHONETIC SYMBOL	AS IN:
i	each, machine	e	able, they
I	sieve, system	ɛ	said, guest
æ	at, plaid	o	load, foe
ə	about, son	ɔ	raw, fought
u	move, ooze	a	father, honor
ʊ	book, full	ay	sigh, buy
		aw	shout, cow
		oy	soy, lawyer

PHONETIC TRANSCRIPTION

One of the first things you must learn is how to represent words phonetically; that is, how to write words using the symbols of our phonetic alphabet. This is easy; all it requires is a little practice and a willingness to think phonetically rather than orthographically (in terms of standard spelling). Once you learn to transcribe words, you can explore more interesting areas, such as how a language organizes sounds and how sounds fit into general patterns as defined by the rules of that language.

In order to transcribe phonetically, you first need to determine how many sounds there are in a particular word. Then you need to determine the phonetic symbol from the previously provided lists that represents each of these sounds. Remember, there are exactly the same number of symbols as there are sounds. Use the word *shake* as an example. It has five letters, but only three sounds, so use three symbols to write it phonetically. From the consonant list you see that [š] represents the first sound, [e] represents the vowel, and [k] represents the final sound, so the word transcription is [šek]. (Remember that phonetic symbols are enclosed in square brackets.) As a second example, the word *knee*, although spelled with four letters, is transcribed [ni] because it is composed of two sounds.

EXERCISE 1

Transcribe each of the following words using the appropriate phonetic symbols from the consonant and vowel lists.

Group 1: Monosyllabic Words

shut	noise	scene	juice
eye	guess	owe	piece
wrong	ouch	phrase	school
gym	who	those	friend
tight	tongue	now	was
quick	rhyme	rough	those
shook	why	ache	one
axe	cheese	month	lounge
doubt	debt	of	off
says	moist	cheese	

Group 2: Bisyllabic Words

echo	unique	many	okay
hygiene	onion	penguin	champagne
biscuit	extinct	antique	although
chronic	healthy	physics	croquet
monkey	caffeine	issue	

The pronunciation of the words in these two groups varies little; generally, they are pronounced the same way throughout the country and in most situations. But many words have more than one pronunciation; one pronunciation is used in some parts of the country while another pronunciation is used in other parts. For example, large sections of the country pronounce *don* and *dawn* the same way, while other large sections do not. Most often, however, different pronunciations are the result of different contexts; we pronounce a word one way in one social setting and another way in a different social setting. For instance, the word *literature* is likely to be pronounced one way when we are talking informally with our friends and another way when we are giving a formal class presentation. The words *candidate* and *history*, as well, usually have formal and informal pronunciations. Can you describe them?

Unfortunately, Americans have long labored under the misguided assumption, especially where language is concerned, that there is one right way to do something, and all other ways are wrong. This is regrettable since, just as we wear different clothes for different occasions and use different words in different circumstances (you might say "shucks" or "darn it" when talking with your parents or other elders; this might differ from what you would say to your dormitory friends!), we use different pronunciations for different occasions. One is not right and the others wrong; each pronunciation is appropriate in its place, and to use variations of pronunciation interchangeably might label us as snooty, pretentious, or ignorant of the English language. It is impossible to over-stress this point, since many people, no matter how well educated or well intentioned, honestly believe that informal pronunciation is sloppy, slovenly, ungrammatical, illiterate, lazy, and ignorant, or all of these. This is not true: most Americans pronounce the word *today* at least two ways, [təde] and [tude], and the phonetic alphabet also expresses both pronunciations. In addressing a formal gathering we might say "I am pleased to be here [tude]." But outside such a setting we are more likely to say "It's good to be here [təde]."

In the exercises below, it is important that you transcribe each of the words as you generally would pronounce them in informal American English. You may not use the informal pronunciations all the time or even most of the time; you may even regard some pronunciations as "wrong," but be aware of the fact that they are characteristic of American English. And be particularly wary of schwa. This exercise will seem artificial, since usually you do not pronounce in isolation; otherwise you might tend to substitute a different vowel for schwa. For instance, it is tempting to transcribe a word like *polite* as [polayt]. But it is important to recognize that, informally, it is usually pronounced [pəlayt]. Is it wrong to transcribe the word *salami* as [salami]? Or should it be [səlami]? The answer is yes—and no. It depends upon the pronunciation you want to represent. If you want to indicate the pronunciation used by your third grade teacher while giving a spelling test, [salami] is correct; if you want to represent the pronunciation of *salami* used by most Americans in general conversation, then [səlami] is correct. The differences will become clearer to you with practice.

<hr />

EXERCISE 2

In this exercise, transcribe to represent informal American pronunciation.

Group 3

among	column	extra	achieve
Asia	supply	fatigue	command
succeed	Canada	mosquito	iguana
kangaroo	Miami	Achilles	apathy
bungalow	cathedral	odyssey	coincide
Hiawatha	macaroni	alfalfa	oxygen
business	brilliant	moustache	baloney

Group 4

zucchini	postpone	family	chestnut
buzzed	seconds	consumes	trucks
clothes	Wednesday	atom	atomic
relaxed	adjective	coughed	physicist

ARTICULATORY PHONETICS

In order to understand how language uses sounds, it is important to understand how sounds are produced by the human vocal apparatus; in other words, to know something about *articulatory phonetics*, so called because sounds are described by the actions (articulations) of the vocal tract as they are produced. Figure 6.1 is a diagram of the human vocal tract, with those areas that are especially important in speech production labeled. Refer to this diagram while reading this chapter as often as necessary and try to locate the relevant areas of your own vocal tract with your tongue or finger.

We produce speech sounds by modifying a stream of air as we push it by the lungs through the trachea and ultimately out of the oral or nasal cavities, or both. We modify the airstream by changing the size or shape, or both, of the cavities in which the airstream resonates. Just as we produce sounds of different pitches when we blow over the openings of different size bottles, we produce different sounds by changing the size and shape of the resonating cavities. With [i], for instance, we use a tiny resonating cavity, and the result is a high-pitched sound; the opposite is true for [a], where we open our mouth fully.

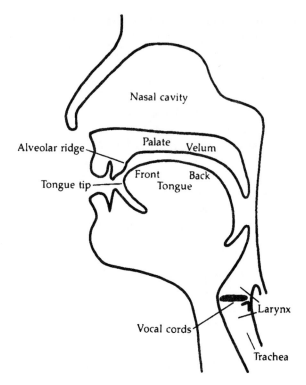

FIGURE 6.1   Human Vocal Tract.

Stated this way the production of speech sounds seems trivial, obvious, and incredibly easy. But the facts of articulation prove otherwise. The production of even the simplest sound is the result of a marvelously complex activity that involves the coordination of dozens of muscles, all acting with the precision and timing of a ballet. The fact that this occurs unconsciously, thousands of times a day, is all the more remarkable.

CONSONANTS

Consonants are sounds created by obstructing airflow, either completely as in the first sound of *dine*, or partially, as in the first sound of *fine*. Consonants are classified by three factors: (1) the location of the obstruction within the oral tract; (2) the nature of the obstruction; and (3) the state of the vocal cords. The sites in the vocal tract where we set up obstructions are called the *points of articulation*, and one way of describing consonants is by referring to these points. For English, there are six points of articulation:

1. *Bilabial* (bi, "two" + labia, "lips"). By completely blocking the airstream with both lips you produce [p], [b], or [m]. Therefore,

[p], [b], and [m] are called *bilabial sounds*. Make each of these sounds, as well as those that follow, several times and pay particular attention to the action of your tongue and lips as you do.

2. *Labio-dental*. These sounds are made by bringing your lower lip into contact with your upper teeth. The sounds [f] and [v] are labio-dentals.

3. *Interdental*. As the term suggests, interdental sounds are made by placing your tongue tip between your teeth. There are two interdental sounds in English: [θ] and [ð]; both are usually spelled *th*.

4. *Alveolar*. The alveolar ridge is the bony crest that lies where your teeth join your palate. Most languages have a number of sounds articulated in the alveolar area; English has six: [t], [d], [n], [s], [z], and [l].

5. *Palatal*. The roof of the mouth is made up of two distinct parts: a hard, front part called the palate (from the Latin word for "plate," as in an artist's palette), and a soft, back part, called the velum. You can easily find the dividing line between the palate and the velum by sliding your tongue over your palate. In English there are six palatal sounds: [č], [ǰ], [š], [ž], [r], and [y].

6. *Velar*. As noted, the velum is the soft, fleshy area lying to the rear of the palate. Check its location in figure 6.1. In English, velar sounds are articulated by bringing the back of the tongue into contact with the velum; velar sounds are [k], [g], and [ŋ].

Point of articulation is only one parameter of consonant articulation, however; another is *manner of articulation*. Manner of articulation refers to the way in which the airstream is obstructed at any given point of articulation. In all languages there are several ways to obstruct the airstream; four of the major manners of articulation are:

1. *Stops* (an older term, but one you may still hear, is *plosive*, since these sounds are exploded). As the term suggests, stop refers to a complete blockage of the airstream. There are six stops in English: the bilabials, [p] and [b], in which the lips block the airstream; the alveolars, [t] and [d], where blockage is between the tongue tip and alveolar ridge; and the velars, [k] and [g], where the back of the tongue contacts the velum. (Make these sounds several times.)

2. *Fricatives* (related to the word *friction*). To produce fricatives, you narrow the vocal tract at one point and force air through the opening, setting up a turbulent airstream. In English, there are the labio-dental fricatives, [f] and [v]; the interdental fricatives, [θ] and [ð]; the alveolar fricatives [s] and [z]; and the palatal fricatives, [š] and [ž]. Other languages have different fricatives; if you have studied Spanish, you know that the *b* in *Cuba* is a bilabial fricative, made by bringing both lips close together and forcing air through the narrowing.

3. *Affricates* (not to be confused with fricatives). Affricates are combination sounds made by articulating a stop and a fricative

in rapid succession, almost simultaneously. Affricates are found in the first sounds in *chin* and *gin,* and the final sounds in *itch* and *edge.* The affricate of *chin* is a combination of the stop [t] and the fricative [š], and the affricate of *gin* is a combination of the stop [d] and the fricative [ž]. You can think of affricates as single sounds since they function as single units in English; therefore, you represent them using single characters from the phonetic alphabet.

4. *Nasals.* The velum acts as a kind of drawbridge in articulation, allowing or prohibiting airflow into the nasal cavity when necessary. If the velum is lowered, the pathway to the nasal cavity is open and air can resonate in both the oral and nasal cavities; if the velum is raised, it shuts off access to the nasal cavity. Sounds made with resonance in the nasal cavity are called *nasal sounds;* all other sounds are *oral sounds.* In English there are three nasals: [m], [n], and [ŋ].

The last item to consider in the production of sounds is the action of the vocal cords as a sound is articulated. This action is particularly important, since it is important in phonetic rules. Within the larynx, the cartilaginous structure known as the Adam's apple, lie two sheets of elastic tissue called the *vocal cords,* or *vocal folds* or *vocal bands.* For the purposes of describing speech sounds in this text, we will consider that the vocal cords assume one of two positions: relaxed and relatively far apart, or tensed and drawn close together, so that there is only a narrow opening (called the *glottis*) between them. The vocal cords are in the relaxed position when we make sounds such as [f] or [s], and in the tensed position when we articulate [v] or [z]. When we articulate [s] or [f], the vocal cords remain relatively still, but for [z] and [v] they vibrate rapidly; they open and close several thousand times each second. This vocal cord vibration is called *voice* and sounds produced with vocal cord vibration are called *voiced sounds;* all other sounds are *voiceless.*

You can easily check for the presence of voice by placing your fingers in your ears and articulating first one sound and then another. The buzzing you hear with some sounds but not others is voice. Try making a long *sssssss,* then a long *zzzzzzz.* Now make a long [θ] and a long [ð]. Which of these sounds is voiced, [s] or [z]? [θ] or [ð]? Is [m] voiced? How about [l]?

Each sound can be described as a combination of: (1) its point of articulation (bilabial, palatal, etc.), (2) its manner of articulation (fricative, nasal, etc.), and (3) whether or not it is voiced. For instance, [f] is a voiceless labio-dental fricative; [ǰ] is a voiced palatal affricate.

This information is summarized in figure 6.2, which shows each sound and indicates its point of articulation, its manner of articulation, and whether it is voiced or voiceless. The points of articulation appear as horizontal headings and the manners of articulation appear as vertical

	Bilabial	Labio-dental	Interdental	Alveolar	Palatal	Velar
Stop	p			t		k
	b			d		g
Fricative		f	θ	s	š	
		v	ð	z	ž	
Affricate					č	
					ǰ	
Nasal	m			n	ŋ	

FIGURE 6.2   **English Obstruents.**

headings at the left. Not all consonants are included in figure 6.2, only those called *obstruents*, sounds that result from obstructing airflow: stops, fricatives, affricates, and nasals. Notice that each cell in figure 6.2 is divided into two parts: a top part for the voiceless member of a pair and a bottom part for the voiced member. Since all nasals are voiced, the cells in this row are not divided.

Figure 6.2 shows clearly that sounds are not indivisible units but are made up of the smaller, fundamental components of point of articulation, manner of articulation, and voicing, which combine in unique ways to create different sounds. From this perspective, a phonetic symbol (or the sounds it represents) is merely a convenient way to represent a specific combination of a point of articulation, a manner of articulation, and voicing. Further discussion of this notion follows later, and there are many references to figure 6.2 in the following pages, since it provides information vital to understanding how English organizes its sounds into groups and changes those groups systematically from one context to another. For now, use figure 6.2 to grasp a general sense of how the sounds are arranged and how they relate to one another.

VARIATION IN SOUNDS

The opening paragraphs of this chapter mentioned that determining the number of sounds in a language is not as easy as it might seem; it is, in fact, often difficult and phoneticians argue frequently over what they consider to be a sound in a particular language. The reasons for the debate arise in part because it is difficult in many cases to determine if a sound is basic to the sound system of a language or if it should be considered a variant of another sound. There is a great deal of variability among sounds and, to illustrate the problems involved, consider the "sound" *t*. Notice that there are no brackets around *t*; we will see the reason for this shortly. Look at how we pronounce *t* in the set of words where *t* occurs initially—words like *top* and *tuck*—and contrast this pronunciation with that of *t* in the set of words in which *t* follows [s], such as *stop* and *stuck*.

Put your fingers on your lips as you first say *top* and then *stop, tuck* and then *stuck*. Do this several times. You should notice that the *t* in one of these sets of words is accompanied by a puff of air (called aspiration), while the *t* of the other set is not. Which word has an aspirated *t*? *Top* or *stop, tuck* or *stuck*?

Now consider the *t* in the word *metal*. Is it more like the *t* of *top* or the *t* of *stop*? Is it different from both of these? Say the word to yourself several times and compare your pronunciation of *metal* with your pronunciation of *medal*. Are *metal* and *medal* pronounced identically or differently? In general conversation most Americans pronounce them exactly alike. Remember, if two words are pronounced the same they must be transcribed the same way. Would you say that the medial (middle) sound of both *metal* and *medal* is more like [t] or more like [d]?

As a final example, look at words like *pot* and *right*, where a final *t* occurs. In this case, English provides an option: you can pronounce *pot* with a puff of air accompanying the *t* as with *top*, or you can just block the airstream at the alveolar ridge and not release it at all. (You can see this nonrelease more clearly with a final *p*, as in *cup*, than with final *t*.)

These examples illustrate that *t* can appear in a number of different forms: sometimes it is accompanied by a puff of air and at other times it is not; sometimes it is pronounced more like [d] than [t], and sometimes it is not released at all. So, how many *t* sounds are there? One or four?

All sounds in all languages have variants such as those of *t*; usually these are called *positional variants*; that is, different forms of a sound occur at different positions in a word; in the case of the *t* variants, aspirated *t* occurs only at the beginning of a syllable, unaspirated *t* follows *s*, unreleased *t* can occur at the end of a word, etc. Notice that each of these phonetically different sounds is, in an important way, the "same" sound; each has an essential "t-ness" at its core; even the most different, the *t* of *metal*, appears as aspirated *t* in the related word *metallic*.

Phoneticians explain the relationships among these different sounds by saying that a language consists of a set of basic sounds, technically called *phonemes*, and a set of related variants, technically called *allophones*. The phoneme/allophone distinction is one of the most important concepts in linguistics; an analogy may help you understand it more fully. Among other devices, the English spelling system makes use of uppercase and lowercase letters, and italics—for example, Q, q, *Q*, and *q* (roman and italic). In an obvious way, these are all different, but in another sense they are all expressions of the same letter, since all have a basic "q-ness." We express both their differences and their similarities by the names we give them: capital *q*, lowercase *q*, capital italic *q*, lowercase italic *q*. For our purposes, it is important to remember that each can occur only in specific environments: we use capital italic *q* at the beginning of a sentence or a proper name that we want to emphasize, lowercase italic *q* for other emphasis, capital *q* at the beginning of a nonemphasized sentence or proper name, and lowercase *q* elsewhere. These usages lead us to conclude that there is a relatively abstract component that unites the four *q*s that we represent as Q, q, *Q*, or *q* (uppercase and lowercase roman and italic); the rules of English writing instruct us when to use each. Similarly, the phoneme /t/ includes the allophones aspirated *t*, unaspirated *t*, unreleased *t*, etc., and the rules of English pronunciation tell us when to pronounce each allophone.

Phoneticians call phonemes *contrastive units*, since they can distinguish one word from another: *top* is not *cop* is not *pop*, so /t/, /k/, and /p/ are separate phonemes. The particular variants of a phoneme, however, are not contrastive; substituting one for another does not result in a different word, but only a word that sounds unusual, as if it were spoken by an individual unfamiliar with the rules of the language. Try using the *t* of *top* (aspirated [t]) in the word *city*. It sounds odd, doesn't it? But you still recognize the word as *city*, not as *sissy* or *sicky*, so aspirated *t* and flap *t* (what phoneticians call the /t/ of *city*, *water*, *bitter*, and the like, since your tongue tip flaps once against your alveolar ridge) are variants of the phoneme /t/. Notice that the phoneme /t/ is placed between slant lines, while a particular allophone of [t] is enclosed in square brackets.

SOME ENGLISH ALLOPHONES

All languages have rules for the pronunciation of phonemes; they indicate which variant to use under which circumstances, when to use aspirated [t], when to use flap [t], etc. A study of several of the rules of English pronunciation follows, but first we need a clear definition of the term "rule." One of the problems in phonetics (and language study in general) is its terminology, and one of the more difficult terms is "rule." Linguists use the term "rule" differently from nonlinguists. Linguists regard rules as descriptions of the way language operates and not as evaluations of "good" or "bad" language use. The rules that linguists use concisely state the principles of a language. For instance, one rule in English is that the phoneme /t/, when it occurs between vowels, is usually pronounced as a voiced flap. This is a rule of American English only; the rules of British English are slightly different, and a speaker of British English might pronounce *city* with aspirated /t/. When you violate language rules, you don't necessarily make social errors, you just sound odd, or your words don't form sentences. Violating phonetic rules usually results in odd pronunciations, as if you learned English from a book but never heard it spoken. You can experience this by saying "Betty makes better butter" using all aspirated *t*'s. You were never taught the rules of English; you just picked them up as a child and you know them so well that you apply them repeatedly without a thought. Linguistics attempts to state rules formally in order to illustrate how a language works.

With phonemes, allophones, and rules in mind, let's look again at aspiration and write a descriptive rule that explains, first, which sounds are aspirated and, second, under what circumstances they are aspirated.

In English three phonemes have aspirated allophones: /p/, /t/, and /k/; they are aspirated whenever they occur at the beginning of a syllable—for example, *pin, tin, kin, upon, octane, occur*. We could simply state that /p/, /t/, and /k/ are aspirated at the beginning of a syllable; but we also want the rule to identify the set of which /p/, /t/, and /k/ are members and to specify why these particular phonemes, as opposed to others, should appear together and function as a group. To do this we need to consult figure 6.2 and examine the point of articulation, manner of articulation, and voicing for /p/, /t/, and /k/. We want to reduce these three sounds to a common factor. Notice that figure 6.2 indicates that /p/, /t/, and /k/ are stops and that they are voiceless; in fact, these three sounds are the only sounds that meet this description. We can use this information to conclude that English has a rule that all voiceless stops are aspirated at the beginning of a syllable.

Using figure 6.2, explain why it would be difficult to write a rule that refers to /p/, /m/, and /j/ as a group.

EXERCISE 3

1. Write a rule using the following information. In English, some vowels are held longer in some circumstances than in others. Say the words below out loud several times, paying particular attention to how long you sustain the vowel in each word as you speak. You should be able to put each of these words into one of two groups: a group with "shorter" vowels and a group with "longer" vowels. For instance, the [i] of *heed* is longer than the [i] of *heat*. (The actual length is not important; what is important is to recognize that some vowels are relatively longer than others.)

made	mate	edge	etch
dose	doze	pot	pod
prove	proof	pig	pick
seed	seat	ice	eyes

2. Make a list of those words with the longer vowels and another list of those words with the shorter vowels.
3. Now we need to determine the environment in which a vowel is lengthened. Look at the words with the longer vowels and consider the consonant at the end of each word. Using figure 6.2, determine the common component for all the consonants and write a rule that describes when a vowel is lengthened. Your rule should begin, "A vowel is lengthened when. . . ."

There are many more allophonic rules in English, but these examples give you an appreciation for the systematic variability of sounds and an understanding of how the rules of English transform a phoneme into a related group of sounds that we actually speak and hear.

VARIATION IN MORPHEMES

We can summarize this brief consideration of phonemes and their allophones as follows:

The sound system of language is made up of a relatively small number of abstract items (phonemes) that occur in a variety of forms (allophones), and the phonetic rules of a language describe where each allophone occurs. What is true for phonemes is also true for words, or, more precisely, for the parts of words called *morphemes*. Morpheme is another term with a precise meaning in linguistics. Your teacher can explain it further; for now we define a morpheme as the smallest part of a word that has a meaning. For instance, *lend* is a one-morpheme word; *lender* is a two-morpheme word consisting of *lend+er*; and *lenders* is a three-morpheme word, *lend+er+s*, where *-er* means "one who does" the verb and *-s* means plural. A particular morpheme may be expressed by one group of phonemes in one instance and by a different group of phonemes in another—yet we recognize it as the same morpheme in both instances. A morpheme often is spelled differently depending on the circumstances, but spelling is not a reliable guide to the identification of morphemes.

We are all familiar with morphemes and their different forms, called *alternates*. One common example is the morpheme we spell *the*, which appears as [ði] in the phrase *the apple, the end*, and *the outsider* but as [ðə] in *the city, the quarterback*, and *the visitor*. What determines the form?

The concept of alternates (and alternation) is important in linguistics, so we will consider a second example. There is a group of words in English that is built on the morpheme *pel*, which has the general meaning of "push" or "drive": *compel, repel, expel, propel*. This morpheme appears not only as *pel* but also as *pul* in words such as *compulsive, repulsion*, and *expulsion*. *Pel* and *pul* represent the same morpheme, and the rules of English tell us when to pronounce each (and, in this case, when to spell them differently). This situation is directly analogous to that of *Q* and *q*, in which the rules of English spelling indicate when to use the two representations of the same letter.

Now we can apply these concepts to another morpheme: the morpheme that means "5." (Notice the use of the numeral rather than the letters in order to allow the morpheme to remain rather abstract). In English we assume the spelling of the numeral 5 is *f i v e*. Actually, this is not entirely true. How about when we are using ordinals—*first*, *second, third, fourth, fifth* (*fifth*, not *fiveth*)? When we multiply 5 times 10 we get *fifty*, not *fivety*. Therefore, the morpheme 5 has two different forms: one spelled *five* and pronounced [fayv]; the other spelled *fif* and pronounced [fɪf]. We are concerned here only with the consonant change, so ignore the vowel difference between *five* and *fif*). Thus, the morpheme 5 has two variants that alternate with one another: [fayv] and [fɪf]. We will assume that *five* [fayv] is the basic form, and we want to know exactly what the change is and why it changes. To do this we notice that the only consonant difference between [fayv] and [fɪf] is that *fif* contains [f] where *five* contains [v]. The first thing we need to do is determine the phonetic difference between [f] and [v]. From figure 6.2, we see that the only difference between [f] and [v] is in voicing; [f] is voiceless and [v] is voiced. Notice that [f] occurs only when the morpheme 5 precedes the suffix [θ] or the suffix [ti]; in other words, when we add [θ] or [ti] to *five*, [fayv] changes to [fɪf] (we also change the spelling, which makes the phonetic change easier to see, but many phonetic changes do not include a change in spelling). Why do these words contain [f] rather than [v]? Why does the voiced sound [v] become the voiceless [f] in *fifty* and *fifth*? The reason for the change is *assimilation*, another important concept in linguistics. In phonetics, assimilation refers to the process in which a sound changes in such a way that it becomes more like another (usually neighboring) sound. In this case, the voiced [v] of *five* becomes voiceless in order to become more like the voiceless [θ] or [t] of the suffix; in the process [v] in effect becomes [f]. Whenever there is assimilation, there is one sound (or one group of sounds) that causes the assimilation and another sound that changes, or undergoes the assimilation. In this example, the [t] of *fifty* and the [θ] of *fifth* are the causes of the assimilation, and the final [v] of *five* is the sound that undergoes the assimilation.

Assimilation is a common and natural process that is found in all languages. The reasons for assimilation are simple. As speakers we try, whenever possible, to reduce the effort required for articulation, and we find that it is easier to pronounce some sequences of sounds than others. One way to make articulation easier is to produce one sound as much like a neighboring sound as possible. Consider the articulatory effort required to pronounce fivty (if the [v] were not assimilated). We would have to vibrate the vocal cords for the [v] and quickly stop the vibration for [t]. We can make the articulation easier by anticipating the voicelessness of [t] and extending voicelessness over both sounds. Since voice is the feature involved, this particular instance is an example of assimilation in voice.

The following is another example of assimilation in which the spelling helps to identify the sounds involved.

We have a number of ways of negating adjectives in English; one way is to use a prefix, but the form of the prefix can vary. We say *indecent*, yet we say *impartial*, because the rules of English do not allow us to say *imdecent* or *inpartial*. (Linguists use * to mark nongrammatical forms.) Two forms of this prefix are shown below:

Prefix Form	Examples
im-	imperfect, immature, implausible, improper
in-	indecent, intolerant, innumerable, indistinct

In order to understand why *imperfect* and *indecent* are spelled as they are (as opposed to *imdecent* and *inperfect*), look at the adjectives to which each form is attached and determine specifically what they have in common. Notice that all the adjectives to which *im-* are attached begin with either /m/ or /p/. Comparing /m/ and /p/ by using the articulatory characteristics of these sounds as shown in figure 6.2 indicates that /m/ and /p/ are both bilabial. To determine the characteristics of the adjectives to which *in-* attaches, it is necessary to ask why *im-*, and not *in-*, precedes the first group, while *in-*, and not *im-*, precedes the second group. Using figure 6.2, you will note that /m/, like /p/, is bilabial and /n/, like /t/ and /d/, is alveolar; in other words, the consonant of the prefix must have the same point of articulation as the first consonant of the adjective to which it is attached. This is an example of assimilation in point of articulation.

Many speakers, especially in more relaxed speech situations, use another form, /ɪŋ/ to negate adjectives like *complete*, *corruptible*, and *glorious*. Although spelled *in-*, this prefix is pronounced [ɪŋ] ([ɪŋkəmplit]). Consider [ɪŋ] and the adjectives to which it is attached. How does this group fit into the pattern we saw with *im-* and *in-*? Explain.

Other forms of this prefix are as follows:

Prefix Form	Examples
ir-	irregular, irresponsible, irrelevant
il-	illegal, illegible, illogical

In what ways do *ir-* and *il-* fit the pattern and in what way are they slightly different? Are they actually more assimilated to their adjectives than *im-*, *in-*, or [ɪŋ]?

One way of looking at assimilation is to see it as a kind of phonetic agreement. You are already familiar with grammatical agreement—for example, English subjects and verbs must agree in number and Spanish articles and nouns must agree in gender. Just as there is grammatical agreement, there is phonetic agreement. Sounds must agree in voicing or point of articulation; several sounds must share the same point of articulation, or they must all be voiced (or voiceless). There are other phonetic agreements, but point of articulation and voicing agreement are probably the most common.

We are now ready to examine phonetic agreement and how we form the regular plural in English (there are a number of irregular plurals that do not follow particular patterns). In elementary school you probably learned that to form a plural noun you add "s" or "es." This is indeed how we write most plurals, but this rule obscures the way we actually form plurals when we speak. There is a single plural morpheme, and it takes several different forms.

EXERCISE 4

1. Listed below is a group of plural nouns, most of which you have seen before. Transcribe them, paying particular attention to how the plural is indicated for each word. What two variants are used to indicate the plural? (A discussion of an important third variant follows later.)

caves	tacks	cuffs	tags
smiths	buds	globes	loops
scouts			

2. Make a list of the singular nouns to which each of the two variants is attached and, using figure 6.2, determine the common components for the singulars in each group. Describe the agreement. Is the cause of the assimilation the singular or the plural morpheme? Is the assimilation in point of articulation or in voicing?

3. Transcribe each of the following words, again paying attention to the plural marker of each one:

bees	lambs	cells	cars	tons	sighs

4. Noting the pattern of assimilation you gathered from the words in the first group, what can you say about the sounds /i/, /m/, /l/, /r/, /n/, and /ay/?

MORPHEMES IN CONTEXT

Earlier you transcribed words written in standard spelling using the symbols of our phonetic alphabet. As mentioned then, these were artificial exercises since it is unusual to encounter words in isolation. We don't say one (pause) word (pause) at (pause) a (pause) time (big pause). In normal speech words and sounds run together; one word affects another word, one sound affects another sound, and our everyday encounters with language sound closer to "jeet?" "na chet" and "haef tuh?" "god-duh" than "did you eat?" "not yet" and "have to?" "got to." In real speech there are no spaces between words and no capital letters at the beginning of sentences or periods at the end. When we put one word next to another in context, a number of changes may occur in one word or the other, or both. In addition to the assimilation that changes sounds, sounds may be added to or deleted from words, or several sounds may be blended together. Usually these changes affect the sounds at the beginnings or ends of words. These changes are the result of the normal operation of phonetic rules. But be warned: our schooling and particularly our literacy can delude us into believing that a word is a word is a word (or that it should be). On the contrary, phonetically, a word in one context may be a different (phonetic) word in another context, and yet a different (phonetic) word in still another context. The point is that these differences are anything but arbitrary; they are the natural results of the regular rules of language. As mentioned earlier, there is often a considerable difference between the way we pronounce a word in isolation and the way we pronounce it in context. The word *a* in isolation is [e], but in context it is either [e] or [ə].

DISSIMILATION (SIMPLIFICATION)

We saw earlier that assimilation is a phonetic process that tends to make neighboring sounds more alike. Many phonetic rules are assimilating rules, which minimize the articulatory differences between sounds. However, it does not follow that sequences of sounds that are most alike are always easiest to pronounce. Sounds can be so much alike that they are nearly impossible to pronounce in sequence or even close to one another. Tongue twisters are wonderful examples. Try saying, at normal speed, "the sixth sick sheik's sixth sheep's sick," one of the worst (or best, depending upon your point of view) tongue twisters ever devised, as listed in the *Guinness Book of World Records*. When faced with a sequence of too-similar sounds, speakers regularly break up the sequence in one of two ways: by deleting one of the offending sounds or by inserting a sound (in English, usually schwa) into the sequence so that the troublesome sounds are separated. *Cupboard*, for instance is [kəbərd]; [kəpbɔrd] is non-English. Since there are two bilabial stops adjacent to one another, English speakers simplify the cluster by deleting [p].

English allows a maximum of three consonants at the beginning of a word (*stream, split*) and up to three consonants at the end (*desks*). (Many American dialects, however, allow only two consonants at the end of a word.) As a general rule, and depending on the specific sounds involved and other phonetic, grammatical, and social factors, English speakers tolerate at most two adjacent consonants in the middle of a word. When we form a compound or add a suffix that increases the number to three or more, we are phonetically overwhelmed and usually respond by dropping one of the three consonants. Thus, the word *sand* and the word *box* present no problems but *sandbox* is another matter; the usual pronunciation is [sænbaks], not [sændbaks]. This pronunciation is neither capricious nor idiosyncratic; a rule of English phonetics allows the deletion of this particular consonant only; to delete any of the others would not reflect English phonetics: [*sædbaks] or [*sændaks].

Once again, remember that pronunciations such as [sænbaks] are not "incorrect" and pronunciations such as [sændbaks] are not "correct." It is true that some speakers pronounce more formally than others, but it is misguided to believe that [sændbaks] is a "better" pronunciation than [sænbaks]. It is a social rather than a linguistic judgment to label one person a "better" pronouncer than another, and it ignores the facts of language. The rules of English provide the possibilities; they specify what can and cannot be done within the context of spoken English. Those who participate most fully in the richness of English know the rules and use the rules for their maximum effect.

=

EXERCISE 5

The examples below are either compounds or include suffixes that create three or more consonants medially. But in normal, rapid conversation, one of the consonants is usually deleted. Mark the deleted consonant in each word and state the English rule for deleting the consonant.

| first grade | kindness | government | Christmas |
| second place | handbag | guest towel | waistcoat |

Earlier, you did an exercise on English plurals; there was a discussion of two alternates and a third was mentioned. Words such as *judges, matches, classes,* and *sneezes* illustrate this third alternate. Refresh your memory of the general rule. Which of the two alternates is found in these words? Why does it not attach directly to the singular?

The English past tense marker has three regular variants or *allomorphs*: /t/, /d/, and /əd/ (or [ɪd]). They are illustrated by the words below:

/t/	/d/	/əd/
AS IN:	*AS IN:*	*AS IN:*
coughed	saved	sifted
touched	judged	waded
passed	buzzed	heated
flapped	rubbed	bounded
marked	sagged	divided
mashed	sealed	coated
asked	dimmed	handed
dressed	pleased	directed
faked	played	sorted
moped	labored	provided

In which environment do you find each of the three alternates? Why are they grouped this way? Are assimilation, simplification, or both involved?

This chapter provides you with only the barest outline of phonetics and a brief sample of the kinds of issues with which phoneticians concern themselves. As with all language study, phonetics attempts to understand the dimensions of human language, the kinds of rules that characterize languages, and what people know about their own language—the rules they carry around in their heads. Because these rules are complex, there is much to learn, and phoneticians will be busy for decades to come.

FOR DISCUSSION AND REVIEW

1. Callary says that "many discrepancies between sound and spelling in English exist." Why is this the case?

2. Define the terms *point of articulation, manner of articulation*, and *voicing (sound)*. Give two original examples of how an understanding of these concepts could be helpful to you.

3. Examine the charts of English consonant and vowel phonemes. Explain why it is significant that not every slot (or cell) is filled.

4. Explain the relationship between phonemes and allophones and their differing roles within a language.

5. Both *assimilation* and *dissimilation* are important phonetic processes. Define each term, and give two original examples of each.

6. How could you put phonetics to work in learning a second language?

7. What would be some advantages and disadvantages of changing English spelling to bring it more into line with pronunciation?

8. Do you think spell checkers will increase or decrease the likelihood of spelling reform? What are your reasons?

9. The following sentences were written by elementary school students:

   a. "I haf to go now."

   b. "Why won chew be my friend?"

   c. "I went to see my grampa."

   From what you know about phonetics, how can you explain their spelling errors?

7

The Form of the Message

Nancy Bonvillain

We can think of language as a system of communication for sending and receiving different kinds of meaningful messages. To investigate how language communicates meanings, it is useful to look carefully at the structure of the messages themselves. In this piece, Nancy Bonvillain, a professor at Simon's Rock College and authority on Native American cultures and languages, describes how sounds are produced and explains the features of sounds themselves. She then moves beyond physical descriptions of sound production to discuss how sounds, when formed together in words, create meaning and are governed by specific linguistic rules. From there, Bonvillian illustrates how components of sound—prosodic features—also help express meaning, and she shows how languages use the same prosodic features to different ends. This selection comes from her 1993 book Language, Culture, and Communication.*

Phonology is the study of sound systems in language. It includes *phonetics*, description of sounds occurring in a language, and *phonemics*, analysis of the use of these sounds to differentiate meanings of words.

PHONETICS

The first task is the description of how sounds are produced or *articulated*. Human language is made possible by manipulation of the vocal apparatus, which consists of lungs, pharanx, larynx, glottis, vocal cords, nose, mouth, tongue, teeth, and lips. Figure 7.1 depicts these parts of the physical system.

Components of the vocal apparatus can be modified or affected by speakers to produce sounds of differing qualities. This ability is obviously essential. Speakers must make distinctions among numerous sounds so that meanings of words can be differentiated. Several kinds of contrasts serve to distinguish sounds. They will be discussed in subsequent sections. (Examples given to illustrate linguistic structure have been obtained from a number of sources, including Bonvillain 1973, Bonvillain n.d., Cowan and Rakusan 1987, Finegan and Besnier 1989, Gleason 1955, Ladefoged 1982, and O'Grady et al. 1989.)

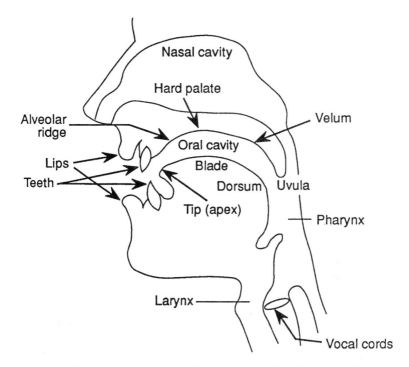

FIGURE 7.1 The Vocal Apparatus. (Adapted from Wardhaugh 1977:33.)

I. Sounds are either voiced or voiceless, depending on the activity of the vocal cords, a pair of small muscular bands in the throat. If the vocal cords are close together when air passes through, the cords vibrate and produce *voiced* sounds; if they are apart and stationary, the resulting sounds are *voiceless*. Voiced/voiceless contrasts can be illustrated by *minimal pairs*, two words composed of sounds that are identical except for one feature of significant difference. The following list contains some voiced/voiceless consonant pairs in English (examples written in standard orthography):

Voiceless	*Voiced*
p: *p*it	b: *b*it
ta*p*	ta*b*
t: *t*en	d: *d*en
bi*t*	bi*d*
f: *f*an	v: *v*an
grie*f*	grie*v*e
s: *s*ap	z: *z*ap
his*s*	hi*s*

Vowels in English are voiced. However, voiceless as well as voiced vowels occur in many languages, including Japanese, Totonac (Mexico),

and Chatino (Mexico). In Totonac, voiceless vowels always occur at the
ends of words (voicelessness is indicated by ̦V beneath a vowel):

/kukṳ/   "uncle"
/mikị̥/   "snow"
/snapapạ̥/   "white"

In both Chatino and Japanese, vowels are voiceless when they occur
between two voiceless consonants. Some examples from Chatino follow
(superscript numbers indicate tones: 2, mid; 3, high).

/kạta³/   "you will bathe"
/kị̥su³/   "avocado"
/tị̥hi²/   "hard"

II. Sounds are either *oral* or *nasal,* the former produced by raising the
velum to the back of the throat, expelling air only through the mouth
(oral cavity), the latter by relaxing the velum and allowing air to pass
through the nose. For instance, *m* and *n* are nasal consonants. All languages have some nasal consonants and many have nasal vowels as well.
This group includes French, Portuguese, Hindi (India), Tibetan, Yoruba
(Nigeria), and Navajo (Native North America).

III. In addition to binary characteristics relevant for all sounds
(voiced/voiceless, oral/nasal), each sound is articulated by manipulation
of parts of the vocal apparatus to produce the diverse sounds of one's
language. Figure 7.2, which illustrates most consonants attested in
human language, classifies sounds according to two dimensions: place
of articulation and manner of articulation. *Place of articulation* refers to
where the sound is formed in the mouth; for example, *bilabial* sounds
are formed by the two lips, and *apico-alveolar* sounds are articulated
with the tip of the tongue (*apico* = apex) and the alveolar ridge. The
second dimension, *manner of articulation,* refers to the degree of interference or modification of the airstream as it passes through the oral
cavity; for example, *stops* are produced by momentary complete blockage of air, *fricatives* by narrowing the vocal channel and thus creating
turbulence of friction in the airstream. Each difference in place and/or
manner of articulation results in a difference in sound quality. Symbols
in the chart are written in phonetic transcription adapted from the
International Phonetic Alphabet, a system of standardized notation
applicable to all languages. . . . In some cases symbols in the chart
correspond to English letters but in others they do not. Note also that
vd = voiced, vl = voiceless.

Vowels are articulated with relatively greater openness of the vocal
tract and relatively less interference with the airstream than is characteristic of consonants. Differences in vocalic quality are produced by movement of the tongue and rounding or unrounding of lips, resulting
in changes in resonance. Additionally, voicing/unvoicing or oral/nasal

Place of Articulation

Manner of Articulation		Bilabial	Labio-dental	Apico-dental	Apico-alveolar	Retroflex	Alveopalatal	Palatal	Dorsovelar	Uvular	Pharyngeal	Glottal
Stops												
Plain	vl.	p			t	ṭ	tʸ	ḳ	k	q		ʔ
	vd.	b			d	ḍ	dʸ	g̣	g	G		
Aspirated	vl.	pʰ			tʰ				kʰ			
	vd.	bʰ			dʰ				gʰ			
Glottalized	vl.	p'			t'				k'			
Labialized	vl.	pʷ			tʷ				kʷ			
	vd.	bʷ			dʷ				gʷ			
Nasals	vl.	m̥			n̥		ñ̥		ŋ̥			
	vd.	m			n	ṇ	ñ		ŋ	N		
Affricates	vl.				c		č	ç				
	vd.						ǰ					
Fricatives	vl.	φ	f	θ	s	ṣ	š		×		ħ	h
	vd.	β	v	ð	z		ž		ɣ		ʕ	
Liquids Laterals					ℓ	ḷ	ƚ					
Central					r	ṛ						
Flaps					ř							
Trills					r̃					R		
Glides							y		w			

FIGURE 7.2   **Consonants.**

contrasts are significant in many, but not all, languages. Figure 7.3 illustrates the physical manipulations involved in vowel production. The tongue positions are depicted for the articulations of three English vowels: [iy] as in the word "beet," [a] as in "pot," and [uw] as in "boot."

Common vocalic segments, represented by phonetic symbols, are classified in Figure 7.4. Dimensions of vowel articulation are: position in the mouth, from front to back, and height, from high to low. Lip rounding or unrounding is also significant.

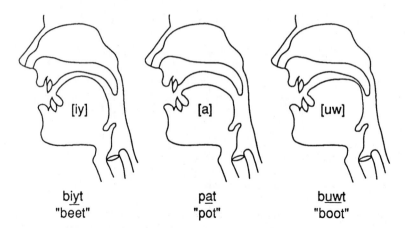

FIGURE 7.3 Tongue Positions for Three English Vowels. (Adapted from O'Grady 1989:28.)

Each language selects its phonetic inventory from among the possible human sounds. No language contains all of them, since requiring speakers to make too many articulatory discriminations or to make them too fine is not feasible. A minimum of perhaps eight variations exist in phonetic inventories, ranging from as few as eight consonants in Hawaiian to as many as 96 in !Kung (spoken in Namibia). Some languages have only three vowels, although about half of all languages contain five vowels, and others, such as English and French, have more than a dozen. Representative English words are given next as illustrations of some symbols in the consonant and vowel charts.

1. Oral stops (complete closure or blockage of airstream):

a. Bilabial:	p:	pɪn	(pin)
	b:	bɪn	(bin)
b. Apico-alveolar:	t:	tɛn	(ten)
	d:	dɛn	(den)

		Front		Central		Back	
		Unrd.	Rd.	Unrd.	Rd.	Unrd.	Rd.
High	Upper	i	ü	ɨ		ɯ	u
	Lower	ɪ	ö	ɨ			ʊ
Mid	Upper	e	ö	ə			o
	Lower	ɛ	œ	ʌ			ɔ
Low		æ		a		ɑ	

FIGURE 7.4 Vowels.

    c. Dorso-velar: k: kat   (cot)
                             g: gat   (got)

2. Nasals (velum is lowered to allow air to pass through the nose):

    a. Bilabial: m: mʌt   (mutt)
    b. Apico-alveolar: n: nʌt   (nut)
    c. Dorso-velar: ŋ: hʌŋ   (hung)

3. Affricates (complete closure followed by narrow opening for air to pass through):

    a. Palatal: č: čɪn   (chin)
                          ǰ: ǰɪn   (gin)

4. Fricatives (narrowing and partial obstruction of vocal passage, resulting in turbulence or friction):

    a. Labio-dental: f: fæn   (fan)
                            v: væn   (van)
    b. Interdental: θ: θay   (thigh)
                            ð: ðay   (thy)
    c. Apico-alveolar: s: sæp   (sap)
                            z: zæp   (zap)
    d. Palatal: š: šap   (shop)
                          ž: ruwž   (rouge)
    e. Glottal: h: hɛd   (head)

5. Liquids (relatively less obstruction of airstream, resulting in modification of air but no turbulence):

    a. Lateral: l: lɛd   (led)
    b. Central: r: rɛd   (red)

6. Glides or semivowels (little obstruction; intermediate between consonants and vowels):

    a. Palatal: y: yɛt   (yet)
    b. Velar: w: wɛt   (wet)

7. Vowels: In English, some vowels are *monophthongs*, articulated in one place in the mouth; others are *diphthongs* or *glides*, involving movement of the sound from one position of another. Diphthongs are noted by a "y" or "w" following the vocalic symbol:

    a. Front (all unrounded):

        iy: bit   (beet)
         ɪ: bɪt   (bit)
      ey: beyt   (bait)
        ɛ: bɛt   (bet)
       æ: bæt   (bat)

    b. Central (all unrounded):

        ʌ: bʌt   (but)
      ay: bayt   (bite)
      aw: bawt   (bout)

c. Back (all rounded):

uw:	buwt	(boot)
ʊ:	bʊk	(book)
ow:	bowt	(boat)
oy:	boy	(boy)
ɔ:	bɔt	(bought)

PHONEMIC ANALYSIS

Every language organizes its phonetic inventory into a system of phonemes. A *phoneme* is the minimal unit of sound that functions to differentiate the meanings of words. It may have only one phonetic representation or it may contain two or more sounds, called *allophones*, which occur in predictable linguistic environments based on rules of allophonic patterning. For example, in English, voiceless stops /p/, /t/, and /k/ each have two allophones: one is *aspirated*, produced with a strong release of air; the other is *unaspirated*. They are illustrated in the following words:

/p/	aspirated:	[pʰɪn]	(pin)
	unaspirated:	[spɪn]	(spin)
/t/	aspirated:	[tʰʌn]	(tun)
	unaspirated:	[stʌn]	(stun)
/k/	aspirated:	[kʰɪn]	(kin)
	unaspirated:	[skɪn]	(skin)

Thus allophones for English voiceless stops are produced with aspiration when they occur initially in a syllable, whereas they are unaspirated following /s/ in the same syllable.

Most native speakers of English are unaware of the fact that the "p"s, "t"s, and "k"s in the words above have slightly different articulations. Speakers learn to make nonconscious allophonic distinctions in early stages of language acquisition. Since the rules are applied consistently thereafter without exception, they become automatic patterns not requiring conscious thought.

Allophony affects liquids and glides in English in accordance with conditioning rules. Voiceless counterparts of /l, r, w, y/ occur following voiceless stops /p, t, k/. In all other environments, liquids and glides are voiced. Compare the following contrasts (voicelessness is indicated by ̥ beneath a consonant):

/r/:	voiceless	[tr̥ɪp]	(trip)
	voiced	[drɪp]	(drip)
/l/:	voiceless	[pl̥ayt]	(plight)
	voiced	[blayt]	(blight)

/w/:	voiceless	[tw̥ɪn]	(twin)
	voiced	[dwɪndl]	(dwindle)
/y/:	voiceless	[ky̥uwt]	(cute)
	voiced	[argyuw]	(argue)

Specific allophonic patterns are not universal but instead, operate within each language according to its own rules. In some languages, the difference between aspirated and unaspirated stops is not allophonic as in English but rather, phonemic. *Phonemic* contrasts signal differences in meanings of words. The following words in Korean constitute minimal pairs for plain /k/ and aspirated /kʰ/ and have separate referents:

/keda/　　"fold"

/kʰeda/　　"dig out"

Similarly, Chinese contrasts /p/ and /pʰ/ (note that high pitch is indicated by V̄ above a vowel):

/pā/	"trumpet"	/pī/	"compare"
/pʰā/	"strip"	/pʰī/	"indigestion"

Finally, aspirated /tʰ/ and unaspirated /t/ are separate phonemes in Hindi (a language of India):

/táli/	"key"	/tóṛna/	"pluck"
/tʰáli/	"dish"	/tʰóṛa/	"little"

Some sounds that have phonemic status in English are allophones in other languages. English distinguishes between voiceless and voiced stops, p/b, t/d, and k/g, but in the Mohawk language (spoken in New York State and Ontario/Quebec, Canada), these sounds are allophones rather than phonemes. They occur in predictable environments. In Mohawk, voiceless stops are produced at the ends of words or preceding other consonants (except glides); voiced stops occur preceding vowels or glides:

/t/ →	[t]/	at ends of words:	[salá:dat]	"pick it up!"
		preceding a consonant:	[ohyótsaʔ]	"chin"
	[d]/	preceding a vowel:	[odáhsaʔ]	"tail"
/k/ →	[k]/	at ends of words:	[wisk]	"five"
		preceding a consonant:	[jiks]	"fly"
	[g]/	preceding a vowel:	[gá:lis]	"stocking"
		preceding a glide:	[á:gwɛks]	"eagle"
			[gyóhdũ]	"nine"

As evidence of the automatic, nonconscious nature of allophones, when Mohawk speakers use English they frequently follow Mohawk allophonic patterns, so that, for example, the English word "chicken" /číkɪn/ is pronounced [čígɪn]. This pronunciation is consistent with

Mohawk rules that require voiced stops preceding vowels. In fact, a "foreign accent" in any language consists, in part, of the application of native allophonic rules when speaking foreign languages.

PROSODIC FEATURES

In addition to consonants and vowels, sound systems make use of *prosodic* or *suprasegmental* features to alter and therefore contrast the sounds or rhythms of speech. Three prosodic features that often affect meaning are stress, pitch, and length.

Stress. In multisyllabic words, *stress* or *accent* is not evenly distributed on every syllable. Rather, different syllables receive different degrees of stress. In some languages, stress rules are automatic; for example, in Czech, Finnish, and Hungarian, every word is accented on the first syllable; in French and Mayan (Mexico), words are accented on the final syllable; and in Polish, Swahili (Africa), and Samoan (Polynesia), the penultimate (next to last) syllable is always stressed. Stress placement in other languages is unpredictable, and therefore changes in stress can serve to differentiate meanings or functions of words. Note the following contrasts between some nouns and verbs in English:

	Noun	*Verb*
"present"	prézɛnt	prezɛ́nt
"object"	ábjɛkt	abjɛ́kt
"construct"	kánstrʌkt	kanstrʌ́kt
"implant"	ímplænt	ɪmplǽnt
"retest"	rítɛst	riytɛ́st

Pitch. *Pitch* or *tone* refers to the voice pitch accompanying a syllable's articulation. Variation in pitch results from changes in relative tension of the vocal cords. Pitch generally occurs with vowels, although some consonants (e.g., /l, r, m, n/) can function as syllable nuclei and carry tone. Many languages throughout the world use pitch to distinguish meanings of words (e.g., Asian languages, such as Chinese and Thai; African languages, including Yoruba, Zulu, and Luganda; Amerindian languages, such as Navajo [U.S. southwest] and Sarcee [western Canada]; and the European Latvian).

The following sets of words from Chinese have separate referents, each signaled by patterns of pitch:

High level:	mā	"mother"	fū	"skin"
High rising:	má	"hemp"	fú	"fortune"
Low falling-rising:	mǎ	"horse"	fǔ	"axe"
Falling:	mà	"scold"	fù	"woman"

In some languages, changes in tone function to signal different grammatical meanings. Compare verbs from Bini, a language spoken in Nigeria:

Low pitch: ìmà "I show" (timeless)

High/low: ímà "I am showing" (continuous)

Low/high: ìmá "I showed" (past)

Pitch is a feature of all languages on units of clauses and/or sentences. It is one of the components of *intonation*. In English, declarative statements and questions are characterized by contrastive pitch contours. Level or falling pitch appears at the ends of statements, whereas rising pitch terminates questions:

Statement: they came in ↘

Question: they came in ↗

Length. The feature of "length" refers to continuation of a sound during its articulation. Some languages employ length to differentiate meanings of words. Short and long vowel contrasts occur in Danish, Czech, Finnish, Arabic, Japanese, Korean, Cree (Canada), Yap (Pacific), and others. Examples from Korean are (long vowels are indicated by V: following a vowel):

/il/   "day"   /i:l/   "work"

/seda/   "to count" /se:da/   "strong"

/pam/   "night"   /pa:m/   "chestnut"

Contrastive length for consonants is less common than for vowels but it is attested in several languages, including Turkish, Finnish, Hungarian, Luganda (Africa), and Arabic. In Luganda, the word /kúlà/, "grow up," contains a short /k/, whereas /kkúlà/, "treasure," has a long /k/. In Classical Arabic, a long consonant in a verb signals the grammatical meaning of "causative" (i.e., making or causing something to happen), as in the following words:

/ʕada/   "he passed"

/ʕadda/   "he made to pass"

/ðakara/   "he remembered"

/ðakkara/   "he reminded" (caused to remember)

/ʕaðaba/   "he abstained"

/ʕaððaba/   "he restrained" (caused to abstain)

Although not all languages make contrasts of length to distinguish referents, changes in the duration of sounds can serve as markers of emphasis or exaggeration. Lengthening a vowel in English can indicate exaggeration, as in

"He is bi-i-i-i-ig!"

This utterance implies greater size than would be conveyed by simply saying "he is big" (Lakoff and Johnson 1980: 127–128).

BIBLIOGRAPHY

Bonvillain, Nancy. 1973. *A Grammar of Akwesasne Mohawk.* Ottawa: National Museum of Canada, Mercury Series No. 8.

_____. n.d. Fieldnotes for Mohawk, Russian, Tagalog, and Turkish.

Cowan, William and Jakomira Rakusan. 1987. *Source Book for Linguistics,* 2nd rev. ed. Philadelphia: John Benjamins.

Finegan, Edward and Niko Besnier. 1989. *Language: Its Structure and Use.* New York: Harcourt Brace Jovanovich.

Gleason, Henry. 1955. *Workbook in Descriptive Linguistics.* New York: Holt, Rinehart & Winston.

Ladefoged, Peter. 1982. *A Course in Phonetics,* 2nd ed. New York: Harcourt Brace Jovanovich.

Lakoff, George and Mark Johnson. 1980. *Metaphors We Live By.* Chicago: University of Chicago Press.

O'Grady, William, Michael Dobrovolsky, and Mark Aronoff. 1989. *Contemporary Linguistics: An Introduction.* New York: St. Martin's Press.

Wardhaugh, Ronald. 1977. *Introduction to Linguistics.* New York: McGraw-Hill.

FOR DISCUSSION AND REVIEW

1. Bonvillain says that human language "is made possible by manipulation of the vocal apparatus." What is the vocal apparatus? List the various parts.

2. What two sets of binary characteristics are relevant for all sounds of language? Give some examples of these characteristics from English and another language.

3. Bonvillain explains that we characterize consonants with three basic features of articulation. What is meant by the term *articulation*? Explain how the sounds of consonants are affected by *voicing*, by the *place of articulation*, and by the *manner of articulation*.

4. Vowels have four significant features. What are they? How is the vowel sound affected when the tongue position changes? What about rounding or unrounding the lips? How significant do these different positions in tongue and lip placement seem to be?

5. What is a *phoneme*? How is a phoneme different from a sound?

6. What is a *minimal pair*? What is "minimal" about it? How do minimal pairs help determine the phonemes of a language?

7. What are *allophones*? How can phonemes in one language be allophones in another? Give an example.

8. What are prosodic features? How do they affect meaning? How can the effects differ from one language to another?

8

What Is Phonology? Language Sounds and Their Rules

The Ohio State University *Language Files*

The Language File *on phonology offers the opportunity to see how sounds are organized in a variety of languages. By working with examples from such different languages as Korean, Ukrainian, and German—as well as English—you will see that two things are at work for speakers of any language: the perception of sound and the sound physically produced, which may differ in slight but significant ways from the perceived sound. In the second half of the essay, you will explore how these two aspects of language allow linguists to deduce the phonological rules of a particular spoken language.*

The exercises at the end of each section of this piece provide the opportunity to try phonological analysis, either on your own or in class. This selection is taken from Files 4.2 and 4.3 of Language Files, *Ninth Edition, published in 2004.*

Both phonetics and phonology can be generally described as the study of speech sounds. *Phonetics* . . . is more specifically the study of how speech sounds are produced, what their physical properties are, and how they are interpreted. *Phonology*, on the other hand, investigates the organization of speech sounds in a particular language. While we might find the same sounds in two or more languages, no two languages organize their sound inventories in the same way. An example will make this point more clearly.

In both Japanese and English we can hear the sounds [s] and [ʃ]. The Japanese word [ʃimasu] 'do' contains both phones, as does the English word [slæʃ] *slash*. The difference between Japanese and English lies in the way the two sounds contribute to the meaning of a word. In English, the two phones can distinguish meaning, as shown by words like [ʃɔr] *shore* and [sɔr] *sore*, where alternating between [ʃ] and [s] affects the meaning of the utterance. In this sense, phonologists say that the occurrence of these two sounds is unpredictable, since we cannot look at the rest of the word and determine which sound will occur. That is, if we know that a word in English ends in [ɔr], we cannot predict whether the word will start with [s] or [ʃ] since both *sore* and *shore* are different, but possible, words.

In Japanese, on the other hand, these two sounds are predictable from their environment. Sounds are predictable when we expect to see one sound or the other based upon the sounds that precede or follow it. If we know that a Japanese word contains the sound [i], we know that it can be preceded by [ʃ], but not by [s]—the combination [si] does not occur in Japanese. However, in English we cannot make this prediction: the sound [s] does appear before the sound [i], as in [si] *see*.

So while Japanese and English contain the phones [s] and [ʃ], the languages differ in that in Japanese we can predict the occurrence of one versus the other and in English we cannot. If someone learning Japanese were to use [s] before [i], the meaning of the word would not change. Instead, a native speaker of Japanese would probably think that the speaker sounded funny or had an accent. On the other hand, if a learner of English were to make the same substitution in English, then the meaning of the word is likely to change. Imagine confusing [s] and [ʃ] and saying "I have to [ʃeyv] more money each month."

Phonologists ask these kinds of questions: What is the organization of sounds in a given language? Of all the sounds in a language, which are predictable and which are unpredictable? What is the phonetic context that allows us to predict the occurrence of certain sounds? Which sounds affect the meaning of words? In the following [sections], we will learn how to answer these questions by examining the sound systems of English as well as other languages. . . .

ALLOPHONES AND PHONEMES

In every language, certain sounds are considered by native speakers to be the "same" sound, even though they may be phonetically distinct. For example, native speakers of English consider the [l] in *lay* to be the same sound as that in *play*, even though the former is voiced and the latter is voiceless. . . . Or, if you ask a native speaker of English how many different sounds are represented by the underlined letters in the words *pin*, *bin*, and *spin*, they will probably say "two," grouping the aspirated [pʰ] of *pin* and unaspirated [p] of *spin* together. Though [pʰ] and [p] are phonetically different sounds, native English speakers typically overlook this difference and consider them to be the "same" sound.

One of the goals of this [discussion] is to understand more clearly the distinction between "same" and "different" sounds. To do this, we will discuss the terms *allophone* and *phoneme*. Since these concepts are the crux of phonological analysis, it is important that they be clearly understood. Perhaps the best way to explain these terms is through examples. On a separate piece of paper, transcribe the following five words:

top	stop	little	kitten	hunter

It is likely that you transcribed all of these words with a [t], like the following:

[tap]   [stap]   [lɪtl̩]   [kɪtn̩]   [hʌntɹ̩]

This is good, since it reflects something that is psychologically real to you. But, in fact, the physical reality (the acoustic phonetic fact) is that the 't' you transcribed in those five examples is pronounced slightly differently from one example to the next. To illustrate this, pronounce the five words again. Concentrate on what the 't' sounds like in each example, but be sure to say them as you normally would if you were talking to a friend.

What differences did you notice? Compare, for example, the /t/ of *top* to that of *stop*. You should be able to detect a short burst or puff of air after the /t/ in *top* that is absent in *stop*. That puff of air is called *aspiration*, which we will transcribe with a superscripted [ʰ]. So while a native speaker would consider the 't' sound in *top* and *stop* to be the same sound, the 't' is actually pronounced differently in each word. This difference can be captured in the transcription, as in [tʰap] and [stap], respectively.

Now say the word *little* and *kitten*. We might say that the 't' in *little* sounds a lot "softer" than the one in *stop*, and is clearly voiced. For most speakers of American English (but not of British English), the 't' in words like *little* is pronounced as a flap, [ɾ], much like the *r* in Spanish in words like [paɾa] 'for' and [toɾo] 'bull'. English *kitten*, on the other hand, is pronounced with the same sound we hear in the expression "uh-oh," a glottal stop [ʔ]. So, we could transcribe *little* and *kitten* as [liɾl̩] and [kiʔn̩], respectively.

For some speakers of American English, in casual speech words like *hunter* are pronounced with no 't' at all, but rather as [hʌnɹ̩]. Try and say it this way and see if it sounds like something you've heard before. In any case, while you may have initially transcribed the five words above with a /t/, they may also be transcribed in a way that reflects the different pronunciations of that sound, as in the following:

[tʰap]   [stap]   [lɪɾl̩]   [kʰɪʔn̩]   [hʌnɹ̩]

To a native speaker, all of the words above have a 't' in them, at least at some psychological level. Proof of that lies in the fact that one may transcribe them all with a 't', at least until trained in transcription. Someone who lacks linguistic training would probably not hesitate to state that all the above words have a 't' and would need to be convinced that subtle differences, like aspiration, exist among them. In this sense, psychologically, the above words do have a 't'. On the other hand, we can observe that the 't' may be pronounced in several different ways.

Unlike a speaker of English, a native speaker of Hindi could not ignore the difference between aspirated and unaspirated sounds when speaking or hearing Hindi. To a speaker of Hindi, the aspirated sound [pʰ] is as different from unaspirated [p], as [pʰ] is from [b] to our ears. The difference between aspirated and unaspirated stops must be noticed by Hindi speakers because their language contains many words that are pronounced in nearly the same way, except that one word will have an aspirated stop where the other has an unaspirated stop. The data in (1) illustrate this.

(1) *Hindi*   *Gloss*
     [pʰəl]   'fruit'
     [pəl]   'moment'
     [bəl]   'strength'

A native speaker of English may not be aware of the difference between aspirated and unaspiratd stops because aspiration will never make a difference in the meanings of English words. If we hear someone say [mæp] and [mæpʰ], we may recognize them as different pronunciations of the same word *map*, but not as different words. Because of the different ways in which [p] and [pʰ] affect meaning distinctions in English and Hindi, these sounds have different values in the phonological systems of the two languages. We say that these two sounds are *noncontrastive* in English, since interchanging the two does not result in a change of meaning. In Hindi, on the other hand, [p] and [pʰ] are *contrastive*, since replacing one sound with the other in a word can change the word's meaning. We will have more to say about this terminological distinction below.

Linguists attempt to characterize these different relations between sounds in language by grouping the sounds in a language's sound inventory into classes. Each class contains all of the sounds that a native speaker considers as the "same" sound. For example, [t] and [tʰ] in English would be members of the same class. But English [tʰ] and [d] are members of different classes because they are contrastive. That is, if you interchange one for the other in a word, you can cause a change in the word's meaning, e.g. [tʰaɪm] *time* vs. [daɪm] *dime*. On the other hand, speakers of Hindi would not classify [t] and [tʰ] as members of the same class because they perceive them as different. That is, they are contrastive.

A class of speech sounds that are judged by a native speaker to be the same sound is called a *phoneme*. Each member of a particular phoneme class is called an *allophone*, which corresponds to an actual phonetic segment produced by a speaker. That is, the various ways that a phoneme is pronounced are called allophones.

In this view, we can say that the 't' sounds in words like *stop, top, little*, and *kitten* all belong to a single class, which we will label by the symbol /t/, characterizing this particular phoneme class. By saying that *stop* and *top*, for example, each have the phoneme /t/, we are saying that the sounds [t] and [tʰ] are related.

In (2) we see how the phoneme /t/ is related to its allophones in English and how the Hindi phonemes /t/ and /tʰ/ are related to their allophones. In English, [t], [tʰ], [ɾ], and [ʔ] are allophones of the same phoneme, which we can label /t/. In this way, we can say that in English the phoneme /t/ has the allophones [t] as in [stap], [tʰ] as in [tʰap], [ɾ] as in [liɾl], and [ʔ] as in [ki?n̩]. On the other hand, in Hindi, [t] and [tʰ] are allophones of different phonemes. Note that symbols representing phonemes are written between slashes; this distinguishes them from symbols representing phones, which are written between square brackets.

(2)	**English**				**Hindi**	
Phonemes:		/t/			/t/	/tʰ/
Allophones:	[t]	[tʰ]	[ʔ]	[ɾ]	[t]	[tʰ]

By providing a description like this, linguists attempt to show that the phonological system of a language has two levels. The more concrete level involves the physical reality of phonetic segments, the allophones, whereas phonemes are something more abstract. In fact, linguists sometimes describe phonemes as the form in which we store sounds in our memory. So, phonemes are abstract psychological concepts, and they are not directly observable in a stream of speech; only the allophones of a phoneme are.

The phoneme is a unit of linguistic structure that is just as significant to the native speaker as the word or the sentence. Native speakers reveal their knowledge of phonemes in a number of ways. When an English speaker makes a slip of the tongue and says [tʃi keɪn] for *key chain*, reversing [tʃ] and [k], he or she has demonstrated that [tʃ] functions mentally as a single unit of sound, just as [k] does. . . . This is not the only way to conceptualize [tʃ]: it is phonetically complex, consisting of [t] followed immediately by [ʃ]. Yet, since [tʃ] represents the pronunciation of a single phoneme /tʃ/ in English, no native speaker would make an error that would involve splitting up its phonetic components; you will never hear [ti kʃen] as a slip of the tongue. . . .

Knowledge of phonemes is also revealed in alphabetic spelling systems. . . . For example, English does not have separate letters for [pʰ] and [p]; they are both spelled with the letter *p*. Examples like this show that the English spelling system ignores the differences in pronunciation that don't result in meaning distinctions. For the most part, the English spelling system attempts to provide symbols for phonemes, not phonetic segments. In general, alphabetic writing systems tend to be phonemic rather than phonetic, though they achieve this goal with varying degrees of success.

Identifying Phonemes and Allophones:
The Distribution of Speech Sounds

In order to determine whether sounds in a given language are allophones of a single phoneme or allophones of separate phonemes we need to consider the distribution of the sounds involved. The *distribution* of a phone is the set of phonetic environments in which it occurs. For example, nasalized vowels in English only occur in the environment of a nasal consonant. More precisely, a linguist would describe the distribution of English [ĩ], [õ], and so on, by stating that the nasalized vowels occur immediately preceding a nasal consonant. In this section, we will mainly be concerned with two types of distribution: contrastive distribution and complementary distribution, though a third distribution, free variation, will also be introduced.

Let us consider *contrastive distribution* first. Recall from above that a pair of phones is contrastive if interchanging the two can change the meaning of a word. This means that the sounds can occur in the same phonetic environment. It also means that the sounds are allophones of different phonemes. Two sounds are noncontrastive if replacing one phone with another does not result in a change of meaning.

Our earlier discussion of the patterning of [p] and [pʰ] in Hindi and English provides a good example of this difference. Recall that we said that in Hindi these two sounds could affect the meaning of a word based on examples like [pəl] *moment* and [pʰəl] *fruit*, where the two meanings are distinguished by the occurrence of [p] of [pʰ]. This means that the two sounds are contrastive in Hindi. In English, on the other hand, simply replacing [p] for [pʰ], or vice versa, will never affect a change in the meaning of a word; the sounds are noncontrastive in English.

We just determined whether or not [p] or [pʰ] are contrastive in Hindi and English by taking into account the distribution of sounds in each individual language. We did this by identifying a *minimal pair*. A minimal pair is defined as a pair of words with different meanings that are pronounced exactly the same way except for one sound that differs. When you find a minimal pair, you know that the two interchangeable sounds are contrastive and, thus, the sounds involved are allophones of different phonemes. If you try, you can think of many minimal pairs in English, or any other language you know well. For example, the minimal pair [tʰiːm] *team* and [tʰiːn] *teen* shows that [n] and [m] are allophones of separate phonemes in English since they can be used to contrast meaning. In Hindi, the words [pʰəl] 'fruit' and [bəl] 'strength' constitute a minimal pair, showing [pʰ] and [b] to be allophones of separate phonemes; [pʰəl] *fruit* and [pəl] *moment* also form a minimal pair in Hindi. But notice that there are no minimal pairs involving [pʰ] and [p] in English; these two sounds are never contrastive with respect to one another. Instead, they are allophones of the same phoneme, /p/.

Consider another example in which two languages make different distinctions using the same set of sounds. In English, it is possible to find minimal pairs in which [l] and [r] are contrasted, e.g., *leaf* [lif] vs. *reef* [rif]; *lack* [læk] vs. *rack* [ræk]. However, [l] and [r] are never contrastive in Korean. Consider the data below ([ɨ] represents a high central unrounded vowel).

Korean	Gloss
[param]	'wind'
[irɨm]	'name'
[pal]	'foot'
[mal]	'horse'

As these examples illustrate, minimal pairs can never be found for [r] and [l] in Korean because these two sounds do not appear in the same positions in words: [r] appears only between two vowels, while [l] does not appear in this position. This observation about the distribution of [r] and [l] is not merely a property of these isolated examples but true of all Korean words containing these sounds. Observations of this sort play an important role in determining which sounds are considered to be the "same" by a native speaker; that is, sounds which are judged by a native speaker to be allophones of a single phoneme.

In addition to contrastive distribution, sounds may also be in *complementary distribution*. Sounds showing this type of distributional pattern are considered to be allophones of a single phoneme. To understand better what we mean by complementary distribution, think about what the term complementary means: two complementary parts of something make up a whole. For example, the set of people in your class at any given moment can be divided into the set of people who are wearing glasses and the set of people who are not. These two sets of people complement each other. They are mutually exclusive, but together they make up the whole class.

Now consider a linguistic example, namely, the distribution of the English sounds [p] and [pʰ].

spat	[spæt]	*pat*	[pʰæt]
spool	[spul]	*pool*	[pʰul]
speak	[spik]	*peek*	[pʰik]

As you can see in the English words just above, [p] and [pʰ] do not occur in the same phonetic environment. As a result, there are no minimal pairs involving a [p]-[pʰ] contrast. In fact, the phones are in complementary distribution: [p] occurs after [s] but never word-initially, while [pʰ] occurs word-initially but never after [s]. Since these sounds appear in different phonetic environments there can be no pair of words composed of identical strings of sounds except for [p] in one and [pʰ] in the other. As stated above, phones that are in complementary distribution are allophones of a single phoneme. In this case, [p] and [pʰ] are both allophones of the phoneme we can represent as /p/. Furthermore, the appearance of one allophone or another in a given context is predictable. For example, we can predict that the allophone [pʰ] (but never [p]) will appear in word-initial position. So even in words not listed above, we know that it will be [pʰ], rather than [p], that will occur at the beginning of a word. Similarly, we can predict that [p] (but never [pʰ]) will follow [s] in other words.

Free Variation

In some phonetic contexts more than one pronunciation of a given sound may be possible. Consider, for example, the following words containing [p] and [p˺] ([p˺] represents an unreleased voiceless bilabial stop).

leap	[lip]	*leap*	[lip˺]
soap	[sop]	*soap*	[sop˺]
troop	[trup]	*troop*	[trup˺]
happy	[hæpi]	—	*[hæp˺i]

It should be clear that these sounds both share some of the same phonetic environments; for example, they can both appear at the ends of words. Unlike the case of English [b] vs. [pʰ], or [m] vs. [n], however, there are no minimal pairs involving these sounds in the language. And note that although there are pairs of words in the list above that differ in only one sound, none of these words contrast in meaning. Thus, the choice between [p] and [p˺] in *leap, soap,* and *troop* does not make a difference in meaning; that is, the sounds are noncontrastive. Rather, they are interchangeable in word-final position. Sounds with this type of patterning are considered to be in *free variation.* To a native speaker, sounds like [p] and [p˺] that are in free variation are perceived as being the "same" sound. Thus, we can conclude that they are allophones of the same phoneme.

Summary

To summarize, a phone's distribution is the collection of phonetic environments in which the phone may appear; when linguists describe a phone's distribution they describe this collection. Relative to each other, two (or more) phones will be in contrastive distribution, complementary distribution, or in free variation. Phones in contrastive distribution may appear in minimal pairs and are allophones of different phonemes. Phones in free variation may also appear in the same phonetic environments but never cause a contrast in meaning; they are allophones of the same phoneme. In either of these two types of distribution, given a particular phonetic environment, one cannot predict which of the phones will occur. If the phones are in complementary distribution, their appearance in particular phonetic environments is predictable; they never appear in minimal pairs and they are allophones of the same phoneme.

EXERCISE 1

Look at the following Ukrainian words containing the sounds [s], [sʲ], [ʃ], and [ʃʲ]. The sounds [sʲ] and [ʃʲ] are palatalized variants of [s] and [ʃ]; palatalization sounds like a [j] sound right after (or on) the consonant and is very close to the [j] sound in the English word [bjuɾi] *beauty*. You might want to review these definitions before you begin: contrastive distribution, complementary distribution, and minimal pair. The words have been arranged to help you identify minimal pairs.

[s]		[sʲ]		[ʃ]		[ʃʲ]	
1. lɪs	'fox'	lɪsʲ	'sheen'	lɪʃ	'lest'		
2. mɪska	'bowl'			mɪʃka	'little mouse'	mɪʃʲi	'mice'
3. sapka	'little hoe'			ʃapka	'hat'		
4. sɪla	'strength'			ʃɪla	'she sewed'	ʃʲistʲ	'six'
5. sum	'sadness'			ʃum	'rustling'		
6. sudɪ	'trials'	sʲudɪ	'hither'			koʃʲi	'baskets'
7. sosna	'pine'	sʲomɪj	'seventh'	ʃostɪj	'sixth'		
8. posadu	'job' (acc.)	posʲadu	'I will occupy'				

a. What minimal pairs can you identify in these words?

b. Is there a minimal triplet (like a minimal pair, but involving three sounds and three words)? What is it?

c. Which three of these four sounds are in contrastive distribution?

d. One of these sounds occurs only before a particular vowel. What is this sound, and what is the vowel? Which words indicate this?

e. Is the consonant you identified in (d) contrastive in Ukrainian, or not?

PHONOLOGICAL RULES

In [the preceding section], we discussed the fact that phonemes and (allo)phones belong to different levels of structure in language—that is, phonemes are mental entities and phones are physical events. In this [section] we consider the connection between these two levels. The mapping between phonemic and phonetic elements is accomplished using *phonological rules* (recall that a rule of grammar expresses a pattern in a language). A speaker's knowledge of phonological rules allows him or her to "translate" phonemes into actual speech sounds; knowledge of these rules forms part of the speaker's linguistic competence. This change from the phonemic underlying form to the actual phonetic form of a word by means of phonological rules can be represented with a diagram:

phonemic form

⇓

rules

⇓

phonetic form

As an example, consider the English word *can* /kæn/. This word has a final /n/ sound in its phonemic form, and in fact it is frequently pronounced with a final [n]. If we listen carefully, however, we find that the final consonant of *can* (especially in casual speech) is often [m] or [ŋ]. The following examples illustrate this. (Here and throughout this file we use a fairly broad transcription style, recording phonetic detail only for the segments under discussion.)

I can ask	[aɪ kæn æsk]	(or [aɪ kn̩ æsk])
I can see	[aɪ kæn si]	(or [aɪ kn̩si])
I can bake	[ai kæm beɪk]	(or [aɪ km̩ beɪk])
I can play	[aɪ kæm pleɪ]	(or [aɪ km̩ pleɪ])
I can go	[aɪ kæŋ goʊ]	(or [aɪ kŋ̩ goʊ])
I can come	[aɪ kæŋ kʌm]	(or [aɪ kŋ̩ kʌm])

As these transcriptions show, /n/ is pronounced as [m] when it precedes a labial consonant and as [ŋ] when it precedes a velar consonant. We can state this fact about English as a descriptive rule:

/n/ is pronounced as   [m] before a labial consonant

[ŋ] before a velar consonant

[n] everywhere else.

(We will be adjusting this rule later on. . . .) Notice that a phonological rule has three parts: the sound(s) affected by the rule, the environment where the rule applies, and the result of the rule. Here /n/ is affected by the rule. The rule applies when /n/ is followed by a labial or velar consonant. The result of the application of the rule is that /n/ acquires the same place of articulation as the following consonant.

Now consider how the phonetic forms of some of the above examples are derived from the phonemic forms:

phonemic form:	/kæn æsk/	/kæn beɪk/	/kæn goʊ/
apply rule:	kæn æsk	kæm beɪk	kæŋ goʊ
phonetic form:	[kæn æsk]	[kæm beɪk]	[kæŋ goʊ]

This illustrates what happens in speaking. In listening, a hearer reverses this process: he or she perceives the phonetic form of an utterance, then sends it "backwards" through the phonological rules, finally obtaining a phonemic form that matches a form stored in memory.

The rule illustrated above applies not only to /n/, but also to /t/ and /d/:

hat trick	[hæt trɪk]
hit batsman	[hɪp bætsmn̩]
night class	[naɪk klæs]
bad dream	[bæd drim]
head band	[hɛb bænd]
bad guy	[bæg gaɪ]

Natural Classes

Can we make one rule to state that /n/, /t/, and /d/ change place of articulation according to what sound follows? Is it random chance that these three sounds all seem to undergo the same phonological rule? To answer these questions, let's first take a look at the articulatory descriptions of these three sounds:

/t/	voiceless alveolar oral stop
/d/	voiced alveolar oral stop
/n/	voiced alveolar nasal stop

Not only are all three sounds alveolar stops, but they are the *only* alveolar stops in English. The description "voiceless alveolar oral stop" can only mean /t/. We can make the description more general by removing some of the properties:

/n/, /t/, /d/	alveolar stop

With respect to English, saying "alveolar stop" is the same as saying /n/, /t/, and /d/. These three sounds are all of the phonemes in English that are produced by stopping the flow of air at the alveolar ridge. Thus, they are the *natural class* of alveolar stops. A natural class is a group of sounds in a language that share one or more articulatory or auditory property, *to the exclusion of all other sounds in that language*. That is, in order for a group of sounds to be a natural class, it must include all of the sounds that share a particular property or set of properties, and not include any sounds that don't.

Properties Used to Describe Natural Classes

All of the properties [that] describe individual sounds can also be used to describe natural classes. For example, in the English vowels the monophthongs [i, u] and the first part of the diphthongs [eɪ] and [oʊ] are tense vowels, and there are no other tense vowels in English. Thus, these vowels are members of the natural class of tense vowels in English. Likewise, the consonants [k, g, ŋ] are all described as velar consonants, and they are the only velar consonants used in English; thus they constitute the natural class of velar consonants in English. [See (3).] Notice that we already referred to the natural class of velar consonants in the formulation of our rule at the beginning of this file. You'll recall that this rule affects the natural class of alveolar stops when followed by a member of either the natural class of velar consonants or the natural class of bilabial consonants. This shows that natural classes can be used to describe both the sounds affected by a rule *and* the environments where a rule applies.

(3) The major natural classes of English consonants

Place of Articulation

Manner of Articulation		Bilabial		Labio-dental		Inter-dental		Alveolar		Palatal		Velar		Glottal	
	Stop	p	b					t	d					ʔ	
	Fricative			f	v	θ	ð	s	z	ʃ	ʒ			h	
	Affricate									tʃ	dʒ				
	Nasal		m						n			ŋ			
	Lateral Liquid								l						
	Retroflex Liquid								r						
	Glide	ʍ	w								j				

Keys: Labials   Sibilants   Obstruents   Sonorants

In talking about groups of sounds, we must use a few properties in addition to those needed to describe individual sounds. For example, . . . the only labiodental consonants in English are the fricatives [f] and [v]. . . . In many situations it is advantageous to refer to [f] and [v] together with [p, b, m, w] and [ʍ] as belonging to the same natural class. For this purpose we use the property *labial*.

Another property used to describe natural classes divides consonants into two groups, *obstruents* and *sonorants*. Obstruents are produced with an obstruction of the airflow. The sounds in this category are stops, fricatives, and affricates. Sonorants, on the other hand, are consonants produced with a relatively open passage for the airflow. Sonorant consonants include nasals, liquids, and glides. Thus, the class of labial obstruents in English is [p, f, b, v], while the class of labial sonorants is [m, w, ʍ]. The class of labial consonants is the union of both sets: [p, f, b, v, m, w, ʍ]. As we will see, being able to divide consonants into obstruents and sonorants is quite useful in stating phonological rules.

Classification of Phonological Rules

In addition to grouping sounds into natural classes, we can classify phonological rules according to the kind of process that they involve. Seven major kinds of processes are discussed here, along with examples from the phonology of English and other languages.

a. Assimilation

Rules of *assimilation* cause a sound to become more like a neighboring sound with respect to some phonetic property. In other words, the segment affected by the rule assimilates or takes on a property from a nearby (usually adjacent) sound. Rules of assimilation are very common in languages. The first rule we considered in this [section] falls into this category. We can call it alveolar stop assimilation because it applies to all alveolar stops (/t/, /d/, and /n/):

> *Alveolar stop assimilation* (English): Alveolar stops assimilate to the place of articulation of a following consonant.

Thus, when a sound having the properties alveolar and stop immediately precedes a labial consonant, this rule causes it to take on the property labial (thereby replacing its specification for alveolar). Similarly, this rule can apply to change the sound's place of articulation feature to dental when it precedes a dental consonant (examples such as *width* [wɪd̪θ] and *in this* [ɪn̪ ðɪs]), and so on for the other places of articulation.

Another common assimilation process is *palatalization*. Palatalization refers to a special type of assimilation in which a consonant becomes like a neighboring sound. For example, when American English speakers say *Did you eat?* rapidly, they very often pronounce it as [dɪdʒa it]. The sound [d] has been turned into a palatal sound [dʒ] because of the influence of the following palatal glide [j]. Vowels such as [i] and [e] also cause this change. The most common types of palatalization occur when alveolar, dental, and velar stops or fricatives appear before a front vowel. So the following are all common types of palatalization: [t] → [tʃ]; [d] → [dʒ]; [s] → [ʃ]; [k] → [tʃ]; [g] → [dʒ]. While there are variants on palatalization and other sounds can be palatalized, the main things to look for are (1) a sound becoming a palatal and/or (2) a sound change conditioned by a front vowel.

The rules of assimilation that we've discussed so far cause sounds to assimilate to *adjacent* sounds. This is a common way that assimilation occurs. However, long-distance assimilation also exists, and a relatively common type of long-distance assimilation is called *vowel harmony*. This typically causes all the vowels in a word to "harmonize" or agree in some property such as rounding or backness.

Finnish has a common type of vowel harmony rule, which can be stated as follows:

Vowel harmony (Finnish): A back vowel becomes front when preceded by a front vowel in the same word.

By this rule, Finnish words have, with few exceptions, either all front vowels or all back vowels, but not both in the same word. We can see the vowel harmony rule in action when a suffix is added to the end of a word. In this case, the suffix vowel changes to match the quality of vowels in the word. For example, the suffix meaning 'in' has the form [-ssa] when added to a word where the last vowel is back, as in [talo] 'house', [talossa] 'in the house'. However, the suffix takes the form [-ssæ] when it attaches to a word with a final front vowel, as in [metsæ] 'forest', [metsæssæ] 'in the forest'. In cases like this, we can say that the vowel of the suffix harmonizes, or assimilates, to the preceding vowel.

b. Dissimilation

Unlike assimilation, which makes sounds more similar, rules of *dissimilation* cause two close or adjacent sounds to become less alike with respect to some property, by means of a change in one or both sounds. An example of dissimilation in Greek is the following:

Manner dissimilation (Greek): A stop becomes a fricative when followed by another stop.

For example, in fast speech especially, the form /epta/ 'seven' can be pronounced as [efta], and /ktizma/ 'building' can be pronounced as [xtizma] ([x] is a voiceless velar fricative).

c. Insertion

Phonological rules of *insertion* cause a segment not present at the phonemic level to be added to the phonetic form of a word. An example of this kind of rule from English is voiceless stop insertion:

Voiceless stop insertion (English): Between a nasal consonant and a voiceless fricative, a voiceless stop with the same place of articulation as the nasal is inserted.

Thus, for instance, the voiceless stop insertion rule may apply to the word *dance* /dæns/ → [dænts], *strength* /strɛŋθ/ → [strɛŋkθ], and *hamster* /hæmstɹ̩/ → [hæmpstɹ̩].

d. Deletion

Deletion rules eliminate a sound. Such rules apply more frequently to unstressed syllables and in casual speech. English examples include:

/h/-Deletion (English): /h/ may be deleted in unstressed syllables.

The /h/-deletion rule would apply to a sentence such as *He handed her his hat* /hi hændəd hɹ hɪz hæt/ to yield [hi hændəd ɹ ɪz hæt]. Deletion is common in fast speech because it saves time and articulatory effort. Sounds like [h] that are not very perceptible are often the "victims" of deletion because speakers can save time and effort by deleting them without sacrificing much information. That is, the listener may not be relying on these sounds in order to understand what the speaker is saying.

e. Metathesis

Rules of *metathesis* change the order of sounds. In many instances, sounds metathesize in order to make words easier to pronounce or easier to understand. In Leti, an Austronesian language, consonants and vowels switch places when a word that ends in a consonant is combined with a word that starts with two consonants. The last two sounds in the first word trade places to avoid having three consonants in a row.

> *CV metathesis* (Leti): When three consecutive consonants occur, the first consonant trades places with the preceding vowel.

By this rule, /danat + kviali/ 'millipede' undergoes metathesis to become [dantakviali], and /ukar + ppalu/ 'index finger' becomes [ukrappalu]. On the other hand, /ukar + lavan/ 'thumb' does not undergo metathesis because there are not three consecutive consonants.

phonemic form:	/danat+kviali/	/ukar+ppalu/	/ukar+lavan/
CV metathesis:	dantakviali	ukrappalu	—
phonetic form:	[dantakviali]	[ukrappalu]	[ukarlavan]

f. Strengthening

Rules of *strengthening* (also called *fortition*) make sounds stronger. The rule of English aspiration, as stated below, provides an example:

> *Aspiration* (English): Voiceless stops become aspirated when they occur at the beginning of a stressed syllable.

The pronunciation of *tap* /tæp/ as [tʰæp] and *cat* /kæt/ as [kʰæt] illustrate the application of the English aspiration rule. Aspirated stops are considered to be stronger sounds than unaspirated stops because the duration of voicelessness is much longer.

g. Weakening

Rules of *weakening* (also called *lenition*) cause sounds to become weaker. The "flapping" rule of English is an example of weakening. [ɾ] is considered to be a weaker sound than [t] or [d] because it is shorter and it obstructs air less.

> *Flapping* (English): An alveolar oral stop is realized as [ɾ] when it occurs after a stressed vowel and before an unstressed vowel.

The pronunciation of *writer* /raɪtɾ̩/ as [raɪɾɾ̩] and *rider* /raɪdɾ̩/ as [raɪɾɾ̩] are examples of the application of this rule. Note that voicing assimilation is involved in the change of /t/ to [ɾ]: the /t/ takes on the "voicedness" of the vowels surrounding it.

Multiple Rule Application

To this point we have seen examples where one phonological rule applies. In reality there is often more than one change that occurs between a given phonemic form and a phonetic output. To illustrate this let's look at how plural nouns are formed in English. When you learned to write in English, you learned that the way to make a noun plural is to add an "s," which is usually pronounced [z]. There are actually three different phonetic forms of the English plural marker: [s], [z], and [əz], seen in the words *cats* [kæts], *dogs* [dagz], and *foxes* [faksəz]. We need only one phonemic form for the plural marker if we use two rules to derive the phonetic forms.

Try to pronounce [kætz] or [dags] in which the voicing quality of the final two consonants differ. You will probably find that it is difficult to produce a consonant cluster if one consonant is voiced and the other is voiceless. It is for this reason that the plural marker changes its voicing specification to match the sound it follows. We will use /-z/ as the phonemic form of the English plural marker, but notice that it doesn't matter whether we choose /-z/ or /-s/. It works out the same in the end.

> *Voicing assimilation* (English): /-z/ takes on the voicing specification of the preceding sound.

Now we can account for the different endings for *dogs* and *cats*, but what about the plurals of words like *fox, ditch, bush, orange, rouge,* and *maze*? What these words have in common is that they end in sounds that have a high-pitched hissing sound quality. These sounds are called *sibilant* consonants. The English sibilants are [tʃ, ʃ, s, dʒ, ʒ, z]. Notice that the plural marker is also a sibilant. Because of the high-pitched hissing sound, it is very difficult to hear two sibilants that are next to each other. Try saying [fakss], [dɪtʃs], [brɪdʒz], etc., and you will get the idea. This is remedied by inserting a schwa between two sibilants.

> *Schwa insertion* (English): Insert [ə] between two sibilants.

With these two rules, we can derive the plural for any English noun (except, of course, for special plurals like *oxen, octopi,* and *cherubim*).

phonemic form:	/kæt+z/	/dag+z/	/faks+z/	/brɪdʒ+z/
schwa insertion:	—	—	faksəz	brɪdʒəz
voicing assimilation:	kæts	—	—	—
phonetic form:	[kæts]	[dagz]	[faksəz]	[brɪdʒəz]

Obligatory and Optional Rules

Notice that phonological rules may be *obligatory* or *optional*. Obligatory English rules include aspiration, vowel nasalization, vowel lengthening, and liquid and glide devoicing. Such a rule always applies in the speech of all speakers of a language or dialect having the rule, regardless of style or rate of speaking. The effects of obligatory rules are often very subtle and difficult to notice, but they are an important part of a native accent. For instance, it may be difficult to tell that a vowel is nasalized in English, but the application of vowel nasalization makes us sound like native speakers of English.

The existence of obligatory rules is what causes people to have foreign accents. It is easier to learn the rules of a new language than to "turn off" the obligatory rules of your native language. The very fact that we are often unaware of these rules causes us to apply them when they are not appropriate. When speakers of American English learn other languages, they often apply rules such as flapping and vowel reduction, even though the other language may not have these rules.

Optional phonological rules, on the other hand, may or may not apply in an individual's speech. Optional rules are responsible for variation in speech; for example, we can pronounce /kæn bi/ *can be* as either [kæm bi] or [kæn bi], depending on whether Alveolar Stop Assimilation is applied or not. The use of optional rules depends in part on rate and style of speech.

Conclusion

In this [section] we have covered seven types of phonological rules: assimilation, dissimilation, insertion, deletion, metathesis, strengthening, and weakening. These phonological rules operate on natural classes of sounds. We have also shown that a natural class is a group of all the sounds in a language that share some articulatory or auditory property(s) to the exclusion of all other sounds in that language. To describe natural classes we have used the properties *consonant, vowel, labial, sibilant, obstruent,* and *sonorant,* as well as properties used to describe individual consonants and vowels.

EXERCISE 2

1. List the members of the following natural classes of English sounds.

   a. alveolar obstruents

   b. voiced labial consonants

    c. velar oral stops

    d. interdental fricatives

    e. high tense vowels

    f. low vowels

    g. palatal sonorants

    h. voiced sibilants

2. Describe the following natural classes of English sounds.

    a. [r, l]

    b. [f, θ, s, ʃ, h]

    c. [w, j, w̥]

    d. [i, u]

    e. [p, b]

    f. [n, r, l]

3. Consider the following paragraphs and answer the questions about natural classes.

    a. The English indefinite article is *a* [ʌ] before most words: *a car, a peanut, a tennis ball*, etc., but it is *an* [æn] before words like *apple, onion, icicle, evening, eagle*, and *honor*. To what natural class do the sounds at the beginning of these words belong?

    b. Some American English speakers (largely in the Midwest and South) pronounce [ɪ] in words like *then, Kenny, pen, Bengals, gem, lengthen, Remington*, and *temperature* (where other speakers have [ɛ]). What natural class of sounds follows these vowels?

    c. Some midwestern American speakers in casual speech drop the unstressed vowel in the first syllable of words like *police, believe, parade, Columbus, pollution, terrific*, and *collision*, but do not drop it in words like *detective, dependent, majestic*, or *pedantic*. What natural class of sounds follows the unstressed vowel in the first syllable in this first group of words?

    d. At some time during a child's language development, he or she might pronounce certain words as follows: *that* [dæt], *these* [diz], *this* [dɪs], and *three* [fri], *think* [fɪŋk], *bath* [bæf]. What natural class of sounds is being affected? Do the sounds used as replacements form a natural class?

4. Identify the phonological rule or rules . . . operating in each of the following derivations.

a. little   /lɪtl̩/   →   [lɪɾl̩]

b. late bell   /leɪt bɛl/   →   [leɪp bɛl]

c. park   /park/   →   [pʰark]

d. lance   /læns/   →   [lænts]

e. It's her car /ɪts hr̩ kar/   →   [ɪts r̩kʰar]

f. ten pages   /tɛn peɪdʒz/   →   [tɛm pʰeɪdʒəz]

g. two cups   /tu kʌpz/   →   [tʰu kʰʌps]

5. Examine the following sets of data, and for each set write a rule to describe the derivation of the phonetic forms from the phonemic ones. (To do so, determine what sound or natural class of sounds is being altered, what the environment is, and what is changing.) Where possible, also explain what kind of process (of the seven types) is involved in the rule.

a. In the speech of some New Yorkers, examples like the following are found.

there	/ðɛr/	→	[ðɛ]	*marry*	/mæri/	→	[mæri]
court	/kɔrt/	→	[kɔt]	*Paris*	/pærɪs/	→	[pærɪs]
large	/larĵ/	→	[laĵ]	*for all*	/fɔr ɔl/	→	[fɔr ɔl]
stores	/stɔrz/	→	[stɔz]	*story*	/stɔri/	→	[stɔri]
cared	/kɛrd/	→	[kɛd]	*caring*	/kɛrɪŋ/	→	[kɛrɪŋ]

b. Examples like the following are very common in English.

OSU	/oɛsju/	[oɛʃu]
did you	/dɪd ju/	[dɪdʒu]
capture	/kæptɪr̩/	[kæptʃr̩]
gracious	/greɪsiəs/	[greɪʃəs]

c. The following data are from German. (The symbol /tˢ/ represents a voiceless alveolar affricate.)

German	Gloss				
Bild	'picture'	/bɪld/	→	[bɪlt]	
blieb	'remained'	/blib/	→	[blip]	
Weg	'way'	/veg/	→	[vek]	
fremd	'foreign'	/frɛmd/	→	[frɛmt]	
gelb	'yellow'	/gɛlb/	→	[gɛlp]	
Zug	'train'	/tˢug/	→	[tˢuk]	
Vogel	'bird'	/fogl̩/	→	[fogl̩]	
Baum	'tree'	/baʊm/	→	[baʊm]	
schnell	'fast'	/ʃnɛl/	→	[ʃnɛl]	

6. In [this section], two rules were used to derive the three phonetic forms of the English plural. Is the order of these rules important? Show what would happen if we applied the Voicing Assimilation rule before the Schwa Insertion rule. Give examples.

FOR DISCUSSION AND REVIEW

1. What is the difference between a *phone* and a *phoneme*? Why might native speakers of a language consider two phonetically different sounds to be the same sound?

2. What does it mean to say that sounds are *"predictable"*?

3. What is the difference between *noncontrastive* and *contrastive* sounds? Explain how contrastive sounds in Hindi might be noncontrastive in English.

4. What is *complementary* distribution? Compare contrastive distribution to complementary distribution. Are the sounds in complementary distribution allophones or phonemes? Give some examples from English. If you can, give examples from other languages.

5. The file suggests that a "speaker's knowledge of phonological rules allows him or her to 'translate' phonemes into actual speech sounds." Explain how this works.

6. What is a natural class of sounds? What are the major natural classes of English consonants? How do /n, t, d/ make up a natural class of English consonants?

7. Explain the difference between *obstruent* and *sonorant*.

8. What is *assimilation*? How does the phonological rule of assimilation work in English?

9. What is *vowel harmony*? How does vowel harmony work in Finnish?

10. What is a deletion rule? Why might deletion rules come into play when a person speaks rapidly?

Projects for "The Sounds of Language: Phonetics and Phonology"

1. Work in small groups to complete this exercise, adapted from Ohio Language File 4.5. Then, in a class discussion each group should compare strategies and answers. Use the cheat sheet below on this page to reach a final resolution.

Mokilese is a language spoken in Micronesia. Examine the distribution of the voiced and voiceless vowel pairs: [i, i̥] and [u, u̥] (voiceless vowels have a circle under the phonetic vowel symbol). For each pair, determine whether they are allophones of different phonemes or allophones of the same phoneme. Provide evidence for your answer. If they are allophones of one phoneme, state the contexts in which each sound occurs and decide which sound is the basic sound. Can any generalizations be made? (Hint: refer to natural classes.)

1. [pi̥san]	'full of leaves'	7. [uduk]	'flesh'
2. [dupu̥kda]	'bought'	8. [kaskas]	'to throw'
3. [pu̥ko]	'basket'	9. [poki]	'to strike something'
4. [ki̥sa]	'we two'	10. [pil]	'water'
5. [su̥pwo]	'firewood'	11. [apid]	'outrigger support'
6. [kamwɔki̥ti]	'to move'	12. [ludʒuk]	'to tackle'

Then, working individually, write a short essay on working with an unfamiliar language. What kinds of data are necessary? What does the ability to work with an unfamiliar language suggest about the structure of language itself?

Mokilese Vowel Pairs Cheat Sheet

Since there are no minimal pairs where [i] and [i̥] are the only different sounds between the pair, and none where [u] and [u̥] are the only different sounds, we proceed to look for complementary distribution. To examine the environments more easily, we can list the sounds which surround the sounds in question.

[i̥]	[i]	[u̥]	[u]
p_s	t_#	p_k	#_d
k_s	p_l	s_p	l_dʒ
k_t	p_d		d_k
	k_#		d_p
			dʒ_k

If these allophones are in complementary distribution, the environment that precedes them does not appear to be the conditioning environment. For the pair [i̥] and [i], there is overlapping distribution, since they both can appear after [p] and [k]. Therefore, we cannot use the environment that precedes [i̥] and [i] to predict which allophone will occur. For the pair [u̥] and [u], the distribution is not overlapping. However, the sounds that precede [u] do not form a natural class, and although the sounds that precede [u̥] are all voiceless consonants, we should not assume that we have found the conditioning environment for [u̥]. This would mean that the conditioning environments for the two pairs of vowels ([u]-[u̥] and [i]-[i̥]) were different. This could happen, of course, but it is more likely that both are conditioned by the same environment, so we should continue to check out others.

The environment that follows the sounds in question also does not appear to be the conditioning environment. The sounds [u̥] and [u] are in overlapping distribution. Both precede [k], and the environments which follow [i̥] form a natural class but present us with the same problem as the sounds following [u̥] (i.e., having to posit different conditioning environments for the two pairs). Before we give up the hypothesis that these pairs of sounds are in complementary distribution, we must examine another possibility: that the environment that surrounds the sounds in question is the conditioning environment.

The sounds that surround [i̥] are voiceless, as are the sounds that surround [u̥]. In addition, the sounds that surround [i] and [u] are voiced. These two sets do not overlap; therefore, we have complementary distribution. This means that [i̥] and [i] are allophones of a single phoneme, as are [u̥] and [u]. We can state a rule that accounts for the distribution of these sounds:

[i] and [u] become voiceless between voiceless consonants

Note that we cannot say that all vowels become voiceless between voiceless consonants as the word [kaskas] illustrates. However, we could make our rule more general by noting that [i] and [u] are both high vowels. Thus our rule becomes:

High vowels become voiceless between voiceless consonants.

2. Many linguists and grammarians complain that the English spelling system contains too many ambiguities and uncertainties with regard to pronunciations. One famous example is the spelling of "fish" by George Bernard Shaw as "g-h-o-t-i." He uses the "gh" from the word "enough," the "o" from the word "women," and the "ti" from the word "nation." In groups of four or five, create lists of the names of the people in your class. How many names are decipherable by others? What does this tell you or reaffirm about the English spelling system?

3. Select an article from your favorite magazine or journal, and bring a copy to class. Form groups. Select a paragraph or two, and simplify the

spelling of the words in the article. Feel free to eliminate unnecessary letters and to shorten as many consonant clusters as you wish. To further simplify the spelling, you may choose to substitute letters for those in the printed words and eliminate others altogether. After your "cleaning" is done, reinsert the paragraph in your article and exchange it with another group. Can your classmates read the passage? Which sounds in English appear to have the greatest variety of spellings? Which letter appears to represent the greatest variety of sounds? What would you propose as a revised alphabet? What have you learned about the English spelling system? As a result of this exercise, what difficulties do you foresee for foreign-language speakers trying to learn English?

4. Phonetic research deals with the features of sounds, while phonology deals with the organization of the sounds within a language. Using data and ideas from the articles in this part as well as those listed in the selected bibliography, write a two- to three-page essay on how understanding or describing a language's sound system appears to include assumptions about the specific sounds in that language.

5. Although most introductions to phonology begin with the phoneme, not all linguists accept the idea of abstract phonemes. Robert Port, for instance, argues against them, whereas Peter Ladefoged suggests that phonemes are primarily useful as a teaching tool (see the following Selected Bibliography). Read and write summaries of three counterarguments to the existence of abstract phonemes. How else do linguists account for "significant" sounds? At the end of each summary, discuss briefly why you find the argument strong or weak.

Selected Bibliography

Ball, Catherine N. *Sounds of the World's Animals*. Dept. of Linguistics, Georgetown University. <www.georgetown.edu/faculty/ballc/animals/animals .html>. [Interesting Web site with examples of how languages worldwide express animal sounds differently.]

Berkeley Linguistics Phonology Lab. University of California at Berkeley. <http://trill.berkeley.edu>. [Accessible Web site useful for both research and teaching, with summaries of latest research on phonology.]

Bland-Stewart, Linda M. "Phonetic Inventories and Phonological Patterns of African American Two-Year-Olds: A Preliminary Investigation." *Communication Disorders Quarterly*. 24.3 (2003): 109–120. [Intended to provide clinicians with basic understanding and appreciation of African American English.]

Chomsky, Noam, and Morris Halle. *The Sound Pattern of English*. Cambridge, MA: M.I.T. P, 1991. [The classic work on the phonology of the English language.]

Denes, Peter, and Elliot Pinson. *The Speech Chain: The Physics and Biology of Spoken Language*. 2nd ed. New York: Worth, 1993. [An accessible explanation of the aspects of spoken communication.]

Dyson, Alice T. "Phonetic Inventories of 2- and 3-Year Old Children." *Journal of Speech and Hearing Disorders*. 53.1 (1998): 89–93. [Studies with two groups of children examining how phonetics evolve during a crucial eighteen-month period.]

Goldsmith, J. A., ed. *Phonological Theory: The Essential Readings*. Oxford: Blackwell, 2000. [Classic and contemporary essays offering an excellent introduction to the sometimes daunting study of theoretical phonology.]

Gussman, Edmund. *Phonology: Analysis and Theory*. Cambridge: Cambridge UP, 2002. [An introductory textbook that assumes no prior experience with linguistics.]

Halle, Morris. "Knowledge Unlearned and Untaught: What Speakers Know about the Sounds of Their Language." *Linguistic Theory and Psychological Reality*. Eds. Morris Halle, Joan Bresnan, and George A. Miller. Cambridge, MA: M.I.T. P, 1981. [Phonology theory from the linguist best known for his work in generative phonology.]

"How to Pronounce *ghoti*." 2006. The Lexiteria Corporation. <www .alphadictionary.com/articles/ling006.html>. [Examination of the regularity and irregularity of English phonology, with emphasis on the "gh" variants.]

Ladefoged, Peter. *A Course in Phonetics*. 4th ed. Belmont, CA: Heinle, 2000. [The hallmark text for the study of phonetics.]

———. *Vowels and Consonants: An Introduction to the Sounds of Language*. 2nd ed. Oxford: Blackwell, 2005. [Accessible text on phonetics that includes a CD with hundreds of examples to illustrate language issues.]

Lieberman, Philip, and Sheila E. Blumstein. *Speech Physiology, Speech Perception, and Acoustic Phonetics*. Cambridge Studies in Speech Science and Communication. Cambridge: Cambridge UP, 1988. [An introduction to the study of speech that assumes no technical background.]

Nilsen, Don L. F., and Alleen Pace Nilsen. *Pronunciation Contrasts in English.* Long Grove, IL: Waveland, 2002. [Particularly helpful to English teachers of non-native English speakers.]

Odden, David. *Introducing Phonology.* Cambridge: Cambridge UP, 2005. [An accessible phonology text aimed at undergraduates.]

Phonetics: The Sounds of Spoken Language. 2005. Depts. of Spanish and Portuguese, German, Speech Pathology and Audiology, and Academic Techonologies, University of Iowa. <www.uiowa.edu/~acadtech/phonetics>. [A phonetics flash animation project with information on American English, German, and Spanish.]

Port, Robert. *Phonology with Rich Memory: A Manifesto.* 26 August 2005. Indiana University. <www.cs.indiana.edu/~port/pap/PhonologyManifesto.htm>. [An argument against the reality of abstract phonemes.]

Pullum, Geoffrey K., and William Ladusaw. *Phonetic Symbol Guide.* Chicago: U of Chicago P, 1996. [A comprehensive encyclopedia of symbols.]

Roach, Peter. *English Phonetics and Phonology.* 3rd ed. Cambridge: Cambridge UP, 2000. [A widely recognized and practical phonology text.]

Roca, I. W. Johnson, and A. Roca. *A Course in Phonology.* Oxford: Blackwell, 2000. [Advanced introductory textbook.]

Serry, T. A., and P. J. Blamey. "A 4-Year Investigation into Phonetic Inventory Development in Young Cochlear Implant Users." *Journal of Speech, Language and Hearing Research.* 42.1 (1999): 141–54. [Studies from spontaneous speech samples of cochlear implant users ages five and younger, before and after implant, suggest development corresponding to that of hearing children.]

Williams, A. Lynn, and Mary Elbert. "A Prospective Longitudinal Study of Phonological Development in Late Talkers." *Language, Speech, & Hearing Services in Schools* 34.2 (2003): 138–54. [Discussion of the early identification and treatment of late-talking children.]

LANGUAGE STRUCTURES: WORDS AND PHRASES

The introduction to Part Two of this book suggests that most linguists describe language in terms of basic components. In this part, we focus on two of these linguistic components: morphology and syntax. The morphology and syntax of a language make the structures for meaning.

The first four selections in Part Three deal with morphology, the study of the structure of words and the processes of forming words. Every word is composed of at least one meaningful unit that cannot be subdivided into smaller units. That unit is called a *morpheme*. A morpheme may be a word that can stand alone, such as *turn*, *desk*, *hope*, *giraffe*, or *walk*; it may combine with other morphemes to derive a new word, for instance, *re*turn, desk*top*, hope*ful*; or it may be attached to another morpheme to give grammatical information, such as the *–s* in giraffe*s* or the *-ed* in walk*ed*.

Part of what it means to know a language is the ability to analyze or divide words into their morphemes. The first piece, "The Minimal Units of Meaning: Morphemes," is from the Ohio State University *Language Files*. This selection introduces the ways we identify morphemes and demonstrates how morphemes combine to form words.

In the next selection, H. A. Gleason Jr. works primarily with data from Hebrew to describe the analytic processes for identifying morphemes in any language. The exercises in Swahili, Ilocano, and Dinka at the end of Gleason's article offer an opportunity to work with languages that may be unfamiliar. Discovering that we can work with them underscores the fact all languages are organized and systematic. For this reason, we can describe the linguistic structure of a language without speaking that language.

The next two articles show how morphology intersects with our everyday lives. In "Understanding Basic Medical Terminology," Janet Romich provides a straightforward application of morphological analysis to the medical profession. Then, in "Mc-: Meaning in the Marketplace," Genine Lentine and Roger Shuy describe how their work on an advertising lawsuit depended on the public's awareness of the social meanings and values associated with certain morphemes.

Finally, we deal with syntax—the study of the rules governing how words are ordered into phrases and sentences. Syntax also encompasses the grammatical classification of words, such as into *noun, verb, adjective,* and so forth. Researchers who study language acquisition in children tell us something remarkable about syntax: very young children just beginning to use language can produce and understand sentences they have never heard before—and they can do this without thinking about it. (In Part Nine, we examine this phenomenon more thoroughly.) Indeed, humans seem predisposed to acquire syntactic rules. Frank Heny, in "Syntax: The Structure of Sentences," uses mainly English examples to examine some important syntactic structures and rules. He then shows how some of these might relate directly to how language is learned.

9

The Minimal Units of Meaning: Morphemes

The Ohio State University *Language Files*

One of the distinguishing features of human language is its multilayered quality. Phonemes, in themselves meaningless, combine to form units that do have meaning—morphemes. All languages use morphemes to construct words. The first part of the following selection uses English to identify the various kinds of morphemes and describe how they function. The second part begins by examining the complex ways English prefixes and suffixes combine with other units. It then explains the hierarchical internal structure of English words that results from these combinations.

A continuous stream of speech can be broken up by the listener (or linguist) into smaller, meaningful parts. A conversation, for example, can be divided into the sentences of the conversation, which can be divided up further into the words that make up each of the sentences. It is obvious to most people that a sentence has a meaning, and that each of the words in it has a meaning as well. Can we go further and divide words into smaller units which still have meanings? Many people think not; their immediate intuition is that words are the basic meaningful elements of a language. This is, however, not the case. Many words can be broken down into still smaller units. Think, for example, of words such as *unlucky*, *unhappy*, and *unsatisfied*. The *un-* in each of these words has the same meaning, loosely, that of "not," but *un* is not a word by itself. Thus, we have identified units—smaller than the word—that have meanings. These are called *morphemes*. Now consider the words *look*, *looks*, and *looked*. What about the *-s* in *looks* and the *-ed* in *looked*? These segments can be separated from the meaningful unit *look*, and although they do not really have an identifiable meaning themselves, each does have a particular function. The *-s* is required for agreement with certain subjects (*she looks*, but not **she look*), and the *-ed* signifies that the action of the verb *look* has already taken place. Segments such as these are also considered morphemes. Thus, a morpheme is the smallest linguistic unit that has a meaning or grammatical function.

Some words, of course, are not composed of other morphemes. *Car*, *spider*, and *race*, for example, are words, but they are also morphemes since they cannot be broken down into smaller meaningful parts. Morphemes that are also words are called *free morphemes* since they can stand alone. *Bound morphemes*, on the other hand, never exist as words themselves, but are always attached to some other morpheme. Some examples of bound morphemes in English are *un-*, *-ed*, and *-s*.

When we identify the number and types of morphemes a given word consists of, we are looking at what is referred to as the *structure of* the word. Morphology is the study of how words are structured and how they are put together from smaller parts. Morphologists not only identify the different classes of morphemes but also study the patterns that occur in the combination of morphemes in a given language. For example, consider the words *rewrite*, *retake*, and *relive*. Notice that *re-* is a bound morpheme that attaches only to verbs, and, furthermore, attaches to the beginning of the verb, not the end. Every speaker of English knows you can't say *write-re* or *take-re* (where *re-* is connected to the end of the free morpheme), nor can you say *rechoice* or *repretty* (where *re-* is connected to a morpheme that is not a verb). In other words, part of a speaker's linguistic competence is knowing, in addition to the meaning of the morphemes of a language, the ways in which the morphemes are allowed to combine with other morphemes.

Morphemes can be classified as either bound or free, as we have seen. There are three additional ways of characterizing morphemes. The first is to label bound morphemes according to whether they attach to the beginning or end of a word. You are most likely familiar with these terms. A *prefix* attaches to the beginning and a *suffix* attaches to the end of a word. The general term for prefixes and suffixes is *affix*, so bound morphemes are also referred to as affixes. The second way of characterizing morphemes is to classify bound morphemes according to their function in the complex words of which they are a part. When some morphemes attach to words, they create, or *derive*, new words, either by changing the meaning of the word or by changing its part of speech. For example, *un-* in *unhappy* creates a new word with the opposite meaning of *happy*. Notice that both *unhappy* and *happy* are adjectives. The suffix *-ness* in *quickness*, however, changes the part of speech of *quick*, an adjective, into a noun, *quickness*. Morphemes that change the meaning or part of speech of a word they attach to are called *derivational* morphemes. Other morphemes do not alter words in this way, but only refine and give extra grammatical information about the word's already existing meaning. For example, *cat* and *cats* are both nouns that basically have the same meaning (i.e., they refer to the same sort of thing), but *cats*, with the plural morpheme *-s*, contains only the additional information that there are more than one of these things referred to. The morphemes that serve a purely grammatical function, never creating a new word but only a different *form* of the same word, are called *inflectional* morphemes.

TABLE 9.1   The Inflectional Suffixes of English

STEM	SUFFIX	FUNCTION	EXAMPLE
wait	-s	3rd per. sg. present	She waits there at noon.
wait	-ed	past tense	She waited there yesterday.
wait	-ing	progressive	She is waiting there now.
eat	-en	past participle	Jack has eaten the Oreos.
chair	-s	plural	The chairs are in the room.
chair	-'s	possessive	The chair's leg is broken.
fast	-er	comparative	Jill runs faster than Joe.
fast	-est	superlative	Tim runs fastest of all.

In every word we find that there is at least one free morpheme. In a morphologically complex word, i.e., one composed of a free morpheme and any number of bound affixes, the free morpheme is referred to as the *stem*, *root*, or *base*. However, if there is more than one affix in a word, we cannot say that all of the affixes attach to the stem. Consider the word *happenings*, for example. When *-ing* is added to *happen*, we note that a new word is derived; it is morphologically complex, but it is a word. The plural morpheme *-s* is added onto the word *happening*, not the suffix *-ing*.

In English the derivational morphemes are either prefixes or suffixes, but, by chance, the inflectional morphemes are all suffixes. Of course, this is not the same in other languages. There are only eight inflectional morphemes in English. They are listed above along with an example of the type of stem each can attach to.

The difference between inflectional and derivational morphemes is sometimes difficult to see at first. Some characteristics of each are listed below to help make the distinction clearer.

Derivational Morphemes

1. Derivational morphemes change the part of speech or the meaning of a word, e.g., *-ment* added to a verb forms a noun (*judg-ment*), and *re-activate* means "activate again."
2. Syntax does not require the presence of derivational morphemes. They typically indicate semantic relations *within* a word, but no syntactic relations outside the word (compare this with item 2 following), e.g., *un-kind* relates *-un* "not" to *kind*, but has no particular syntactic connections outside the word—note that the same word can be used in *he is unkind* and *they are unkind*.
3. Derivational morphemes are usually not very productive; they generally are selective about what they'll combine with. For example, the suffix *-hood* occurs with just a few nouns such as *brother*, *neighbor*, and *knight*, but not with most others, such as *friend*, *daughter*, or *candle*.

4. They typically occur before inflectional suffixes, e.g., *government-s*. -*ment*, a derivational suffix, precedes -*s*, an inflectional suffix.
5. They may be prefixes or suffixes (in English), e.g., *pre-arrange, arrange-ment*.

Inflectional Morphemes

1. They do not change meaning or part of speech, e.g., *big, bigg-er, biggest* are all adjectives.
2. They are required by syntax. They typically indicate syntactic or semantic relations *between* different words in a sentence, e.g., *Nim love-s bananas*. -*s* marks the third-person singular present form of the verb, relating it to the third-person singular subject *Nim*.
3. They are very productive. They typically occur with all members of some large class of morphemes, e.g., the plural morpheme /-s/ occurs with almost all nouns.
4. They occur at the margin of a word, after any derivational morphemes, e.g., *ration-al-iz-ation-s*. -*s* is inflectional, and appears at the very end of the word.
5. They are suffixes only (in English).

There is one final distinction between types of morphemes that is useful. Some morphemes have semantic content. That is, they either have some kind of independent, identifiable meaning or indicate a change in meaning when added to a word. Others serve only to provide information about grammatical function by relating certain words in a sentence to each other (see item 2 about inflectional morphemes, above). The former are called *content* morphemes, and the latter are called *function* morphemes. This might appear at first to be the same as the inflectional and derivational distinction. They do overlap, but not completely. All derivational morphemes are content morphemes, and all inflectional morphemes are function morphemes, as you might have surmised. However, some words can be merely function morphemes. Examples in English of such free morphemes that are also function morphemes are prepositions, articles, pronouns, and conjunctions.

In this file, we have been using conventional spelling to represent morphemes. But it is important to realize that morphemes are pairings of *sounds* with meanings, not spellings with meanings, and representing morphemes phonetically reveals some interesting facts. We find that just as different free morphemes can have the same phonetic representations, as in *ear* (for hearing) and *ear* (of corn), the same is true of bound morphemes. For example, the plural, possessive, and third-person singular suffixes can all sound identical in English (e.g., *cats* [kæts], *Frank's* [fræŋks], and *walks* [waks]). These three suffixes are completely different morphemes, they just happen to be homophonous, or sound alike, in English. Similarly, there are two morphemes in English which sound like [ɪn]. One means "not," as in *inoperable* or *intolerable*, and the other means "in," as in *intake* or *inside*.

One of the more interesting things revealed by transcribing morphemes phonetically is the interaction of phonological and morphological processes. For example, some morphemes have more than one phonetic representation depending on which sounds precede or follow them, but since each of the pronunciations serves the same function or has the same meaning, it is considered to be the same morpheme. In other words, the same morpheme can be pronounced differently depending upon the sounds which follow or precede it. Of course, these different pronunciations will be patterned. For example, the phonetic representation of the plural morpheme is either [s] as in *cats*, [z] as in *dogs*, or [əz] as in *churches*. Each of these three pronunciations is said to be an *allomorph* of the *same* morpheme because [s], [z], and [əz] all have the same function (making some word plural) and because they are similar phonetically. Note that this same phonological process that causes the plural morpheme /s/ to be pronounced as [s] after voiceless sounds, [z] after voiced sounds, and [əz] after sibilants also applies to the possessive morpheme /s/ and the third-person singular morpheme /s/. Consider the morpheme /ɪn/ that means "not" in the words *inoperable, incongruent,* and *impossible.* What are the allomorphs of this morpheme?

We now call your attention to a few pitfalls of identifying morphemes. First, don't confuse morphemes with syllables. A few examples will show that the number of morphemes and syllables in a word are independent of each other. Consider the word *coats*. It is a one-syllable word composed of two morphemes. *Coat* happens to be one morpheme and consist of a single syllable, but *-s* is not even a syllable, although it is a morpheme. Note that *syllable* is a three-syllable word composed only of one morpheme.

Second, note that a given morpheme has a particular sound or sound sequence associated with it, but not every instance of that sound sequence in the language represents that morpheme. For example, take the plural morpheme /s/. When you hear the word [karts] in isolation, you can't determine if the [s] is an instance of this plural morpheme (*the carts are back in the store*), or an instance of the possessive morpheme (*the cart's wheels turn funny*) or of the third-person singular morpheme (*he carts those books around every day*). That sound sequence may not even be a morpheme at all. The [s] in [sun], for example, is not a morpheme. Likewise, the [ɪn] of *inexcusable* is the morpheme that means "not," but the [ɪn] of *print* is not a morpheme.

Third, remember to analyze the phonetic representations of morphemes and not their spellings. A morpheme can have one or more allomorphs, and these allomorphs might be represented by the same or different spellings. The *-er* in *writer* is the same morpheme as the *-or* in *editor,* and the *-ar* in *liar,* since all three mean "one who," but they do not represent separate allomorphs since their pronunciations are identical, namely [ɹ]. On the other hand, the *-s* in *Mark's, John's,* and *Charles's* is the same morpheme, but represents three different allomorphs, since each is pronounced differently.

Finally, we include below a summary list of criteria that might help you to identify the different types of morphemes.

Given a Morpheme,

1. Can it stand alone as a word?

   YES → it's a *free* morpheme (e.g., *bubble, orange*)
   NO → it's a *bound* morpheme (e.g., *-er* in *beater, -s* in *oranges*)

2. Does it have the principal meaning of the word it's in?

   YES → it's the *stem* (e.g., *happy* in *unhappiness*)
   NO → it's an *affix* (e.g., *-or* in *contributor, pre-* in *preview*)

3. Does it create a new word by changing the meaning and/or part of speech?

   YES → it's a *derivational* affix (e.g., *re-* in *rewind, -ist* in *artist*)
   NO → it's an *inflectional* affix (e.g., *-est* in *smartest*)

4. Does it have a meaning, or cause a change in meaning when added to a word?

   YES → it's a *content* morpheme (e.g., *-un* in *untrue*)
   NO → it's a *function* morpheme (e.g., *the, to, or, -s* in *books*)

THE HIERARCHICAL STRUCTURE OF WORDS

When we examine words composed of only two morphemes, we implicitly know two facts about the ways in which affixes join with their stems. First, the stems with which a given affix may combine normally belong to the same part of speech. For example, the suffix *-able* attaches freely to verbs, but not to adjectives or nouns; thus, we can add this suffix to the verbs *adjust, break, compare,* and *debate,* but not to the adjectives *asleep, lovely, happy,* and *strong,* nor to the nouns *anger, morning, student,* or *success.* Second, the words formed by the addition of a given affix to some word or morpheme also normally belong to the same part of speech. For example, the expressions resulting from the addition of *-able* to a verb are always adjectives; thus *adjustable, breakable, comparable,* and *debatable* are all adjectives.

These two facts have an important consequence for determining the way in which words with more than one affix must be formed. What it means is that words are formed in steps, with one affix attaching to a complete word, which can be a free morpheme or a morphologically complex word. Words with more than one affix are not formed in one single step with the affixes and stem just strung together. For example, consider the word *unusable,* which is composed of a prefix *un-,* a stem *use,* and a suffix *-able.* One possible way this morphologically complex word might be formed is all at once, as in: *un* + *use* + *able*, where the prefix and the suffix attach at the same time to the verb stem *use*. However, this cannot be the case, knowing what we know about how affixes attach only to certain parts of speech and create words of certain parts of speech. The prefix *un-*, meaning "not," attaches only to adjectives and creates new words that are also adjectives. (Compare with *unkind*, *unwise*, and *unhappy*.) The suffix *-able*, on the other hand, attaches to verbs and forms words that are adjectives. (Compare with *stoppable*, *doable*, and *washable*.) Therefore, *un-* cannot attach to *use*, since *use* is a verb and not an adjective. However, if *-able* attaches *first* to the stem *use*, then it creates an adjective, *usable*, and the prefix *-un* is allowed to combine with it. Thus the formation of the word *unusable* is a two-step process whereby *use* and *-able* attach first, then *un-* attaches to the word *usable*.

Recall that what we are analyzing is the internal *structure* of words. Words, since they are formed by steps, have a special type of structure characterized as *hierarchical*. This hierarchical structure can be schematically represented by means of a "tree" that indicates the steps involved in the formation of the word, i.e., which morphemes joined together first and so on. The tree for *unusable* is:

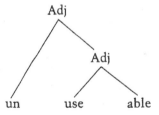

Now consider the word *reusable*. Both the prefix *re-* and the suffix *-able* attach to verbs, but we have already shown that one must attach first. Which is it? Notice that *reusable* cannot be regarded as the result of adding the prefix *re-* to the word *usable* since *re-* attaches only to verbs (compare with *redo*, *relive*, and *refuel*) and *usable* is an adjective. However, *-able* can attach to the verb *reuse* since *-able* attaches to verbs. Thus, our understanding of how the affixes *re-* and *-able* combine with other morphemes allows us to conclude that the verb *reuse*, but not the adjective *usable*, is a step in the formation of the adjective *reusable*.

Interestingly, some words are ambiguous in that they have more than one meaning. When we examine their internal structure, we find an explanation for this: their structure may be analyzed in more than one way. Consider, for example, the word *unlockable*. This could mean either "not able to be locked" or "able to be unlocked." If we made a list to determine the parts of speech the affix *un-* attaches to, we would discover that there are not one but two prefixes that sound like *un-*. The first combines with adjectives to form new adjectives, and means "not."

(Compare with *unaware, unintelligent,* or *unwise.*) The second prefix *un-* combines with verbs to form new verbs, and means "do the reverse of." (Compare with *untie, undo,* or *undress.*)

Even though these prefixes sound alike, they are entirely different morphemes. Because of these two different sorts of *un-* in English, *unlockable* may be analyzed in two different ways. First, the suffix *-able* may join with the verb *lock* to form the adjective *lockable. Un-* may then join with this adjective to form the new adjective *unlockable*, with the meaning "not able to be locked." This way of forming *unlockable* is schematized in the following tree:

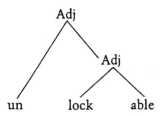

The second way of forming *unlockable* is as follows. The prefix *un-* joins with the verb *lock* to form the verb *unlock*. The suffix *-able* then joins with this verb to form the adjective *unlockable* with the meaning of "able to be unlocked." This manner of forming *unlockable* is represented by the following tree:

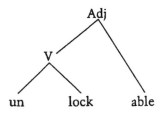

Some Suggestions

There are a few prefixes that do not attach exclusively to one part of speech. For example, consider the prefix *pre-. Pre-* attaches to verbs and does not change the part of speech, as the following examples show:

preexist

predecide

predetermine

predefine

premeditate

However, there are examples of words with the prefix *pre-* that do not follow the same pattern as those cited above:

preseason

predawn

prewar

pregame

In these words *pre-* attaches to a noun and forms an adjective *(the preseason game, the prewar propaganda, the pregame warmup)*. However, the meaning of the prefix is the same as in *preexist, predecide,* etc. (although its function is different). In addition, there are sets such as:

prefrontal

predental

preinvasive

prehistoric

In these words, *pre-* is attaching to an adjective, forming adjectives, and has the same meaning as in *preexist, predecide,* etc. So this is a bit problematic. We don't want to throw out the idea that a given affix attaches only to one part of speech, since the overwhelming majority of affixes adhere to this pattern. Apparently, some morphemes become so productive that their combinatorial possibilities can be extended. Such must be the case with *pre-*. Note, however, that its combinations are nevertheless rule-governed. When *pre-* attaches to verbs, it forms only verbs. When it attaches to nouns, it forms only adjectives, and when it attaches to adjectives, it forms only adjectives. So, it is advisable to consider many examples when attempting to determine the rules by which a given affix combines.

EXERCISES

1. Draw tree diagrams for each of the following words:

a. reconstruction	j. international	s. unmistakable
b. unaffordable	k. misunderstandable	t. insincerity
c. un-American	l. dehumidifier	u. dysfunctional
d. manliness	m. unrespectable	v. inconclusive
e. impersonal	n. nonrefundable	w. premeditatedly
f. irreplaceability	o. mismanagement	x. overgeneralization
g. oversimplification	p. underspecification	y. reformer
h. unhappiness	q. restatement	z. infertility
i. impotency	r. inflammability	aa. dishonesty

2. We said that polar opposite ("not") *un-* attaches only to adjectives, but two exceptions to this rule are *Uncola* and *Uncar*. Why are these exceptions? Why would advertisers have made them up in the first place when the words fail to follow the rule?

FOR DISCUSSION AND REVIEW

1. Explain the difference between derivational morphemes and inflectional morphemes. Illustrate each difference with an example not in the text.
2. What is the difference between content morphemes and function morphemes?
3. Describe the relationship between morphemes and syllables.
4. Explain what an *allomorph* is. Give an example of an English morpheme, in addition to the regular noun plural, that has more than one phonetic representation.
5. Allomorphs, unlike allophones, need not be phonetically similar. The productive plural morpheme in English has the forms /-s/, /-z/, /əz/; the one to be used depends on the final sound of the noun to be made plural. These allomorphs are phonologically conditioned. Some nouns in English, however, do not form regular plurals. List as many "irregular" plurals as you can. Then try to divide them into groups (note: English has five types of morphologically conditioned plurals; four of them derive from Old English).
6. Using an example, explain the statement that "the internal *structure* of words" is "*hierarchical.*"
7. What is the ambiguity of the words *bimonthly* and *biweekly*? Is it similar to or different from the ambiguity of *unlockable*? Explain.

10

The Identification of Morphemes

H. A. Gleason Jr.

If we are native speakers of English, we usually do not find it difficult to identify the morphemes in English words. Most of us rely on our unconscious knowledge of the rules of English and on our familiarity with the English vocabulary. To understand the complexity of morphemic analysis, then, it is useful to examine data from a language that we do not know well. In the following excerpt from his book An Introduction to Descriptive Linguistics, *Professor H. A. Gleason uses some Hebrew verb forms to demonstrate the basic analytical technique for identifying morphemes: comparing groups of utterances that are (1) partially identical in both expression and content, and (2) partially different in both expression and content. Note that both conditions must be met because the smallest change in content (i.e., structure) results in a change in meaning (i.e., expression). At the end of his analysis, Gleason introduces several kinds of morphemes, some of which do not occur in all languages.*

The process of analysis [to identify morphemes] is best shown by detailed discussion of an actual example. For this purpose we will use a series of Hebrew verb forms. The data will be introduced a few words at a time. This is an artificial feature of the presentation. The preceding step is merely implied: namely that we have selected from the corpus those pairs or sets of items that can be profitably compared. The order of presentation is not necessarily that which is most efficient for the analysis of the data, but that which most effectively illustrates the methods used.

1. /zəkartíihuu/ "I remembered him"
2. /zəkartíihaa/ "I remembered her"
3. /zəkartíikaa/ "I remembered thee"

Comparison of items 1 and 2 reveals one contrast in expression, /-uu/:/-aa/, and one in meaning, as shown by translation, and hence presumably in content "him": "her." This may (tentatively!) be considered as a pair of morphemes. However, comparison of 1, 2, and 3 suggests that the first identification was wrong. The contrast now seems to be /-huu/ "him":/-haa/ "her":/-kaa/ "thee." We can be reasonably sure that the morpheme meaning "him" includes the sounds /-uu/ or /-huu/, but until

157

we can identify the remaining parts of the word we cannot be sure how much else is included.

4. /zəkarnúuhuu/   "we remembered him"

5. /zəkarnúuhaa/   "we remembered her"

6. /zəkarnúukaa/   "we remembered thee"

Comparison of 4, 5, and 6 with 1, 2, and 3 reveals a contrast in expression and meaning between /-tíi-/ "I" and /-núu-/ "we." However, as before, we cannot be sure how much is to be included until the remainders of the words are identified. It is conceivable that the morphemes might be /-rtíi-/ "I" and /-rnúu-/ "we." . . .

7. /qəṭaltíihuu/   "I killed him"

8. /qəṭalnúuhuu/   "we killed him"

Comparison of 7 and 8 with the foregoing gives us a basis for identifying /zəkar-/ "remembered" and /qəṭal-/ "killed." By so doing we have tentatively assigned every portion of each word to a tentative morpheme. We have, however, no reason to be certain that each portion so isolated is only a single morpheme. We have only reasonable assurance that by dividing any of these words in a manner similar to /zəkar-tíi-huu/ we have divided between morphemes, so that each piece consists of one or more essentially complete morphemes; that is, each piece is probably either a morpheme or a morpheme sequence.

The problem is somewhat simpler if one sample is identical with another except for an additional item of meaning and of expression:

/koohéen/   "a priest"

/ləkoohéen/   "to a priest"

There can be little doubt as to the most likely place to divide, and we can be rather confident in identifying two tentative morphemes /lə-/ "to" and /koohéen/ "priest." Nevertheless, there are significant possibilities of error so that this sort of division must also be considered tentative. Consider the following English example:

/hím/   "a song used in church"

/hímnəl/   "a book containing /hímz/"

The obvious division is into two morphemes /hím/ and /-nəl/. Reference to the spelling (which is, of course, never conclusive evidence for anything in spoken language!), hymn:hymnal suggests that this is not very certain. Actually the two morphemes are /him ~ himn-/ and /-əl/, as may be shown by comparing additional data: confession:confessional, hymnology:geology, hymnody:psalmody.

9. /zəkaarúuhuu/   "they remembered him"

10. /zəkaaráthuu/   "she remembered him"

If we compare 9 and 10 with the foregoing we find /-huu/ "him," /-úu-/ "they," and /-át-/ "she." But where 1–6 have /zəkar-/, 9 and 10 have /zəkaar-/. There is an obvious similarity of form between /zəkar-/ and /zəkaar-/ and the meaning seems to be identical. We may guess that they are two different allomorphs of one morpheme, and proceed to check whether this hypothesis is adequate. . . . We must leave the question . . . but must anticipate the result. /zəkar-/ and /zəkaar-/ will be shown to be variants of one tentative morpheme.

But though we will proceed on the basis that the hypothesis can be sustained, we must recognize that there are certain other possibilities. (1) /zəkar-/ and /zəkaar-/ may be different morphemes. This seems unlikely because of the similarity of meaning, but we must always remember that English translation may be misleading. (2) A somewhat less remote possibility is that /zəkar-/ and /zəkaar-/ are each sequences of morphemes and contain two contrasting morphemes. We can do nothing with this possibility from the data at hand, because there is no evidence of a contrast in meaning, but this may well be the kind of difference that does not show up clearly in translation. (3) We may have divided wrongly. Perhaps "I" is not /-tíi-/ but /-a-tíi-/ and "they" is similarly /-aa-úu-/. This would mean that the morpheme for "remembered" would have to be /zək-r-/. Our only present reason for rejecting this possibility is the comparative rarity of discontinuous morphemes. We would ordinarily assume that morphemes are continuous sequences of phonemes unless there is cogent reason to believe the contrary.

11. /zəkartúunii/   "you remembered me"

We have as yet no item which forms a wholly satisfactory comparison with 11. We may, however, tentatively divide it into /zəkar-/ + /-túu-/ "you" + /-nii/ "me." We do this because we have come to expect words similar to this to be divisible into three pieces, stem + actor + person acted upon, in that order. A division on such a basis is legitimate if done with caution, though obviously such an identification is not as certain as it would be if based on contrasts for each morpheme separately.

12. /sə̆martúuhaa/   "you guarded him"

13. /ləqaaxúunii/   "they took me"

Even without providing minimal pairs, 12 and 13 pretty well corroborate the conclusion which was drawn from 11. They thus confirm the two morphemes /-túu/ "you" and /-nii/ "me." Words 11, 12, and 13 would be rather unsatisfactory words from which to start an analysis. However, as the analysis proceeds, the requirements for satisfactory samples relax in some respects. This is because we are now able to make our comparisons within the framework of an emerging pattern. This pattern involves certain classes of elements, stems, actor affixes, and affixes stating the person acted upon. It involves certain regular types of arrangement of these elements. In short, the pattern we are uncovering is a portion of the structure of the language at a level a bit deeper than mere details of individual words.

    14. /zəkaaróo/ "he remembered him"

This word cannot be analyzed by comparison with the foregoing only. We can easily identify the stem as /zəkaar-/, identical in form with that of 9 and 10. But the remainder /-óo/ neither seems to consist of the expected two parts (actor and person acted upon), nor to contain the morpheme /-huu/ "him" which meaning would lead us to expect. Since the pattern does not assist us here in the way it did with 11, we must seek some more direct type of evidence.

    15. /zaakártii/   "I remembered"
    16. /zaakárnuu/ "we remembered"
    17. /zaakár/   "he remembered"

These three forms differ from all those examined before in that they do not express a person acted upon. If we compare these words with each other, and if we compare 15 and 16 with 1 and 4, we can easily identify the affixes expressing the actor. These are /-tii/ "I" and /-nuu/ "we," identical with those we found before except for a difference in the stress. In 17, however, there is no affix expressing actor. We will tentatively list Ø (zero) "he" with the other actor affixes. This is intended merely as a convenient notation for our conclusion that the actor "he" is expressed by the absence of any affix indicating some other actor. These three forms also show another variant of the stem: /zaakár/; we shall proceed on the hypothesis that like /zəkar-/ and /zəkaar-/, it is merely another conditioned variant. This proposal should be carefully checked by methods to be discussed later.

    The analysis attained in the last paragraph suggests that item 14 can be considered as divisible as follows: /zəkaar-Ø-óo/. The zero is, of course, a fiction, but it does serve to indicate that the form does show a rather closer parallelism with the others than we could see at first. That is, it contains a stem and a suffix expressing the person acted upon, and these are in the same order that we have found before. Whereas the pattern we had found did not seem to fit this word, closer examination shows that it does fit in with only slight modification. The pattern is therefore valid.

    One problem posed by item 14 is taken care of in this way, but the other remains. We have identified two forms meaning "him," /-huu/ and /-óo/. These are not so obviously similar in form as /zəkar-/ and /zəkaar-/, so the hypothesis that they are allomorphs of one morpheme is not so attractive. Nevertheless, the similarity in meaning, and certain peculiarities in distribution which would be evident in a larger body of data, should induce us to check such a hypothesis. It will be sustained; /-huu ~ -óo/ is one morpheme.

In the course of the discussion we have found four stems: /zəkar-/ "remembered," /qəṭal-/ "killed," /šəmar-/ "guarded," and /ləqaax-/ "took." Comparison of these forms reveals that they all have the same vowels and differ only in consonants. /ləqaax-/ is not an exception, since it compares directly with /zəkaar-/. More data would yield a much longer list of such forms. This similarity in vowels could be a coincidence, but that possibility is slight. Another hypothesis is that these forms consist of two morphemes each. This is very attractive, but there is no means of checking it without a contrast. The following will provide such:

18. /šooméer/   "watchman"
19. /zookéer/   "one who remembers"
20. /qooṭéel/   "killer"

By comparing these with some of the earlier samples we may identify the following morphemes: /z-k-r/ "remember," /q-ṭ-l/ "kill," /š-m-r/ "guard," /l-q-x/ "take," /-oo-ée-/ "one who," and /-ə-a- ~ -ə-aa- ~ -aa-á-/ "-ed." The first four of these are roots; the last two are some sort of affixes.

Note that we were wrong in considering /zəkar-/, /zəkaar-/, and /zaakár/ as allomorphs of a single morpheme. No damage was done, however, since these three forms, each composed of two morphemes, are distributed in exactly the same way as are allomorphs. What we assumed to condition the selection of one of these three (/zəkar-/, etc.) can just as well be considered as conditioning the selection of one of the allomorphs of the affix contained in these stems. Treating larger items as morphemes is, of course, wrong, but not seriously so at preliminary stages, provided the larger units consist of associated morphemes. Ultimate simplification is, however, attained by full analysis in any case like that just discussed.

That the [preceding] analysis . . . should yield morphemes such as /z-k-r/ and /-oo-ée-/ seems at first sight somewhat disconcerting. We expect morphemes to be sequences of phonemes. These, however, are *discontinuous and interdigitated.* Of course there is no reason why such morphemes cannot occur, as in fact our sample has indicated they do. They are much less common than compact sequences of phonemes, but they occur in a wide variety of languages and are quite common in some. Any combination of phonemes which regularly occur together and which as a group are associated with some point in the content structure is a morpheme. We need give no regard to any peculiarity of their arrangement relative to each other and to other phonemes. Rarely do morphemes consist of separate portions widely separated by intervening material. A linguist must always be prepared for such a phenomenon, however, rare as it may be.

Hebrew and related languages are unusual in the large number of discontinuous morphemes they contain. In fact the majority of the roots are similar to {zkr}, consisting of three consonants. Various allomorphs occur: /z-k-r/ in /zaakár/ "he remembered," /-zk-r/ in /yizkóor/ "he was remembering," and /z-kr-/ in /zikríi/ "my remembrance." The three consonants never occur contiguously in any utterance; such roots are discontinuous in all their occurrences.

In other languages, discontinuous allomorphs of otherwise quite usual morphemes occur. These commonly arise as a byproduct of a special type of affix not mentioned before, an *infix*. An infix is a morpheme which is inserted into the stem with which it is associated. In comparison with suffixes and prefixes, infixes are comparatively rare but of sufficiently frequent occurrence to warrant notice. An example is the common Greek stem formative /-m-/ in /lambanɔ•/ "I take" from the root /lab-/. Another is Quileute (Oregon) /-¢-/ "plural" in /ho¢kʷat'/ "white men" from /hokʷat'/ "white person." Such infixes produce discontinuous allomorphs /la-b-/ and /ho-kʷat'/ of the root morphemes with which they occur.

An affix should not be considered as an infix unless there is cogent reason to do so. Of course, any affix which actually interrupts another morpheme is an infix. In Tagalog *ginulay* "greenish blue" is formed from the root *gulay* "green vegetables." The -*in*- is clearly an infix. But it is not justifiable to consider English -*as*- in *reassign* as in infix. This word is made by two prefixes. First *as*- and *sign* form the stem *assign*. Then *re*- is added. The alternative would be to consider *re*- and *sign* as forming a stem *resign* to which an infix -*as*- is added. The latter would be immediately rejected by any native speaker of English, since he would sense that *reassign* has a much closer connection with *assign* than with *resign*. It is always better, unless there is good reason to the contrary, to consider words as being constructed of successive layers of affixes outward from the root.

Most English verbs have a form that is made by the addition of the suffix -*ed*/-d ~ -t ~ -ɨd/. This is usually known as the past. The verbs which lack this formation do, however, have some form which is used in all the same syntactic environments where we might expect such a form, and in comparable social and linguistic contexts. For example, in most of the places where *discover* /dɨskávər/ can be used, *find* /fáynd/ can also. Similarly, where *discovered* /dɨskávərd/ can be used, *found* /fáwnd/ generally can also. *Found* must therefore be considered as the past of *find* in the same sense that *discovered* is the past of *discover*.

Most of the past tenses which lack the -*ed* suffix are clearly differentiated from the base form by a difference of syllable nucleus. We may express the facts by the following equations:

discovered = *discover* + suffix -*ed*
found   = *find*   + difference of syllable nucleus

When it is so stated, it becomes evident that the difference of syllable nucleus functions in some ways like the suffix. We may consider such a difference in phonemes (they are not restricted to nuclei; consider *send:sent*) as a special type of morphemic element called a *replacive*.

We will use the following notation for a replacive: /aw ← (ay)/. This should be read as "/aw/ replaces /ay/." The equation above can be stated in the following form:

found = *find* + *ou* ← (i)

/fáwnd/ = /fáynd/ + /aw ← (ay)/

If this is done, then we must consider /aw ← (ay)/ as another allomorph of the morpheme whose most familiar form is -*ed* and which we can conveniently symbolize {-D_1}. This morpheme has a number of replacive allomorphs. . . . All of them are morphologically conditioned. {-Z_1}, the English noun plural affix, also has replacives among its allomorphs.

It is, of course, possible to describe a language like English without recourse to replacives. Thus, *geese* /gíys/ can be described as containing a root /g-s/ and an infix allomorph of the plural morpheme {-Z_1} of the form /-iy-/. Then the singular would have to be described as containing an infix /-uw-/, an allomorph of a singular morpheme *{X}. Except for the cases under consideration, there are no infixes, nor discontinuous morphemes in the language. To consider plurals like *geese* as formed by an infix turns out to involve many more complications than the alternative of describing replacives. As is often the case, the simpler explanation accords more closely with the native speaker's feeling about his language.

With replacives it is not easy to divide a word into its constituent morphemes. Obviously /gíys/ is two morphemes, but the four phonemes cannot be neatly apportioned between them. A morpheme does not necessarily *consist* of phonemes, but all morphemes are statable in terms of phonemes. A replacive must be described in terms of two sets of phonemes: those that appear when it is present (/iy/ in *geese*) and those that appear when the replacive is absent (/uw/ in *goose*). A morpheme can consist of any recurring feature or features of the expression which can be described in terms of phonemes, without restriction of any sort.

A further, and in some respects more extreme, type of morphemic element can be seen in the past of some other English verbs. Words like *cut* and *hit* parallel such forms as *walked* in meaning and usage. There is, however, no phoneme difference of any kind between the past and the nonpast form. Nevertheless, it is in the interest of simplicity to consider all English past verb forms as consisting of a stem plus an affix. Moreover, the description must in some ways note the lack of any overt marker of the past. An expedient by which both can be done is to consider *cut* "past" as containing a root /kət/ plus a zero affix. (Zero is customarily symbolized Ø to avoid confusion with the letter O.) Ø is therefore another of the numerous allomorphs of {-D_1}.

The plural affix {-Z_1} also has a zero allomorph in *sheep*. The reason that it is necessary to describe these forms in this way rests ultimately in English content structure. Native speakers feel that the dichotomy between singular and plural is a basic characteristic of nouns. Every individual occurrence of any noun must be either singular or plural. *Sheep* is ambiguous, but not indifferent to the distinction. That is, in any given utterance the word is thought of by speaker and hearer as either singular or plural. Sometimes they may disagree, plural being intended and singular being perceived, or vice versa. It requires conscious effort for a person accustomed only to English patterns to conceive of noun referents without consideration of number. To attempt to do so impresses many people as being "too abstract." Yet they feel under no such compulsion to distinguish the exact number if it is more than two.

In other words, there is a covert difference between *sheep* "singular" and *sheep* "plural," and this is linguistically significant as may be seen from the fact that it controls the forms of certain other words in *This sheep is . . . : These sheep are. . . .* The recognition of a Ø allomorph of {-Z₁} is merely a convenient device for entering all this into our description. . . .

FOR DISCUSSION AND REVIEW

The following three exercises by H. A. Gleason Jr. provide practice in morphemic analysis and will help you to assess your understanding of the concepts introduced in the preceding selection. They are taken from a workbook that accompanies his textbook *An Introduction to Descriptive Linguistics*. Commenting on the exercises, Professor Gleason notes that although some inevitable distortion arises in presenting short samples of languages, "All the problems represent real languages" and "the complexities are all genuine."

Swahili (East Africa)

1.	atanipenda	he will like me
2.	atakupenda	he will like you
3.	atampenda	he will like him
4.	atatupenda	he will like us
5.	atawapenda	he will like them
6.	nitakupenda	I will like you
7.	nitampenda	I will like him
8.	nitawapenda	I will like them
9.	utanipenda	you will like me
10.	utampenda	you will like him
11.	tutampenda	we will like him

12. watampenda	they will like him
13. atakusumbua	he will annoy you
14. unamsumbua	you are annoying him
15. atanipiga	he will beat me
16. atakupiga	he will beat you
17. atampiga	he will beat him
18. ananipiga	he is beating me
19. anakupiga	he is beating you
20. anampiga	he is beating him
21. amenipiga	he has beaten me
22. amekupiga	he has beaten you
23. amempiga	he has beaten him
24. alinipiga	he beat me
25. alikupiga	he beat you
26. alimpiga	he beat him
27. wametulipa	they have paid us
28. tulikulipa	we paid you

Note: The forms glossed "he" could as well be glossed "she." The forms glossed "you" are all singular. The plural "you" is omitted from this problem because of a minor complication.

Give the morphemes associated with each of the following meanings:

subjects: _____ I   objects: _____ me
_____ you   _____ you
_____ he   _____ him
_____ we   _____ us
_____ they   _____ them
tenses: _____ future   stems: _____ like
_____ present   _____ beat
_____ perfect   _____ annoy
_____ past   _____ pay

What is the order of the morphemes in a word?

Supply the probable forms for the following meanings:

_____ I have beaten them   _____ you have beaten us
_____ they are beating me   _____ we beat them
_____ they have annoyed me   _____ I am paying him

Supply the probable meanings for the following forms:

atanilipa _____   walikupenda _____
utawapiga _____   nimemsumbua _____

Ilocano (Philippine Islands)

1.	píŋgan	dish	piŋpíŋgan	dishes
2.	tálon	field	taltálon	fields
3.	dálan	road	daldálan	roads
4.	bíag	life	bibíag	lives
5.	nuáŋ	carabao	nunuáŋ	caribao
6.	úlo	head	ulúlo	heads

What type of affix is used to form the plural?

Describe its form and relationship to the stem. Be sure to make clear exactly how much is involved.

Given /múla/ "plant," what would be the most likely form meaning "plants"?

Given /tawtáwa/ "windows," what would be the most likely form meaning "window"?

Dinka (Sudan)

1.	pal	knife	paal	knives	_____
2.	bit	spear	biit	spears	_____
3.	ɣot	hut	ɣoot	huts	_____
4.	čiin	hand	čin	hands	_____
5.	agɔɔk	monkey	agɔk	monkeys	_____
6.	kat	frame	kɛt	frames	_____
7.	mač	fire	mɛ̌č	fires	_____
8.	bɛñ	chief	bañ	chiefs	_____
9.	dom	field	dum	fields	_____
10.	dɔk	boy	dak	boys	_____
11.	gɔl	clan	gal	clans	_____
12.	tuɔŋ	egg	tɔŋ	eggs	_____
13.	muɔr	bull	mior	bulls	_____
14.	buɔl	rabbit	bial	rabbits	_____
15.	met	child	miit	children	_____
16.	jǒŋ	dog	jɔk	dogs	_____
17.	yič	ear	yit	ears	_____

What type of affix is shown in [these] data? List the forms of the affixes in the spaces provided opposite the stems with which they are found. Do not attempt to find conditioning factors; the distribution of allomorphs is morphologically conditioned. This is very frequently true of this type of affix.

11

Understanding Basic Medical Terminology

Janet A. Romich

Training in a technical field such as medicine often involves acquiring new vocabulary. Here, Janet A. Romich, a doctor of veterinary medicine, shows how we can work with unfamiliar words by breaking them down into meaningful parts and making logical assumptions about how those parts are ordered. In doing so, she offers an efficient method for understanding words without having to memorize their specific meanings. Dr. Romich's article, originally published in 1993 in Veterinary Technician, *demonstrates the relevance of morphology as a strategy for dealing with new terminology in any discipline.*

If you work in a veterinary setting, you use medical terminology every day. In addition to using medical terminology on the job, you, as a consumer, are exposed to medical terms and procedures on television, in magazines, and on any public information system. Becoming familiar with how medical terms are organized will enable you to understand words you may encounter at work and will allow you to figure out new words as you are exposed to them.

Studying medical terminology is like learning a new language. At first, the words look different and complicated. By understanding a few important guidelines, however, medical terminology can become interesting and seem like solving a logical puzzle. There are several basic rules to remember in analyzing medical terms; these rules are presented in the following discussion.[1]

When a medical word is first encountered, it should be analyzed structurally and divided into basic components. These components consist of a prefix (an affix occurring at the beginning of a word), a root (the foundation of a word), and a suffix (an affix occurring at the end of a word). For example, the word *hyperglycemia* would be divided into the following parts:

hyper • glyc • emia.

---

[1] Chabner D-E: *Medical Terminology: A Short Course.* Philadelphia: W.B. Saunders Co., 1991, pp. 2–98.

The prefix is *hyper-*, the root is *glyc*, and the suffix is *-emia*. After dividing the word into basic components, the definition can be gleaned by analyzing the suffix, followed by the prefix, and then by the root(s). If two roots are present, the word that occurs first in the word is analyzed first.

In the example of hyperglycemia, *-emia* is the suffix, meaning blood condition; *hyper-* is the prefix, meaning excessive; and *glyc* is the root, meaning sugar. By putting these components together, it becomes apparent that hyperglycemia is a blood condition of excessive sugar. Hyperglycemia is seen in conjunction with several disease processes, including diabetes mellitus.

In some words, a combining vowel may be used between the root and the suffix to make the spoken form of the word flow more easily. The combining vowel is often *o*, but *i* and *a* are also used. If the suffix begins with a vowel, the combining vowel is usually not used. For example, in the word *cystitis*, the suffix is *-itis* (meaning inflammation) and the root is *cyst* (meaning bladder). Cystitis means inflammation of the bladder. A combining vowel is not used in this example because the suffix *-itis* begins with a vowel. In the word *hematology*, the suffix is *-logy* (meaning study of) and the root is *hemat* (meaning blood). Hematology is the study of blood. Because *-logy* does not begin with a vowel, the combining vowel, *o*, appears between the root and the suffix.

In approximately 90% of definitions of medical words, the part of the word that appears first comes last in the definition. In the word *cardiology*, for example, the definition can be gleaned by first analyzing the suffix and then the root. Therefore, cardiology is the study of the heart: *-logy* (meaning study of) and *cardi-* (meaning heart). The letter *o* is the combining vowel.

When defining words describing body systems, the words are usually built in the order in which the organs function. For example, gastroenteritis is divided into the suffix *-itis* meaning inflammation, the two roots *gastr* meaning stomach and *enter* meaning intestine, and the combining vowel *o*. Gastroenteritis is the inflammation of the stomach and intestines. In the digestive system, the stomach comes first structurally and is followed by the intestines; the term *gastroenteritis* is arranged in the same manner.

Some basic rules can be kept in mind to aid in determining the definition of a medical term. Most shorter suffixes mean *pertaining to.* Handouts and textbooks can provide information on basic anatomy and physiology concepts.

In medical writing, the correct spelling of a word is crucial; the slightest spelling error can completely alter the meaning of a word. Consider the words *ileum* and *ilium*. Both words are pronounced the same but have different meanings. *Ileum* is part of the small intestine, and *ilium* is part of the pelvic bone.[2]

---

[2] Chabner D-E: *The Language of Medicine*, 4th ed. Philadelphia: W.B. Saunders Co., 1991, pp. 3–7.

TABLE 1   Suffix List

SUFFIX	DEFINITION	EXAMPLE
-al or -eal	pertaining to	tracheal (pertaining to the trachea)
-ar	pertaining to	hilar (pertaining to a hilus)
-ary	pertaining to	maxillary (pertaining to the maxilla)
-centesis	surgical puncture to remove fluid	cystocentesis (puncture of remove urine)
-cyte	cell	monocyte (a cell with one nucleus)
-ectomy	removal, excision, resection	appendectomy (removal of the appendix)
-emia	blood condition	anemia (lack of blood)
-gram	record	electroencephalogram (a record of brain waves)
-graphy	process of recording	electroencephalography (the recording of brain waves)
-ia	condition, disease	glycosuria (the condition of glucose in the urine)
-ic	pertaining to	icteric (pertaining to jaundice)
-ism	condition, state	aneurysm (state of dilatation of the wall of an artery, a vein, or the heart)
-itis	inflammation	endocarditis (inflammation of the endocardium)
-logist	specialist in the study of	cardiologist (one who studies the heart)
-logy	study of	cardiology (the study of the heart)
-lysis	separation, breakdown, destruction	autolysis (breakdown of tissue after death)
-megaly	enlargement	hepatomegaly (enlargement of the liver)
-oma	tumor, mass	hamatoma (mass of blood)
-osis	abnormal condition	arthrosis (disease of the joints)
-pathy	disease	hepatopathy (disease of the liver)
-plasty	surgical repair	rhinoplasty (surgical repair of the nose)
-rrhea	flow, discharge	amenorrhea (lack of menstruation)
-rrhage	bursting forth of blood	hemorrhage (bleeding)
-scope	instrument to visually examine	laryngoscope (instrument to visualize the larynx)
-scopy	process of visually examining	endoscopy (visual examination of body cavities with an endoscope)
-sis	state of	hemostasis (state of arrested bleeding)
-stomy	opening	urethrostomy (creation of an opening in the urethra)
-therapy	treatment	chemotherapy (therapy with chemicals)
-tomy	process of cutting	urethrotomy (incision into the urethra)
-um	structure	epithelium (structure of tissue that covers the body)
-uria	condition of urine	hematuria (bloody urine)

TABLE 2 Prefix List

PREFIX	DEFINITION	EXAMPLE
a-, an-	no, not, without	atypical (not typical)
ab-	away from	abstain (to stay away from)
ad-	toward, near	adjacent (situated next to)
anti-	against	antimicrobial (active against microorganisms)
bi-	two, both	bipedal (pertaining to or using both feet)
brady-	slow	bradycardia (slow heartbeat)
con-	with, together	concurrent (occurring at the same time)
dys-	bad, painful, difficult	dysfunctional (difficulty in functioning)
ec-	out	ectocytic (outside the cell)
endo-	within, in	endoskeleton (skeleton within the body)
epi-	above, upon	epidural (above the dura mater)
ex-	out	exhale (to breathe out)
hyper-	excessive, above	hyperglycemia (excessive blood sugar)
hypo-	below, deficient	hypoglycemia (deficient blood sugar)
in-	in, into	intubation (insertion of a tube into the body)
infra-	below, beneath	infrapatellar (below the patella)
inter-	between, among	interfemerol (between the thighs)
intra-	within	intraarterial (within an artery)
mal-	bad, abnormal	malocclusion (abnormal occlusion of the maxilla and the mandible)
lumbo-	pertaining to the loins	lumbosacral (pertaining to the loins and sacrum)
meta-	beyond, change	metamorphosis (a striking change)
neo-	new, different	neoplasm (a new, abnormal growth)
para-	near, beside	paraomphilac (beside the umbilicus)
peri-	around, about	periosteum (connective tissue that covers all bones)
poly-	many	polymorphic (occurring in many forms)
post-	after, later	postsurgical (after surgery)
pre-	before, earlier	presynaptic (occurring before a synapse is crossed)
pro-	before, anterior	proleptic (occurring before the usual time)
re-	back, again	reassess (to evaluate again)
sacro-	related to the sacrum	sacrodynia (pain in the sacral region)
sclero-	hardening	sclerostenosis (hardeninng combined with contraction)
sub-	below, under, beneath	subpulmonary (below the lungs)
tachy-	fast	tachycardia (rapid heartbeat)
tri-	three	triamine (compound containing three amino groups)
uni-	one	unilobar (consisting of one lobe)

TABLE 3   Root List

ROOT	DEFINITION	EXAMPLE
abdomin	abdomen (part of the body between the thorax and pelvis)	abdominal (pertaining to the abdomen)
arthr	joint	arthritis (inflammation of the joints)
cardi	heart	cardiovascular (pertaining to the heart and blood vessels)
cervic	neck	cervical (pertaining to the neck)
chem	drug or chemical	chemistry (science of elements and atomic matter)
crani	skull	cranium (upper part of the head)
cyst	urinary bladder	cystalgia (pain in the bladder)
cyt	cell	cytology (the study of cells)
enter	intestine	enteritis (inflammation of the intestine)
epithel	skin, tissue lining surfaces	epithelium (skin)
erythr	red	erythrocyte (red blood cell)
gastr	stomach	gastritis (inflammation of the stomach)
glyc	sugar	glycogenesis (production of sugar)
hem, hemat	blood	hematocrit (tube used to determine the volume of packed red blood cells)
hepat	liver	hepatic (pertaining to the liver)
lapar	abdomen	laparotomy (incision into the abdomen)
later	side	lateral (pertaining to a side)
leuk	white	leukocyte (white blood cell)
nephr	kidney	nephron (functional unit of the kidney)
neur	nerve	neuron (conducting cell of the nervous system)
ophthal	eye	ophthalmology (excision of the eyeball)
oste	bone	osteoplaque (a layer of bone)
ot	ear	otitis (inflammation of the ear)
path	disease	pathogenesis (development of disease)
ren	kidney	reniculus (one of the lobules that forms the kidney)
septic	pertaining to infection	septicemia (infection of organisms in the blood)
thorac	thorax or chest	thoracic (pertaining to the thorax)
vertebr	vertebra or backbone	vertebrate (having a vertebral column)

By keeping these rules in mind, understanding medical terminology can be much easier. The meaning of an unfamiliar word can often be determined simply by dividing it into the suffix, prefix, and root; of course, the meaning can be confirmed by a dictionary. Dividing words to determine meaning and subsequently looking them up in a dictionary is an excellent way for technicians to expand their medical vocabulary. The tables list basic suffixes, prefixes, and roots. Although these lists are not all-inclusive, they are a good starting point for people interested in learning or expanding their medical vocabulary.

FOR DISCUSSION AND REVIEW

1. Dr. Romich argues that morphological analysis is useful outside of linguistic study. What is her argument? How successfully does she prove it?

2. To learn unfamiliar medical terminology, Romich suggests separating an unfamiliar word into its basic parts. What are those parts? Describe how to figure out the definition of the word once you have done this.

3. In most medical definitions, which part of the word comes last in the definition? Give an example.

4. How are medical terms about body systems usually arranged? Give an example.

5. Use the method Romich describes in this article to determine the meaning of the following medical terms : *hepatomegaly, intracranial,* and *neurology.*

   Separate each word into its root, prefix, and suffix parts, and label each part. Refer to the tables in the essay for each morpheme's meaning, and then try writing a definition of each word based on those morphemes.

6. Using the information in "The Minimal Units of Meaning: Morphemes," (pp. 147–56), look again at Romich's tables of medical terms. Are the terms formed with *derivational* or *inflectional* morphemes? Explain.

12

Mc-: Meaning in the Marketplace

Genine Lentine and Roger W. Shuy

Genine Lentine and Georgetown Distinguished Research Professor Emeritus Roger Shuy used morphology as a forensic tool when they were hired as consultants for Quality Inns in a lawsuit filed by fast-food giant McDonald's. In this article, first published in 1990 in American Speech, *Lentine and Shuy discuss their methods of collecting and analyzing words derived from the prefix morpheme* Mc-. *They consider the context for the* Mc- *prefix, the meanings associated with* Mc- *prefixed words, and the public perceptions of things labeled* Mc-. *Their morphological analysis provided a crucial element of the trademark infringement lawsuit. It also demonstrates an important application of linguistics in contemporary public life.*

The lexicon of the English language, or of any language for that matter, responds to constant cultural changes, both subtle and conspicuous. Forces such as technology can add lexical entries with each new advance. Marketing also influences the lexicon when brand names become generic expressions or "normal, everyday names for things" (Cruse 1986, 146); such generic terms then require a specifying modifier for clarity of reference. Expressions like *Panasonic Walkman* and such questions as *What brand of Xerox machine do you have?* do not sound anomalous because the nouns in those expressions have become generic through popular usage (though these trademarks themselves remain vigilantly protected against commercial use). A strong market presence can, in this way, actually introduce new terms into the lexicon. Moreover, the process is not confined to semantic change. Witness, for example, the phonologically deviant (for English) yet common pronunciation of the brand name *Nike* as [nayki]. In no other word in English do the the letters *ike* signal the pronunciation that they do in this word, and yet most American English speakers pronounce the name as it is shown here. Through constant exposure, advertisers thus teach the speech community not only WHAT they want a morpheme or phrase to mean but HOW it should sound.

Corporations do not necessarily mind when their mark becomes a household word—no doubt some cheer! However, when another corporation moves in on their lexical territory by using either the mark or something close to it, they allege TRADEMARK INFRINGEMENT. This paper describes our contribution to a million-dollar trademark infringement suit involving Quality Inns International (QI) and the McDonald's Corporation. At the request of a Washington, DC, law firm,[1] we performed an inductive analysis, based on newspaper and magazine citations, of the place of the *Mc-* formative in the English language. We found that it acts much like a derivational affix, except that, unlike most affixes in this category, it has several senses. More importantly, we found that while large corporations can have great power in generating raw material for lexical change, and while they can prevent other corporations from using specific words in specific ways, they have little effect on stopping the machinery of semantic change once it has begun to operate within the language of everyday spoken and written discourse.

The background of the case is as follows. In the fall of 1987, QI announced plans for a new chain of low-priced hotels to complement their other market categories. They announced that they would call this chain *McSleep Inns*; by 1990, QI planned to open about 200 McSleep franchises. However, only three days after the initial announcement, McDonald's Corporation sent QI a letter, alleging trademark infringement and demanding that QI not use the *McSleep* name. QI responded by seeking a declaratory legal judgment that the mark does not infringe upon any federally registered trademarks, that it does not allege false description or origin, and that it does not infringe upon or violate any common-law rights that McDonald's might have. Preliminary maneuverings lasted for a year, culminating in a seven-day trial in July of 1988 before United States District Judge Paul V. Niemeyer in Baltimore, Maryland. In the end, Judge Niemeyer ruled that QI could not use the prefix in the name of their proposed hotel chain.

Explaining their choice of the name *McSleep* in deposition testimony, QI expressed the belief that the name would project, among other things, an image of thrift and cleanliness. Drawing upon stereotypes of the Scottish character, the president of QI, Robert C. Hazard, said in deposition, "You have got an idea of affordable and you have got an idea that Scots are consistently thrifty, I think they are clean, you know, they are not—like other people—they're considered to be consistently clean, thrifty people."

In a previous, unrelated case, McDonald's had successfully sued "McBagel's," a small restaurant in New York City; the judge ruled that using *Mc-* in combination with a generic food noun did indeed constitute infringement. The use of *Mc-* with a generic term not related to food, however, was not tested. QI's suit against McDonald's asserted that QI had a right to use the name in a non-food industry context, as McSleep Inns were not to contain restaurants. McDonald's claimed to

---

[1] We were engaged by Laurence R. Hefter and Robert Litowitz of the firm of Finnegan, Henderson, Farabow, Garrett, and Dunner.

the contrary that, although it does not own the trademark *Mc-* by itself, it owns a FAMILY of such marks which deserve special trademark protection. They claimed that because McDonald's marks are formulated by combining the *Mc-* or *Mac*-prefix with a generic word to form a "fanciful," "arbitrary" trademark or service mark, they are marks that describe nothing in particular and thus need have no inherent link to the goods or services with which they are linked. The key here is that the marks are formed by combination, and it is that formula for combination that has protection.

Another basic issue in the case was whether or not people would think *McSleep Inns* were somehow related to McDonald's. McDonald's contended that the name *McSleep Inn* was likely to cause confusion and that QI had deliberately selected the word *McSleep* to trade on McDonald's reputation and goodwill. They sought to establish that QI could benefit a great deal from "trading" on the McDonald's name, citing such evidence as that the recognition of Ronald McDonald by children age two to eight was 100%, comparable only to their recognition of Santa Claus.

Precedents with respect to the issue of "confusion" are many. For example, the marks for Notre Dame University and Notre Dame cheese were allowed to coexist, as were the marks for Bulova watches and Bulova shoes and for Alligator raincoats and Alligator shoes. Because these marks occur in widely divergent fields, the public presumably would not make a necessary connection between the two corporate entities. In some cases, however, as Judge Niemeyer points out in his published opinion (1988, 29), "a close affinity of markets for two different products or services can create in the public perception a belief or expectation that one would be expected to go into the other." An important legal principle known as the Aunt Jemima Doctrine concerns related but noncompetitive markets. In this 1917 case, Aunt Jemima Mills Pancake Batter held the trademark, against which the proposed Aunt Jemima Syrup was found to infringe, not only because syrup and flour are both food products but also because they are commonly used together. This doctrine was important to the case at hand: although *McSleep* and *McDonald's* are not in competing areas, there is thought to be a logical connection between the food industry and the lodging industry.

Also central to this case was the issue of generic labels. When a trademark becomes so strong that it becomes the generic label for goods or services associated with another corporation, the owners of the trademark can still protect the mark from corporate use, but they have little influence over its use in everyday language. In some cases, we have lost sight of the original corporate source for certain terms because the owner of the marks surrendered the rights to that mark. Examples of these terms are *aspirin*, *cellophane*, and *escalator*. While this type of generic term is not uncommon, there are also nouns which became generic while the corporation was still protecting its trademark. For example, despite the Xerox Corporation's attempts to encourage speakers into using *pho-tocopy* as a verb instead of *xerox*, the latter can still be heard in offices across America. Similarly, while the Kimberly-Clark corporation still owns the trademark *Kleenex*, many people always ask for a *kleenex* when they need a tissue of any type. The list goes on and on, with examples such as *Q-Tip, Cuisinart,* and *Thermos.*

Mc- shows an unusual mixture of both popular and corporate use. Trademark cases often involve the use of a protected lexical item, in most cases a word or phrase, by one company in a way that allegedly causes confusion with or dilution of another company's mark. One recent example of this is with Toyota's new line of Lexus cars. The Mead Corporation sued Toyota in order to protect their on-line search network called Lexis from trademark dilution. This was fairly straightforward because most English speakers do not frequently use the word *Lexis.* Most speakers could not even produce a definition for *lexis*; its primary dictionary meaning is strongly related to Mead's trademarked name. The case of *Mc-*, however, is not so one-dimensional. To begin with, *Mc-* is not a word at all, nor even a single free morpheme. Rather, it functions as a derivational prefix—a very productive prefix, as we will show below, one that speakers of American English across the country regularly hear, read, and use.

In court, McDonald's suggested that they were themselves responsible for the productivity of the *Mc-* morpheme—indeed, they had even overtly pursued an advertising campaign to that end. Roy T. Bergold, Jr., vice president of advertising for McDonald's, described a campaign in which Ronald McDonald was shown teaching children to put the prefix before many different words, creating *McFries, McShakes,* and *McBest.* The purpose of these commercials was, Bergold said, to create a *McLanguage* specifically associated with McDonald's.

QI made four main arguments in presenting their case that McDonald's cannot claim ownership over every formative of *Mc-* plus a generic word. The first was that there was no likelihood of confusion between *McSleep* and *McDonald's.* The second was that the uses were not competitive: McDonald's marks have been developed in the fast-food business and do not preclude the use of *McSleep Inn* in the lodging business. The third defense involved the fact of extensive third-party uses; having allowed or acquiesced to the extensive use by third parties of a proliferation of words formulated by combining *Mc-* with a generic word, McDonald's should be denied the right to preclude the use of *McSleep Inn*, QI argued. Although there were many such third-party uses listed in the trademark register, rules of evidence permitted QI's attorneys to include only those names for which there was concrete evidence of commercial use. The attorneys found such evidence in telephone directories, credit reports, and newspaper references. They also made phone calls and visited the businesses for purposes of verification. In these names, we find examples mainly of the Scottish association (as in

McDivot's and *McGruff* the crime dog) and of the sense of "basic, convenient, standardized, inexpensive," as in *McLube* automobile service, *McThrift Inn,* and *McMaids* (see the appendix below for the published sources for all cited forms).

The fourth argument was the one for which our testimony was used. QI maintained that *Mc-* has become generic: it has entered into the English language with a recognized meaning of its own. To determine whether or not this argument could be supported within the field of linguistics, we proposed the following analytical procedure and methodology, which served as the basis for testimony.

We surveyed, with the use of a computer search system called Nexis and a national clipping service, a wide sample of sources, looking for words containing the *Mc-* prefix. The data were newspaper and magazine citations collected primarily between March and July 1988. The sources represented a wide range of speech communities within the United States. The sample consisted of about 150 articles in which writers used the prefix *Mc-* with a descriptive or generic term. Our sample included such national magazines as *Forbes, Time,* and *Working Woman,* major newspapers such as the *Los Angeles Times* and the *Washington Post* and local papers such as the *Maple Heights Press,* and technical publications such as *Rubber and Plastics News.* Shuy explained (in his testimony to the court, 1988) the rationale for our choice of a database:

> I wanted a body of data because I did not want to rely upon my own intuitions. I wanted to have an empirical base from which to do the analysis. One can in analysis of any kind sit and think about it and say here's what I know to be true because I am a native speaker of this language and here is how it works, and I know. Or, you can do experiments by, say, bringing people into a laboratory, sitting them down and asking them questions. Or, one can do empirical studies with actually existing natural events, in this case, articles in magazines. . . . Here we have a body of citations and evidence from all over the country and in which the people who wrote it didn't know that they were going to be looked at with this case in mind.

Our goal was to discover inductively how writers, and therefore (with proper respect for the differences between speaking and writing) speakers, use and understand the *Mc-* morpheme. At no point in the trial did we dispute that the *Mc-* prefix has a strong association with McDonald's. We acknowledged this obvious use of the prefix and focused our attention on tracking its spread into other analogous domains. The 94 articles accumulated for our research were gathered together as a two-volume exhibit; excluded from the exhibit were all articles that were specifically about McDonald's restaurants and/or specific McDonald's products.[2]

---

[2] In some of the exhibited stories there was an occasional mention of McDonald's as an illustration of some other point, but by no means as the main focus of the articles.

The range of citations was surprisingly broad. We found an abundance of evidence for the productivity of the morpheme *Mc-*. Writers attached the prefix to words referring to everything from tune-ups to major surgery. We even found examples in which one use would spawn a subsequent use, for example in the case of *McPaper* giving rise to *McTelecast*.

We analyzed each of the 94 citations, drawing from context the senses of the prefix. From this, we produced a rough list of properties associated with the use of *Mc-* and found that *Mc-* had seven distinct senses or functions and that the cues within the articles made clear which senses were intended. Each of the 94 articles fell into one of the seven meaning categories. The seven categories thus grew out of our reading the articles; that is, we did not set up categories and then read the articles to find examples. We found that the prefix was combined mainly with generic nouns, and in some cases with proper nouns, adjectives, adverbs, and verbs. In testimony, illustrative articles were discussed for each of the seven categories of meaning. Following are the senses and functions of *Mc-* that we found represented in the sample:

1. Ethnic associations (includes surnames)
2. Alliterative patternings arising from a proper name
3. Acronyms
4. Products of the McDonald's Corporation
5. Macintosh computer products or related businesses
6. Parodies of a fast-food product or service
7. The meaning "basic, convenient, inexpensive, standardized."

What started out as a simple patronymic prefix has undergone processes of lexical shift, lexical narrowing, and lexical generalization. While the meanings and functions may have been largely set in motion by McDonald's, they now often refer to generalized concepts such as "speed," "efficiency," and "consistency."

The first category, ETHNIC ASSOCIATIONS, included examples in which the prefix was used in order to reinforce a reference to either Scotland or Ireland, especially citations in which the authors made references to thriftiness and other stereotypical attributes associated with the Scottish. Mencken (1963, 388–89) notes that nearly all the words and phrases in English which are based on *Scotch* embody references to the traditional frugality of the Scots, for example, *Scotch Coffee* "hot water flavored with burnt biscuit"; *to play the Scotch organ* "put money in a cash register"; and *Scotch pint* "two-quart bottle." Thus, most of these references were in some way connected with thriftiness. A slightly different example was a crossword puzzle in the *Washington Post Magazine* entitled *McPuzzle*. The theme clues included "Kilted Mystery Writer," "Kilted Gunshot Victim," and "Kilted Racket man." Clearly, the creator of the puzzle was inviting us to make the connection between kilts and Scotland. Another example was an advertisement which drew upon the association with Irish surnames. It read, "McSure it gets there o'ernight," and included such stereotypical tokens of Irishness as the four-leaf clover and the word *blarney.*

The next category, ALLITERATIVE PATTERNINGS ARISING FROM A PROPER NAME, was unlike the other categories in that it was based more on form than on content. In this category, the *Mc-* was not semantically connected in any way to the topic of the article, but rather appeared to have been added for the sheer fun of the repetitive pattern. Examples of this are "McVeto McKernan," "McLish—it rhymes with McDish," and "Jim McMyth" (to refer to Jim McMahon). One article was entitled, "Parents Aided in the 'Mc' of Time." It was about a series of events all involving names beginning with *Mc-*: in Macomb, a town in McDonough County, Illinois, an officer named McBride delivered a baby for a couple named McGrew on St. Patrick's Day (the latter an ethnic reference to things Irish). In these examples there are no clues in the articles that any of the authors is attributing any specific qualities to the noun; rather, the prefix is used playfully in each case—for aesthetic purposes, much in the same way that children play with patterned code languages (Crystal 1987, 58).

The third category, ACRONYMS, was a straightforward one in that it involved the use of initials of the title for something. We had only two examples in this category: *McDap,* which stood for "Mason County Drug Abuse Program," and *McRIDES,* in which the *Mc-* was derived from *Morris County.*

As explained earlier, we did not analyze the articles contained in the fourth category, which were specifically about McDonald's and their products. The fifth category was an obvious one: MACINTOSH COMPUTER PRODUCTS OR RELATED BUSINESSES. These uses were not considered relevant to the *McSleep* case for two reasons. First, McDonald's and Macintosh had apparently ironed out their differences over these names. More importantly, the spelling usually associated with Macintosh computers is *Mac-,* not *Mc-* (although the pronunciation and stress are sometimes the same).

In sorting out the articles, we found that often writers would, in talking about a product or service, create an imaginary set of details about that product or service, making it seem like a fast-food restaurant. This led to the sixth category, PARODIES OF A FAST-FOOD PRODUCT OR SERVICE. The key factor in putting articles into this rather than the final category (described below) is that, in these articles, the author describes something hypothetical or fanciful. For example, in the article *"McSoup* Stirs Dreams of Kitchen Glory," the author, Patti McDonald, dreams of having a soup restaurant:

> "How about McSoup?" I said proudly. . . . "We could even name our restaurant McDonald's and who knows, some day we could even open a chain of them." My husband babbled something about worried about some kind of McSuit if we did such a thing but I didn't understand what he was talking about. . . . I seem to be on my way to McRiches. . . . I will be in my kitchen, making McSoup and dreaming about my pending empire.

In this article, modals such as *could*, the future tense in "I will be in my kitchen," and the author "dreaming" about her "pending" empire all indicate a hypothetical, fanciful concept. In another article, which described the growing popularity of squid, the author said, "Squid McNuggets may be a long way off, but the ugly mollusks are finding their way onto the dinner plates of more and more Americans." This brief reference again indicates a future, hypothetical event.

Another article in this category exaggerated the array of services available to residents of Marin County, California. It reads,

> After paying Bobby Divot a half a hundred for his sage advice, I decided to look for a quick fix for the problems in my upper works. This being Marin County, I didn't know whether to try "Gurus R Me," "Marin County Computerized Psychic Matching Service and Burrito Take Out" or " McMeditation—Over 5,000,000 Mantras Served."

In this example, again, the author uses the *Mc-* prefix to evoke an image of a restaurant or service that would be on a mass-market scale and that would have a "quick-fix" approach. The ridiculous nature of the other names in the list cue the reader to the author's satirical intent.

There was relatively little debate about the first six categories. At issue, and central to the lawsuit, was category seven: THE MEANING "BASIC, CONVENIENT, INEXPENSIVE, STANDARDIZED." Our contention was that not one of the 56 articles presented in this category was specifically about McDonald's or even about hamburgers. Instead, the attachment of the prefix suggested to the reader that the product or service described had the attributes "basic, convenient, inexpensive, standardized." Not all 56 of the articles implied all four of these meanings, but most implied at least three of them.

In arriving at the wording of definition seven, we grouped together related common key words and phrases from the articles and found terms that could subsume the groups. Words and phrases such as *lacks prestige*, *everyday*, *lowbrow*, and *simple* mapped onto the concept "BASIC."

The heading CONVENIENT was suggested by such attributive words as *highly advertised, franchised, easy access, quick, self-service,* and *handy location*. Terms such as *lacks prestige* and *lowbrow* suggested the term INEXPENSIVE. The heading STANDARDIZED had many hyponyms, including *assembly-line precision, high volume, reduces choices, mass merchandising, standardized, state-of-the-art marketing,* and *prepackaged.*

An article that typifies this sense of *Mc-* appeared in *Forbes* magazine. It was called "McArt" and contains phrases such as "mass market art" indicating basic convenience. From the words "mass marketing," "galleries open seven days a week," and "chains," we arrived at a sense of convenience and standardization. These references to the product labelled "McArt" in the article's title tell us essentially what the writer intended when the word *art* was prefixed with *Mc-*.

Another of the articles we cited was called "McLaw: Lawyering for the Masses" (it appeared in *The California Lawyer*). The author describes the easily accessible and inexpensive basic legal services that are cropping up increasingly across the country. Expressions such as "near-omnipresence," "franchise legal clinics," "serving the masses," "everyday legal problems," and "drive-in windows" occur frequently throughout the article. The word *McLaw* appears five times. There is no mention of McDonald's and no direct or indirect reference to hamburgers. It is clear that all four of the characteristics of this final category are described in this article: "basic," "standard," "inexpensive," and "convenient." *Near omnipresence* and *drive-in windows* indicate "convenience." The article notes that these clinics serve the masses and that consultation fees are $20 to $25, indicating that they are "inexpensive." *Everyday legal problems* and *franchised legal clinics* map on to both "standardized" and "basic." Another line from the article suggesting "basic" is "McLaw attorneys lack the prestige, comforts, and salary that come with other types of private practice." Clearly, it is the productive morpheme *Mc-* that is imparting these senses, for if we remove the *Mc-*, leaving *Law attorneys lack the prestige, comforts . . .* , the sentence makes no sense. In linguistic terms, the pair of sentences is a sort of MINIMAL PAIR in that the presence or absence of only one element, *Mc-*, creates a contrast in meaning.

Similarly, an article called *McMiz* about the marketing of the musical *Les Miserables* also used *Mc-* in this way. The following paragraph is revealing in that the author lumps all fast food restaurants together, indicating a generalization of the prefix:

> Maybe it's unfair to link the epic (and epically expensive) "Les Miserables" with fast food. But it's not an entirely unapt allusion, either. Producer Cameron Mackintosh and his organization have perfected elaborate and elegantly aggressive marketing, merchandising and standardized production techniques that the burger giants might envy.

Significantly, the author refers to "fast food" and "the burger giants" rather than specifically to McDonald's, thus suggesting that the comparison is being made to the whole category of large fast-food corporations. The comparison is further broadened when the author comments that the productions are "multiplying like Mrs. Field's cookie boutiques at an unprecedented speed,"—interesting because again *Mc-* is being used to refer to the larger phenomenon of fast food, not just specifically to McDonald's.

Many other references suggest this more general use of the prefix. For example, in an article about the newspaper *USA Today*, Marti Ahern says, "Some call it McPaper—fast news for the fast-food generation." Another article about *USA Today* discusses the editor John Neuharth's decision to print as the lead story the report of death of Princess Grace of Monaco instead of one about the assassination of a Lebanese president-elect.

Neuharth was faulted for this by editors at the more established papers, who then dubbed the paper *McPaper*. Clearly what was operating here was not a direct comparison to McDonald's, but rather a more abstract connection of the similar properties of "giving the people what they want."

Similarly, Erma Bombeck used the prefix in its mass-market, "panderous" sense when she referred to "McStory on the paper's front page" in a column she wrote about the media's preoccupation with the wardrobes of Nancy Reagan and Raisa Gorbachev. In this article, she talked of reading a "McStory," without making any mention even of fast food, much less McDonald's. Furthermore, she does not even use quotes around the expression, suggesting that she does not feel obliged to alert the reader to an unusual word or to an unusual use of an ordinary word.

CONCLUSION

Based upon our analysis, then, we found that the prefix *Mc-* acts like any ambiguous lexical item, in that a reader or hearer must rely on context to determine which of the possible senses the author is intending. At trial, we emphasized the point that meaning is flexible, determined by context. We used the example of the polysemous/ambiguous word *green*, which has a number of related and distinct senses. We argued that when a word is ambiguous, placing it within a specific context often disambiguates it. For example, *green* in the sentence *Give me the green* has a very different sense if the sentence is uttered by one speaker holding the other at gunpoint than it does when uttered by an artist gesturing to his assistant. Sometimes we have to look no further than the sentence itself to conclude which sense of an ambiguous word is intended, as in the sentence *The new cowhand was still a little green*, in which the words *new* and *still* cue us that the intended sense is most likely "inexperienced." In a sentence such as *The young sailor was green*, however, we entertain two possible senses, "seasick" and "inexperienced." In such a case, the hearer or reader would look for evidence elsewhere in the context to determine which sense is intended.

We argued that with the prefix *Mc-* there were several factors suggesting that a person reading the prefix in many of these articles could dismiss the possible association with McDonald's. Placing the prefix in the context of hotel marketing—in other words, situating an abstract *Mc-* name within an actual usage situation unrelated to fast food—it becomes unlikely that one would immediately associate *Mc-* with McDonald's. We argued that the entire package of *McSleep* marketing materials provided contextual cues to the consumer in a manner that is analogous to the way in which words in a sentence or utterance provide cues to the reader or hearer. The samples of marketing materials for the

hotel chain routinely included the QI four-chain logo, firmly contextualizing it within that corporation rather than within McDonald's.
Additionally, the logo was to include a stylized setting sun, an element
common to all of QI's logos. The franchisees were also to be required to
display the legend "by QI" underneath the McSleep Inn logo on their
main exterior signs. Again, the combination of these elements would
draw the viewer's attention from the McDonald's association, much as
we would rule out the prototypical sense of "green color" in the sentence *The girl went green at the thought of drinking sour milk*, even
though it may be true that the primary sense of "green" referring to the
color gives rise to the metaphorical extension of it to the sense of "nauseated." That is, we quickly move from the literal level, when it is
apparent that that level is not relevant, and seek a metaphorical meaning. This metaphorical process is what we found overwhelmingly in the
citations using *Mc-*.

Independent of the analysis we performed for QI, McDonald's
Corporation enlisted the advertising firm of Leo Burnett to conduct a survey of the public's perception of the *Mc-* formative. Because their study
was not based on actual usage data, but rather on a survey taken at a
McDonald's office location, we felt that their results revealed a marked
bias, which is reflected in the following definitions taken from their
results. One description of the meaning read "a kid's product . . . a product children will like better because it's associated with McDonald's."
Another meaning presented in the Leo Burnett survey is "reliable, at a
good price." Still another was "prepackaged, consistent, fast, and easy."
The most negative of the definitions provided in the study was "processed, simplified, has the punch taken out of it." Their study further
acknowledged that ten to twenty percent of the people surveyed had an
even more negative view, saying that *Mc-* connotes "junk food, processed, not real, pre-made, uniform, cheap, bland, a gimmick, etcetera."
Still, their optimistic view of the prefix's connotations is best represented
by a quote taken from one of their own documents: "By virtue of extensive advertising and sales effort and expense and maintenance of the
highest standards of quality and service by McDonald's, 'McDonald's'
and its 'Mc' formative marks have come to be so distinctive and well
recognized that the vast majority of consumers upon seeing the marks
identify them with McDonald's."

Throughout the case we conceded McDonald's Corporation's original
association with the prefix; our results differ from those of the Leo
Burnett survey in that we noted the relatively tiny degree to which writers still make that association explicit. Furthermore, we found that its
use is today predominantly pejorative. Writers in our corpus used the prefix in such a way that suggested that the prefix has come into its own,
with any metaphorical connection to McDonald's fading very fast. It is
the sheer market presence of McDonald's that keeps the name and all it
stands for current in our consciousness; however, it appears that the

prefix has broken loose from those associations and has taken on a life of its own, with the senses intact, but with the original literal connotation becoming considerably less strong. Based upon the evidence of what we found in the citations, we argued that the prefix is at an intermediary phase in its history. It has taken on associations from McDonald's, but it is proceeding to shed those associations and keep the abstract senses that have evolved.

The question of why this prefix has such a strong attraction for speakers and writers remains. One explanation is that it exerts a purely aesthetic appeal in cases where the speaker is clearly doing it for the fun of it, as in the case of "McVeto McKernan." In a similar way, the attorneys' support staff during the case called their office the *McCommand Center*. Judge Niemeyer himself glibly expressed the hope in his published opinion that he would not be considered *a McJudge*. The main appeal of *Mc-*, however, lies in the fact that the prefix has an undeniable economy, a property fundamental to linguistic codes. Just as it is more elegant to say *zipper* than to say *hookless fastening device*, it is easier to say *McSurgery* than to say, periphrastically, *standardized, assembly-line surgery*. To attribute recognized and accepted general characteristics to an otherwise neutral word, people have learned, simply attach *Mc-* to it. Whether the connotation is pejorative or ameliorative is conditioned by the appropriateness to the enterprise of the implied concepts; clearly, *a McLube* should be a fast and efficient place to get one's automobile serviced, but the prospect of going under the knife of a *McSurgeon* is rather daunting.

In the two years since the case, we have continued to see and hear many words formed with this prefix. Writers and speakers continue to get more creative with its use; in cases such as *McPinion, McNificent,* and *McStake* it is even being used as a lexical root. The data we analyzed and the citations we continue to see demonstrate that while McDonald's can be effective in preventing commercial use of the prefix, the two injunctions against its commercial use have done very little to stall its rapid expansion into the popular lexicon.

APPENDIX

List of Citations for *Mc-* and *Mac-*

1. Ethnic Associations (Includes Surnames)

McDuff   1. Computer discount store with a Scottish motif   *Computer & Software News* 7 Dec 1987; 2. Local police search dog   *Western Real Estate News* 20 Nov 1987, Waukesha, WI *Freeman* 2 Mar 1988

McGruff   Public service mascot for crime prevention, dressed as a bloodhound in a trenchcoat   Louisville, KY *Courier-Journal* 8 Apr 1988, *Jersey Journal*

McNificent, McSure   Overnight mail advertisement using a leprechaun and a four-leaf clover   *USA Today* 17 Mar 1989

McPuzzle   Crossword puzzle with clues pertaining to Scotland   *Washington Post Magazine* 17 Apr 1988

MacThrift   Budget office supply store with a Scottish motif   Greensboro *News & Record* 28 Feb 1988

McThrift Motor Inn   Budget motel with a Scottish motif   Norfolk, VA *LedgerStar* 17 Feb 1989

2. Alliterative Patternings Based on a Proper Name

McAuto   Subsidiary, of the McDonnell-Douglas Corporation   *Capital District Business Review* 11 Apr 1988

McBooks   Bookstore named after its owners, McCarthy and McGovern   DeWitt, NY *Business Journal* Feb 1988

McCrazy   Tennis player John McEnroe, known for wild fits of anger   *Sports Illustrated* 16 Aug 1986

McDance   Collaborative work involving musician Bobby McFerrin   Ogden, UT *Standard Examiner* [n.d.] Apr 1988

McLish—it rhymes with McDish   Female body-builder, Rachel McLish   *Los Angeles Times* 26 Jun 1987

Air McMail   Football coach David McWilliams   AP Sep 1986

Jim McMyth   Football player Jim McMahon   *Washington Post* 15 Jan 1988

Spuds McPuppies   Miniature bull terrier puppies named after Budweiser mascot Spuds McKenzie   [source omitted]

McSpeedport   Racetrack in McKeesport, PA   *Pittsburgh Press* 6 Mar 1988

Quick Thaw McStraw   Milkshake named after the Hanna-Barbera animated character, Quick Draw McGraw   Phoenix, AZ *Republic* [n.d.]

Mc of Time   Police officer named McBride, who delivered a baby for a couple named McGrew in McDonough County in the town of Macomb   Taunton, MA *Gazette* 22 Mar 1988

McVeto McKernan   Name given to Maine governor John McKernan by protesting union workers   Bangor, ME *News* 27 Feb 1988; Portland, ME *Press Herald* 12 Feb 1988; Augusta, ME *Kennebec Journal* 23 Feb 1988

3. Acronyms

McDap   Manson County Drug Abuse Program   *USA Today* 2 Mar 1988

McRIDES   Morris County RIDES, a ride-sharing program   *Mt. Olive Chronicle* 18 Feb 1988; Morristown, NJ *Daily Record* 6 Feb 1988

4. Products of the McDonald's Corporation [not analyzed in this study]

5. Macintosh Computer Products or Related Businesses

McBike   Electronically controlled exercise bicycle   Midland, MI *News* 17 Dec 1988

McConsociates, Inc.   Computer consulting firm   Beverly, MA *Times* 14 Mar 1988

McTek   Computer discount store specializing in Macintosh products   *Micro Cornucopia* Feb 1988

McToy   Computer accessory for accelerating processing time   *Incider* [n.d.]

6. Parodies of a Fast-Food Product or Service

McChowMein   Hypothetical name for a Chinese fast-food restaurant Philadelphia *Inquirer* 22 Feb 1988

McFido's   Hypothetical name for an actual restaurant for dogs   Chicago *Herald* 9 May 1988

McFoam   Burger boxes in a science fiction film parody, *The Attack of the Burger Pods*   Minneapolis *Star Tribune* 5 May 1988

McMania   Hypothetical drive-through therapy clinic   Gastonia, NC *Gazette* [n.d.]

McMeditation   Hypothetical fast-service meditation center   Pacific *Sun* 29 Jan 1988

Lamb McNuggets   What the author of the article imagines that an animated wolf should eat   *Comic Buyer's Guide* 2 May 1988

McPaper McNuggets   Detroit *News* 16 Feb 1988

News McNuggets   *AOPA Pilot* Jan 1988

Squid McNuggets   Hypothetical squid tidbits   Bremerton, WA *Sun* [n.d.]

McShaft   Hypothetical fast-service drive shaft mechanics shop   Santa Ana, CA *Register* 8 Feb 1988

Sausage McSouffle   Chicago *Sun-Times* 4 Feb 1988

McSoup   Hypothetical soup restaurant empire name   Ansonia, CT *Sentinel* 20 Nov 1987

7. The Meaning "Basic, Convenient, Inexpensive, Standardized"

McAmerica   *American Politics* Jan 1988

McArt   "mass market art"   *Forbes* 7 Mar 1988

McBimbo   *American Politics* Jan 1988

McBook   "A book so slender and so filled with fast-food humor that his [Cosby's] detractors have called it McBook."   Los Angeles *Times* 25 Sep 1987

McCaviar   "It's for people who like caviar, but don't want to go broke eating it." *Crain's* 27 Jun 1988

McChekhov   "makes fast food from the great Russian writer Anton Chekhov's short stories . . . not so much based on his stories, . . . but looted from them." Baltimore *Sun* 23 Dec 1987

McChic   *American Politics* Jan 1988

McCinema   "quick fix films, hastily written, overly sentimental, contrived and silly."   North Kingstown, RI *Standard-Times* [n.d.]

McDigest   "a daily digest of news, polls, punditry, & gossip."   *Regardie's* Apr 1988

McDome   "a multipurpose stadium."   St. Louis *Construction News & Review* Nov 1987

McDrive-thru   "retreat to the nearest McDrive-thru."   Toledo, OH *Blade* 21 Feb 1988

McDuck's   Used in a cartoon showing an employer arranging to "cater" the company Christmas party at a drive-in window with the name McDuck's on the menu.   *Rubber & Plastics News* 14 Dec 1987

McEconomics Economic policies of the Ronald Reagan administration *American Politics* Jan 1988

McEverything "This is the era of instant gratification, of pop tops, quick wash, fast fix, frozen foods, McEverything." Fort Myers, FL *News-Press* 17 Feb 1988

McFashion "kids are drawn by smaller 'express' stores the same way they're attracted to fast food." *Entrepreneur* Mar 1988

McFood "It's a push-button, do-it-yourself, convenience-oriented world. . . . We can zap a lean cuisine in the micro, or order McFood from a drive-in McSpeaker." Burlington, NJ County *Times* 10 Apr 1988

McFuneral "The industry even has its own 'McFuneral' in Service Corp. International of Texas, which . . . now owns and operates more than 300 cemeteries and more than 600 funeral homes nationwide." *Puget Sound Business Journal* 7 Mar 1988

McGlobe "People shouldn't travel halfway around the world only to find the same hamburger joints they've got back home. . . . We are on the brink of becoming McGlobe." Charleston, WV *Mail* 11 Mar 1988

McGod The God of TV evangelists *American Politics* Jan 1988

McHairpiece "The Aderans Co. [a hairpiece marketer] plans to create a vast franchise network throughout this country beginning this spring." Hagerstown, MD *Herald* [n.d.]

McHealth Care "large for-profit hospital and HMO chains have earned the industry epithet 'McHealth Care.'" UPI 5 Sep 1986

McHistory "In its fast food vending of McHistory" Butte, MT *Standard* [n.d.]

McJobs "They are McJobs that are low-paying and require little if any skill." Hillsbory, OH *Press Gazette* 7 Apr 1988

McJournaled "If the very subject that should have been treated thoughtfully is McJournaled, abbreviated to the trivial, . . . then isn't the editor saying to the reader that it really isn't worth his or her attention?" *Folio* Dec 1987

McLaw "The near omnipresence . . . and the homogeneity of their 340 offices have prompted pundits to dub the franchise phenomenon 'McLaw' suggesting that legal advice is dispensed through drive-in windows." *California Lawyer* Dec 1987

McLife Results of genetic engineering *American Politics* Jan 1988

McLifestyle "What we need and have come to expect in this, our McLifestyle is speed. Speed and easy access." Lewiston-Auburn, ME *Sun-Journal* 7 Feb 1988

McLube "Little drive-in shops offering a 10-minute oil change and chassis lubrication are about to become a supercharged market." Augusta, ME *Kennebec Journal* Feb 1988

McLunch "Cheap, filling, and child-friendly meals." Columbia, MD *Flier* 11 Feb 1988

McMaids [source omitted]

McMail "If the U.S. Postal Service were sold today to a private business we'd see changes overnight. The first thing we would notice is that U.S. Post Offices would be replaced by 'McMail.'" Centerville, OH *Times* 28 Mar 1988

McMarines *American Politics* Jan 1988

McMarketing "creative, successful marketing and advertising strategies should be available as quickly—and be priced as inexpensively—as high-volume, fast-food lunch option. . . . Naturally this type of venture would emphasize speed and low price, rather than good quality." Bradenton, FL *Herald* 4 Apr 1988

McMedia ". . . education delivered via the mass media of cable TV, videocassettes, and radio." [source omitted]

McMedicine "Its critics sometimes refer to it as 'McMedicine,' but proponents of primary care medical centers growing in number say they fill a community's need for prompt and inexpensive care for minor problems." Maple Heights, OH *Press* 18 Feb 1988

McMed Students UPI 5 Sep 1986

McMiz "elaborate and elegantly aggressive marketing, merchandising and standardized production techniques that the burger giants might envy." *Washington Post* 3 Jul 1988

McMoral Majority *American Politics* Jan 1988

McMovie ". . . like fast food, it satisfies the appetite and tastes good. . . . a film hallmarked by a monumental vacuity; a central impoverishment of means, ends and ideology which cuts across genre." *Psychiatric News* Apr 1988

McMovies "instant videos of both the NY Giants & Denver Broncos" Denver *Post* [n.d.]

McMovie, TV "Flat and naggingly ersatz, the film proves roughly as memorable as a fast-food restaurant. It's another TV McMovie" *Washington Post* 29 Apr 1988

McNews "McNews, a mere tidbit of information, . . ." Columbus, OH *Dispatch* 24 Apr 1988

McNewspaper Champaign-Urbana, IL *News-Gazette* 8 Apr 1988

McOffice Supply ". . . fears the existence of a 'McOffice Supply' dealership, if dealers do not create an individuality for their customers." *American Office Dealer*, southwestern ed. Apr 1988

McOil Change *Forbes* 11 Aug 1986

McPaper "fast news for the fast-food generation" *Phoenix Business Journal* [n.d.], "you could sell a whole lot of papers and make a whole lot of money" Grand Island, NE *Independent* [n.d.]; see also quote S.V. MCTELECAST

McPaper Epithet for the newspaper *USA Today* *Christian Science Monitor* 1 Dec 1987, *American Politics* Jan 1988

McPaper Caper Reference to the development of the newspaper *USA Today* York, PA *Dispatch* 29 Jan 1988

McParticles "A truly American sport. Participants motor through 24 fast-food windows, gulping down burgers, fries, fish sandwiches and various McParticles en route." Framingham, MA Middlesex *News* 22 Feb 1988

McPost Office "What we really need is a McPost Office. . . . Anyone who has ever been to the post office knows how poor the service can be." Elgin, IL *Courier News* 21 Jan 1988

McPreachers *American Politics* Jan 1988

McPrisons "Prison franchises: another alternative to prison overcrowding." [source omitted]

McProgram The television equivalent of the newspaper, *USA Today*. Albany, NY *Knickerbocker News* 4 Mar 1988

McRather "Like its print model, the *USA Today* TV show will be a fast-paced potpourri of news and features, divided into four sections, money, sports, life and USA" *Time* 11 Apr 1988

McRead(s)   "Three 'McReads' just right for an airport layover or the beach." *Christian Science Monitor* 29 Jul 1986

McRobot   *Newsweek* 28 Mar 1988

McService   *American Politics* Jan 1988

McShopping   "The impersonal McShopping of the giant, corporate-owned malls is here to stay."   Syracuse, NY *Herald Journal* 1 Feb 1988

McSimplification   *American Politics* Jan 1988

McSouth   *American Politics* Jan 1988

McSpeaker   see quote S.V. MCFOOD   Burlington, NJ County *Times* 10 Apr 1988

McStory   "I read a McStory on the paper's front page that detailed what the American public needed to know were the real differences between Russia and America: Raisa Gorbachev uses Henna Hair Dye . . . Nancy Reagan . . . uses Clairol Chestnut and Moonlight Blond highlights"   Dubois, PA *Courier-Express* 9 Jan 1988

McSuperpowers   *American Politics* Jan 1988

McSurgery   "An increase in the number of surgical procedures that can be done without overnight hospital stays has been predicted because of the approval of a new anesthesia"   Asbury Park, NJ *Press* 27 Dec 1987

McSweater   "The main goal [of Benetton] was to make garments that could be fashionable but at the same time on an industrial scale so everyone could buy them."   *Working Woman* May 1986

McTax Chain   "the seasonal storefront tax preparers."   *Working Woman* Mar 1988

McTelecast   "I know people call the newspaper 'McPaper.' I have no problem with them calling the television version 'McTelecast.' The paper is a quick read; we will be a quick watch."   *Christian Science Monitor* 1 Dec 1987

McTelevangelism   *American Politics* Jan 1988

McTelevision   Detroit *News* 7 Apr 1988

McTrash   *American Politics* Jan 1988

McVideo   Champaign-Urbana, IL *News-Gazette* 8 Apr 1988

McYear   Headline for an article reviewing major news stories for the year 1987 "a fast-food, service-with-a smile, prefabricated, standardized, marketing-dominated [nightmare]."   *American Politics* Jan 1988 (The article contains 23 different terms using the *Mc*-prefix.)

McZippy Burger   West Covina, CA *Highlander* [n.d.]

REFERENCES

Cruse, D. Alan. 1986. *Lexical Semantics*. New York: Cambridge UP.

Crystal, David. 1987. *The Cambridge Encyclopedia of Language*. New York: Cambridge UP.

Mencken, H. L. 1963. *The American Language*. Abridged ed. Ed. Raven I. McDavid, Jr. New York: Knopf.

Niemeyer, Paul V. 1988. Opinion. *Quality Inns International v. McDonald's Corporation*. Civil No. PN-87-2606. U.S. District Court, District of MD.

Shuy, Roger W. 1988. Testimony. *Quality Inns International v. McDonald's Corporation*. Civil No. PN-87-2606. U.S. District Court, District of MD.

≡

FOR DISCUSSION AND REVIEW

1. The lawsuit depended on whether the public associated the morpheme *Mc-* with McDonald's or whether *Mc-* had become generic. Why did public perception of *Mc-* matter to determining trademark infringement?

2. How is the morpheme *Mc-* different from most other derivational prefixes? Give some examples to support your answer.

3. What is the "Aunt Jemima Doctrine," and how was the issue of "confusion" part of the lawsuit between McDonald's and Quality Inns?

4. By collecting data from many sources, the authors discovered a variety of words based on the morpheme *Mc-*. Into what categories did they put their examples? Which category was particularly important in the lawsuit? Why?

5. McDonald's hired an advertising firm to conduct its own survey of the public perception of the prefix *Mc-*. What were the result of this survey? How did they differ from the conclusions of Lentine and Shuy? What might account for the differences?

6. In the appendix at the end of their article, Lentine and Shuy include citations for *Mc-* and *Mac-*. What does this list suggest about whether trademark owners can influence or control everyday language use?

13

Syntax: The Structure of Sentences

Frank Heny

A sentence is not just a string of words; it is a string of words in a certain order, a string that has structure. Thus, cat dog the the chased *is not a sentence; it is just a list of English words. But* The dog chased the cat *is a sentence (as is* The cat chased the dog*). A sentence, then, is more than the sum of its words: it is words ordered in a particular way, in this case according to the rules of English syntax. But how do we learn these rules—rules, generally, we are unaware of?*

In the following article, written for this book in 1985 and revised in 1997, Professor Frank Heny suggests an answer to the question and examines some of the basic syntactic rules of English. He also demonstrates that children come to language learning with an inborn mechanism that "severely limit[s] what the language learner needs to take into account," one of the crucial concepts in contemporary linguistic theory.

LEARNING LANGUAGE IS LEARNING STRUCTURE

It is easy to think of your language as a vast collection of words—like *easy* and *think* and *language* and *vast*. But as soon as you try to take this idea seriously, you realize that it can't be the whole truth. String together the words of the previous sentence in another order:

1. you to that as take idea this try realize truth the be soon it but can't whole seriously you as

The obvious difference between (1) and *But as soon as you try to take this idea seriously, you realize that it can't be the whole truth* is the order of the words; and it is almost equally obvious that what happens when you change the order is that you change how the words themselves interact with each other. Certain words now form coherent groups, like *the whole truth* or *as soon as you try to take this idea seriously.* Saying or writing the words in a particular order structures them into groups: they stop being just isolated words and turn into real language.

English is not just a huge dictionary. Learning it is not simply committing a vast list of words to memory. This may be more obvious if you think about a foreign language. To be able to speak German or French you must do much more than just learn the sounds and meanings of a whole lot of words! Of course you have to know vocabulary, but you could learn dozens of German words from a dictionary every day for the rest of your life and still never approach being able to speak the language.

Despite this fact, that language is so much more than just a huge store of isolated words, what you remember of learning your own native language is likely to be limited to memories of just that—the learning of new words. Think back as far as you can, and see if you can recall starting to learn English. You may well remember occasions in which you learned what a new word meant—perhaps even as far back as when you were two years old. (Indeed, it is probably still an everyday occurrence to learn the meaning of a new word.) But you will not remember a thing about learning how to form the structures those words are set in, the structures that make your language what it is. No native speaker of English remembers learning how to make different kinds of sentences (questions, commands, passive sentences and so on)—or even how to form phrases like *the whole truth*. To a typical native speaker of English, the sentence structure, the way phrases are built up and joined together, seems often so natural that it is hard to conceive of putting words together in any other way—almost as if the structure of the language itself had never had to be learned.

It will take only a moment to verify this. There are kinds of sentences that we use every day yet have never thought about consciously. In the previous paragraph, the expression "passive sentences" appears. Here is a group of English sentences. Try to pick out all the passive ones and jot down the numbers. (Don't worry if you can't do this; just read on after you have tried.)

2. a. I watched the prisoner from the tower.
   b. The tower was where I watched the prisoner from.
   c. The prisoner was being watched from the tower.
   d. I was watching the prisoner.
   e. Who was watching the prisoner?
   f. Who was being watched from the tower?

Unless you happen to have studied traditional grammar, or some linguistics, it is not likely that you were comfortable with this task. The sentences are perfectly simple. You use sentences similar in form to all of them every day. Examples (c) and (f) in fact are passive—but you certainly didn't need to know that in order to use them or others like them.

The purpose of showing you the examples above was not to test your knowledge of traditional grammar. In fact, we assumed that the expression "passive sentence" might be a little unfamiliar, and wanted to show that even if you had no idea which of the examples were passives you would find the sentences perfectly ordinary: you would have absolutely no difficulty using and understanding such structures. If you happened to be familiar with the term "passive" you would not normally be at all conscious of the construction itself, even when you used it, and you would not be in any way helped in your use of passive sentences by being able to identify them. Furthermore, whether or not you picked out (c) and (f), many readers would have failed to do so—yet would not have been less able than you to use and understand passives. Conscious knowledge about the passive construction seems unrelated to the native speaker's ability to deal with passive sentences.

Do not confuse learning the basic structure of your language (which had taken place before you were five years old) with the attempts of teachers, for example, to get you to say "It is I" instead of "It's me" or to distinguish nouns from adjectives. That kind of learning *about* language was a collection of facts or opinions about your language and how it is used. Compared to your original achievement in learning the language itself, this added knowledge was really quite insignificant. Your high school and college English teachers may have taught you a good deal about how to use the language effectively. In particular, they may well have contributed significantly to your ability to write effectively. Written language is an added, in part artificial, skill built upon the oral language that you developed for yourself. Writing you had to learn consciously, just as you have had to learn math or music. In contrast, you had some-how mastered, quite unconsciously, and without any formal teaching, before you first went to grade school, a system so complex that linguists have still not figured out how it works—your native language itself. How did you do it?

At the present time no one really knows for sure. However, some very interesting ideas are now being explored, which seem to come rather close to the truth. It is likely that you developed the structures of your native language so easily because there was actually very little you had to *learn*. Even learning the words was not a matter of learning thousands of quite arbitrary items piece by piece. You learned the words as parts of structures and the structures you did not really have to learn at all. For they were already there before you learned the language—much as the eye is there, with all the appropriate structure, waiting within the womb for the light and the sights it will see.

The underlying patterns of language, any language, were waiting within you in some sense, and all you had to do was select from those internally stored structures the ones into which you could fit the sounds and words of the language you heard around you. By the time you were a year or so old, surrounded by English, the sounds of that language had already begun to form themselves into patterns in your mind—not as a result of your own individual attempts to "discover" the structure of English (surely too much for any toddler) but rather through a process in which those sounds began to clothe some of the preexisting structures, the ones matching English. From this perspective, your learning English was no miracle or mysterious feat of super intelligence! Indeed it would have been a miracle if you, as an ordinary, normal human being had not, under normal circumstances, and surrounded by English, become a fluent English speaker.

To repeat: it was not so much that you *learned* your language as that it simply *developed*, fleshing out certain of a number of possible language structures which were in effect already waiting to develop. The language around you merely determined the particular choices among those structures that had to be made. Had you grown up exposed instead to French or Navajo or Japanese, you would have been forced by the patterns made by the sounds and words to select a different set of options. To see what this idea amounts to we need to understand a little more about what kinds of systems languages are. Ideally, this would mean looking at a number of languages. Because that would take too long, this account will be based almost entirely on English. However, it will be aimed at demonstrating not what *English* is like, but what *language* is like.

STRUCTURE IS MORE THAN JUST WORD ORDER

Let us first be quite clear that sentences are not just strings of words in a particular order, but really do have a complex internal structure. In pointing out the rather obvious fact that a sentence is not just a string of words put together in any old order, we noted that when the words are in a particular order they acquire a certain structure—and in doing so fit together to make up a sentence. This structure is more than just order, for a single string of words strung together in just one order can have two quite different meanings. These two distinct meanings correspond to two sentences. An example follows; make sure that you see that (3) is really two quite distinct sentences, with two distinct meanings, before you go further. The bracketing in (a) and (b) should help you to distinguish these meanings clearly.

   3. I watched the prisoner from the tower.
     a. I watched [the prisoner from the tower].
     b. I watched [the prisoner] [from the tower].

The first way of interpreting this string treats [*the prisoner from the tower*] as a unit: it is the [prisoner from the tower] who is seen by the speaker. This same group of words, [*the prisoner from the tower*], functions as a single unit, a *constituent*, in other, similar sentences. In such sentences, the words *the prisoner from the tower* act together to characterize someone as a prisoner from some tower:

   4. a. [The prisoner from the tower] was what I saw.
     b. [The prisoner from the tower] was being watched carefully.
     c. [The prisoner from the tower], I watched carefully.

In each of these examples, the phrase [*the prisoner from the tower*] could be replaced by other constituents such as [*the prisoner from Siberia*], [*a visitor from Mars*], or [*three men in dark glasses*]. Each of these, too, would be acting as a single unit in such sentences. Under this first interpretation, the sentence has nothing at all to say about where the watcher was, but does imply something about the prisoner.

The other interpretation of (3), on the other hand, represented by (3b), does have something to say about where the watcher was, and has nothing to say about the prisoner. The words *from the tower* are not applied to *the prisoner* at all. The two phrases act quite independently, as separate units. This is suggested by the bracketing in (3b). This time, *from the tower* is much more closely associated with the verb *watched*, or with the pronoun *I* than with *the prisoner*. The sentence is not about a prisoner from a tower at all, but reports that the speaker *watched from the tower*. Given this fact, it is not surprising that (3b) is very similar in meaning to another sentence in which the phrase *from the tower* occurs right at the beginning, next to *I*:

5. [From the tower], I watched [the prisoner].

Constructed out of the same English words as (3), this string can be understood only as having a structure in which *the prisoner* and *from the tower* are separate, unrelated constituents. This is also the case in the following rather closely related sentence:

6. [The prisoner], I watched [from the tower].

This last example may seem a little stilted, but there are occasions when most of us use such forms. It is possible that you could more readily use something like: *It was the prisoner that I watched from the tower* or *As for the prisoner, I watched him from the tower* or perhaps even a passive: *The prisoner was watched from the tower by me—and my friend*. (That extra bit added on—*and my friend*—does not change the structure of the sentence and has been added just to help make the sentence sound more natural.) In all these cases, the phrase [*the prisoner*] is separated from [*from the tower*], and the two are quite independent of each other in meaning. Contrast the unambiguous interpretation of (5) and (6), where *from the tower* is not linked to *the prisoner* in any way, with the equally unambiguous interpretation of all the sentences of (4)—where the whole phrase [*the prisoner from the tower*] was always interpreted as a single constituent, i.e., where each sentence is about a prisoner from some tower.

In the examples of (4) the word order somehow forces us to interpret the words *the prisoner* and *from the tower* together as a single constituent whereas in (5) and (6) the word order splits the two parts of this string and they must be interpreted as two distinct, unrelated constituents. In contrast, the order of words in (3) permits either interpretation depending on how we take the words to be structured: as a single constituent or as two. The word order does not force us to choose, as it does in (4) or (5). In a particular instance, when we hear, or utter, a string of words like (3), we determine (generally quite unconsciously) which structure to assign to it and hence which sentence we will regard it as representing, (3a) or (3b). Thus there are two structures associated with that one order of words: word order sometimes forces words to be structured in a particular way, but it doesn't always do so. Structure and word order are not the same thing.

WAYS OF MARKING OUT PHRASES

All languages are built up from phrases; the phrases are small groups of words interacting with each other in various ways to produce sentences. In English, the order of the words limits the ways in which words can interact to form phrases, though as we saw in the case of (3), word order does not determine the phrase structure completely.

In many languages word order plays little role; in Warlpiri, for example, a language spoken in Australia, the words from a single phrase may be scattered around in a sentence. Thus in Warlpiri it is almost (but not quite!) as if one could say *The from watched I prisoner tower the* and mean (3a). Here is an actual Warlpiri sentence:

7. Wawirri   yalumpu   kapi-rna   panti-rni
   kangaroo   *that*   *spear*   *NONPAST*

I will spear that kangaroo.

This sentence means roughly *I will spear that kangaroo*. There is no obvious word meaning *I*, but the meaning is implied. We are not interested in this aspect of (7), but in the order of the words that *do* appear in the sentence. First, let us focus on the words meaning *that kangaroo*. In (7), those two words are next to each other, as in English, but in the order *kangaroo that*. Thus far, Warlpiri might seem to require a different word order from English. Such an impression is consistent with the fact that the verb meaning *to spear* comes near the end of the sentence, whereas in English it would come before the phrase *the kangaroo*. So in English we would have *spear that kangaroo*, while in (7) we have the equivalent Warlpiri words in the order *kangaroo that spear*—with about the same meaning. There are many languages that differ from English in that the order of the words in the various phrases is not the same as the English order.

But Warlpiri is more radically different. The words of (7) (like those of other Warlpiri sentences) can be moved around in all sorts of ways without changing the essential meaning. Thus, the following means the same as (7):

8. Wawirri   kapi-rna   panti-rni   yalumpu
   kangaroo   *spear*   *NONPAST*   *that*

I will spear that kangaroo.

This example contains just the same words as (7), but in a totally different order. Most striking is the fact that the word meaning *that* comes right at the end of the sentence, while the word meaning *kangaroo* is at the beginning—yet the two words are interpreted in such a way that together they form a phrase meaning the same as the English *that kangaroo*. Of course, a language like Warlpiri obviously must have some way of indicating which of the words of a sentence go together; Warlpiri speakers don't know by magic that in this example *wawirri* and *yalumpu* belong together! We cannot describe here how this is achieved because to do so would mean discussing numerous unfamiliar Warlpiri sentences.

Which words go in which phrases is by no means always signaled by word order. In Warlpiri, for example, as suggested by our examples, the order of the words is practically irrelevant. Other languages vary; the word order in French, like that of English, is quite rigidly fixed and serves to group the words into phrases and the phrases into sentences. Latin was quite free, and other devices signaled which words were grouped into phrases or where the phrases belonged in a sentence. Finnish, Russian, and German fall somewhere in between, with some freedom in word order, and a number of devices (patterns of agreement and case marking, for example) that show what belongs with what and where everything fits into a sentence. Still, Warlpiri sentences, and the sentences of all the other languages that we know about, are constructed out of phrases, and for the most part phrases are much the same as English ones, however they are marked.

A child hearing English or Warlpiri, or any other language, will therefore not need to "figure out" that the babble of noise around it consists of phrases. As far as we can tell today (though our knowledge about such matters is still rather fragmentary), the human infant automatically assumes that any noise it interprets as language consists of words grouped, by one of a small number of devices, into meaningful phrases and hence into sentences. Thus, the child has only to discover whether word order or one of those other methods (such as agreement patterns like those you may have met in Latin or German) signals how words group together into phrases.

There is much that we do not know for sure yet about how a child develops a knowledge of syntax. For example, we do not know just what it is that signals that word order is what matters in English, but that some other option must be relevant when Warlpiri is the language to be learned. One possibility is that certain options are, as it were, "favored" or "unmarked," which is to say that unless a child encounters specific indicators to the contrary, it automatically selects the "unmarked" option whenever there is a choice.

Assume for the sake of argument that word order is the "unmarked" way of grouping words into phrases. A child (no matter what language it will eventually acquire) assumes, until that assumption won't work on the language it hears, that it is hearing words grouped together in some fixed order. The child will expect to find words recurring in fixed, ordered patterns, with adjectives occurring consistently either before or after the nouns they go with and so on.

This expectation is met in the case of English. When the word *that* occurs as part of a phrase built up around the word *kangaroo*, as in *that kangaroo*, they have to appear together. In fact, *that* must appear before *kangaroo*. We can't even say **I want kangaroo that* and still be talking English. (An asterisk before a string of words indicates that *that* string is not a proper sentence in the language; we place it before *I want kangaroo that* to indicate that that string is not an English sentence.) So a child growing up hearing English merely needs to discover *which* order works for English. A child growing up hearing Warlpiri, on the other hand, will need to do more "figuring out" to discover how the phrases in that language are grouped together. (In regard to other aspects of language structure, it will be Warlpiri and not English that follows "unmarked" patterns.)

$$\equiv$$

EXERCISE 1

1. Imagine you are a child. You hear some of the following words grouped together to form English phrases like *several monkeys* or *some gold*:

   > books several yellow those that monkeys gold some inadequate little

   Try to form as many phrases as possible using various selections from these words (not all of them can occur together) and then try to give a general account of how the phrases are formed.
   To do this you will need to:

   a. Decide what orders are possible.
   b. Decide which words can occur at the same point in structure (for example, where *gold* can occur, *yellow* can generally occur as well). You will thus be grouping the words into small classes that act alike.
   c. Make up names for the word classes. If you have studied traditional grammar, it may be natural to call *little* and *gold* "adjectives," but what you call the classes matters little. You just need some way to refer to them. List the words that fall into each class.
   d. Add several words to each of the word classes you have identified. Make sure that your examples act like the original members of the class.
   e. Make up general rules for forming phrases that are built up out of the word classes you have named. Which words come before which other words? Are some word classes free to appear in alternative positions?

2. While continuing to deal only with phrases that seem to you to be very similar to those you have been dealing with, like *several monkeys*, add more and more *classes of words*, and decide what order they occur in. Is the order ever free? That is, can English words ever occur in alternative orders while still (as far as you can tell) occurring within these phrases? (Hint: think of strings of adjectives, like *old*, *sick*, or *tired*.) Can you find words that do not ever occur within phrases of the sort you are dealing with? For example, does the word *unfortunately* ever occur as part of one of these phrases? Try to explain precisely what you mean if you claim that it (or some other word) cannot occur within these phrases.

3. If you know another language that seems to have fixed word order, try to find instances where this is (a) the same as in English for some given pair of word classes (e.g., adjectives and nouns), and (b) where it is different.

SOME SIMPLE PHRASES: NP AND PP

So far we have seen that a string of words, like *the prisoner from the tower*, may act as a single phrase or may be two independent phrases, *the prisoner* and *from the tower*, each a constituent adding its own meaning to the sentence—as in (3b). We have seen that English words, when occurring together in a sentence, are interpreted not just as *strings* of words, but as *structures*, i.e., phrases built up out of those words. The order of the words may determine completely how they group into phrases, as in (4), (5), and (6), or it may not, as in (3). It is the phrases rather than the words as such that form constituents of sentences: (3a) and (3b) contain the same words but different phrases—as suggested by the bracketing in those examples—and their distinct meanings. Phrases like [*the prisoner*], [*from the tower*], and [*the prisoner from the tower*] interact as units with the verb *watch* in a sentence like (3) to yield a meaningful sentence. Individual words like *from* or *the* or *prisoner* do not. Thus *the* was not watched, nor was *prisoner*, nor was the watching *from*. Rather it was [the prisoner] or [the prisoner from the tower] who was watched, and if we know anything about where the watching took place from, then we know that it was [from the tower].

We have seen that at the level of the sentence, it is not words but phrases that are significant, and have also seen how certain English phrases require that the words making them up occur in a fixed order. We have begun to build up a picture of how certain kinds of (so far undefined) phrases consist of various classes of words in certain specific orders. Only when those words occur together in a permitted order can they be grouped together to form a phrase. Now it is time to consider the structure of these phrases themselves, generalizing as precisely as possible about how they are constructed. In other words, we need to determine what may occur in such phrases. They can be very complex—or very short and simple. We could replace *the prisoner* in (5) with phrases of increasing complexity, without altering the essential structure of the sentence as a whole:

9. a. From the tower, I watched [*the prisoner with bare feet*].
   b. From the tower, I watched [*the prisoner in the yard with bare feet*].
   c. From the tower, I watched [*the prisoner in the yard with bare feet who was trying to run away*].

But we could also replace these complex phrases with just a single word:

9. d. From the tower, I watched [*John*].

A phrase does not have to be long, and in (9d) it consists of just that one word, *John*. In each example of (9), the phrase in square brackets refers to the person who is said to be being watched; thus the phrase in question, however long or short it may be, plays the same role in the meaning of the sentence as a whole. In (9c), for example, the prisoner is identified by a long and complex description: *the prisoner in the yard with bare feet who was trying to run away*. The length and complexity of this phrase in no way modifies the role of the phrase in the sentence, which is precisely the same as that of *John* in (9d); it identifies the object being watched.

The phrases of (9), despite their very different levels of complexity, are built up in essentially just one way. Each, no matter how complex (or simple), is constructed around a noun: *prisoner* in the first three, and *John* in the last. There are other nouns in these phrases, such as *yard* and *tower*. But these are just helping the main noun to build up the description, to identify precisely which thing or group of things the phrase refers to. We may call the phrase a noun phrase (NP). It is a phrase built up around a noun, the head noun of that phrase, which most directly identifies the kind of thing to which the phrase refers.

The word *John* is a noun that can act alone as a noun phrase. Most nouns can't. So we can't say **I was watching prisoner*; we have to say *I was watching* the *prisoner*. The noun *prisoner*, when it is in the singular, requires a determiner like *the* or *a*, though this is not always essential when the noun is plural, as in a sentence like *I was watching [prisoners] in the yard*. When *John* is used as the name of someone it does not generally even permit a determiner, and if we said *From the tower I was watching the john* we would probably want to spell the word *john* with a small letter—and mean something quite different from (9d)! Nouns differ in all sorts of ways regarding what they require or permit with them in their phrases; they are alike in that they allow an NP to be built around them, serving as its head.

Not every string of words containing a noun can act as an NP. In English (and this should now come as no surprise), the order of the words is significant. Whereas *the prisoner* is a perfectly fine NP, *prisoner the* is not. Nor is *from the tower the prisoner*. Hence a string like *from the tower the prisoner was watched carefully* can only be interpreted as a statement about how a prisoner, not further identified, was *watched from the tower*. Although right next to *the prisoner* and some distance away from the verb *watched*, the string *from the tower* goes unambiguously with *watched* and never with the NP *the prisoner*. There are many restrictions on what can form a noun phrase. Some are general restrictions; others, as we saw in the previous paragraph, depend on the special properties of the head noun.

Some strings simply cannot be rearranged in any way to form a single noun phrase. For example, there is no way at all to rearrange the words in the string *the suddenly prisoner* and end up with a single, well-formed NP. Similarly with strings like *the run prisoner*, or *that the prisoner three*. Noun phrases, like all the parts of a sentence, have a very precise syntax: they are constructed according to exact formulas. Learning the language may consist in part of learning these, though it seems likely that many regular patterns in NPs do not have to be learned, since they derive from principles that determine the very process of language learning in children. (One of the troublesome aspects of learning a language later in life is that we seem to have to learn far more of those word order rules than a young child does—something may be "blocking" our ability to make use of whatever linguistic principles are available to a young child.) How much of the syntax of noun phrases a child has to learn we do not yet know. If, as we have suggested may be the case, the "unmarked" way of grouping words into phrases is to have them occur in some fixed order, then all that an English-speaking child has to determine is the specific order in which the noun, adjectives, and so on have to be placed in the NP.

NPs do not constitute the only phrase-level building blocks of language. There are other phrases, for example, those like *from the tower*. Although not themselves noun phrases, these nevertheless contain noun phrases (*the tower* in this instance). In addition, they contain prepositions like *from*. Prepositions themselves vary greatly in behavior, just as nouns do. But just as the phrases built up around nouns have a great deal in common with each other, both from the point of view of what can occur inside them and from the point of view of where they can act in a sentence, so prepositional phrases (PPs), built up around prepositions, have a good deal in common. We will not deal in any detail with the syntax of prepositional phrases. We turn instead to the unit within which PPs and NPs have to occur—as do all other phrases and apparently isolated words that can occur in English, like *swiftly, perhaps*, or *as big as Peter*. This larger unit, which seems to be central in (virtually?) all languages, is the sentence.

BASIC ENGLISH SENTENCE PATTERNS

Phrases like NPs and PPs are very important constituents: they contribute a great deal to the structure of language. However, they do so only in interaction with verbs. Verbs, and the phrases built up around them, are what really determine the essentials of sentence structure. And ultimately a language consists of sentences rather than either isolated words or even just independent phrases. Sentences consist of phrases grouped together in certain specific ways, and these phrases consist of words grouped together in specific ways. It is sentence structure that we have to learn, over and above vocabulary, when we learn a foreign language. The syntax of our native language, English for most readers of this selection, is never consciously learned, and is often quite difficult for people to think about consciously. We are now attempting to do just that—to understand how sentences are constructed in language, using English as an example.

Generally it seems that a language will have one or two "normal" or "unmarked" sentence patterns, which are embodied in many of the commonest, most ordinary sentences. The verbs of the language are at the center of this structure, each verb occurring in some variant of the basic pattern. Here are some very simple examples of the English unmarked pattern:

10. a. [The cat] <u>slept</u>.
    b. [My friend] <u>likes</u> this puzzle.
    c. [The wanderer] <u>tramped</u> down the road.
    d. [The cat] <u>put</u> the mouse on the mat.

Each sentence in (10) contains a verb, which is underlined, and a phrase preceding it, the subject of the sentence, which is an NP (i.e., a noun phrase). The subjects are enclosed in square brackets.

Although every sentence in (10), and indeed every simple, "normal" English sentence, contains a verb preceded by a subject, there is a good deal of variation in what can *follow* the verb. Because of differences in the properties of the verbs, each sentence in (10) is forced to differ a little in structure from all the others—and these differences always concern what may, must, or must not occur to the right of that verb. So, for example, (10a) cannot incorporate the phrase *this puzzle* after the verb.

11. *The cat slept this puzzle.

The asterisk is again used to indicate that the string *The cat slept this puzzle* is not a well-formed English sentence. The verb *sleep* differs from *like*; it does not permit the phrase *this puzzle* to appear to its right. In fact, it will not permit any other noun phrase to appear there.

Conversely, the verb *like* cannot appear *without* an NP after it, as suggested by the ungrammaticality of the following:

12. *My friend likes.

What can, must, or must not appear to the right of the verb depends directly on that verb. After *sleep*, no phrase like *this puzzle*, no NP, may appear at all, whereas after *like*, an NP must appear.

Those two verbs, *sleep* and *like*, represent the simplest cases. The first will not permit an NP to its right, while the second requires one. There is a name for verbs like *sleep*; they are called intransitive. Verbs like *like* are called transitive. A transitive verb is one that requires an NP directly to its right; an intransitive verb will not permit a plain NP in that position. An NP directly to the right of a verb is called a direct object. Thus, while transitive verbs require a direct object, intransitive verbs do not permit one.

These two classes of verbs are the most basic, but there are many variations in the way English verbs require or permit the presence or absence of NPs and PPs to their right. For example, *put* requires both an NP and a PP. This is shown by the ungrammaticality of both (13a) and (13b). (Compare these two with the grammatical [10d].)

13. a. *The cat *put* the mouse.
     b. *The cat *put* on the mat.

Likewise, the verb *tramp* seems very strange when used without a PP.

14. *The wanderer tramped.

Tramp at least arguably requires a PP to its right. (This does not mean that we call *tramp* transitive, for that term is confined to verbs requiring a direct object, i.e., requiring an NP and not a PP to the right.)

In general, then, a verb is often closely associated with certain phrases that may or must appear to its right; these phrases, which include noun phrases and PPs, are called its complements.

Verbs that never permit any kind of complement at all are rare, and so are verbs which, like *put*, require more than one phrase to occur in their complement structure. Many verbs seem to *prefer* rather than absolutely *require* certain complements. For example, both of the following are perfectly acceptable:

15. a. Bob Dylan sings.
     b. Bob Dylan sings his own compositions.

The first of these examples suggests that *sings* is intransitive; the second that it is transitive—i.e., requires a direct object. Thus, the meaning of the verb *sing* appears to be such that the verb can permit but does not absolutely require an NP in its complement.

When we say that some phrase is a complement of a verb we are not concerned merely with whether it is absolutely required or excluded by that verb, but with whether the phrase in question goes with the verb in such a way that the meaning of the phrase is actually part of the meaning of the verb. When material to the right of the verb is not part of its complement at all, it is not required and, more significantly, does not interact directly with the meaning of the verb so as to form a part of that meaning. Take a sentence like the following:

16. Jane watched your father on the Paris metro.

What are the complements of *watch*? There are at least two quite distinct constituents after the verb. Each can "move around" independently, much as *the prisoner* and *from the tower* could in (3):

17. a. [On the Paris metro], Jane watched your father.
    b. [Your father] Jane watched on the Paris metro.

Of the two phrases *on the Paris metro* and *your father*, one seems to be part of the complement of *watched*, the other does not. Before we say which is which it would be a good thing to think about the meaning of sentence (16). Which of the two phrases interacts most closely with the verb, building up the meaning of *watched*? That will be the one that is its complement.

The answer is the NP *your father* rather than the PP *on the Paris metro*. The latter adds more detail about where the act of seeing occurred, but it is the *seeing of your father* which is the act of seeing. The PP *on the Paris metro*, a *locative adjunct*, adds information about where the seeing took place, its "location"; the NP *your father* fleshes out the meaning of the verb *watched*: the seeing is a seeing of your father.

This account might be confusing if not further supplemented. For there are all manner of adverbs, among them *quickly* and *carefully*, as well as PPs that can act like adverbs, which seem to be much more closely related to verbs than a locative phrase like *on the Paris metro*:

18. a. Jane watched *carefully*.
    b. Jim sang *in a crazy way*.
    c. Jack ate *noisily*.

These expressions are clearly neither direct objects nor locatives. In fact, they can occur with both:

19. a. Jane watched [NP your father] *carefully* [PP on the Paris metro].
    b. Jim sang [NP the ditty] *in a crazy way* [PP in the bar].
    c. Jack ate [NP the sausage] *noisily* [PP behind my back].

They add to the meaning of the sentence something about the manner in which the watching, singing, or eating was performed (and are often in fact called manner adverbials).

Why are such adverbials not part of the complement of the verb? To put the question another way, how does *eating a sausage* differ (structurally) from *eating noisily*? Consider the sausage. It is part of *eating*—in fact, it is consumed in the process. Nothing happens to "noisily." There is no "noisily" to take part in the eating process; only Jack and the sausages are involved in that. At least in the clear cases, it should be possible to see that the complements of a verb refer to things that participate in the verbal activity. They are the phrases (if any) that build up the core meaning of the verb, and along with that verb form part of a higher-level phrase, the verb phrase. So, in example (16), *your father* is part of the verb phrase, along with *watched*, while *on the Paris metro* is not because *on the Paris metro* does not refer to anything that participates in the activity of watching, while *your father* does. *On the Paris metro* simply indicates where that activity takes place; it is a locative adjunct.

If we now put square brackets around the verb plus its complements in (10)—the verb phrase (VP)—then we see immediately that all four sentences have the same basic structure, an NP followed by a VP:

10. a. [NP The cat]   [VP *slept*].
    b. [NP My friend]   [VP *likes* this puzzle].
    c. [NP The wanderer]   [VP *tramped* down the road].
    d. [NP The cat]   [VP *put* the mouse on the mat].

We can summarize what has been shown so far in this section in the following way: English sentences "normally" consist of an NP before the verb, i.e., a subject, followed by the verb itself and then the complements of that verb, if it has any. Whether a verb requires or permits complements, and if it does, then precisely how many—i.e., precisely how many NPs and/or PPs must or may follow it—is a property of the verb itself.

The complement structure of a verb depends largely on how complex the meaning of that verb is—how many distinct participants are involved in the relevant activity. Comparing the sentences of (10) with each other, it is easy to see how far the structure of each is directly dependent on the verb it contains and hence on the complements that must or may follow that verb. Sleeping is an activity that can involve only a single person; hence the verb *sleep* permits no complements in addition to the subject. You can't like without liking something, so there are two participants in the liking relationship. So *like* not only requires a subject (as do all verbs), but must also have an NP as its complement—a direct object. Tramping is an act that requires a place to tramp in (or down, or whatever)—not just fortuitously but as part of what it means to tramp. So *tramp* more or less requires a PP as its complement. Notice that although *down the road* in (10c) is a kind of locative, somewhat like *on the Paris metro* in (16), it is not an adjunct but a complement. It does not *add* to our information about where some activity took place, for part of the core meaning of tramping is that it involves a relationship between a person and a place— it is in fact an activity in which the subject *changes its place*. Finally, the verb *put* requires both an NP and a PP in its complement, reflecting the fact that putting involves a change of place in something which unlike tramping is brought about by some other entity. The subject of sentence (10d) refers to the "putter." The direct object refers to the thing that is put—i.e., the thing that changes place. And the PP *on the mat* characterizes the location to which the thing is moved. Again, this is a locative phrase. In a sentence like *Jane hit Bill on the mat* it would be a locative adjunct. But in (10d) it is a complement.

EXERCISE 2

In the text we said that (14), *The wanderer tramped*, was not a possible English sentence, that *tramped* is a verb that requires a PP complement. That may well be true, but what about:

> The wanderer tramped on and on.
> Sam tramped wearily away.

What is *on and on*? What is *away*? Think of some other sentences based on verbs that seem to act somewhat like *tramp*, and think of other expressions that could occur instead of *on and on* or *away* in these examples. See if you can provide some kind of coherent account of what is happening. You are not likely to find a clear solution; the problem involves some borderline cases. You may find it interesting, nevertheless, to explore it.

BASIC ENGLISH SENTENCES:
A PHRASE STRUCTURE GRAMMAR

If there is a "normal" pattern that English sentences follow, and especially if it is true that the main lines of this pattern develop more or less automatically as a child constructs his or her own version of English, then it must surely be true that each of us who speaks English in some sense *knows* these basic sentence structures. This is one aspect of knowing the language that, in addition to a knowledge of the meanings of the words, is necessary in order to speak a language. Although, as with so much of language, we do not consciously know what the patterns are, it is clear (for example, when we try to learn another language) just how important that knowledge is.

It is still not clear how the patterns of language are stored in the mind. We know too little about how they develop, nor do we yet know exactly how the language user produces sentences that follow the stored patterns or recognizes that utterances conform to those patterns. Indeed it is still not certain what the crucial features of those patterns are. Structures like those in (10) can be represented in many ways, not all of them equivalent. The way of representing them that emphasizes those features that are truly significant is still subject to debate. That the patterns exist and are significant is perfectly clear, though, and linguists are now trying to find ways of representing these and other language patterns so their representations throw light on language development and use—and on other related aspects of human nature. To do this, they build models of sentence structures—much as a physicist builds models of atoms and molecules.

One of the most fruitful ways of modeling the basic structures of English has been by means of a *phrase structure grammar*. This is a way of directly representing the structure of every basic sentence of the language as a *tree*. Each tree corresponds to a particular sentence, being a model of (the structure of) that sentence. Some examples will help clarify this. The following trees might be assigned to the sentences of (10):

20. a.

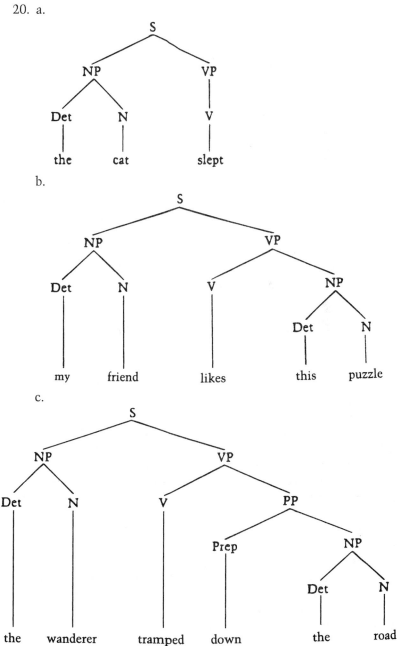

b.

c.

d.

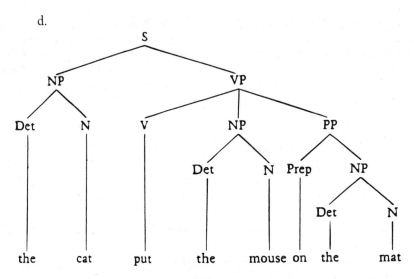

In principle, it is possible to imagine that we might store each sentence of our language independently in the mind, as a tree, like (20a–d), representing the structure of that sentence. However, a little reflection should be enough to make it clear that English cannot be represented in that way. Our knowledge of English cannot be thought of as simply a treelike structure stored with each sentence. We cannot store sentences individually in our brains. Apart from anything else, there are simply too many sentences. (In fact, there is an infinite number of possible sentences in the language, as in any human language.) Each of us deals effortlessly with hundreds of sentences every day that we have never heard before—every one not just a string of words but a structured string. Consequently, in learning English we must have acquired some way of assigning structure to *any* appropriate string of words.

This aspect of our language is represented in a phrase structure grammar by a set of rules that captures the main aspects of English sentence structure in the form of trees like those above, associated appropriately and automatically with every sentence of the language. For every (possible) sentence of English, the rules will construct a tree. The following set of rules would construct the trees of (20)—and others like them:

21. a. S → NP VP
    b. VP → V (NP) (PP)
    c. PP → Prep NP
    d. NP → (Det) N

These rules provide a "recipe" for building a number of related structural skeletons that English sentences of the "normal" pattern will flesh out once appropriate words are linked to the end symbols N, V, Prep, and Det. To yield a way of representing, automatically, a large class of English sentences, those like the sentences in (10), we need only add to the rules of (21) lists of nouns, verbs, prepositions, and determiners that can be linked to the lowest nodes of the trees built by these rules. Before we show precisely how the rules work, you should work through the following exercises.

EXERCISE 3

1. Make up lists of English words that would fall under the symbols N, V, Prep, and Det, and then draw several trees like those in (20), replacing the words in those trees with others from your lists.
2. Describe any problems that arose in completing the previous exercise.
3. If you know another language, try to make lists corresponding to those that you constructed for English, and then try to draw trees for comparable sentences to the ones given for English. Do you meet any problems in carrying out this assignment? If so, describe them.

Each rule in (21) may be thought of as building part of a tree. Let us start with the part built by the rule (21a): S → NP VP. In this tree (for each part of a tree is also itself a tree), the S to the left of the arrow in the rule in question is drawn above the NP and VP that appear to the right of the arrow, and it is linked directly to each of them. The symbols to the right of the arrow (i.e., NP and VP) appear in precisely the same order (from left to right) as they do in the rule itself. So, rule (21a) builds a little piece of structure that looks like this:

22.

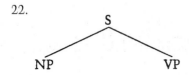

If you find it easier to think in terms of how *you* should interpret the rule, think of it as an instruction to write down the symbol to the left of the arrow and then to write, under it, and in the order in which they appear in the rule, all the symbols to the right of the arrow. And finally, link each of those lower symbols to the one above it. If you follow these instructions precisely, this should enable you to draw (22) as the structure (the *only* structure) resulting from the application of (21a) according to the interpretation we have just given to that rule. First you write down the "S." Then under it you write "NP VP." And finally, you link "NP" to "S," and "VP" to "S." The result is (22).

Now notice that this little tree forms a part of every one of the larger sentence trees given in (20). Make sure you follow this before going further.

Either make a tracing of (22) and lay it over each of the trees given in (20), or simply look carefully at those four earlier trees and satisfy yourself that you *could* lay a tracing of (22) over each of them. (It would cover the S node at the top of each tree, and the NP and VP which are joined to it.)

This is not just a trivial fact, though at first you may not see why it is important. The real significance of having a rule like (21a) in our grammar of English—a rule that draws the sub-tree (22) as a part of every sentence—is that it directly represents an aspect of English structure that has been mentioned several times: the fact that all the "normal" sentence patterns of English contain a subject NP followed by a VP. This rule, (21a), contains NP + VP on the right-hand side, and is the only rule for S in the grammar, so it forces every tree to contain, below the S and connected to it, NP followed by VP. In this way, rule (21a) ensures that the language model of which it forms a central part will include only trees built with the structure NP + VP: every sentence will be associated with the structure NP + VP.

Although of itself quite a small point, it is a typical application of a basic methodology that is central to all current work in theoretical linguistics, and worth following closely for that reason. Let us look at it again from a slightly different angle: in order to discover just how language develops, we need to understand what kinds of structures may be included in a human language. In order to do that, we formulate hypotheses about the structure of language, representing these hypotheses by means of some clear formalism such as a phrase structure grammar. Put this way, the grammar (i.e., the set of rules) in (21) is a step towards understanding how we learn language and must be thought of as an attempt to build a model of the kinds of structure that we, as children, eventually assign to English sentences.

A linguist using the grammar of (21) in an account of English is thereby committed to the claim that a child ends up with a representation of the language that is essentially like that set of rules. The linguist is also committed to the representations for each of the sentences of (10) that are given in the trees drawn by those rules, namely (20a–d). It will be good to try and keep these underlying principles in mind as we proceed. The formal details are important, for it is only by understanding them that you can really grasp the significance of theoretical work on language, but it is all too easy to get bogged down in those formal details and to lose sight of the goals that give them their significance.

We can now fill in additional details, looking briefly at how the rules of (21b–d) provide "recipes" for drawing every aspect of the trees (20). First, we must extend the sub-tree (22). Look at the diagram once again. One branch ends in the symbol "VP." This is the symbol on the left of rule (21b). So when we apply the general instructions for tree-building to this particular rule, "VP" will be the symbol we write down first, just as "S" was with respect to rule (21a). Then we will need to write down, under "VP," the symbols to the right of the arrow in the rule. And so on. In practice, since "VP" is already written down, in (22), we take that as our starting point. We don't write it again. Any time the left-hand symbol of a rule we are applying is already part of an existing tree we proceed in this way: we simply write down the symbols that are on the right of the arrow, placing them under the existing left-hand symbol. So, in this case, we may write down "V NP PP" (all of which appear on the right of the VP rule). We write them immediately under the existing VP in the tree in question, namely (22), in the order they appear in the rule, and we obtain (23):

23.

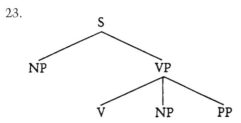

While it is perfectly true that application of rule (21b) to the VP in tree (22) does—and should—produce the above tree (which is a sub-tree of the tree given earlier in [20c]), we have ignored a small but quite significant property of rule (21b), which results in (23) being *not the only tree* drawn by that rule. In (21b) there are two symbols inside parentheses. These parentheses never appear in the trees at all; a tree never contains symbols inside parentheses. The parentheses are in fact not a part of the symbols themselves at all. They simply indicate, in the phrase structure rules, elements that *may*—but *need not*—appear in trees constructed by using those rules.

When we applied (21a), we had no choice but to write down both "NP" and "VP." There was no choice because there were no parentheses around either symbol; and the rule was written without parentheses around these symbols in order to represent English as a language in which every sentence has a subject NP followed by a VP. Rule (21b), on the other hand, allows us a number of choices when we apply it. This reflects the fact that the structure of VP differs from sentence to sentence—that is, not every VP has the same contents. In fact, as we emphasized early on, the structure of the VP of each sentence is dependent on what verb actually appears in it. Our general rules for constructing sentences must therefore permit the appropriate variation. The parentheses in rule (21b) are there, then, because a VP may contain an NP or a PP, both, or neither. Both the NP and the PP are optional, and this is marked by enclosing both symbols in parentheses. When we apply the rule, we have to make a choice; we do not need to write down "V NP PP" under the VP, but may leave out either NP or PP or both. So, under the VP, we may write down just "V NP," omitting the "PP." Or we may write down "V PP," or "V NP PP." Or just "V." We cannot leave out the "V" since that is not inside parentheses. But since everything else is, we may omit any or all of the other symbols.

The operation of the rule may be much easier to follow if we work through each of these possibilities one by one. First, here is the rule itself again:

VP → V (NP) (PP)

Omit both elements in parentheses and we obtain the shortest version of the rule—and, as suggested below, the simplest trees:

24. a. **VP → V**

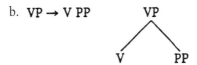

Omit only the NP and we have:

b. **VP → V PP**

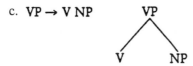

Omit the PP and we have:

c. **VP → V NP**

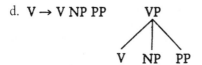

If both NP and PP are selected in applying the rule, so that the longest possible version applies and the right-hand side includes the symbols "V NP PP," then the result is a tree like the one already shown in (23). Using the same format as (24a–c), we obtain:

d. **V → V NP PP**

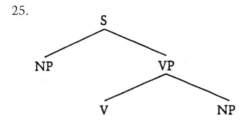

If, when we applied rule (21b) to the VP in tree (22), we had chosen just "V NP," instead of "V NP PP," then the result of applying that rule would not have been (23) but would instead have been:

25.

We could extend this figure so as to turn it into the tree shown in (20b). The structure we have in (25) is a "sub-tree" of (20b). That is to say, you could lay it over (20b) like a tracing, and (perhaps with a little stretching here and there) each symbol and line would match up precisely with a part of that larger, complete tree. To turn (25) into (20b) requires just two applications of rule (21d) to add the proper structure under NP—and then, of course, the right words have to be added at the ends of the branches. In a similar manner, all the sentences of (20) can be obtained from the rules of (21). It would be worth taking the time to try to derive each of these trees by applying those rules in proper order.

≡

EXERCISE 4

1. Construct each of the trees of (20), using the rules in (21) in the manner described in the text.
2. Use the lists of words that you made for the exercise on page 209 to construct other trees for good English sentences having similar patterns to those of (20).
3. Describe briefly any difficulties you have encountered. If you are dissatisfied with the rules or with the way they work, state the problem briefly.

Notice that an un-English string of English words (like *on the mat the cat the mouse put*) will not be assigned a structure by any possible combination of the rules. We need to be clear about that. Why is it true? Here is one way of looking at it: Rule (21a), which starts each derivation off by getting the "S" for "sentence" in position, forces every sentence to consist of an NP followed by a VP. And the rule for VP insists that the verb appear at the beginning of the verb phrase—*followed* by NP or PP or both or neither. There is no rule that will get the verb to appear *preceded by* a string consisting of *on the mat the cat the mouse* since this string consists of PP (*on the mat*) + NP (*the cat*) + NP (*the mouse*). None of the sub-rules of (21) will place PP + NP + NP in that order, let alone place them before the verb. If English included sentences with such a pattern, we would need to add some rules to (21) to generate appropriate trees. For example, we might assign to this string a tree somewhat like the following:

26.

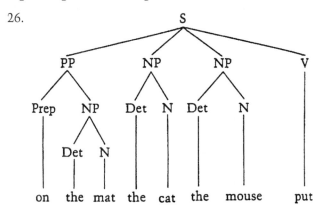

A rule that would generate (26) might, for example, be:

27. S → PP NP NP V

Since English does not permit these structures, of course, we don't add this rule to (21) and hence our grammar, correctly, never generates strings like *on the mat the cat the mouse put*. To that extent, it properly represents the English native speaker's internalized language, generating the sentences of (20) while excluding strings like that shown in (26).

BASIC SENTENCE PATTERNS IN THE MIND

We may regard the rules of (21) as a reasonable first approximation to the way the basic sentence structures of English eventually develop in the mind of a child. However, it is going much too far to conclude from this that rules like these do indeed represent how the English speaker stores those patterns. We cannot, without evidence from many sources, conclude that learning, or developing, a language is in part a matter of constructing a grammar like (21) to define trees for all the sentences of the language. To claim this, that a child acquiring English develops a phrase structure grammar like (21) as a mental representation of the basic patterns of the language, goes far beyond what can be concluded on the basis of the fact that those rules are a "reasonable first approximation" to the representation of English that the child must eventually develop. We have dealt thus far with only a very tiny part of English and there are many other ways of approximating the effect of rules like those in (21).

For a number of years, it seemed likely to most linguists that in learning a language a child does indeed build up a phrase structure grammar providing recipes for constructing all the sentences of the language. The grammar of English, according to this hypothesis about language, would include some rules very much like (21). Recently, it has become clear that a child probably never learns language in terms of rules like these. Rather than trying to discover a set of rules like (21), analyzing for this purpose the language she hears around her (which seemed for a time to be the most likely way for the child to learn language), it now seems probable that a young language learner engages in a much simpler task. To see what this might be, we must consider the task from the point of view of a young child.

Children learn languages other than English. In fact, every child could just as well learn any language, and languages differ from each other in their basic sentence patterns—but not in infinitely many ways. The basic patterns of all languages have much in common. So when a child learns English he needs to determine that the verb goes between the subject and the direct object. Learners of Japanese or Persian need to determine that the verb goes last in the sentence. Young Irish speakers (there are now very few!) find the verb at the very beginning of the sentence. Whether the verb goes at the end or beginning of the sentence or, as in English, after the subject, is probably something that has to be learned. Since the verb is such an important part of every sentence, it needs to be identified.

The position of the verb undoubtedly helps the child to find it. In a language like Warlpiri, of course, where word order is not important, other signals must identify the verb, but generally verbs cannot appear at just any point in a sentence; there are just a very few positions where a verb can be expected to appear. It is likely that when a child begins trying to analyze the language around her, the limitations on word order, etc., which are included in every child's "instinctive" knowledge of what can constitute a language, greatly simplify the task of discovering the verbs of the language to which the child is exposed, and hence of determining those many aspects of structure that depend crucially on the verb.

There seems to be a link, for example, between the position in which the verb appears in a language (first in the sentence, last, or after the subject) and the structure of PPs. A language with the verb in final position, which is to say one whose structure could be represented (in this respect) by a phrase structure rule something like (27), would not have prepositional phrases like those in English, with the preposition before the NP, but would place the preposition *after* the NP. (It would then be called a *postposition* by grammarians, but this difference in name does not reflect any real difference in the function of prepositions and postpositions.) A child exposed to a language in which the verb came last would quickly discover where the verb had to appear. The sentences of the language he heard would follow a rule with "V" on the far right, which we could represent by replacing rules (21a,b) with one like (27) (though probably with an NP in initial position), or perhaps replacing rule (21b) with a rule for VP like this:

VP → NP PP V

A child would not actually have to learn such a rule. Given the fact that language consists of sentences built around verbs having subjects, once the position of the verb was fixed there would be no need to learn, in addition, a specific rule like (27). Nor, given what has just been suggested about the linkage between the position of the verb and the position of prepositions/postpositions, there would be no need to learn a specific rule for PP. There would be only one rule available for PP (*post*positional phrase) in a language with the verb in final position: PP → NP Post. The Post would come last in its phrase, just as the verb comes last. And hence the rule would not need to be learned, let alone stored in the mind.

Now, whether this is indeed a case where the structure of human language is constrained by predetermined limitations built into the human mind is not yet certain. But it does seem very likely that specific rules directly corresponding to phrase structure rules do not often need to be learned by children developing language. In any case, the underlying point seems valid: the patterns of all human languages may well be derived by the application of a few deep, unlearned, "instinctive" principles that make it quite unnecessary to suppose that our native language is learned by constructing explicit grammars like the rules of (21).

Despite this fact, we will continue to present analyses of English in terms of phrase structure rules, just as if such rules really were how speakers of the language represented the patterns of their language. This is partly a matter of convenience: phrase structure rules provide the most transparent way known to us of characterizing the basic structures of a language as a whole. They are, as already pointed out, the best available approximation to those basic structures, even if in fact there is no explicit grammar of this sort that the language learner constructs.

SOME DEVIANT PATTERNS: AUXILIARIES IN ENGLISH QUESTIONS

Not all sentences of English follow patterns that are covered by the rules of (21). In the simplest cases, we would need only to extend those rules. For example, our account of English makes no provision for NPs containing adjectives, such as *little* in *the little cat*. Nor does it allow us to introduce a PP inside an NP, such as (NP *the prisoner* [PP *from the tower*]), one of the very first constructions we noticed, in (3). In both of these instances, it would be quite a simple matter to add extra optional elements at the appropriate points in the rule for NP, (21d). We might, for example, modify the present version, NP → (Det) N, to read NP → (Det) (Adj) N (PP), extending this rule even further to take care of complex NPs like *the man with a huge mouse in one of the three tiniest cages in the world*—and so on!

Among other words that must be introduced into the sentence in this way are the *auxiliaries*. These are the little verblike words that may appear between the subject NP and the VP in any ordinary English statement. When we introduced the idea that there are basic, unmarked patterns in English, we could perfectly well have added one or more auxiliaries to the sentences of (10), for auxiliary verbs are part of the basic sentence structure of the language. We could have used examples like the following (compare them with the corresponding sentences of [10]):

28. a. [The cat] *has* [slept].
    b. [My friend] *could* [likes this puzzle].
    c. [The wanderer] *is* [tramping down the road].
    d. [The cat] *will* [put the mouse on the mat].

In each case, one auxiliary verb appears between the subject and the VP. This is perfectly normal. In fact up to three, and in passive sentences up to four, auxiliaries can appear in this position. They always appear in a fixed sequence. The examples above could have been more complex: *The cat* may have been *sleeping*, or *The wanderer* could be *tramping down the road*, and so on.

In an exhaustive account of the basic structure of English we would need to allow for these auxiliaries. Just as we suggested expanding the rule for NP (i.e., [21d]) to include adjectives (when it would read NP → (Det) (Adj) N (PP)), so we might add an extra symbol, say "AUX," between the NP and the VP of rule (21a) to accommodate auxiliaries: S → NP AUX VP.

Adding such a node would allow us to draw trees like the following:

29.

```
                    S        (=[28b])
         _____/ /        _____
        NP          AUX              VP
       /  \          |             /    \
     Det    N        |            V       NP
      |     |        |            |      /  \
      |     |        |            |    Det    N
      |     |        |            |     |     |
      my   friend  COULD         like  this  puzzle
```

We cannot go into more detail about how to modify the basic structures of English so as to accommodate the auxiliaries in such sentences as these. For we are primarily concerned in this section with the fact that there are many English sentences whose structure differs from that of the "normal" patterns we have seen so far, and does so in ways that suggest that a grammar consisting only of rules like those of (21) does not adequately represent the full structure of a language like English—that human languages exhibit other kinds of structure in addition. The primary reason, therefore, for dealing with the auxiliaries is that in certain kinds of sentences they lead us on to structures that deviate in an interesting way from the "normal" patterns. Corresponding to each of (28a–d) there is a sentence which we may think of as its question counterpart. This question differs from the corresponding nonquestion only in that *the first auxiliary in the nonquestion appears before the subject NP in the question.*

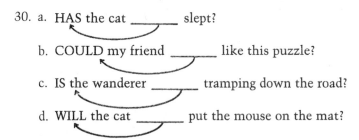

30. a. HAS the cat _____ slept?

    b. COULD my friend _____ like this puzzle?

    c. IS the wanderer _____ tramping down the road?

    d. WILL the cat _____ put the mouse on the mat?

Questions like these are often called "yes-no questions." Each is related to its nonquestion counterpart in a very regular fashion: the first auxiliary verb is not in its "normal" position, but appears to the left of the subject NP. This is suggested by the gaps and arrows in (30). (In fact, there is just a single auxiliary in each of these particular examples, just as there was in their statement counterparts; but it is clear from examination of pairs like *the wanderer* could be *tramping down the road*/could the wanderer _____ be *tramping down the road?* that when there is more than one auxiliary in a sentence, as there often is, then only the *first* auxiliary "moves" to the left of the subject.)

The arrows and gaps in (30), which suggest that the first auxiliary "moves" to a position to the left of the subject NP, imply that the order SUBJECT + AUXILIARY is in some sense normal, primary, or as it is often called, "unmarked," and that when the first of the auxiliaries appears before the subject in questions, this is a "deviation" from the normal order—a "marked" order. There are good reasons for thinking that something along these lines is indeed the case.

We take the order of the auxiliaries in statements as basic, and the order found in questions as in some sense derived from that basic order, because if we do so, then the order of the auxiliaries, and the way they are ordered with respect to the subject NP in a statement and in its corresponding question can be systematically related to each other. Both are taken care of in the basic trees—the ones that questions have before the first auxiliary has moved, which are identical to the trees for the corresponding statements. If we do not take the statement order as basic, then it is hard to relate statements and their corresponding questions in any systematic way. (We do not have the space to show this here, but it is not too difficult to show.) Of course, it could be the case that the order of the auxiliaries in English questions is totally unrelated to their order in statements. But that is rather unlikely; there are simply too many ways in which they can be systematically related—provided we derive the questions from the statements by a *movement rule*, along the lines suggested by the gaps and arrows in (30).

Given an account involving movement of the first auxiliary, a sentence like (28a), *The cat has slept*, would be defined directly by phrase structure rules like those of (21). But its question counterpart, (30a), *Has the cat _____ slept*, would be defined in two steps: first, the phrase structure rules would yield a "normal" sentence, with *has* in the position it occupies in (28a), and then this word would be moved to its eventual position at the front of the sentence.

What stage have we reached in our account of syntactic structure? We began by developing a phrase structure grammar to represent the speaker's knowledge of the general patterns found in certain simple English sentences. We have just seen in outline how phrase structure rules would need to be supplemented by the addition of a movement rule in order to define the structure of English questions. However, we had already seen that there were good reasons for thinking that language learning is not a process by which a phrase structure grammar is constructed. In developing language, a child simply determines such things as the order of the verb and subject, of the verb and direct object, and so on. Speakers of English, Persian, Japanese, Irish and all other languages do not need to construct and store away phrase structure grammars to represent the basic sentence structures; those structures follow automatically once the correct choice is made between a limited number of alternative word orders such as the position of the verb. Now, what about movement rules? Does the English-speaking child learn a movement rule like "In order to form a question, move the first auxiliary in the corresponding statement to the left of the subject NP," and store this rule away in her mind?

The "movement" of the first auxiliary to the beginning of the sentence, which is so characteristic of English questions of all kinds (and occurs in a few other very minor constructions such as, "Boy, *can he* drink beer!"), is actually very rare in the languages of the world. There is probably no other language in which questions are marked by this auxiliary inversion rule—though the Germanic languages generally have the verb in initial position in yes-no questions, making them look superficially very much like (30a–d). It may be that at least certain aspects of this strange little construction do indeed have to be learned specifically by English speakers and stored away. However, there are other kinds of movement that seems so very widespread in the languages of the world that it is likely that they, like the phrase structure grammar which we eliminated as something that has to be learned, develop more or less automatically from general principles governing the structure of human language. In the next section, we look at one such widespread "movement" phenomenon as it appears in English.

WH-MOVEMENT

In addition to questions calling for "yes" or "no" as an answer, there are questions that ask for more detailed information; they are often called information questions. The following simple examples are quite typical:

31. a. Which cake *can* you make?
    b. What *has* Joe put on the table?
    c. Whose mouse *is* the boy looking for?

Like the examples of yes-no questions given earlier, each of these sentences exhibits subject-auxiliary inversion: each contains an auxiliary before the subject. This is perhaps easiest to see if we compare them to similar sentences that are statements rather than questions. Here are some examples that correspond directly to those of (31):

32. a. You *can* make this cake.
    b. Joe *has* put the book on the table.
    c. The boy *is* looking for his mouse.

In (31a) we find the sequence *can you* ("Which cake *can you* make?"); in the corresponding statement (32a), we find *you can* ("*You can* make this cake.") Similarly we find *has Joe* in the question (31b), but *Joe has* in the statement (32b). In the third pair, we find *is the boy* in the question, but *the boy is* in the statement.

These information questions not only exhibit the rather rare, perhaps uniquely English, phenomenon of auxiliary fronting already discussed, but they also begin with a phrase containing a question word—which corresponds to nothing at the beginning of their nonquestion counterparts. It is "movement" of this sort that is so common: the movement of some phrase to the very front of the sentence. In English questions what moves is a phrase containing a special question word. In the following representation of (31) this "*Wh*-phrase" (as it is often called, for reasons that should be obvious) has been set in italic—and for clarity placed in square brackets.

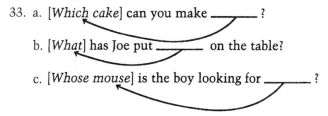

33. a. [*Which cake*] can you make _____ ?

    b. [*What*] has Joe put _____ on the table?

    c. [*Whose mouse*] is the boy looking for _____ ?

The representation in (33) of the sentences of (31) not only isolates the *Wh*-phrase for emphasis, but indicates by means of an arrow and an underlined "gap" where that *Wh*-phrase originated. In these examples, this gap has been placed in the position that would be occupied by an ordinary NP in a corresponding statement. Compare the verb phrases of (31a) and (32a).

34. a. [VP make _____]
    b. [VP make [NP *this cake*]]

What justification is there for representing the question (31a) in this way? Specifically, why must we think of the *Wh*-phrase as linked to that position in the VP, which in the statement (32a) contains the NP *this cake*? Why suppose that there is a rule that in some sense "moves" it from that position?

Intuitively, it seems clear that *which cake* in (31a) is the object of *make*, just as *this cake* is in (32a). There is, in each case, a sentence about some cake that can be made. This alone is not a very clear argument for the precise representation given previously involving movement to the beginning of the sentence from the direct object position. In fact there are clearer indications that the *Wh*-phrase must be regarded as in some sense a part of the verb phrase even though it is not actually inside that phrase in any of these questions. Recall how the verb of a sentence determines what can appear in the VP. The examples of (10–12) are relevant: whereas we can say *The cat slept*, we cannot say *The cat slept the milk*, and similarly, while we can say *My friend likes this puzzle*, *My friend likes* is not acceptable. Now look again at the verb phrases of (31). This time, we will represent them as if they had no gap at all corresponding to the *Wh*-phrase:

35. a. Which cake can you [vp make]?
    b. What has Joe [vp put on the table]?
    c. Whose mouse is the boy [vp looking for]?

If we treat each of these verb phrases as a complete VP, as suggested by this last set of representations, then the VPs should be able to occur independently, forming acceptable sentences when they follow NP subjects. But this is simply not so, as illustrated in (36):

36. a. *You [vp made]
    b. *Joe [vp put on the table]
    c. *The boy [vp looked for]

If we try to use just the words *made, put on the table*, or *looked for* in an independent sentence without an initial *Wh*-phrase and *without a direct object*, the result is quite ungrammatical. This is comparable to ungrammatical examples like (11) and (12). It seems clear that in (31b), the verb phrase is not *put on the table* but *put [what] on the table*, and that the word *what* really is acting as the NP object of *put*. This is similar in the other two examples. So, the "real" structure of (31a) is *You can make [which cake]*. And this is precisely the structure the sentence might have if it were generated directly by the phrase structure grammar of (21). *Wh*-phrases, at least the ones we will look at here, are simply special kinds of NPs, which generally have to appear at the front of the sentence rather than in their "normal" position, for example, as part of the VP.

One way of analyzing such sentences follows closely the lines suggested by the representation in (32): the normal phrase structure rules (i.e., [21]) derive *Wh*-questions just as if they were ordinary statements, with the *Wh*-phrase in the position it would occupy if it were an ordinary NP. In each of our examples, it would be the object of the verb, inside the VP in the position indicated by the underline in (33). Then a rule of *Wh*-movement moves the phrase to the front of the sentence, as suggested by the arrows in those examples. So, for example, *Which cake can you make* starts out as something like *You can make which cake* and then the phrase *which cake* moves to the front, as in (33)—and the auxiliary moves, too, of course, though we are not concerned with that right now.

$$\equiv$$

EXERCISE 5

1. Use the phrase structure grammar of (21) to draw *basic* trees for each of the following sentences:

   a. What picture will you buy for Henry?
   b. Who was Jane talking about?
   c. Which preacher could Jack have seen in Boston?
   d. Whose father could he be thinking of?

2. Now show, by using arrows and gaps, as in the text, how the two movement rules that we have discussed apply to these basic forms to derive the final forms of the sentences.

(Hint: The first sentence should be in the form *You will buy what picture for Henry* when you use the rules of [21] to construct a basic tree for it. This is similar in the others as well.)

Now, how far should we suppose that a child has to learn specific movement rules of this sort in developing knowledge of English? A child must somehow discover that a *Wh*-phrase belongs in its "real" position in the sentence—and must be interpreted as if it still remained there. Yet there is no audible sign of the gap that we underlined in (33); a child simply has to use his knowledge of the language as a whole (in particular, of the basic sentence structures including the properties of verbs and what complements they permit or require) in order to determine where a gap exists. So far, this might not seem too great a feat. The *Wh*-phrase corresponds to one or other of the places where an NP could appear: the subject of the sentence, or somewhere inside the VP. That is all the learner needs to "discover." However, note that in English, and in many other languages, it is possible for the gap to be virtually any distance away from the *Wh*-phrase.

This comes about because sentences can function as parts of other sentences—which can in turn be parts of other sentences. Look at the example that follows:

37. Sam believes [s1 (that) Bill can ride that horse].

The verb *believe* can appear with an ordinary NP object, as in *Sam believes [the child]*, but it can also appear with a whole sentence as its object, as in (37). There, the sentence *Bill can ride the horse* is the object of *believe*. (In [37] the word *that* may precede the embedded sentence, but it need not. It is shown in parentheses to suggest this. In subsequent examples *that* will often be omitted. This makes the sentences sound more natural to some speakers, though others may prefer to put it back in.)

Now we can repeat the process of embedding, setting (37) within another sentence as the object of yet another verb like *believe*. Let us use *think* in this case.

38. Sue will think   [s2 that Sam believes
                         [s1 that Bill can ride that horse]].

The process of embedding sentences inside others can go on indefinitely. The following example consists of (38) embedded as the object of the verb *hope*:

39. Your friend hopes   [s3 that Sue will think
                            [s2 that Sam believes
                            [s1 Bill can ride that horse]]].

We could go on to say *I deny that my friend hopes that Sue will think that Sam believes that Bill can ride that horse*. There is no end.

Now look at what happens when we take complex sentences like these and "remove" one of the NPs, inserting a suitable *Wh*-phrase at the very beginning of the whole thing. Two examples will suffice:

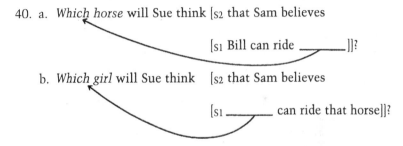

40. a. *Which horse* will Sue think [s2 that Sam believes

[s1 Bill can ride _____]]?

b. *Which girl* will Sue think   [s2 that Sam believes

[s1 _____ can ride that horse]]?

The fact that a *Wh*-phrase can appear indefinitely far away from the position in the sentence that it would occupy if it were an ordinary NP results in deviations from the unmarked NP AUX VP structure imposed by the phrase structure rules of (21) (as modified by the addition of AUX). One NP is not overtly present in its normal place, but appears at the beginning of some sentence, not necessarily even the one that it "really" belongs in.

A child learning the language would be better equipped to grasp the structure of such sentences if he did not have to discover from scratch that *Wh*-movement can occur in language—and better still if there were only certain places to which things could move. There is reason to believe that a child starts out with both advantages: the potential for *Wh*-movement is one of the devices that the learner takes for granted (as we have already suggested)—and there are very strict constraints on how phrases can be moved around. It seems very likely that these constraints are also not things a child has to discover but instead are limitations on the structure of human language that a learner can take for granted. These, at any rate, are the tentative results of recent work. We will now take a brief look at some of the limitations that appear to be placed on how a phrase can be moved.

It is striking that the moved *Wh*-phrase always ends up at the edge of a sentence. This is true not only in English but also in other languages, many quite unrelated to English. It would be strange if all languages had developed this constraint by chance, and there is every reason to believe that it results instead from some essential property of the human mind. This is even more true of some of the other constraints, which, although found in language after language in some form, are very complex and may even be in principle unlearnable.

Here is an example of a kind of structure that is excluded in English and many other languages:

41. *Which horse did Sue ask

                [s2 whether Sam believes [s1 Bill can ride_____]]?

Any English sentence comparable in relevant ways to (41) will be ungrammatical. What are those "relevant" ways? There is just one difference between (41) and (40)—the latter of which was perfectly grammatical. The word *whether* occurs in the former, where *that* appears in the latter. *Whether* introduces a kind of question, and is in fact a special kind of *Wh*-word. It turns out that, in English, *Wh*-phrases, like *which horse* in (41), cannot be moved over a *Wh*-word. As suggested by the arrow in (41), this is precisely what would have to happen for this example to result from *Wh*-movement.

Now notice a very important implication of this fact. No child can learn that forms like (41) are ungrammatical by listening to the language around him. English speakers simply do not use these forms. There is no way, other than, for example, directly asking an adult, for a child to discover that the reason he never hears them is that they are ungrammatical, not part of the English language. Yet all of us know perfectly well that they are extremely bad: totally ungrammatical. And children have no tendency whatever to produce such forms as "mistakes." It is quite impossible that every child learning English is taught, explicitly, that such forms are not to be used; so the only possible explanation of the fact that we all feel them to be ungrammatical is that they are excluded by reason of some part of the inborn mechanism with which we approach the task of learning language. They reflect something quite deep, not learned but innate, which is part of our linguistic makeup.

As a matter of fact, the position is a little more complicated—and even more interesting. If no language permitted forms corresponding to (41), we might be inclined to say that the reason they are bad and never used by even children learning the language is that they simply make no sense. As speakers of English we are inclined to think that this is so. However, although many languages, including English, exclude forms like (41), there are others (those that form questions without making any use of *Wh*-movement) in which questions like (41) are perfectly well formed. Thus, despite our temptation, as native speakers of English, to think that such questions simply "make no sense," they not only make sense but are perfectly normal in languages that use slightly different constructions to form questions. (We can even approximate in English the meaning that [41] would have if it were grammatical, using a clumsy but grammatical sentence like *Of which horse is it true that Sue asked whether Sam believes Bill can ride it?*)

CONCLUSION

The structure of human languages is determined by the nature of the creatures that construct them: human children. Given this fact, we may hope to learn much of interest about human beings by examining the structure of their languages.

Human language consists of far more than just enormous collections of words; this is especially true if we think of words as limited to their meanings and sounds. Languages, including English, are highly structured, and words themselves are a part of that structure. English consists of sentences, which are built up around verbs, which in turn determine the kinds of phrases that make up the sentences. The structure of the sentences of a language is called the syntax of that language.

Every English sentence has a subject NP, but the verb determines what kinds of phrases must occur as its complement. Those phrases are generally NPs and PPs. The internal structure of NPs is determined (at least in part) by their head nouns—and in fact the structure of PPs is determined by the prepositions that head them, though we have not looked at these phrases in detail.

In English, but not, for example, in Warlpiri, word order largely determines the makeup of phrases. The grouping of words into phrases in basic English sentences can be modeled by a phrase structure grammar. There are, nevertheless, reasons for thinking that we do not store those basic patterns as a phrase structure grammar. Many aspects of language structure do not need to be learned. They are fixed, and a child merely has to determine, for example, the order of the verb and its direct object, or of the preposition/postposition and the NP that goes with it. It is these little language-specific facts about order, and not grammars consisting of rules, that have to be learned, and stored in the mind.

In addition to the basic sentence patterns that can be mimicked by a phrase structure grammar, there are patterns that involve the movement of constituents away from their basic positions. Many of these patterns probably do not have to be learned as separate rules. A child expects to find phenomena like *Wh*-movement in a language, and most of the characteristics of this phenomenon are universally constrained to follow set patterns. On the other hand, phenomena like the movement of the auxiliary in English may well have to be learned, assuming that they turn out not to follow solely from general linguistic principles in the way that *Wh*-movement does. There are idiosyncrasies in individual languages; the systematic study of syntax does not simply ignore them but attempts to set limits on them, at the same time concentrating on the universal principles that govern the structure of human language.

Although much remains to be learned about the syntax of human languages, some very significant facts have already been discovered, and syntactic research continues to throw new light on the nature of the mind.

FOR DISCUSSION AND REVIEW

1. Draw trees like those given in (20a–d) for the following sentences. As far as possible, use the same symbols as those used in the example trees (i.e., PP, N, NP, VP, and so on), but where you believe that a word does not fall into any of the classes with symbols given, feel free to invent new ones.
   a. Two beetles crawled over a little leaf.
   b. I can see several old men on the docks.
   c. The goats may eat your straw hat.
   d. Jane drove the new tractor into the barn.
   e. Someone may be asking for assistance.

2. a. Try to give detailed trees for the two interpretations discussed in the text for the string *I watched the prisoner from the tower*. That is, turn the marked sentences (3a and 3b) into proper tree representations. Your two trees should reflect the crucial differences between the two readings discussed in the text. (How should you represent *the prisoner from the tower* in [3a]?)
   b. Do the rules given in (21) provide for trees like those you have constructed? If not, how do the rules need to be modified to do so? (Concentrate on [3a] and consider rule [21d], which draws NP trees.)

3. Your college library has introductory grammar texts for many languages. Look at the grammar of a language unfamiliar to you, preferably one very different from English. Where does the verb occur in statements? (At the end? At the beginning?) What is the structure of the NP? (Where does the N come, the Adj, and so on?) Try to formulate simple phrase structure rules for parts of the language you choose, along the lines of (21a–d) in the text, but with the symbols in the right place to draw appropriate trees for sentences in the language you have chosen. Draw a few trees for this language. Discuss problems that arise in deciding what the rules and trees should be like and anything about language structure that this attempt has taught you.

4. Consider how information questions are formed in a language with which you are somewhat familiar. Use grammar books if necessary to supplement your knowledge, or ask a speaker of the language to help you find examples of these structures in it. Does the language use *Wh*-movement (as English does) for forming these questions? Give detailed arguments for or against your conclusion. (You will have to consider both the form of the questions and the form of ordinary statements in the language.)

5. Consider how far the development of language in children results from the imitation of what they hear and how far it results from factors that are purely internal to the children. Be as specific as possible in your discussion.

6. Summarize the structure of the grammar that, according to Professor Heny, English-speaking children must have internalized as a representation of their language. What kinds of "rules" does this grammar contain? Comment on aspects of sentence structure that seem to have been left out of this selection and that would need to be added for a complete account.

Projects for "Language Structures: Words and Phrases"

1. Using a dictionary published within the past ten years (a *Webster's Unabridged*, for example, or the *American Heritage*), choose a random collection of 100 words. First, divide each word into its morphemes. Then answer the following questions: Which words are derived by combining existing morphemes? Which are composed of a root with at least one derivational morpheme? Which have more than one prefix or more than one suffix? Which have been borrowed from another language? How many began with one meaning but now have a new meaning? How many began as one grammatical category but now have shifted to a new grammatical category? Have any been abbreviated or clipped in some way? Did any begin as an acronym but now exist as a free-standing word?

Once you have accounted for the formation of these words, use your data to write a brief paper discussing the various processes for creating or deriving words in a language. Based on the analysis of your word collection, which processes are more common? Keeping in mind the information in "The Minimal Units of Meaning: Morphemes" (pp. 147–56), discuss how derivational morphemes are used to form or derive new words.

2. Examine the following sentence: "These *foser glipses* have *volbicly merfed* and *wheeple* their *preebs.*"[1] Although you do not know the meaning of any of the italicized words—you can't answer questions like *How does one "merf"?* or *Are "glipses" good to eat?*—you still know a great deal about them.

What can you say about the morphological form of each word? What part of speech would you assign to each? What possible meanings does each word have? How does the structure of the whole sentence help you determine these meanings? How did you apply what you already know about language to these words, which you haven't seen before?

Give the sentence to three students who are not in your class. Ask them to answer the same questions, and then compare the results. How do the results differ? Did anyone use sound or spelling to determine possible meanings?

3. Make a list of ten to twenty acronyms (like *IMHO* or *radar*), blends (like *Panasonic* or *netiquette*), and clips, abbreviations, or shortenings (like *Mac, bot,* or *intel*). Exchange lists with classmates. Do the following with each item on the received list: First, use the item in a sentence. Then write an explanation or description of what the item means.

---

[1] This example comes from Kenneth G. Wilson, "English Grammars and the Grammar of English," which appears in the front matter of *Funk & Wagnalls Standard College Dictionary,* Text Edition (New York: Harcort, Brace & World, 1963).

Then "retrieve" the original words or morphemes used to create the item. Where you can't come up with the original source words, suggest words or morphemes that seem likely or might fit. As a final activity, use some of the "retrieved" morphemes to create three new words. Write definitions of each word based on its parts.

4. Using the three tables from Janet Romich's essay "Understanding Basic Medical Terminology," make a list of twenty medical terms. Then design a questionnaire asking participants to divide the twenty terms into morphemes and label each as a root, prefix, or suffix. Include a space where participants can indicate what they think the word means and what parts of the word lead them to that definition. Ask ten students who have not studied morphology to participate.

Then, analyze your data. How many participants could label and define the terms correctly? Were any terms analyzed correctly by all participants? On which morphemes did participants generally base their definitions? Tally the terms with correct definitions. What overall conclusions could you draw? How do people use their knowledge when faced with new terminology?

5. Below is a list of common derivational suffixes in English.

-al	-ent	-ful	-ness
-able	-ence	-less	-ous
-ly	-ion	-hood	-ist
-ity	-ive	-ize	-er/or

First, for each suffix, come up with three words used in daily, ordinary English. Then, for each word, determine the stem.

6. In "Mc-: Meaning in the Marketplace," Genine Lentine and Roger Shuy make the following statement: "When a trademark becomes so strong that it becomes the generic label for goods or services associated with another corporation, the owners of the trademark can still protect the mark from corporate use, but they have little influence over its use in everyday language." Choose a trademark that, in your opinion, has become generic. Then build a case that it has moved into the general vocabulary. To do so, collect real examples of generic use and interview speakers about the kinds of associations they make with this trademark. Try to incorporate the methodology of Lentine and Shuy, and write up your results in a report.

7. Working individually in class, read the following paragraph:

> The cook arrived home with a bag. In the bag were vegetables. The vegetables were fresh. In the bag was rice. In the bag were spices. The cook had a menu. The cook was happy. The cook had invited a friend for dinner. The friend loved to eat. The friend loved surprises. The friend had a birthday. The dinner was a surprise.

Without changing important words or information, revise this paragraph to eliminate the choppiness and to create a coherent narrative.

Then compare the revised versions written by other class members. Are the paragraphs alike? If not, what are the differences? How, if at all, do differences in sentence structure change meanings? Refer to Frank Heny's discussion of syntax to help explain how you and your classmates produced different meanings from the same set of sentences.

8. Review Frank Heny's "Syntax: The Structure of Sentences" and at least two other introductory sections on syntax in any of the linguistics textbooks listed in the bibliographies here in Part Three and in Part One. Make a list of what linguists focus on when they talk about analyzing the structure of sentences.

9. Record a sample of about ten minutes of speech that contains either extensive technological terminology or speech with a great deal of slang. (Consider taping part of a lecture or a casual discussion between your friends.) Transcribe the sample, and make a list of the technical or slang terms. Then do

- A morphological analysis: How are these words formed? What grammatical categories do they fit into, or what "part of speech" are they?

- A syntactic analysis: What sentence structures can you identify? Label them.

Selected Bibliography

Antony, Louise M., and Norbert Hornstein. *Chomsky and His Critics*. Malden, MA: Blackwell, 2003. [Ten scholars address Chomsky's work on mind and language.]

Barnhard, Robert K., and Sol Steinmetz, eds., *Chambers Dictionary of Etymology*. Edinburgh: Chambers, 1999. [A thorough and fascinating dictionary of the origins of words.]

Bauer, L. *Introducing Linguistic Morphology*. 2nd ed. Washington, D.C.: Georgetown UP, 2004. [A college-level text that addresses changes in word formations in human language.]

Bender, Bryon W. "Essays on Morphology." Dept. of Linguistics, U of Hawaii. <www2.hawaii.edu/~bender/toc.html>. [Collection includes specific focus on Latin inflections and irregularities.]

Berk, Lynn. *English Syntax: From Word to Discourse*. Oxford: Oxford UP, 1999. [Advanced text suitable for linguistics students and TESOL specialists.]

Burton-Roberts, Noël. *Analysing Sentences*. 2nd ed. London: Longman, 1997. [An introductory text on English syntax.]

"But There Are No Such Things as Words." 2006. The Lexiteria Corporation. <http://www.alphadictionary.com/articles/ling005.html>. [A discussion of morphemes that begins with Lewis Carroll's "Jabberwocky."]

"Can Colorless Green Ideas Sleep Furiously?" 2006. The Lexiteria Corporation. <www.alphadictionary.com/articles/ling003.html>. [This accessible article introduces the concept of semantics.]

Chomsky, Noam. "On *Wh*-Movement." *Formal Syntax*. Eds. Peter Culicover, Thomas Wasow, and Adrian Akamajian. New York: Academic Press, 1977. 77–132. [One of the landmark Chomsky studies.]

Coates, Richard. *Word Structure*. London: Routledge, 2000. [A straightforward introduction to morphology.]

Comrie, Bernard. *Aspect: An Introduction to the Study of Verbal Aspect and Related Problems*. Cambridge: Cambridge UP, 1976. [A study of aspectual systems.]

_____. *Tense*. Cambridge: Cambridge UP, 1985. [An introduction to tense systems in multiple languages.]

Cook, V. J., and Mark Newson. *Chomksy's Universal Grammar: An Introduction*. 2nd ed. Malden, MA: Blackwell, 1996. [An integration of Chomsky's theory with recent developments in linguistic study.]

Freivalds, John. "What's in a Name? (Product Names)." *Communication World* 13 (1996): 7–30. [Interesting look at how businesses name products for best effect.]

Greenbaum, Sidney, and Randolph Quirk. *A Student's Grammar of the English Language*. White Plains, NY: Longman, 1990. [Particularly useful to ESL students and teachers.]

Harper, Douglas. *Etymology Dictionary Online*. November 2001. <www.etymonline.com>. [An extensive online word origin resource.]

Haspelmath, Martin. *Understanding Morphology*. Scarborough, ON: Arnold, 2002. [A broad introduction to morphology suitable for beginners.]

Haspelmath, Martin, Matthew S. Dryer, David Gil, and Bernard Comrie, eds. *World Atlas of Language Structures*. New York: Oxford UP, USA, 2005. [Offers a thorough depiction of language structures.]

Huddleston, Rodney, and Geoffrey Pullum. *The Cambridge Grammar of the English Language*. Cambridge: Cambridge UP, 2002. [Solid reference book with careful consideration of language issues.]

Hudson, Richard A. *English Word Grammar*. Oxford: Basil Blackwell, 1990. [A thought-provoking look at grammar and word usage.]

Jackendoff, Ray. *Foundations of Language: Brain, Meaning, Grammar, Evolution*. Oxford: Oxford UP, 2002. [A reinterpretation of Chomsky's theory of universal grammar.]

Klammer, Thomas, Muriel Schultz, and Angela Della Volpe. *Analyzing English Grammar*. 4th ed. White Plains, NY: Longman, 2003. [Combines applications of linguistics theory and learning theory.]

Matthews, Peter H. *Morphology*. 2nd ed. Cambridge: Cambridge UP, 1991. [A significantly revised update of the 1974 first edition.]

Metcalf, Allan. *Predicting New Words: The Secrets of Their Success*. Boston: Houghton Mifflin, 2002. [An engaging look at word and phrase origins.]

Michaelsen, Ove. "Neologisms for the New Millennium." *Word Ways* 37 (2004): 150. [Clever excerpt from Michaelsen's book *Verboddities*.]

Morenberg, Max. *Doing Grammar*. 3rd ed. Oxford: Oxford UP, 2002. [A contemporary approach to grammar within the context of traditional models.]

Shopen, Timothy, ed. *Language Typology and Syntactic Description: Grammatical Categories and the Lexicon*. Vol. 3. Cambridge: Cambridge UP, 1985. 3 vols. [A survey of syntax and morphology in various languages.]

Shuy, Roger. "Discourse Analysis in a Legal Context." *The Handbook of Discourse Analysis*. Eds. Deborah Shiffren, Deborah Tannen, and Heidi E. Hamilton. Malden, MA: Blackwell, 2001. 437–52. [A fascinating look at how language shapes and affects legal proceedings.]

Shuy, Roger. "From Spam to McDonald's in the Trademark Wars." 13 October 2006. *Language Log*. Web log. Geoff Pullum and Mark Lieberman. U Pennsylvania. <http://itre.cis.upenn.edu/~myl/languagelog/archives/003670.html>. [Excellent and insightful discussion about possible trademark infringement over use of "spam," with comparisons to the *Mc*-trademark case.]

Spencer, Andrew, and Arnold N. Zwicky. *The Handbook of Morphology*. Oxford: Blackwell, 1998. [An extensive look at issues in morphology.]

Tallerman, Maggie. *Understanding Syntax*. 2nd ed. London: Arnold, 2005. [Illustrates major concepts in the study of language.]

yourDictionary.com. 2007. yourDictionary.com, Inc. <www.yourdictionary.com>. [Free online dictionary and thesaurus with multilingual resources and a word-of-the-day feature.]

LANGUAGE MEANING
AND LANGUAGE USE

For many of us, meaning is at the heart of language. In Part Four, we investigate what meaning is, suggest explanations for our ability to communicate meaning, and identify the important social contexts and behaviors that affect how we make meaning. The study of meaning is usually divided into semantics and pragmatics. *Semantics* is concerned with the meaning of individual words and how they work in phrases and sentences. *Pragmatics* focuses on how speakers use meaning in specific contexts.

In the first essay, "The Tower of Babel," contemporary linguist Steven Pinker asks one of the oldest and most intriguing questions about humans and language: if humans are born to communicate with language, why do so many languages exist, most so different that the speakers of one can't understand speakers of another? In answer, Pinker suggests that beneath the surface differences among languages are the many precise rules of "Universal Grammar," and he demonstrates that the ways languages differ are trivial compared to their profound structural similarities.

In "Bad Bird and Better Birds: Prototype Theories," Jean Aitchison investigates how we can communicate when we have difficulty establishing exact meanings for the most common words and utterances. Every language includes ambiguity, contradiction, and redundancy; yet, we understand each other. The reason, Aitchison argues, is that meaning relies on how we classify the words we use. Drawing on such word categories as birds, vegetables, furniture, and lies, Aitchison shows "how people are able to cope with word meaning when it is so fuzzy and fluid."

In the next essay, "Pinning Down Semantics," Howard Gregory describes everyday language meaning as something that is built up, layer on layer. Although a word or phrase refers to *something*, Gregory points out that more abstract considerations are also crucial to understanding. For instance, we need to pay attention to the categories of information a word conveys, its various denotations, and whether an expression is true or false in a given situation.

The last two selections in Part Four deal with pragmatics, whereby we look at language as a social phenomenon. In other words, we pay attention to who the speakers and listeners are, their relationships with each other, their goals and preconceived ideas, and, especially, to the discourse itself.

In "Pragmatics," Elaine Chaika examines the social rules of discourse that largely control what we say and how we say it. Her discussion and examples of numerous discourse routines—such as greetings, questions, commands, and compliments—point out the significance of discourse rules in everyday transactions. Indeed, without such routines we may not consider ourselves social beings.

The final essay, Ronald Wardhaugh's "Talk and Action," explains how we use speech to accomplish a range of activities. According to Speech Act theory, when we speak about something, we are doing something as well. For instance, when a police officer says, "You are under arrest," you are no longer free to go home. This is a fairly obvious example, but Wardhaugh also discusses less direct speech acts. For instance, the statement "I'm almost out of gasoline" might imply a question as to where the nearest gas station is or a request for money. Wardhaugh concludes his essay by examining the various ways conversation is cooperative.

14

The Tower of Babel

Steven Pinker

All humans have at least one language, and the number of languages that have existed is vast. How did languages evolve? Are they descendants of a single prototypical language, or did they emerge spontaneously in different parts of the world as the result of a human instinct? How much of a given language is learned after birth, and how much is part of human biology? In the following essay, Steven Pinker, Johnstone Family Professor at Harvard, examines these and other questions about the multiple forms of language. He also identifies the rules of a "Universal Grammar" languages share. This selection is excerpted from Pinker's 1994 book, The Language Instinct: How the Mind Creates Languages, *in which he famously popularized the notion that linguistic capabilities grew out of the process of evolution.*

> And the whole earth was of one language, and of one speech. And it came to pass, as they journeyed from the east, that they found a plain in the land of Shinar; and they dwelt there. And they said one to another, Go to, let us make brick, and burn them thoroughly. And they had brick for stone, and slime had they for mortar. And they said, Go to, let us build us a city and a tower, whose top may reach unto heaven; and let us make us a name, lest we be scattered abroad upon the face of the whole earth. And the Lord came down to see the city and the tower, which the children of men builded. And the Lord said, Behold, the people is one, and they have all one language; and this they begin to do: and now nothing will be restrained from them, which they have imagined to do. Go to, let us go down, and there confound their language, that they may not understand one another's speech. So the Lord scattered them abroad from thence upon the face of all the earth: and they left off to build the city. Therefore is the name of it called Babel; because the Lord did there confound the language of all the earth: and from thence did the Lord scatter them abroad upon the face of all the earth. (Genesis 11:1–9)

In the year of our Lord 1957, the linguist Martin Joos reviewed the preceding three decades of research in linguistics and concluded that God had actually gone much farther in confounding the language of Noah's descendants. Whereas the God of Genesis was said to be content with mere mutual unintelligibility, Joos declared that "languages could differ from each other without limit and in unpredictable ways." That same year, the Chomskyan revolution began with the publication of *Syntactic Structures*, and the next three decades took us back to the literal biblical account. According to Chomsky, a visiting Martian scientist would surely conclude that aside from their mutually unintelligible vocabularies, Earthlings speak a single language.

Even by the standards of theological debates, these interpretations are strikingly different. Where did they come from? The 4,000 to 6,000 languages of the planet do look impressively different from English and from one another. Here are the most conspicuous ways in which languages can differ from what we are used to in English:

1. English is an "isolating" language, which builds sentences by rearranging immutable word-sized units, like *Dog bites man* and *Man bites dog*. Other languages express who did what to whom by modifying nouns with case affixes, or by modifying the verb with affixes that agree with its role-players in number, gender, and person. One example is Latin, an "inflecting" language in which each affix contains several pieces of information; another is Kivunjo, an "agglutinating" language in which each affix conveys one piece of information and many affixes are strung together.

2. English is a "fixed-word-order" language where each phrase has a fixed position. "Free-word-order" languages allow phrase order to vary. In an extreme case like the Australian aboriginal language Warlpiri, words from different phrases can be scrambled together: *This man speared a kangaroo* can be expressed as *Man this kangaroo speared*, *Man kangaroo speared this*, and any of the other four orders, all completely synonymous.

3. English is an "accusative" language, where the subject of an intransitive verb, like *she* in *She ran*, is treated identically to the subject of a transitive verb, like *she* in *She kissed Larry*, and different from the object of the transitive verb, like *her* in *Larry kissed her*. "Ergative" languages like Basque and many Australian languages have a different scheme for collapsing these three roles. The subject of an intransitive verb and the *object* of a transitive verb are identical, and the subject of the transitive is the one that behaves differently. It is as if we were to say *Ran her* to mean "She ran."

4. English is a "subject-prominent" language in which all sentences must have a subject (even if there is nothing for the subject to refer to, as in *It is raining* or *There is a unicorn in the garden*). In "topic-prominent" languages like Japanese, sentences have a special position that is filled by the current topic of the conversation, as in *This place, planting wheat is good* or *California, climate is good*.

5. English is an "SVO" language, with the order subject-verb-object (*Dog bites man*). Japanese is subject-object-verb (SOV: *Dog man bites*); Modern Irish (Gaelic) is verb-subject-object (VSO: *Bites dog man*).

6. In English, a noun can name a thing in any construction: *a banana; two bananas; any banana; all the bananas.* In "classifier" languages, nouns fall into gender classes like human, animal, inanimate, one-dimensional, two-dimensional, cluster, tool, food, and so on. In many constructions, the name for the class, not the noun itself, must be used—for example, three hammers would be referred to as *three tools, to wit hammer.*

And, of course, a glance at a grammar for any particular language will reveal dozens or hundreds of idiosyncrasies.

On the other hand, one can also hear striking universals through the babble. In 1963 the linguist Joseph Greenberg examined a sample of thirty far-flung languages from five continents, including Serbian, Italian, Basque, Finnish, Swahili, Nubian, Masaai, Berber, Turkish, Hebrew, Hindi, Japanese, Burmese, Malay, Maori, Mayan, and Quechua (a descendant of the language of the Incas). Greenberg was not working in the Chomskyan school; he just wanted to see if any interesting properties of grammar could be found in all these languages. In his first investigation, which focused on the order of words and morphemes, he found no fewer than forty-five universals.

Since then, many other surveys have been conducted, involving scores of languages from every part of the world, and literally hundreds of universal patterns have been documented. Some hold absolutely. For example, no language forms questions by reversing the order of words within a sentence, like *Built Jack that house the this is?* Some are statistical: subjects normally precede objects in almost all languages, and verbs and their objects tend to be adjacent. Thus most languages have SVO or SOV order; fewer have VSO; VOS and OVS are rare (less than 1%); and OSV may be nonexistent (there are a few candidates, but not all linguists agree that they are OSV). The largest number of universals involves implications: if a language has X, it will also have Y. If the basic order of a language is SOV, it will usually have question words at the end of the sentence, and postpositions; if it is SVO, it will have question words at the beginning, and prepositions. Universal implications are found in all aspects of language, from phonology (for instance, if a language has nasal vowels, it will have non-nasal vowels) to word meanings (if a language has a word for "purple," it will have a word for "red"; if a language has a word for "leg," it will have a word for "arm").

If lists of universals show that languages do not vary freely, do they imply that languages are restricted by the structure of the brain? Not directly. First one must rule out two alternative explanations.

One possibility is that language originated only once, and all existing languages are the descendants of that proto-language and retain some of its features. These features would be similar across the languages for the same reason that alphabetical order is similar across the Hebrew, Greek, Roman, and Cyrillic alphabets. There is nothing special about alphabetical order; it was just the order that the Canaanites invented, and all

Western alphabets came from theirs. No linguist accepts this as an explanation for language universals. For one thing, there can be radical breaks in language transmission across the generations, the most extreme being creolization, but universals hold for all languages including creoles. Moreover, simple logic shows that a universal implication, like "If a language has SVO order, then it has prepositions, but if it has SOV order, then it has postpositions," cannot be transmitted from parent to child the way words are. An implication, by its very logic, is not a fact about English: children could learn that English is SVO *and* has prepositions, but nothing could show them that *if* a language is SVO, *then* it must have prepositions. A universal implication is a fact about all languages, visible only from the vantage point of a comparative linguist. If a language changes from SOV to SVO over the course of history and its postpositions flip to prepositions, there has to be some explanation of what keeps these two developments in sync.

Also, if universals were simply what is passed down through the generations, we would expect that the major differences between kinds of language should correlate with the branches of the linguistic family tree, just as the difference between two cultures generally correlates with how long ago they separated. As humanity's original language differentiated over time, some branches might become SOV and others SVO; within each of these branches some might have agglutinated words, others isolated words. But this is not so. Beyond a time depth of about a thousand years, history and typology often do not correlate well at all. Languages can change from grammatical type to type relatively quickly, and can cycle among a few types over and over; aside from vocabulary, they do not progressively differentiate and diverge. For example, English has changed from a free-word-order, highly inflected, topic-prominent language, as its sister German remains to this day, to a fixed-word-order, poorly inflected, subject-prominent language, all in less than a millennium. Many language families contain close to the full gamut of variations seen across the world in particular aspects of grammar. The absence of a strong correlation between the grammatical properties of languages and their place in the family tree of languages suggests that language universals are not just the properties that happen to have survived from the hypothetical mother of all languages.

The second counterexplanation that one must rule out before attributing a universal of language to a universal language instinct is that languages might reflect universals of thought or of mental information processing that are not specific to language. Universals of color vocabulary probably come from universals of color vision. Perhaps subjects precede objects because the subject of an action verb denotes the causal agent (as in *Dog bites man*); putting the subject first mirrors the cause coming before the effect. Perhaps head-first or head-last ordering is consistent across all the phrases in a language because it enforces a consistent branching direction, right or left, in the language's phrase structure trees, avoiding difficult-to-understand onion constructions. For example, Japanese is SOV and has modifiers to the left; this gives it constructions like "modifier-SOV" with the modifier on the outside rather than "S-modifier OV" with the modifier embedded inside.

But these functional explanations are often tenuous, and for many universals they do not work at all. For example, Greenberg noted that if a language has both derivational suffixes (which create new words from old ones) and inflectional suffixes (which modify a word to fit its role in the sentence), then the derivational suffixes are always closer to the stem than the inflectional ones. We see this principle in English in the difference between the grammatical *Darwinisms* and the ungrammatical *Darwinsism*. It is hard to think of how this law could be a consequence of any universal principle of thought or memory: why would the concept of two ideologies based on one Darwin be thinkable, but the concept of one ideology based on two Darwins (say, Charles and Erasmus) not be thinkable (unless one reasons in a circle and declares that the mind must find *-ism* to be more cognitively basic than the plural, because that's the order we see in language)? And keep in mind Peter Gordon's experiments showing that children say *mice-eater* but never *rats-eater*, despite the conceptual similarity of rats and mice and despite the absence of either kind of compound in parents' speech. His results corroborate the suggestion that this particular universal is caused by the way that morphological rules are computed in the brain, with inflection applying to the products of derivation but not vice versa.

In any case, Greenbergisms are not the best place to look for a neurologically given Universal Grammar that existed before Babel. It is the organization of grammar as a whole, not some laundry list of facts, that we should be looking at. Arguing about the possible causes of something like SVO order misses the forest for the trees. What is most striking of all is that we can look at a randomly picked language and find things that can sensibly be called subjects, objects, and verbs to begin with. After all, if we were asked to look for the order of subject, object, and verb in musical notation, or in the computer programming language FORTRAN, or in Morse code, or in arithmetic, we would protest that the very idea is nonsensical. It would be like assembling a representative collection of the world's cultures from the six continents and trying to survey the colors of their hockey team jerseys or the form of their harakiri rituals. We should be impressed, first and foremost, that research on universals of grammar is even possible!

When linguists claim to find the same kinds of linguistic gadgets in language after language, it is not just because they expect languages to have subjects and so they label as a "subject" the first kind of phrase they see that resembles an English subject. Rather, if a linguist examining a language for the first time calls a phrase a "subject" using one criterion based on English subjects—say, denoting the agent role of action verbs— the linguist soon discovers that other criteria, like agreeing with the verb in person and number and occurring before the object, will be true of that phrase as well. It is these *correlations* among the properties of a linguistic thingamabob across languages that make it scientifically meaningful to talk about subjects and objects and nouns and verbs and auxiliaries and inflections—and not just Word Class #2,783 and Word Class #1,491—in languages from Abaza to Zyrian.

Chomsky's claim that from a Martian's-eye-view all humans speak a single language is based on the discovery that the same symbol-manipulating machinery, without exception, underlies the world's languages. Linguists have long known that the basic design features of language are found everywhere. Many were documented in 1960 by the non-Chomskyan linguist C. F. Hockett in a comparison between human languages and animal communication systems (Hockett was not acquainted with Martian). Languages use the mouth-to-ear channel as long as the users have intact hearing (manual and facial gestures, of course, are the substitute channel used by the deaf). A common grammatical code, neutral between production and comprehension, allows speakers to produce any linguistic message they can understand, and vice versa. Words have stable meanings, linked to them by arbitrary convention. Speech sounds are treated discontinuously; a sound that is acoustically halfway between *bat* and *pat* does not mean something halfway between batting and patting. Languages can convey meanings that are abstract and remote in time or space from the speaker. Linguistic forms are infinite in number, because they are created by a discrete combinatorial system. Languages all show a duality of patterning in which one rule system is used to order phonemes within morphemes, independent of meaning, and another is used to order morphemes within words and phrases, specifying their meaning.

Chomskyan linguistics, in combination with Greenbergian surveys, allows us to go well beyond this basic spec sheet. All languages have a vocabulary in the thousands or tens of thousands, sorted into part-of-speech categories including noun and verb. Words are organized into phrases according to the X-bar system (nouns are found inside N-bars, which are found inside noun phrases, and so on). The higher levels of phrase structure include auxiliaries (INFL), which signify tense, modality, aspect, and negation. Nouns are marked for case and assigned semantic roles by the mental dictionary entry of the verb or other predicate. Phrases can be moved from their deep-structure positions, leaving a gap or "trace," by a structure-dependent movement rule, thereby forming questions, relative clauses, passives, and other widespread constructions. New word structures can be created and modified by derivational and inflectional rules. Inflectional rules primarily mark nouns for case and number, and mark verbs for tense, aspect, mood, voice, negation, and agreement with subjects and objects in number, gender, and person. The phonological forms of words are defined by metrical and syllable trees and separate tiers of features like voicing, tone, and manner and place of articulation, and are subsequently adjusted by ordered phonological rules. Though many of these arrangements are in some sense useful, their details, found in language after language but not in any artificial system like FORTRAN or musical notation, give a strong impression that a Universal Grammar, not reducible to history or cognition, underlies the human language instinct.

God did not have to do much to confound the language of Noah's descendants. In addition to vocabulary—whether the word for "mouse" is *mouse* or *souris*—a few properties of language are simply not specified in Universal Grammar and can vary as parameters. For example, it is up to each language to choose whether the order of elements within a phrase is head-first or head-last (*eat sushi* and *to Chicago* versus *sushi eat* and *Chicago to*) and whether a subject is mandatory in all sentences or can be omitted when the speaker desires. Furthermore, a particular grammatical widget often does a great deal of important work in one language and hums away unobtrusively in the corner of another. The overall impression is that Universal Grammar is like an archetypal body plan found across vast numbers of animals in a phylum. For example, among all the amphibians, reptiles, birds, and mammals, there is a common body architecture, with a segmented backbone, four jointed limbs, a tail, a skull, and so on. The various parts can be grotesquely distorted or stunted across animals: a bat's wing is a hand, a horse trots on its middle toes, whales' forelimbs have become flippers and their hindlimbs have shrunken to invisible nubs, and the tiny hammer, anvil, and stirrup of the mammalian middle ear are jaw parts of reptiles. But from newts to elephants, a common topology of the body plan—the shin bone connected to the thigh bone, the thigh bone connected to the hip bone—can be discerned. Many of the differences are caused by minor variations in the relative timing and rate of growth of the parts during embryonic development. Differences among languages are similar. There seems to be a common plan of syntactic, morphological, and phonological rules and principles, with a small set of varying parameters, like a checklist of options. Once set, a parameter can have far-reaching changes on the superficial appearance of the language.

If there is a single plan just beneath the surfaces of the world's languages, then any basic property of one language should be found in all the others. Let's reexamine the six supposedly un-English language traits that opened the chapter. A closer look shows that all of them can be found right here in English, and that the supposedly distinctive traits of English can be found in the other languages.

1. English, like the inflecting languages it supposedly differs from, has an agreement marker, the third person singular -*s* in *He walks*. It also has case distinctions in the pronouns, such as *he* versus *him*. And like agglutinating languages, it has machinery that can glue many bits together into a long word, like the derivational rules and affixes that create *sensationalization* and

Darwinianisms. Chinese is supposed to be an even more extreme example of an isolating language than English, but it, too, contains rules that create multipart words such as compounds and derivatives.

2. English, like free-word-order languages, has free ordering in strings of prepositional phrases, where each preposition marks the semantic role of its noun phrase as if it were a case marker: *The package was sent from Chicago to Boston by Mary; The package was sent by Mary to Boston from Chicago; The package was sent to Boston from Chicago by Mary*, and so on. Conversely, in so-called scrambling languages at the other extreme, like Warlpiri, word order is never completely free; auxiliaries, for example, must go in the second position in a sentence, which is rather like their positioning in English.

3. English, like ergative languages, marks a similarity between the objects of transitive verbs and the subjects of intransitive verbs. Just compare *John broke the glass* (glass = object) with *The glass broke* (glass = subject of intransitive), or *Three men arrived* with *There arrived three men*.

4. English, like topic-prominent languages, has a topic constituent in constructions like *As for fish, I eat salmon* and *John I never really liked*.

5. Like SOV languages, not too long ago English availed itself of an SOV order, which is still interpretable in archaic expressions like *Till death do us part* and *With this ring I thee wed*.

6. Like classifier languages, English insists upon classifiers for many nouns: you can't refer to a single square as *a paper* but must say *a sheet of paper*. Similarly, English speakers say *a piece of fruit* (which refers to an apple, not a piece of an apple), *a blade of grass*, *a stick of wood*, *fifty head of cattle*, and so on.

If a Martian scientist concludes that humans speak a single language, that scientist might well wonder why Earthspeak has those thousands of mutually unintelligible dialects (assuming that the Martian has not read Genesis 11; perhaps Mars is beyond the reach of the Gideon Society). If the basic plan of language is innate and fixed across the species, why not the whole banana? Why the head-first parameter, the different-sized color vocabularies, the Boston accent?

Terrestrial scientists have no conclusive answer. The theoretical physicist Freeman Dyson proposed that linguistic diversity is here for a reason: "it was nature's way to make it possible for us to evolve rapidly," by creating isolated ethnic groups in which undiluted biological and cultural evolution can proceed swiftly. But Dyson's evolutionary reasoning is defective. Lacking foresight, lineages try to be the best that they can be, *now*; they do not initiate change for change's sake on the chance that one of the changes might come in handy in some ice age ten thousand years in the future. Dyson is not the first to ascribe a purpose to linguistic diversity. A Colombian Bará Indian, a member of an outbreeding set of tribes, when asked by a linguist why there were so many languages, explained, "If we were all Tukano speakers, where would we get our women?"

As a native of Quebec, I can testify that differences in language lead to differences in ethnic identification, with widespread effects, good and bad. But the suggestions of Dyson and the Bará put the causal arrow backwards. Surely head-first parameters and all the rest represent massive overkill in some design to distinguish among ethnic groups, assuming that that was even evolutionarily desirable. Humans are ingenious at sniffing out minor differences to figure out whom they should despise. All it takes is that European/Americans have light skin and African Americans have dark skin, that Hindus make a point of not eating beef and Moslems make a point of not eating pork, or, in the Dr. Seuss story, that the Star-Bellied Sneetches have bellies with stars and the Plain-Bellied Sneetches have none upon "thars." Once there is more than one language, ethnocentrism can do the rest; we need to understand why there is more than one language.

Darwin himself expressed the key insight:

> The formation of different languages and of distinct species, and the proofs that both have been developed through a gradual process, are curiously parallel. . . . We find in distinct languages striking homologies due to community of descent, and analogies due to a similar process of formation. . . . Languages, like organic beings, can be classed in groups under groups; and they can be classed either naturally, according to descent, or artificially by other characters. Dominant languages and dialects spread widely, and lead to the gradual extinction of other tongues. A language, like a species, when extinct, never . . . reappears.

That is, English is similar though not identical to German for the same reason that foxes are similar though not identical to wolves: English and German are modifications of a common ancestor language spoken in the past, and foxes and wolves are modifications of a common ancestor species that lived in the past. Indeed, Darwin claimed to have taken some of his ideas about biological evolution from the linguistics of his time.

Differences among languages, like differences among species, are the effects of three processes acting over long spans of time. One process is variation—mutation, in the case of species; linguistic innovation, in the case of languages. The second is heredity, so that descendants resemble their progenitors in these variations—genetic inheritance, in the case of species; the ability to learn, in the case of languages. The third is isolation—by geography, breeding season, or reproductive anatomy, in the case of species; by migration or social barriers, in the case of languages. In both cases, isolated populations accumulate separate sets of variations and hence diverge over time. To understand why there is more than one language, then, we must understand the effects of innovation, learning, and migration.

Let me begin with the ability to learn, and by convincing you that there is something to explain. Many social scientists believe that learning is some pinnacle of evolution that humans have scaled from the lowlands of instinct, so that our ability to learn can be explained by our exalted braininess. But biology says otherwise. Learning is found in organisms as simple as bacteria, and, as James and Chomsky pointed out, human intelligence may depend on our having *more* innate instincts, not fewer. Learning is an option, like camouflage or horns, that nature gives organisms as needed—when some aspect of the organisms' environmental niche is so unpredictable that anticipation of its contingencies cannot be wired in. For example, birds that nest on small cliff ledges do not learn to recognize their offspring. They do not need to, for any blob of the right size and shape in their nest is sure to be one. Birds that nest in large colonies, in contrast, are in danger of feeding some neighbor's offspring that sneaks in, and they have evolved a mechanism that allows them to learn the particular nuances of their own babies.

Even when a trait starts off as a product of learning, it does not have to remain so. Evolutionary theory, supported by computer simulations, has shown that when an environment is stable, there is a selective pressure for learned abilities to become increasingly innate. That is because if an ability is innate, it can be deployed earlier in the lifespan of the creature, and there is less of a chance that an unlucky creature will miss out on the experiences that would have been necessary to teach it.

Why might it pay for the child to learn parts of a language rather than having the whole system hard-wired? For vocabulary, the benefits are fairly obvious: 60,000 words might be too many to evolve, store, and maintain in a genome comprising only 50,000 to 100,000 genes. And words for new plants, animals, tools, and especially people are needed throughout the lifespan. But what good is it to learn different grammars? No one knows, but here are some plausible hypotheses.

Perhaps some of the things about language that we have to learn are easily learned by simple mechanisms that antedated the evolution of grammar. For example, a simple kind of learning circuit might suffice to record which element comes before which other one, as long as the elements are first defined and identified by some other cognitive module. If a universal grammar module defines a head and a role-player, their relative ordering (head-first or head-last) could thus be recorded easily. If so, evolution, having made the basic computational units of language innate, may have seen no need to replace every bit of learned information with innate wiring. Computer simulations of evolution show that the pressure to replace learned neural connections with innate ones diminishes as more and more of the network becomes innate, because it becomes less and less likely that learning will fail for the rest.

A second reason for language to be partly learned is that language inherently involves sharing a code with other people. An innate grammar is useless if you are the only one possessing it: it is a tango of one, the sound of one hand clapping. But the genomes of other people mutate and drift and recombine when they have children. Rather than selecting for a completely innate grammar, which would soon fall out of register with everyone else's, evolution may have given children an ability to learn the variable parts of language as a way of synchronizing their grammars with that of the community.

The second component of language differentiation is a source of variation. Some person, somewhere, must begin to speak differently from the neighbors, and the innovation must spread and catch on like a contagious disease until it becomes epidemic, at which point children perpetuate it. Change can arise from many sources. Words are coined, borrowed from other languages, stretched in meaning, and forgotten. New jargon or speech styles may sound way cool within some subculture and then infiltrate the mainstream. Specific examples of these borrowings are a subject of fascination to pop language fanciers and fill many books and columns. Personally, I have trouble getting excited. Should we really be astounded to learn that English borrowed *kimono* from Japanese, *banana* from Spanish, *moccasin* from the American Indians, and so on?

Because of the language instinct, there is something much more fascinating about linguistic innovation: each link in the chain of language transmission is a human brain. That brain is equipped with a universal grammar and is always on the lookout for examples in ambient speech of various kinds of rules. Because speech can be sloppy and words and sentences ambiguous, people are occasionally apt to *reanalyze* the speech they hear—they interpret it as having come from a different dictionary entry or rule than the ones that the speaker actually used.

A simple example is the word *orange*. Originally it was *norange*, borrowed from the Spanish *naranjo*. But at some point some unknown creative speaker must have reanalyzed *a norange* as *an orange*. Though the speaker's and hearer's analyses specify identical sounds for that particular phrase, *anorange*, once the hearer uses the rest of grammar creatively, the change becomes audible, as in *those oranges* rather than *those noranges*. (This particular change has been common in English. Shakespeare used *nuncle* as an affectionate name, a recutting of *mine Uncle* to *my nuncle*, and *Ned* came from *Edward* by a similar route. Nowadays many people talk about *a whole nother thing*, and I know of a child who eats *ectarines* and an adult called *Nalice* who refers to people she doesn't care for as *nidiots*.)

Reanalysis, a product of the discrete combinatorial creativity of the language instinct, partly spoils the analogy between language change on the one hand and biological and cultural evolution on the other. Many linguistic innovations are not like random mutation, drift, erosion, or borrowing. They are more like legends or jokes that are embellished or improved or reworked with each retelling. That is why, although grammars change quickly through history, they do not degenerate, for reanalysis is an inexhaustible source of new complexity. Nor must they progressively differentiate, for grammars can hop among the grooves made available by the universal grammar in everyone's mind. Moreover, one change in a language can cause an imbalance that can trigger a cascade of other changes elsewhere, like falling dominoes. Any part of language can change:

• Many phonological rules arose when hearers in some community reanalyzed rapid, coarticulated speech. Imagine a dialect that lacks the rule that converts *t* to a flapped *d* in *utter*. Its speakers generally pronounce the *t* as a *t*, but may not do so when speaking rapidly or affecting a casual "lazy" style. Hearers may then credit them with a flapping rule, and they (or their children) would then pronounce the *t* as a flap even in careful speech. Taken further, even the underlying phonemes can be reanalyzed. This is how we got *v*. Old English didn't have a *v*; our word *starve* was originally *steorfan*. But any *f* between two vowels was pronounced with voicing turned on, so *ofer* was pronounced "over," thanks to a rule similar to the contemporary flapping rule. Listeners eventually analyzed the *v* as a separate phoneme, rather than as a pronunciation of *f*, so now the word actually is *over*, and *v* and *f* are available as separate phonemes. For example, we can now differentiate words like *waver* and *wafer*, but King Arthur could not have.

• The phonological rules governing the *pronunciation* of words can, in turn, be reanalyzed into morphological rules governing the *construction* of them. Germanic languages like Old English had an "umlaut" rule that changed a back vowel to a front vowel if the next syllable contained a high front vowel sound. For example, in *foti*, the plural of "foot," the back *o* was altered by the rule to a front *e*, harmonizing with the front *i*. Subsequently the *i* at the end ceased being pronounced, and because the phonological rule no longer had anything to trigger it, speakers reinterpreted the *o–e* shift as a morphological relationship signaling the plural—resulting in our *foot–feet, mouse–mice, goose–geese, tooth–teeth,* and *louse–lice.*

• Reanalysis can also take two variants of one word, one created from the other by an inflectional rule, and recategorize them as separate words. The speakers of yesteryear might have noticed that an inflectional *oo–ee* rule applies not to all items but only to a few: *tooth–teeth*, but not *booth–beeth*. So *teeth* was interpreted as a separate, irregular word linked to *tooth*, rather than the product of a rule applied to *tooth*. The vowel change no longer acts like a rule—hence Lederer's humorous story "Foxen in the Henhice." Other sets of vaguely related words came into English by this route, like *brother–brethren, half–halve, teeth–teethe, to fall–to fell, to rise–to raise*; even *wrought,* which used to be the past tense of *work.*

• Other morphological rules can be formed when the words that commonly accompany some other word get eroded and then glued onto it. Tense markers may come from auxiliaries; for example, the English *-ed* suffix may have evolved from *did: hammer-did → hammered.* Case markers may come from slurred prepositions or from sequences of verbs (for example, in a language that allows the construction *take nail hit it, take* might erode into an accusative case marker like *ta-*). Agreement markers can arise from pronouns: in *John, he kissed her, he* and *her* can eventually glom onto the verb as agreement affixes.

• Syntactic constructions can arise when a word order that is merely preferred becomes reanalyzed as obligatory. For example, when English had case markers, either *give him a book* or *give a book him* were possible, but the former was more common. When the case markers eroded in casual speech, many sentences would have become ambiguous if order were still allowed to vary. The more common order was thus enshrined as a rule of syntax. Other constructions can arise from multiple reanalyses. The English perfect *I had written a book* originally came from *I had a book written* (meaning "I owned a book that was written"). The reanalysis was inviting because the SOV pattern was alive in English; the participle *written* could be reanalyzed as the main verb of the sentence, and *had* could be reanalyzed as its auxiliary, begetting a new analysis with a related meaning.

The third ingredient for language splitting is separation among groups of speakers, so that successful innovations do not take over everywhere but accumulate separately in the different groups. Though people modify their language every generation, the extent of these changes is slight: vastly more sounds are preserved than mutated, more constructions analyzed properly than reanalyzed. Because of this overall conservatism, some patterns of vocabulary, sound, and grammar survive for millennia. They serve as the fossilized tracks of mass migrations in the remote past, clues to how human beings spread out over the earth to end up where we find them today.

How far back can we trace the language of this book, modern American English? Surprisingly far, perhaps five or even nine thousand years. Our knowledge of where our language has come from is considerably more precise than the recollection of Dave Barry's Mr. Language Person: "The English language is a rich verbal tapestry woven together from the tongues of the Greeks, the Latins, the Angles, the Klaxtons, the Celtics, and many more other ancient peoples, all of whom had severe drinking problems." Let's work our way back.

America and England first came to be divided by a common language, in Wilde's memorable words, when colonists and immigrants isolated themselves from British speech by crossing the Atlantic Ocean. England was already a Babel of regional and class dialects when the first colonists left. What was to become the standard American dialect was seeded by the ambitious or dissatisfied members of lower and middle classes from southeastern England. By the eighteenth century an American accent was noted, and pronunciation in the American South was particularly influenced by the immigration of the Ulster Scots. Westward expansions preserved the layers of dialects of the eastern seaboard, though the farther west the pioneers went, the more their dialects mixed, especially in California, which required leapfrogging of the vast interior desert. Because of immigration, mobility, literacy, and now the mass media, the English of the United States, even with its rich regional differences, is homogeneous compared with the languages in territories of similar size in the rest of the world; the process has been called "Babel in reverse." It is often said that the dialects of the Ozarks and Appalachia are a relict of Elizabethan English, but this is just a quaint myth, coming from the misconception of language as a cultural artifact. We think of the folk ballads, the hand-stitched quilts, and the whiskey aging slowly in oak casks and easily swallow the rumor that in this land that time forgot, the people still speak the traditional tongue lovingly handed down through the generations. But language does not work that way—at all times, in all communities, language changes, though the various parts of a language may change in different ways in different communities. Thus it is true that these dialects preserve some English forms that are rare elsewhere, such as *afeared*, *yourn*, *hisn*, and *et*, *holp*, and *clome* as the past of *eat*, *help*, and *climb*. But so does *every* variety of American English, including the standard one. Many so-called Americanisms were in fact carried over from England, where they were subsequently lost. For example, the participle *gotten*, the pronunciation of *a* in *path* and *bath* with a front-of-the-mouth "a" rather than the back-of-the-mouth "ah," and the use of *mad* to mean "angry," *fall* to mean "autumn," and *sick* to mean "ill," strike the British ear as all-American, but they are actually holdovers from the English that was spoken in the British Isles at the time of the American colonization.

English has changed on both sides of the Atlantic, and had been changing well before the voyage of the *Mayflower*. What grew into standard contemporary English was simply the dialect spoken around London, the political and economic center of England, in the seventeenth century. In the centuries preceding it, it had undergone a number of major changes, as you can see in these versions of the Lord's Prayer:

CONTEMPORARY ENGLISH: Our Father, who is in heaven, may your name be kept holy. May your kingdom come into being. May your will be followed on earth, just as it is in heaven. Give us this day our food for the day. And forgive us our offenses, just as we forgive those who have offended us. And do not bring us to the test. But free us from evil. For the kingdom, the power, and the glory are yours forever. Amen.

EARLY MODERN ENGLISH (C. 1600): Our father which are in heaven, hallowed be thy Name. Thy kingdom come. Thy will be done, on earth, as it is in heaven. Give us this day our daily bread. And forgive us our trespasses, as we forgive those who trespass against us. And lead us not into temptation, but deliver us from evil. For thine is the kingdom, and the power, and the glory, for ever, amen.

MIDDLE ENGLISH (C. 1400): Our fadir that art in heuenes halowid be thi name, thi kyngdom come to, be thi wille done in erthe es in heuene,

yeue to us this day oure bread ouir other substance, & foryeue to us oure
dettis, as we forgeuen to oure dettouris, & lede us not in to temptacion:
but delyuer us from yuel, amen.

OLD ENGLISH (C. 1000): Faeder ure thu the eart on heofonum, si thin nama
gehalgod. Tobecume thin rice. Gewurthe in willa on eorthan swa swa on
heofonum. Urne gedaeghwamlican hlaf syle us to daeg. And forgyf us ure
gyltas, swa swa we forgyfath urum gyltedum. And ne gelaed thu us on
contnungen ac alys us of yfele. Sothlice.

The roots of English are in northern Germany near Denmark, which
was inhabited early in the first millennium by pagan tribes called the
Angles, the Saxons, and the Jutes. After the armies of the collapsing
Roman Empire left Britain in the fifth century, these tribes invaded what
was to become England (Angle-land) and displaced the indigenous Celts
there into Scotland, Ireland, Wales, and Cornwall. Linguistically, the
defeat was total; English has virtually no traces of Celtic. Vikings invaded
in the ninth to eleventh centuries, but their language, Old Norse, was
similar enough to Anglo-Saxon that aside from many borrowings, the
language, Old English, did not change much.

In 1066 William the Conqueror invaded Britain, bringing with him
the Norman dialect of French, which became the language of the ruling
classes. When King John of the Anglo-Norman kingdom lost Normandy
shortly after 1200, English reestablished itself as the exclusive language
of England, though with a marked influence of French that lasts to this
day in the form of thousands of words and a variety of grammatical
quirks that go with them. This "Latinate" vocabulary—including such
words as *donate*, *vibrate*, and *desist*—has a more restricted syntax; for
example, you can say *give the museum a painting* but not *donate the
museum a painting*, *shake it up* but not *vibrate it up*. The vocabulary
also has its own sound pattern: Latinate words are largely polysyllabic
with stress on the second syllable, such as *desist*, *construct*, and *transmit*, whereas their Anglo-Saxon synonyms *stop*, *build*, and *send* are
single syllables. The Latinate words also trigger many of the sound
changes that make English morphology and spelling so idiosyncratic, like
electric–electricity and *nation–national*. Because Latinate words are
longer, and are more formal because of their ancestry in the government,
church, and schools of the Norman conquerors, overusing them produces
the stuffy prose universally deplored by style manuals, such as *The adolescents who had effectuated forcible entry into the domicile were
apprehended* versus *We caught the kids who broke into the house*.
Orwell captured the flabbiness of Latinate English in his translation of a
passage from Ecclesiastes into modern institutionalese:

I returned and saw under the sun, that the race is not to the swift, nor the
battle to the strong, neither yet bread to the wise, nor yet riches to men
of understanding, nor yet favour to men of skill; but time and chance
happeneth to them all.

Objective consideration of contemporary phenomena compels the conclusion that success or failure in competitive activities exhibits no tendency to be commensurate with innate capacity, but that a considerable element of the unpredictable must invariably be taken into account.

English changed noticeably in the Middle English period (1100–1450) in which Chaucer lived. Originally all syllables were enunciated, including those now represented in spelling by "silent" letters. For example, *make* would have been pronounced with two syllables. But the final syllables became reduced to the generic schwa like the *a* in *allow* and in many cases they were eliminated entirely. Since the final syllables contained the case markers, overt case began to vanish, and the word order became fixed to eliminate the resulting ambiguity. For the same reason, prepositions and auxiliaries like *of* and *do* and *will* and *have* were bled of their original meanings and given important grammatical duties. Thus many of the signatures of modern English syntax were the result of a chain of effects beginning with a simple shift in pronunciation.

The period of Early Modern English, the language of Shakespeare and the King James Bible, lasted from 1450 to 1700. It began with the Great Vowel Shift, a revolution in the pronunciation of long vowels whose causes remain mysterious. (Perhaps it was to compensate for the fact that long vowels sounded too similar to short vowels in the monosyllables that were now prevalent; or perhaps it was a way for the upper classes to differentiate themselves from the lower classes once Norman French became obsolete.) Before the vowel shift, *mouse* had been pronounced "mooce"; the old "oo" turned into a diphthong. The gap left by the departed "oo" was filled by raising what used to be an "oh" sound; what we pronounce as *goose* had, before the Great Vowel Shift, been pronounced "goce." That vacuum, in turn, was filled by the "o" vowel (as in *hot*, only drawn out), giving us *broken* from what had previously been pronounced more like "brocken." In a similar rotation, the "ee" vowel turned into a diphthong; *like* had been pronounced "leek." This dragged in the vowel "eh" to replace it; our *geese* was originally pronounced "gace." And that gap was filled when the long version of *ah* was raised, resulting in *name* from what used to be pronounced "nahma." The spelling never bothered to track these shifts, which is why the letter *a* is pronounced one way in *cam* and another way in *came*, where it had formerly been just a longer version of the *a* in *cam*. This is also why vowels are rendered differently in English spelling than in all the other European alphabets and in "phonetic" spelling.

Incidentally, fifteenth-century Englishmen did not wake up one day and suddenly pronounce their vowels differently, like a switch to daylight saving time. To the people living through it, the Great Vowel Shift probably felt like the current trend in the Chicago area to pronounce *hot* like *hat*, or the growing popularity of that strange surfer dialect in which *dude* is pronounced something like "diiihhhoooood."

=

FOR DISCUSSION AND REVIEW

1. In 1957, Martin Joos and Noam Chomsky wrote "strikingly different" interpretations of the variations in human languages. What were the claims of these two linguists?

2. According to Pinker, what are six obvious ways that other languages differ from English? What does he mean by an "isolating" as opposed to an "inflecting" language? What is the difference between a "fixed-word-order" and a "free-word-order" language? What are SOV and VSO languages? Give an example of each.

3. What does Pinker mean by the term "universals" as it relates to languages? Give an example. What does he mean by a "universal implication"? Give an example.

4. By what arguments does Pinker rule out the idea that all existing languages are descended from a single proto-language?

5. How can Chomsky substantiate the claim, in a world where thousands of languages are spoken, that a visiting Martian scientist would conclude that all humans speak a single language?

6. Name three properties of language that are variable within the framework of Universal Grammar. How does Pinker's analogy between Universal Grammar and an archetypal body plan help clarify the constants and variables of language?

7. Using English as the model, how can it be shown that the basic properties of one language exist in all other languages? Cite examples from Pinker's list.

8. Explain Darwin's important insight into the reasons for the existence of multiple languages.

9. According to Pinker, what are the roles of learning and of innate instincts in the acquisition of language by humans?

10. What does the term "reanalysis" mean in relation to language? In what ways does reanalysis lead to changes in a language?

11. How does the separation or isolation of groups of English speakers lead to different varieties of English?

15

Bad Birds and Better Birds: Prototype Theories

Jean Aitchison

Which of the following colors most closely resembles the color blue: teal blue, peacock blue, sky blue, royal blue, navy blue, or midnight blue? How do we distinguish between such subtle differences in meaning? Semantics is the area of linguistics that analyzes the meaning of individual words and phrases. In this classic piece from the second edition of Words in the Mind *(1994), Professor Jean Aitchison of the University of Oxford examines a peculiar trait of the English language that allows those who speak it to cope with its ambiguous word meanings. Speakers of English use many words with slightly different meanings to convey similar messages. For example, the terms "happy," "excited," "jubilant," "delighted," or "elated" express a positive, pleasant, personal feeling. Aitchison discusses this ambiguous classification of word meaning within the framework of "prototype theory." How we choose words that seem best suited to a specific situation is just one of the questions she attempts to answer.*

The Hatter . . . had taken his watch out of his pocket, and was looking at it uneasily, shaking it every now and then, and holding it to his ear . . .

"Two days wrong?" sighed the Hatter. "I told you butter wouldn't suit the works!" . . .

Alice had been looking over his shoulder with some curiosity. "What a funny watch!" she remarked. "It tells the day of the month, and doesn't tell what o'clock it is!"

–Lewis Carroll, *Alice's Adventures in Wonderland*

If words have a hazy area of application, we are faced with a serious problem in relation to the mental lexicon. How do we manage to cope with words at all? The quotation above from *Alice in Wonderland* gives us a clue. Alice appears to have some notion of what constitutes a "proper watch." This enables her to identify the butter-smeared object owned by the Hatter as a watch, and to comment that it is a "funny" one.

A feeling that some examples of words may be more central than others appears to be widespread, as shown by a dialogue between two small girls in a popular cartoon strip:

252

Reproduced by kind permission of the *London Standard*

Humans, then, appear to find some instances of words more basic than others. Such an observation may shed light on how people understand their meaning. Take birds. Perhaps people have an amalgam of ideal bird characteristics in their minds. Then, if they saw a pterodactyl, they would decide whether it is likely to be a bird by matching it against the features of a bird-like bird, or, in fashionable terminology, a "prototypical" bird. It need not have all the characteristics of the prototype, but if the match was reasonably good, it could be labeled *bird*, though it might not necessarily be a very good example of a bird. This viewpoint is not unlike the checklist viewpoint, but it differs in that, in order to be a bird, the creature in question does not have to have a fixed number of bird characteristics. It simply has to be a reasonable match.

This is an intriguing idea. But, like any intriguing idea, it needs to be tested. How could we find out if people really behave in this way? In fact, psychologists showed quite a long time ago that people treat colors like this (e.g., Lenneberg 1967; Berlin and Kay 1969). However, this type of study has only relatively recently been extended to other types of vocabulary items. Let us consider one of the pioneering papers on the topic.

BIRDY BIRDS AND VEGETABLEY VEGETABLES

About twenty years ago Eleanor Rosch, a psychologist at the University of California at Berkeley, carried out a set of experiments in order to test the idea that people regard some types of birds as "birdier" than other birds, or some vegetables as more vegetable-like or some tools more "tooly."

She devised an experiment which she carried out with more than 200 psychology students: "This study has to do with what we have in mind when we use words which refer to categories," ran the instructions.

> Let's take the word red as an example. Close your eyes and imagine a true red. Now imagine an orangish red . . . imagine a purple red. Although you might still name the orange red or the purple red with the term red, they are not as good examples of red . . . as the clear "true" red. In short, some reds are redder than others. The same is true for other kinds of categories. Think of dogs. You all have some notion of what a "real dog," a "doggy dog" is. To me a retriever or a German shepherd is a very doggy dog while a Pekinese is a less doggy dog. Notice that this kind of judgment has nothing to do with how well you like the thing; you can like a purple red better than a true red but still recognize that the color you like is not a true red. You may prefer to own a Pekinese without thinking that it is the breed that best represents what people mean by dogginess (Rosch 1975, 198).

The questionnaire which followed was ten pages long. On each page was a category name, such as "Furniture," "Fruit," "Vegetable," "Bird," "Carpenter's Tool," "Clothing," and so on. Under each category was a list of fifty or so examples. *Orange, lemon, apple, peach, pear, melon* appeared on the fruit list, and so did most of the other fruits you would be likely to think up easily. The order of the list was varied for different students to ensure that the order of presentation did not bias the results. The students were asked to rate how good an example of the category each member was on a seven-point scale: rating something as "1" meant that it was considered an excellent example; "4" indicated a moderate fit; whereas "7" suggested that it was a very poor example, and probably should not be in the category at all.

The results were surprisingly consistent. Agreement was particularly high for the items rated as very good examples of the category. Almost everybody thought that a *robin* was the best example of a bird, that *pea* was the best example of a vegetable, and *chair* the best example of furniture. On the third list, *sparrow, canary, blackbird, dove,* and *lark* all came out high (figure 15.1). *Parrot, pheasant, albatross, toucan,* and *owl* came somewhat lower. *Flamingo, duck,* and *peacock* were lower still. *Ostrich, emu,* and *penguin* came more than halfway down the seven-point rating, while last of all came *bat,* which probably shouldn't be regarded as a bird at all. Similar results were found for the other categories, that is, *shirts, dresses,* and *skirts* were considered better examples of clothing than *shoes* and *stockings,* which were in turn higher than *aprons* and *earmuffs. Guns* and *daggers* were better examples of weapons than *whips* and *axes,* which were better than *pitchforks* and *bricks.*

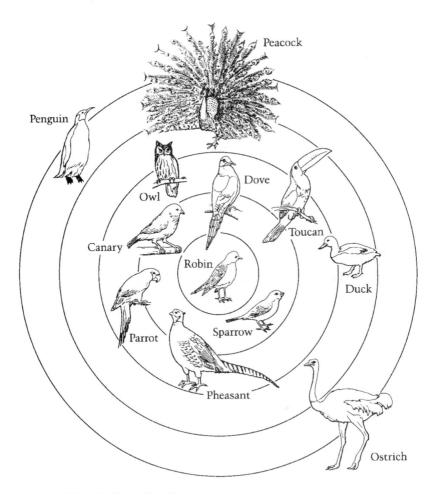

Peacock

Penguin

Owl

Dove

Toucan

Canary

Robin

Duck

Parrot

Sparrow

Pheasant

Ostrich

FIGURE 15.1   Birdiness Rankings.

Saws, hammers, and *screwdrivers* were better examples of carpenters' tools than *crowbars* and *plumblines.*

Psychologists on the other side of America obtained very similar results when they repeated the experiment (Armstrong et al. 1983), so the results are not just a peculiar reaction of Californian psychology students. And Rosch carried out other experiments which supported her original results. For example, she checked how long it took students to verify category membership. That is, she said, "Tell me whether the following is true," and then gave the students sentences such as "A penguin is a bird" or "A sparrow is a bird." She found that good exemplars (her name for examples) of a category were verified faster than less good exemplars, so that it took longer to say "Yes" to "A penguin is a bird" than it did to "A sparrow is a bird" (Rosch 1975).

The results of these experiments are fairly impressive. But there is one obvious criticism: were the students just responding faster to more common words? After all, people come across sparrows far more frequently than penguins, and hammers more often than crowbars. Obviously, frequency of usage is likely to have some effect: in California nectarines and boysenberries are commoner than mangoes and kumquats, so it is not surprising that the former were regarded as "better" exemplars of fruit than the latter. However, the results could not be explained away solely on the basis of word frequency. On the furniture list, rare items of furniture such as *love seat, davenport, ottoman,* and *cedar chest* came out much higher than *refrigerator,* which is a standard part of every American household. On the vegetable list, *pea, carrot,* and *cauliflower* came out higher than *onion, potato,* and *mushroom.* And on the clothes list, *pajamas* and *bathing suit* came out higher than *shoe, tie, hat,* and *gloves.* So people genuinely feel that some things are better exemplars of a category than others, a feeling which is not simply due to how often one comes across the word or object in question.

Furthermore, these judgments were not made primarily on the basis of appearance. Peas, according to Rosch, are prototypical vegetables. If people were simply comparing other vegetables to a visual image of a pea, then we would expect carrots to come out near the bottom of the list. In fact, they come very near the top. And if visual characteristics were important, we would also expect vegetables which look similar, such as carrots, parsnips, and radishes, to be clustered together. But they are not. Nor were judgments made purely in terms of use. If this were so, one would expect benches and stools to come out near the top, since they are closest in function to the prototypical piece of furniture, a chair. But in fact bookcases rank higher than either benches or stools. It is not immediately obvious, therefore, how people came to their conclusions. They were making some type of analysis, though its exact basis was unclear, as the criteria used seemed to be heterogeneous.

To summarize, Rosch's work suggests that when people categorize common objects, they do not expect them all to be on an equal footing. They seem to have some idea of the characteristics of an ideal exemplar— in Rosch's words, a "prototype." And they probably decide on the extent to which something else is a member of the same category by matching it against the features of the prototype. It does not have to match exactly, it just has to be sufficiently similar, though not necessarily visually similar.

Prototype theory is useful, then, for explaining how people deal with untypical examples of a category. This is how unbirdy birds such as pelicans and penguins can still be regarded as birds. They are sufficiently like the prototype, even though they do not share all its characteristics. But it has a further advantage: it can explain how people cope with damaged examples. Previously linguists had found it difficult to explain why anyone could still categorize a one-winged robin that couldn't fly as a bird or a three-legged tiger as a quadruped. Now one just assumes that these get matched against the prototype in the same way as an untypical category member. A one-winged robin that can't fly can still be a bird, even though it's not such a typical one.

Furthermore, the prototype effect seems to work for actions as well as objects: people can, it appears, reliably make judgments that *murder* is a better example of killing than *execute* or *commit suicide*, and that *stare* is a better example of looking than *peer* or *squint* (Pulman 1983).

However, so far we have dealt only with assigning objects and actions to larger categories. We now need to consider whether this is the way in which humans cope with individual words.

DEGREES OF LYING

"Can you nominate in order now the degrees of the lie?" asks a character in Shakespeare's play *As You Like It*, and the clown Touchstone responds by listing seven degrees of lying (Shakespeare, *As You Like It*, 5.4). Obviously the idea that some lies are better lies than others has been around for a long time, and still seems to be relevant today.

A "good" lie, it transpires, has several characteristics (Coleman and Kay 1981). First, the speaker has to assert something that is untrue. However, people often utter untruths without being regarded as liars, particularly in cases of genuine mistakes: a child who argued that six and four make eleven would not be thought of as lying. So a second characteristic of a good lie is that a speaker must believe that what he is saying is false. But even this is insufficient, because a person can knowingly tell untruths without being a liar, as in: "You're the cream in my coffee, you're the sugar in my tea" (metaphor), "He stood so still, you could have mistaken him for a doorpost" (exaggeration or hyperbole), "Since you're a world expert on the topic, perhaps you could tell us how to get the cat out of the drainpipe?" (sarcasm). A third characteristic must therefore be added for a good lie: that the speaker must intend to deceive those addressed. In brief, a fully-fledged or prototypical lie occurs when a speaker:

1. asserts something false
2. which they know to be false
3. with the intention of deceiving.

A prototypical lie, therefore, might be when a child denies having eaten a jam tart which it knows full well it has just scoffed. But consider a situation such as the following: "Schmallowitz is invited to dinner at his boss's house. After a dismal evening enjoyed by no one, Schmallowitz says to his hostess, "Thanks, it was a terrific party." Schmallowitz doesn't believe it was a terrific party, and he isn't really trying to convince anyone he had a good time, but is just concerned to say something to his boss's wife, regardless of the fact that he doesn't expect her to believe it (Coleman and Kay 1981, 31).

Did Schmallowitz lie? The seventy-one people asked this question were quite unsure. They had been told to grade a number of situations on a seven-point scale, from 1 (very sure non-lie) to 7 (very sure lie). For many people, Schmallowitz's situation lay just in the middle between these two extremes, at point 4, where they were unable to decide whether it was a lie or not. Another situation which lay in the middle was the case of Superfan, who got tickets for a championship game, and phoned early in the day to tell his boss that he could not come to work as he was sick. Ironically, Superfan doesn't get to the game, because the mild stomachache he had that morning turned out to be quite severe food poisoning.

Both the Schmallowitz and Superfan cases broke one of the conditions of a good lie, though each broke a different condition. Schmallowitz was not trying to deceive his hostess, he was merely trying to be polite. Superfan did not tell an untruth. Lies, then, like birds, can be graded. Lies can still be lies even when they are not prototypical lies, and they shade off into not being "proper" lies at all.

The realization that individual words need not be used in their prototypical sense can explain a number of puzzling problems, especially cases in which people are unsure of whether they are dealing with the "same" word or not. Consider the following sentences (Jackendoff 1983):

I must have seen that a dozen times, but I never noticed it.

I must have looked at that a dozen times, but I never saw it.

Some people have argued that there are two different verbs *see*, one meaning "my gaze went to an object," as in the first sentence, and the other containing in addition the meaning "something entered my awareness," as in the second. But in a prototypical use of the verb *see*, both conditions are present: one's gaze goes to an object *and* the object enters one's awareness. If awareness is missing, one can stare at something without noticing it. Alternatively, something may enter a person's awareness, such as a dream or a hallucination, even though their gaze has not gone anywhere. These are both "ordinary" uses of the word *see*, but not prototypical ones.

To take another example, look at the following sentences:

The janitor goes from top to bottom of the building.

The staircase goes from top to bottom of the building.

The janitor is clearly moving, but the staircase is not. So are these both instances of the same word *go*? A prototype approach allows *go* to be treated as a single word (Aitchison 1985). In its prototypical use, *go* involves movement, with the mover starting at one point, ending at another, and traversing the distance in between. However, *go* can be used untypically, with the "movement" condition omitted, as happens with staircases and roads. This is a better solution than assuming that two different words *go* are involved, because it avoids the need to make difficult decisions as to which use of *go* is found in sentences such as:

The river Ganges goes from the Himalayas to the Indian Ocean.

The power of prayer goes round the world.

The verb *climb* provides a further example (Fillmore 1982; Taylor 1989; Jackendoff 1990). Consider:

Peter climbed a ladder.

The plane climbed to 30,000 feet.

The temperature climbed to 40°C.

The price of petrol climbed daily.

Mavis climbed down the tree.

Brian climbed into his clothes.

These various uses all sound "normal," even though they differ quite considerably from one another. Prototype theory provides a simple explanation. A prototypical or "default" use of *climb* involves upward movement and clambering—effortful use of limbs, as when Peter shinned up the ladder. If one of these conditions is absent, the result is still a normal use of *climb*, though not a prototypical one. Planes, temperature, and the price of petrol can climb because they are moving upward, even though they are not using any limbs. In contrast, Mavis can climb down the tree, and Peter can climb into his clothes because they are effortfully using their limbs, even though they are not going upward.

But when both upward movement and clambering are absent, the result is weird:

The plane climbed down to 20,000 feet.

The temperature climbed down to 10°C.

Marigold climbed down the stairs.

The snail climbed along the drainpipe.

Judging something against a prototype, therefore, and allowing rough matches to suffice, seems to be the way we understand a number of different words. Furthermore, a general realization that this is how humans probably operate could be of considerable use in real-life situations, as in the example below.

MAD, BAD, AND DANGEROUS TO KNOW

Some years ago a man who specialized in brutal murders of women was brought to trial. The Yorkshire Ripper, as he was called, divided public opinion sharply. Some people argued that he was simply bad, and therefore ought to be punished with a long term of imprisonment. Others claimed that he must be mad, in which case he should be admitted to a hospital and treated as someone who was not responsible for his actions.

Was he mad? Or was he bad? According to newspaper reports, the judge asked the jury to consider whether the Ripper had told the truth to the psychiatrists who examined him. The discrepancies and alterations in the Ripper's story made them conclude that he had told a considerable number of lies. This led them to classify him as "guilty"—bad, not mad. This judgment implies, therefore, that anyone who lies cannot be mad, a somewhat strange conclusion. Perhaps the situation would have been less confusing if the terms *mad* and *bad* had been considered in terms of prototypes (Aitchison 1981).

"To define true madness, What is 't to be nothing else but mad?" asks Polonius, on observing the deranged Hamlet (Shakespeare, *Hamlet*, 2.2). But contrary to Polonius's opinion, madness is not an all or nothing state. A prototypical mad person has several different characteristics. A mad person is, first, someone who thinks and acts abnormally. But this is insufficient, as it would categorize as mentally deranged such people as chess champions. Someone truly mad would, in addition, be unaware that he was thinking and acting abnormally, and furthermore, be unable to prevent himself from behaving oddly. A prototypical lunatic, therefore, might be someone who covers his head with tinfoil because he fears that moon men are about to attack, or someone who walks on her hands because God has supposedly told her not to wear out her feet. On this analysis, the Ripper was partially mad, because he acted strangely and seemed unable to prevent himself from doing so. Yet he was not prototypically mad, because he was perfectly aware that his actions were abnormal.

To turn to badness, someone bad commits antisocial acts, is aware that her actions are antisocial and could control her behavior if she wished. So a prototypical villain might be the pirate Captain Hook in *Peter Pan* or Shakespeare's character Iago. On this reasoning, the Ripper was partially bad, in that he acted antisocially and was aware of it, but not entirely bad, since he apparently could not control his actions.

To modify Caroline Lamb's statement about Lord Byron and reapply it to the Ripper, one could say that he is "around two-thirds mad, two-thirds bad, and certainly dangerous to know." No wonder the jury took so long to decide whether he was mad *or* bad, when he was neither prototypically mad nor prototypically bad.

This example shows that the notion of prototype can be extended beyond nouns and verbs—in this case to the adjectives *mad* and *bad*. But it also hides a problem, that the meaning of adjectives may vary, depending on the noun. Our account of *mad* is fine when accompanied by the word *man* or *woman*, but a *mad dog*, a *mad idea*, or a *mad evening* would require an amended analysis. Such examples suggest that the notion of prototype is not always as straightforward as has been suggested so far. Let us go on to consider this issue.

MUZZINESS OF MULTIPLE MEANINGS?

Pig: "Short-legged and typically stout-bodied mammal . . . with a thick bristly skin and long mobile snout"; "shaped mass . . . of cast crude metal." Both these definitions appear under a single entry in a well-known dictionary (LDEL). The dictionary assumes that both are instances of the "same" word *pig*, as opposed to another type of *pig* which is given a separate entry: *pig* "an earthenware vessel; a crock." But how is a plump farmyard animal related to a lump of metal? Above all, how many words are involved?

Ideally, prototype theory allows us to cut down on the multiple meanings found in many dictionaries, and to say that an understanding of the prototype allows other senses to be predicted. But how does anyone distinguish between one word with nonprototypical usages, such as *climb*, and more than one word, as perhaps with *pig* "farmyard animal" and *pig* "lump of metal"? A word such as *fork* provides a further problem. Is a *fork* you eat with the same word as the *fork* you dig with?

Polysemy—"multiple meanings"—is an age-old problem which has been helped by prototype theory, but by no means solved. Ideally, there should be some agreed test to decide whether a word has more than one meaning (polysemy) or is simply muzzy in its coverage (vagueness). But no one can find one which works.

Various suggestions have been put forward (Geeraerts 1992, 1993; Taylor 1992; Kilgarriff 1992), but none of them are foolproof. Dictionaries often rely on history, and combine items in a single entry if they are descended from the same original word—as seems to be true of *pig*. But this is not very helpful when considering how current-day speakers handle words in their minds.

A *so did* test is sometimes used to distinguish items: "The farmer watched the pig feeding its piglets, and so did the foundry foreman" would be very odd if the foundry foreman was looking at a metal pig (Zwicky and Sadock 1975). But used on *fork*, this test gets weird results. Intuitively, a *fork* is a "pronged implement." Yet the *so did* test would split it up into more than one "word": it would be very odd to say "The glutton used a fork to shovel his potatoes, and so did the farmer" if the glutton was shoveling potatoes into his mouth, and the farmer was digging them out of the ground. Similarly, *sad* in "a *sad* book" would probably be regarded as a different word from *sad* in "a *sad* woman." Each case therefore has to be considered on its merits. Let us look at two puzzling words, *over* and *old*.

MULLING OVER *OVER*

Mulling over *over* has taken up a lot of research time recently (e.g., Lakoff 1987; Taylor 1989; Geeraerts 1992). First, it's hard to identify prototypical *over*. Second, it's unclear how many separate meanings *over* has. Consider:

Virginia's picture is over the fireplace.

The clouds floated over the city.

Doreen pulled the blanket over her head.

Virginia's picture is stationary, but the clouds are moving. The clouds are unlikely to be touching the city, but the blanket is in contact with Doreen's head. Which of these meanings is basic?

There is no agreed solution. Some people argue that Virginia's static picture represents prototypical *over*, others the moving clouds. Still others suggest that *over* is by nature a muzzy word with vagueness built into it: that it means "above, on top of," versus "under," but does not specify whether the "over" item is stationary or moving, in contact with or separated from what's underneath. In this case, all the sentences quoted could be regarded as prototypical. However, all three uses are clearly instances of the same word, even if the prototype is not obvious.

But now look at:

The cow jumped over the moon.

The water flowed over the rim of the bathtub.

Fenella pushed Bob over the balcony.

Sam walked over the bridge.

In all these, there is successful movement to a new location. This cannot easily be accommodated in the primary meaning of *over*. But neither is it completely separate. There seem to be at least two overlapping meanings of *over*: a basic one in which location above is specified and an extended one in which successful movement across occurs (figure 15.2).

Over therefore shows that polysemy is a complex affair, in that different senses of a word may overlap. They cannot easily be related to a

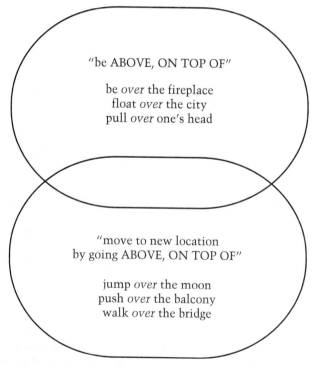

"be ABOVE, ON TOP OF"

be *over* the fireplace
float *over* the city
pull *over* one's head

"move to new location
by going ABOVE, ON TOP OF"

jump *over* the moon
push *over* the balcony
walk *over* the bridge

FIGURE 15.2 *Over.*

prototype, nor do they split neatly into different domains. Let us go on to consider another problem of this type.

OLD PROBLEMS

The word *old* is an old problem (Taylor 1992). Consider:

Pauline was astonished to see
—an old woman (an aged woman)
—an old friend (a long-standing friend)
—her old boyfriend (a former boyfriend)
—old Fred (Fred whom she knew well).

The old woman is aged, but the others may be young. The old friend is still a friend, but the old boyfriend might now be an enemy. Is there a basic usage which can link the others together?

"Aged" in the sense of "in existence for longer than the norm" is arguably the default meaning of *old*. This sense stays the same when the sentence is switched around: *Old* before the noun—"attributive position"—still means the same when moved to after *is*, "predicative position."

Pauline saw an old woman: the woman is old.

This meaning also works with various other words, such as *building*, *tradition*—though a minor complication is that in some cases the opposite of *old* is *young*, as in *young woman*, in others *new*, as in *new building*. The sense "long existence" can also cover *old friend*, though *old* cannot be moved about in the sentence, because the friendship, rather than the friend, is old.

But *old* "former" as in *old boyfriend* does not fit this pattern. Nor does *old Fred*. These have to be regarded as separate, though linked meanings. So how do people know when *old* is used in these funny ways? They have to look for extra clues. A common clue that *old* means "former" is a mark of possession:

Steve's old girlfriend went to Brazil.

An old boyfriend of mine sailed round the world.

Our old house is now divided up into apartments.

In the case of *old Fred*, English speakers have to know that *old* attached to proper names is a mark of friendly affection.

In some cases, then, a basic meaning can be detected by a lack of restrictions on the surrounding syntax, as with *old* "aged." This default meaning can with minor adaptations be extended to other, less prototypical usages, as with *old* "long-standing." But it is impossible to incorporate all meanings under the one prototype. *Old* "former" and *old* "term of affection" need to be recognized as separate words. Their distinctness

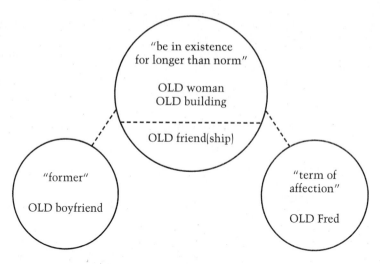

FIGURE 15.3   *Old.*

is signaled by the characteristic nature of the words which accompany them. This situation is shown in figure 15.3.

Old and *over* show that prototypes reduce the polysemy problem, but do not solve it. They also show that prototypes cannot always be handled by looking at words in isolation.

SUMMARY

We have looked at how people are able to cope with word meaning when it is so fuzzy and fluid. They analyze a prototypical exemplar of a word, and then match any new example against the characteristics of the prototype. It does not have to be a perfect match, merely a reasonable fit. This explains how words can be used with slightly different meanings, and how people can recognize new or damaged examples of a category. It also explains how people can deal with verbs.

However, prototype theory only partially solves the polysemy problem—that of cutting down on the apparent multiple meanings of a word. A full understanding of the meaning of many words requires a knowledge of the words which are found with it or related to it.

BIBLIOGRAPHY

Aitchison, J. 1981. "Mad, Bad and Dangerous to Know." *Literary Review* (July): 81–82.

———. 1985. "Cognitive Clouds and Semantic Shadows." *Language and Communication* 5: 69–93.

Armstrong, S. L., L. R. Gleitman, and H. Gleitman. 1983. "What Concepts Might Not Be." *Cognition* 13: 263–308.

Berlin, B., and P. Kay. 1969. *Basic Color Terms: Their Universality and Evolution.* Berkeley and Los Angeles: University of California Press.

Coleman, L., and P. Kay. 1981. "Prototype Semantics: The English Word *lie.*" *Language* 57: 26–44.

Fillmore, C. J. 1982. "Frame Semantics." In Linguistic Society of Korea, *Linguistics in the Morning Calm.* Seoul: Hanshin.

Geeraerts, D. 1992. "Polysemy and Prototypicality." *Cognitive Linguistics* 3: 219–31.

———. 1993. "Vagueness's Puzzles, Polysemy's Vagaries." *Cognitive Linguistics* 4: 223–72.

Jackendoff, R. 1983. *Semantics and Cognition.* Cambridge: MIT Press.

———. 1990. *Semantic Structures.* Cambridge: MIT Press.

Kilgarriff, A. 1992. *Polysemy.* Cognitive Science Research Paper 261. Falmer, Sussex: University of Sussex, School of Cognitive and Computing Sciences.

Lakoff, G. 1987. *Women, Fire and Dangerous Things.* Chicago: University of Chicago Press.

Lenneberg, E. 1967. *Biological Foundations of Language.* New York: Wiley.

Pulman, S. G. 1983. *Word Meaning and Belief.* London: Croom Helm.

Rosch, E. 1975. "Cognitive Representations of Semantic Categories." *Journal of Experimental Psychology: General* 104: 192–233.

Taylor, J. R. 1989. *Linguistic Categorization: Prototypes in Linguistic Theory.* Oxford: Clarendon Press.

———. 1992. "Old Problems: Adjectives in Cognitive Grammar." *Cognitive Linguistics* 3: 1–35.

Zwicky, A., and J. Sadock. 1975. "Ambiguity Tests and How to Fail Them." In *Syntax and Semantics,* ed. J. Kimball, Vol. 4. New York: Academic Press.

FOR DISCUSSION AND REVIEW

1. What is a *prototype*? What is "prototype theory"? Using some examples from the selection, explain how the evidence from Eleanor Rosch and other psychologists support this theory. Then try a modified version of one of Rosch's questions yourself. Say "bird," and write down the names of ten birds. Which are listed first and which last? Compare your list with that of your classmates. Does this exercise seem to show that some birds are "birdier" than others? Now try this with "fish." Are some fish "fishier" than others?

2. Aitchison suggests that prototype theory is useful when trying to account for "damaged" or "untypical examples of a category." Using an original damaged or untypical example, explain why this might be the case.

3. Do you think speakers in different cultures are likely to have different categories and different prototypical exemplars? Why, or why not?

4. How do native English speakers qualify the meaning of "lie"? In what instances are untruths not classified as lies? What kinds of crosscultural complications might arise when more than one "qualification system" is in play, especially among non-native speakers of a language?

5. How do verbs such as "see" and "go" adhere to prototype theory? Compare your results with prototypes of other words.

6. What are the differences between *identification criteria* and *stored knowledge*? How do we communicate successfully if we do not know how identification criteria are interwoven with stored knowledge?

7. What restrictions do we make on the sorting of prototype features? Give some examples to support your answer.

8. What are the difficulties in defining the characteristics of a prototype? Do these weaken prototype theory? Why, or why not?

9. Different languages categorize colors differently, and some languages have more color terms than others. (For a discussion of color categories, see John R. Taylor's *Linguistic Categorization*, in the Selected Bibliography at the end of Part Four.) Do you and your friends have the same color terms? When you say "a brown shirt" or "a pink scarf," do you all mean the same or nearly the same color? How might your different experiences and cultural backgrounds influence the way you categorize colors?

10. In her discussion of the words *over* and *old*, how does Aitchison demonstrate that dealing with words in isolation fails to solve the problem of *polysemy*—of a word having multiple meanings?

16

Pinning Down Semantics

Howard Gregory

The following selection is from the workbook Semantics *(2000) by Howard Gregory, a lecturer in linguistics at the University of Göttingen in Germany. Gregory introduces the basic semantics terminology and issues, and he accompanies the text with a number of useful brief exercises. He makes clear that the meaning of everyday language involves more than simply saying a word and identifying the object it names — that meaning is complex and has several layers. Among the topics Gregory discusses are the relationship between word form and reference, the concept of denotation, and the idea that sentences have meaning in part because they are true or false in specific situations.*

Semantics is 'the study of meaning'. For [our purposes], the object of study is the meaning of human language (sometimes termed 'natural language'). It should not be forgotten, of course, that other structured systems (programming languages, diagrams, rituals, mathematical formulas) all have an appropriate concept of meaning, and hence their own semantics.

So what is meaning? Well, at one level 'meaning' is an ordinary English word, which like most words can be used in a number of different ways. Some of them are illustrated by the sentences in (1).

EXERCISE

1. How else could you describe each of these uses of the word 'mean'?

   a. It's a good [thing] he doesn't know what 'malaka' means.

   b. I'm sure she didn't mean to pour olive oil in your hair.

   c. Mean it? I didn't even *say* it.

   d. I think that means she isn't coming back.

   e. So he's Russian. Does that mean he's good at chess?

   f. 'Irony is the gap between what is said and what is meant'.

But semantics is not about the use of a particular English word, or its correlates in other languages, though these may give us clues about the area under discussion. The Greek word (from which we get 'semantics') conveys the idea of *importance* (compare the English words 'meaningful' or 'significant'). The Chinese equivalent is also used to mean *interest*. This suggests that the subject touches on questions of why people bother to use language in the first place, and why we bother to listen to them. It is certainly a far cry from what people have in mind when they dismiss something as 'a matter of semantics'!

However, semantics as covered [here] is more limited in scope. In terms of the contrast in sentence f above, it is confined largely to the study of 'what is said', leaving aside such interesting issues as irony, metaphor, and social interaction. . . .

FORM AND CONTENT

Take a simple word like 'book'. It can be analyzed at many different levels. First of all we know how it is pronounced and spelt (or spelled?); this is one kind of information. And when we encounter it, we associate it in some way with *books*—either some mental concept of them, or objects in the real world instantiating the concept (never mind which for the moment). The first thing is to distinguish systematically between the first kind of information, which concerns 'book' as an expression in a language, and the second kind, which we can call (very provisionally) the concept of *book*. Typographically, this distinction will be re-inforced by using quotation marks for the former and italics for the latter, as in the previous sentence. (A word of warning: many linguistics books use different conventions.)

It may help to think of situations where words in different languages are said to 'mean the same thing'. For example, 'book', 'livre', 'carte' 'kniga' and 'hon' are expressions in different languages, but are associated with the same concept, *book*. Note that although I have used an English word to label the concept, this is just a matter of convenience. I could have used anything—a word in another language, a number, or a little picture of a book. Equally, I am not implying that speakers of all languages have exactly the same stock of concepts.

Conversely a single word may have more than one meaning. For example the English word 'table' can mean an item of furniture or a kind of chart. To avoid confusing the two meanings (not likely in this case, but it is not always so simple), we should use different labels for the two concepts. Since these labels are arbitrary anyway, one way of doing it is to use *table*$_1$ and *table*$_2$ respectively (rather like in a dictionary). These may be termed word senses, as opposed to word forms.

There is no guarantee that a single word form in another language will cover the same group of word senses. For example in Greek 'trapezi' means what I have called *table*₁, while to express *table*₂ you would have to use a different word form, like 'pinakas'. However, certain clusters of word senses often go together in many languages.

$$\equiv$$

EXERCISES

2. If two word forms share at least one word sense, then they are *synonyms*. Pick out synonyms from the following list, and make sentences illustrating the word sense which they share (note that some of these senses may be specific to colloquial British English). The words may have slightly different connotations—it is quite rare to find *exact* synonyms in language.

store	lies	gift	bottle	porkies	current
guts	shop	hoard	intestines	present	betray

3. Conversely if two distinct word senses correspond to one word form, they are known as *homonyms*. The 'same word form' can of course be defined in terms of sound or spelling, depending which medium is being used. (In the first case they are called 'homophones', in the second case 'homographs'—two different types of homonym.) Make pairs of homonyms of either kind based on the words below.

drag	wrap	wheel	read	polish	practice

4. Investigate whether English word forms with more than one sense correspond to the same word form in some other language known to you; and compare results. (You may be able to do this using a good bilingual dictionary.) Here are a few to start you off:

head	branch	cheek	sex	hard	appointment
black	field	terribly	way	bird	board
miss	pass				

OBJECTS AND THEIR DESCRIPTIONS

One simple approach to meaning is to associate each expression with a particular object in the world. This seems more or less plausible with certain types of expression, such as proper names: 'Bill Clinton' or 'Saddam Hussein', for example seem to refer to recognizable individuals. Similarly phrases like 'the Eiffel Tower' or 'the moon' seem to pick out particular objects. This idea of picking out objects can be termed the *reference* of an expression (the object picked out is its *referent*).

EXERCISE

5. List the words and phrases in this text which have the same referent.

> Einstein College today announced the firing of its director. The chairman of the board of governors said that he had phoned him last night to inform him that his services were no longer .required. This follows overspending on a new residence for students, with resulting cutbacks in academic programs. Their representative, Tracy Sharpe, commented that they now had nice accommodations but no professors.

Reference appears to be an important part of meaning. For example, words like 'it' and 'they', which occur in some form in all languages, depend on it. But it is easy to see that this cannot be the whole story.

EXERCISE

6. What are the referents of the following expressions? (i) 'the president of the USA'; (ii) 'the World Cup winners'; (iii) 'the highest mountain in the world'; (iv) 'the first astronaut'.

These are easy enough to answer, but the problem with this exercise (or pseudo-exercise) is that it reads like part of a trivia quiz, rather than an analysis of meaning. It is possible to be mistaken about the answer to one of these questions (i.e. the referent of the phrase) while understanding perfectly its meaning (in the intuitive sense). Moreover the referent of some of these descriptions changes with time. [When I wrote] this [piece], the referent of the first [was] Bill Clinton (or let's say *bill_clinton*, the same object that is the referent of 'Bill Clinton'). But this [is no longer the case.] On the other hand we would hardly want to say that 'the president of the USA' has changed its meaning.

There are other considerations as well. To take a well-known example, 'the morning star' and 'the evening star' refer to the same object. But it would seem paradoxical to say that they have the same meaning, especially given that 'morning' and 'evening' have (intuitively) opposite meanings. Again, if they had the same meaning, then the discovery that the two phenomena are one planet would hardly be news. It would be like discovering that $1 = 1$. And so with all factual discoveries about the identity of objects.

Thus reference cannot be the whole of meaning. What I have called the 'intuitive sense' of meaning, which remains constant when the referent changes, is often called the *sense* of an expression. If we know its sense, we should be able to pick out its referent in any particular set of circumstances, as long as we know the appropriate facts.

I am going to introduce another terminological distinction, that between reference and *denotation* (though you should note that sometimes these are used almost interchangeably). [Since I am British, if] I use the phrase 'the queen', I am likely to be referring to *queen_elizabeth_II*, the daughter of *george_VI* and the mother of *prince_charles*. On such occasions, she will be the referent of the phrase. But its denotation is something more abstract. It will include all those individuals that could be referred to using the word 'queen'. If you like, it is classifying objects into those which come under the heading 'queen' and those which don't. More precisely, it includes those entities which can be classified by a given sense of the word 'queen'. If you see a pub called 'The Queen's Head' with a picture of Freddie Mercury outside it, a different word sense and hence a different scheme of classification is at work.

EXERCISE

7. For each of these words, distinguish at least two senses. Give two examples of individuals or objects which fall within the denotation of each word sense, and give an example sentence in which they are the intended referent.

   a. bank

   b. star

   c. pig

CONTENT AND CONTEXT

The distinction between denotation and reference brings into focus another crucial aspect of meaning—the context in which an expression is used. To take an obvious example, the phrase 'my wife' can be used by any number of men, normally referring to a different woman in each case. Likewise the referent of 'yesterday's paper' depends when the expression is used (besides the speaker and his or her reading habits). We have to account for the fact that the same expression used in different contexts may have the same meaning in some respects but different in other respects, notably reference.

It is helpful here to distinguish between *token* and *type*. To take some standard non-linguistic examples, two [dimes] are two different objects but they are instances of 'the same thing'. They are two tokens of one type of object. Similarly the 10 a.m. flight to Bucharest is 'the same flight' each day, though the actual aircraft used may be different. (The relevant criteria of sameness or difference depend, of course, on the level of detail required.)

EXERCISE

8. Count the words in the last sentence, first the number of word tokens and then the number of word types.

In language, the same expression, say a sentence, may be used on different occasions. It is 'the same', that is, as far as its phonological and syntactic analysis is concerned, but used at different times or by different speakers (and showing small phonetic variations which may be irrelevant to its linguistics structure). It can be said that it is the same sentence but different utterances of that sentence. The terminology I will adopt here is to say that it comprises one sentence type but several sentence tokens. A token occurs in a context, and this context will normally affect its meaning; especially its reference and that of its subparts.

EXERCISE

9. How many sentence types and tokens are there in this exchange?

   a. 'My theory of X-bar syntax is better than yours.'

   b. 'No it isn't. My theory of X-bar syntax is better than yours.'

   a. 'Look, it's simple. I'm right and you're wrong.'

   b. 'Don't be so childish. I'm right and you're wrong.'

How does the reference change between different tokens of the same sentence type?

As has already been hinted, linguistics in general is more concerned with utterance types than tokens. Suppose in a given situation Mary says to you, 'My computer's crashed.' You can get different kinds of information—that she is still alive, that she speaks English (perhaps with an accent which tells you where she comes from), that she is still talking to you—but linguistic semantics concerns itself with the information offered about her computer. That is derived from the sentence type, in conjunction with *some* contextual information, namely that which identifies the speaker as Mary. The branch of study that concerns itself more extensively with the interpretation of utterances in context is known as *pragmatics*. . . . The exact borderline between semantics and pragmatics is a hazy one, but the relationship between them is certainly a very close one. This must be the case because for many linguistic expressions a crucial part of their meaning (including reference, and hence the truth or falsity of sentences) cannot be determined without looking at context.

WORDS AND SENTENCES

There are two main approaches to linguistic semantics. The first, *lexical semantics,* focuses on the meaning of words. The vocabulary of a language (the 'lexicon') is treated not just as a list of words but as a very rich and complex set of associations. . . . Often this approach overlaps with cognitive psychology. The second approach starts with the meaning of sentences, and borrows heavily from ideas in formal logic and philosophy. This approach is often termed formal or *truth-conditional semantics,* for reasons which will soon become apparent.

The question is sometimes asked which is the basic unit of meaning in language, the word or the sentence. (There are also intermediate levels which seem to have some significance—phrases like 'the girl in the yellow dress', or to 'cook your goose'.) At one extreme, sentences could be regarded as simply combinations of words. After all, many words ('dog', 'apple', 'hot') have an obvious significance of their own, one which can be grasped for example by children before they learn to deal with sentences. Of course such an approach still has to deal with what the Chinese tradition calls 'empty words'—words like 'the' and 'and' which don't have such an obvious reference but which help to glue the sentence together and contribute to its overall meaning. At the other extreme, sentence meaning can be taken as basic and the semantic content of words (whether full or empty) defined in terms of the contribution they make to that of a sentence.

I have no particular axe to grind on this issue of which comes first. . . . The important thing to bear in mind is that sentence meaning is different in kind from the meanings of words or phrases. This is not a matter of length—you can have very long words and very short sentences (compare 'antediluvian' and 'Get out!'). The point is that only a sentence can be true or false. A word or phrase by itself cannot (unless it happens to constitute a complete sentence.).

EXERCISE

10. Say whether or not the following expressions can be true.

    a. 'the man who you saw at the bus-stop yesterday'

    b. 'I miss you'

    c. 'very nice'

    d. 'the truth'

    e. 'it is not true that I burnt the turkey'

    f. 'the fact that they didn't come'

I will assume as a working definition that a sentence is an expression which can be judged true or false (i.e. 'assigned a *truth value*'). Strictly speaking this applies directly only to certain types of sentence, which I will call 'statements'. (Other kinds of sentences, like questions or commands, require a more indirect approach, which is beyond [our scope here]. The truth value does not exhaust the meaning of the sentence (we don't want to arrive at a situation where any two true sentences have the same meaning!). But it is the main thing that distinguishes sentence meanings from the meanings of other expressions. It has been said that 'to know the meaning of a sentence is to know what the world would have to be like for the sentence to be true'. . . .

SUMMARY

This [selection] has taken a preliminary look at the idea of meaning in language, and tried to mark out the area to be covered by 'semantics'. It is concerned mainly with the intrinsic information conveyed by word types and sentence types, in relation to that of other such expressions and to the world which they describe. The closely related field of pragmatics is concerned more with the additional effects associated with the use of an utterance token in a given context.

Sentences are distinguished from other expressions by the fact that they can be judged *true* or *false,* and it was suggested that an important part of the meaning of a sentence involves the ability to assign it one of these truth values on the basis of the facts of the situation it describes.

≡

FOR DISCUSSION AND REVIEW

1. What is the difference between word forms and word senses? Give two examples of each.

2. Gregory notes that reference "appears to be an important part of meaning." Explain the relationship between a word form and its referent. How is it possible for a word form to have more than one referent? Can different word forms have the same referent? Give some examples to back up your answer.

3. According to Gregory, does some sense of an expression's meaning remain the same even when the referent changes? What is the "intuitive sense" of meaning?

4. Explain the concept of denotation, and give some examples of denotative meaning. What is the difference between *reference* and *denotation*?

5. Using an original example, explain the distinction between *token* and *type*.

6. What are the two main approaches to linguistic semantics? Do you think one is more fundamental to semantics than the other? Why, or why not?

7. What is "truth value"? How does truth value separate sentence meaning from other kinds of meaning?

17

Pragmatics: Discourse Routines

Elaine Chaika

The linguistic subfield of pragmatics deals with language as a social phenomenon. In this selection, Elaine Chaika, a linguistics professor at Rhode Island College, examines a variety of ways the norms of social interaction control our language use. She shows how the meaning of an utterance is fully understood only within its social context, which involves the rules and presumptions regarding the event; the participants' relations, roles, and intentions; and how participants have used such language in the past. All of these factors affect the "discourse routines" that come into play in all conversations. Like other forms of language use, discourse routines are rule governed but largely unconscious cultural behaviors that we acquire when we learn a language. Chaika claims that discourse routines are so important that we use them even in very fleeting social contacts. This selection is from her 1982 book, Language: The Social Mirror, *Fourth Edition.*

We control others and they control us by shared discourse routines. By saying certain things, the other party in a dialogue forces certain responses in us. Questions demand answers, and compliments elicit thanks, for instance. In order to understand these routines, one must understand the society in which they occur. Simply knowing the language is not sufficient, for the true meaning often lies not in the actual words uttered but in a complex of social knowledge. Examining such routines can help us understand the unspoken assumptions on which a society is based.

A PARADOX

Language makes us free as individuals but chains us socially. It has already been demonstrated that we are not mere creatures of conditioning when it comes to language. We can say things we never heard before, as well as understand what we have not previously heard.

When we consider discourse rules, however, we find a strange paradox. The social rules of language often force us into responding in certain ways. We are far from free in forming sentences in actual social situations. Frequently we must respond whether we want to or not. Furthermore, we must respond in certain ways (see Givon 1979; Schenkein 1978; Labov and Fanshel 1977).

MEANING AND THE SOCIAL SITUATION

The actual meaning of an utterance depends partially on the social context in which it occurs.

Rommetveit (1971) gives a classic example of this. He tells a story about a man running for political office who is scheduled to give a talk in a school auditorium. When he arrives, he sees that there are not enough chairs. He calls his wife at home. Then he goes to see the janitor. To each, the candidate says, "There aren't enough chairs." To the wife, this means 'Wow! am I popular,' but to the janitor it means 'Go get some more chairs.' The full meaning evoked by the statement "There aren't enough chairs" is largely a product of the context in which it is said, including the relative social statuses, privileges and duties of the speaker and listener. The remainder of this [selection] is concerned with the obligations society places upon us in discourse, as well as the real meaning of utterances in a social context.

A *speech event* is the situation calling forth particular ways of speaking (Gordon and Lakoff 1975). *Genre* refers to the form of speaking. Usually, it has a label, such as *joke, narrative, promise, riddle, prayer,* even *greeting* or *farewell.*

Members of a speech community recognize genres as having beginnings, middles, and ends, and as being patterned. "Did you hear the one about . . . ", for instance, is a recognized opener for the genre *joke* in our society. "Once upon a time . . . " is a recognized opener for the genre *child's story*, and the ending is "They lived happily ever after." The end of *joke* is the *punch line*, often a pun, an unusual or unexpected response to a situation or utterance, or a stupid response by one of the characters in the joke. Typically the stupid response to a situation is one that reveals that the character is lacking in some basic social knowledge or one in which the social meaning of an utterance is ignored and its literal meaning is taken instead. For instance, an old Beetle Bailey cartoon shows Sarge saying to Zero "The wastebasket is full." Instead of emptying the basket, Zero responds "Even I can see that" The joke is that Zero took the words at their face value rather than interpreting them as a command, which was their actual social force.

Sometimes the genre is the entire speech event but not always. Church services are speech events, for instance. *Sermons* are a genre belonging to church, but sermons do not cover the entire speech event. Prayers, responsive readings, hymn singing, and announcements also constitute the speech events of church services.

The way that participants carry out the demands of a genre is their *performance*. In some communities, this is more important than others.

Also, performance is more important in some speech events than others. A professor's performance, for instance, is far more important than that of the students in the classroom. The exception would be those classes in which students have been assigned special speaking tasks.

Perhaps *important* is not quite the right word. The professor's performance will be judged more overtly than a student's and judged according to different criteria. These are the criteria judged in public performance, such as clarity of diction, voice quality, logic of lecture, and coherence. Correct performance in less formal speech events is just as important, but in those judgment is often confined to how appropriate the speech was to the situation. Everyday discourse routines are as much performances as are preaching, joke-telling, and lecturing.

Linguists often use the word *performance* in a more general sense than here. They use it to refer to one's actual speech, which may contain errors, such as slips of the tongue. Since people often realize that they have made speech mistakes, linguists say that there is a difference between *competence* and performance. In this [selection], performance will refer specifically to one's ability to carry out the requirements of a speech event in a given social situation. This, too, may differ from one's competence in that one can be aware of errors in one's performance of a genre. A professor may realize with a sickening thud, for example, that a prepared lecture is boring a class to sleep, or a partygoer may be unable to think of any of the small talk or repartee called for at a party.

Performances in discourse routines are strongly controlled by turn-taking rules that determine who speaks when. Co-occurrence restrictions operate stringently on genres. Often the speech event itself determines them. The genre of sermons occurs in the speech event of church services. Therefore, only features that go with formal style are usually used in sermons. Jokes, in contrast, occur in informal, play situations or as a means of helping someone relax and become more informal. Therefore, formal style features are inappropriate in jokes, so that they are included usually only in the reported conversation of a character in the joke.

INTENTION

In all interaction, the parties assume that each person means what he or she says and is speaking with a purpose. Esther Goody (1978) points out that people impute intentions to others. In fact, she notes, they "positively seek out intentions in what others say and do." What people assume is another's intention colors the meaning they get from messages. How often has someone suspiciously said to a perfectly innocent comment of yours, "Now what did you mean by that?" The question is not asking for literal meaning but for your intention in saying what you did. Presequences rely heavily on our perceiving a speaker's intentions or thinking we do. The child who hears an adult's "Who spilled this milk?" may rightly perceive the question as the precursor to a command "Wipe it up!"

Often, intentions are not perceived correctly, causing misunder-standings as harmless as hearing an honest question as a command or as serious as hearing an innocent comment as an insult. To illustrate the last, consider a man who, in front of his slightly plump wife, looks admir-ingly at a model, "Wow! what a body on that one!" The wife immediately bridles (or dissolves in tears, depending on her personal style) with a "I know I'm too fat. You don't have to rub it in."

The only time that we are freed from the obligation to carry out the socially prescribed roles in speech events is when the other party is inca-pable of acting with a purpose, as when drunk, stoned, or insane (Frake 1964). Perhaps one of the reasons that we get so angry when someone does not act or speak appropriately for the situation is that we can not fig-ure out his or her goals. Without knowing someone's goals, we do not know how to act ourselves when dealing with another person.

SPEECH ACTS

People usually think of speech as a way of stating propositions and conveying information. Austin (1962) also stressed the functions of speech as a way of "doing things with words." Sociolinguists and anthro-pologists have been very concerned with how people use language to manage social interactions. Threatening, complimenting ("buttering someone up"), commanding, even questioning can all be manipulative. Another person's behavior may be affected quite differently from what one might expect from the actual words used. "See that belt?" may be sufficient to restrain a child from wrongdoing. The words themselves are an action. The child, of course, imputes intention to the words. They are heard as a threat of a spanking with the belt.

A CASE IN POINT: THE TELEPHONE

The ritual nature of conversation as well as the role of social conven-tion in determining meaning is easily seen in rules for the telephone (Schegloff 1968). The telephone has been common in American homes only for the past fifty or so years. Yet very definite rules surround its usage. Exactly how such rules arose and became widespread throughout society is not precisely known, any more than we know exactly how a new dialect feature suddenly spreads through a population. All we know is that when-ever a social need arises, language forms evolve to meet the need.

The first rule of telephone conversation in the United States is that the answerer speaks first. It does not have to be so. The rule could as eas-ily be that the caller speaks first. That makes perfectly good sense, as it means that the one who calls is identified at once. Of course, the American way makes equally good sense in that callers are ensured that the receiver is at someone's ear before they start to speak. There are often several equally logical possibilities in conversation rituals, but any one group may adopt just one of the possible alternatives. In other words, if we come across ways different from our own, we should not assume that "theirs" are any better or worse than "ours."

In any event, in the United States, the convention is that the answerer speaks first. If the call could conceivably be for the answerer because he or she is answering the phone in his or her home, the usual first utterance is "Hello."

In places of business or in a doctor's or lawyer's office, wherever secretaries or operators answer the phone, "Hello" is not proper. Rather, the name of the business or office is given, as in "E. B. Marshall Company," "Smith and Carlson," "Dr. Sloan's office" or "George West Junior High." Giving the name in itself means 'This is a business, institution, or professional office.' At one time it was appropriate for servants in a household or even neighbors or friends who happened to pick up the phone to answer "Jones' residence" rather than "Hello," unless the call might conceivably be for the answerer. Increasingly, however, it appears that people answer "Hello" to a residential phone even if the call might not be for them. This situation can lead to complications, especially since the callers still seem to assume that whoever answers "Hello" belongs to that phone.

The British custom of answering with one's name, as "Carl Jones here" seems to be a very efficient solution. Many American callers get thrown off by such a greeting, however. Being impressed with the British rule, I have repeatedly tried to answer my own home phone with "Elaine Chaika here." The result is usually a moment of silence followed by responses like "Uh . . . uh. Elaine?" or "Uh . . . uh. Is Danny there?" The "Uh . . . uh" probably signifies momentary confusion or embarrassment, somewhat different from the "Uh" hesitation that precedes a request to a stranger for directions or the time, as in "Uh, excuse me . . ." Predictably, answering my office phone the same way does not elicit the "Uh . . . uh," although the moment of silence still often occurs.

Godard (1977) recounts the confusion on both her part and callers' in the United States because her native French routine requires that callers verify that the number called is the one reached. Violation of discourse routines, like violations of rules of style, hinders social interaction at least a little even when the violations otherwise fit the situation just fine.

After the answerer says "Hello" or another appropriate greeting, the caller asks, "Is X there?" unless he or she recognizes the answerer's voice as being the one wanted. If the caller recognizes the answerer's voice but wishes to speak to someone else, he or she might say, "Hi, X. Is Y there?" Some do not bother to greet the answerer first. Whether or not hurt feelings result seems to depend on the degree of intimacy involved. Students in my classes report that their mothers often feel hurt if a frequent caller does not say the equivalent of "Hi, Mrs. Jones. Is Darryl there?" Sometimes callers wish to acknowledge the existence of the answerer (phatic communication), but do not wish to be involved in a lengthy conversation so they say the equivalent of "Hi, Mrs. Jones. It's Mary. I'm sorry but I'm in a hurry. Is Darryl there?" On the surface, "I'm sorry but I'm in a hurry" seems to have no relevance. It does, though, because it is an acknowledgment that the caller recognizes acquaintance with the answerer and therefore, the social appropriateness of conversing with her or him.

COMPULSION IN DISCOURSE ROUTINES

In terms of social rules, perhaps what is most interesting is that the person who answers the phone feels compelled to go get the one the caller wants. This compulsion may be so great that answerers find themselves running all over the house, shouting out the windows if necessary to get the one called.

One student of mine, John Reilly, reported an amusing anecdote illustrating the strength of this obligation. He called a friend to go bowling, and the friend's sister answered the phone. She informed John that her brother was cutting logs but that she would go to fetch him. John, knowing that the woodpile was 100 yards away, assured her it was not necessary. All she had to do was to relay the message. Three times she insisted on going. Three times John told her not to. Finally, she said, confusedly, "Don't you want to talk to him?" John repeated that she could extend his invitation without calling the friend to the phone. Suddenly, she just left the phone without responding to John's last remarks and fetched her brother.

As extreme as this may sound, it is actually no more so than the person who leaps out of the tub to answer the phone and, still dripping wet with only a towel for protection, proceeds to run to another part of the house to summon the person for whom the caller asked. It is the rare person who can say, "Yes, X is here, but I don't see her. Call back later." Indeed, there are those who would consider such a response quite rude. It seems as if the person who picks up the phone has tacitly consented to go get whomever is called, regardless of inconvenience, unless the called one is not at home. The sense of obligation, of having to respond in a certain way, is at the core of all social routines, including discourse.

MEANING IN DISCOURSE ROUTINES

Actually, if the one called on the phone is not at home or does not live there any more or never lived there at all, the semantically appropriate response to "Is X there?" should be "No." In fact, however, "No," is appropriate only if X does live there but is not now at home. For example:

If X once lived there, but does not now, an appropriate answer is

1. X doesn't live here any more.
2. X has moved.

or even

3. X lives at _____ now.

Although "no" has the correct meaning, it cannot be used if X no longer lives there.

If X has never lived there, one may answer

4. There is no X here.
5. What number are you calling?
6. You must have the wrong number.

Again, "no" would seem to be a fitting response, but it cannot be used. "No" to "Is X there?" always means that X does belong there but is not there now. Notice that 4 semantically fits for a meaning of 'X no longer lives here', but it never would be used for that meaning by someone socialized into American society.

In discourse routines, frequently an apparently suitable response cannot be used in certain social situations or the response will have a greater meaning than the words used. For instance, one apparently proper response to:

7. Where are the tomatoes? (in a store)

is

8. I don't know.

Most people would find such an honest answer rude, even odd. More likely is

9. I'm sorry, but I don't work here.

or

10. I'm sorry, I'll ask the manager.

If the one asked is an employee, then 10 is appropriate. As with the telephone, the answerer feels obligated. In this instance, the obligation is to supply the answer if he or she is an employee.

PRECONDITIONS

The response 9 would be bizarre except that we all know it is not actually the answer to "Where are the tomatoes?" Rather, it is a response to the preconditions for asking a question of anyone (Labov and Fanshel 1977). These are:

I. The questioner has the right or the duty to ask the question.
II. The one asked has the responsibility or obligation to know the answer.

Preconditions for speech acts are as much a part of their meaning as actual words are. If one asks someone in a store where something is, one probably has categorized that person as an employee, and employees have an obligation to know where things are in their place of work. Hence 9 really means 'You have categorized me erroneously. I don't work here, so I am not obligated to know the answer.'

Sometimes people answer

11. "I don't work here, but the tomatoes are in the next aisle."

The giveaway here is the *but*. It makes no sense in 11 unless it is seen as a response to precondition II. When *but* joins two sentences, it often means 'although,' as in 11, which means 'Although I don't work here, I happen to know that the tomatoes are in the next aisle.' That is, 'Although I am not responsible for knowing or obligated to tell you, since I do not work here, I will anyhow.' Note that the statement "I don't work here" really adds nothing to the pertinent information. It is frequently said anyhow as a way of letting the asker know that he or she miscategorized by assuming that the answerer was an employee.

PRESUPPOSITION

Some meaning in discourse is also achieved by presupposition. This refers to meaning that is never overtly stated but is always presupposed if certain phrases are used. If one says "Even Oscar is going," the use of *even* is possible only if one presupposes that Oscar usually does not go, so that the fact of his going means that everyone is going. Both preconditions and presuppositions are part of the meaning of utterance pairs to be discussed shortly, and both may help constrain the kinds of responses people make to utterances.

UTTERANCE PAIRS

The phenomenon of responsibility which we have already seen as part of telephone routines and answering questions is part of a larger responsibility that adheres to the discourse rules that Harvey Sacks called *utterance pairs* (1964–72, 1970). These are conversational sequences in which one utterance elicits another of a specific kind. For instance,

- Greeting–greeting
- Question–answer
- Complaint–excuse, apology, or denial
- Request/command–acceptance or rejection
- Compliment–acknowledgment
- Farewell–farewell

Whomever is given the first half of an utterance pair is responsible for giving the second half. The first half, in our society, commands the person addressed to give one of the socially recognized appropriate responses.

As with the telephone, these responses often have a meaning different from, less than, or greater than the sum of the words used.

Furthermore, the first half of the pair does not necessarily have to sound like what it really is. That is, a question does not have to be in question form nor a command in command form. All that is necessary for a statement to be construed as a question or a command is for the social situation to be right for questioning or commanding. The very fact that a speech event is appropriate for a question or a command may cause an utterance to be perceived as such, even if it is not in question or command form. As with proper style, situation includes roles and relative status of participants in a conversation. Situation, roles, and social status are an inextricable part of meaning, often as much as, if not more so, than the surface form of an utterance.

QUESTIONS AND ANSWERS

Let us consider questions and answers. Goody (1978) points out that questions, being incomplete, are powerful in forcing responses, at least in our society. . . . We have already seen that certain preconditions exist for questioning and that an answer may be to the precondition rather than to the question itself. In the following discussion, it is always assumed that the preconditions for questioning are fulfilled. We will then be able to gain some insights into how people understand and even manipulate others on the basis of social rules.

There are two kinds of overt questions in English, *yes–no* questions and *wh-* questions. The first, as the name implies, requires an answer of yes or no. In essence, if the *yes–no* question forms are used, one is forced to answer "yes," "no," or "I don't know." There is no way not to answer, except to pretend not to hear. If that occurs, the asker usually repeats the question, perhaps more loudly, or even precedes the repetition with a tap on the would-be answerer's shoulder (or the equivalent). Alternatively, the asker could precede the repeated question with a summons, like "Hey, Bill, I said . . ." or any combination of the three.

It is because members of our society all recognize that they must answer a question and that they must respond "yes" or "no" to a *yes–no* question that the following question is a recognized joke:

12. Have you stopped beating your wife?/your husband?

Since you must know what you do to your spouse, "I don't know" cannot be answered. Only a "yes" or a "no" will do. Either answer condemns. Either way you admit to spouse-beating.

Yes–no questions can also be asked by tags:

13. You're going, *aren't you?*
14. It's five dollars, *right?*

If the preconditions for questioning are present, however, as Labov and Fanshel (1977) point out, a plain declarative statement will be construed as a *yes–no* question, as in

15. Q: You live on 114th Street.
    A: No, I live on 115th.

The *wh-* questions demand an answer that substitutes for the question word. An "I don't know" can also be given. The *wh-* words are *what, when, why, who, where,* and *how* appearing at the start of a question. These words are, in essence, blanks to be filled in.

What has to be answered with the name of a thing or event; *when* with a time; *where* with a location; *why,* a reason; *who,* a person; and *how,* a manner or way something was done. There is actually yet another *wh-* question, "Huh?" which asks in effect, 'Would you repeat the entire sentence you just said?' That is, the "Huh" asks that a whole utterance be filled in, not just a word or phrase.

The answer to any question can be deferred by asking another, creating insertion sequences (Schegloff 1971, p. 76). For instance,

16.
    A: Wanna come to a party?
    B: Can I bring a friend?
    A: Male or female?
    B: Female.
    A: Sure.
    B: O.K.

Note that these questions are answered in reverse order, but all are answered. Occasionally, insertion sequences can lead conversationalists "off the track." When this happens participants may feel a compulsion to get a question answered even if they have forgotten what it was. Hence, comments like:

17. Oh, as you were saying . . .
18. Oh, I forget, what were we talking about?

Note that the "oh" serves as indicator that the speaker is not responding to the last statement, but to a prior one. Such seemingly innocuous syllables frequently serve as markers in conversation.

USING THE RULES TO MANIPULATE

It is easy to manipulate people subtly by plugging them into the presuppositions and preconditions behind statements (Elgin 1980; Labov and Fanshel 1977). For example, a wife might try to get her husband to go to a dance by saying "Even Oscar is going" [see "Presupposition"]. The presupposition is that if Oscar is going, then everyone is. There is a further presupposition that if everyone else is doing something, then so should the person being spoken to. If Oscar is going then everyone is going, ergo, so should the husband. Readers may recognize in this rather common ploy the childhood "Everyone else has one" or "Everyone else is going."

Elgin (1980) also discusses manipulations of the "If you really loved me . . . " variety. These are actually subtle accusations. What they mean is 'You should love me, but you don't. The guilt you feel for not loving me can easily be erased, though, by doing whatever I want.'

Another manipulation is the "Even *you* should be able to do that" type. Here we have *even* again, the word that tells someone that he or she is alone in whatever failing is being mentioned. Its use with *should* is especially clever because it implies that the hearer is stupid or some sort of gross misfit, but it backgrounds that message so that it is not likely to be discussed. Rather, the hearer is made to feel stupid and wrong, so that he or she will be likely to capitulate to the speaker's demands in an effort to prove that if all others can do it, so can the hearer.

One can achieve both manipulation and insult by preceding a comment with "Don't tell me you're going to _____" or "Don't tell me that you believe _____ !" Notice that these are questions in the form of a command. They are actually asking, "Are you really going to _____ ?" or "Do you really believe . . . ?" However, the presuppositions behind these questions in command form are (a) 'You are going to do _____' (or 'You believe _____') and (b) '[your action or belief] _____ is stupid.' For instance,

19. X: Don't tell me that you are going to vote for Murgatroyd!
    Z: Well, I thought I would, but now I'm not so sure.

The really clever manipulation is that Z is instantly made to feel foolish because of presupposition b. However, since X has not overtly accused Z of stupidity, argument is difficult. Z is not even allowed the luxury of anger at the insult, because the insult has not been stated. It is contained only in the presupposition. Z might become immediately defensive but still feel quite stupid because of the implied insult. Not only does X get Z to capitulate, but also X establishes that Z is the stupider of the two. As a manipulatory device, this one is a "double whammy."

Labov and Fanshel (1977) show that some people manipulate in even more subtle ways by utilizing common understanding of social and discourse rules. Using patient-therapist sessions which they received permission to tape, they describe the struggle of a woman named Rhoda for independence from a domineering mother. The mother finally leaves Rhoda at home and goes to visit Rhoda's sister Phyllis. Rhoda cannot cope, but neither can she ask her mother to come home, because that would be an admission that the mother is right in not giving Rhoda more freedom. Rather, Labov and Fanshel say that Rhoda employs an indirect request both to mitigate her asking her mother for help and to disguise her challenge to the power relationship between them. Rhoda calls her mother on the phone and asks,

20. When do you plan to come home?

Since this is not a direct request for help, Rhoda's mother forces an admission by not answering Rhoda's question. Instead, she creates an insertion sequence:

21. Oh, why?

This means 'Why are you asking me when I plan to come home?' In order to answer, Rhoda must admit that she cannot be independent, that the mother has been right all along. Furthermore, as a daughter, Rhoda must answer her mother's question. Her mother has the right to question by virtue of her status, and Rhoda has the duty to answer for the same reason. So, Rhoda responds with

22. Things are getting just a little too much . . . it's getting too hard.

To which the mother replies:

23. Why don't you ask Phyllis [when I'll be home]?

Since, in our society, it is really up to the mother when she will come home, and also, since she has a prior obligation to her own household, "It is clear that Rhoda has been outmaneuvered," according to Labov and Fanshel. The mother has forced Rhoda into admitting that she is not capable, and she has, in effect, refused Rhoda's request for help.

It seems to me that this mother also has conveyed very cleverly to Rhoda that Phyllis is the preferred daughter and has said it so covertly that the topic cannot be discussed openly. Clearly it is the mother's right and duty to come home as she wishes. By palming that decision off on Phyllis, she is actually saying to Rhoda 'No matter what your claim on me is, Phyllis comes first.' That is, for Phyllis's sake, she will suppress her rights as a mother and allow Phyllis to make the decision. Notice that all of this works only because at some level both Rhoda and her mother know the rights and obligations of questioners and answerers.

INDIRECT REQUESTS AND CONFLICT WITH SOCIAL VALUES

All indirect requests do not arise from such hostile situations, although most are used when individual desires conflict with other social rules or values. Classic examples, spoken with an expectant lift to the voice, are:

24. Oh, chocolates.
25. What are those, cigars?

(Sacks, 1964–72)

Assuming that 24 and 25 are spoken by adults who have long known what *chocolate* denotes and are familiar with cigars, these observations are perceived as requests. This is shown by the usual responses to either:

26. Would you like one?
27. I'm sorry, but they aren't mine. (or, I have to save them for X.)

Young toddlers just learning to speak do practice by going about pointing at objects and naming them. Once that stage is past, people do not name items in the immediate environment unless there is an intent, a reason for singling out the item. All properly-socialized Americans know that one should never directly ask for food in another's household or for any possibly expensive goods such as cigars. That would be begging. Therefore, one names the items in another's home or hands so that the naming is construed as an indirect request. There is rarely another reason for an adult to name a common object or food. The responses to 24 and 25 make sense only if the hearer construes those as really meaning 'I want you to offer me some of those chocolates/cigars.'

COMMANDS

Requests for food are not the only discourse routines arising from conflicts between general social rules and the will of the individual. Both commands and compliments, albeit in different ways, run afoul of cultural attitudes.

Commands share virtually the same preconditions as questions.

I. The speaker who commands has the right and/or duty to command.
II. The recipient of the command has the responsibility and/or obligation to carry out the command.

The problem is that, even more than with questioning, the one who has the right to command is usually clearly of higher status than the one who must obey. The United States supposedly is an egalitarian society, but having the right or duty to command implies that some are superior to others. This runs counter to our stated ideals. Therefore, in most actual situations in American speech, commands are disguised as questions. The substitution of forms is possible because both speech acts share the same preconditions. Moreover, phrasing commands as questions maintains the fiction that the one commanded has the right to refuse, even when he or she does not. Consider:

28. Would you mind closing the door?

Even though it is uttered as a *yes–no* question, merely to answer "No" without the accompanying action or "Yes" without an accompanying excuse would either be bizarre or a joke. In the movie *The Return of the Pink Panther*, Peter Sellers asks a passerby if he knows where the Palace

Hotel is. The passerby responds "Yes" and keeps on going. The joke is that "Do you know where X is?" is not really a *yes–no* question but a polite command meaning 'Tell me where X is.'

Direct commanding is allowed and usual in certain circumstances. For instance, parents normally command young children directly. For example,

29. Pick those toys up right away.

Intimates such as spouses or roommates often casually command each other about trivial matters, such as

30. Pick some bread up on your way home.

Often these are softened by "please," "will ya," "honey," or the like.

Direct commanding in command form occurs in the military from those of superior rank to those of inferior. During actual battle it is necessary for combatants to obey their officers without question, unthinkingly, and unhesitatingly. Direct commands yield this kind of obedience so long as those commanded recognize the social rightness of the command or the need. It is no surprise that direct commands are regularly heard in emergency situations, as during firefighting:

31. Get the hose! Put up the ladders!

A great deal of direct commanding is also heard in hospital emergency rooms:

32. Get me some bandages.
    Suture that wound immediately.

In situations that allow direct commands, the full command form need not always be invoked. Just enough has to be said so that the underling knows what to do, as in

33. Time for lunch. (meaning 'Come in for lunch.')
34. Scalpel! Sutures! Dressings!

Note that such commands are contextually bound. They are interpretable as commands only if the participants are actually in a commanding situation. Similarly, Susan Ervin-Tripp's (1972) comment that

35. It's cold in here.

can be interpreted as a command works only in a specific commanding context. The speaker uttering 35 must somehow have the right to ask another to close a window, if that is the cause of the cold, or to ask another to lend his or her coat. In this situation, the fact that one person is closer to an open window may be sufficient reason for him or her to be responsible for closing it. The duty or obligation to carry out a command need not proceed only from actual status but may proceed from the physical circumstances in which the command has been uttered. That is why in the right circumstances ordinary statements or questions may be construed as commands, as in:

36. A: Any more coffee?
    B: I'll make some right away.
    A: No, I wanted to know if I had to buy any.

If is is possible to do something about whatever is mentioned, an utterance may be construed as a command. In 36, it was possible for B to make some coffee, and B must have been responsible for making it at least some of the time. Hence the question about coffee was misinterpreted as a command to make some. The same possibility of misinterpretation can occur in the question

37. Can you swim?

Said by a poolside, it may be interpreted as a command 'Jump in,' but away from a body of water, it will be heard merely as a request for information.

Although questions are often used as polite substitutes for commands, the question command can sometimes be especially imperious:

38. Would you mind being quiet?

Similarly, a command like the following may seem particularly haughty:

39. If you would wait, please.

I suspect that both 38 and 39 carry special force because the high formality signaled by "Would you mind" and "If you would . . . please" contrasts so sharply with the banality of keeping quiet and waiting that the effect of sarcasm is achieved.

COMPLIMENTS

Compliments are another utterance pair type that create conflict. This is because of general social convention and the rule that the first part of an utterance pair must evoke a response. Compliments call for an acknowledgment. The acknowledgment can properly be acceptance of the compliment, as in "Thank you." The problem is that to accept the compliment is very close to bragging, and bragging is frowned upon in middle-class America. Hence, one typical response to a compliment is a disclaimer, like

40. This old rag?
41. I got it on sale.
42. My mother got it for me.

An exception is special occasions when compliments are expected, as when everyone is decked out to go to a prom or a wedding. Then, not only are compliments easily received with "Thank you," but not to compliment can cause offense or disappointment.

Except for such situations, complimenting can lead to social embarrassment. If one persists in complimenting another, the other person often becomes hostile, even though nice things are being said. At the very least the recipient of excessive praise becomes uncomfortable and tries to change the subject. Often he or she becomes suspicious and angry or tries to avoid the person who is heaping praise. The suspicion is either that the complimenter is being patronizing or is trying to get something, to "butter the person up."

Once, I ordered a class to persistently compliment their parents, spouses, or siblings. The most common response was "OK. What do you want this time?" One of the students received a new suit from a friend who owned a men's clothing store, with the friend practically shouting, "OK. If I give you a new suit will that shut you up?"

Many of those complimented became overtly angry. Others quickly found an excuse to leave, and several students found that those on whom they heaped praise shunned them the next time they met. I suspect that the anger results from the social precariousness of being complimented. As with style, when a person is put at a social disadvantage so that he or she does not know how to respond, anger results. It is very uncomfortable to receive too much praise. It is tantamount to continually being asked to tread the line between gracious acceptance and boasting. Most people prefer to ignore anyone who puts them in that situation.

PRESEQUENCES AND SAVING FACE

An interesting class of discourse rules is what Harvey Sacks called *presequences* (lecture, November 2, 1967), particularly preinvitations. Typically, someone wishing to issue an oral invitation, first asks something like

43. What are you doing Saturday night?

If the response includes words like *only* or *just*, as in

44. I'm just washing my hair.
45. I'm only studying.

the inviter can then issue an invitation for Saturday night. If, however, the response is

46. I'm washing my hair.
47. I'm studying.

the potential inviter knows not to issue the invitation. Following a response like 46 or 47, the inviter signals a change in conversation by saying "Uh— — —" and then speaks of something other than Saturday night (or whatever date was mentioned). Issuing of preinvitations is an ego saver like the use of style to signal social class. Having been spared overt refusal, the inviter is able to save face (Goffman 1955).

COLLAPSING SEQUENCES

Sometimes utterance pairs are collapsed (Sacks, November 2, 1967) as in the following exchange at an ice cream counter:

48. A: What's chocolate filbert?
    B: We don't have any.

B's response is to what B knows is likely to come next. If B had explained what chocolate filbert is, then A very likely would have asked for some. Indeed, by explaining what it is, B would be tacitly saying that he or she had some to sell. In a selling situation in our society, explaining what goods or foods are is always an admission that they are available. Imagine your reaction, for instance, if you asked a waiter or waitress what some food was like, and he or she went into detail telling you about it. Then, if you said, "Sounds good. I'll have that," and the response were, "We don't have any," you would think you were being made a fool of.

Another common collapsing sequence is typified by the exchange:

49. A: Do you smoke?
    B: I left them in my other jacket.

Such collapsing sequences speed up social interaction by forestalling unnecessary explanations. They are used for other purposes as well, as when a newcomer joins a discussion in progress:

50. Hi, John. We were just talking about nursery schools.

This either warns John not to join the group or, if he is interested in nursery schools, gives him orientation so that he can understand what is going on.

REPAIRS

If a person uses the wrong style for an occasion, the other party(ies) to the interaction try to repair the error. . . . Schegloff, Jefferson, and Sacks (1977) collected interesting samples of self-correction in discourse, people repairing their own errors. Sometimes this takes the form of obvious correction to a slip of the tongue, as in

51. What're you so *ha*—er un—*un*happy about?

Sometimes speakers make a repair when they have made no overt error, as in

52. Sure enough ten minutes later the bell r—the doorbell rang.

Because such repairs do not show a one-to-one correspondence with actual spoken errors, Schegloff et al. preferred the term *repair* over *correction.* In both 51 and 52, for instance, neither repair was preceded by an error that actually occurred in speech.

Schegloff et al. found an orderly pattern in speech repair. Repairs did not occur just anywhere in an utterance. They occurred in one of three positions: immediately after the error, as in 51 and 52, or at the end of the sentence where another person would normally take the floor:

53. An 'en bud all of the doors 'n things were taped up—I mean y'know they put up y'know that kinda paper stuff, the brown paper.

or right after the other person speaks:

54. *Hannah:*   And he's going to make his own paintings.
    Bea: Mm hm.
    Hannah: And—for I mean his own frames.

If the speaker does not repair an obvious error, the hearer will. Usually this is done by asking a question that will lead the speaker to repair his or her own error. Some examples:

55. A: It wasn't snowing all day.
    B: It *wasn't*?
    A: Oh, I mean it was.
56. A: Yeah, he's got a lot of smarts.
    B: *Huh*?
    A: He hasn't got a lot of smarts.
57. A: Hey, the first time they stopped me from selling cigarettes was this morning.
    B: From *selling* cigarettes?
    A: From buying cigarettes.

Often, the hearer will say "you mean" as in

58. A: We went Saturday afternoon.
    B: You mean Sunday.
    C: Yeah, uhnnn we saw Max . . .

In most of the repairs by hearers, it seems that the hearer knows all along what the intended word was. Still, it is rare, although not impossible, for the hearer actually to supply the word. This seems to be a face saver for the person who made the error. The hearer often offers the correction or the question leading to correction tentatively, as if he or she is not sure. That way, the speaker is not humiliated as he or she might be if the hearer in positive tones asserted that an error was made. Another reason that hearers offer corrections tentatively may be that in doing so, the hearer is in the position of telling someone else what must be going on in his or her mind.

Schegloff et al. (1977, p. 38) state that "the organization of repair is the self-righting mechanisms for the organization of language use in social interaction." In other words, it maintains normal social interaction. We have already seen this in attempted repair of inappropriate style.

The importance of the self-righting mechanism is shown in the following almost bizarre interactions. These involve repairs in greetings and farewells collected as part of a participant observation by a student, Sheila Kennedy. While on guard duty at the door of a dormitory, she deliberately confounded greetings and farewells, with fascinating results.

To a stranger:
59. *Sheila:*   Hi. [pause] Good night.
    Stranger: Hello. [pause] Take it easy.

Note that the stranger also gave both a greeting and a farewell, even matching the pause that Sheila used between them. This is [similar to] exchanges in which subjects [match an] experimenter's style, even when they [question it].

To a female friend:
60. *Friend:* Bye, Sheila.
    Sheila: Hello.
    Friend: Why did you say hello? I said goodbye. [pause] Hi.

Even though the friend questioned the inappropriateness of Sheila's response, she still felt constrained to answer the greeting with a greeting.

To a male friend:
61. *Friend:* Hi!
    Sheila: So long.
           [Both spoke at the same time, so Sheila starts again.]
    Sheila: Hi!
    Friend: Bye. [laughs] Wait a minute. Let's try that again. Hi!
    Sheila: Hello.
    Friend: Bye.
    Sheila: So long.
    Friend: That's better. [laughs and leaves]

What is interesting here is the lengths the subject went to in order that the appropriate pairs were given. Note that he had to get both greeting and farewell matched up before he would leave. The degree to which we are bound by the social rules of discourse is well illustrated in 59–61. The very fact that people go to so much trouble to repair others' responses is highly significant. It shows the importance of discourse routines to social interaction, that one cannot be divorced from the other. Not only must style and kinesics be appropriate for social functioning but so must the discourse itself. Even when people know what the other must mean, as in 55–58, they ask that the discourse be righted. And, even when it makes no difference in a fleeting social contact, as in 59–61, they demand that the right forms be chosen.

NEW RULES OF DISCOURSE

New situations may involve learning new discourse rules. Anthony Wooton (1975, p. 70) gives an example from psychotherapy. Psychiatrists typically do not tell patients what to do. Rather, by asking questions, they try to lead the patient into understanding. The problem is that the questions asked and the answers they are supposed to evoke are different from those already learned as part of normal routines. As an example, Wooton gives:

62. *Patient:*   I'm a nurse, but my husband won't let me work.
    Therapist: How old are you?
    Patient: Thirty-one this December.
    Therapist: What do you mean, he won't let you work?

Here, the patient answers the psychiatrist's first question as if it were bona fide, a real world question. The psychiatrist was not really asking her age, however, as we can see by his next question. What he meant by that question was 'You are old enough to decide whether or not you wish to work.' His question was aimed at leading her to that conclusion.

The patient in therapy has to learn new discourse routines in order to benefit from the therapeutic situation. The therapist uses modes of questioning different from everyday discourse. This is not surprising, since the aim of psychotherapy is for the psychiatrist to lead the patient into self-discovery. Some patients become very annoyed by the questioning, feeling that the therapist is refusing to tell them anything. In traditional psychoanalysis it was accepted that there had to be a period during which the patient 'fought' the analyst by refusing to dredge up the answers from the murky subconscious. It has occurred to me that this period may actually represent a time during which the patient must learn to respond to the new question and answer routines demanded by analysis.

It is very hard to gain insights into oneself by sustained self-questioning, perhaps because questioning is rarely used that way outside the therapeutic situation. Furthermore, repeated questioning in itself is threatening. In many societies, including our own, it is associated with accusation of wrongdoing and ferreting out the truth of one's guilt. It is used as a technique for teaching, to be sure, but even then it is often a way of ferreting out the pupil's lapses in learning.

TOPIC IN NORMAL AND PSYCHOTIC SPEECH

The first half of an utterance pair strongly limits what can come next. It limits both form and subject matter. These are intertwined virtually inseparably: a greeting is both a form and a subject matter. The response to a *wh-* question must use the same words as the question, filling in the missing word signaled by whichever *wh-* word was used. The answer to "Where did you go?" is "I went to [place X]." The answer to "Whom did you see?" is "I saw [person X]."

The larger conversation, beyond utterance pairs, is not so strongly constrained as to form. The entire syntax of the language can be drawn upon to encode new ideas, not just the syntax of greetings or compliments or invitation. The first sentence or so of an answer is predetermined by the question just asked, but the speaker becomes free as soon as an answer is given that fills in the *wh-* word or supplies the *Yes, No,* or *I don't know.* The constraints upon topic, however, remain very strong.

In normal conversation, everything has to be subordinated to topic, whatever is being talked about (see VanDijk 1977). Schegloff (1971) likens this to co-occurrence restrictions such as we saw in style. Once a topic is introduced, it must be adhered to unless some formal indication of change is made. Paradoxically, in American English, this often is "Not to change the subject, but . . ." This disclaimer always changes the topic. Other signals that change topic are "Oooh, that reminds me . . ." or "Oooh, I meant to tell you . . ." The "Oooh" in itself, uttered rapidly on a high pitch with a tense throat, is a warning that an announcement about topic change is coming.

Adherence to a topic is so important that failure to do so is evidence of mental incapacity. A person's mind is said to wander if his or her words wander off topics with no warning. Many observers of patients diagnosed as schizophrenic have noticed peculiarities in their speech, peculiarities traditionally called *thought disorder* (TD). Since not all schizophrenics show these speech disorders, some are termed *non–thought disordered* (NTD). As a result of my own extensive analyses of speech termed TD, I think that such speech differs from normal or NTD speech mainly in that it does not stick to a topic. For instance,

63. My mother's name was Bill and coo. St. Valentine's Day was the start of the breedin' season of the birds.

(Chaika 1974, 1977)

64. Looks like clay. Sounds like gray. Take you for a roll in the hay. Hay day. May day. Help! I just can't. Need help. May day.

(Cohen 1978)

65. I had a little goldfish like a clown. Happy Hallowe'en down.

(Chaika 1974, 1977)

The greatest abnormality in such speech is that the patient is not sticking to a topic. Other than that, each part of the utterance is normal; grammar, word choice, and sounds are correctly used.

The words and phrases chosen do have a connection with one another in each of the samples just given. They are related on the basis of similarity of sound, especially rhyme, and on the basis of shared meaning. "Bill and coo" is an old metaphor for 'love' based upon an image of lovebirds or doves, which bill and coo. Love is also associated with St. Valentine's Day.

"Roll in the hay" means '(sexual) fun'. "Hay day" not only rhymes with "hay," but if, as seems likely, the patient meant 'heyday', it also refers to good times. "Hay day" rhymes with "May day," which is another way of saying "SOS" or "Help!" "Happy Hallowe'en" seems to be an association with "clown," with which "down" is a chance rhyme.

No matter how tightly such associations can be woven into the utterance, still 63–65 are obviously pathological speech. It is topic that determines normal speech, not other kinds of associations between words. Some people have suggested that schizophrenic speech is poetic, because, like poetry, it often rhymes. One major objection to this view is the high interjudge reliability when people are asked to distinguish schizophrenic utterances from others (Maher, McKeon and McLaughlin 1966; Rochester, Martin and Thurston 1977).

The schizophrenic rhyming and figurative speech occurs only because of chance association. Poetic rhyme and artistic language in general seem to be as constrained by a topic as any other kind of normal speech. Rhyming and other features of poetry, such as unusual associations and figurative language, are poetic when they are subordinated to a topic. . . .

In the twentieth century certain authors have deliberately set out to recreate stream of consciousness in their fiction, and some poetry is deliberately formless. Dr. Nancy Andreasen (1973) claims that James Joyce's *Finnegan's Wake* would appear to be schizophrenic to most psychiatrists. Even in such modern literature, however, form is usually subordinated to general topic.

BIBLIOGRAPHY

Andreasen, N. 1973. James Joyce, a portrait of the artist as a schizoid. *Journal of the American Medical Association.* 224: 67–71.

Austin, J. L. 1962. *How to Do Things with Words.* 2nd ed. J. Urmson and M. Sbisa, eds. Cambridge, Mass.: Harvard University Press.

Carswell, E. A., and R. Rommetveit. 1971. *Social Contexts of Messages.* New York: Academic Press.

Chaika, E. 1974. A linguist looks at "schizophrenic" language. *Brain and Language 1:* 257–276.

Chaika, E. 1977. Schizophrenic speech, slips of the tongue, and jargonaphasia: a reply to Fromkin and to Lecours and Vaniers-Clement. *Brain and Language 4:* 464–475.

Cohen, B. D. 1968. Referent communication disturbances in schizophrenia. In S. Schwartz, ed. pp. 1–34.

Cole, P. and J. Morgan, eds. 1975. *Syntax and Semantics,* vol. 3, *Speech Acts.* New York: Academic Press.

Elgin, S. H. 1980. *The Gentle Art of Verbal Self-Defense.* Englewood Cliffs, N.J.: Prentice-Hall.

Ervin-Tripp, S. 1972. On sociolinguistic rules: alternation and co-occurrence. In J. Gumperz and D. Hymes, eds., pp. 213–250.

Frake, C. O. 1964. How to ask for a drink in Subanum. *American Anthropologist* 66: 127–32.

Givon, T., ed. 1979. *Syntax and Semantics*, vol. 12, *Discourse and Syntax*. New York: Academic Press.

Godard, D. 1977. Same setting, different norms: phone call beginnings in France and the United States. *Language in Society 6:* 209–220.

Goffman, E. 1955. On facework. *Psychiatry 18:* 213–231.

Goody, E. N. ed. 1978. *Questions and Politeness*. New York: Cambridge University Press.

Gordon, D., and G. Lakoff. 1975. Conversational postulates. In P. Cole and J. Morgan, eds., pp. 83–106.

Gumperz, J., and D. Hymes, eds. 1972. *Directions in Sociolinguistics*. New York: Holt, Rinehart, and Winston.

Labov, W., and D. Fanshel. 1977. *Therapeutic Discourse*. New York: Academic Press.

Maher, B., K. McKeon, and B. McLaughlin. 1966. Studies in psychotic language. In P. Stone, D. Dunphy, M. Smith, and D. Ogilvie, eds., pp. 469–501.

Rochester, S., J. Martin, and S. Thurston. 1977. Thought process disorder in schizophrenia: the listener's task. *Brain and Language. 4:* 95–114.

Rommetveit, R. 1971. Words, contexts and verbal message transmission. In E. A. Carswell and R. Rommetveit, eds., pp. 13–26.

Sacks, H. 1964–72. Lecture notes. Mimeo.

Sacks, H. 1970. Discourse analysis, untitled mss. mimeo.

Schegloff, E. A. 1968. Sequencing in conversational openings. *American Anthropologist 70:* 1075–1095.

Schegloff, E. A. 1971. Notes on a conversational practice: formulating place. In D. Sudnow, ed., pp. 75–119.

Schegloff, E. A., G. Jefferson, and H. Sacks. 1977. The preference for self-correction in the organization of repair in conversation. *Language 53.* 361–382.

Schenkein, J., ed. 1978. *Studies in the Organization of Conversation*. New York: Academic Press.

Schwartz, S., ed. 1978. *Language and Cognition in Schizophrenia*. Hillsdale, N.J.: Lawrence Erlbaum.

Sudnow, D. ed. 1971. *Studies in Social Interaction*. New York: The Free Press.

Stone, P., D. Dunphy, M. Smith, and D. Ogilvie, eds. 1966. *General Inquirer*. Cambridge, Mass.: MIT Press.

Van Dijk, T. 1977. *Text and Context: Explorations in the Semantics and Pragmatics of Discourse*. New York: Longman.

Wooton, A. 1975. *Dilemmas of Discourse: Controversies about the Sociological Interpretation of Language*. London: Allen and Unwin.

FOR DISCUSSION AND REVIEW

1. Professor Chaika states that language "makes us free as individuals but chains us socially." Explain this apparent paradox.

2. Explain the relationship between a speech event, genre, and performance. Why does this relationship matter?

3. Summarize the rules of telephone conversation in the United States. Are the rules different for land lines versus cell phone use? How is "compulsion," or "sense of obligation," exhibited in telephone discourse? Describe some experiences where assumed "rules" did not apply. How did you figure out other rules?

4. Shared de facto norms of interaction may sometimes work in conflict with the desires of individual participants. Describe an occurrence in your own life that exemplifies this statement.

5. Chaika says that "preconditions for speech acts are as much a part of their meaning as actual words are." Using your own example, explain what Chaika means.

6. Using your own experiences, give an example of each of the six utterance pairs Chaika lists on p. 283. Try to provide examples whose first half of the utterance pair doesn't sound like what it is.

7. What is an "insertion sequence" in a series of questions? Give an example from a conversation with a friend.

8. Explain how we sometimes manipulate others by using the words *even* or *don't*.

9. What do our repairs of other people's responses indicate about discourse routines?

10. Ordinary conversation is partly controlled by a *topic*. What expectations do we have about topics? What might happen when our expectations are not met? How do participants change topic?

11. Chaika suggests that analyzing "abnormal" speech should be done with understanding of what makes speech normal. How does schizophrenic speech differ from normal speech?

18

Talk and Action

Ronald Wardhaugh

In this selection from the fifth edition of An Introduction to Sociolinguistics *(2006), Ronald Wardhaugh, professor emeritus at the University
of Toronto, presents a thorough exploration of speech act theory. According
to this, we use conversation to perform actions in the world, not just to
make statements ("propositions") about the world. In other words, in conversation we accomplish—or fail to accomplish—a variety of social
activities, such as establishing friendships, achieving cooperation, and
creating the basis for future interactions. Wardhaugh begins by discussing the early formulations of speech act theory by Oxford philosopher
John Austin and his student John Searle, including the concept of a*
speech act *and the idea that speech acts have force. Wardhaugh also
explains Paul Grice's* cooperative principle, *which expresses the expectations we uphold in our contributions to a conversation.*

In speaking to one another, we make use of sentences, or, to be more precise, utterances. We can attempt to classify these utterances in any one of
a variety of ways. We can try to classify them by length, e.g., by counting
the number of words in each utterance, but that appears to be of little interest except to those who believe that shorter utterances are more easily
understood than longer ones. We can try to classify them by grammatical
structure along a number of dimensions, e.g., their clausal type and
complexity: active–passive; statement–question–request–exclamatory;
various combinations of these; and so on. We may even try to work out
a semantic or logical structure for each utterance. But it is also possible
to attempt a classification in terms of what sentences do, i.e., to take a
'functional' approach, but one that goes somewhat beyond consideration
of such functions as stating, questioning, requesting, and exclaiming. In
recent years a number of philosophers have had interesting things to say
about what utterances do as well as mean, observing that part of the total
meaning is this very doing.

As soon as we look closely at conversation in general, we see that it
involves much more than using language to state propositions or convey
facts. . . . Through conversation we establish relationships with others,
achieve a measure of cooperation (or fail to do so), keep channels open for
further relationships, and so on. The utterances we use in conversation

enable us to do these kinds of things because conversation itself has certain properties which are well worth examining. Our concern [here] is therefore twofold: we will be concerned both with what utterances do and how they can be used, and, specifically, with how we use them in conversation.

SPEECH ACTS

One thing that many utterances do is make *propositions*: they do this mainly in the form of either statements or questions but other grammatical forms are also possible. Each of the following is a proposition: 'I had a busy day today,' 'Have you called your mother?,' and 'Your dinner's ready!' Such utterances are connected in some way with events or happenings in a possible world, i.e., one that can be experienced or imagined, a world in which such propositions can be said to be either true or false. They have been called *constative utterances.*

A different kind of proposition is the ethical proposition, e.g., 'Big boys don't cry,' 'God is love,' 'Thou shalt not kill,' 'You must tell the truth,' and even 'Beethoven is better than Brahms.' Just like an ordinary proposition, an ethical proposition may be true or false, although not in the same sense. But truth and falsity are not the real purpose of ethical propositions; their real purpose is to serve as guides to behavior in some world or other. 'Big boys don't cry' is obviously value-laden in a way in which 'Your dinner's ready!' definitely is not. Another kind of utterance is the 'phatic' type, e.g., 'Nice day!,' 'How do you do?,' and 'You're looking smart today!' We employ such utterances not for their propositional content but rather for their affective value as indicators that one person is willing to talk to another and that a channel of communication is either being opened or being kept open. Phatic utterances do not really communicate anything; rather, their use allows communication to occur should there be anything of consequence to say. I will have a little more to say on this matter shortly.

Austin (1975), a philosopher, distinguished still another kind of utterance from these, the *performative utterance.* In using a performative utterance, a person is not just saying something but is actually doing something if certain real-world conditions are met. To say 'I name this ship "Liberty Bell"' in certain circumstances is to name a ship. To say 'I do' in other circumstances is to find oneself a husband or a wife—or a bigamist. To hear someone say to you 'I sentence you to five years in jail' in still other circumstances is to look forward to a rather bleak future. Such utterances perform acts: the naming of ships, marrying, and sentencing in these cases. A speech act changes in some way the conditions that exist in the world. It does something, and it is not something that in itself is either true or false. Truth and falsity may be claims made about its having been done, but they cannot be made about the actual doing.

Austin pointed out that the 'circumstances' mentioned above can be prescribed. He mentions certain *felicity conditions* that performatives must meet to be successful. First, a conventional procedure must exist for doing whatever is to be done, and that procedure must specify who must say and do what and in what circumstances. Second, all participants must properly execute this procedure and carry it through to completion. Finally, the necessary thoughts, feelings, and intentions must be present in all parties. In general, the spoken part of the total act, the actual *speech act*, will take the grammatical form of having a first-person subject and a verb in the present tense; it may or may not also include the word *hereby*. Examples are 'I (hereby) name,' 'We decree,' and 'I swear.' This kind of utterance is explicitly performative when it is employed in a conventional framework, such as naming ships, making royal proclamations, and taking an oath in court.

There are also less explicit performatives. Declarations like 'I promise,' 'I apologize,' or 'I warn you' have many of the same characteristics as the previously mentioned utterances but lack any associated conventional procedure; for anyone can promise, apologize, and warn, and there is no way of specifying the circumstances quite so narrowly as in naming ships, proclaiming, or swearing an oath. It is also on occasion possible to use other grammatical forms than the combination of first person and present tense. 'Thin ice,' 'Savage dog,' 'Slippery when wet,' and 'Loitering is forbidden' are all very obviously warnings, so to that extent they are performatives. What we can observe, then, is that, in contrast to constative utterances, that is, utterances which are often used to assert propositions and which may be true or false, they are used either appropriately or inappropriately and, if used appropriately, their very utterance is the doing of the whole or part of an action.

Austin divides performatives into five categories: (1) *verdictives*, typified by the giving of a verdict, estimate, grade, or appraisal ('We find the accused guilty'); (2) *exercitives*, the exercising of powers, rights, or influences as in appointing, ordering, warning, or advising ('I pronounce you husband and wife'); (3) *commissives*, typified by promising or undertaking, and committing one to do something by, for example, announcing an intention or espousing a cause ('I hereby bequeath'); (4) *behabitives*, having to do with such matters as apologizing, congratulating, blessing, cursing, or challenging ('I apologize'); and (5) *expositives*, a term used to refer to how one makes utterances fit into an argument or exposition ('I argue,' 'I reply,' or 'I assume').

Once we begin to look at utterances from the point of view of what they do, it is possible to see every utterance as a speech act of one kind or other, that is, as having some functional value which might be quite independent of the actual words used and their grammatical arrangement. These acts may not be as explicit or direct as 'Out!,' 'I do,' or 'We hereby seek leave to appeal' but there can be little dispute that even to say something like 'I saw John this morning' is an act; at the simplest level it is an act of telling the truth (or what you believe to be the truth) or not. There is also no reason to assume that every language has the same performatives. Although it is unlikely that a language will be without performatives for ordering, promising, and challenging, it is quite easy to see it doing without those for baptizing, naming ships, passing jail sentences, and making bets. Performativity almost certainly varies by culture.

We can now return to expressions like 'Nice day!,' 'How do you do?,' and 'You're looking smart today.' A specific kind of speech is the kind we have referred to previously as *phatic communion*. According to Malinowski (1923, p. 315), phatic communion is a type of speech in which ties of union are created by a mere exchange of words. In such communion words do not convey meanings. Instead, 'they fulfill a social function, and that is their principal aim.' What, therefore, is the function of apparently aimless gossip? Malinowski answers as follows:

> It consists in just this atmosphere of sociability and in the fact of the personal communion of these people. But this is in fact achieved by speech, and the situation in all such cases is created by the exchange of words, by the specific feelings which form convivial gregariousness, by the give and take of utterances which make up ordinary gossip. The whole situation consists in what happens linguistically. Each utterance is an act serving the direct aim of binding hearer to speaker by a tie of some social sentiment or other. Once more, language appears to us in this function not as an instrument of reflection but as a mode of action.

Malinowski himself uses the word *act* in this explanation. In phatic communion, therefore, we have still another instance of language being used to do something, not just to say something. (See also Cheepen, 1988, pp. 14–19.)

According to Searle (1969, pp. 23–4), we perform different kinds of acts when we speak. The utterances we use are *locutions*. Most locutions express some intent that a speaker has. They are *illocutionary acts* and have an *illocutionary force*. A speaker can also use different locutions to achieve the same illocutionary force or use one locution for many different purposes. Schiffrin (1994, ch. 3) has a very good example of the latter. She shows how one form, 'Y'want a piece of candy?' can perform many functions as a speech act, including question, request, and offer. In contrast, we can see how different forms can perform a single function since it is quite possible to ask someone to close the door with different words: 'It's cold in here,' 'The door's open,' and 'Could someone see to the door?' Illocutions also often cause listeners to do things. To that extent they are *perlocutions*. If you say 'I bet you a dollar he'll win' and I say 'On,' your illocutionary act of offering a bet has led to my perlocutionary uptake of accepting it. The *perlocutionary force* of your words is to get me to bet, and you have succeeded.

Searle (1999, pp. 145–6) says that illocutionary acts must be performed 'intentionally.' In order to communicate something in a language that will be understood by another speaker of that language as an utterance it must (1) be correctly uttered with its conventional meaning and (2) satisfy a truth condition, i.e., if it is 'It is raining' it must indeed be raining, and the hearer should recognize the truth of (1) and (2): 'if the hearer knows the language, recognizes my intention to produce a sentence of the language, and recognizes that I am not merely uttering that sentence but that I also mean what I say, then I will have succeeded in communicating to the hearer that it is raining.' Searle also recasts Austin's five categories of performative (here repeated in parentheses) by what he calls their point or purpose: assertives (expositives), which commit the hearer to the truth of a proposition; directives (verdictives), which get the hearer to believe in such a way as to make his or her behavior match the propositional content of the directive; commissives (commissives), which commit the speaker to undertake a course of action represented in the propositional content; expressives (behabitives), which express the sincerity conditions of the speech act; and declaratives (exercitives), which bring about a change in the world by representing it as having been changed.

If we look at how we perform certain kinds of acts rather than at how particular types of utterances perform acts, we can, as Searle (1975) has indicated, categorize at least six ways in which we can make requests or give orders even indirectly. There are utterance types that focus on the hearer's ability to do something ('Can you pass the salt?'; 'Have you got change for a dollar?'); those that focus on the speaker's wish or desire that the hearer will do something ('I would like you to go now'; 'I wish you wouldn't do that'); those that focus on the hearer's actually doing something ('Officers will henceforth wear ties at dinner'; 'Aren't you going to eat your cereal?'); those that focus on the hearer's willingness or desire to do something ('Would you be willing to write a letter of recommendation for me?'; 'Would you mind not making so much noise?'); those that focus on the reasons for doing something ('You're standing on my foot'; 'It might help if you shut up'); and, finally, those that embed one of the above types inside another ('I would appreciate it if you could make less noise'; 'Might I ask you to take off your hat?'). As Searle says (1999, p. 151), 'one can perform one speech act indirectly by performing another directly.'

Searle has concentrated his work on speech acts on how a hearer perceives a particular utterance to have the force it has, what he calls the 'uptake' of an utterance. In particular, what makes a promise a promise? For Searle there are five rules that govern promise-making. The first, the *propositional content rule*, is that the words must predicate a future action of the speaker. The second and third, the *preparatory rules*, require that both the person promising and the person to whom the promise is made must want the act done and that it would not otherwise be done. Moreover, the person promising believes he or she can do what is promised. The fourth, the *sincerity rule*, requires the promiser to intend to perform the act, that is, to be placed under some kind of obligation; and the fifth, the *essential rule*, says that the uttering of the words counts as undertaking an obligation to perform the action.

If this view is correct, it should be possible to state the necessary and sufficient conditions for every illocutionary act. Many of these require that the parties to acts be aware of social obligations involved in certain relationships. They may also make reference to certain other kinds of knowledge we must assume the parties have if the act is to be successful. For example, a command such as 'Stand up!' from A to B can be felicitous only if B is not standing up, can stand up, and has an obligation to stand up if A so requests, and if A has a valid reason to make B stand up. Both A and B must recognize the validity of all these conditions if 'Stand up!' is to be used and interpreted as a proper command. We should note that breaking any one of the conditions makes 'Stand up!' invalid: B is already standing up, is crippled (and A is not a faith healer!), outranks A, or is at least A's equal, or A has no reason that appears valid to B so that standing up appears unjustified, unnecessary, and uncalled for.

These kinds of conditions for illocutionary acts resemble what have been called *constitutive rules* rather than *regulative rules* (Rawls, 1955). Regulative rules are things like laws and regulations passed by governments and legislative bodies: they regulate what is right and wrong and sometimes prescribe sanctions if and when the rules are broken, e.g., 'Trespassing is forbidden' or 'No parking.' Constitutive rules, on the other hand, are like the rules of baseball, chess, or soccer: they actually define a particular activity in the form of 'doing X counts as Y' so that if, in certain prescribed circumstances, you strike a ball in a particular way or succeed in moving it into a certain place, that counts as a 'hit' or a 'goal.' The rules constitute the game: without them the game does not exist. In the same way, speech acts are what they are because saying something counts as something if certain conditions prevail. As Schiffrin (1994, p. 60) says, 'Language can do things—can perform acts—because people share constitutive rules that create the acts and that allow them to label utterances as particular kinds of acts.'

In contrast to Austin, who focused his attention on how speakers realize their intentions in speaking, Searle focuses on how listeners respond to utterances, that is, how one person tries to figure out how another is using a particular utterance. Is what is heard a promise, a warning, an assertion, a request, or something else? What is the illocutionary force of a particular utterance? What we see in both Austin and Searle is a recognition that people use language to achieve a variety of objectives. If we want to understand what they hope to accomplish, we must be prepared to take into account factors that range far beyond the actual linguistic form of any particular utterance. A speaker's intent, or perceived intent, is also important, as are the social circumstances that apparently determine that, if factors X, Y, and Z are present, then utterance A counts as an example of P, but if X, Y, and W are present, then the same utterance counts as an example of Q. We can see that this is the case if we consider promises and threats: these share many of the same characteristics, but they must differ in at least one essential characteristic or there would be no distinction.

COOPERATION

We can view utterances as acts of various kinds and the exchanges of utterances that we call conversations as exchanges of acts, not just exchanges of words, although they are this too. However, we may well ask how we can make such exchanges without achieving some prior agreement concerning the very principles of exchange. In fact, we do not. According to philosophers such as Grice, we are able to converse with one another because we recognize common goals in conversation and specific ways of achieving these goals. In any conversation, only certain kinds of 'moves' are possible at any particular time because of the constraints that operate to govern exchanges. These constraints limit speakers as to what they can say and listeners as to what they can infer.

Grice (1975, p. 45) maintains that the overriding principle in conversation is one he calls the *cooperative principle*: 'Make your conversational contribution such as is required, at the stage at which it occurs, by the accepted purpose or direction of the talk exchange in which you are engaged.' You must therefore act in conversation in accord with a general principle that you are mutually engaged with your listener or listeners in an activity that is of benefit to all, that benefit being mutual understanding.

Grice lists four maxims that follow from the cooperative principle: quantity, quality, relation, and manner. The maxim of *quantity* requires you to make your contribution as informative as is required. The maxim of *quality* requires you not to say what you believe to be false or that for which you lack adequate evidence. *Relation* is the simple injunction: be relevant. *Manner* requires you to avoid obscurity of expression and ambiguity, and to be brief and orderly. This principle and these maxims characterize ideal exchanges. Such exchanges would also observe certain other principles too, such as 'Be polite.'

Grice points out (p. 47) that these maxims do not apply to conversation alone. He says:

> it may be worth noting that the specific expectations or presumptions connected with at least some of the foregoing maxims have their analogs in the sphere of transactions that are not talk exchanges. I list briefly one such analog for each conversational category.
>
> 1. *Quantity.* If you are assisting me to mend a car, I expect your contribution to be neither more nor less than is required; if, for example, at a particular stage I need four screws, I expect you to hand me four, rather than two or six.

2. *Quality.* I expect your contributions to be genuine and not spurious. If I need sugar as an ingredient in the cake you are assisting me to make, I do not expect you to hand me salt; if I need a spoon, I do not expect a trick spoon made of rubber.
3. *Relation.* I expect a partner's contribution to be appropriate to immediate needs at each stage of the transaction; if I am mixing ingredients for a cake, I do not expect to be handed a good book, or even an oven cloth (though this might be an appropriate contribution at a later stage).
4. *Manner.* I expect a partner to make it clear what contribution he is making, and to execute his performance with reasonable dispatch.

What we can observe, therefore, is that the maxims are involved in all kinds of rational cooperative behavior: we assume the world works according to a set of maxims or rules which we have internalized, and we generally do our best to make it work in that way. There is nothing special about conversation when we view it in such a way.

Of course, everyday speech often occurs in less than ideal circumstances. Grice points out that speakers do not always follow the maxims he has described, and, as a result, they may *implicate* something rather different from what they actually say. They may violate, exploit, or opt out of one of the maxims, or two of the maxims may clash in a particular instance. Grice offers the following examples (pp. 51–3). In the first set he says that no maxim is violated, for B's response in each case is an adequate response to A's remark:

A: I am out of petrol.
B: There is a garage round the corner.

A: Smith doesn't seem to have a girlfriend these days.
B: He has been paying a lot of visits to New York lately.

He gives further examples, however, in which there is a deliberate exploitation of a maxim. For example, a testimonial letter praising a candidate's minor qualities and entirely ignoring those that might be relevant to the position for which the candidate is being considered flouts the maxim of quantity, just as does protesting your innocence too strongly. Other examples are ironic, metaphoric, or hyperbolic in nature: 'You're a fine friend' said to someone who has just let you down; 'You are the cream in my coffee'; and 'Every nice girl loves a sailor.' What we do in understanding an utterance is to ask ourselves just what is appropriate in terms of these maxims in a particular set of circumstances. We assess the literal content of the utterance and try to achieve some kind of fit between it and the maxims. Consequently, the answer to the question, 'Why is X telling me this is this way?' is part of reaching a decision about what exactly X is telling me. To use one of Grice's examples (p. 55), if, instead of Smith saying to you that 'Miss X sang "Home Sweet Home,"' he says 'Miss X produced a series of sounds that corresponded closely with the score of "Home Sweet Home,"' you will observe that Smith's failure to be brief helps damn Miss X's performance.

The theory of implicature explains how, when A says something to B, B will understand A's remarks in a certain way because B will recognize that A said more than was required, or gave a seemingly irrelevant reply, or deliberately obfuscated the issue. B will interpret what A says as a cooperative act of a particular kind in the ongoing exchange between A and B, but that cooperation may be shown somewhat indirectly. B will have to figure out the way in which A's utterance is to be fitted into their ongoing exchange, and B's operating assumption will be that the utterance is coherent, that sense can be made of it, and that the principles necessary to do so are available. The task is never an unprincipled one: Grice's maxims provide the necessary interpretive framework within which to establish the relevance of utterances to each other because these 'principles operate even when being flouted' (Levinson, 2001, p. 141). What is left unsaid may be just as important as what is said.

However, when we try to apply any set of principles, no matter what kind they are, to show how utterances work when sequenced into what we call conversations, we run into a variety of difficulties. Ordinary casual conversation is possibly the most common of all language activities. We are constantly talking to one another about this or that. Sometimes the person addressed is an intimate friend, at other times a more casual acquaintance, and at still other times a complete stranger. But we still manage conversation. Because it is such a commonplace activity, we tend not to think about conversation from the point of view of how it is organized, i.e., how particular conversations 'work' is beneath our conscious awareness unless we are one of those who have tried to 'improve' our conversational ability by taking courses in self-improvement or by reading certain books on the topic. Such courses and books have their own focus: they tend to concentrate on the subject matter of talk, on 'correct' pronunciation, diction, and grammar, and on matters of personal taste and behavior. They very rarely tell us anything very informative about how we actually manage conversations, i.e., what makes a particular conversation work. They are examples of what Cameron (1995) calls 'verbal hygiene'. . . .

A commonplace activity is one that occurs frequently and is easily recognizable. It must also conform to certain principles which we may or may not be able to state explicitly. Many activities are commonplace by this definition: eating, sleeping, going to work, passing one another in the street, shopping, and, of course, conversing, to cite but a few. We also recognize that in many cases some people are more successful than others in dealing with the commonplace aspects of life. So far as conversation is concerned, we recognize the fact that some people are better conversationalists than others, but at the same time we may find it difficult to say what makes some better and others worse. In addition, most of us are sensitive to bizarre conversational behavior in others, but we may not always be able to say why a particular piece of speaking strikes us as odd. It is only by attempting to state explicitly the principles that appear to operate in conversations that we can explain these various judgments and reactions.

Above all, conversation is a cooperative activity in the Gricean sense, one that depends on speakers and listeners sharing a set of assumptions about what is happening. If anything went in conversation, nothing would happen. The whole activity would be entirely unpredictable and there would be too much uncertainty to make conversations either worthwhile or pleasant. Not anything goes; indeed, many things do not occur and cannot occur because they would violate the unconscious agreement that holds between speakers and listeners that only certain kinds of things will happen in a normal conversation and that both speakers and listeners will hold to that agreement. Conversation makes use of the cooperative principle; speakers and listeners are guided by considerations of quantity, quality, and so on, and the process of implicature which allows them to figure out relationships between the said and the unsaid. Grice's principles, therefore, form a fundamental part of any understanding of conversation as a cooperative activity. (See Sperber and Wilson, 1995, for an interesting extension of many of these ideas into a cognitively oriented theory of 'relevance' and Clark, 1996, for an approach which has as its thesis that language use is a form of joint action located within social activities.)

Conversation is cooperative also in the sense that speakers and listeners tend to accept each other for what they claim to be: that is, they accept the face that the other offers. . . . That face may vary according to circumstances, for at one time the face you offer me may be that of a 'close friend,' on another occasion a 'teacher,' and on a third occasion a 'young woman,' but it is a face which I will generally accept. I will judge your words against the face you are presenting, and it is very likely that we will both agree that you are at a particular moment presenting a certain face to me and I am presenting a certain face to you. We will be involved in *face-work*, the work of presenting faces to each other, protecting our own face, and protecting the other's face. We will be playing out a little drama together and cooperating to see that nothing mars the performance. That is the norm.

Of course, one party may violate that norm. I can refuse to accept you for what you claim to be, deny your right to the face you are attempting to present, and even challenge you about it. I may also regard your face as inappropriate or insincere, but say nothing, reserving my judgments about your demeanor and words to myself. The second course of action is the more usual; challenging someone about the face he or she is presenting is generally avoided, and those who make a regular practice of it quickly find themselves unwelcome almost everywhere—even to each other! Conversation therefore involves a considerable amount of role-playing: we choose a role for ourselves in each conversation, discover the role or roles the other or the others are playing, and then proceed to construct a little dramatic encounter, much of which involves respecting others' faces. All the world *is* a stage, and we *are* players!

We do get some help in trying to decide what face another is presenting to us and what role is being attempted, but it requires us to have certain skills. As Laver and Trudgill (1979, p. 28) observe, 'Being a listener to speech is not unlike being a detective. The listener not only has to establish what it was that was said, but also has to construct, from an assortment of clues, the affective state of the speaker and a profile of his identity.' The last two phrases, 'the affective state of the speaker' and 'a profile of his identity,' are much the same as what I have called 'face,' for they are concerned with what the speaker is trying to communicate about himself or herself on a particular occasion. Laver and Trudgill add that, 'Fortunately, the listener's task is made a little easier by the fact that the vocal clues marking the individual physical, psychological, and social characteristics of the speaker are numerous.' In other words, there is likely to be a variety of linguistic clues to help the listener. Obviously, listeners will vary in their ability to detect such clues, just as speakers will vary in their ability to present or maintain faces. Consequently, we find here one area of human activity in which there may be a wide range of human abilities so that, whereas X may be said to be 'sensitive' to others, Y may appear 'insincere,' and Z may be completely 'deviant,' and all because of the 'faces' they present to the world and the amount of success they achieve in their chosen roles.

Conversation is cooperative in at least one further way. . . . Human beings make use of commonsense knowledge, which is different in kind from scientific knowledge, and . . . they employ principles of practical reasoning, which are again somewhat different from scientific principles. Moreover, all humans share this orientation and thus cooperate to deal with the world in much the same way. Consequently, we do *not* do certain kinds of things—insist on the literal interpretations of remarks, constantly question another's assumptions, refuse to take things for granted, attack received wisdom, require logical proofs in all reasoning, and so on. There is an unwritten agreement to deal with the world and matters in the world in certain ways; consequently, we put ourselves in serious peril of misunderstanding if we violate that agreement.

BIBLIOGRAPHY

Austin, J. L. (1975). *How to Do Things with Words.* 2nd edn. Oxford: Clarendon Press.
Cameron, D. (1995). *Verbal Hygiene.* London: Routledge.
Cheepen, C. (1988). *The Predictability of Informal Conversation.* London: Pinter.
Clark, H. H. (1996). *Using Language.* Cambridge: Cambridge University Press.
Cole, P. and J. L. Morgan (eds.) (1975). *Syntax and Semantics,* vol. 3: *Speech Acts.* New York: Academic Press.

Duranti, A. (ed.) (2001). *Key Terms in Language and Culture.* Malden, MA: Blackwell.

Grice, H. P. (1975). *Logic and Conversation.* In Cole and Morgan (1975).

Laver, J. and S. Hutcheson (eds.) (1972). *Communication in Face to Face Interaction.* Harmondsworth, England: Penguin Books.

Laver, J. and P. Trudgill (1979). Phonetic and Linguistic Markers in Speech. In Scherer and Giles (1979).

Levinson, S. C. (2001). Maxim. In Duranti (2001).

Malinowski, B. (1923). The Problem of Meaning in Primitive Languages. In C. K. Ogden and I. A. Richards, *The Meaning of Meaning.* London: Routledge & Kegan Paul. In Laver and Hutcheson (1972).

Rawls, J. (1955). Two Concepts of Rules. *Philosophical Review,* 64: 3–32.

Scherer, K. R. and H. Giles (eds.) (1979). *Social Markers in Speech.* Cambridge: Cambridge University Press.

Schiffrin, D. (1994). *Approaches to Discourse.* Oxford: Blackwell.

Searle, J. (1969). *Speech Acts: An Essay in the Philosophy of Language.* London: Cambridge University Press.

Searle, J. (1975). Indirect Speech Acts. In Cole and Morgan (1975).

Searle, J. (1999). *Mind, Language and Society: Doing Philosophy in the Real World.* London: Weidenfeld and Nicolson.

Sperber, D. and D. Wilson (1995). *Relevance.* 2nd ed. Oxford: Blackwell.

FOR DISCUSSION AND REVIEW

1. What is the difference between a constantive or ethical utterance (both are propositions) and a performative utterance? Which of these utterances involve truth or falsity?

2. What is a speech act? What grammatical forms are typically present in a speech act?

3. What *felicity conditions* must be met for an utterance to be a speech act? What does the term *felicity* suggest? Give some examples of utterances that might fail as speech acts because they do not meet felicity conditions.

4. Explain Austin's five kinds of speech acts.

5. Although some speech acts are direct, many are indirect. Using your own example, explain an indirect speech act.

6. John Searle calls some utterances *illocutionary acts* and says they have *illocutionary force.* Explain how this works. How is it possible for a single utterance to express different intentions? After reviewing Deborah Schiffrin's example, "Y'want a piece of candy?" on page 303, create some examples of your own.

7. In *Approaches to Discourse* Deborah Schiffrin (60) says, "Language can do things—can perform acts—because people share constitutive rules that create the acts and that allow them to label utterances as

particular kinds of acts." What are some of the constitutive rules we share?

8. What is Grice's *cooperative principle*? How does it allow us to exchange utterances successfully?

9. What are Grice's four conversational maxims or principles? Give some examples of how each might be met. What are some ways to violate these maxims?

10. Give an example of a speaker *implicating* something different from what he or she is saying.

11. Explain the concept of *face-work*. How does "being a detective" fit into this concept?

Projects for "Language Meaning and Language Use"

1. Steven Pinker begins his "Tower of Babel" discussion by introducing statements about language from two influential linguists, Martin Joos and Noam Chomsky. Do some research on what contemporary linguists have to say about whether all languages have the same basic structures.

Then write a brief research paper about your results. Consider these questions: Do linguists agree that all languages have certain categories or structures in common? If so, what are these categories? Which linguists, if any, disagree about the existence of universals? Try to paraphrase the important issues and summarize the various positions. For your research, read through some of the searchable archives on language-oriented online lists such as funknet.org, (the "funk" is for functional linguistics), where contemporary linguists discuss theories using evidence from biology, genetics, cognitive science, anthropology, and other fields. Some relevant sources listed in the Part Four bibliography are Pinker's *Language Instinct*, Saeed's *Semantics*, Kearns's *Semantics*, Cruse's *Meaning in Language*, and Jackendoff's *Semantics and Cognition*. If you use searchable databases, try "language universals" for a search term.

2. Find a sample of an *agglutinative* language such as Turkish or Finnish. (The Ohio State University *Language Files* is one good source.) Figure our how the grammatical relations are indicated. What does it mean to say that a language is "agglutinating"? How do the morphemes account for many of the grammatical relations between words? Take the same approach with a sample from an *isolative* language such as Mandarin. Ask the same questions of this sample. Is morphology important for indicating relations between words? How important is syntax? Third, take a sample from an *inflected* language such as Latin or Old English. Identify the inflectional morphemes, and briefly explain what they do. Are morphology and syntax important in inflected languages? Explain your answer.

Finally, taking a sample from contemporary English again ask the same questions. Do you find evidence that contemporary English is inflected? What evidence indicates that syntax is important?

3. Write your own definition of the term *grammar*. Then collect up to five definitions from people not in your class. Finally, collect definitions of grammar from a variety of textbooks and usage manuals.

Discuss your findings, and keep these questions in mind: What do these definitions have in common? How do they differ? Do these definitions apply to a specific kind of language? Are labels like *standard* and *nonstandard* used? Do you discover more than one notion of "correct" or "good" grammar? Does any source make a distinction between formal and informal context?

4. Using your findings from the previous project, write a short response to Pinker's argument about the relationship between learning and innate grammar.

5. Using the databases available through your library as well as sources listed in the bibliographies here and in Parts One and Nine, research and write short summaries of two different contemporary theories about whether humans are born with a language "ability." Information from Part Nine, "Language Acquisition and the Brain," will provide some answers. If possible, interview specialists in language acquisition.

6. Study the table "Culinary Semantics," reproduced on the next page, from Dwight Bolinger's *Aspects of Language*, 2nd ed. (New York: Harcourt Brace Jovanovich, 1975, p. 207). Try to develop a similar grid or matrix for another well-defined semantic area.

7. In "Bad Birds and Better Birds," Jean Aitchison examines how we rank words that are members of the same semantic class. She shows, for example, that some birds are more "bird-like" than others. Do some research on prototype theory, and then make your own test. First decide on a distinct, common semantic category. You might use one of Aitchison's categories or something else, if you prefer. Then, gather a group of people who don't know each other well. When you say the name of the category, ask them to immediately write down the item each thinks of first, second, third, and so on. Finally, write up your findings. How did you predict the test results would turn out? Was the prediction accurate?

8. Gregory notes that different words (different word *forms*) may have the same meaning: he gives the examples of 'book,' 'livre,' 'carte,' 'kinga', and 'hon,' which are all associated with the concept of *book* in different languages. Using different languages, try to find at least two sets of different word forms for the same concept. You may want to use some print or online translation dictionaries in your search.

Now look at Pinker's discussion about surface differences and Universal Grammar. Using your own findings as well as Gregory's discussion about form and content, write an essay of about 500 words on Universal Grammar.

9. In "Pragmatics: Discourse Routines," Elaine Chaika mentions the characteristics of schizophrenic speech and how they differ from standard discourse routines. Do some research on schizophrenic speech, and prepare an annotated bibliography of five to seven entries on language and schizophrenic speech. Try to tie your findings to some of the concepts in Chaika's piece.

10. Test Elaine Chaika's description of how people react to persistent compliments. Using the instructions she gave her students, conduct your own experiment. Write up your field notes.

11. Record up to twenty minutes of a typical social interaction, such as dinner with friends or studying with roommates. Be sure to get the permission of the participants first. As you listen to the recording later on,

Culinary Semantics

	Nonfat liquid	Fat	Direct heat	Vigorous action	Long cooking time	Large amt. special substance	Other Relevant Parameters			Collocates With	
							Kind of utensil	Special ingredient	Additional special purpose	Liquids	Solids
cook$_3$										+	+
boil$_1$	+	−								+	+
boil$_2$	+	−		+						+	+
simmer	+	−		−						+	+
stew	+	−		−	+				+soften	−	+
poach	+	−		−					+ preserve shape	−	+
braise	+	−		−			+ lid			−	+
parboil	+	−			−					−	+
steam	+	−		+			+ rack, sieve, etc.			−	+
reduce	+	−		+					+ reduce bulk	+	−
fry	−	+					+ frying pan			−	+
sauté	−	+			−					−	+
pan-fry	−	+					+ frying pan			−	+
French-fry	−	+				+				−	+
deep-fry	−	+				+				−	+
broil	−	−	+							−	+
grill	−	−	+				?(griddle)			−	+
barbecue	−	−	+*					+ BarBQ sauce		−	+
charcoal	−	−	+*							−	+
plank	−	−	+				+ wooden board			−	+
bake^2	−	−	−							−	+
roast	−	−	±							−	+
shirr	−	−	−	−			+ small dish			−	+
scallop	−	−	−				+ shell	+ cream sauce		−	+
brown	−								+ brown surface	−	+
burn	−				+					−	+
toast	−	−	+						+ brown	−	+
rissoler	−	+			+				+ brown	−	+
sear	−	+			−				+ brown	−	+
parch	−	−	−						+ brown	−	+
flambé	−	−	+					+ alcohol	+ brown	−	+
steam-bake	+	−	−							−	+
pot-roast	+	−		−			?(lid)			−	+
oven-poach	+	−	−							−	+
pan-broil	−	−	+				+ frying pan			−	+
oven-fry	−	+	−							−	+

Source: Adapted from Adrienne Lehrer, "Semantic Cuisine," *Journal of Linguistics* 5 (1969): 39–55.
*"Hot coals."

identify utterances as direct or indirect speech acts. Then write up your observations. What specific actions or responses were accomplished by means of speech? Which utterances expressed more than one intention? Were indirect speech acts more typical than direct speech acts? Which utterances might have had a very different meaning in a different context?

12. Write down several jokes you find effective. To do so, you might review some of the television or movie comedies you enjoy. Analyze the jokes using Grice's conversational maxims. Do the jokes appear to violate one or more of the maxims? Where does the humor come in?

13. Working in small groups, each participant should write (a) a definition of what a *lie* is, (b) an example of a lie that she or he would find disturbing, and (c) an example of a lie that might be acceptable. Discuss the various lies as a group. How do violations of the conversational maxims come into play? What are the effects of the specific contexts of the lies?

14. Linguists who specialize in pragmatics have paid a great deal of attention to the idea of *intentionality*. Research the notion of intentionality, and write a summary (up to 500 words) of your findings. Why is intentionality important to the study of discourse? Why is it essential to pay attention to culture when investigating intentionality?

Selected Bibliography

Bakhtin, M. M. *The Dialogic Imagination*. Austin: U of Texas P, 1981. [An introduction to the philosophies of Bakhtin and four of his essays on literature and aesthetics.]

Blakemore, Diane. *Understanding Utterances: An Introduction to Pragmatics*. Oxford: Blackwell, 1992. [From the view-point of Sperber and Wilson's relevance theory.]

Bolinger, Dwight. *Aspects of Language*. 3rd ed. New York: Harcourt Brace, 1981. [Provides a valuable discussion on the importance of contextual meaning in language.]

Brown, Penelope, and Stephen C. Levinson. *Politeness: Some Universals in Language Usage*. Cambridge: Cambridge UP, 1987. [A study about the principles of constructing polite speech.]

Coulthard, Malcolm. *An Introduction to Discourse Analysis*. London: Longman, 1977. [A linguistic approach to the study of conversation.]

Cruse, Alan. *Meaning in Language: An Introduction to Semantics and Pragmatics*. 2nd ed. Oxford: Oxford UP, 2004. [A comprehensive look at meaning.]

DAOL Team. *Discourse Analysis On-Line*. Communication Studies, Sheffield Hallam Univ. <http://extra.shu.ac.uk/daol>. [An international interactive forum for publishing and discussing the latest research using discourse analysis.]

Fairclough, Norm. *Analysing Discourse: Textual Analysis for Social Research*. London: Routledge, 2003. [An accessible introduction to text and discourse analysis.]

Fintel, Kai von. *Semantics etc.* Home page. 2007. <http://semantics-online.org/>. [The M.I.T. professor considers the meaning and function of voicemail and Star Trek science and links to scholarly articles on this blog.]

Goffman, Erving. *Forms of Talk*. Philadelphia: U of Pennylvania P, 1981. [A study of how verbal and nonverbal contact informs communication.]

_____. "On Facework." *Psychiatry* 81 (1955): 213–31. [A classic study of how we represent ourselves in face-to-face contact.]

Grice, H. P. "Meaning." *Semantics: An Interdisciplinary Reader in Philosophy, Linguistics and Psychology*. Eds. David D. Steinberg and Leon A. Jakobovits. Cambridge: Cambridge UP, 1971. 53–59. [A classic study on meaning in discourse and utterances.]

Hudson, Richard. *Word Meaning*. London: Rutledge, 1985. [An introduction to the techniques of lexical semantic analysis.]

Jackendoff, R. "Semantics and Cognition." *Handbook of Contemporary Semantic Theory*. Ed. Shalom Lappin. Malden, MA: Blackwell, 1996. 539–59. [Discussion of semantics as a bridge between theories of language and other cognitive theories.]

Kearns, Kate. *Semantics*. New York: PalgraveMacmillan, 2000. [Good introductory text addressing a wide range of issues in semantics.]

Lappin, Shalom, ed. *Handbook of Contemporary Semantic Theory*. Malden, MA: Blackwell, 1996. [Essays on fundamental issues in semantics.]

Levin, B., and M. Rappaport Hovav. "Lexical Semantics and Syntactic Structure." *Handbook of Contemporary Semantic Theory*. Ed. Shalom Lappin. Malden,

MA: Blackwell, 1996. 487–507. [Formal contemporary approach to semantics and syntax.]

Levinson, S. C. *Pragmatics*. Cambridge: Cambridge UP, 1983. [An introduction to the crucial issues in pragmatics.]

MacCawley, James. *Everything That Linguists Have Always Wanted to Know about Logic but Were Ashamed to Ask*. 2nd ed. Malden, MA: Blackwell, 1993. [Supplement to MacCawley's earlier book on logic in linguistic study.]

Miller, George A. *WordNet: An Electronic Lexical Database*. Cognitive Science Laboratory, Princeton Univ. <wordnet.princeton.edu>. [A lexical reference system inspired by current psycholinguistic theories.]

Modrak, Deborah K. W., *Aristotle's Theory of Language and Meaning*. Cambridge: Cambridge UP, 2000. [Lengthy and comprehensive discussion of Aristotle's theories.]

Peccei, J. *Pragmatics*. London: Routledge, 1999. [A practical introduction that includes exercises and discussion questions.]

Phillips, Nelson, and Cynthia Hardy. *Discourse Analysis: Investigating Processes of Social Construction*. Thousand Oaks, CA: Sage, 2002. [Appropriate for both students and researchers of discourse analysis.]

Pinker, Steven. *The Language Instinct: How the Mind Creates Language*. New York: Perennial Classics, 2000. [Focuses on language development in children.]

Pullum, Geoff, and Mark Liberman. *Language Log*. Web log. U Pennsylvania. <http://itre.cis.upenn.edu/~myl/languagelog>. [Blogging news stories on language myths.]

Saeed, John. *Semantics (Introducing Linguistics)*. 2nd ed. Malden, MA: Blackwell, 2003. [An introduction to semantics for students new to the field.]

Schiffrin, Deborah. *Approaches to Discourse*. Malden, MA: Blackwell. 1994. [Introduction to discourse analysis by leading theorist.]

Schiffrin, Deborah, Deborah Tannen, and Heidi Hamilton, eds. *The Handbook of Discourse Analysis*. Malden MA: Blackwell, 2001. [Essays covering the full range of discourse analysis.]

Searle, John R. "A Classification of Illocutionary Acts." *Language in Society* 5 (1975): 1–23. [Classifying of illocutionary types in English syntax.]

———. *Speech Acts: An Essay in the Philosophy of Language*. Cambridge: Cambridge UP, 1969. [Important development of speech act theory.]

Steinberg, David D., and Leon A. Jakobovits, eds. *Semantics: An Interdisciplinary Reader in Philosophy, Linguistics and Psychology*. Cambridge: Cambridge UP, 1971. [Essays by philosophers, linguists, and psychologists.]

Taylor, John R. *Linguistic Categorization: Prototypes in Linguistic Theory*. 3rd ed. New York: Oxford UP, USA, 2003. [Explores implications of prototype theory, polysemy, and metaphor.]

Verschueren, Jef. *Understanding Pragmatics*. New York & London: Arnold, 1999. [Introduction to theory and methodologies.]

Wierzbicka, Anna. *Cross-Cultural Pragmatics: The Semantics of Human Interaction*. 2nd ed. New York: Gruyter, 2003. [Locates the meaning of human interactions and emotions with different cultures, languages, and speech communities.]

Wodak, Ruth, and Michael Meyer, eds. *Methods of Critical Discourse Analysis: Introducing Qualitative Methods*. London: Sage, 2002. [Essays by leading figures in critical discourse analysis.]

Wood, Linda A., and Rolf O. Kroger. *Doing Discourse Analysis: Methods for Studying Action in Talk and Text*. Thousand Oaks, CA: Sage, 2000. [Theory and applications of discourse analysis.]

PART FIVE

THE HISTORY OF THE LANGUAGE

A living language is always changing. For the most part, we aren't aware of major language changes because they take place slowly over time. Only when we look back at earlier versions do we see how much a language has altered. For instance, English speakers could compare a contemporary story to one of Chaucer's *Canterbury Tales* or to the epic poem *Beowulf*. We would discover that while these are all examples of English, Chaucer's language certainly looks different, and we may not be able to read *Beowulf* without a translation. This type of study of the history and development of languages, which often involves comparing related languages, is called *historical* or *comparative linguistics.*

The first selection, "Comparative and Historical Linguistics," introduces three basic concepts: the theory that some languages share a common ancestor or protolanguage, the premise that languages can be "reconstructed," and the technique known as the comparative method. Using Grimm's Law as an example, Jeanne H. Herndon illustrates the systematic nature of language change and the key role phonology played in the early years of comparative linguistics. The next selection, from the Ohio State University *Language Files*, presents the two primary theories about the development of Indo-European languages: the Family Tree Model and the Wave Model. While neither fully accounts for language change over time and across geographic space, these two models marked the beginning of a new approach to the study of language.

The next three pieces focus specifically on English. In "A Brief History of English," Paul Roberts shows the relationship between socio-historical events and linguistic development of English, from the beginnings of Old English (in approximately 600 C.E.) through Middle English to Early Modern English (starting in about 1600 C.E.). He highlights the main characteristics of the language during each of these periods.

Then, in "Dialects," Lee Pederson introduces us to the major regional dialects of American English and explains how they evolved from the early 1600s to the present. In discussing each dialect, he lists significant sound patterns, grammatical constructions, and words that define the dialect. Pederson also gives attention to the social groups—such as Anglo, African American, and Hispanic communities—that exert important influences on dialects. As Pederson notes in "Regional Patterns of American Speech" (2000), when we study dialects we learn about ourselves because the "shared linguistic features that make up a regional dialect include historical facts of migration and community experience, social facts of ethnic identity, and geographic facts of climate and terrain."

In the final selection, "The Origins of Writing," Celia M. Millward considers writing systems and the relationship between language and the symbols we use to represent it. Although people had been speaking for millions of years before writing was ever invented, literacy is so widespread that it can become, as Millward notes, "almost totally independent of speech." In other words, we can read or write in languages we cannot speak, and we can produce grammatical constructions the we rarely if ever use in conversation. Millward looks briefly at early uses of writing and then gives an overview of various writing systems, with an emphasis on the English alphabet.

19

Comparative and Historical Linguistics

Jeanne H. Herndon

Not until the late eighteenth century did language scholars break from Western tradition and begin to look at language in a different way—to study similarities and differences among many languages and to identify patterns of relationships among languages. Unlike previous work, theirs was entirely descriptive and objective—something new in the Western grammatical tradition. Unfortunately, the work of the great Indian grammarian Pānini (fourth century B.C.E.), who prepared a masterful descriptive grammar of Vedic Sanskrit, was unknown in the West until the beginning of the nineteenth century. In the selection that follows, excerpted from her 1976 book A Survey of Modern Grammars, *Professor Jeanne H. Herndon traces the beginnings of comparative and historical linguistics in the eighteenth century. Using Grimm's Law as an example, she also demonstrates the systematic nature of language change.*

In spite of the fact that most [of the early traditional] grammarians relied upon classical grammarians for method and classical languages for criteria of correctness, some new ideas were stirring in the field of language study in the eighteenth century. These new ideas were not to affect the work of school grammarians for several generations. But among these ideas are to be found the roots of a whole new approach to the problem of analyzing and describing language.

Many language scholars had noted similarities between various European languages; some languages had quite clearly developed from one variety or another of provincial Latin. It remained for an Englishman who was not primarily a language scholar to see relationships among the most widely dispersed of those languages that were later to be recognized as the Indo-European family of languages.

Sir William Jones had served in the colonial government of India and while there had studied Sanskrit. In 1786 he wrote of observing similarities between a remarkable number of vocabulary items in Sanskrit and their equivalents in European and Middle Eastern languages. He suggested that all these languages might have "sprung from some common source, which, perhaps, no longer exists."

Investigation of similarities and differences among languages is called *comparative linguistics*. As language scholars began to establish patterns of relationships among languages, their work came to be called *historical linguistics*. (These scholars were interested primarily in relationships among languages; they were concerned with matters of grammar only insofar as these might indicate relationships among languages and not as a matter of establishing rules of correctness.) Their research was simply a matter of gathering data, sorting, and analyzing it. Their view of change was totally objective. They were interested only in what kinds of changes had occurred, not whether these changes were "right" or "wrong," "good" or "bad."

Among the first linguists to make important comparative studies was a Danish scholar named Rasmus Rask, who compared Icelandic and Scandinavian languages and dialects. Another, Jacob Grimm, carried Rask's studies still further and proposed a theory to account for [some of the regular differences in certain sounds which] he found among languages. Out of these and many other similar studies grew the theory that languages not only change gradually, over long periods of time, but that they change systematically and that the changes are best traced through comparison of the sound systems of languages.

The single most sweeping statement of this kind of sound relationship is often referred to as Grimm's Law or the First Germanic Consonant Shift. It is a systematic comparison of the sound systems of Indo-European languages, which both demonstrates the validity of the theory that these languages sprang from a common source and gives a wealth of information about how they are related.

Grimm concentrated, as had his predecessors, on written forms of words. Actually, he had no choice since he dealt with stages of language development long past. The differences he noted and compared were letters and spellings, but the spelling differences came to be recognized as representative of pronunciation or sound differences. Grimm went even further, and in addition to a simple listing and comparing of differences, he proposed an explanation of the orderly nature of the shift.

According to this theory, three whole sets of sounds in an ancestor of the Germanic languages had shifted from their earlier Indo-European pronunciation. [Figure 19.1 shows] the original sounds and how they changed:

1. The sounds *b*, *d*, and *g* became *p*, *t*, and *k*. (There is only one *kind* of change here—three voiced sounds became silent, or voiceless, sounds.)
2. The sounds that began as *p*, *t*, and *k* became *f*, *th*, and *h*. (Again only one kind of change occurred—three "stops" became three "spirants," or sounds where the air is slowed down but not stopped completely.)
3. The history of the third set of sounds is more complex. These had begun as the breathy voiced stops *bh*, *dh*, and *gh* in early

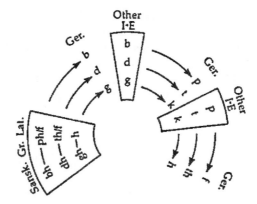

FIGURE 19.1   **Chart of the First Germanic Consonant Shift.**

stages of Indo-European language development and still remain in Sanskrit. They had developed into similar, but not quite the same, sounds *ph* or *f*, *th*, and *h* in later stages of Indo-European language development represented by Latin and Greek. As a part of the Germanic Consonant Shift, this group of sounds shifted to become the voiced stop consonants *b*, *d*, and *g*. The shift of all three sets of consonant sounds—for speakers of the Germanic parent language only—can be seen as something very like a game of phonetic musical chairs.

The boxed letters [in Figure 19.1] represent the sounds that remained in other Indo-European languages; the letters outside the boxes represent the sounds found in Germanic languages as a result of the consonant shift. These correspondences figure prominently in setting the languages derived from the Germanic parent language apart as a distinct branch of the Indo-European family of languages.

These shifts, to repeat, occurred gradually, over very long periods of time. They can be demonstrated by comparing words in a Germanic language, English, which developed after the shift occurred, with items taken from Latin and Greek, languages in which the sounds of these consonants did not shift.

Latin *turba* ⟶ English *thorp*

Latin *dentum* ⟶ English *tooth*

Greek *agros* ⟶ English *acre*

Greek *pous* ⟶ English *foot*

Greek *treis* ⟶ English *three*

Latin *cor* ⟶ English *heart*

Greek *phrater* ⟶ English *brother*

Greek *thygater* ⟶ English *daughter*

Latin *hostis* ⟶ English *guest*

Many words in these languages do not show precisely the same correspondences, but these can be shown to be the result of other shifts or to be related to other factors. Scholars such as Karl Verner noted additional complexities in the nature of the shift and differences resulting from later shifts and proposed theories to explain the apparent "exceptions," until it was possible to trace, in great detail, the development of Indo-European languages over vast stretches of history.

More language samples were gathered, examined, and analyzed; more comparisons were made and new theories proposed. Each new theory could be tested by gathering still more language data and making still more comparisons.

The area of inquiry had been greatly expanded with investigation of Sanskrit and the languages of the Middle East. Sanskrit provided an especially rich body of material for these historical linguists because of the nature of the records open to them. Sanskrit, a literary language of India, had been the subject of grammatical study centuries before Western European scholars had undertaken such investigation of their own languages. As early as the fourth century B.C., an Indian grammarian named Pānini had analyzed Sanskrit and had organized his analysis into a masterful codification of the grammatical units and possible combinations in Sanskrit. For students of historical linguistics, discovery and study of this work were profoundly valuable for two reasons. First, it was a full-fledged grammatical analysis as compared to the fragmentary records of some of the earlier languages they had studied and, second, it represented by far the earliest stage of development of any Indo-European language available to them for study.

Through most of the nineteenth century, linguistic scholarship concentrated primarily on comparative and historical studies. Methods of gathering, classifying, and analyzing data were tested, improved, or discarded, and the improvements tested again.

Comparison of the sound systems of languages was seen to account for only a part of the systematic changes in language. Word forms, inflections, and syntactic differences came to be recognized as important considerations in comparing different stages of the development of languages.

This study of the historical development of a language or languages is sometimes called *diachronic linguistics. Diachronic* is a combination of Greek stems, *dia-* meaning *across*, and *chronos* meaning *time*. For linguists it means that single features of language are traced over long periods of time with changes noted and related to changes in other features of languages over the same periods.

Language researchers gathered data from every nook and cranny of Europe including many dialects peculiar to very small, isolated villages and hamlets. This data led to a major shift of emphasis for some linguists. They moved from the study of historical developments into primary concentration on the similarities and contrasts between contemporary languages and dialects.

After two centuries of enormous amounts of language study, linguists have arrived at some very sweeping theories about the nature of the relationships among the many Indo-European languages. Stated in the simplest possible terms, the important points are these: (1) All these languages developed from a single language which no longer exists. (2) Differences developed when groups of people who spoke this language moved apart and were separated for long periods of time. That is, one group moved into India and their language developed and changed to become Sanskrit; another group moved into southeastern Europe and their language grew into the ancestor of Greek; another group broke off and moved into northern Europe and their language changed in some respects to become the parent language of German, English, Danish, and so on. (3) The fact that all these languages share a common heritage accounts for the fact that some similarities still exist in all of them.

FOR DISCUSSION AND REVIEW

1. What contribution to linguistics did Sir William Jones (1746–94) make?

2. Describe the attitude of historical (or comparative) linguists toward language change. How does this attitude compare with that held by many popular contemporary writers about language usage (e.g., William Safire, Patricia T. O'Connor, and Lynn Truss)?

3. What *kind* of change in language is the most useful to historical linguists? Why?

4. One of the most important characteristics differentiating the Germanic branch of Proto-Indo-European from the languages of all the other branches (see Figure 19.1) is the theory of sound changes called Grimm's Law. Its effects are most easily seen in word-initial sounds. Using the words *tooth*, *foot*, and *three*, show the effect of Grimm's Law in changing these words from their Latin equivalents.

5. Explain how the following sets of words do or do not illustrate Grimm's Law (note: do not consider *only* initial consonants):

	1	2	3
Sanskrit	pitar	bhinádmi	bhrátar
Greek	pater	pheídomai	phráter
Latin	pater	findō	fráter
English	father	bite	brother

6. Why was Sanskrit of special importance to early historical linguists?

7. What were the major conclusions of historical linguists concerning the relationships among the many Indo-European languages?

20

The Family Tree and Wave Models

The Ohio State University *Language Files*

The Indo-European family of languages, of which English is a member, is descended from a prehistoric language, Proto-Indo-European, or Indo-European, which was probably spoken in the fourth millennium B.C.E. in a region that has not been positively identified. However, through the comparative method, we have been able, to learn a great deal about the phonology, morphology, syntax, and semantics of Indo-European, and—because language is an aspect of culture—about the kind of society that its speakers created. In the following 1996 selection, the editors of Language Files *present two popular theories explaining both the relationships among the Indo-European languages and the evolution of their changes and distribution.*

The notion that similar languages are related and descended from an earlier, common language (a protolanguage) goes back to the late eighteenth century when Sir William Jones suggested that the linguistic similarities of Sanskrit to ancient Greek and Latin could best be accounted for by assuming that all three were descended from a common ancestral language. This language was called Proto-Indo-European.

Jones's suggestion was developed in the nineteenth century and gradually came under the influence of Darwin's theory of the evolution of species. Scholars at the time considered language and linguistic development to be analogous in many ways to biological phenomena. Thus, it was suggested that languages, like other living organisms, had "family trees" and "ancestors." A sample "genealogical tree" for the Indo-European (I-E) family of languages appears [in Figure 20.1].

The *family tree theory*, as formulated by August Schleicher in 1871, assumes that languages change in regular, recognizable ways (the *regularity hypothesis*) and that because of this, similarities among languages are due to a "genetic" relationship among those languages (the *relatedness hypothesis*). In order to fill in the particulars of such a relationship, it is necessary to *reconstruct* the hypothetical parent from which the related languages are derived. The principal technique for reconstructing the common ancestor (the protolanguage) of related languages is known as the *comparative method*.

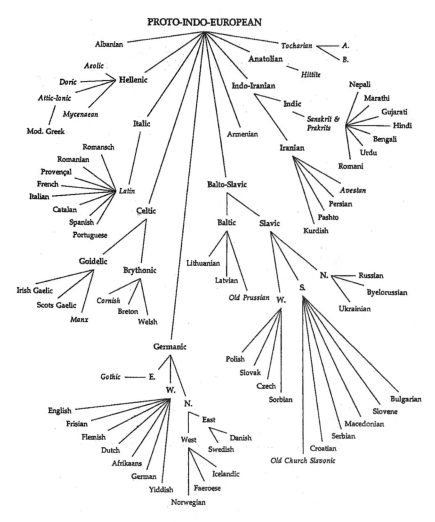

PROTO-INDO-EUROPEAN

FIGURE 20.1   Indo-European Family Tree.

Languages that are no longer spoken are italicized (*Cornish*), and language families are in boldface
(**Baltic**). Indo-European Family Tree adapted from Jeffers and Lehiste, *Principles and Methods for
Historical Linguistics* (1979), p. 302. © 1979 MIT Press. All rights reserved.

In keeping with the analogy of language relationships to human families, the theory makes use of the terms *mother* (or *parent*), *daughter*, and
sister languages. In the family tree of I-E, French and Spanish are sisters,
both are daughters of Latin; Germanic is the mother of English, and so
on. The model clearly shows the direction of change and the relations
among languages, the older stages of the languages being located higher
in the tree and direct descendants being linked to their ancestors through
the straight lines or "branches."

However, a disadvantage exists in that the structure of the family tree may lead people to develop faulty views of two aspects of language change: (1) that each language forms a uniform speech community without internal variation and without contact with its neighbor languages, so that all speakers of Latin, for example, are assumed to have spoken exactly the same way at the time French and Spanish split off; and (2) that the split of a parent language into its daughter languages is a sudden or abrupt occurrence, happening without intermediate stages.

These two views are not supported by the linguistic evidence we have from modern languages. No language is uniform or isolated from others but is always made up of dialects that are still recognized as belonging to the same language, and always shares similarities with other languages in its family, even those belonging to a different subgroup. And as studies of modern language change show, languages do not split apart abruptly but rather drift apart indiscernibly, starting as dialects and ending up as separate languages only after years of gradual change. In fact, the dividing point between two "dialects" and two "languages" is often impossible to locate exactly and is often obscured by nonlinguistic (e.g., political) factors.

To supplement the family tree model and overcome these difficulties, Johannes Schmidt proposed the *wave theory* in 1872. This theory recognizes the gradual spread of change throughout a dialect, language, or a group of languages, much as a wave expands on the surface of a pond from the point where a pebble (i.e., the source of the change) has been tossed in. Dialects are formed by the spread of different changes from different starting points and at different rates; some changes reinforce each other while others only partially overlap or affect only a certain area, much as the waves formed by a scattering of pebbles thrown into a pond may partially overlap. In the wave diagram for I-E [Figure 20.2], the same basic subgroups shown in the family tree are indicated; in addition, however, similarities between various subgroups are also indicated by circles enclosing those languages that share some linguistic feature or set of features, thus cutting across the traditional categories of the family tree. By looking at ever smaller linguistic changes, one can also show the languages within each group and the dialects within each language, indicating clearly how variable languages can be, even though distinct from others. In this way the wave diagram avoids the two faults of the family tree model, though it in turn suffers from disadvantages relating to problems in analyzing the genetic history of the languages displayed.

In fact, neither the family tree model nor the wave model presents entirely adequate or accurate accounts of language change or the relatedness of languages. For example, it is now known that languages can exhibit linguistic similarities without necessarily being related. The similarities may be the result of borrowing from language contact, language drift (that is, independent but identical changes in distinct dialects or languages), similarities in types of morphological structures, syntactic

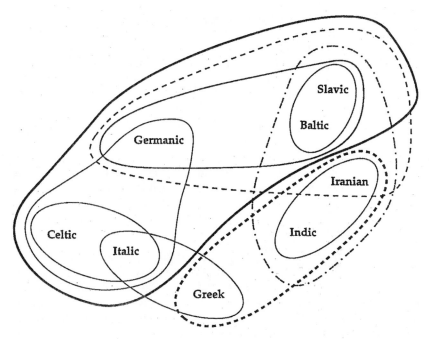

FIGURE 20.2   Indo-European Wave Diagram.

similarities, or other reasons. Nonetheless, the family tree model and the wave model do provide useful frameworks for the discussion of language change.

≡

FOR DISCUSSION AND REVIEW

1. Why is the "family tree theory" so named? What does the family tree theory help to explain?

2. What was found to be inadequate about the family tree theory? How does the wave theory complement the family tree theory?

3. In the wave diagram (Figure 20.2), what is represented by the various lines that enclose languages? Which languages are most closely related, and which are least related?

4. What, if anything, do these two theories leave unexplained about language change?

21

A Brief History of English

Paul Roberts

In this selection from Understanding English *(1958), the late Paul Roberts traces briefly the history of the English language. He places its development in the context of historical events, showing their effects on the language. In general, the grammatical changes from Old English to Modern English have resulted in a change from a highly inflected language (like Latin or Russian) to an analytic language, with few inflectional endings and heavy reliance on word order and function words to signal grammatical meaning. Roberts also discusses some of the major changes in pronunciation and vocabulary from Old English through Middle English to Modern English, commenting especially on the effects of the Great Vowel Shift and on the borrowing of large numbers of foreign words.*

No understanding of the English language can be very satisfactory without a notion of the history of the language. But we shall have to make do with just a notion. The history of English is long and complicated, and we can only hit the high spots.

The history of our language begins a little after A.D. 600. Everything before that is pre-history, which means that we can guess at it but can't prove much. For a thousand years or so before the birth of Christ our linguistic ancestors wandered through the forests of northern Europe. Their language was a part of the Germanic branch of the Indo-European Family (see the previous selection).

At the time of the Roman Empire—say, from the beginning of the Christian Era to around A.D. 400—the speakers of what was to become English were scattered along the northern coast of Europe. They spoke a dialect of Low German. More exactly, they spoke several different dialects, since they were several different tribes. The names given to the tribes who got to England are *Angles*, *Saxons*, and *Jutes*. For convenience, we can refer to them as Anglo-Saxons.

Their first contact with civilization was a rather thin acquaintance with the Roman Empire on whose borders they lived. Probably some of the Anglo-Saxons wandered into the Empire occasionally, and certainly Roman merchants and traders traveled among the tribes. At any rate, this period saw the first of our many borrowings from Latin. Such words as *kettle, wine, cheese, butter, cheap, plum, gem, bishop, church* were borrowed at this time. They show something of the relationship of the Anglo-Saxons with the Romans. The Anglo-Saxons were learning, getting their first taste of civilization.

They still had a long way to go, however, and their first step was to help smash the civilization they were learning from. In the fourth century the Roman power weakened badly. While the Goths were pounding away at the Romans in the Mediterranean countries, their relatives, the Anglo-Saxons, began to attack Britain.

The Romans had been the ruling power in Britain since A.D. 43. They had subjugated the Celts whom they found living there and had succeeded in setting up a Roman administration. The Roman influence did not extend to the outlying parts of the British Isles. In Scotland, Wales, and Ireland the Celts remained free and wild, and they made periodic forays against the Romans in England. Among other defense measures, the Romans built the famous Roman Wall to ward off the tribes in the north.

Even in England the Roman power was thin. Latin did not become the language of the country as it did in Gaul and Spain. The mass of people continued to speak Celtic, with Latin and the Roman civilization it contained in use as a top dressing.

In the fourth century, troubles multiplied for the Romans in Britain. Not only did the untamed tribes of Scotland and Wales grow more and more restive, but the Anglo-Saxons began to make pirate raids on the eastern coast. Furthermore, there was growing difficulty everywhere in the Empire, and the legions in Britain were siphoned off to fight elsewhere. Finally, in A.D. 410, the last Roman ruler in England, bent on becoming emperor, left the islands and took the last of the legions with him. The Celts were left in possession of Britain but almost defenseless against the impending Anglo-Saxon attack.

Not much is surely known about the arrival of the Anglo-Saxons in England. According to the best early source, the eighth-century historian Bede, the Jutes came in 449 in response to a plea from the Celtic king, Vortigern, who wanted their help against the Picts attacking from the north. The Jutes subdued the Picts but then quarreled and fought with Vortigern, and, with reinforcements from the Continent, settled permanently in Kent. Somewhat later the Angles established themselves in eastern England and the Saxons in the south and west. Bede's account is plausible enough, and these were probably the main lines of invasion.

We do know, however, that the Angles, Saxons, and Jutes were a long time securing themselves in England. Fighting went on for as long as a hundred years before the Celts in England were all killed, driven into Wales, or reduced to slavery. This is the period of King Arthur, who was not entirely mythological. He was a Romanized Celt, a general, though probably not a king. He had some success against the Anglo-Saxons, but it was only temporary. By 550 or so the Anglo-Saxons were firmly established. English was in England.

OLD ENGLISH

All this is pre-history, so far as the language is concerned. We have no record of the English language until after 600, when the Anglo-Saxons were converted to Christianity and learned the Latin alphabet. The conversion began, to be precise, in the year 597 and was accomplished within thirty or forty years. The conversion was a great advance for the Anglo-Saxons, not only because of the spiritual benefits but because it reestablished contact with what remained of Roman civilization. This civilization didn't amount to much in the year 600, but it was certainly superior to anything in England up to that time.

It is customary to divide the history of the English language into three periods: Old English, Middle English, and Modern English. Old English runs from the earliest records—i.e., seventh century—to about 1100; Middle English from 1100 to 1450 or 1500; Modern English from 1500 to the present day. Sometimes Modern English is further divided into Early Modern, 1500–1700, and Late Modern, 1700 to the present.

When England came into history, it was divided into several more or less autonomous kingdoms, some of which at times exercised a certain amount of control over the others. In the century after the conversion the most advanced kingdom was Northumbria, the area between the Humber River and the Scottish border. By A.D. 700 the Northumbrians had developed a respectable civilization, the finest in Europe. It is sometimes called the Northumbrian Renaissance, and it was the first of the several renaissances through which Europe struggled upward out of the ruins of the Roman Empire. It was in this period that the best of the Old English literature was written, including the epic poem *Beowulf*.

In the eighth century, Northumbrian power declined, and the center of influence moved southward to Mercia, the kingdom of the Midlands. A century later the center shifted again, and Wessex, the country of the West Saxons, became the leading power. The most famous king of the West Saxons was Alfred the Great, who reigned in the second half of the ninth century, dying in 901. He was famous not only as a military man and administrator but also as a champion of learning. He founded and supported schools and translated or caused to be translated many books from Latin into English. At this time also much of the Northumbrian literature of two centuries earlier was copied in West Saxon. Indeed, the great bulk of Old English writing which has come down to us is in the West Saxon dialect of 900 or later.

In the military sphere, Alfred's great accomplishment was his successful opposition to the Viking invasions. In the ninth and tenth centuries, the Norsemen emerged in their ships from their homelands in Denmark and the Scandinavian peninsula. They traveled far and attacked and plundered at will and almost with impunity. They ravaged Italy and Greece, settled in France, Russia, and Ireland, colonized Iceland and

Greenland, and discovered America several centuries before Columbus. Nor did they overlook England.

After many years of hit-and-run raids, the Norsemen landed an army on the east coast of England in the year of 866. There was nothing much to oppose them except the Wessex power led by Alfred. The long struggle ended in 877 with a treaty by which a line was drawn roughly from the northeast of England to the southeast. On the eastern side of the line Norse rule was to prevail. This was called the Danelaw. The western side was to be governed by Wessex.

The linguistic result of all this was a considerable injection of Norse into the English language. Norse was at this time not so different from English as Norwegian or Danish is now. Probably speakers of English could understand, more or less, the language of the newcomers who had moved into eastern England. At any rate, there was considerable interchange and word borrowing. Examples of Norse words in the English language are *sky, give, law, egg, outlaw, leg, ugly, scant, sly, crawl, scowl, take, thrust.* There are hundreds more. We have even borrowed some pronouns from Norse—*they, their,* and *them.* These words were borrowed first by the eastern and northern dialects and then in the course of hundreds of years made their way into English generally.

It is supposed also—indeed, it must be true—that the Norsemen influenced the sound structure and grammar of English. But this is hard to demonstrate in detail.

A Specimen of Old English

We may now have an example of Old English. The favorite illustration is the Lord's Prayer, since it needs no translation. This has come to us in several different versions. Here is one:

> Fæder ure,
> þu þe eart on heofonum,
> si þin nama gehalgod.
> Tobecume þin rice.
> Gewurþe ðin willa on eorðan swa swa on heofonum.
> Urne gedæghwamlican hlaf syle us to dæg.
> And forgyf us ure gyltas, swa swa we forgyfað urum gyltendum.
> And ne gelæd þu us on costnunge,
> ac alys us of yfele. Soþlice.

Some of the differences between this and Modern English are merely differences in orthography. For instance, the sign æ is what Old English writers used for a vowel sound like that in modern *hat* or *and.* The *th* sounds of modern *thin* or *then* are represented in Old English by þ or ð. But of course there are many differences in sound too. *Ure* is the ancestor of modern *our,* but the first vowel was like that in *too* or *ooze. Hlaf* is modern *loaf;* we have dropped the *h* sound and changed the vowel, which in *hlaf* was pronounced something like the vowel in *father*. Old English had some sounds which we do not have. The sound represented by *y* does not occur in Modern English. If you pronounce the vowel in *bit* with your lips rounded, you may approach it.

In grammar, Old English was much more highly inflected than Modern English is. That is, there were more case endings for nouns, more person and number endings for verbs, a more complicated pronoun system, various endings for adjectives, and so on. Old English nouns had four cases—nominative, genitive, dative, accusative. Adjectives had five—all these and an instrumental case besides. Present-day English has only two cases for nouns—common case and possessive case. Adjectives now have no case system at all. On the other hand, we now use a more rigid word order and more structure words (prepositions, auxiliaries, and the like) to express relationships than Old English did.

Some of this grammar we can see in the Lord's Prayer. *Heofonum*, for instance, is a dative plural; the nominative singular was *heofon*. *Urne* is an accusative singular; the nominative is *ure*. In *urum gyltendum* both words are dative plural. *Forgyfap* is the first person plural form of the verb. Word order is different: "urne gedæghwamlican hlaf syle us" in place of "Give us our daily bread." And so on.

In vocabulary Old English is quite different from Modern English. Most of the Old English words are what we may call native English: that is, words which have not been borrowed from other languages but which have been part of English ever since English was a part of Indo-European. Old English did certainly contain borrowed words. We have seen that many borrowings were coming in from Norse. Rather large numbers had been borrowed from Latin, too. Some of these were taken while the Anglo-Saxons were still on the Continent (*cheese, butter, bishop, kettle,* etc.); a large number came into English after the conversion (*angel, candle, priest, martyr, radish, oyster, purple, school, spend*, etc.). But the great majority of Old English words were native English.

Now, on the contrary, the majority of words in English are borrowed, taken mostly from Latin and French. Of the words in *The American College Dictionary* only about 14 percent are native. Most of these, to be sure, are common, high-frequency words—*the, of, I, and, because, man, mother, road,* etc.; of the thousand most common words in English, some 62 percent are native English. Even so, the modern vocabulary is very much Latinized and Frenchified. The Old English vocabulary was not.

MIDDLE ENGLISH

Sometime between the years 1000 and 1200 various important changes took place in the structure of English, and Old English became Middle English. The political event which facilitated these changes was the Norman Conquest. The Normans, as the name shows, came originally from Scandinavia. In the early tenth century they established themselves in northern France, adopted the French language, and developed a vigorous kingdom and a very passable civilization. In the year 1066, led by Duke William, they crossed the Channel and made themselves masters of England. For the next several hundred years, England was ruled by kings whose first language was French.

One might wonder why, after the Norman Conquest, French did not become the national language, replacing English entirely. The reason is that the Conquest was not a national migration, as the earlier Anglo-Saxon invasion had been. Great numbers of Normans came to England, but they came as rulers and landlords. French became the language of the court, the language of the nobility, the language of polite society, the language of literature. But it did not replace English as the language of the people. There must always have been hundreds of towns and villages in which French was never heard except when visitors of high station passed through.

But English, though it survived as the national language, was profoundly changed after the Norman Conquest. Some of the changes— in sound structure and grammar—would no doubt have taken place whether there had been a Conquest or not. Even before 1066 the case system of English nouns and adjectives was becoming simplified; people came to rely more on word order and prepositions than on inflectional endings to communicate their meanings. The process was speeded up by sound changes which caused many of the endings to sound alike. But no doubt the Conquest facilitated the change. German, which didn't experience a Norman Conquest, is today rather highly inflected compared to its cousin English.

But it is in vocabulary that the effects of the Conquest are most obvious. French ceased, after a hundred years or so, to be the native language of very many people in England, but it continued—and continues still— to be a zealously cultivated second language, the mirror of elegance and civilization. When one spoke English, one introduced not only French ideas and French things but also their French names. This was not only easy but socially useful. To pepper one's conversation with French expressions was to show that one was well-bred, elegant, *au courant*. The last sentence shows that the process is not yet dead. By using *au courant* instead of, say, *abreast of things*, the writer indicates that he is no dull clod who knows only English but an elegant person aware of how things are done in *le haut monde*.

Thus French words came into English, all sorts of them. There were words to do with government: *parliament, majesty, treaty, alliance, tax, government*; church words: *parson, sermon, baptism, incense, crucifix, religion*; words for foods: *veal, beef, mutton, bacon, jelly, peach, lemon, cream, biscuit*; colors: *blue, scarlet, vermilion*; household words: *curtain, chair, lamp, towel, blanket, parlor*; play words: *dance, chess, music, leisure, conversation*; literary words: *story, romance, poet, literary*; learned words: *study, logic, grammar, noun, surgeon, anatomy, stomach*; just ordinary words of all sorts: *nice, second, very, age, bucket, gentle, final, fault, flower, cry, count, sure, move, surprise, plain.*

All these and thousands more poured into the English vocabulary between 1100 and 1500 until, at the end of that time, many people must have had more French words than English at their command. This is not to say that English became French. English remained English in sound structure and in grammar, though these also felt the ripples of French influence. The very heart of the vocabulary, too, remained English. Most of the high-frequency words—the pronouns, the prepositions, the conjunctions, the auxiliaries, as well as a great many ordinary nouns and verbs and adjectives—were not replaced by borrowings.

Middle English, then, was still a Germanic language, but it differed from Old English in many ways. The sound system and the grammar changed a good deal. Speakers made less use of case systems and other inflectional devices and relied more on word order and structure words to express their meanings. This is often said to be a simplification, but it isn't really. Languages don't become simpler; they merely exchange one kind of complexity for another. Modern English is not a simple language, as any foreign speaker who tries to learn it will hasten to tell you.

For us Middle English is simpler than Old English just because it is closer to Modern English. It takes three or four months at least to learn to read Old English prose and more than that for poetry. But a week of good study should put one in touch with the Middle English poet Chaucer. Indeed, you may be able to make some sense of Chaucer straight off, though you would need instruction in pronunciation to make it sound like poetry. Here is a famous passage from the *General Prologue to the Canterbury Tales*, fourteenth century:

> Ther was also a nonne, a Prioresse,
> That of hir smyling was ful symple and coy,
> Hir gretteste oath was but by Seinte Loy,
> And she was cleped Madame Eglentyne.
> Ful wel she song the service dyvyne,
> Entuned in hir nose ful semely.
> And Frenshe she spak ful faire and fetisly,
> After the scole of Stratford-atte-Bowe,
> For Frenshe of Parys was to hir unknowe.

EARLY MODERN ENGLISH

Sometime between 1400 and 1600 English underwent a couple of sound changes which made the language of Shakespeare quite different from that of Chaucer. Incidentally, these changes contributed much to the chaos in which English spelling now finds itself.

One change was the elimination of a vowel sound in certain unstressed positions at the end of words. For instance, the words *name*, *stone*, *wine*, *dance* were pronounced as two syllables by Chaucer but as just one by Shakespeare. The *e* in these words became, as we say, "silent." But it wasn't silent for Chaucer; it represented a vowel sound. So also the words *laughed, seemed, stored* would have been pronounced by Chaucer as two-syllable words. The change was an important one because it affected thousands of words and gave a different aspect to the whole language.

The other change is what is called the Great Vowel Shift. This was a systematic shifting of half a dozen vowels and diphthongs in stressed syllables. For instance, the word *name* had in Middle English a vowel something like that in the modern word *father; wine* had the vowel of modern *mean; he* was pronounced something like modern *hey; mouse* sounded like *moose; moon* had the vowel of *moan*. Again the shift was thoroughgoing and affected all the words in which these vowel sounds occurred. Since we still keep the Middle English system of spelling these words, the differences between Modern English and Middle English are often more real than apparent.

The vowel shift has meant also that we have come to use an entirely different set of symbols for representing vowel sounds than is used by writers of such languages as French, Italian, or Spanish, in which no such vowel shift occurred. If you come across a strange word—say *bine*—in an English book, you will pronounce it according to the English system, with the vowel of *wine* or *dine*. But if you read *bine* in a French, Italian, or Spanish book, you will pronounce it with the vowel of *mean* or *seen*.

These two changes, then, produced the basic differences between Middle English and Modern English. But there were several other developments that had an effect upon the language. One was the invention of printing, an invention introduced into England by William Caxton in the year 1475. Where before books had been rare and costly, they suddenly became cheap and common. More and more people learned to read and write. This was the first of many advances in communication which have worked to unify languages and to arrest the development of dialect differences, though of course printing affects writing principally rather than speech. Among other things it hastened the standardization of spelling.

The period of Early Modern English—that is, the sixteenth and seventeenth centuries—was also the period of the English Renaissance, when people developed, on the one hand, a keen interest in the past and, on the other hand, a more daring and imaginative view of the future. New ideas multiplied, and new ideas meant new language. The English had grown accustomed to borrowing words from French as a result of the Norman Conquest; now they borrowed from Latin and Greek. As we have seen, English had been raiding Latin from Old English times and before, but now the floodgates really opened, and thousands of words from the classical languages poured in. *Pedestrian, bonus, anatomy, contradict, climax, dictionary, benefit, multiply, exist, paragraph, initiate, scene, inspire* are random examples. Probably the average educated American today has more words from French in his vocabulary than from native English sources, and more from Latin than from French.

The greatest writer of the Early Modern English period is of course Shakespeare, and the best-known book is the King James Version of the Bible, published in 1611. The Bible (if not Shakespeare) has made many features of Early Modern English perfectly familiar to many people down to present time, even though we do not use these features in present-day speech and writing. For instance, the old pronouns *thou* and *thee* have dropped out of use now, together with their verb forms, but they are still familiar to us in prayer and in Biblical quotations: "Whither thou goest, I will go." Such forms as *hath* and *doth* have been replaced by *has* and *does*; "Goes he hence tonight?" would now be "Is he going away tonight?"; Shakespeare's "Fie, on't, sirrah" would be "Nuts to that, Mac." Still, all these expressions linger with us because of the power of the works in which they occur.

It is not always realized, however, that considerable changes have taken place between Early Modern English and the English of the present day. Shakespearean actors putting on a play speak the words, properly enough, in their modern pronunciation. But it is very doubtful that this pronunciation would be understood at all by Shakespeare. In Shakespeare's time, the word *reason* was pronounced like modern *raisin*; *face* had the sound of modern *glass*; the *l* in *would, should, palm* was pronounced. In these points and a great many others the English language has moved a long way from what it was in 1600.

RECENT DEVELOPMENTS

The history of English since 1700 is filled with many movements and countermovements, of which we can notice only a couple. One of these is the vigorous attempt made in the eighteenth century, and the rather half-hearted attempts made since, to regulate and control the English language. Many people of the eighteenth century, not understanding very well the forces which govern language, proposed to polish and prune and restrict English, which they felt was proliferating too wildly. There was much talk of an academy which would rule on what people could and could not say and write. The academy never came into being, but the eighteenth century did succeed in establishing certain attitudes which, though they haven't had much effect on the development of the language itself, have certainly changed the native speaker's feeling about the language.

In part, a product of the wish to fix and establish the language was the development of the dictionary. The first English dictionary was published in 1603; it was a list of 2,500 words briefly defined. Many others were published with gradual improvements until Samuel Johnson published his *English Dictionary* in 1755. This, steadily revised, dominated the field in England for nearly a hundred years. Meanwhile in America, Noah Webster published his dictionary in 1828, and before long dictionary publishing was a big business in this country. The last century has seen the publication of one great dictionary: the twelve-volume *Oxford English Dictionary*, compiled in the course of seventy-five years through the labors of many scholars. We have also, of course, numerous commercial dictionaries which are as good as the public wants them to be if not, indeed, rather better.

Another product of the eighteenth century was the invention of "English grammar." As English came to replace Latin as the language of scholarship, it was felt that one should also be able to control and dissect it, parse and analyze it, as one could Latin. What happened in practice was that the grammatical description that applied to Latin was removed and superimposed on English. This was silly, because English is an entirely different kind of language, with its own forms and signals and ways of producing meaning. Nevertheless, English grammars on the Latin model were worked out and taught in the schools. In many schools they are still being taught. This activity is not often popular with schoolchildren, but it is sometimes an interesting and instructive exercise in logic. The principal harm in it is that it has tended to keep people from being interested in English and has obscured the real features of English structure.

But probably the most important force on the development of English in the modern period has been the tremendous expansion of English-speaking peoples. In 1500 English was a minor language, spoken by a few people on a small island. Now it is perhaps the greatest language of the world, spoken natively by over a quarter of a billion people and as a second language by many millions more. When we speak of English now, we must specify whether we mean American English, British English, Australian English, Indian English, or what, since the differences are considerable. The American cannot go to England or the English to America confident that he or she will always understand and be understood. The Alabaman in Iowa or the Iowan in Alabama shows himself or herself a foreigner every time he or she speaks. It is only because communication has become fast and easy that English in this period of its expansion has not broken into a dozen mutually unintelligible languages.

FOR DISCUSSION AND REVIEW

1. Roberts describes in some detail the relationships between historical events in England and the development of the English language. Summarize the most important events, and comment on their relationship to or effect on the English language.

2. What are the three major periods in the history of English? What are the approximate dates of each? On what bases do linguists make these distinctions?

3. During what period was the epic poem *Beowulf* written? Why was this period propitious for the creation of such a work?

4. How did the pronouns *they*, *their*, and *them* come into English? What is unusual about this occurrence?

5. List four important ways that the grammar of Old English differs from that of Modern English. What is the principal difference between the vocabulary of Old English and that of Modern English?

6. When the Anglo-Saxons invaded England, their language became the language of the land, almost completely obliterating the Celtic that had been spoken by the earlier inhabitants. Why did French not become the language of England after the Norman Conquest? Explain Roberts's statement that "English . . . was profoundly changed after the Norman Conquest."

7. How would you characterize in social terms the French words that were brought into English by the Norman Conquest? In what areas of life did French have the greatest influence?

8. Describe the changes the English language underwent as a result of the Great Vowel Shift. What is the importance of this linguistic phenomenon for Modern English?

9. Identify two significant effects that the invention of printing had on the English language.

10. Early English grammars—indeed, almost all English grammars published before 1950—were modeled on Latin grammars. Why was this the case? What problems, if any, did Latin-based grammars cause?

22

Dialects

Lee Pederson

A dialect is a variety of a language that contrasts in systematic, patterned ways with other varieties of that same language. Regional dialects are associated with particular geographic areas, whereas social dialects are associated with particular groups of people. In this selection from the American Heritage Dictionary *(1992), Professor Lee Pederson traces the development of the major dialects of American English from their colonial beginnings in the seventeenth century to the present. Drawing from the dialect research of the past century, Pederson describes the significant features of the four major American dialects. He also notes the need for more research, especially on varieties in the western states. Throughout this piece, Pederson demonstrates that while American dialects differ in systematic ways, they "share essential structural characteristics" with all varieties of Modern English.*

THE BEGINNINGS OF AMERICAN ENGLISH

The fluid structure of Early Modern English underlies the formation of American English. Although the Great Vowel Shift had assigned new values to the long vowels, many British, Scottish, and Irish social dialects were slow to accept all of these emergent features. Morphology and syntax showed inventiveness and flexibility in word formation and adaptations, as with the free use of affixes in word building *(re-, de-, -ish, -ize)*, functional shift of parts of speech (nouns used as verbs, verbs as nouns, and both as adjectival or adverbial modifiers), frequent parenthetical expression, and phrase structures of predication, complementation, and coordination that reflect the intonational contours of the spoken language.

Drawn from that rapidly flowing stream, American English shows a much greater uniformity than its origins might suggest. Einar Haugen has called this evolution of the national language in American "Babel in reverse." The concept of the American melting pot can be found in the writing of St. John de Crèvecoeur, a Norman-French immigrant and the eponym of St. Johnsbury, Vermont. In the *Letters of an American*

Farmer (1782) he provided the logic for a unified American language and culture:

> What attachment can a poor European emigrant have for a country where he had nothing. The knowledge of the language, the love of a few kindred as poor as himself, were the only cords that tied him; his country is now that which gives him land, bread, protection, and consequence: *Ubi panis ibi patria* [where there is bread, there is one's fatherland] is the motto of all emigrants. What is an American, this new man? He is either a European, or the descendant of a European, hence that strange mixture of blood, which you will find in no other country. I could point out to you a family whose grandfather was an Englishman, whose wife was Dutch, whose son married a French woman, and whose present four sons have now four wives of different nations. *He* is an American, who, leaving behind him all of his ancient prejudices and manners, receives new ones from the new mode of life he has embraced, the new government he obeys, and the new rank he holds. He becomes an American by being received in the broad lap of our great *Alma Mater* [Dear Mother]. Here individuals of all nations are melted into a new race of men, whose labors and posterity will one day cause great changes in the world. Americans are the western pilgrims, who are carrying along with them that great mass of art, science, vigor, and industry which began long since in the east; they will finish the great circle. The Americans were once scattered all over Europe; here they are incorporated into one of the finest systems of population which has ever appeared, and which will hereafter become distinct by the power of the different climates they inhabit. The American ought therefore to love this country better than that wherein either he or his forefathers were born.

The first substantial collection of immigrant literature appeared in New England, where writers worked with Elizabethan patterns and recorded a variety of occasional spellings and distinctive forms. In *The History of Plimmoth Plantation* (1620–1647) William Bradford wrote *burthen, fadom, furder, gifen (given), gusle (guzzle), trible (triple), vacabund (vagabond)*, and *woules (wolves)*. Roger Williams rhymed *abode/God, blood/good*, and *America/away* in *A Key to the Language of America* (1643). Ann Bradstreet paired *conceit/great, stood/flood*, and *satisfy/reality* in *The Tenth Muse, Lately Sprung Up in America* (1650). Two generations later Edward Taylor alternated *spoil* and *spile*, as well as *soot* and *sut*, and rhymed *is/kiss, far/cur*, and *vile/soil*.

Early American grammar also showed a great variety of forms. In 1630, aboard the *Arabella* and westward-bound, John Winthrop preached "A Model of Christian Charity" with the line "We must love brotherly without dissimulation: we must love one another with a pure heart fervently." Bradford used *rid, runned* (and *ranne*), *drunk, writ*, and *shrunk* as past forms of *ride, run, drink, write*, and *shrink*, respectively. Williams declared, "My disease is I know not what" and offered the interrogative form "Sleep you?" Mary Rowlandson wrote, "It is not my tongue or pen can express the sorrow of my heart . . ." in her captive narrative of 1675.

During these same years cultural activity all along the Atlantic seaboard produced the first Americanisms. The following native words, among hundreds of others, originated, gained special meaning, or entered the English language through American speech in the seventeenth century: *creek* (stream), *fat pine*, *green corn*, and *papoose* from Massachusetts; *catfish*, *corn* (maize), *mock*[ing]*bird*, *polecat* (skunk), and *raccoon* from Virginia; *Chippewa*, *ground hog*, *Manhattan*, and *Podunk* from New York; *gang* [of birds], *hominy*, *snakeroot*, and *Virginian* from Maryland; *frontier people*, *oyster rake*, *samp*, and *wampum* from Rhode Island; *grocery* (store), *hot cakes* (corn cakes), *peavine* (a climbing plant similar to the pea), and *sunfish* from Pennsylvania; *settlement* and *swampland* from Connecticut; *Dutch grass* (any one of various grasses) and *hickory nut* from South Carolina; *frontier* from New Jersey. Beyond the frontiers *pilot* (a guide over a land route) appeared in what is now Colorado, and *Miami* from what is now Illinois.

NATIVE AMERICAN INFLUENCES

These words suggest the importance of Amerindian loans, especially for artifacts and places. From the Algonquian dialects alone English and French in the New World borrowed more than a hundred terms that remain current in American speech. In addition to *Chippewa*, *hominy*, *Manhattan*, *papoose*, *Podunk*, *samp*, *squash*, and *wampum*, the eastern tribes provided *caribou*, *mackinaw*, *pone*, *Tammany*, *terrapin*, and *toboggan*. These often suggest multiple language contacts; as *caribou* and *toboggan* entered through Canadian French in the north, *barbecue*, *canoe*, and *cushaw* came out of the West Indies through Spanish. Spanish later transmitted *anaqua* (the Texas "knockaway" tree), *coyote*, and *peyote* from the Nahuatl Indian language of Mexico. From Quechua, probably through the cooperative efforts of French and Spanish, New Orleans' *lagniappe* appeared somewhat later. The American place names comprise the greatest Amerindian contribution. From *Appalachia* and the *Alleghenies*, across all five Great Lakes *(Erie, Ontario, Huron, Michigan,* and *Superior)*, from *Chicago* to *Sitka*, Indian words cover the continent. Emblematic of American language and culture are the blends, such as *Bayou La Batre*, Alabama (Choctaw *bayuk* = "creek" + French *de la Batre* = "of the [artillery] battery"), and *Minneapolis*, Minnesota (Dakota *minne* = "water" + Greek/English (a)*polis* = "city"), or the loan translations *Spearfish*, South Dakota, *Warroad*, Minnesota, and *Yellow Dirt Creek*, Georgia, besides the Indian loans of the state names *Alabama* (tribe), *Dakota* (tribe), and *Minnesota* (Dakota *minne* = "water" + *sota* = "white").

LOANS FROM THE EUROPEAN LANGUAGES

Early loans from European languages correspond with Dutch, French, and German settlements in the coastal colonies and along the first interior frontiers. During their New Amsterdam experience the Dutch added to American English the words *boss, Bowery, coleslaw, cookie, sleigh, stoop,* and *waffle.* Later they gave more place names, such as *Catskill, Kinderhook,* and *Schuyler.* Although Thoreau spoke of *Yankee ingenuity* in 1843, the durable nickname probably had its origin in the Dutch diminutive for *John (Johnny), Jan (Janke).* Saint Nicholas, clipped to *Sint Klaas* in a Dutch dialect, became *Santa Claus* before the Revolutionary War.

French loans contrast sharply with the Dutch and later German contributions. Although they also gave English such ordinary household words as *chowder, gopher, pumpkin, sashay, shanty,* and *shivaree,* the enterprising French illustrate their experience in a distinctive set of loans. Explorers, missionaries, and frontier warriors made American words of *bateau, coulee, crevasse, levee, portage, prairie,* and *voyageur.* As the English, Dutch, and Swedes struggled to control the seaboard the French ranged across the interior and left their mark with the names of places at *Bienville, Cape Girardeau, Prairie du Chien,* and *Sault Sainte Marie.*

Early German loans on the frontier are difficult to ascertain. Like the Scandinavians and Anglo-Saxons in England, the Germans and the English spoke languages with a common word stock that still endures in the basic vocabularies of both cultures. For the same reason it is impossible to determine whether *nosh* (snack) and *schlemiel* are of Yiddish or German origin and whether *spook* and *dumb* (stupid) are of Dutch or German origin, because in each case the words occur in both languages. Only when the Germans established discrete territories, as the Dutch had in New York, did the loans begin to appear in significant numbers from Pennsylvania, Cincinnati, Chicago, Milwaukee, St. Louis, and east-central Texas. From early Pennsylvania, American English probably received *smearcase, ponhaws (pannhass = "pan" + hare = "scrapple"), rainworm,* and possibly George Washington's most familiar title, *The Father of His Country,* which first appeared as *Des Landes Vater* on a *Nord Amerikanische Kalender* for 1779.

THE AMERICAN FRONTIER

The frontier contributions of the Swedes and folk speakers of British, Irish, and Scottish dialects are virtually impossible to identify because they were soon united in a common culture. As Crèvecoeur described the people at the outbreak of the Revolution:

> They are a mixture of English, Scotch, Irish, French, Dutch, Germans, and Swedes. From this promiscuous breed, that race now called Americans have risen. The eastern provinces [i.e., the coastal colonies] must needs be expected, as being unmixed descendants of Englishmen.

Early frontier speech probably included the pronouns *hit* (for *it*), *hisn*, *ourn*, *theirn*, and *yourn*, the inflected verb forms *clumb, drug, holp*, and *riz*, the auxiliary construction *mought could* (or *might could*), and a large number of folk pronunciations and lexical items. Scottish forms, also appearing in the poetry of Burns, include *duds* (clothes), *gumption*, *hunkers, mountain billy* (hillbilly), *tow* (cloth), and the distinctive pronunciations reflected in *chimla (chimney), het (heated)*, and *southron (southern)*, as well as the simplification of consonant clusters, as in *kin' (kind)* and *sin' (since)*, and the total assimilation of *l* after back vowels, as in *ca' (call), fu' (full)*, and *howe (hollow)*. From Irish sources probably came *mammy, moonshine*, and *mountain dew*. General English folk forms also included *clean, flat*, and *plumb* (meaning "completely"), *passel* (from *parcel*), and *sass* (from *sauce*). Many of these forms appear in Middle English, and all survive in current American Midland and Southern dialects.

THE EVOLUTION OF DIALECTS IN AMERICAN ENGLISH

During the eighteenth century the principal dialect regions of American English developed. These are the historic cultural areas. Every major regional dialect area, past and present, corresponds almost perfectly with a cultural area delimited by other social systems. The presbyters of Appalachia mark the pattern of Scottish settlement, the Dutch and German barns show a Germanic presence in the eastern and east-central states, the methods of cooking cornmeal in *pones, dodgers*, and *hush puppies* reflect the settlement patterns of various groups, and the superstitions connected with chicken clavicles *(wishbone, pulley bone,* or *lucky bone)* identify social groups, as do the southern greetings *hey* (for *hi*) and *Christmas Gift!* The styles of folk, blues, jazz, and rock music also correspond with cultural areas, contrasting the perfected forms of the Carter Family in Appalachia and Huddie Ledbetter in the Upper Delta, the rural blues of Richard Amerson and the urban blues of Bill Broonzy, the Kansas City jazz of Count Basie and the Chicago jazz of Bud Freeman, or the middle Georgia rock of the Allman Brothers and the southern California rock of the Eagles. All of these are as regionally distinctive as the voices of the musicians are. Wherever clear-cut boundaries of culture can be reconstructed on the basis of historical information from archaeology, music, graphic arts, or the social sciences, dialect differences can be predicted, based on the most persuasive kind of circumstantial evidence: the recorded experience of the forebears of a speech community.

Modern American seaboard dialects preserve the early system from Maine to the Florida Keys and along the Gulf shores to Brownsville, Texas. The coastal communities shared the evolution of urban British pronunciation, grammar, and vocabulary, but very different speech forms developed throughout the interior along the old frontier. Neither of these regions is a uniform cultural area, but remarkable concordances of speech endure. Early centers at Boston, New York, and Philadelphia were quite different from their southern counterparts at Richmond, Charleston, and New Orleans. Along the Atlantic and Gulf coasts, however, the dialects shared important features: the loss of a constricted *r* after vowels (making *popper* homophonous with *Papa*); a contrast of stressed vowels in *Mary, merry,* and *marry*; a most distinctive diphthong in *dues, news,* and *shoes* that approaches that in *few, music,* and *pupil*; the loss of *h* in *whip, white, wheelbarrow,* and similar words; and even a "broad *a*" in *hammer, pasture,* and *Saturday*. Besides the familiar British past form *et* (of *eat*), the coastal dialects also shared lexical features, such as *hog's head cheese, haslets* (or *harslets*), and *piazza* (porch).

The coastal pattern divides near the Potomac. To the north the language and culture drifted away from British influence more quickly than they did in the South, where the early planters of Jefferson's agrarian democracy required close association with British commerce, education, and industry. Southern coastal dialects preserved several other British features: the "clear *l*" of *lean* in *Billy* and *Nelly* as opposed to the "dark *l*" of *load*, a flapped *r* in *three* and *thresh*, as heard in some current British pronunciations of *very* (written humorously as *veddy*), and even an occasional back vowel in *pot* and *crop*. Along the Gulf Coast these forms had mixed currency, largely because of the powerful influence of New Orleans, a cultural center that dominated the entire interior of the South until the Civil War. Basic Northern and Southern contrasts persist from the Potomac to the mouth of the Rio Grande: the Southern drawls (patterns of diphthongs, lengthening, and intonation), the vowel of *ride* [a] (which northerners confuse with *rod* [ɑ]), the vowel of *bird* [ɜɪ] (which northerners associate with Brooklynese), a positional variant [əu] in *house* and *mouse* but not in *rouse* and *cows*, the plural pronoun *you-all* (*y'all*), the past form *drug* (of *drag*), and a large set of vocabulary forms, such as *mosquito hawk* (dragonfly), *crocus sack* (burlap bag), *snap beans* (string beans), and *tote* (carry).

The New Orleans focal area interrupts this pattern, extending its influence from Mobile Bay to beyond the Sabine River. A General Coastal and New Orleans contrast is marked by *serenade, bateau, clabber cheese,* and *mush* along the Southern coast, except in the area of New Orleans dominion, where *shivaree* (*charivari*), *pirogue, cream cheese,* and *cush-cush* prevail. Although *cush* and *cush-cush* have currency throughout the South, nowhere else is there a double form to match the New Orleans usage. Other distinctive terms are *flambeau* (makeshift torch), *(h)armonica* (instead of Southern *harp*), *lagniappe* (something extra, instead of South Carolina *brawtus*, Texas-Spanish *pilon,* and Florida-Minorcan *countra*), *wishbone* (instead of South Midland and Southern *pulley bone*), and *creole tomatoes* (instead of Northern *cherry tomatoes* and Southern *tommytoes*).

Unlike coastal speech, the Midland dialects of that transition area between the North and South grew up in the interior. From Pennsylvania to Georgia the eastern boundary of the Midland dialect area coincides with the geography of the old frontier. Settlers took the land in the great migrations out of Pennsylvania, Maryland, and Virginia during the half century that preceded the Revolutionary War (1725–1775). Thomas' discovery of the Cumberland Gap in 1750 provided a southern gateway to the Middle West, that passage into Kentucky for the ancestors of both Jefferson Davis and Abraham Lincoln. Before the War of 1812 the frontier extended out of Pittsburgh and down the Ohio River in the north and out of the Yadkin Valley of North Carolina in the south, across Tennessee and Kentucky along the Wilderness Trail of Pennsylvania's Daniel Boone.

Like other American dialects, the Midland varieties rose from a British-English base, but on the frontier the social composition was different. Six of the seven ethnic groups mentioned by Crèvecoeur spoke no British English before they arrived in North America. Later those residents of the interior Midland dialect areas were landbound without ports of entry to receive the influence of English culture and to share in the development of the prestigious London forms. More important, the frontier people occupied themselves mainly with survival in a hostile region. Those factors influenced the disparate groups in a uniform way: Midland dialects resisted the phonological changes under way in England and in the coastal colonies to the north and south; English, Irish, and Scottish folk speech reinforced the regional grammar and vocabulary, giving these American dialects identities of their own.

The Midland pattern contrasts most sharply with the interior varieties of Northern and Southern speech. With a domain that in modern times extends from western New England and upstate New York, along the southern shores of the Great Lakes and then northwestward into the upper Middle West, the Inland Northern dialect spread from its eastern source after the War of 1812. With the construction of the Erie Canal, the watercourse from Albany to Buffalo gave upstate New York and New England access to the Great Lakes, as had the construction of the earlier and slower roadways and the later, more efficient railroads. As Northern speech extended out of upper New Jersey and northern Pennsylvania a major dialect boundary was established with the southern limit of *darning needle* (dragonfly), *pail*, and *whiffletree*, contrasting with North Midland *snake feeder*, *bucket*, and *singletree*. From upstate New York and across Ohio, Indiana, Illinois, and Iowa westward, the division of Northern and North Midland remains apparent in the pronunciation of *fog* and *hog*, which are pronounced with the vowel of *father* in the North and the vowel of *dog* in the North Midland, in the pronunciation of the diphthong of *cow*, *house*, and *towel*, which is [æu] in the North Midland, beginning with a higher vowel that is closer to that of *lather*, and the existence of an excrescent *r* in "*warsh*" and "*Warshington*" in some Midland speech. More clearly distinctive are the Northern terms *stone wall, pail, swill, teeter-totter, faucet, pit* [of a cherry or peach], and *fire-fly* contrasting with the Midland terms *stone fence, bucket, slops, seesaw, spicket* (spigot), *seed,* and *lightning bug.* In the West the Northern/Midland distinction is most clearly heard in the pronunciation of *car, yard,* and similar words: the Northern pronunciation is marked by a vowel closer to the vowel of *father*; the Midland pronunciation, by one closer to the vowel of *saw.*

Prior to the Civil War other interior forms spread from south of the Great Lakes to the fringes of the plantation cultures from Virginia to Texas and gave rise to the principal Midland varieties, North and South. Between those contrasting cultures the Midland area is perhaps best divided by a phonological Mason-Dixon Line established by the pronunciation of the medial consonant of *greasy,* with an [s] to the north and a [z] to the south. On the Atlantic Coast the boundary replicates the historic Mason-Dixon Line, the common border of Pennsylvania and Maryland. Philadelphia, with the pronunciation [s], must be considered a Northern territory. Westward, however, this difference in pronunciation marks the division within the Midland territory, from Ohio to Missouri. Heading south, a traveler encounters the line at approximately the same place where grits replace hash browns on the breakfast menu, where greens appear at dinner, and where nice, white rice served with Indiana- or Kentucky-fried chicken are all pronounced with a vowel that northerners confuse with the vowel common to *cat, hat,* and *sat.* With this feature comes the first suggestion of the drawl, indigenous bluegrass music, and stock-car, instead of Indy-type or midget-automobile, racing. Along that same line the northern extent of Southern cultural penetration appears in these contrasts: North Midland *bunk, wishbone, husks, headcheese, fritters, bag,* and *turtle* versus South Midland *pallet, pulley bone, shucks, souse* (or *pressed meat), flitters, sack,* and *terrapin.*

South Midland speech is a Southern dialect, formerly called Hill Southern in contrast with the Upcountry and Lower Southern patterns (Plantation Southern) to the south and east. The principle South Midland/ Southern boundary follows the Blue Ridge Mountains across Virginia, the Carolinas, and Georgia. In South Carolina and Georgia the boundary coincides with the hundred-eighty-day growing season for cotton, the waterways, the soil types, and the cultural organizations inseparable from the plantation systems devoted to the cultivation of indigo, rice, and cane as well as cotton.

Those geographical features and cultural factors underlie the Midland enclaves, as far south as the Florida panhandle, and their Southern counterparts as far north as the St. Francis Basin of Arkansas and the boot heel of Missouri, the cotton country around New Madrid. South Midland is marked by the presence of a constricted *r* after a vowel in *bird, car,* and *horse* and identical vowels in *right* and *ride,* whereas Southern preserves a diphthong in *right* and similar words. Lexical contrasts include South Midland *green beans, red worm, fireboard, French harp* (for *harmonica*), and *tow sack* (for *burlap bag*), versus Southern *snap beans, earthworm, mantelpiece, harp,* and *crocus sack.* In the east South Midland contrasts with Virginia Piedmont Southern with *snake feeder, peanuts,* and *terrapin* versus *snake doctor, goobers,* and *cooter.* In the Mississippi Valley the South Midland dialect occupies the territory by-passed by the plantation cultures as unsuitable for the production of cotton, cane, and rice.

Where the planters extended their operations north and west, as in upper Louisiana, west Tennessee, Arkansas, and east Texas, Lower Southern features outline the area. The Coastal and Gulf Plains were settled from the east, but the deltas of the Mississippi, Atchafalaya, Yazoo, Red, and St. Francis rivers received their populations from the south. As a result interior Southern areas do not show the predictable gradations of uniformity from east to west that are found in the North and North Midland regions.

These Southern dialects are distinguished by coastal forms and by the distinctive contributions of the New Orleans focal area. Coastal Southern pronunciation includes the loss of constricted *r* after vowels, the contrast between the stressed vowels of *Mary, merry,* and *marry,* a "clear *l*" in *Billy* and *Nelly,* and vocabulary items such as *mosquito hawk, crocus sack, hoghead cheese* (or *hog's head cheese*), and *red bug* (instead of *chigger*). Besides *locker* (for *closet*) and *flambeau* (for *makeshift lamp*), the domain of New Orleans is marked by the pervasiveness of *lagniappe, pirogue* (a dugout canoe), *cream cheese* (cottage cheese), *wishbone* (instead of South Midland and Southern *pulley bone*), and *(h)armonica* (instead of South Midland *French harp* or Southern *harp*). Such forms appear as far north as Lake Providence and Monroe, Louisiana, Yazoo City, Mississippi, and along the Gulf Coast beyond the Sabine River into Texas and eastward to Mobile Bay.

The speech of the West is complicated by the blending of Northern, Midland, and Southern forms, as well as by a heavy Spanish influence from Texas to California. The Northern Midland boundary extends over Iowa and cuts across South Dakota in a northwesterly direction. In Montana and Idaho the presence of North and South Midland features reflects the history of the frontier and the enterprises of cattle, agriculture, and mining. Throughout the Rocky Mountains and the urban West Coast the dialects of the early settlers determined the pattern. Seattle and San Francisco speech grew from an Inland Northern base quite similar to old-fashioned Chicago speech. Denver and Los Angeles also developed from that same base, although the Hispanic influence in both places and the successive waves of newcomers from the East, especially in Los Angeles, have obscured the regional pattern that endures with greater stability in Seattle and San Francisco. The Midland influence is strongest west of the Rockies, from Idaho to Arizona, and especially in the conservative speech of Boise, Salt Lake City, and Phoenix. On a train near Yuma, Arizona, during the Great Depression, Woody Guthrie heard the complexity of American speech in the New West as he was going to California:

> There was a big mixture of people here. I could hear the fast accents from the big Eastern joints. You heard the slow, easy-going voices of Southern swamp dwellers, and the people from the Southern hills and mountains. Then another would talk up, and it would be the dry, nosy twang of the folks from the flat wheat plains; or the dialect of the people that come from other countries, whose parents talked another tongue. Then you would hear the slow, outdoor voices of the men from Arizona, riding a short hop to get a job, see a girl, or to throw a little celebration. There was the deep, thick voices of two or three Negroes. It sounded mighty good to me.

THE INFLUENCE OF BILINGUALISM

In just that way, moving across the country, the national idiom grew through languages and dialects in contact. Spanish, French, and German bilingualism marks the regional patterns of Florida, Louisiana, and Pennsylvania, as well as of south Texas. Gullah, an English-based pidgin, developed in the Sea Islands and low country of South Carolina and Georgia. From that source many varieties of American black folk speech are derived, reflecting various stages of creolization as the dialects merge with the dominant patterns. Social dialects grew through urban and rural experiences throughout the country, many of these related to the Americanization of European bilinguals in the urban North and the integration of blacks in all sectors of society. These dialects are further conditioned and refined by formal and situational styles, including slang, ethnic variation, and patterns of usage reflecting socioeconomic class.

Before urban American Spanish gained prominence in San Antonio, Los Angeles, and Miami, that language had already made large contributions to English in the West. Besides the place names, extending from the *Rio Grande* to *Montana*, the Spanish vocabulary marks the cattle country with Western words: *arroyo, bronc(o), chaparral, canyon, cinch, corral, frijoles, hoosegow, lasso, lariat, mesa, mustang, patio, pinto, pronto, ranch, remuda, rodeo, sombrero,* and *tortilla.*

In bilingual communities Spanish speakers of English tend to avoid regional dialect forms in favor of terms from the general vocabulary, despite the distinctive accent and syntax carried over from the parent language. The same tendency appears among the French in Louisiana, who freely use their native loans, such as *banquette* (sidewalk), *boudin* (blood sausage), *faisdodo* (country dance), and *jambalaya,* as well as loan translations and adaptations, such as *coffee black, cream cheese* (cottage cheese), and *(h)armonica.* These same speakers resist the Southern regionalisms *pulley bone* and *snap beans.* German, Italian, Scandinavian,

Slavic, Spanish, and Yiddish speakers reflect the same trend in the urban North, perhaps through learning from books rather than by simple oral acquisition, and perhaps through efforts to translate from their native tongues. In becoming Americans all of these people enriched the national language and culture. If examples are limited to food alone, Germans provided *bock beer* and *pretzels*, Italians brought *antipasto* and *pizza*, Scandinavians added *lingonberries* and *smorgasbord*; Slavs contributed *kolacky* and *kielbasa*, Yiddish-speaking Germans and Slavs gave *bagels* and *gefilte fish*; and Mexican Spanish provided the base for an endless variety of *enchiladas*, *burritos*, and *tacos* as its cooking entered the fast-food industry.

CONTRIBUTIONS FROM THE AFRICAN LANGUAGES

The full impact of African languages through Gullah and Plantation Creole remains to be properly assessed, but evidence suggests the influence is significant. Among African loans these have gained currency in the national language: *chigger, goober, gumbo, jazz, juke (-box, joint,* and *-step)*, *okra, voodoo,* and *yam.* Some are regionally restricted to the South: *cooter* (turtle), *cush* and *cushcush* (mush), and *pinder* (peanut). Others seem limited to the South Carolina and Georgia low country: *buckra* (white man), *det* (heavy), as in *det rain* and *det shower,* and *pinto* (coffin). In addition to the loan-words from Gullah (or "Geechee," the interior Georgia pattern), the creolization of that auxiliary language may have left its mark on American English phonology and grammar as well. As a contact vernacular or language of business (and the probable source of the word *pidgin*), Gullah provided a medium of communication for African slaves and their American supervisors. Thus the pidgin was a language native to neither group. In the development of Plantation Creole (from Portuguese *crioulo* = "white man") the language acquired the highly complex phonological and grammatical rules and complete vocabulary, features necessary in a self-reliant, independent language. General Southern features today include many correspondences with Plantation Creole, the creolized English black folk speech of the plantation cultures of cane, cotton, indigo, and rice. Southern vowel nasality often replaces nasal consonants in *am, been,* and *bacon,* but this feature occurs in Parisian and Louisiana French, as well as in Plantation Creole and West African languages. The simplification of consonant clusters, as in *des* (for *desk* and *desks*) or *tase* (for *taste* and *tastes*), is commonplace in all of those languages, as well as in the Scottish dialect of Robert Burns, who, like American southerners, black and white, often assimilated *l* after back vowels, as in *fa'* (fall) and *saut* (salt). Similarly, the pervasive deletion of articles, copulas, prepositions, and other function words, so characteristic of Gullah and its creolized extensions, is a feature regularly associated with the speech of French, German, and Spanish bilinguals. Nevertheless, this fact remains: large numbers of black and white speakers share those features across the lower South, especially in those areas dominated by the plantation cultures.

THE INFLUENCE OF SOCIAL DIALECTS

As creolization reflects the blending of languages and cultures, so slang, argot, and social dialects mark the activities of subcultures within the basic social structure. Although nothing as widespread as Cockney and Australian rhyming slang has developed in America, inventive usage here has steadily modified native speech. Most slang originates in the specialized conversations of particular groups, in which usage reinforces group identity and develops into private codes that may later gain wide acceptance. These include such now-familiar terms as *clout* and *gerrymander* from politics, *blues* and *jazz* from music, *headline* and *editorial* from journalism, and *by a nose, inside track, front-runner, shoo-in,* and *sure thing* from the vocabulary of horse racing. The distinctive words of other groups—pickpockets, CB operators, and computer specialists— suggest the ways in which the subcultures function and illustrate the ways in which language develops.

Social dialects also underlie the regional patterns of speech, reflecting absolute factors, such as age and ethnic origin, and relative factors, such as education and social position. As a healthy language is always changing, the age and experience of its speakers are recorded by incipient, dominant, and recessive forms, as demonstrated in the vocabulary of automobiles: the emergent *gas guzzler* and *pimpmobile,* the durable *sedan* and *limousine,* and the relic *tin lizzie* and *roadster.* Ethnic terms are the cultural birthrights of individual speakers and great linguistic resources for society at large. Yiddish *schlock, chutzpah, macher,* and *schmaltz* have moved from the Jewish communities to the national language, as have the specialized Sicilian terms *capo, Cosa Nostra,* and *Mafia* in urban American subcultures. Education reinforces language trends with the spread of generalized patterns of pronunciation, grammar, and vocabulary, but these are challenged by migrant accents in Chicago today just as they were in London four hundred years ago. As Latinos made *macho* an American word, blacks have put many Southern regionalisms, such as *funky, up-tight,* and *right on,* into common usage. The language reflects cultural patterns, refined and strengthened through association and social status.

Social dialects also mark the evolution of a language. In America the middle classes have generated great changes. These include the absorption of immigrant cultures at the lower level and influence upon the dominant culture at the higher level. As the linguistic and cultural forms are traditionally conservative in both aristocratic and folk groups, however different their social styles, middle-class society and speech alter those conventional patterns from below and from above. Just as members of the secular and regular clergy, educators, lawyers, politicians, and physicians helped shape the London Standard from the early Middle Ages through the English Renaissance because they were conversant with both the ruling class and the common people, so new patterns of American usage grow today through the influence of upper-middle-class dialects. Even stronger influences appear from the speech of the lower middle class, especially in urban centers, where clerks, cab drivers, and telephone operators come in contact with the entire community in their daily work.

Of these, ethnic dialects preserve the most complicated social varieties of language and reflect the essential spirit of American culture. As frontier societies developed distinctive regional patterns, Spanish, French, Dutch, Scandinavian, and German settlers used their native languages before adopting the dominant English dialect. English, Irish, and Scottish folk speech constituted probably the most influential ethnic varieties on the frontier, but these were modified by the language habits of their neighbors. In the process of Americanization, Europeans, Africans, and Asians gave the language some of its most familiar words: *chop suey, hamburger, hillbilly, juke box, pizza, prairie, rodeo, Santa Claus, smorgasbord,* and *tycoon.*

The national vocabulary reflects the intimacy of conversation and the evolution of democratic social forms. John Adams proposed that Congress establish an American Academy "for refining, correcting, improving, and ascertaining the English language." Later, when asked to preside over such activities, Thomas Jefferson responded:

> There are so many differences between us and England, of soil, climate, culture, productions, laws, religion, and government, that we must be left far behind the march of circumstances, were we to hold ourselves rigorously to their standard. If, like the French Academicians, it were proposed to *fix* our language, it would be fortunate that the step were not taken in the days of our Saxon ancestors, whose vocabulary would illy express the science of this day. Judicious neology can alone give strength and copiousness to language, and enable it to be the vehicle of new ideas.

Instead of rules from a National Academy of English, Americans accepted the common-law customs of intelligent conversation with all of its modifications through time and circumstance. Current usage, for example, may reject *illy express* and *judicious neology*, but history shows the correctness of Jefferson's message. He recognized the certainty of change, the function of language as a cultural tool, and the importance of thoughtful selection. Through common-law customs of speech and writing the national language develops words and records social facts.

FOR DISCUSSION AND REVIEW

1. What four major American dialects does Pederson identify?

2. Which states or parts of states are included in each of the major regional dialects? Name a few contrastive words, grammatical items, and significant sound patterns associated with each of the dialects.

3. Why is it hard to determine the origin of some frontier words, such as those from Dutch, Yiddish, and German?

4. How do agricultural and geographic features—such as soil types— affect the boundaries of the South Midland dialect?

5. According to Pederson, what social groups have had important influences on American dialects? What are the major influences on language in your area?

6. Pederson says that more research is needed to describe the dialects of the western states. Why?

7. How does most slang originate?

8. Give a few of your own examples of incipient, dominant, and recessive forms of words.

23

The Origins of Writing

Celia M. Millward

Speech, as Celia M. Millward notes, is "primary to language." Yet in areas with widespread literacy, the ability to read and write is crucial to survival. Where literacy is limited, however, those with the most power and prestige may decide—and thus control—who is allowed to become literate. In "The Origins of Writing," Millward, a professor of English at Boston University, begins by explaining why written language developed by and for an elite group. She then describes how different writing systems represent languages and how those systems developed. She also provides a detailed history of the alphabetic script and discusses attempts at alphabet reform. This selection is taken from Millward's 1996 book, A Biography of the English Language, *second edition.*

WHY WAS WRITING INVENTED?

Efficient as speech is, it is severely limited in both time and space. Once an utterance has been made, it is gone forever, and the preservation of its contents is dependent on human memory. Writing is as permanent as the materials used in producing it; readers can return to a written record as often as or after as long a period of time as they like. Further, speech is much more limited in space than is writing. Until the invention of electronic media—all of which require supplementary apparatus in the form of transmitters and receivers—speech was spatially limited to the range of the unamplified human voice. Writing can be done on portable materials and carried wherever people can go.

Although it would perhaps be esthetically satisfying to think that the first writing systems were created to preserve literary works, all the evidence indicates that the first true writing was used for far more mundane purposes. Although "creative" literature arose long before the invention of writing, it was orally transmitted, with devices such as alliteration, repetition, and regular meter being used as aids to memory. Writing was invented for the same practical purpose to which, in terms of sheer bulk, most writing today is dedicated, commercial record-keeping—the number of lambs born in a season, the number of pots of oil shipped to a customer, the wages paid to laborers. A second important early use of writing was to preserve the exact wording of sacred texts that would otherwise be corrupted by imperfect memories and changes in the spoken language. For most of the history of writing, literacy has been restricted to a small elite of bookkeepers and priests; often, the two occupations were combined in one scribe. To the illiterate, writing would have seemed a form of magic, an impression that was not discouraged by those who understood its mysteries.

TYPES OF WRITING SYSTEMS

If we can judge by the delight a child takes in its own footprints or scribbles made with any implement on any surface, human beings have always been fascinated by drawing. The urge to create pictures is revealed by the primitive drawings—early forms of graffiti—found in caves and on rocks all over the world. But pictures as such are not writing, although it is not always easy to distinguish pictures from writing. If we define writing as human communication by means of a system of conventional visible marks,[1] then, in many cases, we do not know whether the marks are systematic because we do not have a large enough sample. Nor do we know if the marks were intended to communicate a message. For example, Figure 23.1 is an American Indian *petroglyph* (a drawing or carving on rock) from Cottonwood Canyon, Utah. Conceivably, the dotted lines, wavy lines, spiral, and semicircle had some conventional meaning that could be interpreted by a viewer familiar with the conventions. If so, the petroglyph might be called prewriting, but not actual writing.

Pictograms and Ideograms

More clearly related to writing are the picture stories of American Indians. Like the modern cartoon strip without words, these *pictographs* communicate a message. Further, they often include conventional symbols. Figure 23.2 is from a birch-bark record made by Shahâsh'king (b), the leader of a group of Mille Lacs Ojibwas (a) who undertook a military expedition against Shákopi (e). Shákopi's camp of Sioux (c) was on the St. Peter's River (d). The Ojibwas under Shahâsh'king lost one man (f) at the St. Peter's River, and they got only one arm of an Indian (g).[2]

Although such pictographs do communicate a message, they are not a direct sequential representation of speech. They may include *ideographic* symbols, symbols that represent ideas or concepts but do not stand for

---

[1] The definition is adapted from I. J. Gelb, *A Study of Writing*, rev. ed. (Chicago: University of Chicago Press, 1963), p. 12.

[2] Adapted from Garrick Mallery, "Picture-Writing of the American Indians," in *Tenth Annual Report of the Bureau of Ethnology* (Washington, D.C.: Government Printing Office, 1893), pp. 559–60.

FIGURE 23.1   American Indian Petroglyph.[3]

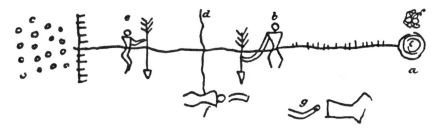

FIGURE 23.2   American Indian Picture Story.

specific sounds, syllables, or words. In Figure 23.2, the drawing at (f) means that the Ojibwas lost one man, but it does not represent a unique series of sounds or words. It could be translated as "We lost one man" or "The Sioux killed a warrior" or "Little Fox died on this expedition" or "One man fell by the river." To take a more familiar example, the picture ▆▆ is an *ideogram;* it does not represent a sequence of sounds, but rather a concept that can be expressed in English in various ways: "go that way" or "in this direction" or "over there" or, combined with words or other ideograms, such notions as "the stairs are to the right" or "pick up your luggage at that place." Ideograms are not necessarily pictures of objects; the arithmetic "minus sign" is an ideogram that depicts not an object, but a concept that can be translated as "minus" or "subtract the following from the preceding" or "negative."

Logograms

Ideograms are not writing, but they are the ancestors of writing. If a particular ideogram is always translated by the same spoken word, it can come to stand for that word and that word alone. At this point,

---

[3] Drawing adapted from Roland Siegrist, ed., *Prehistoric Petroglyphs and Pictographs in Utah* (Salt Lake City: Utah State Historical Society, 1972), p. 62. Reproduced with permission of the Utah State Historical Society.

logograms, or symbols representing a single word, have been invented, and true writing has begun. Indeed, an entire writing system may be based on the logographic principle. This is the case with Chinese, in which each character stands for a word or part of a compound word. In their purest forms, logographic symbols have no relationship to individual sounds, but only to entire words. For example, the Chinese character 吊 stands for a verb meaning "to hang, to suspend"; it is pronounced roughly as [diɑu] in Standard Chinese, but no particular part of the character represents [d] or [i] or [ɑ] or [u]. By itself, the top part of the character, 口, is pronounced [kou], and the bottom part, 巾, is pronounced [jin]. The character 钓 is pronounced in exactly the same way as 吊, but 钓 means "to fish with a hook and line." Like all writing systems actually used for natural languages, Chinese is less than totally pure; many characters contain both ideographic and phonetic components. Still, the Chinese system is basically logographic in that each character stands for an entire word or morpheme, and one cannot determine the pronunciation of an unfamiliar character from its components.

The distinction between ideograms and logograms is somewhat arbitrary. If, within a given language, a symbol is always interpreted as representing one word and one word alone, it is a logogram for that language. However, if it has the same meaning but is represented by different words in other languages, it is, strictly speaking, an ideogram. An example would be the symbol &, which stands only for the word *and* in English, but for *agus* in Irish, *et* in French, *och* in Swedish, *и* in Russian, *na* in Swahili, and so forth. It is a logogram within a given language, but an ideogram across languages.

Syllabaries

Logographic systems are inefficient for most languages because, if every single word in the language is to be represented by a different symbol, an astronomical number of complex symbols is required. Therefore, while the writing is still at the ideographic-logographic stage, scribes may begin to use symbols to represent sounds instead of concepts. They probably begin by punning on existing logograms. For example, assume that English used the logogram ◉ to stand for the word *cell*. Noting that, in speech, the word *cell* sounds like the word *sell*, a clever scribe might decide to use ◉ to mean *sell* as well as *cell* in writing. If the logogram for *fish* were ⋈, then *selfish* could be written ◉ ⋈. Symbols would now represent sound sequences or syllables instead of entire words.

When this kind of punning becomes widely used, the writing system is turning into a **syllabary**, or a system in which each symbol stands for a syllable. Over time, the sound values of symbols become predominant and their picture value less important. As scribes simplify the symbols to save time and space, the original pictures often become unrecognizable. To use our hypothetical example from English again, the logogram for *fish* might change from ⬠ to ◁ to ◁ to ✕ as a syllabic writing system evolved.

The first syllabaries were developed among the Semites of the Middle East, perhaps as long as seven or eight thousand years ago, and the concept of the syllabary rapidly spread over the entire area. Although, strictly speaking, a syllabary represents vowel differences as well as consonant differences among syllables, most of the Semitic syllabaries indicated only consonants. That is, while [ba], [ma], and [ka] were represented by distinct symbols, [ba], [be], and [bi] were all written the same way.

For languages with very simple syllable structures, such as Japanese or Chinese, a syllabary provides an efficient writing system because relatively few symbols are needed to represent every possible syllable in the language. Modern Japanese has two syllabaries, the *katakana* and the *hiragana*. Each of these two syllabaries consists of only 46 basic signs, plus a few diacritical marks. Although the syllabaries are completely adequate for writing anything in Japanese, the prestige of Chinese logograms is so great that contemporary Japanese continues to use a mixture of Chinese characters, called *kanji*, and *kana* syllabic signs—illustrating how cultural factors may outweigh logic and efficiency in determining the written form of a language.

Alphabets

The final step in the phonemicization of writing is the *alphabet*, in which each symbol represents a separate phoneme, not an entire syllable. So far as we know, the alphabet has been invented only once. The Greeks borrowed the Semitic syllabary and, probably over a fairly long period of time, began using unneeded characters to represent vowels separately from consonants. Once there were separate characters for vowels, the originally syllabic characters could always be used for consonants alone, and the alphabet had been invented.

The precise form of the Greek letters, or *graphemes*, changed somewhat over time, and the Romans introduced still further changes when they borrowed the Greek alphabet to write Latin, partly because the sound system of Latin differed in a number of important ways from that of Greek. The Romans did not adopt the Greek letters Θ, Ξ, φ, Ψ, or Ω at all. They modified the most common forms or orientations of Greek Γ, Δ, Λ, Σ to C, D, L, and S, respectively, and then added a tail to C to form G. The archaic Greek letter F had represented [w], but the Romans used it for [f] instead. In Greek, H is a vowel symbol, but it became a consonant symbol in Latin. The grapheme P represents [r] in Greek, but, because the

Romans used P for [p], they had to modify it to R to represent [r]. The Romans adopted the obsolete Greek character Q to represent [k] before [w], as in Latin *quo*. Because Latin used three symbols, C, Q, and K (though K was rarely used) to represent [k], the Latin alphabet almost from the beginning violated the principle of an ideal alphabet, a one-to-one correspondence between phoneme and grapheme.

Primarily through the spread of Christianity from Rome, the Latin version of the alphabet was eventually adopted in all of Western Europe. Because Russia was Christianized by the Eastern Church, whose official language was Greek, its alphabet (the Cyrillic alphabet) was borrowed independently from Greek; in many ways, it is closer to the classical Greek alphabet than the Latin alphabet is. For example, its forms Г, Д, Л, Н, П, Р, Ф, Х for [g, d, l, n, p, r, f, x], respectively, are similar to their Greek originals. However, the Cyrillic alphabet uses В for [v], and Б, a modified form of В, for [b]. С represents [s], and У represents [u]. З, a modified form of Greek Z, is used for [z]. Because Russian is much richer in fricatives and affricates than Greek, new symbols were devised to represent them: Ж, Ц, Ч, Ш, Щ stand for [ž, ts, č, š, šč], respectively. The Cyrillic characters И, Ы, Э, Ю, Я represent the vowels or diphthongs [i, y, ɛ, ju, ja], respectively. Finally, Russian also uses two graphemes as diacritics; they represent no sound of their own, but indicate that a preceding consonant is palatalized (Ь) or not palatalized (Ъ).

English has had two different alphabets. Prior to the Christianization of England, the little writing that was done in English was in an alphabet called the *futhorc* or *runic alphabet*. The futhorc was originally developed by Germanic tribes on the Continent and probably was based on Etruscan or early Italic versions of the Greek alphabet. Its association with magic is suggested by its name, the runic alphabet, and the term used to designate a character or letter, *rune*. In Old English, the word *rūn* meant not only "runic character," but also "mystery, secret." The related verb, *rūnian*, meant "to whisper, talk secrets, conspire." . . .

As a by-product of the Christianization of England in the sixth and seventh centuries, the English received the Latin alphabet. Although it has been modified somewhat over the centuries, the alphabet we use today is essentially the one adopted in the late sixth century. However, its fit to the sound system is much less accurate than at the time of its adoption because many phonological changes have not been reflected in the writing system.

An ideal alphabet contains one symbol for each phoneme, and represents each phoneme by one and only one symbol. In practice, few alphabets are perfect. Even if they are a good match to the sound system when they are first adopted (not always the case), subsequent sound changes destroy the fit. Writing is always much more conservative than speech, and, as the years go by, the fit between phoneme and grapheme becomes worse and worse unless there is regular spelling and even alphabet reform. Such reform has taken place in a number of countries; regular reform is even required by law in Finland. Major reform in the Soviet Union occurred after the 1917 revolution. In 1928, Turkey under Kemal Atatürk switched from the Arabic writing system to the Latin alphabet. However, as the history of Russian and Turkish suggests, resistance to reform is usually so strong that it takes a cataclysmic event like a revolution to achieve it. In general, reform is easier in smaller countries that do not use a language of worldwide distribution and prestige. Even under these circumstances, resistance to reform will be fierce if the country has a long tradition of literacy and literature. Icelandic, for instance, is spoken by fewer than a quarter of a million people, a large proportion of whom are bilingual or trilingual in other European languages. However, pride in their long native literary traditions has to date prevented any significant spelling reform. A person reasonably skilled in Old Norse (c. A.D. 900–c. A.D. 1350) can read modern Icelandic without much difficulty even though the spoken language has undergone vast changes since Old Norse times and even though the present match between grapheme and phoneme is poor indeed. Clearly, people become as emotionally entangled with their writing systems as with their spoken languages.

FOR DISCUSSION AND REVIEW

1. What were the first uses of writing systems? How prevalent was literacy once writing systems developed?
2. Millward gives examples of three systems that might be considered prewriting or "ancestors" of writing systems. Name these systems, and describe how they work.
3. Explain the difference between an ideogram and a logogram. How might an ideogram become a logogram? Name a few writing systems based on logograms.
4. As a syllabic writing system evolves, what happens to the original picture symbols? Why does modern Japanese use two syllabaries?
5. What is an alphabetic writing system? What is each symbol intended to represent—a sound, a syllable, or an idea?
6. How was the alphabet invented?
7. What is an "ideal alphabet," and what is "alphabet reform"? Discuss the effectiveness of alphabet reform in some countries that have tried it.

Projects for "The History of the Language"

1. The two models of the Indo-European language, Family Tree and Wave, are seen as complementary by some and as competing representations by others. Most linguists agree, however, that each shows only part of the story. Analyze one of these models yourself. Select a contemporary Indo-European language with which you are familiar, and try to track its developments using only one model. Begin with the hypothetical "proto-language," and follow the language's various changes to the present. How well does the model describe the historical stages of the language? What kinds of changes don't fit within that model?

2. Some language families such as Polynesian do not have extensive documentation and have only recently been written down. How might you hypothetically reconstruct a language that lacks an extended written history?

3. As the pieces included in Part Five show, English is a member of the Germanic branch of the Indo-European language family. The label *Indo-European* includes languages extending from Europe to the Indian subcontinent of Asia, which means that quite a few other branches besides the Germanic one exist. Select another branch, such as Slavic, Hellenic, or Celtic, and write a research paper on the development of contemporary languages in that family.

4. Of the world's approximately five thousand living languages, only seventy are Indo-European. The Afro-Asiatic, Austronesian, Dravidian, Hmong-Mien, Iroquoian, Na-Dene, Nilo-Saharan, Signed language, Sino-Tibetan, Trans New Guinea, Uralic, and Uto-Aztecan language families each contain a number of languages, some with several million native users. Visit the *Ethnologue* language-family index Web page (www.ethnologue.com/family_index.asp) to find a more comprehensive list of language families.

From a list such as that provided by *Ethnologue*, choose a language family with at least a million native users, and write a report on it. Identify the subfamilies, if it has any, and the languages of each subfamily. You might also create maps showing the geographic distribution of the subfamilies, number of speakers of languages in each subfamily, and language families in the area. Consider these questions as well: What are the important linguistic features of the languages? For example, do they have more or fewer voiced consonants than in English? Do the languages have sounds or even ways of using breath that do not exist in English? Are the languages tonal? How are words and sentences formed?

5. In "A Brief History of English," Paul Roberts notes that people in the eighteenth century were considerably concerned with "correct" English: written guides to pronunciation and grammars and dictionaries

362

became popular. Write a research paper on one aspect of this era. Here are some topics to consider:

- A social climate that encouraged English speakers to notice their pronunciation and language usage
- Military, technological, or territorial changes that required new vocabulary
- The history of dictionaries and how they changed
- What prominent thinkers of the day had to say about "correct" English

6. Roberts mentions that at one time interest arose in establishing an "academy" to monitor and purify the English language. One of those interested was Jonathan Swift (1667–1745). Prepare a report on the arguments for and against establishing such an academy. You might also investigate academies that do exist in other countries, such as in France. How do these academies function? What kinds of authority do they have? Are they effective at purifying the language?

7. *The Oxford English Dictionary (OED)* is one of the most comprehensive historical dictionaries ever prepared, and it continues to come out in new editions and new technological forms. Many people find it both fun and enlightening to read. Become familiar with the *OED* by teaching a classmate to use it. Select an entry, and explain the various parts. What do the abbreviations mean? How does the entry show sound or grammatical changes? What are the different parts of the entry? What kinds of information are included? What is the function of the quotations? How are they organized?

8. The following passages are versions of the Lord's Prayer as they were written during different periods in the history of the English language. (a) Analyze the forms that the various words have in common, and consider how each word changes from the first to the last version and, also, from one version to the next (e.g., Faeder, fadir, father, Father). (b) Do the same kind of analysis on the various syntactical (i.e., word-order) changes that you discover (e.g., Tōcume þīn rīce; Thy kyngdom cumme to; Let they kingdom come; Thy kingdom come). (c) Write an essay commenting on the changes you have discovered in these excerpts. Give as many examples of the changes as are necessary to support your conclusions. Finally, draw some conclusions about the evolution of the English language as revealed in the passages.

(1.) Eornostlīce gebiddaþ ēow þus Fæder ūre þū þe eart on heofonum, sie þin nama gehālgod.

(2.) Tōcume þīn rice. Gewurþe þīn willa on eorþan swā swā on heofonum.

(3.) Ūrne daeghwæmlīcan hlāf syle ūs tōdæg.

(4.) And forgyf ūs ure gyltas swā swā we forgyfaþ ūrum gyltendum.

(5.) And ne gelæd þū ūs on costnunge ac ālys us of yfele.

(6.) Witodlice gyf gē forgyfaþ mannum hyra synna, þonne forgyfþ ēower sē heofonlīca fæder ēow ēowre gyltas.

(7.) Gyf gē sōþlīce ne forgyfaþ mannum, ne ēower fæder ne forgyfþ ēow ēowre synna.

Old English (ca. 1000)

(1.) Forsothe thus ȝe shulen preyen, Oure fadir that art in heuenes, halwid be thi name;

(2.) Thy kyngdom cumme to: be thi wille don as in heuen and in erthe;

(3.) ȝif to vs this day oure breed ouer other substaunce;

(4.) And forȝeue to vs oure dettis, as we forȝeue to oure dettours;

(5.) And leede vs nat in to temptacioun, but delyuere vs fro yuel. Amen.

(6.) Forsothe ȝif ȝee shulen forȝeuve to men her synnys, and ȝoure heuenly fadir shal forȝeue to ȝou ȝoure trespassis.

(7.) Sothely ȝif ȝee shulen forȝeue not to men, neither ȝoure fadir shal forzȝue to ȝou ȝoure synnes.

Middle English (Wycliffe, 1389)

(1.) After thys maner there fore praye ye, O oure father which arte in heven, halowed be thy name;

(2.) Let thy kingdom come; they wyll be fulfilled as well in erth as hit ys in heven;

(3.) Geve vs this daye oure dayly breade;

(4.) And forgeve vs oure treaspases, even as we forgeve them which trespas vs;

(5.) Leede vs not into temptacion, but delyvre vs ffrom yvell. Amen.

(6.) For and yff ye shall forgeve other men there trespases, youre father in heven shal also forgeve you.

(7.) But and ye wyll not forgeve men there trespases, no more shall youre father forgeve youre trespases.

Early Modern English (Tyndale, 1526)

(1.) Pray then like this: Our Father who art in heaven, Hallowed be thy name.

(2.) Thy kingdom come, Thy will be done, On Earth as it is in heaven.

(3.) Give us this day our daily bread;

(4.) And forgive us our debts, As we also have forgiven our debtors;

(5.) And lead us not into temptation, But deliver us from evil.

(6.) For if you forgive men their trespasses, your heavenly Father also will forgive you;

(7.) But if you do not forgive men their trespasses, neither will your father forgive your trespasses.

Modern English (1952)

9. American English shows more uniformity than British English and much more uniformity than many other languages. Thus some commentators say that American English has no dialects. Do some research to counter this position. Collect examples of dialect features, including sounds, grammatical constructions, and words particularly associated with your regional dialect. Then use these examples in a brief (two- to four-page) essay arguing for the existence of distinct dialects in American English.

10. Working in groups of two or three, develop a historical dialect picture of your city, town, county, or state. Perhaps the class could choose the scope, and each group could target one aspect of the dialect's history. Find out who originally settled in the area and what language or languages they spoke. What group(s) settled next, and what languages did they speak? Continue to the present. Lee Pederson's essay "Dialects" and the bibliography at the end of Part Five are good places to start.

11. As an individual project, develop a language history of your own family. Find out what languages are currently in use in your family, and work backwards. Try to determine where the various branches of your family originated, and then do research to see what languages were spoken in those areas at the time.

12. During the nineteenth and twentieth centuries, a number of artificial languages were developed in the hope that a common language would ameliorate causes of conflict in the world. The creators of these languages wanted the languages to be acceptable to everyone and easy to learn. Three of these languages are Volapük, Esperanto, and Interlingual; sometimes Basic English is also included in this group. Write a research paper on an artificial language, and try to cover the following topics: the language's sociohistorical background and the various "real" languages it is based on; its basic linguistic structures; and the motivations for developing an artificial universal language.

13. Using Celia M. Millward's "The Origins of Writing" as a starting point, research the historical stages of the alphabet used for English. A number of scholars suggest that it began when Semitic-speaking merchants transformed hieroglyphics into phonological symbols. Then what happened? What were the forms of the symbols? How did they change? If possible, find photographic images of the different stages and create a visual presentation of your findings using PowerPoint or another multimedia program.

14. Select a logographic writing system—such as Mandarin—that you do not regularly use. What is the relationship between symbols and their meanings? Between symbols and art and calligraphy (if applicable)? Between writing and literacy? Have spelling reforms occurred as the language developed, and if so how did those changes affect these relationships? Write an essay explaining your findings, and compare them with the discussion of logographs in Celia M. Millward's "The Origins of Writing."

15. Research on writing systems often provides insight into cultural change. For this project, choose an alphabet you do not know and a location where it is used. Then investigate the origins and history of that alphabet in that place. Is the writing system associated with a particular language group? Is the current writing system the original one, or did it replace something else? If it was brought by others, who were they? Has it been adapted in any way? What types of literature employ the writing system? Is the alphabet used as an art form? Are any other writing systems used in this area, and if so have they influenced the alphabet you are studying? Create a presentation based on your findings.

Selected Bibliography

Aitchison, Jean. *Language Change: Progress or Decay?* Cambridge: Cambridge UP, 2000. [Nontechnical approach to linguistic history that includes a look at grammatical evolution and concludes that change is neither good nor bad, but understanding changes is essential to understanding language.]

Algeo, John, and Thomas Pyles. *Origin and Development of the English Language.* 5th ed. Belmont, CA: Heinle, 2004. [Updated edition of a classic textbook; includes current research.]

Andresen, Julie. *Linguistics in America 1769–1924.* Oxford: Routledge, 1996. [The study of linguistics placed within American social and political history.]

Bailey, Richard. *Images of English: A Cultural History of the Language.* Ann Arbor: U of Michigan P, 1993. [Focuses on language attitudes within social and cultural contexts.]

Baker, P. *Readings from* Beowulf. U of Virginia. <www.engl.virginia.edu/OE/Beowulf.Readings/Beowulf.Readings.html>. [With audio files of text readings.]

Baker, Peter S. *The Electronic Introduction to Old English.* 2003. Western Michigan U. <www.wmich.edu/medieval/resources/IOE/index.html>. [Online introduction to Old English grammar, meter, and poetic style.]

Ball, Cathy. *Old English Pages.* 30 Dec. 2000. Georgetown U. <www.georgetown.edu/faculty/ballc/oe/old_english.html>. [A compendium of resources for the study of Old English and Anglo-Saxon England.]

Baugh, Albert C., and Thomas Cable. *History of the English Language.* 5th ed. Upper Saddle River, NJ: Prentice Hall, 2001. [This edition of the classic textbook includes Chicano English and Black English.]

Bernstein, Cynthia, Tom Nunnally, and Robin Sabino. *Language Variety in the South Revisited.* Tuscaloosa: U of Alabama P, 1997. [Expanded to include exploration of African American English.]

Burnley, David. *The History of the English Language: A Sourcebook.* 2nd ed. New York: Longman, 2000. [Includes outlines and illustrations documenting language changes from Old English to present-day English.]

Burrow, J. A., and Thorlac Turville-Petre. *A Book of Middle English.* 3rd ed. Malden, MA: Blackwell, 2004. [An examination of Middle English with representative samples of the literature of the time.]

Campbell, Lyle. *Historical Linguistics: An Introduction.* 2nd ed. Cambridge: MIT P, 2004. [Accessible text with examples from a broad range of languages and hands-on exercises for students.]

Cassidy, Frederic G., and Joan Houston Hall, eds. *Dictionary of American Regional English.* 4 vols. Cambridge, MA: Belknap/Harvard UP, 2004. [More than 11,000 entries include local idioms, definitions, and dates of origin. The forthcoming fifth volume will cover the remainder of the alphabet. Audio samples, quizzes, and newsletters are available on the dictionary's Web site, http://polyglot.lss.wisc.edu/dare/dare.html.]

Comrie, Bernard. *The World's Major Languages.* Cambridge: Cambridge UP, 1990. [Extensive look at language families with emphasis on Indo-European languages.]

Coulmas, Florian, ed. *The Blackwell Encyclopedia of Writing Systems.* Malden, MA: Blackwell, 1999. [Includes more than 400 systems with extensive cross-referencing and comprehensive bibliography.]

Crowley, Terry. *An Introduction to Historical Linguistics.* 3rd ed. Auckland: Oxford UP, 1997. [Draws on a wide range of languages with attention to Australia and the Pacific.]

Crystal, David. *Language Death.* Cambridge: Cambridge UP, 2002. [Argues for multilingualism to preserve cultural diversity and minority languages.]

Diringer, David. *The Alphabet: A Key to the History of Mankind.* New York: Funk & Wagnalls, 1976. [Extensive references and bibliographies along with almost 1,000 illustrations.]

Dixon, R. M. W. *The Rise and Fall of Languages.* Cambridge: Cambridge UP, 1997. [Proposes a punctured equilibrium model for language extinction.]

Everhart, Deborah, and Martin Irvine. *Labyrinth Library Middle English Bookcase.* Georgetown U. <www.georgetown.edu/labyrinth/library/me/me.html>. [Links to well- and lesser-known Middle English texts and authors.]

Fennell, Barbara A. *A History of English: A Sociolinguistic Approach.* Malden, MA: Blackwell, 2001. [An overview of major structural changes through various historical eras with examples from classical literature and prose and poetry.]

Fortson, Benjamin W., IV. *Indo-European Language and Culture: An Introduction.* Malden, MA: Blackwell, 2004. [Examines speech and grammar within Indo-European social and cultural contexts.]

"Historical Linguistics." *LSA: Videos on the Web.* Linguistic Society of America. <www.uga.edu/lsava/Topics/Historical%20Linguistics/Historical%20Linguistics.html>. [Video clips tracing word forms and pronunciations through Indo-European languages into English.]

Hock, Hans Heinrich, and Brian D. Josephs. *Language History, Language Change, and Language Relationship: An Introduction to Historical and Comparative Linguistics.* Berlin: Walter de Gruyter, 1996. [Contrasts American and British English using illustrations and literary examples to demonstrate how language diverges.]

Janson, Tore. *Speak: A Short History of Languages.* Oxford: Oxford UP, 2004. [A far-reaching history that includes multiple international languages and maps.]

Johnson, Ellen. *Lexical Change and Variation in the Southeastern United States, 1930–1990.* Tuscaloosa: U of Alabama P, 1996. [An in-depth discussion of language evolution, focusing on the Southeast and how cultural changes influenced linguistic variation through the twentieth century.]

Kastovksy, Deiter, and Arthur Mettinger, eds. *The History of English in a Social Context: A Contribution to Historical Linguistics.* Berlin: Walter de Gruyter, 2000. [Essays by international scholars with particular emphasis on language in Shakespeare and Early Modern literature.]

Katsiavriades, Kryss, and Talaat Qureshi. "Language Families." *The KryssTal Web Site.* 2007. <www.krysstal.com/langfams.html>. [Explores ten major language families in detail, with information about many others.]

Koenig, Ekkehard. *The Germanic Languages.* Oxford: Routledge, 2002. [Includes chapter-length discussions of twelve Germanic languages, including Faroese and Afrikaans.]

Kretzschmar, William. *Linguistic Atlas Projects.* 10 June 2006. University of Georgia. <http://us.english.uga.edu>. [Maps and links to current dialect projects, with access to global dialect information.]

Labov, William, Sharon Ash, and Charles Bobick. *Atlas of North American English.* <www.ling.upenn.edu/phonoatlas>. [Comprehensive language survey of urban areas in the United States and Canada with an emphasis on phonological data establishing regional dialect boundaries.]

Lehmann, Winfred. "Some Proposals for Historical Linguistic Grammars." *Southwest Journal of Linguistics.* 23.2 (2004): 145–57. [Available as digital download.]

Leith, Dick. *A Social History of English.* 2nd ed. London: Routledge, 1997. [A look at what the author terms "New Englishes" around the world and discussions of how gender issues have changed language usage.]

Masica, Colin. *The Indo-Aryan Languages.* Cambridge: Cambridge UP, 1993. [Detailed history, with useful appendices and extensive bibliography.]

McWhorter, John. *The Power of Babel: A Natural History of the Language.* New York: Harper Perennial, 2003. [Detailed illustrated discussion of the family tree of languages and the ways languages evolve.]

Medieval Calligraphy. Harvard U. <http://courses.dce.harvard.edu/~humae105/fall97/twest>. [Ancient calligraphic scripts, scripts from the first to the fifteenth centuries, development of modem letter forms, and other developments.]

Mitchell, Bruce, and Fred C. Robinson. *A Guide to Old English.* 7th ed. Malden, MA: Blackwell, 2007. [Includes presentation of grammatical mood in Old English as well as the "Cotton Gnomes" and Wulfstan's *Sermo Lupi ad Anglos.*]

Morris, Tim. "Sites Devoted to Old English." History and Development of the English Language Course home page. Aug.–Dec. 1998. Dept. of English, U of Texas at Arlington. <www.uta.edu/english/tim/courses/4301f98/linglinx/oe.html>. [Links to Old English Web sites.]

Mosser, Dan. *History of the English Language.* 23 May 2005. <http://ebbs.english.vt.edu/hel/hel.html>. [Portal to sites on the history of English (HEL) and to HEL discussion groups.]

Nakanishi, Akira. *Writing Systems of the World: Alphabets, Syllabaries, Pictograms.* North Clarendon, VT: Charles E. Tuttle, 1990. [Concise dictionary of writing systems supplemented with extensive illustrations and examples.]

Nunberg, Geoffrey. "Lingo, Jingo: English Only and the New Jingoism." *The American Prospect.* 8.33. <www.prospect.org/print/V8/33/nunberg-g.html>. [Includes discussion of the controversial theory of English as an endangered language.]

"Old English Aerobics." 1999. Briery Creek Software. U. of Virginia. <www.engl.virginia.edu/OE/OEA>. [Provides a wealth of exercises in Old English.]

Page, R. I. *An Introduction to English Runes.* 2nd ed. Rochester, NY: Boydell P, 2006. [A practical guide to the runic alphabet with recently discovered historical documents.]

Readings of Old English Poetry. <www.kami.demon.co.uk/gesithas/readings/readings.html>. [Old English verse with Modern English translation and audio files for Old English readings.]

Renfrew, Colin. *Archaeology and Language: The Puzzle of Indo-European Origins.* Cambridge: Cambridge UP, 1990. [A synthesis of linguistic and anthropological research that reconsiders the issues of language origin and ethnic affiliation.]

Rickford, John Russell. *Spoken Soul: The Story of Black English.* Hoboken, NJ: Wiley & Son, 2000. [Discussion of Ebonics with examples from Langston Hughes and Maya Angelou.]

Robinson, Andrew. *The Story of Writing.* New York: Thames and Hudson, 1999. [Examines international and historic scripts as well as communication through logograms and pictographic symbols.]

Rogers, William E., and Diana Ervin. "The History of English Phonemes." 19 March 2001. Furman University. <http://alpha.furman.edu/~wrogers/phonemes>. [Examines each stage of English development, with links to additional information on each historical era.]

Sacks, David. *Letter Perfect: The Marvelous History of Our Alphabet from A to Z.* New York: Random House-Broadway, 2004. [An eclectic volume about each alphabet letter with anecdotes about language and the people who define it.]

Sampson, Geoffrey. *Writing Systems: A Linguistic Introduction.* 1986. North Clarendon, VT: Charles E. Tuttle, 1990. [A general look at writing systems with examples from Japanese, Chinese, and Korean.]

Schneider, Edgar. *Focus on USA.* Amsterdam: John Benjamins, 1996. [A collection of essays on regional and social usage, "American College Slang."]

Science. 27 Feb. 2004: 1319–31. [See the following five articles: "Searching for the Indo-Europeans," Michael Balter; "From Heofonum to Heavens," Yudhijit Bhattacharjee; "The Future of Language," David Graddol; and "The First Language?" Elizabeth Pennisi.]

Sledd, James, and Wilma R. Ebbitt. *Dictionaries and THAT Dictionary: A Casebook on the Aims of Lexicographers and the Targets of Reviewers.* Glenview, IL: Scott, Foresman and Co., 1962. [Essays on the history and theory of lexicography and dictionary making.]

Trask, R. L. *Historical Linguistics: An Introduction.* New York: St. Martin's Press, 1996. [Study of language change and comparison.]

Turville-Petre, Thorlac. *Reading Middle English Literature.* Malden, MA: Blackwell, 2006. [Texts of religious piety and love and marriage in Middle English.]

Wagner, Jennifer. *European Languages: A Comparative Analysis.* Indo-European Languages. <www.ielanguages.com/eurolang.html>. [Explores translation, spelling, grammar, and other topics.]

Watkins, Calvert. *The American Heritage Dictionary of Indo-European Roots.* Boston: Houghton Mifflin, 2000. [Collection of 13,000 words together with 1,350 reconstructed roots.]

Wright, Linda. *The Development of Standard English, 1300–1800: Theories, Descriptions, Conflicts.* Cambridge: Cambridge UP, 2000. [Examines the development of Standard English as it relates to the transition from Middle to Modern English.]

LANGUAGE VARIATION AND SOCIAL INTERACTION

All species have communication systems, but human language is particularly complex and interesting. In this volume, we have looked at human language as an abstract system, progressing from the smallest units of sound—phonemes and morphemes—to the larger units of words, phrases, and sentences. We also have examined the properties of meaning, how languages change over time, and how dialects develop. In Part Six, we turn directly to the study of language variation and how it influences social interaction, values, and policies.

The first selection, "Speech Communities" by the late Paul Roberts, explains the idea that language variation is a social reality. In other words, each of us belongs both successively and simultaneously to a number of different speech communities, some based on age, some on social class and education, and some on the places where we have lived. We find that we are always members of multiple speech communities, both regional and social.

Next, in "Regional Dialects and Social Class," Ronald Macaulay uses examples from British and American English dialects to describe how language varies from one geographic region to another. Then he discusses how differences in social dialect may affect not just academic and professional success. Citing a number of studies, Macauley shows how we make judgments reflecting prejudice and stereotypes based on language variation and warns us that such life-changing judgments based on relatively small differences in speakers' pronunciation or grammar reflect prejudice and stereotypes.

In the third selection, "Standards and Vernaculars," Walt Wolfram and Natalie Schilling-Estes present the myths and realities regarding formal, informal, and vernacular speech in the United States. They note that we define informal standard and vernacular English by disfavored features—that is, variations that deviate from "correct" formal language.

Like Macaulay, they illustrate that commonly held notions about vernacular speech can reveal underlying regional or ethnic biases, and throughout *American English Dialects and Variations* they point to a "significant discrepancy between the public perception of linguistic difference and the linguistic reality."

The next three selections focus on language variation and social interaction in North America. They help us understand that language prestige and status have significant social outcomes.

The most researched dialect of American English is African American English (AAE), a variety that began in the earliest days of the United States. In the past three decades, linguists have tried to establish a full linguistic description of AAE and to comprehend its historical development. Although AAE is an influential social dialect, it has lacked the high prestige of other important varieties, as Lee Pederson notes in Part Five. In 1996, the status of AAE as a dialect of American English became a matter of public debate when the Oakland, California, School Board passed its Oakland Resolution on Ebonics. This resolution was intended primarily to help AAE-speaking students master Standard English. It recommended training teachers to work with the structural differences between AAE and Standard English. The Oakland Resolution received a great deal of public attention and generated considerable debate, particularly among those who saw it as a proposal to replace Standard English with AAE. Here, we include the amended version of the Oakland Resolution on Ebonics, followed by John Rickford's essay, "Suite for Ebony and Phonics," that rejects the idea that Ebonics is either slang or "lazy English." Ebonics, Rickford shows us, is a naturally occurring, systematic, and rule-governed variety of English.

In the last selection, "Endangered Native American Language," James Crawford warns us that of the approximately 6,000 languages in the world today, perhaps 90 percent are moribund or without the likelihood of existing beyond the present generation of speakers. Many languages native to the Americas already have become extinct, and many others, from the Arctic to Tierra del Fuego, are disappearing as their speakers switch to more dominant languages, such as English, Spanish, or Portuguese. As we'll see in Part Ten of this volume, language extinction appears to be one of the repercussions of globalization. Here, Crawford argues that we should recognize the importance of maintaining languages, and he uses the endangered Native American languages to discuss why language diversity matters.

24

Speech Communities

Paul Roberts

The concept of speech communities is basic to an understanding of regional and social variation in language, otherwise known as dialects. In the following excerpt from his 1958 book Understanding English, *the late Paul Roberts introduces the concept of speech communities and argues that they "are formed by many features: age, geography, education, occupation, social position." He could have added that the characteristics of racial or ethnic identity and gender also lead to membership in speech communities. In addition to the effects of speech communities, all speakers of a language use a variety of jargons and a range of styles, the latter varying in terms of levels of formality. (For a discussion of these kinds of variations, see Harvey A. Daniels's "Nine Ideas about Language" in Part One.) Finally, Roberts emphasizes that language variation is a natural phenomenon that is not necessarily good or bad. He notes that value judgments about language are often value judgments about people.*

Imagine a village of a thousand people all speaking the same language and never hearing any language other than their own. As the decades pass and generation succeeds generation, it will not be very apparent to the speakers of the language that any considerable language change is going on. Oldsters may occasionally be conscious of and annoyed by the speech forms of youngsters. They will notice new words, new expressions, "bad" pronunciations, but will ordinarily put these down to the irresponsibility of youth, and decide piously that the language of the younger generation will revert to decency when the generation grows up.

It doesn't revert, though. The new expressions and the new pronunciations persist, and presently there is another younger generation with its own new expressions and its own pronunciations. And thus the language changes. If members of the village could speak to one another across five hundred years, they would probably find themselves unable to communicate.

Now suppose that the village divides itself and half the people move away. They move across the river or over a mountain and form a new village. Suppose the separation is so complete that the people of New Village have no contact with the people of Old Village. The language of

373

both villages will change, drifting away from the language of their common ancestors. But the drift will not be in the same direction. In both villages there will be new expressions and new pronunciations, but not the same ones. In the course of time the languages of Old Village and New Village will be mutually unintelligible with the language they both started with. They will also be mutually unintelligible with one another.

An interesting thing—and one for which there is no perfectly clear explanation—is that the rate of change will not ordinarily be the same for both villages. The language of Old Village changes faster than the language of New Village. One might expect that the opposite would be true—that the emigrants, placed in new surroundings and new conditions, would undergo more rapid language changes. But history reports otherwise. American English, for example, despite the violence and agony and confusion to which the demands of a new continent have subjected it, is probably essentially closer to the language of Shakespeare than London English is.

Suppose one thing more. Suppose Old Village is divided sharply into an upper class and a lower class. The sons and daughters of the upper class go to preparatory school and then to the university; the children of the lower class go to work. The upper-class people learn to read and write and develop a flowering literature; the lower-class people remain illiterate. Dialects develop, and the speech of the two classes steadily diverges. One might suppose that most of the change would go on among the illiterate, that the upper-class people, conscious of their heritage, would tend to preserve the forms and pronunciations of their ancestors. Not so. The opposite is true. In speech, the educated tend to be radical and the uneducated conservative. In England one finds Elizabethan forms and sounds not among Oxford and Cambridge graduates but among the people of backward villages.

A village is a fairly simple kind of speech community—a group of people steadily in communication with one another, steadily hearing one another's speech. But the village is by no means the basic unit. Within the simplest village there are many smaller units—groupings based on age, class, occupation. All these groups play intricately on one another and against one another, and a language that seems at first a coherent whole will turn out on inspection to be composed of many differing parts. Some forces tend to make these parts diverge; other forces hold them together. Thus the language continues in tension.

THE SPEECH COMMUNITIES OF THE CHILD

The child's first speech community is ordinarily his family. The child learns whatever kind of language the family speaks—or, more precisely, whatever kind of language it speaks to him. The child's language learning, now and later, is governed by two obvious motives: the desire to communicate and the desire to be admired. He imitates what he hears. More or less successful imitations usually bring action and reward and tend to be repeated. Unsuccessful ones usually don't bring action and reward and tend to be discarded.

But since language is a complicated business it is sometimes the unsuccessful imitations that bring the reward. The child, making a stab at the word *mother*, comes out with *muzzer*. The family decides that this is just too cute for anything and beams and repeats *muzzer*, and the child, feeling that he's scored a bull's eye, goes on saying *muzzer* long after he has mastered *other* and *brother*. Baby talk is not so much invented by the child as sponsored by the parent.

Eventually the child moves out of the family and into another speech community—other children of his neighborhood. He goes to kindergarten and immediately encounters speech habits that conflict with those he has learned. If he goes to school and talks about his *muzzer*, it will be borne in on him by his colleagues that the word is not well chosen. Even *mother* may not pass muster, and he may discover that he gets better results and is altogether happier if he refers to his female parent as his ma or even his old lady.

Children coming together in a kindergarten class bring with them language that is different because it is learned in different homes. It is all to some degree unsuccessfully learned, consisting of not quite perfect imitations of the original. In school all this speech coalesces, differences tend to be ironed out, and the result differs from the original parental speech and differs in pretty much the same way.

The pressures on the child to conform to the speech of his age group, his speech community, are enormous. He may admire his teacher and love his mother; he may even—and even consciously—wish to speak as they do. But he *has* to speak like the rest of the class. If he does not, life becomes intolerable.

The speech changes that go on when the child goes to school are often most distressing to parents. Your little Bertram, at home, has never heard anything but the most elegant English. You send him to school, and what happens? He comes home saying things like "I done real good in school today, Mom." But Bertram really has no choice in the matter. If Clarence and Elbert and the rest of the fellows customarily say "I done real good," then Bertram might as well go around with three noses as say things like "I did very nicely."

Individuals differ of course, and not all children react to the speech community in the same way. Some tend to imitate and others tend to force imitation. But all to some degree have their speech modified by forces over which neither they nor their parents nor their teachers have any real control.

Individuals differ too in their sensitivity to language. For some, language is always a rather embarrassing problem. They steadily make boners, saying the right thing in the wrong place or the wrong way. They have a hard time fitting in. Others tend to change their language slowly, sticking stoutly to their way of saying things, even though their way differs from that of the majority. Still others adopt new language habits almost automatically, responding quickly to whatever speech environment they encounter.

Indeed some children of five or six have been observed to speak two or more different dialects without much awareness that they are doing so. Most commonly, they will speak in one way at home and in another on the playground. At home they say, "I did very nicely" and "I haven't any"; these become at school, "I done real good" and "I ain't got none."

THE CLASS AS A SPEECH COMMUNITY

Throughout the school years, or at least through the American secondary school, the individual's most important speech community is his age group, his class. Here is where the real power lies. The rule is conformity above all things, and the group uses its power ruthlessly on those who do not conform. Language is one of the chief means by which the school group seeks to establish its entity, and in the high school this is done more or less consciously. The obvious feature is high school slang, picked up from the radio, from other schools, sometimes invented, changing with bewildering speed. Nothing is more satisfactory than to speak today's slang; nothing more futile than to use yesterday's.

There can be few tasks more frustrating than that of the secondary school teacher charged with the responsibility of brushing off and polishing up the speech habits of the younger generation. Efforts to make *real* into *really*, *ain't* into *am not*, *I seen him* into *I saw him*, *he don't* into *he doesn't* meet at best with polite indifference, at worst with mischievous counterattack.

The writer can remember from his own high school days when the class, a crashingly witty bunch, took to pronouncing the word *sure* as *sewer*. "Have you prepared your lesson, Arnold?" Miss Driscoll would ask. "Sewer, Miss Driscoll," Arnold would reply. "I think," said Miss Driscoll, who was pretty quick on her feet too, "that you must mean 'sewerly,' since the construction calls for the adverb not the adjective." We were delighted with the suggestion and went about saying "sewerly" until the very blackboards were nauseated. Miss Driscoll must have wished often that she had left it lay.

CONFRONTING THE ADULT WORLD

When the high school class graduates, the speech community disintegrates as the students fit themselves into new ones. For the first time in the experience of most of the students the speech ways of adult communities begin to exercise real force. For some people the adjustment is a relatively simple one. A boy going to work in a garage may have a good deal of new lingo to pick up, and he may find that the speech that seemed so racy and won such approval in the corridors of Springfield High leaves his more adult associates merely bored. But a normal person will adapt himself without trouble.

For others in other situations settling into new speech communities may be more difficult. The person going into college, into the business world, into scrubbed society may find that he has to think about and work on his speech habits in order not to make a fool of himself too often.

College is a particularly complicated problem. Not only does the freshman confront upperclassmen not particularly disposed to find the speech of Springfield High particularly cute, but the adult world, as represented chiefly by the faculty, becomes increasingly more immediate. The problems of success, of earning a living, of marriage, of attaining a satisfactory adult life loom larger, and they all bring language problems with them. Adaptation is necessary, and the student adapts.

The student adapts, but the adult world adapts too. The thousands of boys and girls coming out of the high schools each spring are affected by the speech of the adult communities into which they move, but they also affect that speech. The new pronunciation habits, developing grammatical features, different vocabulary do by no means all give way before the disapproval of elders. Some of them stay. Elders, sometimes to their dismay, find themselves changing their speech habits under the bombardment of those of their juniors. And then of course the juniors eventually become the elders, and there is no one left to disapprove.

THE SPACE DIMENSION

Speech communities are formed by many features besides that of age. Most obvious is geography. Our country was originally settled by people coming from different parts of England. They spoke different dialects to begin with and as a result regional speech differences existed from the start in the different parts of the country. As speakers of other languages came to America and learned English, they left their mark on the speech of the sections in which they settled. With the westward movement, new pioneers streamed out through the mountain passes and down river valleys, taking the different dialects west and modifying them by new mixtures in new environments.

Today we are all more or less conscious of certain dialect differences in our country. We speak of the "southern accent," the "Brooklyn accent," the "New England accent." Until a few years ago it was often said that American English was divided into three dialects: Southern American (south of the Mason-Dixon line); Eastern American (east of the Connecticut River); and Western American. This description suggests certain gross differences all right, but recent research shows that it is a gross oversimplification.

The starting point of American dialects is the original group of colonies. We had a New England settlement, centering in Massachusetts; a Middle Atlantic settlement, centering in Pennsylvania; a southern settlement, centering in Virginia and the Carolinas. These colonies were different in speech to begin with, since the settlers came from different parts of England. Their differences were increased as the colonies lived for a century and a half or so with only thin communication with either Mother England or each other. By the time of the Revolution the dialects were well established. Within each group there were of course subgroups. Richmond speech differed markedly from that of Savannah. But Savannah and Richmond were more like each other than they were like Philadelphia or Boston.

The Western movement began shortly after the Revolution, and dialects followed geography. The New Englanders moved mostly into upper New York State and the Great Lakes region. The Middle Atlantic colonists went down the Shenandoah Valley and eventually into the heart of the Midwest. The southerners opened up Kentucky and Tennessee, later the lower Mississippi Valley, later still Texas and much of the Southwest. Thus new speech communities were formed, related to the old ones of the seaboard, but each developing new characteristics as lines of settlement crossed.

New complications were added before and after the Revolution by the great waves of immigration of people from countries other than England: Swedes in Delaware, Dutch in New York, Germans and Scots-Irish in Pennsylvania, Irish in New England, Poles and Greeks and Italians and Portuguese. The bringing in of black slaves had an important effect on the speech of the South and later on the whole country. The Spanish in California and the Southwest added their mark. In [the twentieth and twenty-first centuries], movement of peoples goes on: the trek of southern blacks to northern and western cities, the migration of people from Arkansas, Oklahoma, and Texas to California. All these have shaped and are shaping American speech.

We speak of America as the melting pot, but the speech communities of this continent are very far from having melted into one. Linguists today can trace very clearly the movements of the early settlers in the still-living speech of their descendants. They can follow an eighteenth century speech community west, showing how it crossed this pass and followed that river, threw out an offshoot here, left a pocket there, merged with another group, halted, split, moved on once more. If all other historical evidence were destroyed, the history of the country could still be reconstructed from the speech of modern America.

SOCIAL DIFFERENCES

The third great shaper of speech communities is social class. This has been, and is, more important in England than in America. In England, class differences have often been more prominent than those of age or place. If you were the blacksmith's boy, you might know the son of the local baronet, but you didn't speak his language. You spoke the language of your social group, and he that of his, and over the centuries these social dialects remained widely separated.

England in the twentieth century has been much democratized, but the language differences are far from having disappeared. One can still tell much about a person's family, his school background, his general position in life by the way he speaks. Social lines are hard to cross, and language is perhaps the greatest barrier. You may make a million pounds and own several cars and a place in the country, but your vowels and consonants and nouns and verbs and sentence patterns will still proclaim to the world that you're not a part of the upper crust.

In America, of course, social distinctions have never been so sharp as they are in England. We find it somewhat easier to rise in the world, to move into social environments unknown to our parents. This is possible, partly, because speech differences are slighter; conversely, speech differences are slighter because this is possible. But speech differences do exist. If you've spent all your life driving a cab in Philly and, having inherited a fortune, move to San Francisco's Nob Hill, you will find that your language is different, perhaps embarrassingly so, from that of your new acquaintances.

Language differences on the social plane in America are likely to correlate with education or occupation rather than with birth—simply because education and occupation in America do not depend so much on birth as they do in other countries. A child without family connection can get himself educated at Harvard, Yale, or Princeton. In doing so, he acquires the speech habits of the Ivy League and gives up those of his parents.

Exceptions abound. But in general there is a clear difference between the speech habits of the college graduate and those of the high-school graduate. The cab driver does not talk like the Standard Oil executive, the college professor like the carnival pitch man, or an Illinois merchant like a sailor shipping out of New Orleans. New York's Madison Avenue and Third Avenue are only a few blocks apart, but they are widely separated in language. And both are different from Broadway.

It should be added that the whole trend of modern life is to reduce rather than to accentuate these differences. In a country where college education becomes increasingly everybody's chance, where executives and refrigerator salesmen and farmers play golf together, where a college professor may drive a cab in the summertime to keep his family alive, it becomes harder and harder to guess a person's education, income, and social status by the way he talks. But it would be absurd to say that language gives no clue at all.

GOOD AND BAD

Speech communities, then, are formed by many features: age, geography, education, occupation, social position. Young people speak differently from old people, Kansans differently from Virginians, Yale graduates differently from Dannemora graduates. Now let us pose a delicate question: aren't some of these speech communities better than others? That is, isn't better language heard in some than in others?

Well, yes, of course. One speech community is always better than all the rest. This is the group in which one happens to find oneself. The writer would answer unhesitatingly that the noblest, loveliest, purest English is that heard in the Men's Faculty Club of San Jose State College, San Jose, California. He would admit, of course, that the speech of some of the younger members leaves something to be desired; that certain recent immigrants from Harvard, Michigan, and other foreign parts need to work on the laughable oddities lingering in their speech; and that members of certain departments tend to introduce a lot of queer terms that can only be described as jargon. But in general the English of the Faculty Club is ennobling and sweet.

As a practical matter, good English is whatever English is spoken by the group in which one moves contentedly and at ease. To the bum on Main Street in Los Angeles, good English is the language of other L.A. bums. Should he wander onto the campus of UCLA, he would find the talk there unpleasant, confusing, and comical. He might agree, if pressed, that the college man speaks "correctly" and he doesn't. But in his heart he knows better. He wouldn't talk like them college jerks if you paid him.

If you admire the language of other speech communities more than you do your own, the reasonable hypothesis is that you are dissatisfied with the community itself. It is not precisely other speech that attracts you but the people who use this speech. Conversely, if some language strikes you as unpleasant or foolish or rough, it is presumably because the speakers themselves seem so.

To many people, the sentence "Where is he at?" sounds bad. It is bad, they would say, in and of itself. The sounds are bad. But this is very hard to prove. If "Where is he at?" is bad because it has bad sound combinations, then presumably "Where is the cat?" or "Where is my hat?" are just as bad, yet no one thinks them so. Well, then, "Where is he at?" is bad because it uses too many words. One gets the same meaning from "Where is he?" so why add the *at*? True. Then "He going with us?" is a better sentence than "Is he going with us?" You don't really need the *is*, so why put it in?

Certainly there are some features of language to which we can apply the terms *good* and *bad, better* and *worse*. Clarity is usually better than obscurity; precision is better than vagueness. But these are not often what we have in mind when we speak of good and bad English. If we like the speech of upper-class Englishmen, the presumption is that we admire upper-class Englishmen—their characters, culture, habits of mind. Their sounds and words simply come to connote the people themselves and become admirable therefore. If we heard the same sounds and words from people who were distasteful to us, we would find the speech ugly.

This is not to say that correctness and incorrectness do not exist in speech. They obviously do, but they are relative to the speech community— or communities—in which one operates. As a practical matter, correct speech is that which sounds normal or natural to one's comrades. Incorrect speech is that which evokes in them discomfort or hostility or disdain.

FOR DISCUSSION AND REVIEW

1. Identify the factors that, according to Roberts, are responsible for the development of speech communities and contribute to internal differences within each community. Trace the changing speech communities of an individual, using age as the only variable.

2. Change has occurred less rapidly in American English than in British English; change also occurs more rapidly in both countries among the educated than among the uneducated. Identify three reasons why this is so.

3. Explain Roberts's statement that "baby talk is not so much invented by the child as sponsored by the parent." Describe two examples of this phenomenon in your family.

4. Roberts writes of the "pressures on the child to conform to the speech" of his or her age group, class, and speech community. Discuss such pressures you felt while growing up.

5. Roberts believes that marked differences exist between the speech communities of one generation and the next. Observe and describe speech differences between students and faculty in your school. Compare your findings with those of your instructor. Is age the only factor here? What kinds of differences exist between your speech and that of your parents? Between your speech and that of your grandparents? What, in general, are people's attitudes toward these differences?

6. Explain the geographic basis from which American regional dialects originated. Do you agree with Roberts's statement, "If all other

historical evidence were destroyed, the history of the country could still be reconstructed from the speech of modern America"? Why, or why not?

7. Roberts writes that "language differences on the social plane in America are likely to correlate with education or occupation rather than with birth." Discuss the implications of this statement. Do your experiences support it? Explain your answer.
   (Note: Before answering questions 8 through 10, you should review Harvey A. Daniels's "Nine Ideas about Language" in Part One, pp. 3–20.)

8. Note three distinctive characteristics or functions, or a combination of both, of the consultative style.

9. In what ways does the casual style differ from the consultative?

10. Note five distinctive characteristics of the formal style. To what extent do you think most Americans have learned to speak in this style? Give specific examples.

25

Regional Dialects and Social Class

Ronald K. S. Macaulay

The issue of how language use influences social identity has become a major avenue of research in sociolinguistics and other fields. In this selection from The Social Art: Language and Its Uses *(1996), Professor Ronald Macaulay examines the ranges of language differences that occur in dialects. Drawing examples primarily from British and American English—including dialects of his own Scots English— Macaulay shows that where a number of language differences come together, we tend to find dialect boundaries. He also explains that where we find major dialect separation other kinds of separation may exist, such as distinct social identities or difference in educational success, and these differences aren't neutral. Social judgments about variation in pronunciation or grammar affect opportunities in school and throughout adult life.*

REGIONAL DIALECTS

It is impossible to think back to a time when any language was homogeneous. Even when, if it was the case, there were very small groups speaking the same language, there must have been some variety. Language is heterogeneous by its very nature and the existence of differences creates the possibility of combining certain features into new groupings. To take a parallel from another field, there are now several hundred recognized breeds of dog but all dogs have as their common ancestor the wolf. Through centuries of selective breeding, the wolf has evolved into such different creatures as the Great Dane, the dachshund, the poodle, and the Lakeland terrier. Certain features of size, color, temperament, and so on have been selectively reinforced or suppressed. So it is with language. Although we have no idea what the ur-language was, or even whether there was only one, we know enough about language diversification to know that languages can change dramatically with changing circumstances. Most European languages can be traced back to a hypothetical single ancestor..., yet speakers of Russian, Greek, Welsh, French, and English do not consider themselves as speaking the same language, though they will find occasional resemblances among the words of the different languages.

As [you know], there are several sources of linguistic differences and one of them is geography. The nineteenth-century French scholar Gaston Paris observed:

> Varieties of common speech blend into one another by imperceptible gradations. A villager who might know only the speech of his village would easily understand that of the neighbouring village, with a bit more difficulty that of the village he would come to by walking on in the same direction, and so on, until finally he reached a point where he would understand the local speech only with great difficulty.

Because of this notion of gradual variation, many linguists have despaired of using the term *dialect* in any well-defined sense. Yet there are often linguistic features that show clear regional variation. For example, the Old English vowel in such words as *stān* and *bān* has become the vowel in *stone* and *bone* in most varieties of modern English. North of the River Humber in northeast England, however, this vowel developed differently so that Scottish children may be heard saying:

> Sticks and stanes may break my banes
> But names will never hurt me.

The line dividing two areas that differ by a single feature such as this is called an *isogloss*. Where a number of isoglosses coincide there is a strong likelihood of a dialect boundary. For example, there are more isoglosses at the border between England and Scotland than for a considerable distance on either side of that border. In this case the language differences coincide with a difference in national identity. Similarly, it is not surprising that there should be a number of features that distinguish the speech of the South in the United States from that of the North. Noah Webster, fifty years after the United States gained its independence from Britain, was at pains to show the independence of American English by spellings such as *theater, color, defense,* and *jeweler* in contrast to *theatre, colour, defence,* and *jeweller.* There are nowadays many forms and expressions that distinguish the two varieties. For example:

British	American
pavement	sidewalk
petrol	gasoline
boot (of a car)	trunk
motorway	freeway
goods van	freight car
biscuit	cookie
lift	elevator
queue	line
handbag	purse

There are also morphological differences. The past tense of the verb *fit* is *fitted* in British English and *fit* in American English; the past participle of *got* is *gotten* in the United States and *got* in Britain. Britons say *different from* in contrast to American *different than*. With increased travel and two-way traffic in television entertainment, many people are aware of such differences, but I find that my students in California do not understand the British colloquial expression *ticked off* as in *The supervisor called me in and I was ticked off* (that is, "reprimanded") because for them it means "annoyed." In England when I tell people that my daughter *went to school in Santa Cruz*, they are surprised to learn that she went to university there. Most Americans, however, have learned that in Britain *public school* refers to an exclusive private school. There may still be confusion with *grammar school*, which in the United States is for younger children and in Britain for older pupils, and *prep school*, which prepares pupils for a public school in England and for college in the United States. Finally, *colleges* in Britain, unlike those in the United States, do not grant baccalaureate degrees.

Does this mean that British English and American English are different dialects? In one sense, yes, but the term seems inappropriate for such large areas that have a great deal of geographical variation within them. Languages and dialects have both a unifying function and a separatist function. They help a group of people see what they have in common with each other and how they differ from "others." In the past, before the existence of passports or other identifying documents, language was one way of distinguishing not only friend from foe but also those from whom a suitable marriage partner could be chosen. Dialects still serve this function. It is part of what it means to be English or American to speak in a certain way, just as it is part of what it means to be Scots, Welsh, Texan, or a New Yorker.

Dialects can differ with respect to any characteristic of language. The most obvious is pronunciation. In the Old Testament it is recorded that the men of Gilead asked the Ephraimites to say the word *Shibboleth*; if they could not say it correctly but said *Sibboleth* instead, they were killed. Things are not usually so serious nowadays, but a Carribean woman who was attempting to enter the United States illegally from Canada at Niagara Falls was stopped when she claimed to have been born in "Booffalo" on the grounds that anyone who was born in Buffalo would know how to say it. Single sounds, however, can give an important clue as to geographical origin. In England north of a line approximately from the Wash to the Bristol channel, the vowel in words such as *come* and *much* is pronounced as if spelled *coom* and *mooch*. This was an important factor when advertisements for traveling salesmen often contained the warning *Northcountrymen need not apply*. In the United States the word *greasy* is usually pronounced with an [s] north of the Mason-Dixon line and with a [z] south of it. In Scottish dialects, where the effects of the Great Vowel Shift are different from its impact in England, words such as *down* and *mouse* are pronounced *doon* and *moose*.

In the Potteries area of England, according to Peter Trudgill, there is an interesting pattern of vowels:

bait is pronounced like beat

beat is pronounced like bait

bought is pronounced like boat

boat is pronounced like boot

boot is pronounced like bout

bout is pronouced like bite

bite is pronounced like "baht"

According to Trudgill, in this dialect, *it seems the same* is pronounced like *it sames the seem*. In practice, even substantial differences like this need not always cause difficulty in understanding because it will often be clear from the context which word is being used. Only occasionally does a word occur in an ambiguous context. I once bought a freezer from someone who had grown up in New Jersey. He warned me that there was *a plastic pen* in it that sometimes rattled. Knowing that he had young children who were quite lively, the presence of a plastic pen did not seem surprising to me. It was years later that I realized that he had been talking about *a plastic pan*.

There can also be morphological differences between dialects, for example, in negation. In Scottish dialects the contracted negative is frequently *-nae* rather than *-n't* as in *the foreman there he didnae want a lassie* and *it cannae be broken*. In some dialects *ain't* is used for all contracted forms of the negative with *be* and *have*, instead of *isn't*, *aren't*, *hasn't*, and *haven't*. For example, *there ain't nothing over there* and *I ain't got one single flea in my hair, they're all married*. In Somerset dialect *I be* can occur for *I am* as in *he's older than what I be* and *I ben't taking her down there*. In both England and the United States there is variation in the past tense *of see* in local dialects. In the north and part of the southwest of England *seed* is used, in the southeast *seen* is more common, while in many places *see* is used as a past tense. A similar kind of distribution is found in dialects in the eastern United States with *see* (for the past tense) commonest in northern parts, *seen* in midland areas, and *seed* in the southern part.

Syntactic differences in dialects have been studied less than other aspects, partly because it is more difficult to collect information on syntax. In Ayr in Scotland I recorded speakers using emphatic forms of syntax such as *he was some man him, it was Jimmy Brown was the fireman, it was him that led the band*, and *that's me seen it*. In Irish English there are similar but different constructions: *it was a great race was that, it is looking for more land a lot of them are, it's badly she'd do it now*. In Alabama speakers have a distinctive verb form with *done* as in *I think that Mr. K has done passed away* and *they had done operated on her for appendicitis*, where the sense is like "already." In Hawick in Scotland double modals are found as in *he might could do it for you* where the use of both *might* and *could* reinforces the notion of possibility. Such combinations are also found in the southern United States: *I might should turn over to Ann* and *it shouldn't oughta take us very long*. The persistence of such forms despite the efforts of teachers and other authorities to discourage them is a reminder that the actual standards for "correctness" are set by the people who speak the language.

The greatest differences, however, are found in vocabulary, particularly in the kinds of words that are learned directly from other people rather than in school or from books. Words for farm equipment, birds, animals, and plants have traditionally varied from region to region. For example, in different parts of Scotland the foxglove is known as *bloody finger, fairy finger, witch's pap, trowie glove, bloody man's finger, lady's finger, witch's thimble, fairy thimble, dead man's bell*, and *dead man's finger*. The references to *finger* translate its Latin technical name *digitalis purpurea*.

When I was growing up in Ayrshire, I often got a *skelf* in my finger and I thought that was the word all Scots used for a splinter. When the first volume of the *Linguistic Atlas of Scotland* came out, I found that this word was only one of many; those in the north of Scotland called it a *stab* or a *stob*, while further south it was known as a *spale* or a *spelk*. When I went to California, I learned a number of new words. It took me some time to find out that *submarine* was a special kind of sandwich, but even longer to discover that the same sandwich had other names in other parts of the United States—a *hoagie* in Philadelphia, a *po' boy* in New Orleans, a *grinder* in New England, a *hero* in New York City, a *wedge* or a *torpedo* in other parts of New York State, and a *zep* in Norristown, Pennsylvania.

Local customs can also give rise to local words. In Scotland the last corn sheaf cut at harvest was considered important enough to justify its own name. In the northeast it is known as the *clyack*, further south it is the *maiden*, in central Scotland it is the *kirn*, and in the southwest it is the *hare*. It does not have a special name south of the Scottish-English border.

There is one dialect that is not usually considered such and that is the standard dialect. There is probably no expression referring to a variety of language that is more liable to misuse and misinterpretation than *Standard English*.

Part of this is because of the ambiguity in the word *standard*. It can be used in reference to a model for imitation or as a basis for comparison, as in *setting a standard*, but it can also be used in the sense of "normal, average" as in *standard model*. Use of the term Standard English can imply that it is both the measure of excellence and the normal form of language to be used. Consequently, forms of language that are labeled "nonstandard" are assumed to be inferior and abnormal, and thus this label is simply a euphemism for "substandard."

There are many people who will insist that Standard English is the best possible form of English because it is (1) the most logical, (2) the most regular, and (3) the most beautiful. Each of these views is questionable. (1) Languages are neither logical nor illogical, though the users of the language can be. (2) Those dialects in which the third-person singular -s inflexion has been lost are more regular (in this respect) than Standard English. (3) There is no objective criterion by which the beauty of a language can be measured.

Beliefs in the superiority of Standard English in these terms would be harmless were it not that they can lead to prejudice against a large proportion of the population in both the United States and Great Britain. Standard English is a form of language based on that used by the educated minority in both countries. It is promulgated through the educational system and sustained largely through the editorial staff of the media and major publishing houses. Dennis Preston has clearly expressed the value of such a variety:

> Surely one of the functions of a standard is to convey serious information in a variety which implies that the speaker or writer is well-informed and which disallows a caricature of the message itself on the grounds that it is delivered in "incorrect" language.

It is as a "neutral" variety that Standard English is useful, to avoid the distracting impact of local variants. In this sense, Standard English is a nonregional dialect and that is why it is being considered [here]. However, it also has social class associations since it is identified with the speech of the middle and upper classes, and in that sense belongs in the next [section]. I once suggested that a better term would be *Common English*, and then deviations would be examples of *Uncommon English*, which they often are in the case of local dialect expressions, though none the worse for that.

There is another reason for considering Standard English [now]. It had its origin in a regional dialect. There were major dialect differences in Old English, which continued into Middle English. In the fourteenth century the administrative center of England moved to London, taking with it an East Midland form of speech that became the basis of what is known as Chancery English, the form in which official documents were written. This written form laid the foundation for the administrative language of the court and ultimately led to what we now call Standard English. Even today it is largely the written form that determines what is accepted as standard.

John Earl Joseph points out that the common view puts a high value on the notion of a standard language:

> The myth of a Golden Age that is so deeply embedded in Western culture includes as one of its facets that in the harmonious time all people shared a common tongue, and that the subsequent diversity of language and dialects accords with a diminution of all positive virtues from their

primeval absoluteness. In so far as standardization represents a cultural effort to restore language to its pristine state, its goal will be to overcome dialectal diversity by providing the ideal medium for communication among all members of the unit of loyalty.

The importance of standard English in the educational system has been a controversial subject. James Sledd expresses one view forcefully: "Upward mobility is impossible for underdogs who have not learned middle-dog barking." The importance of attitudes to language will be examined [next].

SOCIAL CLASS

Over the past thirty years it has been shown quite clearly that in socially stratified societies there are systematic differences in the way people from different backgrounds speak. This is not a new phenomenon but goes back at least as far as Chaucer's time. The invention of the portable tape recorder, however, has made it possible to investigate social differences in language more closely and to show exactly which features vary and under what circumstances. Briefly, the most common method has been to record samples of speech from people of different social backgrounds in a single community and to search the tapes for features of language that vary. Such features are labeled *linguistic variables*. For example, in New York City it is common to hear [t] instead of [θ] in words such as *think* and *three*. This usage is not equally frequent among people from all social backgrounds but is more common among those lower down the social scale. The extent to which this is true can be shown by taking the contexts in which a choice is possible between [t] and [θ] and counting the number of times [t] occurs. By converting this score to an average, it is possible to produce an index for this variable for each individual whose speech has been recorded. The indexes for individuals at the same socioeconomic level can then be combined and averaged to produce a score for that section of the community. The results for the (th) variable can be seen in Figure 25.1.

It can be seen from Figure 25.1 that the line slopes downward from the lowest socioeconomic level to the highest. In other words, as you go up the social ladder you are less likely to find people using [t] for [θ]. There is thus a correlation between socioeconomic level and the use of the (th) variable. Other correlations may appear. For example, in Glasgow the use of a glottal stop for [t], particularly before a vowel or a pause, is generally condemned by teachers and others in positions of authority. However, most Glaswegians use glottal stops to some extent as Table 25.1 shows. The roman numerals refer to three social class groupings based on occupation. I is the professional and managerial level; II the lower white-collar occupations; and III the manual workers. It can be seen that the use of glottal stops increases from Group I to Group III. It can also be seen that

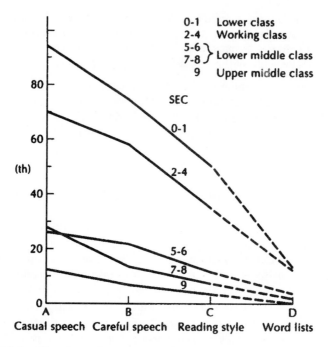

FIGURE 25.1   Class Stratification of /th/. (From Labov, 1966. By permission of the Center for Applied Linguistics.)

in each group women use fewer glottal stops than men. This is most obvious in Group II . . . . There is also an interesting difference depending upon the age of the speaker as shown in Table 25.2. At ten years old the children I interviewed in Glasgow speak more like each other regardless of family background than the fifteen-year-olds or the adults. In other words, social

TABLE 25.1   Percentage of Glottal Stops

	I	II	III
All adults	10.3	27.1	84.0
Men	11.3	41.6	90.7
Women	9.3	12.5	77.2

TABLE 25.2   Percentage of Glottal Stops

	I	II	III
Adults	10.3	27.1	84.0
15-year-olds	14.9	69.2	87.4
10-year-olds	57.5	84.3	83.9

differences in language increase with age rather than decrease. If this is true elsewhere, then it would mean that education, far from having a leveling effect actually has a stratifying effect.

There is no evidence that normal human beings are significantly different at birth in their potential for developing language. The language children learn does not depend upon any characteristics of their genetic parents but on the language they hear around them at the time they are learning to speak. Infants adopted soon after birth into families speaking a totally different language from that of their natural parents will learn the language of their adoptive parents. The language, education, race, and social position of the natural parents are totally irrelevant. It is therefore rather surprising that there is such a close relationship between family background and success on language tests in school.

A large number of studies in different countries have shown that family background is a very important factor in predicting success at school. Children from lower social-class groups on average do worse at school than those from higher social-class groups and part of the reason appears to be language. In the United States most high school students applying for admission to colleges and universities take a standardized achievement test (SAT) administered by the College Entrance Board. Every year statistics are compiled showing the average SAT scores achieved by students according to family income. Figure 25.2 shows that there is an almost perfect match between the rise in parental income and the rise in average scores. These figures are based on nearly a million responses and

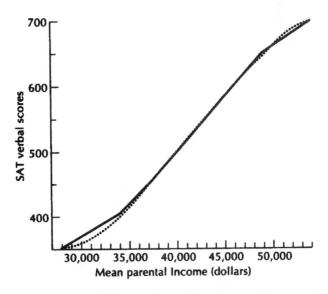

FIGURE 25.2 Average SAT Scores Versus Mean Parental Income (Calculated from SDQ Questions 27, 41–43 [1983–84]).

the correlation has remained constant over a number of years, so it is not a matter of chance.

A large-scale survey of seven-year-olds in Britain found that children in the lowest social-class group were twenty months behind those in the highest social-class group in reading skills. Moreover, the chances of an unskilled manual worker's child being a poor reader were six times greater than those of a professional worker's child, and the chances that the manual worker's child would be a nonreader were fifteen times greater.

It should be stressed that there is no evidence to show that this lack of success among children from certain kinds of backgrounds has anything to do with natural ability. On the contrary, there is considerable evidence to show that many of those children who fail at school are as capable as many of those that succeed. One study in the United States failed to find any differences in intelligence among newly born children that could be related to social class differences among the parents. It is also important to emphasize that a poor score on a language test need not indicate that a child is nonverbal. All normal children develop normal skills under normal conditions but the kinds of topics they talk about and the ways in which they will talk about them depend upon the environment in which they are growing up. A test that classifies as nonverbal a child who can be heard communicating effectively through language with other children outside of the classroom has simply failed to tap that child's linguistic competence.

Some Italian adolescents who had been considered failures in the state school system were taken into an "alternative" school. As a group project, they wrote a book in which they commented on the shortcomings of the educational system in their country. It is a book that is full of perceptive and insightful comments. One of their remarks refers to the importance of language: "Languages are created by the poor, who go on renewing them for ever. The rich crystalize them in order to put on the spot anybody who speaks in a different way. Or in order to make him fail exams" (*Letter to a Teacher*, by the School of Barbiana). Language tests may prove to be discriminatory for a variety of reasons having to do with linguistic, cultural, and social differences.

However, the influence of language differences on success in the school is not limited to tests. Teachers' expectations may affect a child's academic progress and such expectations are often based on the child's use of language. Children who speak up, articulate clearly, speak fluently, use the same language forms as the teacher, both answer and ask questions, and appear to understand what is said to them are generally judged to be brighter and more likely to succeed, and most teachers would be able to point to many examples where their judgment had been confirmed by the child's subsequent success. However, the teacher's judgment, expectations, and consequent behavior may have been an important ingredient in that success. This is fortunate for the child rewarded in this way but unfortunate for those of the child's peers who have been judged less favorably, for whom the expectations have been lower and for whom the teacher's attitude may have produced less positive results.

Unfortunately, there are cultural and social differences in the use of language that may mislead the teacher in judging the child's potential. In some cultures, children are not encouraged to question adults or volunteer remarks in their presence. A child from such a background might easily appear sullen, uncooperative, or dull to a teacher who has different expectations about "normal" speech behavior from a child of that age. Conversely, in other cultures children may be encouraged to show off in front of adults and they may seem to be impudent and undisciplined to a teacher who does not expect this.

Differences in "good manners" and what is considered appropriate behavior should not and probably would not affect success in school were it not for the important fact that so much of language development is cumulative. The more you know, the easier it is to increase that knowledge. The better you read, the easier it will be to read more widely and more quickly. Learning one thing is often the essential springboard to learning something else. Thus the child's early experiences in school may be of critical importance for future linguistic and intellectual development. It is tragic if differences between the child's form of speech and the teacher's either create serious problems of communication between them or lead the teacher to underestimate the child's potential.

Since the teacher's expectations can affect children's progress in academic subjects, the dangers inherent in making superficial judgments are obvious. Unfortunately, it is too easy to find evidence of negative attitudes toward certain forms of speech. One investigator in the United States asked a group of trainee teachers to evaluate the speech of some Anglo-American, African-American, and Mexican-American children. They saw the children on videotape and heard them on an accompanying audiotape. What the trainee teachers did not know was that excerpts from the same speech sample were played with the videotapes of the three different groups of children. Not altogether surprisingly (but very revealingly) the trainee teachers rated the speech of the African-American and Mexican-American children as less "standard" than that of the Anglo-American children, although in fact the actual quality of speech was the same for all three groups of children. Thus what the trainee teachers were reacting to was not what they heard but what they expected to hear from children from a particular kind of background. Although the trick played on the trainee teachers was rather unfair, the experiment reveals the existence of preconceived notions of speech among people who were hoping to become teachers. It is not only children whose speech is the subject of prejudice.

The ability to distinguish tiny variations in speech allows people to make superficial judgments about someone from the way he or she speaks. Just as people are often favorably or unfavorably judged on the basis of the length of their hair, the neatness of their clothes, or the state of their shoes, similarly they may be judged on the basis of their way of speaking. It has been shown in experiments that people are willing to judge their fellow citizens on the evidence of quite short samples of recorded speech. Listeners have been able to make consistent judgments about a speaker's social status, suitability for various jobs, education, race, personality, physical toughness, and the possibility of becoming a friend of the listener's. Such judgments are often inaccurate, reflecting the prejudices and stereotypes that exist in the community. The judgments are also likely to vary with the age, sex, education, race, and social background of the listener.

For example, a study in Canada showed that listeners judged speakers to be different in personality depending upon whether they were speaking English or French; the speakers were judged to be more intelligent and dependable when they were speaking English than when they were speaking French. (The listeners did not know that they were listening to the same people speaking in the two languages.) The listeners also judged the English speakers to be taller and better looking than the French speakers, thus revealing stereotypes associated with the two types of speaker in Canada. The judgments varied somewhat depending upon whether the listener was a member of the English-speaking community or of the French-speaking community, but the overall pattern of the responses was similar. In this study the speakers used two distinct languages, French and English, but similar results have been obtained when different dialects (regional and/or social) of the same language have been used.

The features of language upon which social judgments are based are often relatively small differences in pronunciation or grammar. For example, dialects of English differ according to whether the /r/ is pronounced at the end of words such as *car* and *four* or before another consonant as in *card* or *fourth*. In some communities (for example, in most of southern and midland England and in the southern United States), it is considered correct to omit the /r/ in such words. In other communities (the rest of the United States and in Scotland) it is considered correct to pronounce the /r/ in these words. Judgments about what is correct are based upon the speech of those members of the community whose way of speaking has a particular kind of prestige so that it is generally taken as the norm for educated middle-class speakers. However, there is nothing inherently better about either kind of pronunciation, as is obvious from the fact that the prestige forms are exactly reversed in New York and London, two cities with large numbers of educated, middle-class speakers. Nor is it more correct to pronounce the /r/ because it is the older form or because it is there in the spelling. In few communities is the sound corresponding to the *gh* in words such as *night* and *thought* pronounced, although it was always pronounced some seven hundred years ago and it still is in some Scottish dialects.

There is also no reason to believe that one variety of language is inherently more logical than another. In many dialects of English it is normal to use more than one indicator of negation in an utterance such as *I never touched none of them* where speakers of another dialect might say *I didn't touch any of them.* There is nothing illogical about the first form. Such multiple marking of negation was normal in English until about Shakespeare's time, though its use at the present time is restricted to certain dialects. Another example of the arbitrariness of value judgments in language can be seen in the difference between French and English as regards the marking of negation. In English multiple marking of negation, as in *I ain't done nothing,* is stigmatized. In French it is the reduction of negative marking to a single form that is stigmatized. In "correct" (that is, socially approved) French the simple negative consists of two parts, *ne* and *pas,* as in *Je ne sais pas* ("I don't know"). Many French people now use simply *pas* alone for the negative in everyday conversation, much to the disgust of purists. Nor is it illogical to say *Me and John did it* instead of *John and I did it* or to say *They big* instead of *They're big.* What is considered grammatical in the standard language is the result of a process whereby certain forms used by the dominant elite have been identified as correct in the educational system and in the media, while different forms used by other groups are labeled incorrect (ungrammatical). This is not because there is anything inherently better about either kind of form. Nor does it follow from this that use of the nonstandard forms is careless or random. Dialects of a language differ from one another in a number of ways for historical and social reasons, but all dialects are highly organized, abstract systems with their own complex rules. The reasons for valuing one dialect more highly than another are social, not linguistic, but there is no doubt that many people feel very strongly about such matters.

The importance of attitudes toward language is considerable. In many situations it is important to make a good impression when first meeting a stranger, and the way one speaks may contribute significantly to the impression created. In an interview for a job this may even be of crucial importance. As was pointed out [earlier], the way children speak may affect the teacher's view of their intelligence and ability. It is particularly unfortunate if children are made to feel that their way of speaking is inferior in any way, and this can happen when the child's form of speech differs considerably from that of the teacher. The attitude of teachers toward language in the classroom is particularly important. This has been exceptionally well expressed by John Macnamara: "The teacher believes that language is to be respected and caressed for its own sake, that one needs to do penance and prepare oneself to capture the fine points of pronunciation and grammar as Sir Galahad prepared himself to seek the Holy Grail." Macnamara believes that many children are baffled by this attitude since they see language as merely a modest tool for communicating. He argues that the best way to encourage them to make use of their language learning ability is by getting the children vitally engaged in communicating.

It would be wrong to say that small differences in pronunciation and grammar are unimportant since people pay attention to such things and often attach great significance to them, but in themselves they are trivial. A rather simple metaphor may help to emphasize this point. Drinking vessels come in many shapes and sizes and are made of diverse materials and, other things being equal, we often value one more than the other. If we are thirsty, however, it is not the vessel itself but what it contains that is important.

The grammatical structure of language is like the shape of the drinking vessel and pronunciation is like the material it is made out of, but the meaning is what the cup contains. When we are thirsty we are more likely to be interested in the drink itself than in the beauty of the cup.

There are two further parallels. The first is the appropriateness for a particular situation, which is often a matter of convention. Wedgwood fine bone-china cups are often highly valued, but it is not usually considered correct to serve brandy or champagne in them. Second, what is appropriate in one situation may not be so in another. When one goes mountaineering, a plastic or metal cup may be more serviceable than a thin-stemmed wineglass. Similarly with language there is no reason to believe that any single form will be suitable for all situations, which is why so many different forms can exist within a speech community. Such diversity is to be welcomed and enjoyed rather than condemned or eradicated.

FOR DISCUSSION AND REVIEW

1. What is an isogloss, and how do groups of isoglosses indicate a dialect boundary? Are you aware of dialect boundaries in your area? Explain.

2. When Macaulay says that "languages and dialects have both a unifying function and a separatist function," what does he mean? Examining his examples of British and American English, do you see them as separate languages, varieties of the same language, or both? Give some examples from your own experience.

3. How do you respond to differences in pronunciation, and to what extent does the type of speaker—stranger, acquaintance, child, and so on—alter that response? What words did you pronounce differently when you were a child? Do any of your pronunciations now differ from those of your peers? Explain.

4. In television or movies, how is social difference indicated by dialect difference? Provide examples from familiar films or shows.

5. Macaulay suggests that syntactic differences in pronunciation have received less attention than other types of difference. Why does that seem to be the case? How do you feel about or respond to differences in "grammar" among your friends, relatives, or those from other regions of the country?

6. What three reasons does Macauley give to back up his belief that Standard English is not superior to other forms?

7. How has modern technology expanded the possibilities for investigating social differences in language? What are linguistic variables, and how are they obtained?

8. Macaulay provides data from a New York City study of the occurrence of either [t] or [θ] (such as the difference in pronouncing *think* as either "tink" or "think") and a Glasgow study of the occurrence of either a glottal stop or a [t]. In these studies, how does social class relate to the occurrence of the nonstandard pronunciation? What pronunciations are you aware of that show a relationship to social class?

9. Macaulay gives examples from several countries that appear to relate social class to educational achievement. How do language differences seem to influence student success? To influence teachers' expectations? How do you feel about standardized testing? What is your experience with such testing?

10. How are prejudice and stereotypes intertwined with language use in aspects of our lives other than in education? Give some examples from your own experience.

26

Standards and Vernaculars

Walt Wolfram and Natalie Schilling-Estes

Walt Wolfram is William C. Friday Distinguished Professor at North Carolina State University. He has spent more than thirty years research-ing vernacular dialects of American English, including African American, Appalachian, Vietnamese, and the Outer Banks. A highly respected expert on language variation in North America, he was one of the first to bring such knowledge and the concept of standard language into the classroom. Co-author, Natalie Schilling-Estes, associate professor of lin-guistics at Georgetown University, writes extensively on language vari-ation in American English, especially that based on region, ethnicity, gender, and style.

Wolfram and Schilling-Estes assert in American English: Dialects and Variations *(2006) that language differences, which they call "facts of life," are "unavoidable in a society composed of a variety of social groups." In this selection from the second edition of the book, Wolfram and Schilling-Estes discuss the difficulties of defining formal and informal standard English as well as vernacular varieties. They also note that we usually associate standard dialects with respected or socially favored groups but tend to link vernaculars with socially dis-favored groups.*

STANDARDS AND VERNACULARS

The notion of a widespread, normative variety, or "standard dialect" is an important one, but it is not always easy to define in a precise way, espe-cially for English. In some countries, such as France and Spain, language academies have been established and these institutions are responsible for determining what forms are considered acceptable for the normative "standard." They determine, for example, what new words are allowed to be included in official dictionaries and what grammatical forms and pro-nunciations are included as standard. In the United States we do not have such an institution, and various attempts to establish this type of agency have failed (Heath 1976). Labels such as standard English and popular terms such as "correct English" or "proper English" are commonly used but not without some ambiguity. At best, we can discuss how the notion of stan-dard English is used and then offer a reasonable definition of the term based on how it seems to operate in our society. . . .

Before we get too far into this discussion, we should note that whether or not there are specific institutions set up to guide the establishment of a standard variety, language standardization of some type seems inevitable. Ultimately, we can attribute this to underlying principles of human behavior in which certain ways of behaving (dressing, speaking, treating elders, and so forth) are established as normative for the society.

As a starting point, it is helpful to distinguish between the operation of standard English on a formal and informal level. In formal standardization, language norms are prescribed by recognized sources of authority, such as grammar and usage books, dictionaries, and institutions like language academies. In the United States, we don't have a language academy, but we have many grammar and usage books that people turn to for the determination of standard forms. The key words in this definition are "prescribed" and "authority" so that the responsibility for determining standard forms is largely out of the hands of most speakers of the language. Whenever there is a question as to whether or not a form is considered standard English, we can turn to authoritarian guides to usage. If, for example, we have a question as to where to use *will* and *shall*, we simply look it up in our usage guide, which tells us that *shall* is used for first person questions (*Shall I go?*) and *will* is used in other contexts (*He will go*). At that point, the question of a particular usage is often settled.

FORMAL STANDARD ENGLISH, or PRESCRIPTIVE STANDARD ENGLISH, tends to be based on the written language of established writers and is typically codified in English grammar texts. It is perpetuated to a large extent in formal institutions, such as schools, by those responsible for English language education. It also is very conservative and often resistant to changes taking place within the language. For some features, the prescribed usage will border on obsolescence. For example, the subjunctive use of *be* in sentences such as *If this be treason, I am a traitor* is a structure that is largely obsolete, yet this use can still be found in some prescriptive grammar books. Similarly, the maintenance of the singular form of *data* as *datum*, or even the *shall/will* distinction, has largely disappeared from spoken language, but it is still prescribed in many usage guides and maintained in written language. Without an official agency responsible for the maintenance of a uniform formal standard English in the United States, there will be some disagreement among prescriptive grammarians, but in most cases, there is fairly strong agreement. As set forth, formal standard English is most likely to be exemplified in impersonal written language and the most formal kinds of spoken language occasions, especially where spoken language has been written first.

If we took a sample of everyday conversational speech, we would find that there are virtually no speakers who consistently speak formal standard English as prescribed in the grammar books. In fact, it is not unusual for the same person who prescribes a formal standard English form to violate standard usage in ordinary conversation. For example, one of the prescribed formal standard English rules prohibits the use of a pronoun following a subject noun, as in *My mother, she took me to the movies,* and many teachers will correct children who use this form. Yet we have documented these same teachers using sentences such as *The students who returned late from recess yesterday and today,* **they** *will have to remain after school* within a few minutes of correcting children for using similar types of sentences. The point of these illustrations is not to expose as hypocrites those who assume responsibility for perpetuating standard English norms, but to show that the prescribed formal variety is, in reality, not always maintained consistently in natural spoken language. Does this mean that standard English does not exist in our society, and that we should stop talking about this variety as if it were a real entity? On the contrary, there is plenty of evidence that people in our society make judgments about other people's speech, including an evaluation of standardness, based on everyday, natural speech. So there appears to be another, more informal level, of standardness that operates in American society.

INFORMAL STANDARD ENGLISH, without recourse to prescriptive authority, is much more difficult to define than formal standard English, and a realistic definition will have to take into account the actual kinds of assessments that members of American society make as they judge other speakers' standardness. As a starting point, we must acknowledge that the informal notion of standard English exists on a continuum, with speakers ranging along the continuum between the standard and nonstandard poles. Informal standard English is a continuous rather than categorical notion and speakers may be judged as more or less standard. For example, speakers may be placed at different points on a standard–nonstandard continuum as in figure 26.1 with Speaker **A** using few, if any, nonstandard forms, and Speaker **E** using many.

Ratings of standardness not only exist on a continuum; they can be fairly subjective as well. Based on different experiences as well as different regional and social dialect backgrounds, one listener may rate a particular speaker as standard while another listener rates the same speaker as nonstandard. For example, a Northern-born middle-class African American might rate a Southern white as nonstandard, while a native of the region might rate the same speaker as a standard speaker. By the same token, a person from the Midwest might rate a native of New York City as nonstandard while another New Yorker might rate the same speaker as standard. Further, preconceptions and prejudices about how different groups of people are expected to speak come into play as well. For example, researchers (e.g. Williams 1973) have shown that people may judge the *same voice* as "standard" or "nonstandard" depending on

FIGURE 26.1   **A Continuum of Standardness.**

which video image it is paired with (e.g. a European American vs. African American face).

Though there is certainly a subjective dimension to the notion of standardness, there is, at the same time, a consensus in rating speakers at the more extreme ranges of the continuum. Thus, virtually all listeners will rate Speaker **A** in figure 26.1 as a standard English speaker and Speaker **E** as a nonstandard English speaker. On the other hand, there might be considerable difference in the ratings which Speakers **B** and **C** receive in terms of a simple classification into standard or nonstandard categories. Furthermore, we have found that the classification of speakers at the extreme poles of the continuum (such as Speakers **A** and **E**) tends to be consistent regardless of the socioeconomic class of the person making the judgment.

Classifications of standardness will also be somewhat flexible with respect to the specific features of the regional variety being judged. Thus, the *r*-less pronunciations which characterize Eastern New England or Southeastern American pronunciation (as in *cah* for *car* or *beah* for *bear*) may be judged as standard English, as will the *r*-ful pronunciations that characterize certain other dialects. And people may be judged as standard English speakers whether they *go to the beach, go to the shore,* or *go to the ocean* for a summer vacation. On this informal level, standard English is a pluralistic notion, at least with respect to pronunciation and vocabulary differences. That is, there are regional standards recognized within the broad and informal notion of standard American English. For example, there are regional standards for the South, for the Midwest, and for New England, though they may differ in terms of the particular items included in each standard.

What is it about a speaker's dialect that is critical in determining whether the speaker will be judged as standard or nonstandard? There is no simple answer to this question, and people tend to give overall impressions, such as "quality of voice," "tone of expression," or "correct grammar," when they are asked to explain their judgments of standardness and nonstandardness. Despite the vagueness of such responses, there do seem to be a few relatively specific criteria that people use in judging a person's speech as standard. For one, standard American English seems to be determined more by what it is *not* than by what it is. To a large extent, American English speech samples rated as standard English by a cross-section of listeners exhibit a range of regional variation in pronunciation and vocabulary items, but they do *not* contain grammatical structures that are socially stigmatized. If native speakers from Michigan, New England, and Arkansas avoid the use of socially stigmatize'd grammatical structures such as "double negatives" (e.g. *They didn't do nothing*), different verb agreement patterns (e.g. *They's okay*), and different irregular verb forms (e.g. *She done it*), there is a good chance they will be considered standard English speakers even though they may have distinct regional pronunciations. In this kind of assessment, informal standard

English is defined in more of a negative than a positive way. In other words, if a person's speech is free of socially disfavored structures, then it is considered standard.

The definition of informal standard English as a variety free of stigmatized features tends to be supported by an additional observation about Americans' attitudes toward dialects. For the most part, Americans do not assign strong positive, or prestige, value to any particular dialect of American English. The basic contrast in the US exists between negatively valued dialects and those without negative value, not between those with prestige value and those without. Curiously, Americans still assign positive value to British dialects, which are not even viable options for wide-scale use in the United States and Canada. It is difficult to say exactly why Americans look upon British English so favorably, but one possibility is a lingering colonial effect, thus showing the enduring influence of traditional language attitudes a couple of centuries after the US gained its independence from British rule. Americans, in commenting on different dialects of American English, are much more likely to make comments about nonstandardness ("That person doesn't talk correct English") than they are to comment on standardness (e.g. "That person really speaks correct English"). The notion of standard English is certainly operative in American society on an informal level, but it differs considerably from the formal standard English norm that is often taught as *the* standard. For the purposes of our discussion . . . , we will refer to this more informal definition of the standard language rather than the formal one, since it is the informal version that has a more direct bearing on our everyday lives.

EXERCISE 1

There are a couple of levels of standards that seem to be noticeable to people when they listen to speech. We don't usually comment on informal standard English, but we may comment on a person's speech if it is nonstandard. It is, however, possible to call attention to speech because it sounds too formal or "proper." Forms that are too standard for everyday conversation are sometimes referred to as SUPERSTANDARD ENGLISH. In the following sets of sentences, identify which sentences characterize (1) nonstandard English, (2) informal standard English, and (3) superstandard English. What forms in the sentences are responsible for your assessment? Are there any sentences you're not sure about? Why?

1. a. He's not as smart as I.
   b. He's not so smart as I.
   c. He ain't as smart as me.
   d. He not as smart as me.

2. a. He's not to do that.
   b. He not supposed to do that.
   c. He don't supposed to do that.
   d. He's not supposed to do that.
3. a. I'm right, ain't I?
   b. I'm right, aren't I?
   c. I'm right, am I not?
   d. I'm right, isn't I?
4. a. If I was going to do that, I would start right now.
   b. If I were going to do that, I would start right now.
   c. Were I to do that, I would start right now.
   d. I would start right now, if I was going to do that.
5. a. A person should not change her speech.
   b. One should not change one's speech.
   c. A person should not change their speech.
   d. A person should not change his or her speech.

Why do people sometimes comment about other people's speech because it sounds too proper?

VERNACULAR DIALECTS

At the other end of the continuum of standardness is nonstandardness. Varieties that seem to be typified by the use of nonstandard forms are often referred to as VERNACULAR DIALECTS. The term vernacular is used here simply to refer to varieties of a language that are not classified as standard dialects. It is used in much the same way that the term *vernacular language* is used to refer to local or native languages of common communication which contrast with the official language of a multilingual country. Other researchers may refer to these vernacular varieties as NONSTANDARD DIALECTS or nonmainstream dialects, but we have chosen to use the term *vernacular* because it seems more neutral than these alternatives.

As with standard dialects of English, there are a number of different social and regional factors that go into the labeling of a vernacular, and any attempt to define a vernacular dialect on a single dimension is problematic. Ultimately, each dialect is delimited according to a complex array of factors, including matters related to social class, region, ethnicity, situation, and so forth. Furthermore, vernacularity, like standardness, exists on a continuum so that particular speakers may exhibit speech which is more or less vernacular. Thus, Speaker **D** in figure 26.1 may or may not be classified as a vernacular dialect speaker, but we can expect a consensus of people (from the same and different dialects) to recognize Speaker **E** as a representative of some vernacular variety. Nonetheless, it is possible for both vernacular and non-vernacular speakers of English to identify paradigmatic speakers of vernacular varieties in a way that is analogous to the way that we can identify representatives of standard dialects.

Unlike standard dialects, which are largely defined by the *absence* of socially disfavored structures of English, vernacular varieties seem to be characterized by the *presence* of socially conspicuous structures—at least to speakers of informal standard English who do not typically use them. In other words, vernacular varieties are the converse of standard dialects in that an assortment of marked nonstandard English structures sets them apart as being vernacular. Although each vernacular dialect seems to have its own core of vernacular structures, we have to be careful saying that all speakers of a given variety will exhibit these core features. Not all speakers of a given dialect necessarily use the entire set of structures associated with their dialect, and there may be differing patterns of usage among speakers of the variety. In fact, attempts to isolate *the* common core of structures for a particular vernacular often lead to heavily qualified, imprecise descriptions. Such qualification is typified in the attempt of Walt Wolfram and Donna Christian to delimit "Appalachian English."

> There may be some question as to whether it is justifiable to differentiate an entity such as AE [Appalachian English] from other (equally difficult to define precisely) varieties of American English, particularly some of those spoken in the South. Quite obviously, there are many features we have described which are not peculiar to speakers within the Appalachian range. On the other hand, there also appears to be a small set of features which may not be found in other areas. Even if this is not the case, we may justify our distinction of AE on the basis of the combination of features.... Fully cognizant of the pitfalls found in any attempt to attach terminological labels to the varieties of English, we shall proceed to use the designation AE as a convenient, if loosely-defined notion. (Wolfram and Christian 1976: 29–30)

Language scholars sometimes have difficulty defining the set of features that uniquely distinguishes a given vernacular variety, but it is easy to demonstrate that both professionals and non-professionals identify and classify quite accurately speakers representing the vernacular pole on the continuum. Vernacular dialects are identifiable entities in American society, despite our inability to come up with precise sets of structures characterizing them....

We can summarize the features that set apart standard dialects and vernacular dialects as follows:

> FORMAL STANDARD: applied primarily to written language and the most formal spoken language situations; objective standards prescribed by language "authorities"; standards codified in usage books, dictionaries, and other written texts; conservative outlook on language forms.

INFORMAL STANDARD: applied to spoken language; determined by actual usage patterns of speakers; listener judgment essential in determining socially acceptable norms; multiple norms of acceptability, incorporating regional and social considerations; defined negatively by the avoidance of socially stigmatized linguistic structures.

VERNACULAR: applied to spoken language; determined by usage patterns of speakers; listener judgment essential in determining social unacceptability; usually defined by the presence of a set of socially stigmatized linguistic structures.

Since both formal and informal standard varieties are usually associated with socially favored, mainstream groups, they are socially respected in American society, but since vernacular varieties are associated with socially disfavored groups, they are not considered socially respectable. This association, of course, simply reflects underlying values about different social groups in our society and is hardly dependent on language differences alone.

Before concluding our discussion of definitions of "standard" and "vernacular," it is important to note that notions of standardness and prestige can operate quite differently in different societies. Although the US doesn't really have one single language variety that is accorded great social prestige, there are prestige varieties in some other countries and other societies, and these varieties may or may not be used as widespread norms or "standards." For example, Classical Arabic is not widely used in everyday communication in the Arabic-speaking world; instead, there exist a number of national and regional standards that are used in communicative interactions where a widespread norm is needed (e.g. in business situations). In such cases the standards may actually be somewhat devalued rather than socially favored (as in the US), since they do not correspond with the prestige variety. Hence, the widespread standards in use in the Arabic-speaking world tend to be considered "lesser" forms of the language than classical Arabic, despite their widespread usage. Even in Great Britain, where "proper" British English, or "Received Pronunciation" (RP), seems the logical choice as a standard variety for daily interaction, evidence indicates increasing usage of several widespread standards that are quite different from RP and which do not have the same prestige value (e.g. Britain 2001; Milroy and Gordon 2003: 88–115).

LABELING VERNACULAR DIALECTS

Although the choice of a label for a particular vernacular dialect such as African American English or Appalachian English may seem relatively unimportant, it can become a very important consideration when the broader social, political, and cultural considerations associated with naming are taken into account. For example, in the past half century, the vernacular dialect associated with African Americans has had the following labels, given here in approximate chronological sequence: *Negro Dialect, Substandard Negro English, Nonstandard Negro English, Black English, Afro-American English, Ebonics, Vernacular Black English, African American (Vernacular) English,* and *African American Language.* And believe it or not, this is not a complete list. On one level, one can correlate some of these name changes with changes in names for ethnic groups themselves that have taken place in American society. But there are also more subtle dimensions, such as the choice between African American Language versus African American English. In this instance, the term "language" is used because of the legitimacy ascribed to languages as opposed to dialects. Furthermore, there are often strong affective associations related to particular labels. For example, the label *Ebonics,* originally introduced in the early 1970s, gained great notoriety in the mid-1990s in connection with a highly publicized resolution by the Oakland Unified School District Board of Education. As a result of the controversy, the label evoked many negative comments and derogatory parodies. In contrast, the synonymous terms typically used by linguists, African American English or African American Language, do not typically evoke such parodies. Labels are always tricky because it can be difficult to delimit their referents in a precise way and because they may carry such strong affective connotations. Terms for vernacular dialects, like other aspects of behavior, do not exist in an ideological vacuum and often reflect underlying attitudes about sociolinguistic asymmetries and linguistic subordination as well as the social inequities underlying this subordination.

In this [selection], we use the term AFRICAN AMERICAN ENGLISH (often abbreviated AAE) to refer to that variety spoken by and considered to be a key part of the ethnic heritage and cultural identity of many people of African descent in the US. The term actually encompasses a number of sub-varieties, since there is variation in African American English based on region, social class, and style, among other factors. We choose this label chiefly because of its neutrality and its widespread usage in current linguistic scientific studies, while recognizing that other labels may be equally appropriate, or perhaps more so, for different purposes (e.g. for promoting African American cultural heritage or sociopolitical equality). Our choice of label should not be taken as any sort of statement regarding whether AAE should be considered a "language" or a "dialect," since the distinction between "language" and "dialect" cannot be made on purely linguistic grounds but is intricately tied to sociopolitical and sociocultural considerations. In addition, decisions as to whether a particular variety constitutes a language in its own right can change over time. For example, in recent decades in the former Yugoslavia, Serbo-Croatian, once regarded as a single language, has come to be regarded as at least three separate languages: Serbian, Bosnian, and Croatian, largely as a result of recent political rather than linguistic changes.

Parallel to the term "African American English," we use the term "African American" to refer to people of African descent in the US, most often those with historic or cultural ties to the slave trade. It is not easy to determine the precise population(s) covered by the label "African American." For example, it is unclear whether the term should be applied to recent immigrants from Africa and their families; it is also not clear whether it includes those from North Africa (e.g. Egypt) or only those from Sub-Saharan Africa. In addition, many African Americans self-identify as "Black" rather than, or in addition to, "African American." Further, the classification of particular people as "African American" may be different in different regions or among different social groups and may change over time; and people may even feel different degrees of "African-American-ness" in different situations—for example, when talking with family members about ethnically sensitive issues vs. participating in a classroom discussion about linguistics with people of various ethnicities.

Another label employed widely . . . is EUROPEAN AMERICAN, used to refer to speakers popularly labeled "White" in American society. The term "White" defies precise definition and indeed often seems to be a catch-all to refer to anyone who does not consider themselves, or is not considered by others, to have a marked "ethnic" identity. In reality, everyone is of *some* ethnicity. It's just that many people of European descent, especially of British or Northern European descent, have been dominant in American society for so long that they have come to be seen (or to uphold themselves) as the "default" or "normal" group (e.g. Hill 1998) against which everyone who is different must be compared (and, sadly, often judged lacking). The widespread belief that European Americans are not "ethnic" parallels in many ways the belief, in discussions of language and gender, that only women's gender matters and that men's linguistic and other behavior is "neutral" rather than influenced by gender in any way. . . . To the extent that we can apply any degree of precision to the term "European American," we intend it to refer to those people in US society of British or Continental European (especially Northern European) descent who would label themselves or be labeled by others as "White." When a group identifies itself with an ethnic label (e.g. Jewish American), [it is appropriate to] use that term when relevant to the discussion at hand (but see, e.g., Modan 2001 on the complex and shifting relation between "Jewishness" and "Whiteness"). Again, "European American" is no easier to define than "African American," and again the definition is relative in that who is considered "White" can change over time or vary according to a variety of factors such as region, class, and speech situation. . . . There is no single European American English any more than there is a single African American English. In fact, research indicates that European American varieties differ more widely from one another than do the different varieties of African American English.

... Despite the prominence of the Black–White distinction in American society historically and currently, America has always been a country of rich ethnic and social diversity, and it is important to recognize and gain greater understanding of the many other cultures and language varieties that have shaped American society and continue to shape it today.

BIBLIOGRAPHY

Britain, David (2001) Space and spatial diffusion. In J. K. Chambers, Peter Trudgill, and Natalie Schilling-Estes (eds.), *The Handbook of Language Variation and Change*, Oxford: Blackwell, 603–37.

Heath, Shirley Brice (1976) A national language academy? Debate in the new nation. *International Journal of the Sociology of Language* 11: 8–43.

Hill, Jane (1998) Language, race, and White public space. *American Anthropologist* 100 (3): 680–9.

Milroy, Lesley, and Matthew Gordon (2003) *Sociolinguistics: Method and Interpretation*. Oxford: Blackwell.

Modan, Gabriella (2001) White, whole wheat, rye: Jews and ethnic categorization in Washington, DC. *Journal of Linguistic Anthropology* (special issue titled *Discourses of Whiteness*, guest ed. by Mary Bucholtz and Sara Trechter) 11 (1): 116–30.

Williams, Frederick (1973) Some research notes on dialect attitudes. In Roger W. Shuy and Ralph W. Fasold (eds.), *Language Attitudes: Current Trends and Prospects*. Washington, DC: Georgetown University Press, 113–28.

Wolfram, Walt, and Donna Christian (1976) *Appalachian Speech*. Washington, DC: Center for Applied Linguistics.

FOR DISCUSSION AND REVIEW

1. Wolfram and Schilling-Estes describe myths and realities regarding dialect. Do you agree with their characterization? Why, or why not? Do you ever find that what you know or have been taught about dialect differs from what you believe?

2. What is "Formal Standard English" as defined by Wolfram and Schilling-Estes? How do circumstances affect the use of Formal Standard English?

3. What do the authors mean when they say English features are socially favored or disfavored? Can you give examples? Do people agree about what these are? Would this be the case with other languages?

4. Why is Informal Standard English so difficult to define? Give a few examples of how "ratings of standardness . . . can be fairly subjective."

5. The authors suggest that even though Informal Standard English includes a range of possibilities, it is recognizable for the lack of

"disfavored" features. Do you find this to be the case? When you notice variation in spoken English, do you notice some differences more than others? What about your own speech? Do you speak an informal variety of Standard English? How would you label it?

6. Do you think of Formal Standard English as more correct or grammatical than other varieties of English? When do you use it? Do grammars or usage manuals influence what you consider correct?

7. The authors suggest in their exercise that we notice when people sound too formal. Give some original examples of "superstandard" English or hypercorrectness. If you haven't done so yet, try the exercise in this selection. How do you assess these sentences?

8. Discuss how the labeling of a vernacular dialect can reflect underlying attitudes.

9. Are some varieties of English considered standard because the groups associated with them have more power or prestige? Wolfram and Schilling-Estes suggest elsewhere in their book that a dialect's value is "derived strictly from the social position of their communities of speakers." Do you think that is accurate? Is that a reality you find in your community?

27

Oakland School Board Resolution on Ebonics (Amended Version)

Oakland School Board

On December 18, 1996, the Oakland School Board passed its original Resolution on Ebonics, which was intended to help African American students in the school district develop fluency in Standard English. The school board, in consultation with linguists and scholars, argued that the African American Vernacular English (AAVE) was a distinct social dialect, exhibiting features of its African language ancestry. It further suggested that training teachers to recognize and use the linguistic differences between AAVE ("Ebonics") and Standard English would help students master the latter. Although the original resolution did not propose teaching Ebonics in the schools, the media presented the resolution as if it did. Public response was largely negative, with some people calling Ebonics "corrupt" and "street slang." This selection, the amended resolution, is the Oakland School Board's attempt to clarify its argument.

Resolution of the Board of Education Adopting the Report and Recommendations of the African American Task Force; A Policy Statement and Directing the Superintendent of Schools to Devise a Program to Improve the English Language Acquisition and Applications Skills of African-American Students (No. 9697-0063) WHEREAS, numerous validated scholarly studies demonstrate that African-American students as a part of their culture and history as African people possess and utilize a language described in various scholarly approaches as "Ebonics" (literally "Black sounds") or "Pan-African Communication Behaviors" or "African Language Systems;" and

WHEREAS, these studies have also demonstrated that African Language Systems have origins in West and Niger-Congo languages and are not merely dialects of English; and

WHEREAS, these studies demonstrate that such West and Niger-Congo African languages have been recognized and addressed in the educational community as worthy of study, understanding or application of their principles, laws and structures for the benefit of African-American students both in terms of positive appreciation of the language and these students' acquisition and mastery of English language skills; and

WHEREAS, such recognition by scholars has given rise over the past fifteen years to legislation passed by the State of California recognizing the unique language stature of descendants of slaves with such legislation being vetoed repeatedly by various California state governors; and

WHEREAS, judicial cases in states other than California have recognized the unique language stature of African-American pupils, and such recognition by courts has resulted in court-mandated educational programs which have substantially benefitted African-American children in the interest of vindicating their equal protection of the law rights under the Fourteenth Amendment to the United States Constitution; and

WHEREAS, the Federal Bilingual Education Act (20 U.S.C. 1402 et seq.) mandates that local educational agencies "build their capacities to establish, implement and sustain programs of instruction for children and youth of limited English proficiency;" and

WHEREAS, the interests of the Oakland Unified School District in providing equal opportunities for all of its students dictate limited English proficient educational programs recognizing the English language acquisition and improvement skills of African-American students are as fundamental as is application of bilingual or second language learner principles for others whose primary languages are other than English. Primary languages are the language patterns children bring to school; and

WHEREAS, the standardized tests and grade scores of African-American students in reading and language arts skills measuring their application of English skills are substantially below state and national norms and that such deficiencies will be remedied by application of a program featuring African Language Systems principles to move students from the language patterns they bring to school to English proficiency; and

WHEREAS, standardized tests and grade scores will be remedied by application of a program with teachers and instructional assistants who are certified in the methodology African Language Systems principles used to transition students from the language patterns they bring to school in English. The certified teachers of these students will be provided incentives including, but not limited to salary differentials;

NOW, THEREFORE, BE IT RESOLVED that the Board of Education officially recognized the existence, and the cultural and historic bases of West and Niger-Congo African Language Systems, and these are the language patterns that many African-American students bring to school; and

BE IT FURTHER RESOLVED that the Board of Education hereby adopts the report, recommendations and attached Policy Statement of the District's African-American Task Force on language stature of African-American speech; and

BE IT FURTHER RESOLVED that the Superintendent in conjunction with her staff shall immediately devise and implement the best possible academic program for the combined purposes of facilitating the acquisition and mastery of English language skills, while respecting and embracing legitimacy and richness of the language patterns whether they are known as "Ebonics," "African Language Systems," "Pan-African Communication Behaviors" or other description; and

BE IT FURTHER RESOLVED that the Board of Education hereby commits to earmark District general and special funding as is reasonably necessary and appropriate to enable the Superintendent and her staff to accomplish the foregoing; and

BE IT FURTHER RESOLVED that the Superintendent and her staff shall utilize the input of the entire Oakland educational community as well as state and federal scholarly and educational input in devising such a program; and

BE IT FURTHER RESOLVED that periodic reports on the progress of the creation and implementation of such an educational program shall be made to the Board of Education at least once per month commencing at the Board meeting of December 18, 1996.

Passed by the following vote:

AYES: Hodge, Cook, Rice, Harrison, Gallo, Vice President Spencer, President Quan
    NOES: None
    ABSTAINING: None
    ABSENT: None

(Received from Oakland Unified School District, Office of the Board of Education, January 22, 1998)

≡

FOR DISCUSSION AND REVIEW

1. What are the primary reasons the Oakland School Board formally passed a resolution about a specific variety of English? Are you aware of similar situations in your own schools or elsewhere? Explain.

2. What specific statements does the resolution make about the history and linguistic features of Ebonics? Why would the school board see these as important?

3. Why did the resolution focus especially on linguistic training for teachers? How might understanding dialect variation help in teaching Standard English in a diverse classroom?

4. The resolution proposed using the features of Ebonics as part of the strategy for developing proficiency in Standard English. This kind of approach uses contrastive analysis, which is typical for teaching English as a second, foreign, or new language. Does your state have any such programs? What approaches were used in teaching Standard English at your schools?

5. The stated motivation for addressing the language needs of African American students in the Oakland School District was to help Ebonics speakers develop their Standard English skills by "using the vernacular to teach the standard," as John Rickford put it in a speech of the same name given at the California State University Long Beach Conference on Ebonics on March 29, 1997. Do you think this would be effective for students of other vernaculars? How would this differ from the kind of grammar or language arts training you had in school?

6. Immediately after passage of the original Oakland School Board Resolution on Ebonics, negative responses occurred in the mainstream media from both sides of the political spectrum. Why might that have happened?

28

Suite for Ebony and Phonics

John Rickford

John Rickford, Martin Luther King Jr. Centennial Professor and director of the Program in African and Afro-American Studies at Stanford, is one of the foremost experts in the history and development of African American English. His research on language variation and its links to ethnicity and social class has influenced current theories about the formation and development of African American Vernacular English (AAVE). Rickford often interweaves his scholarship with community concerns. This essay, originally published in the December 1997 issue of Discover *magazine, is one of several of his applying a linguistic under-standing of AAVE to issues in American education. Rickford first reviews the public outrage over Ebonics following passage of the Oakland School Board Resolution. He then uses linguistic analysis to refute the accusation that Ebonics is slang by explaining what dialects are, how they differ from slang, and how Ebonics exhibits all the system-atic, rule-governed characteristics of a dialect.*

To James Baldwin, writing in 1979, it was "this passion, this skill, . . . this incredible music." Toni Morrison, two years later, was impressed by its "five present tenses," and felt that "The worst of all possible things that could happen would be to lose that language." What these African American novelists were talking about was Ebonics, the vernacular or informal speech of many African Americans, which rocketed to public attention after the Oakland School Board approved a resolution in December 1996 recognizing it as the primary language of African American students.

The reaction of most people across the country—in the media, at holiday gatherings, and on electronic bulletin boards—was overwhelm-ingly negative. In the flash-flood of email on America Online, Ebonics was variously described as "lazy English," "bastardized English," "poor grammar," and "fractured slang." Oakland's decision to recognize Ebonics and use it to facilitate mastery of Standard English [SE] also elicited superlatives of negativity: "ridiculous, ludicrous," "VERY, VERY STUPID," "a terrible mistake." Linguists—the scientists who carefully study the sounds, words, and grammars of languages and dialects—were less rhapsodic about Ebonics than the novelists, but much more positive than most of the media and the general public. At their January 1997 annual meeting, members of the Linguistic Society of America [LSA] unanimously approved a resolution describing Ebonics as "systematic and rule-governed like all natural speech varieties," and referring to the Oakland resolution as "linguistically and pedagogically sound." In order to understand how linguists could have had such a different take on the Ebonics issue, we need to understand how linguists study language and what their studies of Ebonics over the past thirty years have led them to agree on (and what it has not).

Although linguists approach the study of language from different perspectives—some are keener on language change, for instance, while others are more interested in language as a formal system, in what language tells us about human cognition, or how language reflects social divisions—we agree on a number of general principles. One of these is that linguistics is descriptive rather than prescriptive, our goal being to describe how language works rather than to prescribe how people should or shouldn't speak. A second principle is that all languages have dialects— regional or social varieties which develop when people are separated by geographical or social barriers and their languages change along different lines, as they develop their own pronunciations, for instance, or their own ways of referring to things. When linguists speak of "dialects" they don't do so in the pejorative way that many non-linguists do. A dialect is just a variety of a language; everyone speaks at least one. A third principle, vital for understanding linguists' reactions to the Ebonics controversy, is that all languages and dialects are systematic and rule- governed. To some extent, this is a theoretical assumption—for if indi- viduals made up their own sounds and words and did NOT follow a common set of rules for putting them together to express meaning, they would be unable to communicate with each other, and children would have a hard time acquiring the "language" of their community. But it is also an empirical finding. Every human language and dialect which we have studied to date—and we have studied thousands—has been found to be fundamentally regular, although its rules may differ from those of other varieties.

Now is Ebonics just "slang," as so many people have characterized it? Well, no, because slang refers just to the vocabulary of a language or dialect, and even so, just to the small set of new and (usually) short-lived words like *chillin* ("relaxing") or *homey* ("close friend") which are used primarily by young people in informal contexts. Ebonics includes non- slang words like *ashy* (referring to the appearance of dry skin, especially in winter) which have been around for a while, and are used by people of all age groups. Ebonics also includes distinctive patterns of pronuncia- tion and grammar, the elements of language on which linguists tend to concentrate because they are more systematic and deep-rooted.

But is Ebonics a different language from English or a different dialect of English? Linguists tend to sidestep questions like these, noting, as the 1997 LSA resolution did, that the answers often depend on sociohistorical and political considerations rather than on linguistic ones. For instance, spoken Cantonese and Mandarin are mutually unintelligible, but they are usually regarded as "dialects" of Chinese because their speakers use the same writing system and see themselves as part of a common Chinese tradition. By contrast, although Norwegian and Swedish share many words and their speakers can generally understand each other, they are usually regarded as different languages because they are the autonomous varieties of different political entities (Norway, Sweden). Despite this, most linguists might agree that Ebonics is more of a dialect of English than a separate language, insofar as it shares most of its vocabulary and many other features with other informal varieties of American English, and insofar as its speakers can understand and be understood by speakers of most other American English dialects.

At the same time, Ebonics is one of the most distinctive varieties of American English, differing from Standard English [SE]—the educated standard—in several ways. Consider, for instance, its verb tenses and aspects. ("Tense" refers to WHEN an event occurs, e.g. present or past, and "aspect" to HOW it occurs, e.g. habitually or not.) When Toni Morrison referred to the "five present tenses" of Ebonics, she didn't give examples, but it is probably usages like these—each one different from SE—which she had in mind:

1. Present progressive: He Ø runnin. (=SE "He is running" or "He's running.")
2. Present habitual progressive: He be runnin. (=SE "He is usually running.")
3. Present intensive habitual progressive: He be steady runnin. (=SE "He is usually running in an intensive, sustained manner.")
4. Present perfect progressive: He bin runnin. (=SE "He has been running.")
5. Present perfect progressive with remote inception: He BIN runnin. (=SE "He has been running for a long time, and still is.")

The distinction between events which are non-habitual or habitual, represented in 1 and 2 respectively by the non-use or use of an invariant *be* form, can only be expressed in SE with adverbs like "usually." Of course, SE can use simple present tense forms (e.g. "He runs") for habitual events, but then the meaning of an ongoing or progressive action signalled by the "-ing" suffix is lost. Note too that *bin* in 4 is unstressed, while *BIN* in 5 is stressed. The former can usually be understood by non-Ebonics speakers as equivalent to "has been" with the "has" deleted, but the stressed BIN form can be badly misunderstood. Years ago, I presented the Ebonics sentence "She BIN married" to twenty-five Whites and twenty five Blacks from various parts of the US, and asked them, individually, if they understood the speaker to be still married or not.

While almost all the Blacks (23, or 92%) said "Yes," only a third of the whites (8, or 32%) gave this correct answer. In real life, a misconstrual of this type could be disastrous!

OK, so it's not just slang, but an English dialect, sharing a lot with other English varieties, but with some pretty distinctive features of its own. What of characterizations of Ebonics as "lazy" English, as though it were the result of snoozing in a hammock on a Sunday afternoon, or the consequences of not knowing or caring about the rules of "proper" English? Well, if you remember the linguistics principle that all languages are rule-governed, you'll probably be ready to reject these characterizations as a matter of general principle, but you can also challenge them on specific grounds.

One problem with statements like these is that they fail to recognize that most of the "rules" we follow in using language are below the level of consciousness, unlike the rules that we're taught in grammar books or at school. Take for instance, English plurals. Although grammar books tell us that you add "s" to a word to form a regular English plural, as in "cats" and "dogs," that's only true for writing. (Let's ignore words that end in s-like sounds, like "boss," which add "-es," and irregular plurals like "children.") In speech, what we actually add in the case of "cat" is an [s] sound, and in the case of "dog" we add [z]. (Linguists use square brackets to represent how words are pronounced rather than how they are spelled.) The difference is that [s] is voiceless, with the vocal cords in the larynx or voice box in our throats (the Adams apple) spread apart, and that [z] is voiced, with the vocal cords held closely together and noisily vibrating. You can hear the difference quite dramatically if you put your fingers in your ears and produce a "ssss" sequence followed by a "zzzz" sequence followed by a "ssss" sequence: sssszzzzssss. Everytime you switch to "zzzz" your voice box switches on (voiced), and everytime you switch to "ssss" your voice box switches off (voiceless). Now, how do you know whether to add [s] or [z] to form a plural when you're speaking? Easy. If the word ends in a voiceless consonant, like "t," add voiceless [s]. If the word ends in a voiced consonant, like "g," add voiced [z]. Since all vowels are voiced, if the word ends in a vowel, like "tree," add [z]. Because we spell both plural endings with "s," we're not aware that English speakers make this systematic difference every day, and I'll bet your English teacher never told you about "voiced" [z] and "voiceless" [s]. But you follow the "rules" for using them anyway, and anyone who didn't—for instance, someone who said "book[z]"—would strike an English speaker as sounding funny.

One reason people might regard Ebonics as "lazy English" is its tendency to omit word-final consonants, especially if they come after another consonant, as in "tes(t)" and "han(d)." But if one were just being lazy or cussed or both, why not also leave out the final consonant in a word like "pant"? This is NOT permitted in Ebonics, and the reason (building on your newly acquired knowledge about voicing) is that

Ebonics does not allow the deletion of the second consonant in a word-final sequence unless both consonants are either voiceless, as with "st," or voiced, as with "nd." In the case of "pant," the final "t" is voiceless, but the preceding "n" is voiced. Not only is Ebonics systematic in following this rule, but even its exceptions to the rule—negative forms like "ain'," and "don'"—are non-random. In short, Ebonics is no more lazy English than Italian is lazy Latin. To see the (expected) regularity in both we need to see each in its own terms, appreciating the complex rules that native speakers follow effortlessly and unconsciously in their daily lives.

Talking about native speakers naturally brings up the question of who speaks Ebonics. If we made a list of all the ways in which the pronunciation or grammar of Ebonics differs from that of SE, we probably couldn't find anyone who uses all of them 100% of the time. There is certainly no gene that predisposes one to speak Ebonics, so while its features are found most commonly among African American speakers ("Ebonics" is itself derived from "Ebony" and "phonics," meaning "Black sounds"), not all African Americans speak it. Ebonics features, especially distinctive tense-aspect forms like those in examples 1–5 above, are more common among working class than among middle class speakers, among adolescents than among the middle aged, and in informal contexts (a conversation in the street) rather than formal ones (a sermon at church) or writing. These differences are partly the result of differences in environment and social network (recall our point about geographical and social conditions forging dialects), and partly the result of differences in identification. Lawyers and doctors and their families have more contact than blue collar workers and the unemployed do with Standard English speakers, in their schooling, their work environments, and their neighborhoods. Moreover, working class speakers, and adolescents in particular, often embrace Ebonics features as markers of Black identity, while middle class speakers (in public at least), tend to eschew them.

What about Whites and other ethnic groups? Some Ebonics pronunciations and grammatical features are also found among other vernacular varieties of English, especially Southern White dialects, many of which have been significantly influenced by the heavy concentration of African Americans in the South. But other Ebonics features, including copula absence, habitual *be*, and remote *BIN* are rarer or non-existent in White vernaculars. When it comes to vocabulary, the situation is different. Partly through the influence of rap and hip hop music, a lot of African American slang has "crossed over" to whites and other ethnic groups, particularly among the young and the "hip" (derived from Wolof *hipi* "be aware"). Expressions like *givin five* ("slapping palms in agreement or congratulation") and *Whassup*? are so widespread in American discourse that many people don't realize they originated in the African American community. This is also true of older, non-slang words like *tote* ("carry," derived from Kongo -*tota*, Swahili -*tuta*).

By this point, some readers of this article might be fuming. It's one thing to talk about the distinctiveness and regularity of Ebonics and its value as a marker of Black identity and hipness, you might say, but don't linguists realize that nonstandard dialects are stigmatized in the larger society, and that Ebonics speakers who cannot shift to SE are less likely to do well in school and on the job front? Well, yes. As the January 1997 LSA resolution emphasized, "there are benefits in acquiring Standard English." But there is experimental evidence both from the United States and Europe that the goal of mastering the standard language might be better achieved by approaches that take students' vernaculars into account and teach them explicitly to bridge the gap to the standard than by conventional approaches which ignore the vernacular altogether. (Most conventional approaches show a shockingly poor success rate, I should add.) To give only one example: At Aurora University, outside Chicago, African American inner-city students taught by a Contrastive Analysis approach in which SE and Ebonics features were systematically contrasted through explicit instruction and drills showed a 59% REDUCTION in their use of Ebonics features in their SE writing after eleven weeks, while a control group taught by conventional methods showed an 8.5% INCREASE in such features. Despite ambiguities in their original wording, what the Oakland school board essentially wanted to do is help their students increase their mastery of SE and do better in school through an extension of the Standard English Proficiency program, a contrastive analysis approach widely used in California and already in use in some Oakland schools. It was considerations like these that led the Linguistic Society of America to endorse the Oakland proposal as "linguistically and pedagogically sound."

Let us turn now to the issue of the origins of Ebonics, on which there is much less agreement among linguists. The Oakland resolution referred to the influence of West African languages as the source of Ebonics' distinctive features, and as one reason for its recognition. The African ancestors of today's African Americans came to America mostly as slaves, and mostly between 1619 and 1808, when the slave trade officially ended. Like the forebears of many other Americans, these waves of African "immigrants" spoke languages other than English. Their languages were from the Niger-Congo language family, especially the West Atlantic, Mande and Kwa subgroups spoken from Senegal and Gambia to the Cameroons (e.g. Wolof, Mandingo, Twi, Ewe, Yoruba, Igbo), and the Bantu subgroup spoken further south (e.g. Kimbundu, Umbundu, Kongo). Arriving in an American milieu in which English was dominant, the slaves learned English. But how quickly and completely they did so, and with how much influence from their African languages, are matters of dispute.

One view, the Afrocentric or Ethnolinguistic view, is that most of the distinctive pronunciation and grammatical features of Ebonics represent transfers or continuities from Africa, since West Africans acquiring

English as slaves restructured it according to the patterns of Niger-Congo languages. On this view, Ebonics simplifies word final consonant clusters ("pas'") and omits linking verbs like *is* and *are* ("He Ø happy") because these features are generally absent from Niger-Congo languages, and Ebonics creates verbal forms like habitual *be* and remote BIN because these tense-aspect categories are present in Niger-Congo languages. However, most Afrocentrists don't specify the particular West African languages and examples which support their argument, and given the wide array of languages in the Niger-Congo family, some historically significant Niger-Congo languages don't support them. For instance, while Yoruba does indeed lack a linking verb like *is* for some adjectival constructions, it has another linking verb *rí* for other adjectives, and SIX other linking verbs for non-adjectival constructions where English would use *is* or *are*. Moreover, features like consonant cluster simplification are also found among other English vernaculars (for instance, in England) which had little or no West African influence, and this weakens the Afrocentric argument. Many linguists acknowledge continuing African influences in some Ebonics and American English words (direct loans like *hip* and *tote* were cited earlier, and we can add to these loan-translations of West African concepts into English words, as with *cut-eye* "a glance of derision or disgust"). But when it comes to Ebonics pronunciation and grammar, they want more specific proof.

A second view, the Eurocentric or dialectologist view, is that African slaves learned English from White settlers, and that they did so relatively quickly and successfully, with little continuing influence from their African linguistic heritage. Vernacular or non-SE features of Ebonics, including consonant cluster simplification and habitual *be*, are seen as transfers from vernacular dialects spoken by colonial English, Irish, or Scotch Irish settlers, many of whom were indentured servants, or as features which developed in the 20th century, after African Americans became more isolated in urban ghettoes. (Habitual *be* appears to be commoner in urban than in rural areas.) However, as with Afrocentric arguments, we still don't have enough details of the putative source features in British and settler English varieties, and crucial Ebonics features like the absence of linking *is* appear to be rare or non-existent in them, so they're unlikely to have been the source. Moreover, even with relatively low proportions of Blacks to Whites in the early colonial period, and the fact that they worked alongside each other in households and fields, particularly in the North, the assumption that slaves rapidly and successfully acquired the dialects of the Whites around them requires a rosier view of their social relations and interactions than the historical record and contemporary evidence suggest.

A third view, the Creolist view, is that many African slaves, in acquiring English, developed a simplified fusion of English and African languages which linguists call a pidgin or creole, and that this influenced the subsequent development of Ebonics. A *pidgin* is a contact vernacular, used to facilitate communication between speakers of two or more languages. Native to none of its speakers, a pidgin is a mixed language, incorporating elements of its users' native languages, and it is also has a less complex grammar and a smaller vocabulary than its input languages. A *creole*, as traditionally defined, is a pidgin which has become the primary or native language of its users (e.g. the children of pidgin speakers), expanding its vocabulary and grammatical machinery in the process, but still remaining simpler than the original language inputs in some respects. Most creoles, for instance, don't use inflectional suffixes to mark tense ("he walk*ed*"), plurality ("boys") or possession ("John's house").

Where are creoles common? All over the world, but particularly on the islands of the Caribbean and the Pacific, where large plantations brought together huge groups of slaves or indentured laborers, speaking various ethnic languages, and smaller groups of colonizers and settlers whose European languages (English, French, Dutch) the former had to learn. Under such conditions, with minimal access to European speakers, new restructured varieties like Haitian Creole French and Jamaican Creole English arose. These do show African influence, as the Afrocentric theory would predict, but where the patterns of various African languages were conflicting, the Creolist theory would provide for elimination or simplification of more complex alternatives, like the seven linking verbs of Yoruba referred to above. Within the United States, one well-established English creole is Gullah, spoken on the Sea Islands off the coast of South Carolina and Georgia, where Blacks constituted 80% to 90% of the local population in places. When I did research on one of the South Carolina Sea Islands some years ago, I recorded the following creole sentences, much like what one would hear in Caribbean Creole English today:

6. E.M. *run an gone* to *Suzie* house. (=SE "EM went running to Suzie's house.")
7. But I *does* go to see people when they Ø sick. (=SE "But I usually go to see people when they are sick.")
8. De mill *bin* to Bluffton *dem time*. (=SE "The mill was in Bluffton in those days.")

Note the characteristically creole absence of past tense and possessive inflections in 6, the absence of linking verb *are* and the presence of unstressed habitual *does* in 7, and the use of unstressed *bin* for past and *dem time* (without s, but with pluralizing dem) in 8.

What about creole origins for Ebonics? One way in which creole speech might have been introduced to many of the American colonies is through the large numbers of slaves who were imported in the 17th and 18th centuries from Caribbean colonies like Jamaica and Barbados where creoles definitely did develop. Some of those who came directly from Africa may also have brought with them pidgins or creoles which developed around West African trading forts. Moreover, some creole varieties—apart from well-known cases like Gullah—might have developed on American soil. While the percentages of Blacks in the local population might have been too low in 18th century New England and Middle Colonies for creoles to develop (3% and 7% respectively, compared with 50% to 90% in the early Caribbean), they were higher in the South (40% overall, 61% in south Carolina), where the bulk of the Black population in America was concentrated. There are also observations from travelers and commentators through the centuries to Black speech being different from White speech (contra the Eurocentric scenario), and repeated textual attestations of Black speech with creole-like features. Even today, certain features of Ebonics, like the absence of linking *is* and *are*, are widespread in Gullah and Caribbean English creoles, while rare or nonexistent in British dialects.

My own view, perhaps evident from the preceding, is that the creolist hypothesis most neatly incorporates the strengths of the other hypotheses, while avoiding their weaknesses. But there is no current consensus among linguists on the origins issue, and research from these competing perspectives is proceeding at fever pitch. One of the spinoffs of this kind of research is the light it sheds on aspects of American history which we might not otherwise consider. Whatever the final resolution of the origins issue, we should not forget that linguists from virtually all points of view agree on the systematicity of Ebonics, and on the potential value of taking it into account in teaching Ebonics speakers to read and write. That position may strike non-linguists as unorthodox, but that is where our science leads us.

FOR DISCUSSION AND REVIEW

1. Professor Rickford identifies three principles guiding the study of language. What are they?

2. According to Rickford, what are some differences between slang and a dialect? Can you think of others?

3. Is Ebonics a separate language from English or a dialect of English?

4. On what does Professor Rickford base his claim that Ebonics is not just "lazy English"? Why do we not recognize the rules of Ebonics grammar?

5. What are some phonological comparisons Rickford makes between Ebonics and other varieties of English?

6. Explain the Afrocentric or Ethnolinguistic view of the distinctive features of Ebonics. Explain the Eurocentric view.

7. Why does Professor Rickford support the Creolist view regarding the development of Ebonics?

8. Professor Rickford was one of the recognized expert linguists who spoke in support of the Oakland Resolution that Ebonics was a distinct, "systemic and rule-governed" variety of English. Despite such support, a strong negative response arose in the media and much of the public appeared to be unconvinced. Would statements by linguists matter to you in determining language status? Why, or why not?

9. How does the Ebonics controversy demonstrate that the idea of language has political and social dimensions?

29

Endangered Native American Language: What Is to Be Done and Why

James Crawford

James Crawford, former executive director of the National Association for Bilingual Education, often writes on language policy issues. A long-time proponent of what he calls an "English +" language design for education, he believes that all American students should become bilingual and that schools should foster bilingualism through curriculum design.

Crawford opens this 1998 essay with a discussion of the extinction of languages worldwide. Within this framework, he then reexamines the history and effect of different social policies on Native American languages. Throughout, Crawford deals with three major issues that continue to be relevant today: why languages become extinct, whether the decline of a language can be turned around, and why saving or reviving language is important.

The threat to linguistic resources is now recognized as a worldwide crisis. According to Krauss (1992a), as many as half of the estimated 6,000 languages spoken on earth are "moribund"; that is, they are spoken only by adults who no longer teach them to the next generation. An additional 40 percent may soon be threatened because the number of children learning them is declining measurably. In other words, 90 percent of existing languages today are likely to die or become seriously embattled within the next century. That leaves only about 600 languages, 10 percent of the world's total, that remain relatively secure—for now. This assessment is confirmed, with and without such detailed estimates, by linguists reporting the decline of languages on a global scale, but especially in the Americas, Africa, Australia, and Southeast Asia (Robins & Uhlenbeck, 1991; Brenzinger, 1992; Schmidt, 1990).

In formulating a response to this crisis, there are three questions that need to be explored: (1) What causes language decline and extinction? (2) Can the process be reversed? And (3) why should we concern ourselves with this problem? Before attempting to provide answers, it would be helpful to look in detail at the situation of Native American languages in the United States.

THE CRISIS

Language loss has been especially acute in North America. No doubt scores, perhaps hundreds, of tongues indigenous to this continent have vanished since 1492. Some have perished without a trace. Others survived long enough for 20th century linguists to track down their last speakers and partially describe their grammars—for example, Mohican in Wisconsin, Catawba in South Carolina, Yahi in California, Natchez in Louisiana, and Mashpi in Massachusetts (Swadesh, 1948).

While Krauss (1995) estimates that 175 indigenous languages are still spoken in the United States, he classifies 155 of these—89 percent of the total—as moribund. Increasingly, young Native Americans grow up speaking only English, learning at best a few words of their ancestral tongue. Out of 20 native languages still spoken in Alaska, only Central Yupik and St. Lawrence Island Yupik are being transmitted to the next generation.

Similarly, in Oklahoma only two of 23 are being learned by children. All of the nearly 50 languages indigenous to California are moribund; most are kept alive by small groups of elders (Hinton, 1994). Few of Washington State's 16 Indian vernaculars are spoken by anyone under the age of 60. Krauss (1995) projects that, nationwide, 45 of today's Native American languages will lose their last native speakers by the year 2000; 125 by 2025; and 155 by 2050. Most of the 20 that remain, while viable at present, will soon be fighting to survive.

The imminence and scale of language extinction are well illustrated by the Census Bureau's (1993) estimate that more than one-third of American Indian and Alaska Native tongues had fewer than 100 home speakers in 1990.[1] And this is probably a conservative estimate of the threat, since the Census has no way of knowing whether these are fluent speakers. It simply asks the rather vague and ambiguous question: "Does this person speak a language other than English at home?" But not "How well?" "How often?" or "Under what circumstances?"[2]

Rapid shift to English is evident even among speakers of the healthiest indigenous languages such as Navajo, a group that was historically isolated and thus among the slowest to become bilingual. As late as 1930, 71 percent of Navajos spoke no English, as compared with only 17 percent of all American Indians at the time (Census Bureau, 1937). The number who speak Navajo in the home remains substantial—148,530 in 1990, or 45 percent of all Native American language speakers (Census Bureau, 1993). But the percentage of Navajos who speak only English is growing, predictably among those who have migrated from their tribal homeland, but also among those who have remained. For Navajos living

TABLE 29.1   Tribal Population and Home Language Speakers, Age 5+, Navajo Reservation and Trust Lands (Arizona, New Mexico, and Utah), 1980–1990

	AGE 5–17	%	AGE 18+	%	TOTAL	%
1980						
Population	43,121	100.0	65,933	100.0	109,054	100.0
Speak only English	*5,103*	*11.8*	*2,713*	*4.1*	*7,816*	*7.2*
Speak other language	38,018	88.2	63,220	95.9	101,238	92.8
1990						
Population	42,994	100.0	81,301	100.0	124,295	100.0
Speak only English	*12,207*	*28.4*	*6,439*	*7.9*	*18,646*	*15.0*
Speak other language	30,787	71.6	74,862	92.1	105,649	85.0

Source: Census Bureau, 1989; 1994.

on the reservation, aged 5 and older, the proportion of English-only speakers rose from 7.2 percent in 1980 to 15.0 percent in 1990. For those aged 5–17, the increase was even more dramatic: from 11.8 percent to 28.4 percent (see Table 29.1). Among school-age children living on the reservation, the number of monolingual English speakers more than doubled, from 5,103 to 12,207.

A 1992 tribal survey suggests even more rapid erosion. Among 3,328 Navajo kindergartners at 110 schools on or near the reservation, 32 percent spoke Navajo well, while 73 percent spoke English well. Only 16 percent were rated higher in Navajo than in English (Holm, 1993). These figures are quite ominous for the future viability of Navajo, long considered the most secure indigenous tongue in the United States.

The crisis of Native American languages can be summarized as follows: unless current trends are reversed, and soon, the number of extinctions seems certain to increase. Numerous tongues—perhaps one-third of the total—are on the verge of disappearing along with their last elderly speakers, and many others are not far behind. Even the most vigorous 10 percent have a weakening hold upon the young. In short, Native American languages are becoming endangered species.

WHAT CAUSES LANGUAGE DEATH?

Obvious parallels have been drawn between the extinction of languages and the extinction of plants and animals. In all probability, like the majority of creatures in natural history, the majority of languages in human history have passed from the scene:[3] they have fallen victim to predators, changing environments, or more successful competitors. Moreover, the pace of extinction is clearly accelerating both for languages and for biological species. In the past, despite a few exceptional periods (e.g., the late Mesozoic era, when the dinosaurs died out), the process has proceeded discretely and locally. Today, by contrast, it is proceeding generically and globally. We appear to have entered a period of mass extinctions—a threat to diversity in our natural ecology and also in what might be called our cultural ecology.

Wilson (1992) has estimated that before industrialism began to affect tropical rain forests, roughly one in a million plants and animals there became extinct each year; today the rate is between one in a thousand and one in a hundred. Instead of individual species facing difficulties in particular habitats, suddenly we are seeing a generalized threat to many species, such as the well-publicized extinction of frogs in diverse environments.

Naturally, we do not have similar estimates for the rate of language extinction. Because languages leave no fossil record, there is no way to calculate the rate at which they died out in the past. But the phenomenon of language death is strikingly similar—and causally linked—to the death of biological species. Modern cultures, abetted by new technologies, are encroaching on once-isolated peoples with drastic effects on their way of life and on the environments they inhabit. Destruction of lands and livelihoods; the spread of consumerism, individualism, and other Western values; pressures for assimilation into dominant cultures; and conscious policies of repression directed at indigenous groups—these are among the factors threatening the world's biodiversity as well as its cultural and linguistic diversity.

How does a language die? One obvious way is that its speakers can perish through disease or genocide. This was the fate, for example, of most languages spoken by the Arawak peoples of the Caribbean, who disappeared within a generation of their first contact with Christopher Columbus. But such cases are relatively rare. More often language death is the culmination of language shift, resulting from a complex of internal and external pressures that induce a speech community to adopt a language spoken by others. These may include changes in values, rituals, or economic and political life resulting from trade, migration, intermarriage, religious conversion, or military conquest. Some describe these as "changes in the ecology of languages" (Wurm, 1991)—continuing the comparison with natural species—a Darwinian model suggesting that languages must adapt or perish.

Here the analogy begins to become misleading. Unlike natural species, languages have no genes and thus carry no mechanism for natural selection. Their prospects for survival are determined not by any intrinsic traits, or capacity for adaptation, but by social forces alone. As a practical matter, in discussing language shift it is probably impossible to avoid biomorphic metaphors like *ecology, survival, death, extinction,* and *genocide* (certainly if one judges from this paper thus far). But unless we remain vigilant, such metaphors can lead us into semantic traps, and these traps have political consequences.

Conceiving language loss as a Darwinian process implies that some languages are fitter than others, that the "developed" will survive and the "primitive" will go the way of the dinosaurs. While I know of no linguist who makes such an argument, there are plenty of laypersons who do. (And such voices are heeded by legislators, as testified by the advance of the English Only movement since the mid-1980s.) Some scholars of "language death" have helped to perpetuate this misunderstanding by ignoring its social and historical causes. By focusing exclusively on "structural-linguistic" factors, they imply "that a language can 'kill itself' by becoming so impoverished that its function as an adequate means of communication is called into question" (Sasse, 1992, pp. 10–11). The research literature demonstrates precisely the opposite: such structural changes are the result, not the cause, of language decline.

In a related vein, several writers have raised the question: "Language murder or language suicide?" (e.g., Edwards, 1985)—as if it were possible to separate external and internal factors in language loss and thereby assess blame. According to the "suicide" model, a language community (say, the Irish) opts to abandon its native tongue out of self-interest (to enjoy the superior opportunities open to English speakers) rather than in response to coercion. As Denison (1977, p. 21) asserts, a speech community

> sometimes "decides," for reasons of functional economy, to suppress a part of itself. . . . [T]here comes a point when multilingual parents no longer consider it necessary or worthwhile for the future of their children to communicate with them in a low-prestige language variety, and when children are no longer motivated to acquire active competence in a language which is lacking in positive connotations such as youth, modernity, technical skills, material success, education. The languages at the lower end of the prestige scale retreat from ever increasing areas of their earlier functional domains, displaced by higher prestige languages, until there is nothing left for them to be appropriately used about. In this sense they may be said to "commit suicide."

Certainly language choices are made, in the final analysis, by speakers themselves. But this "explanation" of language death explains little about the social forces underlying such choices. Whether deliberate or not, the notion of language suicide fosters a victim-blaming strategy. It reinforces the ethnocentric prejudice, all too common among dominant groups, that certain languages are unfit to survive in the modern world. At best, it encourages the prevalent worldwide response to threatened cultures: malign neglect.

Yet "murder," too, has been overrated as a cause of language extinction. This is due in part to the popular notion that conquerors "naturally" force their languages on others. But scholars, too, have favored the murder hypothesis, for example, in explaining the spread of Indo-European languages. The traditional account is that, over a relatively brief period—roughly the 4th millennium B.C.—bands of warriors armed with superior technology (and in some versions, with superior "racial" traits) charged out of the Russian steppes (or Asia Minor or Northern Europe) to defeat indigenous peoples from India to Ireland and impose their own Proto-Indo-European vernacular(s).[4]

Renfrew (1987) has recently cast strong doubts on this hypothesis. Invoking archaeological as well as linguistic evidence, he argues that Proto-Indo-European advanced more gradually through the expansion of agriculture, beginning as early as 6500 B.C. Farming supports considerably larger populations than hunting and gathering, but also requires constant migration in search of arable land. Thus, instead of spreading their language(s) primarily by conquest, it is more likely that Indo-Europeans overwhelmed other language communities with superior numbers. Europe's original inhabitants (with exceptions, e.g., the Basques) either adopted the newcomers' way of life, including their speech, or perished trying to compete with it. In this scenario demographic, cultural, and economic changes, rather than military factors played the key roles in language extinction. While the debate over Indo-European origins continues, Renfrew's hypothesis is more consistent with sociolinguistic evidence about language shift.

In sum, the murder vs. suicide dichotomy is simplistic in the extreme. And it lends support to those who would either justify the colonizer's prerogative to coerce assimilation or blame the victims for acquiescing. Languages die from both internal and external causes, operating simultaneously. On the one hand, the process always reflects forces beyond its speakers' control: repression, discrimination, or exploitation by other groups (and, in many situations, all three). On the other hand, except in the case of physical genocide, languages never succumb to outside pressures alone. There must be complicity on the part of speech community itself, changes in attitudes and values that discourage teaching its vernacular to children and encourage loyalty to the dominant tongue.

Take the example of Native American languages, which were targeted by the U.S. government in a campaign of linguistic genocide. In 1868, a federal commission on making peace with the plains Indians concluded: "In the difference of language to-day lies two-thirds of our trouble. . . . Schools should be established, which children should be required to attend; their barbarous dialects should be blotted out and the English language substituted" (quoted in Atkins, 1887).

By the 1880s this policy was institutionalized in the boarding school system established by the Bureau of Indian Affairs (BIA). Under strict English Only rules, students were punished and humiliated for speaking their native language as part of a general campaign to erase every vestige of their Indianness. A BIA teacher in the early 1900s explained that the schools "went on the assumption that any Indian custom was, per se, objectionable, whereas the customs of whites were the ways of civilization. . . . [Children] were taught to despise every custom of their forefathers, including religion, language, songs, dress, ideas, methods of living"

(Albert H. Kneale, quoted in Reyhner, 1992, p. 45). Lieutenant Richard Henry Pratt, architect of the BIA school system, summed up its educational philosophy succinctly: "Kill the Indian . . . and save the man" (Pratt, 1973 [1892], p. 261).

When John Collier was appointed commissioner of Indian Affairs in 1933, he condemned and prohibited these ethnocentric practices, going so far as to experiment with vernacular instruction in Navajo and other languages (Szasz, 1977). Nevertheless, English Only rules and punishments persisted unofficially for another generation, as many former students can attest.

In the short term, the coercive assimilation policy met with limited success in eradicating Indian languages. Brutality of this kind naturally breeds resistance and determination to defend the culture under attack. Moreover, the isolation and exclusion of most Indians from the dominant society made assimilation seem like a poor bargain indeed. Even when students excelled in BIA schools and embraced the dominant culture, on graduation they were usually shunned by white society.

Over time, however, the English Only policy did take a toll on the pride and identity of many Indians, alienating them from their cultural roots and from their tribes, and giving them little or nothing in return. Being punished for speaking the ancestral language often devalued it in their own minds, and some accepted the dominant society's judgments. This has left a legacy of opposition to bilingual education among not a few Indian parents, who vividly remember the pain they suffered in school and hope to shield their children from the same experience (Crawford, 1995).

Yet while the English Only boarding schools did damage to the status of indigenous languages within their own communities, other factors may have exerted a stronger influence. The advent of a cash economy, government services, and in some cases industrial employment, along with the penetration of once-remote reservations by English-language media (especially television and VCRs), have created new pressures and enticements for Native Americans to enter the wider society, or at least to abandon their old ways.

Returning again to the example of the Navajo, we can see that language shift began to accelerate after the BIA abandoned its punitive English Only policy. That is, linguistic assimilation seems to have proceeded more efficiently on a laissez-faire basis than it did through coercion. Pragmatic parents tend to see advantages in raising their children mostly or entirely in English, the language of social and economic mobility. Thus every step toward modernization puts the indigenous tongue at a greater disadvantage. Gradually its sphere of usage contracts to home and hearth, religious rituals, and traditional ceremonies. In theory, stable bilingualism (diglossia) offers a possible antidote to language loss, but the odds for maintaining this balance decline to the extent that traditional cultures decline, thereby shrinking the domains of the ancestral tongue.

How should we conceptualize the causes of language shift? Rather than rely on Darwinian metaphors, Fishman (1991, pp. 55–67) offers criteria with fewer semantic pitfalls. In place of changing "ecology," he cites "dislocations"—physical, economic, social, and cultural—affecting a language community. These include a group's dispersal from its historic homeland, subordination to a socioeconomic system in which its tongue commands limited power and prestige, and the weakening of traditional bonds through contact with modern, atomized democracies that elevate individual freedom over communal values. While a comprehensive theory of language loss remains to be developed, Fishman's categories provide a useful framework for investigation.

IS THERE A CURE?

What, if anything, can be done to cope with this crisis? Is it possible to rescue languages now on the brink of extinction, or perhaps even to resuscitate some that are no longer spoken? This latter idea is not so far-fetched when one considers the example of Hebrew—a "dead" language for nearly 2,000 years when it was brought back to life in modern Israel; Hebrew today has several million speakers. Some Native American groups have expressed interest in doing the same thing. Recently the Coquille tribe of Oregon sought funding for a project to revive the Miluk language, using tape recordings from the 1930s of its last living speakers (Farley, 1992).

Of course, it would be hard to find a community whose language is threatened today that commands the level of resources the State of Israel devoted to the cause of reviving Hebrew. So the question of whether this kind of effort can succeed is very relevant. If there is little hope of preventing the extinction of a language, a revitalization project may be illadvised; scarce funds might be better spent on other social and educational programs. On the other hand, if endangered languages can be saved, there is little time for delay in the name of budgetary constraints.

In the 1980s several tribes recognized the urgency of this task. The Navajo, Tohono O'odham, Pasqua Yaqui, Northern Ute, Arapaho, and Red Lake Band of Chippewa were among those that adopted policies designed to promote the use of their ancestral tongues in reservation schools and government functions. Ironically, in most cases the English Only movement sounded the alarm bells that energized Indian leaders (Crawford, 1992b).

While these tribal language policies were an important first step, their implementation has been uneven. To succeed, language renewal projects require not only good intentions but enormous practical efforts. Some tribes still need expert help to complete orthographies, grammar books, and dictionaries. Virtually all need assistance in developing and publishing curriculum materials. Bilingual education programs—for example, at community-run schools like Rough Rock on the Navajo reservation—are a major (if underutilized) tool for promoting native-language literacy (McLaughlin, 1992). Another key task is teacher-training, complicated by the fact that Indian language speakers often lack academic credentials, while outsiders lack essential cultural and linguistic knowledge. As a result, these projects must draw on cultural resources available on reservations, relying especially on elders, the true experts in these languages.

Tribal initiative and control are essential to the success of revitalization efforts because language choices are a matter of consensus within each community. They are very difficult to impose from without. "All-important is the peoples' will to restore their native languages," Krauss (1992b) maintains, citing his experiences at the Alaska Native Language Center in Fairbanks. "You cannot from the outside inculcate into people the will to revive or maintain their languages. That has to come from them, from themselves." If endangered languages are to be saved, it is crucial for native speakers to see the value of doing so and get actively involved in the process.

At the same time language renewal faces a perennial barrier to social progress on Indian reservations: scarce resources. Such projects must compete with other, usually more pressing priorities like health care, housing, schooling, and economic development. Most tribes, lacking a local tax base, have historically relied on federal funding for these needs. But since 1980 the federal government has cut back substantially on its support of Indian programs generally. . . .

Congress . . . passed the Native American Languages Acts of 1990 and 1992, laws that, respectively, articulate a government policy of protecting indigenous languages and authorize a grant program for that purpose. While some federal help was previously available through the National Science Foundation, the National Endowment for the Humanities, and the Department of Education, for the first time the 1992 Act made tribes eligible for funding to carry out language conservation and renewal. Yet Congress has been slow to fund the program. Finally, in the fall of 1994, the Clinton Administration awarded $1 million in grants to launch 18 language revitalization projects nationwide—a meager amount but still a beginning.[5]

Implementation of the 1990 Act has also been disappointing. Among other things, it called upon all agencies of the federal government—including the Departments of Interior, Education, and Health and Human Services—to review their activities in consultation with tribes, traditional leaders, and educators to make sure they comply with the policy of conserving Native American languages. By the fall of 1991, the president was required to report back to Congress on what was being done and to recommend further changes in law and policy. But [recent administrations have] failed to conduct the mandated review[s]. . . . So, although the federal government now has a strong policy statement on file favoring the preservation of indigenous tongues, its real-world impact has thus far been limited.

So the question remains: Is there a realistic chance of reversing the erosion of Native American languages? In theory, this goal is quite possible to achieve, as we know from the miraculous revival of other languages. Heroic efforts are now being made on behalf of languages with only a few elderly speakers, for example, by the Advocates for Indigenous California Language Survival (Hinton, 1994; Feldman, 1993). For other languages, especially those still being learned by children, taught in bilingual education programs, and receiving tribal support, there is considerable hope. In practice, however, limited progress is being made in retarding the pace of language shift overall. This bleak situation is unlikely to change without a stronger commitment at all levels and without a substantial infusion of new resources. To put it bluntly, the decisive factor in the survival of Native American languages will be politics—the final subject of this paper.

WHY SHOULD WE CARE?

Why concern ourselves with the problem of endangered Native American languages, to the extent of investing the considerable time, effort, and resources that would be needed to save even a handful of them? Posing the question in this way may seem callous, considering the shameful history of cultural genocide practiced against indigenous peoples in this country. But, for many non-Indians, who tend to view linguistic diversity as a liability rather than an asset, the value of these languages is not self-evident. Knowledge about Native American issues in general is limited. Meanwhile assimilationist biases remain strong; hence the symbolic opposition these days to any kind of public expenditure aimed at preserving "ethnic" cultures (Crawford, 1992b). Until such attitudes are changed—by effectively answering the question, "Why should we care about preserving Native American languages?"—there will be limited progress in conservation and renewal.

Advocates have advanced a variety of answers. Let us consider them on their scientific merits and on their political appeal.

1. Linguists, who are increasingly vocal on this issue, have warned that the death of any natural language represents an incalculable loss to their science. "Suppose English were the only language available as a basis for the study of general human grammatical competence," writes Hale (1992, p. 35). While "we could learn a great deal . . . we also know enough about linguistic diversity to know that we would miss an enormous amount." No doubt few who are acquainted with this

problem would disagree: from a scientific standpoint, the destruction of data is always regrettable. Losing a language means losing a rare window on the human mind. But from the perspective of the public and policymakers, this argument smacks of professional self-interest; it is hardly a compelling justification for new spending in times of fiscal austerity.

2. Others have argued that the loss of linguistic diversity represents a loss of intellectual diversity. Each language is a unique tool for analyzing and synthesizing the world, incorporating the knowledge and values of a speech community. Linguistic "categories [including] number, gender, case, tense, mode, voice, 'aspect,' and a host of others . . . are not so much discovered in experience as imposed upon it" (Sapir, 1931). Thus to lose such a tool is to "forget" a way of constructing reality, to blot out a perspective evolved over many generations. The less variety in language, the less variety in ideas. Again, a Darwinian analogy:

> Evolutionary biologists recognize the great advantage held by species that maintain the greatest possible diversity. Disasters occur when only one strain of wheat or corn, a "monoculture," is planted everywhere. With no variation, there is no potential to meet changing conditions. In the development of new science concepts, a "monolanguage" holds the same dangers as a monoculture. Because languages partition reality differently, they offer different models of how the world works. There is absolutely no reason why the metaphors provided in English are superior to those of other languages. [Schrock, 1986.]

Theoretically this sounds plausible; yet such effects are impossible to quantify. Who can say whether a concept that evolved in one language would never have evolved in another? The extreme version of the Sapir-Whorf hypothesis that perception and cognition are determined by the structure of whatever language one happens to speak—has been demolished by Chomskyan linguistics (see, e.g., Pinker, 1994). Its more flexible version, "linguistic relativity," is another matter. Few would dispute that culture, influenced by language, influences thought. Yet the impact remains too elusive, too speculative, to rally public concern about language loss.

3. Then there is the cultural pluralist approach: language loss is "part of the more general loss being suffered by the world, the loss of diversity in all things" (Hale, 1992, p. 3). While this argument is politically potent—with lots of cosmopolitan appeal—it is scientifically dubious. For at least one linguist working to save endangered languages, such "statements . . . are appeals to our emotions, not to our reason" (Ladefoged, 1992, p. 810). Again the biological analogy breaks down. From the loss of natural species scientists are continually documenting ripple effects that harm our global ecosystem. No such evidence is available for the loss of linguistic species, which are not

physically interdependent and which "evolve" in very different ways. No doubt it would be interesting to know more about extinct languages like Sumerian, Hittite, Etruscan, and even Anglo-Saxon. But how can we regard their disappearance as a global "catastrophe"? As for the threat to human diversity in general, "the world is remarkably resilient . . . ; different cultures are always dying while new ones arise" (Ladefoged, 1992, p. 810). Indeed, this resilience is the basis for linguistic diversity itself.

4. A final—and, in my view, the most effective—line of argument appeals to the nation's broader interest in social justice. We should care about preventing the extinction of languages because of the human costs to those most directly affected. "The destruction of a language is the destruction of a rooted identity" (Fishman, 1991, p. 4) for both groups and individuals. Along with the accompanying loss of culture, language loss can destroy a sense of self-worth, limiting human potential and complicating efforts to solve other problems, such as poverty, family breakdown, school failure, and substance abuse. After all, language death does not happen in privileged communities. It happens to the dispossessed and the disempowered, peoples who most need their cultural resources to survive.

In this context, indigenous language renewal takes on an added significance. It becomes something of value not merely to academic researchers, but to native speakers themselves. This is true even in extreme cases where a language seems beyond repair. As one linguist sums up a project to revive Adnyamathanha, an Australian Aboriginal tongue that had declined to about 20 native speakers:

> It was not the success in reviving the language—although in some small ways [the program] did that. It was success in reviving something far deeper than the language itself—that sense of worth in being Adnyamathanha, and in having something unique and infinitely worth hanging onto. [D. Tunbridge, quoted in Schmidt, 1990, p. 106.]

NOTES

1. "Native North American languages" comprised 136 different groupings; of these, 47 were spoken in the home by fewer than 100 persons; an additional 22 were spoken by fewer than 200.

2. Without an interviewer to explain the purpose of the home-language question, it has elicited unintended responses. The extent of language shift may be understated through misinterpretations, such as: "Can this person speak, at any level of proficiency, a language other than English?" and "Does this person ever speak another language at home?" So persons with limited proficiency, such as those who have studied a foreign language in school, are often counted as minority language speakers. E.g., the 1980 Census found

that a substantial minority of "Spanish speakers" in the home were not of Hispanic ethnicity—a "totally untenable . . . conclusion," according to Veltman (1988, p. 19). Moreover, self-reports have been shown to be unreliable when compared with objective measures of language proficiency (see, e.g., Hakuta & D'Andrea, 1992), often contaminated by ethnic feelings, such as pride in the native language. Ambiguous questions provide even more room for subjective assessments. On the other hand, the Census has acknowledged a significant undercount of minority groups, including Native Americans. Those living in remote areas are least likely to be counted; in the past, large numbers of census forms have piled up, unclaimed, at reservation trading posts. Such Indians are less likely to speak only English in the home; so undercounting them tends to overstate the extent of language shift. Another possible distortion, especially for small populations, is that language estimates are based on a 12 percent sample. A survey conducted by linguists and indigenous speakers in California turned up several Indian languages missed entirely by the 1990 Census (Hinton, 1994).

On balance, however, the last two decennial censuses probably overstate the extent of proficiency in (and usage of) languages other than English. Fortunately, the questions were asked consistently in 1980 and 1990. So at least the trends of language shift may be reliably plotted on the basis of comparable data. Unfortunately, no home language question was asked before 1980.

3. Krauss speculates that 10,000 years ago, there may have been as many as 15,000 languages worldwide—2.5 times as many as today (Schwartz, 1994).

4. Of course, this idea predates the advent of linguistic archaeology. In 1492, Antonio de Nebrija completed a Castilian grammar book, the first ever completed of a European language. When he presented it to Queen Isabella and she asked, "What is it for?" the Bishop of Avila answered for him: "Your Majesty, language is the perfect instrument of empire." Thus began a 300-year attempt by Spanish monarchs to repress and replace indigenous languages in the New World. Yet despite repeated edicts from Madrid, the policy was frequently ignored by Spanish priests and civil officials, who found it easier to pursue their work through indigenous lingua francas like Nahuatl and Quechua (Heath, 1972). A U.S. Commissioner of Indian Affairs similarly invoked the conqueror's prerogative to justify linguistic repression in North America:

> All are familiar with the recent prohibitory order of the German Empire forbidding the teaching of the French language in either public or private schools in Alsace and Lorraine. Although the population is almost universally opposed to German rule, they are firmly held to German political allegiance by the military hand of the Iron Chancellor. If the Indians were in Germany or France or any other civilized country, they should be instructed in the language there used. As they are in an English-speaking country they must be taught the language which they must use in transacting business with the people of this country. No unity or community of feeling can be established among different peoples unless they are brought to speak the same language, and thus become imbued with like ideas of duty. [Atkins, 1887.]

5. The Administration for Native Americans, a branch of the Department of Health and Human Services, issued regulations governing this grant program in the Federal Register on March 25, 1994.

BIBLIOGRAPHY

Atkins, J. D. C. (1887). *Report of the commissioner of Indian affairs.* House Exec. Doc. No. 1, Pt. 5, 50th Cong., 1st Sess. Washington, DC: U.S. Government Printing Office.

Brenzinger, M. (Ed.). (1992). *Language death: Factual and theoretical explorations with special reference to East Africa.* Berlin: Mouton de Gruyter.

Census Bureau, U.S. (1937). *The Indian population of the United States and Alaska.* Washington, DC: U.S. Government Printing Office.

Census Bureau, U.S. (1989). *1980 census of population: Characteristics of American Indians by tribes and selected areas.* PC80-2-1C. Washington, DC: U.S. Government Printing Office.

Census Bureau, U.S. (1993). Number of non-English language speaking Americans up sharply in 1980s, Census Bureau says. [Press release] April 28.

Census Bureau, U.S. (1994). *1990 census of population: Social and economic characteristics for American Indian and Alaska Native areas.* 1990 CP-2-1A. Washington, DC: U.S. Government Printing Office.

Crawford, J. (Ed.). (1992a). *Language loyalties: A source book on the Official English controversy.* Chicago: University of Chicago Press.

Crawford, J. (1992b). *Hold your tongue: Bilingualism and the politics of "English Only."* Reading, MA: Addison-Wesley.

Crawford, J. (1995). *Bilingual education History, politics theory, and practice.* 3rd ed. Los Angeles: Bilingual Educational Services.

Denison, N. (1977). Language death or language suicide? *International Journal of the Sociology of Language, 12,* 13–22.

Edwards, J. (1985). *Language, society, and identity.* Oxford: Basil Blackwell.

Farley, J. (1992). Statement of Jerry Farley, executive vice president, Coquille Economic Development Co. In U.S. Senate, *Native American Languages Act of 1991: Hearing before the Select Committee on Indian Affairs* (p. 29). Washington, DC: U.S. Government Printing Office.

Feldman, P. (1993). Breathing new life into dying languages. *Los Angeles Times,* July 12, pp. A1, A20–21.

Fishman, J. A. (1991). *Reversing language shift: Theoretical and empirical foundations of assistance to threatened languages.* Clevedon, England: Multilingual Matters.

Hakuta, K., & D'Andrea, D. (1992). Some properties of bilingual maintenance and loss in Mexican background high-school students. *Applied Linguistics, 13,* 72–99.

Hale, K. (Ed.). (1992). Endangered languages. *Language, 68,* 1–42.

Heath, S. B. (1972). *Telling tongues: Language policy in Mexico, colony to nation.* New York: Teachers College Press.

Hinton, L. (1994). *Flutes of fire: Essays on California Indian languages.* Berkeley, CA: Heyday Books.

Holm, W. (1993). *A very preliminary analysis of Navajo kindergartners' language abilities.* Window Rock, AZ: Navajo Division of Education, Office of Diné Culture, Language and Community Services.

Krauss, M. (1992a). The world's languages in crisis. *Language, 68,* 6–10.

Krauss, M. (1992b). Statement of Mr. Michael Krauss, representing the Linguistic Society of America. In U.S. Senate, *Native American Languages Act of 1991: Hearing before the Select Committee on Indian Affairs* (pp. 18–22). Washington, DC: U.S. Government Printing Office.

Krauss, M. (1995). Endangered languages: Current issues and future prospects. Keynote address, Dartmouth College, Hanover, NH. Feb. 3.

Ladefoged, P. (1992). Another view of endangered languages. *Language, 68,* 809–11.

McLaughlin, D. (1992). *When literacy empowers: Navajo language in print.* Albuquerque: University of New Mexico Press.

Pinker, S. (1994). *The language instinct: How the mind creates language.* New York: Morrow.

Pratt, R. H. (1973). Official report of the nineteenth annual Conference of Charities and Correction [1892]. In F. P. Prucha (Ed.), *Americanizing the American Indians: Writings by the "Friends of the Indian," 1880–1900* (pp. 260–71). Cambridge, MA: Harvard University Press.

Renfrew, C. (1987). *Archaeology and language: The puzzle of Indo-European origins.* Chicago: University of Chicago Press.

Reyhner, J. (1992). Policies toward American Indian languages: A historical sketch. In Crawford, J. (Ed.), *Language Loyalties: A Source Book on the Official English Controversy* (pp. 41–47). Chicago: University of Chicago Press.

Robins, R. H., & Uhlenbeck, E. (Eds.). (1991). *Endangered languages.* Oxford: Berg.

Sapir, E. (1931). Conceptual categories in primitive languages. *Science, 74,* 578.

Sasse, H.-J. (1992). Theory of language death. In Brenzinger, M. (Ed.), *Language death: Factual and theoretical explorations with special reference to East Africa* (pp. 7–30). Berlin: Mouton de Gruyter.

Schmidt, A. (1990). *The loss of Australia's Aboriginal language heritage.* Canberra: Aboriginal Studies Press, 1990.

Schrock, J. R. (1986). The science teacher and foreign languages. *Kansas Science Teacher, 3,* 12–15.

Schwartz, J. (1994). Speaking out and saving sounds to keep native tongues alive. *Washington Post,* March 14 (p. A3).

Senate, U.S. (1992). *Native American Languages Act of 1991: Hearing before the Select Committee on Indian Affairs.* Washington, DC: U.S. Government Printing Office.

Swadesh, M. (1948). Sociologic notes on obsolescent languages. *International Journal of American Linguistics, 14,* 226–35.

Szasz, M. C. (1977). *Education and the American Indian: The road to self-determination since 1928.* 2nd ed. Albuquerque: University of New Mexico Press.

Veltman, C. (1988). *The future of the Spanish language in the United States.* Washington, DC: Hispanic Policy Development Project.

Wilson, E. O. (1992). *The diversity of life.* Cambridge, MA: Harvard University Press.

Wurm, S. A. (1991). Language death and disappearance: Causes and circumstances. In Robins, R. H., & Uhlenbeck, E. (Eds.), *Endangered languages* (pp. 1–18). Oxford: Berg.

===

FOR DISCUSSION AND REVIEW

1. Crawford uses a "biomorphic metaphor" to draw a parallel between language extinction and extinction of a biological species. Discuss whether language death is a "natural" phenomenon. How are these processes analogous? How are they different?

2. What effects did English Only policies have on Native American languages? How did assimilation and other factors affect language shift? In regard to new language groups in the United States today, do you think assimilation necessarily entails language shift? Why, or why not?

3. Crawford calls for policies and their implementation to keep existing Native American languages from extinction. What kinds of tribal government policies might help preserve endangered languages? How do you feel about using federal or state funds to save languages?

4. Discuss Crawford's reasons for why we should be concerned over the loss of Native American languages.

5. How is linguistic diversity important? Can it ever be a liability? Explain.

Projects for "Language Variation and Social Interaction"

1. Linguistic atlas and dictionary projects have been crucial in showing the language variation that exists among English speakers in North America. For this project, prepare a report on the purposes and methods of one of these projects. Choose one of the following:

- *Linguistic Atlas of the United States and Canada* (available at www.lap.uga.edu)

- *Linguistic Atlas of New England* (available at www.lap.uga.edu)

- *Linguistic Atlas of the Middle and South Atlantic States* (available at www.lap.uga.edu)

- *Linguistic Atlas of the Gulf States* (available at www.lap.uga.edu)

- *Dictionary of American Regional English* (DARE, available at http://polyglot.lss.wisc.edu/dare/dare.html)

- *Atlas of North American English* (ANAE, available at www.ling.upenn.edu/phonoatlas)

Each has a wealth of maps, statistics, and supplementary material describing the background, fieldwork methods, and types of analysis used with the project. (See the Selected Bibliography for a more complete list.)

2. The names of cities, towns, rivers, and mountains often provide clues to settlement and migration patterns. Using a map of your area, select three place names and discuss their significance. For each, try to discover the name's origin, if its meaning or pronunciation has changed, and whether it is used elsewhere in the United States or in other countries. A helpful source for this project is the American Name Society (ANS), available at www.wtsn.binghamton.edu/ANS. Other sources are Kelsie B. Hardner's *Illustrated Dictionary of Place Names* (1976) and George R. Stewart's *American Place-Names* (1970). Depending on where you live, you may also find useful information in publications by local historians at historical societies, museums, and public libraries. Create an oral presentation (with visuals) or a report discussing your findings.

3. In "Sense and Nonsense about American Dialects" (*PMLA* 81 [1966]:7–17), Raven I. McDavid Jr. says that "the surest social markers in American English are grammatical forms." To test McDavid's claim, collect about a dozen examples of marked grammatical forms in your community. Do you find differences in subject-verb agreement? Differences in pronoun choice? Different forms of past-tense verbs? Different ways of expressing negation or completion? As you collect your examples, keep notes about where you are and who is speaking. Then write up your findings. Which differences in grammatical forms are regional? Which are

social? What forms would be included within Formal Standard English, Informal Standard English, or Vernacular Nonstandard English as defined by Wolfram and Schilling-Estes in "Standards and Vernaculars"?

4. The concept of Standard English has given rise to misunderstanding and debate. For many Americans, "standard" implies that one variety of English is more correct than other varieties. Using Wolfram and Schilling-Estes's essay, "Standards and Vernaculars," as a starting point, write a brief paper on the history of the concept of Standard English. How did the concept develop? How do various linguists define it? Why do discussions about Standard English often include the notions of power and social class?

5. This project is derived from a project suggested in the "American Dialects" chapter of the Ann Curzan and Michael Adams textbook *How English Works* (Pearson-Longman, 2006, p. 434). Using the *Dictionary of American Regional English* (*DARE*), the *Oxford English Dictionary* (*OED*), and, if available, the *Dictionary of Smoky Mountain English* and the *National Scottish Dictionary*, identify the Appalachian English terms in the following passage by Tony Earley (1998, 80). Once you have a list of terms, try to determine the approximate first use of each term and where it originated. You'll find *DARE* and the *OED* particularly useful for this part. Here is the passage:

> Nor is "quare" the only word still hiding out in my grandmother's house which dictionaries assure us lost currency years ago. If I brought a quare person to Sunday dinner at Granny's and he ate something that disagreed with him, we might say he look a little peaked. Of course, we might decide that he was peaked not because he had eaten something that disagreed with him but because he had eaten a bait of something he liked. We would say, Why, he was just trifling to leave the table. He ate almost the whole mess by himself. And now we have this quare, peaked, trifling person on our hands. How do we get him to leave? Do we job him in the stomach? Do we hit him with a stob? No, we are kinder than that. We tell him, "Brother, you liked to have stayed too long." We put his dessert in a poke and send him on his way. — Tony Earley

Now, rewrite the passage twice. The first time, write it in Formal Standard American English. Then write a version using your own most informal English. In this second version, use your own idioms, slang, and regional dialect.

6. As we have seen, dialect differences in pronunciation abound. The following list contains words with distinct regional pronunciations. Compare your pronunciation of these items with those of others in your class:

collar	cot	wash
car	apricot	paw
empty	dog	tomato
door	clientele	marry

garage	mangy	Mary
oil	house	roof
can	very	sorry
greasy	either	fog
lot	caller	water
caught	horse	almost
hurry	class	idea.

What pronunciation differences do you note among the members of your class? Are any regional patterns of pronunciation evident? Any differences that correlate with age? Compare your results to discussions of regional pronunciation such as in Lee Pederson's "Dialects" in Part Five, in Walt Wolfram and Natalie Schilling-Estes's book *American English* (2006), and the introduction to Volume I of the *Dictionary of American Regional English.*

7. Several of the readings in Part Six deal with variations in speech among people of different regions and social groups. Compile a list of slang and idiomatic phrases from the students in your class. Your list may include some of the following: ways of indicating refusal ("no way") or desirability ("hot" or "swe-et!"); forms of address ("dude"); and expressions of difference ("the hooyah"), disapproval ("cold"), fear ("squicks me out"), or amazement ("shut *up*"). Some expressions depend on phonology ("ew") and some on idiomatic word order or use ("she is so not invited" or "he got drunk married"). Because the *Oxford Dictionary of Slang* and the *Oxford Dictionary of Modern Slang* are arranged thematically, they may help you decide on categories. (See the bibliography at the end of this section.)

Using your list of words and phrases, conduct a survey in your community or within your family. Before asking any questions, record the participant's age, level of education, sex, and place of origin. Then ask each participant whether he or she (a) has heard the term, (b) uses the term, and (c) knows other expressions that have the same meaning. After gathering your data, write a report of your survey results. What does the survey tell you about language variation?

8. William Safire of the *New York Times* called the *Dictionary of American Regional English* "the most exciting linguistic project going on in the United States." To date, four volumes of the five volumes have been published, bringing the project up through *Sk-*. Spend some time examining *DARE*, as it is called, in preparation for writing a report about it. At the beginning of Volume I, you will find short essays about regional variation in the United States; the nature of "folk" linguistics; a description of the fieldwork, collection, and organizing processes for the words and phrases included in *DARE*; and an explanation of the way to read entries. You might consider these questions for your report: What is the purpose of this dictionary? What kinds of information does it contain? What kinds

of sources were used? How were the people interviewed selected? What kinds of uses would this dictionary have?

9. In 1977, well before the Oakland Ebonics Resolution, a lawsuit was brought against the Ann Arbor, Michigan, School Board on behalf of fifteen African American children. The lawsuit argued that the children's poor achievement scores resulted in part from the school failing to account for language and cultural differences. (See *Martin Luther King Junior Elementary School Children, et al.* v *Ann Arbor School District Board*, 473 F. Supp. 1371 [1979]). The "Ann Arbor Decision" continues to generate controversy and misunderstanding. Using library and database resources, prepare a report discussing one of the following: (a) the origins of the lawsuit, (b) the findings of the court, or (c) the effects of the decision on the Ann Arbor schools. One useful reference is *Black English: Educational Equity and the Law*, edited by John W. Chambers Jr. (Karoma Publishers, 1983).

10. In 1973, Professor Robert Williams, a social psychologist at George Washington University, coined the term *Ebonics*—a blend of *ebony* and *phonics*—referring especially to the phonology of black college students. For this project, first review the public statements made about the Oakland Resolution in the media, and note how the term *Ebonics* is used by various speakers. The "Dialects: African American Vernacular English" Web page and Theresa Perry and Lisa Delpit's *The Real Ebonics Debate* are good places to start your research. (See the Selected Bibliography.) You will find a range of responses about Ebonics and the resolution from across the political and social spectrum. Once you feel familiar with the various positions, write an essay articulating one of them.

11. The issue of language death is a hot topic among linguists and also among those involved in social and educational policy making. Research and write a position paper about language death in the contemporary world. Do endangered languages exist in similar social or political situations? Does population size matter? Do social or political or economic conditions contribute to language extinction? How have globalization and technology contributed to language death? To what extent do you think language death is good or bad? To develop your position, you might look back to Part Four, where Steven Pinker asserts that language endangerment matters in "Tower of Babel," and at James Crawford's essay "Endangered Native American Language," which describes the rising extinction rate of languages.

12. James Crawford urges his readers to be concerned about language death. Choose a specific language that is currently in danger of extinction, and create a multimedia presentation about the language itself and its speakers. A number of languages in Australia and Africa are in various stages of extinction, as are some languages in the Americas. Here are some questions you might consider in developing your presentation: How has the language been documented? Does it have an alphabet or

writing system? How many people speak the language, and to what extent is it used (for example, only at home or among family members)? How many people spoke the language in, say, the past fifty years? What changes in the social, cultural, and economic situation have influenced the use of the language? What other languages are in use with this group of people? What attempts, if any, are people making to protect or revive the language? Consider using photographs, maps, video, and audio clips in your presentation.

Selected Bibliography

American FactFinder. United States Census Bureau. <http://factfinder.census.gov>. [U.S. population data with links to geographic and language information.]

American Languages: Our Nation's Many Voices. U of Wisconsin System Board of Regents. <http://digicoll.library.wisc.edu/AmerLangs/>. [University of Wisconsin search engine with access to digitized audio recordings "documenting linguistic diversity in the United States."]

Baugh, John. *Beyond Ebonics: Linguistic Pride and Racial Prejudice.* Oxford: Oxford UP, 2000. [An interdisciplinary look at the origins and politics of African American language in the wake of the 1996 ruling by the Oakland School Board.]

Bhatia, Tej. *The Handbook of Bilingualism.* Malden, MA: Blackwell, 2004. [Examines the influence of bilingualism on learning processes and on community politics.]

Bilingual Research Journal. 19 (Winter 1995). [Special issue on indigenous language education and literacy focused on the history of and issues in bilingual education since the 1960s.]

Campbell, Lyle. *American Indian Languages: The Historical Linguistics of Native America.* Oxford: Oxford UP, 2000. [An extensive discussion of Native American languages and a lengthy index of languages and language families.]

Cantoni, Gina, ed. *Stabilizing Indigenous Languages.* Flagstaff: Center for Excellence in Education, Northern Arizona U, 1996. [Collection of conference papers, with discussions of policy changes, educational reforms, and community initiatives.]

Carver, Craig. *American English Dialects.* Ann Arbor: U of Michigan P, 1987. [With 2,000 words and phrases, a comprehensive description of the historical and cultural development of American dialects that redefines the boundaries of regional dialects.]

Center for the Study of Upper Midwest Culture. 18 May 2006. U of Wisconsin–Madison. <http://csumc.wisc.edu>. [Web site with live links to information about preservation, celebration, education, and ethnic organizations, among other things.]

Cran, William, and Robert MacNeil. *Do You Speak 'American'?* 2005. Public Broadcasting Services. <www.pbs.org/speak>. [Companion to the PBS television series on American English.]

Crawford, James. *Educating English Learners: Language Diversity in the Classroom.* 5th ed. Los Angeles: Bilingual Educational Services, 2004. [Updated introduction to language-minority education, including a discussion of the No Child Left Behind Act and other policies that impact ESL education.]

"Dialects: African American Vernacular English." 2007. Center for Applied Linguistics. <www.cal.org/ebonics>. [Bibliographic references and links to numerous articles.]

Dictionary of American Regional English (DARE). 9 Jan 2007. U of Wisconsin–Madison. <http://polyglot.lss.wisc.edu/dare/dare.html>. [Updated Web site for *DARE* that allows users to access the dictionary's text and maps, pose questions, take fun dialect quizzes, and listen to audio samples of people from every region of the United States.]

Fillmore, Charles. "Speech at the American Cultures Center." Feb. 1997. 2007. Center for Applied Linguistics. <www.cal.org/topics/dialects/fillmore.html>. [A history of Ebonics and the aftermath of the Oakland School Board decision.]

Finegan, Edward, ed. *Language in the USA: Themes for the Twenty-First Century.* Cambridge: Cambridge UP, 2004. [Essays on varieties of American English in social and cultural contexts.]

Gordon, Matthew. "Phonological Correlates of Ethnic Identity: Evidence of Divergence?" *American Speech* 75.2 (2000), 115–36. [Examines relationships between marked phonological features and ethnic identity.]

Green, Lisa J. *African-American English: A Linguistic Introduction.* Cambridge: Cambridge UP, 2002. [Presents AAE as a language and discusses its representation in secular, religious public contexts.]

Johnson, Ellen. *Lexical Change and Variation in the Southeastern United States, 1930–1990.* Tuscaloosa: U of Alabama P, 1996. [Discussion of language development in the southeastern United States during cultural changes of the twentieth century.]

Labov, William, Sharon Ash, and Charles Boberg. *Altas of North American English.* Linguistics Laboratory, U of Pennsylvania. <www.ling.upenn.edu/phonoaltas>. [Comprehensive language survey of urban United States and Canada, with emphasis on phonological data establishing regional dialect boundaries.]

Lighter, Jonathan E., *Historical Dictionary of American Slang.* Oxford: Oxford UP, 2006. [Covers more than 300 years of American slang with examples from various historical eras and contexts.]

———. *Random House Historical Dictionary of American Slang.* Vols. 1–3. New York: Reference Publications, 1997–2002. [Catalogs slang in both canonical literature and popular culture, from Shakespeare to Seuss.]

Linguistic Atlas Projects. 2005. U of Georgia. <www.lap.uga.edu>. [Provides access to the various atlas projects that study dialects of English as spoken in the United States.]

Linguistic Society of America. Linguistics Society of America. <www.lsadc.org>. [Links to the publications *LSA Bulletin, Language,* and *e-language,* along with student resources and information about meetings.]

The Linguist List. 18 Apr 2007. Eastern Michigan U and Wayne State U. <www.linguistlist.org>. [Language discussion list with a comprehensive menu of relevant events, archives of academic language communities, and information on jobs and conferences.]

Lippi-Green, Rosina. *English with an Accent: Language, Ideology and Discrimination in the United States.* Oxford: Routledge, 1997. [An examination of American attitudes toward language differences and the discrimination and stigmatization resulting from these.]

Macaulay, Ronald K. S. *The Social Art: Language and Its Users.* Oxford: Oxford UP, 1994. [Provides insight into conversation, advertising, notions of standard language, and other relevant topics.]

McGoff, Michael F. *American Name Society.* State U of New York at Binghamton. <www.wtsn.binghamton.edu/ANS/>. [Scholarly society devoted to the study of naming practices plus links to *NAMES: The Journal of Onomastics.*]

Mithun, Marianne. *The Languages of Native North America.* Cambridge: Cambridge UP, 2001. [Considers genetic and geographic differences among Native American language families and individual characteristics.]

Mufwene, Salikoko. "African American English." *The Cambridge History of the English Language.* Vol. 6. Cambridge: Cambridge UP 2001. [Discusses current research in AAE, with essays by noted scholars on topics such as the Oakland School Board controversy and the language of rap music.]

Mufwene, Salikoko, John Rickford, Guy Bailey, and John Baugh. *African-American English: Structure, History and Use.* Oxford: Routledge, 1998. [Examines grammatical and social issues of AAE, providing a chapter on educational reform for minority students.]

Murray, Thomas E., and Beth Lee Simon. *Language Variation and Change in the American Midland.* Amsterdam: John Benjamins, 2006. (Varieties of English around the World Ser.) [A collection of essays by sociolinguists discussing significant language issues and changes associated with the Midwest variety of American English; with maps and data.]

Nichols, Joanna. *Linguistic Diversity in Space and Time.* Chicago: U of Chicago P, 1999. [Examines the impact of genetics and geography on language, voice systems, and structural features.]

North Carolina Language and Life Project. Linguistics Department, NC State U. <www.ncsu.edu/linguistics/code/Research%20Sites/ncllp2.htm>. [Links to NCLLP research sites, audio recordings, and maps.]

Oxford Dictionary of Modern Slang. New York: Oxford UP, USA. 2005. [Focuses on twentieth-century slang throughout the English-speaking world.]

Pederson, Lee. "Regional Patterns of American English." 2005. *Bartleby.com: Great Books Online.* Ed. Steven van Leeuwen. 2006 <www.bartleby.com/61/5.html>. [Originally appearing in *American Heritage Dictionary of English*, 4th ed.; historical development of major American regional dialects.]

Perry, Theresa, and Lisa Delpit. *The Real Ebonics Debate.* Ypsilanti, MI: Beacon 1998. [Discusses the reality and perceptions of Ebonics and how media misrepresentations have informed public opinion about its legitimacy.]

Poplack, Shana. *The English History of African American English.* Malden, MA: Blackwell, 1999. [Explores AAE as a hybrid of multiple early varieties of English rather than as a derivative of plantation creole.]

Redd, Teresa M., and Karen Schuster Webb. *A Teacher's Introduction of African American English: What a Writing Teacher Should Know.* Urbana, IL: National Council of Teachers of English, 2005. [A guide to AAE and to teaching writing skills for mainstream expectations.]

Rickford, John. "The Ebonics Controversy in My Backyard: A Sociolinguist's Experiences and Reflections." *John Rickford's Writings on the "Ebonics" Issue.* Stanford U. <www.stanford.edu/~rickford/ebonics>. [Rickford's essay about his attempts to provide a linguist's view of the Oakland Resolution on Ebonics; available with his other writings on AAVE at his Web site.]

———. "Variation and Change in Our Living Language." 2005. *Bartleby.com: Great Books Online.* Ed. Steven van Leeuwen. <www.bartleby.com/61/6.html>. [First appearing in *American Heritage Dictionary of English*, 4th ed., this discusses the dichotomy of "standard language" in the face of constant change and persistent dynamism in all languages that survive and thrive.]

Schneider, Edgar. *Focus on USA.* Amsterdam: John Benjamins, 1996. (Varieties of English around the World General Ser.) [A collection of essays on variation in American English, including "American College Slang."]

Slobin, Dan I., Julie Gerhardt, Amy Kyratzis, Jiansheng Guo, and Susan Ervin-Tripp. *Social Interaction, Social Context, and Language: Essays in Honor of Susan Ervin-Tripp.* Mahwah, NJ: Lawrence Erlbaum Associates, 1996. [Examines a wide range of historical and contemporary topics, such as language acquisition, bilingualism, and narrative discourse.]

Spears, Richard. *McGraw-Hill's Dictionary of American Idioms and Phrasal Verbs.* New York: McGraw-Hill, 2006. [Comprehensive guide with discussion of issues like sexist language, bilingual education, and child language acquisition.]

Teaching Indigenous Languages. 2007. Northern Arizona U. <http://jan.ucc.nau.edu/%7Ejar/TIL.html>. [Provides links to more than 100 full-text papers from Stabilizing Indigenous Languages Conferences, 1997–2003, and related topics.]

Varieties of English. 2001. Language Samples Project, Arizona U. <www.ic.arizona.edu/~lsp/index.html>. [Provides background on various forms of English and includes related exercises.]

Washington, Dorothy Ann. *Ebonics: A Selected Bibliography.* Purdue U. <www.purdue.edu/bcc/library/ebonics.htm>. [Provides dozens of sources for such topics as politics, education, mathematics, sciences, media, and slang.]

Wolfram, Walt, and Natalie Schilling-Estes. *American English.* 2nd ed. Malden MA: Blackwell, 2006. [Examines regional differences in language, contrasts rural and urban dialects, and explores differences in minority dialects like Cajun, Latino, and Native American.]

Wolfram, Walt, and Erik Thomas. *The Development of African American English.* Malden, MA: Blackwell, 2002. [Focusing on a biracial coastal community in North Carolina, this book examines the history and future of AAE.]

Wolfram, Walt, and Ben Ward, eds. *American Voices: How Dialects Differ from Coast to Coast.* Malden, MA: Blackwell, 2005. [Focuses on dialects in the North, South, and Midwest regions of the United States and on settlement of groups that populate those regions.]

LANGUAGE AND CULTURE

Beginning in the twentieth century, many scholars have looked at language as a key to understanding culture and society. In Part Seven, we examine how language shapes belief systems and patterns of thinking and how culture is, in fundamental ways, a product of language.

In the opening essay, "Pidgins and Creoles," David Crystal discusses the dynamics of what may happen when people who share no common language must communicate with each other. In some situations, a simplified language called a *pidgin* develops so that people can conduct trade or business or talk for other reasons. Because speakers use a pidgin for specific purposes, they are not, at first, likely to acquire it at home, but when a pidgin is passed on to the next generation of users, it then becomes a *creole*. As Crystal explains, "a creole is a pidgin language which has become the mother tongue of a community—a definition which emphasizes that pidgins and creoles are two stages in a single process of linguistic development."

In the second selection, "Metaphors We Live By," George Lakoff and Mark Johnson examine the relationship between fundamental cultural concepts such as time, space, and action and the metaphors we use that encode these concepts. Johnson and Lakoff are interested in the connections among language, cognition, and meaning and in how we use metaphor to express our understanding of the world in language. For instance, in English, we commonly express the concept of time as a commodity that can be saved, lost, or wasted. In fact, this metaphor is so ingrained in our culture we do not even notice how it shapes and restricts our experience of the world.

Nicholas Evans's essay, "A Myth: Aborigines Speak a Primitive Language," contests the notion that the Aboriginal languages of Australia have no grammar, use minimal vocabularies, and are inadequate for dealing with the contemporary world. With numerous examples from these languages, Evans demonstrates that Aboriginal languages are indeed complex and able to adapt to a changing universe. He leads us to believe that no such thing as a primitive language may exist.

In "Rearing Bilingual Children in a Monolingual Culture: A Louisiana Experience," Stephen J. Caldas and Suzanne Caron-Caldas face head-on the challenges posed by both the hazards of bilingual education and the desire to preserve and perpetuate a valued culture. To raise children who are fluent in both French and English, they call on the resources of a proud but perhaps dying heritage in their Louisiana community and on the wisdom of linguistic scholarship.

In the last two essays, Nancy Lord and Laura Bohannan describe what happened when they chose to immerse themselves in cultures and languages other than their own. When Lord moved to Alaska, she was delighted by the wisdom and humor of the words used by the local Dena'ina tribe; at the same time, she was distressed to learn that Dena'ina was a language on the edge of extinction. Lord is alarmed by the rapid loss of native languages all over the world. When a language disappears, she says in "Native Tongues," the knowledge of place and origin specific to that culture disappears with it.

Laura Bohannan, an anthropologist, lived among the Tiv people of Nigeria for several years to learn their language and customs. When tribal elders, in turn, asked her to share with them one of the great stories of her own culture—*Hamlet*—Bohannan saw this as an opportunity to prove that human nature is universal. What happened when Bohannan tried to tell Shakespeare's story in a different culture forced her to confront her ideas about human nature and the role language plays in building a community.

30

Pidgins and Creoles

David Crystal

In the seventeenth century, a South American trader would have landed on the shores of Africa with wares to trade but no common language for communication. To conduct business, some means of communication had to be developed. The trader would have created a pidgin *language, which incorporates vocabulary elements from two languages and simplifies grammatical forms from one or both languages. Typically used by speakers of two or more languages, pidgins are defined as rudimentary languages with simplified grammars and limited lexicons. Because people do not learn pidgins as native speakers, a pidgin language is called an auxiliary language. In contrast,* creoles, *which develop from pidgins, are learned by native speakers and are considered fully developed languages. In the following selection from the* Cambridge Encyclopedia of Language *(1997), David Crystal, honorary professor at University College of North Wales, examines the differences between pidgin and creole languages and points out that creole languages throughout the world exhibit remarkable structural uniformities.*

PIDGIN LANGUAGES

A pidgin is a system of communication which has grown up among people who do not share a common language, but who want to talk to each other, for trading or other reasons. Pidgins have been variously called "makeshift," "marginal," or "mixed" languages. They have a limited vocabulary, a reduced grammatical structure, and a much narrower range of functions, compared to the languages which gave rise to them. They are the native language of no one, but they are nonetheless a main means of communication for millions of people, and a major focus of interest to those who study the way languages change.

It is essential to avoid the stereotype of a pidgin language, as perpetrated over the years in generations of children's comics and films. The "Me Tarzan, you Jane" image is far from the reality. A pidgin is not a language which has broken down; nor is it the result of baby talk, laziness, corruption, primitive thought processes, or mental deficiency. On the contrary, pidgins are demonstrably creative adaptations of natural languages, with a structure and rules of their own. Along with creoles, they are

451

evidence of a fundamental process of linguistic change, as languages come into contact with each other, producing new varieties whose structures and uses contract and expand. They provide the clearest evidence of language being created and shaped by society for its own ends, as people adapt to new social circumstances. This emphasis on processes of change is reflected in the terms *pidginization* and *creolization*.

Most pidgins are based on European languages—English, French, Spanish, Dutch, and Portuguese—reflecting the history of colonialism. However, this observation may be the result only of our ignorance of the languages used in parts of Africa, South America, or Southeast Asia, where situations of language contact are frequent. One of the best-known non-European pidgins is Chinook Jargon, once used for trading by American Indians in northwest U.S.A. Another is Sango, a pidginized variety of Ngbandi, spoken widely in west-central Africa.

Because of their limited function, pidgin languages usually do not last for very long—sometimes for only a few years, and rarely for more than a century. They die when the original reason for communication diminishes or disappears, as communities move apart, or one community learns the language of the other. (Alternatively, the pidgin may develop into a creole.) The pidgin French which was used in Vietnam all but disappeared when the French left; similarly, the pidgin English which appeared during the American Vietnam campaign virtually disappeared as soon as the war was over. But there are exceptions. The pidgin known as Mediterranean Lingua Franca, or Sabir, began in the Middle Ages and lasted until the twentieth century.

Some pidgins have become so useful as a means of communication between languages that they have developed a more formal role, as regular auxiliary languages. They may even be given official status by a community, as lingua francas. These cases are known as *expanded pidgins*, because of the way in which they have added extra forms to cope with the needs of their users, and have come to be used in a much wider range of situations than previously. In time, these languages may come to be used on the radio, in the press, and may even develop a literature of their own. Some of the most widely used expanded pidgins are Krio (in Sierra Leone), Nigerian Pidgin English, and Bislama (in Vanuatu). In Papua New Guinea, the local pidgin (Tok Pisin) is the most widely used language in the country.

CREOLE LANGUAGES

A creole is a pidgin language which has become the mother tongue of a community—a definition which emphasizes that pidgins and creoles are two stages in a single process of linguistic development. First, within a community, increasing numbers of people begin to use pidgin as their principal means of communication. As a consequence, their children hear it more than any other language, and gradually it takes on the status of a mother tongue for them. Within a generation or two, native language use becomes consolidated and widespread. The result is a creole, or "creolized" language.

The switch from pidgin to creole involves a major expansion in the structural linguistic resources available—especially in vocabulary, grammar, and style, which now have to cope with the everyday demands made upon a mother tongue by its speakers. There is also a highly significant shift in the overall patterns of language use found in the community. Pidgins are by their nature auxiliary languages, learned alongside vernacular languages which are much more developed in structure and use. Creoles, by contrast, are vernaculars in their own right. When a creole language develops, it is usually at the expense of other languages spoken in the area. But then it too can come under attack.

The main source of conflict is likely to be with the standard form of the language from which it derives, and with which it usually coexists. The standard language has the status which comes with social prestige, education, and wealth; the creole has no such status, its roots lying in a history of subservience and slavery. Inevitably, creole speakers find themselves under great pressure to change their speech in the direction of the standard—a process known as *decreolization*.

One consequence of this is the emergence of a continuum of several varieties of creole speech, at varying degrees of linguistic "distance" from the standard—what has been called the *post-creole continuum*. Another consequence is an aggressive reaction against the standard language on the part of creole speakers, who assert the superior status of their creole, and the need to recognize the ethnic identity of their community. Such a reaction can lead to a marked change in speech habits, as the speakers focus on what they see to be the "pure" form of creole—a process known as *hypercreolization*. This whole movement, from creolization to decreolization to hypercreolization, can be seen at work in the recent history of Black English in the U.S.A.

The term *creole* comes from Portuguese *crioulo*, and originally meant a person of European descent who had been born and brought up in a colonial territory. Later, it came to be applied to other people who were native to these areas, and then to the kind of language they spoke. Creoles are now usually classified as "English based," "French based," and so on—though the genetic relationship of a creole to its dominant linguistic ancestor is never straightforward, as the creole may display the influences of several contact languages in its sounds, vocabulary, and structure.

Today, the study of creole languages, and of the pidgins which gave rise to them, attracts considerable interest among linguists and social historians. To the former, the cycle of linguistic reduction and expansion which they demonstrate, within such a short time-scale, provides fascinating evidence of the nature of language change. To the latter, their

TABLE 30.1

FRENCH	GUYANESE CRÉOLE	KRIO	ENGLISH
Mangez	Mãʒe	Chɔp	Eat
J'ai mangé	Mo mãʒe	A chɔp	I ate
Il/Elle a mangé	Li mãʒe	I chɔp	He/She ate
Je mange/Je suis en train de manger	Mo ka mãʒe	A de chɔp	I am eating
J'avais mangé	Mo te mãʒe	A bin chɔp	I ate/had eaten
Je mangeais	Mo te ka mãʒe	A bin de chɔp	I was eating
Je mangerai	Mo ke mãʒe	A go chɔp	I shall eat
Il/Elle est plus grand que vous	Li gros pas u	I big pa yu	He/She/It is bigger than you

development is seen to reflect the process of exploration, trade, and conquest which has played such a major part in European history over the past 400 years.

WHERE DO PIDGINS AND CREOLES COME FROM?

The world's pidgins and creoles display many obvious differences in sounds, grammar, and vocabulary, but they have a remarkable amount in common. Two opposed theories have attempted to explain these differences.

Many Sources?

A long-standing view is that every creole is a unique, independent development, the product of a fortuitous contact between two languages. On the surface, this polygenetic view is quite plausible. It seems unlikely that the pidgins which developed in Southeast Asia should have anything in common with those which developed in the Caribbean. And it is a general experience that these varieties come into use in an apparently spontaneous way—as any tourist knows who has faced a souvenir seller. Would not the restricted features of the contact situations (such as the basic sentence patterns and vocabulary needed in order to trade) be enough to explain the linguistic similarities around the world?

The view is tempting, but there are several grounds for criticism. In particular, it does not explain the *extent* of the similarities between these varieties. Common features such as the reduction of noun and pronoun inflections, the use of particles to replace tenses, and the use of repeated forms to intensify adjectives and adverbs are too great to be the result of coincidence. Why, then, should the pidginized forms of French, Dutch, German, Italian, and other languages all display the same kind of modifications? Why, for example, should the English-based creoles of the Caribbean have so much in common with the Spanish-based creoles of the Philippines? How could uniformity come from such diversity?

One Source?

The opposite view argues that the similarities between the world's pidgins and creoles can be explained only by postulating that they had a common origin (i.e., are monogenetic), notwithstanding the distance which exists between them. Moreover, a clear candidate for a "protolanguage" has been found—a fifteenth-century Portuguese pidgin, which may in turn have descended from the Mediterranean lingua franca known as Sabir. The Portuguese are thought to have used this pidgin during their explorations in Africa, Asia, and the Americas. Later, it is argued, as other nations came to these areas, the simple grammar of this pidgin came to be retained, but the original Portuguese vocabulary was replaced by words taken from their own languages. This view is known as the *relexification* hypothesis.

There is a great deal of evidence to support the theory, deriving from historical accounts of the Portuguese explorations, and from modern analyses of the languages. For instance, every English-based pidgin and creole has a few Portuguese words, such as *savi* "know," *pikin* "child," and *palava* "trouble." In Saramaccan, an English-based creole of Suriname, 38% of the core vocabulary is from Portuguese. Early accounts of Chinese pidgin refer to a mixed dialect of English and Portuguese. And on general grounds, relexification of a single "proto-pidgin" seems a more plausible hypothesis than one which insists on a radical parallel restructuring of several languages.

The shift in approach, implicit in the relexification theory, is fundamental: it is not the case that English, and the other languages, were creolized, but that an original (Portuguese) creole was anglicized. However, not all the facts can be explained in this way. Pitcairnese creole has no Portuguese influence, and yet has much in common with other varieties. What accounts for those similarities? Then there are several pidgins and creoles which have developed with little or no historical contact with European languages—Sango and Chinook, for instance. And there seem to be many structural differences between European and non-European pidgins and creoles, which the common origin hypothesis finds difficult to explain.

The evidence is mixed. Disentangling the structural similarities and differences between these varieties is a difficult task, and the evidence could be taken to support either a monogenetic or a polygenetic theory. Far more descriptive studies are needed before we rule out one view or the other.

Table 30.2　Pidgins Compared

ENGLISH	TOK PISIN	CHINESE PIDGIN	SANGO	CHINOOK JARGON
bell	bɛl	bell	ngbéréná	tíntin
big	bɪgfɛlə	big	kótá	hyás
bird	pɪǧɪn	bird(ee)	ndɛkɛ	kalákala
bite	kajkajɪm	bitee	tɛ	múckamuck
black	blækfɛlə	black	(zo)vɔkɔ	klale
blood	blʊt	blood	méné	pilpil
cold	kilfɛlə	colo	dé	cole, tshis
come	kəm	li	ga	chahko
die	daj	dielo	kúi	mémaloost
dog	dɔg	doggee	mbo	kámooks
drink	drɪŋk	dlinkee, haw	yç	muckamuck
ear	ir	ear	mé	kwolánn
earth	grawn	glound	sése	illahie
eat	kajkaj	chowchow	kóbe, tɛ	múckamuck
fat	gris	fat, glease	mafuta	glease
feather	gras bɪlɔŋ pɪǧɪn	fedder	kɔá tí ndɛkɛ	kalákala yaka túpso
fish	fiš	fishee	susu	pish
give	gɪvɪm	pay	fú	pótlatch
green	grinfɛlə	gleen, lu	vɔkɔ kété	pechúgh
hair	gras bɪlɔŋ hɛd	hair	kɔá	yákso
hand	hæn	hand, sho	mabɔkɔ	le mah
head	hɛd	headee	li	la tet
heart	klak	heart	coeur	túmtum
know	save	savvy	hínga	kumtuks
man	mæn	man	kɔlǐ	man
no	no	na	non	wake
nose	nos	peedza	hɔ	nose
one	wənfɛlə	one piecee	ɔkɔ	ikt
small	lɪklɪk	likki	kété	ténas
sun	sən	sun	lá	sun, ótelagh
talk	tɔk	talkee	tɛnɛ	wáuwau
two	tufɛlə	two	óse	mokst
warm	hɔtfɛlə	warm	wá	waum

Lexical similarities and differences between pidgins are clearly illustrated in this list of items collected by F. G. Cassidy in the 1960s, taken from the set of "basic words" used in glotto-chronology. The English element predominates in Tok Pisin and Chinese Pidgin; in Sango, the vast majority of the words are African; in Chinook, most words are from Chinook or other Amerindian languages (but note the influence of both French and English). French names for parts of the body have emerged in Sango and Chinook. Though there is no historical connection between the languages, note also the coincidences of thought which have produced the figurative phrases for feather (grass-of-bird [Tok Pisin], hair-of-bird [Sango], and leaf-of-bird [Chinook]), and the words for heart in Tok Pisin and Chinook, both of which stress the notion of heartbeat.

Meanwhile, other theories have been proposed, in an attempt to explain these similarities and differences. Other forms of simplified speech have been noted, such as those used by children, in telegrams and headlines, and in talking to foreigners. It is possible that the processes underlying pidgins and creoles reflect certain basic preferences in human language (such as fixed word order, or the avoidance of inflections). In this connection, these languages provide fresh and intriguing evidence in the search for linguistic universals.

≡

FOR DISCUSSION AND REVIEW

1. How does Crystal define pidgins and creoles?
2. What misconceptions surround the study of pidgins?
3. How do pidgins develop? Why is it likely that a pidgin would become extinct?
4. What does Crystal mean by "expanded pidgins"? At what point do pidgins become expanded?
5. How do creoles develop? What does Crystal mean when he says that a language becomes "creolized"? How might a creole language come into conflict with other forms of language?
6. Crystal claims that Black English or African American English shows *creolization, decreolization,* and *hypercreolization.* What do these terms mean?
7. Crystal's isn't the only view on the recent history of African American English. How might John Rickford and the other linguists included in Part Six explain the development of African American English?
8. Crystal says, "The world's pidgins and creoles display many obvious differences in sounds, grammar, and vocabulary, but they have a remarkable amount in common." What are two opposing theories that attempt to explain these differences? Which theory do you favor? Why?
9. According to some linguists, a relexification process may occur in pidgin languages. Describe that process.
10. Why is it important to study both pidgins and creoles? What is their value in the ongoing study of language?

31

Metaphors We Live By

George Lakoff and Mark Johnson

George Lakoff is a professor of linguistics at the University of California, Berkeley, and a Senior Fellow at the Rockridge Institute. He worked with Mark Johnson, a professor of philosophy at the University of Oregon, in examining how language, cognition, and meaning are interrelated. In Metaphors We Live By *(1980), from which this selection is taken, they argue that metaphor is at the heart of language and consequently at the heart of how we understand our world. According to Lakoff and Johnson, metaphor is not a poetic device we use occasionally but is "pervasive in everyday life." In this selection, the authors offer examples to show the importance of metaphor to language and our perception of the world. As Lakoff and Johnson put it elsewhere in their book, "Metaphor is as much a part of our functioning as our sense of touch, and as precious."*

CONCEPTS WE LIVE BY

Metaphor is for most people a device of the poetic imagination and the rhetorical flourish—a matter of extraordinary rather than ordinary language. Moreover, metaphor is typically viewed as characteristic of language alone, a matter of words rather than thought or action. For this reason, most people think they can get along perfectly well without metaphor. We have found, on the contrary, that metaphor is pervasive in everyday life, not just in language but in thought and action. Our ordinary conceptual system, in terms of which we both think and act, is fundamentally metaphorical in nature.

The concepts that govern our thought are not just matters of the intellect. They also govern our everyday functioning, down to the most mundane details. Our concepts structure what we perceive, how we get around in the world, and how we relate to other people. Our conceptual system thus plays a central role in defining our everyday realities. If we are right in suggesting that our conceptual system is largely metaphorical, then the way we think, what we experience, and what we do every day is very much a matter of metaphor.

But our conceptual system is not something we are normally aware of. In most of the little things we do every day, we simply think and act more or less automatically along certain lines. Just what these lines are is by no means obvious. One way to find out is by looking at language. Since communication is based on the same conceptual system that we use in thinking and acting, language is an important source of evidence for what that system is like.

Primarily on the basis of linguistic evidence, we have found that most of our ordinary conceptual system is metaphorical in nature. And we have found a way to begin to identify in detail just what the metaphors are that structure how we perceive, how we think, and what we do.

To give some idea of what it could mean for a concept to be metaphorical and for such a concept to structure an everyday activity, let us start with the concept ARGUMENT and the conceptual metaphor ARGUMENT IS WAR. This metaphor is reflected in our everyday language by a wide variety of expressions:

ARGUMENT IS WAR

Your claims are *indefensible.*

He *attacked every weak point* in my argument.

His criticisms were *right on target.*

I *demolished* his argument.

I've never *won* an argument with him.

You disagree? Okay, *shoot!*

If you use that *strategy,* he'll *wipe you out.*

He *shot down* all of my arguments.

It is important to see that we don't just *talk* about arguments in terms of war. We can actually win or lose arguments. We see the person we are arguing with as an opponent. We attack his positions and we defend our own. We gain and lose ground. We plan and use strategies. If we find a position indefensible, we can abandon it and take a new line of attack. Many of the things we *do* in arguing are partially structured by the concept of war. Though there is no physical battle, there is a verbal battle, and the structure of an argument—attack, defense, counterattack, etc.—reflects this. It is in this sense that the ARGUMENT IS WAR metaphor is one that we live by in this culture; it structures the actions we perform in arguing.

Try to imagine a culture where arguments are not viewed in terms of war, where no one wins or loses, where there is no sense of attacking or defending, gaining or losing ground. Imagine a culture where an argument is viewed as a dance, the participants are seen as performers, and the goal is to perform in a balanced and aesthetically pleasing way. In such a culture, people would view arguments differently, experience them differently, carry them out differently, and talk about them differently. But *we* would probably not view them as arguing at all: they would simply be doing something different. It would seem strange even to call what they were doing "arguing." Perhaps the most neutral way of describing this difference between their culture and ours would be to say that we have a discourse form structured in terms of battle and they have one structured in terms of dance.

This is an example of what it means for a metaphorical concept, namely, ARGUMENT IS WAR, to structure (at least in part) what we do and how we understand what we are doing when we argue. *The essence of metaphor is understanding and experiencing one kind of thing in terms of another.* It is not that arguments are a subspecies of war. Arguments and wars are different kinds of things—verbal discourse and armed conflict—and the actions performed are different kinds of actions. But ARGUMENT is partially structured, understood, performed, and talked about in terms of WAR. The concept is metaphorically structured, the activity is metaphorically structured, and, consequently, the language is metaphorically structured.

Moreover, this is the *ordinary* way of having an argument and talking about one. The normal way for us to talk about attacking a position is to use the words "attack a position." Our conventional ways of talking about arguments presuppose a metaphor we are hardly ever conscious of. The metaphor is not merely in the words we use—it is in our very concept of an argument. The language of argument is not poetic, fanciful, or rhetorical; it is literal. We talk about arguments that way because we conceive of them that way—and we act according to the way we conceive of things.

The most important claim we have made so far is that metaphor is not just a matter of language, that is, of mere words. We shall argue that, on the contrary, human *thought processes* are largely metaphorical. This is what we mean when we say that the human conceptual system is metaphorically structured and defined. Metaphors as linguistic expressions are possible precisely because there are metaphors in a person's conceptual system. Therefore, whenever . . . we speak of metaphors, such as ARGUMENT IS WAR, it should be understood that *metaphor* means *metaphorical concept.*

THE SYSTEMATICITY OF
METAPHORICAL CONCEPTS

Arguments usually follow patterns; that is, there are certain things we typically do and do not do in arguing. The fact that we in part conceptualize arguments in terms of battle systematically influences the shape arguments take and the way we talk about what we do in arguing. Because the metaphorical concept is systematic, the language we use to talk about that aspect of the concept is systematic.

We saw in the ARGUMENT IS WAR metaphor that expressions from the vocabulary of war, e.g., *attack a position, indefensible, strategy, new line of attack*, *win*, *gain ground*, etc., form a systematic way of talking about the battling aspects of arguing. It is no accident that these expressions mean what they mean when we use them to talk about arguments. A portion of the conceptual network of battle partially characterizes the concept of an argument, and the language follows suit. Since metaphorical expressions in our language are tied to metaphorical concepts in a systematic way, we can use metaphorical linguistic expressions to study the nature of metaphorical concepts and to gain an understanding of the metaphorical nature of our activities.

To get an idea of how metaphorical expressions in everyday language can give us insight into the metaphorical nature of the concepts that structure our everyday activities, let us consider the metaphorical concept TIME IS MONEY as it is reflected in contemporary English.

TIME IS MONEY

You're *wasting* my time.

This gadget will *save* you hours.

I don't *have* the time to *give* you.

How do you *spend* your time these days?

That flat tire *cost* me an hour.

I've *invested* a lot of time in her.

I don't *have enough* time to *spare* for that.

You're *running out* of time.

You need to *budget* your time.

Put aside some time for ping pong.

Is that *worth your while*?

Do you *have* much time *left*?

He's living on *borrowed* time.

You don't *use* your time *profitably*.

I *lost* a lot of time when I got sick.

Thank you for your time.

Time in our culture is a valuable commodity. It is a limited resource that we use to accomplish our goals. Because of the way that the concept of work has developed in modern Western culture, where work is typically associated with the time it takes and time is precisely quantified, it has become customary to pay people by the hour, week, or year. In our culture TIME IS MONEY in many ways: telephone message units, hourly wages, hotel room rates, yearly budgets, interest on loans, and paying your debt to society by "serving time." These practices are relatively new in the history of the human race, and by no means do they exist in all cultures. They have arisen in modern industrialized societies and structure our basic everyday activities in a very profound way. Corresponding to the fact that we *act* as if time is a valuable commodity—a limited resource, even money—we *conceive of* time that way. Thus we understand and experience time as the kind of thing that can be spent, wasted, budgeted, invested wisely or poorly, saved, or squandered.

TIME IS MONEY, TIME IS A LIMITED RESOURCE, and TIME IS A VALUABLE COMMODITY are all metaphorical concepts. They are metaphorical since we are using our everyday experiences with money, limited resources, and valuable commodities to conceptualize time. This isn't a necessary way for human beings to conceptualize time; it is tied to our culture. There are cultures where time is none of these things.

The metaphorical concepts TIME IS MONEY, TIME IS A RESOURCE, and TIME IS A VALUABLE COMMODITY form a single system based on subcategorization, since in our society money is a limited resource and limited resources are valuable commodities. These subcategorization relationships characterize entailment relationships between the metaphors. TIME IS MONEY entails that TIME IS A LIMITED RESOURCE, which entails that TIME IS A VALUABLE COMMODITY.

We are adopting the practice of using the most specific metaphorical concept, in this case TIME IS MONEY, to characterize the entire system. Of the expressions listed under the TIME IS MONEY metaphor, some refer specifically to money (*spend, invest, budget, profitably, cost*), others to limited resources (*use, use up, have enough of, run out of*), and still others to valuable commodities (*have, give, lose, thank you for*). This is an example of the way in which metaphorical entailments can characterize a coherent system of metaphorical concepts and a corresponding coherent system of metaphorical expressions for those concepts.

METAPHORICAL SYSTEMATICITY: HIGHLIGHTING AND HIDING

The very systematicity that allows us to comprehend one aspect of a concept in terms of another (e.g., comprehending an aspect of arguing in terms of battle) will necessarily hide other aspects of the concept. In allowing us to focus on one aspect of a concept (e.g., the battling aspects of arguing), a metaphorical concept can keep us from focusing on other aspects of the concept that are inconsistent with that metaphor. For example, in the midst of a heated argument, when we are intent on attacking our opponent's position and defending our own, we may lose sight of the cooperative aspects of arguing. Someone who is arguing with you can be viewed as giving you his time, a valuable commodity, in an effort at mutual understanding. But when we are preoccupied with the battle aspects, we often lose sight of the cooperative aspects.

A far more subtle case of how a metaphorical concept can hide an aspect of our experience can be seen in what Michael Reddy has called the "conduit metaphor." Reddy observes that our language about language is structured roughly by the following complex metaphor:

Ideas (or meanings) are objects.

Linguistic expressions are containers.

Communication is sending.

The speaker puts ideas (objects) into words (containers) and sends them (along a conduit) to a hearer who takes the idea/objects out of the word/containers. Reddy documents this with more than a hundred types of expressions in English, which he estimates account for at least 70 percent of the expressions we use for talking about language. Here are some examples:

The CONDUIT Metaphor

It's hard to *get* that idea *across to* him.

I *gave* you that idea.

Your reasons *came through* to us.

It's difficult to *put* my ideas *into* words.

When you *have* a good idea, try to *capture* it immediately *in* words.

Try to *pack* more thought *into* fewer words.

You can't simply *stuff* ideas *into* a sentence any old way.

The meaning is right there *in* the words.

Don't *force* your meanings *into* the wrong words.

His words *carry* little meaning.

The introduction *has* a great deal of thought *content.*

Your words seem *hollow.*

The sentence is *without* meaning.

The idea is *buried in* terribly dense paragraphs.

In examples like these it is far more difficult to see that there is anything hidden by the metaphor or even to see that there is a metaphor here at all. This is so much the conventional way of thinking about language that it is sometimes hard to imagine that it might not fit reality. But if we look at what the CONDUIT metaphor entails, we can see some of the ways in which it masks aspects of the communicative process.

First, the LINGUISTIC EXPRESSIONS ARE CONTAINERS FOR MEANINGS aspect of the CONDUIT metaphor entails that words and sentences have meanings in themselves, independent of any context or speaker. The MEANINGS ARE OBJECTS part of the metaphor, for example, entails that meanings have an existence independent of people and contexts. The part of the metaphor that says LINGUISTIC EXPRESSIONS ARE CONTAINERS FOR MEANING entails that words (and sentences) have meanings, again independent of contexts and speakers. These metaphors are appropriate in many situations—those where context differences don't matter and where all the participants in the conversation understand the sentences in the same way. These two entailments are exemplified by sentences like

The meaning is *right there in* the words,

which, according to the CONDUIT metaphor, can correctly be said of any sentence. But there are many cases where context does matter. Here is a celebrated one recorded in actual conversation by Pamela Downing:

Please sit in the apple-juice seat.

In isolation this sentence has no meaning at all, since the expression "apple-juice seat" is not a conventional way of referring to any kind of object. But the sentence makes perfect sense in the context in which it was uttered. An overnight guest came down to breakfast. There were four place settings, three with orange juice and one with apple juice. It was clear what the apple-juice seat was. And even the next morning, when there was no apple juice, it was still clear which seat was the apple-juice seat.

In addition to sentences that have no meaning without context, there are cases where a single sentence will mean different things to different people. Consider:

We need new alternative sources of energy.

This means something very different to the president of Mobil Oil from what it means to the president of Friends of the Earth. The meaning is not right there is the sentence—it matters a lot who is saying or listening to the sentence and what his social and political attitudes are. The CONDUIT metaphor does not fit cases where context is required to determine whether the sentence has any meaning at all and, if so, what meaning it has.

These examples show that the metaphorical concepts we have looked at provide us with a partial understanding of what communication, argument, and time are and that, in doing this, they hide other aspects of these concepts. It is important to see that the metaphorical structuring involved here is partial, not total. If it were total, one concept would actually *be* the other, not merely be understood in terms of it. For example, time isn't really money. If you *spend your time* trying to do something and it doesn't work, you can't get your time back. There are no time banks. I can *give you a lot of time*, but you can't give me back the same time, though you can *give me back the same amount of time*. And so on. Thus, part of a metaphorical concept does not and cannot fit.

On the other hand, metaphorical concepts can be extended beyond the range of ordinary literal ways of thinking and talking into the range of what is called figurative, poetic, colorful, or fanciful thought and language. Thus, if ideas are objects, we can *dress them up in fancy clothes, juggle them, line them up nice and neat,* etc. So when we say that a concept is structured by a metaphor, we mean that it is partially structured and that it can be extended in some ways but not others.

FOR DISCUSSION AND REVIEW

1. Lakoff and Johnson claim that "our concepts structure what we perceive, how we get around in the world, and how we relate to other people." Do you find this to be true? What kind of evidence do they give to prove this claim? Try to create some counterexamples to this claim.

2. The authors claim that our everyday language is full of the metaphors expressing our most basic concepts. Explain this idea in terms of their first example, *argument is war.* In what other ways can you think of argument? Are they metaphors? Is it possible to think of argument without metaphor? Why, or why not?

3. Using an original example, explain the authors' statement that "the essence of metaphor is understanding and experiencing one kind of thing in terms of another."

4. According to Lakoff and Johnson, we talk about a concept in a certain way because we think about it that way. What is the relationship among metaphoric expression, thought, and action? How is this relationship revealed in the metaphoric concept *time is money?*

5. What might happen if you try to change a particular metaphor? We think of sadness or depression in terms of color (blue) or direction (down), but could we use different metaphors for these concepts in our culture? Why, or why not?

6. Lakoff and Johnson say that comprehending "one aspect of a concept in terms of another . . . will necessarily hide other aspects of the concept." Using an example, explain how this works.

7. In addition to the metaphors mentioned in the selection, what are some other metaphors we live by? How do these metaphors influence how you understand and use the concept(s)?

8. What had been your definition or idea of metaphor before you read this selection? Has it changed? In what ways?

32

A Myth: Aborigines Speak a Primitive Language

Nicholas Evans

Nicholas Evans, a professor of linguistics at Melbourne University, is an expert on the languages of Aboriginal Australia. He not only researches and writes about these languages, but he has learned a number of them as well. The following selection is from the 1999 anthology Language Myths, *edited by Laurie Bauer and Peter Trudgill. Here Evans refutes the idea that the Aboriginal languages of Australia are primitive. Drawing examples from a variety of these languages, Evans shows that they are grammatically complex; have extensive, finely tuned vocabularies; and are fully adaptable to a changing world. By the end of the selection, he makes us question whether a "primitive" language even exists. As Evans notes, Aboriginal languages extend "our notions of what complex organizing principles can be found in human languages."*

As a linguist who spends much time researching Australian Aboriginal languages, I have often been informed by people I have met in my travels that 'You must have an easy job—it must be pretty simple figuring out the grammar of such a primitive language.' If you go further and ask your travelling companions over a beer or six why they hold this belief, you encounter a number of sub-myths:

There is just one Aboriginal language.

Aboriginal languages have no grammar.

The vocabularies of Aboriginal languages are simple and lack detail; alternatively, they are cluttered with details and unable to deal with abstractions.

Aboriginal languages may be all right in the bush, but they can't deal with the [twenty-first] century.

I'll deal with each of these individually below. . . .

So, you can speak Aborigine?

The first white arrivals in Botany Bay came equipped with an Aboriginal vocabulary recorded by Captain Cook and others in Cooktown, north

Queensland but soon found this was of no more use in communicating with the owners of the Botany Bay region than a Lithuanian phrasebook would be in London: Captain Cook recorded the Guugu Yimidhirr language (giving us the word *kangaroo* in the process), while the language of the Sydney region was Dhaaruk, only distantly related. In fact, Aboriginal Australia displays striking linguistic diversity and, traditionally, around 250 languages, further subdivisable into many dialects, were spoken over the continent. Many Aboriginal communities would prefer to count these dialects as distinct languages. If we did this, we would have to elevate this figure to about 600.

Some languages are, of course, more closely related than others. In Western Arnhem Land, for example, such languages as Mayali and Dalabon are as closely related as English and Dutch, so that 'I will eat fish' is *ngangun djenj* and *ngahnguniyan djenj* respectively. Others, such as Ilgar, are only very distantly related (more distant from Mayali and Dalabon than English is from Bengali, although Mayali and Ilgar are spoken only a couple of hundred kilometres apart), so that 'I will eat fish' in Ilgar is *anyarrun yihab*.

With so many languages spoken by a population of at most three quarters of a million, you can easily work out that the average language would only have a couple of thousand speakers. But, of course, people's social universes were much larger than this. This meant that by adulthood it was normal to be multilingual; this was made easier by the fact that most people married spouses with a different language to their own, so that children grew up speaking both the mother's and the father's languages, as well as other languages their grandparents, for example, may have spoken. For example, my Ilgar teacher, Charlie Wardaga, learned Ilgar from his father, as well as Marrgu from older people in the area he grew up in, Garig and Manangkari from other relatives, Gunwinygu from one grandparent (and he took a Gunwinygu-speaking wife and frequently sings at ceremonial gatherings where Gunwinygu is the common language) and Iwaidja through living in the Minjilang community where it is the dominant language.

There's no grammar—you can just chuck the words together in any order

In the first difficult weeks when I was beginning to learn the Kayardild language of Bentinck Island in Queensland I experienced the usual language-learner's nightmare of failing to understand most of what was said. One of my more considerate teachers, Pluto Bentinck, would help me by repeating each sentence, working his way through all possible orderings of its words: *dangkaa bangaya kurrija, dangkaa kurrija bangaya, bangaya dangkaa kurrija, dangkaa kurrija ngada*, and so on. Given that *dangkaa* means. 'the/a man', *kurrija* 'see(s)', and *bangaa* 'the/a turtle', how could he put the words in any order without changing the meaning from 'the man sees the turtle' to 'the turtle sees the man'?

Speakers of a language like Kayardild have this freedom because the identification of who does what is carried out by so-called case markers on the ends of words: the *-ya* on *bangaya* marks it as the object of the verb and hence the thing seen, while the *-a* on the end of *dangkaa* marks it as the subject and hence the seer. So while it is true that words can be put in any order, it does not indicate lack of grammar—grammar, as a code for expressing meaning, can take many forms in different languages, and here (as in Latin or Russian) the work is done by word endings rather than word ordering.... You should be able to work out for yourself six ways of saying 'the turtle sees the man'; see answer 1 at the end of this [essay].

This system of case endings is so efficient that it allows parts of sentences to be specific in ways that aren't always clear in English. Consider the sentence 'The man saw the turtle on the beach.' Who is on the beach—the man, the turtle or both? Kayardild expresses each of these meanings differently—where it is the turtle on the beach, the 'associative' suffix *-nurru* is added to *ngarn-* 'beach', and the resultant *ngarnnurru* receives a further *-ya* to link it clearly to the object, giving *dangkaa bangaya kurrija ngarnnurruya* (or any other of the 4 × 3 × 2 possible word orderings). If it is the man on the beach, *-nurru* is used again, plus *-wa* to link it with 'man' (*a* cannot directly follow *u*, so a *w* is inserted): *dangkaa bangaya kurrija ngarrnnurruwa*, and the other orderings. And if both are on the beach, a different suffix *-ki* is used, giving *dangkaa bangaya kurrija ngarnki*, and so forth.

Not all grammars of Aboriginal languages work in the same way as Kayardild, of course—any more than English and Russian work in the same way. For example, Mayali from Western Arnhem Land is a 'polysynthetic' language that builds up highly complex verbs able to express a complete sentence, such as *ngabanmarneyawoyhwarrgahganjginjeng* 'I cooked the wrong meat for them again,' which can be broken down into *nga-* 'I', *ban-* 'them', *marne-* 'for', *yawoyh-* 'again', *warrgah-* 'wrongly directed action', *ganj-* 'meat', *ginje-* 'cook' and *-ng* 'past tense'.

Australian Aboriginal pronoun systems are in some ways more explicit than English as well. The main way of showing number in Dalabon from Western Arnhem Land is through the pronoun prefixed to the verb. So we find:

> *biyi*   *kah-boninj*
> man   he-went
> 'The man went.'
>
> *biyi*   *barrah-boninj*
> man   they two-went
> 'The two men went.'
>
> *biyi*   *balah-boninj*
> man   they-went
> 'The men went.'

But that is not all. Another way of saying 'the two men went' would be *biyi keh-boninj*. This would be appropriate if the men were related 'disharmonically'—i.e. in odd-numbered generations, like father and son, or uncle and nephew, e.g. *be-ko keh-boninj* 'they two, father and son, went.' The 'harmonic' form, *barrah-boninj*, is only appropriate for people in even-numbered generations, such as brothers, spouses or grandparents with grandchildren, e.g. *winjkin-ko barrah-boninj* 'they two, grandmother and grandchild, went.'

In a short article like this we can only scratch the surface, but it should be clear by now that Aboriginal grammars have plenty to engage your analytic powers.

Just a few hundred words and you've got it all

However complicated the grammars, surely the vocabularies are pretty simple? After all, there are no words for 'neutron', 'virus' or 'terra nullius', so that's three down already. Assertions like this usually take one of two forms—either the languages are supposed to have a welter of detailed words but be incapable of generalizing, or they are just said to have very general words with too few to be precise. On both counts such sub-myths are wildly wrong.

The fine detail and nuanced observation of Aboriginal vocabularies is so great that I will only have space to consider a few words for the natural world, though one could make similar points with terms for emotions, or smells and fragrances, or ways of moving. Many plant and animal species had distinct names in the Aboriginal languages in whose territories they are found well before they had been recognized as species by Western taxonomic biology. The Oenpelli python, for example, has had the long-established Kunwinjku name *nawaran* but was only identified as a distinct species in the 1960s, whereupon it received the Linnean name *Morelia oenpelliensis*.

To get an idea of the degree of conciseness and detail in the biological vocabulary of a typical Aboriginal language, compare the Kunwinjku kangaroo terms with their English equivalents, in the table . . .

Language Myths

LINNEAN AND ENGLISH NAMES	MALE	FEMALE	CHILD
Macropus antilopinus (antilopine wallaroo)	karndakidj kalaba (large individual male)	karndayh	djamunbuk (juvenile male)
Macropus bernardus (black wallaroo)	nadjinem baark	djukerre	
Macropus robustus (wallaroo)	kalkberd kanbulerri (large male)	wolerrk	narrobad (juvenile male)
Macropus agilis (agile wallaby)	warradjangkal/kornobolo nakurdakurda (very large individual)	merlbbe/ kornobolo	nakornborrh nanjid (baby)

In addition to the various detailed terms just given, Kunwinjku also has a general term, *kunj*, to cover all the macropods, i.e. all kangaroos and wallabies; in English we only have the scientific term *macropod* to denote this category. And in addition to these different nouns, Kunwinjku also has different verbs to describe the different manners of hopping of these various macropods—*kamawudme* for the hopping of male antilopine wallaroo, *kadjalwahme* for the hopping of the corresponding female, *kanjedjme* for the hopping of the wallaroo, *kamurlbardme* for the hopping of the black wallaroo, and *kalurlhlurlme* for the hopping of the agile wallaby. This focus on identifying macropods by the peculiarities of their gait is particularly interesting in the light of recent work on computer vision programs able to identify wallaby species, which had far more success doing this on the basis of their movement than their static appearance.

Quite apart from finely classifying different entities, vocabularies of Aboriginal languages often also show the ecological links between particular plant and animal species. For example, the Mparntwe Arrernte language of the Alice Springs area, where various types of grub are an important source of food, has a method of naming grubs after the bushes where you can find them: *tnyeme* 'witchetty bush' yields the *tnyematye* 'witchetty grub', *utnerrenge* 'emu bush' yields the grub known as *utnerrengatye*, and you can work out for yourself the name of the grub found in *thenge*, the ironwood tree (see answers).

Sometimes there is no term in the ordinary language to cover certain more general categories, but special language varieties learned in adulthood and used under restricted circumstances possess the more abstract terms. The most extreme example of special abstract language is found on Mornington Island, where second-degree initiates, to become full men, had to learn a special initiation language known as Demiin, which had only about 200 words and hence needed to be highly abstract. For example, the complex Lardil pronoun system, where there are nineteen distinct pronouns in the ordinary language, is collapsed to two in Demiin—*n!aa* 'group containing me—i.e. I or we' and *n!uu* 'group not containing me, i.e. you, he, she, they'. (*n!* denotes a 'clicked' *n*-sound, for Demiin also has special sounds not used in the everyday language.)

They might be OK in the bush, but there's no way they can deal with the modern world

Languages tend to have the richest vocabulary in those areas in which their speakers have been interested long enough to develop specialized terms. In the early Middle Ages it was widely believed that only Latin had a sufficiently sophisticated vocabulary to discuss law, theology, medicine and science, but as various nations began to use their mother tongues more widely, each modern European language (English, French, German and so on) soon developed its own terms. Aboriginal languages are at a similar point today—they lack many terms, but their rich grammars give them the capacity to develop them when they are needed. . . .

It is natural that Aboriginal languages should have developed their vocabularies most in such realms as the Australian biota and geography, kinship and so on and not in areas that have not traditionally been a central part of Aboriginal culture—such as financial transactions, nautical terminology or nuclear physics. However, just as English has responded to the encounters between its speakers and the Australian continent by coining new terms, such as the macropod terms we discussed above, so have speakers of Aboriginal languages responded by creating new terms to deal with the proliferation of novel concepts that contact with Europeans and with late-twentieth-century technology more generally, has brought.

Making up a new word from scratch is not a usual method of doing this in any language. Instead, the usual three methods are to build up new words from the existing resources of the language for compounding or affixation (e.g. *downsize* in English), to borrow words from other languages (e.g. *sputnik*) and to extend the meanings of existing words (e.g. *surfing the net*). Each of these methods has been widely employed by Aboriginal languages.

As an example of compounding, Kayardild has created the words *wadubayiinda* for 'tobacco', by compounding *wadu* 'smoke' with the root *bayii-* 'be bitten', literally 'that by means of which the smoke is bitten', and, for 'car', the word *duljawinda*, literally 'ground-runner'.

Many languages have borrowed their words for days and months, higher numbers, government institutions and Western medicine from English. Often the pronunciations of borrowed words are changed to the point where their original source is not recognizable: the English word 'hospital' ends up as *wijipitirli* in Warlpiri.

Extending existing word meanings has been a common solution to the problem of coining new vocabulary for automobiles. In Kunwinjku, for example, *kun-denge* 'foot' also means 'wheel', *kun-rakmo* 'hip' also means 'wheel housing', and the term for 'to get a flat tyre' compounds *kun-rakmo* with the verb *belngdan* 'to settle, as of mud stirred up in water' to give *rakmo-belngdanj* 'it has a flat tyre' (literally 'its hip has settled'). Combinations of compounding and extension of meaning are a common way of dealing with novel concepts—when a text on nuclear physics had to be translated into Warlpiri, for example, a new compound verb was coined to mean 'cause nuclear fission' by using a root meaning 'hit' and an element meaning 'be scattered'. The fact that Warlpiri can now be used to discuss central concepts of nuclear physics is clear testimony to the adaptability of Aboriginal languages.

A Last Word

Linguists would love to have primitive languages to study in order to understand how human language has evolved. But, as I hope to have shown, Aboriginal languages certainly do not fit the bill—in fact, their complexities have played an important role in linguistics over the last three decades in extending our notions of what complex organizing principles can be found in human languages.

Answers

1. *bangaa dangkaya kurrija, bangaa kurrija dangkaya, dangkaya bangaa kurrija, dangkaya kurrija bangaa, kurrija bangaa dangkaya, kurrija dangkaya bangaa*
2. *thengatye*

FOR DISCUSSION AND REVIEW

1. According to Evans, multilingualism is the norm in Aboriginal Australia. Why do individuals there speak so many languages? What might be some possible outcomes of this kind of widespread multilingualism?

2. Evans compares English with Kayardild—a language that relies on case endings, another way of saying suffixes or functional morphemes. Why do case endings make sentence meaning clearer? Write an original English sentence that is ambiguous because of the lack of case endings. What does the exercise tell you about English grammar? How does it change your perception of Aboriginal languages like Kayardild?

3. How do Aboriginal pronoun systems differ from English?

4. Many of the Australian Aboriginal languages have rich vocabularies for the natural world. Why would this be the case? When you consider your own languages, which aspects of life have rich vocabularies and which have poor ones? Jot down some words to back up your opinion.

5. What three word-making processes are used in Australian Aboriginal languages for creating new words? How are new words created in English or other languages you speak? How are novel concepts often coined? Do you think that any language can adapt to changes in knowledge, culture, and technology? Why, or why not?

6. Is it possible for a language to be "primitive"? When a language is described as "primitive," what might be meant? Are some languages more sophisticated or complex than others? If so, in what ways?

33

Rearing Bilingual Children in a Monolingual Culture: A Louisiana Experience

Stephen J. Caldas
Suzanne Caron-Caldas

When the authors of this study married, they brought together two French-language subcultures on the North American continent, those of Quebec and southern Louisiana. Ironically, Caldas, descended directly from the French-speaking Acadians (Cajuns), spoke only English when he met the French-speaking Quebec woman who was to become his wife. Because of the difficulty these two educators experienced in attempting to learn each other's languages, they decided to raise their children to be bilingual. This 1992 essay, originally published in American Speech, *is an account of their efforts. With their knowledge of linguistics and appreciation for the French heritage of their Louisiana community, Caldas and Caron-Caldas carefully monitored their children's exposure to both languages. They found that the children made equal gains in French at home and in English in their preschool and neighborhood.*

Rearing children to be bilingual in a culture which is overwhelmingly monolingual is a formidable task. There are a multitude of obstacles to achieving this goal which arise from the constant invasion on all sides of the dominant culture's language. These obstacles seem to be particularly magnified in North America, where there has been a long history of intolerance to any language but English. According to one linguist, the dominant attitude seems to be, "It would be so much simpler if we all spoke the same language, namely English" (Darbelnet, 1976, 5).

This article is a descriptive ethnography of a genre similar to Heath's study (1983) of language acquisition and usage in two small Carolina piedmont communities. We attempt to describe a particular family's experience in a specific social milieu. Though we feel as though there are certain universal principles of language acquisition, we caution against the generalizibility of our study experiences.

Our story begins in 1980 with our marriage, and Stephen's exposure for the first time to French Canada. Stephen stepped off an airplane in Québec City and into the middle of the "separatist" movement. Though never taking sides in this heated issue, the experience sensitized him to the threatened French culture and language of his own state and planted the seed for our family project.

The French-speaking Acadians (Cajuns) of South Louisiana, originally exiled from Nova Scotia in the mid-eighteenth century, successfully resisted linguistic assimilation for almost two centuries. However, even this exceptionally close-knit culture has not been able to withstand the onslaught of American English. As a testament to this fact, though Stephen is the son of an Acadian woman, he spoke no French before marrying his Québecoise co-author. Suzanne likewise spoke no English. Our initial attempts to communicate were centered around a French-English paperback dictionary which was quickly reduced to tatters by our romantically inspired efforts to understand each other. In this work we outline our efforts to achieve bilingualism ourselves, and our subsequent project to raise our three children to be French/English bilinguals in the increasingly monolingual culture of South Louisiana.

The decline of French in Louisiana dates to the early 1920s, when a wave of isolationist anti-foreign sentiment swept across the United States. This mood resulted in the passage of legislation by several states restricting the language of instruction to English (Alexander, 1980). The state legislature of Louisiana passed a law which made utilizing French as the language of instruction in Louisiana's schools illegal (Mazel, 1979). Acadian children who spoke French while at school were often harshly disciplined. Though anti-French-speaking sentiment has all but disappeared in Louisiana, so has the French language among this generation of Cajuns. Remarking on the current situation, one historian laments, "It is monstrous that people who speak English with an unmistakable French accent should have to be taught French" (Taylor, 1976, 184).

But this was exactly Suzanne's mission when she was hired by CODOFIL (Council for the Development of French in Louisiana) in 1980: to help in the revival of the French language in Louisiana. She was soon teaching French in the first elementary-school immersion program in the state.

Suzanne was as anxious to improve her English as Stephen was to improve his French. Since she was now immersed in an English-speaking culture, it was agreed that we should speak as much French as possible at home. Though the tendency to speak English was strong, Stephen daily forced himself to communicate with his new wife in her native tongue. Since we were both educators, we had the opportunity to spend several of our summer and winter vacations in Québec, where Stephen had no choice but to speak French.

By 1983 Stephen felt confident enough to minor in French as he worked on his master's degree at Louisiana State University, eventually becoming certified to teach French at the primary and secondary levels. Still, bilingualism seemed an elusive goal to both of us. We adopted Darbelnet's definition (1976, 4) of *bilingual* "being equally at home and equally effective in two languages," though among scholars there is little consensus as to precisely how the term is to be defined (Fraser and Mougeon, 1990). Our mutual efforts notwithstanding, as we struggled to master each other's language, it was becoming clear to both of us that the goal of bilingualism was truly difficult to achieve.

Or so we thought. Our perception of bilingualism changed as a result of two factors. The first was a scene we witnessed while crossing the English Channel during a summer trip to Europe in 1982. Seated across from us on the ferry was a couple with a three-year-old child. The father spoke to him in French, and the mother spoke to him in English. The child not only understood both of his parents, but he replied to both of them in their respective tongues and without an accent! The second factor was Suzanne's experience as an elementary French immersion teacher. In short, her fourth graders, in their first year of French, progressed rapidly enough to hold a conversation in French after only a few months. We resolved to spare our future offspring all of the effort we were expending to acquire a second language—we were going to *rear* our children bilingually from birth.

Suzanne became pregnant in 1984. We had already devised our strategy—Suzanne was to address our first-born only in French, while Stephen was to speak to our child only in English. We implemented our plan with the birth of John in May of 1985.

One of our first instinctual concerns was that we would confuse our newborn son. We countered this fear by continually reminding ourselves of the Channel-crossing episode as well as of the fact that a majority of the world's population is, after all, multilingual (Lambert et al., 1981). Secondly, we were initially very self-conscious of the fact that among our family, friends, and acquaintances, we were the only parents who spoke to their child in two different languages. However, we realized soon enough that there was no basis for concern on either count. As John grew, his capacity to understand our French and English seemed perfectly normal for a child his age. Also, rather than being regarded strangely by our fellow Louisianians, we were often encouraged and praised by the many Cajuns we encountered who wished that their French-speaking parents and grandparents had raised them bilingually. Stephen's mother, herself of Acadian descent, regretted that her French-speaking mother had never spoken to her in French. Members of Suzanne's Québecois family, who were particularly sensitive to the importance of speaking both French and English, were clearly pleased by our efforts to raise John bilingually.

John spent about eight hours a day, five days a week, in English-speaking day care from the time he was three months old until we enrolled him in preschool at age four. As he grew, we slowly became aware that Suzanne's French communication represented a fraction of the

English John was exposed to in his environment (via day care, TV, relatives, neighbors, etc.). Thus when John was 18 months old, we resolved that both of us had to speak to him only in French to more equally balance his exposure to the two languages. Also, given that our home communications had grown a bit sloppy over the preceding years, with our communicating to each other in a mixture of French and English, or "Franglais," we fervently resolved to speak to each other only in French. Thus French became the exclusive language of our home from the time John was 18 months old.

Though he understood both languages equally well, John had still barely begun to speak by the time he was 21 months old. We were aware that bilingual children might begin speaking later than monolingual children (Saunders, 1984), so we were hoping that this was the case with John. It was. By his second birthday, to our great relief and astonishment, John exploded in language! He initially mixed French and English words together (e.g., "Look at the maison"), referred to as *code switching* (Commins and Miramontes, 1989), but within several months he could clearly differentiate between the two languages. He rarely mixed French and English thereafter.

In May of 1987, just as John turned two, Suzanne gave birth to a set of identical twin girls. Given the success we were having with John, we extended our practice of only speaking French to Valérie and Stéphanie as well. Consequently, unlike John, they were never addressed in English at home.

In the meantime, John's French and English vocabulary continued to expand, though he seemed to have a preference for English. Research emphasizes the importance of exposing children to the culture of their second language to facilitate their acquisition of it (Harding and Riley, 1986). Thus, in order to show him that his parents were not the only people in the world speaking French, John spent two weeks in Québec with Suzanne not long after his third birthday.

Upon their return from Québec we noted a decided preference for and improvement in our son's French. This preference lasted several months until he returned to day care in the fall, at which time English again became his dominant mode of communication. In fact throughout his third year, the bulk of his utterances to both us, and his twin sisters, were in English. We doggedly continued our practice of speaking only French to each other, and to the children. The twins, like John, understood our French, and everyone else's English, with equal facility. However, they were even slower to speak than John had been. We were somewhat encouraged to discover through research that twins, on average, speak later than do singletons (Savić, 1980). We were also concerned with John's practice of speaking to his sisters only in English. By their second birthday, the twins were beginning to imitate John's speech.

We concluded that another trip to Québec was necessary. During the summer of 1989, when John was four and the twins two, we left on our two-week summer vacation to Lac Trois Saumons, a resort lake community northeast of Québec city. Upon arriving, John's aunt offered to keep John with her and his nine-year-old French-speaking cousin during the entire two-week period. John would have no recourse to English. This proved to be a watershed event in our bilingual family experiment.

Following this two weeks of total immersion in French, our son completely abandoned his use of English in the home. In the fall of 1989, we enrolled John in a university preschool in Baton Rouge, where all communication was in English. During the first parent/teacher conference in November, where Stephen assumed that the teacher already knew that John spoke only French at home, he casually mentioned this fact to her. To our mutual surprise, John had never mentioned his bilingualism to her. He spoke English, the teacher informed Stephen, as well as any other four-year-old in his class.

In May of 1990 at the conclusion of his preschool year, and as John turned five years old, his teacher administered the Houghton Mifflin Reading Program Readiness Test to each student in the class. The test is widely used to determine a child's readiness for kindergarten. John scored above the readiness level in all 10 subtests. The absence of English at home clearly had not impaired his performance in an English-speaking preschool.

Following the example of their brother upon returning from Québec, the twins quickly abandoned the few English utterances they were capable of articulating and began speaking only French words at home. In day care, however, where they spent 8 hours a day five days a week, their developing language was English. Interestingly enough they spoke not only to others but also to each other mostly in English while at day care, but switched to French as their interpersonal language upon returning home.

In May of 1990 when they turned three years old, we took Valérie and Stéphanie for a speech screening test provided by our local school district. In order to get as objective an assessment as possible, we did not inform the speech pathologist that only French was spoken in the home. Both girls were individually screened. We were informed that except for their pronunciation of the /ɪ/ phoneme, their speech was developing normally for children their age. Our speculation is that their constant exposure to the French uvular [ʀ] may be slowing their acquisition of the English /ɪ/ sound.

In conclusion, it seems that our efforts to raise our children bilingually, guided by research, determination, and a desire to preserve Louisiana's unique French heritage, are succeeding. Nevertheless, it must be emphasized that the process is ongoing, and consequently the verdict is in a sense still out. John scored well on an English measure of his kindergarten readiness, but he was not administered a parallel test in French. Though our subjective impression is that he speaks French as well as he speaks English, at this time we lack objective evidence to confirm this.

We anticipate continuing challenges in our struggle. First, as the children become more aware of their unique linguistic status, it's conceivable that their current spontaneous French communication with us in public will be replaced by a self-conscious reluctance to speak differently from everyone else (Commins and Miramontes, 1989). Thus we deem it important not only to educate them to speak French, but to be proud of their French-speaking heritage as well. Second, there is the equally challenging task of ensuring that they learn to read and write French as well as speak it. We may be able to accomplish this by enrolling them in a French immersion program, teaching them at home, or some combination of the two. Frequent trips to Québec could help out on both counts.

We caution against the generalizibility of our particular experience. Our setting is somewhat unique in that the negative stereotype once associated with French-speaking Louisianians has been largely replaced by nostalgia for the disappearing French language. In many other parts of the United States, minority language speakers are still negatively stereotyped, resulting in a reluctance by the bilingual child to speak in his or her minority tongue (Commins and Miramontes, 1989). We find this unfortunate, to say the least, especially in light of research which indicates that bilingual students score higher on both verbal and nonverbal measures of intelligence than do their monolingual classmates (Lambert, 1972).

Based on our experience and the experience of Louisiana, however particularistic, the current xenophobic mood among some in the United States who insist on making English the "official" language for fear it may decline in importance seems completely unfounded. We have made virtually no attempt to teach English to our children, yet they are obtaining fluency in it like any other American child. We concur with Melendez (1989, 71) who notes that ". . . learning English—developing a common [national] language does not require unlearning or not learning other languages."

BIBLIOGRAPHY

Alexander, Kern. *School Law*. St. Paul: West, 1980.

Commins, Nancy L., and Ofelia B. Miramontes. "Perceived and Actual Linguistic Competence: A Descriptive Study of Four Low-Achieving Hispanic Bilingual Students." *American Educational Research Journal*, 26 (1989), 443–72.

Darbelnet, Jean. *Le Français en contact avec l'Anglais en Amérique du Nord*. Québec: Les Presses de L'Université Laval, 1976.

Fraser, Carol A., and François Mougeon. "Developing a Test of Advanced Bilingualism: The Glendon Experience." *The Canadian Modern Language Review/La Revue canadienne des langues vivantes*, 46 (1990), 779–93.

Harding, Edith, and Philip Riley. *The Bilingual Family: A Handbook for Parents*. Cambridge: Cambridge University Press, 1986.

Heath, Shirley Brice. *Ways with Words: Language, Life, and Work in Communities and Classrooms*. Cambridge: Cambridge University Press, 1983.

Lambert, Wallace E. *Bilingual Education of Children: The St. Lambert Experiment.* Rowley, MA: Newbury, 1972.

Lambert, Wallace E., Catherine E. Snow, Beverly A. Goldfield, Anna Uhl Chamot, and Stephen R. Cahir. *Faces and Facets of Bilingualism.* Bilingual Education Series 10. Washington: National Clearinghouse for Bilingual Education, 1981.

Mazel, Jean. *Louisiane: Terre d'aventure.* Paris: Laffont, 1979.

Melendez, Sarah F. "A Nation of Monolinguals, a Bilingual World." *NEA Today* 7, 6 (1989), 70–74.

Saunders, George. *Bilingual Education: Guidance for the Family.* Avon, England: Multilingual Matters, 1984.

Savić, Svenka. *How Twins Learn to Talk.* Trans. Vladislava Felbabov. New York: Academic, 1980.

Taylor, Joe Gray. *Louisiana: A Bicentennial History.* New York: Norton, 1976.

FOR DISCUSSION AND REVIEW

1. Caldas and Caron-Caldas warn the reader against generalizing from their experience. Of what value to a broad field like linguistics is a first-person account such as theirs?

2. What prompted the authors to raise their children to be bilingual?

3. What were the two primary concerns the parents faced in attempting to raise a bilingual child? How were they resolved? What characteristics of the authors' particular situation were helpful? Might parents attempting to raise bilingual children in different circumstances face more difficult problems; if so, how might they be overcome?

4. Why did the parents resolve to speak only French at home when John became eighteen months old? Why did they feel it was important to take him for visits to Quebec?

5. What is code switching?

6. According to the authors, what are the advantages of growing up bilingual?

7. What challenges do the parents anticipate as the children grow older? Which of these challenges is primarily linguistic? Which cultural?

8. In what ways is the situation of the Caron-Caldas children different from that of bilingual Native American or Hispanic American children? In what ways is it similar?

9. Do you think it is likely that the Caron-Caldas children will eventually leave behind their private French-speaking lives?

34

Native Tongues

Nancy Lord

Linguists know that the unique qualities of a particular language reflect the characteristics of its place of origin and the cultural context of the people who speak it. When professional writer Nancy Lord set out to learn the "native tongue" of her chosen home in Homer, Alaska—that is, the language of the aboriginal dwellers—she made a number of discoveries. She learned that the Dena'ina language is exquisitely attuned to a landscape marked by rivers, mountains, and wildlife; she deepened her ability to appreciate both the landscape and the seminomadic people who lived in harmony with it; and she became aware of the truth of Benjamin Whorf's assertion that, in Lord's words, "there are no primitive languages, only languages with varying emphases." To her sorrow, she also learned that Dena'ina, like hundreds of native languages all over the world, is on the edge of extinction. Lord argues that the death of a language prevents us from knowing the world through the ancient accumulated wisdom of its native speakers. This essay first appeared in Sierra *magazine in 1996.*

As I walk one day through the woods above my Alaska fishcamp, I find myself thinking of the stream that slips by me in the brush. Though I only glimpse it in one spot, I know its twists and turns as contours of the place, its flow not just as water but as map. This is the traditional way by which the people of this place know where they are and where they are going.

Before the invention of the compass, people in most parts of the world marked direction by the sun and stars. In the far north, though, the sun crosses the sky in greatly varied locations depending on the season, and summer nights are brighter than starlight. Eskimos developed directional systems based on positions relative to the coastline, while Athabaskans developed theirs according to the flow of rivers.

The logic of this—even for me, who came to this Alaska shore from afar and only as an adult—is obvious, and truly lovely. The old, meandering trail I follow keeps the creek on one side, connecting the beach on Cook Inlet with the forested uplands. Downstream the creek takes me home; upstream it takes me to ponds and a lake, then farther inland to another lake. Since the beginning of our lives here my partner and I have referred to Cook Inlet itself in upstream and downstream terms, because of the way the water flows in and rushes out on the tides. When I learned that the Dena'ina Athabaskans who first inhabited the Cook Inlet area called the inlet something that translated to "Big-Water River" and marked its directions as upstream, downstream, and across, I understood with new clarity how the language was confirming the landscape, the landscape shaping the language. The way of speaking about the inlet was given by the inlet itself.

As I learned a little Dena'ina, I began to see its profound dependence on locations. Athabaskan languages layer prefixes and suffixes onto root words in a way that emphasizes directions, distances, and relative positionings—very important for a semi-nomadic culture where people needed to be very clear about where they were and where they needed to go for food and other necessities. (This might be compared to the complexity of verb tenses in the languages of cultures oriented more toward considerations of timing.) Dena'ina, which builds into one word locational information that would take an entire sentence in English, serves life in this place both efficiently and elegantly.

Languages, of course, belong to environments in the same way that living creatures do, shaped by and shaping the places that spawn them, both in the words needed to identify and address the particulars of those places and in the structures needed to survive in them. And so I want to learn what I can of the language of this place where I live, just as I want to know its plants and wildlife. Its very name—Kustatan, "point of land"—describes it perfectly. The brown bear's name—*ggagga*—is used sometimes to refer to animals in general and indicates how significant the bear was in Dena'ina culture; it also reminds me that bears are still largely in charge here. The raven's name is *ggugguyni*, pronounced to match the watery gurgle the bird makes in the back of its throat, and the golden-crowned sparrow *tsik'ezlagh* all summer sings the three descending minor-key notes that sound out its name. My experience of what I see and hear around me is vastly enriched by being able to identify even a small bit of it in its native, coevolutionary tongue.

It is only because of one remarkable man that I know anything about it. The last Dena'ina to speak the dialect of this area, Peter Kalifornsky, died in 1993, but only after committing his last years to preserving his native tongue. With the help of a linguist, Kalifornsky worked out a written form of the language and then became its first author, writing several books of traditional and personal stories. He also developed language lessons and began to teach the Dena'ina language to the people who owned it and had lost it—or, rather, had it taken from them. This linguistic recovery coincided with a lively cultural revival—even if Dena'ina is listed by the University of Alaska as a "foreign" language.

To identify mountains, Kalifornsky used single words for "ridge broken up into knolls, almost bare," "ridge with knolls pointing up," "ridge sloping to a point," "pointed up mountain," and "sloping mountain." He listed words for the way trees grow on the mountains: "they grow on the upper mountain slope"; "they grow up the mountain in strips"; "they grow up the mountainsides"; "they grow through the pass." The translations are awkward but precise. They make me look more attentively at mountainsides now, see with more exactness their shapes against the sky and the patterns of their vegetation.

There's poetry in Dena'ina, too. The volcanic mountain known as Redoubt I now think of by the translation of its native name—"the one with wrinkled forehead." Sixty-Foot Rock has metamorphosed before my eyes, particularly in the warm-weather mirages that are so common here, as "soles of feet waving." A distant mountain is known as "ridge where we cry," because from it the Dena'ina could look down and think about their mothers and fathers and brothers—all their people who went there before them, all their sad and beautiful history, all their connections to one another and to the place that was home. The Roman culture behind the names of our months has its own attractions, but June, September, and January can never suit this land as do "king salmon month," "the month leaves turn yellow," and "the month we sing."

A late part of the European "discovery" of America was the discovery of the fit between a native language and its place of origin. On his trips into the Maine woods, Thoreau made a point of learning the Penobscot and Abenaki names of birds, plants, and places from his Indian guides. He learned that the native name for the fish he knew as "pout" described its habit of leading its young as a hen leads her chicks— something he had himself observed but never found in any book. From the Abenaki words for fir branches (*sedi*) and the act of spreading fir branches on the ground for a bed (*sediak*), he understood not only a relationship, but a different way of seeing.

"It was a new light when my guide gave me Indian names for things for which I had only scientific ones before," Thoreau wrote in his journal. "In proportion as I understood the language, I saw them from a new point of view. . . . A dictionary of the Indian language reveals another and wholly new life to us."

The idea that language shapes the way we see and understand the world was popularized in the 1930s as "linguistic relativity" by linguist Benjamin Lee Whorf. "We cut nature up, organize it into concepts, and ascribe significances as we do, largely because we are parties to an agreement to organize it in this way," Whorf explained. "All observers are not led by the same physical evidence to the same picture of the universe, unless their linguistic backgrounds are similar, or can in some way be calibrated." Every language, he said, has its own pattern-system by which its speakers not only communicate but also analyze nature, notice or neglect certain relationships, and channel reasoning. Without the words or structure to articulate a concept, that concept won't occur. Likewise, if a language is rich in ways to express certain sorts of ideas, then its speakers will habitually think along those linguistic paths. The picture of the universe, Whorf insisted, shifts from tongue to tongue.

Much of Whorf's work was centered on Hopi, which differs dramatically from Indo-European languages in its treatment of time. Instead of rigid past-present-future tenses, Hopi divides time into two modes: objective (the manifest, or things that exist now) and subjective (the unmanifest, things that can be thought about or are in a state of becoming). In Hopi, as in many Native American languages, fixed temporal points are less important than process, possibility, and the cyclical nature of time. This linguistic structure reflects and reinforces Hopi cultural values, so that a person living in that language understands and responds to the world differently than does an English speaker who attaches *-ed* or *-ing* to verbs.

Whorf's somewhat circular theory—that a person speaks this way because he thinks this way because he speaks this way—turned out not to be provable by scientific methods, and has since been largely discredited. But it did change the way we think about language. In Whorf's time, many people still believed that the languages of "primitive" cultures were "undeveloped." Whorf demonstrated that there are no primitive languages, only languages with varying emphases. "Many American Indian and African languages abound in finely wrought, beautifully logical discriminations about causation, action, result, dynamic or energetic quality, directness of experience, etc., all matters of the function of thinking, indeed the quintessence of the rational," he wrote. "In this respect they far outdistance the European languages." He cited, for example, the Native American rendering as verbs many words we know in English as nouns; this system, he argued, was better suited for understanding dynamic states and what we might think of as the science of physics. He pointed as well to the four persons of Algonkian pronouns, which allow clear and compact reference to complex social relationships, an African tense distinction between events with and without present results or influences, and, among the Coeur d'Alene Indians of Idaho, the use of three verb forms that discriminate between different causal processes.

Similarly, although the Wintun Indians of California disregard tense, they tag their verbs with suffixes to specify whether what they're conveying is known by direct experience or hearsay. Certain Australian languages that appear to lack the words for describing spatial relationships—no "in front of" or "beside"—rely on an absolute frame of reference, coordinates that establish the world as one big grid.

Although every person with normal vision sees the same spectrum of light, not all cultures recognize the same colors. Some languages, like that of the Dani of New Guinea, identify only two—black and white, or dark and light. Navajo, like Latin, distinguishes between the black of darkness and the black of coal; it has one word for gray and brown, includes some of what we would call "green" in its word for blue, and others in its word for yellow. Experiments have demonstrated that people from cultures with large and precise color vocabularies are better able to remember and pick out colors they have been previously shown. Having words for colors helps us remember them.

Everyone knows the axiom that Eskimos have hundreds of words for snow. Although this has been overstated—actually, Eskimo languages don't have all that many root words for different kinds of snow, but form specialized words by building on root words—it is still true that people in northern climates speak of (and thus also see and consider) their ice- and snowbound environments with a keen precision. There are important survival distinctions to be made between a snow that can easily be cut into blocks for building shelter and one that will soon turn to rain. Alaska's Aleuts have a word that translates as "the snow that melts the snow," to designate the wet snowfall of spring—that which hastens the melt of the old snow beneath it. (Since I learned this concept, I've come to think of spring snow with a new appreciation, a more accepting attitude toward winter's end.) In sharp contrast, the Aztec language has a single word—with different endings—for snow, ice, and cold.

Here at home, the Dena'ina have an entire lexicon with which to describe kinds of streams and trails. It makes a difference if a stream is a river, a tributary, the outlet of a lake, a straight stretch of water, a place of fast or slow current, covered with slush ice or overflow ice. Likewise, a trail is not just a trail; it's a packed-snow trail or a trail with snow drifted over, an animal trail, a snowshoe or sled trail, a trapline trail, or a trail used for getting wood.

The same wealth of Dena'ina language applies to salmon and other fish—not only the names of the fish but specialized words to distinguish between dried fish, half-dried fish, a bundle of dried fish, fish dried in one day's wind, fish dried with eggs inside, fish dried ungutted, fish dried flat, smoked fish, half-smoked fish, the backbone of the fish, the fish belly, the fat, the fatty part just in front of the king's dorsal fin, the roe, dried roe, fermented roe, frozen roe, salted roe, and roe soup. To know these words is to share in the universe of salmon.

Along my trail in Dena'ina country, I try to imagine how differently— or more clearly—I might see my world if I had the Dena'ina language precision with which to know my surroundings and my place in them. I look at a fern and think "fern." But if instead I thought of *uh t'una*, I would know that I was seeing and thinking about the leafy part of the plant, in contrast to *uh*, its underground parts used for food. And if I thought of another part of the plant, *elnen tselts'egha* (literally "ground's coiled rectum"), I would find humor in the fiddlehead fern.

Unfortunately, few of these words are spoken anymore, one person to another in the course of daily living. Of the original five dialects of Dena'ina Athabaskan, one is long gone, the second's fluency died with Peter Kalifornsky, and two of the other three are spoken only by elders. Only one, in an isolated village, is still spoken by young adults. What remains of the various dialects has been assembled in dictionary form by linguist James Kari of the University of Alaska's Native Language Center.

If not for Kari, Dena'ina words would be scattering silently and irretrievably into the winds.

Once there were between 10,000 and 15,000 languages in the world. Today there are barely 6,000, and half of those are no longer being learned by children and will probably become extinct within the next century. "They are beyond endangerment," says University of Alaska linguist Michael Krauss. "They are the living dead."

Of North America's 300-some Native languages, about 210 are still spoken. (About 50 of those are in California, the world's most linguistically diverse region after New Guinea and the Caucasus.) Very few of the 210 are, however, still spoken by children. Even Navajo, by far the largest language group with 200,000 speakers, appears to be in trouble. A generation ago, 90 percent of Navajo children entering school spoke their language; today, the reverse is true—90 percent of Navajo children entering school speak English, but not Navajo. In Alaska, only two of the 20 Native languages are still spoken by children and one language— Eyak—has one remaining elderly speaker. Krauss believes that despite bilingual programs in schools, all Native American languages are today threatened.

The cause, of course, is the unfinished conquest of Native peoples and the eradication of their cultures. Even after the wars and removals ended and were replaced with assimilation policies, most white Americans believed that Natives would be best off abandoning their "inferior" cultures and adopting the English-only, mainstream American one. Until the 1960s, Natives were forbidden to speak their own languages in schools, and children were punished for doing so. Parents were told that they were holding their children back by speaking their languages at home, and so they too were silenced.

Even the best bilingual programs can't compensate for traditional family-to-child language learning. Language loss is further exacerbated by the influence of television and "global culture." At this late date, perhaps the best that can be done is to teach Native languages as second or even third languages, so that coming generations can learn enough of their ancestral tongues to maintain respect for them and for their heritage, and to continue some ceremonial and artistic uses.

Preservation, Tlingit oral historians Richard and Nora Marks Dauenhauer remind us, is what we do to berries in jam jars and salmon in cans. Preserved foods are different from thriving berry patches and surging runs of salmon, and dictionaries are not the same as speech. Books and recordings can preserve languages, but only people and communities can keep them alive.

Most people are now aware of and concerned about the mass extinction of animals and plants. We understand the need for diversity, and the imperative to protect what we can. As with species, once a language is lost it is gone forever. Every extinguished language diminishes the world by robbing us of the ability to know that world with the millennia of accumulated wisdom of groups such as California's Pomo, or the New Guinea Dani, or the Gwich'in of Alaska.

Back at my fishcamp, the sky opens, and a hard, dumping rain pounds onto the metal roof, the alders, the squally inlet. When the rain stops I walk behind the cabin to pick fireweed shoots for a salad. The air is fragrant with plant oils and wet earth, and all the leaves and grasses are magnified by the droplets caught in their creases and dangling from their tips. A warm white light suffuses the breaking clouds; its shafts pierce the mosaic of green and gray inlet waters. There's a Dena'ina word for this— this fresh-scrubbed, brightened, new-world look. *Htashtch'ul*. The world everywhere after a rain looks fresh and lovely, but to have a word to put to it—a word that came from this land, that is as native as the blue-backed salmon and alder thickets, that tells me what the first people saw and what significance they gave by naming it—makes me feel even more a part of this place.

Words have power. Languages connected to place help us to respect local knowledge, to ask and answer the tough questions about how the human and nonhuman can live together in a tolerant and dignified way. They can help us extend our sense of community; what we hold ourselves responsible for, what we must do to live right and well.

The Dena'ina greeting is *Yaghali du?* "Is it good?" Not, "How are you?" but, "Is it good?" There is, in the question, the assumption that something larger is at stake than the feelings of the two speakers, something less anthropocentric, less egocentric. If it is good, then we shall all—me, you, our community, the larger world—prosper together, not the one individual at the expense of others.

Yaghali du? Yaghali du? The answer we want is *Aa'yaghali*. Yes, it is good. It is all good.

FOR DISCUSSION AND REVIEW

1. Why do native Alaskans use waterways instead of the sun and the stars to define direction and location? How does this affect the structure of their languages?

2. What parallel may be drawn between the use of prefixes and suffixes in Dena'ina and verb tenses in English?

3. Why does Lord refer to the native language of her chosen home as coevolutionary? What relationships exist between a place and the human language spoken there? How are these relationships revealed in the Dena'ina words for mountains and fish?

4. Why did Thoreau value the Abenaki names of things for which he already knew the English scientific names?

5. What is the central idea in Whorf's theory of "linguistic relativity"? What lasting effect, according to Lord, did his theory have on our understanding of the nature of languages?

6. How does the Hopi concept of time, as Whorf describes it, differ from ours? What role does language play in a person's development and understanding of concepts?

7. Do you think Lord would agree with Lakoff and Johnson's view on metaphoric concepts (see "Metaphors We Live By," pp. 458–65)? Why, or why not?

8. Give several reasons why the number of living languages in the world is shrinking so rapidly.

9. According to Lord, the loss of a language "diminishes the world." Why?

10. What specific powers does Lord ascribe to words?

35

Shakespeare in the Bush

Laura Bohannan

Are all peoples subject to the same feelings and driven by the same motivations? Do great stories of human endeavor carry identical messages to every audience, regardless of its background? In the early 1950s, Laura Bohannan, an anthropologist at the University of Illinois at Chicago, attempted to retell the story of Hamlet while staying with the Tiv of Nigeria. In doing so, she found that it was very difficult to translate a classic tale from one language and culture to another. Indeed, Bohannan found that the "universals" of Shakespeare's Hamlet—*power, betrayal and madness—were interpreted very differently by the Tiv. Although written over fifty years ago, Bohannan's epiphany about culture and language is still valid today. This essay was originally published in* Natural History *in 1966.*

Just before I left Oxford for the Tiv in West Africa, conversation turned to the season at Stratford. "You Americans," said a friend, "often have difficulty with Shakespeare. He was, after all, a very English poet, and one can easily misinterpret the universal by misunderstanding the particular."

I protested that human nature is pretty much the same the whole world over; at least the general plot and motivation of the greater tragedies would always be clear—everywhere—although some details of custom might have to be explained and difficulties of translation might produce other slight changes. To end an argument we could not conclude, my friend gave me a copy of *Hamlet* to study in the African bush: it would, he hoped, lift my mind above its primitive surroundings, and possibly I might, by prolonged meditation, achieve the grace of correct interpretation.

It was my second field trip to that African tribe, and I thought myself ready to live in one of its remote sections—an area difficult to cross even on foot. I eventually settled on the hillock of a very knowledgeable old man, the head of a homestead of some hundred and forty people, all of whom were either his close relatives or their wives and children. Like the other elders of the vicinity, the old man spent most of his time performing ceremonies seldom seen these days in the more accessible parts of the tribe. I was delighted. Soon there would be three months of enforced isolation and leisure, between the harvest that takes place just before the rising of the swamps and the clearing of new farms when the water goes down. Then, I thought, they would have even more time to perform ceremonies and explain them to me.

I was quite mistaken. Most of the ceremonies demanded the presence of elders from several homesteads. As the swamps rose, the old men found it too difficult to walk from one homestead to the next, and the ceremonies gradually ceased. As the swamps rose even higher, all activities but one came to an end. The women brewed beer from maize and millet. Men, women, and children sat on their hillocks and drank it.

People began to drink at dawn. By midmorning the whole homestead was singing, dancing, and drumming. When it rained, people had to sit inside their huts: there they drank and sang or they drank and told stories. In any case, by noon or before, I either had to join the party or retire to my own hut and my books. "One does not discuss serious matters when there is beer. Come, drink with us." Since I lacked their capacity for the thick native beer, I spent more and more time with *Hamlet*. Before the end of the second month, grace descended on me. I was quite sure that *Hamlet* had only one possible interpretation, and that one universally obvious.

Early every morning, in the hope of having some serious talk before the beer party, I used to call on the old man at his reception hut—a circle of posts supporting a thatched roof above a low mud wall to keep out wind and rain. One day I crawled through the low doorway and found most of the men of the homestead sitting huddled in their ragged cloths on stools, low plank beds, and reclining chairs, warming themselves against the chill of the rain around a smoky fire. In the center were three pots of beer. The party had started.

The old man greeted me cordially. "Sit down and drink." I accepted a large calabash full of beer, poured some into a small drinking gourd, and tossed it down. Then I poured some more into the same gourd for the man second in seniority to my host before I handed my calabash over to a young man for further distribution. Important people shouldn't ladle beer themselves.

"It is better like this," the old man said, looking at me approvingly and plucking at the thatch that had caught in my hair. "You should sit and drink with us more often. Your servants tell me that when you are not with us, you sit inside your hut looking at a paper."

The old man was acquainted with four kinds of "papers": tax receipts, bride price receipts, court fee receipts, and letters. The messenger who brought him letters from the chief used them mainly as a badge of office, for he always knew what was in them and told the old man. Personal letters for the few who had relatives in the government or mission stations were kept until someone went to a large market where there was a letter writer and reader. Since my arrival, letters were brought to me to be read. A few men also brought me bride price receipts, privately, with requests to change the figures to a higher sum. I found moral arguments were of no avail, since in-laws are fair game, and the technical hazards of forgery difficult to explain to an illiterate people. I did not wish them to think me silly enough to look at any such papers for days on end, and I hastily explained that my "paper" was one of the "things of long ago" of my country.

"Ah," said the old man. "Tell us."

I protested that I was not a storyteller. Story telling is a skilled art among them; their standards are high, and the audiences critical—and vocal in their criticism. I protested in vain. This morning they wanted to hear a story while they drank. They threatened to tell me no more stories until I told them one of mine. Finally, the old man promised that no one would criticize my style "for we know you are struggling with our language." "But," put in one of the elders, "you must explain what we do not understand, as we do when we tell you our stories." Realizing that here was my chance to prove *Hamlet* universally intelligible, I agreed.

The old man handed me some more beer to help me on with my storytelling. Men filled their long wooden pipes and knocked coals from the fire to place in the pipe bowls; then, puffing contentedly, they sat back to listen. I began in the proper style, "Not yesterday, not yesterday, but long ago, a thing occurred. One night three men were keeping watch outside the homestead of the great chief, when suddenly they saw the former chief approach them."

"Why was he no longer their chief?"

"He was dead," I explained. "That is why they were troubled and afraid when they saw him."

"Impossible," began one of the elders, handing his pipe on to his neighbor, who interrupted, "Of course it wasn't the dead chief. It was an omen sent by a witch. Go on."

Slightly shaken, I continued. "One of these three was a man who knew things"—the closest translation for scholar, but unfortunately it also meant witch. The second elder looked triumphantly at the first. "So he spoke to the dead chief saying, 'Tell us what we must do so you may rest in your grave,' but the dead chief did not answer. He vanished, and they could see him no more. Then the man who knew things—his name was Horatio—said this event was the affair of the dead chief's son, Hamlet."

There was a general shaking of heads round the circle. "Had the dead chief no living brothers? Or was this son the chief?"

"No," I replied. "That is, he had one living brother who became the chief when the elder brother died."

The old men muttered: such omens were matters for chiefs and elders, not for youngsters; no good could come of going behind a chief's back; clearly Horatio was not a man who knew things.

"Yes, he was," I insisted, shooing a chicken away from my beer. "In our country the son is next to the father. The dead chief's younger brother had become the great chief. He had also married his elder brother's widow only about a month after the funeral."

"He did well," the old man beamed and announced to the others, "I told you that if we knew more about Europeans, we would find they really were very like us. In our country also," he added to me, "the younger brother marries the elder brother's widow and becomes the father of his children. Now, if your uncle, who married your widowed mother, is your father's full brother, then he will be a real father to you. Did Hamlet's father and uncle have one mother?"

His question barely penetrated my mind; I was too upset and thrown too far off balance by having one of the most important elements of *Hamlet* knocked straight out of the picture. Rather uncertainly I said that I thought they had the same mother, but I wasn't sure—the story didn't say. The old man told me severely that these genealogical details made all the difference and that when I got home I must ask the elders about it. He shouted out the door to one of his younger wives to bring his goatskin bag.

Determined to save what I could of the mother motif, I took a deep breath and began again. "The son Hamlet was very sad because his mother had married again so quickly. There was no need for her to do so, and it is our custom for a widow not to go to her next husband until she has mourned for two years."

"Two years is too long," objected the wife, who had appeared with the old man's battered goatskin bag. "Who will hoe your farms for you while you have no husband?"

"Hamlet," I retorted without thinking, "was old enough to hoe his mother's farms himself. There was no need for her to remarry." No one looked convinced. I gave up. "His mother and the great chief told Hamlet not to be sad, for the great chief himself would be a father to Hamlet. Furthermore, Hamlet would be the next chief: therefore he must stay to learn the things of a chief. Hamlet agreed to remain, and all the rest went off to drink beer."

While I paused, perplexed at how to render Hamlet's disgusted soliloquy to an audience convinced that Claudius and Gertrude had behaved in the best possible manner, one of the younger men asked me who had married the other wives of the dead chief.

"He had no other wives," I told him.

"But a chief must have many wives! How else can he brew beer and prepare food for all his guests?"

I said firmly that in our country even chiefs had only one wife, that they had servants to do their work, and that they paid them from tax money.

It was better, they returned, for a chief to have many wives and sons who would help him hoe his farms and feed his people; then everyone loved the chief who gave much and took nothing—taxes were a bad thing.

I agreed with the last comment, but for the rest fell back on their favorite way of fobbing off my questions: "That is the way it is done, so that is how we do it."

I decided to skip the soliloquy. Even if Claudius was here thought quite right to marry his brother's widow, there remained the poison motif, and I knew they would disapprove of fratricide. More hopefully I resumed, "That night Hamlet kept watch with the three who had seen his dead father. The dead chief again appeared, and although the others were afraid, Hamlet followed his dead father off to one side. When they were alone, Hamlet's dead father spoke."

"Omens can't talk!" The old man was emphatic.

"Hamlet's dead father wasn't an omen. Seeing him might have been an omen, but he was not." My audience looked as confused as I sounded. "It *was* Hamlet's dead father. It was a thing we call a 'ghost.'" I had to use the English word, for unlike many of the neighboring tribes, these people didn't believe in the survival after death of any individuating part of the personality.

"What is a 'ghost'? An omen?"

"No, a 'ghost' is someone who is dead but who walks around and can talk, and people can hear him and see him but not touch him."

They objected. "One can touch zombis."

"No, no! It was not a dead body the witches had animated to sacrifice and eat. No one else made Hamlet's dead father walk. He did it himself."

"Dead men can't walk," protested my audience as one man.

I was quite willing to compromise. "A 'ghost' is the dead man's shadow."

But again they objected. "Dead men cast no shadows."

"They do in my country," I snapped.

The old man quelled the babble of disbelief that arose immediately and told me with that insincere, but courteous, agreement one extends to the fancies of the young, ignorant, and superstitious, "No doubt in your country the dead can also walk without being zombis." From the depths of his bag he produced a withered fragment of kola nut, bit off one end to show it wasn't poisoned, and handed me the rest as a peace offering.

"Anyhow," I resumed, "Hamlet's dead father said that his own brother, the one who became chief, had poisoned him. He wanted Hamlet to avenge him. Hamlet believed this in his heart, for he did not like his father's brother." I took another swallow of beer. "In the country of the great chief, living in the same homestead, for it was a very large one, was an important elder who was often with the chief to advise and help him. His name was Polonius. Hamlet was courting his daughter, but her father and her brother . . . [I cast hastily about for some tribal analogy] warned her not to let Hamlet visit her when she was alone on her farm, for he would be a great chief and so could not marry her."

"Why not?" asked the wife, who had settled down on the edge of the old man's chair. He frowned at her for asking stupid questions and growled, "They lived in the same homestead."

"This was not the reason," I informed them. "Polonius was a stranger who lived in the homestead because he helped the chief, not because he was a relative."

"Then why couldn't Hamlet marry her?"

"He could have," I explained, "but Polonius didn't think he would. After all, Hamlet was a man of great importance who ought to marry a chief's daughter, for in his country a man could have only one wife. Polonius was afraid that if Hamlet made love to his daughter, then no one else would give a high price for her."

"That might be true," remarked one of the shrewder elders, "but a chief's son would give his mistress's father enough presents and patronage to more than make up the difference. Polonius sounds like a fool to me."

"Many people think he was," I agreed. "Meanwhile Polonius sent his son Laertes off to Paris to learn the things of the country, for it was the homestead of a very great chief indeed. Because he was afraid that Laertes might waste a lot of money on beer and women and gambling, or get into trouble by fighting, he sent one of his servants to Paris secretly, to spy out what Laertes was doing. One day Hamlet came upon Polonius's daughter Ophelia. He behaved so oddly he frightened her. Indeed"—I was fumbling for words to express the dubious quality of Hamlet's madness— "the chief and many others had also noticed that when Hamlet talked one could understand the words but not what they meant. Many people thought that he had become mad." My audience suddenly became much more attentive. "The great chief wanted to know what was wrong with Hamlet, so he sent for two of Hamlet's age mates [school friends would have taken long explanation] to talk to Hamlet and find out what troubled his heart. Hamlet, seeing that they had been bribed by the chief to betray him, told them nothing. Polonius, however, insisted that Hamlet was mad because he had been forbidden to see Ophelia, whom he loved."

"Why," inquired a bewildered voice, "should anyone bewitch Hamlet on that account?"

"Bewitch him?"

"Yes, only witchcraft can make anyone mad, unless, of course, one sees the beings that lurk in the forest."

I stopped being a storyteller, took out my notebook and demanded to be told more about these two causes of madness. Even while they spoke and I jotted notes, I tried to calculate the effect of this new factor on the plot. Hamlet had not been exposed to the beings that lurk in the forests. Only his relatives in the male line could bewitch him. Barring relatives not mentioned by Shakespeare, it had to be Claudius who was attempting to harm him. And, of course, it was.

For the moment I staved off questions by saying that the great chief also refused to believe that Hamlet was mad for the love of Ophelia and nothing else. "He was sure that something much more important was troubling Hamlet's heart."

"Now Hamlet's age mates," I continued, "had brought with them a famous storyteller. Hamlet decided to have this man tell the chief and all his homestead a story about a man who had poisoned his brother because he desired his brother's wife and wished to be chief himself. Hamlet was sure the great chief could not hear the story without making a sign if he was indeed guilty, and then he would discover whether his dead father had told him the truth."

The old man interrupted, with deep cunning, "Why should a father lie to his son?" he asked.

I hedged: "Hamlet wasn't sure that it really was his dead father." It was impossible to say anything, in that language, about devil-inspired visions.

"You mean," he said, "it actually was an omen, and he knew witches sometimes send false ones. Hamlet was a fool not to go to one skilled in reading omens and divining the truth in the first place. A man-who-sees-the-truth could have told him how his father died, if he really had been poisoned, and if there was witchcraft in it; then Hamlet could have called the elders to settle the matter."

The shrewd elder ventured to disagree. "Because his father's brother was a great chief, one-who-sees-the-truth might therefore have been afraid to tell it. I think it was for that reason that a friend of Hamlet's father—a witch and an elder—sent an omen so his friend's son would know. Was the omen true?"

"Yes," I said, abandoning ghosts and the devil; a witch-sent omen it would have to be. "It was true, for when the storyteller was telling his tale before all the homestead, the great chief rose in fear. Afraid that Hamlet knew his secret, he planned to have him killed."

The stage set of the next bit presented some difficulties of translation. I began cautiously. "The great chief told Hamlet's mother to find out from her son what he knew. But because a woman's children are always first in her heart, he had the important elder Polonius hide behind a cloth that hung against the wall of Hamlet's mother's sleeping hut. Hamlet started to scold his mother for what she had done."

There was a shocked murmur from everyone. A man should never scold his mother.

"She called out in fear, and Polonius moved behind the cloth. Shouting, 'A rat!' Hamlet took his machete and slashed through the cloth." I paused for dramatic effect. "He had killed Polonius!"

The old men looked at each other in supreme disgust. "That Polonius truly was a fool and a man who knew nothing! What child would not know enough to shout, 'It's me!'" With a pang, I remembered that these people are ardent hunters, always armed with bow, arrow, and machete; at the first rustle in the grass an arrow is aimed and ready, and the hunter shouts "Game!" If no human voice answers immediately, the arrow speeds on its way. Like a good hunter Hamlet had shouted, "A rat!"

I rushed in, to save Polonius's reputation. "Polonius did speak. Hamlet heard him. But he thought it was the chief and wished to kill him earlier that evening. . . ." I broke down, unable to describe to these pagans, who had no belief in individual after-life, the difference between dying at one's prayers and dying "unhousell'd, disappointed, unaneled."

This time I had shocked my audience seriously. "For a man to raise his hand against his father's brother and the one who has become his father—that is a terrible thing. The elders ought to let such a man be bewitched."

I nibbled at my kola nut in some perplexity, then pointed out that after all the man had killed Hamlet's father.

"No," pronounced the old man, speaking less to me than to the young men sitting behind the elders. "If your father's brother has killed your father, you must appeal to your father's age mates; *they* may avenge him. No man may use violence against his senior relative." Another thought struck him, "But if his father's brother had indeed been wicked enough to bewitch Hamlet and make him mad that would be a good story indeed, for it would be his fault that Hamlet, being mad, no longer had any sense and thus was ready to kill his father's brother."

There was a murmur of applause. *Hamlet* was again a good story to them, but it no longer seemed quite the same story to me. As I thought over the coming complications of plot and motive, I lost courage and decided to skim over dangerous ground quickly.

"The great chief," I went on, "was not sorry that Hamlet had killed Polonius. It gave him a reason to send Hamlet away, with his two treacherous mates, with letters to a chief of a far country, saying that Hamlet should be killed. But Hamlet changed the writing on their papers, so that the chief killed his age mates instead." I encountered a reproachful glare from one of the men whom I had told undetectable forgery was not merely immoral but beyond human skill. I looked the other way.

"Before Hamlet could return, Laertes came back for his father's funeral. The great chief told him Hamlet had killed Polonius. Laertes swore to kill Hamlet because of this, and because his sister Ophelia, hearing her father had been killed by the man she loved, went mad and drowned in the river."

"Have you already forgotten what we told you?" The old man was reproachful. "One cannot take vengeance on a madman; Hamlet killed Polonius in his madness. As for the girl, she not only went mad, she was drowned. Only witches can make people drown. Water itself can't hurt anything. It is merely something one drinks and bathes in."

I began to get cross. "If you don't like the story, I'll stop."

The old man made soothing noises and himself poured me some more beer. "You tell the story well, and we are listening. But it is clear that the elders of your country have never told you what the story really means. No, don't interrupt! We believe you when you say your marriage customs are different, or your clothes and weapons. But people are the same everywhere; therefore, there are always witches and it is we, the elders, who know how witches work. We told you it was the great chief who wished to kill Hamlet, and now your own words have proved us right. Who were Ophelia's male relatives?"

"There were only her father and her brother." *Hamlet* was clearly out of my hands.

"There must have been many more; this also you must ask of your elders when you get back to your country. From what you tell us, since Polonius was dead, it must have been Laertes who killed Ophelia, although I do not see the reason for it."

We had emptied one pot of beer, and the old men argued the point with slightly tipsy interest. Finally one of them demanded of me, "What did the servant of Polonius say on his return?"

With difficulty I recollected Reynaldo and his mission. "I don't think he did return before Polonius was killed."

"Listen," said the elder, "and I will tell you how it was and how your story will go, then you may tell me if I am right. Polonius knew his son would get into trouble, and so he did. He had many fines to pay for fighting, and debts from gambling. But he had only two ways of getting money quickly. One was to marry off his sister at once, but it is difficult to find a man who will marry a woman desired by the son of a chief. For if the chief's heir commits adultery with your wife, what can you do? Only a fool calls a case against a man who will someday be his judge. Therefore Laertes had to take the second way: he killed his sister by witchcraft, drowning her so he could secretly sell her body to the witches."

I raised an objection. "They found her body and buried it. Indeed Laertes jumped into the grave to see his sister once more—so, you see, the body was truly there. Hamlet, who had just come back, jumped in after him."

"What did I tell you?" The elder appealed to the others. "Laertes was up to no good with his sister's body. Hamlet prevented him, because the chief's heir, like a chief, does not wish any other man to grow rich and powerful. Laertes would be angry, because he would have killed his sister without benefit to himself. In our country he would try to kill Hamlet for that reason. Is this not what happened?"

"More or less," I admitted. "When the great chief found Hamlet was still alive, he encouraged Laertes to try to kill Hamlet and arranged a fight with machetes between them. In the fight both young men were wounded to death. Hamlet's mother drank the poisoned beer that the chief meant for Hamlet in case he won the fight. When he saw his mother die of poison, Hamlet, dying, managed to kill his father's brother with his machete."

"You see, I was right!" exclaimed the elder.

"That was a very good story," added the old man, "and you told it with very few mistakes. There was just one more error, at the very end. The poison Hamlet's mother drank was obviously meant for the survivor of the fight, whichever it was. If Laertes had won, the great chief would have poisoned him, for no one would know that he arranged Hamlet's death. Then, too, he need not fear Laertes' witchcraft; it takes a strong heart to kill one's only sister by witchcraft.

"Sometime," concluded the old man, gathering his ragged toga about him, "you must tell us some more stories of your country. We, who are elders, will instruct you in their true meaning, so that when you return to your own land your elders will see that you have not been sitting in the bush, but among those who know things and who have taught you wisdom."

====

FOR DISCUSSION AND REVIEW

1. In the opening paragraph, Bohannan quotes her English friend as saying, "one can easily misinterpret the universal by misunderstanding the particular." How does this comment relate to Bohannan's own interpretation of *Hamlet*? How does it relate to the response to *Hamlet* of her African audience?

2. For what reason does Bohannan agree to tell the story of Hamlet to the tribespeople?

3. At one point, Bohannan abandons *Hamlet* for a few moments in order to take notes. Both she and the elders are authorities in their own culture; when it comes to storytelling, however, they behave very differently. Discuss these differences and the reasons for them.

4. Near the end of the essay, the old man remarks that "people are the same everywhere." What do both the comment and this theme have to do with language?

5. Bohannan noticed that translating "scholar" into "man who knew things" fundamentally changed the concept being translated. Explain.

6. The words "father," "wife," "widow," and "ghost" appear to have culture-specific meanings. Discuss how this is possible.

7. At crucial points in the story-telling, Tiv audience members resist Bohannan's explanations for Hamlet's actions. What alternate motivations do they give?

8. Does this essay support the Sapir-Whorf hypothesis that language shapes our understanding of the world?

Projects for "Language and Culture"

1. Following his selection "Pidgins and Creoles" in *The Cambridge Encyclopedia of Language,* David Crystal lists one hundred different pidgin and creole languages of the world along with a map to illustrate their locations. Some of the most prominent or most widely used of those listed include the following:

- Hawaiian Pidgin/Creole, estimated 500,000 speakers
- Gullah, estimated 150,000–300,000 speakers
- Louisiana Creole French
- Papiamentu (Papiamento), estimated 200,000 speakers
- Haitian French Creole, estimated four million speakers
- Sranan, estimated 800,000 speakers
- Cocoliche
- Bagot Creole English
- Australian Pidgin
- Cameroon Pidgin English, estimated two million speakers
- Tok Pisin (Neo-Malaysian), estimated one million speakers
- Congo Pidgins

Choose one of these pidgin or creole languages, or go to the selection and choose one. Keep in mind that some languages with "pidgin" in the name, like Zaire Pidgin English, have become creoles. After doing library research, prepare a report on the language and share what you have discovered with the class. Where and why did the pidgin or creole language originate? What groups of people started speaking it? What other languages or dialects does it influence? What appears to be the future of the language? After your class has shared their reports, create a list of characteristics all pidgins and creoles have in common.

2. As an alternative to the previous project, look at Crystal's list, "100 pidgins and creoles" in *The Cambridge Encyclopedia of Language.* It shows that a significant number of people worldwide speak at least one creole language. When we look at the world map, we see that many of the creole languages developed in coastal or port areas where trade occurred or in areas that underwent colonization. Select one of the creole languages from Crystal's list, and write a research paper on the origins and development of this language.

3. Pidginized languages have been described as "reduced" or "minimal," yet where they exist, they serve as the basis for communication in significant arenas of life. As Ronald Wardhaugh notes in *An Introduction to Sociolinguistics*, fifth edition, a pidginized language is often "highly

functional in the lives of those who use them and are important for that reason if for no other" (p. 62). First, research the *uses* of a pidginized variety, such as the pidgin German of the Gastarbeiters ("guest-workers") in the 1970s and 1980s, Nigerian Pidgin English, or Juba Arabic of Southern Sudan. After you have gathered information about the origins, speakers, and uses of the language, write an expository essay demonstrating the value of the language in the cultures that use it.

4. Lakoff and Johnson argue that metaphors play a key role in language, thought, and action. Try to determine whether your experience provides evidence for this claim. First, select one of the following conceptual metaphors:

- Ideas are plants.
- Understanding is seeing.
- Knowledge is a landscape.
- Sadness *or* happiness has a direction.
- Importance has size.

Then collect a number of specific everyday expressions that reflect this metaphor. You might use news media, literary works, advertising, product labels, television or movie dialogue, or music lyrics, along with your own typical expressions. Now write up your findings. How many different expressions of the underlying metaphor did you discover? What do the variations indicate? What connections do you find between how you think about this concept and the expressions you use for it?

5. Nicholas Evans's essay refutes the idea that some languages are simple or primitive. He mentions several language myths, such as the idea that some languages don't have grammar, have limited vocabularies, or are not suitable for modern technology or science. Other language myths include the notion that some languages are more beautiful or logical than others or that television makes everyone sound the same. Choose one of these language myths, or select another you are aware of, and write a persuasive essay making a case for or against the myth. Include examples to provide evidence for your argument. Laurie Bauer and Peter Trudgill's collection, *Language Myths,* may give you some ideas for your own argument (see Selected Bibliography).

6. Many writers who grew up in bilingual households or with two or more languages have examined how this linguistic dualism affected their sense of identity and shaped their perceptions of the world around them. Select the memoir pieces or essays on this topic by two different writers, and write a paper discussing their experiences. You might look at the work of American writers for whom English is not the first or dominant language, such as Richard Rodriguez and Gloria Anzaldua. You might also select writers, such as Leila Sebbar or Asia Djabar, who grew up in a colonized or postcolonial nation where a European language competed with an existing language.

7. In Part Six, James Crawford calls for the preservation of endangered Native American languages, and in this part, Nancy Lord argues that the loss of a language "diminishes the world." Each is writing from a position of personal commitment. For this project, research one of the endangered languages that has been discussed in the selections or another endangered language. Then write an essay exploring the ways that this endangered language does and/or doesn't embody the culture of the people who speak it.

8. Nancy Lord in "Native Tongues" discusses the Sapir-Whorf hypothesis of linguistic relativity, also known as the Whorfian hypothesis, which proposes that language determines how we know or experience the world and that differences in language result in differences in worldviews. Although this hypothesis, formulated by Edward Sapir and Benjamin Whorf in the 1930s, has been criticized over the years, it continues to be influential. Write a research paper on the Sapir-Whorf hypothesis. What were the historical contexts of this hypothesis? What cultures did Sapir and Whorf work with? What kinds of evidence provide the basis for the hypothesis?

9. Although the theory of linguistic relativity remains controversial, more recent research on early cognition suggests that linguistic categories may indeed influence how we understand the world. For this class project, divide into two groups. Each group should prepare a presentation about the idea of linguistic relativity. Discuss the scholarly arguments and evidence for and against this theory, and read some works that call linguistic relativity into question. For an overview of the theory, you might consult "The Linguistic Relativity Hypothesis" (http://plato.stanford.edu/entries/relativism/supplement2.html). These pieces should also help you form your argument: Geoffrey Pullum's essay "The Great Eskimo Vocabulary Hoax," in his book by the same title; Steven Pinker's "Mentalese" in *The Language Instinct*; John J. Gumperz and Stephen C. Levinson's collection, *Rethinking Linguistic Relativity*; and Anthony Woodbury's "Counting Eskimo Words for Snow: A Citizen's Guide," available online at www.princeton.edu/~browning/snow.html.

10. Oral culture has been an important part of almost every tradition. Before print was widespread in Europe, the bard, minstrel, skald, or troubadour played a role similar to that of the storyteller in an oral culture such as that of the Tiv. Research and write a descriptive paper about the role of the teller of news or stories in early Greece or medieval Europe. Alternatively, research and write a brief paper about the power bestowed on storytellers in a particular community. How are storytellers identified or chosen? What responsibilities do they have? What are their daily social and formal ceremonial functions? Does the role of storyteller include any culturally defined types of power?

11. Laura Bohannan may have been "quite sure that *Hamlet* had only one possible interpretation, and that one universally obvious," but she is not the only interpreter of the play to struggle with her audience

over concepts such as ghosts, madness, and incest. English-speaking audiences experience the same problems with a 400-year-old story about a quasi-historical event obscured in the mists of medieval Europe, though perhaps not to the extent the Tiv did.

For this project, keep a film journal noting how these culture-based concepts—ghosts, madness, incest—are interpreted in performance. First read Shakespeare's *Hamlet* if you are not already familiar with it. Then go to the movies. Several accessible versions of *Hamlet* are available on film, notably those featuring the performances of Laurence Olivier, Mel Gibson, Kenneth Branagh, and Ethan Hawke in the title role. View the Olivier version, followed by one or more of the others, and analyze their differences in interpreting the three concepts.

Selected Bibliography

Anzaldua, Gloria. *Borderlands/La Frontera: The New Mestiza.* 2nd ed. San Francisco: Aunt Lute, 1999. [In this part memoir, part poetry collection, part culture study, the author uses personal experience as a Tejana/American to critique the intersection of language, culture, and identity.]

Basso, Keith, H. *Western Apache Language and Culture: Essays in Linguistic Anthropology.* Tucson: U of Arizona P, 1990. [Essays spanning Basso's twenty-five years of experience with the Western Apache; includes his well-known discussions of silence, place naming, and metaphor.]

Bauer, Laurie, and Peter Trudgill. *Language Myths.* London: Penguin Books, 1998. [Essays studying topics and misconceptions about language, including the media's impact on language and reactions to various accents and speech among international speakers.]

Berlin, Brent, and Paul Kay. *Basic Color Terms: Their Universality and Evolution.* Berkeley and Los Angeles: U of California P, 1969. [Updated report on research begun at a Berkeley graduate seminar in 1967 and spanning more than thirty years of linguistic change via the process of color perception.]

Blount, Ben. *Language, Culture, and Society: A Book of Readings.* Long Grove, IL: Waveland, 1995. [Twenty-four essays spanning classic linguistics and contemporary language study from an individual, social, and cultural perspective.]

Bourdieu, Pierre. *Language and Symbolic Power.* Cambridge: Polity, 1991. [Critique of traditional linguistic theory, suggesting that language defines individuals rather than just providing a means for communicating with others.]

Crystal, David. *The Cambridge Encyclopedia of Language.* Cambridge: Cambridge UP, 1997. [Exhaustive consideration of language, covering theoretical and applied subfields of linguistics and topics ranging from alphabets to the Kurzweil Reading Machine.]

Duranti, Alessandro. *Linguistic Anthropology: A Reader.* Malden, MA: Blackwell, 2001. [Essays covering speech community and communicative competence, language performance, language socialization and literacy practices, and language and power.]

Duranti, Alessandro, Joan Bresnan, and Bernard Comrie. *Linguistic Anthropology.* Cambridge: Cambridge UP, 1997. [Combines historical and contemporary theory to address cultural systems, diversity, and ethnological methods.]

García, O., and Otheguy, R., eds. *English across Cultures; Cultures across English: A Reader in Cross-Cultural Communication.* Berlin: Mouton de Gruyter, 1989. [Essays about intercultural communication in globalized classrooms, with discussions of English in Ireland, Black English in Britain, and Puerto Rican English in New York.]

Gumperz, John J., and Stephen C. Levinson, eds. *Rethinking Linguistic Relativity.* Cambridge: Cambridge UP, 1996. [Essays addressing contemporary theories of linguistic relativity and the Sapir-Whorf hypothesis.]

Holm, John. *Pidgins and Creoles.* Cambridge Language Surveys. Vols. 1 and 2. Cambridge: Cambridge UP, 1988. [Volume 1 focuses on linguistic structure and theory, while Volume 2 provides a sociohistorical discussion of approximately 100 pidgins and creoles.]

Kuipers, Joel C., and Judith Irvine. *Language, Identity, and Marginality in Indonesia: The Changing Nature of Ritual Speech on the Island of Sumba.* Cambridge: Cambridge UP, 1998. [Discussion of the impact of Indonesian on local and regional languages and the social and political consequence of the shift, focusing on Weyewa society on Sumba Island.]

Lakoff, George. *Women, Fire and Dangerous Things: What Categories Reveal about the Mind.* Chicago: U of Chicago P, 1990. [A study of cognitive linguistics and its impact on social science studies.]

Lakoff, George, and Mark Johnson. *Metaphors We Live By.* 2nd ed. Chicago: U of Chicago P, 2003. [Examination of the central role of metaphor to cognition and expression.]

Lawler, John. "Metaphors We Compute By." 1999. Home page. 4 Apr. 2007. U of Michigan. <www-personal.umich.edu/~jlawler/meta4compute.html>. [Meaning and uses of metaphor as applied to computer language.]

Leach, Edmund. *Culture and Communication: The Logic by Which Symbols Are Connected: An Introduction to the Use of Structuralist Analysis in Social Anthropology.* Cambridge: Cambridge UP, 1976. [Addresses issues pertaining to structuralist writing, especially Levi-Strauss's work.]

Le Page, Robert. *Acts of Identity: Creole-Based Approaches to Language and Ethnicity.* Cambridge: Cambridge UP, 1985. [Examines, through extensive fieldwork with Creole communities, the understanding and perceptions of language within the community and of those outside the community.]

Lucy, John Arthur. *Language Diversity and Thought: A Reformulation of the Linguistic Relativity Hypothesis.* Cambridge: Cambridge UP, 1992. [Reconsiders Sapir-Whorf theories of relativity, using comparisons between American English and Maya of southeastern Mexico.]

Mühlhäusler, Peter. *Pidgin and Creole Linguistics.* Oxford: Basil Blackwell, 1986. [The study of pidgins and creoles with discussion of grammaticalization.]

Parkin, David, *Semantic Anthropology.* Burlington, VT: Academic, 1983. [Foundational essys that explore how meaning is generated during significant interactions concerning illness among Aborigines, politics in Mali, Christian greetings that distinguish the saved from the unsaved in Kasigau Kenya, and more.]

Pidgin and Creole Languages: A Guide to Green Library Collections. 27 June 2005. Stanford U. <www-sul.stanford.edu/depts/ssrg/pidgins/pidgin.html>. [Online resource on pidgins and creoles, with glossaries, references, maps, catalogs, and checklists.]

Pullam, Geoffrey K. *The Great Eskimo Vocabulary Hoax and Other Irreverent Essays on the Study of Language.* Chicago: U of Chicago P, 1991. [An entertaining collection that examines the myths and notions of language.]

Romaine, Suzanne. *Pidgin and Creole Languages.* London: Longman, 1988. [Examination of the history and linguistic structures of pidgins and creoles.]

Salzman, Zdenek. *Language, Culture, and Society: An Introduction to Linguistic Anthropology.* 3rd ed. Boulder: Westview, 2003. [Updated edition of a comprehensive introduction that now includes consideration of language and gender, ethnicity, and diversity.]

Scollon, Ron, and Suzanne Wong Scollon, "Discourse and Intercultural Communication," in *The Handbook of Discourse Analysis.* Malden, MA:

Blackwell, 2001, 538–47. [Demonstrates how discourse analysis can be applied to deconstruct, interpret, and delimit cultural categories. Rejecting "culture" as a preexistent, examines how identities and meaning are constructed within and by means of interaction.]

Swoyer, Chris. "The Linguistic Relativity Hypothesis." *Stanford Encyclopedia of Philosophy*. 2003. Stanford U. <http://plato.stanford.edu/entries/relativism/supplement2.html>. [Hypothesizes about differences in language in relation to differences in perception.]

Thomason, Sarah G., and Terrence Kaufman. *Language Contact, Creoliation, and Genetic Linguistics*. Berkeley and Los Angeles: U of California P, 1988. [Introduction to the impact of social and political factors on language change and viability.]

Todd, Loreto. *Some Day Been Dey: West African Pidgin Folktales*. London: Routledge and Kegan Paul, 1971. [West African tales from author's massive collection of oral and written literatures, including pidgin texts from Africa.]

PART EIGHT

LANGUAGE AND GENDER

The study of language and gender combines two related concerns: how language expresses gender and how language shapes gender. Linguists studying social dialects have long noted that women and men appear to use language differently and, fueled by recent theoretical developments in related fields, that these differences influence how we understand what it is to be feminine or masculine. As Stanford professor Penelope Eckert says, "Gender is not independent of other aspects of social identity." Today, we understand *gender* not as an abstract biological category or an innate personality trait we are born with, but as something we make or *do* in specific contexts. In the study of language and gender, we ask how language is used to construct gender and how language encodes specific ideas of gender.

In the first selection, "Language and Gender," Mary Talbot introduces the idea of *gender*. It is, she tells us, a social construct, not a fixed biological category. She begins by presenting early research on sex differences in language that focus on how, in some cultures, women and men use distinctly different sounds, pronouns, or vocabulary items, while in other cultures differences involve kinds of language use. For instance, among British and American English speakers, women use more standard grammatical forms than men. These differences reflect what it means to be *female* or *male* in that culture. In general, Talbot suggests, gendered language not only reflects social differences between men and women, but also to a certain extent creates or maintains these differences.

Next, in "Discourse Patterns of Males and Females," Fern L. Johnson examines language use from a cultural perspective. Focusing on the United States, she finds that "we all speak culturally." In other words, our conversations, like other aspects of culture, express our shared histories and traditions. As Johnson looks at various discourse patterns, she finds that even in early childhood play, girls reproduce the softer, polite, higher-pitched voices considered feminine and boys the more forceful, straightforward, lower-pitched voices associated with masculinity.

As adults, women and men also seem to use qualitatively different strategies for conducting conversation. Although, as Johnson notes, much of the research on gendered discourse has been limited to those of European background, she finds substantial evidence that we make or construct gender by means of language.

In the last two classic selections, Deborah Tannen explores how men's and women's language behaviors differ and why the differences often lead to communication problems. Tannen claims that women and men misunderstand each other because they grow up in and continue to live in what amounts to different worlds. In "'I'll Explain It to You': Lecturing and Listening," she argues that women and men have different goals in conversation and that the conversational strategies men use, such as interruption, help to establish their own status and authority. In "Ethnic Style in Male–Female Conversation," Tannen analyzes how ethnic differences between married partners affect their conversation. Looking particularly at the strategy of indirectness, she finds that different cultural backgrounds further complicate communication between men and women.

36

Language and Gender

Mary Talbot

Dr. Mary Talbot, in the Department of Language and Culture at Sunderland University in England, is interested in the relationships among language, gender, and power and in how these play out in advertising and related media. In this selection from her 1998 text Language and Gender: An Introduction, *she first reviews some early language and gender studies. This research reveals that in some languages, Japanese for instance, sex differentiation is absolute—women use one sound or word and men use another. In others, differences are in frequency, that is, in how often particular words or language patterns are used. Talbot then distinguishes between biologically determined sex and the sociological idea of gender and notes the pitfalls of treating sex and gender as the same thing. Language use, she stresses, is part of gender identity— something we learn along with our other cultural behaviors.*

Gender is an important division in all societies. It is of enormous significance to human beings. Being born male or female has far-reaching consequences for an individual. It affects how we act in the world, how the world treats us. This includes the language we use, and the language used about us. I want . . . to make you more conscious of the social category of gender, of the divisions made on the basis of it and, not least, of the part language plays in establishing and sustaining these divisions. In linguistics and language learning, the label 'language and gender' sometimes causes a bit of confusion because people naturally think of gender as a grammatical category. . . . Gender, in the sense I am using it here, is a social category, not a grammatical one.

LINGUISTIC SEX DIFFERENTIATION

The earliest work on men, women and language attended to 'sex differentiation'. Studies of such differences were carried out by Europeans (and other 'Westerners') with an interest in anthropology. They have tended to concentrate on phonological and lexicogrammatical 'exotica' (sound patterns, words and structures). A great deal of this kind of study has focused on the existence of different pronouns or affixes specific for

men and women, whether as speakers, spoken to or spoken about. Sex differentiation of this kind is uncommon in languages of European origin.
The pronoun systems of Germanic languages—such as English and
Danish—only distinguish sex in third person singular reference (*he/him*,
she/her or *it*). That is, when one individual is speaking to a second one
about a third, the sex of the third person is specified. The pronoun systems
of Romance languages—such as French, Italian and Spanish—are similar,
except that they mark sex in the third person *plural* (*ils/elles*, etc.) as well.
Colloquial Arabic also has sex-marking in the second person singular
(*you*); so that in addressing a person as *you*, the pronoun you use will
depend on whether that person is male (*ʔinta*) or female (*ʔinti*). (The
symbol *ʔ* represents a glottal stop.)

Other languages have very different pronoun systems. The Japanese
one is complicated by the existence of distinct levels of formality and the
need to take into account the status of the person you are talking to in
deciding which level to use. There is a range of different words for the
first person pronoun, *I*, for instance. There are formal pronouns which
can be used by both women and men: *watashi* and the highly formal
watakushi. Less formally, *atashi* is used only by women, *boku* traditionally only by men (there is also another form, *ore*, available to men if they
want to play up their masculinity). Choice of pronoun depends here on
the sex of the speaker not the addressee. That is, if you are a woman you
must use the 'female' pronoun form and if you are a man you must
choose from the 'male' forms. Japan does appear to be undergoing change.
Girls in Japanese high schools say that they use the first-person pronoun
boku, because if they use *atashi* they cannot compete with the boys
(Jugaku 1979, cited in Okamoto 1995: 314). Feminists have been reported
using another form, *boke*, to refer to themselves (Romaine 1994: 111).

In some traditional, tribal societies, men and women have a whole
range of different vocabularies that they use (while presumably understanding 'male' and 'female' forms but not using both). An extreme
example of this phenomenon was in the language used by the Carib
Indians (who inhabited what is now Dominica, in the Lesser Antilles).
When explorers from Europe first encountered these people, they thought
the women and the men were speaking distinct languages. A European
writer-traveller in the seventeenth century had this to say about them:

> the men have a great many expressions peculiar to them, which the
> women understand but never pronounce themselves. On the other hand,
> the women have words and phrases which the men never use, or they
> would be laughed to scorn. Thus it happens that in their conversations it
> often seems as if the women had another language than the men.
> (Rochefort, cited in Jespersen 1922: 237)

This linguistic situation is more likely in stable, conservative cultures, where male and female social roles are not flexible. However, a
contemporary tribal people in Brazil, the Karajá—whose language has

TABLE 36.1   Differences in Male and Female Speech in Karajá

MALE SPEECH	FEMALE SPEECH	PORTUGUESE	ENGLISH
heto	hetoku		house
otu	kotu		turtle
bisileta	bisikreta	bicicleta	bicycle
nobiotxu	nobikutxu	domingo	Sunday

Source: Fortune and Fortune 1987: 476.

more differences between male and female speech than any other language—are currently coping with rapid and profound cultural changes affecting every aspect of their society. In Karajá speech, sex of speaker is marked phonologically. There are systematic sound differences between male and female forms of words, even occurring in loan words from Portuguese. There are some examples in table 36.1. Notice the absence of /k/ and /ku/ in male speech.

Traditionally, the Karajá speakers have very clearly defined social roles for women and men. The distinct male and female forms contribute to marking these two domains, a central aspect of Karajá tribal identity. Since young people are now learning to read and write in their mother-tongue of Karajá, these distinct forms will be retained. As a consequence, they will be less likely to lose their sense of cultural identity in the process of assimilation into the larger, Portuguese-speaking Brazilian society than if they had to acquire literacy through Portuguese.

Sex differences in language of the kind we have been considering were grouped together as *sex-exclusive* differentiation in the 1970s. A distinction between sex-exclusive and *sex-preferential* differentiation—first suggested by an American linguist, Ann Bodine—became popular for labelling two different kinds of feature under investigation. Unlike sex-exclusive differences, sex-preferential differences are not absolute; they are matters of degree. While sex-exclusive differentiation is fairly uncommon in languages of European origin, the same cannot be said of sex-preferential differentiation. [It has been argued, for instance, that] women use forms of language that are closer to the prestige 'Standard' than men do (that is, speak more 'correctly'), and . . . that [they] use a cooperative style in conversation while men use a style based on competitiveness.

Both sex-exclusive and sex-preferential differences are highly culture-specific. Acquiring them is an important part of learning how to behave as 'proper' men and women in a particular culture. Failure to acquire appropriate forms and their usage can have serious, even devastating, consequences for the individuals concerned. Gretchen Fortune, an American linguist in Brazil who co-produced the original writing system which is still used by the Karajá, has told of one young Karajá speaker whose use of women's forms was not corrected by his parents (Fortune 1995). This individual's collision with the linguistic norms of his community meant that he became a type of 'misfit' and source of ridicule within the community. For him, as a 'misfit', Portuguese provided a new identity and a kind of liberation.

Linguistic sex differentiation can become a location of social struggle within a society, not just the struggle of one individual. Japanese men's and women's forms are ceasing to be sex exclusive, that is, forms used exclusively by one sex.

SEX VERSUS GENDER

This brings me to the distinction between sex and gender. It was first articulated in detail by a British feminist in the early seventies (Oakley 1972). It does not exist in all languages—it's absent from French, Norwegian and Danish, for example—but for us, as language scholars, it is an important distinction.

Sex is biologically founded. It is a matter of genes, gonads and hormones. Female ova contain the female sex chromosome X; a male sperm contains either a female X chromosome or a male Y chromosome. Ultimately whether you have ended up male or female is all down to whether your father gave you an X or a Y. It is these chromosomes which determine the development of the gonads (embryonic sex glands) into either ovaries or testes. At around eight weeks old, the gonads of a fetus with one X and one Y chromosome start to produce the 'male' hormone testosterone, after which the fetus begins to develop male genitalia. Without the production of this hormone, the fetus continues as normal; that is, it carries on developing as a female. Sex is essentially binary. One is either male or female (of course, hermaphrodites confuse the picture; I'll come to that in the next section).

Gender by contrast is socially constructed; it is learned. People acquire characteristics which are perceived as masculine and feminine. In everyday language, it makes sense to talk of a 'masculine' woman or a 'feminine' man. Unlike sex, gender is not binary; we can talk about one man being more masculine (or feminine) than another. This contrast is reflected in the grammar of English. Grammatically we can have *masculine, more masculine, most masculine* but not *male, *maler, *malest* (the asterisk is marking the ungrammatical forms, a convention in linguistics). People are 'gendered' and actively involved in the process of their own gendering. . . .

From the above it is clear that what have been called sex-exclusive and sex-preferential differentiations are in fact ways of *doing gender.* They are part of behaving as 'proper' men and women in particular cultures. If they were genuinely matters of biological sex, they would not display the extraordinary diversity that they do. They would be the same everywhere.

So it would be misleading, and not at all helpful, to conflate sex and gender. Accounts differ, however, over the extent to which differences between the sexes are biologically determined or learned. For instance, there is a good deal of evidence indicating that men tend to be more aggressive than women. There are many more men than women convicted of violent crime. The presence of higher levels of testosterone in men than in women is often used to account for this difference (testosterone is known as the male hormone and is crucial in the development of the male fetus, but it is found in women as well).

The research evidence is far from being conclusive, however. There seems to be a connection between high testosterone levels and aggression, but it certainly is not possible to claim a definite *causal* link between them. That is, we cannot say for sure that testosterone makes people aggressive. After all, there is a lot of research evidence documenting boys' tendency to be more aggressive than girls, even at pre-school age; different levels of aggression between boys and girls cannot be put down to hormone differences, since children's hormone levels are negligible. In fact, there is some research to suggest that it might be the other way around: a person's aggressiveness might cause an increase in their testosterone level. We have a chicken-and-egg situation, in fact. And the problem doesn't end there. What do we mean by aggression anyway? The term is notoriously imprecise (see, for example, the Australian feminist Lynne Segal's account of it being used synonymously with 'dominance' (1994: 182)). It can be used to refer to very different phenomena, from assertiveness in seminars to serial killing.

So, is men's tendency for greater aggression a biological (that is, sexual) characteristic, or is it an aspect of masculine gender and therefore socially constructed? Or is it perhaps both? Well, it is probably best to concede that people's behavior patterns come about in an interplay of biology and social practices, so that ultimately it is not really possible to separate the biological from the social. For the record, a causal link between testosterone and aggression has been established in rats and mice, not in humans or other primates. In some primate species, but not all, greater levels of aggression have been found among males than among females. Even where this is the case, there is no need for a biological explanation (Bem 1993: 34–5). As Segal observes:

> The biological alone is . . . never wholly determining of experience and behavior. For example, all people must eat, but what we eat, how, when and where we eat, the phenomena of vegetarianism, dieting, dietary rules, obesity, anorexia, indeed any human practice or problem surrounding eating cannot even be adequately conceived of, let alone understood, only by talk of biological propensities. (1994: 186)

In making claims about the relation between sex and gender, then, we need to be careful. When gender is mapped on to sex, as it frequently is, there is an implicit assumption that socially determined differences between women and men are natural and inevitable. The confusion of sex and gender has political underpinnings: it often accompanies a reassertion of traditional family roles, or justifications for male privileges. Consider a few examples. Here are some comments I have heard fairly recently. They probably sound all too familiar:

> Women aren't allowed to do what's natural these days. Normal women want to have babies, they want to stay at home, but they can't.

> Well, I suppose the boys do dominate in class. Oh, they hog the computers, naturally. No, the girls just aren't interested.

> You women always complain. So now it's 'competitive work environments', is it? You get what you want and you're never bloody satisfied. Always whingeing about something. 'Competitive work environments', 'harassment in the workplace'—what a load of crap! Not up to the job, more like.

> If you can't take the heat, sweetheart, go back to kitchen.

And so on. The last one was intended as a witty put-down, of course. (See Spender (1995) for Australian equivalents of the remark about boys in classrooms.) When the distinction between sex and gender is erased, restricted possibilities open to women and girls may be excused as biologically necessary and received ideas about differences in male and female capacities, needs and desires left unchallenged.

So claiming that sex and gender are essentially the same is a conservative argument. As Ann Oakley has observed, 'in situations of social change, biological explanations may assume the role of an ethical code akin in moral persuasiveness to religion' (1982: 93). An extreme, and hence comical, expression of this in operation was in a magazine article in the late seventies dealing with a perceived threat to humanity in enormous numbers of women choosing the independence of a working wage over domesticity and dependency. The article was headed 'Ambition, stress, power, work—IS IT ALL TURNING WOMEN INTO MEN?' In it a 'top endocrinologist and Professor of Medicine' appealed to women to 'recognize their limits before it's too late' (cited in Kramarae 1981: v–vi). Too late for what, I wonder?

I wish it was always so easy to laugh at, though. There is a popular and influential field of research devoted to reducing human behavior to biology. Sociobiology, as it is known, tries to establish a genetic basis for behavior. A recent contribution to this field claims to provide evidence that black Americans' relatively poor educational achievement is genetically based (Murray and Herrnstein 1994); in other words, that black people are genetically inferior. It is rather startling to find similar biological fundamentalism among feminists. Consider, for example, the American feminist Andrea Dworkin's dogmatic and frighteningly reductive assertion that 'violence is male and the male is the penis' (1979: 515).

Claims about direct biological influences on language are just as contentious. There has been a huge amount of research attempting to establish sex-related differences in brain capacity, a lot of it in recent years by sociobiologists. It is politically highly sensitive. Disputed claims about cognitive differences are that women are born to be better with language than men, and men are innately better than women with visual and spatial things. There are indeed some fairly well-documented differences:

1. Girls statistically go through the stages of language development a little earlier than boys.
2. Girls are less likely to have language-related disturbances, such as stuttering and reading difficulties.
3. The right and left hemispheres of the brains of girls and women tend to be less specialized in function than in boys and men (less lateralized). This means that the speech centres are not so exclusively established in the left hemisphere; women process speech on the right side more than men do. The upshot of this is that if a woman's left hemisphere is injured (through a stroke, for example) she will probably show less impairment of speech than a man would.

Difference 3 is often used to account for 1 and 2. There is a major problem with this, however. We have a chicken-and-egg situation again. How can we assume that the difference in lateralization is innate? Newborn babies don't fit the pattern at all. In fact, some researchers have discovered that *boys'* brains tend to be less lateralized. Environmental influence seems a far more plausible way of accounting for the differences. There is plenty of evidence indicating that boys and girls are spoken to differently. Apparently we talk to baby girls more, for instance. Might this not stimulate greater facility with language? It seems highly likely. To cut a long story short, after vast amounts of research trying to prove fundamental biological differences in the mental capacities of women and men, results have been inconclusive. What intrigues me is that people want to find such differences at all. As British linguist Deborah Cameron has observed, 'studies of "difference" are not just disinterested quests for the truth, but in an unequal society inevitably have a political dimension' (Coates and Cameron 1988: 5–6).

   In dealing with learned kinds of activity, such as linguistic interaction, we can only speak with any certainty about gendered behavior. Linguistic interaction is obviously behavior which has been learned, and there is little point in trying to account for it by talking about innate qualities. In societies with sex-exclusive differences in language use, choice from among a range of lexicogrammatical options is part of gender performance. The word 'choice' is perhaps not the right one, since the forms for use by women and men are enforced by prescriptive rule. They can be compared with prescriptive rules in English such as 'two negatives make a positive', 'never end a sentence with a preposition', or 'don't say "him and me", say "he and I"'. Speakers are corrected, one way or another, if they produce inappropriate forms. The consequences of transgressing the rules are probably more dire than they would be for an

English speaker these days, however. Occasionally there are exceptions when speakers are not corrected and suffer as a result, as we know from Fortune's research among the Karajá in Brazil.

Gender, then, is not biological but psycho-social; it should always be considered in the context of social relations between people.

SEX AND GENDER AS TROUBLESOME DICHOTOMIES

A recent collection on language and gender research opens with the observation that 'Just as we rarely question our ability to breathe, so we rarely question the habit of dividing human beings into two categories: females and males' (Bergvall, Bing and Freed 1996: 1). The authors of this first chapter, American linguists Janet Bing and Victoria Bergvall, go on to consider how human beings need to impose categories and boundaries on experience in order to understand it. This is something very familiar to linguists. Boundaries in our experiences can be quite fuzzy and vague; language puts things into clear-cut categories, imposing boundaries, limits and divisions on reality. Bing and Bergvall observe, for example, that we have the distinct categories of 'day' and 'night', but the actual boundaries between them are indistinct. We cannot identify precisely when it stops being daytime and becomes night. Day and night are bipolar categories that language imposes; the reality is a continuum. Similarly, sociolinguists interested in dialect continua are used to dealing with indistinct boundaries. It can be very difficult to determine where one variety of a dialect or language ends and another begins. The point Bing and Bergvall are making is that a lot of experience is best described as a continuum and bipolar categories are not always accurate.

I have already observed that gender is a continuum. It makes sense to talk about degrees of masculinity and femininity. We can say that one person is more feminine than another. But surely male and female are clear-cut categories, aren't they? Well, usually yes, but not always. It turns out that sex is also a continuum. In the last section I presented the basic determinants of fetal sexual development. Sometimes things happen differently, however. For instance, a fetus with X and Y chromosomes may not receive its crucial dose of the 'male' hormone testosterone at eight weeks. It may not be enough. Or if enough, it may be at the wrong time. 'Mistakes' like these mean intersexed development of the fetus. Not all individuals are born male or female. Some are born as both, some as neither, and some are indeterminate. According to figures cited by Bing and Bergvall, for every 30,000 births there is one intersexed infant. 'Although the birth of intersexed individuals is not rare,' as they observe, 'it *is* unmentionable, even in tabloids that regularly report such outrageous topics as copulation with extraterrestrials and the reappearance of Elvis.' In industrialized societies, the binary distinction between male and female is medically enforced. Exceptions are 'corrected', surgically and with hormone treatment. Since this is the case, it should be no surprise that physicians acknowledge that sex as well as gender is socially constructed (Bing and Bergvall 1996: 8–9).

In some writing on language and gender there is a tendency to treat the pyscho-social categories of masculine and feminine as bipolar. This is particularly true of work on distinct interactional styles of men and women. . . . Such studies put essentialism out through the front door, only to let it in again at the back. That is to say, they do away with biological essentialism, just to replace it with a kind of social essentialism, which is just as bad. . . . Bing and Bergvall pessimistically predict that, despite our increasing awareness of the problems of gender polarization and stereotyping, 'there will probably be no decline in the number of students who begin their term-paper research with the question, "How is the language of men and women different?" Such questions strengthen deeply held certainties that mere facts cannot dislodge' (1996: 6). I sincerely hope they are mistaken.

BIBLIOGRAPHY

Bem, Sandra Lipsitz (1993) *The Lenses of Gender: Transforming the Debate on Sexual Inequality*. New Haven: Yale University Press.

Bergvall, Victoria L., Bing, Janet M. and Freed, Alice F. (eds) (1996) *Rethinking Language and Gender Research: Theory and Practice*. London: Longman.

Bing, Janet M. and Bergvall, Victoria L. (1996) The question of questions: beyond binary thinking. In Bergvall, Bing and Freed 1996.

Coates, Jennifer and Cameron, Deborah (eds) (1998) *Women in their Speech Communities*. London: Longman.

Dworkin, Andrea (1979) *Pornography: Men Possessing Women*. New York: Dutton.

Fortune, Gretchen (1995) Gender marking in Karajá. Paper presented at Lancaster University (Linguistics Dept), 10 March.

Hall, Kira, and Mary Bucholtz, eds. (1995) *Gender Articulated: Language and the Socially Constructed Self*. New York: Routledge.

Jespersen, Otto (1992) *Language: Its Nature, Development and Origin*. London: Allen & Unwin.

Jugaku, Akiko (1979) *Nihongo to onna* (The Japanese language and women). Tokyo: Iwanami.

Kramarae, Cheris (1981) *Women and Men Speaking*. Rowley, Mass.: Newbury House.

Murray, Charles and Herrnstein, Richard (1994) *The Bell Curve: Intelligence and Class Structure in American Life*. New York: Free Press.

Oakley, Ann (1972) *Sex, Gender and Society*. London: Temple Smith.

Oakley, Ann (1982) *Subject Women*. London: Fontana.

Okamoto, Shigeko (1995) 'Tasteless' Japanese: less 'feminine' speech among young Japanese women. In Hall and Bucholtz 1995.

Romaine, Suzanne (1994) *Language in Society: An Introduction to Socio-linguistics*. Oxford: Oxford University Press.

Segal, Lynne (1994) *Is the Future Female? Troubled Thoughts on Contemporary Feminism*. First published 1987. London: Virago.

Spender, Dale (1995) *Nattering on the Net: Women, Power and Cyberspace*. Melbourne: Spinifex.

FOR DISCUSSION AND REVIEW

1. Talbot gives several examples of sex differentiation in specific languages. What are the first-person pronoun differences in Japanese? How does the pronoun relate to the speaker? What might it mean that pronoun choice is changing in Japan? Why would girls in Japanese high schools choose *boku* rather than *atashi*?

2. Germanic and Romance languages have less sex differentiation than others that Talbot mentions. Does this mean that gender identity is less important in English-, Danish-, or French-speaking cultures? Why, or why not?

3. Distinguish between sex-exclusive and sex-preferential differences in language. What examples of these differences does Talbot provide? Jot down some examples of gender-specific words, grammatical forms, pitch, or intonation in your own culture. Are these examples of sex-exclusive or sex-preferential differences?

4. According to Talbot, what is the difference between sex and gender? List some behavioral differences between men and women. How might you account for these differences?

5. What kinds of problems can occur when sex and gender are considered the same?

6. Talbot observes that "gender is a continuum" and that it "makes sense to talk about degrees of masculinity and femininity." What does she mean by these statements? How can language be more or less masculine or fiminine?

37

Discourse Patterns of Males and Females

Fern L. Johnson

Fern L. Johnson, professor of English at Clark University, brings a "language-centered perspective on culture" to her discussion of gendered discourses in this selection, taken from her book Speaking Culturally: Language Diversity in the United States *(2000). Because gender is part of cultural identity, she believes that examining our patterns of language behaviors helps us understand how gender is constructed. Here, Johnson asks us to pay attention to the conversations of our everyday lives. Using the research of the past thirty years, she discusses the complexities of gendered language among children and among adults. Dispelling some myths along the way, Johnson explains a number of important concepts, including folk linguistics, topic selection, talkativeness, topic control, and interruptions.*

As cultural beings, women and men discursively display their gender identities across the life span. From birth onward, how men and women speak, how they are spoken about and to, and their more general relation to discourse are profoundly fashioned through social experience. In this section, I first consider the concept of gendered folk linguistics and then evidence documenting the impact of gender on children's and adult language-in-use.

Folk Linguistics

I begin with the notion that, as cultural beings, all of us learn and carry in our heads certain ideas about men's and women's speech. These ideas about speech (whether verifiable or not) comprise *folk linguistics*, or the ideas about speech held by those who are not specialists in the analysis of language. I frequently ask students in my class on language diversity to characterize the language and communication style of males and females by using words and phrases that come to mind quickly. Over more than a decade, women and men alike consistently characterize men in comparison to women as more direct, harsher, less willing to reveal emotions, more

517

impersonal, more likely to use slang and swear words, more assertive, more likely to promote their own ideas, more sports-oriented, and so forth. When it comes to characterizing women's communication, they say that women tend to be less forceful, softer in voice, more personal, likely to talk a lot, oriented to trivia and gossip, more polite, more grammatically correct, less inclined to promote the self, and so forth. These consistencies convey a commonality in the folk linguistics of gendered language use for mass U.S. culture. What my students said in the late 1990s and what they said in the 1980s also mirror the results of studies accessing the perceptions and stereotypes of men's and women's speech done back in the mid-1970s (Kramer, 1977 [later citations to the same person are under the name of Kramarae]; Siegler & Siegler, 1976).

Although certainly a mixture of fact and fiction, folk linguistics guide individuals in framing perceptions, social expectations, and personal evaluations. For example, a folk linguistic perception might hold that soft voices are nonassertive or that gossip is trivial. Moreover, folk linguistics guide the training of girls and boys in the "ought-ness" of their language use: Girls "ought" to speak politely; boys "ought" to speak confidently.

THE LANGUAGE OF BOYS AND GIRLS

As preschoolers, my two sons took great delight in an enactment that I call "We're girls." They presented themselves with dishtowels on their heads to signify long hair and gleefully exclaimed in unnaturally high-pitched, whiney voices, "We're girls! We're girls!" Naming many girls (and women) who had neither long hair nor high voices failed to dampen the boys' enactment; it was repeated many times, revealing their own folk linguistics of gendered (in this case girls') speech. Where had they gotten this representation of girls? Was it from friends? If so, from boys or girls? From teachers? From stories that had been read to them? From watching cartoons? Although we smugly exonerated the nuclear family as a teacher in this case, cultural learning about gender enactments spoke powerfully in their play behavior. The precise locale of learning is impossible to pinpoint simply because gender models abound. Our boys were already gender-saturated.

The tacit knowledge possessed by children about gendered language has been the focus of intriguing academic research. Elaine Andersen (1986) looked at children's folk linguistics when she studied the discourse produced in puppet situations where the children played the role of father, mother, or child in family, school, or medical situations. She found that 5-year-old girls and boys clearly distinguish the language of mothers and fathers in their enactments. Mothers' speech was portrayed as softer; more talkative, polite, and qualified; and filled with more endearments and baby talk; compared with fathers' speech, which was louder; more straightforward, forceful, and unqualified; and pitched more deeply. This research corresponds with what one hears from young children when they are play-acting: They force their voices into lower-pitched ranges when playing dads and men and into higher-pitched ranges when playing moms and women.

But how does gender manifest itself in the more mundane day-to-day discourse of young children? The picture appears to be one of early encul-turation into gendered language patterns for topics spoken about, styles in same-sex interactions, and sex role-linked language in situations where girls and boys interact with one another.

Same-Sex Interaction

A number of studies compare the language patterns of preschool and early school-age boys and girls when interacting among themselves. In one study (Austin, Salehi, & Leffler, 1987), the interactions in preschool of 3- to 5-year-old children from middle- and working-class backgrounds revealed different speech characteristics for girls and boys. Girls' speech exhibited more devices that served to facilitate interaction and to reinforce what others said, both of which provide continuity for the interaction. Boys' speech was replete with devices to get attention and to initiate a line of activity. Similarly, Cook, Fritz, McCornack, and Visperas (1985) found preschool-age boys to be more assertive than girls in their spontaneous language use while playing together with non-sex-typed toys, such as puzzles. Topics also emerge in this age group in sex-typical fashion. Boys as young as 4 years have been found to talk more about sports and particular locations and places for things compared to girls, who talk more about identity, wishes, needs, and preschool activity itself (Haas, 1979). The studies of young children also show the greater proclivity of females for talking as an activity in itself and of males for concrete activities and physical action. Deborah Tannen (1990) observed that second-grade girls easily talked together and shared personal stories; boys were uncomfortable being placed in a situation with nothing to do but talk. In a study of African American youth, Marjorie Harness Goodwin (1990) documented that girls from preschool onward spent more time talking than in any kind of play activity, which was not the case for boys.

An interesting set of analyses of "conflict talk" has been undertaken by Amy Sheldon (1990, 1992, 1993, 1996), who studied the discourse of 3- to 5-year-olds in day care centers. Although she found girls as well as boys to engage in conflict, their verbal strategies sounded quite different. The boys she observed handled conflict in a more heavy-handed fashion, expressing more self-assertive statements and dominance, whereas the girls used more collaborative discourse and negotiation as strategies to mitigate conflict (Sheldon, 1990, 1993).

Boys and Girls Together

There is less research that directly assesses the language behavior of boys and girls when they are together in interaction, but what does exist points to sex-role patterns that are strikingly conventional. Anita Esposito (1979) looked at mechanisms of dominance in the language of 3- and 4-year-olds playing together in a day care center. She found that boys interrupted girls twice as often as girls interrupted boys—a finding that will be of interest when adult language use is discussed. Haas (1979) found in studying 4-, 8-, and 12-year-olds that girls laughed more when interacting with boys than with each other. Almost 10 years later, Jacqueline Sachs (1987) reported that preschool girls soften their statements with an accompaniment of smiles.

It appears, then, that little girls and little boys demonstrate gender-linked language behaviors at an early age. They tend to gravitate toward same-sex play, and their verbal displays in that context reveal different patterns for what it means to engage in interpersonal discourse. Many toys and activities are sex-specific: Consider the proliferation of Barbie and other dolls for girls and road construction vehicles and combative action figures for boys. And clothing seems to be an escalating field for gender marking: Baby girls wear ribbons in their hair and little socks rimmed in lace, and although girls do wear pants, dresses and tights are currently *de rigueur*; boys' jeans come in styles with names like "Tough Skins," and pink, even if occasionally worn in combination with other colors during infancy, disappears in boys' clothing as they reach school age. Kids are often verbally enjoined by grown-ups—especially their parents—to behave in gender appropriate ways: Boys are told to "toughen up" and to "stand up for yourself" and "don't be a sissy"; girls are told to "act like a lady," "sit up properly," and "keep your dress down where it belongs." One incident I observed starkly exemplifies the parental role in verbally shaping gendered behavior. A mother, whose 3-year-old daughter was jumping down some steps in a public place with a 3-year-old boy, told her little girl several times to stop. Having no effect, she finally shouted, "Emily, stop that! Girls don't jump like that!"

Clearly, kids learn the implications of these many-gendered things early in life, as the cultural gendered worlds of men and women begin to take shape in guiding their thought, action, and language. In a provocative and widely cited essay, Daniel Maltz and Ruth Borker (1982) discuss the ways in which girls and boys learn to express friendliness differently—ways that implicate different cultural assumptions and not simply lack of precision in communication. They summarize the discursive world of girls as centered in friendships that are formed through talk, expressive of criticism without being overly aggressive, and reliant on deciphering cues about the motives of others. They characterize the discursive world of boys as centered in establishing the self as dominant, maintaining the attention of others, and asserting the self when others are the focus of attention. These patterns form the foundation for gender cultures that mature over time.

One fascinating aspect of children's enculturation into gendered identities and discourses is the persistence of gender dualisms alongside the greater fluidity of some cultural practices across boys and girls. Little boys, for instance, play with child-size cooking utensils and engage in pretend meal preparation; and little girls are on the soccer and T-ball fields as early as boys. Yet, *at the same time*, the clothing, the array of activities, and the verbal strategies all replicate the gender status quo, re-creating dualities, polarities, and the dominant ideology of gender relations. Along with changes (sometimes called "advances" in gender equality or gender freedom), it seems that "everything old is new again."

I turn now to several vantage points on gendered language use in adult society.

GENDERED LANGUAGE PATTERNS IN ADULTHOOD

The considerable amount of scholarship now available on gender and language points to distinctive ways of speaking among women and men and to a range of explanations for the role of gender in shaping discourse (see Cameron, 1992; Coates, 1998). Questions about gendered language can be grouped into two categories. First are questions of fact about women's and men's communication: Do men and women talk about different topics? Do they participate differently in conversations with members of the same sex contrasted to the opposite sex? Do they differ in their styles of speaking? Does one sex or the other tend to talk more? Interrupt more? Second are questions focused on interpreting those facts in the context of various theories about gender differences in language use: Why do women and men use language differently? Do they communicate interculturally from the perspective of co-equal cultures, or are men culturally dominant and therefore dominant in their discourse?

Topics in Discourse

Topicality, or the subject matter of conversation, is a good starting point in our consideration of women's and men's language-in-use because most of us can easily recognize at least the surface content of speech. Yet, although we can usually summarize the topics covered in a conversation (e.g., what movie to see, what you did last night, why you forgot your lover's birthday, your fight with your partner about who should be doing the laundry, a decision about buying a car, and dealing with parents about financial responsibilities), we are less able to characterize topic patterns in our discourses with others.

In the area of gender and topics, an early study by Elizabeth Aries (1976) continues to be cited as a foundation piece. Her content analysis of group discussions among same-sex and mixed-sex college students who were brought together to get to know one another revealed several patterns. First, all-male groups focused on themes of superiority and aggression through sarcastic teasing and talking about movies, books, current events, politics, sports, and travel. Second, all-female groups shared information about themselves, their feelings, their homes, and their relationships with others. Third, when females and males talked together, women talked less about home and family and males talked more about themselves and their feelings; in other words, each sex modified its topicality in the presence of the other sex. In a subsequent study, Aries (1982) reported that in mixed-sex college groups assembled to discuss a case study involving an ethical dilemma, females engaged in more socioemotional talk and men in more task-oriented talk.

In another study, Pamela Kipers (1987) studied 470 conversations that occurred in the faculty room of a middle school in New Jersey. Kipers's findings also confirmed a gender pattern in topics. In order of frequency, the primary conversation topics among women were focused on (a) home and family, (b) social issues, and (c) personal and family finances. For men, the most frequent topics were (a) work-related topics about specific educational programs, summer jobs, and pay and (b) recreation. The findings for the women are particularly interesting because the setting is the workplace, where one might expect more work-related talk. Yet, women seemed to reflect on their dual responsibilities for home and work by talking about their children, child care arrangements, and cooking. Men simply did not discuss these topics with one another. A number of the social issues discussed by women also related to children—drug abuse, child abuse, the effects of television violence on children, juvenile suicide—none of which were featured in the men's conversations. When men and women conversed together, the top two topics were (a) work related and (b) home and family. In sum, the most frequent topic for each sex was drawn into the mixed-sex conversations, suggesting cross-gender topical accommodations. These results, including the percentages for topics, are displayed in Table 37.1.

TABLE 37.1 Most Frequent Topics for All-Women, All-Men, and Mixed-Sex Conversations from the Kipers Study of Informal Teachers' Conversations

ALL-WOMEN GROUPS	ALL-MEN GROUPS	MIXED-SEX GROUPS
Home and family, 28%		Home and family, 22%
Social issues, 21%		
Personal and family finances, 12%		
	Work related, 39%	Work related, 25%
	Recreation, 21%	

Gender divisions in topicality also emerged in research conducted by Monica Hiller and myself (Hiller & Johnson, 1996), which focused on conversations in two coffee shops (one frequented by young adults and the other by middle-aged and older customers). An analysis of topics showed that whereas both men and women talked about work and social issues, women talked about personal issues, unlike the older men, who virtually never discussed personal issues.

This sampling of studies suggests a broad distinction in what women and men are likely to focus on in conversation, especially when those conversations are with members of the same sex. Women favor more personal and domestic topics. Men stick more to external subject matter and sociable discourse.

What men and women talk about in the more informal context of close friendship also shows gendered patterns for topics of conversation. Johnson and Aries (1983a) asked college students to indicate what they talked about with their closest same-sex friends. Young women reported that they talked more frequently about themselves, their problems, and their close relationships than did young men, although they too reported conversations on these topics. As we might expect, young men talked much more about sports than did young women. A companion study of adults in their 40s and 50s (Aries & Johnson, 1983) found that women, compared to men, reported more frequent talk about their doubts and fears, personal and family problems, and intimate relationships; only for the topic of sports did men report significantly more frequent conversations than women.

These topic patterns, in addition to the proclivity of women to define talk itself as an essential agenda in their personal relationships with other women (Johnson, 1996; Johnson & Aries, 1983b), point to different subject matter domains for language use that may well emerge from different levels of cultural abstractions pertaining to what is salient and of value. These subject matter domains interrelate with experience to create different ways in which women and men come to "voice" their existence and relatedness to others. And although women and men frequently talk to one another, their cross-gender talk differs in topic focus from that of either man-to-man or woman-to-woman talk.

Talkativeness

The folk linguistic "theories" of Eurowhites in the United States are replete with references to the greater talkativeness of women in comparison to men. Culturally symbolic phrases such as "yackety-yack," "jibber-jabber," "cackling hens," "blabber-mouth," "chit-chat," and "idle chatter" all convey a distinctly female image of the talker. These phrases capture not only a belief that women talk more than men but that the substance of their talk is generally unimportant. Within mainstream U.S. culture, the "chatty woman" and the "gossip" contrast to the "taciturn man" and "man of few words" in representing two orders of discourse—one characterized by excess and one by restraint. But is the folk linguistic knowledge fact or fiction?

One way in which women typically differ from men is in their greater valuing of conversation as a legitimate activity in itself—especially talk with one another. When Elizabeth Aries and I (Johnson & Aries, 1983b) interviewed a broad range of women about their close friendships, we found uniformity in their reports that talk is the most important aspect of these relationships. In contrast, men tend to view activity as a more central focus of friendship. In some cultural groups, such as the white, urban, working-class Chicago neighborhood studied by Philipsen (1975), extensive talk among men is even frowned on. In other groups, such as urban African Americans, verbal performance such as rapping or doing the dozens may be a significant part of male identity (Folb, 1980; Kochman, 1972), but such performances focus on creativity rather than conversation.

Many studies have assessed the sheer amount of talk (usually measured in clock time) by men and women in various circumstances. A comprehensive review by Deborah James and Janice Drakich (1993) of 63 studies conducted between 1951 and 1991 concludes that "the bulk of research findings indicate that men talk more than women" (p. 281).

This pattern in the research of more talk by men than by women in cross-gender conversations is anecdotally evident across a range of situations. Especially in work settings, women report that in discussions with men they are often the ones who have difficulty getting a word in edgewise. I have observed a number of community meetings about policy or problem issues where women's attendance is high but their proportion of talk low. In my own teaching over a number of years, I have observed that male students usually emerge as the main talkers in class, even when the women outnumber the men. More women seem to be speaking up in class, but the pattern remains one of asymmetry. In the classroom context, this and other patterns of discouragement for women students have been termed the "chilly climate"—a climate that is cool toward women and that tends to discourage participation (Hall & Sandler, 1982).

Patterns of Control in Male-Female Discourse

Most people have at some time or another felt totally overwhelmed by the talk of others. Sometimes, we cannot get a word in edgewise; sometimes, we simply want the other person to shut up; sometimes, we sense that a conversation with another person or in a group situation unfolds in an unbalanced way. Although the greater quantity of talk by men compared to women in cross-gender situations implicitly points to discourse control, other research deals more directly with the question of how discourse patterns systematically establish control. Two areas of scholarship on conversation are considered: (a) topic control and (b) turn-taking. Even though the research in this domain raises as many questions as it answers, it also suggests ways in which women and men participate differently in conversation.

Topic dominance, achieved by introducing topics and controlling the flow of topics within a conversation, sets the agenda for what people in a conversation will discuss. Topic control functions to regulate the content of discourse. Sometimes, the right to control the topic of conversation exists through social convention, as when a boss controls talk about an employee's job performance or an attorney controls the topic when examining a witness. Often, however, topic control is an open issue to be subtly negotiated by the participants. But is it open when it comes to gender? Unfortunately, little research exists to address this question, but what there is suggests possible patterns.

The studies by Aries (1976, 1982) pinpoint patterns in topic control among college student groups. First, when women talked with one another, topics were much more distributed among participants than was the case with men. Women also talked in greater depth on the topics they initiated than did men, which is consistent with what men and women report about their conversations with same-sex friends (Aries & Johnson, 1983; Johnson & Aries, 1983a). The comparison can be visualized as shown in Figure 37.1.

In this illustration, the male conversation has five different topics, three with one follow-up comment, one with two follow-up comments, and one with none. The female conversation has only two topics, but each gets developed more extensively: one with five follow-up comments and the other with three. One possible explanation for this pattern is that the males are asserting content control by continuously changing topics whereas the females facilitate the development of a topic in a balanced way prior to initiating new subject matter. In my discussions with students and groups with whom I have consulted, these patterns always ring true to

Male Pattern	*Female Pattern*
T¹_____	T¹_____
x	x
T²_____	x
T³_____	x
x	x
x	x
T⁴_____	T²_____
x	x
T⁵_____	x
x	x

FIGURE 37.1 **Illustration of Male and Female Topic Patterns.** NOTE: T = a topic; x = a comment made on that topic.

what both women and men think they experience in conversation. Women typically say "that's exactly what happens when I get together with my girlfriends," and men note something such as "guys really don't do much discussing but they like to joke and one-up each other."

In Aries's (1982) second study, the women talked more than the men in mixed-sex groups, but the functionality of their utterances differed: Males gave opinions, suggestions, and information in a proactive fashion, whereas females more often responded to what the males said by agreeing, disagreeing, or asking questions.

West and García (1988) looked at topic control by analyzing how topic shifts occur in conversation. They found that all instances of unilateral topic shifts were initiated by men. Their research is limited because of its restriction to a small sample of college students, but, again, the findings suggest a possible pattern of gender-skewed topic control.

One of the most provocative approaches to examining discourse control in conversations was undertaken by Carol Edelsky (1981/1993), who studied what she calls the conversational *floor* or "the acknowledged what's-going-on within a psychological time/space" (p. 209). Edelsky distinguished *collaborative floors* in which participants jointly develop and sustain the topic from *singly developed floors* in which one person holds forth, thereby controlling the topic, or manages to keep the topic focused even if others comment on it. Floor is a more complex notion than topic in the sense that one might introduce a topic and even develop it without "having the floor." Imagine a conversation among five people focused on mortgage rates, during which two individuals briefly comment on the possibility of buying vacation homes; this topic is heard by the others but never becomes the focus of the group's discourse. Or think about a situation I observed in which a group of parents were discussing their children's use of the Internet; one parent talked at length about why his kids are not allowed to use the home computer, only to have his remarks politely ignored as the group quickly returned to Internet use.

Edelsky's (1981/1993) analysis of conversations among a faculty committee revealed that men and women participate essentially as equals in collaborative floor segments of conversation but that men and not women control singly developed floors. In fact, she found no singly developed floor segments where a woman spoke.

The second topic pertinent to discourse control is *turn-taking.* Consider conversation to be the give-and-take of utterances that are jointly developed by the participants. That give-and-take, however, can occur through the full range of egalitarian to lopsided distribution of the conversational speaking turns.

Neatly ordered turn-taking occurs when one participant completes an utterance before the next person beings speaking. Such discourse might be described as polite, civil, formal, considerate, or stilted depending on the context of the conversation and the cultural background of the participants.

Another form of turn-taking moves the turn more abruptly from speaker to speaker by (a) overlapping one utterance onto the end of another person's utterance or (b) interrupting the progress of another's utterance, which is like a conversational tackle tactic. Overlaps are less intrusive but still can cut off another speaker. Interruptions, if successful, take control of talk, as shown in the example below; here, B cuts off A mid-sentence (// marks the point of interruption):

A: I really don't care what we do so let's//

B: //I guess I really don't want to go to a movie again tonight.

Although a prevailing view in U.S. linguistics has been that the normal state of affairs is for one person to speak at a time (Sacks et al., 1974), that view is culturally biased and does not reflect the normal state of affairs in many ethnic discourses, where interruption and overlap are common. Schiffrin (1984), for example, shows instances of interruption as part of sociable Jewish argument. Whether normative or not, interrupting and overlapping function to assert control over discourse. The key question is whether men compared to women are more likely to exercise this kind of control.

The early studies of interruptions and overlaps were conducted by Candace West and Don Zimmerman (West & Zimmerman, 1983; Zimmerman & West, 1975), who investigated these devices in mixed-sex interactions. In their first study, they found that 96% of all interruptions were initiated by men who interrupted women; in the second study, 75% were male initiated. These data suggest that males are overwhelmingly more likely to interrupt females than vice versa, but subsequent studies show varied results.

Based on reviewing 33 studies conducted between 1965 and 1991, James and Clarke (1993) concluded that no pattern exists between gender and interruptions. Their analysis resulted in the following breakdown:

17 studies with no gender differences

11 studies with significantly more male interruptions

5 studies with significantly more female interruptions

James and Clarke's conclusion of no gender effect is, however, misleading. Even though half of the studies show no gender differences, the other half are weighted 2:1 toward the males; that is, males are found to interrupt more often than are females in twice the number of studies where there are gender differences—certainly not a trivial pattern.

James and Clarke (1993) did raise important questions about the function served by interruptions, noting that some are disruptive whereas others serve a supportive function; Kennedy and Camden (1983) refer to these two types of interruptions as *confirming* and *disconfirming*. Several studies point to the greater use of confirming interruptions by women, but the data are sparse. Furthermore, as with any body of research, methods and situation vary greatly, which makes it more difficult to determine whether any trends exist.

In addition to what we know about interruptions from research studies, self-report of perceptions provides another vantage point. Over the years, I have asked numerous students, colleagues, and individuals in training sessions whether they believe there is a gender pattern to interruption behavior. Although many men report that there "probably is," women more emphatically assert that they frequently experience being interrupted by males. What is not clear is whether these reports arise from frequency alone, from a greater sensitivity among women to interruptions when they occur (which might be part of the pragmatic rule system for women but not men), or to folklinguistic perceptions. Some women also report that they "fight back" by interrupting men or refusing to let men interrupt them. This might explain why Kennedy and Camden (1983) found female graduate student teaching assistants to out-interrupt their male peers. Yet, the women in this study were interrupted more than the men, even by women.

BIBLIOGRAPHY

Andersen, E. S. (1986). The acquisition of register variation by Anglo-American children. In B. B. Schieffelin & E. Ochs (Eds.), *Language socialization across cultures* (pp. 153–161). Cambridge, UK: Cambridge University Press.

Aries, E. (1976). Interaction patterns and themes of male, female, and mixed groups. *Small Group Behavior, 7,* 7–18.

Aries, E. J. (1982). Verbal and nonverbal behavior in single-sex and mixed-sex groups: Are traditional sex roles changing? *Psychological Reports, 51,* 127–134.

Aries, E. J., & Johnson, F. L. (1983). Close friendship in adulthood: Conversational content between same-sex friends. *Sex Roles, 9,* 1183–1196.

Austin, A. M., Salehi, M., & Leffler, A. (1987). Gender and developmental differences in children's conversations. *Sex Roles, 16,* 497–510.

Cameron, D. (1992). *Feminism and linguistic theory* (2nd ed.). New York: St. Martin's.

Coates, J. (Ed.). (1998). *Language and gender: A reader.* Oxford/Malden, MA: Blackwell.

Cook, A. S., Fritz., J. J., McCornack, B. L., & Visperas, C. (1985). Early gender differences in the functional usage of language. *Sex Roles, 12,* 909–915.

Edelsky, C. (1993). Who's got the floor? In D. Tannen (Ed.), *Gender and conversational interaction* (pp. 189–227). New York: Oxford University Press. (Original work published 1981)

Esposito, A. (1979). Sex differences in children's conversation. *Language and Speech, 22,* 213–220.

Folb, E. (1980). *Runnin' down some lines: The language and culture of black teenagers.* Cambridge, MA: Harvard University Press.

Goodwin, M. H. (1990). *He-said she-said: Talk as social organization among black children.* Bloomington: Indiana University Press.

Haas, A. (1979). Male and female spoken language differences: Stereotypes and evidence. *Psychological Bulletin, 86,* 616–626.

Hall, R., & Sandler, B. (1982). *The classroom climate: A chilly one for women?* (Project on the Status and Education of Women). Washington, DC: Association of American Colleges.

Hiller, M., & Johnson, F. L. (1996, November). *Gender and generation in conversational topics: A case study of two coffee shops.* Paper presented at the annual meeting of the Speech Communication Association, San Diego, CA.

James, D., & Clarke, S. (1993). Women, men, and interruptions: A critical review. In D. Tannen (Ed.), *Gender and conversational interaction* (pp. 231–280). New York: Oxford University Press.

James, D., & Drakich, J. (1993). Understanding gender differences in amount of talk: A critical review of research. In D. Tannen (Ed.), *Gender and conversational interaction* (pp. 281–312). New York: Oxford University Press.

Johnson, F. L. (1996). Friendships among women: Closeness in dialogue. In J. Wood (Ed.), *Gendered relationships* (pp. 79–94). Mountain View, CA: Mayfield.

Johnson, F. L., & Aries, E. J. (1983a). Conversational patterns among same-sex pairs of late-adolescent close friends. *Journal of Genetic Psychology, 142,* 225–238.

Johnson, F. L., & Aries, E. J. (1983b). The talk of women friends. *Women's Studies International Forum, 6,* 353–361.

Kennedy, C. W., & Camden, C. (1983). A new look at interruptions. *Western Journal of Speech Communication, 47,* 45–58.

Kipers, P. S. (1987). Gender and topic. *Language and Society, 16,* 543–557.

Kochman, T. (1972). *Rappin' and stylin' out: Communication in urban black America.* Chicago: University of Illinois Press.

Kochman, T. (1981). *Black and white styles in conflict.* Chicago: University of Chicago Press.

Kramer, C. (1977). Perceptions of female and male speech. *Language and Speech, 20,* 151–161.

Maltz, D. N., & Borker, R. A. (1982). A cultural approach to male-female miscommunication. In J. J. Gumperz (Ed.), *Language and social identity* (pp. 196–216). Cambridge, UK: Cambridge University Press.

Philipsen, G. (1975). Speaking "like a man" in Teamsterville: Culture patterns of role enactment in an urban neighborhood. *Quarterly Journal of Speech, 61,* 13–22.

Sachs, J. (1987). Preschool boys' and girls' language use in pretend play. In S. U. Philips, S. Steele, & C. Tanz (Eds.), *Language, gender, and sex in comparative perspective* (pp. 178–188). New York: Cambridge University Press.

Sacks, H., Schegloff, E. A., & Jefferson, G. (1974). A simplest systematic for the organization of turn-taking in conversation. *Language, 50,* 696–735.

Schiffrin, D. (1984). Jewish argument as sociability. *Language in Society, 13,* 311–335.

Sheldon, A. (1990). Pickle fights: Gendered talk in preschool disputes. *Discourse Processes, 13,* 5–31.

Sheldon, A (1992). Conflict talk: Sociolinguistic challenges to self-assertion and how young children meet them. *Merrill-Palmer Quarterly, 38,* 95–117.

Sheldon, A. (1993). Preschool girls' discourse competence: Managing conflict. In M. Bucholtz, K. Hall, & B. Moonwomon (Eds.), *Locating power: Proceedings of the 1992 Berkeley Women and Language Conference* (Vol. 2, pp. 528–539). Berkeley, CA: Berkeley Linguistic Society.

Sheldon, A. (1996). You can be the baby brother but you aren't born yet: Preschool girls' negotiation for power and access in pretend play. *Research on Language in Social Interaction, 29,* 57–80.

Siegler, D. M., & Siegler, R. S. (1976). Stereotypes of males' and females' speech. *Psychological Reports, 39,* 167–170.

Tannen, D. (1990). Gender differences in topical coherence: Creating involvement in best friends' talk. *Discourse Processes, 13,* 73–90.

West, C., & García, A. (1988). Conversational shift work: A study of topical transitions between women and men. *Social Problems, 35,* 551–575.

West, C., & Zimmerman, D. H. (1983). Small insults: A study of interruptions in cross-sex conversations between unacquainted persons. In B. Thorne, C. Kramarae, & N. Henley (Eds.), *Language, gender, and society* (pp. 102–117). Rowley, MA: Newbury House.

Zimmerman, D. H., & West, C. (1975). Sex roles, interruptions, and silences in conversations. In B. Thorne & N. Henley (Eds.), *Language and sex: Difference and dominance* (pp. 105–129). Rowley, MA: Newbury House.

FOR DISCUSSION AND REVIEW

1. When Johnson asks her students to characterize the language and communication styles of males and females, what responses does she consistently receive? Do these responses agree with how you would characterize male and female language behaviors? Why does Johnson call these ideas *folk linguistics*?

2. What does Johnson mean by the "ought-ness" of language use?

3. When Johnson tells about her own preschool-age sons play-acting "We're girls," what does she describe them doing? Why was Johnson ineffective in countering her young sons' ideas about girls?

4. Many research studies show that children become aware of gender at an early age. How might this awareness affect a young boy's interaction with a girl or a young girl's interaction with a boy? Give some specific examples.

5. According to the research cited in the selection, how do topics of adult conversation vary in all-female groups vs. all-male groups? How might these topics change in a mixed-sex group? What kinds of topics do you discuss with different groups of friends? How important is gender in determining the topics in these conversation?

6. Discuss the folk linguistic theory of "talkativeness." How well does this theory hold up against research studies?

7. Why is "topic control" significant for understanding gendered discourse? What is meant by the *conversational floor*? How do interruptions and turn-taking affect conversation control? What is your experience with topic control in mixed-sex conversations? In same-sex conversation?

38

"I'll Explain It to You": Lecturing and Listening

Deborah Tannen

In her scholarly work and her best-selling books, Deborah Tannen, professor of linguistics at Georgetown University, has encouraged millions of readers to take conversation seriously. According to Tannen, understanding how we talk to one another helps us understand who we are as social beings and why we act the way we do. Some of her most popular books include Talking 9 to 5: Women and Men at Work *(2001),* You're Wearing That? Understanding Mothers and Daughters in Conversation *(2006), and* You Just Don't Understand *(1990), the source of the following selection. Here Tannen claims that women and men have different goals and strategies when they participate in conversation. Although problems arise from such differences, Tannen believes that men and women can improve their communication by understanding each other's goals and using each other's strategies.*

At a reception following the publication of one of my books, I noticed a publicist listening attentively to the producer of a popular radio show. He was telling her how the studio had come to be built where it was, and why he would have preferred another site. What caught my attention was the length of time he was speaking while she was listening. He was delivering a monologue that could only be called a lecture, giving her detailed information about the radio reception at the two sites, the architecture of the station, and so on. I later asked the publicist if she had been interested in the information the producer had given her. "Oh, yes," she answered. But then she thought a moment and said, "Well, maybe he did go on a bit." The next day she told me, "I was thinking about what you asked. I couldn't have cared less about what he was saying. It's just that I'm so used to listening to men go on about things I don't care about, I didn't even realize how bored I was until you made me think about it."

I was chatting with a man I had just met at a party. In our conversation, it emerged that he had been posted in Greece with the RAF during 1944 and 1945. Since I had lived in Greece for several years, I asked him about his experiences: What had Greece been like then? How had the Greek villagers treated the British soldiers? What had it been *like* to be a British soldier in wartime Greece? I also offered information about how Greece had changed, what it is like now. He did not pick up on my remarks about contemporary Greece, and his replies to my questions quickly changed from accounts of his own experiences, which I found riveting, to facts about Greek history, which interested me in principle but in the actual telling left me profoundly bored. The more impersonal his talk became, the more I felt oppressed by it, pinned involuntarily in the listener position.

At a showing of Judy Chicago's jointly created art work *The Dinner Party*, I was struck by a couple standing in front of one of the displays: The man was earnestly explaining to the woman the meaning of symbols in the tapestry before them, pointing as he spoke. I might not have noticed this unremarkable scene, except that *The Dinner Party* was radically feminist in conception, intended to reflect women's experiences and sensibilities.

While taking a walk in my neighborhood on an early summer evening at twilight, I stopped to chat with a neighbor who was walking his dogs. As we stood, I noticed that the large expanse of yard in front of which we were standing was aglitter with the intermittent flickering of fireflies. I called attention to the sight, remarking on how magical it looked. "It's like the Fourth of July," I said. He agreed, and then told me he had read that the lights of fireflies are mating signals. He then explained to me details of how these signals work—for example, groups of fireflies fly at different elevations and could be seen to cluster in different parts of the yard.

In all these examples, the men had information to impart and they were imparting it. On the surface, there is nothing surprising or strange about that. What is strange is that there are so many situations in which men have factual information requiring lengthy explanations to impart to women, and so few in which women have comparable information to impart to men.

The changing times have altered many aspects of relations between women and men. Now it is unlikely, at least in many circles, for a man to say, "I am better than you because I am a man and you are a woman." But women who do not find men making such statements are nonetheless often frustrated in their dealings with them. One situation that frustrates many women is a conversation that has mysteriously turned into a lecture, with the man delivering the lecture to the woman, who has become an appreciative audience.

Once again, the alignment in which women and men find themselves arrayed is asymmetrical. The lecturer is framed as superior in status and expertise, cast in the role of teacher, and the listener is cast in the role of student. If women and men took turns giving and receiving lectures, there would be nothing disturbing about it. What is disturbing is the imbalance. Women and men fall into this unequal pattern so often because of the differences in their interactional habits. Since women seek to build rapport, they are inclined to play down their expertise rather than display it. Since men value the position of center stage and the feeling of knowing more, they seek opportunities to gather and disseminate factual information.

If men often seem to hold forth because they have the expertise, women are often frustrated and surprised to find that when they have the expertise, they don't necessarily get the floor.

FIRST ME, THEN ME

I was at a dinner with faculty members from other departments in my university. To my right was a woman. As the dinner began, we introduced ourselves. After we told each other what departments we were in and what subjects we taught, she asked what my research was about. We talked about my research for a little while. Then I asked her about her research and she told me about it. Finally, we discussed the ways that our research overlapped. Later, as tends to happen at dinners, we branched out to others at the table. I asked a man across the table from me what department he was in and what he did. During the next half hour, I learned a lot about his job, his research, and his background. Shortly before the dinner ended there was a lull, and he asked me what I did. When I said I was a linguist, he became excited and told me about a research project he had conducted that was related to neurolinguistics. He was still telling me about his research when we all got up to leave the table.

This man and woman were my colleagues in academia. What happens when I talk to people at parties and social events, not fellow researchers? My experience is that if I mention the kind of work I do to women, they usually ask me about it. When I tell them about conversational style or gender differences, they offer their own experiences to support the patterns I describe. This is very pleasant for me. It puts me at center stage without my having to grab the spotlight myself, and I frequently gather anecdotes I can use in the future. But when I announce my line of work to men, many give me a lecture on language—for example, about how people, especially teenagers, misuse language nowadays. Others challenge me, for example questioning me about my research methods. Many others change the subject to something they know more about.

Of course not all men respond in this way, but over the years I have encountered many men, and very few women, who do. It is not that speaking in this way is *the* male way of doing things, but that it is *a* male way. There are women who adopt such styles, but they are perceived as speaking like men.

IF YOU'VE GOT IT, FLAUNT IT—OR HIDE IT

I have been observing this constellation in interaction for more than a dozen years. I did not, however, have any understanding of *why* this happens until fairly recently, when I developed the framework of status and connection. An experimental study that was pivotal in my thinking shows that expertise does not ensure women a place at center stage in conversation with men.

Psychologist H. M. Leet-Pellegrini set out to discover whether gender or expertise determined who would behave in what she terms a "dominant" way—for example, by talking more, interrupting, and controlling the topic. She set up pairs of women, pairs of men, and mixed pairs, and asked them to discuss the effects of television violence on children. In some cases, she made one of the partners an expert by providing relevant factual information and time to read and assimilate it before the videotaped discussion. One might expect that the conversationalist who was the expert would talk more, interrupt more, and spend less time supporting the conversational partner who knew less about the subject. But it wasn't so simple. On the average, those who had expertise did talk more, but men experts talked more than women experts.

Expertise also had a different effect on women and men with regard to supportive behavior. Leet-Pellegrini expected that the one who did not have expertise would spend more time offering agreement and support to the one who did. This turned out to be true—*except* in cases where a woman was the expert and her nonexpert partner was a man. In this situation, the women experts showed support—saying things like "Yeah" and "That's right"—far *more* than the nonexpert men they were talking to. Observers often rated the male nonexpert as more dominant than the female expert. In other words, the women in this experiment not only didn't wield their expertise as power, but tried to play it down and make up for it through extra assenting behavior. They acted as if their expertise were something to hide.

And perhaps it was. When the word *expert* was spoken in these experimental conversations, in all cases but one it was the man in the conversation who used it, saying something like "So, you're the expert." Evidence of the woman's superior knowledge sparked resentment, not respect.

Furthermore, when an expert man talked to an uninformed woman, he took a controlling role in structuring the conversation in the beginning *and* the end. But when an expert man talked to an uninformed man, he dominated in the beginning but not always in the end. In other words, having expertise was enough to keep a man in the controlling position if he was talking to a woman, but not if he was talking to a man. Apparently, when a woman surmised that the man she was talking to had more information on the subject than she did, she simply accepted the reactive role. But another man, despite a lack of information, might still give the expert a run for his money and possibly gain the upper hand by the end.

Reading these results, I suddenly understood what happens to me when I talk to women and men about language. I am assuming that my acknowledged expertise will mean I am automatically accorded authority in the conversation, and with women that is generally the case. But when I talk to men, revealing that I have acknowledged expertise in this area often invites challenges. I *might* maintain my position if I defend myself successfully against the challenges, but if I don't, I may lose ground.

One interpretation of the Leet-Pellegrini study is that women are getting a bum deal. They don't get credit when it's due. And in a way, this is true. But the reason is not—as it seems to many women—that men are bums who seek to deny women authority. The Leet-Pellegrini study shows that many men are inclined to jockey for status, and challenge the authority of others, when they are talking to men too. If this is so, then challenging a woman's authority as they would challenge a man's could be a sign of respect and equal treatment, rather than lack of respect and discrimination. In cases where this is so, the inequality of the treatment results not simply from the men's behavior alone but from the differences in men's and women's styles: Most women lack experience in defending themselves against challenges, which they misinterpret as personal attacks on their credibility.

Even when talking to men who are happy to see them in positions of status, women may have a hard time getting their due because of differences in men's and women's interactional goals. Just as boys in high school are not inclined to repeat information about popular girls because it doesn't get them what they want, women in conversation are not inclined to display their knowledge because it doesn't get them what they are after. Leet-Pellegrini suggests that the men in this study were playing a game of "Have I won?" while the women were playing a game of "Have I been sufficiently helpful?" I am inclined to put this another way: The game women play is "Do you like me?" whereas the men play "Do you respect me?" If men, in seeking respect, are less liked by women, this is an unsought side effect, as is the effect that women, in seeking to be liked, may lose respect. When a woman has a conversation with a man, her efforts to emphasize their similarities and avoid showing off can easily be interpreted, through the lens of status, as relegating her to a one-down position, making her appear either incompetent or insecure.

A SUBTLE DIFFERENCE

Elizabeth Aries, a professor of psychology at Amherst College, set out to show that highly intelligent, highly educated young women are no longer submissive in conversations with male peers. And indeed she found that the college women did talk more than the college men in small groups she set up. But what they said was different. The men tended to set the agenda by offering opinions, suggestions, and information. The women tended to react, offering agreement or disagreement. Furthermore, she found that body language was as different as ever: The men sat with their legs stretched out, while the women gathered themselves in. Noting that research has found that speakers using the open-bodied position are more likely to persuade their listeners, Aries points out that talking more may not ensure that women will be heard.

In another study, Aries found that men in all-male discussion groups spent a lot of time at the beginning finding out "who was best informed about movies, books, current events, politics, and travel" as a means of "sizing up the competition" and negotiating "where they stood in relation to each other." This glimpse of how men talk when there are no women present gives an inkling of why displaying knowledge and expertise is something that men find more worth doing than women. What the women in Aries's study spent time doing was "gaining a closeness through intimate self-revelation."

It is crucial to bear in mind that both the women and the men in these studies were establishing camaraderie, and both were concerned with their relationships to each other. But different aspects of their relationships were of primary concern: their place in a hierarchical order for the men, and their place in a network of intimate connections for the women. The consequence of these disparate concerns was very different ways of speaking.

Thomas Fox is an English professor who was intrigued by the differences between women and men in his freshman writing classes. What he observed corresponds almost precisely to the experimental findings of Aries and Leet-Pellegrini. Fox's method of teaching writing included having all the students read their essays to each other in class and talk to each other in small groups. He also had them write papers reflecting on the essays and the discussion groups. He alone, as the teacher, read these analytical papers.

To exemplify the two styles he found typical of women and men, Fox chose a woman, Ms. M., and a man, Mr. H. In her speaking as well as her writing, Ms. M. held back what she knew, appearing uninformed and uninterested, because she feared offending her classmates. Mr. H. spoke and wrote with authority and apparent confidence because he was eager to persuade his peers. She did not worry about persuading; he did not worry about offending.

In his analytical paper, the young man described his own behavior in the mixed-gender group discussions as if he were describing the young men in Leet-Pellegrini's and Aries's studies:

> In my sub-group I am the leader. I begin every discussion by stating my opinions as facts. The other two members of the sub-group tend to sit back and agree with me. . . . I need people to agree with me.

Fox comments that Mr. H. reveals "a sense of self, one that acts to change himself and other people, that seems entirely distinct from Ms. M.'s sense of self, dependent on and related to others."

Calling Ms. M.'s sense of self "dependent" suggests a negative view of her way of being in the world—and, I think, a view more typical of men. This view reflects the assumption that the alternative to independence is dependence. If this is indeed a male view, it may explain why so many men are cautious about becoming intimately involved with others: It makes sense to avoid humiliating dependence by insisting on independence. But there is another alternative: *inter*dependence.

The main difference between these alternatives is symmetry. Dependence is an asymmetrical involvement: One person needs the other, but not vice versa, so the needy person is one-down. Interdependence is symmetrical: Both parties rely on each other, so neither is one-up or one-down. Moreover, Mr. H.'s sense of self is also dependent on others. He requires others to listen, agree, and allow him to take the lead by stating his opinions first.

Looked at this way, the woman and man in this group are both dependent on each other. Their differing goals are complementary, although neither understands the reasons for the other's behavior. This would be a fine arrangement, except that their differing goals result in alignments that enhance his authority and undercut hers.

DIFFERENT INTERPRETATIONS—AND MISINTERPRETATIONS

Fox also describes differences in the way male and female students in his classes interpreted a story they read. These differences also reflect assumptions about the interdependence or independence of individuals. Fox's students wrote their responses to "The Birthmark" by Nathaniel Hawthorne. In the story, a woman's husband becomes obsessed with a birthmark on her face. Suffering from her husband's revulsion at the sight of her, the wife becomes obsessed with it too and, in a reversal of her initial impulse, agrees to undergo a treatment he has devised to remove the birthmark—a treatment that succeeds in removing the mark, but kills her in the process.

Ms. M. interpreted the wife's complicity as a natural response to the demand of a loved one: The woman went along with her husband's lethal schemes to remove the birthmark because she wanted to please and be appealing to him. Mr. H. blamed the woman's insecurity and vanity for her fate, and he blamed her for voluntarily submitting to her husband's authority. Fox points out that he saw her as individually responsible for her actions, just as he saw himself as individually responsible for his own actions. To him, the issue was independence: The weak wife voluntarily took a submissive role. To Ms. M., the issue was interdependence: The woman was inextricably bound up with her husband, so her behavior could not be separated from his.

Fox observes that Mr. H. saw the writing of the women in the class as spontaneous—they wrote whatever popped into their heads. Nothing could be farther from Ms. M.'s experience as she described it: When she knew her peers would see her writing, she censored everything that popped into her head. In contrast, when she was writing something that only her professor would read, she expressed firm and articulate opinions.

There is a striking but paradoxical complementarity to Ms. M.'s and Mr. H.'s styles, when they are taken together. He needs someone to listen and agree. She listens and agrees. But in another sense, their dovetailing purposes are at cross-purposes. He misinterprets her agreement, intended in a spirit of connection, as a reflection of status and power: He thinks she is "indecisive" and "insecure." Her reasons for refraining from behaving as he does—firmly stating opinions as facts—have nothing to do with her attitudes toward her knowledge, as he thinks they do, but rather result from her attitudes toward her relationships with her peers.

These experimental studies by Leet-Pellegrini and Aries, and the observations by Fox, all indicate that, typically, men are more comfortable than women in giving information and opinions and speaking in an authoritative way to a group, whereas women are more comfortable than men in supporting others. . . .

LISTENER AS UNDERLING

Clearly men are not always talking and women are not always listening. I have asked men whether they ever find themselves in the position of listening to another man giving them a lecture, and how they feel about it. They tell me that this does happen. They may find themselves talking to someone who presses information on them so insistently that they give in and listen. They say they don't mind too much, however, if the information is interesting. They can store it away for future use, like remembering a joke to tell others later. Factual information is of less interest to women because it is of less use to them. They are unlikely to try to pass on the gift of information, more likely to give the gift of being a good audience.

Men as well as women sometimes find themselves on the receiving end of a lecture they would as soon not hear. But men tell me that it is most likely to happen if the other man is in a position of higher status. They know they have to listen to lectures from fathers and bosses.

That men can find themselves in the position of unwilling listener is attested to by a short opinion piece in which A. R. Gurney bemoans being frequently "cornered by some self-styled expert who harangues me with his considered opinion on an interminable agenda of topics." He claims that this tendency bespeaks a peculiarly American inability to "converse"—that is, engage in a balanced give-and-take—and cites as support the French observer of American customs Alexis de Tocqueville, who wrote, "An American . . . speaks to you as if he was addressing a meeting." Gurney credits his own appreciation of conversing to his father, who "was a master at eliciting and responding enthusiastically to the views of others, though this resiliency didn't always extend to his children. Indeed, now I think about it, he spoke to us many times as if he were addressing a meeting."

It is not surprising that Gurney's father lectured his children. The act of giving information by definition frames one in a position of higher status, while the act of listening frames one as lower. Children instinctively sense this—as do most men. But when women listen to men, they are not thinking in terms of status. Unfortunately, their attempts to reinforce connections and establish rapport, when interpreted through the lens of status, can be misinterpreted as casting them in a subordinate position— and are likely to be taken that way by many men.

WHAT'S SO FUNNY?

The economy of exchanging jokes for laughter is a parallel one. In her study of college students' discussions groups, Aries found that the students in all-male groups spent a lot of time telling about times they had played jokes on others, and laughing about it. She refers to a study in which Barbara Miller Newman found that high school boys who were not "quick and clever" became the targets of jokes. Practical joking—playing a joke *on* someone—is clearly a matter of being one-up: in the know and in control. It is less obvious, but no less true, that *telling* jokes can also be a way of negotiating status.

Many women (certainly not all) laugh at jokes but do not later remember them. Since they are not driven to seek and hold center stage in a group, they do not need a store of jokes to whip out for this purpose. A woman I will call Bernice prided herself on her sense of humor. At a cocktail party, she met a man to whom she was drawn because he seemed at first to share this trait. He made many funny remarks, which she spontaneously laughed at. But when she made funny remarks, he seemed not to hear. What had happened to his sense of humor? Though telling jokes and laughing at them are both reflections of a sense of humor, they are very different social activities. Making others laugh gives you a fleeting power over them: As linguist Wallace Chafe points out, at the moment of laughter, a person is temporarily disabled. The man Bernice met was comfortable only when he was making her laugh, not the other way around. When Bernice laughed at his jokes, she thought she was engaging in a symmetrical activity. But he was engaging in an asymmetrical one.

A man told me that sometime around tenth grade he realized that he preferred the company of women to the company of men. He found that his female friends were more supportive and less competitive, whereas his male friends seemed to spend all their time joking. Considering joking an asymmetrical activity makes it clearer why it would fit in with a style he perceived as competitive. . . .

MUTUAL ACCUSATIONS

Considering these dynamics, it is not surprising that many women complain that their partners don't listen to them. But men make the same complaint about women, although less frequently. The accusation

"You're not listening" often really means "You don't understand what I said in the way that I meant it," or "I'm not getting the response I wanted." Being listened to can become a metaphor for being understood and being valued.

In my earlier work I emphasized that women may get the impression men aren't listening to them even when the men really are. This happens because men have different habitual ways of showing they're listening. As anthropologists Maltz and Borker explain, women are more inclined to ask questions. They also give more listening responses—little words like *mhm, uh-uh,* and *yeah*—sprinkled throughout someone else's talk, providing a running feedback loop. And they respond more positively and enthusiastically, for example by agreeing and laughing.

All this behavior is doing the work of listening. It also creates rapport-talk by emphasizing connection and encouraging more talk. The corresponding strategies of men—giving fewer listener responses, making statements rather than asking questions, and challenging rather than agreeing—can be understood as moves in a contest by incipient speakers rather than audience members.

Not only do women give more listening signals, according to Maltz and Borker, but the signals they give have different meanings for men and women, consistent with the speaker/audience alignment. Women use "yeah" to mean "I'm with you, I follow," whereas men tend to say "yeah" only when they agree. The opportunity for misunderstanding is clear. When a man is confronted with a woman who has been saying "yeah," "yeah," "yeah," and then turns out not to agree, he may conclude that she has been insincere, or that she was agreeing without really listening. When a woman is confronted with a man who does *not* say "yeah"—or much of anything else—she may conclude that *he* hasn't been listening. The men's style is more literally focused on the message level of talk, while the women's is focused on the relationship or metamessage level.

To a man who expects a listener to be quietly attentive, a woman giving a stream of feedback and support will seem to be talking too much for a listener. To a woman who expects a listener to be active and enthusiastic in showing interest, attention, and support, a man who listens silently will seem not to be listening at all, but rather to have checked out of the conversation, taken his listening marbles, and gone mentally home.

Because of these patterns, women may get the impression that men aren't listening when they really are. But I have come to understand, more recently, that it is also true that men listen to women less frequently than women listen to men, because the act of listening has different meanings for them. Some men really *don't* want to listen at length because they feel it frames them as subordinate. Many women do want to listen, but they expect it to be reciprocal—I listen to you now; you listen to me later. They become frustrated when they do the listening now and now and now, and later never comes.

MUTUAL DISSATISFACTION

If women are dissatisfied with always being in the listening position, the dissatisfaction may be mutual. That a woman feels she has been assigned the role of silently listening audience does not mean that a man feels he has consigned her to that role—or that he necessarily likes the rigid alignment either.

During the time I was working on this book, I found myself at a book party filled with people I hardly knew. I struck up a conversation with a charming young man who turned out to be a painter. I asked him about his work and, in response to his answer, asked whether there has been a return in contemporary art to figurative painting. In response to my question, he told me a lot about the history of art—so much that when he finished and said, "That was a long answer to your question," I had long since forgotten that I had asked a question, let alone what it was. I had not minded this monologue—I had been interested in it—but I realized, with something of a jolt, that I had just experienced the dynamic that I had been writing about.

I decided to risk offending my congenial new acquaintance in order to learn something about his point of view. This was, after all, a book party, so I might rely on his indulgence if I broke the rules of decorum in the interest of writing a book. I asked whether he often found himself talking at length while someone else listened. He thought for a moment and said yes, he did, because he liked to explore ideas in detail. I asked if it happened equally with women and men. He thought again and said, "No, I have more trouble with men." I asked what he meant by trouble. He said, "Men interrupt. *They* want to explain to *me*."

Finally, having found this young man disarmingly willing to talk about the conversation we had just had and his own style, I asked which he preferred: that a woman listen silently and supportively, or that she offer opinions and ideas of her own. He said he thought he liked it better if she volunteered information, making the interchange more interesting.

When men begin to lecture other men, the listeners are experienced at trying to sidetrack the lecture, or match it, or derail it. In this system, making authoritative pronouncements may be a way to begin an *exchange* of information. But women are not used to responding in that way. They see little choice but to listen attentively and wait for their turn to be allotted to them rather than seizing it for themselves. If this is the case, the man may be as bored and frustrated as the woman when his attempt to begin an exchange of information ends in his giving a lecture. From his point of view, she is passively soaking up information, so she must not have any to speak of. One of the reasons men's talk to women frequently turns into lecturing is *because* women listen attentively and do not interrupt with challenges, sidetracks, or matching information.

In the conversations with male and female colleagues that I recounted at the outset of this chapter, this difference may have been crucial. When

I talked to the woman, we each told about our own research in response to the other's encouragement. When I talked to the man, I encouraged him to talk about his work, and he obliged, but he did not encourage me to talk about mine. This may mean that he did not want to hear about it—but it also may not. In her study of college students' discussion groups, Aries found that women who did a lot of talking began to feel uncomfortable; they backed off and frequently drew out quieter members of the group. This is perfectly in keeping with women's desire to keep things balanced, so everyone is on an equal footing. Women expect their conversational partners to encourage them to hold forth. Men, who do not typically encourage quieter members to speak up, assume that anyone who has something to say will volunteer it. The men may be equally disappointed in a conversational partner who turns out to have nothing to say.

Similarly, men can be as bored by women's topics as women can be by men's. While I was wishing the former RAFer would tell me about his personal experiences in Greece, he was probably wondering why I was boring him with mine and marveling at my ignorance of the history of a country I had lived in. Perhaps he would have considered our conversation a success if I had challenged or topped his interpretation of Greek history rather than listening dumbly to it. When men, upon hearing the kind of work I do, challenge me about my research methods, they are inviting me to give them information and show them my expertise—something I don't like to do outside of the classroom or lecture hall, but something they themselves would likely be pleased to be provoked to do.

The publicist who listened attentively to information about a radio station explained to me that she wanted to be nice to the manager, to smooth the way for placing her clients on his station. But men who want to ingratiate themselves with women are more likely to try to charm them by offering interesting information than by listening attentively to whatever information the women have to impart. I recall a luncheon preceding a talk I delivered to a college alumni association. My gracious host kept me entertained before my speech by regaling me with information about computers, which I politely showed interest in, while inwardly screaming from boredom and a sense of being weighed down by irrelevant information that I knew I would never remember. Yet I am sure he thought he was being interesting, and it is likely that at least some male guests would have thought that he was. I do not wish to imply that all women hosts have entertained me in the perfect way. I recall a speaking engagement before which I was taken to lunch by a group of women. They were so attentive to my expertise that they plied me with questions, prompting me to exhaust myself by giving my lecture over lunch before the formal lecture began. In comparison to this, perhaps the man who lectured to me about computers was trying to give me a rest.

The imbalance by which men often find themselves in the role of lecturer, and women often find themselves in the role of audience, is not the creation of only one member of an interaction. It is not something that men do to women. Neither is it something that women culpably "allow" or "ask for." The imbalance is created by the difference between women's and men's habitual styles. . . .

HOPE FOR THE FUTURE

What is the hope for the future? Must we play out our assigned parts to the closing act? Although we tend to fall back on habitual ways of talking, repeating old refrains and familiar lines, habits can be broken. Women and men both can gain by understanding the other gender's style, and by learning to use it on occasion.

Women who find themselves unwillingly cast as the listener should practice propelling themselves out of that position rather than waiting patiently for the lecture to end. Perhaps they need to give up the belief that they must wait for the floor to be handed to them. If they have something to say on a subject, they might push themselves to volunteer it. If they are bored with a subject, they can exercise some influence on the conversation and change the topic to something they would rather discuss.

If women are relieved to learn that they don't always have to listen, there may be some relief for men in learning that they don't always have to have interesting information on the tips of their tongues if they want to impress a woman or entertain her. A journalist once interviewed me for an article about how to strike up conversations. She told me that another expert she had interviewed, a man, had suggested that one should come up with an interesting piece of information. I found this amusing, as it seemed to typify a man's idea of a good conversationalist, but not a woman's. How much easier men might find the task of conversation if they realized that all they have to do is listen. As a woman who wrote a letter to the editor of *Psychology Today* put it, "When I find a guy who asks, 'How was your day?' and really wants to know, I'm in heaven."

FOR DISCUSSION AND REVIEW

1. Tannen begins her essay by recounting several anecdotes that illustrate her main point or thesis. State her thesis in your own words. How do her anecdotes support it? What experiences from your own life support or refute her thesis?

2. Tannen often speaks about her research to both men and women. What are the typical responses of each gender?

3. According to Tannen, what do men primarily seek through conversation and what do women seek? What roles do men and women

characteristically adopt as a result, and how do these different roles lead to inequality?

4. According to the findings of Leet-Pellegrini, what happens in a conversation when a woman is the expert and a man is the nonexpert? When the expert and nonexpert are both men? How would you interpret these findings?

5. In Aries's study, how do all-female groups seek to establish camaraderie? How do all-male groups try to do so? Do you find evidence of these different approaches in your own world? Explain.

6. Why are telling jokes and laughing at them "very different social activities"? How might joking be understood as an "asymmetrical" activity? What kind of joking occurs in your ordinary conversation? Is it asymmetrical?

7. According to Maltz and Borker, what characterizes the listening response of women? Of men?

8. What suggestions does Tannen offer to overcome the imbalance between the male "lecturer" and the female "listener"?

39

Ethnic Style in Male–Female Conversation

Deborah Tannen

In this selection, Deborah Tannen, professor of linguistics at Georgetown University, looks at how ethnic background affects men's and women's conversations. In considering Greek, American, and Greek-American speakers of English, Tannen focuses on indirectness as a communication strategy between married partners of different cultural backgrounds. She finds that both ethnicity and gender play important roles in how participants interpret a conversation. She also learns that the strategy of indirectness may persevere for a generation or more after the language in which it originated is unknown to the user. Tannen's study illustrates that communication is complicated by many factors. This essay was originally published in Language and Social Identity *(1982), edited by John J. Gumperz.*

This [selection] focuses on indirectness in male–female discourse, seen as a feature of conversational style. The present analysis investigates social, rather than individual, differences in the context of conversation between married partners; however, the phenomena eludicated operate in individual style as well. Investigation of expectations of indirectness by Greeks, Americans, and Greek-Americans traces the process of adaptation of this conversational strategy as an element of ethnicity.

Misunderstandings due to different uses of indirectness are commonplace among members of what appear to (but may not necessarily) be the same culture. However, such mixups are particularly characteristic of cross-cultural communication. There are individual as well as social differences with respect to what is deemed appropriate to say and how it is deemed appropriate to say it.

It is sharing of conversational strategies that creates the feeling of satisfaction which accompanies and follows successful conversation: the sense of being understood, being "on the same wave length," belonging, and therefore of sharing identity. Conversely, a lack of congruity in conversational strategies creates the opposite feeling: of dissonance, not being understood, not belonging, and therefore of not sharing identity.

This is the sense in which conversational style is a major component of what we have come to call ethnicity.

As has been [noted by other researchers], conversational control processes operate on an automatic level. While it is commonly understood that different languages or different dialects have different words for the same object, in contrast, ways of signalling intentions and attitudes seem self-evident, natural, and real.

Much recent linguistic research has been concerned with the fact that interpretation of utterances in conversation often differs radically from the meaning that would be derived from the sentences in isolation. Robin Lakoff (1973) observes that sociocultural goals, broadly called *politeness*, lead people to express opinions and preferences in widely varying linguistic forms. Lakoff's (1979) recent work demonstrates that characteristic choices with respect to indirectness give rise to personal style, and that an individual's style is a mixture of strategies which shift in response to shifting situations. Ervin-Tripp (1976) has shown the great variation in surface form which directives may take in American English. Brown and Levinson (1978) argue that the form taken by utterances in actual interaction can be seen as the linguistic means of satisfying the coexisting and often conflicting needs for *negative face* (the need to be left alone) and *positive face* (the need to be approved of by others). As a result, people often prefer to express their wants and opinions *off record*—that is, indirectly.

Indirectness is a necessary means for serving the needs for *rapport* and *defensiveness*, associated respectively with Brown and Levinson's positive and negative face. *Rapport* is the lovely satisfaction of being understood without explaining oneself, of getting what one wants without asking for it. *Defensiveness* is the need to be able to save face by reneging in case one's conversational contribution is not received well—the ability to say, perhaps sincerely, "I never said that," or "That isn't what I meant." The goals of rapport and defensiveness correspond to Lakoff's politeness rules "Maintain camaraderie" and "Don't impose."

An individual learns conversational strategies in previous interactive experience, but chooses certain and rejects other strategies made available in this way. In other words, the range of strategies familiar to a speaker is socially determined, but any individual's set of habitual strategies is unique within that range. For example, research has shown that New Yorkers of Jewish background often use overlap—that is, simultaneous talk—in a cooperative way; many members of this group talk simultaneously in some settings without intending to interrupt (Tannen 1979, 1981). This does not imply that all New Yorkers of Jewish background use overlap cooperatively. However, a speaker of this background is more likely to do so than someone raised in the Midwest. And it is even more unlikely that such simultaneous talk will be used by an Athabaskan raised in Alaska, according to the findings of Scollon, who has shown that Athabaskans highly value silence and devalue what they perceive as excessive talk.

The present analysis and discussion seeks to investigate social differences in expectations of indirectness in certain contexts by Greeks, Americans, and Greek-Americans, tracing the process of adaptation of this conversational strategy as an element of ethnicity. The research design is intended to identify patterns of interpretation, not to predict the styles of individual members of these groups.

A Greek woman of about 65 told me that, before she married, she had to ask her father's permission before doing anything. She noted that of course he never explicitly denied her permission. If she asked, for example, whether she could go to a dance, and he answered,

(1) An thes, pas. (If you want, you can go.)

she knew that she could not go. If he really meant that she could go, he would say,

(2) Ne. Na pas. (Yes. You should go.)

The intonation in (1) rises on the conditional clause, creating a tentative effect, while the intonation in (2) falls twice in succession, resulting in an assertive effect. This informant added that her husband responds to her requests in the same way. Thus she agrees to do what he prefers without expecting him to express his preference directly.

This example is of a situation in which interlocutors share expectations about how intentions are to be communicated; their communication is thus successful. To investigate processes of indirectness, however, it is useful to focus on interactions in which communication is not successful (Gumperz and Tannen 1979). Such sequences are the discourse equivalents of starred sentences in syntactic argumentation. They render apparent processes which go unnoticed when communication is successful.

[This essay] focuses on communication between married partners. Interactions between couples reveal the effects of differing uses of indirectness over time. People often think that couples who live together and love each other must come to understand each other's conversational styles. However, research has shown that repeated interaction does not necessarily lead to better understanding. On the contrary, it may reinforce mistaken judgments of the other's intentions and increase expectations that the other will behave as before. If differing styles led to the earlier impression that the partner is stubborn, irrational, or uncooperative, similar behavior is expected to continue. This has been shown for group contact among Greeks and Americans (Vassiliou et al. 1972) and can be seen in personal relations as well. Misjudgment is calcified by the conviction of repeated experience.

Systematic study of comparative communicative strategies was made by asking couples about experiences in which they become aware of differing interpretations of conversations. It became clear that certain types of communication were particularly given to misinterpretation— requests, excuses, explanation: in short, verbalizations associated with getting one's way. One couple recalled a typical argument in which both maintained that they had not gone to a party because the other had not wanted to go. Each partner denied having expressed any disinclination to go. A misunderstanding such as this might well go undetected between casual acquaintances, but, between couples, ongoing interaction makes it likely that such differences will eventually surface.

In this case, the mixup was traced to the following reconstructed conversations:

(3)   Wife: John's having a party. Wanna go?
      Husband: OK.
      (Later)
      Wife: Are you sure you want to go to the party?
      Husband: OK, let's not go. I'm tired anyway.

In this example the wife was an American native New Yorker of East European Jewish extraction. It is likely that this background influenced her preference for a seemingly direct style. (This phenomenon among speakers of this background is the focus of analysis in Tannen 1979, 1981.) In discussing the misunderstanding, the American wife reported she had merely been asking what her husband wanted to do without considering her own preference. Since she was about to go to this party just for him, she tried to make sure that that was his preference by asking him a second time. She was being solicitous and considerate. The Greek husband said that by bringing up the question of the party, his wife was letting him know that she wanted to go, so he agreed to go. Then when she brought it up again, she was letting him know that she didn't want to go; she had obviously changed her mind. So he came up with a reason not to go, to make her feel all right about getting her way. This is precisely the strategy reported by the Greek woman who did what her father or husband wanted without expecting him to tell her directly what that was. Thus the husband in example (3) was also being solicitous and considerate. All this considerateness, however, only got them what neither wanted, because they were expecting to receive information differently from the way the other was sending it out.

A key to understanding the husband's strategy is his use of "OK." To the wife, "OK" was a positive response, in free variation with other positive responses such as "yes" or "yeah." In addition, his use of *anyway* is an indication that he agrees. Finally, the husband's intonation, tone of voice, and nonverbal signals such as facial expression and kinesics would have contributed to the impact of his message. Nonetheless, the wife asserted that, much as she could see the reasoning behind such interpretations in retrospect, she still missed the significance of these cues at the time. The key, I believe, is that she was not expecting to receive her husband's message through subtle cues; she was assuming he would tell her what he wanted to do directly. To the listener, a misunderstanding is indistinguishable from an understanding; one commits to an interpretation and proceeds to fit succeeding information into that mold. People will put up with a great deal of seemingly inappropriate verbal behavior before questioning the line of interpretation which seems self-evident. Direct questioning about how a comment was meant is likely to be perceived as a challenge or criticism.

This example demonstrates, furthermore, the difficulty of clearing up misunderstandings caused by stylistic differences. In seeking to clarify, each speaker continues to use the very strategy that confused the other in the first place. In this way, interaction often results in increasing divergence rather than convergence of style. That is, each partner's characteristic style leads the other to apply increasingly extreme forms of the conflicting strategy. In example (3), the wife's strategy for clarifying was to go "on record," through a direct question, as inquiring about her husband's preference, and to ask her husband to go on record about his preference. Since the husband did not expect preferences to be directly expressed, his wife's second question seemed to him an even more recondite hint. He responded with an even more subtle use of indirectness: to allow her to get her way and to offer a reason of his own in justification. And so it goes. Expectations about how meaning will be communicated are so compelling that information intended in a different mode is utterly opaque.

A key parameter here is setting. Does a participant define an interaction as one in which it is appropriate to hint? Numerous discussions triggered by the presentation of these findings have suggested possible male–female differences among Americans in this regard. An audience member commented, "When I first started going out with my boyfriend, we never had misunderstandings about where we should go and what we should do. Now that we've been going together for two years, it seems to happen all the time. How come?" My hypothesis is that, at the beginning of their acquaintance, both partners deemed it appropriate to watch out for the other's hints, to give options. However, as the relationship was redefined, the woman expected increased use of indirectness, reasoning, "We know each other so well, you will know what I want without my telling you." The man, on the other hand, expected less indirectness, reasoning, "We know each other so well that we can tell each other what we want." As the context of their relationship changed, they differed in how they expected their communicative strategies to change. In addition, when partners interact over time, they become more rather than less likely to react, perhaps negatively, to each other's subtle cues, as repeated experience leads them to expect such behavior.

Another example of a reported conversation between a married couple follows.

(4) Husband: Let's go visit my boss tonight.
     Wife: Why?
     Husband: All right, we don't have to go.

Both husband and wife agreed that the husband's initial proposal was an indication that he wanted to visit his boss. However, they disagreed on the meaning of the wife's question, "Why?" The wife explained that she meant it as a request for information. Therefore she was confused and frustrated and couldn't help wondering why she married such an erratic man who suddenly changed his mind only a moment after making a request. The husband, for his part, explained that his wife's question clearly meant that she did not want to go, and he therefore rescinded his request. He was frustrated, however, and resentful of her for refusing. In discussion, the wife, who was American, reported that she systematically confronted this strange reaction to her asking "Why?" Certainly, the use of this question can be either a request for information or an indirect way of stalling or resisting compliance with a perceived request. The key here is which meaning of "why" is likely to be used in this context.

In order to determine to what extent cross-cultural differences are operating in patterns of interpretation of indirectness, further systematic questioning of Greeks, Americans, and Greek-Americans was undertaken. The remainder of this [essay] reports results of that research.

The Greek sample was taken from native Greeks living in the Bay Area of California. Most were young men who had come to the United States for graduate study or women contacted through church organizations. Therefore the age and educational levels differed sharply for men and women. In all cases, Greek respondents had been exposed to American communicative systems. That differences emerged nonetheless is a testament to the reality of the effect.

Greek-Americans were contacted in New York City because it was not possible to find California Greek-Americans who had grown up in distinctly Greek communities. The fact that Greek-Americans from New York are compared with Americans from California is now seen as a weakness; subsequent research (Tannen 1979) has indicated that New Yorkers are less likely to expect indirectness than Californians. Again, the fact that differences do emerge is testimony to the effect of ethnicity. Finally, Americans with Greek-born parents and grandparents are lumped together in this study. There is some indication that those with Greek parents show the effect of ethnicity more strongly than do those of Greek grandparents and American-born parents.

A questionnaire was designed to present the Greek, American, and Greek-American respondents with the conversation about going to a party. The questionnaire elicited their interpretations by presenting paraphrase choices and then asked for explanations of those choices in order to identify the interpretive strategies motivating them. The first part of the questionnaire reads:

(5) A couple had the following conversation:
    Wife: John's having a party. Wanna go?
    Husband: OK.
    Wife: I'll call and tell him we're coming.

Based on this conversation only, put a check next to the statement which you think explains what the husband really meant when he answered "OK."

[1–I] My wife wants to go to this party, since she asked. I'll go to make her happy.

[1–D] My wife is asking if I want to go to a party. I feel like going, so I'll say yes.

What is it about the way the wife and husband spoke, that gave you that impression?

What would the wife or husband have had to have said differently, in order for you to have checked the other statement?

The first choice, here referred to as 1–I (Indirect), represents roughly what the Greek husband reported he had meant by "OK." 1–D (Direct) represents what the American wife reported she had thought he meant. A comparison of the percentage of respondents in the three groups who opted for Paraphrase 1–I turns out looking much like a continuum, with Greeks the most likely to take the indirect interpretation, Americans the least likely, and Greek-Americans in the middle, somewhat closer to Greeks (see Table 39.1).

In example (5), and throughout the present discussion, I refer to one interpretation as direct and the other as indirect. These labels reflect the two possible functions of the question: as a request for information (its literal sense) and as an off-record show of resistance (an indirect speech act). This is not to imply, however, that anyone's conversational style is categorically direct. In a sense, all interpretation in context is indirect. What are variable are the modes of indirectness—when and how it is deemed appropriate to hint, that is, to signal unstated contextual and interpersonal information.

It has been suggested (Lakoff 1975) that American women tend to be more indirect than American men. As seen in Tables 39.2 and 39.3, percentages of respondents taking the indirect interpretation are more or less the same for Greek men and women and for Greek-American men and women, while, for Americans, separating male and female respondents

TABLE 39.1   Respondents Choosing 1–I

GREEKS (27)	GREEK-AMERICANS (30)	AMERICANS (25)
48% (13)	43% (13)	32% (8)

TABLE 39.2   Male Respondents Choosing 1–I

GREEKS (10)	GREEK-AMERICANS (9)	AMERICANS (11)
50% (5)	44% (4)	27% (3)

TABLE 39.3   Female Respondents Choosing 1–I

GREEKS (17)	GREEK-AMERICANS (21)	AMERICANS (14)
47%	43%	36%
(8)	(9)	(5)

yields quite different percentages, with fewer men and more women choosing Paraphrase 1–I. If these samples are representative, they are intriguing in suggesting a stylistic gulf between American men and women which does not exist between Greek men and women.

The second part of the questionnaire presents the second part of the conversation, followed by paraphrase choice and questions about interpretive strategies. It reads:

(6)   Later, the same couple had this conversation:
      Wife: Are you sure you want to go to the party?
      Husband: OK, let's not go. I'm tired anyway.
      Based on *both* conversations which you read, put a check next to the statement that you think explains what the husband really meant when he spoke the second time:
      [2–I]   It sounds like my wife doesn't really want to go, since she's asking about it again. I'll say I'm tired, so we don't have to go, and she won't feel bad about preventing me from going.
      [2–D]   Now that I think about it again, I don't really feel like going to a party because I'm tired.
      What is it about the way the husband or wife spoke that gave you that impression?
      What would they have had to have said differently, in order for you to have checked the other statement?

The two paraphrases presented in the second part of the questionnaire represent the respective interpretations reported by the Greek husband (the one here labeled 2–I, Indirect) and the American wife (here labeled 2–D, Direct) in the actual interchange. This also highlights an aspect of the questionnaire which is different for male and female respondents. Women and men are both asked to interpret the husband's comments, while it is likely that women identify with the wife and men with the husband. Furthermore, the indirect interpretation is favored by the fact that the husband's response indicates that he took that interpretation.

The choice of both 1–I and 2–I reveals the most indirect interpretive strategy, by which both the wife's questions are taken to indicate her hidden preferences—or at least that the husband's reply is taken to show that he interprets them that way. Again, results fall out on a continuum with Greeks the most likely to take the indirect interpretation, Americans the least likely, and Greek-Americans in between, slightly closer to the Greeks (see Table 39.4).

TABLE 39.4   Respondents Choosing 1–I and 2–I

GREEKS (27)	GREEK-AMERICANS (30)	AMERICANS (25)
26%	20%	12%
(7)	(6)	(3)

Quantitative results, then, tended to corroborate the impression that more Greeks than Americans opted for the indirect interpretation of questions, and that Greek-Americans were in between, slightly closer to Greeks. However, the pilot study questionnaire was not designed primarily to yield quantitative data. The main function of the paraphrase choices was to serve as a basis for short answers and extended discussion about the patterns of interpretation which prompted one or the other choice, and the linguistic and contextual factors influencing them. Results of the short answer and interview/discussion components follow.

Patterns of interpretation emerged from respondents' explanations of their choice of paraphrase and from alternative linguistic forms they reported would have led them to the other choice. Following paraphrase choices, the questionnaire asked, "What is it about the way the wife and the husband spoke, that gave you that impression?" and then, "What would the wife or husband have had to have said differently, in order for you to have checked the other statement?" Differences in explanations of interpretations were systematic in reference to two aspects of the conversation: the wife's asking of questions, and the form of the husband's responses.

Paraphrase 1–I indicates that the wife's question means she wants to go to the party. The reasoning reported by Greeks to explain their choice of 1–I is that if the wife didn't want to go, she would not have brought it up in the first place. Greeks, Americans, and probably members of any cultural group are capable of interpreting a question either as a request for information or as an expression of some unstated meaning. However, members of one culture or another may be more likely to interpret a question in a particular context in one way or another. Much recent research in pragmatics has elaborated on the indirect speech act function of questions as requests for action, or commands. Esther Goody (1978:40) set out to discover why natives of Gonja do not ask questions in teaching and learning situations. She concluded that Gonjans are "trained early on to attend above all to the command function of questioning. The pure information question hasn't got a chance!" Similarly, I suggest, in the context under consideration, natives of Greece are more disposed to attend to the indirect request function of questions.

Respondents' comments explaining why they chose one or the other paraphrase often focused on the husband's choice of OK. Americans who thought the husband really wanted to go to the party explained that "OK" = "yes" (24% of the Americans said this). But if they thought the husband was going along with his wife's preference, the Americans still focused on "OK" as the cue. In this case they explained that "OK" lacks enthusiasm (20% of the Americans said this).

The expectation of enthusiasm was stronger for Greeks than for Americans. Whereas 24% of the Americans pointed to the affirmative nature of "OK," not a single Greek did so. In contrast, fully half of the Greeks who explained their choices referred to the fact that "OK" (in Greek, *endaxi*) was an unenthusiastic response. This is more than double the percentage of Americans (20%) who said this. The *enthusiasm constraint* is in keeping with findings of Vassiliou, Triandis, Vassiliou, and McGuire (1972), who conclude that Greeks place value on enthusiasm and spontaneity (as opposed to American emphasis on planning and organization). Vassiliou et al. observe that such differences in "subjective culture" may contribute to the formation of ethnic stereotypes.

Related to the enthusiasm constraint—perhaps another aspect of it— is the *brevity effect*. Many respondents referred to the brevity of the husband's response when they explained their paraphrase choices. However, if Americans made reference to his brevity, it was in explanation of their choice of paraphrase 1–D, the direct interpretation. Their reasoning was that brevity evidenced informality, casualness, and hence sincerity. This explanation is based on a strategy which assumes that people will express preferences directly in this context. More than a quarter (28%) of the American respondents took this approach. In stark contrast, any Greeks who mentioned the brevity of the husband's answer "OK" (*endaxi*) pointed to it as evidence that he was reluctant to go to the party. To them, brevity is a sign of unwillingness to comply with another's perceived preference. This interpretation presupposes that resistance to another's preference, in this context, will not be verbalized directly; 20% of Greek respondents took this approach.

The explanations given by Greek-Americans for their paraphrase choices were a blend of typical Greek and typical American explanations. They explained that brevity reveals lack of enthusiasm, whereas no Americans did, and they explained that brevity is casual, whereas no Greeks did, in roughly the same proportions (23% and 20%, respectively). Only two (7%) said that "OK" = "yes," whereas no Greeks and 24% of Americans said this. Thus Greek-Americans were closer to Greeks than to Americans in their interpretive style.

Further corroborative results came in the form of comments volunteered by respondents following their completion of the questionnaire; the suggestion that Greeks tend to be more indirect in the context of an intimate relationship "rang true" for respondents.

What are the implications of such differences for cross-cultural communication? It is possible that a good bicultural, like a good bilingual, sees both possibilities and code-switches. For example, an

American-born woman of Greek grandparents said that she had to check both paraphrases on the questionnaire. She explained that if she projected herself into the position of the wife, she would take the indirect interpretation, but if she imagined her non-Greek husband asking, she would take the direct paraphrase. In other words, she was aware of both possible strategies. She commented that she tends to be indirect because she picked it up from her mother, who was influenced by her own mother (i.e., the grandmother born in Greece). In the same spirit, another Greek-American woman laughed when she read paraphrase 2–I, saying, "That sounds just like my grandmother."

It is far from certain, however, that awareness of the existence of differences in communicative strategies makes them less troublesome, since their operation remains unconscious and habitual. Again, a personal testimony is most eloquent: that of a professional man living in New York City, whose grandparents were from Greece. He seemed fully assimilated, did not speak Greek, had not been raised in a Greek neighborhood, and had few Greek friends. In filling out the questionnaire, he chose paraphrase 1–I, the initial indirect interpretation. In later discussion he said that the notion of indirectness "rang such a bell." He commented, " . . . to a great extent being Greek implies a certain feeling of differentness with regard to understanding others which I have some trouble with." He elaborated on what he meant: "I was trying to get at the idea of . . . this very thing that we talked about [indirectness] and I see it as either something heroically different or a real impediment . . . Most of the time I think of it as a problem. And I can't really sort it out from my family and background . . . I don't know if it's Greek. I just know that it's me. And it feels a little better to know that it's Greek."

CONCLUSIONS

These results indicate how respondents report they would interpret a conversation. In actual interaction, intonation, facial expression, past experience with these and other speakers, and a myriad of other factors influence interpretation. Moreover, whenever people communicate, they convey not only the content of their message, but an image of themselves (Goffman 1959). Thus respondents must have referred for their answers not only to their interactive experience but also to their notion of social norms.

Eventually such an approach must be combined with tape-recording and videotaping of actual interaction, to determine not only what speakers expect but what they do.

Conversational style—the ways it seems natural to express and interpret meaning in conversation—is learned through communicative experience and therefore is influenced by family communicative habits.

As the Greek-American quoted above put it, one "can't really sort it out from . . . family and background." In other words, conversational style is both a consequence and indicator of ethnicity. Conversational style includes both how meaning is expressed, as seen in patterns of indirectness, and what meaning is expressed, as in how much enthusiasm is expected. All of these conversational strategies create impressions about the speaker—judgments which are made, ultimately, not about how one talks but about what kind of person one is. Conversational style, therefore, has much to do with the formation of ethnic stereotypes.

Conversational style is more resistant to change than more apparent marks of ethnicity such as retention of the parents' or grandparents' language. Seaman (1972:204) demonstrates that the modern Greek language is "practically extinct" among third-generation Greek-Americans and will be "totally extinct in the fourth generation." However, those very third-generation Greek-Americans who have lost the Greek language may not have lost, or not lost entirely, Greek communicative strategies. Understanding these strategies, and the patterns of their retention or loss, can offer insight into the process of cultural assimilation at the same time that it provides insight into discourse processes in a heterogeneous society.

BIBLIOGRAPHY

Brown, P. and Levinson, S. 1978. "Universals in Language Usage: Politeness Phenomena." In *Questions and Politeness*. E. N. Goody, ed. Cambridge: Cambridge University Press.

Ervin-Tripp, S. 1976. "Is Sybil There? The Structure of Some American English Directives." *Language in Society* 5: 25–66.

Goffman, Erving. 1959. *The Presentation of Self in Everyday Life*. Garden City, NJ: Doubleday.

Goody, Esther N. 1978. Towards a theory of questions. In Esther N. Goody (Ed.), *Questions and Politeness: Strategies in Social Interaction*. Cambridge: Cambridge University Press, pp. 17–43.

Gumperz, J. J. and Tannen, D. 1979. "Individual and Social Differences in Language Use." In *Individual Differences in Language Ability and Language Behavior*. W. Wang and C. Fillmore, eds. New York: Academic Press.

Lakoff, R. 1973. "The Logic of Politeness; or, Minding Your P's and Q's." *CLS* 10: Chicago Linguistics Society.

Lakoff, R. 1975. *Language and Women's Place*. New York: Harper and Row.

Lakoff, R. 1979. "Stylistic Strategies within a Grammar of Style." In *Language, Sex, and Gender*. J. Orasanu, M. Slater, and L. Loeb Adler, eds. *Annals of the New York Academy of Sciences* 327: 53–78.

Seaman, P. D. 1972. *Modern Greek and American English in Contact*. The Hague: Mouton.

Tannen, D. 1979. Processes and Consequences of Conversational Style. Ph.D. dissertation. University of California, Berkeley.

Tannen, D. 1981. "New York Jewish Conversational Style." *International Journal of the Sociology of Language* 30: 133–49.

Vassiliou, V., Triandis, H., Vassiliou, G. and McGuire, H. 1972. "Interpersonal Contact and Stereotyping." In *The Analysis of Subjective Culture*. H. Triandis, ed. New York: Wiley.

≡

FOR DISCUSSION AND REVIEW

1. Tannen implies that at least three dynamics may come into play in conversation between married partners. What are they?

2. What does Tannen mean by *indirectness*? Define the term in your own words, and compare your definition with those of classmates. When a speaker uses indirectness, what needs are likely motivating him or her?

3. What is the role of ethnicity in successful conversation?

4. What characterizes a situation with successful communication? What may happen when married couples do not understand each other's conversational styles?

5. In Tannen's example, what chief difference characterized the misunderstanding between members of a couple made up of one of Greek heritage and the other not? How was the cause of this misunderstanding reinforced in a subsequent study of Greek-Americans and their partners? According to the study, are Greeks or Americans more likely to expect indirectness in conversation?

6. Explain the roles of *enthusiasm constraint* and *brevity effect* in respondents' interpretations of the misunderstanding.

7. In an American setting, is the male or female more likely to expect indirectness in conversation? On what evidence do you base your response?

8. Comment on Tannen's observation that "conversational style is both a consequence and indicator of ethnicity."

Projects for "Language and Gender"

1. In his article "Girl Talk–Boy Talk" published in *Science* in 1985, John Pfeiffer introduces at least three differences in the communication styles of boys and girls. Read this article, and then make your own contemporary observations. First you will need to obtain permission to observe and ideally record at a preschool or kindergarten, an elementary school, and a junior high or middle school. Select three ages of boys and girls to observe, such as four–five, eight–nine, and eleven–twelve. Take notes on the interactions you observe.

Then play the recordings (audio or video) in class, and make a list of the communication goals and strategies of the girls and the boys. Where did you observe distinct differences, and where did you see girls and boys using the same strategies? Did the children communicate differently in mixed-sex groups than in same-sex groups? What about communication styles in different culture groups?

2. A number of writers argue that language is sexist, and one solution to this problem is to create gender-neutral linguistic forms. Write a research essay on the various approaches to identifying, removing, or neutralizing sexist forms. Some of the entries in the bibliography for Part Eight, such as the Dubois and Crouch or the Nilsen essays in the Joyce Penfield collection or the volume by Deborah Cameron, will provide you with theoretical discussions and numerous examples of proposed new forms.

3. Using the idea of folk linguistics, conduct a face-to-face survey similar to what Professor Johnson describes in "Discourse Patterns of Males and Females." Prepare a questionnaire about the language behaviors and discourse styles of male and females, and interview at least ten people, recording their immediate responses. Ask participants (who should include both men and women) to give a simple characterization of women's speech and of men's speech. Then ask some specific questions: Who uses insults, jokes, or obscenities? Who uses commands? Who uses suggestions? Who is more polite or assertive? Who is more talkative? Who interrupts the most? For more ideas, look again at Johnson's selection on pages 517–30.

Then write up your findings. Which responses are consistent? To what extent do these responses seem to reflect popular ideas about gender and language? Which responses surprised you? Compare your findings to those of your classmates and to what Johnson or other researchers have discovered.

4. Select a television show, such as a crime or medical drama, whose main female and male characters have fairly equal qualifications and occupations. Record at least one episode or borrow one from the library so that you can review, replay, and pause it. Analyze the gendered language

behaviors and discourse patterns of the main characters. Pay attention to a number of items: Does the female character have a higher pitch or softer voice than the male character? Does one character tend to use more suggestions while the other issues more commands or makes direct requests? Try to keep track of who introduces topics as well as what part of the storyline (subplot or "issue") belongs to which character. Depending on the show, you may find that one character tells jokes while the other only responds to them. Notice who issues insults and who interrupts. Also pay attention to how characters interact in mixed-sex groups or same-sex groups.

Using your findings, write a paper discussing how gender is expressed and represented in this show. Consider whether the show's writers have worked with or against preexisting stereotypes about gender. Use the data from your analysis as evidence.

5. A number of popular books seek to identify or claim to resolve communication problems between men and women. One of these is John Gray's *Men Are from Mars, Women Are from Venus: A Practical Guide for Improving Communication and Getting What You Want in Your Relationships* (1992). Read this book or another popular book, such as Suzette Haden Elgin's *Genderspeak: Men, Women, and the Gentle Art of Verbal Self-Defense* (1993), about communication between the sexes. (See the Selected Bibliography.) Write an analytical essay discussing how the writer popularizes gender research by linguists and social scientists. Are the author's interpretations valid, useful, or insightful? Why, or why not? Do the interpretations seem to be culture specific? Why, or why not? Does the author use *sex* and *gender* as synonyms or as distinct ideas?

6. Deborah Tannen's work is based on the idea that girls and boys are raised in different cultures and that they continue to live in different cultures. Her "difference model" is one of three approaches to understanding women's and men's language use. Another approach is the "deficit model," which takes male language as the norm and examines how female language differs from it. Robin Lakoff's book, *Language and Woman's Place* (1975) first introduces this idea. A third view, the "dominance model," suggests that differences in power play out in the different ways we conduct conversations. This view can be found in Deborah Cameron's *Feminism and Linguistic Theory* (1985) and in an article by Elinor Oaks and Carolyn Taylor, "The 'Father Knows Best' Dynamic in Dinnertime Narratives" (see Hall and Bucholtz in Selected Bibliography). Write a paper on one of these three approaches, and address some of these questions: Who uses this particular approach? What are the presumptions of the model? What kinds of evidence are provided to validate the model? What are the arguments against it? Does this approach seem to be a useful way to understand gender differences in conversation? Why, or why not?

7. Sociolinguists such as Deborah Tannen and Jennifer Coates (see Selected Bibliography) work with different models, yet both agree that women and men appear to have different conversational goals and

strategies. Make your own observations, and see whether or not they match those described by Tannen and Coates.

Record the conversations of a set of female friends who regularly talk with each other and a set of male friends who regularly talk to each other, both in same-sex groups. Try to record each conversation for at least twenty minutes or long enough for the participants to relax and talk naturally. If necessary, provide them with a topic to talk about. After you have usable recordings, analyze the conversations in regard to the conversational goals, strategies, or styles discussed in Part Eight. Here are some things to pay attention to: If the participants establish camaraderie, how do they do so? What strategies do they use to indicate interest, create relationships, compete, or express mutual concerns? Keep track of how often speakers change and what techniques they use to get a turn to speak. Who asks questions, offers confirmation, asserts opinions, or establishes expertise or experience? What gender differences do you find in how women and men use conversation? How do your results compare with the claims made by Johnson or Tannen? Present your findings in class.

8. For this project, first divide into small groups and obtain reading textbooks for elementary grades one to three from three different decades—for instance, from the 1930s, the 1960s, and from the 1990s or later. Then use the following steps to analyze the gender representations and language features for each era.

a. *Do a character analysis.* Determine the ratio of male to female characters. Which characters initiate activity, which participate, and which are fairly inactive? Does this change depending on the target age group?

b. *Look at pronouns.* Where is *he* used as a generic pronoun? Do any textbooks use a form that combines or includes both *he* and *she*? Is *they* used instead of singular third-person pronouns?

c. *Look at other kinds of language features or use.* For instance, are character names associated with boys or girls? Are names gender neutral? What kinds of titles or forms of address (*Mr., Mrs., Ms., Dr., Mother, Sir, Ma'am,* etc.) are used for adults? What kinds of verbs and adjectives are linked to males vs. females? Are men and women given professions, and, if so, do they differ based on gender?

Discuss your group's findings with the rest of the class.

9. Select a new name for yourself that is either gender specific or distinctly gender neutral. Tell your friends, family members, and coworkers that you will have this name for a week. Keep a journal or create a blog while you live with this new name. At the end, present your new self to the class. Record how you chose the name, your feelings about it, and the cultural associations you have with it. Using information from the U.S. Census Bureau (www.census.gov) and other sources such as the American Name Society (www.wtsn.binghamton.edu/ANS), find out how popular your new name is or was. Interview family members to

learn how your birth name was chosen and to test their responses to your new name. In some cultures, people change names as their lives change. How did your sense of identity change as you lived with your new name? Did your new name come to seem more or less feminine or masculine as you lived with it?

10. The language and imagery used in advertising is intended to reflect the worldview of the target audience. Write an expository essay on how advertising appeals to cultural notions of gender. Collect some recent ads—from television, the Internet, and magazines—promoting an item that appears to be gender specific. Analyze the language, images, and conversational strategies used in the set of ads. How do these reflect, counter, or reinterpret the intended audience's ideas and beliefs about gender? Does advertising in the different types of media seem to assume different audiences?

Selected Bibliography

Baron, Dennis. *Grammar and Gender.* New Haven, CT: Yale UP, 1987. [Argues that sexual attitudes and differences of both men and women have informed linguistic models and attempts to get beyond norms and expectations to understand gender issues in language.]

Brown, Penelope, and Stephen C. Levinson. *Politeness: Some Universals in Language Usage.* 1978. Cambridge: Cambridge University Press, 1987. [Identifies politeness as organizing principle of social interaction and offers politeness model as a way of understanding social relations.]

Bucholtz, Mary. *Reinventing Identities: The Gendered Self in Discourse.* New York: Oxford UP USA, 1999. [Essays by scholars investigating language and gender in relation to class, teenage notions of femininity, African American drag queens, and so on.]

———. *Resources for Language and Gender Studies.* 19 June 2004. Linguistics Department, U of California Santa Barbara. <www.linguistics.ucsb.edu/faculty/bucholtz/lng>. [Useful links for language and gender; provides access to latest information on resources, conferences, publications, and organizations.]

Cameron, Deborah. *Verbal Hygiene: Politics of Language.* London: Routledge, 1995. [Discussion of how language and writing style are "corrected" through internal censoring and external editing.]

Coates, Jennifer. *Language and Gender: A Reader.* Oxford: Blackwell. 1998. [Essays that include studies of gender differences in mechanics, grammar, and pronunciation and in same-sex and mixed-sex talk.]

———. *Women, Men and Language: A Sociolinguistic Account of Gender Differences in Language.* 2nd ed. New York: Longman, 1983. [Discusses gender differences in childhood development, influences on language change, and effects in the classroom and the workplace.]

Crawford, Mary. *Talking Difference: On Gender and Language.* London: Sage, 1997. [Discusses gendered differences in various genres of talk, including wit and humor and storytelling.]

Dubois, Betty Lou, and Isabel Crouch. "Linguistic Disruption: He/She, S/He, He or She, He-She." In Joyce Penfield (ed.), *Women and Language in Transition.* New York: State U of New York P, 1987. [Description of attempts to eliminate gender bias through use of gender-neutral pronouns.]

Elgin, Suzette Haden. *Genderspeak: Men, Women, and the Gentle Art of Verbal Self-Defense.* New York: John Wiley, 1993. [Argues that language is a means to bridge the gaps in men and women's perceptions of the world.]

Goodwin, Marjorie Harness. *He-Said-She-Said: Talk as Social Organization among Black Children.* 5th ed. Indianapolis: Indiana UP, 1990. [Foundational study exploring gender differences in the language of African American children in various contexts, such as neighborhood interaction, disputes, and gossip.]

Goueffic, Louise. *Breaking the Patriarchal Code: The Linguistic Basis of Sexual Bias.* Manchester, CT: Knowledge Ideas and Trends, 1996. [Exploration of gender differences in Indo-European languages, supplemented by charts and lists of words that suggest bias within language.]

Graddol, David, and Joan Swann, *Gender Voices*. Oxford: Blackwell, 1990. [Focuses on many areas of difference in language between genders, examining biological, psychological, and political influences in varied communication contexts.]

Gray, John. *Men Are from Mars, Women Are from Venus: A Practical Guide for Improving Communication and Getting What You Want from Your Relationship*. New York: HarperCollins, 1993. [Popular book describing gender differences in language used by married men and women and offering advice on navigating resulting communication problems.]

Hall, Kira, and Mary Bucholtz, eds. *Gender Articulated: Language and the Socially Constructed Self*. New York: Routledge, 1995. [Essays on topics such as lesbian discourse, cybercommunication, and the Anita Hill/Clarence Thomas hearings.]

Henton, Caroline. "Fact and Fiction in the Description of Female and Male Pitch." *Language and Communication* 9.4 (1989): 299–311. [A contemporary examination of stereotypical views of male and female pitch, range, and expressiveness and the realities that go beyond those perceptions.]

Kiesling, Scott. "Power and the Language of Men." *Language and Masculinity*. Eds. Sally Johnson and Ulrike Meinhof. Oxford: Blackwell, 1997. 65–85. [Examines the impact of power strategies in male communication through the study of language use during a college fraternity meeting.]

Lakoff, Robin. *Language and Woman's Place*. Oxford: Oxford UP, 2004. [Revised edition of the pioneering 1975 classic that first brought together the studies of gender and language, with updated discussions of the impact of sexuality, politics, and power.]

Lawler, John. *Council on the Status of Women and Language, Part of the Linguistic Society of America*. 1993. Home page. U of Michigan. <www-personal.umich.edu/~jlawler/gender.html>. [Provides sample syllabi, sample exams, fieldwork exercises, and bibliographies.]

Lehrer, Adrienne. *Wine and Conversation*. Bloomington, IN: Indiana UP, 1983. [Using wine tasting as a model, this examines establishing communication norms in relation to word meaning, intention, and perception of expertise.]

Livia, Anna, and Kira Hall, eds. *Queerly Phrased: Language, Gender, and Sexuality*. New York: Oxford UP, 1997. [Essays examining language use in specific communities including the Deaf, Jews, Japanese, and hermaphrodites.]

McConnell-Ginet, Sally, and Penelope Eckert. *Language and Gender*. Cambridge: Cambridge UP, 2003. [Introductory textbook, with discussions of communicative norms and gender roles.]

Nilsen, Alleen Pace. "Guidelines against Sexist Language: A Case History." *Women and Language in Transition*. Ed. Joyce Penfield. Albany: State U of New York P, 1987. [Examines the role of style guidelines and editorial boards in academic publications; includes a useful appendix.]

Penelope, Julia. *Speaking Freely: Unlearning Lies of the Father's Tongues*. New York: Elsevier Science, 1990. [Views language as a human-made construct with male-centered bias that can be unlearned.]

Penfield, Joyce, ed. *Women and Language in Transition*. Albany: State U of New York P, 1987. [Essays examining how language expresses gender and how changes in gender roles and social perceptions are and are not reflected in language change.]

Pfeiffer, John. "Girl Talk–Boy Talk." *Science* (Feb. 1985): 58–63. [Examination of differences between male and female speech and how they reflect American conceptions of the sexes.]

Romaine, Suzanne. *Communicating Gender.* Mahwah, NJ: Lawrence Erlbaum, 1999. [Examines gendered communication, focusing on grammar and societal perceptions of language use.]

Schiffman, Harold. "Gender Bibliography." 18 Apr. 2004. Home page of Harold F. Schiffman. Dept. of South Asia Studies, U of Pennsylvania. <http://ccat.sas .upenn.edu/%7Eharoldfs/popcult/bibliogs/gender/gendbibs.html>. [Links to information on gender and Chinese language, discussions of social markings in language, and general bibliographies.]

Sheldon, Amy. "Pickle Fights: Gendered Talk in Preschool Disputes." *Gender and Conversational Interaction.* Ed. Deborah Tannen. New York and Oxford: Oxford UP, 1993. 83–106. [Analyzes conflict resolution among preschool-age children and finds gendered differences in resolution strategies.]

Syllabi on the Web for Women- and Gender-Related Courses. 8 July 2006. Center for Women and Information Technology, U of Maryland, Baltimore County. <www.umbc.edu/cwit/syl_ling.html>. [Sample syllabi and course outlines for introductory and advanced courses.]

Tannen, Deborah. *Conversational Style: Analyzing Talk among Friends.* New York: Oxford UP, 2005. [Examines different speech style in the discourse of participants in a Thanksgiving dinner.]

———. *You Just Don't Understand: Women and Men in Conversation.* New York: Harper, 2001. [Widely read book discussing gendered differences in conversational styles and goals.]

Thorne, Barrie, Cheris Kramarae, and Nan Henley, eds. *Language, Gender and Society.* Rowley, MA: Newbury, 1983. [Annotated essays addressing a range of topics, from interpersonal communication to gender differences in language maintenance of the only North American creole.]

LANGUAGE ACQUISITION AND THE BRAIN

The acquisition of language is considered to be an extraordinary achievement. As psycholinguist Jean Berko Gleason (2004) points out, by the age of three or four, human children "typically have acquired thousands of vocabulary words, complex grammatical and phonological systems, and equally complex rules for how to use their language appropriately in many social settings." This is the case for almost all children in all cultures and in every society.

The subfields of linguistics that deal with how humans acquire language are *psycholinguistics*, which studies language acquisition from before birth through early childhood, and *neurolinguistics*, which focuses on the organization of language and the brain. Although there are a number of hypotheses about language acquisition, we still do not fully understand the types of interactions involved, the stages that are gone through, the linguistic features children acquire at each stage, or even why humans develop language at all.

The selections in Part Nine are classic articles that introduce the long-standing questions about language acquisition. In recent years, other researchers have challenged some of the specific claims within these articles. Nevertheless, the questions and ideas discussed here lie at the heart of studying human language development.

In "Brain and Language," Jeannine Heny traces the major developments in twentieth-century neurolinguistic research and explores the probable reasons for brain lateralization—the process whereby each side of the brain becomes dedicated to certain cognitive functions. She then describes the different ways to measure which hemisphere does what. The right hemisphere, Heny explains, has a number of important cognitive functions, including some that are crucial to normal language processing. She notes, however, that language capabilities in terms of hemispheres may be assigned differently in some people. She expands on this point in her discussion of bilinguals, deaf users of sign language, the left-handed, females, and others.

Then, in "Signals, Signs, and Words: From Animal Communication to Language," William Kemp and Roy Smith explore the similarities and differences between nonhuman and human communication. As this essay points out, animal communication systems are fascinating in and of themselves. The primate research of the late twentieth century attempted to determine the ability of primates to learn human language. Acknowledging that some primate research has been fraught with design problems and ethical issues, Kemp and Smith survey the evidence and conclude that work with primates may have achieved less than some advocates claim but certainly more than many critics allow.

In the third selection, "The Acquisition of Language," Breyne Arlene Moskowitz provides an overview of the language acquisition process. She shows how children, in learning all the systems of grammar, use the same basic technique: they formulate a general rule, test it, and then modify it gradually until near mastery is achieved.

Next is Eric H. Lenneberg's presentation—in a chart format—titled "Developmental Milestones in Motor and Language Development." Lenneberg, who was concerned with the biological foundations of language, juxtaposes the stages of motor and language development for children ages twelve weeks to four years. At this latter point, most children can hop, jump over things, balance, and catch, and they have also achieved a rich vocabulary and complex grammar.

George A. Miller and Patricia M. Gildea note, in "How Children Learn Words," that "the average child learns at the rate of 5,000 words per year, or about thirteen per day." Miller and Gildea discuss the processes and stages of word learning and the strategies children use to make associations between words and concepts. They also explain why some teaching techniques, such as assigning dictionary exercises, are not very effective.

In "The Development of Language in Genie: A Case of Language Acquisition beyond the 'Critical Period,'" the late Victoria L. Fromkin and her colleagues report in detail on the linguistic development of Genie, a thirteen-year-old girl found in 1970 who had suffered extreme physical and social isolation and deprivation. Genie's case provided evidence for the idea that language acquisition has a "critical period." It also greatly aided researchers' understanding of the relationship between linguistic and cognitive development.

In the final essay, "American Sign Language: 'It's Not Mouth Stuff— It's Brain Stuff,'" Richard Wolkomir finds proof that signed language is exactly that, true language. As he reviews the history and development of American Sign Language (ASL), he learns that even at Gallaudet University—the only university for the deaf and the hearing impaired— controversy over teaching signed languages continues to this day. Wolkomir also discusses the work of psycholinguist Ursula Bellugi and her research group, who have investigated many aspects of signed language and its relationship to sound-based languages.

Brain and Language

Jeannine Heny

In the following selection, Jeannine Heny, professor of English at Indiana University of Pennsylvania, examines the evolution of the human brain and some possible causes of brain lateralization. She traces the research involving aphasia and the attempts to "map out" the language functions of the cortex. Describing the many ways to measure hemispheric activity, Heny demonstrates that both the left and right hemispheres of the brain are important in language processing and that they probably differ in the type of processing. Curiously, though, people do not all use the same hemisphere for language tasks. As Heny points out, our understanding of the complex relationship between language and the brain has increased enormously in recent years, but it is still tantalizingly incomplete. This article, updated in 1997, was originally published in the fourth edition of this book in 1985.

About five million years ago, early hominid brain size began to increase dramatically. After about ten million years of relatively stable weight, the human brain was embarking on a growth phase that would see it more than triple its volume to reach today's proportions. Five million years may seem very long; but, as Figure 40.1 shows, it can represent a phenomenal rate of growth on an evolutionary scale.

At the same time, other changes were taking place as well: our forebears became predominantly right-handed, made use of increasingly sophisticated tools, and organized their culture in ever more complex ways. The result of this evolution, *Homo sapiens*, looked rather unimpressive: a puny, almost hairless animal, with a bent windpipe that reduced breathing efficiency to nearly half of its original capacity. The creature's teeth were practically useless for chewing; it had nothing to match the sharp incisors of rats or the long canine teeth of wolves, lions, and other primates. Even inside the nervous system, the human species had taken risks, giving up a potentially useful insurance policy: the two halves of the brain were no longer identical, as in many lower species; thus, there was little chance of "backup" from one half of the brain if the other suffered damage. But the animal did have at least one feature that more than compensated for all it had lost: the most highly developed communication system on Earth—human language.

In fact, human brain evolution involved much more than increased size, as Figure 40.2 reveals. In lower mammals such as the rat, the brain

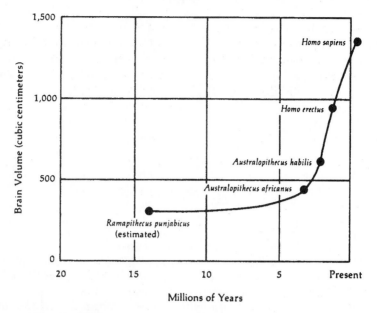

FIGURE 40.1   Human Evolution: Brain Size.

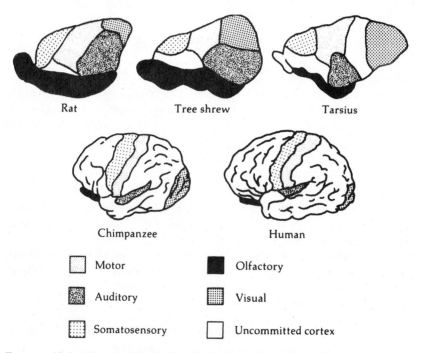

FIGURE 40.2   Human Evolution: Brain Function. These figures show the approximate space devoted to sensory and motor functions in various mammalian brains. The white areas, called *association cortex*, represent neural tissue not committed to basic functions. As shown, the increase in brain size is accompanied by a dramatic increase in the proportion of association cortex in humans.

is almost wholly taken up with sensory and motor functions. In contrast, the primate brain has a greatly enlarged outer layer or *cortex*, resulting in a dramatic increase in "uncommitted" cortical tissue not needed for basic functions. A high degree of asymmetry, or hemispheric specialization, nearly doubles this available space in humans (by the way, one estimate suggests that the human cortex contains more nerve connections than there are people on Earth!).[1] This essay focuses on the way in which the brain's powerful outer layer handles language.

DISCOVERING THE BRAIN

The Classical Language Areas

For centuries, the nature of the brain was shrouded in mystery. Aristotle is said to have thought it was a cold sponge, whose main task was to cool the blood.[2] Later, Leonardo da Vinci represented the brain as a curious void filled by three tiny bulbous structures arranged in a straight line behind the eyeball, whose functions he defined according to commonly held assumptions of his time.[3]

Not all early theories were quite so misguided, however. From the first studies on language deficits in the Greco-Roman era, it was suspected that the brain played some direct part in language use. Still, modern scholarship on this question dates only to the early nineteenth century. At that stage, scientific opinion was divided; some believed that language resided in the frontal lobes, while Franz Gall, the founder of phrenology, drew language in Area XV on his now famous map of the brain. Neither theory contained any hint that language might be handled more actively in one hemisphere than the other.

In 1836 an obscure French country doctor, Marc Dax, attended a medical conference in Montpelier, France, and presented the only scientific paper of his life. Dax claimed that, in forty aphasic patients he had seen in his practice, loss of language ability always correlated with damage to the left half of the brain. The paper went unnoticed at the time, and its remarkable insight was soon forgotten.

It was the French surgeon Paul Broca who, in 1864, dramatically proved Dax's original claim (about which, by the way, he knew nothing). Broca described his patient "Tan," named after the only word he could say. Tan could write normally, and seemed to understand everything said to him; he could move his lips or tongue in any direction when asked to

---

[1] Trevarthen (1983, 60).

[2] Comment (cited from work by Clarke and O'Mally) in Arbib, Caplan, and Marshall (1982, 6); this article provides an interesting overview of neurolinguistic history.

[3] Harth (1982, 37–42).

do so, but he was totally incapable of meaningful speech. Broca hypothesized that his patient suffered from a pure disturbance of language, resulting from left-hemisphere injury. Soon, his claim was proven: at autopsy, patients like Tan were found to have brain damage in the rear portion of the left frontal lobe, just above the left ear. Equivalent damage to the right hemisphere seemed to have little effect on speech. The area Broca isolated, and the aphasia associated with it, now bear his name: the term *Broca's aphasia* (also called *nonfluent* or *motor* aphasia) has come to stand for a complex of symptoms, ranging from extreme difficulty in articulation to *agrammatic* speech, where a patient produces halting strings of words without grammatical markers (e.g., inflections on verbs) or function words (such as articles and prepositions). The passage below gives an example of speech by a patient with Broca's aphasia. The patient is trying to describe a picture showing a little boy stealing cookies from a cookie jar while his chair is tipping over; a little girl is helping him. Their mother stands at the window staring into space while the sink in front of her overflows.

> Cookie jar . . . fall over . . . chair . . . water . . . empty . . . ov . . . ov . . . [Examiner: "overflow?"] Yeah.[4]

Another agrammatic patient, asked to tell the story of Cinderella, responded as follows:

> Cinderella . . . poor . . . um 'dopted her . . . scrubbed floor, um, tidy . . . poor, um . . . 'dopted . . . si-sisters and mother . . . ball. Ball, prince um, shoe.[5]

Ten years after Broca's discovery, Karl Wernicke, a twenty-six-year-old researcher in Germany, made yet another startling breakthrough. The patients who especially attracted his interest had no damage to Broca's area. Nor did they have obvious physical difficulty producing speech: in some cases, they could produce a stream of speech with no trouble in pronunciation and no significant loss of grammatical morphemes. But the content of their utterances ranged from puzzling to meaningless.

The Wernicke's aphasic who produced the following passage was also trying to describe the cookie theft picture described above. His flowing speech contrasts sharply with the hesitant, ungrammatical answer of the first patient. Yet, despite his fluency, he seems to make very little sense of the situation he sees:

> Well, this is . . . mother is away here working out o'here to get her better, but when she's working, the two boys looking in the other part. One their small tile into her time here. She's working another time because she's getting, too.[6]

---

[4] Cited from earlier work by Goodglass and Kaplan, in Blumstein (1982, 205).
[5] Schwartz, Linebarger, and Saffran (1985, 84).
[6] Blumstein (1982, 205).

The symptoms of Wernicke's aphasia are diverse and complex: a particularly striking form, called *jargon aphasia,* is marked by super-fluent speech and *neologisms,* that is, nonwords whose origin is unknown. The excerpt below is taken from a long spontaneous monologue:

> And I say, this is wrong, I'm going out and doing things and getting ukeleles taken every time and I think I'm doing wrong because I'm supposed to take everything from the top so that we do four flashes of four volumes before we get down low . . . Face of everything. This guy has got to this thing, this thing made out in order to slash immediately to all of the windpails . . . This is going right over me from there, that's up to five station stuff form manatime, and with that put it all in and build it all up so it will all be spent with him conversing his condessing . . .[7]

Wernicke's aphasics typically have great problems finding the simplest, everyday words, especially names for things. One patient, shown a knife, tried to tell what it was:

> That's a resh. Sometimes I get one around here that I can cut a couple regs. There's no rugs around here and nothing cut right. But that's a rug, and I had some nice rekebz. I wish I had one now. Say how Wishi idaw, uh windy, look how windy. It's really window, isn't it?[8]

As a result of studying such patients, the young Wernicke managed not only to isolate a new area, but also to present the first coherent model of language processing in the brain. According to Wernicke, a speaker first draws the words from Wernicke's area where meanings are stored, located near the primary auditory cortex (just above and behind the left ear). A bundle of nerves called the *arcuate fasciculus* then transmits the idea to Broca's area, where it picks up sound structure before being sent to the motor cortex. There, the message is encoded into commands to the tongue, lips, and other articulators, and emerges as speech. Wernicke's model, illustrated in Figure 40.3, still stands at the center of current research.

The discovery of Broca's and Wernicke's areas in the left hemisphere soon inspired others to seek the remaining pieces of the neurolinguistic puzzle. Scientists reasoned that all brain function must follow a clear, if complex, mapping system. Indeed, a few striking cases turned up to fuel the prevailing enthusiasm, where highly circumscribed damage caused specific, clearly identifiable symptoms. In 1892, for example, the French neurologist Dejerine observed a patient who could not read, although his visual skills, writing, and speech were normal. On autopsy, it was found that his left visual area was destroyed, along with the nerves connecting visual regions in the two hemispheres. Thus, only the right, nonverbal hemisphere could "see"—and it could not perceive what it saw as *language.* Hence, of course, it could not "read" what it saw. Nor could it

---

[7] Brown (1981, 170–171).
[8] Adapted from Buckingham (1981, 59).

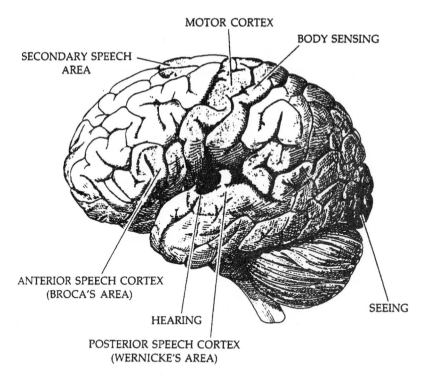

MOTOR CORTEX

BODY SENSING

SECONDARY SPEECH
AREA

ANTERIOR SPEECH CORTEX
(BROCA'S AREA)

SEEING

HEARING

POSTERIOR SPEECH CORTEX
(WERNICKE'S AREA)

FIGURE 40.3 The Classical Language Areas of the Brain. Note the proximity of Broca's area to the "motor cortex," where instructions to speech articulators originate. The proximity of Wernicke's area to neural centers for sight and hearing is also important, because this arrangement seems to allow the spoken and written word to be available for semantic processing in Wernicke's area as soon as they are perceived.

transmit the image it received to the language centers on the left for interpretation.

But the diagram-makers ran into problems from the outset. For one thing, it had long been known that severe aphasics, with extensive left-hemisphere lesions and with no ability to produce a normal spontaneous utterance, can often sing, curse, and produce fixed expressions such as "How are you?" This suggested that the right hemisphere (despite its absence on the neurolinguistic "map") might have some linguistic potential. More serious, however, was the elusive task of pinning down symptoms to points on the cortex. Exhaustive study by neurologists such as Henry Head in the 1920s showed that, at best, only a rough correlation could be found between symptom types and broad cortical areas. (Imagine a map of the United States in which the best one could do was place Boston "somewhere in the New England–New York State area." One could indeed capture the distinction between San Francisco and Boston with such a picture, but it could hardly be termed a useful guide for getting to Boston!)

These problems led many to abandon mapmaking altogether, on the grounds that language may be too complex to be broken down into discrete subprocesses, each assigned its own cortical territory. Now, the trend has again partially reversed, with recent research combining the spirit of both approaches. Scientists still search for the locus of specific verbal capacities, sometimes with painstaking accuracy, as in electrical stimulation research. Yet neurologists generally agree that this search is not likely to yield a one-to-one correspondence between units of grammatical knowledge and points on the brain's surface. The cortical areas that handle higher cognitive activity are too closely intertwined to be clearly teased apart and mapped out. And, within this system, linguistic and nonlinguistic capacity must be linked: a patient with a general impairment affecting, for example, memory or the ability to carry out purposeful actions, will have trouble speaking normally—but not because his grammatical knowledge is impaired.

Linguistics and Aphasia

When Broca and Wernicke made their discoveries about the brain, modern cognitive linguistics was unknown, and the terminology used to describe the functions of the language areas was vague; neurologists spoke of "sensory images" and "motor images" of words as being stored in Wernicke's and Broca's areas, respectively. Only now, after a century of brain research, has linguistic theory become rich enough to make a significant contribution to the understanding of aphasic syndromes. Three examples will help illustrate how this is happening.

First, consider the concept of "agrammatism." On the surface, it seems simple to describe. Take a sentence, like *A girl is playing in the yard*, and remove all the little particles, function words, and verb endings (*a, is, -ing,* etc.), and you have a plausible agrammatic sentence, right? (In this case, *girl . . . play . . . yard.*) Unfortunately, the answer is no. Broca's aphasics do not produce perfect language with a few predictable parts missing. For one thing, it may not be accurate to say that parts are *missing* at all: note that, in English, where both the bare stem *play* and the past tense *played* are fully acceptable forms, one *could* say that the aphasic simply chooses one form over another in saying *play* and not *played*. As it turns out, in languages where there is no "bare verb stem" form, such as *play*, this does seem to be what happens. In these languages, agrammatic speakers produce fully acceptable verb forms, but they use them in the wrong places. This suggests that the original "missing parts" description was prejudiced by the form of English, where the simple, unsuffixed verb form (e.g., *like*) happens to be the one agrammatics overuse most. This makes a critical difference in the linguistic interpretation of agrammatism. The earlier description implied that Broca's aphasics cannot form words properly; their *morphological*, or word-formation, rules for language do not function as they should. But under this new view things look very different: the rules that put elements like *play* and *-ed* together might be quite intact; it could be the *choice* of word forms, not their construction, that fails in these patients.

In fact, Broca's aphasic symptoms are not limited to word formation. Broca's aphasics produce too many nouns (recall the aforementioned sentence of *ball, prince um, shoe*). They often omit the verb altogether in a sentence, or use a related noun (e.g., *discussion* instead of *discuss*). Sentence patterns seem generally disrupted, as can be easily seen from agrammatic sentences cited in the literature, such as *the girl is flower the woman* and *the boy and the girl is valentine*. Researchers are now focusing on this question, trying to learn just how sensitive Broca's aphasics are to syntactic patterns, and where their attempts to put words together in the right order might be failing.

Other related work tries to interpret the classical description itself in linguistic terms. The trick is to characterize neatly the cluster of little elements lost: prepositions, articles, the *-ed* ending of the verb *walked*, the *'s* of *John's here*. What do all these have in common? Some represent whole words, and some represent parts of words. The preposition plays a major part in grammar, but articles don't. Just what part of linguistic *knowledge* would be missing in a patient whose only deficit was the omission of these elements? Mary-Louise Kean (1977) first proposed that these elements are all *unstressed*; hence, the agrammatic's problem, claimed Kean, is phonological (i.e., related to the sound system of the language). Since then, equally interesting suggestions have linked agrammatism to syntax, morphology, and language processing.[9] Although the final answer remains to be found, it is exciting that careful work on aphasic speech is finally able to yield such clear proposals.

A second line of research suggests that Wernicke's aphasia, too, may have been described in overly simplistic terms: it has been assumed that a Broca's aphasic has access to the meaning of words, while a Wernicke's aphasic does not. One recent study challenges this notion, emphasizing the case of a Wernicke's aphasic who could neither read words nor identify pictures of an object, but could nevertheless say what category the object belongs to (girl's name, tool, animal, etc.). This suggests that a more careful view of "meaning" must be identified if Wernicke's aphasia is to be fully understood.[10] A similar note of caution comes from a recent study on meaning. When normal subjects are given series of letter-strings and asked to say whether they are real words, most respond more quickly if the current word is semantically related to one they have just heard. So, if the subject has just heard the word *barn*, he will react faster to, say,

---

[9] A detailed discussion and references to these theories can be found in Caplan (1987).

[10] Warrington and Shallice (1979), and later ongoing research cited in Caplan (1987).

horse than to an unrelated word like *fry*. Amazingly enough, it is *Wernicke's* aphasics, and not Broca's, who react as normal subjects in this so-called semantic priming experiment,[11] suggesting that some kind of semantic access functions normally in these patients. Again, this kind of study can lead to important results, not only in defining aphasic types, but in understanding the nature of meaning itself.

A third exciting question being raised is this: is there a common denominator, some factor or cluster of factors that all aphasia types share? Goodglass and Menn (1985) found that *all* aphasics, regardless of type, had difficulty with sorting out the proper relationships between the underlined pairs of words in these sentences:

Point to the spoon with the pencil.
Point to the pencil with the spoon.

The trainer's dog is here
The dog's trainer is here.[12]

Others have suggested that certain sentence patterns or even word forms may cause difficulty for virtually all aphasics. If such a common denominator can be found, it will obviously contribute a great deal to the task of defining classical aphasia types. And, again, it will help flesh out Wernicke's model of how the brain processes language.

TWO BRAINS OR ONE: HEMISPHERIC ASYMMETRIES AND THEIR ORIGIN

The realization that one important mental faculty seemed to belong to one side of the brain raised a host of intriguing questions from the start. Does a human being have two consciousnesses or one? Is the mute right hemisphere teeming with unsatisfied desires and ideas that will never be expressed due to its dominant, talkative left twin? If the connections between the two halves were severed, would the result be a creature with two quite distinct personalities, each having its own thoughts, world-view, and feelings? The famous nineteenth-century psychologist William McDougall thought not. In fact, so deep was his conviction that he offered to have his brain anatomically split should he develop a terminal illness. He never did, and the experiment was left undone in his lifetime.[13]

To the more prosaic, however, other questions arose: what else does the left hemisphere do? And what, if anything, is the special domain of the right hemisphere? Hypotheses meant to capture the brain's left-right dichotomy have sprung up in abundance, especially in the past fifteen years. These include the short list given in Table 40.1.

---

[11] Milberg et al. (1987).
[12] Goodglass and Menn (1985, 22).
[13] Springer and Deutsch (1985, 26).

TABLE 40.1   **The Two Brains and What They Do**

LEFT BRAIN	RIGHT BRAIN
Analytic processing	Holistic processing (dealing with overall patterns, or "gestalt" forms)
Temporal relations	Spatial relations
Speech sounds	Nonspeech sounds
Mathematics	Music
Intellectual	Emotional

At its most fanciful, the contrast implied in the last pair of terms has led to global claims about "Eastern" and "Western" modes of thought, which, fascinating as they may be, are unsubstantiated. This speculation often comes uncomfortably close in spirit to the now-discounted claims of phrenologists in the early nineteenth century that bumps on each person's skull mirror "bumps on the brain," which in turn reveal personality traits.

But serious scientific questions arise from Table 40.1 as well. First, what counts as "language"? Most would agree that the word *cow*, printed on a card, should be perceived as language, but what about the single letter *c*? Or, for that matter, what about groups of letters that don't spell a word? There is some evidence that we perceive sequences like *kug, zeb*, or *bem* as language while sequences like *nku, lke*, and *okl* are perceived more as though they were simply geometric shapes (Young et al. 1984). Pronounceability seems to be the cue here; one could imagine Dr. Seuss creating a character called a *Zeb*, if he [hadn't] already done so, but a name like *Lke* would take some getting used to, even for the most imaginative child.

More puzzling still, the very same linguistic material presented in two forms may be handled differently. Subjects seem to use the left hemisphere to read text in standard print such as this, but the right hemisphere is called upon to handle elaborate lettering styles, which presumably require more visual skill (Bryden and Allard 1976). Likewise, mirror-image writing, or blurred or incomplete text, seems to be processed on the right.

In fact, subtleties of this sort abound. Japanese readers show some tendency for right-hemisphere activity when reading in the *kanji* script, where each character represents a word. But in the phonetically based *kana* script, where a letter usually stands for a syllable, the expected left-hemisphere dominance reemerges. Aphasia types distinguish between the two writing systems as well. Japanese aphasics often seem to retain some ability to read *kanji* script, while no longer able to comprehend the sound-based *kana* system. This again suggests that the processing of *kanji* characters can be mediated by areas outside the normal language centers, possibly in the right hemisphere.

Thus, some seemingly verbal tasks may be handled by the right hemisphere. And the converse seems also to be true: some spatial work seems to be done on the left, especially if it involves comparison or association between pairs of shapes. To further complicate matters, in an interesting study done in 1980, Gur and Reivich found no hemispheric advantage for a spatial (gestalt completion) test, suggesting that it can be handled equally well by either hemisphere. But there was a significant difference in how well the job was done: subjects who "chose" to use the right, spatially adept, hemisphere performed with significantly greater efficiency. But those who used the left hemisphere also achieved reasonable results; this suggests that, in some cases, the unspecialized hemisphere may be like an untrained worker who manages to succeed at a job although he may not be the ideal person to do it.

In the light of these and similar findings, researchers now believe that it is the type of processing, not the type of material processed, that distinguishes the two hemispheres; in other words, the first entry in Table 40.1 can be thought of as the only true difference. The left hemisphere is called upon whenever detailed analysis is in order, whereas the right hemisphere goes into action if holistic processing is needed. Language and mathematics typically involve sequential analysis or other kinds of analytical thinking, whereas pictures and faces are usually taken in all at once, as are musical patterns.

Under this more subtle view of lateralization, the Gur and Reivich results can be more plausibly explained. If, for some reason, a task does not clearly identify itself as requiring a right- or left-hemisphere approach, the job might be shunted off to different halves of the brain in different people—or even in the same person at different times, depending on which hemisphere happens to be more active. But it is quite reasonable to expect that the hemisphere with a more appropriate approach to the task will get better results.

Interesting support for the "processing strategy" approach comes from several experiments showing that trained musicians (who analyze as they listen) actually process music in the *left* hemisphere. Only the musically unsophisticated layperson, who hears music as holistic patterns, shows the expected right-hemisphere dominance. Layperson and musician hear the same patterns, but their reaction, their *way of listening*, differs.

Finally, once lateralization is seen in this more abstract way, another seemingly unrelated fact may tie in as well: the ability for fine, sequenced hand movements, called *manual praxis*, is also linked to the left hemisphere. Although hand movement and language seem very different on the surface, it is reasonable to suppose that a similar type of neural mechanism might be needed to orchestrate fine hand movements and to fashion complex sentence patterns.

This last point brings us back to the opening theme of this article: where did brain asymmetry come from? Was language the first activity to move into the analytical left hemisphere? Some think not. As a species, they argue, we must have developed fine manual coordination before language as we now know it. The need to make a rock into a sharp arrowhead or scraping tool calls for complex techniques involving fingers, wrist, and hand; this, many believe, is the left hemisphere's original specialty. If so, language may have been drawn to the left hemisphere simply because the neural circuitry available there for complex tool use was somehow suited to take on linguistic calculations.

This hypothesis remains open for debate. But tantalizing pieces of evidence seem to support it. For instance, in aphasia, fine hand coordination is often impaired along with language. Furthermore, the human species has been overwhelmingly right-handed for a long time, suggesting that asymmetry for handedness came early in human evolution. CroMagnon hand tracings were virtually always of the left hand; thus, the artists must have been drawing with the right. The skulls of prehistoric animals provide mute evidence as well; archeologists tell us that the earliest hunting hominids must have used tools held in the right hand to slay game, judging from the position of fractures and marks on the skulls of ancient animals.

Other hints scattered along our evolutionary trail lead to a quite different view. Brain asymmetry has been found elsewhere in the animal kingdom—in rodents, in other primates, and especially in birds. Even the most imaginative of scientists has yet to suspect a song sparrow of being an effective tool user, yet sparrows and chaffiniches have song strongly lateralized in the left hemisphere. Looking at such species makes it seem plausible to some scientists that tool use is not necessarily the answer. In fact, it may have been the right brain, not the left, that first specialized. In the struggle for survival, even a rat can use an acute eye and a quick emotional response to avoid becoming dinner for a hungry hawk. Some would argue that, for humans too, the demands of survival and the hunt preceded the impulse toward language. If so, the right hemisphere's visual and emotional roles may have taken their place *before* left-hemisphere functions. Language may have simply migrated to the left hemisphere by default, as it were.

TESTING THE BRAIN

The careful reader will by now wonder how all the claims in Table 40.1 can be made with certainty. How do we know what a single hemisphere is doing? There are, of course, the aphasia studies, but studies of brain malfunction are not ideally reliable. Suppose you wanted to find out what a specific transformer does in a radio: would you remove the transistor or break it, turn the radio on, and see what happens? Relying on aphasia as an indicator of localized function comes remarkably close to this intuitively unsatisfactory method. In fact, matters are even worse than a simple analogy would suggest. It is well known that brain tissue (unlike radio components) can "reorganize." That is, if one area of the brain is damaged, especially at an early age, other areas may take over the original tissue's function. Clearly, information from aphasia must be treated with caution.

The "Split Brain"

A surgical technique known as *commissurotomy*, used to treat severe cases of epilepsy, seems at first sight to provide perfect subjects for studying brain lateralization. Commissurotomy involves severing the corpus callosum, the main bundle of fibers connecting the brain's two hemispheres, as shown in Figure 40.4. With patients who have undergone this operation, neurologists can communicate with each cerebral hemisphere separately. Thus, using specialized techniques, one can show a picture or a written text to a single hemisphere and see how it responds.

These patients have been studied intensely, and with interesting results; but the general implications of these studies are controversial. Epilepsy is clearly accompanied by abnormal brain activity, often from an early age. Thus, as with aphasics, the brain tissue of split-brain patients may have reorganized in ways that make them atypical. For decades, researchers have grappled with these problems by searching for tests that can be used with normal subjects.

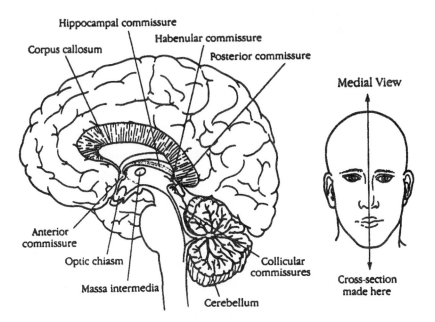

FIGURE 40.4   The Corpus Callosum.

Behavioral Tests

A widely used technique called *tachistoscopic presentation* represents one attempt to learn what one hemisphere does more efficiently or more accurately than the other. A subject is asked to fix her gaze on a central point directly in front of her. An image is then flashed to her right or left visual field. The subject does not know which side will display the image, and the flash is too brief (less than one-fifth of a second) to allow eye movement to one side or the other. Because of the human nervous system's organization, the image is perceived primarily by one side of the brain—the one *opposite* the visual field involved. If a subject handles stimuli presented on the right side of the screen better, she is assumed to be using the left hemisphere more actively.

Doreen Kimura at the Montreal Neurological Institute has adapted this principle to auditory stimuli in the *dichotic listening test*. The ear, like the eye, conveys messages most effectively via the so-called contralateral nerve pathway to the opposite hemisphere of the brain. Thus, if two different words are played to a subject's two ears, the left hemisphere will hear the word played to the right ear, and vice versa. As it turns out, many subjects consistently hear words more accurately with their right ear, but identify tunes played to the left ear more accurately. As with tachistoscopic data, dichotic listening results have played an important role in confirming the assumptions underlying Table 40.1.

The lateral eye movement (or LEM) provides a more indirect, and more controversial, way to look at brain activity via behavior. When answering a question, we tend to look left or right, rather than directly into the eyes of the asker. This sideways glance is said to show which hemisphere is providing the answer: activity on one side of the brain is said to trigger an automatic response to eye movement, in the opposite direction from the locus of mental activity. So, an emotional question should trigger an automatic eye shift leftwards; a verbal or intellectual question should cause the eyes to drift toward the right, while the analytical left hemisphere computes the necessary answer.

Unfortunately, behavioral tests have their drawbacks. A single subject tested twice with one week intervening may show different results. Furthermore, hemispheric activation at any given moment is fickle enough to be disrupted by seemingly minor factors, as in the phenomenon called *priming*. Subjects are asked to memorize a list of words, thus presumably "turning on" the left hemisphere's circuits. If asked immediately afterwards to perform some spatial task that normally yields right-hemisphere dominance, they will often fail to show the expected result. Instead, they will perform the spatial task with the left hemisphere, presumably using the "wrong" processing strategy. To use a rough analogy, people seem to use the calculator which is already turned on, rather than the one specialized for the task at hand. Obviously, the success of lateralization tests demands control of such outside factors, which is no simple matter.

Physiological Measures

The cerebral cortex is highly asymmetrical, even to the naked eye. The Sylvian fissure, a deep cleft running through the cortex, rises more sharply on the right, and is longer on the left. Its rear inner surface (called the *planum temporale*), which includes Wernicke's area, is usually larger on the left, even in fetal brains. In fact, the human skull, the brain's outer casing, protrudes noticeably in the left rear area, pushed out by the bulging left hemisphere. But despite a long and heated debate in the nineteenth century about the relationship between brain size and intelligence (Broca believed a large brain meant high intelligence), no detailed conclusions have resulted from gross measurement of brain tissue. More subtle methods are needed to deal with the brain in physiological terms.

Scientists have learned to observe chemical and electrical activity in different regions of the brain. Sophisticated devices for accomplishing this include computerized axial tomography (CT or CAT) scan, positron emission tomography (PET) scan, electroencephalogram (EEG), and measures of regional cerebral bloodflow (rCBF). Also useful is the famous Wada test, named after its developer, Juhn Wada.

In the Wada test, the powerful barbiturate sodium amytal is injected into the carotid artery leading to one hemisphere in patients about to undergo brain surgery, to determine whether language is affected. When the drug enters the language hemisphere, the patient's speech is arrested within seconds; thus, the surgeon can be sure which hemisphere should be protected during the operation. Yet another surgical technique involves direct stimulation of the brain. Pioneered in the 1950s by the surgeon Wilder Penfield, this method has recently attracted renewed interest with the advent of improved techniques.

ARE WE ALL ALIKE?

What, the reader may ask, about *my* brain? Where do I store math, physics, music, or for that matter, language? Can one make a reliable guess for any individual brain as to how closely it approximates the classical model? The answer is yes—but only if you are a healthy monolingual, English-speaking, right-handed, hearing, adult male who can read. Beyond this class, caution is in order: some believe that the ideal classical pattern may apply to only about one person in four. The following sections show how populations may diverge from the picture given so far.

Babies

Babies, and even unborn fetuses, have physically enlarged language areas in their left hemispheres. Behaviorally, too, the very young show signs of asymmetry: by monitoring factors such as sucking response and changed heartbeat, one can determine the responses of infants to stimuli around them. Studies using such measures have found clear lateralization for speech sounds in the left hemisphere of infant brains, as opposed to chirps or nonspeech sounds, which the babies seem to process in the right hemisphere—this exists even in preterm babies born in about the thirty-sixth week of gestation.

However, until about age ten, child aphasia cases differ markedly from adult ones. Most young children show symptoms of something like Broca's aphasia regardless of where brain injury occurs within the left hemisphere. Thus, although language may be situated on the left by age five, localization within the left hemisphere may come later; hence, the classical diagram in Figure 40.3 may be only partially spelled out in children.

The question of infant asymmetry raises interesting questions. How can a brain that has no language be "specialized" for language? What kind of processing is the infant brain doing, and how does it assign a stimulus to a given hemisphere? Research on this intriguing topic may ultimately show which prelinguistic faculties lead to the development of language in children.

Bilinguals

A child's brain may in fact be like an electronic board with only some minimal (albeit highly significant) circuits provided at the outset. The details of the remaining circuitry may be up to the user to determine—in this case, the child, whose experiences in growing up "reconfigure" the brain's circuits. If so, different people may wire their neural boards in quite different ways, provided, that is, that they stay within the bounds imposed by the initial connections (which, in this case, ensure that some variant of wiring for human language emerges, and not binary code or birdsong).

Seen via this analogy, a bilingual speaker might be like a computer buff trying to do with one central processing unit the job normally done by two. Hence, one would expect the details of his processing machinery to be quite different. In fact, for some time, it has been noted that polyglot speakers (people with more than one language) produce unexpected aphasia types, perhaps because their experiences have led to special neural patterns. In about half the reported cases of polyglot aphasia, any recovery that takes place affects both (or all) languages at the same rate. Still, many patients recover one language earlier or more perfectly than others, and about one-fourth never regain one or more of their languages.[14] Physicians cannot predict which language will be recovered first or more fully, although some generalization is possible. The language best recovered is likely to be the last one used before injury, or the best known, or the one that is heard most during the recovery period.

---

[14] Grosjean (1982, 259).

Some rare cases pose especially perplexing challenges. One such case reported in 1980 involved a French-Arabic bilingual nun in Morocco who had a moped accident and became severely aphasic, losing speech altogether. Four days later, she could speak a few words of Arabic, but no French. After two weeks, she could speak French again fluently, but in the space of one day, her French fluency quite disappeared. She astounded observers by being able to converse fluently only in Arabic.[15]

The occurrence of bilingual aphasia suggests quite clearly that bilinguals have more right-hemisphere linguistic activity than monolinguals. Aphasia is about five times more likely to result from right-hemisphere damage in a polyglot speaker than in a monolingual. This can only be explained if some of a bilingual's linguistic ability is stored on the right side of the brain, or at least in areas not affected by damage to the classical language areas on the left. Research involving electrical stimulation of brain sites also gives some support for differential storage of two languages in a single brain: when the brain is stimulated at a given point, a patient may have trouble naming familiar objects. For bilinguals, naming difficulties in the two languages arise from stimulation at *different* points. Furthermore, electrical stimulation disturbs a patient's ability to name things in the less proficient language over a broader range of sites, suggesting that the second or nondominant language takes up more neural space than the first language.

Finally, some believe that the right hemisphere plays a major role in second-language learning, especially in the early stages when memory for stock phrases is essential to the learner. Can the very experience of learning a second language alter cerebral patterns in unexpected ways? Some early research suggests that bilingual children think differently—more independently and more creatively—and that this may extend to nonverbal areas. The significance of such intriguing findings has yet to be fully worked out.

The fact that languages can be stored, learned, or lost in different areas of the brain suggests strongly that the neural anatomy for two languages within a single brain can be different. Unfortunately, the relationship between gross anatomy and brain function remains mysterious. At best, we can turn to another analogy: Multilingual speakers may be telling us that the cerebral cortex is like a computer in some respects— highly complex, rigid in its basic setup, yet also versatile and subject to "programming" (here, unconscious) by the user.

Speakers versus Signers

Users of American Sign Language (ASL or Ameslan) depend on manual activity, not speech, to encode basic meanings. If experience molds neural

---

[15] Op. cit., 260.

patterns, then the very nature of ASL raises some fascinating questions. Do the deaf generate and process signs in the left hemisphere? Can Broca's area, with its ability to interface with commands to the tongue and lips, also handle a system based on hand signals?

Early lateralization studies for ASL showed inconsistent results; some seemed to indicate right-hemisphere language processing, which could be explained by the visual nature of signing. Others concluded that signers had no cerebral asymmetry at all. The key may lie in the researchers' conception of signing: most early studies used static photographs to test asymmetry. But ASL signers do not communicate by flashing pictures at one another. In normal situations, signers deal with a number of dimensions at once: hand position, orientation, and crucially, movement. It makes intuitive sense to claim, as some have done, that signers in action do indeed make crucial use of the traditional left-brain language centers; we simply need more sophisticated techniques to verify this hypothesis.

Recent studies of impaired signers (see Bellugi 1983) yield important evidence for the claim that signers may process language as oral speakers do: injury to the classical language areas on the left has been found to produce strikingly similar aphasia types in ASL and oral languages.

Here, too, experience may be crucial. Deaf people whose schools used different training methods show consistently different patterns in the usual asymmetry tests. In fact, one startling finding about signers suggests that experience may be an even more potent force on the brain's map than previously suspected. Neville (1977) reported that he observed evoked potential (that is, electrical activity) in the *auditory* cortex of native signers in response to flashes of light. For oral speakers, the auditory cortex is the center, near Wernicke's area, where sound is first perceived. If Neville's claim is substantiated, the term *auditory cortex* may prove quite inappropriate for signers.

Readers, Japanese, and Others

The theme of experience leads neatly to the next point, which has implications for anyone reading this article. Where signing and multiple languages may cause a person's brain to diverge from the classical pattern, some believe that the experience of literacy may have a significant effect in *reinforcing* left-hemisphere dominance for language. Some studies report that illiterates show a much lower incidence of aphasia following left-hemisphere brain damage, and may even develop aphasia from right-hemisphere injury. If this is true, it suggests that language ability is more symmetrical in this group. Dealing with the written word may involve the left hemisphere's analytical techniques in such an intense way as to strengthen the ties between language and the left brain.

This claim, however, has been controversial (it is challenged in Caplan 1987), and the aphasia data have proven difficult to confirm.

Yet another suggestion about early experience comes from Japanese. Normally, Americans tend to treat pure vowel sounds as "nonlanguage" in dichotic listening tests (sounds like "ah" and "ooooh" are likely to be interpreted as emotional utterances rather than as words). Japanese speakers, in contrast, seem to process single-vowel sounds on the left, as normal linguistic material. Professor Tadanoku Tsunoda of Tokyo's Medical and Dental University blames this on the "vowel dominant" nature of his language, which may influence the way Japanese children perceive the boundary between language and other sounds.[16]

This recalls a widely accepted claim about tone languages, based on lateralization for tone in Thai. Native speakers of Thai, who must make use of the pitch levels in a word to understand its meaning, tend to perceive tone as linguistic material. To most English speakers, the complex pitch patterns of a tone language like Thai or Vietnamese simply sound like some kind of puzzling singsong effect overlayed on speech; hence, they are likely to filter out the tone and send it off to the right hemisphere. Given this, it is not surprising that English speakers have substantial difficulty in learning tone languages!

Left-Handers and Women

Two more groups stand out as neurologically different: left-handers and women. This time, the difference obviously cannot be linked to experience: genetics must play an important role.

This history of left-handers is fraught with myths and misleading ideas. In some societies, left-handed people have been viewed as clumsy and awkward, *gauche* if not downright *sinister*, to cite two words owing their origin to French and Latin forms meaning "left." In China, India, and in Arab countries, left-handers are said to have been banned from the dinner table. To many, however, reversed hand preference is seen as a sign of eminence: Michelangelo, Benjamin Franklin, Alexander the Great, and Einstein are cited as examples.

In their widely read book *Left Brain, Right Brain*, Sally Springer and Georg Deutsch include one chapter entitled "The Puzzle of the Left-Hander." They point out that it is difficult to even identify a left-hander for sure since many people use the left hand for some activities and the right for others. Even supposedly unconscious tests for handedness (e.g., how a person crosses his arms, or draws a horse in profile, etc.) invariably yield mixed results.

---

[16] Brabyn (1982, 11).

Springer and Deutsch go on to trace opposing claims on the cause of handedness (genetic versus environmental), and many claims of smaller scope, such as the notion that the characteristic "inverted" writing position found in some left-handers may indicate left-hemisphere language, and that this may be part of a more general pattern for detecting "like-hemisphere" language and handedness. Supporters point to one isolated right-handed "inverter" who showed right-hemisphere language dominance.

But the puzzles of handedness remain. Scientists no longer believe that the left-handed person is simply a mirror image of a right-hander, with speech on the right and spatial abilities on the left. As many as 70 percent of left-handers have a dominant left hemisphere for language, just as do right-handers. Of the rest, half are thought to have bilateral language representation, with no clearly dominant hemisphere. This leaves a mere 15 percent of left-handers with language dominant on the right. Even this picture may not be accurate; one recent study reanalyzes data from aphasia and concludes that bilateral speech representation may be more common than previously believed, perhaps occurring in as high as 40 percent of all left-handed people (cited in Segalowitz and Bryden 1983, 348).

Aphasia tends to be less severe and to last a shorter time for left-handers, and even for right-handers in families with left-handed members. Moreover, left-handed speakers are eight times more likely than right-handers to suffer from aphasia after damage to the right hemisphere only. This must mean that they store more linguistic knowledge in the non-dominant hemisphere than do right-handers. Since there is no clear evidence for bilateral speech in right-handed monolinguals, this points to handedness as a clear indication of cerebral difference.

On women, our last interesting population, in 1879 the then-eminent social psychologist Gustave LeBon wrote:

> In the most intelligent races, as among the Parisians, there are a large number of women whose brains are closer in size to those of gorillas than to the most developed male brains . . . All psychologists who have studied the intelligence of women . . . recognize that they . . . represent the most inferior form of human evolution and that they are closer to children and savages than to an adult, civilized man.[17]

LeBon, following Broca, felt that bigger meant better in cerebral terms, and thus justified his sexist views by biological argument.

None but the most irrational antifeminist would today accept LeBon's comments. But we do know that women's brains are distinctive. For one thing, the gross physiological differences noted between the

---

[17] Gould (1980, 155).

hemispheres are less obvious in women than in men. And other strong indicators of cerebral asymmetry are equally hard to confirm in women. Like left-handers, women may tend toward more symmetrical, evenly balanced, language capacities in the two hemispheres. Again, the aphasia statistics are revealing: women are less likely than men to become aphasic from unilateral damage to the left hemisphere. This suggests that, at the very least, the right hemisphere in women can take over language functions readily if the language centers on the left become disabled. More likely, the right hemisphere in women takes a more active role in language processing even in the absence of injury.

Behavioral tests yield supporting evidence. In dichotic listening tests, men outnumber women nearly 2 to 1 in showing right-ear advantage for verbal material. In fact, some early attempts to find cerebral asymmetries seem to have failed simply because they included too many female subjects! It is clear that neurological lateralization patterns must be considered in understanding the biological distinction between the sexes. Hopefully, further research will clarify and explain these differences.

WHERE DO WE GO FROM HERE?

The human brain still shelters the fundamental mystery of our existence: what does it mean to be human? Clearly, language must be an important part of the answer, and we have come a long way from the Egyptian physicians who attributed language disorders to the "breath of an outside god."[18] As this essay shows, much progress has been made in finding the answers to an ancient and fundamental question: how does the *Homo sapiens* in Figure 40.1 differ from his Australopithecine ancestors? How does this creature manage to handle such a highly complex communication system in the three pounds or so of gray matter lodged in the human skull?

To fully understand the neurology of language, researchers will have to answer the questions raised above, and many more not yet even hinted at. How is language related to other cognitive skills? What goes on behind the scenes, in the subcortical tissue beneath the language areas? It is clear that the thalamus, for instance, plays an important role in language. The complexity of the issues involved, and the way they touch on many disciplines at once, is clearly reflected in recent publications. The coming years are sure to see an ever-increasing crop of journals and books devoted to the mysteries of language, brain, and cognition.

---

[18] Arbib et al. (1982).

BIBLIOGRAPHY

Arbib, M. A., D. Caplan, and J. C. Marshall. "Neurolinguistics in Historical Perspective." In *Neural Models of Language Processes*, eds. M. Arbib, D. Caplan, and J. Marshall. New York: Academic Press, 1982.

Bellugi, U. "Language Structure and Language Breakdown in American Sign Language." In *Psychobiology of Language*, ed. M. Studdert-Kennedy. Cambridge: MIT Press, 1983.

Blumstein, S. E. "Language Dissolution in Aphasia: Evidence for Linguistic Theory." In *Exceptional Language and Linguistics*, eds. L. Obler and L. Menn. New York: Academic Press, 1982.

Brabyn, H. "Mother Tongue and the Brain." *UNESCO Courier* (February 1982), 10–13.

Brown, J. W. "Case Reports of Semantic Jargon." In J. W. Brown, ed., 1981.

——, ed. *Jargonaphasia*. New York: Academic Press, 1981.

Bryden, M. P., and F. Allard. "Visual Hemifield Differences Depend on Typeface." *Brain and Language* 3 (1976), 41–46.

Buckingham, H. "Where Do Neologisms Come From?" In J. W. Brown, ed., 1981.

Caplan, D. *Neurolinguistics and Linguistic Aphasiology: An Introduction*. New York: Cambridge University Press, 1987.

Caramazza, A., J. Gordon, E. G. Zurif, and D. De Luca. "Right Hemisphere Damage and Verbal Problem Solving Behavior." *Brain and Language* 3 (1976), 41–46.

Dennis, M. "Language Acquisition in a Single Hemisphere: Semantic Organization." In *Biological Studies of Mental Processes*, ed. D. Caplan. Cambridge: MIT Press, 1980.

Gardner, H., J. Silverman, W. Wapner, and E. Zurif. "The Appreciation of Antonymic Contrasts in Aphasia." *Brain and Language* 6 (1978), 301–317.

Goodglass, H., and L. Menn. "Is Agrammatism a Unitary Phenomenon?" In M.-L. Kean, ed., 1985.

Gould, S. J. *The Panda's Thumb: More Reflections in Natural History*. New York: Norton, 1980.

Grosjean, F. *Life with Two Languages*. Cambridge: Harvard University Press, 1982.

Gur, R. C., and N. Reivich. "Cognitive Task Effects on Hemispheric Blood Flow in Humans: Evidence for Individual Differences in Hemispheric Activation." *Brain and Language* 9 (1980), 78–92.

Harth, E. *Windows on the Mind: Reflections on the Physical Basis of Consciousness*. New York: Morrow, 1982.

Kean, M.-L. "The Linguistic Interpretation of Aphasic Syndromes: Agrammatism in Broca's Aphasia, an Example." *Cognition* 5 (1977), 9–46.

——, ed. *Agrammatism*. New York: Academic Press, 1985, 1977.

Milberg, W., S. Blumstein, and B. Dworetzky. "Processing of Lexical Ambiguities in Aphasia." *Brain and Language* 31 (1987), 138–150.

Neville, H. J. "Electroencephalographic Testing of Cerebral Specialization in Normal and Congenitally Deaf Children: A Preliminary Report." In *Language Development and Neurological Theory*, eds. S. Segalowitz and F. Gruber. New York: Academic Press, 1977.

Schwartz, M., M. Linebarger, and E. Saffran. "The Status of the Syntactic Theory of Agrammatism." In M.-L. Kean, ed., 1985.

Segalowitz, S., and M. Bryden. "Individual Differences in Hemispheric Representation of Language." In *Language Functions and Brain Organization*, ed. S. Segalowitz. New York: Academic Press, 1983.

Springer, S. P., and G. Deutsch. *Left Brain, Right Brain*, rev. ed. San Francisco: W. H. Freeman and Company, 1985.

Trevarthen, C. "Development of the Cerebral Mechanisms for Language." In *Neuropsychology of Language, Reading, and Spelling*. New York: Academic Press, 1983.

Wapner, W., S. Hamby, and H. Gardner. "The Role of the Right Hemisphere in the Apprehension of Complex Linguistic Materials." *Brain and Language* 14 (1981), 15–33.

Warrington, E. K., and T. Shallice. "Semantic Access Dyslexia." *Brain* 102 (1979), 43–63.

Winner, E., and H. Gardner. "The Comprehension of Metaphor in Brain-Damaged Patients." *Brain* 100 (1977), 719–727.

Young, A. W., A. W. Ellis, and P. L. Birn. "Left Hemisphere Superiority for Pronounceable Nonwords, But Not for Unpronounceable Letter Strings." *Brain and Language* 22 (1984), 14–23.

≡

FOR DISCUSSION AND REVIEW

1. What is the difference between Broca's area and Wernicke's area? How does each area seem to contribute to language production or understanding? Why are the relationships between these areas and the cortical centers for sight, hearing, and motor function important in terms of language?

2. Heny says that "in some cases, the unspecialized hemisphere may be like an untrained worker who manages to succeed at a job although he may not be the ideal person to do it." What exactly does she mean by this remark?

3. Why might studies done on aphasics and split-brain subjects yield misleading information on brain lateralization?

4. Why is it difficult to clearly label a person as left- or right-handed? Do you know people who use different hands for different tasks? If so, which hand is used for which specific tasks? What pattern(s), if any, can you suggest?

5. Divide the following activities into two columns (left and right), according to which hemisphere you think is likely to be dominant for performing each. In cases where you are unsure, explain the aspects of the task that led you to list it tentatively on one side rather than the other:

   a. distinguishing between the syllables *ba* and *pa*
   b. choosing the right answer in a multiplication problem

    c. defining the word *independence*
    d. recognizing a friend's face
    e. singing the "Star Spangled Banner"
    f. deciding whether your employer is in a good mood
    g. recognizing the string of letters *ZBQ*
    h. playing the guitar
    i. recognizing a grasshopper's chirp
    j. understanding the utterance "The girl was bitten by the dog."
    k. finding a word to rhyme with *inch*

6. How do dichotic listening and tachistoscopic tests work? How might *priming* affect the results of such tests? If a subject sees or hears more accurately on the left, which cerebral hemisphere must be involved? Why?

7. Why is aphasia much more likely to result from right-hemisphere damage in a bilingual speaker than in a monolingual speaker? What does research on bilinguals tell us about the versatility of the brain?

8. How blind people process Braille characters is somewhat uncertain. In tests, it seems that subjects with good vision, when they first encounter the raised characters, can make them out best with the left hand. But it is very difficult to get clear-cut results for experienced Braille readers. How do you explain this? How might this situation be comparable to how trained and untrained people process music? How does the Braille situation relate to Heny's discussion of sign language? How would nonsigners be likely to process signs?

9. In general terms, how do women and left-handers seem to differ from other individuals in terms of brain asymmetry?

10. Suppose you constructed an experiment asking people to choose a picture that matches the sentence "He's really gotten himself into a nice pickle now!" Their choices are illustrations of:

    a. A man who has just dug his way into a giant pickle.
    b. A man with a bewildered look on his face standing near a disabled car on an isolated road. His clothes are covered with grease, and strewn around him on the ground are what appear to be the parts of his engine.
    c. A man sitting in an armchair reading a book.

What pictures(s) would you expect each of the following groups to choose, and why?

    a. Broca's aphasics
    b. Wernicke's aphasics
    c. right-hemisphere–damaged patients
    d. normal "control" subjects

41

Signals, Signs, and Words: From Animal Communication to Language

William Kemp and Roy Smith

For many years and for many reasons, people have studied the communication of "talking" horses, dophins, bees, whales, monkeys, and chimpanzees. Some researchers have tried to discover if only humans possess language, while others have sought to understand both the similarities and differences between animal communication and human language. In this selection, Professor Emeritus William Kemp and Professor Roy Smith, both of the University of Mary Washington, survey the research on animal communication. They explain the difficulties of doing such research as well as its importance. They describe the elaborate communication systems of bees, birds, and nonhuman primates. Discussing the extensive work with chimpanzees and gorillas conducted in the 1970s, 1980s, and 1990s, Kemp and Smith argue convincingly that apes can learn to make semantic associations with a great many arbitrary symbols. This essay, which the authors revised in 1997, originally appeared in their book Speaking Act in Natural Words: Animals, Communication, and Language.

> The sound of the waterfall
> has for a long time
> ceased,
> yet with its name
> we can hear it still.
>
> —Fujiwaro No Kinto, d. 1041

Haiku is human language at its peak: stunning images from a few carefully chosen syllables. Despite claims for remarkable communication and even language among the many animals around us, no one has offered an example of haiku by a humpback whale or a chimpanzee. This is not to say that animals do not communicate effectively; they certainly do. Still, most humans use language as something qualitatively different from other forms of communication, at least some of the time.

Because language is so important to the experience of being human, most who study language reserve to humans the ability to use and understand language. As a result, the possibility of animal language has become a challenge to our unique position in the natural world. But evolutionary theory, the organizing framework of the biological and social sciences, warns that we must examine any behavior in its context. Behaviors develop from the interaction over many generations of subtle and not-so-subtle alterations in the physical and physiological conformation of an organism. If these changes allow their bearers to develop behaviors to exploit better the world they live in, they are more fit than other individuals and reproduce more successfully. The new behaviors then become the baseline for further changes. These adaptive changes cumulatively alter the nature of a group of organisms and the way it fits into the environment.

Given the essential dependence of human personal, social, and cultural experience on language, its mastery clearly changes the way we deal with our world. And most linguists agree that language is based on just the sorts of inherited physical capacities that an evolutionary understanding of language requires. But then where are the precursors of human language? Can we recognize in the communication systems of other animals analogies to the pieces that gave birth to human language? Do other animals have communication systems with characteristics parallel to our own? Are there examples of animal language?

An easy answer might be that humans use language to communicate while nonhumans use animal signaling. Unfortunately, this view implies that a loving glance from your mother is part of language while a loving glance from your dog is not. Humans use language layered atop other forms of communication, such as body language, and the nonlanguage signals often contain the more important messages. At the very least, we share with other species an impressive degree of nonlingual communication. Examining animal communication reveals important ways in which language differs from communication in other animals. It also suggests that language is not an aberration that appeared suddenly, without evolutionary precursors.

Ethologists treat animal communication under three headings. The first is *form*. For an animal's behavior to have value as a signal, it must be in a constant form that others can recognize and connect reliably to some future behavior by the signaler. Ethologists call such stereotyped behavior a *display*. The second part of animal communication is *context*; it includes the general environment in which an animal is displaying as well as simultaneous displays it sends through sensory modes or channels. Thus, a dog's bark may convey one message about future behavior when its tail is wagging, another when its tail is stiff. Context usually resolves such ambiguities. The third part of animal communication is the *response* to the signal. Communication is valuable because it increases the likelihood of one animal's choosing behavior that fits with the behavior of others. The choice by the receiving animal must be clear to be sure it has actually communicated. Otherwise, we can't tell the difference between ruffling feathers to get them straight and ruffling feathers to signal an impending conflict.

Consider one of the elaborate prairie dog cities on the western plains. Alarm calls announce a stranger's approach and send nearby animals scurrying to holes from which they cautiously peer. Can there be any doubt that sentries are telling their comrades about the intruder? Patient observation and careful analysis suggest that this alarm, like other prairie-dog vocalizations, is a display. Prairie dogs apparently give this signal whenever they become aroused enough to stop what they are doing and scan the environment, but not scared enough to run for cover immediately. They give the same call during territorial disputes when the caller is unsure whether to attack or retreat. Other prairie dogs, upset by the signaler, give their own version of the display, spreading agitation through the colony. The alarm system works very effectively; knowing that your neighbor is aroused is important. But the prairie dog's display contains information about the caller, not about the source of the alarm. Each prairie dog must sit up and look for himself.

Distinctive behavior that reliably indicates what an animal will do promotes cooperation and reduces conflict, because it allows neighbors to adjust their actions according to what the display predicts. Few animals seriously injure one another in disputes over territory, food, or mates, because displays allow rivals to establish which one is dominant without resorting to combat. Crudely put, the meaning of an agonistic display is, "I feel like attacking you ferociously very soon." The individual whose display is more convincing usually wins. We need not imagine animals computing the combat odds or planning their displays. Sending and comprehending displays are parts of each animal's (and human's) automatic behavior. In human interactions, smiling usually elicits a responding smile and a frown prompts a frown, without any planning by anyone.

In discussing human language, linguists use concepts similar to the ethologist's form, context, and response. Linguists work with *syntax*, which emphasizes form; *semantics*, which emphasizes meaning (defined partly by context); and *pragmatics*, which emphasizes how context modifies or replaces the meaning of an utterance. Linguists also analyze human speech into meaning units called *morphemes* and sound units called *phonemes*—units that seem unique to spoken language. But particular manifestations of phonemes (called *allophones*) share with displays an invariant surface form guided by a stable program in the central nervous system. Both allophones and displays are examples of unvarying sets of motor movements that ethologists call *fixed action patterns.*

As displays become language, several things change. The form of communication shifts from a limited number of lengthy, stereotyped displays to a very large number of very short displays (allophones) that can be combined in many ways according to hierarchical rules. The importance of context also changes. Displays begin as indications of an animal's response to its environment; they are more about the animal itself than about the world. In contrast, humans frequently use language to describe environment(s), while their displays signal much of the accompanying affective content. Although the context of a sentence usually colors its meaning, the sentence has meaning independent of context. Displays have only contextual meaning.

While the response to a display is how we know its meaning, the response of others to language may be unimportant. Although Fujiwaro wrote his haiku for others to read, and probably would be delighted to know that people appreciate it nine hundred years after his death, he must have written it partly or perhaps chiefly for the delight of capturing his experience in words. We have no clear evidence that nonhumans play with their communication systems simply to revel in the workings of the system itself.

Language is also capable of abstraction, a power that seems to have few natural parallels in animal communication. Of course, many animals can create general concepts; some dogs understand that *all* cars are to be chased. And some higher primates, having learned artificial sign systems from humans, clearly use and understand some abstract signs. But even in the cleverest animals, natural displays have no way of presenting abstract propositions about either the animal or its world. The human abilities conferred by language to plan for the future and control our environment are without parallel in other species. Language is far removed from the simple fixed action patterns of affective displays. A hierarchy of rule systems, from phonetics to semantics, transforms language from a set of environmental responses to a self-contained, generative symbol system operating simultaneously on several independently structured levels. Thus our thoughts are at least partly dissociated from our feelings.

Despite clear differences, animal communication systems have a lot to tell us about language. For one thing, displays have evolved in every species out of environmental demands and adaptations to meet those demands. The more carefully we study how other animals exchange signals, the more clearly we see how closely communication systems connect to other elements of behavior. We also find that many creatures are a good deal more clever than we suppose.

For example, we usually regard insects as just barely sentient, doing their business by instinct and incapable of significant mental activity, yet we marvel at the architectural achievements of social insects (ants, bees, termites, and wasps). In fact, the architecture of a termite mound or an ant nest is genetically designed. Each insect responds to the chemical and tactile signals around it with a set of fixed action patterns programmed into its simple brain. In a real sense no member of this miniature corps of engineers has any plan at all; the genetic repository of the whole community contains the blueprint for building the nest, and for other activity besides. More marvelous still are the systems of communication by which social insects manage their collective lives, using emitted chemicals (called *pheromones*), sound, and physical activity to exchange information and coordinate their behavior.

The best understood insect communication system is the dance of the honeybee (*Apis mellifera*). Humans have been interested for centuries in honeybees, but until the 1920s no one noticed that bees returning from a successful foray convey to hivemates important information, which concentrates hive activity on the best sources of nectar. In 1919 Karl von Frisch set out to discover how hundreds of foraging bees could arrive as if by magic at a rich food source recently discovered by a single bee. The result of his experiment was striking:

> I attracted a few bees to a dish of sugar water, marked them with red paint and then stopped feeding for a while. As soon as all was quiet, I filled the dish again and watched a scout which had drunk from it . . . after her return to the hive. I could scarcely believe my eyes. She performed a round dance on the honeycomb which greatly excited the marked foragers around her and caused them to fly back to the feeding place.
>
> (von Frisch 1967, 72–73)

In a series of elegant experiments over the next twenty years, von Frisch established that the round dance conveys three pieces of information: the presence of a food source, its richness, and the type of food available (see Figure 41.1). The scent clinging to the dancer's body, along with droplets of nectar regurgitated from her honey stomach, tell nearby bees of her find. If she dances vigorously, other recruits follow her dance, then

FIGURE 41.1   Round Dance.

promptly leave the hive and search busily for the odors she carries, completely ignoring all other food sources. They may also be guided by a "Here it is!" pheromone the scout releases as she visits the source a second time. Returning to the hive, the recruits will also dance vigorously and spread the odor. Soon, hundreds of hivemates will be exploiting the recently discovered trove.

In 1944 von Frisch began exploring how honeybees deal with food sources far from their hive. He discovered that bees use a "tail-wagging" dance to communicate the distance and direction of remote food sources (see Figure 41.2). "In the tail-wagging dance," he reported (1967), "they run in a straight line wagging their abdomen to and fro, then return to the starting point in a semicircle, repeat the tail-wagging run, return in a semicircle on the other side, and so on." Bees responding to this dance would completely ignore food sources near the hive—even those with identical odors—in their flight to the distant goal.

Von Frisch also discovered that the tail-wagging dance tells the recruit bees which direction to fly and how far to go before starting their search. The scout bee does her dance on a vertical comb inside the dark hive. The angle between an imaginary vertical line running up the comb surface and the tail-wagging run of her dance corresponds to the angle

FIGURE 41.2   Tail-Wagging Dance.

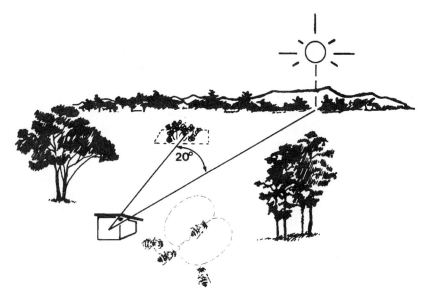

FIGURE 41.3   Angle of Wagging Dance Showing the Sun's Position.

between the sun and the food source (see Figure 41.3). So if the food source is twenty degrees to the left or right of the sun as seen from the opening of the hive, her waggle run will be offset twenty degrees to the left or right of the vertical. If the food source is directly away from the sun, she will start at the top of the comb, dancing straight down, and so on. Later experiments established that this directional information is extremely accurate. In a typical trial lasting fifty minutes, 42 of 54 bees (78%) found the target food source, 7 missed by an angle of fifteen degrees to the right or left, 4 by thirty degrees, and 1 directionally challenged bee by forty-five degrees. The scout bees also compensate for detours, direct-ing hivemates to fly straight toward the goal. Having reasonably accurate internal clocks, they can even adjust their waggle dance for the sun's movement across the sky. While the angle of the waggle run indicates the direction of the goal, its tempo indicates the distance; the farther the source, the more waggle runs the dancer makes per unit of time.

Not all honeybees use exactly the same set of dances. Von Frisch's students have established that different honeybee strains set the bound-aries between the round and tail-wagging dances at different distances, and encode like distances by different tempos. For example, Italian bees (*Apis m. ligustica*) dance slower for any given distance than did von Frisch's Austrian bees (*Apis m. carnica*). When Boch, a student of von Frisch, put both kinds of bees into one hive, miscommunication ran ram-pant. In response to Italian bees, the Austrians flew too far; in response to the Austrian scouts, Italians did not fly far enough. One can accurately say that the bee "language" has genetic dialects.

But is the bee dance really language? It certainly conveys information in an arbitrary code about parts of the world outside the bee herself and remote from where she dances. The dance thus satisfies several of the design features by which Hockett and Altmann (see page 64) attempted to distinguish between animal communication and human language. But von Frisch himself found significant limits to the bee's communication system. He put a hive beneath a radio tower, placed a very rich sugar-water solution high up in the tower, and showed several scouts where it was. After they returned to the hive and danced heroically, their mates searched busily all around the hive—but not up the tower. Evolved for foraging across horizontal landscapes, the powerful communication system of honeybees has no way of indicating up or down. Unlike human language, bee displays are not productive; they do not recombine bits of the code to produce novel messages. Bee messages are essentially the same message, differing only in a few details, uttered almost mechanically, over and over again in response to a narrow band of stimuli. This rigidity prevents the bees in mixed hives from learning each others' dialects, despite repeated attempts to communicate.

Because birds are larger than bees and interact over longer distances, one might suppose they use even more complicated communication systems. Their behavior certainly seems more varied than that of insects, and more vocal. Calls and songs are embedded in a rich context of elaborate visual displays. Their messages to mates, rivals, or neighbors arise from a coordinated package of activities, not any single element within the package. Still, to linguists the sounds birds make are the most interesting part of their behavior because, like humans, birds are physiologically and behaviorally specialized to produce and respond to streams of meaningful sound.

Ornithologists divide bird vocalizations into two categories: *calls* and *songs*. Calls tend to be brief, simple in structure, and confined to a particular context. As a result, some calls elicit sharp reactions from nearly every bird hearing them. The contrasting *alarm* and *mobbing* calls that many birds produce when they spot a predator are often shared across species; many birds make similar acoustic distinctions between the two calls. Alarms, given when the predator is airborne and thus able to strike promptly, have acoustic properties that make it difficult for the predator to find the bird emitting them. In contrast, mobbing calls, which summon neighbors to attack a stationary predator, have acoustic features that make the sound easy to locate, so that every bird responding will know where to attack. The survival value of differing calls is obvious.

But only a predator, rival, or prospective mate shows interest in the information contained in birdsong. Song is usually loud, sustained, complex in structure, seasonal, confined to males, and prompted by mating or territorial concerns. Some species, of course, sing no songs at all, using calls instead for territorial and breeding information; in strictest terms a song is simply an especially elaborate call. Still, the distinction between the two has a practical value to us because song seems musical to us and calls do not. Certainly, if a male songbird is to breed, he must learn to sing the right tune: it attracts females and keeps rival males away. And if a female is to breed, she must recognize the tune of an appropriate male.

A major function of birdsong is to establish and maintain breeding territories. Each resident male spends much of his time patrolling his boundaries and declaring his presence in song. The "message" of the song indicates the singer's probable behavior. Roughly translated, a territorial song says that the singer will attack any adult male of the same species who enters his territory. But as the singer's probable behavior changes across the spring, so does the meaning of the song. Early in the season, when pairs are still forming, a male chaffinch (*Fringilla coelebs*) will not attack adult females entering his territory. At that time of year, his song is all invitation. But later on, when eggs are incubating, he will attack strange females. The song does not change, but its meaning does. Other birds know the meaning from the time of year.

Of even greater interest to linguists than the purpose of birdsong is that they learn to repeat sometimes long and complex songs with great precision. In fact, most do not *learn* their songs in the strict meaning of the word. Only four of the twenty-nine avian orders have complex song repertoires or dialects and clearly must acquire their songs after birth. In the other twenty-five orders, the appropriate calls or songs appear to be part of each bird's genetic heritage.

Even within the largest family of songbirds, learning strategies differ sharply from one species to the next. Young song sparrows (*Melospiza melodia*), for example, must hear themselves sing to produce their full repertoire; song sparrows deafened when young fail to develop normal song, unlike individuals merely isolated when young. In contrast, young finches of several species learn the song of the adult male who helps care for them, even if he is of another species. White-crowned sparrows (*Zonotrichia leucophyrs*) and chaffinches must hear adults of their own species sing during the first spring of their lives; white-crowned sparrows raised in isolation until their second spring never perform properly, even after hearing adult song. In such species, it appears that each male is born with a generalized template for his species song. The length and timing of his critical learning period differ according to species, but the pattern is similar. The point of crystallization, when the template has become rich enough to support full adult song during the coming year, varies with the species, but the necessity of a passive learning period does not. This template is analogous to Chomsky's hypothesis of a genetic template supporting universal grammar in humans.

Although genetics establishes dialects of bees, learning appears to produce regional dialects in birds, as it does in human speech. In many species, birds of one area develop shared variations of the species song. These variations persist for several generations at least, and are clearly differences in learning rather than in the genetic template; fledglings from one area transported to another sing the new dialect, not that of their parents.

Because birds are more like humans than bees, are they closer in communicative ability as well? Probably not. Insect communication and behavior are in many ways as complex as our own. The impressive achievements of insect communities depend on reliable communication systems to coordinate the behavior of thousands, even millions. In contrast, bird vocalizations seem ambiguous. It may even be useful to see birdsong as a simpler form of communication than either the stereotyped, meaning-packed movements and chemical signals of bees or the more variable multichannel displays of some mammals.

But the complexity and variability of mammalian signaling may disguise the rather limited range of subjects of their signal. If most mammals communicate about the same limited set of subjects, and if those subjects are part of an environment shared by humans, it is not surprising that humans understand their mammalian pets—or that the pets appear to understand humans.

Four activities account for almost all the displays of mammals: mating, rearing young, resolving conflict, and maintaining group organization. In many species, from insects to birds, elaborate courtship rituals supplement the basic chemical signals of sexual readiness. Still, the rituals give only redundant information about the sexual condition and identity of the displaying animal. Mammals are no different, although their sexual displays are rather ordinary compared to the courtship of other animals. In contrast, the other three display categories show extensive expansion, reflecting specific mammalian adaptations.

Communication between mother and offspring is unimportant in sea turtles, which abandon their newly laid eggs and return to the sea. Even birds, many of which are good and faithful parents, communicate with their young through a simple set of calls and several kinds of specialized physical contact until the young are ready to fly. Then the fledgling is on its own to find food, avoid predators, and maybe migrate. Young turtles are genetically programmed to run for the sea as soon as they hatch. In ways we do not fully understand, migratory birds are programmed to find their way accurately across immense distances. Neither turtles nor birds learn much from their parents. So it is hardly surprising that all turtles and most birds produce multiple offspring as insurance that the species will continue. Although the casualty rate may be high, some offspring are bound to survive and keep the species going.

In contrast, most mammalian parents invest a remarkable amount of energy and time in a few offspring. Maternal care over a long period involves elaborate and sustained interaction between mothers and their young. The displays guiding this interaction are no more complex than those controlling mating. In fact, to a casual human observer they may not seem to be displays at all, because we behave very similarly in caring for our own infants: feeding, cleaning, restraining, warning, punishing, and petting.

Still, the fundamental feature of animal communication persists in even the most social mammals: the value of displays does not depend on a desire to tell another animal something. And even the most highly social mammals send messages with great redundancy. Such redundancy, together with a fairly limited number of messages, perhaps only a couple of dozen, is important because it means that pulling one sensory channel from the display for some other purpose need not seriously disrupt the message. In developing language, humans appear to have reserved the acoustic channel for complex spoken language. But the original display system still functions in human behavior, as the expanding literature on kinesics testifies.

Representatives of another group of mammals, the cetaceans, have also adapted the auditory channel for special communication. Water as a medium for chemical, visual, or acoustic signals is considerably different from air. Because a liquid veil shields the individual and social lives of water-based vertebrates from casual observation, we lack much of the behavioral context to understand their communication systems. For years scientists studied the sonar signals of dolphins as a model for artificial sonar systems. Various explanations for dolphin sonar have included stunning or killing prey, forming acoustic images of their surroundings, identifying individuals, and, according to one author, deliberately communicating with each other and with humans. A decade of intensive work with captive dolphins showed both the refinement of dolphin sonar and the flexibility with which the animals apply it to solving problems. Early behavioral studies using trained animals also suggested that dolphin problem-solving ability stems from a high level of intelligence but failed to find a useful way of measuring their cognitive skills.

More recently, Louis Herman and his colleagues have shown that dolphins are capable of responding to unique sequences of learned signals that identify various objects and actions; his subjects can execute accurately an interesting range of instructions. While the resulting claims for dolphin syntax and sentence comprehension are based on linguistically questionable definitions, this carefully described work illustrates again the remarkable cognitive capacities of the animals.

The humpback whales, another group of cetaceans (*Megaptera novaeangliae*), have been extensively studied in their breeding grounds off Hawaii and Baja California, and in their Alaskan hunting grounds. The animals seem to live in social aggregations without discernible structure. During their summer feeding season off Alaska, stable groups (most often chiefly female) sometimes hunt together in clearly coordinated ways, and even in the same areas from one year to the next. But during the winter breeding season, when the animals do little if any hunting, the only stable social groups are pairs of cows and calves, often followed by an interested adult male or three.

Like other cetaceans, humpback whales make a variety of sounds, but they are famous for singing. (Shortly after the discovery of this behavior in the 1960s, an album of whale songs was briefly popular.) In several ways whale and birdsongs are similar: males do the singing only during the breeding season, and the whale song is learned. Each song consists of several discrete *themes*, usually sung in the same sequence. The themes in turn contain *phrases*, the phrases contain *subphrases*, and the subphrases contain *units*. Complex birdsong can be analyzed using the same concepts. Whale song is also dialectical; Atlantic and Pacific humpbacks sing clearly different songs.

The most interesting feature of whale song is that within a given breeding population it changes rapidly over time. Analyzing the singing of Pacific whales for two breeding seasons, Payne, Tyack, and Payne (1983) found "dramatic monthly evolution following set rules of change. Substitution, omission, and addition occur at different rates in different times, but at any one time all songs are similar." We know almost nothing about what constitutes "good" whale singing; since no one has been able to identify the offspring of any male humpback, we cannot correlate a specific performance of a whale song with success at breeding. But it appears that a singing male must do two things simultaneously: produce the complex song and listen to the songs of his competitors. Nothing else can explain the fact that although the song changes steadily, nearly all males sing the same song all the time. The acoustic transactions among humpback whales exemplify a special kind of reciprocity in which the singing of each animal simultaneously shapes and is shaped by the singing of his neighbors.

Unfortunately, we do not know the meaning of this behavior. Since nearly all males seem to be singing the same song, females may choose mates on the basis of their troubadorial gifts. Possibly the songs are addressed entirely to other males as a way of spacing out individuals in the breeding territory. Given our ignorance about how aquatic creatures spend their time, we might construct several models to explain whale singing, based on the behavior of various land creatures.

To understand the basis of human language in animal communication, it seems wise to study our closest surviving biological relatives, the other primates. Although the similarities hold obvious promise for advancing understanding of humans, they make valid, objective research with primates difficult. Anne Premack writes:

> Aside from a human baby, I can think of no creature which can arouse stronger feelings of tenderness than an infant chimpanzee. It has huge round eyes and a delicate head and is far more alert than a human infant of the same age. When you pick up a young chimp, it encircles your body with its long, trembling arms and legs, and the effect is devastating— you want to take it home! (1967, 17).

Early studies, some using human infants as controls, investigated whether raising chimpanzees in a completely human environment (*cross-fostering*) would produce humanlike behavior, including spoken language. Although the chimps learned rapidly to respond to a variety of spoken commands, none acquired speech or even clearly intelligible word sounds. This result is hardly surprising; other primates do not share the subtle genetic adaptations of the human vocal track that enable speech. So, beginning in the mid sixties, several research teams began exploring other means of communicating with the animals.

Although these studies used different methodologies, they had two important goals in common. First, they focused on teaching the animals to produce symbols. Whether making signs, placing plastic tokens, or pushing computer keys, the animals were to create recognizable utterances to obtain reinforcement from their human trainers. Second, researchers hoped that the animals would produce strings of signs that would show meaning not only in the individual symbols but also in the order of the signs. Linguists have always emphasized the importance of syntax in human language, and sequence, or word order, is certainly important in the grammars of many languages—including English, the native language of these researchers. So ape language projects followed the lead of linguists.

Allen and Beatrice Gardner (1969) chose American Sign Language (ASL) and began teaching it to a female chimp whom they named Washoe. ASL is a complex, flexible system of hand signs developed for the deaf. A language in its own right rather than a facsimile of English, ASL uses the shape of the hand(s), their relative position, and their movement to convey ideas. Since home-raised chimps had shown excellent motor control at an earlier age than human infants, the Gardners felt confident that chimps could master ASL. Certain that a chimpanzee could readily learn arbitrary signs to obtain food, drink, and other things, they set a larger goal: "We wanted Washoe not only to ask for objects but to answer questions about them and also to ask us questions. We wanted to develop behavior that could be described as conversation" (Gardner and Gardner 1969). Just under two years into the project, Washoe had acquired 34 signs. By the end of the third year, she knew 85 signs. Her mature vocabulary reached approximately 180 signs (see Figure 41.4).

In later years the Gardners acquired other animals and offered them similar training, with similar results. Changes in funding transported this small colony of signing chimpanzees from Nevada to the University of Oklahoma for several years and finally to Central Washington University, where Roger Fouts, who began working with the animals as a graduate student of the Gardners, presided over a number of chimps living in a laboratory approximation of a social group. In the seventies, Herbert Terrace directed a Gardner-like program with one animal, Nim Chimsky. Penny Patterson carried on a similar project with two gorillas, Koko and Michael, and Lynn Miles did similar work with an orangutan named Chantek.

Not all investigators used adaptations of ASL. Even before the Gardners' first reports, Anne and David Premack (1983) had begun training a chimp named Sarah to answer simple questions using plastic tokens affixed to a sticky board, and their first publications nearly coincided with the Gardners'. Sarah's tokens were completely arbitrary shapes and colors (a blue triangle meant "apple," for instance), and the Premacks gave her very elaborate, step-by-step training in both definitions and sequence of tokens within a statement (see Figure 41.5).

Inspired by both the Gardners and the Premacks, Duane Rumbaugh developed an arbitrary language called Yerkish (after the Yerkes Primate Center in Atlanta) to communicate first with a female chimp named

FIGURE **41.4**   Washoe Signing "Tickle."

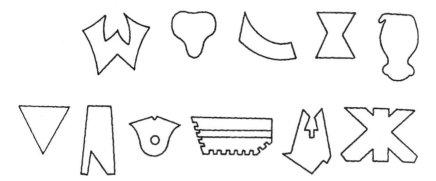

FIGURE **41.5**   Sarah's Symbols.

Lana, then with two males named Sherman and Austin. Its symbols, called lexigrams, are arbitrary designs displayed on the backlit keys of a large computer-controlled keyboard (see Figure 41.6). They are moved randomly from key to key so the animals will learn to select the designs rather than locations on the board. The lexigrams of the current message appear on a screen above the board, and the computer records all input.

FIGURE 41.6   Yerkish: Sample Lexigrams.

The Gardners themselves no longer work with chimps. The Premacks' project continued, focusing on the cognitive rather than linguistic abilities of their animals. Rumbaugh and his wife Sue Savage-Rumbaugh have extended their lexigram system to work with profoundly retarded humans and with bonobos, another species of ape. Fouts and Patterson continue their ASL research programs. Fouts has given Washoe an adopted son, Loulis, and studies the transfer of signing from one generation to the next.

Through the seventies and eighties, these projects attracted some popular attention—Washoe, for example, appeared in two different programs of the PBS science series *NOVA*. The projects also provoked considerable controversy about methodology, the nature of the animals' capabilities, and what it means to be "human." [Forty] years ago, humans were often defined as "the tool-making animal." But then Jane Goodall (1986) and other field scientists demonstrated that wild chimpanzees make and use a variety of tools, which constitutes a kind of protoculture for particular groups of animals. Not all groups make or use the same tools, and within a given group toolmaking and use are passed from one generation to the next. By the early seventies, only language conspicuously separated humans from other higher primates. However, the images of Washoe, Sarah, and Lana apparently engaging in communicative transactions with humans through arbitrary symbolic signs called into question even that distinction. No one denied that the animals were performing arbitrary and "unnatural" behavior. At issue was the meaning of that behavior. What was going on in the animals' minds? Was it language? Was it a kind of protolanguage, which could give a shadowy glimpse into our own evolutionary past? Or were the primate communication researchers overinterpreting their data? Criticism took two main forms: attacks on the accuracy of data, and alternative analyses of what the accumulating data means.

The most severe critics charged that the researchers were either dishonest or unable to avoid providing behavioral cues to their animals, which could explain away any instance of symbol use. Led by Thomas Sebeok, these critics campaigned to discredit all the ape language projects and deny funding to the investigators. Interestingly, even the first studies by the Gardners had used a standard technique to avoid just the sort of cuing their critics attributed to them. They used the double-blind design developed by social psychologists to control the influence of extraneous information on the behavior of human subjects in experiments.

In a double-blind design, no one in direct contact with the subjects knows which experimental condition is in effect at any time. Consider, for example, a study to test for the effects of hypnosis on suggestibility. The chief experimenter decides on the design of the experiment but does not interact with the subjects. In turn, the hypnotist, having been told perhaps that the experiment is about pain perception, is blind to the hypotheses, so neither the hypnotized nor the control subjects can gather relevant cues from the person they actually work with. The experimenter gathering data, not knowing which of the subjects have been hypnotized and which are in the control group, is blind to the experimental manipulation and cannot provide distorting cues either.

The Gardners early established a reliable double-blind system for testing Washoe's vocabulary. They report that in a typical double-blind testing session Washoe correctly named 91 or 92 of 128 items. The obvious meaning of these experiments, confirmed by the Premacks and Rumbaughs using different symbol systems, is that chimpanzees can learn to use arbitrary signs within the problem/reward structure of a behavioral experiment. The animals earned their treats honestly, by learning the symbols the experimenters asked them to learn.

Still, critics have rejected the significance of this achievement, offering a limited interpretation of the data: that the animals are simply using a learned maneuver—whether making a gesture, selecting a plastic token, or punching a computer key—to get something they want. The claim, in other words, is that the animals are not performing a cognitive function even vaguely analogous to naming familiar objects and actions; they are simply doing tricks for reward, just as a pet mynah bird will say "come in" when it hears a knock on the door. This area of controversy developed into a discussion of whether strings of symbols produced by the animals constitute syntax. To demonstrate the point, pigeons were trained to peck four colors in rigid sequence to obtain food. Labeling the four colors with words to produce English sentences like "please give me corn," "start give corn stop," or "dammit, where's the corn" does not mean that pigeons have learned language. The "messages" they produce are artifacts of the experimental apparatus, not constructions of the pigeons' minds. Although the process is laborious, careful conditioning of sequenced responses can produce such behavior in a variety of animals.

In the late eighties, Sue Savage-Rumbaugh realized that a fundamental feature in the design of all the projects had simultaneously fed the controversy and made it unresolvable: all projects had concentrated on training animals to produce signs, using their comprehension of signs only as evidence of reliable mastery of production. This emphasis gave all the projects similar features:

- long training periods before significant results appeared
- communicative transactions that interested the experimenters more than the animals

Emphasis on positive reinforcement—getting a treat for the right answer—meant that critics could always claim the animals were simply doing tricks to get rewards. Transactions interesting chiefly to the experimenters meant that the animals sometimes performed erratically, throwing the reliability of their mastery into question. It also meant that the animals' interests were not the focus of using signs.

Benefitting from the results and problems of earlier ape studies, Savage-Rumbaugh has carefully built a program of research into the basic language capacities of chimps and their cousins, bonobos. These two species certainly are the most closely related to humans genetically, and an evolutionary understanding of human nature suggests studying them for insight into the underpinnings of human language. Based on work in parallel programs for encouraging language development in apes and mentally retarded individuals, Savage-Rumbaugh has presented important and challenging results on just how both groups acquire the use of signs.

Starting with the program for teaching Lana to use Yerkish for acquiring rewards, Savage-Rumbaugh began a series of experiments with Sherman and Austin designed to make symbolic communication functional for them as well as for her. In one experiment, for example, she required Sherman and Austin to exchange information through lexigrams so they could use appropriate tools to extricate food from various containers. The animals were placed in different rooms, and one was allowed to watch a human put food into one of six kinds of container. After the human left, whichever animal knew where the food was hidden could use the keyboard to ask his comrade for the appropriate tool. If they completed the transaction successfully, they could share the prize. Allowed to use lexigrams, each would readily ask for or provide the appropriate tool; deprived of lexigrams, each would present the available tools in random order, or persistently offer the same tool. Having or not having access to the arbitrary symbols of Yerkish completely changed how they solved their problem. Having reframed the problem to be studied from production of syntactic utterances to comprehension of symbols for objects of value and use to a chimp, Savage-Rumbaugh clearly demonstrated that chimps and bonobos both possess cognitive capacities to comprehend and use arbitrary symbols for communication.

This new orientation, combined with access to another species of ape, has led to the most interesting results from ape language research. Kanzi, a bonobo raised from infancy in a symbol-rich environment, spontaneously acquired a small set of symbols. Constantly present in tutoring sessions with his mother, the young bonobo was never the focus of training; he acquired his first symbols through observation, much as a young human learns early words through constant exposure and observation. Kanzi's ability became obvious only when he started using the Yerkish keyboards to get desired objects (food or toys) and initiate desired play activities. Thereafter, Kanzi learned a large set of symbols quite rapidly.

Savage-Rumbaugh has shown convincingly that after intensive language exposure Kanzi can also understand spoken words and has the ability to respond to at least some aspects of word order. As she notes: "Such an ape can also understand the intentions of others as expressed through language, though the nonlinguistic expression of intent must match the linguistic one or the words will be ignored" (1994, xi–xii). Analysis by a developmental linguist, Patricia Greenfield, suggests that Kanzi may well be using Yerkish lexigram combinations in a systematic way—one similar to the simple grammar that governs the two-word stage in young humans. Further, the replication of these results with two other bonobos and a common chimpanzee imply that this basic ability is generally available to both species, though bonobos seem more proficient at this kind of learning.

These results justify Savage-Rumbaugh's shift in experimental focus from production to comprehension. Certainly neither Kanzi nor any other ape has *produced* utterances or sign strings that match the complexities of human grammar. And although Kanzi responds appropriately to requests, commands, and even embedded identifiers, verb modifiers and conditionals leave him completely confused. Still, the basic ability to comprehend ordered symbol strings and extract the information about the world they convey appears in nonhuman as well as human primates. Chimps, bonobos, and possibly gorillas and orangutans have the basic cognitive ability that humans use in language comprehension. The unique ability is the control humans exert over modified vocal, breathing, and swallowing structures.

Although primate studies have not uncovered systems that closely parallel human language, they have certainly provided insight into the variety of ways that animals exchange meaningful and useful information about their environments and their actions and intentions in relation to them. Attempts to elicit ordered communication by signs in apes may have failed in their original objective, but they have given us evidence of cognitive capacities in apes that are far beyond our expectations. And we are closer to understanding the basic abilities from which our ancestors developed the language capacity that shapes the world we inhabit.

What are we to take away from a quarter century of ape language work? A combination of classic experimental research, informed observation, and quasi-ethological research on the relationship between symbol use and environmental consequences reveals that apes comprehend even when their spontaneous production of signs is limited. But of course this is also true for young children. Indeed, examined objectively, the corpus of evidence for early language usage in Kanzi is more convincing than that in many linguistic development studies of children. Like young humans, apes are capable of using arbitrary symbol systems to manipulate their environment and relationships with others. Unlike bees and most birds, apes are not limited to a neurologically programmed set of behavioral signals.

What does this tell us about apes and about ourselves? The basic cognitive and neurological abilities that underlie language exist in our closest biological relatives. But full comprehension of syntax and the production of syntactic utterances appear limited to humans. This difference correlates interestingly with human brain lateralization. Among all nonhuman higher primates, handedness is evenly distributed—approximately fifty percent of chimpanzees are right-handed and fifty percent left-handed. In contrast, something like ninety percent of human beings are right-handed—that is, left hemisphere dominant. It begins to seem increasingly significant that the brain areas most concerned with the intricate processes of speech and syntax production are typically located in the left hemisphere. If this level of syntactic competence is beyond the mastery of nonhuman primates, then syntax production becomes a promising candidate for one dimension of language capability that only humans as a species have developed.

The expanding body of information on animal communication in general and the acquisition of symbol systems by primates in particular is valuable to students of human language in several ways. First, it helps us to understand, however vaguely, the mental worlds of animals we often consider mindless if not senseless. And for linguists particularly, the study of ape communication provides a rare contrast to normal human language competence. Parallels between teaching the Yerkish lexigram system to severely mentally retarded humans as well as chimps and bonobos have already proved instructive. Last, because language does not leave fossils, we are unlikely to resolve all our questions about its evolution. We might resolve some of them by examining the closest thing to language fossils: the communicative and cognitive capacities of our nearest biological relatives. Although the other higher primates are not in any sense our linguistic ancestors, their evolutionary history may have conserved the cognitive abilities shared by our common prelingual ancestors.

Careful study has shown the degree of human communication that takes place on the level of affective displays using fixed action patterns. The same studies, however, have shown how great a gap separates animal and human use of symbols. Human language is an additional symbolic layer, extremely rich in hierarchical rule systems, superimposed on an existing pattern of communication that we share with other animals. This new layer has led to rapid alteration of every facet of human social structure and even to changes in human perception of the world.

To continue to acquire information about communication systems in a broad range of animals, investigators need to rethink older data, integrate new studies, and reexamine some operating assumptions. Communication within social groups is a fundamental part of animal life, and particular features of a species' communication system have long been seen as defining that species' unique social and even biological nature. The human capacity to appreciate multiple levels of meaning in a set of auditory or written signals clearly separates the cognitive worlds of humans and other primates. Advances in fields such as neurophysiology, linguistics, cognitive science, and comparative psychology seem to be converging on new and exciting conceptions that will challenge much of our understanding of the role language plays in human cognition and behavior.

While current information does not show that any other animals have even a close approximation of formal language systems, such formal language (as opposed to other verbal and nonverbal communication systems) plays a relatively small role in the majority of our everyday lives.

By changing the focus of primate research from the study of formal language skills to cognitive strategies, several investigators have shown that chimps have cognitive mapping skills very similar to those of humans. The differences in the basic perceptual skills of higher primates may be slight indeed; genetic data suggest that the physical differences are minimal. The similarity of the cognitive world of great apes and humans, in contrast to their seemingly absolute difference in syntactic ability, suggests the decisiveness of the world-constructing power of language. The linguistic differences between human and animal may, in the case of higher primates, represent only small cognitive differences. Yet the power of language, once unleashed, has magnified them into an unbridgeable gulf.

BIBLIOGRAPHY

Gardner, B. T., and R. A. Gardner. "Teaching Sign Language to a Chimpanzee." *Science* 165 (1969), 664–672.

Hockett, C. F., and S. A. Altmann. "A Note on Design Features." In *Animal Communication*, ed. T. A. Sebeok. Bloomington: University of Indiana Press, 1968.

Payne, K., P. Tyack, and R. Payne. "Progressive Changes in the Songs of Humpback Whales (*Megaptera novaeangliae*): A Detailed Analysis of Two Seasons in Hawaii." In *Communication and Behavior of Whales*, ed. R. Payne. AAAS Selected Symposia Series. Boulder: Westview Press, 1983.

Premack, Anne. *Why Chimps Can Read*. New York: Harper & Row, 1976.

Savage-Rumbaugh, E. Sue, and Roger Lewin. *Kanzi: The Ape at the Brink of the Human Mind*. New York: John Wiley and Sons, 1994.

Von Frisch, Karl. *A Biologist Remembers*. Trans. Lisbeth Gombrich. Oxford: Pergamon Press, 1967.

SUGGESTED READINGS

General

Griffin, D. R. *The Question of Animal Awareness: Evolutionary Continuity of Mental Experience*. Los Altos, CA: William Kaufmann, 1981. [In this important book Griffin opened the way to a reconsideration of cognitive capacities and functions in animals.]

Peters, R. *Mammalian Communication: A Behavioral Analysis of Meaning*. Monterey, CA: Brooks/Cole, 1980. [A well-written, clearly organized analysis of nonverbal communication from moles to man.]

Smith, W. John. *The Behavior of Communicating*. Cambridge: Harvard University Press, 1977. [A good general introduction to communication as a kind of behavior that fits into other behavior and environment.]

Bees

Gould, J. L., and C. G. Gould. "Can a Bee Behave Intelligently?" *New Scientist* 98 (1983), 84–87. [An interesting update on bee language research.]

Von Frisch, K. *Bees: Their Vision, Chemical Senses, and Language.* Rev. ed. Ithaca, NY: Cornell University Press, 1971. [The classic story of von Frisch's seminal work on honeybee communication.]

Whales

Payne, R., ed. *Communication and Behavior of Whales.* AAAS Selected Symposia Series. Boulder: Westview Press, 1983. [A compendium of papers that explore the communicative behavior of whales.]

Schusterman, R. J., J. A. Thomas, and F. G. Wood, eds. *Dolphin Cognition and Behavior: A Comparative Approach.* Hillsdale, NJ: Lawrence Erlbaum Associates, 1986. [The editors collected an array of reports on dolphin communication and placed it in the larger context of communicative behavior in other species.]

Birds

Catchpole, C. K., and P. J. B. Slater. *Bird Song: Biological Themes and Variations.* Cambridge: Cambridge University Press, 1995. [A comprehensive survey of research on birdsong.]

Apes

de Luce, J., and H. T. Wilder, eds. *Language in Primates: Perspectives and Implications.* New York: Springer-Verlag, 1983. [This third compendium is somewhat more balanced, definitely more philosophical, and less polemic than the first two.]

Goodall, J. *The Chimpanzees of the Gombi: Patterns of Behavior.* Cambridge: Belknap, 1986. [Among the observations in this summary of decades of meticulous work are several on the nature of chimp vocalization and its role in their social organization.]

Premack, D., and A. Premack. *The Mind of an Ape.* New York: W. W. Norton, 1983. [An entertaining and informative summary of a more cognition-oriented line of research with chimps.]

Savage-Rumbaugh, E. Sue, and Roger Lewin. *Kanzi: The Ape at the Brink of the Human Mind.* New York: John Wiley and Sons, 1994. [The most recent book on the subject, it offers a clear overview and details the shift in emphasis from language production to cognitive capacities of primates.]

Sebeok, T. A., and J. Umiker-Sebeok, eds. *Speaking of Apes: A Critical Anthology of Two-Way Communication with Man.* New York: Plenum Press, 1980. [This anthology is largely an outgrowth of a conference spearheaded by Sebeok and Terrace to publicize their doubts about ape language research.]

Sebeok, T. A., and R. Rosenthal, eds. *The Clever Hans Phenomenon: Communication with Horses, Whales, Apes, and People.* Annals of the New York Academy of Sciences, vol. 364. New York: New York Academy of Sciences, 1981. [A second anthology covers areas and commentators left out of the first volume, but with the same intent and purpose.]

Terrace, H. *Nim: A Chimp Who Learned Sign Language.* New York: Alfred Knopf, 1979. [Terrace presents in detail his work with Nim and the basis for his reinterpretation of his results.

=====

FOR DISCUSSION AND REVIEW

1. Why do ethologists and linguists believe that studying different kinds of animal communication is important? When you have observed or interacted with cats or dogs or other animal species on a regular basis, what have you noticed about how they communicate?

2. In analyzing animal communication, ethologists use the terms *form*, *context*, and *response*. Define and give an original example of each term. How do these concepts correspond to communication between humans?

3. Kemp and Smith state that "distinctive behavior that reliably indicates what an animal will do promotes cooperation and reduces conflict, because it allows neighbors to adjust their actions according to what the display predicts." Drawing on your own experience, write a brief description of at least one situation involving a nonhuman species that illustrates this principle. What example involving humans might also demonstrate this principle?

4. Explain the similarities and differences between the *allophones* of human speech and animal *displays*. You might also consider hand position, shape, and movement in a human signed language such as ASL. How do signed languages differ from animal displays?

5. According to Kemp and Smith, how are bee displays different from those of humans? What problems do bees have in communicating with one another?

6. Explain the differences between bird calls and bird songs, noting the separate functions of each.

7. Kemp and Smith say that "the fundamental feature of animal communication persists in even the most social mammals: the value of displays does not depend on a desire to tell another animal something." What does this statement imply about human language versus animal communication?

8. What design "problems" did Savage-Rumbaugh discover in early primate research? How did she set about to correct these problems, and how have her changes affected more recent research?

9. What have researchers learned by working with Kanzi, a bonobo primate?

10. In the final pages of their essay, what conclusions do Kemp and Smith reach about the ape-language research of the past forty years?

42

The Acquisition of Language

Breyne Arlene Moskowitz

The image of parents urging their infant to repeat the words "mama" and "dada" is an American stereotype. The acquisition of language, however, follows quite a different path, as linguistics professor Breyne Arlene Moskowitz describes in this 1978 article from Scientific American. *Moskowitz explores a number of areas, including the prerequisites for language learning; the one-word, two-word, and telegraphic stages; the acquisition of function words; and the processes of rule formation and semantics. She shows that children are active learners who consistently follow the same basic procedure: hypothesizing rules, trying them, and modifying them. Although the examples discussed here concern children learning English, researchers have observed the same process in children learning other languages. While reading this selection, considered a classic, think about the language development of any young children you know and try to identify the stages Moskowitz describes.*

An adult who finds herself in a group of people speaking an unfamiliar foreign language may feel quite uncomfortable. The strange language sounds like gibberish: mysterious strings of sound, rising and falling in unpredictable patterns. Each person speaking the language knows when to speak, how to construct the strings, and how to interpret other people's strings, but the individual who does not know anything about the language cannot pick out separate words or sounds, let alone discern meanings. She may feel overwhelmed, ignorant, and even childlike. It is possible that she is returning to a vague memory from her very early childhood, because the experience of an adult listening to a foreign language comes close to duplicating the experience of an infant listening to the "foreign" language spoken by everyone around her. Like the adult, the child is confronted with the task of learning a language about which she knows nothing.

The task of acquiring language is one for which the adult has lost most of her aptitude but one the child will perform with remarkable skill. Within a short span of time and with almost no direct instruction the child will analyze the language completely. In fact, although many subtle refinements are added between the ages of five and ten, most children have completed the greater part of the basic language-acquisition process by the age of five. By that time a child will have dissected the language into its minimal separable units of sound and meaning; she will have discovered the rules for recombining sounds into words, the meanings of individual words, and the rules for recombining words into meaningful sentences, and she will have internalized the intricate patterns of taking turns in dialogue. All in all she will have established herself linguistically as a full-fledged member of a social community, informed about the most subtle details of her native language as it is spoken in a wide variety of situations.

The speed with which children accomplish the complex process of language acquisition is particularly impressive. Ten linguists working full time for ten years to analyze the structure of the English language could not program a computer with the ability for language acquired by an average child in the first ten or even five years of life. In spite of the scale of the task and even in spite of adverse conditions—emotional instability, physical disability, and so on—children learn to speak. How do they go about it? By what process does a child learn language?

WHAT IS LANGUAGE?

In order to understand how language is learned it is necessary to understand what language is. The issue is confused by two factors. First, language is learned in early childhood, and adults have few memories of the intense effort that went into the learning process, just as they do not remember the process of learning to walk. Second, adults do have conscious memories of being taught the few grammatical rules that are prescribed as "correct" usage, or the norms of "standard" language. It is difficult for adults to dissociate their memories of school lessons from those of true language learning, but the rules learned in school are only the conventions of an educated society. They are arbitrary finishing touches of embroidery on a thick fabric of language that each child weaves for herself before arriving in the English teacher's classroom. The fabric is grammar: the set of rules that describe how to structure language.

The grammar of language includes rules of phonology, which describe how to put sounds together to form words; rules of syntax, which describe how to put words together to form sentences; rules of semantics, which describe how to interpret the meaning of words and sentences; and rules of pragmatics, which describe how to participate in a conversation, how to sequence sentences, and how to anticipate the information needed by an interlocutor. The internal grammar each adult has constructed is identical with that of every other adult in all but a few superficial details. Therefore each adult can create or understand an infinite number of sentences she has never heard before. She knows what is acceptable as a word or a sentence and what is not acceptable, and her judgments on these issues concur with those of other adults. For example, speakers of English generally agree that the sentence "Ideas green sleep colorless furiously" is ungrammatical and that the sentence "Colorless green ideas sleep furiously" is grammatical but makes no sense semantically. There is similar agreement on the grammatical relations represented by word order. For example, it is clear that the sentences "John hit Mary" and "Mary hit John" have different meanings although they consist of the same words, and that the sentence "Flying planes can be dangerous" has two possible meanings. At the level of individual words all adult speakers can agree that "brick" is an English word, that "blick" is not an English word but could be one (that is, there is an accidental gap in the adult lexicon, or internal vocabulary), and that "bnick" is not an English word and could not be one.

How children go about learning the grammar that makes communication possible has always fascinated adults, particularly parents, psychologists, and investigators of language. Until recently diary keeping was the primary method of study in this area. For example, in 1877 Charles Darwin published an account of his son's development that includes notes on language learning. Unfortunately most of the diarists used inconsistent or incomplete notations to record what they heard (or what they thought they heard), and most of the diaries were only partial listings of emerging types of sentences with inadequate information on developing word meanings. Although the very best of them, such as W. F. Leopold's classic *Speech Development of a Bilingual Child*, continue to be a rich resource of contemporary investigators, advances in audio and video recording equipment have made modern diaries generally much more valuable. In the 1960s, however, new discoveries inspired linguists and psychologists to approach the study of language acquisition in a new, systematic way, oriented less toward long-term diary keeping and more toward a search for patterns in a child's speech at any given time.

An event that revolutionized linguists was the publication in 1957 of Noam Chomsky's *Syntactic Structures*. Chomsky's investigation of the structure of grammars revealed that language systems were far deeper and more complex than had been suspected. And of course if linguistics was more complicated, then language learning had to be more complicated. In the . . . years since the publication of *Syntactic Structures* the disciplines of linguistics and child language have come of age. The study of the acquisition of language has benefited not only from the increasingly sophisticated understanding of linguistics but also from the improved understanding of cognitive development as it is related to language. The improvements in recording technology have made experimentation in this area more reliable and more detailed, so that investigators framing new and deeper questions are able to accurately capture both rare occurrences and developing structures.

The picture that is emerging from the more sophisticated investigations reveals the child as an active language learner, continually analyzing what she hears and proceeding in a methodical, predictable way to put together the jigsaw puzzle of language. Different children learn language in similar ways. It is not known how many processes are involved in language learning, but the few that have been observed appear repeatedly, from child to child and from language to language. All the examples I shall discuss here concern children who are learning English, but identical processes have been observed in children learning French, Russian, Finnish, Chinese, Zulu, and many other languages.

Children learn the systems of grammar—phonology, syntax, semantics, lexicon, and pragmatics—by breaking each system down into its smallest combinable parts and then developing rules for combining the parts. In the first two years of life a child spends much time working on one part of the task, disassembling the language to find the separate sounds that can be put together to form words and the separate words that can be put together to form sentences. After the age of two the basic process continues to be refined, and many more sounds and words are produced. The other part of language acquisition—developing rules for combining the basic elements of language—is carried out in a very methodical way: the most general rules are hypothesized first, and as time passes they are successively narrowed down by the addition of more precise rules applying to a more restricted set of sentences. The procedure is the same in any area of language learning, whether the child is acquiring syntax or phonology or semantics. For example, at the earliest stage of acquiring negatives a child does not have at her command the same range of negative structures that an adult does. She has constructed only a single very general rule: Attach "no" to the beginning of any sentence constructed by the other rules of grammar. At this stage all negative sentences will be formed according to that rule.

Throughout the acquisition process a child continually revises and refines the rules of her internal grammar, learning increasingly detailed subrules until she achieves a set of rules that enable her to create the full array of complex, adult sentences. The process of refinement continues at least until the age of ten and probably considerably longer for most children. By the time a child is six or seven, however, the changes in her grammar may be so subtle and sophisticated that they go unnoticed. In general children approach language learning economically, devoting their energy to broad issues before dealing with specific ones. They cope with clear-cut questions first and sort out the details later, and they may adopt any one of a variety of methods for circumventing details of a language system that they have not yet dealt with.

PREREQUISITES FOR LANGUAGE

Although some children verbalize much more than others and some increase the length of their utterances much faster than others, all children overgeneralize a single rule before learning to apply it more

(1)	(2)	(3)	(4)	(5)	(6)
boy		boys	boysəz	boys	boys
cat		cats	catsəz	cats	cats
			catəz		
man	men	mans	mansəz	mans	men
			menəz		
house		house	housəz	houses	houses
foot		foots	footsəz	feets	feet
feet		feets	feetsəz		

TABLE 42.1 Sorting out of competing pronunciations that result in the correct plural forms of nouns takes place in the six stages shown in this table. Children usually learn the singular forms of nouns first (1), although in some cases an irregular plural form such as "feet" may be learned as a singular or as a free variant of a singular. Other irregular plurals may appear for a brief period (2), but soon they are replaced by plurals made according to the most general rule possible: To make a noun plural add the sound "s" or "z" to it (3). Words such as "house" or "rose," which already end in an "s"- or "z"-like sound, are usually left in their singular forms at this stage. When words of this type do not have irregular plural forms, adults make them plural by adding an "əz" sound. (The vowel "ə" is pronounced like the unstressed word "a.") Some children demonstrate their mastery of this usage by tacking "əz" endings indiscriminately onto nouns (4). That stage is brief and use of the ending is quickly narrowed down (5). At this point only irregular plurals remain to be learned, and since no new rule-making is needed, children may go on to harder problems and leave final stage (6) for later.

narrowly and before constructing other less widely applicable rules, and all children speak in one-word sentences before they speak in two-word sentences. The similarities in language learning for different children and different languages are so great that many linguists have believed at one time or another that the human brain is preprogrammed for language learning. Some linguists continue to believe language is innate and only the surface details of the particular language spoken in a child's environment need to be learned. The speed with which children learn language gives this view much appeal. As more parallels between language and other areas of cognition are revealed, however, there is greater reason to believe any language specialization that exists in the child is only one aspect of more general cognitive abilities of the brain.

Whatever the built-in properties the brain brings to the task of language learning may be, it is now known that a child who hears no language learns no language, and that a child learns only the language spoken in her environment. Most infants coo and babble during the first six months of life, but congenitally deaf children have been observed to cease babbling after six months, whereas normal infants continue to babble. A child does not learn language, however, simply by hearing it spoken. A boy with normal hearing but with deaf parents who communicated by the American Sign Language was exposed to television every day so that he would learn English. Because the child was asthmatic and was confined to his home he interacted only with people at home, where his family and all their visitors communicated in sign language. By the age of three he was fluent in sign language but neither understood nor spoke English. It appears that in order to learn a language a child must also be able to interact with real people in that language. A television set does not suffice as the sole medium for language learning because, even though it can ask questions, it cannot respond to a child's answers. A child, then, can develop language only if there is language in her environment and if she can employ that language to communicate with other people in her immediate environment.

CARETAKER SPEECH

In constructing a grammar children have only a limited amount of information available to them, namely the language they hear spoken around them. (Until about the age of three a child models her language on that of her parents; afterward the language of her peer group tends to become more important.) There is no question, however, that the language environments children inhabit are restructured, usually unintentionally, by the adults who take care of them. Recent studies show that there are several ways caretakers systematically modify the child's environment, making the task of language acquisition simpler.

Caretaker speech is a distinct speech register that differs from others in its simplified vocabulary, the systematic phonological simplification of some words, higher pitch, exaggerated intonation, short, simple sentences, and a high proportion of questions (among mothers) or imperatives (among fathers). Speech with the first two characteristics is formally designated Baby Talk. Baby Talk is a subsystem of caretaker speech that has been studied over a wide range of languages and cultures. Its characteristics appear to be universal: in languages as diverse as English, Arabic, Comanche, and Gilyak (a Paleo-Siberian language) there are simplified vocabulary items for terms relating to food, toys, animals, and body functions. Some words are phonologically simplified, frequently by the duplication of syllables, as in "wawa" for "water" and "choochoo" for "train," or by the reduction of consonant clusters, as in "tummy" for "stomach," and "scambled eggs" for "scrambled eggs." (Many types of phonological simplification seem to mimic the phonological structure of an infant's own early vocabulary.)

Perhaps the most pervasive characteristic of caretaker speech is its syntactic simplification. While a child is still babbling, adults may address long, complex sentences to her, but as soon as she begins to utter meaningful, identifiable words they almost invariably speak to her in very simple sentences. Over the next few years of the child's language

(1)	(2)	(3)	(4)	(5)	(6)
walk		walked	walkedəd	walked	walked
play		played	playedəd	played	played
need		need	needəd	needed	needed
come	came	comed	camedəd comedəd	comed	came
go	went	goed	goed wentəd	goed	went

TABLE 42.2   Development of past-tense forms of verbs also takes place in six stages. After the present-tense forms are learned (1) irregular past-tense forms may appear briefly (2). The first and most general rule that is postulated is: To put a verb into the past tense, add a "t" or "d" sound (3). In adult speech, verbs such as "want" or "need," which already end in a "t" or "d" sound, are put into the past tense by adding an "əd" sound. Many children go through a brief stage in which they add "əd" endings to any existing verb forms (4). Once the use of the "əd" ending has been narrowed down (5), only irregular past-tense forms remain to be learned (6).

development the speech addressed to her by her caretakers may well be describable by a grammar only six months in advance of her own.

The functions of the various language modifications in caretaker speech are not equally apparent. It is possible that higher pitch and exaggerated intonation serve to alert a child to pay attention to what she is hearing. As for Baby Talk, there is no reason to believe the use of phonologically simplified words in any way affects a child's learning of pronunciation. Baby Talk may have only a psychological function, marking speech as being affectionate. On the other hand, syntactic simplification has a clear function. Consider the speech adults address to other adults; it is full of false starts and long, rambling, highly complex sentences. It is not surprising that elaborate theories of innate language ability arose during the years when linguists examined the speech adults addressed to adults and assumed that the speech addressed to children was similar. Indeed, it is hard to imagine how a child could derive the rules of language from such input. The wide study of caretaker speech conducted [in the 1970s] has shown that children do not face this problem. Rather it appears they construct their initial grammars on the basis of the short, simple, grammatical sentences that are addressed to them in the first year or two they speak.

CORRECTING LANGUAGE

Caretakers simplify children's language-analysis task in other ways. For example, adults talk with other adults about complex ideas, but they talk with children about the here and now, minimizing discussion of feelings, displaced events, and so on. Adults accept children's syntactic and phonological "errors," which are a normal part of the acquisition process. It is important to understand that when children make such errors, they are not producing flawed or incomplete replicas of adult sentences; they are producing sentences that are correct and grammatical with respect to their own current internalized grammar. Indeed, children's errors are essential data for students of child language because it is the consistent departures from the adult model that indicate the nature of a child's current hypotheses about the grammar of language. There are a number of memorized, unanalyzed sentences in any child's output of language. If a child says, "Nobody likes me," there is no way of knowing whether she has memorized the sentence intact or has figured out the rules for constructing the sentence. On the other hand, a sentence such as "Nobody don't like me" is clearly not a memorized form but one that reflects an intermediate stage of a developing grammar.

Since each child's utterances at a particular stage are from her own point of view grammatically correct, it is not surprising that children are fairly impervious to the correction of their language by adults, indeed to any attempts to teach them language. Consider the boy who lamented to his mother, "Nobody don't like me." His mother seized the opportunity to correct him, replying, "Nobody likes me." The child repeated his original version and the mother her modified one a total of eight times until in desperation the mother said, "Now listen carefully! Nobody likes me." Finally her son got the idea and dutifully replied "Oh! Nobody don't likes me." As the example demonstrates, children do not always understand exactly what it is the adult is correcting. The information the adult is trying to impart may be at odds with the information in the child's head, namely the rules the child is postulating for producing language. The surface correction of a sentence does not give the child a clue about how to revise the rule that produced the sentence.

It seems to be virtually impossible to speed up the language-learning process. Experiments conducted by Russian investigators show that it is extremely difficult to teach children a detail of language more than a few days before they would learn it themselves. Adults sometimes do, of course, attempt to teach children rules of language, expecting them to learn by imitation, but Courtney B. Cazden of Harvard University found that children benefit less from frequent adult correction of their errors than from true conversational interaction. Indeed, correcting errors can interrupt that interaction, which is, after all, the function of language. (One way children may try to secure such interaction is by asking "Why?" Children go through a stage of asking a question repeatedly. It serves to keep the conversation going, which may be the child's real aim. For example, a two-and-a-half-year-old named Stanford asked "Why?" and was given the nonsense answer: "Because the moon is made of green cheese." Although the response was not at all germane to the conversation, Stanford was happy with it and again asked "Why?" Many silly answers later the adult had tired of the conversation but Stanford had not. He was clearly not seeking information. What he needed was to practice the form of social conversation before dealing with its function. Asking "Why?" served that purpose well.)

In point of fact adults rarely correct children's ungrammatical sentences. For example, one mother, on hearing "Tommy fall my truck down," turned to Tommy with "Did you fall Stevie's truck down?" Since imitation seems to have little role in the language-acquisition process, however, it is probably just as well that most adults are either too charmed by children's errors or too busy to correct them.

Practice does appear to have an important function in the child's language learning process. Many children have been observed purposefully practicing language when they are alone, for example in a crib or a playpen. Ruth H. Weir of Stanford University hid a tape recorder in her son's bedroom and recorded his talk after he was put to bed. She found that he played with words and phrases, stringing together sequences of similar sounds and of variations on a phrase or on the use of a word: "What color . . . what color blanket . . . what color mop . . . what color glass . . . what color TV . . . red ant . . . fire . . . like lipstick . . . blanket . . . now the blue blanket . . . what color TV . . . what color horse . . . then what color table . . . then what color fire . . . here yellow spoon." Children who do not have much opportunity to be alone may use dialogue in a similar fashion. When Weir tried to record the bedtime monologues of her second child, whose room adjoined that of the first, she obtained through-the-wall conversations instead.

THE ONE-WORD STAGE

The first stage of child language is one in which the maximum sentence length is one word; it is followed by a stage in which the maximum sentence length is two words. Early in the one-word stage there are only a few words in a child's vocabulary, but as months go by her lexicon expands with increasing rapidity. The early words are primarily concrete nouns and verbs; more abstract words such as adjectives are acquired later. By the time the child is uttering two-word sentences with some regularity, her lexicon may include hundreds of words.

When a child can say only one word at a time and knows only five words in all, choosing which one to say may not be a complex task. But how does she decide which word to say when she knows 100 words or more? Patricia M. Greenfield of the University of California at Los Angeles and Joshua H. Smith of Stanford have suggested that an important criterion is informativeness, that is, the child selects a word reflecting what is new in a particular situation. Greenfield and Smith also found that a newly acquired word is first used for naming and only later for asking for something.

Superficially the one-word stage seems easy to understand: a child says one word at a time, and so each word is a complete sentence with its own sentence intonation. Ten years ago a child in the one-word stage was thought to be learning word meanings but not syntax. [Since that time,] however, students of child language have seen less of a distinction between the one-word stage as a period of word learning and the subsequent period, beginning with the two-word stage, as one of syntax acquisition. It now seems clear that the infant is engaged in an enormous amount of syntactic analysis in the one-word stage, and indeed that her syntactic abilities are reflected in her utterances and in her accurate perception of multiword sentences addressed to her.

Ronald Scollon of the University of Hawaii and Lois Bloom of Columbia University have pointed out independently that important patterns in word choice in the one-word stage can be found by examining larger segments of children's speech. Scollon observed that a nineteen-month-old named Brenda was able to use a vertical construction (a series of one-word sentences) to express what an adult might say with a horizontal construction (a multiword sentence). Brenda's pronunciation, which is represented phonetically below, was imperfect and Scollon did not understand her words at the time. Later, when he transcribed the tape of their conversation, he heard the sound of a passing car immediately preceding the conversation and was able to identify Brenda's words as follows:

BRENDA: "Car [pronounced 'ka']. Car. Car. Car."
SCOLLON: "What?"
BRENDA: "Go. Go."
SCOLLON: [Undecipherable.]
BRENDA: "Bus [pronounced 'baish']. Bus. Bus. Bus. Bus. Bus. Bus. Bus."
SCOLLON: "What? Oh, bicycle? Is that what you said?"
BRENDA: "Not ['na']."
SCOLLON: "No?"
BRENDA: "Not."
SCOLLON: "No. I got it wrong."

Brenda was not yet able to combine two words syntactically to express "Hearing that car reminds me that we went on the bus yesterday. No, not on a bicycle." She could express that concept, however, by combining words sequentially. Thus the one-word stage is not just a time for learning the meaning of words. In that period a child is developing hypotheses about putting words together in sentences, and she is already putting sentences together in meaningful groups. The next step will be to put two words together to form a single sentence.

THE TWO-WORD STAGE

The two-word stage is a time for experimenting with many binary semantic-syntactic relations such as possessor-possessed ("Mommy sock"), actor-action ("Cat sleeping"), and action-object ("Drink soup").

When two-word sentences first began to appear in Brenda's speech, they were primarily of the following forms: subject noun and verb (as in "Monster go"), verb and object (as in "Read it"), and verb or noun and location (as in "Bring home" and "Tree down"). She also continued to use vertical constructions in the two-word stage, providing herself with a means of expressing ideas that were still too advanced for her syntax. Therefore once again a description of Brenda's isolated sentences does not show her full abilities at this point in her linguistic development. Consider a later conversation Scollon had with Brenda:

> BRENDA: "Tape corder. Use it. Use it."
> SCOLLON: "Use it for what?"
> BRENDA: "Talk. Corder talk. Brenda talk."

Brenda's use of vertical constructions to express concepts she is still unable to encode syntactically is just one example of a strategy employed by children in all areas of cognitive development. As Jean Piaget of the University of Geneva and Dan I. Slobin of the University of California at Berkeley put it, new forms are used for old functions and new functions are expressed by old forms. Long before Brenda acquired the complex syntactic form "Use the tape recorder to record me talking" she was able to use her old forms—two-word sentences and vertical construction—to express the new function. Later, when that function was old, she would develop new forms to express it. The controlled dovetailing of form and function can be observed in all areas of language acquisition. For example, before children acquire the past tense they may employ adverbs of time such as "yesterday" with present-tense verbs to express past time, saying "I do it yesterday" before "I dood it."

Bloom has provided a rare view of an intermediate stage between the one-word and the two-word stages in which the two-word construction—a new form—served only an old function. For several weeks Bloom's daughter Alison uttered two-word sentences all of which included the word "wida." Bloom tried hard to find the meaning of "wida" before realizing that it had no meaning. It was, she concluded, simply a placeholder. This case is the clearest ever reported of a new form preceding new functions. The two-word stage is an important time for practicing functions that will later have expanded forms and practicing forms that will later expand their functions.

TELEGRAPHIC SPEECH

There is no three-word stage in child language. For a few years after the end of the two-word stage children do produce rather short sentences, but the almost inviolable length constraints that characterized the first two stages have disappeared. The absence of a three-word stage has not been satisfactorily explained as yet; the answer may have to do with the fact that many basic semantic relations are binary and few are ternary. In any case a great deal is known about the sequential development in the language of the period following the two-word stage. Roger Brown of Harvard has named that language telegraphic speech. (It should be noted that there is no specific age at which a child enters any of these stages of language acquisition and further that there is no particular correlation between intelligence and speed of acquisition.)

Early telegraphic speech is characterized by short, simple sentences made up primarily of content words: words that are rich in semantic content, usually nouns and verbs. The speech is called telegraphic because the sentences lack function "words": tense endings on verbs and plural endings on nouns, prepositions, conjunctions, articles, and so on. As the telegraphic-speech stage progresses, function words are gradually added to sentences. This process has possibly been studied more thoroughly than any other in language acquisition, and a fairly predictable order in the addition of function words has been observed. The same principles that govern the order of acquisition of function words in English have been shown to operate in many other languages, including some such as Finnish and Russian, that express the same grammatical relations with particularly rich systems of noun and verb suffixes.

In English many grammatical relations are represented by a fixed word order. For example, in the sentence "The dog followed Jamie to school" it is clear it is the dog that did the following. Normal word order in English requires that the subject come before the verb, and so people who speak English recognize "the dog" as the subject of the sentence. In other languages a noun may be marked as a subject not by its position with respect to the other words in the sentence but by a noun suffix, so that in adult sentences word order may be quite flexible. Until children begin to acquire suffixes and other function words, however, they employ fixed word order to express grammatical relations no matter how flexible adult word order may be. In English the strong propensity to follow word order rigidly shows up in children's interpretations of passive sentences such as "Jamie was followed by the dog." At an early age children may interpret some passive sentences correctly, but by age three they begin to ignore the function words such as "was" and "by" in passive sentences and adopt the fixed word-order interpretation. In other words, since "Jamie" appears before the verb, Jamie is assumed to be the actor, or the noun doing the following.

FUNCTION WORDS

In spite of its grammatical dependence on word order, the English language makes use of enough function words to illustrate the basic principles that determine the order in which such words are acquired. The progressive tense ending "-ing," as in "He going," is acquired first,

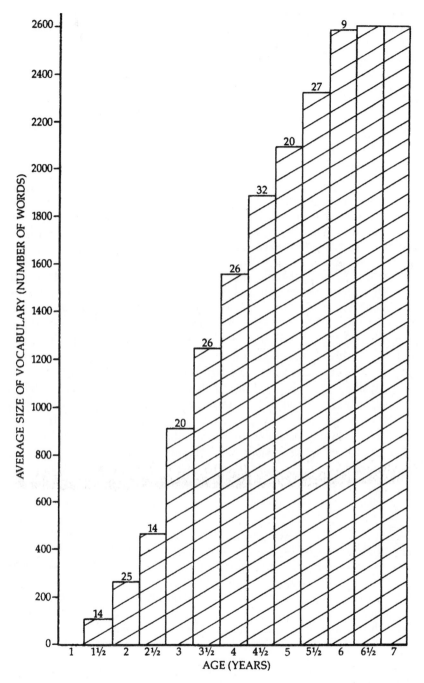

FIGURE 42.1 Children's average vocabulary size increases rapidly between the ages of one-and-a-half and six-and-a-half. The numbers over the first ten columns indicate the number of children tested in each sample age group. Data are based on work by Madorah E. Smith of the University of Hawaii.

(1) Laura (2:2) Her want some more. Her want some more candy.	(4) Andrew (2:0) Put that on. Andrew put that on.
(2) Laura (2:2) Where my tiger? Where my tiger book?	(5) Andrew (2:1) All wet. This shoe all wet.
(3) Laura (2:2) Let's dooz this. Let's do this. Let's do this puzzle.	(6) Benjy (2:3) Broke it. Broke it. Broke it I did.

TABLE 42.3   Children correct their speech in ways that reflect the improvements they are currently making on their internal grammar. For example, Laura (1–3) is increasing the length of her sentences, encoding more information by embellishing a noun phrase. Andrew (4, 5) and Benjy (6) appear to be adding subjects to familiar verb-phrase sentences.

long before the present-tense third-person singular ending "-s," as in "He goes." The "-s" itself is acquired long before the past tense endings, as in "He goed." Once again the child proves to be a sensible linguist, learning first the tense that exhibits the least variation in form. The "-ing" ending is pronounced only one way, regardless of the pronunciation of the verb to which it is attached. The verb endings "-s" and "-ed," however, vary in their pronunciation: compare "cuts (s)," "cuddles (z)," "crushes (əz)," "walked (t)," "played (d)," and "halted (əd)." (The vowel "ə," called "schwa," is pronounced like the unstressed word "a.") Furthermore, present progressive ("-ing") forms are used with greater frequency than any other tense in the speech children hear. Finally, no verb has an irregular "-ing" form, but some verbs do have irregular third-person present-tense singular forms and may have irregular past-tense forms. (The same pattern of learning earliest those forms that exhibit the least variation shows up much more dramatically in languages such as Finnish and Russian, where the paradigms of inflection are much richer.)

The past tense is acquired after the progressive and present tenses, because the relative time it represents is conceptually more difficult. The future tense ("will" and a verb) is formed regularly in English and is as predictable as the progressive tense, but it is a much more abstract concept than the past tense. Therefore it is acquired much later. In the same way the prepositions "in" and "on" appear earlier than any others, at about the same time as "-ing," but prepositions such as "behind" and "in front of," whose correct usage depends on the speaker's frame of reference, are acquired much later.

It is particularly interesting to note that there are three English morphemes that are pronounced identically but are acquired at different times. They are the plural "-s," the possessive "-s," and the third-person singular tense ending "-s," and they are acquired in the order of listing. Roman Jakobson of Harvard has suggested that the explanation of this

(7) Jamie (6:0)

Jamie:	Why are you doing that?
Mother:	What?
Jamie:	Why are you writing what I say down?
Mother:	What?
Jamie:	Why are you writing down what I say?

(8) Jamie (6:3)

Jamie:	Who do you think is the importantest kid in the world except me?
Mother:	What did you say, Jamie?
Jamie:	Who do you think is the specialest kid in the world not counting me?

(9) Jamie (6:6)

Jamie:	Who are you versing?
Mother:	What?
Jamie:	I wanted to know who he was playing against.

(10) Jamie (6:10)

Jamie:	I figured something you might like out.
Mother:	What did you say?
Jamie:	I figured out something you might like.

TABLE 42.4 Jamie (7–10) seems to be working on much more subtle refinements such as the placement of verb particles, for example the "down" of "writing down." (Each child's age at time of correction is given in years and months.) Corrections shown here were recorded by Judy S. Reilly of University of California at Los Angeles.

phenomenon has to do with the complexity of the different relations the morphemes signal: the singular-plural distinction is at the word level, the possessive relates two nouns at the phrase level, and the tense ending relates a noun and a verb at the clause level.

The forms of the verb "to be"—"is," "are," and so on—are among the last of the function words to be acquired, particularly in their present-tense forms. Past- and future-tense forms of "to be" carry tense information, of course, but present-tense forms are essentially meaningless, and omitting them is a very sensible strategy for a child who must maximize the information content of a sentence and place priorities on linguistic structures still to be tackled.

PLURALS

When there are competing pronunciations available, as in the case of the plural and past tenses, the process of sorting them out also follows a predictable pattern. Consider the acquisition of the English plural, in which six distinct stages can be observed. In English, as in many other (but not all) languages, nouns have both singular and plural forms. Children usually use the singular forms first, both in situations where the singular form would be appropriate and in situations where the plural form would be appropriate. In instances where the plural form is irregular in the adult model, however, a child may not recognize it as such and may use it in place of the singular or as a free variant of the singular. Thus in the first stage of acquisition, before either the concept of a plural or the linguistic devices for expressing a plural are acquired, a child may say "two cat" or point to "one feet."

When plurals begin to appear regularly, the child forms them according to the most general rule of English plural formation. At this point it is the child's overgeneralization of the rule, resulting in words such as "mans," "foots," or "feets," that shows she has hypothesized the rule: Add the sound /s/ or /z/ to the end of a word to make it plural. (The slashes indicate pronounced sounds, which are not to be confused with the letters used in spelling.)

For many children the overgeneralized forms of the irregular nouns are actually the earliest /s/ and /z/ plurals to appear, preceding "boys," "cats," and other regular forms by hours or days. The period of overgeneralization is considered to be the third stage in the acquisition of plurals because for many children there is an intermediate second stage in which irregular plurals such as "men" actually do appear. Concerned parents may regard the change from the second-stage "men" to the third-stage "mans" as a regression, but in reality it demonstrates progress from an individual memorized item to the application of a general rule.

In the third stage the small number of words that already end in a sound resembling /s/ or /z/, such as "house," "rose," and "bush," are used without any plural ending. Adults normally make such words plural by adding the suffix /əz/. Children usually relegate this detail to the remainder pile, to be dealt with at a later time. When they return to the problem, there is often a short fourth stage of perhaps a day, in which the child delightedly demonstrates her solution by tacking /əz/ endings indiscriminately onto nouns no matter what sound they end in and no matter how many other plural markings they may already have. A child may wake up one morning and throw herself into this stage with all the zeal of a kitten playing with its first ball of string.

Within a few days the novelty wears off and the child enters a less flamboyant fifth stage, in which only irregular plurals still deviate from the model forms. The rapid progression through the fourth stage does not mean that she suddenly focused her attention on the problem of /əz/ plurals. It is more likely that she had the problem at the back of her mind throughout the third stage. She was probably silently formulating hypotheses about the occurrence of /əz/ and testing them against the plurals she was hearing. Finding the right rule required discovering the phonological specification of the class of nouns that take /əz/ plurals.

Arriving at the sixth and final stage in the acquisition of plurals does not require the formulation of any new rules. All that is needed is the simple memorizing of irregular forms. Being rational, the child relegates such minor details to the lowest-priority remainder pile and turns her attention to more interesting linguistic questions. Hence a five-year-old may still not have entered the last stage. In fact, a child in the penultimate stage may not be at all receptive to being taught irregular plurals. For example, a child named Erica pointed to a picture of some "mouses," and her mother corrected her by saying "mice." Erica and her mother each repeated her own version two more times, and then Erica resolved the standoff by turning to a picture of "ducks." She avoided the picture of the mice for several days. Two years later, of course, Erica was perfectly able to say "mice."

NEGATIVE SENTENCES

One of the pioneering language-acquisition studies of the 1960s was undertaken at Harvard by a research group headed by Brown. The group studied the development in the language of three children over a period of several years. Two members of the group, Ursula Bellugi and Edward S. Klima, looked specifically at the changes in the children's negative sentences over the course of the project. They found that negative structures, like other subsystems of the syntactic component of grammar, are acquired in an orderly, rule-governed way.

When the project began, the forms of negative sentences the children employed were quite simple. It appeared that they had incorporated the following rule into their grammar: To make a sentence negative attach "no" or "not" to the beginning of it. On rare occasions, possibly when a child had forgotten to anticipate the negative, "no" could be attached to the end of a sentence, but negative words could not appear inside a sentence.

In the next stage the children continued to follow this rule, but they had also hypothesized and incorporated into their grammars more complex rules that allowed them to generate sentences in which the negatives "no," "not," "can't," and "don't" appeared after the subject and before the verb. These rules constituted quite an advance over attaching a negative word externally to a sentence. Furthermore, some of the primitive imperative sentences constructed at this stage began with "don't" rather than "no." On the other hand, "can't" never appeared at the beginning of a sentence, and neither "can" nor "do" appeared as an auxiliary, as they do in adult speech: "I can do it." These facts suggest that at this point "can't" and "don't" were unanalyzed negative forms rather than contractions of "cannot" and "do not," but that although "can't" and "don't" each seemed to be interchangeable with "no," they were no longer interchangeable with each other.

In the third stage of acquiring negatives many more details of the negative system had appeared in the children's speech. The main feature of the system that still remained to be worked out was the use of pronouns in negative sentences. At this stage the children said "I didn't see something" and "I don't want somebody to wake me up." The pronouns "somebody" and "something" were later replaced with "nobody" and "nothing" and ultimately with the properly concorded forms "anybody" and "anything."

Many features of telegraphic speech were still evident in the third stage. The form "is" of the verb "to be" was frequently omitted, as in "This no good." In adult speech the auxiliary "do" often functions as a dummy verb to carry tense and other markings; for example, in "I didn't see it," "do" carries the tense and the negative. In the children's speech at this stage "do" appeared occasionally, but the children had not yet figured out its entire function. Therefore in some sentences the auxiliary "do" was omitted and the negative "not" appeared alone, as in "I not hurt him." In other sentences, such as "I didn't did it," the negative auxiliary form of "do" appears to be correct but is actually an unanalyzed, memorized item; at this stage the tense is regularly marked on the main verb, which in this example happens also to be "do."

Many children acquire negatives in the same way that the children in the Harvard study did, but subsequent investigations have shown that there is more than one way to learn a language. Carol B. Lord of U.C.L.A. identified a quite different strategy employed by a two-year-old named Jennifer. From twenty-four to twenty-eight months Jennifer used "no" only as a single-word utterance. In order to produce a negative sentence she simply spoke an ordinary sentence with a higher pitch. For example, "I want put it on" spoken in a high pitch meant "I don't want to put it on." Lord noticed that many of the negative sentences adults addressed to Jennifer were spoken with an elevated pitch. Children tend to pay more attention to the beginning and ending of sentences, and in adult speech negative words usually appear in the middle of sentences. With good reason, then, Jennifer seemed to have hypothesized that one makes a sentence negative by uttering it with a higher pitch. Other children have been found to follow the same strategy. There are clearly variations in the hypotheses children make in the process of constructing grammar.

SEMANTICS

Up to this point I have mainly discussed the acquisition of syntactic rules, in part because in the years following the publication of Chomsky's *Syntactic Structures* child-language research in this area flourished. Syntactic rules, which govern the ordering of words in a sentence, are not all a child needs to know about language, however, and after the first flush of excitement over Chomsky's work investigators began to ask questions about other areas of language acquisition. Consider the development of the rules of semantics, which govern the way words are interpreted. Eve V. Clark of Stanford reexamined old diary studies and noticed

STAGE 1	STAGE 2	STAGE 3
No . . . wipe finger.	I can't catch you.	We can't make another broom.
No a boy bed.	I can't see you.	I don't want cover on it.
No singing song.	We can't talk.	I gave him some so he won't cry.
No the sun shining.	You can't dance.	No, I don't have a book.
No money.	I don't want it.	I am not a doctor.
No sit there.	I don't like him.	It's not cold.
No play that.	I don't know his name.	Don't put the two wings on.
No fall.	No pinch me.	**A**
Not . . . fit.	Book say no.	I didn't did it.
Not a teddy bear.	Touch the snow no.	You didn't caught me.
More . . . no.	This a radiator no.	I not hurt him.
Wear mitten no.	No square . . . is clown.	Ask me if I not made mistake.
	Don't bite me yet.	**B**
	Don't leave me.	Because I don't want somebody to wake me up.
	Don't wake me up . . . again.	I didn't see something.
	He not little, he big.	**C**
	That no fish school.	I isn't . . . I not sad.
	That no Mommy.	This not ice cream.
	There no squirrels.	This no good.
	He no bite you.	I not crying.
	I no want envelope.	That not turning.
	I no taste them.	He not taking the walls down.

TABLE 42.5 Three stages in acquisition of negative sentences were studied by Ursula Bellugi of the Salk Institute for Biological Studies and Edward S. Klima of the University of California at San Diego. They observed that in the first stage almost all negative sentences appear to be formulated according to the rule: Attach "no" or "not" to the beginning of a sentence to make it negative. In the second stage additional rules are postulated that allow the formation of sentences in which: "no," "not," "can't," and "don't" appear after the subject and before the verb. In the third stage several issues remain to be worked out, in particular the agreement of pronouns in negative sentences (B), the inclusion of the forms of the verb "to be" (C), and the correct use of the auxiliary "do" (A). In adult speech the auxiliary "do" often carries tense and other functional markings such as the negative; children in the third stage may replace it by "not" or use it redundantly to mark tense that is already marked on the main verb.

that the development in the meaning of words during the first several months of the one-word stage seemed to follow a basic pattern.

The first time children in the studies used a word, Clark noted, it seemed to be as a proper noun, as the name of a specific object. Almost immediately, however, the children generalized the word based on some feature of the original object and used it to refer to many other objects. For example, a child named Hildegard first used "tick-tock" as the name for her father's watch, but she quickly broadened the meaning of the word, first to include all clocks, then all watches, then a gas meter, then a firehose wound on a spool, and then a bathroom scale with a round dial. Her generalizations appear to be based on her observation of common features of shape: roundness, dials, and so on. In general the children in the diary studies overextended meanings based on similarities of movement, texture, size, and, most frequently, shape.

As the children progressed, the meanings of words were narrowed down until eventually they more or less coincided with the meanings accepted by adult speakers of the language. The narrowing-down process has not been studied intensively, but it seems likely that the process has no fixed end point. Rather it appears that the meanings of words continue to expand and contract through adulthood, long after other types of language acquisition have ceased.

One of the problems encountered in trying to understand the acquisition of semantics is that it is often difficult to determine the precise meaning a child has constructed for a word. Some interesting observations have been made, however, concerning the development of the meanings of the pairs of words that function as opposites in adult language. Margaret Donaldson and George Balfour of the University of Edinburgh asked children from three to five years old which one of two cardboard trees had "more" apples on it. They asked other children of the same age which tree had "less" apples. (Each child was interviewed individually.) Almost all the children in both groups responded by pointing to the tree with more apples on it. Moreover, the children who had been asked to point to the tree with "less" apples showed no hesitation in choosing the tree with more apples. They did not act as though they did not know the meaning of "less"; rather they acted as if they did know the meaning and "less" meant "more."

Subsequent studies have revealed similar systematic error making in the acquisition of other pairs of opposites such as "same" and "different," "big" and "little," "wide" and "narrow," and "tall" and "short." In every case the pattern of learning is the same: one word of the pair is learned first and its meaning is overextended to apply to the other word in the pair. The first word learned is always the unmarked word of the pair, that is, the word adults use when they do not want to indicate either one of the opposites. (For example, in the case of "wide" and "narrow," "wide" is the unmarked word: asking "How wide is the road?" does not suggest that the road is wide, but asking "How narrow is the road?" does suggest that the road is narrow.)

Clark observed a more intricate pattern of error production in the acquisition of the words "before" and "after." Consider the four different types of sentence represented by (1) "He jumped the gate before he patted the dog," (2) "Before he patted the dog he jumped the gate," (3) "He patted

CHILD'S LEXICAL ITEM	FIRST REFERENTS	OTHER REFERENTS IN ORDER OF OCCURRENCE	GENERAL AREA OF SEMANTIC EXTENSION
mooi	moon	cake round marks on windows writing on windows and in books round shapes in books tooling on leather book covers round postmarks letter "o"	shape
bow-wow	dog	fur piece with glass eyes father's cufflinks pearl buttons on dress bath thermometer	shape
kotibaiz	bars of cot	large toy abacus toast rack with parallel bars picture of building with columns	shape
bébé	reflection of child (self) in mirror	photograph of self all photographs all pictures all books with pictures all books	shape
vov-vov	dog	kittens hens all animals at a zoo picture of pigs dancing	shape
ass	goat with rough hide on wheels	things that move: animals, sister, wagon . . . all moving things all things with a rough surface	movement texture
tutu	train	engine moving train journey	movement
fly	fly	specks of dirt dust all small insects child's own toes crumbs of bread a toad	size
quack	ducks on water	all birds and insects all coins (after seeing an eagle on the face of a coin)	size
koko	cockerel's crowing	tunes played on a violin tunes played on a piano tunes played on an accordion tunes played on a phonograph all music merry-go-round	sound
dany	sounds of a bell	clock telephone doorbells	sound

TABLE 42.6 Children overgeneralize word meanings, using words they acquire early in place of words they have not yet acquired. Eve V. Clark of Stanford University has observed that when a word first appears in a child's lexicon, it refers to a specific object but the child quickly extends semantic domain of the word, using it to refer to many other things. Eventually meaning of the word is narrowed down until it coincides with adult usage. Clark found that children most frequently base the semantic extension of a word on the shape of its first referent.

the dog after he jumped the gate," and (4) "After he jumped the gate he patted the dog." Clark found that the way the children she observed interpreted sentences such as these could be divided into four stages.

In the first stage the children disregarded the words "before" and "after" in all four of these sentence types and assumed that the event of the first clause took place before the event of the second clause. With this order-of-mention strategy the first and fourth sentence types were interpreted correctly but the second and third sentence types were not. In the second stage sentences using "before" were interpreted correctly, but an order-of-mention strategy was still adopted for sentences that used "after." Hence sentences of the fourth type were interpreted correctly, but sentences of the third type were not. In the next stage both the third and the fourth sentence types were interpreted incorrectly, suggesting that the children had adopted the strategy that "after" actually meant "before." Finally, in the fourth stage both "before" and "after" were interpreted appropriately.

It appears, then, that in learning the meaning of a pair of words such as "more" and "less" or "before" and "after" children acquire first the part of the meaning that is common to both words and only later the part of the meaning that distinguishes the two. Linguists have not yet developed satisfactory ways of separating the components of meaning that make up a single word, but it seems clear that when such components can be identified, it will be established that, for example, "more" and "less" have a large number of components in common and differ only in a single component specifying the pole of the dimension. Beyond the studies of opposites there has been little investigation of the period of semantic acquisition that follows the early period of rampant overgeneralization. How children past the early stage learn the meanings of other kinds of words is still not well understood.

PHONOLOGY

Just as children overgeneralize word meanings and sentence structures, so do they overgeneralize sounds, using sounds they have learned in place of sounds they have not yet acquired. Just as a child may use the word "not" correctly in one sentence but instead of another negative word in a second sentence, so may she correctly contrast /p/ and /b/ at the beginnings of words but employ /p/ at the ends of words, regardless of whether the adult models end with /p/ or /b/. Children also acquire the details of the phonological system in very regular ways. The ways in which they acquire individual sounds, however, are highly idiosyncratic, and so for many years the patterns eluded diarists, who tended to look only at the order in which sounds were acquired. Jakobson made a major advance in this area by suggesting that it was not individual sounds children acquire in an orderly way but the distinctive features of sound, that is, the minimal differences, or contrasts, between sounds. In other words, when a child begins to contrast /p/ and /b/, she also begins to contrast all the other pairs of sounds that, like /p/ and /b/, differ only in the absence or presence of vocal-cord vibration. In English these pairs include /t/ and /d/, and /k/ and the hard /g/. It is the acquisition of this contrast and not of the six individual sounds that is predictable. Jakobson's extensive examination of the diary data for a wide variety of languages supported this theory. Almost all current work in phonological theory rests on the theory of distinctive features that grew out of his work.

My own recent work suggests that phonological units even more basic than the distinctive features play an important part in the early acquisition process. At an early stage, when there are relatively few words in a child's repertory, unanalyzed syllables appear to be the basic unit of the sound system. By designating these syllables as unanalyzed I mean that the child is not able to separate them into their component consonants and vowels. Only later in the acquisition process does such division into smaller units become possible. The gradual discovery of successively smaller units that can form the basis of the phonological system is an important part of the process.

At an even earlier stage, before a child has uttered any words, she is accomplishing a great deal of linguistic learning, working with a unit of phonological organization even more primitive than the syllable. That unit can be defined in terms of pitch contours. By the late babbling period children already control the intonation, or pitch modulation, contours of the language they are learning. At that stage the child sounds as if she is uttering reasonably long sentences, and adult listeners may have the impression they are not quite catching the child's words. There are no words to catch, only random strings of babbled sounds with recognizable, correctly produced question or statement intonation contours. The sounds may accidentally be similar to some of those found in adult English. These sentence-length utterances are called sentence units, and in the phonological system of the child at this stage they are comparable to the consonant-and-vowel segments, syllables, and distinctive features that appear in the phonological systems of later stages. The syllables and segments that appear when the period of word learning begins are in no way related to the vast repertory of babbling sounds. Only the intonation contours are carried over from the babbling stage into the later period.

No matter what language environment a child grows up in, the intonation contours characteristic of adult speech in that environment are the linguistic information learned earliest. Some recent studies suggest that it is possible to identify the language environment of a child from her babbling intonation during the second year of life. Other studies suggest that children can be distinguished at an even earlier age on the basis of whether or not their language environment is a tone language, that is, a language in which words spoken with different pitches are identifiable as different words, even though they may have the same sequence of consonants and vowels. To put it another way, "ma" spoken with a high pitch and "ma" spoken with a low pitch can be as different to someone speaking a tone language as "ma" and "pa" are to someone speaking English. (Many African and Asian languages are tone languages.) Tones are learned very early, and entire tone systems are mastered long before other areas of phonology. The extremely early acquisition of pitch patterns may help to explain the difficulty adults have in learning the intonation of a second language.

PHONETICS

There is one significant way in which the acquisition of phonology differs from the acquisition of other language systems. As a child is acquiring the phonological system she must also learn the phonetic realization of the system: the actual details of physiological and acoustic phonetics, which call for the coordination of a complex set of muscle movements. Some children complete the process of learning how to pronounce things earlier than others, but differences of this kind are usually not related to the learning of the phonological system. Brown had what has become a classic conversation with a child who referred to a "fis." Brown repeated "fis," and the child indignantly corrected him, saying "fis." After several such exchanges Brown tried "fish," and the child, finally satisfied, replied, "Yes, fis." It is clear that although the child was still not able to pronounce the distinction between the sounds "s" and "sh," he knew such a systematic phonological distinction existed. Such phonetic muddying of the phonological waters complicates the study of this area of acquisition. Since the child's knowledge of the phonological system may not show up in her speech, it is not easy to determine what a child knows about the system without engaging in complex experimentation and creative hypothesizing.

Children whose phonological system produces only simple words such as "mama" and "papa" actually have a greater phonetic repertory than their utterances suggest. Evidence of that repertory is found in the late babbling stage, when children are working with sentence units and are making a large array of sounds. They do not lose their phonetic ability overnight, but they must constrain it systematically. Going on to the next-higher stage of language learning, the phonological system, is more important to the child than the details of facile pronunciation. Much later, after the phonological system has been acquired, the details of pronunciation receive more attention.

In the period following the babbling period the persisting phonetic facility gets less and less exercise. The vast majority of a child's utterances fail to reflect her real ability to pronounce things accurately; they do, however, reflect her growing ability to pronounce things systematically. (For a child who grows up learning only one language the movements of the muscles of the vocal tract ultimately become so overpracticed that it is difficult to learn new pronunciations during adulthood. On the other hand, people who learn at least two languages in early childhood appear to retain a greater flexibility of the vocal musculature and are more likely to learn to speak an additional language in their adult years without the "accent" of their native language.)

In learning to pronounce, then, a child must acquire a sound system that includes the divergent systems of phonology and phonetics. The acquisition of phonology differs from that of phonetics in requiring the creation of a representation of language in the mind of the child. This representation is necessary because of the abstract nature of the units of phonological structure. From only the acoustic signal of adult language the child must derive successively more abstract phonological units: first intonations, then syllables, then distinctive features, and finally consonant-vowel segments. There are, for example, few clear segment boundaries in the acoustic signal the child receives, and so the consonant-and-vowel units could hardly be derived if the child had no internal representation of language.

At the same time that a child is building a phonological representation of language she is learning to manipulate all the phonetic variations of language, learning to produce each one precisely and automatically. The dual process of phonetics and phonology acquisition is one of the most difficult in all of language learning. Indeed, although a great deal of syntactic and semantic acquisition has yet to take place, it is usually at the completion of the process of learning to pronounce that adults consider a child to be a full-fledged language speaker and stop using any form of caretaker speech.

ABNORMAL LANGUAGE DEVELOPMENT

There seems to be little question that the human brain is best suited to language learning before puberty. Foreign languages are certainly learned most easily at that time. Furthermore, it has been observed that people who learn more than one language in childhood have an easier time learning additional languages in later years. It seems to be extremely important for a child to exercise the language-learning faculty. Children who are not exposed to any learnable language during the crucial years, for example children who are deaf before they can speak, generally grow up with the handicap of having little or no language. The handicap is unnecessary: deaf children of deaf parents who communicate by means of the American Sign Language do not grow up without language.

They live in an environment where they can make full use of their language-learning abilities, and they are reasonably fluent in sign language
by age three, right on the developmental schedule. Deaf children who
grow up communicating by means of sign language have a much easier
time learning English as a second language than deaf children in oral-
speech programs learning English as a first language.

The study of child language acquisition has made important contributions to the study of abnormal speech development. Some investigators of child language have looked at children whose language development is abnormal in the hope of finding the conditions that are
necessary and sufficient for normal development; others have looked at
the development of language in normal children in the hope of helping
children whose language development is abnormal. It now appears that
many of the severe language abnormalities found in children can in
some way be traced to interruptions of the normal acquisition process.
The improved understanding of the normal process is being exploited to
create treatment programs for children with such problems. In the past
therapeutic methods for children with language problems have emphasized the memorizing of language routines, but methods now being
developed would allow a child to work with her own language-learning
abilities. For example, the American Sign Language has been taught
successfully to several autistic children. Many of these nonverbal and
antisocial children have learned in this way to communicate with therapists, in some cases becoming more socially responsive. (Why sign
language should be so successful with some autistic children is unclear;
it may have to do with the fact that a sign lasts longer than an auditory
signal.)

There are still many questions to be answered in the various areas I
have discussed, but in general a great deal of progress has been made in
understanding child language over the past 20 years. The study of the
acquisition of language has come of age. It is now a genuinely interdisciplinary field where psychologists, neurosurgeons, and linguists work
together to penetrate the mechanisms of perception and cognition as well
as the mechanisms of language.

BIBLIOGRAPHY

Bloom, Lois. *One Word at a Time*. The Hague: Mouton, 1975.
Brown, Roger. *A First Language: The Early Stages*. Cambridge: Harvard
    University Press, 1973.
Dil, Anwar S., ed. *Language Structure and Language Use: Essays by Charles A.
    Ferguson*. Stanford: Stanford University Press, 1971.
McNeill, David. *The Acquisition of Language: The Study of Developmental
    Psycholinguistics*. New York: Harper & Row, 1970.

FOR DISCUSSION AND REVIEW

1. Moskowitz states that "children approach language learning economically, devoting their energy to broad issues before dealing with specific ones." Explain how the tables showing the development of correct noun plural forms and of correct past-tense forms of verbs support this claim.

2. What are the characteristics of "caretaker speech"? Why is its use important to children in their acquisition of language? How has the recognition of caretaker speech modified linguists' thinking about the process of language acquisition?

3. Explain how and why children in the one-word and two-word stages of language acquisition use vertical constructions. How is this linguistic strategy typical of what children do in all areas of cognitive development?

4. Children's acquisition of function words (including inflectional affixes such as noun plurals and the -*ing* and past-tense forms of verbs) in English and in other languages follows a very predictable order. Using examples from English, explain what principles govern the sequence of function-word acquisition.

5. How and why might English-speaking children use high pitch to make negative statements? What does this use of pitch reveal about how children learn grammar?

6. Discuss how children expand their semantic understanding and use of a word. What features of the referent are most important? Explain how a child might narrow down the word *lion* or *pencil*.

7. With regard to how children learn pairs of words with opposite meanings (e.g., *more* vs. *less*), explain the statement that "children acquire first the part of the meaning that is common to both words and only later the part that distinguishes the two."

8. What part of the language system do children learn first? What are some implications of this very early learning for adults who are trying to learn a new language?

9. Explain the statement that "in learning to pronounce ..., a child must acquire a sound system that includes the divergent systems of phonology and phonetics."

43

Developmental Milestones in Motor and Language Development

Eric H. Lenneberg

All normal children go through the same stages of language acquisition and motor development, although not all progress at the same rate. However, the relationship between language acquisition and sensorimotor development is not clear. Some researchers believe that some level of sensorimotor knowledge must precede language acquisition, whereas others argue that cortical maturation is the essential prerequisite for both language and motor development. The issue is whether language is an autonomous cognitive system or whether it is only one way of manifesting cognitive ability. The following chart, developed by the late Eric H. Lenneberg, originally appeared in his 1967 book Biological Foundations of Language. *It juxtaposes the stages of motor and language development typically reached by children from twelve weeks through four years of age.*

AT THE COMPLETION OF:	MOTOR DEVELOPMENT	VOCALIZATION AND LANGUAGE
12 weeks	Supports head when in prone position; weight is on elbows; hands mostly open; no grasp reflex	Markedly less crying than at 8 weeks; when talked to and nodded at, smiles, followed by squealing-gurgling sounds usually called *cooing*, which is vowel-like in character and pitch-modulated; sustains cooing for 15–20 seconds
16 weeks	Plays with rattle placed in his hands (by shaking it and staring at it), head self-supported; tonic neck reflex subsiding	Responds to human sounds more definitely; turns head; eyes seem to search for speaker; occasionally some chuckling sounds
20 weeks	Sits with props	The vowel-like cooing sounds begin to be interspersed with more consonantal sounds; labial fricatives, spirants, and nasals are common; acoustically, all vocalizations are very different from the sounds of the mature language of the environment

(continued)

AT THE COMPLETION OF:	MOTOR DEVELOPMENT	VOCALIZATION AND LANGUAGE
6 months	Sitting: bends forward and uses hands for support; can bear weight when put into standing position, but cannot yet stand with holding on; reaching: unilateral; grasp: no thumb apposition yet; releases cube when given another	Cooing changing into babbling resembling one-syllable utterances; neither vowels nor consonants have very fixed recurrences; most common utterances sound somewhat like *ma*, *mu*, *da*, or *di*
8 months	Stands holding on; grasps with thumb apposition; picks up pellet with thumb and fingertips	Reduplication (or more continuous repetitions) becomes frequent; intonation patterns become distinct; utterances can signal emphasis and emotions
10 months	Creeps efficiently; takes side steps, holding on; pulls to standing position	Vocalizations are mixed with sound-play such as gurgling or bubble-blowing; appears to wish to imitate sounds, but the imitations are never quite successful; beginning to differentiate between words heard by making differential adjustment
12 months	Walks when held by one hand; walks on feet and hands—knees in air; mouthing of objects almost stopped; seats self on floor	Identical sound sequences are replicated with higher relative frequency of occurrence and words (*mamma* or *dadda*) are emerging; definite signs of understanding some words and simple commands (show me your eyes)
18 months	Grasp, prehension, and release fully developed; gait stiff, propulsive, and precipitated; sits on child's chair with only fair aim; creeps downstairs backward; has difficulty building tower of three cubes	Has a definite repertoire of words—more than three, but fewer than fifty; still much babbling but now of several syllables with intricate intonation pattern; no attempt at communicating information and no frustration for not being understood; words may include items such as *thank you* or *come here*, but there is little ability to join any of the lexical items into spontaneous two-item phrases; understanding is progressing rapidly
24 months	Runs, but falls in sudden turns; can quickly alternate between sitting and stance; walks stairs up or down, one foot forward only	Vocabulary of more than 50 items (some children seem to be able to name everything in the environment); begins spontaneously to join vocabulary items into two-word phrases; all phrases appear to be own creations; definite increase in communicative behavior and interest in language

(continued)

AT THE COMPLETION OF:	MOTOR DEVELOPMENT	VOCALIZATION AND LANGUAGE
30 months	Jumps up into air with both feet; stands on one foot for about two seconds; takes few steps on tiptoe; jumps from chair; good hand and finger coordination; can move digits independently; manipulation of objects much improved; builds tower of six cubes	Fastest increase in vocabulary with many additions every day; no babbling at all; utterances have communicative intent; frustrated if not understood by adults; utterances consist of at least two words, many have three or even five words; sentences and phrases have characteristic child grammar, that is, they are rarely verbatim repetitions of an adult utterance; intelligibility is not very good yet, though there is great variation among children; seems to understand everything that is said to him
3 years	Tiptoes three yards; runs smoothly with acceleration and deceleration; negotiates sharp and fast curves without difficulty; walks stairs by alternating feet; jumps 12 inches; can operate tricycle	Vocabulary of some 1000 words; about 80% of utterances are intelligible even to strangers; grammatical complexity of utterances is roughly that of colloquial adult language, although mistakes still occur
4 years	Jumps over rope; hops on dominant foot; catches ball in arms; walks line	Language is well-established; deviations from adult norm tend to be more in style than in grammar

FOR DISCUSSION AND REVIEW

1. According to Lenneberg's table, do motor and language development seem to progress at similar rates—that is, do children develop more rapidly in one area than in the other?

2. Jean Piaget has argued that children acquire meanings as an extension of sensorimotor intelligence and that the development of vocabulary categories, for example, depends on motor development (things can be "graspable" or "suckable"). Thus, abilities in different areas (e.g., motor skills and language) that appear at the same age should be similar because they are based on the same cognitive knowledge. Can you support or refute this argument on the basis of Lenneberg's table? If you need additional information, describe the kind(s) of data you would want to have.

44

How Children Learn Words

George A. Miller and Patricia M. Gildea

In looking at how children learn words, we find that we do not teach them as many words, or as much language overall, as we think we do. In fact, children have the remarkable ability to learn many more words than they are actually taught. This well-known selection first appeared in Scientific American *in October 1987. Here psychology professor George A. Miller, emeritus of Princeton University, and social scientist Patricia M. Gildea, a professor at Rutgers University, examine how children learn new words. They suggest that the process has two stages, and they discuss children's tendency to "overextend" meaning as new words are acquired. Miller and Gildea also evaluate the various strategies for teaching new words—through reading, dictionary exercises, social interaction, and computer technology.*

Listening to a child who is just learning to talk, one is most aware of the child's limited command of the language. What one tends to overlook is the sheer magnitude of the child's achievement. Simply learning the vocabulary is an enormous undertaking. The fact is that for many years after starting to talk a child learns new words at a rate of more than ten per day! Yet little is known about how children do it. Certainly they do not do it by memorizing dictionary entries. Our findings and those of other workers suggest that formal efforts to build vocabulary by sending children to the dictionary are less effective than most parents and teachers believe. We are exploring the possibility that a computer program providing lexical information about new words encountered in the context of a story might be more effective.

When adults set out to learn a new language, they know what is in store. They realize they will have to learn a new pronunciation, a new grammar, a new vocabulary, and a new style of using language. They know they will have to spend many hours every day for years before they can call themselves fluent in the new language. They also know, however, that they will be able to rely on teachers to explain, in their first language, everything they need to learn about the second language.

How different it is for infants. Having no language, they cannot be told what they need to learn. Yet by the age of three they will have mastered the basic structure of their native language and will be well on their way to communicative competence. Acquiring their first language is the most impressive intellectual feat many people will ever perform.

Students of how children learn language generally agree that the most remarkable aspect of this feat is the rapid acquisition of grammar. Nevertheless, the ability of children to conform to grammatical rules is only slightly more wonderful than their ability to learn new words.

How many words must one know in order to use English effectively? The answer depends on several variables, including the definition of "word." For the purpose of counting, a word can be defined as the kind of lexical unit a person has to learn; all the derivative and compound forms that are merely morphological variations on the conceptual theme would not be counted as separate words. For example, *write* is a word and its morphological variants (*writes, writ, wrote, written, writing, writer,* and so on) are relatives in the same family. If such a family is counted as a single word and knowing a word is defined as being able to recognize which of four definitions is closest to the meaning, the reading vocabulary of the average high school graduate should consist of about 40,000 words. If all the proper names of people and places and all the idiomatic expressions are also counted as words, that estimate would have to be doubled.

This figure says something about the ability of children to learn words. If the average high school graduate is 17 years old, the 80,000 words must have been learned over a period of 16 years. Hence the average child learns at the rate of 5,000 words per year, or about 13 per day. Children with large vocabularies probably pick up new words at twice that rate. Clearly, a learning process of great complexity goes on at a rapid rate in every normal child.

No one teaches children 13 or more words a day. Children must have a special talent for this kind of learning. Some valuable hints as to how they do it were uncovered a decade ago by Susan Carey and Elsa J. Bartlett, who were then at Rockefeller University. They worked with the names of colors. First they established that a group of three-year-olds did not know the color olive. Most of the children called it green and some of them called it brown.

Carey and Bartlett taught the children a nonsense name for olive—a name they would not have heard anywhere else. They took two cafeteria trays and painted one tray olive and the other blue. Each child was then told casually, "Hand me the chromium tray. Not the blue one, the chromium one." The child would pause and perhaps point to the olive tray. "This one?" "Yes, that one. Thank you."

A week later, with no further guidance, the children were again asked to name the colors. When olive was presented, they paused. They did not remember *chromium*, but now they knew that this color was not called green or brown. A single exposure was enough to begin a reorganization of their color lexicon.

This simple experiment demonstrated some important points about how children learn words. First, in order to learn a word a child must be able to associate its sound with its meaning. Mastering the mechanics of uttering and recognizing a word and mastering the concept that it expresses are separate learning processes. After their experience with the trays the children knew that olive has a special name—that it is not called green or brown—but they did not remember the particular spoken sound associated with that perceived color. Many repetitions may be necessary before the sound of a new word becomes familiar.

Second, a child's appreciation of the meaning of a word seems to grow in two stages, one rapid and the other much slower. Children are quick to notice new words and to assign them to broad semantic categories. After hearing *chromium* just once the three-year-olds assigned it to the semantic field of color names. Children are able to keep such fields separate even before they know what the individual words mean. Asked the color of something, they may respond with almost any color term at random, but they never answer *round* or *five* or *lunch.*

The slow stage entails working out the distinctions among words within a semantic category. A child who has correctly assigned *red, green, yellow,* and *blue* to the semantic field of color terms still has to learn the differences between and relations among those words. This stage ordinarily takes much longer than the first and may never be completely finished; some adults, for example, correctly assign *delphinium* and *calceolaria* to the semantic field of flowering-plant names but have not learned what plants the words denote and cannot identify the flowers on sight. At any given time many words will be in this intermediate state in which they are known and categorized but still not distinguished from one another.

A related aspect of word learning by preschoolers that has attracted wide attention is called overextension. For example, a small child learning the word *apple* may apply it to a tomato. *Apple* is thought to mean, say, round, red, and of a certain size; without further qualification those attributes define ripe tomatoes as well as ripe apples. Overextension can occur when a child's conception of a word's meaning is incomplete.

The opposite error also occurs, but it is revealed only by special questioning. For example, a child who thinks that being round, red, and of a certain size defines *apple* might fail to use *apple* to refer to green or yellow apples. The only way to identify such an underextension is to show the child green or yellow apples and ask what they are called.

The ability of preschoolers to soak up words has attracted increasing attention in recent years. Much more is known about it than was known when Carey and Bartlett did their pioneering study with color names. The word-learning process becomes even more complex, however, during the school years.

In the early grades schoolchildren are expected to learn to read and write. At first they read and write familiar words they have already learned by means of conversation. In about the fourth grade they begin to see written words they have not heard in conversation. At this point it is generally assumed that something special must be done to teach children these unfamiliar words.

This educational assumption runs into serious problems. Although children can recognize that they have not seen a word before, learning it well enough to use it correctly and to recognize it automatically is a slow process. Indeed, learning a new word entails so much conceptual clarification and phonological drill that there simply is not enough classroom time to teach more than 100 or 200 words a year in this way. Since learning runs so far ahead of teaching—some 5,000 words learned in a year compared with 200 taught—it is hard to avoid the question: How do schoolchildren learn so much more than they are taught?

Many words are acquired through reading. Children learn words at school in the same way as they do at home: by observing how the words are used in intelligible contexts. The difference is that the academic environment depends more on written contexts. Both public opinion and scientific evidence are converging on the view that the best way to facilitate vocabulary growth in schoolchildren is to have them read as much as possible.

Learning words by reading them in context is effective but not efficient. Some contexts are uninformative, others misleading. If the word in question expresses an unfamiliar concept, a single context of use will seldom support more than one hypothesis about the word's meaning. In order for reading to have any substantial effect on vocabulary a great deal of reading must be done.

How much? A child who spent fifty minutes of every school day reading at, say, 200 words per minute would read one million words in a 100-day school year. A million running words of English prose would typically contain no more than 50,000 distinct word types, representing roughly 10,000 word families. Schoolbooks would probably contain fewer different words. Even among 10,000 different words, it is unlikely that more than 1,000 would be totally new lexical items. Since multiple encounters are required in order to learn a new word, it is clear that reading one million words per year is not enough. In order to account for a growth rate of 5,000 words in a year it seems necessary to think about continued learning from conversational interactions supplemented by reading several million words per year. Indeed, children who read little outside the classroom generally do poorly on vocabulary tests.

The fact that children learn many more words than anyone has time to teach them also carries implications for the role of teachers in this learning process. Learning new words from purely literary contexts of use—from the contexts provided on the printed page—is harder than learning them through interaction with a person. In conversation it is usually possible to ask the speaker what an unfamiliar word means. Moreover, in most conversations visual information supplements the linguistic information. Such help is missing from the printed page.

Given this additional difficulty, it seems reasonable to ask teachers to help children to be more efficient in learning new words from context. If they cannot teach all the words children need to know, perhaps teachers could help their students learn how to work out such things for themselves.

One way to figure out what an unfamiliar word means is to use a dictionary. In about the fourth grade, therefore, most schools begin to teach dictionary skills: spelling, alphabetizing, pronunciation, parts of speech, and a little morphology and etymology. The idea, which is perfectly reasonable, is that children should learn how to find unfamiliar words in a dictionary and how to understand what they read there.

One trouble with this approach is that most healthy, right-minded children have a strong aversion to dictionaries. There may be good reason. We have looked at some of the tasks teachers assign in order to get students to use dictionaries. In our opinion these exercises do not merit the faith that teachers and parents have in them.

Two tasks are often assigned when children are being taught how to use a dictionary. One task entails disambiguation: the child is given a sentence that contains an ambiguous word—a word with two or more senses—and told to find it in the dictionary and to decide which sense the author of the sentence had in mind. The other task calls for production: the child is given a word and told to look it up in the dictionary and to write a sentence incorporating it. On the face of it both tasks look as though they should be instructive. It is therefore surprising to discover how ineffectual they are.

Learning from a dictionary requires considerable sophistication. Interrupting your reading to find an unfamiliar word in an alphabetical list, all the while keeping the original context in mind so that you can compare it with the alternative senses given in the dictionary, then selecting the sense that is most appropriate in the original context—that is a high-level cognitive task. It should not be surprising that children are not good at it. Even when most of the complications are removed, children are still not good at it. On a simplified disambiguation task, in which fourth-grade students were given just two senses and asked to choose the one that was intended in a particular sentence, the students did little better than chance.

The second task, producing a sentence incorporating a new word, has the virtue of requiring the student to use the word and so, presumably, to think about its meaning. We have studied this production task extensively. After reading several thousand sentences that were written by children in the fifth and sixth grades we have concluded that it too is a waste of time.

Typical of the curious sentences we encountered was "Mrs. Morrow stimulated the soup." It illustrates the most frequent kind of error made by children in that age range. If they already know the word, their sentences are usually all right. If the word is unfamiliar, however, the results are often mystifying. In order to understand what the child did, you have to read carefully the same dictionary definitions the child read. The child who looked up *stimulate* found *stir up* among the definitions.

The example provides a key to what happens when children consult a dictionary. They find the unfamiliar word and then look for a familiar word or phrase among the definitions. Next they compose a sentence using the familiar word or phrase and substitute the new word for it. One of our favorite examples came from a fifth-grader who looked up the unfamiliar word *erode*, found the familiar phrases *eat out* and *eat away* in the definition, and thought of the sentence "Our family eats out a lot." She then substituted *erode* for *eats out*; the resulting sentence was "Our family erodes a lot."

If children are so good at learning new words when they hear or see them used in context, why do they have trouble learning new words when they see them in a dictionary? We decided to look more closely at what goes on when an unfamiliar word is encountered in the context of a typical sentence. A preliminary study indicated that children can write better sentences when they are given a model sentence employing the word than when they are given a definition of the word. Since many of the sentences they wrote were patterned on the models, this result could not be interpreted to mean that the children learned more about the meaning of a word from illustrative sentences than they learned from definitions. Nevertheless, the observation was encouraging, and we pressed on.

The next step was simple: if one example is good, three should be better. When we made this comparison, however, we found that the number of examples made little difference. The acceptability ratings of sentences written after seeing one model sentence were the same as the ratings of sentences written on the basis of three examples.

That observation made us think again about what was going on. Apparently three unrelated sentences are hard for children to integrate, and so they simply focus on one of three examples and ignore the others. This behavior resembles what children do in reading dictionary definitions.

We were surprised by one result, although perhaps in retrospect we should have expected it. Mistakes resembling simple substitutions appeared even when model sentences were given instead of dictionary definitions. For example, given the model sentence "The king's brother tried to usurp the throne" to define the unfamiliar word *usurp*, the children wrote such sentences as "The blue chair was usurped from the room," "Don't try to usurp that tape from the store," "The thief tried to usurp the money from the safe," and so on. They had gathered from the model sentence that *usurp* means *take*, and so they composed sentences using *take* and then substituted *usurp* for it.

Children can appreciate at least part of the meaning of an unfamiliar word from its context, as in the case of *take* as one component of the meaning of *usurp*. Just as younger children may overextend *apple* because they know only part of its meaning, so this partial definition of *usurp* resulted in its being overextended. That is to say, if *usurp* is incompletely defined as *take*, it can be said of anything takable: chairs, tape, money, or whatever. When it is seen from this perspective, the behavior of these children in the fifth and sixth grades is merely a later stage in the development of a word-learning process employed by preschool children.

The substitution strategy therefore seems to be quite general. In the context of a model sentence, however, something more than a simple substitution error appears. The children cannot search through an illustrative sentence for a familiar word as they could in a dictionary definition. First they must abstract a familiar concept from the context of the unfamiliar word. Only then can they apply the substitution rule.

Might there be a better way to foster the growth of vocabulary? What we and others have found out about the word-learning process will support some plausible suggestions. Put at the front of your mind the idea that a teacher's best friend in this endeavor is the student's motivation to discover meaning in linguistic messages. Then the problems with the traditional modes of instruction will begin to make sense. Drill on arbitrarily preselected lists of words seldom takes place at a time when the student feels a need to know those words; it fails to draw on the natural motivation for learning the associations between word and meaning. Learning through reading faces the opposite problem; not enough information about the word is available at the moment the student is motivated to learn its meaning.

What is needed is reading, which can make students curious about unfamiliar words, supplemented by immediate information about the meaning and use of those words. The important thing is to provide the information while the reader still wants it. Dictionaries are too slow. Recourse to a dictionary may help a mature and well-motivated student, but for the average child in the elementary grades it is likely to compound interruption with misunderstood information. A human tutor— someone immediately available to detect and resolve lexical misunderstandings—would be much better than a dictionary.

Given the shortage of attentive tutors to sit at every young reader's elbow, it is natural to wonder how much of the tutoring task might be carried out by a suitably programmed computer. For example, suppose reading material was presented to the student by a computer that had been programmed to answer questions about the meanings of all the words in the material. No alphabetical search would be needed: the student would simply point to a word and information about it would appear. No sophisticated disambiguation would be necessary: the computer would know in advance which particular sense of a word was appropriate in the context. Indeed, no definition would be necessary: the phrase or sentence containing the word could be rephrased to show what the word meant in the context.

As a case in point, imagine what such a computer might do with *erode* and *usurp*. It might present a text containing the sentence

"The president's popularity was eroded by his bad relations with Congress." If the student asked for information about *erode*, the computer might state: "Things can erode; when soil is eroded by rain or wind, it breaks up and so is slowly destroyed and removed. Someone's power or authority can erode too, being slowly destroyed or removed by unfavorable developments. That kind of erosion is meant in the sentence about the president."

Suppose that for *usurp* the computer presented a text containing the sentence "The king's brother failed in his effort to usurp the throne." Asked for information, the computer might say: "When you usurp a title, job, or position from someone else, you seize it or take it away even though you have no right to it. In the sentence about the king's brother, *throne* means not just the piece of furniture the king sits on; it also stands as a symbol of the king's authority."

Providing such explanations almost instantly is well within the range of currently available computer technology. It is even possible to add a voice that pronounces the target word and explains it, or to show pictures indicating what the word denotes in the context.

We are exploring some of these possibilities with a setup in which children in the fifth and sixth grades interact with a video display. They are asked to read a text that describes an episode from a motion picture they have just seen. Included in the text are certain marked words the reader is expected to learn. When one of them comes up, the child can ask for information about its meaning in any or all of three forms: definitions, sentences, and pictures.

For some children illustrative sentences are more informative than definitions or pictures. When such children are given a definition, they read it and quickly return to the story. When they are given a sentence that is relevant to the story and uses the word in the same context, they interpret it as a puzzle to be solved. They spend more time thinking about the meaning of the word and remember it better a week later.

We found that providing information when it is wanted can significantly improve the children's grasp of unfamiliar words, as is demonstrated by their ability to recognize the meanings and to write acceptable sentences incorporating the words. The results reinforce our belief that much can be done with computers to make learning words easier.

=

FOR DISCUSSION AND REVIEW

1. At the beginning of the article, the authors suggest that we compare how we learned or were taught words as a child with how we learn new words now. What early memories can you recall of learning or being taught new words? Compare your memories to those of your classmates.

2. What early word-learning processes were demonstrated by Carey and Bartlett? Do you use these processes now?

3. Miller and Gildea suggest that as children learn new words, they pass through two stages of development. What are these stages, and how would you describe them? Are these stages limited to early language acquisition, or do you think they apply to you today?

4. What is meant by the term "overextension"? Describe some instances of a young child overextending the meaning of a word. When, if at all, have you used overextension to figure out meaning?

5. Psycholinguists and others have observed that children learn much more language than they are taught. What explanations can you offer for this phenomenon? What theories of language do your explanations support?

6. Miller and Gildea suggest that children learn new words by reading them in context, through social interaction, and by using dictionaries. What difficulties are associated with using textual context and dictionaries for word learning? Why is it easier to learn words through social interaction?

7. How might contemporary technologies alleviate some of the problems children have in learning new words?

45

The Development of Language in Genie: A Case of Language Acquisition beyond the "Critical Period"

Victoria Fromkin, Stephen Krashen, Susan Curtiss,
David Rigler, and Marilyn Rigler

UCLA linguistics professor Victoria Fromkin (1923–2000) was a prominent researcher in psycholinguistics, with particular interest in language and the brain. In this selection, Fromkin and her colleagues describe the tragic case of Genie, a girl who experienced extreme neglect and isolation for most of her childhood. They also discuss in detail the impact such isolation had on her linguistic development. From the age of twenty months to age fourteen, Genie was kept in a small, dark room, neglected physically and emotionally. After her discovery in 1970 and continuing until 1979, Genie's linguistic development was observed regularly. As a result, researchers increased their understanding of many aspects of language acquisition, cognitive development, and brain lateralization.

When this article first appeared, in Brain and Language *in 1974, the authors were guardedly optimistic about the possibility of Genie's continued linguistic advancement. By 1979, however, her language progress had clearly slowed, and an earlier prediction of dysphasia was deemed to be correct. Nevertheless, Genie's cognitive development continued to advance, and she could communicate effectively using a variety of nonverbal techniques, including her own drawings. Because of their work with Genie, Victoria Fromkin and Susan Curtiss went on to examine normal language development in those with other types of cognitive impairments. As Maya Pines concludes in her postscript, "the ordeal of an abused child may help us understand some of the most puzzling but important aspects of our humanity."*

Notes: The research reported on in this paper was supported in part by a grant from the National Institutes of Mental Health, U.S. Department of Health, Education and Welfare, No. MH-21191-03.

This is a combined and expanded version of a number of papers presented before the American Psychological Association, the Linguistic Society of America, the Acoustical Society of America, and the American Speech and Hearing Association, including S. Curtiss (1972); Curtiss et al. (1972, 1973); Krashen et al. (1972a, 1972b); Fromkin (1972); D. Rigler (1972).

Genie, the subject of this study, is an adolescent girl who for most of her life underwent a degree of social isolation and experiential deprivation not previously reported in contemporary scientific history. It is a unique case because the other children reported on in contemporary literature were isolated for much shorter periods and emerged from their isolation at much younger ages than did Genie. The only studies of children isolated for periods of time somewhat comparable to that of this case are those of Victor (Itard 1962) and Kaspar Hauser (Singh and Zingg 1966).

All cases of such children reveal that experiential deprivation results in a retarded state of development. An important question for scientists of many disciplines is whether a child so deprived can "catch up" wholly or in part. The answer to this question depends on many factors including the developmental state achieved prior to deprivation, the duration, quality, and intensity of the deprivation, and the early biological adequacy of the isolated child. In addition, the ability of such "recuperation" is closely tied to whether there is a "critical period" beyond which learning cannot take place. The concept of a "critical period" during which certain innately determined faculties can develop derived from experimental embryology. It is hypothesized that should the necessary internal or external conditions be absent during this period, certain developmental abilities will be impossible.

Lenneberg (1967) presents the most specific statement about critical periods in humans as it concerns the acquisition of language. He starts with the assumption that language is innately determined, that its acquisition is dependent upon both necessary neurological events and some unspecified minimal exposure to language. He suggests that this critical period lasts from about age two to puberty: language acquisition is impossible before two due to maturational factors, and after puberty because of the loss of "cerebral plasticity" caused by the completion of the development of cerebral dominance, or lateralized specialization of the language function.

The case of Genie is directly related to this question, since Genie was already pubescent at the time of her discovery, and it is to this question that the discussion is primarily directed. The case also has relevance for other linguistic questions such as those concerning distinctions between the comprehension and production of language, between linguistic competence and performance, and between cognition and language.

There are many questions for which we still have no answers. Some we may never have. Others must await the future developments of this remarkable child. The case history as presented is therefore an interim report.

CASE HISTORY

Genie was first encountered when she was thirteen years, nine months. At the time of her discovery and hospitalization she was an unsocialized, primitive human being, emotionally disturbed, unlearned, and without language. She had been taken into protective custody by the police and, on November 4, 1970, was admitted into the Children's Hospital of Los Angeles for evaluation with a tentative diagnosis of severe malnutrition. She remained in the Rehabilitation Center of the hospital until August 13, 1971. At that time she entered a foster home, where she has been living ever since as a member of the family.

When admitted to the hospital, Genie was a painfully thin child with a distended abdomen who appeared to be six or seven years younger than her age. She was 54.5 inches tall and weighed 62.25 pounds. She was unable to stand erect, could not chew solid or even semisolid foods, had great difficulty in swallowing, was incontinent of feces and urine, and was mute.

The tragic and bizarre story which was uncovered revealed that for most of her life Genie had suffered physical and social restriction, nutritional neglect, and extreme experiential deprivation. There is evidence that from about the age of twenty months until shortly before admission to the hospital Genie had been isolated in a small closed room, tied into a potty chair where she remained most or all hours of the day, sometimes overnight. A cloth harness, constructed to keep her from handling her feces, was her only apparel of wear. When not strapped into the chair she was kept in a covered infant crib, also confined from the waist down. The door to the room was kept closed and the windows were curtained. She was hurriedly fed (only cereal and baby food) and minimally cared for by her mother, who was almost blind during most of the years of Genie's isolation. There was no radio or TV in the house and the father's intolerance of noise of any kind kept any acoustic stimuli which she received behind the closed door to a minimum. (The first child born to this family died from pneumonia when three months old after being put in the garage because of noisy crying.) Genie was physically punished by the father if she made any sounds. According to the mother, the father and older brother never spoke to Genie although they barked at her like dogs. The mother was forbidden to spend more than a few minutes with Genie during feeding.

It is not the purpose of this paper to attempt to explain the psychotic behavior of the parents which created this tragic life for Genie, nor to relate the circumstances which led to the discovery. (See Hansen 1972; D. Rigler 1972.) It is reported that Genie's father regarded her as a hopelessly retarded child who was destined to die at a young age and convinced the mother of this. His prediction was based at least in part on Genie's failure to walk at a normal age. Genie was born with a congenital dislocation of the hips which was treated in the first year by the application of a Frejka pillow splint to hold both legs in abduction, and the father placed the blame for her "retardation" on this device.

On the basis of what is known about the early history, and what has been observed so far, it appears that Genie was normal at the time of birth and that the retardation observed at the time of discovery was due principally to the extreme isolation to which she was subjected, with its accompanying social, perceptual, and sensory deprivation. Very little evidence exists to support a diagnosis of early brain damage, primary mental deficiency, or infantile autism. On the other hand, there is abundant evidence of gross environmental impoverishment and of psychopathological behavior on the part of the parents. This is revealed to some extent in Genie's history and equally by the dramatic changes that have occurred since her emergence. (See D. Rigler 1972; M. Rigler 1972.)

Genie's birth was relatively normal. She was born in April 1957, delivered by Caesarian section. Her birth problems included an Rh negative incompatibility for which she was exchange transfused (no sequelae were noted), and the hip dislocation spoken of above. Genie's development was otherwise initially normal. At birth she weighed 7 pounds, 7.5 ounces. By three months she had gained 4.5 pounds. According to the pediatrician's report, at six months she was doing well and taking food well. At eleven months she was still within normal limits. At fourteen months Genie developed an acute illness and was seen by another pediatrician. The only other medical visit occurred when Genie was just over 3.5 years of age.

From the meager medical records at our disposal, then, there is no indication of early retardation. After admission to the hospital, Genie underwent a number of medical diagnostic tests. Radiology reported a "moderate coxa valga deformity of both hips and a narrow rib cage" but no abnormality of the skull. The bone age was reported as approximately eleven years. Simple metabolic disorders were ruled out. The neurologist found no evidence of neurological disease. The electroencephalographic records reported a "normal waking record." A chromosomal analysis was summarized as being "apparently normal."

During the first few months of her hospitalization additional consultations were undertaken. The conclusion from among all of these evaluative efforts may be summarized briefly. Functionally Genie was an extremely retarded child, but her behavior was unlike that of other mentally defective children. Neither, apparently, was she autistic. Although emotionally disturbed behavior was evident there was no discernible evidence of physical or mental disease that would otherwise account for her retarded behavior. It therefore seems plausible to explain her retardation as due to the intensity and duration of her psychosocial and physical deprivation.

The dramatic changes that have occurred since Genie's emergence reinforce this conclusion. Approximately four weeks after her admission to the hospital a consultant described a contrast between her admission status and what he later observed (Shurley, personal communication). He wrote that on admission Genie

> was pale, thin, ghost-like, apathetic, mute, and socially unresponsive. But now she had become alert, bright-eyed, engaged readily in simple social play with balloons, flashlight, and toys, with familiar and unfamiliar adults. . . . She exhibits a lively curiosity, good eye–hand coordination, adequate hearing and vision, and emotional responsivity. . . . She reveals much stimulus hunger. . . . Despite her muteness . . . Genie does not otherwise use autistic defenses, but has ample latent affect and

responses. There is no obvious evidence of cerebral damage or intellectual stenosis—only severe (extreme) and prolonged experiential, social,
and sensory isolation and deprivation during her infancy and childhood . . . Genie may be regarded as one of the most extreme and prolonged cases of such deprivation to come to light in this century, and as
such she is an "experiment in nature."

GENIE'S LINGUISTIC DEVELOPMENT

Important elements in Genie's history are still unknown and may
never be known. We have no reliable information about early linguistic
developments or even the extent of language input. One version has it
that Genie began to speak words prior to her isolation and then ceased.
Another is that she simply never acquired language at all beyond the
level observed on hospital entry. One thing is definite: when Genie was
discovered she did not speak. On the day after admission to the hospital
she was seen by Dr. James Kent who reports (Kent 1972):

> Throughout this period she retained saliva and frequently spit it out into
> a paper towel or into her pajama top. *She made no other sounds except
> for a kind of throaty whimper.* . . . (Later in the session) . . . she imitated
> "back" several times, as well as "fall" when I said "The puppet will
> fall." . . . She could communicate (her) needs nonverbally, at least to a
> limited extent. . . . Apart from a peculiar laugh, frustration was the only
> other clear affective behavior we could discern. . . . When very angry she
> would scratch at her own face, blow her nose violently into her clothes
> and often void urine. During these tantrums *there was no vocalization.*
> . . . We felt that the eerie silence that accompanied these reactions was
> probably due to the fact that she had been whipped by her father when
> she made noise.

At the outset of our linguistic observations, it was not clear whether
Genie's inability to talk was the result solely of physiological and/or emotional factors. We were unable to determine the extent of her language
comprehension during the early periods. Within a few days she began to
respond to the speech of others and also to imitate single words. Her
responses did not however reveal how heavily she was dependent on
nonverbal, extralinguistic cues such as "tone of voice, gestures, hints,
guidance, facial and bodily expressions" (Bellugi and Klima 1971). To
determine the extent of her language comprehension it was necessary to
devise tests in which all extralinguistic cues were eliminated.[1] If the comprehension tests administered showed that Genie did comprehend what
was said to her, using linguistic information alone, we could assume that
she had some knowledge of English, or had acquired some linguistic
"competence." In that case, the task facing Genie would not be one of

---

[1] The tests were designed, administered, and analyzed by S. Curtiss.

language learning but of learning how to use that knowledge—adding a performance modality—to produce speech. If the tests, on the other hand, in addition to her inability to speak, showed that she had little ability to understand what was said to her when all extralinguistic cues were eliminated, she would be faced with true first-language acquisition.

LINGUISTIC COMPREHENSION

The administration of the comprehension tests which we constructed had to wait until Genie was willing and able to cooperate. It was necessary to develop tests which would not require verbal responses since it was her comprehension not her active production of speech to be tested at this stage. The first controlled test was administered in September 1971, almost eleven months after Genie's emergence. Prior to these tests Genie revealed a growing ability to understand and produce individual words and names. This ability was a necessary precursor to an investigation of her comprehension of grammatical structure, but did not in itself reveal how much language she knew since the ability to relate the sounds and meanings of individual lexical items, while necessary, is not a sufficient criterion for language competence.

It was quite evident that at the beginning of the testing period Genie could understand individual words which she did not utter herself, but, except for such words, she had little if any comprehension of grammatical structures. Genie was thus faced with the complex task of primary language acquisition with a postpubescent brain. There was no way that a prediction could be made as to whether she could or would accomplish this task. Furthermore, if she did not learn language it would be impossible to determine the reasons. One cannot draw conclusions about children of this kind who fail to develop. One can, however, draw at least some conclusions from the fact that Genie has been acquiring language at this late age. The evidence for this fact is revealed in the results of the seventeen different comprehension tests which have been administered almost weekly over the last two years. A slow but steady development is taking place. We are still, of course, unable to predict how much of the adult grammar she will acquire.

Among the grammatical structures that Genie now comprehends are singular-plural contrasts of nouns, negative-affirmative sentence distinctions, possessive constructions, modifications, a number of prepositions (including *under, next to, beside, over,* and probably *on* and *in*), conjunction with *and,* and the comparative and superlative forms of adjectives. (For further details on the comprehension tests, see Curtiss et al. 1973.)

The comprehension tests which are now regularly administered were designed by Susan Curtiss, who has been most directly involved in the research of Genie's linguistic development. (New tests are constantly being added.) The nouns, verbs, and adjectives used in all of the tests are used by Genie in her own utterances (see below for discussion on Genie's spontaneous speech production). The response required was primarily a "pointing" response. Genie was familiar with this gesture prior to the onset of testing. One example can illustrate the kinds of tests and the procedures used.

To test Genie's singular/plural distinction in nouns, pairs of pictures are used—a single object on one picture, three of the identical objects on the other. The test sentences differ only by absence or presence of plural markers on the nouns. Genie is asked to point to the appropriate picture. The words used are: balloon(s), pail(s), turtle(s), nose(s), horse(s), dish(es), pot(s), boat(s). Until July 1972, the responses were no better than chance. Since July 1972, Genie gives 100 percent correct responses. It is important to note that at the time when she was not responding correctly to the linguistically marked distinction, she could appropriately use and understand utterances including numbers ("one," "two," "three," etc.) and "many," "more," and "lots of."

SPEECH PRODUCTION AND PHONOLOGICAL DEVELOPMENT

Genie's ability to comprehend spoken language is a better indication of her linguistic competence than is her production of speech because of the physical difficulties Genie has in speaking. At the age when normal children are learning the necessary neuromuscular controls over their vocal organs to enable them to produce the sounds of language, Genie was learning to repress any and all sounds because of the physical punishment which accompanied any sounds produced. This can explain why her earliest imitative and spontaneous utterances were often produced as silent articulations or whispered. Her inability to control the laryngeal mechanisms involved in speech resulted in monotonic speech. Her whole body tensed as she struggled to speak, revealing the difficulties she had in the control of air volume and air flow. The intensity of the acoustic signal produced was very low. The strange voice quality of her vocalized utterances is at least partially explainable in reference to these problems.

Because of her speech difficulties, one cannot assess her language competence by her productive utterances alone. But despite the problems which still remain, there has been dramatic improvement in Genie's speech production. Her supraglottal articulations have been more or less normal, and her phonological development does not deviate sharply from that observed in normal children. In addition, she is beginning, both in imitations and in spontaneous utterances, to show some intonation and her speech is now being produced with greater intensity.

Like normal children, Genie's first one-word utterances consisted of Consonant-Vowel (CV) monosyllables. These soon expanded into a more complex syllable structure which can be diagrammed as (C) (L/G) V (C), where L stands for liquid, G, glide, and the parenthesized elements optional.

Words of two and three syllables entered into her productive vocabulary and in these words stress was correctly marked by intensity and/or duration of the vowel as well as vowel quality (with the unstressed vowel being ə). To date, all of the consonants of Standard American English are included in her utterances (with the interdental fricatives occurring only in imitations, and the affricates occurring inconsistently). She still deletes final consonants more often than not. Their correct sporadic presence, however, shows them to be part of her stored representation of the words in which they occur. Consonant clusters were first simplified by the deletion of the /s/ in initial /sp/ /sk/ /st/ clusters; at the present time, in addition to this method of preserving the CV syllable structure, she sometimes adds an epenthetic schwa between the two consonants.

Other changes in Genie's phonological system continue to be observed. At an earlier stage a regular substitution of /t/ for /k/, /n/, and /s/ occurred in all word positions: this now occurs only word medially. /s/ plus nasal clusters are now being produced.

What is of particular interest is that in imitation Genie can produce any English sound and many sound sequences not found in her spontaneous speech. It has been noted by many researchers on child language that children have greater phonetic abilities than are revealed in their utterances. This is also true of Genie; her output reflects phonological constraints rather than her inability to articulate sounds and sound sequences.

Neither Genie nor a normal child learns the sound system of a language totally independent from the syntactic and semantic systems. In fact, the analysis of the syntactic and semantic development of Genie's spontaneous utterances reveals that her performance on the expressive side is paralleling (although lagging behind) her comprehension.

As stated above, within a few weeks after admission to the hospital Genie began to imitate words used to her, and her comprehension of individual words and names increased dramatically. She began to produce single words spontaneously after about five months.

SENTENCE STRUCTURE

For normal children perception or comprehension of syntactic structures exceeds production; this is even more true in Genie's case possibly for the reasons given above. But even in production it is clear that Genie is acquiring language. Eight months after her emergence Genie began to produce utterances, two words (or morphemes) in length. The structures of her earliest two-word "sentences" were Modifier + Noun and Noun + Noun genitive constructions. These included sentences like "more soup," "yellow car," "Genie purse," and "Mark mouth." After about two months she began to produce strings with verbs—both Noun (subject) + Verb, and Verb + Noun (object), e.g., "Mark paint" (N + V), "Curtiss cough" (N + V), "want milk" (V + N), and "wash car" (V + N). Sentences with a noun followed by a predicate adjective soon followed, e.g., "Dave sick."

In November 1971, Genie began to produce three- and four-word strings, including subject + verb + object strings, like "Tori chew glove," modified noun phrases like "little white clear box," subject-object strings, like "big elephant long trunk," and four-word predications like "Marilyn car red car." Some of these longer strings are of interest because the syntactic relations which were only assumed to be present in her two-word utterances were now overtly expressed. For example, many of Genie's two-word strings did not contain any expressed subject, but the three-word sentences included both the subject and object: "Love Marilyn" became "Genie love Marilyn." In addition, Modifier-noun Noun Phrases and possessive phrases which were complete utterances at the two-word sentence stage are now used as constituents of her longer strings, e.g., "more soup" occurred in "want more soup" and "Mark mouth" became a constituent in "Mark mouth hurt."

In February 1972, Genie began to produce negative sentences. The comprehension test involving negative/affirmative distinctions showed that such a distinction was understood many months earlier. (In the tests she had no difficulty in pointing to the correct picture when asked to "show me 'The girl is wearing shoes'" or "Show me the bunny that has a carrot" vs. "Show me the bunny that does not/doesn't have a carrot.") The first negative morpheme used by Genie was "no more." Later she began to use "no" and "not." To date, Genie continues to negate a sentence by attaching the negative morpheme to the beginning of the string. She has not yet acquired the "negative movement transformation" which inserts the negative morpheme inside the sentence in English.

About the same time that the negative sentences were produced, Genie began to produce strings with locative-nouns, such as "cereal kitchen" and "play gym." In recent months prepositions are occurring in her utterances. In answer to the question "Where is your toy radio?" she answered "On chair." She has also produced sentences such as "Like horse behind fence" and "Like good Harry at hospital."

In July 1972, Verb plus Verb-phrase strings were produced: "Want go shopping," "Like chew meat." Such complex VPs began to emerge in sentences that included both a complex Noun-phrase and a complex Verb-phrase, e.g., "Want buy toy refrigerator" and "Want go walk (to) Ralph." Genie has also begun to add the progressive aspect marker "ing" to verbs, always appropriately to denote ongoing action: "Genie laughing," "Tori eating bone."

Grammatical morphemes that are phonologically marked are now used, e.g., plurals as in "bears," "noses," "swings," and possessives such as "Joe's room," "I like Dave's car."

While no definite-indefinite distinction has appeared, Genie now produces the definite article in imitation, and uses the determiner "another" spontaneously, as in "Another house have dog."

At an earlier stage, possession was marked solely by word order; Genie now also expresses possession by the verb "have," as in "bears have sharp claw," "bathroom have big mirror."

A most important syntactic development is revealed by Genie's use of compound NPs. Prior to December 1971, she would only name one thing at a time, and would produce two sentences such as: "Cat hurt" followed by "dog hurt." More recently she produced these two strings, and then said "Cat dog hurt." This use of a "recursive" element is also shown by the sentence "Curtiss, Genie, swimming pool" in describing a snapshot.

Genie's ability to combine a finite set of linguistic elements to form new combinations, and the ability to produce sentences consisting of conjoined sentences, shows that she has acquired two essential elements of language that permit the generation of an infinite set of sentences.

This is of course an overly sketchy view of the syntactic development evidence in Genie's utterances. (For further details see Curtiss et al. 1972.) It is clear even from this summary that Genie is learning language. Her speech is rule-governed—she has fixed word-order of basic sentence elements and constituents, and systematic ways of expressing syntactic and semantic relations.

LINGUISTIC DEVELOPMENT IN RELATION TO NORMALS

Furthermore it is obvious that her development in many ways parallels that of normal first-language acquisition. There are, however, interesting differences between Genie's emerging language and that of normal children. Her vocabulary is much larger than that of normal children whose language exhibits syntactic complexity parallel to Genie's. She has less difficulty in storing lists than she does learning the rules of the grammar. This illustrates very sharply that language acquisition is not simply the ability to store a large number of items in memory.

Genie's performance on the active/passive comprehension test also appears to deviate from that of normal children. Bever (1970) reports on experiments aimed at testing the capacity in young children "to recognize explicitly the concept of predication as exemplified in the appreciation of the difference between subject-action and action-object relations." The children in these experiments were requested to act out using both simple active sentences and reversible passive sentences, such as "The cow kisses the horse" and simple passives such as "The horse is kissed by the cow." He reports that "children from 2.0 to 3.0 act out simple active sentences 95 percent correctly, (and) . . . do far better than 5 percent on simple passives." He concludes that "since they perform almost randomly on passives . . . they can at least distinguish sentences they can understand from sentences they cannot understand. Thus, the basic linguistic capacity evidenced by the two-year-old child includes the notion of reference for objects and actions, the notion of basic functional internal relations, and at least a primitive notion of different sentence structures." Genie was similarly tested but with the "point to" response rather than the "acting out" response. That is she was asked to point to "The boy pulls/is pulling the girl" or "The girl is pulled by the boy." For each such test sentence she was presented with two pictures, one depicting the boy as agent, the other with the girl as agent. Unlike the children tested by Bever, Genie's responses to both active and passive sentences have been random, with no better than a chance level of correct responses for either the active or the passive sentences. This is particularly strange when compared with Genie's own utterances which show a consistent word order to indicate Subject Verb Object relations. While she never produces passive constructions, her active sentences always place the object after the verb and the subject before the verb (when they are expressed).

Another difference between Genie and normal children is in the area of linguistic performance. Genie's linguistic competence (her grammar, if we can speak of a grammar at such an early stage of development) is in many ways on a par with a two- or two-and-a-half-year-old child. Her performance—particularly as related to expressive speech—is much poorer than normal children at this level. Because of her particular difficulties in producing speech, however, a number of relatively successful efforts have been directed to teaching her written language. At this point she recognizes, names, and can print the letters of the alphabet, can read a large number of printed words, can assemble printed words into grammatically correct sentences, and can understand sentences (and questions) constructed of these printed words. On this level of performance, then, she seems to exceed normal children at a similar stage of language development.

Genie's progress is much slower than that of normals. Few syntactic markers occur in her utterances; there are no question words, no demonstratives, no particles, no rejoinders. In addition, no movement transformations are revealed. Such rules exist in the adult grammar and in normal children's grammars as early as two years. Transformational rules are those which, for example, would move a negative element from the beginning of the sentence to the position after an auxiliary verb. Such a transformational rule would change *I can go* in its negative form from *Neg + I + can + go* to *I + can + neg* (can't) *+ go*. As stated above, Genie continues to produce negative sentences only by the addition of the negative element to the beginning of the sentence, e.g., *No more ear hurt, No stay hospital, No can go.*

Cognitively, however, she seems to be in advance of what would be expected at this syntactic stage. Her earliest productive vocabulary included words cognitively more sophisticated than one usually finds in the descriptions of first vocabulary words. Color words and numbers, for example, were used which usually enter a child's vocabulary at a much later grammatical stage (Castner 1940; Denckla 1972).

At the time that Genie began to produce utterances of two words (June 1971) she had an active vocabulary of 200 words, which far exceeds the size of the normal children's lexicon at this stage (about fifty words). This development seems to parallel that found in aphasic children (Eisenson and Ingram 1972). She comprehends all the *wh-* questions; normal children ordinarily learn *how, why,* and *when* questions later than *who, what,* and *where* (Brown 1968), although syntactically such questions are similar. Her comprehension of the comparative and superlative, and the differences between *more* and *less* also indicates cognitive sophistication not revealed by her syntax, suggesting at least a partial independence of cognition and language.

COGNITIVE DEVELOPMENT

The attempt to assess Genie's cognitive development is extremely difficult. All tests purported to measure cognitive abilities, in fact, measure knowledge that has been acquired through experience. In addition, many tests are substantially dependent on verbal response and comprehension. The distinction between cognition and language development is therefore not always possible. A number of tests have, however, been utilized.

Genie could not easily be psychologically tested by standard instruments at the time of her admission. It is still difficult to administer many of the standard tests. On the Vineland Social Maturity Scale, however, she averaged about fifteen months at the time of admission, and on a Gesell Developmental Evaluation, a month and a half later, scores ranged from about one to about three years of age. There was a very high degree of scatter when compared to normal developmental patterns. Consistently, language-related behavior was observed to occur at the lower end of the range of her performance and was judged (by the psychologists at the hospital) to be at about the fifteen months level.

Her cognitive growth, however, seemed to be quite rapid. In a seven-month span her score had increased from fifteen to forty-two months, and six months after admission, on the Leiter International Performance Scale (which depends relatively little on culturally based, specific knowledge, and requires no speech) she passed all the items at the four year level, two at the five year level, and two out of four at the seven year level. In May 1973 her score on this test was on the six to eight year level. At the same time, the Stanford Binet Intelligence Scale elicited a mental age of five to eight. In all the tests, the subsets which involved language were considerably lower than those assessing other abilities.

From this brief summary of Genie's linguistic development we can conclude the following: (1) When she first emerged from isolation, Genie, a child of thirteen years, nine months had not acquired language; (2) Since there is no evidence of any biological deficiencies, one may assume this was due to the social and linguistic isolation which occurred during eleven years of her life; (3) Since her emergence she has been acquiring her first language primarily by "exposure" alone (this is revealed both by her own speech and by her comprehension of spoken language); (4) Her cognitive development has exceeded her linguistic development.

THE "CRITICAL AGE" HYPOTHESIS AND LANGUAGE LATERALIZATION

As mentioned above, Genie's ongoing language acquisition is the most direct test of Lenneberg's critical age hypothesis seen thus far. Lenneberg (1967) has presented the view that the ability to acquire primary language (and the acquisition of second languages "by mere exposure") terminates with the completion of the development of cerebral dominance, or lateralization, an event which he argues occurs at around puberty. As we have demonstrated above, however, while Genie's language acquisition differs to some extent from that of normal children, she is in fact in the process of learning language, as shown by the results of tests and by the observations of her spontaneous and elicited speech. Thus, at least some degree of first-language acquisition seems to be possible beyond the critical period.

Genie also affords us the opportunity to study the relationship of the development of lateralization and language acquisition.

Lateralization refers to the fact that each hemisphere appears to be specialized for different cognitive functions; that is, some functions seem to be "localized" primarily on one side of the brain. . . . [The various monaural and dichotic listening tests given to Genie suggested a pronounced right-hemisphere dominance for language as well as for environmental sounds.]

In trying to assess this unusual situation it is important to note that Genie seems very proficient in what are considered right-hemisphere functions. . . . [In] psychological tests her development can be comprehended more meaningfully when performances on two kinds of test tasks are distinguished: those that require analytic or sequential use of symbols, such as language and number; and those that involve perception of spatial configurations or Gestalts. On the first group of tasks Genie's performance is consistently in the low range, presently approximating an age of two-and-a-half to three years, approximately the age level of her linguistic performance using comparative linguistic criteria. On configurational tests, however, her performance ranges upwards, lying somewhere between eight years and the adult level, depending on the test. . . . The rate of growth on these tests has been very rapid. . . .

It would appear then that Genie is lateralized to the right for both language and nonlanguage functions. This assumes that these nonlinguistic abilities, which have been shown to be right-hemisphere lateralized, are indeed functions of Genie's right hemisphere. We are now in the process of designing tests involving other modalities which will hopefully provide more conclusive evidence on this question.

If this proves to be the case, one tentative hypothesis to explain how this developed is as follows: At the time of her isolation, Genie was a "normal" right-handed child with potential left-hemisphere dominance. The inadequate language stimulation during her early life inhibited or interfered with language aspects of left hemisphere development. This would be tantamount to a kind of functional atrophy of the usual language centers, brought about by disuse or suppression. Apparently, what meager stimulation she did receive was sufficient for normal right-hemisphere development. (One can imagine her sitting, day after day, week after week, year after year, absorbing every visual stimulus, every crack in the paint, every nuance of color and form.) This is consistent with the suggestion (Carmon et al. 1972) that the right hemisphere is the first to develop since it is more involved with the perception of the environment. Genie's current achievements in language acquisition, according to this reasoning, are occurring in that hemisphere which somehow did mature more normally.

The hypothesis that Genie is using a developed right hemisphere for language also predicts the dichotic listening results. The undeveloped language areas in the left hemisphere prevent the flow of (just language) impulses from the left primary auditory receiving areas to the right hemisphere. This explains why Genie's scores are so similar to split-brain and hemispherectomized subjects; the only auditory pathways that are functional for *verbal* stimuli are the right ipsilateral and left contralateral. The low right score is due to the suppression that occurs under the dichotic condition. Her perfect monotic scores are predicted, since suppression only takes place dichotically.

If this hypothesis is true it modifies the theory of the critical period: while the normal development of lateralization may not play a role in the critical period, lateralization may be involved in a different way; the left hemisphere must perhaps be linguistically stimulated during a specific period of time for it to participate in normal language acquisition. If such stimulation does not take place during this time, normal language acquisition must depend on other cortical areas and will proceed less efficiently due to the previous specialization of these areas for other functions.

A comparison of Genie's with the other instances of right (minor) hemisphere speech in adults implies that Genie's capacity for language acquisition is limited and will cease at some time in the near future. Such cases are rare and not well described from a linguistic point of view. A. Smith's (1966) description of a left hemispherectomized man is the best of these. This man could not speak at all after his left hemisphere was removed but did begin to communicate in "propositional language" ten weeks later. The patient continued to make linguistic progress but remained severely aphasic eight months after surgery (see also Bogen 1969). Similarly, Hillier (1954) reported a left hemispherectomy performed on a fourteen-year-old boy for a tumor whose onset was one year previous to surgery. Again, there was early progress in language learning but after nineteen months progress ceased and the deficit became stable.

It is unfortunate that there is no information concerning cerebral dominance for other cases of isolated children—those that acquired language as well as those that didn't. Itard suggests that Victor was about twelve years of age when he was found in the woods of Aveyron, and that "It is . . . almost proved that he had been abandoned at the age of four or five years" (Itard 1962). If, in those first years he was not genetically deficient, lateralization should have been complete and language should have been acquired. Itard states further that "if, at this time, he already owed some ideas and some words to the beginning of an education, this would all have been effaced from his memory in consequence of his isolation." How, why, and if such "memory effacement" occurs are questions open to speculation. Despite this "effacement," Victor "did acquire a very considerable reading vocabulary, learning, by means of printed phrases, to execute such simple commands as to pick up a key" (Itard 1962, xii), but he never learned to speak. The scar "which (was) visible on his throat" may have damaged his larynx. It is impossible to tell from Itard's reports the exact extent of Victor's comprehension of spoken language.

Another case, similar to some extent to that of Genie, is that of a child who was not exposed to language until she was six-and-a-half years old because of her imprisonment with a mute and totally uneducated aphasic mother (Mason 1942). Within twenty-two months, she progressed from her first spoken words ("ball," "car," "bye," "baby") to asking such questions as "Why does the paste come out if one upsets the jar?" The rapidity with which she acquired the complex grammar of English provides some support for the hypothesis that the language learning mechanism is more specific than general.

This case is also consistent with a two-to-puberty critical period theory. The language learning capacity of the right hemisphere, then, may be limited either in time or amount of learning. Because we have no grammatical descriptions of right-hemisphere speech, we cannot predict how far Genie will progress from comparisons with such cases. On the other hand, Genie's progress in language acquisition impressionistically seems to have far exceeded that of the other reported cases. We intend to continue administering dichotic listening tests to see if the left hemisphere begins to show increasing language function. If this occurs, one plausible conclusion would be that language acquisition and use are a precondition for such lateralization to occur. We note, of course, that this would be contrary to the Krashen and Harshman position that later-alization *precedes* language acquisition. There is also some evidence of laterality differences in neonates (Wada, quoted in Geschwind 1970; Molfese 1972).

It is clear from this report that we have more questions than answers. We are hopeful that Genie's development will provide some of these answers.

As humanists we are hopeful that our tentative prognosis of a slow-ing down of language and permanent dysphasia will prove to be wrong. For despite the predictions of our hypothesis, Genie continues to make modest but steady progress in language acquisition and is providing us with data in an unexplored area, first-language acquisition beyond the "critical period." After all, a discarded hypothesis is a small price to pay for confirmation of the astonishing capabilities and adaptability of the human mind. (See the postscript by Maya Pines on page 669.)

BIBLIOGRAPHY

Bellugi, U., and E. Klima. Consultation Report, March 1971.

Bever, T. G. "The cognitive basis for linguistic structures." In *Cognition and the Development of Language*. ed. J. R. Hayes. New York: John Wiley, 1970, 279–362.

Bogen, J. E. "The other side of the brain I: Dysgraphia and dyscopia following cere-bral commissurotomy." *Bulletin of the Los Angeles Neurological Societies* 34 (July 1969), 73–105.

Brown, R. "The development of WH questions in child speech." *Journal of Verbal Learning and Verbal Behavior* 7 (1968), 279–290.

Carmon, A., Y. Harishanu, R. Lowinger, and S. Levy. "Asymmetries in hemispheric blood volume and cerebral dominance." *Behavioral Biology*, 1972.

Castner, B. M. *Language Development in the First Five Years of Life.* ed. A. Gesell. New York: Harper & Row, 1940.

Chomsky, N. "Explanatory models in linguistics." In *Logic, Methodology, and the Philosophy of Science*. ed. E. Nagel, P. Suppes, and A. Taiski. Stanford: Stanford University Press, 1962.

Clarke, A. D. B., and A. M. Clarke. "Some recent advances in the study of early deprivation." *Child Psychology and Psychiatry* 1, 1960.

Curtiss, S. "The development of language in Genie." Paper presented to the 1972 Annual Convention of the American Speech and Hearing Association, San Francisco, November 1972, 18–20.

Curtiss, S., V. Fromkin, and S. Krashen. "The syntactic development of Genie." Paper presented to the annual meeting of the Linguistic Society of America, Atlanta, Georgia, December 1972.

Curtiss, S., V. Fromkin, S. Krashen, D. Rigler, and S. Spitz. "Language Laterali-zation in a Case of Extreme Psychosocial Deprivation." *Journal of the Acoustical Society of America* 53, no. 1 (1973), 367–368.

Davis, K. "Extreme social isolation of a child." *American Journal of Sociology* 45 (1940), 554–565.

————. "Final note on a case of extreme isolation." *American Journal of Sociology* 52 (1947), 432–437.

Denckla, M. B. "Performance on color tasks in kindergarten children." *Cortex* 8 (1972), 177–190.

Dennis, W., and P. Najarian. "Infant development under developmental handicap." *Psychological Monographs* 71, no. 7 (1957).

Eisenson, J., and D. Ingram. "Childhood aphasia—an updated concept based on recent research." *Papers and Reports on Child Language Development.* Stanford University (1972), 103–120.

Fraiberg, S., and D. A. Freedman. "Studies in the ego development of the congenitally blind child." *The Psychoanalytic Study of the Child* 19 (1964), 113–169.

Fromkin, V. "The development of language in Genie." Paper presented at the 80th Annual Convention of the American Psychological Association, Honolulu, Hawaii, September 1–8, 1972.

Geschwind, N. "The organization of language and the brain." *Science* 170 (1970), 940–944.

Haggard, M., and A. Parkinson. "Stimulus and task factors as determinants of ear advantage." *Quarterly Journal of Experimental Psychology* 23 (1971), 168–177.

Hansen, H. "The first experiences and the emergence of 'Genie.'" Paper presented at the 80th Annual Convention of the American Psychological Association, Honolulu, Hawaii, September 1–8, 1972.

Hillier, F. "Total left hemispherectomy for malignant glaucoma." *Neurology* 4 (1954), 718–721.

Howe, M., and F. G. Hall. *Laura Bridgeman.* Boston: Little, Brown, 1903.

Itard, J. *The Wild Boy of Aveyron.* New York: Appleton-Century-Crofts, 1962.

Kent, J. "Eight months in the hospital." Paper presented at the 80th Annual Convention of the American Psychological Association, Honolulu, Hawaii, September 1–8, 1972.

Koluchova, J. "Severe deprivation in twins." *Child Psychology and Psychiatry* 13 (1972).

Krashen, S. "Language and the left hemisphere." *Working Papers in Phonetics* 24 (1972), UCLA.

————. "Lateralization, language learning, and the critical period: Some new evidence." *Language Learning* 23 (1973a), 63–74.

————. "Mental abilities underlying linguistic and non-linguistic functions." *Linguistics* (1973b).

Krashen, S., V. Fromkin, S. Curtiss, D. Rigler, and S. Spitz. "Language lateralization in a case of extreme psychological deprivation." Paper presented to the 84th meeting of the Acoustical Society of America, 1972a.

Krashen, S., V. Fromkin, and S. Curtiss. "A neurolinguistic investigation of language acquisition in the case of an isolated child." Paper presented to the Linguistic Society of America. Winter meeting, Atlanta, Georgia, December 27–29, 1972b.

Krashen, S., and R. Harshman. "Lateralization and the critical period." *Working Papers in Phonetics* 23 (1972), 13–21. UCLA (Abstract in *Journal of the Acoustical Society of America* 52, 174).

Lenneberg, E. H. *Biological Foundations of Language.* New York: Wiley, 1967.

Mason, M. K. "Learning to speak after six and one-half years." *Journal of Speech Disorders* 7 (1942), 295–304.

Milner, B., L. Taylor, and R. Sperry. "Lateralized suppression of dichotically presented digits after commissural section in man." *Science* 161 (1968), 184–186.

Molfese, D. L. "Cerebral asymmetry in infants, children and adults: Auditory evoked responses to speech and musical stimuli." *Journal of the Acoustical Society of America* 53 (1972), 363 (A).

Rigler, D. "The Case of Genie." Paper presented to the 1972 Annual Convention of the American Speech and Hearing Association, San Francisco, California. November 18–20, 1972.

Rigler, M. "Adventure: At home with Genie." Paper presented at the 80th Annual Convention of the American Psychological Association, Honolulu, Hawaii, September 1–8, 1972.

Singh, J. A. L., and R. M. Zingg. *Wolf-Children and Feral Man*. Archon Books, 1966.

Skinner, B. F. *Verbal Behavior*. New York: Appleton-Century-Crofts, 1957.

Smith, A. "Speech and other functions after left (dominant) hemispherectomy." *Journal of Neurology, Neurosurgery and Psychiatry* 29 (1966), 467–471.

Spitz., R. A. "The role of ecological factors in emotional development." *Child Development* 20 (1949), 145–155.

Von Feuerbach, A. *Kasper Hauser*. (Translated from the German) London: Simpkin and Marshall, 1833.

Zurif, E. B., and M. Mendelsohn. "Hemispheric specialization for the perception of speech sounds: The influences of intonation and structure." *Perception and Psychophysics* 11 (1972), 329–332.

Genie: A Postscript

Maya Pines

In 1978, Genie's mother became her legal guardian. During all the years of Genie's rehabilitation, her mother had also received help. An eye operation restored her sight, and a social worker tried to improve her behavior toward Genie. Genie's mother had never been held legally responsible for the child's inhuman treatment. Charges of child abuse were dismissed in 1970, when her lawyer argued that she "was, herself, a victim of the same psychotic individual"—her husband. There was "nothing to show purposeful or willful cruelty," he said.

Nevertheless, for many years the court assigned a guardian for Genie. Shortly after Genie's mother was named guardian, she astounded the therapists and researchers who had worked with Genie by filing a suit against Curtiss and the Children's Hospital among others—on behalf of herself and her daughter—in which she charged that they had disclosed private and confidential information concerning Genie and her mother for "prestige and profit" and had subjected Genie to "unreasonable and outrageous" testing, not for treatment, but to exploit Genie for personal and economic benefits. According to the *Los Angeles Times*, the lawyer who represents Genie's mother estimated that the actual damages could have totaled $500,000. [*Editor's note:* The case was settled out of court, with no damages awarded.]

[In the years since the] case was filed, Genie has been completely cut off from the professionals at Children's Hospital and UCLA. Since she is too old to be in a foster home, she apparently is living in a board-and-care home for adults who cannot live alone. The *Los Angeles Times* reported that as of 1979 her mother was working as a domestic servant. All research on Genie's language and intellectual development has come to a halt. However, the research Genie stimulated goes on. Much of it concerns the relationship between linguistic ability and cognitive development, a subject to which Genie has made a significant contribution.

Apart from Chomsky and his followers, who believe that fundamental language ability is innate and unrelated to intelligence, most psychologists assume that the development of language is tied to—and emerges from—the development of nonverbal intelligence, as described by Piaget. However, Genie's obvious nonverbal intelligence—her use of tools, her drawings, her knowledge of causality, her mental maps of space—did not lead her to an equivalent competence in the grammar normal children acquire by the age of five.

Puzzled by the discrepancy between Genie's cognitive abilities and her language deficits, Curtiss and Fromkin wondered whether they could find people with the opposite pattern—who have normal language ability despite cognitive deficits. That would be further evidence of the independence of language from certain aspects of cognition.

In recent months, they have found several such persons among the mentally retarded, as well as among victims of Turner's syndrome, a chromosomal defect that produces short stature, cardiac problems, infertility, and specific learning difficulties in females. With help from the National Science Foundation (which had also funded some of Curtiss's research on Genie), Fromkin and Curtiss have identified and started working with some children and adolescents who combine normal grammatical ability with serious defects in logical reasoning, sequential ability, or other areas of thinking.

"You can't explain their unimpaired syntax on the basis of their impaired cognitive development," says Curtiss, who is greatly excited by this new developmental profile. She points out that in the youngsters studied, the purely grammatical aspect of language—which reflects Chomsky's language universals—seems to be isolated from the semantic aspect of language, which is more tied to cognition. "Language no longer looks like a uniform package," she declares. "This is the first experimental data on the subject." Thus the ordeal of an abused child may help us understand some of the most puzzling but important aspects of our humanity.

FOR DISCUSSION AND REVIEW

1. Noting that all children who suffer serious experiential deprivation show slowed development, Fromkin and her colleagues state that "An important question for scientists of many disciplines is whether a child so deprived can 'catch up' wholly or in part." List the various factors to consider in answering this question.

2. Describe as fully as you can the condition (physical, emotional, developmental, etc.) of Genie at the time she was discovered and hospitalized. What appear to be the effects of the conditions under which she lived? Why do the authors conclude that although "functionally Genie was an extremely retarded child," the most plausible explanation for such retardation was "the intensity and duration of her psychosocial and physical deprivation"?

3. Genie's linguistic and cognitive development was monitored from the time she was found until several years later. Why was it important to devise tests for ascertaining her language comprehension at the beginning of the monitoring?

4. After stating that Genie is learning language, the authors point out differences between her linguistic development and that of "normals." What are these differences, and why are they significant? What stage has Genie reached in the acquisition of sentence negation? What are the implications of her achieving this stage?

5. Compare Genie's linguistic development with Lenneberg's Developmental Milestones (pp. 640–42). Explain how her linguistic development has been a test of Lenneberg's critical age hypothesis, as described on page 653.

6. The authors form a tentative hypothesis to account for Genie's being "lateralized to the right for both language and nonlanguage functions." What does Genie's case tell us about the relationship between language acquisition and brain lateralization? If they are correct in their prediction, how would this information affect the critical age hypothesis?

7. Even though Genie was slowly acquiring language, why did Fromkin and her colleagues predict in 1974 that Genie probably would have permanent dysphasia?

8. When Fromkin and Curtiss began working with people who had "normal language ability despite cognitive deficits," what did they discover? How did their findings support Chomsky's theory of language ability?

46

American Sign Language: "It's Not Mouth Stuff— It's Brain Stuff"

Richard Wolkomir

During his career, Richard Wolkomir has written numerous essays on a variety of topics, including mobile robots, endangered species, and noise in the workplace. In this article, which first appeared in the Smithsonian *in July 1992, he takes a careful look at the issues and current research involving American Sign Language. Wolkomir first delves into the controversy over whether ASL is truly a language—and whether it should even be taught to deaf children. He traces the history of ASL and features the comments of specialists from Gallaudet University, the only university for the deaf and hearing impaired in North America. Wolkomir also introduces the research of Ursula Bellugi and her colleagues, who continue to investigate the acquisition of signed languages and how it differs from—or is similar to—the acquisition of sound languages. Agreeing with the findings of many specialists, Wolkomir concludes that ASL is indeed a language that has all the essential characteristics of English, French, or any other spoken language. The controversies over the nature of signed languages and teaching ASL involve issues about culture, literacy, and personal identity that remain current today.*

In a darkened laboratory at the Salk Institute in San Diego, a deaf woman is signing. Tiny lights attached to her sleeves and fingers trace the motions of her hands, while two special video cameras whir.

Computers will process her hands' videotaped arabesques and pirouettes into mathematically precise three-dimensional images. Neurologists and linguists will study these stunning patterns for insight into how the human brain produces language.

Sign has become a scientific hot button. Only in the past 20 years have linguists realized that signed languages are unique—a speech of the hand. They offer a new way to probe how the brain generates and understands language, and throw new light on an old scientific controversy: whether language, complete with grammar, is innate in our species, or whether it is a learned behavior. The current interest in sign language has roots in the pioneering work of one renegade teacher at Gallaudet

University in Washington, D.C., the world's only liberal arts university for deaf people.

When Bill Stokoe went to Gallaudet to teach English, the school enrolled him in a course in signing. But Stokoe noticed something odd: among themselves, students signed differently from his classroom teacher.

"HAND TALK": A GENUINE LANGUAGE

Stokoe had been taught a sort of gestural code, each movement of the hands representing a word in English. At the time, American Sign Language (ASL) was thought to be no more than a form of pidgin English. But Stokoe believed the "hand talk" his students used looked richer. He wondered: Might deaf people actually have a genuine language? And could that language be unlike any other on Earth? It was 1955, when even deaf people dismissed their signing as "slang." Stokoe's idea was academic heresy. It is 37 years later. Stokoe—now devoting his time to writing and editing books and journals and to producing video materials on ASL and the deaf culture—is having lunch at a cafe near the Gallaudet campus and explaining how he started a revolution. For decades educators fought his idea that signed languages are natural languages like English, French and Japanese. They assumed language must be based on speech, the modulation of sound. But sign language is based on the movement of hands, the modulation of space. "What I said," Stokoe explains, "is that language is not mouth stuff—it's brain stuff."

It has been a long road, from the mouth to the brain. Linguists have had to redefine language. Deaf people's self-esteem has been at stake, and so has the ticklish issue of their education.

"My own contribution was to turn around the thinking of academics," says Stokoe. "When I came to Gallaudet, the teachers were trained with two books, and the jokers who wrote them gave only a paragraph to sign language, calling it a vague system of gestures that looked like the ideas they were supposed to represent."

Deaf education in the '50s irked him. "I didn't like to see how the hearing teachers treated their deaf pupils—their expectations were low," he says. "I was amazed at how many of my students were brilliant." Meanwhile, he was reading the work of anthropological linguists like George Trager and Henry Lee Smith Jr. "They said you couldn't study language without studying the culture, and when I had been at Gallaudet a short time, I realized that deaf people had a culture of their own."

When Stokoe analyzed his students' signing, he found it was like spoken languages, which combine bits of sound—each meaningless by itself—into meaningful words. Signers, following similar rules, combine individually meaningless hand and body movements into words. They choose from a palette of hand shapes, such as a fist or a pointing index finger. They also choose where to make a sign; for example, on the face or on the chest. They choose how to orient the hand and arm. And each sign has a movement—it might begin at the cheek and finish at the chin. A shaped hand executing a particular motion creates a word. A common underlying structure of both spoken and signed language is thus at the level of the smallest units that are linked to form words.

Stokoe explained his findings on the structure of ASL in a book published in 1960. "The faculty then had a special meeting and I got up and said my piece," he says. "Nobody threw eggs or old vegetables, but I was bombarded by hostility." Later, the university's president told Stokoe his research was "causing too much trouble" because his insistence that ASL was indeed a language threatened the English-based system for teaching the deaf. But Stokoe persisted. Five years later he came out with the first dictionary of American Sign Language based on linguistic principles. And he's been slowly winning converts ever since.

"WHEREVER WE'VE FOUND DEAF PEOPLE, THERE'S SIGN"

Just as no one can pinpoint the origins of spoken language in prehistory, the roots of sign language remain hidden from view. What linguists do know is that sign languages have sprung up independently in many different places. Signing probably began with simple gestures, but then evolved into a true language with structured grammar. "In every place we've ever found deaf people, there's sign," says anthropological linguist Bob Johnson. But it's not the same language. "I went to a Mayan village where, out of 400 people, 13 were deaf, and they had their own Mayan Sign—I'd guess it's been maintained for thousands of years." Today at least 50 native sign languages are "spoken" worldwide, all mutually incomprehensible, from British and Israeli Sign to Chinese Sign.

Not until the 1700s, in France, did people who could hear pay serious attention to deaf people and their language. Religion had something to do with it. "They believed that without speech you couldn't go to heaven," says Johnson.

For the Abbe de l'Epee, a French priest born into a wealthy family in 1712, the issue was his own soul: he feared he would lose it unless he overcame the stigma of his privileged youth by devoting himself to the poor. In his history of the deaf, *When the Mind Hears*, Northeastern University psychologist Harlan Lane notes that, in his 50s, de l'Epee met two deaf girls on one of his forays into the Paris slums and decided to dedicate himself to their education.

The priest's problem was abstraction: he could show the girls a piece of bread and the printed French word for "bread." But how could he show them "God" or "goodness"? He decided to learn their sign language as a teaching medium. However, he attempted to impose French grammar onto the signs.

"Methodical signing," as de l'Epee called his invention, was an ugly hybrid. But he did teach his pupils to read French, opening the door to education, and today he is a hero to deaf people. As his pupils and disciples proliferated, satellite schools sprouted throughout Europe. De l'Epee died happily destitute in 1789 surrounded by his students in his Paris school, which became the National Institution for Deaf-Mutes under the new republic.

Other teachers kept de l'Epee's school alive. And one graduate, Laurent Clerc, brought the French method of teaching in sign to the United States. It was the early 1800s; in Hartford, Connecticut, the Rev. Thomas Hopkins Gallaudet was watching children at play. He noticed that one girl, Alice Cogswell, did not join in. She was deaf. Her father, a surgeon, persuaded Gallaudet to find a European teacher and create the first permanent school for the deaf in the United States. Gallaudet then traveled to England, where the "oral" method was supreme, the idea being to teach deaf children to speak. The method was almost cruel, since children born deaf—they heard no voices, including their own—could have no concept of speech. It rarely worked. Besides, the teachers said their method was "secret." And so Gallaudet visited the Institution for Deaf-Mutes in Paris and persuaded Laurent Clerc to come home with him.

During their 52-day voyage across the Atlantic, Gallaudet helped Clerc improve his English, and Clerc taught him French Sign Language. On April 15, 1817, in Hartford, they established a school that became the American School for the Deaf. Teaching in French Sign Language and a version of de l'Epee's methodical sign, Clerc trained many students who became teachers, too, and helped spread the language across the country. Clerc's French Sign was to mingle with various "home" signs that had sprung up in other places. On Martha's Vineyard, Massachusetts, for example, a large portion of the population was genetically deaf, and virtually all the islanders used an indigenous sign language, the hearing switching back and forth between speech and sign with bilingual ease. Eventually, pure French Sign would blend with such local argots and evolve into today's American Sign Language.

After Clerc died, in 1869, much of the work done since the time of de l'Epee to teach the deaf in their own language crumbled under the weight of Victorian intolerance. Anti-Signers argued that ASL let the deaf "talk" only to the deaf; they must learn to speak and to lip-read. Pro-Signers pointed out that, through sign, the deaf learned to read and write English. The Pros also noted that lipreading is a skill that few master. (Studies estimate that 93 percent of deaf schoolchildren who were either born deaf or lost their hearing in early childhood can lip-read only one in ten everyday sentences in English.) And Pros argue correctly that the arduous hours required to teach a deaf child to mimic speech should be spent on real education.

"Oralists" like Horace Mann lobbied to stop schools from teaching in ASL, then the method of instruction in all schools for the deaf. None was more fervent than Alexander Graham Bell, inventor of the telephone and husband of a woman who denied her own deafness. The president of the National Association of the Deaf called Bell the "most to be feared enemy of the American deaf." In 1880, at an international meeting of educators of the deaf in Milan, where deaf teachers were absent, the use of sign language in schools was proscribed.

After that, as deaf people see it, came the Dark Ages. Retired Gallaudet sociolinguist Barbara Kannapell, who is cofounder of Deafpride, a Washington, D.C., advocacy group, is the deaf daughter of deaf parents from Kentucky. Starting at age 4, she attended an "oral" school, where signing was outlawed. "Whenever the teacher turned her back to work on the blackboard, we'd sign," signs Kannapell. "If the teacher caught us using sign language, she'd use a ruler on our hands."

Kannapell has tried to see oralism from the viewpoint of hearing parents of deaf children. "They'll do anything to make their child like themselves," she signs. "But, from a deaf adult's perspective, I want them to learn sign, to communicate with their child."

In the 1970s, a new federal law mandated "mainstreaming." "That law was good for parents, because they could keep children home instead of sending them off to special boarding schools, but many public schools didn't know what to do with deaf kids," signs Kannapell. "Many of these children think they're the only deaf kids in the world."

Gallaudet's admissions director, James Tucker, an exuberant 32-year-old, is a product of the '70s mainstreaming. "I'd sit in the back, doing work the teacher gave me and minding my own business," he signs. "Did I like it? Hell no! I was lonely—for years I thought I was an introvert." Deaf children have a right to learn ASL and to live in an ASL-speaking community, he asserts. "We learn sign for obvious reasons—our eyes aren't broken," he signs. Tucker adds: "Deaf culture is a group of people sharing similar values, outlook and frustrations, and the main thing, of course, is sharing the same language."

Today, most teachers of deaf pupils are "hearies" who speak as they sign. "Simultaneous Communication," as it is called, is really signed English and not ASL. "It looks grotesque to the eye," signs Tucker, adding that it makes signs too "marked," a linguistic term meaning equally stressed. Hand movements can be exaggerated or poorly executed. As Tucker puts it: "We have zealous educators trying to impose weird hand shapes." Moreover, since the languages have entirely different sentence structures, the effect can be bewildering. It's like having Japanese spoken to English-speaking students with an interpreter shouting occasional English words at them.

New scientific findings support the efforts of linguists such as Bob Johnson, who are calling for an education system for deaf students based on ASL, starting in infancy. Research by Helen Neville, at the Salk Institute, shows that children must learn a language—any language—during their first five years or so, before the brain's neural connections are locked in place, or risk permanent linguistic impairment. "What suffers is the ability to learn grammar," she says. As children mature, their brain organization becomes increasingly rigid. By puberty, it is largely complete. This spells trouble because most deaf youngsters learn language late; their parents are hearing and do not know ASL, and the children have little or no contact with deaf people when young.

Bob Johnson notes that more than 90 percent of all deaf children have hearing parents. Unlike deaf children of deaf parents, who get ASL instruction early, they learn a language late and lag educationally. "The average deaf 12th-grader reads at the 4th-grade level," says Johnson. He believes deaf children should start learning ASL in the crib, with schools teaching in ASL. English, he argues, should be a second language, for reading and writing: "All evidence says they'll learn English better." It's been an uphill battle. Of the several hundred school programs for the deaf in this country, only six are moving toward ASL-based instruction. And the vast majority of deaf students are still in mainstream schools where there are few teachers who are fluent in ASL.

Meanwhile, researchers are finding that ASL is a living language, still evolving. Sociolinguist James Woodward from Memphis, who has a black belt in karate, had planned to study Chinese dialects but switched to sign when he came to Gallaudet in 1969. "I spent every night for two years at the Rathskeller, a student hangout, learning by observing," he says. "I began to see great variation in the way people signed."

Woodward later concentrated on regional, social and ethnic dialects of ASL. Visiting deaf homes and social clubs in the South, he found that Southerners use older forms of ASL signs than Northerners do. Southern blacks use even more of the older signs. "From them, we can learn the history of the language," he says.

Over time, signs tend to change. For instance, "home" originally was the sign for "eat" (touching the mouth) combined with the sign for "sleep" (the palm pillowing the cheek). Now it has evolved into two taps on the cheek. Also, signs formerly made at the center of the face migrate toward its perimeter. One reason is that it is easier to see both signs and changes in facial expressions in this way, since deaf people focus on a signer's face—which provides crucial linguistic information—taking in the hands with peripheral vision.

Signers use certain facial expressions as grammatical markers. These linguistic expressions range from pursed lips to the expression that results from enunciating the sound "th." Linguist Scott Liddell, at Gallaudet, has noted that certain hand movements translate as "Bill drove to John's." If the signer tilts his head forward and raises his eyebrows while signing, he makes the sentence a question: "Did Bill drive to John's?" If he also makes the "th" expression as he signs, he modifies the verb with an adverb: "Did Bill drive to John's inattentively?"

Sociolinguists have investigated why this unique language was for so long virtually a secret. Partly, Woodward thinks, it was because deaf people wanted it that way. He says that when deaf people sign to the hearing, they switch to English-like signing. "It allows hearing people to be identified as outsiders and to be treated carefully before allowing any interaction that could have a negative effect on the deaf community," he says. By keeping ASL to themselves, deaf people—whom Woodward regards as an ethnic group—maintain "social identity and group solidarity."

A KEY LANGUAGE INGREDIENT: GRAMMAR

The "secret" nature of ASL is changing rapidly as it is being examined under the scientific microscope. At the Salk Institute, a futuristic complex of concrete labs poised on a San Diego cliff above the Pacific, pioneer ASL investigator Ursula Bellugi directs the Laboratory for Cognitive Neuroscience, where researchers use ASL to probe the brain's capacity for language. It was here that Bellugi and associates found that ASL has a key language ingredient: a grammar to regulate its flow. For example, in a conversation a signer might make the sign for "Joe" at an arbitrary spot in space. Now that spot stands for "Joe." By pointing to it, the signer creates the pronoun "he" or "him," meaning "Joe." A sign moving toward the spot means something done to "him." A sign moving away from the spot means an action by Joe, something "he" did.

In the 1970s, Bellugi's team concentrated on several key questions that have been of central concern ever since MIT professor Noam Chomsky's groundbreaking work of the 1950s. Is language capability innate, as Chomsky and his followers believe? Or is it acquired from our environment? The question gets to the basics of humanity since our language capacity is part of our unique endowment as a species. And language lets us accumulate lore and pass it on to succeeding generations. Bellugi's team reasoned that if ASL is a true language, unconnected to speech, then our penchant for language must be built in at birth, whether we express it with our tongue or hands. As Bellugi (above) puts it: "I had to keep asking myself, 'What does it mean to be a language?'"

A key issue was "iconicity." Linguistics has long held that one of the properties of all natural languages is that their words are arbitrary. In English, to illustrate, there is no relation between the sound of the word "cat" and a cat itself, and onomatopoeic words like "slurp" are few and far between. Similarly, if ASL follows the same principles, its words should not be pictures or mime. But ASL does have many words with transparent meanings. In ASL, "tree" is an arm upright from the elbow, representing a trunk, with the fingers spread to show the crown. In Danish Sign, the signer's two hands outline a tree in the air. Sign languages are rife with pantomimes. But Bellugi wondered: Do deaf people perceive such signs as iconic as they communicate in ASL?

One day a deaf mother visited the lab with her deaf daughter, not yet 2. At that age, hearing children fumble pronouns, which is why parents say, "Mommy is getting Tammy juice." The deaf child, equally confused by pronouns, signed "you" when she meant "I." But the sign for such pronouns is purely iconic: the signer points an index finger at his or her own torso to signify "I" or at the listener to signify "you." The mother corrected the child by turning her hand so that she pointed at herself. Nothing could be clearer. Yet, as the child chattered on, she continued to point to her mother when she meant "I."

Bellugi's work revealed that deaf toddlers have no trouble pointing. But a pointing finger in ASL is linguistic, not gestural. Deaf toddlers in the "don't-understand-pronouns" stage do not see a pointing finger. They see a confusing, abstract word. ASL's roots may be mimetic, but— embedded in the flow of language—the signs lose their iconicity.

By the 1980s, most linguists had accepted sign languages as natural languages on an equal footing with English, Italian, Hindi and others of the world. Signed languages like ASL were as powerful, subtle and intricately structured as spoken ones.

The parallels become especially striking in wordplay and poetry. Signers creatively combine hand shapes and movements to create puns and other humorous alterations of words. A typical pun in sign goes like this: a fist near the forehead and a flip of the index finger upward means that one understands. But if the little finger is flipped, it's a joke meaning one understands a little. Clayton Valli at Gallaudet has made an extensive study of poetry in ASL. He finds that maintenance or repetition of hand shape provides rhyming, while meter occurs in the timing and type of movement. Research with the American Theater of the Deaf reveals a variety of individual techniques and styles. Some performers create designs in space with a freer movement of the arms than in ordinary signing. With others, rhythm and tempo are more important than spatial considerations. Hands may be alternated so that there is a balance and symmetry in the structure. Or signs may be made to flow into one another, creating a lyricism in the passage. The possibilities for this new art form in sign seem bounded only by the imagination within the community itself.

The special nature of sign language provides unprecedented opportunities to observe how the brain is organized to generate and understand language. Spoken languages are produced by largely unobservable movements of the vocal apparatus and received through the brain's auditory system. Signed languages, by contrast, are delivered through highly visible movements of the arms, hands and face, and are received through the brain's visual system. Engagement of these different brain systems in language use makes it possible to test different ideas about the biological basis of language.

The prevailing view of neurologists is that the brain's left hemisphere is the seat of language, while the right controls our perception of visual space. But since signed languages are expressed spatially, it was unclear where they might be centered.

To find out, Bellugi and her colleagues studied lifelong deaf signers who had suffered brain damage as adults. When the damage had occurred in their left hemisphere, the signers could shrug, point, shake their heads and make other gestures, but they lost the ability to sign. As happens with hearing people who suffer left-hemisphere damage, some of them lost words while others lost the ability to organize grammatical sentences, depending on precisely where the damage had occurred.

Conversely, signers with right-hemisphere damage signed as well as ever, but spatial arrangements confused them. One of Bellugi's right-hemisphere subjects could no longer perceive things to her left. Asked to describe a room, she reported all the furnishings as being on the right, leaving the room's left side a void. Yet she signed perfectly, including signs formed on the left side. She had lost her sense of topographic space, a right-hemisphere function, but her control of linguistic space, centered in the left hemisphere, was intact. All of these findings support the conclusion that language, whether visual or spoken, is under the control of the left hemisphere.

One of the Salk group's current efforts is to see if learning language in a particular modality changes the brain's ability to perform other kinds of tasks. Researchers showed children a moving light tracing a pattern in space, and then asked them to draw what they saw. "Deaf kids were way ahead of hearing kids," says Bellugi. Other tests, she adds, back up the finding that learning sign language improves the mind's ability to grasp patterns in space.

THINKING AND DREAMING IN SIGNS

Salk linguist Karen Emmorey says the lab also has found that deaf people are better at generating and manipulating mental images. "We found a striking difference in ability to generate mental images and to tell if one object is the same as another but rotated in space, or is a mirror image of the first," she says, noting that signers seem to be better at discriminating between faces, too. As she puts it: "The question is, does the language you know affect your other cognitive abilities?"

Freda Norman, formerly an actress with the National Theater of the Deaf and now a Salk research associate, puts it like this: "English is very linear, but ASL lets you see everything at the same time."

"The deaf think in signs," says Bellugi. "They dream in signs. And little children sign to themselves."

At McGill University in Montreal, Psychologist Laura Ann Petitto recently found that deaf babies of deaf parents babble in sign. Hearing infants create nonsense sounds like "bababababa," first attempts at language. So do deaf babies, but with their hands. Petitto watched deaf infants moving their hands and fingers in systematic ways that hearing children not exposed to sign never do. The movements, she says, were their way of exploring the linguistic units that will be the building blocks of language—their language.

Deaf children today face a brighter future than the generation of deaf children before them. Instruction in ASL, particularly in residential schools, should accelerate. New technologies, such as the TDD (Telecommunications Device for the Deaf) for communicating over telephones, relay services and video programs for language instruction, and the recent Americans with Disabilities Act all point the way to a more supportive environment. Deaf people are moving into professional jobs, such as law and accounting, and more recently into computer-related work. But it is not surprising that outside of their work, they prefer one another's company. Life can be especially rewarding for those within the ASL community. Here they form their own literary clubs, bowling leagues and gourmet groups.

As the Salk laboratory's Freda Norman signs: "I love to read books, but ASL is my first language." She adds, smiling: "Sometimes I forget that the hearing are different."

FOR DISCUSSION AND REVIEW

1. Why might the idea that ASL is a "genuine language" be controversial?
2. Bill Stokoe noticed important similarities between his students' signing and the structure of words in sound-based language. What were these similarities, and why are they significant?
3. Anthropological linguist Bob Johnson says that "in every place we've ever found deaf people, there's sign." What might this statement suggest about humans and language? Does it surprise you that the sign languages of different cultures are "mutually incomprehensible"? Why, or why not?
4. Why is the French priest Abbe de l'Epee considered a hero to deaf people? How did his teachings influence American Sign Language?
5. What are some of the arguments for and against teaching deaf children a signed language? Are these linguistic arguments of social ones? Why do the hearing parents of deaf children sometimes favor oralism?
6. How do singers use facial markers as grammatical expressions? When such markers change, are the changes similar to what happens in spoken languages? In what way?
7. What is "iconicity"? What evidence did Ursula Bellugi's research team find that indicated signs were perceived as abstract or linguistic and not iconic? Why is it important that signs are perceived as abstract?

Projects for "Language Acquisition and the Brain"

1. Some findings on neural asymmetry suggest that the kind of notation or code (alphabets, symbols, etc.) used in a given task influences how quickly a person accomplishes a task. Recall, for example, Jeannine Heny's comments on the use of two types of Japanese script. Using examples from your own experience, think about how using one set of symbols rather than another might influence your performance on a given task. For instance, try to multiply using Roman rather than Arabic numerals. Which can you process faster: "XIX times III" or "19 times 3" or "19 × 3"? Another example would be the speed (or accuracy) of reading and understanding a text in print, in handwriting, or in calligraphy. If you are someone who can use different alphabets, do you process one more quickly than another, for instance Cyrillic versus Roman or Perso-Arabic versus Devanagiri? Try to read a text with many abbreviations, and then read the same text with everything written out fully. If you do math regularly, try understanding a proof that is entirely in math notation versus one mixed with English or another language.

Have a classmate devise a task using one of the preceding suggestions, or a different one, for you. Then, try to accomplish the task using at least two different notations or codes. Write a brief essay describing your task, and discuss the results of your experiment. How does notation or code affect your approach to a task, your efficiency in working on it, and your success in accomplishing it? Do you bring specific expectations to a task based on the type of notation or code you use? How might your experience with this task affect your approach to other code-related tasks?

2. Write a report on a recent *nonprimate* communication research study that attempts to understand the communicative behaviors of a particular species. To do so, be sure to include research from a field other than linguistics, such as psychology, cognitive science, zoology, or biology. Do the researchers' conclusions differ from those discussed by Kemp and Smith? What new insights are revealed about communication among bees or birds or other species? Some possible sources are included in the bibliography at the end of this part. In addition, the *Animals and Language* Web site, www.laits.utexas.edu/hebrew/personal/language/animals/resources.html, provides a general listing of articles by category. The reference librarians at your campus library will also be helpful in finding reliable sources.

3. Research and give a presentation on a *primate* communication research study. You might choose one of the studies mentioned in the Kemp and Smith essay, or you may want to investigate a more contemporary project, such as the Orang Utan Project based at the National Zoo

in Washington, D.C., or the project at Central Washington University's Chimpanzee and Human Communication Institute. At the beginning of your presentation, be sure to inform your audience about the specific questions the researchers asked in that particular project. Also explain how the project was designed.

4. This project is adapted from an activity in Jean Berko Gleason and Nan Bernstein Ratner's chapter on language acquisition in the second edition of *Psycholinguistics*. Test the hypothesis that a parent speaks differently to children of different ages. First, choose a family with children of a range of ages. Then obtain permission to record the interactions of one of the parents with the children. Once you have documented the interactions (with audio or video recording), analyze the conversations. How does the parent's speech differ depending on the age of the child? List specific differences. Do you think the parent's speech potentially encourages language development or hinders it? Why? What words or phrases seem typical of parental speech? Which seem atypical? Compare your sample data with the predictions in the selections by Moskowitz and by Lenneberg. Present your findings in class, and then discuss the following question: what generalizations can you and your classmates make about how parents speak to children of different ages?

5. Because children can make meaningful gestures before they can verbalize, some child psychologists have encouraged parents to develop signed communication with their infants. In recent years, psychologists have developed a number of specific systems for signing with infants, and some of these systems have been marketed commercially to the general public. Write a researched essay on infant learning and baby signing. How did it develop? Who is the target audience? Consider how baby sign differs from a signed language such as American Sign Language and why this is the case. To begin your research, look at *Baby Signs: How to Talk with Your Baby before Your Baby Can Talk*, by Linda Acredolo, Susan Goodwin, and Douglas Abrams, and the *Handspeak* and *Makaton* Web sites. (See this part's Selected Bibliography.)

6. Examine the following conversation (documented by Ursula Bellugi in 1970) between Eve, a twenty-four-month-old child, and her mother:

EVE: Have that?
MOTHER: No, you may not have it.
EVE: Mom, where my tapioca?
MOTHER: It's getting cool. You'll have it in just a minute.
EVE: Let me have it.
MOTHER: Would you like to have your lunch right now?
EVE: Yeah. My tapioca cool?
MOTHER: Yes, it's cool.
EVE: You gonna watch me eat my lunch?
MOTHER: Yeah, I'm gonna watch you eat your lunch.
EVE: I eating it.

MOTHER: I know you are.
EVE: It time Sarah take a nap.
MOTHER: It's time for Sarah to have some milk, yeah. And then she's
   gonna take a nap and you're gonna take a nap.
EVE: And you?
MOTHER: And me too, yeah.

Compare the grammar of Eve's speech with that of her mother. What grammatical features are systematically missing from Eve's speech? Now look at a conversation between Eve and her mother recorded only three months later:

MOTHER: Come and sit over here.
EVE: You can sit down by me. That will make me happy. Ready to
   turn it.
MOTHER: We're not quite ready to turn the page.
EVE: Yep, we are.
MOTHER: Shut the door, we won't hear her then.
EVE: Then Fraser won't hear her too. Where he's going? Did you
   make a great big hole there?
MOTHER: Yes, we made a great big hole in here; we have to get a new
   one.
EVE: Could I get some other piece of paper?
MOTHER: You ask Fraser.
EVE: Could I use this one?
MOTHER: I suppose so.
EVE: Is Fraser goin take his pencil home when he goes?
MOTHER: Yes, he is.

When you compare Eve's speech at twenty-four months to her speech at twenty-seven months, what changes do you notice? Try to describe the grammatical rules Eve seems to have acquired. What pieces of speech provide evidence for the grammar she has learned?

   Using these conversations and your comparisons of Eve's grammatical constructions, write a short paper of one to two pages about Eve's language learning process.

   7. Psycholinguistic research shows that children acquire the social skills of language use simultaneously with their acquisition of other language skills. That is, they learn *how* to use language in specific situations as they acquire language itself. Prepare a presentation on the social skills aspect of language acquisition. An early but useful article on this topic is Susan Ervin-Tripp's "Social Backgrounds and Verbal Skills" in Renira Huxley and Elizabeth Ingram's *Language Acquisition: Models and Methods* (1971). You could begin with an introductory textbook on linguistics, which will include a chapter on psycholinguistics or child language. Some possible sources are listed in this part's bibliography.

   8. Research and write a paper on someone who had cognitive deficits or failed to fully develop language as a result of isolation during critical

periods of the language acquisition processes. In your paper, use the information from your own research as well as from Eric Lenneberg, "Developmental Milestones in Motor and Language Development" (pp. 640–42) and Victoria Fromkin et al., "The Development of Language in Genie: A Case of Language Acquisition beyond the 'Critical Period'" (pp. 652–71) to formulate a set of principles about the stages of "ordinary" language acquisition and the kinds of stimuli and interactions necessary for full acquisition.

9. Research and write a paper on the possible effects of stroke or dementia on language-related brain function. In your paper, address the following questions: Where are the different language centers in the brain? What kinds of language abilities can be lost with certain types of strokes? Is it possible to regain language abilities after a stroke? What therapies focus on language-related brain damage? In your conclusion, discuss what the effects of strokes might tell us about how language is organized in the brain.

10. In recent decades, many effective therapies have emerged to improve the language capabilities of people who experience aphasia—the loss of language skills as a result of brain damage. Research and prepare a report describing the development, testing, and goals of one of the following therapeutic techniques:

- *Melodic Intonation Therapy (MIT)* uses the singing of music to engage the nondominant hemisphere of the brain in language production. Two useful articles about MIT are available at http://aphasiology.pitt.edu.

- *Promoting Aphasic's Communicative Effectiveness (PACE)* uses conversation between the patient and therapist, who participate as equals. To find information on PACE, you might start with Patrick McCaffrey's material titled "Asphasia: Therapy" at *Neuroscience on the Web* (www.csuchico.edu/~pmccaffrey//index.html).

- *Schuell's Stimulation Approach (SSA)* uses multiple modalities to stimulate language responses. Originally, SSA relied on intense auditory stimulation. See Roberta Chapey's *Language Intervention Strategies in Aphasia and Related Neurogenic Communication Disorders* (in the bibliography at the end of this part) for one place to start.

- *Thematic Language Stimulation (TLS)*, developed by Shirley Morganstein and Marilyn Certner Smith in the 1970s, is an approach that can be used by professionals and nonprofessionals. Workbooks offer familiar topics with a core set of vocabulary items to stimulate typical syntactic and discourse structures.

11. The process of learning a second language after age eleven or twelve is different from doing so at a young age. Some of the difference involves brain function, and some involves the contexts for learning.

Young children learn languages by using them in "natural" contexts, but adults (and older children) tend to learn new languages in formal situations.

Prepare a researched presentation on adult second-language learning, focusing on *either* the neurological aspects or the social contexts. If you investigate the neurolinguistic aspects, you might look at how the adult brain stores, organizes, or accesses information and compare that to the brain processes of an infant or young child. If you focus on social contexts, you might investigate methods of teaching language in public high school or at the university level, the use of language labs, or commercial language immersion courses.

12. In many areas of the world, people learn several languages, often acquiring them naturally as children. Nonetheless, people continue to question whether growing up bilingual adversely affects a child's development. In 1995, the *New York Times* sparked a debate about possible language problems for toddlers who are raised by nannies who speak a different tongue. In response, UCLA linguistics professor Victoria Fromkin made the following statement in a letter to the editor: "Years of linguistic research show that children will learn any language to which they are exposed before puberty, and that learning or being exposed to a second or third or fourth language will not negatively affect the acquisition of any of them." Research Fromkin's assertion, and write a position paper arguing for or against it. Use evidence to support your claim.

13. In most urban areas in the world, people use at least two languages on a daily basis. The United States, however, has a history of resistance to bilingualism. In fact, despite the increasing cultural diversity in this country, only about 10 percent of U.S. citizens speak a language other than English. Have a class debate on whether or not American adults should be fluent in at least one language besides English. To prepare for the debate, gather statistics about language, immigration, and settlement in the United States. For the latest data, you will find the U.S. Census Web site, www.census.gov, quite useful. (The "American FactFinder" section will be particularly helpful.) Your university library and public libraries should be able to provide current state and local information.

14. Richard Wolkomir notes in his "American Sign Language: 'It's Not Mouth Stuff—It's Brain Stuff'" (pp. 672–81) that controversy continues over learning a signed language, over the contexts of using it, and even over whether a nonverbal system of communication is a true language. Write a research paper on the development of ASL or another signed language and the controversies surrounding it. Wolkomir's essay and Oliver Sacks's *Hearing Voices* (in this part's Selected Bibliography) are two places to begin your research.

15. The question of official acceptance or classification of a signed language such as ASL or FSL (French Signed Language) affects many people. In the United States, states provide different services to people depending on whether ASL is recognized as a foreign language, an independent

language, or something else. Some universities in the United States accept ASL (and other signed languages) for foreign-language credit, while others do not. For this project, write a three- to four-page persuasive paper arguing that your university or your state legislature should either accept or not accept ASL as a foreign language. To find out the present status of ASL in your state and at your school, go to the Web site for the Laurent Clerc National Deaf Education Center at Gallaudet University (http://infotogo.gallaudet.edu/051ASL.html). Dr. Sherman Wilcox, of the University of New Mexico, provides a list of universities that accept ASL for foreign-language credit on his Web site (http://web.mac.com/swilcox/iWeb/UNM/univlist.html). Boston University's College of Arts and Sciences describes its policy regarding ASL, as well as a record of its policy shift and links to other relevant materials (www.bu.edu/asllrp/fl/#issue).

Selected Bibliography

Acredolo, Linda, Susan Goodwin, and Douglas Abrams. *Baby Signs: How to Talk with Your Baby before Your Baby Can Talk.* New York: McGraw, 2002. [A practical guide to teaching baby sign language to encourage communication before speech.]

Albert M. L., R. W. Sparks, and N. A. Helm. "Melodic Intonation Therapy for Aphasia." *Archives of Neurology* 29 (1973): 130–31. [Examines how MIT can help restore verbal communication in aphasia patients and what kind of patient might have the most success with the method.]

Armstrong, David F. "Some Notes on ASL as a 'Foreign' Language." *Sign Language Studies* 59 (1998): 231–39. [Discussion of ASL as an independent language.]

Bar-Adon, Aaron, and W. F. Leopold. *Child Language: A Book of Readings.* Englewood Cliffs, NJ: Prentice, 1971. [Essays examining issues in child language and development, including intonation, the arbitrariness of word classification, and the integration of phonology and grammar.]

Baron, Naomi S. *Growing Up with Language: How Children Learn to Talk.* Reading, MA: Addison, 1992. [Focuses on language development in children from birth to age six through representation of three different types of language learners.]

Berko, Jean. "The Child's Learning of English Morphology." *Word* 14 (1958): 46–56. [An early examination of basic questions regarding the acquisition of morphology.]

Berko Gleason, Jean. *The Development of Language.* 6th ed. Boston: Allyn, 2004. [Articles examining language development from infancy through adulthood, focusing on various developmental stages.]

Bonvillian, J., M. Orlansky, and L. Novack. "Developmental Milestones: Sign Language Acquisition and Motor Development." *Child Development* 54 (1983): 1435–45. [Studies the impact on children of deaf parents in motor development, and signed and spoken language acquisition.]

Bowerman, Melissa, and Steven Levinson. *Language Acquisition and Conceptual Development.* Cambridge: Cambridge UP, 2001. [Essays focusing on the relationship between child language acquisition and cognitive development in a variety of ethnolinguistic contexts.]

Brown, Roger. *A First Language: The Early Stages.* Cambridge, MA: Harvard UP, 1973. [Examines language development in preschool children.]

Chapey, Roberta, ed. *Language Intervention Strategies in Aphasia and Related Neurogenic Communication Disorders.* 4th ed. Baltimore: Lippincott, Williams, and Wilkins. [Discusses rehabilitation for aphasia patients with particular attention to language and communication assessments and intervention approaches.]

Clark, Eve B. *First Language Acquisition.* Cambridge: Cambridge UP, 2002. [Respected psycholinguist presents social and cognitive approaches to the study of language acquisition, with discussions of bilingualism and dialect.]

Culicover, Peter, and Ray Jackendoff. *Simpler Syntax.* New York: Oxford UP, 2005. [The integration of the studies of syntax and semantics.]

Curtiss, Susan. *Genie: A Psycholinguistic Study of a Modern-Day "Wild Child."* New York: Academic, 1977. [Famous study of Genie, a young girl raised without adequate sensory or social contacts during her formative years; denied language interaction, she faced severe challenges in learning to speak.]

Emmorey, Karen, and Harlan L. Lane, eds. *The Signs of Language Revisited: An Anthology in Honor of Ursula Bellugi and Edward Klima.* Mahwah, NJ: Erlbaum, 2000. [Essays documenting research on signed language and includes personal reminiscences of Bellugi and of Klima.]

Fantini, Alvino. *Language Acquisition of a Bilingual Child.* London: Taylor, 1985. [Case study examining the first fifteen years of a boy raised in two languages.]

Fletcher, Paul, and Brian MacWhinney, eds. *The Handbook of Child Language.* Cambridge: Blackwell, 1995. [Twenty-five essays from experts on all aspects of child language acquisition, including sociolinguistic contexts of grammar development and processes of bilingual acquisition.]

Foster-Cohen, Susan H. *An Introduction to Child Language Development.* Learning about Language. Ser. eds. Geoffrey Leech and Mick Short. Upper Saddle River, NJ: Pearson, 1999. [Explores philosophical theory and empirical data pertaining to language acquisition and processing in children.]

Gardner, Howard. *Intelligence Reframed: Multiple Intelligences for the 21st Century.* New York: Basic, 2000. [Expanded theory of multiple intelligences as first articulated in Gardner's *Frames of Mind*; examines how education can be adapted to individual differences in intelligence.]

Goldberg, Adele. *Constructions at Work: The Nature of Generalizations in Language.* New York: Oxford UP, 2006. [A constructionist approach to how and why language is acquired and how internal processes and the external applications of language intersect.]

Halliday, Morris. *Learning How to Mean: Explorations in the Development of Language.* New York: Arnold, 1975. [Discusses the linguistic process in the very young, who have not yet developed a framework for acquiring meaning.]

Lapiak, Jolanta A. *Handspeak* 2007. <www.handspeak.com>. [An online service providing resources, dictionaries, and lessons in Baby Sign.]

Lenneberg, Eric. *The Biological Foundations of Language.* New York: Wiley, 1967. [Enormously influential presentation of stages of language acquisition correlated with motor development.]

Loritz, Daniel. *How the Brain Evolved.* New York: Oxford UP, 2006. [An evolutionary approach to the development of language in the brain.]

Lucas, Ceil. *The Sociolinguistics of Sign Languages.* Cambridge: Cambridge UP, 2001. [Addresses issues in signed languages, including multilingualism, language policy, and discourse analysis.]

Luria, A. R. *The Man with the Shattered World: The History of a Brain Wound.* Trans. Lynn Solotaroff. 1972. Cambridge, MA: Harvard UP, 2004. [An account of a soldier wounded in a 1943 battle whose traumatic head wound affected his memory and ability to speak and write.]

Lust, Barbara, and Clare Foley. *First Language Acquisition: The Essential Readings.* Malden, MA: Blackwell, 2004. [Essays by noted theorists, such as Noam Chomsky, providing historical context and a framework for the study of language acquisition.]

MacWhinney, Brian. *Child Language Data Exchange System.* <http://childes.psy.cmu.edu>. [Resource providing links to databases, manuals, dictionaries, and topics related to language development.]

Makaton. 29 Apr. 2007. Makaton Vocabulary Development Project. <http://makaton.org>. [A language development program that uses signs to support speech development in children.]

Marcus, Gary F., Steven Pinker, M. Ullman, M. Hollander, T. J. Rosen, and F. Xu. *Overregularization in Language Acquisition.* Chicago: U of Chicago P, 1997.

[Examines the frequency and likelihood of overregularization of irregular verbs in children's language learning.]

McCaffrey, Patrick. "Unit Ten, Aphasia: Therapy." *Neuroscience on the Web*. 2001. California State U, Chico. <www.csuchico.edu/~pmccaff/syllabi/SPPA336/336unit10.html>. [Overview of various therapeutic approaches to aphasia, including behavior modification, cognitive therapy, and combinations of the two.]

Nakamura, Karen. *Deaf Culture and Language*. 11 Feb. 2007. <www.deaflibrary.org>. [A virtual library containing links to resources pertaining to deaf and hearing-impaired cultures in the United States and Japan.]

Obler, Loraine K., and J. Gjerlow. *Language and the Brain*. 1999. Cambridge: Cambridge UP, 2002. [Discussion of the relationship between areas of the brain and language functions, with emphasis on neurolinguistic development and affects of psychophysical disorder on language abilities.]

Ochs, Elinor. "Talking to Children in Western Samoa." *Language and Society* 11 (1982): 77–104. [Examines the impact of cultural values and beliefs on the communication between young children and their caregivers.]

Padden, Carol, and Tom Humphries. *Inside Deaf Culture*. Cambridge, MA: Harvard UP, 2005. [A thorough introduction to deaf culture.]

Poizner, Howard, Edward Klima, and Ursula Bellugi. *What the Hands Reveal about the Brain*. 1987. Cambridge, MA: Bradford/MIT Press, 1990. [Examines language as symbolic communication, with discussion of visual modalities and deaf communities.]

Ritchie, William, and Tej Bhatia. *Handbook of Child Language Acquistion*. San Diego: Academic, 1998. [Essays with case studies examining language acquisition in children.]

Sacks, Oliver. *Seeing Voices*. New York: Vintage Ed., 2000. [Study of children with prelingual deafness and how they learn to communicate.]

"Secret of the Wild Child." *NOVA*. Public Broadcast Corporation. <www.pbs.org/wgbh/nova/transcripts/2112gchild.html>. [Study of Genie, the young girl who was without language skills due to severe sensory and social deprivation, and how she acquired communication skills as a teenager.]

Shipley, Elizabeth F., Carlota S. Smith, and Lila R. Gleitman. "A Study in the Acquisition of Language: Free Responses to Commands." *Language* 45 (1969): 322–42. [Examines language understanding in children.]

Slobin, Dan, ed. *The Crosslinguistic Study of Language Acquisition*. Mahwah, NJ: Erlbaum, 1997. [Multivolume set with studies of children speaking various languages and living in different cultures.]

Sparks, R., and A. L. Holland. "A Melodic Intonation Therapy." *Journal of Speech and Hearing Disorders* 41 (1976): 287–97. [Discussion of MIT theory, which suggests that melody and rhythm can be useful in language acquisition, particularly in aphasia patients.]

Tomasello, Michael. *Constructing a Language: A User-Based Theory of Language Acquisition*. Cambridge, MA: Harvard UP, 2005. [Argues against the "language instinct," suggesting that children acquire language with existing cognitive abilities and exposure to use.]

Valdman, Albert. *Studies in Second Language Acquisition: A Publication of Cambridge University Press*. Indiana U. <www.indiana.edu/~ssla>. [Online resource with access to journal issues and links to related conferences and journals in applied linguistics.]

Valli, Clayton, and Ceil Lucas. *The Linguistics of American Sign Language*. Washington, D.C.: Gallaudet UP, 1992. [A critical source on ASL.]

PART TEN

GLOBAL ENGLISH

In this part, we look at English as a global language—an international code that creates global connections and serves important roles far beyond its original territory of use. By the 1990s, approximately 375 million people were native speakers of English, and another 375 million spoke English as their second language, a number that continues to increase. In addition, approximately 750 million use English as a foreign language. How did there come to be so many non-native users of English? What has made English "global," and the language of choice in so many situations? The following selections address these questions. They also look at how the globalization of English may fuel complex social, economic, and political tensions and at how, as English spreads across the globe, new Englishes emerge.

In the first selection, "Why a Global Language?" David Crystal explains that a global language has "a special role that is recognized in every country," and he discusses the factors necessary for such a role to develop. Crystal also addresses the various dangers of a global language, presenting evidence to counter some critics' claims. He believes that this is a time when languages can become global and that English is likely to be one global language.

Next, in "Attitudes toward English: The Future of English in South Asia," Richard W. Bailey looks at how English-educated members of the South Asian creative and intellectual elite feel about English. Like people in other areas of the world that underwent colonialism, South Asians are ambivalent toward English and resentful over the cultural and national traditions it replaced. Bailey's piece provides a forum for a number of writers and thinkers to examine their own language use. He also includes predictions from educators about the future of English in specific South Asian nations.

Although we sometimes talk about English as if it were one identifiable language, English is actually a set of historically and structurally related varieties, some of them mutually unintelligible. In the final piece, "Natural Seasonings: The Linguistic Melting Pot," John McWhorter explains what happens when languages come into contact with one another. Noting that "the world's languages rub shoulders much more than a Rand McNally view of things would suggest," he uses a four-level division to represent the various effects of language contact. Through numerous examples, McWhorter reveals how words and grammatical structures are borrowed and how totally new languages may arise.

47

Why a Global Language?

David Crystal

*In his teaching and in over one hundred publications, David Crystal,
now Honorary Professor of Linguistics at the University of Wales,
Bangor, has been explaining language and especially the development of
English since 1964. In* English as a Global Language, *2nd edition (2003),
from which this selection is taken, Crystal examines what it means for
English to have global status, and he looks at its special roles in many
countries. He notes that English is often recognized as a global language,
but not because so many have it as a first language. Rather, he says, people consider English global because approximately one-quarter of the
world's population uses English with some competence for economic,
political, or social reasons. Crystal also discusses whether or not the
world needs a global language and the possible dangers of having one.
Focusing directly on the issues of linguistic power, complacency, and
death, he argues convincingly that a global language does not automatically harm other languages, cultures, or nations.*

'English is the global language.'

A headline of this kind must have appeared in a thousand newspapers and
magazines in recent years. 'English Rules' is an actual example, presenting to the world an uncomplicated scenario suggesting the universality of
the language's spread and the likelihood of its continuation.[1] A statement
prominently displayed in the body of the associated article, memorable
chiefly for its alliterative ingenuity, reinforces the initial impression:
'The British Empire may be in full retreat with the handover of Hong
Kong. But from Bengal to Belize and Las Vegas to Lahore, the language of
the sceptred isle is rapidly becoming the first global lingua franca.'
Millennial retrospectives and prognostications continued in the same
vein, with several major newspapers and magazines finding in the subject
of the English language an apt symbol for the themes of globalization,
diversification, progress and identity addressed in their special editions.[2]
Television programmes and series, too, addressed the issue, and achieved

---

[1] *Globe and Mail*, Toronto, 12 July 1997.
[2] Ryan (1999).

world-wide audiences.[3] Certainly, by the turn of the century, the topic must have made contact with millions of popular intuitions at a level which had simply not existed a decade before.

These are the kinds of statement which seem so obvious that most people would give them hardly a second thought. Of course English is a global language, they would say. You hear it on television spoken by politicians from all over the world. Wherever you travel, you see English signs and advertisements. Whenever you enter a hotel or restaurant in a foreign city, they will understand English, and there will be an English menu. Indeed, if there is anything to wonder about at all, they might add, it is why such headlines should still be newsworthy.

But English *is* news. The language continues to make news daily in many countries. And the headline *isn't* stating the obvious. For what does it mean, exactly? Is it saying that everyone in the world speaks English? This is certainly not true, as we shall see. Is it saying, then, that every country in the world recognizes English as an official language? This is not true either. So what does it mean to say that a language is a global language? Why is English the language which is usually cited in this connection? How did the situation arise? And could it change? Or is it the case that, once a language becomes a global language, it is there for ever?

These are fascinating questions to explore, whether your first language is English or not. If English is your mother tongue, you may have mixed feelings about the way English is spreading around the world. You may feel pride, that your language is the one which has been so successful; but your pride may be tinged with concern, when you realize that people in other countries may not want to use the language in the same way that you do, and are changing it to suit themselves. We are all sensitive to the way other people use (it is often said, abuse) 'our' language. Deeply held feelings of ownership begin to be questioned. Indeed, if there is one predictable consequence of a language becoming a global language, it is that nobody owns it any more. Or rather, everyone who has learned it now owns it—'has a share in it' might be more accurate—and has the right to use it in the way they want. This fact alone makes many people feel uncomfortable, even vaguely resentful. 'Look what the Americans have done to English' is a not uncommon comment found in the letter-columns of the British press. But similar comments can be heard in the USA when people encounter the sometimes striking variations in English which are emerging all over the world.

---

[3] For example, *Back to Babel*, a four-part (four-hour) series made in 2001 by Infonation, the film-making centre within the British Foreign and Commonwealth Office, had sold to sixty-four countries by 2002. The series was notable for its range of interviews eliciting the attitudes towards English of users in several countries. It was also the first series to devote a significant part of a programme to the consequences for endangered languages (...). The series became available, with extra footage, on DVD in 2002: www.infonation.org.uk.

And if English is not your mother tongue, you may still have mixed feelings about it. You may be strongly motivated to learn it, because you know it will put you in touch with more people than any other language; but at the same time you know it will take a great deal of effort to master it, and you may begrudge that effort. Having made progress, you will feel pride in your achievement, and savour the communicative power you have at your disposal, buy may none the less feel that mother-tongue speakers of English have an unfair advantage over you. And if you live in a country where the survival of your own language is threatened by the success of English, you may feel envious, resentful or angry. You may strongly object to the naivety of the populist account, with its simplistic and often suggestively triumphalist tone.

These feelings are natural, and would arise whichever language emerged as a global language. They are feelings which give rise to fears, whether real or imaginary, and fears lead to conflict. Language marches, language hunger-strikes, language rioting and language deaths are a fact, in several countries. Political differences over language economics, education, laws and rights are a daily encounter for millions. Language is always in the news, and the nearer a language moves to becoming a global language, the more newsworthy it is. So how does a language come to achieve global status?

WHAT IS A GLOBAL LANGUAGE?

A language achieves a genuinely global status when it develops a special role that is recognized in every country. This might seem like stating the obvious, but it is not, for the notion of 'special role' has many facets. Such a role will be most evident in countries where large numbers of the people speak the language as a mother tongue—in the case of English, this would mean the USA, Canada, Britain, Ireland, Australia, New Zealand, South Africa, several Caribbean countries and a sprinkling of other territories. However, no language has ever been spoken by a mother-tongue majority in more than a few countries (Spanish leads, in this respect, in some twenty countries, chiefly in Latin America), so mother-tongue use by itself cannot give a language global status. To achieve such a status, a language has to be taken up by other countries around the world. They must decide to give it a special place within their communities, even though they may have few (or no) mother-tongue speakers.

There are two main ways in which this can be done. Firstly, a language can be made the official language of a country, to be used as a medium of communication in such domains as government, the law courts, the media, and the educational system. To get on in these societies, it is essential to master the official language as early in life as possible. Such a language is often described as a 'second language', because it is seen as a complement to a person's mother tongue, or 'first language'.[4] The role of an official language is today best illustrated by English, which now has some kind of special status in over seventy countries, such as Ghana, Nigeria, India, Singapore and Vanuatu. . . . This is far more than the status achieved by any other language—though French, German, Spanish, Russian and Arabic are among those which have also developed a considerable official use. New political decisions on the matter continue to be made: for example, Rwanda gave English official status in 1996.

Secondly, a language can be made a priority in a country's foreign-language teaching, even though this language has no official status. It becomes the language which children are most likely to be taught when they arrive in school, and the one most available to adults who—for whatever reason—never learned it, or learned it badly, in their early educational years. Russian, for example, held privileged status for many years among the countries of the former Soviet Union. Mandarin Chinese continues to play an important role in South-east Asia. English is now the language most widely taught as a foreign language—in over 100 countries, such as China, Russia, Germany, Spain, Egypt and Brazil—and in most of these countries it is emerging as the chief foreign language to be encountered in schools, often displacing another language in the process. In 1996, for example, English replaced French as the chief foreign language in schools in Algeria (a former French colony).

In reflecting on these observations, it is important to note that there are several ways in which a language can be official. It may be the sole official language of a country, or it may share this status with other languages. And it may have a 'semi-official' status, being used only in certain domains, or taking second place to other languages while still performing certain official roles. Many countries formally acknowledge a language's status in their constitution (e.g. India); some make no special mention of it (e.g. Britain). In certain countries, the question of whether the special status should be legally recognized is a source of considerable controversy—notably, in the USA. . . .

Similarly, there is great variation in the reasons for choosing a particular language as a favoured foreign language: they include historical tradition, political expediency and the desire for commercial, cultural or technological contact. Also, even when chosen, the 'presence' of the language can vary greatly, depending on the extent to which a

---

[4] The term 'second language' needs to be used with caution—as indeed do all terms relating to language status. The most important point to note is that in many parts of the world the term is not related to official status, but simply reflects a notion of competence or usefulness. There is a long-established tradition for the term within the British sphere of influence, but there is no comparable history in the USA.

government or foreign-aid agency is prepared to give adequate financial support to a language-teaching policy. In a well-supported environment, resources will be devoted to helping people have access to the language and learn it, through the media, libraries, schools and institutes of higher education. There will be an increase in the number and quality of teachers able to teach the language. Books, tapes, computers, tele-communication systems and all kinds of teaching materials will be increasingly available. In many countries, however, lack of government support, or a shortage of foreign aid, has hindered the achievement of language-teaching goals.

Distinctions such as those between 'first', 'second' and 'foreign' language status are useful, but we must be careful not to give them a simplistic interpretation. In particular, it is important to avoid interpreting the distinction between 'second' and 'foreign' language use as a difference in fluency or ability. Although we might expect people from a country where English has some sort of official status to be more competent in the language than those where it has none, simply on grounds of greater exposure, it turns out that this is not always so. We should note, for example, the very high levels of fluency demonstrated by a wide range of speakers from the Scandinavian countries and the Netherlands. But we must also beware introducing too sharp a distinction between first-language speakers and the others, especially in a world where children are being born to parents who communicate with each other through a lingua franca learned as a foreign language. In the Emirates a few years ago, for example, I met a couple—a German oil industrialist and a Malaysian—who had courted through their only common language, English, and decided to bring up their child with English as the primary language of the home. So here is a baby learning English as a foreign language as its mother tongue. There are now many such cases around the world, and they raise a question over the contribution that these babies will one day make to the language, once they grow up to be important people, for their intuitions about English will inevitably be different from those of traditional native speakers.

These points add to the complexity of the present-day world English situation, but they do not alter the fundamental point. Because of the three-pronged development—of first-language, second-language and foreign-language speakers—it is inevitable that a global language will eventually come to be used by more people than any other language. English has already reached this stage. [Current statistics] suggest that about a quarter of the world's population is already fluent or competent in English, and this figure is steadily growing—in the early 2000s that means around 1.5 billion people. No other language can match this growth. Even Chinese, found in eight different spoken languages, but unified by a common writing system, is known to 'only' some 1.1 billion.

WHAT MAKES A GLOBAL LANGUAGE?

Why a language becomes a global language has little to do with the number of people who speak it. It is much more to do with who those speakers are. Latin became an international language throughout the Roman Empire, but this was not because the Romans were more numerous than the peoples they subjugated. They were simply more powerful. And later, when Roman military power declined, Latin remained for a millennium as a the international language of education, thanks to a different sort of power—the ecclesiastical power of Roman Catholicism.

There is the closest of links between language dominance and economic, technological and cultural power. . . . Without a strong power-base, of whatever kind, no language can make progress as an international medium of communication. Language has no independent existence, living in some sort of mystical space apart from the people who speak it. Language exists only in the brains and mouths and ears and hands and eyes of its users. When they succeed, on the international stage, their language succeeds. When they fail, their language fails.

This point may seem obvious, but it needs to be made at the outset, because over the years many popular and misleading beliefs have grown up about why a language should become internationally successful. It is quite common to hear people claim that a language is a paragon, on account of its perceived aesthetic qualities, clarity of expression, literary power or religious standing. Hebrew, Greek, Latin, Arabic and French are among those which at various times have been lauded in such terms, and English is no exception. It is often suggested, for example, that there must be something inherently beautiful or logical about the structure of English, in order to explain why it is now so widely used. 'It has less grammar than other languages', some have suggested. 'English doesn't have a lot of endings on its words, nor do we have to remember the difference between masculine, feminine, and neuter gender, so it must be easier to learn'. In 1848, a reviewer in the British periodical *The Athenaeum* wrote:

> In its easiness of grammatical construction, in its paucity of inflection, in its almost total disregard of the distinctions of gender excepting those of nature, in the simplicity and precision of its terminations and auxiliary verbs, not less than in the majesty, vigour and copiousness of its expression, our mother-tongue seems well adapted by *organization* to become the language of the world.

Such arguments are misconceived. Latin was once a major international language, despite its many inflectional endings and gender differences. French, too, has been such a language, despite its nouns being masculine or feminine; and so—at different times and places—have the heavily inflected Greek, Arabic, Spanish and Russian. Ease of learning has nothing to do with it. Children of all cultures learn to talk over more or less the same period of time, regardless of the differences in the grammar of their languages. And as for the notion that English has 'no grammar'—a claim that is risible to anyone who has ever had to learn it as a foreign language—the point can be dismissed by a glance at any of the large twentieth-century reference grammars. The *Comprehensive grammar of the English language,* for example, contains 1,800 pages and some 3,500 points requiring grammatical exposition.[5]

This is not to deny that a language may have certain properties which make it internationally appealing. For example, learners sometimes comment on the 'familiarity' of English vocabulary, deriving from the way English has over the centuries borrowed thousands of new words from the languages with which it has been in contact. The 'welcome' given to foreign vocabulary places English in contrast to some languages (notably, French) which have tried to keep it out, and gives it a cosmopolitan character which many see as an advantage for a global language. From a lexical point of view, English is in fact far more a Romance than a Germanic language. And there have been comments made about other structural aspects, too, such as the absence in English grammar of a system of coding social class differences, which can make the language appear more 'democratic' to those who speak a language (e.g. Javanese) that does express an intricate system of class relationships. But these supposed traits of appeal are incidental, and need to be weighed against linguistic features which would seem to be internationally much less desirable—notably, in the case of English, the accumulated irregularities of its spelling system.

A language does not become a global language because of its intrinsic structural properties, or because of the size of its vocabulary, or because it has been a vehicle of a great literature in the past, or because it was once associated with a great culture or religion. These are all factors which can motivate someone to learn a language, or course, but none of them alone, or in combination, can ensure a language's world spread. Indeed, such factors cannot even guarantee survival as a living language— as is clear from the case of Latin, learned today as a classical language by only a scholarly and religious few. Correspondingly, inconvenient structural properties (such as awkward spelling) do not stop a language achieving international status either.

A language has traditionally become an international language for one chief reason: the power of its people—especially their political and military power. The explanation is the same throughout history. Why did Greek become a language of international communication in the Middle

---

[5] Largely points to do with syntax, of course, rather than the morphological emphasis which is what many people, brought up in the Latinate tradition, think grammar to be about. The figure of 3,500 is derived from the index which I compiled for Quirk, Greenbaum, Leech and Svartvik (1985), excluding entries which related solely to lexical items.

East over 2,000 years ago? Not because of the intellects of Plato and Aristotle: the answer lies in the swords and spears wielded by the armies of Alexander the Great. Why did Latin become known throughout Europe? Ask the legions of the Roman Empire. Why did Arabic come to be spoken so widely across northern Africa and the Middle East? Follow the spread of Islam, carried along by the force of the Moorish armies from the eighth century. Why did Spanish, Portuguese and French find their way into the Americas, Africa and the Far East? Study the colonial policies of the Renaissance kings and queens, and the way these policies were ruthlessly implemented by armies and navies all over the known world. The history of a global language can be traced through the successful expeditions of its soldier/sailor speakers. And English . . . has been no exception.

But international language dominance is not solely the result of military might. It may take a militarily powerful nation to establish a language, but it takes an economically powerful one to maintain and expand it. This has always been the case, but it became a particularly critical factor in the nineteenth and twentieth centuries, with economic developments beginning to operate on a global scale, supported by the new communication technologies—telegraph, telephone, radio—and fostering the emergence of massive multinational organizations. The growth of competitive industry and business brought an explosion of international marketing and advertising. The power of the press reached unprecedented levels, soon to be surpassed by the broadcasting media, with their ability to cross national boundaries with electromagnetic ease. Technology, chiefly in the form of movies and records, fuelled new mass entertainment industries which had a worldwide impact. The drive to make progress in science and technology fostered an international intellectual and research environment which gave scholarship and further education a high profile.

Any language at the centre of such an explosion of international activity would suddenly have found itself with a global status. And English, . . . was apparently 'in the right place at the right time'. . . . By the beginning of the nineteenth century, Britain had become the world's leading industrial and trading country. By the end of the century, the population of the USA (then approaching 100 million) was larger than that of any of the countries of western Europe, and its economy was the most productive and the fastest growing in the world. British political imperialism had sent English around the globe, during the nineteenth century, so that it was a language 'on which the sun never sets'.[6] During the twentieth century, this world presence was maintained and promoted almost single-handedly through the economic supremacy of the new American superpower. Economics replaced politics as the chief driving force. And the language behind the US dollar was English.

---

[6] An expression adapted from the nineteenth-century aphorism about the extent of the British Empire. It continued to be used in the twentieth century, for example by Randolph Quirk (1985: 1).

WHY DO WE NEED A GLOBAL LANGUAGE?

Translation has played a central (though often unrecognized) role in human interaction for thousands of years. When monarchs or ambassadors met on the international stage, there would invariably be interpreters present. But there are limits to what can be done in this way. The more a community is linguistically mixed, the less it can rely on individuals to ensure communication between different groups. In communities where only two or three languages are in contact, bilingualism (or trilingualism) is a possible solution, for most young children can acquire more than one language with unselfconscious ease. But in communities where there are many languages in contact, as in much of Africa and South-east Asia, such a natural solution does not readily apply.

The problem has traditionally been solved by finding a language to act as a *lingua franca*, or 'common language'. Sometimes, when communities begin to trade with each other, they communicate by adopting a simplified language, known as a *pidgin*, which combines elements of their different languages.[7] Many such pidgin languages survive today in territories which formerly belonged to the European colonial nations, and act as lingua francas; for example, West African Pidgin English is used extensively between several ethnic groups along the West African coast. Sometimes an indigenous language emerges as a lingua franca—usually the language of the most powerful ethnic group in the area, as in the case of Mandarin Chinese. The other groups then learn this language with varying success, and thus become to some degree bilingual. But most often, a language is accepted from outside the community, such as English or French, because of the political, economic or religious influence of a foreign power.

The grographical extent to which a lingua franca can be used is entirely governed by political factors. Many lingua francas extend over quite small domains—between a few ethnic groups in one part of a single country, or linking the trading populations of just a few countries, as in the West African case. By contrast, Latin was a lingua franca throughout the whole of the Roman Empire—at least, at the level of government (very few 'ordinary' people in the subjugated domains would have spoken much Latin). And in modern times Swahili, Arabic, Spanish, French, English, Hindi, Portuguese and several other languages have developed a major international role as a lingua franca, in limited areas of the world.

The prospect that a lingua franca might be needed for the *whole* world is something which has emerged strongly only in the twentieth century, and since the 1950s in particular. The chief international forum for political communication—the United Nations—dates only from 1945. Since then, many international bodies have come into being, such

---

[7] For the rise of pidgin Englishes, see Todd (1984).

as the World Bank (also 1945), UNESCO and UNICEF (both 1946), the World Health Organization (1948) and the International Atomic Energy Agency (1957). Never before have so many countries (around 190, in the case of some UN bodies) been represented in single meeting-places. At a more restricted level, multinational regional or political groupings have come into being, such as the Commonwealth and the European Union. The pressure to adopt a single lingua franca, to facilitate communication in such contexts, is considerable, the alternative being expensive and impracticable multi-way translation facilities.

Usually a small number of languages have been designated official languages for an organization's activities: for example, the UN was established with five official languages—English, French, Spanish, Russian and Chinese. There is now a widespread view that it makes sense to try to reduce the numbers of languages involved in world bodies, if only to cut down on the vast amount of interpretation/translation and clerical work required. Half the budget of an international organization can easily get swallowed up in translation costs. But trimming a translation budget is never easy, as obviously no country likes the thought of its language being given a reduced international standing. Language choice is always one of the most sensitive issues facing a planning committee. The common situation is one where a committee does not have to be involved—where all the participants at an international meeting automatically use a single language, as a utilitarian measure (a 'working language'), because it is one which they have all come to learn for separate reasons. This situation seems to be slowly becoming a reality in meetings around the world, as general competence in English grows.

The need for a global language is particularly appreciated by the international academic and business communities, and it is here that the adoption of a single lingua franca is most in evidence, both in lecture-rooms and board-rooms, as well as in thousands of individual contacts being made daily all over the globe. A conversation over the Internet . . . between academic physicists in Sweden, Italy and India is at present practicable only if a common language is available. A situation where a Japanese company director arranges to meet German and Saudi Arabian contacts in a Singapore hotel to plan a multi-national deal would not be impossible, if each plugged in to a 3-way translation support system, but it would be far more complicated than the alternative, which is for each to make use of the same language.

At these examples suggest, the growth in international contacts has been largely the result of two separate developments. The physicists would not be talking so conveniently to each other at all without the technology of modern communication. And the business contacts would be unable to meet so easily in Singapore without the technology of air transportation. The availability of both these facilities in the twentieth century, more than anything else, provided the circumstances needed for a global language to grow.

People have, in short, become more mobile, both physically and electronically. Annual airline statistics show that steadily increasing numbers are finding the motivation as well as the means to transport themselves physically around the globe, and sales of faxes, modems and personal computers show an even greater increase in those prepared to send their ideas in words and images electronically. It is now possible, using electronic mail, to copy a message to hundreds of locations all over the world virtually simultaneously. It is just as easy for me to send a message from my house in the small town of Holyhead, North Wales, to a friend in Washington as it is to get the same message to someone living just a few streets away from me. In fact, it is probably easier. That is why people so often talk, these days, of the 'global village'.

These trends would be taking place, presumably, if only a handful of countries were talking to each other. What has been so impressive about the developments which have taken place since the 1950s is that they have affected, to a greater or lesser extent, every country in the world, and that so many countries have come to be involved. There is no nation now which does not have some level of accessibility using telephone, radio, television and air transport, though facilities such as fax, electronic mail and the Internet are much less widely available.

The scale and recency of the development has to be appreciated. In 1945, the United Nations began life with 51 member states. By 1956 this had risen to 80 members. But the independence movements which began at that time led to a massive increase in the number of new nations during the next decade, and this process continued steadily into the 1990s, following the collapse of the USSR. There were 190 member states in 2002—nearly four times as many as there were fifty years ago. And the trend may not yet be over, given the growth of so many regional nationalistic movements worldwide.

There are no precedents in human history for what happens to languages, in such circumstances of rapid change. There has never been a time when so many nations were needing to talk to each other so much. Three has never been a time when so many people wished to travel to so many places. There has never been such a strain placed on the conventional resources of translating and interpreting. Never has the need for more widespread bilingualism been greater, to ease the burden placed on the professional few. And never has there been a more urgent need for a global language.

WHAT ARE THE DANGERS OF A GLOBAL LANGUAGE?

The benefits which would flow from the existence of a global language are considerable; but several commentators have pointed to possible risks.[8] Perhaps a global language will cultivate an elite monolingual

---

[8] These risks, and all the associated points discussed in this section, are given a full treatment in the companion volume to this one, *Language death* (Crystal 2000).

linguistic class, more complacent and dismissive in their attitudes towards other languages. Perhaps those who have such a language at their disposal—and especially those who have it as a mother-tongue—will be more able to think and work quickly in it, and to manipulate it to their own advantage at the expense of those who do not have it, thus maintaining in a linguistic guise the chasm between rich and poor. Perhaps the presence of a global language will make people lazy about learning other languages, or reduce their opportunities to do so. Perhaps a global language will hasten the disappearance of minority languages, or—the ultimate threat—make *all* other languages unnecessary. 'A person needs only one language to talk to someone else', it is sometimes argued, 'and once a world language is in place, other languages will simply die away'. Linked with all this is the unpalatable face of linguistic triumphalism— the danger that some people will celebrate one language's success at the expense of others.

It is important to face up to these fears, and to recognize that they are widely held. There is no shortage of mother-tongue English speakers who believe in an evolutionary view of language ('let the fittest survive, and if the fittest happens to be English, then so be it') or who refer to the present global status of the language as a 'happy accident'. There are many who think that all language learning is a waste of time. And many more who see nothing wrong with the vision that a world with just one language in it would be a very good thing. For some, such a world would be one of unity and peace, with all misunderstanding washed away—a widely expressed hope underlying the movements in support of a universal artificial language (such as Esperanto). For others, such a world would be a desirable return to the 'innocence' that must have been present among human beings in the days before the Tower of Babel.[9]

It is difficult to deal with anxieties which are so speculative, or, in the absence of evidence, to determine whether anything can be done to reduce or eliminate them. The last point can be quite briefly dismissed: the use of a single language by a community is no guarantee of social harmony or mutual understanding, as has been repeatedly seen in world history (e.g. the American Civil War, the Spanish Civil War, the Vietnam War, former Yugoslavia, contemporary Northern Ireland); nor does the presence of more than one language within a community necessitate civil strife, as seen in several successful examples of peaceful multilingual coexistence (e.g. Finland, Singapore, Switzerland). The other points, however, need to be taken more slowly, to appreciate the alternative perspective.

---

[9] The Babel myth is particularly widely held, because of its status as part of a biblical narrative (Genesis, chapter 11). Even in biblical terms, however, there is no ground for saying that Babel introduced multilingualism as a 'curse' or 'punishment'. Languages were already in existence before Babel, as we learn from Genesis, chapter 10, where the sons of Japheth are listed 'according to their countries and each of their languages'. See Eco (1995).

The arguments are each illustrated with reference to English—but the same arguments would apply whatever language was in the running for global status.

Linguistic Power. Will those who speak a global language as a mother tongue automatically be in a position of power compared with those who have to learn it as an official or foreign language? The risk is certainly real. It is possible, for example, that scientists who do not have English as a mother tongue will take longer to assimilate reports in English compared with their mother-tongue colleagues, and will as a consequence have less time to carry out their own creative work. It is possible that people who write up their research in languages other than English will have their work ignored by the international community. It is possible that senior managers who do not have English as a mother tongue, and who find themselves working for English-language companies in such parts of the world as Europe or Africa, could find themselves at a disadvantage compared with their mother-tongue colleagues, especially when meetings involve the use of informal speech. There is already anecdotal evidence to suggest that these things happen.

However, if proper attention is paid to the question of language learning, the problem of disadvantage dramatically diminishes. If a global language is taught early enough, from the time that children begin their full-time education, and if it is maintained continuously and resourced well, the kind of linguistic competence which emerges in due course is a real and powerful bilingualism, indistinguishable from that found in any speaker who has encountered the language since birth. These are enormous 'ifs', with costly financial implications, and it is therefore not surprising that this kind of control is currently achieved by only a minority of non-native learners of any language; but the fact that it is achievable (as evidenced repeatedly by English speakers from such countries as Denmark, Sweden and the Netherlands) indicates that there is nothing inevitable about the disadvantage scenario.

It is worth reflecting, at this point, on the notion that children are born ready for bilingualism. Some two-thirds of the children on earth grow up in a bilingual environment, and develop competence in it. There is a naturalness with which they assimilate another language, once they are regularly exposed to it, which is the envy of adults. It is an ability which seems to die away as children reach their teens, and much academic debate has been devoted to the question of why this should be (the question of 'critical periods').[10] There is however widespread agreement that, if we want to take the task of foreign language learning seriously, one of the key principles is 'the earlier the better'. And when that task *is* taken seriously, with reference to the acquisition of a global language, the elitism argument evaporates.

---

[10] For bilingual acquisition, see De Houwer (1995), Baker and Prys Jones (1998).

Linguistic Complacency. Will a global language eliminate the motivation for adults to learn other languages? Here too the problem is real
enough. Clear signs of linguistic complacency, common observation suggests, are already present in the archetypal British or American tourist
who travels the world assuming that everyone speaks English, and that it
is somehow the fault of the local people if they do not. The stereotype of
an English tourist repeatedly asking a foreign waiter for tea in a loud 'read
my lips' voice is too near the reality to be comfortable. There seems
already to be a genuine, widespread lack of motivation to learn other languages, fuelled partly by lack of money and opportunity, but also by lack
of interest, and this might well be fostered by the increasing presence of
English as a global language.

It is important to appreciate that we are dealing here with questions
of attitude or state of mind rather than questions of ability—though it is
the latter which is often cited as the explanation. 'I'm no good at languages' is probably the most widely heard apology for not making any
effort at all to acquire even a basic knowledge of a new language.
Commonly, this self-denigration derives from an unsatisfactory language
learning experience in school: the speaker is perhaps remembering a
poor result in school examinations—which may reflect no more than an
unsuccessful teaching approach or a not unusual breakdown in teacher–
adolescent relationships. 'I never got on with my French teacher' is
another typical comment. But this does not stop people going on to generalize that 'the British (or the Americans, etc.) are not very good at learning languages'.

These days, there are clear signs of growing awareness, within English-
speaking communities, of the need to break away from the traditional
monolingual bias.[11] In economically hard-pressed times, success in boost-
ing exports and attracting foreign investment can depend on subtle factors,
and sensitivity to the language spoken by a country's potential foreign
partners is known to be particularly influential.[12] At least at the levels of
business and industry, many firms have begun to make fresh efforts in this
direction. But at grass-roots tourist level, too, there are signs of a growing
respect for other cultures, and a greater readiness to engage in language
learning. Language attitudes are changing all the time, and more and more
people are discovering, to their great delight, that they are not at all bad at
picking up a foreign language.

In particular, statements from influential politicians and administrators are beginning to be made which are helping to foster a fresh

---

[11] The awareness is by no means restricted to English-speaking communities, as
was demonstrated by the spread of activities associated with the European Year of
Languages, 2001 (European Commission (2002)).
[12] For economic arguments in support of multilingualism and foreign language
learning, see the 1996 issue of the *International Journal of the Sociology of Language*
on 'Economic Approaches to Language and Language Planning'; also Coulmas (1992).

climate of opinion about the importance of language learning. A good example is an address given in 1996 by the former secretary-general of the Commonwealth, Sir Sridath Ramphal. His title, 'World language: opportunities, challenges, responsibilities', itself contains a corrective to triumphalist thinking, and his text repeatedly argues against it:[13]

> It is all too easy to make your way in the world linguistically with English as your mother tongue . . . We become lazy about learning other languages . . . We all have to make a greater effort. English may be the world language; but it is not the world's only language and if we are to be good global neighbours we shall have to be less condescending to the languages of the world—more assiduous in cultivating acquaintance with them.

It remains to be seen whether such affirmations of good will have long-term effect. In the meantime, it is salutary to read some of the comparative statistics about foreign language learning. For example, a European Business Survey by Grant Thornton reported in 1996 that 90 per cent of businesses in Belgium, The Netherlands, Luxembourg and Greece had an executive able to negotiate in another language, whereas only 38 per cent of British companies had someone who could do so. In 2002 the figures remained high for most European countries in the survey, but had fallen to 29 per cent in Britain.[14] The UK-based Centre for Information on Language Teaching and Research found that a third of British exporters miss opportunities because of poor language skills.[15] And English-monolingual companies are increasingly encountering language difficulties as they try to expand in those areas of the world thought to have greatest prospects of growth, such as East Asia, South America and Eastern Europe—areas where English has traditionally had a relatively low presence. The issues are beginning to be addressed—for example, many Australian schools now teach Japanese as the first foreign language, and both the USA and UK are now paying more attention to Spanish (which, in terms of mother-tongue use, is growing more rapidly than English)—but we are still a long way from a world where the economic and other arguments have universally persuaded the English-speaking nations to renounce their linguistic insularity.

Linguistic Death. Will the emergence of a global language hasten the disappearance of minority languages and cause widespread language death? To answer this question, we must first establish a general perspective. The processes of language domination and loss have been known throughout linguistic history, and exist independently of the emergence of a global language. No one knows how many languages have died since humans became able to speak, but it must be thousands. In many

---

[13] Ramphal (1996).
[14] Grant Thornton (2002).
[15] For a recent statement, see CILT (2002).

of these cases, the death has been caused by an ethnic group coming to be assimilated within a more dominant society, and adopting its language. The situation continues today, though the matter is being discussed with increasing urgency because of the unprecedented rate at which indigenous languages are being lost, especially in North America, Brazil, Australia, Indonesia and parts of Africa. At least 50 per cent of the world's 6,000 or so living languages will die our within the next century.[16]

This is indeed an intellectual and social tragedy. When a language dies, so much is lost. Especially in languages which have never been written down, or which have been written down only recently, language is the repository of the history of a people. It is their identity. Oral testimony, in the form of sagas, folktales, songs, rituals, proverbs and many other practices, provides us with a unique view of our world and a unique canon of literature. It is their legacy to the rest of humanity. Once lost, it can never be recaptured. The argument is similar to that used in relation to the conservation of species and the environment. The documentation and—where practicable—conservation of languages is also a priority, and it was good to see in the 1990s a number of international organizations being formed with the declared aim of recording for posterity as many endangered languages as possible.[17]

However, the emergence of any one language as global has only a limited causal relationship to this unhappy state of affairs. Whether Sorbian survives in Germany or Galician in Spain has to do with the local political and economic history of those countries, and with the regional dominance of German and Spanish respectively, and bears no immediate relationship to the standing of German or Spanish on the world stage.[18] Nor is it easy to see how the arrival of English as a global language could directly influence the future of these or many other minority languages. An effect is likely only in those areas where English has itself come to be the dominant first language, such as in North America, Australia and the Celtic parts of the British Isles. The early history of language contact in these areas was indeed one of conquest and assimilation, and the effects

---

[16] This is an average of the estimates which have been proposed. For a detailed examination of these estimates, see Crystal (2000: chapter 1).

[17] These organizations include The International Clearing House for Endangered Languages in Tokyo, The Foundation for Endangered Languages in the UK and The Endangered Language Fund in the USA. Contact details for these and similar organizations are given in Crystal (2000: Appendix).

[18] The point can be made even more strongly in such parts of the world as Latin America, where English has traditionally had negligible influence. The hundreds of Amerindian languages which have disappeared in Central and South America have done so as a result of cultures which spoke Spanish and Portuguese, not English. Chinese, Russian, Arabic and other major languages have all had an impact on minority languages throughout their history, and continue to do so. The responsibility for language preservation and revitalization is a shared one.

on indigenous languages were disastrous. But in more recent times, the emergence of English as a truly global language has, if anything, had the reverse effect—stimulating a stronger response in support of a local language than might otherwise have been the case. Times have changed. Movements for language rights (alongside civil rights in general) have played an important part in several countries, such as in relation to the Maori in New Zealand, the Aboriginal languages of Australia, the Indian languages of Canada and the USA and some of the Celtic languages. Although often too late, in certain instances the decline of a language has been slowed, and occasionally (as in the case of Welsh) halted.

The existence of vigorous movements in support of linguistic minorities, commonly associated with nationalism, illustrates an important truth about the nature of language in general. The need for mutual intelligibility, which is part of the argument in favour of a global language, is only one side of the story. The other side is the need for identity—and people tend to underestimate the role of identity when they express anxieties about language injury and death. Language is a major means (some would say the chief means) of showing where we belong, and of distinguishing one social group from another, and all over the world we can see evidence of linguistic divergence rather than convergence. For decades, many people in the countries of former Yugoslavia made use of a common language, Serbo-Croatian. But since the civil wars of the early 1990s, the Serbs have referred to their language as Serbian, the Bosnians to theirs as Bosnian and the Croats to theirs as Croatian, with each community drawing attention to the linguistic features which are distinctive. A similar situation exists in Scandinavia, where Swedish, Norwegian and Danish are largely mutually intelligible, but are none the less considered to be different languages.

Arguments about the need for national or cultural identity are often seen as being opposed to those about the need for mutual intelligibility. But this is misleading. It is perfectly possible to develop a situation in which intelligibility and identity happily co-exist. This situation is the familiar one of bilingualism—but a bilingualism where one of the languages within a speaker is the global language, providing access to the world community, and the other is a well-resourced regional language, providing access to a local community. The two functions can be seen as complementary, responding to different needs. And it is because the functions are so different that a world of linguistic diversity can in principle continue to exist in a world united by a common language.

None of this is to deny that the emergence of a global language can influence the structure of other languages—especially by providing a fresh source of loan-words for use by these other languages. Such influences can be welcomed (in which case, people talk about their language being 'varied' and 'enriched') or opposed (in which case, the metaphors are those of 'injury' and 'death'). For example, in recent years, one of the healthiest languages, French, has tried to protect itself by law against what is widely perceived to be the malign influence of English: in official contexts, it is now illegal to use an English word where a French word already exists, even though the usage may have widespread popular support (e.g. *computer* for *ordinateur*). Purist commentators from several other countries have also expressed concern at the way in which English vocabulary—especially that of American English—has come to permeate their high streets and TV programmes. The arguments are carried on with great emotional force. Even though only a tiny part of the lexicon is ever affected in this way, that is enough to arouse the wrath of the prophets of doom. (They usually forget the fact that English itself, over the centuries, has borrowed thousands of words from other languages, and constructed thousands more from the elements of other languages— including *computer*, incidentally, which derives from Latin, the mother-language of French.)[19]

The relationship between the global spread of English and its impact on other languages attracted increasing debate during the 1990s. The fact that it is possible to show a correlation between the rate of English adoption and the demise of minority languages has led some observers to reassert the conclusion that there is a simple causal link between the two phenomena, ignoring the fact that there has been a similar loss of linguistic diversity in parts of the world where English has not had a history of significant presence, such as Latin America, Russia and China. A more deep-rooted process of globalization seems to be at work today, transcending individual language situations. Anachronistic views of linguistic imperialism, which see as important only the power asymmetry between the former colonial nations and the nations of the 'third world', are hopelessly inadequate as an explanation of linguistic realities.[20] They especially ignore the fact that 'first world' countries with strong languages seem to be under just as much pressure to adopt English, and that some of the harshest attacks on English have come from countries which have no such colonial legacy. When dominant languages feel they are

---

[19] English has borrowed words from over 350 other languages, and over three-quarters of the English lexicon is actually Classical or Romance in origin. Plainly, the view that to borrow words leads to a language's decline is absurd, given that English has borrowed more words than most. Languages change their character, as a result of such borrowing, of course, and this too upsets purists, who seem unable to appreciate the expressive gains which come from having the option of choosing between lexical alternatives, as in such 'triplets' as (Anglo-Saxon) *kingly*, (French) *royal* and (Latin) *regal*. For further examples, see the classic source, Serjeantson (1935), also Crystal (1995). See also Görlach (2002).

[20] Two prominent positions are Phillipson (1992) and Pennycook (1994).

being dominated, something much bigger than a simplistic conception of power relations must be involved.[21]

These other factors, which include the recognition of global inter-dependence, the desire to have a voice in world affairs and the value of multilingualism in attracting trade markets, all support the adoption of a functionalist account of English, where the language is seen as a valuable instrument enabling people to achieve particular goals. Local languages continue to perform an important set of functions (chiefly, the expression of local identity) and English is seen as the primary means of achieving a global presence. The approach recognizes the legacy of colonialism, as a matter of historical fact, but the emphasis is now on discontinuities, away from power and towards functional specialization.[22] It is a model which sees English playing a central role in empowering the subjugated and marginalized, and eroding the division between the 'haves' and the 'have nots'. Those who argue for this position have been dismissed as dis-playing 'naive liberal idealism' and adopting a 'liberal laissez-faire atti-tude'.[23] Rather, it is the linguistic imperialism position which is naive, disregarding the complex realities of a world in which a historical con-ception of power relations has to be seen alongside an emerging set of empowering relationships in which English has a new functional role, no longer associated with the political authority it once held.

If working towards the above goal is idealism, then I am happy to be an idealist; however, it is by no means laissez-faire, given the amount of time, energy and money which have been devoted in recent years to lan-guage revitalization and related matters. Admittedly, the progress which has been made is tiny compared with the disastrous effects of globaliza-tion on global diversity. But to place all the blame on English, and to ignore the more fundamental economic issues that are involved, is, as two recent commentators have put it, 'to attack the wrong target, to indulge in linguistic luddism'.[24] Solutions are more likely to come from

---

[21] The point is also made by Lysandrou and Lysandrou (2003): 'The pace of English language adoption over the past decade or so has been so explosive as to make it diffi-cult if not impossible to accept that those accounts of the phenomenon which focus on power asymmetries can bear the burden of explanation.' It is reinforced by the litera-ture on language endangerment, which has made it very clear that the survival of a lan-guage depends largely on factors other than political power (e.g. Brenzinger (1998), Crystal (2000)). Focusing on Africa, for example, Mufwene (2001, 2002) has drawn attention to the many African languages which have lost their vitality because speak-ers have adopted peer languages that have guaranteed a surer economic survival.

[22] For example, Fishman, Conrad and Rubal-Lopez (1996).

[23] The name-calling is Pennycook's (2001: 56), who uses these phrases with refer-ence to the first edition of the present ('overmarketed' (sic)) book. For a further exam-ple of what might euphemistically be called 'debate', see Phillipson (1998/1999) and Crystal (1999/2000).

[24] Lysandrou and Lysandrou (2003).

the domain of economic policy, not language policy. As Lysandrou and Lysandrou conclude:

> If English can facilitate the process of universal dispossession and loss, so can it be turned round and made to facilitate the contrary process of universal empowerment and gain.

COULD ANYTHING STOP A GLOBAL LANGUAGE?

Any discussion of an emerging global language has to be seen in the political context of global governance as a whole. In January 1995, the Commission on Global Governance published its report, *Our global neighbourhood*.[25] A year later, the Commission's co-chairman, Sridath Ramphal, commented (in the paper referred to [previously]):

> There were, for the most part, people who were pleased that the Report had engaged the central issue of a global community, but they took us to task for not going on—in as they thought in a logical way—to call for a world language. They could not see how the global neighbourhood, the global community, which they acknowledged had come into being, could function effectively without a world language. A neighbourhood that can only talk in the tongues of many was not a neighbourhood that was likely to be cohesive or, perhaps, even cooperative . . . And they were right in one respect; but they were wrong in the sense that we *have* a world language. It is not the language of imperialism; it is the language we have seen that has evolved out of a history of which we need not always be proud, but whose legacies we must use to good effect.

And at another place, he comments: 'there is no retreat from English as the world language; no retreat from an English-speaking world'.

Strong political statements of this kind immediately prompt the question, 'Could anything stop a language, once it achieves a global status?' The short answer must be 'yes'. If language dominance is a matter of political and especially economic influence, then a revolution in the balance of global power could have consequences for the choice of global language.[26] There is no shortage of books—chiefly within the genre of science fiction—which foresee a future in which, following some cataclysmic scenario, the universal language is Chinese, Arabic or even some Alien tongue. But to end up with such a scenario, the revolution would indeed have to be cataclysmic, and it is difficult to speculate sensibly about what this might be.[27] Smaller-scale revolutions in the world order

---

[25] Commission on Global Governance (1995).

[26] Graddol (1998) explores this scenario.

[27] Speculation about the political state of the world leads Dalby (2002) to envision 200 languages remaining in 200 years' time. Janson (2002) takes linguistic speculation to an even more apocalyptic point, reflecting on the state of human language 2 million years from now.

would be unlikely to have much effect, given that . . . English is now so widely established that it can no longer be thought of as 'owned' by any single nation.

A rather more plausible scenario is that an alternative method of communication could emerge which would eliminate the need for a global language. The chief candidate here is automatic translation ('machine translation'). If progress in this domain continues to be as rapid as it has been in the past decade, there is a distinct possibility that, within a generation or two, it will be routine for people to communicate with each other directly, using their first languages, with a computer 'taking the strain' between them. This state of affairs can already be seen, to a limited extent, on the Internet, where some firms are now offering a basic translation service between certain language pairs. A sender types in a message in language X, and a version of it appears on the receiver's screen in language Y. The need for post-editing is still considerable, however, as translation software is currently very limited in its ability to handle idiomatic, stylistic, and several other linguistic features; the machines are nowhere near replacing their human counterparts. Similarly, notwithstanding the remarkable progress in speech recognition and synthesis which has taken place in recent years, the state of the art in real-time speech-to-speech automatic translation is still primitive. The 'Babel fish', inserted into the ear, thus making all spoken languages (in the galaxy) intelligible, is no more than an intriguing concept.[28]

The accuracy and speed of real-time automatic translation is undoubtedly going to improve dramatically in the next twenty-five to fifty years, but it is going to take much longer before this medium becomes so globally widespread, and so economically accessible to all, that it poses a threat to the current availability and appeal of a global language. And during this time frame, all the evidence suggests that the position of English as a global language is going to become stronger. By the time automatic translation matures as a popular communicative medium, that position will very likely have become impregnable. It will be very interesting to see what happens then—whether the presence of a global language will eliminate the demand for world translation services, or whether the economics of automatic translation will so undercut the cost of global language learning that the latter will become otiose. It will be an interesting battle 100 years from now.

A CRITICAL ERA

It is impossible to make confident predictions about the emergence of a global language. There are no precedents for this kind of linguistic growth, other than on a much smaller scale. And the speed with which a

---

[28] Explored by Douglas Adams (1979: chapter 6).

global language scenario has arisen is truly remarkable. Within little more than a generation, we have moved from a situation where a world language was a theoretical possibility to one where it is an evident reality.

No government has yet found it possible to plan confidently, in such circumstances. Languages of identity need to be maintained. Access to the emerging global language—widely perceived as a language of opportunity and empowerment—needs to be guaranteed. Both principles demand massive resources. The irony is that the issue is approaching a climax at a time when the world financial climate can least afford it.

Fundamental decisions about priorities have to be made. Those making the decisions need to bear in mind that we may well be approaching a critical moment in human linguistic history. It is possible that a global language will emerge only once. Certainly, as we have seen, after such a language comes to be established it would take a revolution of world-shattering proportions to replace it. And in due course, the last quarter of the twentieth century will be seen as a critical time in the emergence of this global language.

For [a number of reasons], all the signs suggest that this global language will be English. But there is still some way to go before a global lingua franca becomes a universal reality. Despite the remarkable growth in the use of English, at least two-thirds of the world population do not yet use it. In certain parts of the world (most of the states of the former Soviet Union, for example), English has still a very limited presence. And in some countries, increased resources are being devoted to maintaining the role of other languages (such as the use of French in several countries of Africa). Notwithstanding the general world trend, there are many linguistic confrontations still to be resolved.

Governments who wish to play their part in influencing the world's linguistic future should therefore ponder carefully, as they make political decisions and allocate resources for language planning. Now, more than at any time in linguistic history, they need to adopt long-term views, and to plan ahead—whether their interests are to promote English or to develop the use of other languages in their community (or, of course, both). If they miss this linguistic boat, there may be no other.

BIBLIOGRAPHY

Adams, Douglas. 1979. *The hitch-hiker's guide to the galaxy.* London: Pan.

Baker, Colin and Prys Jones, Sylvia. 1998. *Encyclopedia of bilingualism and bilingual education.* Clevedon: Multilingual Matters.

Brenzinger, Matthias. Ed. 1998. *Endangered languages in Africa.* Cologne: Rüdiger Köper.

CILT [Centre for Information on Language Teaching and Research]. 2002. *Speaking up for languages.* London: CILT.

Commission on Global Governance. 1995. Ingvar Carlsson and Sridath Ramphal (co-chairmen), *Our global neighbourhood.* New York: United Nations.

Coulmas, Florian. 1992. *Language and economy.* Oxford: Blackwell.

Crystal, David. 1995. *The Cambridge encyclopedia of the English language.* Cambridge: Cambridge University Press.

1999/2000. On trying to be crystal-clear: a response to Phillipson. *European English Messenger* 8 (1), 1999, 59–65; expanded in *Applied Linguistics* 21, 2000, 415–23.

2000. *Language death.* Cambridge: Cambridge University Press.

Dalby, Andrew. 2002. *Language in danger.* Harmondsworth: Penguin.

De Houwer, Annick. 1995. Bilingual language acquisition. In Paul Fletcher and Brian MacWhinney (eds.), *The handbook of child language.* Oxford: Blackwell, 219–50.

Eco, Umberto. 1995. *The search for the perfect language.* Oxford: Blackwell

European Commission. 2002. *European Year of Languages 2001: some highlights.* Brussels: European Commission, Language Policy Unit.

Fishman, Joshua A., Conrad, Andrew and Rubal-Lopez, Alma. Eds. 1996. *Post-imperial English.* Berlin and New York: Mouton de Gruyter.

Görlach, Manfred. 2002. Ed. *English in Europe.* Oxford: Oxford University Press.

Graddol, David. 1998. *The future of English.* London: The British Council.

Grant Thornton. 2002. *European business survey.* London: Grant Thornton.

Janson, Tore. 2002. *Speak: a short history of languages.* Oxford: Oxford University Press.

Lysandrou, Photis and Lysandrou, Yvonne. 2003. Global English and proregression: understanding English language spread in the contemporary era. *Economy and Society* 32 (2), 207–33. Paper given to conference on 'The cultural politics of English as a world language', Freiburg, June 2001.

Mufwene, Salikoko S. 2001. *The ecology of language evolution.* Cambridge: Cambridge University Press.

2002. Colonization, globalization, and the future of languages in the twenty-first century. Translated paper based on a contribution to a UNESCO debate, Paris, September 2001.

Pennycook, Alistair. 1994. *The cultural politics of English as an international language.* London: Longman.

2001. *Critical applied linguistics.* New York: Erlbaum.

Phillipson, Robert. 1992. *Linguistic imperialism.* Oxford: Oxford University Press.

1998/1999. Review of Crystal (1997). *European English Messenger* 7 (2), 1998, 53–6. Expanded in *Applied Linguistics* 20, 1999, 265–76.

Quirk, Randolph. 1985. The English language in a global context. In Randolph Quirk and H. G. Widdowson (eds.), *English in the world.* Cambridge: Cambridge University Press, 1–6.

Quirk, Randolph, Greenbaum, Sydney, Leech, Geoffrey and Svartvik. Jan. 1985. *A comprehensive grammar of the English language.* London: Longman.

Ramphal, Sridath. 1996. World language: opportunities, challenges, responsibilities. Paper given at the World Members' Conference of the English-Speaking Union, Harrogate, UK.

Ryan, Keith. Ed. 1999. *The official commemorative album for the millennium.* London: Citroen Wolf Communications.

Serjeantson, Mary. 1935. *A history of foreign words in English.* London: Routledge and Kegan Paul.

Todd, Loreto. 1984. *Modern Englishes: pidgins and creoles.* Oxford: Blackwell.

=

FOR DISCUSSION AND REVIEW

1. How does Crystal define a global language? What does he mean by its "special role," and what two primary factors affect that role?

2. Why might one language become global—or international—rather than another? To what extent, if at all, do the following factors come into play: the number of people who speak the language, its cultural influence, and its inherent linguistic qualities? How important are military and economic power to the creation of a global language?

3. Explain how the growth of technology in the twentieth and twenty-first centuries has spurred the globalization of English.

4. What is a lingua franca? Why does a lingua franca develop?

5. What are some of the dangers of a global language? What arguments does Crystal offer to counter these risks? Does evidence that Crystal is wrong exist?

6. Does borrowing words from another language lead to the decline of the original language? Why, or why not? Use examples to back up your answer.

7. Why does Crystal say it is inevitable that English will become a global language? Could another language such as Chinese, Arabic, or Spanish emerge as a global language? Why, or why not? Is more than one global language possible?

8. Why does Crystal say, "It is possible that a global language will emerge only once"?

48

Attitudes toward English: The Future of English in South Asia

Richard W. Bailey

In a wide range of writings, University of Michigan linguistics professor Richard W. Bailey has looked at what people think about the English language and how they relate it to issues of status and social identity. In this essay, taken from his South Asian English: Structure, Use, and Users *(1996), Bailey discusses English as an imposed colonial inheritance in South Asia, an area of the world with many native languages and ancient intellectual and literary traditions. He listens to South Asian writers, thinkers, and educators in an attempt to gauge the extent of the ongoing resentment against English. How, he asks, have negative or ambivalent attitudes affected individual language choice or influenced government policies toward learning English? Among South Asian writers, Bailey discovers, as Sinhalese literary editor Gamini Haththotuwegama says, that "writing in English is one of the crimes and contradictions of the English-educated elite." Bailey finds contradictions as well among professional educators, who offer varied predictions about the future of English in their own nations.*

Attitudes toward a foreign language are the most important predictors of learners' success. Having a strong motivation to learn the new language outweighs the learner's age, aptitude, and the pedagogical method used in the process of acquiring it, and thus attitudes toward English merit our particular consideration. What makes the measurement of attitudes difficult, of course, is that it is nearly impossible to analyze, on a large scale, the views of people who do not declare what their attitudes are. School enrollments, book and newspaper production, and broadcasting are all indicators of language preferences, but they often are directed to "influential" members of the community rather than to the population at large. Political manifestos and government policies provide further evidence of attitudes, but it is often difficult to discern how effective and far-reaching they are in practice. With little consensus on the appropriate measures to use, it is instructive to examine the opinions of persons whose influence shapes the climate of belief.

Yasmine Gooneratne reminds us of something that in the interests of civility and tact is seldom mentioned in the international conversation about world English: "There is still a deep-seated resentment in countries such as India, Pakistan and Sri Lanka—perhaps in Africa, too, but certainly in regions that possess and ancient written literature, and a creative literary tradition of their own—against English, which was the principal tool used by their nineteenth-century rulers in the process of their deracination" (Gooneratne 1980:3). This deep-seated resentment is of particular interest because it is passed along from one generation to the next. Political colonialism in South Asia came to an end almost fifty years ago, but these memories endure, remain part of the collective mythology, and influence the present climate for language choice and language learning. All around the anglophone world we find obituaries for English or, if *obituaries* is too strong a word, accounts of a language suffering a terminal illness.

LITERARY EXPRESSION AND THE FUTURE OF ENGLISH

In postcolonial times resentment against English and the institutions fostered by English speakers has been freely expressed in literature. The title of Austin Clarke's (1980) autobiography vividly expresses what it meant to be young in colonial Barbados: *Growing up Stupid under the Union Jack*. Another Caribbean writer, Jamaica Kincaid, makes English the center of her indictment of colonial rule:

> I cannot tell you how angry it makes me to hear people from North America tell me how much they love England, how beautiful England is, with its traditions. All they see is some frumpy, wrinkled-up person passing by in a carriage waving at a crowd. But what I see is the millions of people, of whom I am just one, made orphans: no motherland, no fatherland, no gods, no mounds of earth for holy ground, no excess of love which might lead to the things that an excess of love sometimes brings, and worst and most painful of all, no tongue. For isn't it odd that the only language I have in which to speak of this crime is the language of the criminal who committed the crime? And what can that really mean? For the language of the criminal can contain only the goodness of the criminal's deed. . . . (Kincaid 1988:32–33)

Still another example from the Caribbean shows a way out of the dilemma for a people whose "real mother tongue" has been stolen from them. (These are the views of Guyanese novelist and poet Jan Carew.)

> We have no standardised language, we have a fluid situation. The "book language" here is one that nobody ever spoke, and the colloquial language, the Creole language, was never institutionalised by the authorities. So obviously, some synthesis of these different languages and a rationalisation of these conflicts must come from a concrete base. I find, for example, people saying: "You can't use a Creole language, you must

use a sophisticated language or how are you going to deal with science?"
You can deal with science. And as the people develop science they will
find the words to name and a language to deal with the science they are
developing. (quoted in Searle 1984:241–42)

Literary expression of this same view is frequent and eloquent, and it is
not always made from the perspective of what "must come" or of the language the people "will find":

> I have crossed an ocean
> I have lost my tongue
> from the root of the old one
> a new one has sprung.
>   (Nichols 1984:64)

Writers who offer these views represent an important force in the creation of a constellation of attitudes that by no means favors English, at
least in its "internationally accepted" variety.

If we return to the South Asian context, we can see how the possibility of an alternative language provides an easier choice than that faced by
writers for whom English is their only language. Writers in the Caribbean
must choose English (in some form) or silence. Writers in South Asia
have many possibilities, and this choice among languages is itself a topic
for fiction and poetry.

Zulfikar Ghose, for instance, characterizes his thoughts thus when
asked on a train, "Are you going to marry an Indian girl, then?": "And
what am I to say to that? Oh my people, how can I tell you that I woo the
English language each morning and that she divorces me each night? No,
I say, I have no fixed plans yet. No fixed plans, I tell myself, tearing up
page after page of manuscript" (Ghose 1965:138). Some of the same pain
appears in these stanzas (the second and last) of his poem "One Chooses
a Language":

> The English alphabet dangled its A
> *for Apple* when I was eight in Bombay.
> I stuttered and chewed almonds for a cure.
> My tongue, rejecting a vernacular
> for a new language, resisted utterance.
> Alone, I imitated the accents
> of English soldiers, their pitch and their tone.
> They were the mouths to my tongue's microphone.
>
> Back on the ferry, connecting two shores,
> on the stateless sea among anecdotes
> and duty-free liquor, I've nothing to say
> who said little between Dunkirk and Marseille.
> There's England, my dictionary my ignorance
> brings me back to. I give poetry readings
> where people ask at the end (just to show
> their interest) how many Indian languages I know.
>   (Ghose 1967:5–6)

The autobiography and the book of poems from which I have drawn these extracts were written more than twenty years ago. Few young South Asian writers today are pursuing an anguished love affair with English with the same ardor or continue to regard England as the dictionary to which their ignorance brings them back. Poems of this sort are not so much about deracination as about a failure of transplantation to take hold and bring the writer to life in English soil.

But this topic (in Aristotle's sense of that term) has a remarkable staying power. Consider this poem, from the 1970s, by Rajagopal Parthasarathy from Tamil Nadu:

> My tongue in English chains,
> I return, after a generation, to you.
> I am at the end
>
> of my dravidic tether
> hunger for you unassuaged.
> I falter, stumble.
>
> Speak a tired language
> wrenched from its sleep in the *Kural*,[1]
> teeth, palate, lips still new
>
> to its agglutinative touch.
> Now, hooked on celluloid, you reel
> down plush corridors.
>   (Parthasarathy 1977:49)

Although he may have returned to the Dravidic tether of Tamil, Parthasarathy still celebrates that return in elegant English verse full of English wordplay: "hooked on celluloid" showing a tricky turn on current slang, and "reel" expressing the accidental convergence of a drunken stagger and the metal frame that holds the coil of film. Such craft in the use of English contradicts the idea that the poet (and others less articulate than he) are unwillingly bound in "English chains." Like Ghose's, Parthasarathy's poem relies on the trope of dramatic irony: the complaint about the speaker's inadequate English is expressed artfully in skillful English verse.[2]

The paradox of writing *against* English *in* English has been a source of anguish among South Asian writers like Ghose and Parthasarathy. The Sri Lankan poet Lakdasa Wikkramasinha (1940–78) declared in his first book of poetry: "To write in English is a form of cultural treason. I have had for the future to do this by making my writing entirely immoralist and destructive" (Wikkramasinha 1965:51). Far from destructive, however, his six volumes of poetry were all written in English and incorporated allusions to Western writers from Horace to Mandelstam. In a memorial tribute written shortly after the poet's accidental death, a friend evaluated this aspect of Wikkramasinha's career:

> Lakdasa was an eminent bilingual and it used to be my unfailing quarrel
> with him that he did not devote his enormous gifts to writing more and
> more poetry in Sinhala, less and less in English. . . . It is one of the crimes
> and contradictions in which the English-educated are caught up that
> they cannot help but continue to write in English while, perhaps, resent-
> ing the urge to do so; and among all our literary artists Lakdasa was one
> who, ironically enough, could not resist the temptation to write in
> English and enrich the tonality of English here and extend its poetic life,
> though not its range, for Lakdasa has tended to limit his range rather
> willfully. (Haththotuwegama 1988:118)

The idea that writing in English is one of the crimes and contradictions
of the English-educated elite appears again and again in postindepen-
dence South Asian literature.

So far I have considered attitudes toward English as a matter of personal choice, but of course it is the social context that is crucial for the
future of English, both as a literary language and in other domains.
Resentment toward English is not, after all, the exclusive property of literary folk.

In Yasmine Gooneratne's poem "Post-Office Queue" the feelings of
those who do not use English are highlighted in a monologue spoken by
a wealthy woman, a member of Sri Lanka's anglicized elite suddenly
forced to confront an unanglicized world:

> There is not very much that we can share,
> Sister, although I know you are standing
> Here next to me, and your curious stare
> Touches me though it carries no understanding.
> Let me say quickly, before you criticise
> Me, that it isn't really my fault.
> For all my shortcomings I humbly apologise,
> That your life lacks salt.
>
> Rustling cotton betrays the ironing hands,
> Oil of sandal and jasmine conspire to give me away.
> You suspect a cook in my kitchen, and shining pans;
> But in extenuation, I would like to say
> He isn't a very good cook, his soups could be better,
> Though pastry and *pilau*, thank Heaven! he's competent at.
> And an ayah, it can't be denied, gives one leisure for letters
> And civilised chat.
>
> I realise, of course, that all this is ephemeral,
> And I would (how I *do* wish I could!) come near, but confess
> That visiting the non-paying wards at the General
> Wasn't a success.
> Well, I've tried to do my share
> And now it's up to you.
> Why don't you show in some way that *you* care?
> It seems to me you've got to make an effort too.

I suppose you know you really stand to win
And I know who is going to be hurt.
But to ask in English for a stamp is not yet a mortal sin;
Your insular virtue need not make me dirt.

(Gooneratne 1971:59)

The "curious stare" of the woman in the queue sets off in the speaker a paroxysm of liberal guilt, as if the stare were a look of hatred. This satiric poem shows this member of the elite facing her own insignificance in a postcolonial world (and, of course, the irrelevance of her letters and civilized chat). Of the two women, the one who does not know English will win in the end.

Let me conclude this sketch of English as a literary subject in South Asia with this extract from a poem by Bangladeshi writer Abdul Ghani Hazari (1925–76), "Wives of a Few Bureaucrats":

On the pages of the British magazine
Maggie's amour, Jacqueline's hymn,
Flirtations of Liz Taylor. BB's bust,
And Marilyn's suicide
And suicide
And suicide
And the evening invitation.
And then, Oh Lord,
Our body insipid at night,
The bloodless moon at the window;
The used body—snoring husband
Sleepless night
And tranquilizer.

O Lord, with no other means left
We turn our face to you;
Give us some work, mirror in vanity bags,
Foundation and lipstick, and social service.

(in Rashid 1986:38)[3]

The uncomfortable anglicized Sri Lankan woman in Gooneratne's poem is here manifested in the despairing Bangladeshi women with their unsatisfying Western gear and sterile lives. What is to the purpose for my argument is that this poem is written not in English but in Bangla.

UNIVERSITIES AND THE FUTURE OF ENGLISH

As English-using colleges and universities in South Asia prepare teachers and other graduates, they set a standard for English, whether a localized variety or an international one. Yet from time to time English-medium higher education has been supplemented or replaced by education through a local language, although English may enjoy a special status as a foreign language. (Medicine, engineering, and other technical subjects often continue to be taught in English, both in South Asia and elsewhere, even during periods when English-medium education has been discouraged.) Government policies supporting or suppressing English-medium primary and secondary schools have a great deal to do with the skill and fluency of students entering the colleges and universities, and these policies vary from place to place in the region.[4] Obviously the future of English will depend in large measure on the consistent availability of English-medium schools for the young, and although India has sustained support for them for many years, Bangladesh, Pakistan, and Sri Lanka have had inconsistent policies on English in schools—sometimes encouraging it and sometimes discouraging or even forbidding it.

The views of university teachers of English seem to me to be a good index of the present state and future development of English in South Asia. In 1977 Professor S. Nagarajan (now of Hyderabad) presented a valedictory lecture on the occasion of his relinquishing the chair in English at Poona University. For slightly different published versions of this lecture, he chose two titles: "Children of Macaulay" and "Some Historical Notes on the Decline of English." In opening his remarks he declared: "The English language in India has been . . . steadily declining for a long while, but we are resolved to let it neither die nor flourish" (Nagarajan 1977:341). As he concluded, he promised to expatiate on the subject further in "the valedictory lecture some twelve years hence which I shall no doubt deliver when I make my final bow as a teacher" (1977:349).

Professor Nagarajan has yet to give that final valedictory, but he responded recently to my questions about the decline of English: "I am afraid the standard of English in India, in spite of the proliferation of schools and colleges in which English is the medium of education, continues its melancholy, long, withdrawing roar" (personal communication, November 10, 1988). To see whether this gloomy prediction reflected the views of others in similar positions, I invited influential persons knowledgeable about South Asia[5] to comment on the statement (without identifying Professor Nagarajan as the source of the remark). Here are some of their responses:

Bangladesh
English is "withdrawing" in its use and as a medium of instruction, though it remains a compulsory or optional subject in schools. As literacy is increasing in Bangladesh, more people are coming into contact with English, but that is no pointer to the popularity of English. The use of English (in speaking and writing) is going down the graph. (Sadrul Amin, University of Dhaka)

This is a very simplistic statement about a complex linguistic situation. Necessary English is expanding or spreading in India (and Bangladesh) and unnecessary English is giving way to vernaculars. A reallocation of functions of languages is taking place. (A. M. Md. Abu Musa, University of Dhaka)

This is generally true. But efforts are being made to improve the teaching of English, setting realistic goals and producing relevant materials. (A. M. M. Hamidur Rahman, University of Dhaka)

The first statement fits Bangladesh perfectly as is evident in the general decline in linguistic proficiency needed for academic and occupational purposes (the two felt needs). Policy has kept it as a compulsory subject from primary to higher secondary but with no effective results. Recently, some clandestine English-medium schools have been officially recognized—with strings attached naturally. And there's talk of allowing students the option of studying at tertiary level in either English or the Bengali medium. Most recently, a news item declared "English shall be compulsory from primary to university level!" To be fair, then, efforts are afoot to right certain wrongs of the past. Therefore, "its melancholy, long, withdrawing roar" perhaps could be stemmed with policy makers making proper decisions—not arbitrarily, but by consulting experts on the subject. Too hopeful for a third-world administration? Perhaps. (Arifa Rahman, University of Dhaka)

India
Nonsense. Certainly standards do vary from University to University, but it should be remembered that these are not the only centres where English is taught. All the major cities have numerous private institutions charging high fees—which those who can afford to gladly pay—teaching English, conversation particularly. "Indian English" is laughed at by the purists, but so was "American English" a hundred years ago. I suppose it's all a question of economic power. As and when India becomes not just culturally important but also economically powerful, "Indian English" will develop a respectability of its own. (R. W. Desai, University of Delhi)

The Arnoldian quotation illustrates the style of the professor under reference. The lament on the decline of standards in English started almost at the same time as English was introduced into the school curriculum in India. (Ayyappa Paniker, University of Kerala, Trivandrum)

The English language in India is not declining. It is progressing as would be evident from the growing demand for early English education and the proliferation of English-medium schools. The declining proficiency is a myth. The top 20 percent and the bottom 20 percent are still comparable. The growth in the number gives the impression of a declining standard. (D. P. Pattanayak, Central Institute for Indian Languages, Mysore)

I don't agree either that the English language in India is or has been "steadily declining" or that the standard of English in India is making a "withdrawing" roar. I think the language is well-established and is in no danger of disappearance. (N. S. Prabhu, National University of Singapore)

The standards are no worse than they were earlier. As another writer has said, the rumors about the death of English on the subcontinent are vastly exaggerated. Too often obituaries for English have been written and as often they have had to be withdrawn. If anything, English is flourishing on an unprecedented scale and the demand seems to be insatiable. It will be learnt and used in a way suited to the conditions of India. It won't be *native* English but that is irrelevant. (S. N. Sridhar, State University of New York at Stony Brook)

I prefer to disagree with my compatriot and colleague. As long as India continues to be a free country with its multiplicity of linguistic states, English is bound to continue as a link language. It may be a matter of many more years before English can be replaced as the language of jurisprudence and medium of instruction in higher education. (T. K. Subramaniam, College of Engineering, Anna University, Madras)

As the language proliferates, there is bound to be some dilution of quality except in some pockets which might preserve fairly high standards despite their erosion elsewhere. (Caleekal T. Thomas, University of Calicut)

Nepal
Broadly speaking the statement is true. This also applies to South Asia in general including Nepal. However, there are contrary trends too. The English language teaching-learning situation, people's growing strong desire to learn English and such other factors need careful analysis before coming to any definite conclusion. (Professor Y. P. Verma, Tribhuvan University)

Comparisons over time are problematic. My guess is (and we have some evidence from our *Survey of English Teaching in Nepal* [Davies, Glendinning, and McLean 1984]) that similar numbers have adequate, often good, English as thirty or forty years ago. The problem is the dissemination of that adequate English to others. This has been the official finding in these last years (with a brief withdrawal in the 70s) but the means and resources have not been available. What this may mean—and still means—is that for the majority English has only a symbolic role. (Alan Davies, University of Edinburgh)

Pakistan
The English language is not "declining"; it still is what it was before. However, proficiency in English is declining, and its educational uses may be said to be shrinking for various reasons. (M. Ismail Bhatti, Punjab University, Lahore)

In 1987, Professor Karrar Husain said, "Ever since the teaching and learning of English became a fatigue of slavery rather than a labour of love, the standard of language proficiency has, not surprisingly, declined." I agree with that view. I see the English teaching profession attracting fewer and fewer men. Therefore, as the stratum of English-language speakers and writers thins out, and the profession turns over exclusively (almost) to women, a valuable resource of English in the community will be lost. (Abbas M. Husain, University of Karachi)

The standard of English language has been slowly declining here. The increasing number of private schools are much concerned about teaching

English, and it gives some hope for the future. Frequent films and plays on TV also stimulate interest among the young people. Most of the student population has a burning wish to learn more and more English, but the traditional methods of teaching are inadequate. The students have a need to learn because it is still the language of government and higher education. (Ramat Ullah Khan, Government College, Nowshera)

It seems to me that there is a grain of truth in what the professor has said. The only thing I wish to say to counter his point is that I do not see how we can dispense with English. We will have to retain English as an important and necessary second language. For example, colleges and universities cannot do without English. (Kalim-Ur-Rahman, University of Karachi)

There is no denying the fact that the standard of English is deteriorating here. But who's to blame? The policy-makers as well as the educationists. The importance of English as a vehicle for the acquisition of scientific knowledge and exposure to the world can't be over-emphasized. (Zafar Hussain Zaidi, Government Post-Graduate College, Rawalpindi)

Sri Lanka
Unlike India, Sri Lanka has one predominant national language, Sinhalese; and only one other main language, Tamil. English-medium schools therefore no longer exist. In Arts faculties of universities too, there is no English-medium education. In employment and public life, however, particularly at higher levels, the use of English continues. The variety is changing; confidence in using it has reduced. Melancholy? To some people, yes. Perhaps the place of English is best viewed in relation to the tremendous elaboration of the national languages over the past forty years. As a result, English is increasingly used now as a supplement to a healthy use of Sinhalese or Tamil. This changes the role of English, and it is this change in role that is often misinterpreted as recession. It can also be misinterpreted as an increase. The reality is the change, rather than recession or increase. (Siromi Fernando, University of Colombo)

Sri Lankan English is very much alive among the people I know best — those that grew up with me. On account of short-sighted administrative policies, the interest in English did wane during the 60s and 70s. This however is merely a temporary lapse. I have no doubt that English would be very much alive in the future. The lion *will* roar but in a decidedly Sri Lankan voice! (L. A. Gunewardena, University of Peradeniya)

In Sri Lanka, English is *not* the language of education, though the sciences at university level (including medicine) are taught in English. In the past two or three years, attempts have been made to re-introduce English as a medium of education, but this is only in a very limited number of schools and only in the capital, Colombo. But though English will never become a major language of education, it is increasingly becoming important as a second language in education. Just two days ago, on 10th December 1988, the government officially proclaimed English as a link language between the two major communities [Sinhalese and Tamil], whose languages were declared national languages—the first time English has been given such status in independent Sri Lanka. (Ryhana Raheem, University of Colombo)

I certainly hope it does. It is not happening right now, but what he/she said in essence will happen with our peoples' movement towards socialism. (Malinda Seneviratne, Harvard College)

The general decline in the immediate post-independence period, which saw the removal of English as a medium of instruction, appears to have been countered in recent years by (a) a general awareness, born of the growth of tourism, emigrant labour, technological advances, etc., of the benefits a knowledge of English can bring; and (b) government keenness to raise standards. As such, conceivably more people now have access to some form of English, even though at what used to be the top layers, proficiency has declined. (Rajiva Wijesinha, The British Council, Colombo)

Like South Asian creative writers, some of these academic leaders find themselves in an ambivalent position. Is English a proper South Asian language? Is it mainly an important additional language for the region? Or is it inimical to the aspirations of the people?

Most popular journalism and many scholarly studies accept unquestioningly that English is (or is about to be) a universal world language. Evidence in support of such claims is usually drawn from the use of English in science, technology, and development; maritime and air transportation; diplomacy and multinational manufacture and distribution of goods; computer data bases and "high-level" programming languages; and broadcasting, film, pop music, and other allurements of anglophone popular culture. Certainly English *is* used more and more widely in all these fields, and there is no obvious reason to imagine another world language soon competing with English in these domains of human endeavor.

Nevertheless, these remarkable developments in the use of English obscure an important fact: English is proportionally diminishing in use. A minority language to begin with, English use will shrink to an even smaller share of the world population by the end of [the twentieth] century. As I have argued elsewhere, English is becoming the language of the powerful few at the expense of the powerless many (see Bailey 1983, 1990). "Anglo*phobia* is a lower-class attitude," writes the Indian poet Paul Jacob (in Lal 1969:216), and other creative writers and academic leaders in South Asia detect a perplexing and perilous problem in the class stratification of access to English.[6] As long as people believe that English is a vehicle for their own aspirations (or those of their children), English will continue to be an important language. Whether English learning and democracy are compatible in South Asia remains to be seen.

NOTES

1. "Tamil classic of the third or fourth century A.D. by Valluvar" (author's note).

2. For a more direct expression of his views, see Parthasarathy (1982).

3. Hazari himself translated this poem into English. I am grateful to Professor M. Harunur Rashid for presenting me with a copy of the anthology containing it.

4. Consider the following report: "The language debate continues, is in fact a little more intense, and the government policies continue to discourage the use of English at all levels. For instance, the Government of Punjab announced plans toward the end of the year (1979) to establish three hundred new schools in the private sector but warned against the adoption of English as the medium of instruction, an order which the new schools will have to comply with so that they can qualify for registration with the Department of Education. The government had to repeat warnings to this effect because, in the cities, there is a great parent-pressure for English-medium schools" (Hashmi 1980:151).

5. A mailed questionnaire was supplemented by a briefer version circulated to the conferees in Islamabad, January 7, 1989. The extracts that follow are published with the permission of their authors.

6. See Pattanayak (1987) and (1989).

BIBLIOGRAPHY

Bailey, Richard W. 1983. Literacy for life: An international perspective. In *Literacy for life: The demand for reading and writing*, ed. Richard W. Bailey and Robin Melanie Fosheim, 30–44. New York: Modern Language Association.

———. 1990. The English language at its twilight. In *The state of the language*, 2d ed., ed. Leonard Michaels and Christopher Ricks, 83–94. Berkeley: University of California Press.

Clarke, Austin C. 1980. *Growing up stupid under the Union Jack: A memoir.* Toronto: McCleland and Stewart.

Ghose, Zulfikar. 1965. *Confessions of a native-alien.* London: Routledge and Kegan Paul.

———. 1967. *Jets from orange.* London: Macmillan.

Goffin, R. C. 1934. *Some notes on Indian English.* S.P.E. Tract no. 41. Oxford: Clarendon.

Gooneratne, Yasmine. 1971. *Word, bird, motif: Poems.* Kandy, Sri Lanka: T.B.S. Godamunne and Sons.

———. 1980. *Diverse inheritance: A personal perspective on commonwealth literature.* Adelaide, Australia: Centre for Research in the New Literatures in English.

Hashmi, Alamgir. 1980. Appendix I: Pakistan. *Journal of Commonwealth Literature* 15 (2): 151–56.

Haththotuwegama, Gamini. 1988. The poetry of Lakdasa Wikkramasinha: A memorial tribute. In *An anthology of contemporary Sri Lankan poetry in English*, ed. Rajiva Wijesinha, 116–24. Colombo, Sri Lanka: The British Council in collaboration with the English Association of Sri Lanka.

Kincaid, Jamaica. 1988. *A small place.* New York: Farrar, Straus, Giroux.

Lal, P., ed. 1969. *Modern Indian poetry in English.* Calcutta: Writers' Workshop.

Nagarajan, S. 1977. Some historical notes on the decline of English. *Journal of Higher Education* (New Delhi), 2 (3): 341–9.

Nichols, Grace. 1984. Epilogue. In *The fat black woman's poems*. London: Virago.

Parthasarathy, R. 1977. *Rough passage*. Delhi: Oxford University Press.

———. 1982. Whoring after English gods. In *Writers in East-West encounter: New cultural bearings*, ed. Guy Amirthanayagam, 65–84. London: Macmillan.

Pattanayak, D. P. 1987. *Multilingualism and multiculturalism: Britain and India*. Occasional Paper no. 6. London: Centre for Multicultural Education.

———. 1989. English and language conflict in South Asia. Paper presented at the International Conference on English in South Asia, Islamabad, Pakistan.

Rashid, M. Harunur, ed. 1986. *A choice of contemporary verse from Bangladesh*. Dhaka, Bangladesh: Bangla Academy.

Searle, Chris. 1984. *Words unchained: Language and revolution in Grenada*. London: Zed.

Wikkramasinha, Lakdhasa. 1965. *Lustre poems*. Kandy, Sri Lanka: Ariya.

FOR DISCUSSION AND REVIEW

1. Yasmine Gooneratne says that there continues to be "deep-seated resentment in countries such as India, Pakistan and Sri Lanka" toward English. Why is this so? Where else in the world might such resentment occur? How is growing up as an English speaker in the United States different from growing up with English in India, Barbados, or Jamaica?

2. In terms of language choice, how might Caribbean writers differ from writers in South Asia?

3. Why is "writing against English in English" a paradox? Why has writing in English been "a source of anguish" for some South Asian writers? What does their experience reveal about the psychological aspects of language and identity?

4. Why is it significant to Bailey that the Bangladeshi poem by Hazari, "Wives of a Few Bureaucrats," is written in Bangla?

5. When Professor S. Nagarajan of India says "we are resolved to let [English] neither die nor flourish," what does he mean? Do you think he would distinguish, as Professor Musa of Bangladesh does, between "necessary" and "unnecessary English"? Explain.

6. Using statements from the selection, discuss why some educators think proficiency in English is declining in South Asia.

7. After reviewing the "remarkable developments in the use of English," Bailey writes that "English is proportionally diminishing in use." Does this surprise you? Why, or why not? What does he mean by this statement? How does the importance of a language differ from its proportionate use? Does Bailey's claim contradict Crystal's claims in the preceding selection about English use?

49

===

Natural Seasonings: The Linguistic Melting Pot

John McWhorter

John McWhorter, a Senior Fellow at the Manhattan Institute, looks at language change as a dynamic, complex phenomenon influenced by race, ethnicity, and cultural issues. In this selection, from his 2001 book The Word on the Street: Debunking the Myth of "Pure" Standard English, *McWhorter refutes the idea that a language is a monolithic set of words and grammatical structures. Instead, he says, languages are melting pots, and change is natural. According to McWhorter, one of the most unavoidable causes of such change is contact, and he suggests a four-level schema for describing what can happen when languages come into contact. Using examples from numerous languages, he explains how languages borrow words and grammatical structures. Dealing with more complex mixtures, he also shows us how creoles and intertwined languages develop. As McWhorter puts it, "languages have always profoundly influenced one another—often just sharing words, but sometimes even sharing word order and endings and becoming new languages entirely."*

There are about 170 countries in the world today. Because administrative and cultural necessity lead countries to declare one or two languages "official," it would be a natural conclusion that there exist roughly two hundred-odd languages in the world, each more or less contained by the tidy outlines of the countries we see on a map. (Only four countries currently recognize more than two languages as official: Spain—Spanish, Catalan, Basque; Singapore—Chinese, Malay, Tamil, English; India— English, Hindi, and fourteen regional languages; and Luxembourg— French, German, and a German dialect called Letzebuergisch.)

Yet, in fact, there are no fewer than about 5,000 languages spoken in the world. This is an automatic indication that the world's languages rub shoulders much more than a Rand McNally view of things would suggest. For example, there are about 150 languages spoken in India, 250 languages spoken in Nigeria, and an astounding 1,000—one-fifth of the world's languages—in little New Guinea. Specifically, as a natural result of this geographical proximity between languages, as many people in the world are bi- or multilingual as not.

Many Americans find bilingualism rather exotic, rather like a particular flair for dress or a pentatonic scale. In fact, associating being American with speaking a single language, English, is due in part to most early settlers being willing immigrants, committed to a bracing new experiment in democracy and to a common language. Even so, large groups in the United States speaking other languages alongside English were much more common well into the 1800s than they are today. This behavior began to go by the wayside when cultural and political policy began to explicity discourage people from speaking other languages. For example, as hard as it is to believe, German was once the "second language of the United States" the way Spanish is today, but the vilification of Germans during World War I discouraged parents from passing the language on to their children. Native Americans were physically punished for speaking their languages in reservation schools until as recently as 1950, and even today the English Only movement, discouraging bilingual education, inherently casts speaking Spanish in a suspicious light. Finally, global domination has encouraged people in other countries to learn English, depriving Americans of a prime driving force for learning other languages well—necessity. For example, despite the cute scenes in Berlitz books of "Mr. Smith" reserving hotel rooms in Paris in French and buying train tickets in Rome in Italian, it is quite possible for an English speaker to make their way through most of Europe without learning a word of anything because most public servants are required to speak at least functional English.

Many foreigners are amused that Americans find bilingualism exotic, especially as it shades into outright astonishment when Americans encounter people who speak more than two languages. For example, if you meet East Africans, you will presumably communicate with them in English; meanwhile, they more than likely also speak not only Swahili, East Africa's linguistic coin of the realm, but also the local language of the area where they were born—and often, yet another local language. Finally, if they are from a country once colonized by a power other than England, they probably speak that power's official language as well—French if from Burundi, Portuguese if from Mozambique, etc. East Africans think nothing of this, yet they have to get used to being treated as if they glowed in the dark or could breathe underwater because they are multilingual. One East African I know from Mozambique speaks English, Portuguese, Swahili, and the local languages Yao and Nyanja and thinks no more of this than I do of my ability to boil water.

When two or more languages are rolled around the same mouths over long periods, they have a natural tendency to merge, sometimes only affecting each other's edges, but just as often blending so thoroughly that brand new languages result. Linguists have found that there is no such thing as languages coexisting without affecting one another. Nowhere on earth have two languages been spoken together for longer than ten minutes with each remaining pristine. Finally, besides undergoing their private erosions, renewals, and drifts, most languages also change because of influence from other languages. For example, French is spoken alongside English in Canada and is full of English influences, from words like *badloque* for "bad luck" to expressions some have been found to use like *sur la télévision* for "on TV," using the word *sur* "on" where in Parisian French the preposition would be *à* "at." Similarly, the German of the Pennsylvania Dutch is full of English influences, while the Afrikaans spoken by South Africans is what happened to Dutch when spoken by the Khoi people (the "bushman" in *The Gods Must Be Crazy* was one) as much as by the Dutch.

It is as natural as hair growing that languages change within themselves, and just as natural that languages also change because of words and even structures brought in from other languages. In other words,

Languages spoken together change one another.

STAIRWAY TO HEAVEN: THE LEVELS OF LANGUAGE MIXTURE

Once again, we are all aware of how languages mix to an extent: *macho* from Spanish, *Angst* from German. However, many languages take not only colorful expressions like *macho* and *Angst*, but even many of their most basic, everyday words from other languages. For example, an Old English speaker did not sit on a chair, but on a *setl. Chair* was borrowed from French by Middle English, when the Norman French temporarily governed England from 1066 until the thirteenth century. The words *judge, prayer, soldier, pork, boots, stable, pain, porch, mountain, safe, satisfy* and boatloads of others were similarly borrowed from French. In fact, between the French vocabulary, a similarly massive amount of words we inherited from Latin, and other foreign words here and there, a mere one percent of the words in modern English trace back to Anglo-Saxon itself (they tend to be kitchen-sink words that define the heart of an existence, like *father, sister, fight, and, but, love,* and *die,* and they are therefore 62 percent of the words most actually used). All the rest were imported from elsewhere.

As with erosion, renewal, and drift, however, in real life such influences from other languages are often resisted, treated as the invasion of "impurities" from other systems, rather than as part of an eternal, unremarkable process. The Office de la Langue Française in Quebec, for example, is currently waging a war against the influx of English terms into Canadian French, desperately coining French equivalents as the population goes on gaily using the English terms. A particularly memorable example was the call to use *hambourgeois* in place of *hamburger;* a similar language police in France have actually been under the impression that the French would call marketing *la mercatique.* However, no one felt this way when French terms pervaded Middle English, an invasion just as unremarkable and, crucially, inevitable.

This kind of reaction neglects our basic fact that languages spoken together always affect one another, and that this is no more resistible than rain or snow—and ultimately just as beautiful in its own way. This traffic in linguistic material is more crossfertilization than contamination. For example, one could certainly have made a ringing argument that English before the Norman Conquest combined a glorious vocabulary with a grammar capable of expressing the finest subtleties, and indeed this was true—*Beowulf* is a majestic piece of prose. However, who would argue that modern English, complete with its French "contamination," does not combine a glorious vocabulary with a grammar capable of expressing the finest subtleties? More to the point, we do not even realize what a bastard vocabulary we are using unless we learn this in school or from a book like this one. In the same way, the basic vocabulary of modern Vietnamese is over a third Chinese, inherited during the one thousand years that China occupied Vietnam. Yet the Vietnamese are intensely proud of their language and its literature, and rightly so—again, the fact that so much of the vocabulary is Chinese is a mere academic point; the originally Chinese word *ngu* "language" feels no more "alien" to a Vietnamese person than the French-derived word *language* does to us.

We can call this kind of word sharing "Level One" of language mixture. We gain further perspective on all of this when we see that vocabulary exchange is but the tip of an iceberg when it comes to the ways that languages affect one another. Quite often, languages even borrow whole sentence structures from other languages. For example, in the English spoken in Ireland, there are not only Irish Gaelic words like *cleeve* for *basket, prockus* for *mixture,* and *spalpeen* for *rascal,* but sentences like *Is it out of your mind you are?* are used everyday. This is because in Irish Gaelic, the language spoken in Ireland before English, this word order is normal, and Irish Gaelic and English have been spoken in Ireland by many people bilingually for centuries. Another example is *They're after leaving* meaning *They just left,* which is based on the fact that the Irish Gaelic word for *after* is used in this meaning. Similarly, the reason that the definite article *ul* wound up at the end of the noun in Romanian (*om* **ul** "the man") instead of at the beginning, like in other Romance languages (*l'homme, el hombre*), is that Romania is a region that has been shared by a great many different language groups over the ages. Throughout history, Romanian speakers were so often bilingual in Romanian and a language that placed its definite article after the noun, like Bulgarian or Albanian, that Romanian speakers began using not only some words from those languages, but even their word order, in their own language. This kind of mixing, by which a language takes in not only some words but even some sentence structures from another language, is what we will call "Level Two" of language mixture.

As a matter of fact, when all a language takes from another one is mere words (Level One), it is usually because only a small number of speakers of the first language are bilingual in the second—usually the ruling classes and the educated. In such cases, most speakers are not using the second language alongside the first one on a daily basis—instead, influence from the second language "trickles down" from the elite class to the masses. In cases like this, what trickles down most easily are isolated words, rather than the things that are harder to pick up from a foreign language, such as word order and endings, which require actual use of the second language to get the hang of. This was the situation, for example, in England when it was occupied by the Norman French: The Normans were the rulers but the masses continued happily using English. It is for this reason that so many of the words we inherited from French have to do with concepts of government (*reign*), fashion (*attire*), art (*pen*), cuisine (*poultry*), and, actually, the very words *government*, *fashion*, *art*, and *cuisine*. Just as often, however, geography and history have it that many, most, or all of a language's speakers speak another one alongside, and the result is the likes of *Is it out of your mind you are?* and *om ul*. In fact, *most* languages have had some Level Two–type influence on their structure from other languages at some point in their history.

Yet languages can transform one another even more deeply than in the Irish English and Romanian cases, to such a profound degree that the result is a new language entirely. Cases like this, which will be our Level Three of language mixture, are called *creole languages*.

Most creole languages emerged during the European-driven slave trade in the middle of the second millennium, in plantation colonies such as Jamaica, Haiti, Louisiana, and Suriname. On a plantation, a large gang of African slaves often spoke too many different African languages for any one of them to be of much use, but meanwhile had little direct interaction with speakers of the European language spoken by their masters, even though this language, being the language of power and the language of the land, was the natural choice as a common tongue. The slaves therefore only learned the language of their masters partially—a basket of sine qua non nouns, verbs, and adjectives; a preposition or two; some set expressions; and otherwise, at best a bit of this and a tad of that.

The first result was a rudimentary "lingo," with a small vocabulary and little structure per se, capable of communicating only basic ideas and relying as much on surrounding context as on language itself. This is called a *pidgin*. An example of a pidgin was the English spoken by many Native Americans early in the colonial history of the United States, when Native American communities were still thriving and most contact with Europeans was strictly utilitarian and brief. Continuing to speak their native languages (of which there were about 300 in America before Europeans came) in their daily lives, they only learned as much English as was necessary to negotiate relations with the foreign invaders.

Here is a sample of American Indian Pidgin English, an entertaining put-down by a Native American woman of a white man:

> You silly. You weak. You baby-hands. No catch horse. No kill buffalo.
> No good but for sit still—read book.

(This went both ways: Europeans also learned pidgin versions of Native American languages.)

This woman certainly got her point across, but obviously this kind of speech can only take one so far. Speech at this level can convey only the broadest, most concrete of concepts—subtleties of feeling or argument, such as discussing just why you don't want to see someone again after a perfect date, or defending your right to have a midlife crisis at 32—would be all but impossible. Many of us have felt handicapped in this fashion in a foreign country, where we had only hesitant command of the language. Nevertheless, in a quick week of trading across a river, to bring up one's first kiss or the meaning of a sunset would be rather marginal to the proceedings, and therefore in many places pidgins have stayed at this stage indefinitely.

However, unlike the Native American trader, or ourselves on a junior year abroad, African slaves were condemned to live in the new language for life. They had neither the opportunity to return to using their mother tongues, nor did they have enough contact with whites to acquire English more fully. Nevertheless, the basic human need for communication beyond the level of "you baby-hands" remained.

What does one do in such a situation? What African slaves did was supplement their stock of European words and the rudiments of the language's structure with structures from their native African languages, as well as with certain linguistic strategies that we can see in all languages in one way or another. The result was brand-new languages with, roughly speaking, words from one language and structure from others—in other words, creole languages.

"Creole" is often thought to refer specifically to Louisiana, but in fact creole languages have emerged through this process in dozens of places. In English colonies, this process created Jamaican patois, Gullah of South Carolina, and Tok Pisin in Papua New Guinea (*Pisin* is from business, not what you may be thinking). In French colonies, the results were Haitian Creole, Martiniquan Creole, Mauritian Creole, and others. Papiamentu of Curaçao is a Spanish creole, Cape Verdeans speak a Portuguese one, slaves in the Virgin Islands spoke a Dutch one (now unfortunately extinct), and so on.

Slaves were brought to the Caribbean from a long section of the western coast of Africa, which stretches from modern-day Senegal down to Angola. Therefore, it is the structures of the languages spoken along this coast that Caribbean creoles are based on. There are hundreds of languages spoken along the West African coast, with as much difference between many of them as between English and Japanese. However, because of where Europeans established most of their trade settlements to gather slaves

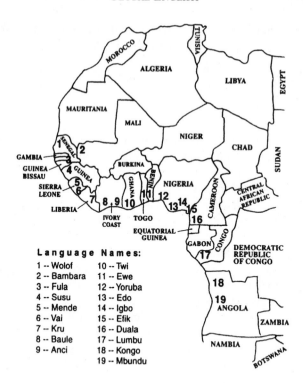

Language Names:
1 -- Wolof   10 -- Twi
2 -- Bambara   11 -- Ewe
3 -- Fula   12 -- Yoruba
4 -- Susu   13 -- Edo
5 -- Mende   14 -- Igbo
6 -- Vai   15 -- Efik
7 -- Kru   16 -- Duala
8 -- Baule   17 -- Lumbu
9 -- Anci   18 -- Kongo
                19 -- Mbundu

from, one group of languages had a particularly strong impact on Caribbean creoles. These languages are spoken on the coast of what is today Ghana, Togo, Benin, and Nigeria, and include Twi, Ewe, Yoruba, and Igbo.

Here, for example, is one paragraph of a story in Sranan, an English creole developed by slaves in Suriname in South America and now spoken there by the whole society:

> Di Shirley doro na oso baka, en mama taki wan brifi de na tafa tapu gi en. Wantewante Shirley bigin aksi ensrefi, taki suma na a suma di seni en, bika a sabi taki suma no de fu seni wan brifi gi en. So Shirley, a teki a brifi opo. Di a opo en, a man si taki wan Valentine-karta de na ini, dan a si taki a nen fu Charles skrifi na ondro.

> When Shirley got home, her mother said there was a letter for her on the table. Right away Shirley started wondering who it could be from, because she knew that she was not expecting anyone to send her a letter. So Shirley opened the envelope. When she did, she saw that there was a Valentine card inside, and she saw that Charles' name was written on the bottom.

The first passage barely looks like English, and you could spend days listening to Sranan before even noticing that it had anything to do with English. Sranan is indeed, broadly speaking, English words used in a West African sound system and sentence structure. It is so different from English that word-for-word translation is needed:

Di   Shirley doro na oso   baka, en   mama   taki
when S   come to house back her mother say

wan brifi de na tafa tapu gi en.
a   letter is on table top give her

Wantewante Shirley bigin aksi ensrefi,
immediately S   start ask herself

taki suma na suma   di   seni en, bika   a   sabi
that who   is person that send it because she know

taki suma no de fu seni wan brifi gi   en. So
that person not is for send   a   letter give her so

Shirley, a   teki   a   brifi opo. Di   a   opo en,
S   she take the letter open when she open it

a   man si   taki wan Valentine -karta de na ini,
she can see that a   V   card   is at inside

dan a   si   taki a   nen   fu Charles skrifi
then she see that the name of   C   written

na ondro.
on bottom

We can immediately see that this, unlike the "baby-hands" passage, is a full language, capable of expressing precision and nuance. We have articles like *wan* 'a' and *a* 'the'; phrase linkers like *di* 'when', *dan* 'then', *taki* 'that', and *bika* 'because'; and words that specify something's exact position in relation to something else like *tapu* 'on,' *ondro* 'bottom', etc.

The African roots of this language run broad and deep. The Gaelic sentence structures in Irish English are exotic to our ear, but nevertheless still sound like English to us—*Is it out of your mind you are*? and *They're after leaving* may sound odd at first, but we can manage to shoehorn them into our sense of what English can be. However, the African influence on Sranan transforms the English source material so profoundly that we know we aren't in Kansas anymore.

Note, for example, that Yoruba (YAW-roo-bah), like many West African languages, runs verbs together without a conjunction, as in "I take machete cut tree," where in English we would have to say "I take the machete *and* cut the tree" or "I take the machete *to* cut the tree":

Mo fi   ada   ge   igi   na.
I   take machete cut tree the
I cut the tree with a machete.

Sranan does this as well, as in the earlier passage, **seni** *wan brifi* **gi** *en* '**send** a letter **give** her.'

Another example of this is that in many West African languages, where we use prepositions, a noun of position is placed after the main noun, such as in Ewe (EH-vay) of Togo:

E le xo   me.

he is house interior
He is in the house.

Sranan has the same sentence structure, as in the story, where the letter is *na tafa* **tapu** 'at table **on**.'

Even further, however, in Sranan not only the West African sentence patterns, but even the sound patterns are applied to English. For example, in many West African languages, clusters of consonants are rare, and words tend to be made up of syllables consisting of a consonant plus a vowel, or just one vowel, as in the earlier Yoruba sentence. Sranan takes English words and applies this sound structure to them, and thus *talk* is *taki*, *top* is *tapu*, *in* is *ini*. To be sure, there is some Gaelic-derived sound patterning in Irish English—the source of the wonderful Irish accent. However, like the sentence structures, this sound pattern influence is light enough that we can easily fit it into a conception of English. On the other hand, *opo* for *open* and *ensrefi* for *himself* are clearly another matter—that is, another language.

We see similar examples of profound West African influence in many creole languages. For example, a Haitian Creole speaker says,

Pran-l ba   mwen.

take-it give me
Bring it to me.

This sentence runs two verbs together just as Sranan does because its creators spoke the same West African languages (*pran* is from *prendre* 'to take'; *ba* is from an obsolete French word for "give," *bailler*).

Because colonial plantations entailed throwing together slaves speaking so many different West African languages into a situation in which they had limited contact with a language they needed to use, plantation colonies were natural places for creoles to emerge. Because the European powers naturally concentrated their colonies in subequatorial regions most suitable for large-scale agriculture, today most creoles are spoken in the postcolonial nations of the Caribbean and surrounding areas (e.g., Jamaican patois, Sranan, Haitian, Papiamentu), West Africa (e.g., Krio of Sierra Leone, Cape Verdean Portuguese Creole), and Oceania (e.g., Tok Pisin). However, creoles have emerged in a great many other places. For example, in southern Sudan in the late 1800s, slaves speaking various local languages were recruited into occupying Turco-Egyptian armies under Arabic-speaking commanders. Arabic was the language the soldiers used among themselves. As on plantations, this was a situation where the Arabic spoken was at first mostly a pidgin variety, which quickly expanded into a creole. Expelled from the country by nationalist forces, these soldiers were resettled permanently in Uganda and Kenya, where their descendants still speak this creole Arabic called Nubi, unintelligible to speakers of Arabic itself. There are also creole varieties of Swahili, Malay, Zulu, and many other languages.

Yet just as English is not "contaminated" by its massive amount of French vocabulary, and Romanian is not "tainted" by structures like *om ul* 'man-the,' Sranan's miscegenational history has led not to "bad English" but to a complex, nuanced language in its own right. Indeed, creoles are so different from the languages that provided their words that they have gone beyond being dialects of that language, but are instead whole new languages—Brooklyn English is a dialect of English, but Sranan is a separate language, for which English happens to have been a springboard as a vocabulary source.

It is easy to suppose that creoles are in fact just bizarre bastardizations of the languages that provided their words, and this has often been asserted not only by Europeans, but by creole speakers themselves— Jamaican newspapers, for example, are full of denunciations of Jamaican patois by educators, politicians, and other people in power. This is often a response to the fact that creoles do not use the systems of word endings that European languages use. Indeed, where English has *I walk, you walk, he walks*, Sranan has *mi waka, yu waka, a waka*, with the same form for all three pronouns. Similarly, English has *I walked*, but Sranan instead has *mi bin waka*, using a separate word instead of an ending.

From our perspective, speaking a European language and usually learning closely related ones like French, Spanish, and German, this lack of endings quite naturally looks "primitive" and "simple," and indeed the endings are missing because the creators of the creole did not learn them. Endings are one of the hardest things to learn in a language—imagine how much easier Spanish would be if 'I speak' were just *yo hablar*, with there being no need to cram lists like *yo hablo* 'I speak,' *tu hablas* 'you speak,' *él habla* 'he speaks,' *nosotros hablamos* 'we speak,' etc. into our heads. The situation in which the first slaves found themselves, with so little contact with actual native English speakers, did not allow them to pick up this "final frontier" aspect of the European language that whites spoke on the plantation.

However, endings are but one of a dazzling array of ways in which a language can be complex. A great many of the world's languages use no endings whatsoever, and yet are maddeningly difficult for nonnative speakers to learn; the Chinese languages are a particularly useful example. The Chinese languages and others that use no endings utilize a number of other structures which are as elaborate and subtle as any in languages that are not creoles.

Creole speakers, needing a full language, made full use of such strategies. Indeed, anyone learning a creole cannot help but notice immediately that creoles are tricky and complex in a number of ways. There are lengthy and complex grammars and self-teaching courses on Haitian Creole, just as there are for Greek and Chinese, for example. Haitians are quite proud of their language, to the extent of being as amazed at foreigners who become fluent in Haitian Creole as Japanese are to see foreigners get the hang of their language. Haitians have even been heard to assume that Adam and Eve spoke in Haitian Creole, which is no more tenuous an assumption than that they spoke a Germanic tongue that arose among humble invaders drinking from skulls on a wet little island!

Here is an example of how creoles can be as prickly as other languages. Saramaccan is a creole language spoken by members of rain forest communities in Suriname, who are descended from slaves who escaped the plantations on the coast (where Sranan developed) and established successful, thriving settlements that survive to this day. In Saramaccan, to say *I am your father*, one says,

Mi da i   tatá.
I   am your father
I am your father.

(The accents indicate that these syllables are pronounced on a higher tone than the others, something else that takes some doing for an English-speaking person to wrap their mouths around.)

Based on this example, if we were learning Saramaccan, we would naturally assume that *da* was the word for *be*. Therefore, if we learned that *at home* is *a wósu* (*wósu* is from *house*, believe it or not), we would expect that the way to say *I am at home* would be as follows:

Mi da a wósu.
I   am at house
I am at home.

But laughter would echo through the canopies of the forest if you said this. In fact, there is a separate word for *be* when one is discussing *where* one is as opposed to *what* one is. *Da* is only used when something is actually the direct equivalent of something else—if you are someone's father, then automatically their father is presumably you. When what is being specified about something is its location, then the verb is not *da* but *de*, and thus our proper sentence would be as follows:

Mi de a wósu.
I   am at house
I am at home.

Thus *mi da a wósu*, using the verb *to be* of equating, would mean roughly "I embody the state of being at home," which is the sort of thing only the most profound of us usually find ourselves uttering.

Even knowing this, however, it is easy to screw up when learning Saramaccan. Based on what we just saw, one would think that the way to say that "a dog is an animal" would be as follows:

Dágu da wan mbéti.

dog   is an   animal
A dog is an animal.

(*Mbéti* is from *meat*, which was used as the word for *animal* by the first slaves in Suriname because in many African languages, the words for *animal* and *meat* are the same—in these languages one eats "animal," as opposed to our rather fastidious way of distancing ourselves from the issue by calling animal flesh which we are consuming by another word, "meat." Learning the word *meat*, these Africans naturally extended its meaning to also signify living creatures, just as it did in their native languages, since they did not have enough contact with whites to have much use for the *animal/meat* distinction.)

However, that sentence *dágu da wan mbéti* would be rather odd. A Saramaccan speaker would usually say,

Dágu de wan mbéti.

dog   is an   animal
A dog is an animal.

To us this seems almost willfully frustrating—maybe we can accept that animals are actually "meats" running around, but surely an animal isn't a place! However, within Saramaccan structure, in sentences like this, the dog is seen as occupying a place within a field of concepts comprising animals, and thus in an extended sense dogs are "in" "animalness."

We see things like this in all creoles, and it shows that creoles are as tricky as the languages we are used to speaking and learning. As we can see, one cannot speak Saramaccan—or Sranan—by simply stripping English of its endings; nor could we speak Haitian by simply speaking French pidgin style. On the contrary, not only can creoles be spoken downright incorrectly (*Mi da a wósu*), but it can even be spoken in such a way that the speaker, while managing to achieve basic communication, is nevertheless detectable as a nonnative speaker in not having quite mastered the accent, *mots justes*, and particular ways of putting things that mark a native speaker. In other words, creoles are *languages*. There is heartbreaking poetry written in Sranan, richly considered novels in Haitian, and newspapers in Papiamentu and Tok Pisin.

Thus what we see is that languages are constantly mixing to various extents, and yet the results are always intricate tool kits with explicit rules, capable of expressing the full range of human experiences.

And it doesn't even stop here. Finally, there are cases where languages mix even more intimately than in creoles. For example, the native language of the Indians in Ecuador is Quechua. When a railroad was built between the town of Salcedo and the capital, Quito, young male Indians from the town began working in Quito for long periods, where they learned Spanish. Gradually, they began to identity with urban life to an extent that set them apart within their Indian communities, while remaining an integral part of these communities nonetheless. As a linguistic expression of this, they developed a way of speaking among themselves that used Spanish vocabulary within Quechua structure right down to not only the Quechua sentence structure, but also the Quechua word endings. The result was a new language that they call Media Lengua 'middle language.'

Here, for example, is a Spanish sentence:

Vengo para pedir un favor.

come-I for ask a favor
I come to ask a favor.

Here is the same sentence in Quechua:

Shuk fabur-da maña-nga-bu shamu-xu-ni.

one favor-ACC ask-NOM-"to" come-"-ing"-I
I come to ask a favor.

Notice that Quechua, like Latin, uses endings on nouns to indicate the function of a word in the sentence. ACC stands for "accusative," like the ending in Latin that marks something as an object . . . ; in Quechua, this ending is -da. NOM stands for nominative or "subject," the "default" case. In Latin, the way you know something is the subject is when it has no ending. On the other hand, in Quechua, even the nominative has an ending, -nga. Furthermore, the nominative ending can be put on a verb rather than just on nouns, as in Latin. The fact that it is "I" who is asking the favor is signaled with an ending -ni, just as the ending -o does this in Spanish (veng-o 'I come'). The ending -bu expresses the notion that the separate word to would in the Spanish or English version of the sentence.

Here is the sentence in Media Lengua:

Unu fabur-**ta** pidi-**nga-bu** bini-**xu-ni**.

a favor-ACC ask-NOM-BEN come-PROG-I
I come to ask a favor.

In some ways, the Media Lengua case reminds us of creoles like Sranan. For example, Media Lengua uses Quechua sentence structure—as in Quechua, Media Lengua puts the object first (a favor to ask I come). Also, it uses a Quechua sound system like Sranan uses a West African one. For example, Quechua has no e or o but just a, i, and u, and thus pidi rather than pedir, fabur rather than favor, etc.

However, Media Lengua goes a step further in mixing than creoles. In creoles, the words from one language are mixed with the things that most of the languages spoken by the people exposed to the new language happen to have in common, such as the verb-stringing in some West African languages. We saw it in Yoruba; it is also found in Ewe, Twi, and many of the other languages that Caribbean slaves spoke. However, there are a great many things that any single West African language has that we do not find in a creole because things this language-specific would not have been comprehensible to the people who spoke other West African languages. For example, while in English we express the future with a word, *will*, in one language spoken by the first slaves in Suriname, Ewe, the future is expressed with a prefix, as in the following:

Mí-á-do

we-will-talk
We will talk.

Another one of the slaves' languages, Twi, has a different prefix for the future, *be-*. Igbo has *ga-*. Each West African language has a different one. We do not see any of these prefixes in Sranan because since there were so many languages spoken by the slaves in Suriname, if slaves speaking one language had tried to tack their particular future prefix onto an English verb, only the few speakers of that African language would have understood what it meant—*mí á-waka* would only mean "I will walk" to an Ewe speaker; to a Twi speaker it would be as meaningless as it is to us.

Indeed, endings are one of the most idiosyncratic aspects of any language, and no two regular languages have all of the same ones, even when closely related. For example, the English past tense ending is *-ed*, as in *walked*. German is a close relative, but nevertheless has *-te*, as in *ich lern-**te** 'I learned,' while another close relative, Swedish, has *-de*, as in *ja kalla-**de** 'I called.' Therefore, the contribution of the West African languages stayed on the level of the broad aspects of sentence structure as a whole like verb-stringing, which all of the languages had in common, many of them being relatives. In the same way, for example, even if each Romance language has different endings ("We talk" is *parl-**ons*** in French, *habl-**amos*** in Spanish, and *parl-**iamo*** in Italian), all of them have the sentence-level trait of placing the adjective after the noun ("black cat" is *chat noir* in French, *gato negro* in Spanish, and *gatto nero* in Italian). Therefore, a slave could pass the "verb-stringing" feature from an individual language into Sranan and still be understood by most of the others, since so many of the Africans' native languages had this feature as well.

Media Lengua is different from creoles in that the people learning Spanish all spoke the same language, Quechua. As a result, they could bring not only Quechua sentence structure to the new language that they were creating, but even the idiosyncratic, persnickety little things like endings. Languages like Media Lengua, called *intertwined languages*, are our Level Four of language mixture, being the closest two languages can mingle (intertwined languages could be described as two languages doing exactly what you may be thinking).

While the young men who created Media Lengua spoke both Spanish and Quechua; today there are young people whose first and best language is Media Lengua, who barely speak Quechua at all, and speak Spanish only as a second language to be used with outsiders and in Quito. In other words, Media Lengua has become the language of the community.

Media Lengua is but one example of an intertwined language. In the western prairie provinces of Canada and across the border in Montana and North Dakota, a hybrid of Canadian French and the Native American language Cree (called Michif) is spoken by communities of Métis (MEH-tiss, or if you want a French sound, may-TEE), progeny of unions between French Canadians and Cree (as early as the 1700s) who feel neither French Canadian nor Cree, but something poised neatly in-between. In the 1800s, on Copper Island off the east coast of Russia in the Bering Strait, Russian seal trappers cohabitated with Eskimo women who spoke the language Aleut. They left behind children who created a language using Russian words and Aleut endings, Mednyj Aleut (MED-nee ah-LOOT). There are many other examples of intertwined languages, all of them are as rich and expressive and complex as any other.

All of these examples show us that not only is language mixture common and inevitable, but that to whatever extent it proceeds in any given case, the result is always a systematic, nuanced, and complex tool.

FUZZY LOGIC: THE NONDISCRETE NATURE OF LANGUAGE MIXTURE

It is important that we realize, as we pass from mere borrowing of words (*government, fashion, art,* and *cuisine*) through borrowing of scattered sentence patterns (*Is it out of your mind you are?* from Irish Gaelic) through creoles (Sranan's *seni wan brifi gi en* 'send her a letter') and finally to intertwined languages (Media Lengua's *unu fabur-ta pidi-nga-bu bini-xu-ni* 'I come to ask you a favor'), that there are no discrete boundaries between these levels of mixture. The examples we have seen are all useful points on what is a continuum of language mixture, and in real life a language mixture can occupy just about any point on that continuum, depending on the situation in which the language arises.

For example, often there is no discrete line between a European language and a creole using its words. Instead, the European language and the creole are poles at the ends of a spread of dialects that gradually shade from European language through Level Two mixture to the Level Three of a creole. For example, in Guyana in South America, an English creole developed among plantation slaves which is rather similar to Sranan:

Mi bin gee am wan.

I "-ed" give him one
I gave him one.

This creole is a typical example of Level Three mixture. However, it was spoken primarily by field slaves who had the very least contact with whites and English. Meanwhile, slaves who worked in the house, such as cooks, laundresses, and artisans, as well as slaves owned individually or in twos and threes who worked in towns, had more contact with English, and thus they developed a speech form that was not as profoundly influenced by West African languages as the creole, but which nevertheless was distinct enough from English to be perceptible as a thing apart, barely comprehensible to a European English speaker.

In this type of intermediate variety, the earlier creole sentence would be roughly: *Ah did give ee wan. Ah* is closer to *I* than *mi, did give* is closer to what we know as English than *bin gee.* However, there are still West African influences; for example, the use of *ah* for *I* reflects the consonant-vowel tendency in West African languages, which make sequences of vowel sounds like *ah-ee* (*I*) unfamiliar to their speakers. This is roughly a Level Two mixture, leaning closer to Level Three than *They're after leaving,* but not a creole in the sense of Sranan *seni wan brifi gi en.* Thus we have a sequence of dialects increasingly close to European English:

Mi bin gee am wan.
Ah did give ee wan.
I gave him one.

Even this, however, waters down the actual picture, because there are a whole range of dialects between even these, the results of slaves having slightly less or slightly more contact with English. A more accurate picture would be this:

Mi bin gee am wan.
Mi di gi ee wan.
Ah did give ee wan.
Ah give im wan.
I gave him one.

A truly representative illustration of this simple statement would show about 15 varieties, but our schematic depiction should suffice to show that language mixture is a matter of degree. Today, people with the least education, usually in rural areas, speak the full-blown creole the most. Standard English is spoken by those with the most education: often urban dwellers in positions of influence. People speak the varieties in the middle depending on education and place of residence.

EX UNO PLURES: MANY LANGUAGES OUT OF ONE

Just as a lowly shrewish-looking, cat-sized creature evolved into mammals as different as horses, dogs, elephants, and whales, one language gradually evolves into several. Just as the first horse, a schnauzer-sized, five-toed little critter, evolved into horses, zebras, and donkeys, a language evolves into various dialects. Just as we don't see horses, dogs, and elephants as perversions of their unmourned homely, nervous, buck-toothed little ancestor, we do not see languages as degraded versions of their ancestors. By the same token, just as we do not see horses, zebras, and asses as decayed versions of the five-toed little critter, nor Saint Bernards, Chihuahuas, and Labradors as unfortunate detours from the ancestral dog, no dialect of a language is inherently unfit or inadequate (although I must admit I occasionally have my doubts about Chihuahuas).

When it comes to language mixture, however, the analogy with evolution stops because among nature's organisms, the progeny of different species are indeed deficient organisms. Sometimes a hybrid can be pulled off, but always with a price—mules, hybrids of horses and donkeys, are sterile, not to mention cranky, for example. And were genetics to allow us to breed, say, a rabbit and a rhinoceros, we can be sure that the result would be a misbegotten Picasso painting of an animal that would not live long or well.

However, when languages mix, the result is not a galumphing, perplexed rabboceros, but a new language as vital and vibrant as its parents. Languages mix not like animals but like colors—when red and blue mix the result is purple, a color that obviously is in no way "weaker" or "less representative" than red or blue.

Zero in on almost any one of the world's five thousand or so languages, and you will see that it is actually a bundle of different varieties, with the grand, unitary-sounding name of English or Japanese or Swahili actually serving as a convenient umbrella term for all of them. Look a little closer, and you see that where these languages—or more properly, dialects of these languages—rub up against one another, they always mix, sometimes mixing so deeply that the very notion of whether the variety is Spanish or Russian or Turkish starts to become as irrelevant an issue as whether teal is green or blue. And yet, all of these tens of thousands of dialects of five thousand languages are rich, subtle tapestries, be they spoken in a tiny, preliterate village; in huts behind a mountain on a wind-swept plain; on a steamy Carribean island; or in a bustling urban newsroom.

This is well illustrated by taking a last, final bird's-eye view of what Spanish is in the real world. Spanish, of course, arose in Spain, but is now spoken by more people in its former colonies in Latin America than in Spain itself. In Latin America, Spanish has first of all undergone our Level One of language mixture. Just as English acquired many words from French and Vietnamese many words from Chinese, in Latin America even the standard Spanish spoken by the educated classes contains a great many words taken from languages spoken by the Indians who the Spaniards encountered there. For example, in Ecuador, the word for potato is not *patata*, as in Spain, but *papa*, the word for potato in Quechua; similarly, "dirty" is *carcoso* instead of *sucio*, "orphan" is *guácharo* instead of *huérfano*, etc.

As we saw, however, there is also Level Two language mixture: Languages can also inherit not just words but sentence patterns from other languages, while remaining quite recognizable nevertheless, such as Irish English's *Is it out of your mind you are?*, based on Irish Gaelic. For example, in Ecuador, Quechuas who speak Spanish and Quechua often transfer Quechua sentence patterns into Spanish, creating a Spanish dialect subtly different from the Spanish of educated Ecuadorans, but still Spanish nonetheless. For example, in the educated Spanish of Ecuador, as across the Spanish-speaking world, "Juan's hat" would be *el sombrero de Juan* "the hat of Juan." However, a Quechua will often, in the midst of Spanish little different from the casual speech of educated Ecuadorans, say something like *de Juan su sombrero* "of Juan his hat." This pattern sounds a little odd to the ear of a Spaniard, but in fact it is based upon the Quechua version of the phrase, which is

> Huwan-pa ch'uku-n.
>
> Juan-of   hat-his

De Juan su sombrero keeps *de* and *su* before the nouns, following the Spanish pattern, but uses the word order of Quechua, and also has the "redundant" *his* that Quechua uses (redundance is not "primitive"—in the French *les hommes petits* 'the small men,' *les* alone would do just fine to make the phrase plural; the -*s*'s at the ends of the other two words are redundant).

This, however, is still Spanish, not a new language. However, elsewhere, Spanish mixes with other languages on the next level, the result being Spanish creoles (Level Three). Here, for example, is Papiamentu for *We fly to Holland*:

> Nos ta bula bai Hulanda.
>
> we   be fly   go   Holland

Notice the verb-string *fly-go* here, which is based on the same West African languages as the similar pattern in Sranan and Haitian Creole. Also, all endings are gone—where Spanish would have *vol-**amos*** 'we fly,' Papiamentu has a bare verb that is the same with all pronouns. Finally, there is the tendency toward consonant-vowel sound patterning—where Spanish has *volar* for *fly*, Papiamentu recasts this as *bula*. Here, then, Spanish has mixed so deeply with West African languages that we have a new language entirely.

Yet language mixture operates on a continuum. In this light, it is useful to point out that creole though it is, Papiamentu is not as far away from Spanish as, say, Sranan is from English, or Haitian is from French. It actually uses a few endings from Spanish in some parts of its structure (not shown here) and does not make as much use of the African verb-stringing, among other things, as many other creoles do. This is because while it was forming, slaves usually worked on small farms or in towns, and thus they had much more contact with Spanish than, say, Haitian slaves had with French, working in gangs of as much as 500 on massive plantations. However, just as there is a range of creole varieties in Guyana, some light-years from English and others quite close, there are creoles based on Spanish that are further from Spanish than Papiamentu. For example, in the early 1600s, slaves in Colombia escaped into the interior and developed a community called El Palenque de San Basilio, where their descendants still live today, speaking a Spanish creole called Palenquero. Here is a sentence:

> Suto kelé-ba ngopiá abué ele.
>
> we want-ed hit   father his
> We wanted to hit his father.

(In this language, the accents signify stress, not higher tone as in Saramaccan.)

All of these words are from Spanish, but are so thoroughly transformed by West African sound patterns and sentence structures as to be all but unrecognizable to any Spanish speaker who doesn't happen to also speak Palenquero. *Suto* is from *nosotros*, shortened and then recast into the West African consonant-vowel pattern we are familiar with. *Kelé* is from *querer* 'to want.' The *ba* is from the verb *acabar* 'to finish,' which has been shortened (ah-ka-BAR became simply BA) and turned into a brand-new past ending: The first slaves ran two verbs, *querer* and *acabar*, together in our West African verb-stringing pattern. *Ngopiá* is from *golpear* (goal-pay-AR) 'to hit'; the *ng* sound is found in African languages. The placement of *ele* 'his' after the noun instead of before is also a West African word order, similar to the "house-in" order we saw in Sranan and Ewe. Thus Papiamentu and Palenquero show that creole-type mixture is a matter of degree.

And then finally, we return to Ecuador, where because the people learning Spanish speak only one language, Quechua, they can mix their native language with Spanish even more specifically than African slaves did, creating Media Lengua. Even here, however, Media Lengua is but the most extreme example of a process that actually occurs in degrees. For example, there are Quechuas who speak a type of Spanish that is basically a Level Two mixture, using constructions like *De Juan su sombrero*. But, in addition, these Quechuas pepper their speech with a little ending from Quechua, *-ca*, which means roughly "you know." They do not use any of the other endings from Quechua that we see in Media Lengua, but with its *-ca*, this kind of Spanish is a step further along the way to Media Lengua than that of speakers who would say *De Juan su sombrero* but never use this *-ca*—call it Level Two plus. On the other hand, further along the way to Media Lengua but not yet there, there are Quechuas who speak a variety that is basically Media Lengua, but that uses a few Spanish endings instead of Quechua ones, and uses many of the Quechua endings only optionally rather than obligatorily. This variety is indeed Level Four mixing, an intertwined language, but is closer to Spanish than the Media Lengua we have already seen.

The Spanish that we learn from textbooks is but one of a whole array of forms that it takes worldwide—not only is Spanish actually a cover term for various dialects, but the very notion of Spanish shades into a range of varieties mixed in degrees with other languages to the point that they can no longer even be called Spanish. Yet they remain languages in their own right.

There are many languages in the world whose names stand for what, when viewed close up, is a continuum of mixed language varieties—English, French, Spanish, Portuguese, Dutch, Arabic, Turkish, Indonesian, and Swahili, as well as lesser-known languages like Afrikaans (of South Africa), Assamese (of India), and Bemba (of Zambia). For other languages, many if not all of their varieties are mixed to at least Level Two, a situation that is increasingly widespread with the ever-growing influence of certain geopolitically dominant languages on the world stage. The lesson from all of this is that not only are all languages bundles of dialects, but that languages have always profoundly influenced one another—often just sharing words, but sometimes even sharing word order and endings and becoming new languages entirely—the result of billions of people jostling for space on our small planet.

≡

FOR DISCUSSION AND REVIEW

1. What reasons does McWhorter give to explain why most Americans speak only English?

2. When languages borrow words from each other, McWhorter says the process is "more crossfertilization than contamination." What does he mean by this remark?

3. What kinds of borrowing take place in McWhorter's Levels One and Two? Give some examples from borrowed words you're familiar with, from the English spoken in Ireland, or from other languages.

4. Why might a language take only words from another language—and nothing else? How do some of the English words borrowed from French illustrate this phenomenon?

5. In McWhorter's Level Three, an entirely new language is created. Explain how creole languages develop. How is a pidgin language part of this process?

6. Could you understand the Sranan passage? How, if at all, has McWhorter's discussion of creoles and mixed languages changed your thinking about English?

7. Explain intertwined language. How does a language such as Media Lengua differ from a creole?

Projects for "Global English"

1. Use one of the following quotations from David Crystal's selection in this part (pp. 693–716) as your starting point, and develop an argument supporting this proposition: English as a global language provides increased access and opportunity to everyone no matter where they are or what languages they speak.

> Shortly after I became Secretary-General of the Commonwealth in 1975, I met Prime Minister Sirimavo Bandaranaike in Colombo and we talked of ways in which the Commonwealth Secretariat could help Sri Lanka. Her response was immediate and specific: "Send us people to train our teachers to teach English as a foreign language." . . . The Prime Minister went on to explain that the policies her husband had put into place twenty years earlier to promote Sinhalese as the official language had succeeded so well that in the process Sri Lanka—so long the pearl of the English-speaking world in Asia—had in fact lost English, even as a second language save for the most educated Sri Lankan. Her concern was for development. Farmers in the field, she told me, could not read the instructions on bags of imported fertiliser—and manufacturers in the global market were not likely to print them in Sinhalese. Sri Lanka was losing its access to the world language of English. –Sridath Ramphal, "World Language: Opportunities, Challenges, Responsibilities," 1996.

> To study molecular genetics, all you need to get into the Harvard University Library, or the medical library at Sweden's Karolinksa Institute, is a phone line and a computer. And, it turns out, a solid command of the English language. Because whether you are a French intellectual pursuing the cutting edge of international film theory, a Japanese paleobotanist curious about a newly discovered set of primordial fossils, or an American teen-ager concerned about Magic Johnson's jump shot, the Internet and World Wide Web really only work as great unifiers if you speak English. . . . Anatoly Voronov, director of Russian Internet provider Glasnet, says, "[The Internet] is the ultimate act of intellectual colonialism. The product comes from America so we must either adapt to English or stop using it. That is the right of business. But if you are talking about a technology that is supposed to open the world to hundreds of millions of people you are joking. This just makes the world into new sorts of haves and have nots." –Michael Spector, "World Wide Web: 3 English Words," 1996.

2. First, consider this statement by linguists Ann Curzon and Michael Adams in *How English Works* (2006):

> English certainly offers opportunities for wider readership and shared conversation, as well as perhaps unity in countries with multiple local languages, but what gets lost? This debate raises the important question of whether the use of English as a global language and the maintenance of native languages and multilingualism are truly at odds. In other words, does a global language require or necessarily result in the reduction of local languages?

Then, select a country with multiple native or local languages and with English as an officially recognized language. Research the use of languages in that country, and then use your findings to write an argumentative essay. You may want to make a case that the presence of English causes the loss of native or local languages. Or you may argue that such loss is due to the political or cultural dominance of another native language—and not English. You might also discover—and argue—that major disruptions are not taking place among local languages despite the use of English for economic or social reasons.

3. The various Englishes in the world each have their own history. Using resources such as Jan Svartik and Geoffrey Leech's *English: One Tongue, Many Voices*; Peter Trudgill and Jean Hannah's fourth edition of *International English*; or Tom McArthur's *Oxford Guide to World English*, write a research paper on English in a region of the world you do not associate with English speakers. Consider who first brought English into the area, who used it initially, and for what purposes. Were official mandates or rules created for use or excluding or giving access to English? Has the use of English increased or decreased over time? The bibliography at the end of this part also contains listings for several introductory volumes on World Englishes, including Cambridge University Press's and John Benjamins Press's series on specific varieties of English.

4. In considering the future of English in South Asia, David Crystal notes that commercially, the "English language teaching (ELT) business has become one of the major growth industries round the world in the last half century." Research and write a paper on English language teaching as a business. How many Teaching English as a Second Language (TESOL) programs are available at universities in your state? How many private training programs are available in your area? Look into the training pedagogy, how teachers are recruited, where they are placed, and what they are typically paid. Include discussion of how ELT differs from academic TESOL training.

5. In *The Future of English?*, David Graddol asks whether the Internet is "the electronic 'flagship'" of global English. Similarly, Geoffrey Nunberg asks whether the Internet will always speak English. (See the bibliography at the end of this part.) Conduct a class debate over the questions raised by these two linguists.

6. University of Illinois linguist Braj Kachru describes how English spreads around the world as three concentric circles, with the Inner Circle at the center, the Outer Circle in the middle, and the Expanding Circle as outermost. Write a research paper on Kachru's Three Circles. Briefly explain the three circles, and then consider some of these questions: How have linguists and language policy makers used this approach? What criticisms have they made about Kachru's theory, and what modifications to his theory have they suggested? What issues seem to come up regarding the role(s) of English in the Outer Circle countries? What other hypotheses have been put forth to explain the spread of English? To start, read

David Crystal's *Global English* 2003: 60–61, where he summarizes Kachru's ideas with the Circles; David Graddol's *The Future of English* (mentioned above); and Kachru's own "The Sacred Cows of English" (in *English Today*, 16: 3–8). For more information, check the bibliography at the end of this part for volumes with "World English" in the title. Also look for responses to Kachru's ideas in issues of *English Today* from the past decade.

7. Collect at least five advertisements that include print or writing from one of the countries considered "Outer Circle" countries—that is, countries where English was not native but where it now has official recognition, serves important functions, and is a second language for a portion of the population. Outer Circle countries include Singapore, India, and Malawi. (See David Crystal's *English as a Global Language* for more.) You will also need to discover what other languages are in use in that country.

Once you have the ads, examine the language used in each, and write a brief report about whether and how this country incorporates different languages into its advertising. Look, for example, at spelling, pronunciation, types of grammatical constructions, specific words and phrases, and abbreviations. Do you find language switching? Do you recognize English word forms that have changed meanings or grammatical functions? Do the visuals seem more representative of one language than another? Also consider what sorts of social knowledge or shared cultural experience are presumed by the producers of the ads. Can you fully understand or appreciate the ad? Why, or why not? If possible, include in your report some of the ads you discuss.

8. For this project, small groups will make presentations on government policies and official roles for English in countries where English is not a predominant first language. Each group should choose one country from a region such as the Caribbean, East Africa, or Southeast Asia. Then determine the arenas of English language use for that country, such as education, government, or law. Also consult Lexis/Nexis and other databases to find media coverage of language policies and public concerns. Finally, check the various government and tourist Web sites for public or official stands on the roles and status of native languages and of English.

9. Since at least the seventeenth century, a number of universal or constructed languages have been put forward to foster international harmony and communication. Among these are Esperanto, Interlingua, Volapük, and Novial. Most of these languages have been short lived (the Interlingua Institute explains the demise of Interlingua as a result of the globalization of English), but each has a particular history, grammar, and purpose. Research and write a brief history of one constructed international language.

10. John McWhorter describes the process of contact and change that leads to development of an English-based creole. For this project, research

and write a history of a creole based on English. Use www.ethnologue.com and other World English sources listed in the bibliography at the end of this part to choose an active English-based creole. In addition to Sranan, a creole McWhorter discusses in his essay, Singapore English, Gullah, Bay Islands Creole English of Honduras, Krio of Sierra Leone, and Kriol of Australia have a substantial number of speakers. To begin thinking about how creoles develop, you might look at David Crystal's "Pidgins and Creoles" in Part Seven (pp. 451–57).

Selected Bibliography

Baumgardner, Robert U. "The Indigenization of English in Pakistan." *English Today* 21 (1990): 59–65. [Cultural and linguistic development of Pakistani English with discussion of Urdu influences.]

Cheshire, Jenny, ed. *English around The World: Sociolinguistic Perspectives.* Cambridge: Cambridge UP, 1991. [Articles discussing the growth of English as a global language, its variations, and its social context.]

Crystal, David. *The Cambridge Encyclopedia of the English Language.* 2nd ed. Cambridge: Cambridge UP, 2003. [Extensively illustrated and comprehensive encyclopedia about the English language, with in-depth discussions of regional and social dialects and issues such as political correctness.]

———. *English as a Global Language.* 2nd ed. Cambridge: Cambridge UP, 2003. [Examines the rise of English as a global language and considers the history and effects of globalization.]

D'Souza, Jean. "Contextualizing Range and Depth in Indian English." *World Englishes* 20 (2001): 145–59. [Discusses uses and varieties of English in India, with insights into language globalization in relation to South Asia.]

Easton, Eva L. "English around the World." *English Online.* 13 April 2007. <http://eleaston.com/world-eng.html>. [Extensive resource for information about varieties of English.]

English Today. Cambridge: Cambridge UP. [A journal available in print and online at the Cambridge University Press Web site; reports on all aspects of English.]

Ethnologue. 2007. SIL Int. <www.ethnologue.com>. [Catalog of nearly 7,000 known living languages, with social and demographic information and bibliographic references.]

Graddol, David. *The Future of English?: A Guide to Forecasting the Popularity of English in the 21st Century.* 2000. The British Council. <www.britishcouncil.org/learning-elt-future.pdf>. [Discusses the trends that impact language changes and makes forecasts about the future of English.]

"Grammar Safari." *Intensive English Institute.* U of Illinois at Urbana–Champaign. <www.iei.uiuc.edu/student_grammarsafari.html>. [Resource of non-typical grammar, with activities and exercises.]

Honna, Nobuyuki, ed. *Asian Englishes: An International Journal of the Sociolinguistics of English in Asia.* 2006. ALC Press. <www.alc.co.jp/asian-e>. [Focuses on the growing use of English, English language education, and the social contexts of English throughout Asia.]

International Association for World Englishes. 2005. <www.iaweworks.org>. [Information about IAWE articles, conferences, and memberships.]

Jenkins, J. *World Englishes: A Resource Book for Students.* London: Routledge, 2003. [Resources and activities for the study of world Englishes.]

Kachru, Braj. *The Other Tongue: English across Cultures.* 2nd ed. Urbana, IL: U of Illinois P, 1992. [Articles examining the international uses of English, including English testing of non-native speakers, World English in the classroom, and literary creativity.]

Kachru, Yamuna, and Cecil L. Nelson. *World Englishes in Asian Contexts.* Aberdeen, HK: Hong Kong UP, 2006. [Examines theoretical and pedagogical issues, including the intersection of English and Asian languages.]

Knowles, Gerry. *A Cultural History of the English Language*. London: Arnold, 1997. [Provides a history of English through social and cultural contexts, covering topics such as discourse analysis and literacy.]

Lim, Lisa. *Singapore English: A Grammatical Description*. Amsterdam: Benjamins, 2004. [Examines the grammar of Spoken Singapore English and issues of education and policy making related to it.]

Mair, Christian, ed. *The Politics of English as a World Language: New Horizons in Postcolonial Cultural Studies* (Cross/Cultures 65). Amersterdam: Rodopi, 2003. [Selected conference papers discussing English as a world language, new Englishes, postcolonial literatures, and other related topics.]

McArthur, Tom. *The Oxford Guide to World English*. Oxford: Oxford UP, 2003. [Comprehensive presentation of all varieties of World English, organized by geographic region.]

———. "World or International or Global English—And What Is It Anyway?" *English Today*. Georgetown U Round Table on Languages and Linguistics Archive, Digital Georgetown and Georgetown UP. <http://digital.georgetown.edu/gurt/1999/gurt_1999_30.pdf>. [World Englishes expert discusses the emergence of an authentically universal language.]

McWhorter, John. *Word on the Street: Debunking the Myth of Pure "Standard" English*. New York: Perseus, 2001. [Argues that all languages are always changing naturally and that popular culture is not destroying English.]

Meier, Paul. *International Dialects of English Archive*. Dept. of Theatre and Film, Kentucky U. <www.ku.edu/~idea>. [Provides sound files for dialects of English with examples from specific locales.]

Melcher, Gunnel, and Phillip Shaw. *World Englishes: An Introduction*. London: Arnold, 2003. [Examines varieties of World Englishes with examples from popular culture.]

Nihalani, Paroo, Ray K. Tongue, Priya Hosali, and Jonathan Crowther. *Indian and British English: A Handbook of Usage and Pronunciation*. 2nd ed. Oxford: Oxford UP, 2006. [A dictionary of Indian English.]

Nunberg, Geoffrey. "Will the Internet Always Speak English?" *The American Prospect* 27 Mar 2000. <www.prospect.org/print/V11/10/nunberg-g.html>. [University of California–Berkeley linguistics professor's examination of English as the dominant language on the Internet.

Patil, Z. N. "On the Nature and Role of English in Asia." *The Linguistics Journal*. June 2006. <www.linguistics-journal.com/June2006_zn.php>. [Discusses issues pertaining to English in Asia, including intelligibility and the legitimacy of variations in the language.]

Patrick, Peter L. *Linguistics Human Rights: A Sociolinguistic Introduction*. 2 Nov. 2005. Dept. of Linguistics, U of Essex. <http://privatewww.essex.ac.uk/~patrickp/lhr/lhrengonlywork.htm>. [Features case law pertaining to English-only policies in the American workplace.]

Pennycook, Alistair. *The Cultural Politics of English as an International Language*. London: Longman, 1994. [Examines the political and social implications of the global spread of English and suggests that the classroom is a political arena for using English as a language of protest; outlines "critical pedagogy."]

Phan Le Ha. "Toward a Critical Notion of Appropriation of English as an International Language." *The Asian EFL Journal Quarterly* 7.3 (2005): 34–46. <www.asian-efl-journal.com/September_05_plh.php>. [Suggests a TESOL pedagogy deriving from multiple cultures.]

Phillipson, Robert. *Linguistic Imperialism*. Oxford: Oxford UP, 1992. [Examines social, political, and ideological implications of English as a world language.]

Prendergast, D. "Views on Englishes: A talk with Braj B. Kachru, Salikoko Mufwene, Rajendra Singh, Loreto Todd, and Peter Trudgill." *Links & Letters* 5 (1998): 225–41. <www.raco.cat/index.php/LinksLetters/issue/view/1905/showToc>. [Five international scholars address social, political, and cultural issues pertaining to World Englishes.]

Qiong, Hu Xiao. "Why China English Should Stand Alongside British, American, and Other 'World Englishes.'" *English Today* 20.2 (2004): 26–33. [Proposes that Chinese students learn a form of English unique to China as opposed to British or American English.]

Romaine, Suzanne, ed. *The Cambridge History of the English Language, Vol. 4: 1776–1997*. Cambridge: Cambridge UP, 1998. [Essays discussing English in North America from the American Revolution to contemporary American English.]

Schneider, Edgar, gen. ed. *Varieties of English around the World*. Amsterdam: Benjamins. [An ongoing series of scholarly studies.]

Siegel, Jeff, and Ermile Hargrove. *Language Varieties*. 30 March 2007. School of Languages, Cultures, and Linguistics, U of New England, Australia. <www.une.edu.au/langnet>. [Provides links to information on varieties of English, pidgins and creoles, and regional, minority, and localized dialects.]

Stanlaw, James. *Japanese English: Language and Culture Contact*. Aberdeen, HK: Hong Kong UP, 2005. [Uses archival material and anthropological fieldwork to examine Japanese English, including issues and ramifications of its use.]

Svartik, Jan, and Geoffrey Leech. *English: One Tongue, Many Voices*. Basingstoke, UK: Palgrave, 2006. [Covers the origins, development, variation, and globalization of English; the development of international Englishes; and the politics of language change.]

Trudgill, Peter, and Jean Hannah. *International English: A Guide to the Varieties of Standard English*. 4th ed. London: Arnold, 2002. [Updated edition of an accessible guide to English worldwide with new information on the English of Bangladesh, Pakistan, and the Philippines.]

Welsh, Irvine. *Trainspotting*. New York: Norton, 2002. [Scottish writer's black comic portrait of working-class heroin addicts in Edinburgh, written in the 1980s. Includes glossary to help understand vernacular and slang in the dialogue.]

World Englishes. Malden, MA: Blackwell. [Publication devoted to the study of international English.]

LANGUAGE IN THE CLASSROOM

In this part, we look at the relationship between language and literacy, the ability to read and write. Although the title of Part Eleven puts language "in the classroom," we begin to be literate before we ever enter school. The skills required for writing and reading, for describing and interpreting our worlds, and even for learning how to learn are strongly influenced by the communities where we grow up. The following selections shed light on this and several other issues. How, for instance, should we teach children to read and write? What are the best ways to balance the rules of grammar and the ongoing changes in living languages? Why was the development of the alphabet so important?

In the first selection, "Languages and Writing," John P. Hughes lays the groundwork for discussing literacy by explaining the derivation of alphabetic writing systems. He contends that the original phonemic alphabet arose by a great stroke of luck and that its dissemination through succeeding cultures has altered the course of history. The phonemic alphabet, Hughes claims, took the capability of written communication out of the exclusive province of the educated elite and moved it into the public arena.

Is it necessary or even possible to define a standard of quality for English language usage? In "What Makes Good English Good?" John Algeo takes aim at some of the most cherished notions of scholars and grammarians and finds no absolutes. "Because good English is so diverse," he writes, "to use it in more than a few circumstances requires an equally diverse knowledge and a fine sense of what is appropriate under varying conditions."

Although children acquire spoken language naturally, learning to write and read requires instruction and conscious effort. In the third selection, "Reading, Writing and Speech," Victoria Fromkin, Robert Rodman, and Nina Hyams make the point that teaching methods for reading and writing should "take advantage of the child's innate linguistic knowledge." Stressing the importance of teaching phonics, they also discuss the various uses of punctuation and why English words are spelled the way they are.

In the now classic "What No Bedtime Story Means," Shirley Brice Heath discusses the development of literacy in preschool and primary-grade children. The children Heath researched in three Carolina Piedmont communities are involved in what she calls *literacy events*—occasions for learning to take meaning from written language—but they do not all prosper in school. As it turns out, the *kinds* of literacy events children experience affect in significant ways what they accomplish in a typical classroom environment.

Finally, in "English Language Learners in School," Suzanne F. Peregoy and Owen F. Boyle describe how teachers can put the diverse backgrounds of what they call new English learners at the center of teaching design. The authors discuss the importance of knowing students' personal history and culture and how to apply that knowledge in the classroom. They also present some of the current education programs that teachers use for English language learners, including those based on the home language, those based on English, and those that put students in the general classroom with little special assistance.

50

Languages and Writing

John P. Hughes

Most Americans take mass literacy for granted. They find it difficult to imagine that many adults in the United States cannot read and write. They are also surprised to learn that even today a significant proportion of the world's five thousand spoken languages lack writing systems. In the following selection from his 1962 book The Science of Language: An Introduction to Linguistics, *Professor John P. Hughes suggests the limitations that the lack of a writing system can impose. He traces in detail the evolution of writing systems, sometimes logical and sometimes not, from the earliest Cro-Magnon cave drawings to present-day systems. Note his explanation of the advantages of alphabetic systems and the unique nature of their origin.*

It has been said that the two oldest and greatest inventions of man were the wheel and the art of controlling fire. This is probable enough: and if one wished to make a group of three, surely the development of writing must claim the third place. Without a system of writing, no matter how wise or sublime the thought, once uttered it is gone forever (in its original form, at least) as soon as its echoes have died away.

Indeed, it would seem that without a means of preserving wisdom and culture, civilization, which depends on the passing on of a heritage from generation to generation, could not develop. The facts, however, are otherwise: noteworthy civilizations *have* arisen and flourished without possession of any form of writing, usually by forming a class of society whose duty and profession it was to keep in memory what we write down in books (and, too often, subsequently forget). Even the average citizen in such a society took as a matter of course demands upon his memory which we today would consider beyond human capacity.

All the same, one may question whether a really complex civilization—one capable of governing large areas, for instance—could be supported by such a system. If there ever was one, we may be sure it has been grossly slighted by history—which, after all, depends almost entirely on written records. Who, for example, has ever heard the Gaulish version of Caesar's campaigns?

There seems to be no reason to doubt that the many systems of writing which have been developed at different times by various peoples during mankind's long history all grew, by steps which we can and shall trace, out of man's ability to draw pictures.

Suppose you wish to preserve a record of your catching a twenty-pound trout, but happen to be illiterate. The obvious thing to do would be to draw and hang a picture of yourself catching the big fish. It was, apparently, an equally obvious thing to do some fifty thousand years ago, for the caves which yielded us the remains of the Cro-Magnon man first attracted attention because of their beautifully drawn pictures of a procession, perhaps a hunt, of animals. We shall never know whether this was a mere decoration or a record.

Given the ability to draw well enough so that your representations of persons and objects can be readily recognized, it is, of course, not difficult to tell a complete story in one panoramic picture, or in a series of uncaptioned sketches. The range of information that can be conveyed in this way can be greatly extended if a few simple conventions are agreed upon between the artist and his prospective audience: the use of a totem-sign for a certain tribe; considering a prone man to be sick or wounded if his eyes were open, dead if they are closed, and so on. Several tribes of North American Indians made use of this kind of communication (figure 50.1).

In these circumstances, it will be noted, pictures act as a means for the communication of thought, and thus are somewhat like a language in themselves. Indeed, some authorities include this kind of communication among various forms of "language," but we have deliberately excluded it from our definition. It is common and conventional to call this kind of writing *ideographic writing*, and while the term is convenient, this is properly in no sense either language or writing, as we shall proceed to show.

FIGURE 50.1 An Indian Pictographic Message. This message of friendship was sent from an American Indian chief to the president of the United States—the figure in the White House. The chief, identified by the lines rising from his head, who is sending the message, and the four warriors behind him, belong to the eagle totem; the fifth warrior is of the catfish totem. The figure at lower left is evidently also a powerful chief. The lines joining the eyes indicate harmony, and the three houses indicate the willingness of the Indians to adopt white men's customs. (From Henry R. Schoolcraft, *Historical and Statistical Information Respecting the Indian Tribes of America*, I, 418.)

Note, first, that the kind of communication achieved in figure 50.1 is totally independent of the language or languages of the persons who make the drawing and of those who read it. The "text" may be correctly "read" in any language. It is not an effort to record the *language* in which the event is described, but, like language itself, to record the *original events*: we might even say it is a system alternative to language for symbolizing events. And therefore it is not strictly writing; for writing is always a *record or representation of language*.

Ideographic "writing" cannot be strictly language either, for it has two limitations which would make it unworkable as a system for expressing human thought. First, it is not within everyone's competence: some of us have no talent for drawing. This, however, could be offset by conventionalizing the characters to a few simple strokes, not immediately recognizable as the original picture except by previous knowledge of the convention (see figure 50.2).

But then the second, more serious objection still remains: even with such conventionalization, the system cannot adequately express the whole range of human thought; and to do so even partially will require thousands of characters and a system of such complexity that exceedingly few in the society could master it.

The Chinese people have an ancient and beautiful script which was originally, and still is largely, ideographic. The characters have been conventionalized, but it is still quite easy to recognize their origin, as is shown in figure 50.2. Although there are many mutually unintelligible dialects of Chinese, the same written text can be read by any native (each in his own dialect), and the gist can even be made out by one who knows the principles of the system, but little of the language. Chinese writing is thus one of the strongest forces toward Chinese cultural unity. . . . But it is estimated that 70,000 to 125,000 characters exist (not all, of course, used with equal frequency), and it is said that a scholar takes seven years to learn to read and write Chinese if he already speaks it, while over 80 percent of the native speakers of Chinese are illiterate in their own language.

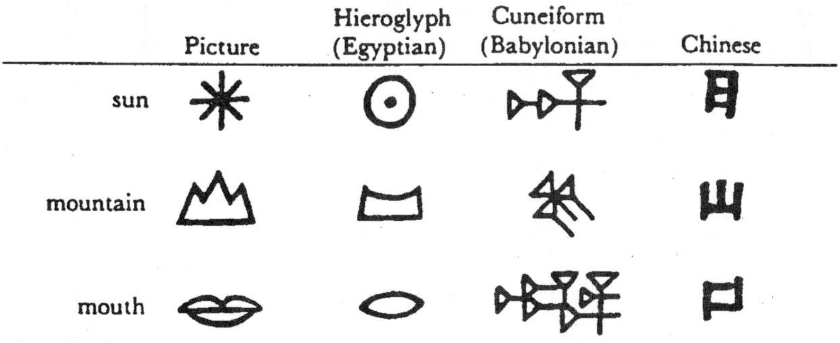

	Picture	Hieroglyph (Egyptian)	Cuneiform (Babylonian)	Chinese
sun				
mountain				
mouth				

FIGURE 50.2   Conventionalized Symbols.

Where there is considerable divergence between a language and its written representation, as in the case of Chinese or Italian, where many different dialects are written with the same spelling, or in French or English, where the language has changed considerably since the stage for which the writing was devised, a tendency may arise to consider the written language the "correct" language, of which the spoken language is a deformation which should be "corrected" to agree with the writing. This is particularly true when the writing either records, or once recorded, or is believed to record, the speech of a class of society which enjoys prestige, to which many native speakers would like to assimilate themselves.

This, however, always obscures things and puts the cart before the horse. Actually, the prestige class of any society probably least conforms its speech consciously to writing: sure of their status, its members do not worry about betraying an inferior origin in speech or behavior. It is said that if a man's table manners are absolutely disgusting, he is either a peasant or a duke. Writing is, in its essence, nothing but a means of recording language with some degree of efficiency. Whether one form or another of the language is "good" or "correct" is an entirely different question; a system of writing is good or bad according to how it records, accurately or otherwise, whatever form of the language it is aiming to record.

However, because of the prestige of letters in largely illiterate populations (which is so great that *gramarye* has even been thought to have magic power), the opposite tendency to "correct" language according to written forms has been so strong as to lead to such things as the creation of a word like "misle" from a misreading of the word "misled."[1] Many similar examples could be given.

PICTOGRAPHIC WRITING

Any nation which finds occasion to use a form of ideographic writing with any regularity, even if all the writing is the job of one relatively small social group, will probably sooner or later take the simple and logical step to *pictographic writing*. In this case, the written sign, which in ideographic writing is the symbol for an *idea*, becomes the symbol of a *word*. For example, a device like

which represents the floor-plan of a house, now becomes a sign for *per*, the Egyptian word for "house," or of *beyt'*, the Hebrew word for "house."

---

[1] This is an extreme case of what is called "spelling pronunciation." More typical examples are the pronunciation, by Americans in England, of words like *twopence* and *halfpenny* as written.

Another example: the picture

conventionalized to

which of course represented the snout of an ox, now becomes a sign for *alep*, the ancient Hebrew word for "ox."

The advantages of this step for the improvement of communication are evident. The written sign now symbolizes, not an idea, but a word, and a word is a far more precise symbol of a mental concept than any other which can be devised. With a sufficient stock of symbols of this new type, the writer can distinguish among a house, a stable, a barn, a shed, and a palace; whereas with ideographic writing he is pretty well limited to "house" vs. "big house" or "small house" (as there is no separate symbol for the adjective, the bigness or smallness cannot be specified and can range from "largish" to "enormous"). Much ambiguity is avoided: if you have tried to convey messages ideographically . . . you know how easy it is for an intended message "the king is angry" to be interpreted "the old man is sick."

Pictographic writing is, moreover, true writing, since it is a means of recording language, not just an alternative way of expressing the concepts which language expresses.

All pictographic writing systems that we know have developed from ideographic systems, and show clear traces of this, notably in their tendency to preserve ideographic symbols among the pictographic. Thus, the ancient Egyptians had an ideograph for water, a representation of waves or ripples:

$$\text{∿∿∿∿}$$

Eventually they derived from this a sign

$$\begin{matrix}\text{∿∿∿∿}\\\text{∿∿∿∿}\\\text{∿∿∿∿}\end{matrix}$$

standing for the word *mu*, which meant "water." But they often wrote the word *mu* as follows:

$$\text{∿∿∿}\ \underset{\text{9}}{\quad}\qquad \begin{matrix}\text{∿∿∿∿}\\\text{∿∿∿∿}\\\text{∿∿∿∿}\end{matrix}$$

And in writing of a river, the word for which was *atur*,

they also added the water sign: *atur* was written

$$\begin{matrix}\end{matrix}$$

The purpose of these ideographic "determinants" was probably to help the reader who did not know the particular word or sign by giving an indication of its general connotation. Nouns denoting persons were usually given the "determinant" of a little man—

or a little woman—

For, despite the noteworthy increases in efficiency which pictographic writing represents, thousands of characters are still necessary; and one advantage of the ideographic system has been lost—the characters are no longer self-explanatory. (This is only a theoretical advantage on behalf of ideographic script, since, while the ideographic character for a bird should presumably be readily recognized as a bird, in practice the characters have to be conventionalized for the sake of those who do not draw well.)

A considerable number of pictographic writing systems have been developed at different times in different parts of the world, but, Sunday-supplement science to the contrary notwithstanding, quite independently of one another, so that we have no ground for talking about the "evolution" by man of the art of writing. There is no evidence whatever for a First Cave Man who sat with hammer and chisel and stone and figured out how to chisel the first message, after which man made improvement after improvement, until the peak (represented, of course, by English orthography of the present day) was reached. Actually, nations once literate have been known to lapse into illiteracy as a result of ruinous wars and social disorganization.

SYLLABIC WRITING, UNLIMITED AND LIMITED

The step from pictographic to syllabic writing is an easy, logical, and, it might very well seem, self-evident one; yet there have been several nations which developed the first without ever proceeding to the second. It would probably be safe to say, however, that a majority of those who came as far as pictographic writing took the step to syllabic script.

In pictographic writing it is, of course, as easy to develop a stock of thousands of characters as in ideographic; yet, strange as it might seem, there is still always a shortage. This shortage arises because it is extremely difficult or impossible to represent some words in pictures. Take "velocity," for example. Is there any picture you could draw to express this that might not be read as, say, "the man is running"? Or, if you think you could picture "velocity," how would you handle "acceleration"? If you still think you could manage this one, what sort of picture, pray, would you draw for the word "the"?

The first step toward syllabic writing is taken when you permit yourself to cheat a little and take advantage of homophones. There is, let us say, a good pictograph for "the sea"; you use it to express the Holy "See," or "I see" (writing, perhaps, the characters for *eye* and *sea*).

When you have expressed the word "icy" by the characters for *eye* and *sea*, or *belief* by the characters for *bee* and *leaf*, you have turned the corner to syllabic writing. Any relationship whatever between the character and the *meaning* of the syllable it stands for is henceforth entirely irrelevant. The character expresses nothing but a sequence of sounds— the sounds making up one of the syllables of the language.

The first result of this is a gain of efficiency: a decrease in the number of possible characters (since more than one word or syllable can be written with the same syllabic character—in fact a great number can be written with varying sequences and combinations of a rather small number of characters). This gain is largely theoretical, however, for there will still be several thousand characters. The superiority of syllabic writing over pictographic from the point of view of efficiency will largely depend on the structure of syllables in the language using it. If syllables are generally or always simple in structure, a syllabic system of writing may work extremely well.

In every type of language, however, ambiguity and duplication are likely to be discovered in this kind of *unlimited syllabic* writing. It is often uncertain which of various homonymous readings is intended (e.g., does a character for "deep" joined to one for "end" mean "deep end" or "depend"?). And conversely, there are almost always two or more ways to say the same thing.

If the users of a syllabic system have a sense of logic, they will soon tend to adopt the practice of always writing the same syllable with the same character. The immediate result of this is for the first time to reduce the number of signs to manageable proportions: the sequence *baba* will always be expressed by signs expressing BA BA—never by signs for syllables such as BAB HA, BA ABA, 'B AB HA. Hence the number of signs is not so great as not to be within the capacity of the more or less average memory.

Since many languages have only one syllable-type—CV (i.e., consonant followed by vowel)—application of the principle above to the syllabic writing of such a language results in a very simple, logical and efficient system, next to alphabetic writing the most efficient writing possible.

The simplicity and efficiency are likely to prove elusive, however, when applied to languages of more complex syllabic structure. Even so, one almost inevitably arrives at the idea of having a series of signs representing syllables in which each consonant of the language is paired with each vowel: BA, BE, BI, BO, BU; DA, DE, DI, DO, DU; FA, FE, FI, FO, FU; and so on. A list of such signs is called a *syllabary*.

Some time after this stage of limited *syllabic writing* has been reached, the thought may occur that the inventory of signs can be further reduced by taking one form, without any specification, as the form for, say, BA; and then simply using diacritic marks to indicate the other possible syllable structures: something like the following:

△ **BA**   △ **BI**   △- **BU**
△ **BE**   -△ **BO**

This brings us very close to alphabetic writing. The last step in syllabic writing and the first in alphabetic writing might come about by accident; suppose a class of words ends in a syllable -*ba*, and in the course of time the vowel ceases to be pronounced. Now the syllabic sign △ stands for B alone, not BA; and some sign (in Sanskrit *virāma*, in Arabic *sukūn*) is invented to express this situation: e.g., △ will express BA, and △ will express B. By use of this sign the vowel of any syllabic sign can be suppressed, and any sign in the syllabary can be made alphabetic.

A situation like that just described is seen in the Semitic writing systems (Arabic, Hebrew), of which it is often said that they "write only the consonants." Actually, all the Arabic and Hebrew letters were originally syllabic signs, representing the consonant *and* a vowel (see figure 50.3).

ALPHABETIC WRITING

As will be clear by now, true alphabetic writing consists in having a sign for each sound (technically each phoneme) of the language, rather than one for each word or one for each syllable. This is the most efficient writing system possible, since a language will be found to have some thousands of words and at least a couple of hundred different syllables, but the words and syllables are made up of individual speech sounds which seldom exceed sixty to seventy in number, and sometimes number as few as a dozen. Hence an alphabetic writing system can, with the fewest possible units (a number easily within anyone's ability to master), record every possible utterance in the language.

It would seem that the different stages we have traced, from drawing pictures to ideographs, to pictographic and syllabic writing, so logically follow each other as inevitably to lead a nation or tribe from one to the next until ultimately an alphabetic writing would be achieved. But such is simply not the case. Many great nations, for example the Japanese, have come as far as syllabic writing, and never seemed to feel a need to go beyond it. Indeed, in all the history of mankind, alphabetic writing has been invented only once, and all the alphabets in the world that are truly so called are derived from that single original alphabet. It seems likely that but for a certain lucky linguistic accident, man would never have discovered the alphabetic principle of writing. Had that been the case, the history of mankind would certainly have been very, very different.

There is a strong probability that it was the ancient Egyptians who first hit on the alphabetic principle; but we cannot prove it, for we cannot show that all or even a majority of the characters which ultimately

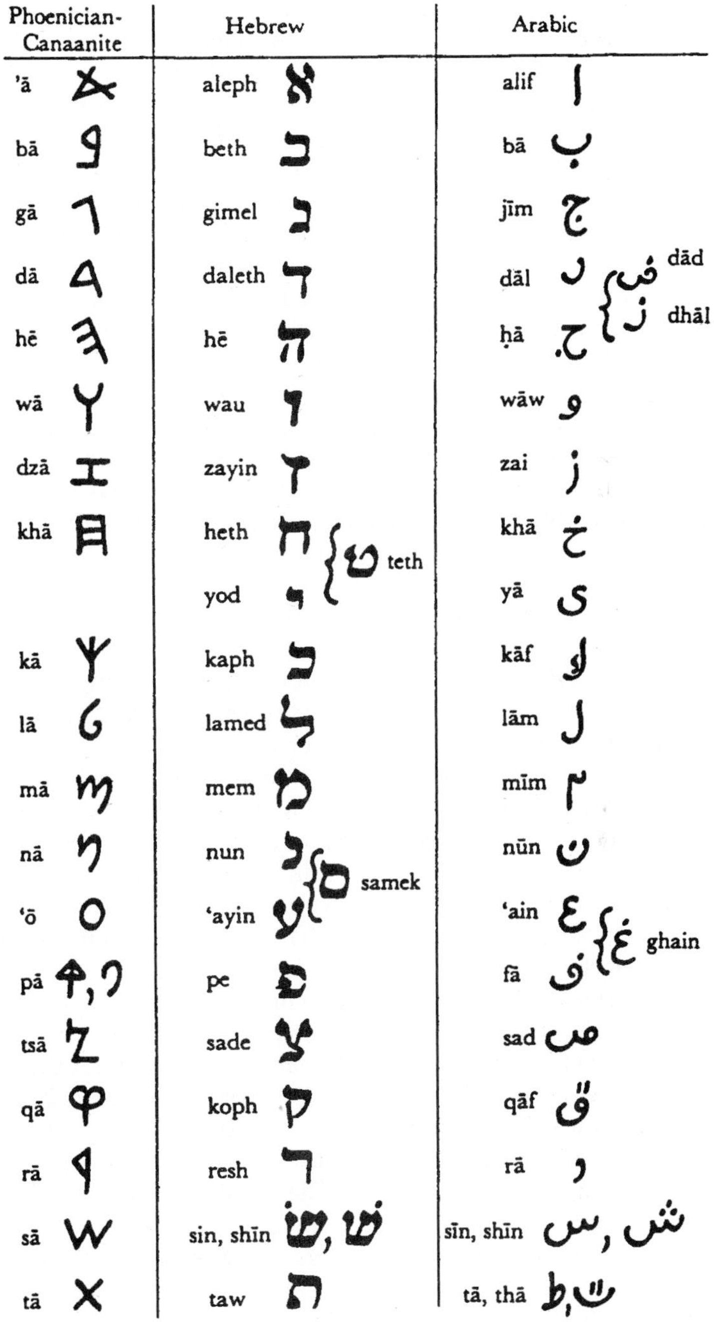

Phoenician-Canaanite	Hebrew	Arabic
ʼā	aleph	alif
bā	beth	bā
gā	gimel	jīm
dā	daleth	dāl · dād · dhāl
hē	hē	ḥā
wā	wau	wāw
dzā	zayin	zai
khā	heth, teth	khā
	yod	yā
kā	kaph	kāf
lā	lamed	lām
mā	mem	mīm
nā	nun, samek	nūn
ʻō	ʻayin	ʻain · ghain
pā	pe	fā
tsā	sade	sad
qā	koph	qāf
rā	resh	rā
sā	sin, shīn	sīn, shīn
tā	taw	tā, thā

FIGURE 50.3 Semitic Alphabets. The names of the letters of the Phoenician-Canaanite (Old Semitic) alphabet are surmises. Letters in one alphabet which do not have correlatives in the others are set off to the side. The traditional order of the Arabic letters has been modified slightly to stress parallels.

became the alphabet we know were used in Egyptian texts of any period (though an apparently sound pedigree can be made for a few of them).

Of course, the hieroglyphic writing had a stock of thousands of characters, and might well have included the ones we are looking for in texts which have disappeared or not yet been discovered. What is harder to explain, however, is that when the Egyptians wrote alphabetically, they gave alphabetic values to an entirely different set of characters (figure 50.4). Yet the Egyptians had been using a writing system for literally thousands of years, and had gone through all the stages. It does not seem likely that some other nation came along just as the Egyptians were on the point of discovering the alphabetic principle, snatched the discovery from under the Pharaohs' noses—and then taught *them* how to write alphabetically! There is certainly a mystery here which is still to be solved, and much fame (in learned circles) awaits him [or her] who solves it. If the Egyptians did indeed fail, after three thousand years, to discover the principle of alphabetic writing, it is striking evidence that man might never have had this art except for the lucky accident which we shall now proceed to describe.

Not being able to prove a connection between the alphabet and Egyptian writing, for the present we have to say that the oldest known genuine alphabet was the Old Semitic, ultimate ancestor of the scripts used today to write Arabic and Hebrew. This alphabet had, of course, been a syllabic script. How had it turned that all-important corner into alphabetic writing? It seems probable that it was prompted in this direction by the structure of the Semitic languages.

To us, the "root" of our verb *ask* is the syllable *ask*, to which various other syllables are prefixed or suffixed to make the various verbal forms, for example the past tense (*ask-ed*), the progressive present tense (*is asking*), the third-person singular present (*ask-s*), and so on.

With verbs like *drive* or *sing*, however, we might say that the root is a syllable *dr-ve* or *s-ng*, where the dash indicates some vowel, but not always the same vowel, since we have *drive, drove, driven, sing, sang, sung.* Something is expressed by the alternation of these vowels, to be sure . . . , but the root of the verb is still a *syllable*, even with a variable vowel.

It was probably some kind of (alternating vowel) system like this which led to the situation now characteristic of Semitic languages (which is really just a further step in this direction), whereby the meaning of "driving" would inhere in the consonants D-R-V, that of "asking" in '-S-K. In Semitic languages the "root" of a word is really a *sequence of consonants* (usually three), modifications of the root being effected by kaleidoscopic rearrangements of the vowels intervening.

Thus, anything to do with writing shows the consonants K-T-B, but "he wrote" = *KaTaBa*, "it is written" = *meKTūB*, "he got it written" = *KaTtaBa*, "scribes" = *KuTtaBūn*, and so on. Words which seem to us quite unrelated turn out to be, in this system, derived from each other, like *SaLāM*, "peace," *iSLāM*, "the Mohammedan [sic] religion," *muSLiM*, "a Mohammedan." (From *salām* we get *'aslāma*, "he pacified, subjugated";

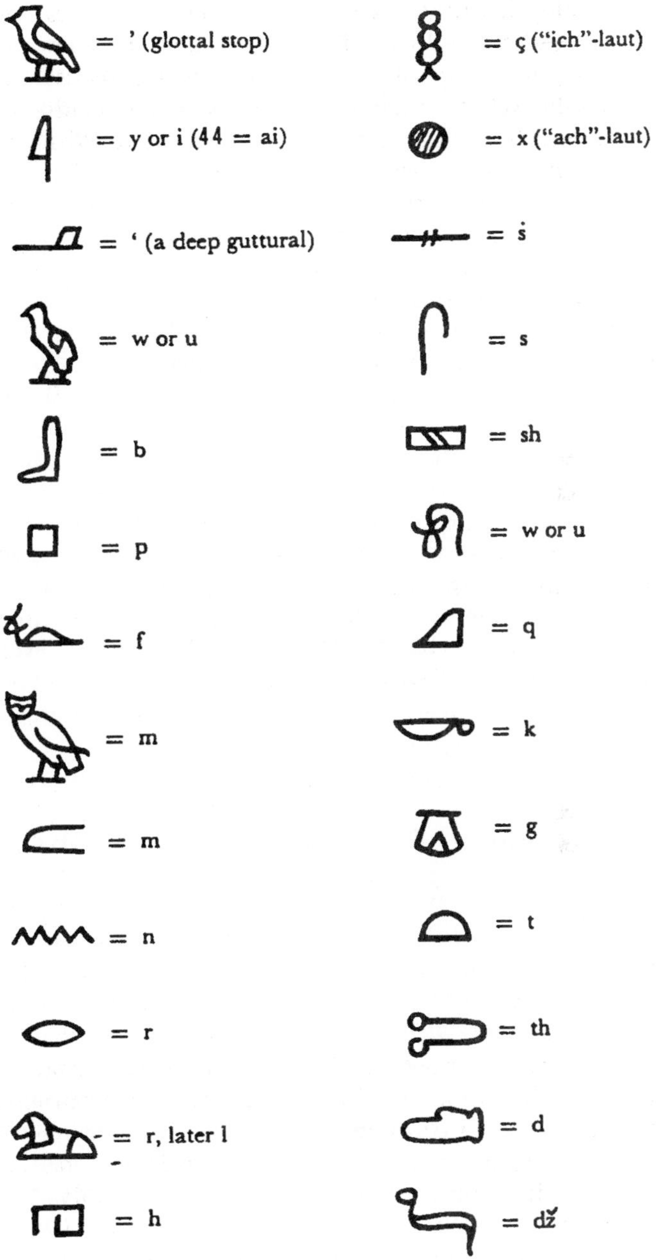

🦅	= ' (glottal stop)	𝄞	= ç ("ich"-laut)
𝄴	= y or i (44 = ai)	◓	= x ("ach"-laut)
⌐▱	= ' (a deep guttural)	┈╫	= ṡ
🦅	= w or u	∫	= s
⌡	= b	▭	= sh
▢	= p	𝄢	= w or u
⤳	= f	◁	= q
🦉	= m	⌣	= k
⊂	= m	⟁	= g
⋀⋀⋀	= n	⌒	= t
⬭	= r	⌐	= th
🦁 = r, later l		⌅	= d
⊓▢	= h	⤿	= dž

FIGURE 50.4   Egyptian Alphabetic Characters.

islām is "subjugation, submission" to God, and *muslim* is "one who has submitted.")

Obviously, no other type of language is better adapted to suggest to its speakers that there is a unit of word structure below the syllable; that

BA is in turn composed of B- and -A. This is precisely what other nations might never have guessed. In Semitic, where BA alternates constantly with BI and BU, and sometimes with B- (the vowel being silenced), it is almost inevitable that every user of the language should develop a concept of the phoneme—a notion which is fundamental to the development of true alphabetic writing.

The structural nature of the Semitic languages is, therefore, in all probability the happy accident which became the key that unlocked for mankind, for the first and only time, the mystery of how to record speech by the method of maximum efficiency—one which does not have so many characters as to make learning it a complex art demanding years of training nor require a skill in drawing which few possess, nor consume large volumes of material for a relatively small amount of recorded message.

The consequences of this lucky accident are truly tremendous. If we did not have the alphabet, it would be impossible to hope for universal literacy, and therefore (if Thomas Jefferson's view was correct) for truly representative government. Writing could have been kept a secret art known only to a privileged few or to a particular social class which would thus have an undue advantage over the others. Information could not nearly so easily be conveyed from nation to nation, and the levels of civilization achieved by the Romans and ourselves might still be only goals to strive for. Truly, Prometheus did not do more for human progress than the unnamed scribe who first drew an alphabetic sign.

THE WANDERINGS OF THE ALPHABET

Let us here stress again that as far as can be ascertained from the available records, the principle of alphabetic writing has only been discovered once—hence, in the whole world *there is only one alphabet*. It follows that any people which writes in alphabetic signs has learned and adapted the use of the alphabet from another people who, in turn, had done the same. When the wanderings of this most potent cultural innovation are plotted, it makes an impressive odyssey. But the same would no doubt be true of every other discovery which has figured in an advance of civilization, if the same means existed for following its trail.

The earliest preserved inscriptions in alphabetic script date to about 1725 B.C. and were found in and around Byblos, in the country then known as Phoenicia (now Lebanon). It would seem that an alphabetic script which we might call Old Semitic was fairly familiar in that region at that time, though, as we have said, we cannot establish precisely where this script was invented, or by which Semitic tribe. It has been suggested that several Semitic peoples might have hit on the alphabetic principle at around the same time; but, if so, they seem to have soon adopted a common set of symbols.

This Old Semitic alphabet is of course the ancestor of the Hebrew, Phoenician, and Aramaic systems of writing. From these northern Semites, the knowledge of the alphabet appears to have passed, on the one hand, to the Greeks of Asia Minor, and on the other, to the Brahmans of ancient India, who developed from it their *devanagari*, the sacred script in which the religious rituals and hymns of the ancient Hindus were recorded.

With this exception, it seems that the genealogy of every other alphabetic system of writing goes through the Greeks. And it was because of the structure of *their* language that the Greeks were responsible for the greatest single improvement in the system: the origination of signs for the vowels.

The Semitic dialects had certain sounds which did not exist in Greek. The symbols for some of these, such as *qoph* (Q), the sign for the velar guttural which had existed in Indo-European but had everywhere been replaced by *p* in Attic Greek, were simply discarded by the Greeks (except in their use as numbers, but that is a different story). In other cases, however, the Greeks kept and used the symbol for a syllable beginning with a non-Greek sound, but pronounced it *without the foreign consonant*—so that the symbol became a sign for the syllable's vowel.

Thus, the first sign in the alphabet originally stood for the syllable 'A, where the sign ' represents the "glottal stop," a contraction and release of the vocal cords—not a phoneme in English, but used often enough as a separator between vowels (e.g., oh-'oh), and you have heard it in Scottish dialect as a substitute for T: *bo'le* for *bottle*, *li'le* for *little*. Some dialects of Greek had this sound, and others did not. Those which did ultimately lost it, so that the sign ∀ (by now written in a different direction, A) everywhere became the sign, not for 'A, but for the vowel *A*.

Other Semitic gutturals had had the tendency to influence adjacent vowels in the direction of O or U, and they accordingly, by the process just described, became the signs for those vowels.

A rather good illustration of what was going on is found in the sign H, standing for the syllable HE. In Ionic Greek, where the sound *h* was eventually eliminated, H became the sign for the vowel *e*. In Sicilian Greek, however, where syllables beginning with *h* still remained, the same H became the sign for *h*—which is our usage also, because we got the alphabet from the Romans, who got it from the Greeks, who followed the Sicilian tradition.

This fact explains deviations in *our* values for the alphabetic signs as compared with those of the standard (Attic) Greek alphabet (see figure 50.5). Since the alphabet had not been invented as a tool for writing Greek, each Greek dialect which adopted it had to modify it a little—to assign different values to some of the signs, and discard the excess signs or use them in new ways, according to the phonology of their own speech.

While practically all modern nations which have alphabetic writing got it directly or indirectly from the Romans, there are a few to whom the tradition passes directly from the Greeks, in some cases concomitantly

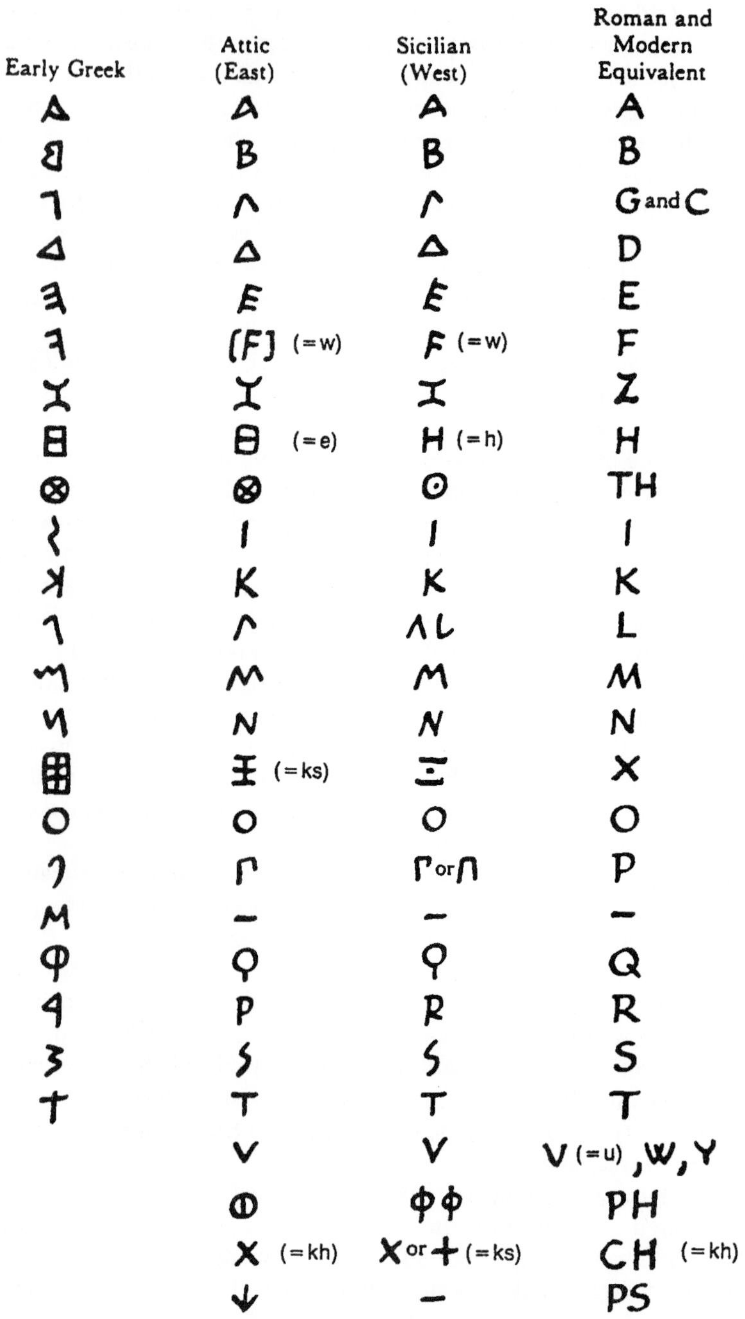

Early Greek	Attic (East)	Sicilian (West)	Roman and Modern Equivalent
Δ	Α	Α	A
Β	B	B	B
Γ	Λ	Γ	G and C
Δ	Δ	Δ	D
Ε	E	Ė	E
Ϝ	(F) (=w)	F (=w)	F
X	I	I	Z
B	Θ (=e)	H (=h)	H
⊗	⊗	⊙	TH
ζ	I	I	I
K	K	K	K
L	Λ	ΛL	L
M	M	M	M
N	N	N	N
⊞	Ξ (=ks)	Ξ	X
O	O	O	O
Γ	Γ	Γ or Π	P
M	–	–	–
φ	Ϙ	Ϙ	Q
Ϙ	P	R	R
Ϟ	Ϟ	Ϟ	S
T	T	T	T
	V	V	V (=u), W, Y
	Φ	Φφ	PH
	X (=kh)	X or + (=ks)	CH (=kh)
	↓	–	PS

FIGURE 50.5   Greek Alphabets. Note changes in direction of writing and variation of values between Attica and Sicily (after E. M. Thompson).

with direct northern Semitic influence. Between the third and fifth centuries A.D., the spread of Christianity occasioned the devising of the ornamental and highly efficient Armenian, and the intriguing, delicate Georgian alphabets. And when the feared Goths were marauding throughout Latin Christendom, Ulfilas, child of a Gothic father and a Greek mother, became the St. Patrick of the Goths, Christianizing them and translating the Bible into their language, writing it with an alphabet which, according to repute, he invented, basing it on Greek. Ulfilas' lucky bilingualism not only gave us our oldest extensive records of any Germanic language, but also, it is believed, served as the basis of the Scandinavian "runic" writing, although some think it was the other way around.

Later, in the ninth century, when Christianity reached the Slavic peoples, two principal alphabets, the "glagolitic" and the "Cyrillic" (the latter named in honor of one of its reputed inventors, St. Cyril, who died 869 A.D.; the other inventor was his brother, St. Methodius, d. 855 A.D.), were devised to represent the then most generally used Slavic dialect. From these developed in the course of time the national alphabets of those Slavic peoples who were evangelized from Byzantium—the Russians, the Ukrainians, the Bulgarians, and the Serbs (figure 50.6). (In contemporary Russia the Cyrillic alphabet has in turn been adapted for writing many non–Indo-European languages of the Soviet Union.)

Slavs who got their religion from Rome had to struggle to put their complex Slavic phonology into the Latin alphabet, with what often seem (to English speakers) jaw-breaking results, as seen in names like Przemyśl, Szczepiński, and Wojciechowicz. The name Vishinsky, as a rough transcription from the Cyrillic, is identical with the Polish name Wyszyński.

From the great Roman empire the art of alphabetic writing passed, by inheritance or adoption, to virtually all the peoples who know it today. They were responsible for many interesting and important innovations in the basic system which there is not space to detail here, but which may be found in any thorough and complete history of the alphabet. We shall just point out a few of the most significant ones.

The Romance-speaking peoples simply inherited their alphabet; in many cases, they did not realize that they were not still speaking, as well as writing, genuine but perhaps rather careless Latin. When they made an effort to write Latin more correctly, only then did they realize that theirs was actually a different language.

It was during the time when Latin was still spoken, however, that the first modifications had to be made in the alphabet—leading to the first diacritic signs. The sound *h* became silent in colloquial Latin in the first century B.C. and in standard Latin by the second century A.D. Thereafter the letter was a zero, expressing nothing, and hence could be used with other letters to express variations: TH for something like T that was not quite a T; GH for something like G that was not a G, and so on.

Cyrillic	Russian	Equivalent	Cyrillic	Russian	Equivalent
ⰀⰀ	а	a	Ȣ	у	u
Б	б	b	Ф	ф	f
В	в	v	Ѳ	ѳ*	f (originally th)
Г	г	g	Х	х	kh
Д	д	d	Ѡ		ō
Є	е	ye	Ш	ш	sh
Ж	ж	zh	Ѱ	щ	shch
Ѕ		dz	Ч	ц	ts
Ꙁ	з	z	Ỿ	ч	ch
Н	и	i	Ъ	ъ*	"hard sign"
І	і*	i	Ꙑ	ы	y̆
Ћ		d', t'	Ь	ь	"soft sign"
К	к	k	Ѣ	я	ya
Ʌ	л	l	Ю	ю	yu
М	м	m	Ѥ	ѣ*	ye
N	н	n	Ѧ, Ꙗ		ĕ, yĕ
О	о	o	Ѫ, Ѭ		ō, yō
П	п	p	Ѯ		ks
Р	р	r	Ѱ		ps
С	с	s	Ѵ		ü
Т	т	t			

* These letters were abolished in 1918.

FIGURE 50.6 Slavic Alphabets. (Some of the Modern Russian letters are given out of standard order for purpose of matching.)

Another early diacritic, perhaps the earliest, was the letter G. Words like *signum* had shifted in pronunciation at a very early period from SIG-NUM to SING-NUM to, probably, [seɲo] (where the sign ɲ stands for what is technically a "palatized n," as *gn* in French *mignon* or *ñ* in Spanish *cañón*). This made the G, in this particular position, another zero: and the idea logically arose that any sound could be distinguished from a palatalized correlative by prefixing G to the latter: N/GN; L/GL. Hence Romance languages blossomed with forms like *egli*, *Bologna*, *segno*, *Cagliari*. But Portuguese used the faithful H to express these sounds (*filho*, *senhor*), and Spanish, which had divested itself of doubled consonants, used a doubled letter (*castillo*, *suenno*), and later used an abbreviation for a doubled *n* (*sueño*)—for the Spanish *tilde* is nothing other than the well-known medieval Latin MS. abbreviation for an M or N (*tā*, *dōinū*, *ītētiōē*). Thus, the American who reads the Italian name *Castiglione* as *Cas-tig-li-o-ni* is murdering the harmonious genuine sound, since the spelling stands for *Ca-sti-lyo-ne*.

When the practice ceased of using as names of the letters the names of the objects they had pictured (or some meaningless derivative thereof, like *alpha*, *beta*), there arose the custom of naming a letter by giving (in the case of a vowel) its *sound*, or (in the case of a consonant), its sound *preceded* or *followed by [e]*. (In English this latter sound has uniformly shifted to [i], so we say the letters of the alphabet [e], [bi], [si], but Frenchmen say [a], [be], [se].) In some exceptional cases, however, phonetic shift has eliminated the letter's sound from its name. Our name for R is [ar] (from earlier [er] by the same change which gives us *heart*, *hearth*, *sergeant*). In English pronunciation, however, R is silent after a vowel, so the name of the letter R is *ah*—with no R in it.

Again, our name for *h* is *aitch*, a meaningless word in English but a preservation of French *la hache* "the hatchet"—suggested by the letter's appearance, to be sure.

$$\mathfrak{F} = h$$

—but originally containing its sound; no [h] has been pronounced in French, however, for over a century, so the name of this letter, too, fails to contain its sound . . .

Our present letters J and W are known to have been invented in the sixteenth century. In Latin, since all W's had become V's by the second century A.D., the letter U, however written (V, U), expressed that sound—the choice between the rounded and the angular form being purely a matter of calligraphy. The English language, however, had both the V sounds and the W sounds; so, to express the latter, English printers of the sixteenth century "doubled" the former, writing vv (or uu).

Latin also lacked any sound like English J; but this sound appeared in Old French in words where Latin had had *i*, either as *ee* or as *y* (𝔉*anuarius* > *janvier*; *iuvenis* > *jeune*), and printers traditionally used *i* for it. Medieval scribes often extended this letter downwards in an ornamental flourish at the end of a number (thus: xiiij), and no doubt it was this which suggested the adoption in English printing of this alternative form of *i* for the *j*-sound. For quite a while, however, many printers continued to regard i/j and u/w/v as interchangeable and to print *Iohn, starres aboue, A Vvinter's Tale,* **F***nterlude,* and so on.

We have been able to mention here only a few of the vicissitudes undergone by the alphabet—*the* alphabet, only one, always the same— in its long journey through space and time from the eastern shores of the Mediterranean to the far islands of the Pacific.

FOR DISCUSSION AND REVIEW

1. According to Hughes, "ideographic writing" is "properly in no sense either language or writing." How does he support this statement? Do you agree or disagree? Defend your answer.

2. In general, each character of written Chinese represents one morpheme or one word. Explain the advantages of such a system, which does not involve linking sound to written characters, to the Chinese culture. What are the disadvantages?

3. Justify Hughes's statement that "Pictographic writing is . . . true writing."

4. Describe the development of syllabic writing systems from pictographic systems. What are the advantages of the former? How might a limited syllabic system develop into an alphabetic system? Is such a logical progression more-or-less inevitable? Why, or why not?

5. Why does Hughes claim that alphabetic writing is "the most efficient writing system possible"?

6. Explain how the structure of the Semitic languages and the development of the phoneme concept led to the development of the alphabet.

7. Summarize chronologically what Hughes calls "the wanderings of the alphabet." Be sure to explain the important contribution made by the Greeks and how the structure of their language affected this alphabet.

8. What is a diacritic sign? Give three examples (draw them from at least two languages). Describe the development of diacritic signs as part of alphabetic writing.

9. Hughes describes the development of an alphabetic writing system as a "lucky accident" and as "truly tremendous." Describe the kind(s) of cultures that might have developed had an alphabetic writing system not evolved.

51

What Makes Good English Good?

John Algeo

Even though language is constantly changing, people will always attempt to mandate what is acceptable in speech and writing. For more than 300 years, a battle has been waging over what constitutes good English. Many scholars have insisted on the distinction between imply *and* infer, *have refused to split an infinitive, and have bemoaned the use of* between you and I *instead of the truly correct* between you and me. *The following tongue-in-cheek essay first appeared in P. C. Boardman's* The Legacy of Language: A Tribute to Charlton Laird *(1987). Here, John Algeo, professor emeritus from The University of Georgia, reviews the ten key criteria that usage experts and grammarians have used for determining what constitutes good English. As you read, ask yourself which criteria you use for judging correct usage, including your own.*

Human beings are a peculiar species. We have a rage for order: out of the great booming chaos of the world around us, we obsessively make pattern and regularity. Out of the wilderness, we make cities. Out of experience, we make histories. Out of speech, we make grammars. And in the process of turning chaos into order, we create values.

The human species has been called *homo sapiens*, the earthy one who knows or experiences. But we might as well be called *homo judex*, the judge, because an inescapable human impulse is to distinguish between good and bad. For us, the good is its own warrant. As Mammy Yokum was wont to instruct her physically sound and morally pure, if intellectually disadvantaged, offspring, Li'l Abner: "Good is better than evil because it's so much nicer." Or, as *Webster's New World Dictionary of the American Language*, with which Charlton Laird was associated, defines the word, *good* is "a general term of approval or commendation, meaning 'as it should be.'"

Should is a powerful and distinctly human concept. Wars have been fought over it. Among English speakers, the Grammar Wars began in the seventeenth century, when pedagogues fell out over why and how to teach Latin. One camp wanted to teach grammar as an end in itself, because knowing grammar is good. Another camp wanted to teach grammar only so that young English scholars could read the great works of Latin literature. The two camps were roughly the equivalents three hundred years ago of scientific linguists and literary humanists (if I may use the word *humanist* without calling down the wrath of the Reverend Jerry Falwell). The equivalence is only approximate, however, because the grammar-as-an-end-in-itself advocates of the 1600s had a strong bent toward logic and neatening up the language, whereas the grammar-as-a-tool-for-literature advocates argued that the ancients could hardly have been wrong in the way they used their own language and thus needed no help from grammarians intent on regularizing and improving Latin.

Joseph Webbe, a doughty combatant in the lists of the Grammar Wars, scored against the grammarians in his 1622 book, *An Appeale to Truth*, by writing that

> they haue not onely weakened and broken speech, by reducing it vnto the poore and penurious prescript of Grammar-rules; but haue also corrupted it with many errors, in that they haue spoken otherwise than they ought to doo: well, in respect of rules; but ill in respect of custome, which is the *Lady and Mistress* of speaking.[1]

Our modern Grammar Wars (chronicled by Edward Finegan in his *Attitudes toward English Usage: The History of a War of Words*) have seen a curious realignment of forces. Today it is those whose principal concern is with studying language as an end in itself who are most in sympathy with Webbe's position "that we can neither in the Latine, nor in any other Tongue, be obedient vnto other rules or reasons, than Custome and our sense of hearing,"[2] whereas it is some contemporary men and women of letters who ignore custom and their sense of hearing in favor of "the poore and penurious prescript of Grammar-rules." And so we have spawned a new subspecies, variously called *pop-grammarians* or *usageasters* (the latter by Thomas L. Clark).[3]

The Grammar Wars go on. And, as they were more than three hundred years ago, they are still concerned with the question of what good English is. What makes good English good? A variety of answers have been given to that question, and since the question has been so long with us, it is useful occasionally to summarize the answers that have been given.

What I propose to do briefly in this essay is to look at ten of the grounds that have been proposed for deciding what good English is. I focus on grounds proposed by Theodore M. Bernstein, mentioning a few other writers on usage to show that Bernstein is not a linguistic sport. I single out Bernstein, not because he is particularly better or worse than others of the tribe, but because he wrote a good bit on the subject of usage, because he is typical of the modern man of letters, and because he was kind enough to provide a handy list of criteria for determining good usage.

---

[1] Joseph Webbe, *An Appeale to Truth, in the Controuersie betweene Art, & Vse; about the Best and Most Expedient Course in Languages* (1622). Reprinted in *English Linguistics, 1500–1800*, ed. R. C. Alston, no. 42 (Menston, England: Scolar Press, 1967), 22.

[2] Ibid., 46.

[3] Thomas L. Clark, "The Usageasters," *American Speech* 55 (1980): 131–136.

COMMUNICATIVE CRITERION

In *The Careful Writer* (1965), Bernstein equates good English with successful communication: "What good writing can do . . . is to assure that the writer is really in communication with the reader, that he is delivering his message unmistakably."[4] Porter Perrin has a similar criterion for good English: "So far as the writer's language furthers his intended effect, it is good; so far as it fails to further that effect, it is bad, no matter how 'correct' it may be."[5]

These are pious statements, which, like promises never to curtail Social Security benefits, are made to be broken. Bernstein does not even get out of the introduction to his book before he fractures the ideal of communication: "Let us insist that *disinterested* be differentiated from *uninterested*."[6] He urges this difference as essential to the existence of good English, with no concern for communicating with those readers for whom the two words are synonyms. If Bernstein had been really concerned about successful communication, he would not have advised his readers to avoid *disinterested* in the sense "uninterested" but rather told them not to use it at all, because the word is ambiguous. Bernstein's point about the need for communication is obviously well made, but it is seldom taken seriously by those who make it.

Bernstein goes on to enumerate six other sources for determining good English. It is worth looking at them seriatim.

LITERARY CRITERION

Bernstein adduces "the practices of reputable writers, past and present."[7] This criterion, like that of successful communication, is practically de rigueur in any discussion of usage. It is also a criterion of respectable antiquity. Webbe in 1622 had cited authors like Cicero as models of good Latin, in distinction to the grammarians among his contemporaries who invented rules that imposed more order on Latin than was to be found in classical authors. The authority of the literati was also invoked by Thomas Lounsbury, who used an elegant chiasmus in his *Standard of Usage in English*: "The best, and indeed the only proper, usage is the usage of the best."[8]

---

[4] Theodore M. Bernstein, *The Careful Writer: A Modern Guide to English Usage* (New York: Atheneum, 1965), vii.

[5] Porter G. Perrin, *Writer's Guide and Index to English*, 4th ed. rev. Karl W. Dykema and Wilma R. Ebbitt (Chicago: Scott Foresman, 1965), 27.

[6] Bernstein, xv.

[7] Ibid., viii.

[8] Thomas R. Lounsbury, *The Standard of Usage in English* (New York: Harper, 1908), vi.

As appealing as it may be to English teachers, the literary criterion suffers from several weaknesses. One is the difficulty of deciding which authors are reputable or best and which are not; there is a danger of circularity—writers who do not use good English (as the decider conceives it) are clearly not reputable or best, however widely read they may be. Another difficulty is that of deciding how far past or present one will look for models of good English: Joyce Carol Oates? Virginia Woolf? Ralph Waldo Emerson? Fanny Burney? Shakespeare? Chaucer? the Beowulf poet? In fact, popular writers on usage cite reputable writers as exemplifiers of good English rather infrequently. They are rather more apt to quote the words of famous authors as examples of blunders by the mighty, Homer nodding, and all that. Since the days of Bishop Lowth, citing errors from the works of great writers (or of one's opponents) has been a game rivaled only by the current popularity of Trivial Pursuit.

SCHOLARLY CRITERION

Bernstein's next criterion for good English is from "the observations and discoveries of linguistic scholars."[9] He carefully qualifies this criterion in two ways, however. First, "the work of past scholars has, when necessary, been updated," and second, "the work of contemporary scholars has been weighed judiciously." That is, *homo judex* is free to change (update) or to ignore (weigh judiciously) whatever he does not like. Although clearly subordinate to reputable writers, linguistic scholars seem like an authoritative group to invoke, especially if you don't have to pay any attention to them. We like being told that the message we are getting is backed by authorities: 9 out of 10 doctors, 64 percent of economists, any and all linguistic scholars. However, the fact that something is said to be recommended by doctors or economists or linguistic scholars is of no importance. What is important is the evidence on which doctors, economists, and linguistic scholars speak. And therefore this criterion is no criterion at all. It is not evidence, but publicity hype.

PEDAGOGICAL CRITERION

The following criterion is even phonier. It is "the predilections of teachers of English, wherever—right or wrong, like it or not—these predilections have become deeply ingrained in the language itself."[10] It is not at all clear that any predilections of any teachers of English have ever become deeply ingrained in our language. There may be one or two trivial matters for which the sweat of English teachers has dripped so incessantly

---

[9] Bernstein, viii.
[10] Ibid., viii.

on the stone of real language that it has finally worn a small indentation—
the pronunciation of the *t* in *often* is probably one—but on the whole, not
only are English teachers overworked, underpaid, and poorly educated,
they are also ineffective.

The archetype of the starched schoolmarm who has devoted her
life, at the sacrifice of all personal comfort and happiness, to upholding
standards and educating into self-awareness the pliable young minds
entrusted to her charge is as mythological as Parson Weems's George
Washington. Bernstein seems to be remembering with ambivalent nostalgia some Miss Thistlebottom from the eighth grade, who, in the haze
of fifty intervening years, has taken on the epic proportions of Candida,
Martin Joos's Muse of Grammar.[11] The reality is likely to have been thin-
ner and more wizened. The predilections of teachers of English that have
become deeply ingrained in our language are probably a null set.

LOGICAL CRITERION

Bernstein's next criterion is "what makes for clarity, precision, and
logical presentation."[12] This is another mom-and-apple-pie criterion.
However important clarity, precision, and logic are, our impression of
them in language is likely to be a function of our familiarity with particular words or grammatical structures. Those for whom *disinterested*
means "uninterested" find that use perfectly clear and precise. The difference between *She be here* and *She here* is clear and logical to anyone
who understands it. Those who find such expressions muddled, vague,
and illogical have got a problem. But the problem is theirs; it is not one
for those who use the expressions. Talk about clarity and logic in language is often an unconscious confession of ignorance and ethnocentrism. What we know, we think logical; what we don't, illogical.

This criterion is often expressed by saying that good writing is the
expression of good thinking. Ambrose Bierce, for example, held such a
position in his delightfully quirky little book *Write It Right*, subtitled
A Little Blacklist of Literary Faults, in which he says that good writing
"is clear thinking made visible."[13] Bierce is probably best known for his
advice to "prefer *ruined* to *dilapidated* since the latter—coming from
Latin *lapis* "a stone"—cannot properly be used of any but a stone structure."[14] That is an example of diaphanous, rather than clear, thinking.

A similar standard was adopted by Richard Mitchell, whose *Underground Grammarian* announced in its first issue: "Clear language

---

[11] Martin Joos, *The Five Clocks* (New York: Harcourt, 1967).
[12] Bernstein, viii–ix.
[13] Ambrose Bierce, *Write It Right: A Little Blacklist of Literary Faults* (New York:
Neale, 1909; New York: Union Library Association, 1934), 5.
[14] Ibid., 23.

engenders clear thought and clear thought is the most important benefit of education."[15] One may subscribe to the idea that clear thought is the best possible result of education, while finding the proposition that clear language produces clear thought to be muddled. However, one can forgive almost any amount of Mitchell's muddling for the sake of his épée, for example, his palpable hit in saying that "so many [college administrators] seem to be born aluminum-siding salesmen who took a wrong turn somewhere along the line."[16]

The link between good language and clear or exact thinking has been made by many writers on usage. One more example, an older one, will have to suffice. John O'London, who dedicated his book *Is It Good English?* To "Men, Women, and Grammarians," thereby expressing his opinion of our tribe, wrote: "Good English follows clear thinking rather than that system of rules called Grammar which youth loathes and maturity forgets."[17]

A problem with the equivalence of good language and clear thinking is that the latter might be defined as thinking that arrives logically at correct conclusions. T. S. Eliot and John Steinbeck, whom one might suppose to use rather good language, have thought themselves into rather different conclusions. It is hard to see how Eliot and Steinbeck can each be said to be clear thinking on social questions. Or, as Jim Quinn points out, "If good thought made good writing, and good writing made good thought, then Immanuel Kant, Hegel, and Ludwig Wittgenstein are not worth reading."[18]

PERSONAL CRITERION

Bernstein's penultimate criterion is the personal preference of the author, of which he asks rhetorically: "And why not? . . . After all, it's my book."[19] Why not, indeed. This is the most honest criterion Bernstein has set forward. By asserting it, he agrees with a cartoon that appeared shortly after the publication of Nancy Mitford's *Noblesse Oblige*, a popular treatment of the difference between U (upper class) and non-U language.[20] In the cartoon, a tweedy, horsy-looking woman says to her companion at the tea table, "I always say, if it's me it's U."

Everyone is certainly entitled to a choice among linguistic options. And if you can get people to buy a book in which you state your choices, why not? First amendment, free enterprise, and all that. Right on, Ted! Let's throw out all that malarkey about communicating unmistakably,

---

[15] Richard Mitchell, *The Graves of Academe* (Boston: Little, Brown, 1981), 27.

[16] Ibid., 28.

[17] John O'London, *Is It Good English?* (New York: Putnam's, 1925), xi.

[18] Jim Quinn, *American Tongue and Cheek: A Populist Guide to Our Language* (New York: Pantheon, 1980), 76.

[19] Bernstein, ix.

[20] Nancy Mitford, ed. *Noblesse Oblige* (New York: Harper & Row, 1956).

reputable writers, linguistic scholars, English teachers, and logic, and just hunker down with good old ipse dixit. If it's me, it's U. As H. L. Mencken said, "No one ever went broke underestimating the intelligence of the American public."

PROFESSIONAL CRITERION

Bernstein's last criterion is a letdown from the preceding high point. He cites his experience in working with language as an editor of the *New York Times* and congratulates himself on the newspaper's "precision, accuracy, clarity, and—especially in recent years [under Bernstein's editorship, presumably]—good writing."[21] All this criterion does is to establish Bernstein's credentials for ipse-dixiting. It is a sad anticlimax. How much better to finish off with a glorious burst of egotistic self-assertion. Well, we can't all be perfect.

People who earn their living by the word, particularly the written word, know how to use words effectively. If they did not, they would not earn much of a living. But effective journalism and even great literature are obviously not the same thing as good English. If they were, only effective journalists and great writers would be using good English. That Bernstein spent many years as an editor, worrying about the language of others, explains how he came to write five books on usage; it does not warrant his claiming special authority to determine what is good language.

STYLISTIC CRITERION

Other writers have offered still further criteria for good English. Some have identified the stylistic characteristics of bad writing and thus by inference defined what is good. Richard Mitchell, the Underground Grammarian, for example, focuses on the sins of wordiness, weasel words (*attempt to, may*), passive verbs with no agent, and "needless neologism"[22] Similarly, Edwin Newman castigates clichés, jargon, voguish words, redundancy, and innovations—or what he imagines to be innovations (they frequently are nothing of the kind).

A digression: the subtitle of Newman's first book (*Strictly Speaking: Will America Be the Death of English?*)[23] identifies him as a disciple of the Armageddon school of usageasters. He, like John Simon, whose *Paradigms Lost*[24] is subtitled *Reflections on Literacy and Its Decline*, sees us as living in the time of the end. It is ironic that the demise of

---

[21] Bernstein, ix.

[22] Mitchell, 27, 49.

[23] Edwin Newman, *Strictly Speaking: Will America Be the Death of English?* (New York: Warner Books, 1974, 1975).

[24] John Simon, *Paradigms Lost: Reflections on Literacy and Its Decline* (New York: Potter, 1980).

English should be predicted at a time when the language is being used by more people for more purposes in more places around the globe than ever before. Thomas Lounsbury expressed an ironic insight that is as applicable today as it was in 1908, when he wrote it:

> There seems to have been in every period of the past, as there is now, a distinct apprehension in the minds of very many worthy persons that the English tongue is always approaching collapse, and that arduous efforts must be put forth, and put forth persistently, in order to save it from destruction.[25]

In a generation between Lounsbury and Newman-Simon, the anonymous "Vigilans" was another of the Dying-Declining-Doomsters. In his book *Chamber of Horrors* he castigated jargon, which he characterized as involving circumlocutions; long, abstract, unfamiliar words using classical roots; phrases where single words will do; padding; cautious wording and euphemism; vagueness and woolliness; and esoteric expressions.[26]

Our thoughts and our language are certainly intimately related, if they are not in fact the same thing. And pompous language is fair game. It is great sport to expose and snicker at egregious examples of linguistic bombast and thick-headedness, as the Armageddon usageasters are wont to do. But such sport is easy to overdo. The cannons of Mitchell-Newman-Simon- "Vigilans" tend to produce, not a bang, but a whimper—kvetching against petty violations of an idiosyncratic standard of style. It is remarkable that so much has been written, so seriously, about such trivia.

DEMOCRATIC CRITERION

A refreshingly different approach to the subject is that of Jim Quinn, whose *American Tongue and Cheek* is a lusty defense of many of the bugbears of contemporary usageasters. Quinn delights in showing that usageasters frequently do not know what they are talking about and that their criteria for defining good language are nonsense. Quinn is straightforward in stating his own criterion: "For me, the only sensible standard of correctness is usage by ordinary people."[27]

And yet Quinn's own usage populism is also nonsense if taken at face value. Ordinary people and extraordinary people alike make mistakes in using language; mistakes are a part of usage. When people notice mistakes—their own or others'—they correct them. Editing language is just as natural as producing it, and so is passing judgment on some forms of language as better than others. The values we attach to our linguistic options are just as much a part of the language as the options themselves.

---

[25] Lounsbury, 2.
[26] "Vigilans," *Chamber of Horrors: A Glossary of Official Jargon Both English and American*, intro. Eric Partridge (New York: British Book Centre, 1952).
[27] Quinn, 11.

We are value-ridden, judgmental beings. As a piece of rhetoric, a sortie in the Grammar Wars, Quinn's position is great tactics, but it is weak strategy.

ELITIST CRITERION

In America we have no official aristocracy, whose speechways might provide a standard for the commoners of the realm. So we make do with a less well-defined group: educated, respected, important people in the community. Their usage is sometimes held up as a model for the hoi polloi of the citizenry. Bergen and Cornelia Evans in their *Dictionary of Contemporary American Usage* write: "Respectable English . . . means the kind of English that is used by the most respected people, the sort of English that will make readers or listeners regard you as an educated person."[28] William and Mary Morris echo the theoretical sentiment, if not the practical sensibleness, of the Evanses. The Morrises define *standard* (which is not the same as *good*, but is related) as "word usage occurring in the speech and writing of literate, educated users of the language."[29]

Another digression: the *Harper Dictionary of Contemporary Usage,* which the Morrises edited, deserves special acknowledgment as among the most ignorant usage guides to have made the big time. My favorite lapse is their explanation of the use of the objective case for the subject of an infinitive. Under the heading "infinitive, subject of the," they write:

> The confusion about the use of "I" and "me" is reflected in such statements as "The first thing for somebody like you or I to do. . . ." *The subject of the infinitive* "to do" must be in the accusative or objective case. Since the objective case of the first personal pronoun is "me," the statement should be "The first thing for somebody like you or me to do. . . ."[30]

The Morrises tripped over their own grammatical razzle-dazzle. In the example they cite, the subject of the infinitive is *somebody*; *you or me* is the object of the preposition *like*. So the example is irrelevant to the point for which it is cited. The Morrises are educated users of the language, but grammatically they are booboisie.

CONCLUSION

There are other criteria we might identify. But these ten are enough to show what the tendency has been. In deciding what makes good English good, commentators have tried to correlate variation with some outside factor—success in communication, literary excellence, scholarly

---

[28] Bergen and Cornelia Evans, *A Dictionary of Contemporary American Usage* (New York: Random House, 1957), v.

[29] William and Mary Morris, with the assistance of a panel of 136 distinguished consultants on usage, *Harper Dictionary of Contemporary Usage* (New York: Harper & Row, 1975), xxii.

[30] Ibid., 338.

authority (at least nominally), pedagogical effort, logic, personal authority, professional expertise, esthetic style, a democratic majority, or an elite model. The unspoken assumption is that good English ought to be good for something.

Efforts to correlate goodness in language with something else are all flawed. Good English is simply what English speakers, in a particular situation, agree to regard as good. There are as many kinds of good English as there are situations in which English is used and sorts of participants who use it. Standard English is one sort of good English—good, that is, in the circumstances that call for it—but it is not the only sort.

Robert Pooley says something similar in *The Teaching of English Usage*:

> The English language is full of possible variations. The term "good usage" implies success in making choices in these variations such that the smallest number of persons (and particularly persons held in esteem) are distracted by the choices.[31]

Good English is the cellophane man—you can see right through it. It does not distract because in any given circumstance it is what the participants expect.

To paraphrase Mammy Yokum, "Good English is so much nicer than bad English because it's better." There is no external criterion by which we can judge what is good in language, either standard English or any other kind. Good language is just what the users of the language have decided is good. Their judgments are exasperatingly inconsistent and unpredictable. Moreover, the bounds they assign to the good are disconcertingly fuzzy; those bounds keep changing, as users of the language push this way and that way against them, continually altering the limits of acceptability. Finally, what is good is wholly relative to the circumstances and the speakers. Despite Wilson Follett's asseveration in *Modern American Usage* that "there is a [i.e., one] right way to use words and construct sentences, and many wrong ways,"[32] good in language is multivalent (that's *mul'ti-va'lent* or *mul-tiv'a-lent*, depending on the circumstances).

Because good English is so diverse, to use it in more than a few circumstances requires an equally diverse knowledge and a fine sense of what is appropriate under varying conditions. Charlton Laird made one of the most sensible comments ever written about usage when he observed, in his introductory essay to *Webster's New World Dictionary*, that "good usage requires wide knowledge and tasteful discrimination; it cannot be learned easily."[33] It is appropriate, especially here, for Laird to have the last word.

---

[31] Robert C. Pooley, *The Teaching of English Usage* (Urbana, IL: National Council of Teachers of English, 1974), 5.

[32] Wilson Follett, *Modern American Usage: A Guide* (New York: Hill and Wang, 1966), 3.

[33] Charlton Laird, "Language and the Dictionary." In *Webster's New World Dictionary of the American Language,* Second College Edition. Ed. David B. Guralnik (New York and Cleveland: World, 1970), xxv.

FOR DISCUSSION AND REVIEW

1. Which of the criteria that Algeo discusses sound very familiar? To what extent has your speech or writing been influenced by any of them?

2. Algeo says that "*should* is a powerful and distinctly human concept." What does he mean? How does each of the criteria Algeo discusses pay homage to the notion of "should"?

3. What is Algeo's attitude toward so-called usage experts?

4. What, according to Algeo, is the problem with the relationship between "good language and clear or exact thinking"?

5. What does Algeo mean when he states that "good English is the cellophane man"?

6. Discuss examples from your experience or observation that support Algeo's conclusion that "because good English is so diverse, to use it in more than a few circumstances requires an equally diverse knowledge and a fine sense of what is appropriate under varying conditions."

52

Reading, Writing and Speech

Victoria Fromkin, Robert Rodman, and Nina Hyams

At the conclusion of their seventh edition of An Introduction to
Language, *the late Victoria Fromkin (professor of linguistics at
University of California, Los Angeles), Robert Rodman (professor of
computer science, North Carolina State University), and Nina Hyams
(professor of linguistics, University of California, Los Angeles) provide a
number of insights into the connections between spoken language and
reading and writing. They begin by discussing the uses of punctuation
and how we "replace" punctuation when we speak. Then Fromkin and
her colleagues stress the importance of teaching phonics, noting that
educators need to take advantage of children's innate sound-symbol
knowledge. They also offer a brief overview of English spelling and
explain how and why it has changed over the centuries—sometimes by
adding or dropping letters and pronouncing them or not. They comment
as well on why spelling and pronunciation must often differ. Ultimately,
the authors conclude that our written language does have some effect on
how we speak. But for the most part, they remind us, our writing is a
reflection of "the grammar that every speaker knows."*

> . . . Ther is so great diversite
> In English, and in wryting of oure tonge,
> So prey I god that non myswrite thee . . .
>
> —GEOFFREY CHAUCER, Troilus and Cressida

The development of writing freed us from the limitations of time and
geography, but spoken language still has primacy, and is the principal
concern of most linguists. Nevertheless, writing systems are of interest
for their own sake.

The written language reflects, to a certain extent, the elements and
rules that together constitute the grammar of the language. The letters of
the alphabet represent the system of phonemes, although not necessarily
in a direct way. The independence of words is revealed by the spaces
between them in most writing systems. Japanese and Thai do not require
spaces between words, although speakers and writers are aware of the
individual words. On the other hand, no writing system shows the individual morphemes within a word in this way, even though speakers
know what they are.

Many languages use punctuation, including capitalization, to indicate sentences, phrases, questions, intonation, stress, and contrast, but the written forms of other languages do not make use of punctuation.

Consider the difference in meaning between (1) and (2):

1. The Greeks, who were philosophers, loved to talk a lot.
2. The Greeks who were philosophers loved to talk a lot.

The relative clause in (1), set off by commas, is nonrestrictive because it means that all the Greeks were philosophers. It may be paraphrased as (1'):

1'. The Greeks were philosophers, and they loved to talk a lot.

The meaning of the second sentence, without the commas, can be paraphrased as:

2'. Among the Greeks, it was the philosophers who loved to talk a lot.

Similarly, by using an exclamation point or a question mark, the intention of the writer can be made clearer.

3. The children are going to bed at eight o'clock. (a simple statement)
4. The children are going to bed at eight o'clock! (an order)
5. The children are going to bed at eight o'clock? (a question)

These punctuation marks reflect the pauses and the intonations that would be used in the spoken language.

In sentence 6 *he* can refer to either John or someone else, but in sentence 7 the pronoun must refer to someone other than John:

6. John said he's going.
7. John said, "He's going."

The apostrophe used in contractions and possessives also provides syntactic information not always available in the spoken utterance.

8. My cousin's friends (one cousin)
9. My cousins' friends (two or more cousins)

Writing, then, somewhat reflects the spoken language, and punctuation may even distinguish between two meanings not revealed in the spoken forms, as shown in sentences 8 and 9.

In the normal written version of sentence 10,

10. John whispered the message to Bill and then he whispered it to Mary

he can refer to either John or Bill. In the spoken sentence, if *he* receives extra stress (called *contrastive stress*), it must refer to Bill; if *he* receives normal stress, it refers to John.

A speaker can usually emphasize any word in a sentence by using contrastive stress. Writers sometimes attempt to show emphasis by using all capital letters, italics, or underlining the emphasized word. This is nicely illustrated by the Garfield cartoon below.

In the first panel we understand Garfield as meaning, "I didn't do it, someone else did." In the second panel the meaning is "I didn't do it, even though you think I did." In the third, the contrastive stress conveys the meaning "I didn't do it, it just happened somehow." In the fourth panel Garfield means, "I didn't do it, though I may be guilty of other things." In each case the boldfaced word is contrasted with something else.

Although such visual devices can help in English, it is not clear that they can be used in a language such as Chinese. In Japanese, however, this kind of emphasis can be achieved by writing a word in katakana [the Japanese syllabay derived from Chinese characters].

The use of italics has many functions in written language. One use is to indicate reference to the italicized word itself, as in "*the dog* is a noun article." A children's riddle, which is sung aloud, plays on this distinction:

Railroad crossing, watch out for cars

How do you spell it without any *r*'s?

The answer is "i-t." The joke is that the second line, were it written, would be:

How do you spell *it* without any *r*'s?

Written language is more conservative than spoken language. When we write we are more apt to obey the prescriptive rules taught in school than when we speak. We may write "it is I" but we say "it's me." Such informalities abound in spoken language, but may be "corrected" by copy editors, diligent English teachers, and careful writers. A linguist wishing to describe the language that people regularly use therefore cannot depend on written records alone.

READING

Children learn to speak instinctively without being taught. Learning to read and write is not like learning to speak. Recently, however, the Whole Language approach to reading has suggested that children can learn to read just as they learn to talk, through "constant interaction with family and friends, teachers and classmates." This view is given in a National Council of Teachers of English brochure that appears on the World Wide Web. It opposes the view that children be taught to segment speech into individual sounds and relate these sounds to the letters of the alphabet, which is sometimes referred to as *teaching phonics*.

As we have seen . . . , most written languages are based on oral language. The Whole Language advocates do not understand the way that children acquire language. They deny the fact that the ability to learn language is an innate, biologically determined aspect of the human brain, whereas reading and writing are not. Otherwise, one would not find so many people who speak so many languages that have no written form.

Many studies have shown that deaf children who have fully acquired a sign language have difficulty learning to read. This is understandable since the alphabetic principle in a system like English requires an understanding of sound-symbol regularities. Hearing children should therefore not be deprived of the advantage they would have if their unconscious knowledge of phonemes is made conscious.

In developing teaching methods for reading and writing, it is important to understand the interactions of speech, reading, and writing. Whatever methods are adopted, however, it should take advantage of the child's innate linguistic knowledge, and include helping the child relate sounds to letters.

SPELLING

"Do you spell it with a 'v' or a 'w'?" inquired the judge.
"That depends upon the taste and fancy of the speller, my Lord," replied Sam.

–CHARLES DICKENS, The Pickwick Papers

If writing represented the spoken language perfectly, spelling reforms would never have arisen. . . . [S]ome of the problems in the English orthographic system . . . prompted George Bernard Shaw to write:

> . . . It was as a reading and writing animal that Man achieved his human eminence above those who are called beasts. Well, it is I and my like who have to do the writing. I have done it professionally for the last sixty

years as well as it can be done with a hopelessly inadequate alphabet devised centuries before the English language existed to record another and very different language. Even this alphabet is reduced to absurdity by a foolish orthography based on the notion that the business of spelling is to represent the origin and history of a word instead of its sound and meaning. Thus an intelligent child who is bidden to spell *debt*, and very properly spells it *d-e-t*, is caned for not spelling it with a *b* because Julius Caesar spelt the Latin word for it with a *b*.[1]

The irregularities between graphemes (letters) and phonemes have been cited as one reason "why Johnny can't read." Homographs such as *lead* /lid/ and *lead* /lɛd/ have fueled the flames of spelling reform movements. Different spellings for the same sound, silent letters, and missing letters also are cited as reasons that English needs a new orthographic system. The following examples illustrate the discrepancies between spelling and sounds in English:

Same Sound, Different Spelling	*Different Sound, Same Spelling*		*Silent Letters*	*Missing Letters*
/aj/	thought	/θ/	listen	use/juz/
	though	/ð/	debt	fuse/fjuz/
aye	Thomas	/t/	gnome	
buy			know	
by	ate	/e/	psychology	
die	at	/æ/	right	
hi	father	/a/	mnemonic	
Thai	many	/ɛ/	science	
height			talk	
guide			honest	
			sword	
			bomb	
			clue	
			Wednesday	

The spelling of most English words today is based on English as spoken in the fourteenth, fifteenth, and sixteenth centuries. Spellers in those times saw no need to spell the same word consistently. Shakespeare spelled his own name in several ways. In his plays, he spelled the first person singular pronoun variously as *I*, *ay*, and *aye*.

---

[1] G. B. Shaw. 1948. Preface to R. A. Wilson, *The Miraculous Birth of Language*, New York: Philosophical Library.

When the printing press was introduced in the fifteenth century, archaic and idiosyncratic spellings became widespread and more permanent. Words in print were frequently misspelled outright because many of the early printers were not native speakers of English.

Spelling reformers saw the need for consistent spelling that correctly reflected the pronunciation of words. To that extent, spelling reform was necessary. But many scholars became overzealous. Because of their reverence for Classical Greek and Latin, these scholars changed the spelling of English words to conform to their etymologies. Where Latin had a *b*, they added a *b* even if it was not pronounced. Where the original spelling had a *c* or *p* or *h*, these letters were added, as shown by these few examples:

Middle English Spelling		*Reformed Spelling*
indite	→	indict
dette	→	debt
receit	→	receipt
oure	→	hour

Such spelling habits inspired Robert N. Feinstein to compose the following poem, entitled *Gnormal Pspelling:*[2]

Gnus and gnomes and gnats and such—
Gnouns with just one G too much.
Pseudonym and psychedelic—
P becomes a psurplus relic.
Knit and knack and knife and knocked—
Kneedless Ks are overstocked.
Rhubarb, rhetoric and rhyme
Should lose an H from thyme to time.

Even today spelling reform is an issue. Advertisers often spell *though* as *tho*, *through* as *thru*, and *night* as *nite*. The *Chicago Tribune* once used such spellings, but it gave up the practice in 1975. Spelling habits are hard to change, and many people regard revised spelling as substandard.

The current English spelling system is based primarily on the earlier pronunciations of words. The many changes that have occurred in the sound system of English since then are not reflected in the current spelling, which was frozen due to widespread printed material and scholastic conservatism.

For these reasons, modern English orthography does not always represent what we know about the phonology of the language. The disadvantage is partially offset by the fact that the writing system allows us to read and understand what people wrote hundreds of years ago without the need for translations. If there were a one-to-one correspondence between our spelling and the sounds of our language, we would have difficulty reading the *U.S. Constitution* or the *Declaration of Independence*, let alone the works of Shakespeare and Dickens.

Languages change. It is not possible to maintain a perfect correspondence between pronunciation and spelling, nor is it 100 percent desirable. For instance, in the case of homophones, it is helpful at times to have different spellings for the same sounds, as in the following pair:

The book was red. The book was read.

Lewis Carroll makes the point with humor:

"And how many hours a day did you do lessons?" said Alice.
     "Ten hours the first day," said the Mock Turtle, "nine the next, and so on."
     "What a curious plan!" exclaimed Alice.
     "That's the reason they're called lessons," the Gryphon remarked, "because they lessen from day to day."

There are also reasons for using the same spelling for different pronunciations. A morpheme may be pronounced differently when it occurs

---

[2] "Gnormal Pspelling" by Robert N. Feinstein from *National Forum: The Phi Kappa Phi Journal,* Summer, 1986. Reprinted with permission.

in different contexts. The identical spelling reflects the fact that the different pronunciations represent the same morpheme. This is the case with the plural morpheme. It is always spelled with an *s* despite being pronounced [s] in *cats* and [z] in *dogs*. The sound of the morpheme is determined by rules, in this case and elsewhere.

Similarly, the phonetic realizations of the vowels in the following forms follow a regular pattern:

aj/ɪ	i/ɛ	e/æ
divine/divinity	serene/serenity	sane/sanity
sublime/sublimate	obscene/obscenity	profane/profanity
sign/signature	hygiene/hygienic	humane/humanity

These considerations have led some scholars to suggest that in addition to being phonemic, English has a *morphophonemic orthography*. To read English correctly morphophonemic knowledge is required. This contrasts with a language such as Spanish, whose orthography is almost purely phonemic.

Other examples provide further motivation for spelling irregularities. The *b* in *"debt"* may remind us of the related word *debit*, in which the *b* is pronounced. The same principle is true of pairs such as *sign/signal*, *bomb/bombardier*, and *gnosis/prognosis/agnostic*.

There are also different spellings that represent the different pronunciations of a morpheme when confusion would arise from using the same spelling. For example, there is a rule in English phonology that changes a /t/ to an /s/ in certain cases:

democrat → democracy

The different spellings are due in part to the fact that this rule does not apply to all morphemes, so that *art + y* is *arty*, not **arcy*. Regular phoneme-to-grapheme rules determine in many cases when a morpheme is to be spelled identically and when it is to be changed.

Other subregularities are apparent. A *c* always represents the /s/ sound when it is followed by a *y, i,* or *e*, as in *cynic, citizen,* and *censure*. Because it is always pronounced [k] when it is the final letter in a word or when it is followed by any other vowel (*coat, cat, cut*, and so on), no confusion results. The *th* spelling is usually pronounced voiced [ð] between vowels (the result of an historical intervocalic voicing rule), and in function words such as *the, they, this,* and *there*. Elsewhere it is the voiceless [θ].

There is another important reason why spelling should not always be tied to the phonetic pronunciation of words. Different dialects of English have divergent pronunciations. Cockneys drop their "(h)aitches" and Bostonians and southerners drop their *r*'s; *neither* is pronounced [niðər], [najðər], and [niðə] by Americans, [najðə] by the British, and [neðər] by the Irish; some Scots pronounce *night* [nɪxt]; people say "Chicago" and "Chicawgo," "hog" and "hawg," "bird" and "boyd"; *four* is pronounced [f:ɔ] by the British, [fɔr] in the Midwest, and [foə] in the South; *orange* is pronounced in at least two ways in the United States: [arənĵ] and [ɔrənĵ].

While dialectal pronunciations differ, the common spellings indicate the intended word. It is necessary for the written language to transcend local dialects. With a uniform spelling system, a native of Atlanta and a native of Glasgow can communicate through writing. If each dialect were spelled according to its pronunciation, written communication among the English-speaking peoples of the world would suffer.

SPELLING PRONUNCIATIONS

For pronunciation, the best general rule is to consider those as the most elegant speakers who deviate least from written words.
                                                              −SAMUEL JOHNSON (1755)

Despite the primacy of the spoken over the written language, the written word is often regarded with excessive reverence. The stability, permanency, and graphic nature of writing cause some people to favor it over ephemeral and elusive speech. Humpty Dumpty expressed a rather typical attitude: "I'd rather see that done on paper."

Writing has affected speech only marginally, however, most notably in the phenomenon of *spelling pronunciation*. Since the sixteenth century, we find that spelling has to some extent influenced standard pronunciation. The most important of such changes stem from the eighteenth century under the influence and decrees of the dictionary-makers and the schoolteachers. The struggle between those who demanded that words be pronounced according to the spelling, and those who demanded that words be spelled according to their pronunciation, generated great heat in that century. The preferred pronunciations were given in the many dictionaries printed in the eighteenth century, and the "supreme authority" of the dictionaries influenced pronunciation in this way.

Spelling also has influenced pronunciation of words that are infrequently used in normal daily speech. In many words that were spelled with an initial *h*, the *h* was silent as recently as the eighteenth century. Then, no [h] was pronounced in *honest, hour, habit, heretic, hotel, hospital*, and *herb*. Common words like *honest* and *hour* continued *h*-less, despite the spelling. The other less frequently used words were given a "spelling pronunciation," and the *h* is sounded today. *Herb* is currently undergoing this change. In British English the *h* is pronounced, whereas in American English it generally is not.

Similarly, the *th* in the spelling of many words was once pronounced like the /t/ in *Thomas*. Later most of these words underwent a change in pronunciation from /t/ to /θ/, as in *anthem, author*, and *theater*. Nicknames may reflect the earlier pronunciations: "Kate" for "Catherine," "Betty" for "Elizabeth," "Art" for "Arthur." *Often* is often pronounced with the *t* sounded, though historically it is silent, and up-to-date dictionaries now indicate this pronunciation as an alternative.

The clear influence of spelling on pronunciation is observable in the way place-names are pronounced. *Berkeley* is pronounced [bʊrkli] in California, although it stems from the British [baːkli]; *Worcester* [wʊstər] or [wʊstə] in Massachusetts is often pronounced [wʊrčɛstər] in other parts of the country. *Salmon* is pronounced [sæmən] in most parts of the United States, but many southern speakers pronounce the [l] and say [sælmən].

Although the written language has some influence on the spoken, it does not change the basic system—the grammar—of the language. The writing system, conversely, reflects, in a more or less direct way, the grammar that every speaker knows.

═══

FOR DISCUSSION AND REVIEW

1. Fromkin and her colleagues begin with the assertion that "the development of writing freed us from the limitations of time and geography." Using some examples, explain what this statement means.

2. What different kinds of information does punctuation provide? How does spoken language show the same kinds of information? In two of your own written sentences, demonstrate how punctuation might change their meaning. If you were speaking these sentences, how could you use contrastive stress to change the meaning?

3. When the authors note that "written language is more conservative than spoken language," what do they mean? How different is your own spoken language from your writing? When, if at all, do you edit what you say? In what circumstances are you likely to edit what you write?

4. What is the Whole Language approach to reading? Why, specifically, do the authors refute it? Do you agree with them that the teaching of phonics—or relating sounds to letters—is important to children's learning how to read and write? Why, or why not?

5. Why did spelling reformers centuries ago often add a letter to an English word even though the letter was not pronounced? Give a few examples of this phenomenon.

6. Why is it sometimes advantageous to have "different spellings for the same sounds"—and the "same spelling for different pronunciations"? Support your answer with some original examples.

7. The authors say that "it is necessary for written language to transcend local dialects." Explain this remark by using some common expressions from your area of the country and elsewhere.

53

What No Bedtime Story Means

Shirley Brice Heath

Shirley Brice Heath is professor emeritus of linguistics and English at Stanford University and currently teaches at Brown University. In her research over the years, she has focused primarily on the development of literacy among young people in low-income communities. Heath believes that identifying cultures as either "literate" or "oral" is a false dichotomy, and she argues instead for recognizing the culturally diverse ways of becoming literate. In this influential 1982 piece, originally published in Language in Society, *Heath discusses her research in three Carolina Piedmont communities. "Maintown" children, she discovers, are likely to be well prepared for school because their early "literacy events" are geared to the standard classroom approach. Children in "Roadville" or "Trackton," however, learn about the world and how to use written language in different ways, so they often encounter serious difficulties in school. Yet some of these children have strengths, in areas such as storytelling, that children in "Maintown" do not. All young students could benefit, Heath suggests, if educators would take into account communities' varied "ways of knowing."*

In the preface to *Introduction to S/Z*, Roland Barthes's work on ways in which readers read, Richard Howard writes: "We require an education in literature . . . in order to discover that *what we have assumed*—with the complicity of our teachers—*was nature is in fact culture, that what was given is no more than a way of taking*" (emphasis not in the original; Howard 1974:ix).[1] This statement reminds us that the *culture* children learn as they grow up is, in fact, "ways of taking" meaning from the environment around them. The means of making sense from books and relating their contents to knowledge about the real world is but one "way of taking" that is often interpreted as "natural" rather than learned. The quote also reminds us that teachers (and researchers alike) have not recognized that ways of taking from books are as much a part of learned behavior as are ways of eating, sitting, playing games, and building houses.

As school-oriented parents and their children interact in the preschool years, adults give their children, through modeling and specific instruction, ways of taking from books that seem natural in school and in numerous institutional settings such as banks, post offices, businesses, and government offices. These *mainstream* ways exist in societies around the world that rely on formal educational systems to prepare children for participation in settings involving literacy. In some communities these ways of schools and institutions are very similar to the ways learned at home; in other communities the ways of school are merely an overlay on the home-taught ways and may be in conflict with them.[2]

Yet little is actually known about what goes on in storyreading and other literacy-related interactions between adults and preschoolers in communities around the world. Specifically, though there are numerous diary accounts and experimental studies of the preschool reading experiences of mainstream middle-class children, we know little about the specific literacy features of the environment upon which the school expects to draw. Just how does what is frequently termed "the literate tradition" envelop the child in knowledge about interrelationships between oral and written language, between knowing something and knowing ways of labeling and displaying it? We have even less information about the variety of ways children from *nonmainstream* homes learn about reading, writing, and using oral language to display knowledge in their preschool environment. The general view has been that whatever it is that mainstream school-oriented homes have, these other homes do not have it; thus these children are not from the literate tradition and are not likely to succeed in school.

A key concept for the empirical study of ways of taking meaning from written sources across communities is that of *literacy events*: occasions in which written language is integral to the nature of participants' interactions and their interpretive processes and strategies. Familiar literacy events for mainstream preschoolers are bedtime stories; reading cereal boxes, stop signs, and television ads; and interpreting instructions for commercial games and toys. In such literacy events, participants follow socially established rules for verbalizing what they know from and about the written material. Each community has rules for socially interacting and sharing knowledge in literacy events.

This paper briefly summarizes the ways of taking from printed stories families teach their preschoolers in a cluster of mainstream school-oriented neighborhoods of a city in the southeastern region of the United States. I then describe two quite different ways of taking used in the homes of two English-speaking communities in the same region that do not follow the school-expected patterns of bookreading and reinforcement of these patterns in oral storytelling. Two assumptions underlie this paper and are treated in detail in the ethnography of these communities (Heath 1983): (1) Each community's ways of taking from the printed word and using this knowledge are interdependent with the ways children learn to talk in their social interactions with caregivers; (2) there is little or no validity to the time-honored dichotomy of "the literate tradition" and "the oral tradition." This paper suggests a frame of reference for both the community patterns and the paths of development children in different communities follow in their literacy orientations.

MAINSTREAM SCHOOL-ORIENTED BOOKREADING

Children growing up in mainstream communities are expected to develop habits and values that attest to their membership in a "literate society." Children learn certain customs, beliefs, and skills in early enculturation experiences with written materials: The bedtime story is a major literacy event that helps set patterns of behavior that reoccur repeatedly through the life of mainstream children and adults.

In both popular and scholarly literature, the bedtime story is widely accepted as a given—a natural way for parents to interact with their child at bedtime. Commercial publishing houses, television advertising, and children's magazines make much of this familiar ritual, and many of their sales pitches are based on the assumption that in spite of the intrusion of television into many patterns of interaction between parents and children, this ritual remains. Few parents are fully conscious of what bedtime storyreading means as preparation for the kinds of learning and displays of knowledge expected in school. Ninio & Bruner (1978), in their longitudinal study of one mainstream middle-class mother–infant dyad in joint picturebook reading, strongly suggest a universal role of bookreading in the achievement of labeling by children.

In a series of "reading cycles," mother and child alternate turns in a dialogue: The mother directs the child's attention to the book and/or asks what-questions and/or labels items on the page. The items to which the what-questions are directed and labels given are two-dimensional representations of three-dimensional objects, so that the child has to resolve the conflict between perceiving these as two-dimensional objects and as representations of a three-dimensional visual setting. The child does so "by assigning a privileged, autonomous status to pictures as visual objects" (1978:5). The arbitrariness of the picture, its decontextualization, and its existence as something that cannot be grasped and manipulated like its "real" counterparts are learned through the routines of structured interactional dialogue in which mother and child take turns playing a labeling game. In a "scaffolding" dialogue (cf. Cazden 1979), the mother points and asks "What is x?" and the child vocalizes and/or gives a nonverbal signal of attention. The mother then provides verbal feedback and a label. Before the age of 2, the child is socialized into the initiation–reply–evaluation sequences repeatedly described as the central structural feature of classroom lessons (e.g., Sinclair & Coulthard 1975; Griffin & Humphry 1978; Mehan 1979). Teachers ask their students questions to which the answers are prespecified in the mind of the teacher.

Students respond, and teachers provide feedback, usually in the form of an evaluation. Training in ways of responding to this pattern begins very early in the labeling activities of mainstream parents and children.

Maintown Ways

This patterning of "incipient literacy" (Scollon & Scollon 1979) is similar in many ways to that of the families of fifteen primary-level schoolteachers in Maintown, a cluster of middle-class neighborhoods in a city of the Piedmont Carolinas. These families (all of whom identify themselves as "typical," "middle-class," or "mainstream") had preschool children, and the mother in each family was either teaching in local public schools at the time of the study (early 1970s) or had taught in the academic year preceding participation in the study. Through a research dyad approach, using teacher-mothers as researchers with the ethnographer, the teacher-mothers audiorecorded their children's interactions in their primary network—mothers, fathers, grandparents, maids, siblings, and frequent visitors to the home. Children were expected to learn the following rules in literacy events in these nuclear households:

1. As early as 6 months of age, children *give attention to books and information derived from books*. Their rooms contain bookcases and are decorated with murals, bedspreads, mobiles, and stuffed animals that represent characters found in books. Even when these characters have their origin in television programs, adults also provide books that either repeat or extend the characters' activities on television.

2. Children, from the age of 6 months, *acknowledge questions about books*. Adults expand nonverbal responses and vocalizations from infants into fully formed grammatical sentences. When children begin to verbalize about the contents of books, adults extend their questions from simple requests for labels ("What's that?" "Who's that?") to ask about the attributes of these items ("What does the doggie say?" "What color is the ball?")

3. From the time they start to talk, children *respond to conversational allusions to the content of books; they act as question-answerers who have a knowledge of books*. For example, a fuzzy black dog on the street is likened by an adult to Blackie in a child's book: "Look, there's a Blackie. Do you think *he's* looking for a boy?" Adults strive to maintain with children a running commentary on any event or object that can be book-related, thus modeling for them the extension of familiar items and events from books to new situational contexts.

4. Beyond 2 years of age, children *use their knowledge of what books do to legitimate their departures from "truth."* Adults encourage and reward "book talk," even when it is not directly relevant to an ongoing conversation. Children are allowed to suspend reality, to tell stories that are not true, to ascribe fiction-like features to everyday objects.

5. Preschool children *accept book and book-related activities as entertainment.* When preschoolers are "captive audiences" (e.g., waiting in a doctor's office, putting a toy together, or preparing for bed), adults reach for books. If there are no books present, they talk about other objects as though they were pictures in books. For example, adults point to items and ask children to name, describe, and compare them to familiar objects in their environment. Adults often ask children to state their likes or dislikes, their view of events, etc. at the end of the captive-audience period. These affective questions often take place while the next activity is already under way (e.g., moving toward the doctor's office, putting the new toy away, or being tucked into bed), and adults do not insist on answers.

6. Preschoolers *announce their own factual and fictive narratives* unless they are given in response to direct adult elicitation. Adults judge as most acceptable those narratives that open by orienting the listener to setting and main character. Narratives that are fictional are usually marked by formulaic openings, a particular prosody, or the borrowing of episodes in storybooks.

7. When children are about 3 years old, adults discourage the highly interactive participative role in bookreading children have hitherto played and children *listen and wait as an audience.* No longer does either adult or child repeatedly break into the story with questions and comments. Instead, children must listen, store what they hear, and, on cue from the adult, answer a question. Thus children begin to formulate "practice" questions as they wait for the break and the expected formulaic questions from the adult. It is at this stage that children often choose to "read" to adults rather than be read to.

A pervasive pattern of all these features is the authority that books and book-related activities have in the lives of both the preschoolers and members of their primary network. Any initiation of a literacy event by a preschooler makes an interruption, an untruth, a diverting of attention from the matter at hand (whether it be an uneaten plate of food, a messy room, or an avoidance of going to bed) acceptable. Adults jump at openings their children give them for pursuing talk about books and reading.

In this study, writing was found to be somewhat less acceptable as an "anytime activity," since adults have rigid rules about times, places, and materials for writing. The only restrictions on bookreading concern taking good care of books: They should not be wet, torn, drawn on, or lost. In their talk to children about books and in their explanations of why they buy children's books, adults link school success to "learning to love books," "learning what books can do for you," and "learning to entertain yourself and to work independently." Many of the adults also openly expressed a fascination with children's books "nowadays." They generally judged them as more diverse, wide-ranging, challenging, and exciting than books they had as children.

The Mainstream Pattern

A close look at the way bedtime-story routines in Maintown taught children how to take meaning from books raises a heavy sense of the familiar in all of us who have acquired mainstream habits and values. Throughout a lifetime, any school-successful individual moves through the same processes described above thousands of times. Reading for comprehension involves an internal replaying of the same types of questions adults ask children about bedtime stories. We seek *what-explanations*, asking what the topic is, establishing it as predictable and recognizing it in new situational contexts by classifying and categorizing it in our minds with other phenomena. The what-explanation is replayed in learning to pick out topic sentences, write outlines, and answer standardized tests that ask for the correct titles to stories, and so on. In learning to read in school, children move through a sequence of skills designed to teach what-explanations. There is a tight linear order of instruction that recapitulates the bedtime-story pattern of breaking down the story into small bits of information and teaching children to handle sets of related skills in isolated sequential hierarchies.

In each individual reading episode in the primary years of schooling, children must move through what-explanations before they can provide *reason-explanations* or *affective commentaries*. Questions about why a particular event occurred or why a specific action was right or wrong come at the end of primary-level reading lessons, just as they come at the end of bedtime stories. Throughout the primary-grade levels, what-explanations predominate, reason-explanations come with increasing frequency in the upper grades, and affective comments most often come in the extra-credit portions of the reading workbook or at the end of the list of suggested activities in textbooks across grade levels. This sequence characterizes the total school career. Highschool freshmen who are judged poor in compositional and reading skills spend most of their time on what-explanations and practice in advanced versions of bedtime-story questions and answers. They are given little or no chance to use reason-giving explanations or assessments of the actions of stories. Reason-explanations result in configurational rather than hierarchical skills, are not predictable, and thus do not present content with a high degree of redundancy. Reason-giving explanations tend to rely on detailed knowledge of a specific domain. This detail is often unpredictable to teachers, and is not as highly valued as is knowledge that covers a particular area of knowledge with less detail but offers opportunity for extending the knowledge to larger and related concerns. For example, a primary-level student whose father owns a turkey farm may respond with reason-explanations to a story about a turkey. His knowledge is intensive and covers details perhaps not known to the teacher and not judged as relevant to the story. The knowledge is unpredictable and questions about it do not continue to repeat the common core of content knowledge of the story. Thus such configured knowledge is encouraged only for the "extras" of reading—an extra-credit oral report or a creative picture and story about turkeys. This kind of knowledge is allowed to be used once the hierarchical what-explanations have been mastered and displayed in a particular situation and, in the course of one's academic career, only when one has shown full mastery of the hierarchical skills and subsets of related skills that underlie what-explanations. Thus reliable and successful participation in the ways of taking from books that teachers view as natural must, in the usual school way of doing things, precede other ways of taking from books.

These various ways of taking are sometimes referred to as "cognitive styles" or "learning styles." It is generally accepted in the research literature that they are influenced by early socialization experiences and correlated with such features of the society in which the child is reared as social organization, reliance on authority, male–female roles, and so on. These styles are often seen as two contrasting types, most frequently termed "field independent–field dependent" (Witkin et al. 1966) or "analytic–relational" (Kagan, Sigel & Moss 1963; Cohen 1968, 1969, 1971). The analytic/field-independent style is generally presented as that which correlates positively with high achievement and general academic and social success in school. Several studies discuss ways in which this style is played out in school—in preferred ways of responding to pictures and written text and selecting from among a choice of answers to test items.

Yet we know little about how behaviors associated with either of the dichotomized cognitive styles (field-dependent/relational and field-independent/analytic) were learned in early patterns of socialization. To be sure, there are vast individual differences that may cause an individual to behave so as to be categorized as having one or the other of these learning styles. But much of the literature on learning styles suggests that a preference for one or the other is learned in the social group in which the child is reared and in connection with other ways of behaving found in that culture. But how is a child socialized into an analytic/field-independent style? What kinds of interactions does he enter into with his parents and the stimuli of his environment that contribute to the development of such a style of learning? How do these interactions mold selective attention practices such as "sensitivity to parts of objects," "awareness of obscure, abstract, nonobvious features," and identification of "abstractions based on the features of items" (Cohen 1969:844–5)? Since the predominant stimuli used in school to judge the presence and extent of these selective attention practices are written materials, it is clear that the literacy orientation of preschool children is central to these questions.

The foregoing descriptions of how Maintown parents socialize their children into a literacy orientation fit closely those provided by Scollon & Scollon for their own child, Rachel. Through similar practices, Rachel was "literate before she learned to read" (1979:6). She knew, before the age of 2, how to focus on a book and not on herself. Even when she told a story about herself, she moved herself out of the text and saw herself as author, as someone different from the central character of her story. She learned to pay close attention to the parts of objects, to name them, and to provide a running commentary on features of her environment. She learned to manipulate the contexts of items, her own activities, and language to achieve booklike, decontextualized, repeatable effects (such as puns). Many references in her talk were from written sources; others were modeled on stories and questions about these stories. The substance of her knowledge, as well as her ways of framing knowledge orally, derived from her familiarity with books and bookreading. No doubt this development began by labeling in the dialogue cycles of reading (Ninio & Bruner 1978), and it will continue for Rachel in her preschool years along many of the same patterns described by Cochran Smith (1984) for a mainstream nursery school. There teacher and students negotiated storyreading through the scaffolding of teachers' questions and running commentaries that replayed the structure and sequence of storyreading learned in their mainstream homes.

Close analyses of how mainstream school-oriented children come to learn to take from books at home suggest that such children learn not only how to take meaning from books, but also how to talk about it. In doing the latter, they repeatedly practice routines that parallel those of classroom interaction. By the time they enter school, they have had continuous experience as information givers; they have learned how to perform in those interactions that surround literate sources throughout school. They have had years of practice in interaction situations that are the heart of reading—both learning to read and reading to learn in school. They have developed habits of performing that enable them to run through the hierarchy of preferred knowledge about a literate source and the appropriate sequence of skills to be displayed in showing knowledge of a subject. They have developed ways of decontextualizing and surrounding with explanatory prose the knowledge gained from selective attention to objects.

They have learned to listen, waiting for the appropriate cue that signals it is their turn to show off this knowledge. They have learned the rules for getting certain services from parents (or teachers) in the reading interaction (Merritt 1979). In nursery school, they continue to practice these interaction patterns in a group rather than in a dyadic situation. There they learn additional signals and behaviors necessary for getting a turn in a group and for responding to a central reader and to a set of centrally defined reading tasks. In short, most of their waking hours during the preschool years have enculturated them into: (1) all those habits associated with what-explanations, (2) selective attention to items of the written text, *and* (3) appropriate interactional styles for orally displaying all the know-how of their literate orientation to the environment. This learning has been finely tuned and its habits are highly interdependent. Patterns of behaviors learned in one setting or at one stage reappear again and again as these children learn to use oral and written language in literacy events and to bring their knowledge to bear in school-acceptable ways.

ALTERNATIVE PATTERNS OF LITERACY EVENTS

But what corresponds to the mainstream pattern of learning in communities that do not have this finely tuned, consistent, repetitive, and continuous pattern of training? Are there ways of behaving that achieve other social and cognitive aims in other sociocultural groups?

The data below are summarized from an ethnography of two communities—Roadville and Trackton—located only a few miles from Maintown's neighborhoods in the Piedmont Carolinas. Roadville is a white working-class community of families steeped for four generations in the life of the textile mill. Trackton is a working-class black community whose older generations have been brought up on the land, either farming their own land or working for other landowners. However, in the past decade, they have found work in the textile mills. Children of both communities are unsuccessful in school; yet both communities place a high value on success in school, believing earnestly in the personal and vocational rewards school can bring and urging their children "to get ahead" by doing well in school. Both Roadville and Trackton are literate communities in the sense that the residents of each are able to read printed and written materials in their daily lives, and on occasion they produce written messages as part of the total pattern of communication in the community. In both communities, children go to school with certain expectancies of print and, in Trackton especially, children have a keen sense that reading is something one does to learn something one needs to know (Heath 1980). In both groups, residents turn from spoken to written uses of language and vice versa as the occasion demands, and the two modes of expression seem to supplement and reinforce each other. Nonetheless there are radical differences between the two communities in the ways in which children and adults interact in the preschool years; each of the two communities also differs from Maintown. Roadville and Trackton view children's learning of language from two radically different perspectives: In Trackton, children "learn to talk"; in Roadville, adults "teach them how to talk."

Roadville

In Roadville, babies are brought home from the hospital to rooms decorated with colorful, mechanical, musical, and literacy-based stimuli. The walls are decorated with pictures based on nursery rhymes, and from an early age children are held and prompted to "see" the wall decorations.

Adults recite nursery rhymes as they twirl the mobile made of nursery-rhyme characters. The items of the child's environment promote exploration of colors, shapes, and textures: A stuffed ball with sections of fabrics of different colors and textures is in the crib; stuffed animals vary in texture, size, and shape. Neighbors, friends from church, and relatives come to visit and talk to the baby and about him to those who will listen. The baby is fictionalized in the talk to him: "But this baby wants to go to sleep, doesn't he? Yes, see those little eyes gettin' heavy." As the child grows older, adults pounce on wordlike sounds and turn them into "words," repeating the "words," and expanding them into well-formed sentences. Before they can talk, children are introduced to visitors and prompted to provide all the expected politeness formulas, such as "Bye, bye," "Thank you," and so forth. As soon as they can talk, children are reminded about these formulas, and book or television characters known to be "polite" are involved as reinforcement.

In each Roadville home, preschoolers first have cloth books, featuring a single object on each page. They later acquire books that provide sounds, smells, and different textures or opportunities for practicing small motor skills (closing zippers, buttoning buttons, etc.). A typical collection for a 2-year-old consisted of a dozen or so books—eight featured either the alphabet or numbers; others were books of nursery rhymes, simplified Bible stories, or "real-life" stories about boys and girls (usually taking care of their pets or exploring a particular feature of their environment). Books based on Sesame Street characters were favorite gifts for 3- and 4-year-olds.

Reading and reading-related activities occur most frequently before naps or at bedtime in the evening. Occasionally an adult or older child will read to a fussy child while the mother prepares dinner or changes a bed. On weekends, fathers sometimes read with their children for brief periods of time, but they generally prefer to play games or play with the children's toys in their interactions. The following episode illustrates the language and social interactional aspects of these bedtime events; the episode takes place between Wendy (2;3 at the time of this episode) and Aunt Sue, who is putting her to bed.

> [Aunt Sue (AS) picks up book, while Wendy crawls about the floor, ostensibly looking for something]
> W: Uh uh
> AS: Wendy, we're gonna read, uh, read this story, come on, hop up here on this bed. [Wendy climbs up on the bed, sits on top of the pillow, and picks up her teddy bear. Aunt Sue opens book, points to puppy]
> AS: Do you remember what this book is about? See the puppy? What does the puppy do? [Wendy plays with the bear, glancing occasionally at pages of the book, as Aunt Sue turns. Wendy seems to be waiting for something in the book]
> AS: See the puppy?

[Aunt Sue points to the puppy in the book and looks at Wendy to see if she is watching]

W: Uh huh, yea, yes ma'am

AS: Puppy sees the ant, he's a li'l [Wendy drops the bear and turns to book] fellow. Can you see that ant? Puppy has a little ball.

W: Ant bite puppy [Wendy points to ant, pushing hard on the book]

AS: No, the ant won't bite the puppy, the [turns page] puppy wants to play with the ant, see? [Wendy tries to turn the page back; AS won't let her, and Wendy starts to squirm and fuss]

AS: Look here, here's someone else, the puppy [Wendy climbs down off the bed and gets another book]

W: Read this one

AS: Okay, you get back up here now. [Wendy gets back on bed]

AS: This book is your ABC book. See the A, look, here, on your spread, there's an A. You find the A. [The second book is a cloth book, old and tattered, and long a favorite of Wendy's. It features an apple on the cover, and its front page has an ABC block and ball. Through the book, there is a single item on each page, with a large representation of the first letter of the word commonly used to name the item. As AS turns the page, Wendy begins to crawl about on her quilt, which shows ABC blocks interspersed with balls and apples. Wendy points to each of the A's on the blanket and begins talking to herself. AS reads the book, looks up, and sees Wendy pointing to the A's in her quilt]

AS: That's an A, can you find the A on your blanket?

W: There it is, this one, there's the hole too. [Pokes her finger through a place where the threads have broken in the quilting]

AS: [Points to ball in book] Stop that, find the ball, see, here's another ball.

This episode characterizes the early orientation of Roadville children to the written word. Bookreading time focuses on letters of the alphabet, numbers, names of basic items pictured in books, and simplified retellings of stories in the words of the adult. If the content or story plot seems too complicated for the child, the adult tells the story in short, simple sentences, frequently laced with requests that the child give what-explanations.

Wendy's favorite books are those with which she can participate; that is, those to which she can answer, provide labels, point to items, give animal sounds, and "read" the material back to anyone who will listen to her. She memorizes the passages and often knows when to turn the pages to show that she is "reading." She holds the book in her lap, starts at the beginning, and often reads the title—"Puppy."

Adults and children use either the title of the book (or phrases such as "the book about a puppy") to refer to reading material. When Wendy acquires a new book, adults introduce the book with phrases such as

"This is a book about a duck, a little yellow duck. See the duck. Duck goes quack quack." On introducing a book, adults sometimes ask the child to recall when they have seen a real specimen of the one treated in the book: "Remember the duck on the College lake?" The child often shows no sign of linking the yellow fluffy duck in the book with the large brown and gray mallards on the lake, and the adult makes no effort to explain that two such disparate-looking objects go by the same name.

As Wendy grows older, she wants to "talk" during the stories and Bible stories, and carry out the participation she so enjoyed with the alphabet books. However, by the time she reaches $3\frac{1}{2}$, Wendy is restrained from such wide-ranging participation. When she interrupts, she is told: "Wendy, stop that, you be quiet when someone is reading to you" or "You listen; now sit still and be quiet." Often Wendy will immediately get down and run away into the next room, saying "No, no." When this happens, her father goes to get her, pats her bottom, and puts her down hard on the sofa beside him. "Now you're gonna learn to listen." During the third and fourth years, this pattern occurs more and more frequently; only when Wendy can capture an aunt who does not visit often does she bring out the old books and participate with them. Otherwise, parents, Aunt Sue, and other adults insist that she be read a story and that she "listen" quietly.

When Wendy and her parents watch television, eat cereal, visit the grocery store, or go to church, adults point out and talk about many types of written material. On the way to the grocery, Wendy (3;8) sits in the back seat, and when her mother stops at a corner, Wendy says, "Stop." Her mother says, "Yes, that's a stop sign." Wendy has, however, misread a yield sign as a stop. Her mother offers no explanation of what the actual message on the sign is, yet when she comes to the sign she stops to yield to an oncoming car. Her mother, when asked why she had not given Wendy the word "yield," said it was too hard, Wendy would not understand, and "It's not a word we use like *stop*."

Wendy recognized animal-cracker boxes as early as 10 months, and later, as her mother began buying other varieties, Wendy would see the box in the grocery store and yell, "Cook cook." Her mother would say, "Yes, those are cookies. Does Wendy want a cookie?" One day Wendy saw a new type of cracker box, and screeched, "Cook cook." Her father opened the box and gave Wendy a cracker and waited for her reaction. She started the "cookie," then took it to her mother, saying, "You eat." The mother joined in the game and said, "Don't you want your *cookie?*" Wendy said, "No cookie. You eat." "But Wendy, it's a cookie box, see?" and her mother pointed to the C of "crackers" on the box. Wendy paid no attention and ran off into another room.

In Roadville's literacy events, the rules for cooperative discourse around print are repeatedly practiced, coached, and rewarded in the preschool years. Adults in Roadville believe that instilling in children the proper use of words and understanding of the meaning of the written word are important for both their educational and religious success. Adults repeat aspects of the learning of literacy events they have known. as children. In the words of one Roadville parent, "It was then that I began to learn . . . when my daddy kept insisting I *read* it, *say* it right. It was then that I *did* right, in his view."

The path of development for such performance can be described in three overlapping stages. In the first, children are introduced to discrete bits and pieces of books—separate items, letters of the alphabet, shapes, colors, and commonly represented items in books for children (apple, baby, ball, etc.). The latter are usually decontextualized, and they are represented in two-dimensional, flat line drawings. During this stage, children must participate as predictable information givers and respond to questions that ask for specific and discrete bits of information about the written matter. In these literacy events, specific features of the two-dimensional items in books that are different from their real counterparts are not pointed out. A ball in a book is flat; a duck in a book is yellow and fluffy; trucks, cars, dogs, and trees talk in books. No mention is made of the fact that such features do not fit these objects in reality. Children are not encouraged to move their understanding of books into other situational contexts or to apply it in their general knowledge of the world about them.

In the second stage, adults demand an acceptance of the power of print to entertain, inform, and instruct. When Wendy could no longer participate by contributing her knowledge at any point in the literacy event, she learned to recognize bookreading as a performance. The adult exhibited the book to Wendy: She was to be entertained, to learn from the information conveyed in the material, and to remember the book's content for the sequential follow-up questioning, as opposed to ongoing cooperative, participatory questions.

In the third stage, Wendy was introduced to preschool workbooks that provided story information and was asked questions or provided exercises and games based on the content of the stories or pictures. Follow-the-number coloring books and preschool push-out-and-paste workbooks on shapes, colors, and letters of the alphabet reinforced repeatedly that the written word could be taken apart into small pieces and one item linked to another by following rules. She had practice in the linear, sequential nature of books: Begin at the beginning, stay in the lines for coloring, draw straight lines to link one item to another, write your answers on lines, keep your letters straight, match the cutout letter to diagrams of letter shapes.

The differences between Roadville and Maintown are substantial. Roadville adults do not extend either the content or the habits of literacy events beyond bookreading. They do not, upon seeing an item or event in the real world, remind children of a similar event in a book and launch a running commentary on similarities and differences. When a game is played or a chore done, adults do not use literate sources. Mothers cook without written recipes most of the time; if they use a recipe from a written source, they do so usually only after confirmation and alteration by friends who have tried the recipe. Directions to games are read, but not carefully followed, and they are not talked about in a series of questions and answers that try to establish their meaning. Instead, in the putting together of toys or the playing of games, the abilities or preferences of one party prevail. For example, if an adult knows how to put a toy together, he does so; he does not talk about the process, refer to the written material and "translate" for the child, or try to sequence steps so the child can do it.[3] Adults do not talk about the steps and procedures of how to do things; if a father wants his preschooler to learn to hold a miniature bat or throw a ball, he says, "Do it this way." He does not break up "this way" into such steps as "Put your fingers around here," "Keep your thumb in this position," "Never hold it above this line." Over and over again, adults do a task and children observe and try it, being reinforced only by commands such as "Do it like this" and "Watch that thumb."

Adults at tasks do not provide a running verbal commentary on what they are doing. They do not draw the attention of the child to specific features of the sequences of skills or the attributes of items. They do not ask questions of the child, except questions which are directive or scolding in nature ("Did you bring the ball?" "Didn't you hear what I said?"). Many of their commands contain idioms that are not explained: "Put it up" or "Put that away now" (meaning "Put it in the place where it usually belongs") or "Loosen up," said to a 4-year-old boy trying to learn to bat a ball. Explanations that move beyond the listing of names of items and their features are rarely offered by adults. Children do not ask questions of the type "But I don't understand? What is that?" They appear willing to keep trying, and if there is ambiguity in a set of commands, they ask a question such as "You want me to do this?" (demonstrating their current efforts), or they try to find a way of diverting attention from the task at hand.

Both boys and girls during their preschool years are included in many adult activities, ranging from going to church to fishing and camping. They spend a lot of time observing and asking for turns to try specific tasks, such as putting a worm on the hook or cutting cookies. Sometimes adults say, "No, you're not old enough." But if they agree to the child's attempt at the task, they watch and give directives and evaluations: "That's right, don't twist the cutter." "Turn like this." "Don't try to scrape it up now, let me do that." Talk about the task does not segment its skills and identify them, nor does it link the particular task or item at hand to other tasks. Reason-explanations such as "If you twist the cutter, the cookies will be rough on the edge" are rarely given—or asked for.

Neither Roadville adults nor children shift the context of items in their talk. They do not tell stories that fictionalize themselves or familiar events. They reject Sunday school materials that attempt to translate Biblical events into a modern-day setting. In Roadville, a story must be invited or announced by someone other than the storyteller, and only certain community members are designated good storytellers. A story is recognized by the group as a story about one and all. It is a true story, an actual event that happened to either the storyteller or someone else present. The marked behavior of the storyteller and audience alike is seen as exemplifying the weaknesses of all and the need for persistence in overcoming such weaknesses. The sources of stories are personal experience. They are tales of transgressions that make the point of reiterating the expected norms of behavior of man, woman, fisherman, worker, and Christian. They are true to the facts of the event.

Roadville parents provide their children with books; they read to them and ask questions about the books' contents. They choose books that emphasize nursery rhymes, alphabet learning, animals, and simplified Bible stories, and they require their children to repeat from these books and to answer formulaic questions about their contents. Roadville adults also ask questions about oral stories that have a point relevant to some marked behavior of a child. They use proverbs and summary statements to remind their children of srories and to call on them for simple comparisons of the stories' contents to their own situations. Roadville parents coach children in their telling of a story, forcing them to tell about an incident as it has been precomposed or pre-scripted in the head of the adult. Thus in Roadville children come to know a story as either an accounting from a book or a factual account of a real event in which some type of marked behavior occurred and there is a lesson to be learned. Any fictionalized account of a real event is viewed as a *lie*; reality is better than fiction. Roadville's church and community life admit no story other than that which meets the definition internal to the group. Thus children cannot decontextualize their knowledge or fictionalize events known to them and shift them about into other frames.

When these children go to school they perform well in the initial stages of each of the three early grades. They often know portions of the alphabet, some colors and numbers, and can recognize their names and tell someone their address and their parents' names. They will sit still and listen to a story, and they know how to answer questions asking for what-explanations. They do well in reading workbook exercises that ask for identification of specific portions of words, items from the story, or the linking of two items, letters, or parts of words on the same page. When the teacher reaches the end of storyreading or the reading circle and asks questions such as "What did you like about the story?" relatively few Roadville children answer. If asked questions such as "What would you have done if you had been Billy [a story's main character]?" Roadville children most frequently say, "I don't know" or shrug their shoulders.

Near the end of each year, and increasingly as they move through the early primary grades, Roadville children can handle successfully the initial stages of lessons. But when they move ahead to extra-credit items or to activities considered more advanced and requiring more independence, they are stumped. They turn frequently to teachers, asking, "Do you want me to do this? What do I do here?" If asked to write a creative story or tell it into a tape recorder, they retell stories from books; they do not create their own. They rarely provide emotional or personal commentary on their accounting of real events or book stories. They are rarely able to take knowledge learned in one context and shift it to another; they do not compare two items or events and point out similarities and differences. They find it difficult either to hold one feature of an event constant and shift all others or to hold all features constant but one. For example, they are puzzled by questions such as "What would have happened if Billy had not told the policemen what happened?" They do not know how to move events or items out of a given frame. To a question such as "What habits of the Hopi Indians might they be able to take with them when they move to a city?" they provide lists of features of life of the Hopi on the reservation. They do not take these items, consider their appropriateness in an urban setting, and evaluate the hypothesized outcome. In general, they find this type of question impossible to answer, and they do not know how to ask teachers to help them take apart the questions to figure out the answers. Thus their initial successes in reading, being good students, following orders, and adhering to school norms of participating in lessons begin to fall away rapidly about the time they enter the fourth grade. As the importance and frequency of questions and reading habits with which they are familiar decline in the higher grades, they have no way of keeping up or of seeking help in learning what it is they do not even know they don't know.

Trackton

Babies in Trackton come home from the hospital to an environment that is almost entirely human. There are no cribs, car beds, or carseats, and only an occasional highchair or infant seat. Infants are held during their waking hours, occasionally while they sleep, and they usually sleep in the bed with parents until they are about 2 years of age. They are held, their faces fondled, their cheeks pinched, and they eat and sleep in the midst of human talk and noise from the television, stereo, and radio. Encapsulated in an almost totally human world, they are in the midst of constant human communication, verbal and nonverbal. They literally feel the body signals of shifts in emotion of those who hold them almost continuously; they are talked about and kept in the midst of talk about topics that range over any subject. As children make cooing or babbling sounds, adults refer to this as "noise," and no attempt is made to interpret these sounds as words or communicative attempts on the part of the baby. Adults believe they should not have to depend on their babies to tell them what they need or when they are uncomfortable; adults know, children only "come to know."

When a child can crawl and move about on his or her own, he or she plays with the household objects deemed safe for him or her—pot lids, spoons, plastic food containers. Only at Christmastime are there special toys for very young children; these are usually trucks, balls, doll babies, or plastic cars, but rarely blocks, puzzles, or books. As children become completely mobile, they demand ride toys or electronic and mechanical toys they see on television. They never request nor do they receive manipulative toys, such as puzzles, blocks, take-apart toys or literacy-based items, such as books or letter games.

Adults read newspapers, mail, calendars, circulars (political and civic-events-related), school materials sent home to parents, brochures advertising new cars, television sets, or other products, and the Bible and other church-related materials. There are no reading materials especially for children (with the exception of children's Sunday school materials), and adults do not sit and read to children. Since children are usually left to sleep whenever and wherever they fall asleep, there is no bedtime or naptime as such. At night, they are put to bed when adults go to bed or whenever the person holding them gets tired. Thus going to bed is not framed in any special routine. Sometimes in a play activity during the day an older sibling will read to a younger child, but the latter soon loses interest and squirms away to play. Older children often try to "play school" with younger children, reading to them from books and trying to ask questions about what they have read. Adults look on these efforts with amusement and do not try to persuade the small child to sit still and listen.

Signs from very young children of attention to the nonverbal behaviors of others are rewarded by extra fondling, laughter, and cuddling from adults. For example, when an infant shows signs of recognizing a family member's voice on the phone by bouncing up and down in the arms of the adult who is talking on the phone, adults comment on this to others present and kiss and nudge the child. Yet when children utter sounds or combinations of sounds that could be interpreted as words, adults pay no attention. Often by the time they are 12 months old, children approximate words or phrases of adults' speech; adults respond by laughing or giving special attention to the child and crediting him with "sounding like" the person being imitated. When children learn to walk and imitate the walk of members of the community, they are rewarded by comments on their activities: "He walks just like Toby when he's tuckered out."

Children between the ages of 12 and 24 months often imitate the tune or "general Gestalt" (Peters 1977) of complete utterances they hear around them. They pick up and repeat chunks (usually the ends) or phrasal and clausal utterances of speakers around them. They seem to remember fragments of speech and repeat these without active production. In this first stage of language learning, the *repetition* stage, they imitate the intonation contours and general shaping of the utterances they repeat. Lem (1;2) in the following example illustrates this pattern.

> MOTHER [talking to neighbor on porch while Lem plays with a truck on the porch nearby]: But they won't call back, won't happen=
> LEM: =call back
> NEIGHBOR: Sam's going over there Saturday, he'll pick up a form=
> LEM: =pick up on, pick up on [Lem here appears to have heard "form" as "on"]

The adults pay no attention to Lem's "talk," and their talk, in fact, often overlaps his repetitions.

In the second stage, *repetition with variation*, Trackton children manipulate pieces of conversation they pick up. They incorporate chunks of language from others into their own ongoing dialogue, applying productive rules, inserting new nouns and verbs for those used in the adults' chunks. They also play with rhyming patterns and varying intonation contours.

> MOTHER: She went to the doctor again.
> LEM (2;2): Went to de doctor, doctor, tractor, dis my tractor, [in a singsong fashion] doctor on a tractor, went to de doctor.

Lem creates a monologue, incorporating the conversation about him into his own talk as he plays. Adults pay no attention to his chatter unless it gets so noisy as to interfere with their talk.

In the third stage, *participation*, children begin to enter the ongoing conversations about them. They do so by attracting the adult's attention with a tug on the arm or pant leg, and they help make themselves understood by providing nonverbal reinforcements to help recreate a scene they want the listener to remember. For example, if adults are talking, and a child interrupts with seemingly unintelligible utterances, the child will make gestures or extra sounds, or act out some outstanding features of the scene he is trying to get the adult to remember. Children try to create a context, a scene, for the understanding of their utterance.

This third stage illustrates a pattern in the children's response to their environment and their ways of letting others know their knowledge of the environment. Once they are in the third stage, their communicative efforts are accepted by community members, and adults respond directly to the child instead of talking to others about the child's activities as they have done in the past. Children continue to practice for conversational participation by playing, when alone, both parts of dialogues, imitating gestures as well as intonation patterns of adults. By 2;6 all children in the community can imitate the walk and talk of others in the community or of frequent visitors such as the man who comes around to read the gas meters. They can feign anger, sadness, fussing, remorse, silliness, or any of a wide range of expressive behaviors. They often use the same chunks of language for varying effects, depending on nonverbal support to give the language different meanings or cast it in a different key

(Hymes 1972). Girls between 3 and 4 years of age take part in extraordinarily complex stepping and clapping patterns and simple repetitions of handclap games played by older girls. From the time they are old enough to stand alone, they are encouraged in their participation by siblings and older children in the community. These games require anticipation and recognition of cues for upcoming behaviors, and the young girls learn to watch for these cues and to come in with the appropriate words and movements at the right time.

Preschool children are not asked for what-explanations of their environment. Instead, they are asked a preponderance of analogical questions that call for nonspecific comparisons of one item, event, or person with another: "What's that like?" Other types of questions ask for specific information known to the child but not the adults: "Where'd you get that from?" "What do you want?" "How come you did that?" (Heath 1982b). Adults explain their use of these types of questions by expressing their sense of children: They are "comers," coming into their learning by experiencing what knowing about things means. As one parent of a 2-year-old boy put it: "Ain't no use me tellin' 'im, 'Learn this, learn that, what's this, what's that?' He just gotta learn, gotta know; he see one thing one place one time, he know how it go, see sump'n like it again, maybe it be the same, maybe it won't." Children are expected to learn how to know when the form belies the meaning, and to know contexts of items and to use their understanding of these contexts to draw parallels between items and events. Parents do not believe they have a tutoring role in this learning; they provide the experiences on which the child draws and reward signs of their successfully coming to know.

Trackton children's early stories illustrate how they respond to adult views of them as "comers." The children learn to tell stories by drawing heavily on their abilities to render a context, to set a stage, and to call on the audience's power to join in the imaginative creation of story. Between the ages of 2 and 4 years, the children, in a monologue-like fashion, tell stories about things in their lives, events they see and hear, and situations in which they have been involved. They produce these spontaneously during play with other children or in the presence of adults. Sometimes they make an effort to attract the attention of listeners before they begin the story, but often they do not. Lem, playing off the edge of the porch, when he was about $2\frac{1}{2}$ years of age, heard a bell in the distance. He stopped, looked at Nellie and Benjy, his older siblings, who were nearby, and said:

Way

Far

Now

It a churchbell

Ringin'

Dey singin'

Ringin'

You hear it?

I hear it

Far

Now.

Lem had been taken to church the previous Sunday and had been much impressed by the churchbell. He had sat on his mother's lap and joined in the singing, rocking to and fro on her lap, and clapping his hands. His story, which is like a poem in its imagery and linelike prosody, is in response to the current stimulus of a distant bell. As he tells the story, he sways back and forth.

This story, somewhat longer than those usually reported from other social groups for children as young as Lem,[4] has some features that have come to characterize fully developed narratives or stories. It recapitulates in its verbal outline the sequence of events being recalled by the story-teller. At church, the bell rang while the people sang. In the line "It a churchbell," Lem provides his story's topic and a brief summary of what is to come. This line serves a function similar to the formulas often used by older children to open a story: "This is a story about (a church bell)." Lem gives only the slightest hint of story setting or orientation to the listener; where and when the story took place are capsuled in "Way / Far." Preschoolers in Trackton almost never hear "Once upon a time there was a——" stories, and they rarely provide definitive orientations for their stories. They seem to assume listeners "know" the situation in which the narrative takes place. Similarly, preschoolers in Trackton do not close off their stories with formulaic endings. Lem poetically balances his opening and closing in an *inclusio*, beginning "Way / Far / Now" and ending "Far / Now." The effect is one of closure, but there is no clearcut announcement of closure. Throughout the presentation of action and result of action in their stories, Trackton preschoolers invite the audience to respond or evaluate the story's actions. Lem asks, "You hear it?" which may refer either to the current stimulus or to yesterday's bell, since Lem does not productively use past tense endings for any verbs at this stage in his language development.

Preschool storytellers have several ways of inviting audience evaluation and interest. They may themselves express an emotional response to the story's actions; they may have another character or narrator in the story do so, often using alliterative language play; or they may detail actions and results through direct discourse or sound effects and gestures. All these methods of calling attention to the story and its telling distinguish the speech event as a story, an occasion for audience and story teller to interact pleasantly and not simply to hear an ordinary recounting of events or actions.

Trackton children must be aggressive in inserting their stories into an ongoing stream of discourse. Storytelling is highly competitive.

Everyone in a conversation may want to tell a story, so only the most aggressive wins out. The content ranges widely, and there is "truth" only in the universals of human experience. Fact is often hard to find, though it is usually the seed of the story. Trackton stories often have no point— no obvious beginning or ending; they go on as long as the audience enjoys and tolerates the storyteller's entertainment.

Trackton adults do not separate out the elements of the environment around their children to tune their attentions selectively. They do not simplify their language, focus on single-word utterances by young children, label items or features of objects in either books or the environment at large. Instead, children are continuously contextualized, presented with almost continuous communication. From this ongoing, multiple-channeled stream of stimuli, they must themselves select, practice, and determine rules of production and structuring. For language, they do so by first repeating, catching chunks of sounds and intonation contours, and practicing these without specific reinforcement or evaluation. But practice material and models are continuously available. Next, the children seem to begin to sort out the productive rules for the speech and practice what they hear about them with variation. Finally, they work their way into conversations, hooking their meanings for listeners into a familiar context by recreating scenes through gestures, special sound effects, and so on. These characteristics continue in their story-poems and their participation in jump-rope rhymes. Because adults do not select out, name, and describe features of the environment for the young, children must perceive situations, determine how units of the situations are related to each other, recognize these relations in other situations, and reason through what it will take to show their correlation of one situation with another. The children can answer questions such as "What's that like?" ("It's like Doug's car"), but they can rarely name the specific feature or features that make two items or events alike. For example, in saying a car seen on the street is "like Doug's car," a child may be basing the analogy on the fact that this car has a flat tire and Doug's also had one last week. But the child does not name (and is not asked to name) what is alike between the two cars.

Children seem to develop connections between situations or items not by specification of labels and features in the situations but by configuration links. Recognition of similar general shapes or patterns of links seen in one situation and connected to another seems to be the means by which children set scenes in their nonverbal representations of individuals, and later of their verbal chunking, and then their segmentation and production of rules for putting together isolated units. They do not decontextualize; instead they heavily contextualize nonverbal and verbal language. They fictionalize their "true stories," but they do so by asking the audience to identify with the story through making parallels from their own experiences. When adults read, they often do so in a group. One person, reading aloud, for example, from a brochure on a new car decodes the text and displays illustrations and photographs, and listeners relate the text's meaning to their experiences, asking questions and expressing opinions. Finally, the group as a whole synthesizes the written text and the negotiated oral discourse to construct a meaning for the brochure (Heath 1982a).

When Trackton children go to school, they face unfamiliar types of questions that ask for what-explanations. They are asked as individuals to identify items by name and to label features such as shape, color, size, number. The stimuli to which they are to give these responses are two-dimensional flat representations that are often highly stylized and bear little resemblance to the real items. Trackton children generally score in the lowest percentile range on the Metropolitan Reading Readiness tests. They do not sit at their desks and complete reading workbook pages; neither do they tolerate questions about reading materials that are structured in the usual lesson format. Their contributions are in the form of "I had a duck at my house one time"; "Why'd he do that?" or they imitate the sound effects teachers may produce in stories they read to the children. By the end of the first three primaty grades, their general language-arts scores have been consistently low, except for those few who have begun to adapt to and adopt some of the behaviors they have had to learn in school. But the majority not only fail to learn the content of lessons, but also do not adopt the social-interactional rules for school literacy events. Print in isolation bears little authority in their world. The kinds of questions asked about reading books are unfamiliar. The children's abilities to link metaphorically two events or situations and to recreate scenes are not tapped in the school; in fact, *these abilities often cause difficulties*, because they enable children to see parallels teachers did not intend and, indeed, may not recognize until the children point them out (Heath 1978).

By the end of the lessons or by the time in their total school career when reason-explanations and affective statements call for the creative comparison of two or more situations, it is too late for many Trackton children. They have not picked up along the way the composition and comprehension skills they need to translate their analogical skills into a channel teachers can accept. They seem not to know how to take meaning from reading; they do not observe the rules of linearity in writing, and their expression of themselves on paper is very limited. Taped oral stories are often much better, but these rarely count as much as written compositions. Thus Trackton children continue to collect very low or failing grades, and many decide by the end of the sixth grade to stop trying and turn their attention to the heavy peer socialization that usually begins in these years.

FROM COMMUNITY TO CLASSROOM

A recent review of trends in research on learning pointed out that "learning to read through using and learning from language has been less systematically studied than the decoding process" (Glaser 1979:7).

Put another way, how children learn to use language to read to learn has been less systematically studied than decoding skills. Learning how to take meaning from writing before one learns to read involves repeated practice in using and learning from language through appropriate participation in literacy events such as exhibitor/questioner and spectator/respondent dyads (Scollon & Scollon 1979) or group negotiation of the meaning of a written text. Children have to learn to select, hold, and retrieve content from books and other written or printed texts in accordance with their community's rules or "ways of taking," and the children's learning follows community paths of language socialization. In each society, certain kinds of childhood participation in literacy events may precede others, as the developmental sequence builds toward the whole complex of home and community behaviors charactetistic of the society. The ways of taking employed in the school may in turn build directly on the preschool development, may require substantial adaptation on the part of the children, or may even run directly counter to aspects of the community's pattern.

At Home

In *Maintown* homes, the construction of knowledge in the earliest preschool years depends in large part on labeling procedures and what-explanations. Maintown families, like other mainstream families, continue this kind of classification and knowledge construction throughout the child's environment and into the school years, calling it into play in response to new items in the environment and in running commentaries on old items as they compare to new ones. This pattern of linking old and new knowledge is reinforced in narrative tales that fictionalize the teller's events or recapitulate a story from a book. Thus for these children the bedtime story is simply an early link in a long chain of interrelated patterns of taking meaning from the environment. Moreover, along this chain the focus is on the individual as respondent and cooperative negotiator of meaning from books. In particular, children learn that written language may represent not only descriptions of real events, but decontextualized logical propositions, and the occurrence of this kind of information in print or in writing legitimates a response in which one brings to the interpretation of written text selected knowledge from the real world. Moreover, readers must recognize how certain types of questions assert the priority of meanings in the written word over reality. The "real" comes into play only after prescribed decontextualized meanings; affective responses and reason-explanations follow conventional presuppositions that stand behind what-explanations.

Roadville also provides labels, features, and what-explanations, and prescribes listening and performing behaviors for preschoolers. However, Roadville adults do not carry on or sustain in continually overlapping and interdependent fashion the linking of ways of taking meaning from books to ways of relating that knowledge to other aspects of the environment. They do not encourage decontextualization; in fact, they proscribe it in their own stories about themselves and their requirements of stories from children. They do not themselves make analytic statements or assert universal truths, except those related to their religious faith. They lace their stories with synthetic (non-analytic) statements that express, describe, and synthesize real-life materials. Things do not have to follow logically so long as they fit the past experience of individuals in the community. Thus children learn to look for a specific moral in stories and to expect that story to fit their facts of reality explicitly. When they themselves recount an event, they do the same, constructing the story of a real event according to coaching by adults who want to construct the story as they saw it.

Trackton is like neither Maintown nor Roadville. There are no bedtime stories; in fact, there are few occasions for reading to or with children specifically. Instead, during the time these activities would take place in mainstream and Roadville homes, Trackton children are enveloped in different kinds of social interactions. They are held, fed, talked about, and rewarded for nonverbal, and later verbal, renderings of events they witness. Trackton adults value and respond favorably when children show they have come to know how to use language to show correspondence in function, style, configuration, and positioning between two different things or situations. Analogical questions are asked of Trackton children, although the implicit questions of structure and function these embody are never made explicit. Children do not have labels or names of attributes of items and events pointed out for them, and they are asked for reason-explanations, not what-explanations. Individuals express their personal responses and recreate corresponding situations with often only a minimal adherence to the germ of truth of a story. Children come to recognize similarities of patterning, though they do not name lines, points, or items that are similar between two items or situations. They are familiar with group literacy events in which several community members orally negotiate the meaning of a written text.

At School

In the early reading stages, and in later requirements for reading to learn at more advanced stages, children from the three communities respond differently, because they have learned different methods and degrees of taking from books. In contrast to Maintown children, Roadville children's habits learned in bookreading and toy-related episodes have not continued for them through other activities and types of reinforcement in their environment. They have had less exposure to both the content of books and ways of learning from books than have mainstream children. Thus their need in schools is not necessarily for an intensification of presentation of labels, a slowing down of the sequence of introducing what-explanations in connection with bookreading. Instead they need *extension of these habits to other domains* and to opportunities for practicing habits such as producing running commentaries, creating exhibitor/questioner and spectator/respondent roles, etc. Perhaps, most important, Roadville children need to have articulated for them *distinctions in discourse strategies and structures*. Narratives of real events have certain strategies and structures; imaginary tales, flights of fancy, and affective expressions have others. Their community's view of narrative discourse style is very narrow and demands a passive role in both creation of and response to the account of events. Moreover, these children have *to be reintroduced to a participant frame of reference to a book*. Though initially they were participants in bookreading, they have been trained into passive roles since the age of 3 years, and they must learn once again to be active information givers, taking from books and linking that knowledge to other aspects of their environment.

Trackton students present an additional set of alternatives for procedures in the early primary grades. Since they usually have few of the expected "natural" skills of taking meaning from books, they must not only learn these but also *retain their analogical reasoning practices* for use in some of the later stages of learning to read. They must *learn to adapt the creativity in language, metaphor, fictionalization, recreation of scenes, and exploration of functions and settings of items they bring to school*. These children already use narrative skills highly rewarded in the upper primary grades. They distinguish a fictionalized story from a real-life narrative. They know that telling a story can be in many ways related to play; it suspends reality and frames an old event in a new context; it calls on audience participation to recognize the setting and participants. They must now *learn as individuals to recount factual events in a straightforward way* and *recognize appropriate occasions for reason-explanations and affective expressions*. Trackton children seem to have skipped learning to label, list features, and give what-explanations. Thus they need to *have the mainstream or school habits presented in familiar activities with explanations related to their own habits of taking meaning* from the environment. Such "simple," "natural" things as distinctions between two-dimensional and three-dimensional objects may need to be explained to help Trackton children learn the stylization and decontextualization that characterize books.

To lay out in more specific detail how Roadville's and Trackton's ways of knowing can be used along with those of mainstreamers goes beyond the scope of this paper. However, it must be admitted that a range of alternatives to ways of learning and displaying knowledge characterizes all highly school-successful adults in the advanced stages of their careers. Knowing more about how these alternatives are learned at early ages in different sociocultural conditions can help the schools to provide opportunities for all students to avail themselves of these alternatives early in their school careers. For example, mainstream children can benefit from early exposure to Trackton's creative, highly analogical styles of telling stories and giving explanations, and they can add the Roadville true story with strict chronicity and explicit moral to their repertoire of narrative types.

In conclusion, if we want to understand the place of literacy in human societies and ways children acquire the literacy orientations of their communities, we must recognize two postulates of literacy and language development:

1. Strict dichotomization between oral and literate traditions is a construct of researchers, not an accurate portrayal of reality across cultures.
2. A unilinear model of development in the acquisition of language structures and uses cannot adequately account for culturally diverse ways of acquiring knowledge or developing cognitive styles.

Roadville and Trackton tell us that the mainstream type of literacy orientation is not the only type even among Western societies. They also tell us that the mainstream ways of acquiring communicative competence do not offer a universally applicable model of development. They offer proof of Hymes's assertion a decade ago that "it is impossible to generalize validly about 'oral' vs. 'literate' cultures as uniform types" (1974:54).

Yet in spite of such warnings and analyses of the uses and functions of writing in the specific proposals for comparative development and organization of cultural systems (cf. Basso 1974:432), the majority of research on literacy has focused on differences in class, amount of education, and level of civilization among groups having different literacy characteristics.

"We need, in short, a great deal of ethnography" (Hymes 1973) to provide descriptions of the ways different social groups "take" knowledge from the environment. For written sources, these ways of taking may be analyzed in terms of *types of literacy events*, such as group negotiation of meaning from written texts, individual "looking things up" in reference books, writing family records in Bibles, and the dozens of other types of occasions when books or other written materials are integral to interpretation in an interaction. These must in turn be analyzed in terms of the specific *features of literacy events*, such as labeling, what-explanation, affective comments, reason-explanations, and many other possibilities. Literacy events must also be interpreted in relation to the *larger sociocultural patterns* that they may exemplify or reflect. For example, ethnography must describe literacy events in their sociocultural contexts, so we may come to understand how such patterns as time and space usage, caregiving roles, and age and sex segregation are interdependent with the types and features of literacy events a community develops. It is only on the basis of such thoroughgoing ethnography that further progress is possible toward understanding cross-cultural patterns of oral and written language uses and paths of development of communicative competence.

NOTES

1. First presented at the Terman Conference on Teaching at Stanford University, 1980, this paper has benefited from cooperation with M. Cochran Smith of the University of Pennsylvania. She shares an appreciation of the relevance of Roland Barthes's work for studies of the socialization of young children into literacy; her research (1984) on the storyreading practices of a mainstream school-oriented nursery school provides a much-needed detailed account of early school orientation to literacy.

2. Terms such as *mainstream* and *middle-class* are frequently used in both popular and scholarly writings without careful definition. Moreover, numerous studies of behavioral phenomena (for example, mother–child interactions in language learning) either do not specify that the subjects being described are drawn from mainstream groups or do not recognize the importance of this limitation. As a result, findings from this group are often regarded as universal. For a discussion of this problem, see Chanan & Gilchrist 1974; Payne & Bennett 1977. In general, the literature characterizes this group as school-oriented, aspiring toward upward mobility through formal institutions, and providing enculturation that positively values routines of promptness, linearity (in habits ranging from furniture arrangement to entrance into a movie theatre), and evaluative and judgmental responses to behaviors that deviate from their norms. In the United States, mainstream families tend to locate in neighborhoods and suburbs around cities. Their social interactions center not in their immediate neighborhoods but in voluntary associations across the city. Thus a cluster of mainstream families (and not a community—which usually implies a specific geographic territory as the locus of a majority of social interactions) is the unit of comparison used here with the Trackton and Roadville communities.

3. Behind this discussion are findings from cross-cultural psychologists who have studied the links between verbalization of task and demonstration of skills in a hierarchical sequence, e.g., Childs & Greenfield 1980. See Goody 1979 on the use of questions in learning tasks unrelated to a familiarity with books.

4. Cf. Umiker-Sebeok's (1979) descriptions of stories of mainstream middle-class children, ages 3–5, and Sutton-Smith 1981.

BIBLIOGRAPHY

Basso, K. (1974). The ethnography of writing. In R. Bauman & J. Sherzer (eds.), *Explorations in the Ethnography of Speaking*. Cambridge: Cambridge University Press, pp. 425–32.

Cazden, C. B. (1979). Peekaboo as an instructional model: Discourse development at home and at school. *Stanford Papers and Reports in Child Language Development* 17:1–29.

Chanan, G. & Gilchrist, L. (1974). *What School Is For*. New York: Praeger.

Childs, C. P. & Greenfield, P. M. (1980). Informal modes of learning and teaching. In N. Warren (ed.), *Advances in Cross-Cultural Psychology*, vol. 2. London: Academic Press, pp. 269–316.

Cochran Smith, M. (1984). *The Making of a Reader.* Norwood, N.J.: Ablex.

Cohen, R. (1968). The relation between socio-conceptual styles and orientation to school requirements. *Sociology of Education* 41:201–20.

Cohen, R. (1969). Conceptual styles, culture conflict, and nonverbal tests of intelligence. *American Anthropologist* 71, 5:828–56.

Cohen, R. (1971). The influence of conceptual rule-sets on measures of learning ability. In C. L. Brace, G. Gamble, & J. Bond (eds.), *Race and Intelligence.* Anthropological Studies, no. 8. Washington, D.C.: American Anthropological Association, pp. 41–57.

Glaser, R. (1979). Trends and research questions in psychological research on learning and schooling. *Educational Researcher* 8, 10:6–13.

Goody, E. (1979). Towards a theory of questions. In E. N. Goody (ed.), *Questions and Politeness: Strategies in Social Interaction.* Cambridge: Cambridge University Press, pp. 17–43.

Griffin, P. & Humphry, F. (1978). Task and talk. In *The Study of Children's Functional Language and Education in the Early Years.* Final report to the Carnegie Corporation of New York. Arlington, Va.: Center for Applied Linguistics.

Heath, S. (1978). *Teacher Talk: Language in the Classroom.* Language in Education 9. Arlington, Va.: Center for Applied Linguistics.

Heath, S. (1980). The functions and uses of literacy. *Journal of Communication* 30, 1:123–33.

Heath, S. (1982a). Protean shapes: Ever-shifting oral and literate traditions. In Deborah Tannen (ed.), *Spoken and Written Language: Exploring Orality and Literacy.* Norwood, N.J.: Ablex, pp. 91–118.

Heath, S. (1982b). Questioning at home and at school: A comparative study. In George Spindler (ed.), *Doing Ethnography: Educational Anthropology in Action.* New York: Holt, Rinehart, & Winston, pp. 102–31.

Heath, S. (1983). *Ways with Words: Language, Life and Work in Communities and Classrooms.* Cambridge: Cambridge University Press.

Howard, R. (1974). A note on S/Z. In R. Barthes, *Introduction to S/Z*, trans. Richard Miller. New York: Hill & Wang, pp. ix–xi.

Hymes, D. H. (1972). Models of the interaction of language and social life. In J. J. Gumperz & D. Hymes (eds.), *Directions in Sociolinguistics.* New York: Holt, Rinehart, & Winston, pp. 35–71.

Hymes, D. H. (1973). Speech and language: On the origins and foundations of inequality among speakers. *Daedalus* 102:59–85.

Hymes, D. H. (1974). Speech and language: On the origins and foundations of inequality among speakers. In E. Haugen & M. Bloomfield (eds.), *Language as a Human Problem.* New York: Norton, pp. 45–71.

Kagan, J., Sigel, I., & Moss, H. (1963). Psychological significance of styles of conceptualization. In J. Wright & J. Kagan (eds.), *Basic Cognitive Processes in Children.* Monographs of the Society for Research in Child Development 28, 2:73–112.

Mehan, H. (1979). *Learning Lessons.* Cambridge, Mass.: Harvard University Press.

Merritt, M. (1979). Service-like Events during Individual Work Time and Their Contribution to the Nature of the Rules for Communication. NIE Report EP 78-0436.

Ninio, A. & Bruner, J. (1978). The achievement and antecedents of labelling. *Journal of Child Language* 5:1–15.

Payne, C. & Bennett, C. (1977). "Middle class aura" in public schools. *Teacher Educator* 13, 1:16–26.

Peters, A. (1977). Language learning strategies. *Language* 53:560–73.

Scollon, R. & Scollon, S. (1979). *The Literate Two-Year-Old: The Fictionalization of Self.* Working Papers in Sociolinguistics. Austin: Southwest Regional Laboratory.

Sinclair, J. M. & Coulthard, R. M. (1975). *Toward an Analysis of Discourse.* New York: Oxford University Press.

Sutton-Smith, B. (1981). *The Folkstories of Children.* Philadelphia: University of Pennsylvania Press.

Umiker-Sebeok, J. D. (1979). Preschool children's intraconversational narratives. *Journal of Child Language* 6, 1:91–110.

Witkin, H., Faterson, F., Goodenough, R., & Birnbaum, J. (1966). Cognitive patterning in mildly retarded boys. *Child Development* 37, 2:301–16.

FOR DISCUSSION AND REVIEW

1. Using a few examples, explain what Heath means by "literacy events." How do these events influence the way children in different communities learn to interact with caregivers? What early literacy events do you remember from your childhood?

2. Why is story reading between a parent and young child so important in mainstream families? What do *what-questions* help a young child achieve?

3. Which rules or behaviors of Maintown preschoolers coincide with reading instruction in primary-level classrooms? How do these rules apply to education throughout a person's life? Why are students usually expected to provide what-explanations before they can give reason-explanations or affective commentaries?

4. How are Roadville preschoolers socialized for literacy differently from Maintown children? What literacy events are typical for Roadville children?

5. Why would Roadville children initially do well in school but perhaps become less successful in later grades? What is the "pattern of linking old and new knowledge"? What does it mean that a child becomes a "respondent and cooperative negotiator of meaning"? Why do these become increasingly important as children advance in school?

6. What are some typical literacy events for Trackton children? What types of interactive questioning do adults use with them? How does this questioning differ from the questioning practices used with Maintown and Roadville children?

7. Even though Trackton children can draw parallels between events or situations and tell imaginative stories, many of them do not perform well in school. Why is this the case?

8. Because children use different "ways of taking" knowledge from the environment, what does Heath suggest schools do to improve the learning opportunities for all students?

9. Heath argues against the "time-honored dichotomy of 'the literate tradition' and 'the oral tradition.'" How does her research show that this is a false dichotomy?

54

English Language Learners
in School

Suzanne F. Peregoy and Owen F. Boyle

In the fourth edition of their textbook, Reading, Writing, and Learning in ESL: A Resource Book for K–12 *(2005), Suzanne F. Peregoy, professor of education at San Francisco State University, and Owen F. Boyle, professor of education at San Jose State University, offer sound advice to teachers about creating classroom environments for actively involving ESL students in learning English. In this excerpt from their text, Peregoy and Boyle first provide a number of practical tips to help teachers learn about their students' personal history, literacy experiences, and culture. They also address specific classroom issues—such as using small-group formats, making eye contact, and improving questioning techniques— that may improve a teacher's ability to communicate with English learners. The second half of this piece presents an overview of the various kinds of bilingual programs and English language instructional programs that exist for English language learners. Throughout their discussion, Peregoy and Boyle emphasize learning as a social process and encourage educators to know and capitalize on the "richly diverse backgrounds" of their student English learners.*

In this [selection], we address the concerns of teachers when they first encounter students who are new to English in their classrooms, discussing such questions as the following:

1. Who are English language learners?
2. How can I get to know my English learners when their language and culture are new to me?
3. How do cultural differences affect the way my students respond to me and to my efforts to teach them?
4. How can I ease newcomers into the routines of my class when they understand very little English?
5. How do current policy trends affect English learners?
6. What kinds of programs exist to meet the needs of English language learners?

First, come with us into Buzz Bertolucci's classroom. It is the first day of school in Mr. Bertolucci's first grade. All the children are seated on the rug and have just finished the opening routines with the calendar. After introducing the children to each other through a song, Buzz places a Big Book of *The Gingerbread Man* in front of the class. With its large print and colorful illustrations, the 30-inch-tall Big Book not only captures the children's attention but also helps them understand the story's events. Mr. Bertolucci reads the book to the entire class, points to the pictures, puts on a gingerbread man mask, and acts out words such as "Run, run as fast as you can. You can't catch me. I'm the Gingerbread Man!" The entire book is "read" and acted out by members of the class on this, their first day of school. When the story is finished, one of the school cooks enters the room and hands a note to Mr. Bertolucci. He reads it to the class: "I jumped out of your book and ran to the cafeteria. Come and meet me! The Gingerbread Man." Teacher and children leave for the cafeteria but cannot find the Gingerbread Man there. They ask the cooks if they've seen the Gingerbread Man, but they haven't. Finally, one cook suggests that they look in the oven, and there they find another note from the Gingerbread Man: "I've gone to the janitor's storeroom by the bathrooms. See you there!" The class finds the janitor and asks if he's seen the Gingerbread Man, but he replies that the Gingerbread Man has gone to the nurse's office. When they meet the nurse, the children learn that the Gingerbread Man has gone to the counselor's office and then to the principal's office. Finally, the principal reports that the Gingerbread Man has returned to their classroom. When the children return to the classroom, each one finds a Gingerbread Man cookie at his or her desk.

As the children eat their cookies, Mr. Bertolucci reads *The Gingerbread Man* again. He has introduced his children to literature in an involving way. In addition, he has introduced the new children to their school and to the many people and places in the school they will need to know. He has also presented the literature and its simple theme in a concrete and interesting manner. His children will look forward to the next book he reads in class, and they will look forward to reading and writing themselves.

It may surprise you to learn that more than half the children in Mr. Bertolucci's class are new to the English language, coming from homes in which languages such as Spanish, Cantonese, and Japanese are spoken. Such linguistic variety was not always the case, but changes in the neighborhood over the past ten years have been dramatic. Mr. Bertolucci has responded to these changes by keeping many of his favorite teaching routines, such as the Gingerbread Man, but modifying them to meet the needs of his English language learners. You may be facing similar changes in your school, given today's immigration patterns. In this [selection, we first] want to introduce you to the great diversity among the children who are called English language learners, to help you better understand and integrate them into your classroom and school. We use the terms *English language learners* and *English learners* to refer to non-native English speakers who are learning English in school.

Typically, English learners speak a primary language other than English at home, such as Spanish, Cantonese, Russian, Hmong, and French. English learners vary in their proficiency in their primary languages. Of course, they vary in English language proficiency as well. Those who are beginners to intermediates in English are often referred to as *limited English proficient (LEP)*, a term that is used in federal legislation and other official documents. We will use the terms *English learners, English language learners, non-native English speakers,* and *second language learners* synonymously . . . to refer to students who are in the process of learning English as a new language. Our main concern is with those who are at the beginning or intermediate stages of English language acquisition. The terms *English as a Second Language (ESL)* and *English for Speakers of Other Languages (ESOL)* are often used to refer to the acquisition of English as a non-native language. We continue to use the former term because it is widely used and descriptive, even though what we refer to as a "second language" might actually be a student's third or fourth language. A synonym for ESL . . . is *English Language Development (ELD)*.

WHO ARE ENGLISH LANGUAGE LEARNERS?

Students who speak English as a non-native language live in all areas of the United States. The number of English language learners has steadily increased in recent decades, nearly doubling between 1992 and 2002 when survey results estimated that 4,747,763 English language learners were enrolled in U.S. public schools in grades pre-K through 12. During that time, English learner enrollment increased at almost eight times the rate of total student enrollment (Padolsky, 2002a, 2002b). Many English learners are sons and daughters of immigrants who have left their home countries to seek a better life. Some recent immigrants have left countries brutally torn by war or political strife in regions such as Southeast Asia, Central America, the Middle East, and Eastern Europe. Others have immigrated for economic reasons. Still others come to be reunited with families who are already here or or to seek educational opportunities they may find in the United States. Finally, many English learners were born in the United States, and some of them, such as Native Americans of numerous tribal heritages, have roots in American soil that go back for countless generations.

Whether immigrant or native born, each group brings its own history and culture to the enterprise of schooling (Heath, 1986). Furthermore, each group contributes to the rich tapestry of languages and cultures that form the basic fabric of the United States. Our first task as teachers, then, is to become aware of our students' personal histories and cultures, so as to understand their feelings, frustrations, hopes, and aspirations. At the same time, as teachers we need to look closely at ourselves to discover how our own culturally ingrained attitudes, beliefs, assumptions, and communication styles play out in our teaching and affect our students' learning. By developing such understanding, we create the essential foundation for meaningful instruction, including reading and writing instruction. As understanding grows, teacher and students alike can come to an awareness of both diversity and universals in human experience, as shared in this poem by a high school student who emigrated with her parents from Cambodia (Mullen & Olsen, 1990).

You And I Are The Same
You and I are the same
but we don't let our hearts see.
Black, White and Asian
Africa, China, United States and all other
countries around the world
Peel off their skin
Like you peel an orange
See their flesh
like you see in my heart
Peel off their meat
And peel my wickedness with it too
Until there's nothing left
but bones.
Then you will see that you and I
are the same.

> –by Kien Po (Kien Po, "You and I Are the Same," 1990, San Francisco: California Tomorrow. Reprinted with permission of the author.)

HOW CAN I GET TO KNOW MY ENGLISH LEARNERS?

Given the variety and mobility among second language groups, it is likely that most teachers, including specialists in bilingual education or ESL, will at some time encounter students whose language and culture they know little about. Perhaps you are already accustomed to working with students of diverse cultures, but if you are not, how can you develop an understanding of students from unfamiliar linguistic and cultural backgrounds? Far from a simple task, the process requires not only fact finding but also continual observation and interpretation of children's behavior, combined with trial and error in communication. Thus, the process is one that must take place gradually.

Getting Basic Information When a New Student Arrives

When a new student arrives, we suggest three initial steps. First of all, begin to find out basic facts about the child: What country is the child from? How long has he or she lived in the United States? Where and with whom is the child living? What language or languages are spoken in the home? If the child is an immigrant, what were the circumstances of immigration? Some children have experienced traumatic events before and during immigration, and the process of adjustment to a new country may represent yet another link in a chain of stressful life events (Olsen, 1998).

Second, obtain as much information about the student's prior school experiences as possible. School records may be available if the child has already been enrolled in a U.S. school. However, as you are not likely to receive a cumulative folder forwarded from another country, you may need to piece the information together yourself, a task that requires resourcefulness, imagination, and time. Some school districts collect background information on students when they register, as well as administer English language proficiency tests. Thus, your own district office is one possible source of information. In addition, you may need the assistance of someone who is familiar with the home language and culture, such as another teacher, a paraprofessional, or a community liaison, who can ask questions of parents, students, or siblings. Keep in mind that some children may have had no previous schooling, despite their age, or perhaps their schooling has been interrupted. Other students may have attended school in their home countries. Students with prior educational experience bring various kinds of knowledge to school subjects and may be quite advanced. Be prepared to validate your students for their special knowledge. We saw how important this was for fourth-grader Li Fen, a recent immigrant from mainland China who found herself in a regular English language classroom, knowing not a word of English. Li Fen was a bright child, but naturally somewhat reticent to involve herself in classroom activities during her first month in the class. She made a real turnaround, however, the day the class was studying long division. Li Fen accurately solved three problems at the chalkboard in no time at all, though her procedure differed slightly from the one in the math book. Her classmates were duly impressed with her mathematical competence and did not hide their admiration. Her teacher, of course, gave her a smile with words of congratulations. From that day forward, Li Fen participated more readily, having earned a place in the class.

When you are gathering information on your students' prior schooling, it's important to find out whether they are literate in their home language. If they are, you might encourage them to keep a journal using their native language, and if possible, you should acquire native language books, magazines, or newspapers to have on hand for the new student. In this way, you validate the student's language, culture, and academic competence, while providing a natural bridge to English reading. *Make these choices with sensitivity, though, building on positive responses from your students.* Bear in mind, for example, that some newcomers may not wish to be identified as different from their classmates. We make this caveat because of our experience with a 7-year-old boy, recently arrived from Mexico, who attended a school where everyone spoke English only. When we spoke to him in Spanish, he did not respond, giving the impression that he did not know the language. When we visited his home and spoke Spanish with his parents, he was not pleased. At that point in his life, he may have wanted nothing more than to blend into the dominant social environment, in this case an affluent, European American neighborhood saturated with English.

The discomfort felt by this young boy is an important reminder of the internal conflict experienced by many youngsters as they come to terms with life in a new culture. As they learn English and begin to fit into school routines, they embark on a personal journey toward a new cultural identity. If they come to reject their home language and culture, moving toward maximum assimilation into the dominant culture, they may experience alienation from their parents and family. A moving personal account of such a journey is provided, for example, by journalist Richard Rodriquez in his book *Hunger of Memory* (1982). Even if English learners strive to adopt the ways of the new culture without replacing those of the home, they will have departed significantly from many traditions their parents hold dear. Thus, for many students the generation gap necessarily widens to the extent that the values, beliefs, roles, responsibilities, and general expectations differ between the home culture and the dominant one. Keeping this in mind may help you empathize with students' personal conflicts of identity and personal life choices.

The third suggestion, then, is to become aware of basic features of the home culture, such as religious beliefs and customs, food preferences and restrictions, and roles and responsibilities of children and adults (Ovando, Collier, & Combs, 2003; Saville-Troike, 1978). These basic bits of information, though sketchy, will guide your initial interactions with your new students and may help you avoid asking them to say or do things that may be prohibited or frowned upon in the home culture, including such common activities as celebrating birthdays, pledging allegiance to the flag, and eating hot dogs. Finding out basic information also provides a starting point from which to interpret your newcomer's responses to you, to your other students, and to the ways you organize classroom activities. Just as you make adjustments, your students will also begin to make adjustments as they grow in the awareness and acceptance that ways of acting, dressing, eating, talking, and behaving in school are different to a greater or lesser degree from what they may have experienced before.

Classroom Activities That Let You Get to Know Your Students

Several fine learning activities may also provide some of the personal information you need to help you know your students better. One way is to have all your students write an illustrated autobiography, "All About Me" or "The Story of My Life." Each book may be bound individually, or all the life stories may be bound together and published in a class book, complete with illustrations or photographs. Alternatively, student stories may be posted on the bulletin board for all to read. This assignment lets you in on the lives of all your students and permits them to get to know, appreciate, and understand each other as well. Of particular importance, this activity does not single out your newcomers because all your students will be involved.

Personal writing assignments like the one mentioned lend themselves to many grade levels because personal topics remain pertinent across age groups even into adulthood. Students who speak little or no English may begin by illustrating a series of important events in their lives, perhaps to be captioned with your assistance or that of another student. In addition, there are many ways to accommodate students' varying English writing abilities. For example, if students write more easily in their native tongue than in English, allow them to do so. If needed, ask a bilingual student or paraprofessional to translate the meaning for you. Be sure to publish the student's story as written in the native language, because you will thereby both validate the home language and expose the rest of the class to a different language and its writing system. If a student knows some English but is not yet able to write, allow her or him to dictate the story to you or to another student in the class.

Another way to begin to know your students is to start a dialogue journal with them. Provide each student with a blank journal and allow the student to draw or write in the language of the student's choice. You may then respond to the students' journal entries on a periodic basis. Interactive dialogue journals . . . have proven useful for English learners of all ages (Kreeft, 1984). Dialogue journals make an excellent introduction to literacy and facilitate the development of an ongoing personal relationship between the student and you, the teacher. As with personal writing, this activity is appropriate for all students, and if you institute it with the entire class you provide a way for newcomers to participate in a "regular" class activity, Being able to do what others do can be a source of great pride and self-satisfaction to students who are new to the language and culture of the school.

Finally, many teachers start the school year with a unit on themes such as "Where We Were Born" or "Family Origins." Again, this activity is relevant to all students, whether immigrant or native-born, and it gives teacher and students alike a chance to know more about themselves and each other. A typical activity with this theme is the creation of a world map with a string connecting each child's name and birthplace to your city and school. Don't forget to put your name on the list along with your birthplace! From there, you and your students may go on to study more about the various regions and countries of origin. Clearly, this type of theme leads in many directions, including the discovery of people in the community who may be able to share information about their home

> **Example 54.1 A Few Important Books on Multicultural Teaching**
>
> Banks, J. A. (2003). *Teaching strategies for ethnic studies* (7th ed.). Boston: Allyn and Bacon.
> Garcia, E. (2001). *Understanding and meeting the challenge of student cultural diversity* (3rd ed.). Boston: Houghton Mifflin.
> Igoa, C. (1995). *The inner world of the immigrant child.* New York: St. Martin's Press.
> Nieto, S. (2004). *Affirming diversity: The sociopolitical context of multicultural education* (4th ed.). Boston: Allyn and Bacon.
> Tiedt, P. L., & Tiedt, I. M. (2002). *Multicultural teaching: A handbook of activities, information, and resources* (6th ed.). Boston: Allyn and Bacon.

countries with your class. Your guests may begin by sharing food, holiday customs, art, or music with students. Through such contact, through theme studies, through life stories, and through reading about cultures in books such as those listed in Example 54.1 you may begin to become aware of some of the more subtle aspects of the culture, such as how the culture communicates politeness and respect, or how the culture views the role of children, adults, and the school. If you are lucky enough to find such community resources, you will not only enliven your teaching but broaden your cross-cultural understanding as well (Ada & Zubizarreta, 2001).

Not all necessary background information will emerge from these classroom activities. You will no doubt want to look into cultural, historical, and geographical resources available at your school or community library. In addition, you may find resource personnel at your school including paraprofessionals and resource teachers, who can help with specific questions or concerns. In the final analysis, though, your primary source of information is the students themselves as you interrelate on a day-to-day basis.

HOW DO CULTURAL DIFFERENCES AFFECT TEACHING AND LEARNING?

The enterprise of teaching and learning is deeply influenced by "culture" in a variety of ways. To begin with, schools themselves reflect the values, beliefs, and practices of the larger society. In fact schools represent a major socializing force for all students, albeit a somewhat foreign one for many English learners. In addition, teachers and students bring to the classroom particular cultural orientations that affect how they perceive and interact with each other in the classroom. As teachers of

English learners, most of us will encounter students whose languages and cultures differ from our own. Thus we need to learn about our students and their cultures while at the same time reflecting on how our own culturally rooted behaviors may facilitate or interfere with teaching and learning (Trumbull, Rothstein-Fisch, & Greenfield, 2000). In this section we define basic aspects of culture in the classroom as a starting point for looking at ourselves and our students in this light.

In order to learn about your students through personal interactions. you may need to hone your skills in observing and interpreting their behavior. Such skills are especially important when you first meet your students, whether at the beginning of the school year or when they first enroll in your class. One procedure to help focus your observations is to keep a journal in which you jot notes at the end of each day concerning how your new student is doing. Does she understand basic school rules such as hand raising? Is he starting to form friendships? What activities does your new student seem to be happiest doing: small-group activities, individual seatwork, listening to stories, drawing pictures? In which activities is the student reluctant? By noticing activities that are most comfortable for students, you can make sure that your newcomer has frequent opportunities to participate in them. In this way, you build a positive attitude toward what may as yet be an alien environment: school. From there, you may gradually draw the student into other school routines.

Culture in the Classroom Context

When you make observations in your classroom, you are actually using some of the tools used by anthropologists when they study another culture through ethnography (e.g., introspection, interviewing, observation, and participant observation). As the teacher, you are automatically both participant and observer in the classroom culture. However, you will need to step back at times to reflect introspectively on how your classroom operates. In addition, you may want to take time to observe your students during independent and small-group activity. In this way, you will have the opportunity to give full attention to how your students are functioning socially in your classroom.

In order to make the most of your introspective reflections and observations, you may need some concepts to guide interpretations. In other words, it's one thing to notice that Nazrene "tunes out" during whole-class lessons but quite another to figure out why, so that you can alter your instruction to reach her. To provide you with some interpretive touchstones, we suggest you consider for a moment some of the aspects that constitute culture, because these represent potential sources of overt conflict or silent suffering if your classroom rules and structures conflict with those already culturally engrained in your students.

Definitions of Culture and Its Content

Culture may be defined as the shared beliefs, values, and rule-governed patterns of behavior that define a group and are required for group membership (Goodenough, 1981; Saville-Troike, 1978). Thus defined, culture comprises three essential aspects: what people know and believe, what people do, and what people make and use. Every child is born into the culture of a particular group of people, and through the culture's child-rearing practices every child is socialized, to a greater or lesser extent, toward becoming first a "good boy" or "good girl" and ultimately a "good man" or "good woman" in the eyes of the culture. Thus, culture may be thought of as the acquired knowledge people use both to interpret experience and generate behavior (Spradley, 1980).

For the purposes of understanding your students, we summarize in Table 54.1 cultural content with questions outlined by Saville-Troike (1978). The content of culture may be categorized into various components, including (1) family structure; (2) definitions of stages, periods, or transitions during a person's life; (3) roles of children and adults and corresponding behavior in terms of power and politeness; (4) discipline; (5) time and space; (6) religion; (7) food; (8) health and hygiene; and (9) history, traditions, holidays, and celebrations. Table 54.1 provides a number of questions that you might ask yourself about these aspects of culture. As you read the questions, try to answer them for your own culture as well as for a different cultural group in order to get a sense of similarities and differences across cultures.

When students in our university classes discuss the questions in Table 54.1 according to their family traditions, interesting patterns emerge. Although many students identify with middle-class, European American cultural values, such as punctuality, some also add special traditions passed down from immigrant grandparents or great-grandparents, including special foods and holiday traditions. Other students come from families who have been in this country for centuries, yet maintain particular regional traditions such as herbal healing practices. In addition, some students have maintained strong religious traditions, such as Buddhist, Catholic, Greek Orthodox, Judaic, Muslim, and traditional Native American beliefs. From these discussions, we find that each individual actually embodies a variety of cultures and subcultures.

One student found the cultural questions an interesting way to look at her own family. Her parents had met and married in Germany, her father an Egyptian and Coptic Christian, her mother a German Catholic. From there they moved with their three young children to the United States. Najia reflected, with some amusement, on how different her German relatives were from her Egyptian relatives. For example, her German relatives visited once or twice a year, making plans well in advance and staying a short, predetermined amount of time. Her Egyptian relatives, in contrast, "couldn't seem to get enough of each other." They loved long

TABLE 54.1   Cultural Content and Questions

CULTURAL CONTENT	QUESTIONS
Family structures	What constitutes a family? Who among these or others live in one house? What are the rights and responsibilities of each family member? What is the hierarchy of authority? What is the relative importance of the individual family member in contrast to the family as a whole?
The life cycles	What are the criteria for defining stages, periods, or transitions in life? What rites of passage are there? What behaviors are considered appropriate for children of different ages? How might these conflict with behaviors taught or encouraged in school? How is the age of the children computed? What commemoration, if any, is made of the child's birth and when?
Roles and interpersonal relationships	What roles are available to whom, and how are they acquired? Is education relevant to learning these roles? How do the roles of girls and women differ from those of boys and men? How do people greet each other? What forms of address are used between people of differing roles? Do girls work and interact with boys? Is it proper? How is deference shown and to whom and by whom?
Discipline	What is discipline? What counts as discipline and what doesn't? Which behaviors are considered socially acceptable for boys versus girls at different ages? Who or what is considered responsible if a child misbehaves? The child? Parents? Older siblings? The environment? Is blame even ascribed? Who has authority over whom? To what extent can one person impose his or her will on another? How is behavior traditionally controlled? To what extent and in what domains?
Time and space	How important is punctuality? How important is speed in completing a task? Are there restrictions associated with certain seasons? What is the spatial organization of the home? How much space are people accustomed to? What significance is associated with different locations or directions, including north, south, east, west?
Religion	What restrictions are there concerning topics discussed in school? Are dietary restrictions to be observed, including fasting on particular occasions? When are these occasions? What restrictions are associated with death and the dead?
Food	What is eaten? In what order and how often is food eaten? Which foods are restricted? Which foods are typical? What social obligations are there with regard to food giving, reciprocity, and honoring people? What restrictions or proscriptions are associated with handling, offering, or discarding food?
Health and hygiene	How are illnesses treated and by whom? What is considered to be the cause? If a student were involved in an accident at school, would any of the common first aid practices be considered unacceptable?
History, traditions, holidays	Which events and people are sources of pride for the group? To what extent does the group in the United States identify with the history and traditions of the country of origin? What holidays and celebrations are considered appropriate for observing in school? Which ones are appropriate only for private observance?

visits, with as many of the family together as possible. Najia's German mother emphasized orderliness and punctuality in the home, with carefully scheduled and planned meals. The family ate at the specified hour, and all were expected to be there on time. With such differences concerning time and space, Najia wondered that her parents were able to make a highly successful marriage. She attributed their success in part to their individual personalities: her mother, an artist, is by nature easy-going and flexible; her father, an electronic engineer, is an organized thinker and planner. As individuals, they seemed compatible with many of each other's cultural ways. Najia's reflections are a reminder that people's behavior combines both cultural and individual differences.

Sociolinguistic Interactions in the Classroom

One particularly important aspect of culture that can affect teaching and learning has to do with the ways you use language during instruction. Because teaching and learning depend on clear communication between teacher and students, the communicative success of teacher–student interactions is crucial. Early on, difficulties may arise from lack of a common language. However, communication difficulties may persist even after students have acquired the basics of English if the student and teacher are following different sociocultural rules about how to use language (Cazden, 1986). For example, if the home culture values strict authority of adults over children and if children are only supposed to speak when spoken to, then these same children may be reluctant to volunteer an answer in class. You might quite logically interpret this reluctance as disinterest or lack of knowledge, when in fact the student may simply be waiting for you to invite him or her to respond. On the other hand, some students may not want to answer your questions because displaying knowledge in class amounts to showing off, causing them to stand out like a sore thumb (Philips, 1983). Some students consider enthusiastic knowledge display impolite because it could make their friends appear ignorant. These examples illustrate how cultural values affecting language use may impede teacher–student communication in either English or the home language.

Language use differences can be especially confusing in the realm of teacher questioning. Research has shown that teachers often do not allow much "wait time" after asking a question in class (Rowe, 1974). It turns out that what is considered enough wait time in normal conversations varies across cultures, as do rules concerning how and when to interrupt and the number of people who may speak at once (Bauman & Scherzer, 1974; Ochs & Schieffelin, 1984; Schieffelin & Eisenberg, 1984; Shultz, Erickson, & Florio, 1982). In addition, students must learn what the teacher's rules are regarding who can speak with whom and when (Mehan, 1979). These rules may vary with the activity structure (e.g., teacher-led lesson versus small-group projects). Another aspect of teacher questioning that may be problematic is that teachers typically ask questions with a particular answer in mind, in order to assess what students know or have learned. For some students, these "known-answer" questions might be considered odd or of dubious purpose (Heath, 1983; Mehan, 1979), resulting in student reluctance to participate in such interrogations. You might want to reflect on your own questioning practices in terms of wait time, question types, and the actual phrasing you use. If your questions are greeted with blank stares, try altering your questioning style. Another possibility is to introduce question/answer sessions with a brief explanation of what you are trying to accomplish and why. That way, if students are unaccustomed to your question types, you will at least help them understand your purpose for asking them.

Culturally Related Responses to Classroom Organization

There are other cultural differences that may interfere with student participation in learning activities in the classroom. One of these is the social organization of lessons (Mehan, 1979). Within the constraints of time and adult assistance, teachers typically utilize whole-class, small-group, and individualized formats for instruction. It is important to recognize that these formats represent distinctly different types of *participation structures* (Philips, 1983), each with its own rules about when to speak and how. Students may experience various degrees of comfort or discomfort with these various formats, based on both cultural and individual differences (Au & Jordan, 1981). For example, the use of small groups for cooperative learning has become a major thrust toward increasing learning for all students but especially for ethnic minority students (Kagan, 1986). The rationale is that many ethnic minority cultures instill strong values of group cooperation, and, therefore, such instruction will build on home experience. In addition, cooperative groups provide students with practice in getting along with people different from themselves to the extent that groups consist of students with different backgrounds. We are convinced that cooperative group learning is a valuable tool for teachers, for the reasons described. However, it is important to keep in mind that some students may feel that the teacher, as the academic authority, is the only proper person to learn from in the classroom. One way to accommodate such students is to balance your use of group work with necessary teacher-directed instruction. When you do ask students to work in cooperative groups, you need to explain your reasons for doing so, thereby showing that group learning is valid academically. In fact, parents may need to hear your reasons as well. We knew one child who was functioning beautifully in cooperative groups, yet during parent conferences, his father politely asked when we were going to start teaching! Cultural differences in teaching practices thus present challenges to teachers, students, and parents alike.

In summary, we know that different students may be more comfortable with some instructional formats than with others and that their feelings stem from both cultural and individual preferences. We suggest you *use a variety of formats to meet the multiple needs of your diverse students*. Your best route is to be aware of how you create the participation structures of learning (i.e., grouping formats) in order to observe and interpret student responses with thoughtful sensitivity, making modifications as needed.

Literacy Traditions from Home and Community

As you approach the teaching of reading and writing to English learners, you will want to be aware of the literacy knowledge your students bring with them. Literacy knowledge will stem not only from prior schooling but also from experiences with the ways reading and writing are used in the home and community (Au & Jordan, 1981; Boggs, 1972; Heath, 1983). It is helpful to become aware of how reading and writing are traditionally used in the community because these traditional literacy uses will influence your students' ideas, beliefs, and assumptions about reading and writing. You will want to build on these ideas and make sure to expand them to include the functions of literacy required by U.S. schools and society. Let us make this concept more clear through some examples.

Gustavo, age 7, entered the first grade of an urban elementary school in February, halfway through the academic year. He had come from rural Mexico, and this was his first time in school. He didn't even know how to hold a pencil. At first, he was so intimidated that he would refuse to come into the classroom at the beginning of the school day. With persistent coaxing from the teacher and her assistant, he reluctantly complied. Once in, Gustavo was anxious to fit into the normal class routines. He loved to wave his hand in the air when the teacher asked a question, although at first he didn't know what to do when called on. That part of the routine took a little time to master.

One day, as we were chatting with Gustavo, he began to tell us all about his little town in Michoacán, about the travails of the trip *pa' 'l norte* (to the north), and then about an incident when his 2-year-old sister became critically ill. His mother, he recounted, knew what medicine the baby needed, but it was only available in Mexico. So they had to "find someone who could write" to send to Mexico for the medicine. They did, and Gustavo's baby sister recovered.

What does this story tell us about the concept of literacy that Gustavo offers for the teacher to build on? First, we can surmise that

Gustavo has not had extensive opportunities to explore reading and writing at home. He probably has not been read to much, nor has he been provided with paper and pencils for dabbling in drawing and writing—the very activities so highly recommended today as the foundation of literacy development. On the other hand, he is well aware of how important it is to be able to write—it was a matter of life and death for his sister! Furthermore, he is aware of the inconveniences, not to say dangers, of illiteracy. Thus, Gustavo, at the tender age of 7, brings a deeper understanding of the importance of literacy than many children whose rich early literacy experiences allow them to take such things for granted. Gustavo's motivation and understanding provide the foundation for the teacher to build on. Gustavo needs daily exposure to the pleasures and practical functions of print through stories, poems, rhymes, labels, letters, notes, recipes, board games, instructions, and more. With practice and hard work, his proudest moment will come when he himself writes the next letter to Mexico.

In contrast to Gustavo, students who immigrate when older often bring substantial experience and skill in reading and writing in their home language. These experiences and skills provide a good foundation for learning to read and write in English. Students who read in their home language already know that print bears a systematic relationship to spoken language, that print carries meaning, and that reading and writing can be used for many purposes. Moreover, literate students know that they are capable of making sense of written language. Such experience and knowledge will transfer directly to learning to read and write in English, given English language development and appropriate literacy instruction (Cummins, 1981; Hudelson, 1987; Odlin, 1989). Thus, when students arrive with home language literacy skills, teachers do not have to start all over again to teach reading and writing (Goodman, Goodman, & Flores, 1979; Peregoy, 1989; Peregoy & Boyle, 1991, Peregoy & Boyle, 2000). Rather, they can build on a more sophisticated base of literacy knowledge, adding the specifics for English as needed. . . .

CURRENT POLICY TRENDS AFFECTING THE EDUCATION OF ENGLISH LEARNERS

Whether you are new or experienced in the field of education, media reports have no doubt introduced you to various reform efforts in education, many of which have been promoted by federal and state education policy. Because disparate needs and interests are served by education policy, and because there are always divergent points of view as to how any problem may be solved, the arena of educational policy is filled with controversy and debate. In this section, we briefly discuss education policies affecting English learners across the nation and offer additional resources on this complex topic.

Academic Standards and Assessment

The implementation of academic standards and assessment permeates all levels of education today. If you are in a teaching credential program, for example, chances are your coursework is organized to teach and assess what you should know and be able to do to be an effective teacher. Similarly, standards have been delineated for K–12 students that specifically define the knowledge and skills that students must attain for promotion and graduation in subjects such as reading, math, science, social science, and English language arts. In addition, standards have been developed that specifically address English language development for students new to English (e.g., Teachers of English to Speakers of Other Languages, 1997; California State Department of Education, 2002). Teachers generally need to become familiar with the standards of the content areas they teach, as well as with standards specific to English learners. In this section, we introduce you to basic issues in standards-based reforms. . . .

The standards and assessment movement traces its origins to *A Nation at Risk* (National Commission on Excellence in Education, 1983), a national report funded by the U.S. Congress that called for improvement in education across the country. Among the outcomes of the report was the development of the National Assessment of Education Progress (NAEP), a large scale, national assessment program that permits comparisons among states on student achievement in reading, writing, and mathematics. By conducting periodic assessments of students in grades 4, 8, and 12, NAEP is able to provide the public with a "report card" on how well students are doing across the nation. NAEP findings have been used to spur education reforms, such as the reading instruction reforms of the 1990s, aimed at increasing student achievement. The current focus on rigorous academic standards, assessment, and accountability can all be traced back to the reforms called for in *A Nation at Risk*.

In recent years the push for high academic standards and achievement has gained momentum. In order for students to achieve high academic standards, Congress encouraged national education organizations and state departments of education to develop rather detailed descriptions of curriculum content to be taught across the grades in subjects such as reading, mathematics, social science, science, and English language arts. Standards documents are generally structured to include (1) content standards that delineate what students should know and be able to do, (2) benchmarks that specify expected knowledge and skills for each content standard at different grade levels, and (3) progress indicators that describe how well students need to do in order to meet a given content standard (Laturnau, 2003). Criteria for achievement are thus built in to the standards.

High-Stakes Testing

Hand in glove with the use of curriculum standards is the implementation of high-stakes, standardized testing to measure how well standards are being met. Serious consequences may be applied when standards are not met, supposedly to motivate achievement and increase accountability (Ananda & Rabinowitz, 2000). For example, performance on a high school exit exam may determine whether a student will receive a high school diploma, regardless of passing grades in all required high school coursework. Similarly, standardized test performance may play a part in deciding grade retention or promotion of students in elementary, middle, and high school. School funding may depend on raising test scores. Furthermore, teachers and principals may be held directly accountable for student achievement (Afflerbach, 2002). Low-achieving schools, for example, may be subject to restaffing measures, in which teachers and principal are moved elsewhere and a totally new staff brought in.

The teeth in the jaws of high-stakes testing have been sharpened by the *No Child Left Behind Act of 2001* (NCLB Act), federal legislation reauthorizing the *Elementary and Secondary Education Act* (ESEA) originally passed in 1965 to improve academic performance among lower-achieving, "economically disadvantaged" students. While standardized tests have long been used to identify students who qualify for educational assistance, the new law raises standardized testing to a higher pitch, requiring states to implement "accountability systems" covering all public schools and students. All students in grades 3 through 8 are to be tested by rigorous standards in reading and math. In addition, states are to establish and meet "progress objectives" ensuring that *all* groups of students reach academic proficiency within 12 years. In order to monitor the progress of "all groups,' "test results are to be broken out by poverty, race, ethnicity, disability and limited English proficiency" (U.S. Office of Elementary and Secondary Education, 2002, p. 1). Schools that meet or exceed their progress objectives will be eligible for an "achievement award," whereas those who fall below must improve or be subject to "corrective action," such as restaffing. The Act thus places tremendous pressures on schools serving groups who tend to score lower on standardized tests than their middle- and upper-class, white counterparts.

Over the decades *socioeconomic status* has proven to be one of the strongest predictors of standardized test performance. Children from low-income families consistently score lower than those in more affluent circumstances, and racial, ethnic, and language minority students are overrepresented in the lower income brackets. Unfortunately, it is not clear that mandating achievement will improve learning or even raise test scores, especially with the high-pressure atmosphere it creates. For example, we have heard young children anxiously voice concern that their test performance might cause their favorite teacher to be moved to another school.

Equally problematic is the danger that test scores may be used inappropriately either to retain students or to sort them into less challenging instructional programs. Even worse, high-stakes testing may actually increase the already high dropout rate among racial, ethnic, and language minority students. Because of the lifelong consequences of educational decisions based on high-stakes testing, it is essential that these tests be proven both fair and valid for all students, especially those living in poverty. Therefore, constant scrutiny is needed to monitor the effects of high-stakes testing to ensure that all students are provided meaningful and equitable access to a high-quality education, one that welcomes them in rather than pushing them out, one that broadens their life choices rather than narrowing them (Escamilla, Mahon, Riley-Bernal, & Ruteledge, 2003; Valdez Pierce, 2003).

In addition to issues related to socioeconomic status, testing and progress mandates such as those in NCLB pose special problems for many students new to English. First of all, *English proficiency* affects student performance and may render test results inaccurate if not totally invalid (Abedi, 2001; Abedi, Leon, & Mirocha, 2001). If performance is low, it may not be clear whether the cause is limited English knowledge, insufficient content knowledge, or a combination of both. In addition to English language proficiency, other factors may affect English learners' preparedness for successful performance, including the amount, quality, content, and continuity of prior schooling relative to the content and format of the test.

Furthermore, the NCLB actually requires an *accelerated learning pace* for English learners in order to close the achievement gap between them and the general student population. With research showing that it takes five to ten years to development academic language proficiency (Thomas & Collier, 1997, 2002), this progress mandate is ill-informed and highly unrealistic for many English learners. Finally, it is important to remember that English proficiency is necessary but not sufficient for academic achievement in an English language curriculum. It takes more than knowledge of the language to make progress in school. Quality instruction, a safe and supportive school environment, student motivation, and parental support are also factors that come into play.

In summary, in recent decades we have witnessed a tidal wave of movement calling for high educational standards and assessment. In the past, curriculum content has been generally similar in schools across the country, but states and local communities have always retained control over the specifics. However, the national standards and assessment movement is leading toward a standardized, uniform national curriculum. Whether these reforms will finally help or hinder learning among *all* students remains to be seen. More problematic is the implementation of high-stakes testing, the effects of which have the potential to create larger divisions between rich and poor, between those with power and those without.

Education Policy Specific to English Learners

While English learners are affected by general education policy, they are also subject to policies specific to their English proficiency status. Federal law requires schools to identify and serve students in need of educational support based on English language proficiency. The purpose of such educational support is twofold: (1) to promote English language development and (2) to provide meaningful instruction so that students may learn academic content appropriate to their grade level. Schools are free to choose the kind of program that will best meet the needs of their students, including whether students' primary language will be used for instruction or not. Since 1968 when the ESEA Title VII Bilingual Education Act was passed, bilingual education programs have been developed throughout the country, utilizing such languages as Spanish, Vietnamese, Chinese, Japanese, French, and Portuguese. In addition, bilingual programs have served numerous Native American languages such as Navajo, Cherokee, and Crow. However, with the passage of the NCLB Act, the bilingual education provisions of ESEA Title VII have *not* been reauthorized for the first time in history. The current reauthorization of the ESEA thus effectively eliminates federal support for (but does not prohibit) bilingual instructional programs.

Instead of supporting bilingual instruction, the comprehensive NCLB Act places heavy emphasis on English language proficiency, not only for students but also for teachers, who must be certified as proficient in written and oral English. While leaving schools choice of program type, the Act requires them to use instructional methods that research has proven effective. In order to increase accountability, the Act requires states to establish standards and benchmarks for English language proficiency and academic content. Academic content standards are to be aligned with those established for the general K–12 student population.

The elimination of federal support for bilingual education represents the culmination of several decades of heated debate, not just among lawmakers and educators, but among the general public as well. Arguments against bilingual education have often centered on the effectiveness of bilingual instruction in teaching English, with no attention given to potential benefits to bilingualism or to primary language use and maintenance. Proponents and opponents both cite research and statistics to support their cases regarding the effectiveness of bilingual instruction (cf. Crawford, 1999; Faltis & Hudelson, 1998; Lessow-Hurley, 2000; Ovando, 2003; Ovando, Collier, & Combs, 2003). However, research seldom provides absolute, unequivocal findings. Instead, results have to be interpreted based on the research method, including background information on students and teachers in the study, the type of program implemented, the extent to which teachers follow the program model, and many other variables. Because it is difficult to control for these variables, research results are usually open to criticism on either side of the debate.

Example 54.2 Useful Resources on Bilingual Education

Crawford, J. (1999). *Bilingual education: History, politics, theory and practice* (4th ed.). Los Angeles, CA: Bilingual Educational Services.

Cummins, J. (2001). *Negotiating identities: Education for empowerment in a diverse society* (2nd ed.). Los Angeles: California Association for Bilingual Education.

Faltis, C. J., & Hudelson, S. J. (1998). *Bilingual education in elementary and secondary school communities: Toward understanding and caring.* Boston: Allyn and Bacon.

Lessow-Hurley, J. (2000). *The foundations of dual language instruction* (3rd ed.). New York: Addison-Wesley Longman.

Moraes, M. (1996). *Bilingual education: A dialogue with the Bakhtin Circle.* Albany: State University of New York Press.

Ovando, C. (2003, Spring). Bilingual education in the United States: Historical development and current issues. *Bilingual Research Journal, 27*(1), 1–24. (Available online at http://brj.asu.edu.)

In the final analysis, research findings tend to play a smaller role than attitudes, values, beliefs, and ideology in the effectiveness debate. We offer additional resources on bilingual education in Example 54.2.

In addition to the effectiveness issue, anti–bilingual-education sentiment is fueled by the belief that, in order to unify diverse groups, in public life English should be used exclusively. The use of languages other than English in hospitals, social service agencies, schools, voting booths, and other public venues is considered anathema by members of the "English only" movement, promoted by groups such as U.S. English and English First. Resentment against immigrants and resources allocated to serve them adds fuel to the "English only" movement. These sentiments have found their way into a variety of ballot initiatives in states such as California and Arizona aimed at (1) eliminating bilingual education, (2) restricting public services to immigrants, and (3) requiring English as the "official language" to the exclusion of all others. Whether such initiatives are upheld in the courts or not, they send a chilly message that finds its way into our classrooms as we attempt to create positive learning environments for English learners (Gutierrez, Asato, Pacheco, Moll, Olson, Horng, Ruiz, Garda, & McCarty, 2002).

In summary, English learners are subject to both *general* education policy and to policy *specific* to their English learner status. Educational reform in the U.S. has become extremely politicized in recent decades. Now more than ever, state and federal legislators are mandating not only the content of the curriculum, but at times even the method of instruction. Greater and greater emphasis is being placed on English as the primary language of instruction. These trends are leading to greater uniformity and standardization in curriculum and instruction. The current emphasis on detailed and specific curriculum standards and concomitant high-stakes testing has placed tremendous pressure on students, teachers, and principals to get students to test well. These trends existed prior to the passage of NCLB and are likely to continue when the ESEA comes up again for reauthorization. Now as never before educators need to form a strong voice in the political processes that create education policy.

WHAT KINDS OF PROGRAMS EXIST TO MEET THE NEEDS OF ENGLISH LANGUAGE LEARNERS?

If you are fairly new to the enterprise of educating English language learners, you might be interested in the kinds of programs in place throughout the country to serve them. We offer such information in the following sections so that you will have an idea of what some school districts are doing. If your school has just begun to experience growth in English learner populations, these general descriptions may provide a starting point for considering a more formalized English language support program. It is important to reiterate that *federal law* requires that all English learners be provided with an educational program that provides them (1) *access to the core curriculum* and (2) *opportunities for English language development*. Districts are given substantial latitude in selecting program types and choosing whether to use the students' home language for instruction. *State laws govern program requirements at a more specific level.* Thus, as you consider program development for your English learners, you will want to seek information from your state and local offices of education.

Bilingual Education Programs

English language learners find themselves in a wide variety of school programs, from those carefully tailored to meet their specific linguistic and cultural needs to programs in which very little is done differently to accommodate them. Perhaps the simplest distinction among programs is whether two languages or one is used for instruction. Bilingual education programs are defined as educational programs that use two languages, one of which must be English, for teaching purposes. Bilingual education programs have taken many forms, but two goals are common to all: (1) to teach English and (2) to provide access to the core curriculum through the home language while students are gaining English language proficiency (Lessow-Hurley, 2000).

The following are brief sketches of some of the most prevalent bilingual program models. As you read these descriptions, think of them as skeletons that may vary considerably in the flesh as differences in communities, students, teachers, and administrators affect program implementation. In addition, bear in mind that some program models may overlap and that a single model may be called by a different name from the one given here.

In the program model descriptions we indicate whether the program serves language minority students, language majority students, or both. In the United States and other English-speaking countries, *language minority students* are those who speak a language other than English at home. In other words, their home language is a minority group language such as Cantonese, Crow, or Spanish. *Language majority students* are those whose primary language is English, the predominant national language or majority language. In this [selection], we are concerned with language minority students who are learning English in school, thus the term English learners. However, a discussion of bilingual program models would be incomplete without some mention of the immersion model developed in Canada, in which language majority students learn a minority group language in school. The extensively researched Canadian immersion model, discussed subsequently, has been highly successful and has influenced instructional development in second language teaching throughout the world (Lessow-Hurley, 2000).

Transitional Bilingual Education. Transitional bilingual education programs are designed to serve language minority students who are limited English proficient. Primary language instruction is provided for one to three years. The purpose of primary language instruction is to build a foundation in literacy and academic content that will facilitate English language and academic development as students acquire the new language. After the transition to English instruction, no further instruction in the home language is offered. The goal is to develop English language proficiency for limited English proficient students as soon as possible.

Maintenance Bilingual Education. Maintenance bilingual education is designed to serve language minority students who are limited English proficient. It differs from transitional bilingual education in that primary language instruction is provided *throughout* the elementary grades and in some cases continues in middle and high school. English language instruction is also provided throughout the grades. The purpose of the maintenance model is to help language minority students develop and maintain their primary language as well as become fully proficient in oral and written English. Thus the program goals include full bilingualism and biliteracy for English learners.

Immersion Education. Originally developed in Canada, immersion programs are designed to teach a minority language to language majority students. For example, in Canada, native English-speaking students often learn French as a second language. In the United States, native English-speaking students learn languages such as Spanish or Cantonese. In immersion programs, students receive subject matter instruction through their second language to develop second language proficiency while learning academic content. Special techniques are used to help them understand, participate, and learn in the new language. Language, content, and literacy instruction take place in the students' new language in the early grades, with the gradual introduction of English language arts as students progress up the grades. The ultimate goal is full bilingualism and biliteracy in English and the minority language for native English-speaking students. Immersion programs are therefore *bilingual* programs designed to serve language majority students. Canadian immersion programs have been extensively studied and evaluated by the Ontario Institute for Studies in Education (Genesee, 1984, 1987; Swain & Lapkin, 1989). The success of the Canadian immersion model has influenced program development in two-way immersion described below as well as structured English immersion, and sheltered instruction (cf. Krashen, 1984) discussed in a subsequent section.

Two-Way Immersion Programs. Two-way immersion programs, also called developmental bilingual education (Christian, 1994), combine elements of Canadian immersion and maintenance bilingual education to serve *both* language majority and language minority students. Two-way immersion programs group more or less equal numbers of native English-speaking students and native speakers of a minority language together for instruction. In the early grades the non-English language (e.g., Spanish) is used for instruction in an immersion approach, that is, second language acquisition through content instruction in the second language. This procedure provides second language development for English speakers and intensive primary language development for the native speakers of the minority language early on. Instruction through English, including reading and writing, begins with about 20 minutes a day in kindergarten and is gradually increased as students move up the grades until approximately equal time is given for each language (Reynolds, Dale, & Moore, 1989). As English language instruction increases, native English speakers develop their primary language (English) skills, and native Spanish speakers develop their second language (English) skills. At the same time, both groups develop skills in the minority language. Alternatively, some two-way programs use both languages from kindergarten on up the grades in approximately equal proportions. In any case, the goal is full bilingualism and biliteracy for *both* language minority and language majority students. For example, the English speakers acquire Spanish or Cantonese and the Spanish or Cantonese speakers acquire English. Both groups develop and maintain their home languages. Emphasis on primary language maintenance for language minority students is a goal shared by the maintenance bilingual education model. The two-way program model has been carefully developed, researched, and evaluated in school districts throughout the United States with positive results (cf. Christian, 1994; Lindholm, 1990; Lindholm & Gavlek, 1994; Lindholm-Leary, 2001; Peregoy, 1991; Peregoy & Boyle, 1990a).

Newcomer Programs. Newcomer programs are designed to support the initial adjustment of immigrant students to the language, culture, and schooling of their new country. All students in newcomer programs are recent arrivals from other countries. Newcomer programs emphasize the integration of academic and personal-social support to help students adjust (Chang, 1990). Newcomer programs may make use of students' home languages for instruction, but they also emphasize systematic English language instruction. Newcomer programs are short-term, often only one year, and are intended to prepare students to succeed in regular schooling situations, where they may continue to receive bilingual instruction, English language development, and sheltered English content instruction, also referred to as Specially Designed Academic Instruction in English (SDAIE). . . .

English Language Instructional Programs

Bilingual education programs serve only a small percentage of eligible students. Much more common are instructional programs that make use of only one language, English, for teaching. In many urban and suburban areas today, classrooms include students from several language groups, making bilingual instruction difficult to implement. Among program types that use only English for instruction are the following.

Sheltered English or Specially Designed Academic Instruction in English (SDAIE). In these programs, students are taught subject matter entirely in English. Subject matter instruction is organized to promote second language acquisition while teaching cognitively demanding, grade-level-appropriate material. Special teaching techniques are used to help students understand English instruction even though they are still limited in English language proficiency. Sheltered instruction, or SDAIE, is most effective for students who have already achieved intermediate English language proficiency. Primary language support may be provided separately according to district resources and student needs.

ESL Pull-out. In these programs, English learners receive the majority of their instruction in regular classrooms alongside their monolingual English-speaking peers. However, they are "pulled out" of the classroom on a regular basis to receive additional help from an ESL teacher or aide. The help they receive consists of English language development activities as well as reinforcement of subject matter being taught in the regular classroom. The goal is to help students get by while becoming proficient in oral and written English.

English Language Development (ELD). In these programs, English learners are taught all subject matter using English as the language of instruction in a class taught by a teacher with special knowledge of second language development. The majority of students in such classes are usually non-native English speakers with various levels of English language proficiency. At the elementary school level, English language development teachers are responsible for teaching students English language and literacy skills as well as the full elementary school core curriculum, including mathematics, science, and social studies. The goal is full English language, literacy, and academic development. At the secondary level, English language development teachers are primarily responsible for English language and literacy development; content is taught by subject matter specialists using sheltering or SDAIE techniques. The term *English Language Development* (ELD) is sometimes used synonymously with ESL, English as a Second Language, and ESOL, English for Speakers of Other Languages.

Structured English Immersion. In these programs English learners are taught all content through English using sheltering techniques to make instruction understandable. It is important to distinguish structured English immersion from the Canadian immersion model described earlier. Specifically, structured English immersion does not promote primary language literacy, whereas the Canadian model does. Therefore, the goal of structured English immersion is language, literacy, and content learning in English only; whereas the Canadian model aims for full bilingualism and biliteracy.

English Language Learners in the "General Education" Classroom

Although various bilingual and monolingual English support programs have been designed specifically for English language learners, many students find themselves in classrooms where little, if any, special assistance is provided. These students face a "sink-or-swim" situation. Increasingly, however, sound practices in second language teaching are reaching the general education or "regular" classroom teacher. . . . We believe that [such practices] can be applied by teachers, regardless of the type of program: bilingual, ELD, or English only. Just as our students bring diverse backgrounds, so also will programs exhibit diversity as we all join forces to move our students toward educational success and integration into the larger society.

Quality Indicators to Look for in Programs Serving English Learners

We have seen that English learner programs vary widely. However, there are certain basic elements recognized by professionals in English learner education that any quality program should include. These elements are summarized in the following statement on the education of

K–12 language minority students in the United States issued by TESOL (Teachers of English to Speakers of Other Languages), the international, professional organization for educators working with English learners (TESOL, 1992).

> TESOL supports programs which promote students' growth in English language proficiency, enhance cognitive growth, facilitate academic achievement, and encourage cultural and social adjustment. Such programs include:
>
> - comprehensive English as a Second Language instruction for linguistically diverse students which prepares them to handle content area material in English.
> - instruction in the content areas which is academically challenging, but also is tailored to the linguistic proficiency, educational background and academic needs of students.
> - opportunities for students to further develop and/or use their first language in order to promote academic and social development.
> - professional development opportunities for both ESOL and other classroom teachers which prepare them to facilitate the language and academic growth of linguistically and culturally different children.*

SUMMARY

In this [selection], we have highlighted the rich diversity among students who are learning English as a second language in school. In our descriptions, we focus on children's different experiential backgrounds and strengths, while pointing out particular challenges they face in school. Because we believe strongly in building on each student's prior knowledge and experience, we suggest a variety of ways you can get to know your English learners, even though you may not yet share a common language. These activities include personal writing topics, interactive journal writing, and writing by students in their home language. Knowing that cultural differences can create an initial source of miscommunication, we have pointed out various components of culture defined by anthropologists, while suggesting ways to recognize and honor cultural differences among students in the classroom. We have also discussed how classroom organization and language use may be more or less comfortable for students as a result of both cultural and individual differences. We suggest cooperative group learning as one strategy for integrating students into the classroom fabric and promoting English language acquisition. . . . Finally, we offered an overview of the kinds of classrooms and programs in which English language learners find themselves.

BIBLIOGRAPHY

Abedi, J. (2001, Summer). Assessment and accommodations for English Language Learners: Issues and recommendations. *Policy Brief 4.* Los Angeles, CA: National Center for Research on Evaluation, Standards, and Student Testing, University of California.

Abedi, J., Leon, S., & Mirocha, J. (2001). *Impact of student's language background on standardized achievement test results: Analyses of extant data.* Los Angeles: National Center for Research on Evaluation, Standards, and Student Testing, University of California.

Ada, A. F., & Zubizarreta, R. (2001). Parent narratives: The cultural bridge between Latino parents and their children. In M. de la Luz Reyes & J. Halcon (Eds.), *The best for our children: Critical perspectives on literacy for Latino students.* New York: Teachers College Press.

Afflerbach, P. (2002). The road to folly and redemption: Perspectives on the legitimacy of high stakes testing. *Reading Research Quarterly, 37*(3), 348–360.

Ananda, S., & Rabinowitz, S. N. (2000). The high stakes of high stakes testing. West Ed Policy Brief. Retrieved August 14, 2003, from http://www.wested .org/cs/wew/view/rs/181

Au, K. H., & Jordan, C. (1981). Teaching reading to Hawaiian children: Finding a culturally appropriate solution. In H. Trueba, G. P. Guthrie, & K. H.-P. Au (Eds.), *Culture and the bilingual classroom: Studies in classroom ethnography* (pp. 139–152). Rowley, MA: Newbury House.

Bauman, R., & Scherzer, J. (1974). *Explorations in the ethnography of speaking.* New York: Cambridge University Press.

Boggs, S. (1972). The meaning of questions and narratives to Hawaiian children. In C. B. Cazden, V. P. Johns, & D. Hymes (Eds.), *The functions of language in the classroom.* New York: Teachers College Press.

California State Department of Education (2002). *English-language development standards for California public schools: Kindergarten through grade twelve.* Sacramento, CA: Author.

Cazden, C. (1986). Classroom discourse. In M. C. Wittrock (Ed.), *Handbook of research on teaching* (pp. 432–463). New York: Macmillan.

Chang, H. N.-L. (1990). *Newcomer programs.* San Francisco: California Tomorrow Immigrant Students Project.

Christian, D. (1994). *Two-way bilingual education: Students learning through two languages.* (Educational Practice Rep. No. 12). Santa Cruz, CA, and Washington, DC: National Center for Research on Cultural Diversity and Second Language Learning.

Crawford, J. (1999). *Bilingual education: History, politics, theory and practice* (4th ed.). Los Angeles, CA: Bilingual Educational Services.

Cummins, J. (1981). The role of primary language development in promoting educational success for language minority students. In California State Department of Education (Ed.), *Schooling and language minority students: A theoretical frame-work* (pp. 3–49). Los Angeles: Evaluation, Dissemination and Assessment Center, California State University.

Escamilla, K., Mahon, E., Riley-Bernal, H., & Rutledge, D. (2003). High-stakes testing, Latinos, and English language learners: Lessons from Colorado. *Bilingual Research Journal, 27*(1), 25–49.

Faltis, C. J., & Hudelson, S. J. (1988). *Bilingual education in elementary and secondary school communities: Toward understanding and caring.* Boston: Allyn and Bacon.

Genesee, F. (1984). *Studies in immersion education.* Sacramento, CA: California State Department of Education.

Genesee, F. (1987). *Learning through two languages: Studies of immersion and bilingual education.* Cambridge, MA: Newbury House.

Goodenough, W. H. (1981). *Language, culture and society.* New York: Cambridge University Press.

Goodman, K., Goodman, Y., & Flores, B. (1979). *Reading in a bilingual classroom.* Rosslyn, VA: National Clearinghouse for Bilingual Education.

Gutierrez, K., Asato, J., Pacheco, M., Moll, L. C., Olson, K., Horng, K. L., Ruiz, R., Garcia, E., & McCarty, T. L. (2002). "Sounding American": The consequences of new reforms on English language learners. *Reading Research Quarterly, 37*(3), 328–347.

Heath, S. B. (1983). *Ways with words: Language, life and work in communities and classrooms.* New York: Cambridge University Press.

Heath S. B. (1986). Sociocultural contexts of language development. In California State Department of Education (Ed.), *Beyond language: Social and cultural factors in schooling language minority students* (pp. 143–186). Los Angeles: Evaluation, Dissemination and Assessment Center, California State University.

Hudelson, S. (1987). The role of native language literacy in the education of language minority children. *Language Arts, 64,* 827–841.

Kagan, S. (1986). Cooperative learning and sociocultural factors in schooling. In California State Department of Education (Ed.), *Beyond language: Social and cultural factors in schooling language minority students* (pp. 231–298). Los Angeles: Evaluation, Dissemination and Assessment Center, California State University.

Krashen, S. D. (1984). Immersion: Why it works and what it has taught us. *Language in Society, 12,* 61–64.

Kreeft, J. (1984). Dialogue writing—Bridge from talk to essay writing. *Language Arts, 61,* 141–150.

Laturnau, J. (2003). Standards-based instruction for English language learners. In G. G. Garcia (Ed.), *English learners reaching the highest level of English literacy* (pp. 286–305). Newark, DE: International Reading Association.

Lessow-Hurley, J. (2000). *The foundations of dual language instruction* (2nd ed.). New York: Addison-Wesley Longman.

Lindholm, K. J. (1990). Bilingual immersion education: Criteria for program development. In A. Padilla, H. Fairchild, & C. Valadez (Eds.), *Bilingual education: Issues and strategies* (pp. 91–105). Newbury Park, CA: Sage.

Lindholm, K. J., & Gavlek, K. (1994). *California DBE projects: Project-wide evaluation report, 1992–1993.* San Jose, CA: Author.

Lindholm-Leary, K. (2001). *Dual language education.* Clevedon, England: Multilingual Matters.

Mehan, H. (1979). *Learning lessons.* Cambridge, MA: Harvard University Press.

Mullen, N., & Olsen, L. (1990). You and I are the same. In J. A. Cabello (Ed.), *California perspectives* (pp. 23–29). San Francisco: California Tomorrow.

National Commission on Excellence in Education (1983). *A nation at risk.* Washington, DC: U.S. Government Printing Office.

Ochs, E., & Schieffelin, G. G. (1984). Language acquisition and socialization: Three developmental stories and their implications. In R. Shweder & R. LeVine (Eds.), *Culture theory: Essays on mind, self, and emotion* (pp. 276–322). Cambridge: Cambridge University Press.

Odlin, T. (1989). *Language transfer: Cross-linguistic influence in language learning.* Cambridge: Cambridge University Press.

Olsen, L. (1998). *Made in America: Immigrant students in our public schools.* New York: The New Press.

Ovando, C. (2003, Spring). Bilingual education in the United States: Historical development and current issues. *Bilingual Research Journal, 27*(1), 1–24. Retrieved on July 7, 2003, from http://brj.asu.edu

Ovando, C. J., Collier, V. P., & Combs, M. C. (2003). *Bilingual and ESL classroom: Teaching in multicultural contexts* (3rd ed.). Boston: McGraw-Hill.

Padolsky, D. (2002a). AskNCELA no. 1: How many school-aged English language learners (ELLs) are there in the U.S.? Retrieved on June 18, 2003, from http://www.ncela.gwu.edu/askncela/01leps.htm

Padolsky, D. (2002b). AskNCELA no. 8: How has the English language learner population changed in recent years? Retrieved on June 18, 2003, from http://www.ncela.gwu.edu/askncela/08leps.htm

Peregoy, S. (1989, Spring). Relationships between second language oral proficiency and reading comprehension of bilingual fifth grade students. *Journal of the National Association for Bilingual Education, 13*(3), 217–234.

Peregoy, S. (1991). Environmental scaffolds and learner responses in a two-way Spanish immersion kindergarten. *Canadian Modern Language Review, 47*(3), 463–476.

Peregoy, S., & Boyle, O. (1990a). Kindergartners write! Emergent literacy of Mexican American children in a two-way Spanish immersion program. *Journal of the Association of Mexican American Educators,* 6–18.

Peregoy, S., & Boyle, O. (1990b). Reading and writing scaffolds: Supporting literacy for second language learners. *Educational Issues of Language Minority Students: The Journal, 6,* 55–67.

Peregoy, S., & Boyle, O. (1991). Second language oral proficiency characteristics of low, intermediate, and high second language readers. *Hispanic Journal of Behavioral Sciences, 13*(1), 35–47.

Peregoy, S., & Boyle, O. (2000). English learners reading in English: What we know, what we need to know. In L. Meyer (Ed.), *Theory into Practice, 39*(4), 237–247.

Philips, S. U. (1983). *The invisible culture: Communication in classroom and community on the Warm Springs Indian Reservation.* White Plains, NY: Longman.

Reynolds, J., Dale, G., & Moore, J. (1989). *How to plan and implement a two-way Spanish immersion program.* Sacramento, CA: California State Department of Education.

Rodriguez, R. (1982). *Hunger of memory.* New York: Godine.

Rowe, M. B. (1974). Wait time—Is anybody listening? *Journal of Psycholinguistic Research, 3,* 203–224.

Saville-Troike, M. (1978). *A guide to culture in the classroom.* Rosslyn, VA: National Clearinghouse for Bilingual Education.

Schieffelin, B. B., & Eisenberg, A. (1984). Cultural variation in children's conversations. In R. L. Schiefelbusch & J. Pickar (Eds.), *The acquisition of communicative competence* (pp. 377–420). Baltimore: University Park Press.

Shultz, J., Erickson, F., & Florio, S. (1982). "Where's the floor?": Aspects of social relationships in communication at home and at school. In P. Gilmore & A. Glatthorn (Eds.), *Children in and out of school: Ethnography and education* (pp. 88–123). Washington, DC: Center for Applied Linguistics.

Spradley, J. P. (1980). *Participant observation.* New York: Holt, Rinehart & Winston.

Swain, M., & Lapkin, S. (1989). *Evaluating bilingual education: A Canadian case study.* Clevedon, England: Multilingual Matters.

Teachers of English to Speakers of Other Languages (1992). *TESOL statement on the education of K–12 language minority students in the United States.* Washington, DC: Author.

Teachers of English to Speakers of Other Languages (1997). *ESL Standards for Pre-K–12 Students.* Alexandria, VA: Author.

Thomas, W., & Collier, V. (1997, December). *School effectiveness for language minority students.* National Clearinghouse for Bilingual Education (NCBE) Resource Collection Series, No. 9. http://www.gwu.edu/ncbepubs/resource/effectiveness/index.html

Thomas, W., & Collier, V. (2002). *A national study of school effectiveness for language minority students' long-term academic achievement.* Santa Cruz: Center for Research on Education, Diversity and Excellence, University of California, Santa Cruz. http://www.crede.ucsc.edu/research/llaa/1.1 final.html

Trumbull, E., Rothstein-Fisch, C., & Greenfield, P. (2000). *Bridging cultures in our schools: New approaches that work.* West Ed Knowledge Brief. Retrieved June 17, 2003, from http://web.wested.org/online pubs/bridging/aboutbc.shtml

U.S. Office of Elementary and Secondary Education (2002). The No Child Left Behind Act, Executive Summary. Available at http://www.ed.gov/offices/OESE/esea/exec-summ.html

Valdez Pierce, L. (2003, March/April/May). Accountability and equity: Compatible goals of high-stakes testing? *TESOL Matters* 13(2). Alexandria, VA: Teachers of English to Speakers of Other Languages.

FOR DISCUSSION AND REVIEW

1. Why do Peregoy and Boyle think it is important to make use of English language learners' cultural backgrounds?

2. To obtain information about new English learners, what three steps do the authors suggest for teachers? Why would knowing about students' literacy in their home language be helpful?

3. Jot down several classroom activities that can provide teachers with important biographical information. How might you adapt these activities for high school or adult students?

4. The authors suggest using an anthropological approach to classroom observations. What is involved in anthropological observations?

5. In a classroom with English language learners, why should teachers pay particular attention to their own questioning practices? How can wait time, question types, and phrasing cause problems?

6. Briefly describe the various kinds of bilingual education programs, mentioning whether they are for language minority students, language majority students, or both. How does funding affect program selection and development?

7. How do structured English immersion programs in the United States differ from those in Canada? Which approach seems more beneficial to you? What advantages, if any, do you see in two-way immersion programs?

8. Why are bilingual education programs sometimes difficult to implement in today's classrooms?

9. Briefly describe the predominant English language instructional programs, noting how they differ.

Projects for "Language in the Classroom"

1. The Japanese language is unique in having three functioning writing systems: a pictographic writing system, Kanji, and two syllabic writing systems, Hiragana and Katakana. Write a paper on the history and use of each writing system. How did each develop, and how do they overlap and differ? Use interviews, either personal or online, with native writers of Japanese to investigate how they learned the writing systems and how they use them in daily life. Ask users whether they think the use of more than one writing system has advantages or complications.

2. Write a brief history and description of the Cyrillic alphabet. What languages were originally represented by the Cyrillic alphabet, and what languages are now? Like the Roman alphabet, Cyrillic is phonemic. Try to determine how adequate Cyrillic is for representing the sounds of the languages that use it. In your paper, address the possibility of using Cyrillic for English and for Japanese.

3. Write a data-based paper on perceptions of "language abuses." To collect your data, either use a written questionnaire or recorded interviews compiling a list of twelve to fifteen language "abuses" from your friends. What do they consider "bad" English or incorrect grammar? Then compile a list from adults of your parents' generation. If your participants have additional comments about particular kinds of "bad" English, record these as well. For each participant, be sure to note age, sex, and level of education. Then consult at least two usage manuals or grammar books. One should be published between 1960 and 1989, the other between 1990 and the current year. Which abuses named by your participants match entries in either of the manuals? What differences, if any, do you notice between the responses of your friends and those of your parents' generation? Do responses vary by sex and education? After you have analyzed all of your data, write up your findings.

4. Write a personal memoir of approximately 2,000 words about learning the grammar of your home, first, or native language. Try to use several approaches to collecting information: mine your own memory; talk with family, friends, and former schoolmates, if possible; look at some of the textbooks and exercises from the years you were in school; and, if possible, talk with your former teachers. In your memoir, discuss what was taught and what you remember learning. Describe the social, physical, and psychological circumstances of your language education. Since this is a personal piece of writing, feel free to express how you felt, what you do and do not remember, and whether your idea of "grammar" has changed. You may want to take a multigenre approach. For instance, you might include examples from your work or textbooks or include other images.

5. Prepare a research paper on the phonics approach to reading. As you do your research, consider these questions: What is the theoretical basis for this approach? In what ways does phonics or a sound-based approach presume that humans have "innate linguistic knowledge"? How well would this approach work with writing systems that are not based on sound-symbol relations? Do most current reading programs include the teaching of phonics? What reading methods does the school system in your area endorse? If some schools have turned away from a phonics approach, what was their rationale for doing so?

6. After doing some research, prepare a report on how spelling is taught in one of the elementary schools in your area. Review the theoretical bases and dominant approaches for teaching spelling. Try to get permission to visit a classroom during a spelling lesson. What instructional methods and materials are teachers using? What other approaches have they tried? Do they find their current method more successful than other ones? Why, or why not? Also talk with teachers to find out how spelling fits in with the rest of the curriculum. For instance, are students expected to use new spelling words in their language and reading classes?

7. Research and prepare a report on how ESL teachers take account of the cultural backgrounds of their students. Begin by reviewing the textbooks used in TESOL programs at your school, especially those for the Methods and Materials, and in the Second Language Acquisition courses. If possible, interview instructors who teach in the TESOL program. Ask whether coursework or the practicum includes ways to incorporate ESL students' backgrounds. A further step would be to contact graduates of the TESOL program currently teaching and ask them about their actual practices now that they have experience. A good way to write up your findings would be to begin with proposed approaches and then follow through to actual application and real-world experiences.

8. For this project, assume you are an anthropologist. Using the table developed by Muriel Saville-Troike and included in "English Language Learners in School" by Suzanne Peregoy and Owen Boyle (p. 838), conduct research with your family to answer the questions. Interview some family members, and also use firsthand observation and participation to develop a detailed description of your family's culture. If you have photographic, video, or audio documentation of family traditions or events, review these with the questions in mind. You may find you have other questions to add to those suggested by Saville-Troike. Once you have answered the questions, write a detailed description of your family culture.

9. Peregoy and Boyle note in "English Language Learners in School" that it is a matter of federal law "that all English learners be provided with an educational program" offering "(1) *access to the core curriculum* and (2) *opportunities for English language development.*" (p. 848). For this project, find out what program or programs your city, county, or state is actually providing. Begin with Peregoy and Boyle's list of types of programs (pp. 848–52), and divide the class so that at least one student

researches each program type. For the program you research, include information on the following: Where is it in use? How was it selected? What are the funding sources? Who is the target population? How are teachers trained? How is the program assessed? To get a better general understanding of each program, look for Web sites such as the Center for Applied Linguistics's Newcomers: Language and Academic Programs for Recent Immigrants (www.cal.org/crede/newcomer.htm), which provides valuable resources for further research.

Selected Bibliography

Adams, M. J. *Beginning to Read: Thinking and Learning about Print*. Cambridge, MA: MIT, 1990. [An approach integrating phonics with reading for meaning.]

Algeo, John, and Thomas Pyles. *The Origins and Development of the English Language*. 5th ed. Belmont, CA: Heinle, 2004. [Respected history-of-English textbook covering all historical periods of English development, with new materials on contemporary usage.]

The American Heritage® Dictionary of the English Language. 4th ed. Boston: Houghton, 2000. Bartleby.com. <www.bartleby.com/61>. [Includes discussion on regionalisms, Indo-European word origins, and other contextualizing information.]

Amis, Kingsley. *The King's English: A Guide to Modern Usage*. New York: St. Martin's, 1999. [A witty take on the English language and Americans' use of it.]

Au, Kathyrn H. *Multicultural Issues and Literacy Achievement*. Mahwah, NJ: Erlbaum, 2005. [Teachers' resource on literacy theory, research, and historical perspectives.]

Beard, Robert. *Language Fun*. 1996. Bucknell U. <http://web.archive.org/web/19970714062251/www.bucknell.edu/~rbeard/fun.html>. [Links to information on phonology, morphology, syntax and semantics, historical linguistics, and assorted dictionaries.]

Biber, Douglas. *Variation across Speech and Writing*. Cambridge: Cambridge UP, 1988. [An empirical study of variation in English spoken and written texts.]

Boyd, Fenice B., Cynthia H. Bock, and Mary S. Rozendal, eds. *Multicultural and Multilingual Literacy and Language: Contexts and Practices*. New York: Guilford, 2003. [Essays examining relationships between classroom learning and development of literacies in complex linguistic and cultural contexts.]

Bryson, Bill. *The Mother Tongue: English and How It Got That Way*. New York: Harper, 1991. [Humorous, popular history of the English language.]

Byram, M. *Routledge Encyclopedia of Language Teaching and Language Learning*. London: Routledge, 2004. [Includes materials on teaching English, testing and assessment, and important figures in language education.]

Chambers, Tyler. *I Love Languages*. 2007. <www.ilovelanguages.com>. [Links to useful materials, including dictionaries, translations, software, and language schools.]

Cleary, Linda Miller. *From the Other Side of the Desk: Students Speak Out about Writing*. Portsmouth, NH: Boynton, 1991. [Student writing and interviews documenting responses to teacher and peer evaluations; includes ESL students.]

Coulmas, Florian. *The Writing Systems of the World*. Cambridge, MA: Blackwell, 1989. [An illustrated discussion and analysis of writing systems and the significance of those systems to the study of language.]

Crystal, David. "The Prescriptive Tradition." *The Cambridge Encyclopedia of Language*. Cambridge: Cambridge UP, 1997. [Explores arguments in the debate between prescriptive and descriptive approaches to language.]

Daniels, Peter T., and William Bright, eds. *The World's Writing Systems.* New York: Oxford UP, 1996. [Comprehensive examination by eighty scholars in dictionary presenting world's writing systems.]

Diamond, Barbara J., and Margaret A. Moore. *Multicultural Literacy: Mirroring the Reality of the Classroom.* White Plains, NY: Longman, 1995. [Integration of multicultural literacy into all aspects of curriculum.]

English Usage, Style and Composition. 2005. Bartleby.com. <www.bartleby.com/usage>. [Links include *The Elements of Style* and *The King's English.*]

Fathman, Ann K., and David T. Crowther. *Science for English Language Learners: K–12 Classroom Strategies.* Arlington, VA: NSTA, 2006. [Suggests integrating the teaching of science and language as an approach for success with culturally diverse classrooms.]

Fennell, Barbara. *A History of English: A Sociolinguistic Approach.* Malden, MA: Blackwell, 2001. [Innovative sociolinguistic approach to the standard study of the history of English.]

Ferguson, Charles A., and Shirley Brice Heath, eds. *Language in the U.S.A.* New York: Cambridge UP, 1981. [Classic essays written expressly for the volume, including examinations of several American Indian languages.]

Fowler, H. W., and F. G. Fowler. *The King's English.* 1908. Oxford: Oxford UP, 2003. [Explanations of vocabulary, syntax, and punctuation reflecting early twentieth-century usage.]

Goodenough, W. H. *Language, Culture and Society.* New York: Cambridge UP, 1981. [Covers basic issues of language, such as syntax and semantics, as well as issues of how the individual and cultural contexts impact language.]

"Grammar Safari." *Intensive English Institute.* U of Illinois, Urbana-Champaign. <www.iei.uiuc.edu/student_grammarsafari.html>. [Open-access Web resource for grammar studies, including grammar and usage activities and exercises.]

Grant, Carl A., ed. *Education for Diversity: An Anthology of Multicultural Voices.* Boston: Allyn, 1995. [Articles in support of diversity in the classroom that explore the social and educational ramifications for schools and communities.]

Heath, Shirley Brice. *Ways with Words: Language, Life and Work in Communities and Classrooms.* Cambridge: Cambridge UP, 1983. [Classic and influential study of language development in children from adjacent working-class white and black communities.]

Kreft, J. "Dialogue Writing—Bridge from Talk to Essay Writing." *Language Arts* 61 (1984): 141–50. [Using dialogue writing as communication combining essay writing and oral communication.]

Lederer, Richard. *The Revenge of Anguished English: More Accidental Assaults upon Our Language.* New York: St. Martin's, 2005. [One in the Anguished English series of humorous books examining the language errors of children and adults.]

Linguist List—Ask a Linguist. 18 Apr 2007. Eastern Michigan U and Wayne State U. <www.linguistlist.org> [Online resource for language questions, with links to FAQs on topics in linguistics.]

Maggio, Rosalie. *How to Say It: Choice Words, Phrases, Sentences, and Paragraphs for Every Situation.* Upper Saddle River, NJ: Prentice, 2001 [Guide to writing meaningful and effective business and personal letters.]

Ovando, Carlos J., Mary Carol Combs, and Virginia P. Collier. *Bilingual and ESL Classrooms: Teaching in Multicultural Contexts with PowerWeb.* New York:

McGraw, 2005. [Comprehensive guide providing teachers theoretical and practical information for working with students, including those with special needs.]

Pullam, Geoff, and Mark Liberman. *Language Log*. Web log. U of Pennsylvania. [Ongoing blog with postings pertaining to language issues, quirks, and puzzles and links to language events in media and to other blogs.]

Rodriguez, Richard. *Hunger of Memory*. New York: Godine, 1982. [Autobiographical account of growing up as a Mexican-American in Sacramento.]

Ruddell, R. B., and M. R. Ruggell. *Teaching Children to Read and Write: Becoming an Influential Teacher*. Boston: Allyn, 1995. [Theory, strategies, and examples for developing effective teaching.]

Saville-Troike, Muriel. *A Guide to Culture in the Classroom*. Rosslyn, VA: NCBE, 1978. [Explores the relationship among language, culture, and education in bilingual classrooms.]

Truss, Lynn. *Eats, Shoots and Leaves: The Zero Tolerance Approach to Punctuation*. New York: Gotham, 2004. [Popular book discussing grammar and punctuation with numerous instances of errors in public usages.]

Waite, Maurice, ed. *The Oxford Dictionary and Usage Guide to the English Language*. New York: Oxford UP, 1996. [Combines more than 45,000 entries; expanded to include changes in language.]

Wells, G. *The Meaning Makers: Children Learning and Using Language to Learn*. Portsmouth, NH: Heinemann, 1986. [Follows the development of children's language, literacy, and education from infancy through elementary school.]

Glossary

acoustic phonetics.   The study of how sound is transmitted in human speech. See also *articulatory phonetics.*

affix.   A *bound morpheme* (prefix, infix, suffix) that, when attached to a base, modifies the meaning of the base word. Sometimes it changes the base's grammatical category.

affricate.   A speech sound made by articulating first a *stop* and then a *fricative* (e.g., in English, the initial sounds in *chain, gerbil,* or *Jane*).

agglutinative language.   A language with words composed of series of bound morphemes. These words' meanings are comparable to phrases or sentences in English.

allophone.   A variant of a phoneme.

alveolar.   A sound made by placing the tip or blade of the tongue on the bony ridge (the alveolar ridge) behind the upper teeth (e.g., the initial sounds of the English words *tin, sin, din, zap, nap,* and *lap*); also, a point of articulation.

ambiguity.   The linguistic quality of having more than one meaning. Ambiguity may be lexical (Meet me at the *bank*), structural (I like *chocolate cake and pie*), or both (Janet <u>made the robot</u> *fast*).

American Sign Language (ASL, Ameslan).   A linguistic system of gesture-based communication associated with deaf culture. Like other signed languages, relies on hand shape, position, and movement and the symbolic values associated with those. Users may also communicate with finger spelling or with other systems of signed languages.

aphasia.   Partial to total impairment of ability to produce or understand language as a result of brain damage (usually from a stroke or trauma).

applied linguistics.   Application of linguistic theory, methods, and results to fields such as language teaching and pedagogy, advertising, communication, lexicography, law, etc.

articulatory phonetics.   The study of human speech sounds that focuses on how sound is produced and the physiology of sound production. See *acoustic phonetics.*

aspiration.   The puff of air following articulation of a speech sound. In English, the voiceless stop consonants /p, t, k/ are aspirated at the beginning of a word (e.g., *pot, top, kit*).

assimilation.   A phonological process whereby a sound changes to become more like another, often adjacent, sound.

back formation.   A word formation process that derives a new base by removing presumed added affixes (*edit* is a back formation from *editor*).

base.   A free or bound morpheme to which affixes are added to form new words (*cat* is a free base; *-ceive* is a bound base).

bilabial.   A sound made by constriction of the two lips (e.g., the first sound in *pet, bet,* and *met*).

bilingual education program.   An educational program that uses two languages, one the target language, for new language learners.

Black English.   A label loosely used in nonscholarly discussion about features or varieties of American English associated with or imputed to African American speakers. See also *Ebonics.*

blending.   A word formation process *compounding* two or more words and clipping at least one. The classic is *sm(oke) + (f)og = smog.*

borrowing.   A process whereby words are adopted or otherwise incorporated from one language into another; also, the result of that process.

bound morpheme.   A morpheme that cannot appear alone. In English, prefixes and suffixes are bound morphemes, as are some bases.

Broca's area.   An area at the base of the motor cortex in the left hemisphere of the human brain concerned with forming comprehensible utterances.

caretaker speech.   A register characterized by simplified vocabulary; slow and clear articulation; short, simple sentences; and sometimes repetition.

central.   A sound, usually a vowel, made with the tongue body neither front nor back.

clipping.   A word formation process of shortening a word; not always predictable (e.g., *taxi* or *cab* from *taxicab*).

coinage.   A relatively infrequent process of word formation when speakers deliberately create new words.

comparative linguistics.   The method of comparing apparent similarities of word forms and meaning across languages presumed to be related; used to determine historical relationships.

complementary distribution.   An organization of sounds in a language such that *allophones* (variants) of the same *phoneme* do not occur in the same phonological environment. See also *free variation.*

compounding.   A word formation process of combining two or more words to form a new word. For example, *book + bag = bookbag* and *head + set = headset.*

connotative meaning.   Word meaning that depends on linguistic and other associations made by language users.

consonant.   A speech sound produced by significantly obstructing or constricting air flow.

cooperative principle. The principle (proposed by philosopher H. P. Grice) that at any given moment, participants in conversation make their utterances in concert with the presumed goals of the conversation. See *Maxims of Conversation*.

copula. A linking verb.

creole. A full language arising from contact between two or more languages (often developing from a pidgin stage) that has become the natural first language of a community of speakers.

critical period. A widely accepted idea that exposure to and interaction with language during childhood is necessary for complete language acquisition.

derivation. A word formation process producing a new word by adding one or more *morphemes* to an existing word or *base*.

descriptivism. An approach to grammar that describes and accounts for language characteristics and usage as they currently exist. See *prescriptivism*.

diachronic linguistics. The study and analysis of language change over time.

dialect. A variety of a language, usually regional or social, set off from other varieties of the same language by differences in phonology, grammatical structures, and lexical items.

dichotic listening. A research technique of presenting two different sounds simultaneously, through earphones, to an individual's left and right ears.

diphthong. A complex vowel sound having one beginning point of articulation and a different ending point (the English words *high*, *house*, and *hoist* have diphthongs).

discourse. A continuous stretch of language use (spoken, written, etc.) going beyond a sentence.

dissimilation. A change in one or more adjacent sounds that serves to make a string of similar sounds less similar.

downgrading. A historical process through which the value of a word declines. Also known as *pejoration*, *devaluation*, and *depreciation*.

Early Modern English. The English spoken in England from about C.E. 1450 to 1700.

Ebonics. A 1970s *coinage* that came to popular prominence in the 1990s for American English associated with urban African Americans.

ethnocentricity. The belief that one's culture (including language) is normative, logical, natural, or superior while others are peripheral, irrational, less explicable, or inferior.

etymology. The study of word history; the history of specific words.

finger spelling. The use of hand gestures to symbolize letters of an alphabet.

free variation. Two or more allophones occurring in the same phonological position without affecting meaning. See also *complementary distribution*.

fricative. A sound produced by causing nearly complete obstruction of the air flow, creating friction; a *manner of articulation*.

front. A vowel feature where the tongue is forward (in the front) of the mouth (*oral cavity*).

function words. Words indicating grammatical relations (e.g., articles, prepositions, conjunctions) but with little semantic meaning or outside world reference.

functional shift. A word formation process of shifting from one grammatical category to another without changing form (e.g., verb, to *walk* → noun, a *walk*).

gender. In grammar, a category that marks nouns, pronouns, and adjectives as masculine, feminine, or neuter, without reference to the gender of persons in the world.

generative grammar. The set of productive rules used to generate a potentially infinite number of sentences within a human language.

glide. A vowel-like speech sound that provides a transition between other sounds (the English words *yet* and *wet* begin with a glide; *my* and *cow* end with a glide).

Global English. The worldwide spread and reliance on English as an international code of communication, especially among non-native users of English.

globalization. Increased types of contact among people not possible earlier in human history because of geographic separation; usually attributed to changes in technologies, transportation, and the interconnectedness of economies.

glottal stop. A speech sound produced by constriction in the glottis (American English informal pronunciation of *button* and the refusal *uh-uh* have a glottal stop).

glottis. The space, within the larynx, between the vocal folds.

grammar. The systems of a language—phonology, morphology, syntax, semantics, and lexicon—necessary to form and interpret sentences.

Great Vowel Shift. A long-term set of changes affecting the long vowels of English, beginning in the *Middle English* period, that resulted in discrepancies between spelling and pronunciation of modern English.

Grimm's law. A statement of the regular sound changes that took place in Proto-Germanic but not in other Indo-European languages.

high. A vowel feature whereby the tongue is relatively high in the oral cavity.

historical linguistics. The study of change in language over time.

holophrastic phase. The stage of language acquisition when children produce one-word utterances.

ideograph. A character in a writing system that stands for an idea and is, or was, pictorial. See also *pictograph*.

ideolect. The variety of language spoken by one person. See also *dialect*.

illocutionary force. The intentions of a speaker, as far as those listening can discern from the context. *Implicit* illocutionary force is unstated; *explicit* illocutionary force is stated. See *Speech Act Theory*.

immersion program. A category of language learning whereby students receive subject matter instruction in the target language to develop language proficiency while learning academic content.

Indo-European. A group of languages descended from a common ancestor and now widely spoken in Europe, North and South America, Australia, New Zealand, and parts of India.

inflection.   In grammar, an affix that signals a grammatical relationship, such as case or tense. In phonetics, a change of emphasis or pitch during speech.

interdental.   A sound made by placing the tongue tip between the teeth (e.g., the initial sounds of the English words *thin* and *then*).

International Phonetic Alphabet (IPA).   A set of symbols and diacritical marks that permits the unambiguous recording of any perceivable differences in speech sounds; an alphabet with a different symbol for every sound in the world's languages.

labial.   A manner-of-articulation term that includes the bilabials and the labiodentals.

labiodental.   A *place of articulation*; the lower lip in contact with the upper teeth (e.g., the first sound of the English words *fat* and *vat*).

larynx.   Cartilaginous musculature at the top of the trachea containing the vocal folds; the "voicebox."

lateralization.   Distribution of a cognitive or other function to the left or right hemisphere of the brain.

lexicon.   The mental list of words in a language, including pronunciation, meaning, and grammatical function; also, the collection of all the vocabulary of a language.

linguist.   A person who studies language structures, language use, or language users.

linguistic relativity.   The hypothesis that a culture's worldview is influenced by the structure of its language.

linguistic relativity hypothesis.   The position that language structure shapes a culture's worldview. Also known as the *Sapir-Whorf Hypothesis* after Edward Sapir and Benjamin Lee Whorf.

liquid.   A consonant produced by less constriction than fricatives but more than glides (American English /l/ and /r/ are liquids).

low.   A vowel feature whereby the tongue is low in the mouth (oral cavity).

manner of articulation.   How the flow of air from the lungs is modified, usually in the mouth, to produce a speech sound. See also *place of articulation*.

Maxims of Conversation.   H. P. Grice's formulation of shared conversational rules constraining participants in a conversation: maxims of manner (avoid obscurity, avoid ambiguity, be brief, be orderly), maxim of quality (have a basis for your statements), maxim of quantity (be sufficiently informative), and maxim of relation (be relevant). See *cooperative principle*.

mean length of utterance (MLU).   A measure of morphemes in the speech of young children; often used to determine the progress of language acquisition.

metalanguage.   A language used for talking about language.

metaphor.   Figurative language; extension of meaning beyond the original or literal; a statement of similarity between things that are dissimilar.

mid.   A vowel feature whereby the tongue position is midway between the roof and the floor of the oral cavity.

Middle English.   The English spoken in England from approximately 1100 to 1450 C.E.

minimal pair. Words distinguished by only one distinctive feature in the same position with different meanings (English *bat/pat*, and *choke/joke* are minimal pairs).

Modern English. English spoken from 1700 to the present.

morpheme. The smallest unit in a language that has meaning or grammatical information; a morpheme may be a stand-alone word or a bound *affix*.

morphology. The study of the composition or structure of words.

nasal. A speech sound produced by stopping airflow out of the mouth and lowering the velum so that air flows out of the nose (nasal cavity). A *manner of articulation*.

native speaker. One who has learned a language as a child and therefore speaks it fluently.

Old English. Also called Anglo Saxon; the Germanic language spoken in England from about 450 to 1100 C.E.

orthography. Any writing system widely used in society.

palatal. A speech sound produced by the tongue coming into contact with the hard palate of the roof of the mouth (initial sounds of English *church*, *ship*, *judge*, *rim*, and *yet*, and the medial sound of *measure*).

palate. The hard front part of the roof of the mouth.

perceptual phonetics. The study of the perception and identification of speech sounds by a listener.

performative verb. In *Speech Act Theory*, a verb used to perform the act it names (in the sentence, "I *tell* you I won't," *tell* is a performative verb because saying "tell" performs the act of telling).

phoneme. A distinctive sound of a language; a speech sound native speakers of a language identify as the same sound even though it has more than one variant.

phonetics. The study of speech sounds.

phonics. The method of teaching beginners to read and pronounce words by learning the phonetic values of letters, letter groups, and syllables.

phonology. The study of the sound system of a language.

phrase-structure rule. A rule that generates or shows the possible grammatical relations between constituents of a sentence.

pictograph. A character in a writing system that stands for a word. See also *ideograph*.

pidgin. A language that develops out of contact between speakers who otherwise share no language in common, typically with a simplified grammar and limited lexicon.

place of articulation. The place in the vocal tract where the airflow is modified, usually by constriction, in the production of speech sounds; also called *point of articulation*. See also *manner of articulation*.

pragmatics. The study of speech acts, discourse, and the social contexts of language use.

prescriptivism. An approach to grammar that explains explains how the elements of language should be used. See *descriptivism*.

presuppositions. Implicit assumptions participants in a conversation make about what is explicitly said.

Proto-Indo-European. A hypothetical language posited from documented languages from South Asia (the "Indo-") to Europe; a reconstruction of a hypothetical language from which these languages are believed to descend.

psycholinguistics. The study of the relationship between language and psychological processes, especially the integrated study of neurological, physiological, and psychological developments related to language acquisition.

register. A subset of the language associated with a particular occupation or activity; group who engage in that activity.

Sapir-Whorf hypothesis. See *linguistic relativity hypothesis*.

semantics. The study of meaning in language, with a focus on word or lexical meaning and sentence or compositional meaning.

semiotics. The study of signs and symbols as they are found in all human populations.

sibilants. *Fricatives* characterized by a hissing sound.

sociolinguistics. The study of language use, with focus on patterns of language variation in relation to social groups.

speech act. An utterance whereby saying something is doing what is said (to say, "*I promise* to take you to dinner" is to perform the act of promising).

Speech Act Theory. An approach focusing on the intentions and effects of language use by participants in conversation.

speech community. A group of people who regularly communicate with one another, who share norms for language use and other types of interaction, and who may share feelings of community membership.

Standard English. A form of English taught in schools, considered "correct," often perceived as representing the speech of higher socioeconomic classes, and used for public communication in domains such as government, national media, and law.

stop. A speech sound produced by completely blocking the airstream; a manner of articulation.

syntax. The study of the structure of sentences and of the interrelationships of their parts.

telegraphic stage. During language acquisition, the stage when children compose short utterances primarily with content words.

trachea. The tubal area extending from the larynx through the back of the mouth and the nasal cavity to the lungs and through which air travels; the "windpipe."

transformation. A grammatical operation that changes an existing syntactic structure (e.g., a passive sentence) into a related syntactic structure (an active sentence) using formal rules of correspondence.

transliterate. To represent or spell a word from one language in the characters of the alphabet of another language.

universal grammar. A hypotheical set of language properties common to all human languages.

usage. How words and phrases are actually used in a language community. See *descriptivism* and *prescriptivism*.

velar. A speech sound produced when the back of the tongue is in contact with the *velum* (in English, the final sound in *sick*, *rig*, and *sing* are velar).

velum.   The soft back part of the roof of the mouth.

vocal folds.   Thin sheets of muscle tissue within the larynx.

vocal tract.   The air passage above the larynx, including the pharynx, the nasal cavity, and the mouth cavity.

voice-onset-time (VOT).   The time between moving the lips and vibrating the vocal cords (in English, /b/ has a VOT of 0 milliseconds; /p/ has a VOT of +40 milliseconds).

voicing.   A characteristic of articulation. A *voiced sound* occurs when the vocal folds vibrate; a *voiceless sound* occurs when the vocal folds do not vibrate. See *articulatory phonetics, manner of articulation, place of articulation.*

vowel.   A speech sound produced with a relatively free flow of air; vowel sounds are determined by the shape of the vocal tract and the position of the tongue.

Wernicke's area.   An area in the cortex of the left hemisphere of the brain involved with meaning.

Acknowledgments

Jean Aitchison. "Chimps, Children and Creoles." From *The Biology of Language*, edited by S. Puppel, pp. 1–17. Copyright © 1995. With kind permission by John Benjamins Publishing Company, Amsterdam/Philadelphia. www.benjamins.com. "Bad Birds and Better Birds." From *Words in the Mind: An Introduction to the Mental Lexicon*, 3rd Edition by Jean Aitchison. Copyright © 1994 Jean Aitchison. Published by Blackwell Publishers: Oxford UK and Cambridge, MA USA. Reprinted by permission of Blackwell Publishers UK and the author.

John Algeo. "What Makes Good English Good?" From Phillip C. Boardman, *The Legacy of Language: A Tribute to Charlton Laird.* Copyright © 1987 by University of Nevada Press. Reprinted with the permission of the University of Nevada Press.

Richard W. Bailey. "Attitudes toward English: The Future of English in South Asia." From *South Asian English: Structure, Use, and Users*, edited by Robert J. Baumgardner. Copyright © 1996 by the Board of Trustees of the University of Illinois. Used with permission of the University of Illinois Press.

Laura Bohannan. "Shakespeare in the Bush." From *Natural History*, August/September 1966. Copyright © 1966 by Laura Bohannan. Reprinted by permission of Denis Bohannan, as representative for the author's estate.

Dwight Bolinger. "Culinary Semantics." From *Aspects of Language*, Third Edition. Copyright © 1981. Reprinted with permission of Heinle, a division of Thomson Learning: www.thomsonrights.com. Fax 800-730-2215.

W. F. Bolton. "Language: An Introduction." From *A Living Language*, First Edition. Copyright © 1982. Reprinted by permission of the McGraw-Hill Companies.

Nancy Bonvillain. "The Form of the Message." From Bonvillain, Nancy, *Language, Culture and Communication: The Meaning of Messages*, 1st Edition. Copyright © 1993. Reprinted by permission of Pearson Education, Inc., Upper Saddle River, NJ.

Stephen J. Caldas and Suzanne Caron-Caldas, "Rearing Bilingual Children in a Monolingual Culture." From *American Speech*, Volume 67, no. 3, Fall 1992. Copyright © 1992 Duke University Press. All rights reserved. Used by permission of the publisher.

Edward Callary. "Phonetics." (Including tables, exercises and graphics.) Copyright © 1981 by R. E. Callary. Revised 1984 by R. E. Callary. Reprinted by permission of the author.

Elaine Chaika. "Discourse Routines." From *Language: The Social Mirror*, 1st Edition by Elaine Chaika. Copyright © 1982. Reprinted with permission of Heinle, a division of Thomson Learning: www.thomsonrights.com. Fax 800-730-2215.

James Crawford. "Endangered Native American Languages." Copyright © 1998 by James Crawford. Reprinted by permission of the author. All rights reserved.

David Crystal. "Pidgins and Creoles." Including tables, plus 12 of 100 pidgin and creole languages listed at the end of the selection. From *The Cambridge Encyclopedia of Language*, 2/e. Copyright © 1997 Cambridge University Press. "Why a Global Language?" From *English as a Global Language*, 2nd Edition. Copyright © 2003 by Cambridge University Press. Reprinted with permission of Cambridge University Press.

Harvey A. Daniels. "Nine Ideas about Language." From *Famous Last Words: The American Language Crisis Reconsidered*. Copyright © 1983 by the Board of Trustees, Southern Illinois University. Reprinted with the permission of Southern Illinois University Press.

Tom Earley. "The Quare Gene: What Will Happen to the Secret Language of the Appalachians?" From *The New Yorker*, September 21, 1998, p. 80. Copyright © 1998. Reprinted by permission of The New Yorker.

Karen Emmorey. "Sign Language." Reprinted from *Encyclopedia of Human Behavior*, vol. 4, Ed., V. S. Ramachandran, pp. 193–204. Copyright © 1994 by Academic Press, Inc. Reprinted with permission from Elsevier.

Nicholas Evans. "Aborigines Speak a Primitive Language." From *Language Myths*, edited by Laurie Bauer and Peter Trudgill. Copyright © 1998 by Laurie Bauer and Peter Trudgill. Reproduced by permission of Penguin Books, Ltd.

Robert N. Feinstein. "Gnormal Pspelling." First published in *National Forum: The Phi Kappa Phi Journal* (Summer 1986). Reprinted with permission from the Estate of Robert Ann Levis Feinstein.

Victoria Fromkin, Stephen Krashen, Susan Curtiss, David Rigler, and Marilyn Rigler, "The Development of Language in Genie: A Case of Language Acquisition beyond the 'Critical Period.'" From *Brain and Language*, vol. 1, no. 1, 1974, pp. 81–107. Copyright © 1974. Reprinted with permission from Elsevier.

Victoria Fromkin, Robert Rodman, and Nina Hymans. "Reading, Writing and Speech." From *An Introduction to Language*, 7th Edition by Fromkin/Rodman/Hyams. Copyright © 2003. Reprinted with permission of Heinle, a division of Thomson Learning: www.thomsonrights.com. Fax 800-730-2215.

"Garfield" cartoon. Copyright © 1993 Paws, Inc. Reprinted with the permission of Universal Press Syndicate. All rights reserved.

Zulfikar Ghose. "One Chooses a Language." First published in *Jets from Orange* by Zulfikar Ghose. Copyright © 1967. Published by Macmillan. Reprinted with permission of Aitken Alexander Associates, agents for the author.

H. A. Gleason, Jr. "Identification of Morphemes." From *Introduction to Descriptive Linguistics*, Rev. 2nd Edition by Gleason. Copyright © 1961. Reprinted with permission of Heinle, a division of Thomson Learning: www.thomsonrights.com. Fax 800-730-2215. Three exercises providing practice in morphemic analysis. Originally published in *A Workbook in Descriptive Linguistics* by H. A. Gleason, Jr. Copyright © 1955, 1961 by Holt, Rinehart and Winston, Inc. and renewed 1983, 1989 by H. A. Gleason, Jr. Reprinted with permission from the publishers.

Yasmine Gooneratne. "Post Office Queue." Originally published in *Word, Bird, Motif: Poems*. Kandy, Sri Lanka: TBS. Godamunne and Sons. Reprinted with permission of the author.

Howard Gregory. "Pinning Down Semantics." From *Semantics*, by Howard Gregory. Copyright © 2000 by Routledge. Reproduced by permission of Taylor & Francis Books UK.

Abdul Ghani Hazari. "Wives of a Few Bureaucrats." Originally published in *A Choice of Contemporary Verse*, edited by M. Harumur Rashid. Copyright © 1986. Dhaka, Bangladesh, Bangla Academy. Reprinted by permission of the publisher.

Shirley Brice Heath. "What No Bedtime Story Means: Narrative Skills at Home and School." From *Language in Society*, 1982, 11: 49–75. Copyright © 1982 by Shirley Brice Heath. Reprinted with the permission of Cambridge University Press and the author.

Frank Heny. "Syntax: The Structure of Sentences." From *Language in Society* by Frank Heny. Copyright © 1985 by Frank Heny. Revised 1997 by Frank Heny. Reprinted with permission of the author.

Jeannine Heny Fontaine. "Brain and Language." Copyright © 1985 by Jeannine Heny. Revised 1997 by Jeannine Heny. Reprinted by permission of the author.

Jeanne H. Herndon. "Comparative and Historical Linguistics." From *A Survey of Modern Grammars*, 2nd Edition by Herndon. Copyright © 1976. Reprinted with permission of Heinle, a division of Thomson Learning: www.thomsonrights.com. Fax 800-730-2215.

John P. Hughes, Ph. D., "Languages and Writing," pp. 116–143, from *The Science of Language: An Introduction to Linguistics*. New York: Random House, 1962. Copyright © 1962 and renewed 1990 by John P. Hughes. Reprinted with permission of Megadot Communications, Inc., Upper Montclair, NJ 07043, Literary and Business Agents for John P. Hughes, Ph.D., and Author's Estate.

Robert J. Jeffers and Isle Lehiste. "Indo-European Family Tree." Adapted from *Principles and Methods for Historical Linguistics*, figure on p. 302. Copyright © 1979 Massachusetts Institute of Technology. Reprinted by permission of MIT Press.

Fern L. Johnson. "Discourse Patterns of Males and Females." From *Speaking Culturally: Language Diversity in the United States*, by Fern L. Johnson, pp. 91–106. Copyright © 2000, reprinted by permission of Sage Publications Inc.

William Kemp and Roy Smith, "Signals, Signs, and Words: From Animal Communication to Language." From *Speaking Act to Natural Words: Animals, Communication, and*

Language. Copyright © 1985 by William Kemp and Roy Smith. Revised 1997 by William Kemp and Roy Smith. Used with permission of the authors.

Jamaica Kincaid. Excerpt from *A Small Place.* Copyright © 1988 by Jamaica Kincaid. Reprinted by permission of Farrar, Straus & Giroux, LLC.

William Labov. "Class Stratification of /th/." From *The Social Stratification of English in New York City.* Published by the Washington, D.C. Center for Applied Linguistics, 1966. Reprinted by permission of the Center for Applied Linguistics, 1966.

George Lakoff and Mark Johnson. Excerpt from *Metaphors We Live By* by George Lakoff and Mark Johnson. Copyright © 1980 by George Lakoff and Mark Johnson. Reprinted by permission of the University of Chicago Press.

Eric H. Lenneberg. "Developmental Milestones in Motor and Language Development." From *Biological Foundations of Language.* Copyright © 1967 by Eric H. Lenneberg. Reprinted by permission of Roger Lenneberg.

Genine Lentine and Roger W. Shuy, "Mc-: Meaning in the Marketplace," in *American Speech*, Vol. 65, no. 4, pp. 349–366. Copyright © 1990 the American Dialect Society. All rights reserved. Used by permission of the publisher.

Nancy Lord. "Native Tongues." Originally published in *Sierra*, November/December 1996. Reprinted with permission of the author.

Ronald Macaulay, "Regional Dialects and Social Class." From *The Social Art: Language and Its Uses.* Copyright © 1994, 1996 by Ronald Macaulay. Used by permission of Oxford University Press, Inc.

Angus McGill. *Clive* cartoon. From the London *Standard*. Copyright © Clive McGill. Reproduced with kind permission of the Peter Knight Agency.

John McWhorter. "Natural Seasonings: The Linguistic Melting Pot." From *The Word on the Street: Fact and Fable about English*, by John McWhorter. Copyright © 1998 by John McWhorter. Reprinted by permission of the Perseus Books Group.

George A. Miller. "Nonverbal Communication." From *Communication, Language, and Meaning: Psychological Perspectives.* Copyright © 1973 by Basic Books, Inc. Reprinted by permission of Basic Books, a member of Perseus Books, L.L.C.

George A. Miller and Patricia M. Gildea. "How Children Learn Words." From *Scientific American*, September 1987. Copyright © 1987 by *Scientific American*. Reprinted with the permission of the publisher. All rights reserved.

Celia Millward. "The Story of Writing." From *A Biography of the English Language*, 2nd Edition by Millward. Copyright © 1996. Reprinted with permission of Heinle, a division of Thomson Learning: www.thomsonrights.com. Fax 800-730-2215.

Breyne Arlene Moskowitz. "The Acquisition of Language." From *Scientific American*, November 1978. Copyright © 1978 by *Scientific American*. Reprinted with the permission of the publisher. All rights reserved.

Grace Nichols. "I Have Crossed an Ocean." From *The Fat Black Woman's Poems.* Copyright © 1984 Grace Nichols. Reprinted with permission of Little, Brown, U.K.

Oakland School Board. "Revised Oakland Resolution on Ebonics (Amended Version)." January 22, 1998. Reprinted by permission of the Oakland Unified School District Board of Education.

William O'Grady, Michael Dobrovolsky, and Mark Aronoff. "Sample Exercise, Mokilese" and "Appendix A: Answers to Example Exercises." From *Contemporary Linguistics: An Introduction.* Copyright © 1989 by St, Martin's Press. Reprinted by permission.

Ohio State Language Files. "Family Tree and Wave Models." From *Language Files: Material for an Introduction to Language*, Sixth Edition. Copyright © 1994 by the Ohio State University Press. Reprinted with permission of the publisher.

Ohio State Language Files. "Minimal Units of Meaning." From *Language Files: Material for an Introduction to Language*, Sixth Edition. Copyright © 1994 by The Ohio State University Press. Reprinted by permission of the publisher.

Ohio State Language Files. "What Is Phonology, The Value of Sounds: Phonemes and Phonological Rules." From *Language Files: Material for an Introduction to Language*, Sixth Edition. Copyright © 1994 by the Ohio State University Press. Reprinted by permission of the publisher.

Author and Title Index

Subject Index